# Wine Travel Guide to the World

Robert Joseph

“”

In Margaux, I want to tread the warm, well-drained gravel outcrops... I want to see the Andes water gushing down off the mountains into the fertile vineyards of Chile's Maipo Valley. I want to feel the howling mists chill me to the bone in California's Carneros, and then feel the warm winds of New Zealand's Marlborough tugging at my hair. I want it all to make sense.

*Oz Clarke*

# Introduction

Welcome to the first ever book of its kind. A guide specifically conceived and written for anyone who travels and enjoys wine. Lots of books have been published that are devoted to the wine and tourism of specific regions; what sets this guide apart is that it covers the planet, from established wine-producing countries such as France and Australia to new ones like Thailand and India.

The wine world is evolving at a bewildering speed. Vines are being planted and good reds and whites produced in places no one would have dreamed of just a few years ago. But it's not just the origin and flavour of the stuff in the bottle that's changing; today wine tourism is becoming big business. In Rioja, for example, Frank Gehry, the architect behind Bilbao's Guggenheim museum has just designed a similarly iconic building for a joint venture by the Marqués de Riscal bodega and Starwood hotels. At a more modest level, in the southwest of France, you can now stay in a vigneron's cottage and learn at first hand what it's like to make a living out of growing grapes on the same land as one's great-great-grandfather. And, in New Zealand, there's a brilliant new multimedia venture called the Big Picture, where you can sit back in an armchair and enjoy the sensation of a helicopter flight over the Central Otago wine region, with tasting visits to several wineries.

But the Guide is not just about vineyards and wineries. It also includes a wide range of recommended wine-focused restaurants and bars in most of the world's major cities. So, if you are in Boston or Beijing, Sydney or St Petersburg, Dublin or Dubai. You should have a pretty good idea of where to go to find a good glass of red or white. Enjoy!

# Contents



## Essentials

## France

## Spain

## Portugal

## Italy

## Germany

## Rest of Europe

## North America

## Latin America

## Australia

## New Zealand

## Levant & Africa

## Asia

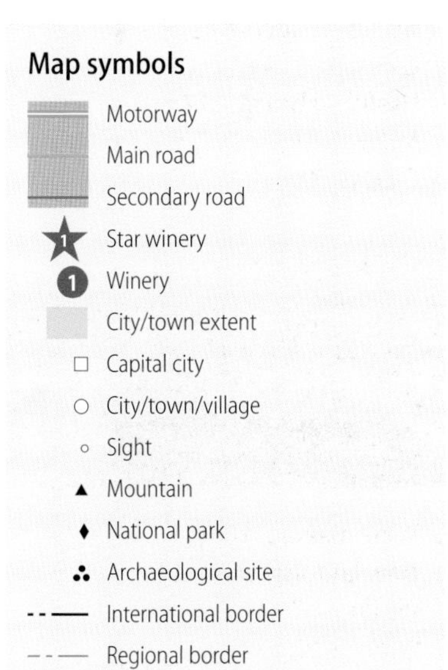

# About the book

This is a book of secrets; a collection of the experiences of hundreds of wine professionals and enthusiasts around the world. As someone who has sometimes spent up to three or four months per year travelling, I've often found myself in a strange city wondering where I might be able to wash down my lunch or dinner with a glass or two of good wine. I've long believed that it would be handy to have a global guide to such places. On the other hand, I've similarly often thought that it would be good to be able to publish in a more permanent form, descriptions of wineries I have contributed to the ephemeral world of newspapers and magazines. And, most particularly, to be able to draw attention to out-of-the-way producers who rarely come under the spotlight.

Out of these ideas was born the notion of a book and website for and by people who enjoy travel and wine. The transformation of the idea into reality came thanks to Footprint, specialist publishers of travel books, and to the sponsorship of Montana Wines (producer of Brancott), the largest, and one of the best, wine companies in New Zealand.

The world of wine is changing at such a pace that it was evident from the outset that if the book was to be up-to-date when it was published, we would need to gather our information from across the globe as rapidly as possible. To achieve this I decided to call on the help of an extraordinary collection of individuals whom I have encountered over the last 25 years of travelling. Some of these are professionals; some are enthusiasts. Some are based in the countries for which they have offered recommendations; some, like me, flit back and forth for our work taking note of the places we have liked, while others, like wine producers Philippe Guigal of the Rhône, Robert Hill-Smith of Yalumba in South Australia and Jean Marie Johnston of Bordeaux, fit into both camps. Many of these people offered far more recommendations than we could possibly have room for in a book of this size. For these, and for the chance to add your own recommendations or to comment on ones that others have made, please go to www.worldwinetravelguide.com.

By its very nature, this is a quirky, and quite personal, guide. It does not claim to include all of the world's very best wine producers (many of whom do not, in any case, welcome non-professional visitors) or all of the very finest restaurants and bars, which are, by definition well covered by countless other guides. Every entry in this book has impressed at least one and often, several wine lovers whose views I respect. I hope the guide gives you as much pleasure as their experiences have given them.

# About the author

Robert Joseph is one of the most widely travelled wine writers in the world. Since living in Burgundy in the early 1980s and returning to the UK to found *Wine International* magazine, he has visited vineyards and wineries on every continent and in out-of-the-way places including Cuba, China, Uruguay and Zimbabwe. Having founded the International Wine Challenge in London and helped to make it the biggest wine competition in the world, he has chaired International Wine Challenges in Moscow, Beijing, Shanghai, Hanoi, Bangkok, Singapore, Hong Kong and Tokyo and been invited to judge at competitions in France, Germany, Australia, Italy, Portugal, New Zealand, Chile, South Africa and the US. He was also one of the first pair of non-Japanese to take part in the annual competition for Japanese wines. The *Wine Travel Guide to the World* is his 28 th book. Previous publications include, *The Good Wine Guide*, *The Complete Encyclopedia of Wine*, *The Wines of the Americas*, *French Wines*, *Bordeaux and its wines* and the *Art of the Wine Label*. Robert Joseph lives in London with his partner, two children and a ludicrous number of bottles of wine.

# Acknowledgements

This book is very much a team effort. The recommendations for the wineries, restaurants, bars, museums and shops were provided by a list of people that is far too long to include here, all of whom deserve a huge vote of thanks. Their names and even more of their recommendations appear on the www.worldwinetravelguide.com website. Other experts who greatly contributed to this book either directly, or through their own works include Ian D'Agata (whose contribution to Italy was crucial), Joel Payne and Charles Metcalfe (who were similarly helpful on Germany and Portugal respectively), Mary Dowey (on Ireland), Tim Johnson (on France), Monty Friendship (on South Africa), Igor Serdyuk (on Russia), Oz Clarke, Tom Stevenson. James Halliday, Jancis Robinson, Hugh Johnson (for wine history), Bob Campbell, Michael Fridjhon, Antonio Terni (editor of *Vinas Bodegas & Vinos*, for information on Central and South America) and John and Erica Platter (for information on wine in Africa). I also owe a particular debt to the online efforts of Jamie Goode (www.wineanorak.com), Jancis Robinson (www.jancisrobinson.com), Bertrand Celce (www.wineterroirs.com) and Britt Karlsson (www.bkwine.com).

Much of the more tedious and thankless research for this book was carried out by Julie Campbell with additional input from Tanya Garnham, while other research and the writing up of most of the recommendations was done by Simon Woods, Hilary Azzam, Josie Butchart, Natasha Hughes, and most particularly Anastasia Edwards. All of their efforts were crucial to the existence of the guide, but the person to whom I am most grateful is Footprint's managing editor Sophie Blacksell who, with her team, did a brilliant, tireless, efficient, rapid and remarkably uncomplaining job of turning a mass of words and pictures into the book you have in your hands. These people all collectively deserve credit for this first edition of the Wine Travel Guide to the World. Any blame should fall on my shoulders alone.

# Using the guide

This guide focuses on wineries, restaurant, bars and hotels around the world that offer a unique, memorable or just plain enjoyable wine-related experience. The very best of these are highlighted with a star. In addition, we have included lists of the best producers in each region, plus background information on the most important wine-producing countries. Turn to the back of the book to find a glossary of wine-related terms and a list of useful websites.

## Symbols

A set of symbols is used to illustrate the facilities and services offered by each featured establishment, as follows:

- Wine tasting
- Tours of the winery, cellars or vineyard
- Wine sold directly to visitors
- Wine museum or wine-related exhibition
- Wine or cookery courses
- Suitable for children
- Biodynamic or organic winery
- Accommodation
- Restaurant
- Wine bar or notable wine list
- Entertainment
- Festival or annual event
- Outdoor activities
- Spa facilities
- Tourist attraction (not wine-related)

## Pricing

We have used a simple price code to indicate the relative expense of establishments.

For hotels:

**$$$** over US$250
**$$** US$150-249
**$** under US$150

Prices are for a double room, not including service charge or meals.

For restaurants:

**$$$** over US$50
**$$** US$25-49
**$** under US$25

Prices are per head for a two course meal without wine.

Every effort has been made to ensure the details in this guide are accurate. However, readers are strongly advised to contact venues in advance to confirm opening hours and other information.

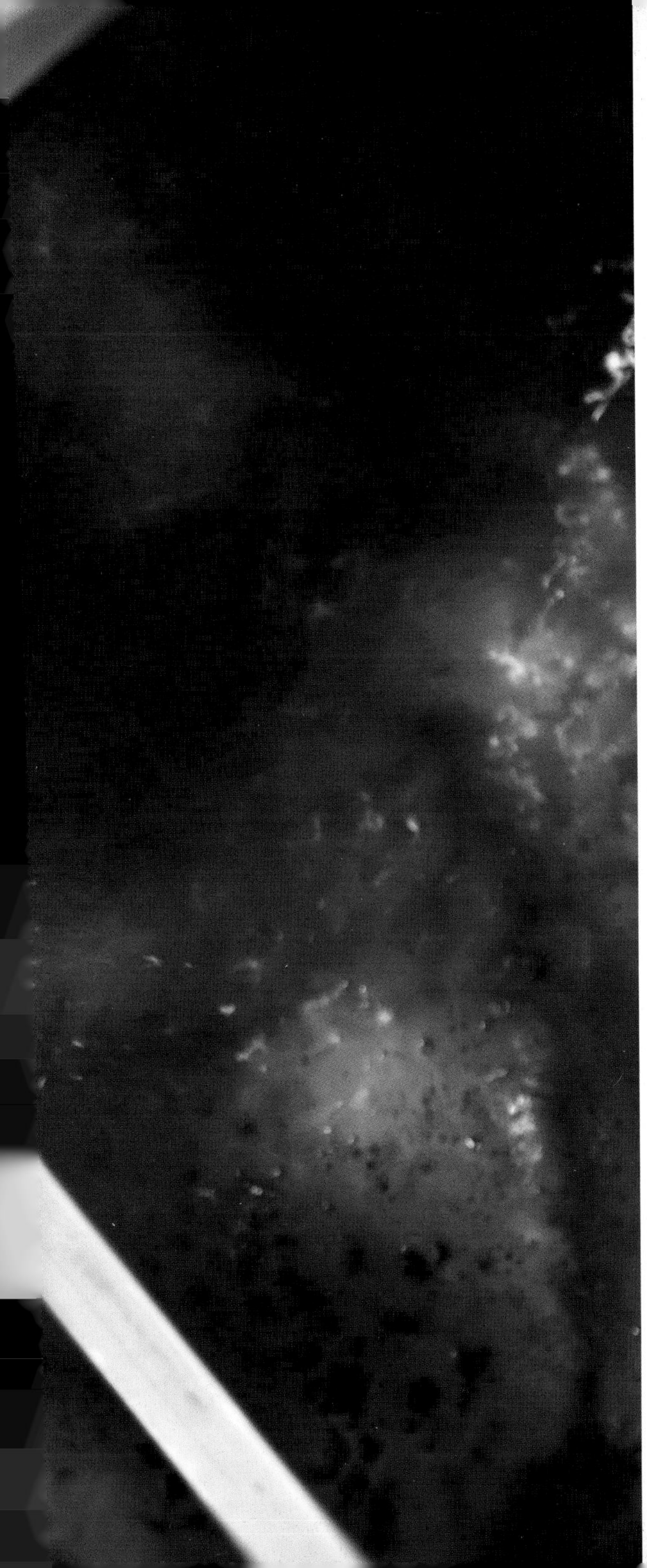

# Essentials

# Making wine



So much romantic prose has been devoted to the subject of how a wine gets its flavour and the supposedly magic properties of particular bits of hillside, that it is probably worth taking a clear-headed look at the roles played by grape varieties, climate, soil, aspect and winemaking. Choosing which of these is the most important is as fascinating or as fruitless as trying to define the influence of nature or nurture on human behaviour.

## Grapes

A wine made from Cabernet Sauvignon should always look and taste different from one made from Pinot Noir because of the intrinsic characters of the two grape varieties. The former will, for example, be darker in colour and more tannic, because it has thicker, blacker skin. But these two grapes also perform better in different soils and climates – and require different styles of winemaking, so you will almost never get to compare Cabernet Sauvignon and Pinot Noir wines that have come from precisely the same piece of land and been produced in precisely the same way. Even so, when wine experts try to guess the identity of an anonymous wine, one of the first things they will try to discern is the grape, or the mixture of grapes from which it is made.

There are at least 60 species and 8000 different types of vines, all of which can be identified from each other by often subtle variations in the shape of their leaves or by analysis of their DNA. At one end of the scale, there are vines, including *muscadine* and *vitis labrusca* that grow wild particularly in North America, which are resistant to cold, diseases and pests and can be good to eat but make wine that reminds people variously of foxes, nail varnish and cheap strawberry ice cream. At the other end of the scale, there are the quality *vitis vinifera*, such as Merlot, Chardonnay and Cabernet Sauvignon – varieties most of us have encountered – and a host of interesting and dull ones whose names will ring no bells at all. In between, there are a few hybrids, made by crossing labrusca with vinifera vines in an effort to combine quality with hardiness. Hybrids are illegal in all of Europe's major wine

regions, but are found in England and parts of North America. To complicate matters slightly further, there are also man-made crosses between vinifera vines – Pinotage (page 355) is a cross between Pinot Noir and Cinsault – and multiple clones of each grape variety. The Chardonnay grown in much of California and Chile has a more melon-like flavour than the nuttier ones to be found in Burgundy, but some Californians take pride in growing Burgundian clones. In Europe, vines sometimes also go under different names depending on where they are grown; this is especially true of the Tempranillo in Spain and the Sangiovese in Italy, for example. The aliases may refer to different clones but this is far from guaranteed.

Most grapes taste relatively similar when they are picked, but the process of fermentation which converts the sugar they contain into ethyl alcohol and carbon dioxide, also accentuates their individual characters. Wine made from Sauvignon Blanc grapes will, for example, have a blackcurrant leaf and gooseberry smell and flavour, while Gewürztraminer will remind tasters of lychees. These hallmarks are so strong, especially when the wine is young, that even a complete beginner will find it easy to spot which is which. Other varietals are less obviously identifiable.

## Climate

Climate – either the natural climate of the region, the microclimate of the vineyard, or the weather conditions of a particular vintage – will also have a major part to play. The wine expert playing a guessing game will focus his or her attention on whether the wine in front of them came from a warm or cool place. As a rule, the more sun the grapes have seen, the richer, riper and fuller the flavour of the wine they will produce. But this is not an absolute rule. Winemakers who overcrop – grow too many grapes per vine – and over-irrigate in a warm country like Chile will produce wine with a thin, underripe flavour that might be reminiscent of efforts from a cooler region elsewhere. Likewise, wine from an unusually hot, dry, European vintage like 2003 and 2005 might bear a stronger resemblance to a wine made from the same grape in, say, California than to one made from a cold, rainy European year like 2002.

Within any region, there are also suntraps and areas where grapes never ripen as well. (In some parts of France, such as Burgundy and parts of Bordeaux, those lucky, sunnier slopes might be allowed to label their wines as Grands). Altitude has a role to play, as does the location: close to the ocean or in the middle of a land mass. Even areas that might be thought of as hot may mitigate the effect on the grapes by having cool nights.

In the 1930s, the Californian professors A J Winkler and Maynard Amerine came up with a way to classify wine regions called 'heat summation' which used a unit of measurement they dubbed 'degree days'. Vines need a temperature of 10°C to grow. Each degree above that figure over 24 hours is counted as one degree day. So, if the average temperature of a day in a given region is 20°F, it will be counted as having 10 degree days (20-10). All of the degree days in a given region between 1 April and 31 October – the northern hemisphere growing season – are then added to produce its total degree days. Champagne, for example, has 1050 degree days, Beaune in Burgundy has 1310 and Healdsburg in California's Sonoma Valley has 1755. As a rule, the more degree days you have, the more sugar your grapes will have and the less acidity. Yields will be high, but flavour and colour will be less intense.

This simple rule of thumb has helped growers in new regions to decide which grapes will perform best: varieties like Pinot Noir, Chardonnay and Riesling are at their best in regions with fewer heat days. Zinfandel and Cabernet Sauvignon need more. However, averages are dangerous. Vintages need to be seen as obstacle races; from the moment the first green life appears on the wooden vine in the spring until the grapes are picked in the autumn, the vine will react to the amount of sunlight, warmth and water. When temperatures are too high, vines simply stop growing.

Water is also essential. Vines don't grow well in drought conditions. In the New World, and now in Spain and in France's Vin de Pays regions, irrigation is allowed. In the denominated regions of France and Italy, however, it is – for illogical reasons – illegal to water a vine even when it is gasping for moisture. On the other hand, a potentially ideal vintage in which the weather conditions have ripened the grapes perfectly can be spoiled by rainstorms during the harvest that dilute the wine. (In France, where irrigation is deemed unacceptably 'industrial', regions including Bordeaux are legally allowed to use clever machines that extract excess water from grape juice by a process of reverse osmosis.)

## Soil

Soil is also important – though less so than is often claimed. The role of the soil is to hold as much moisture as a vine needs to grow and no more, but some vines, like some flowers, prefer particular types of soil. Cabernet Sauvignon does well on gravel, for example, while Merlot likes clay and Chardonnay famously does well on limestone. Subtle variations of soil and subsoil can influence the flavours of wines quite significantly, as can be seen in Burgundy where vineyards producing identifiably different wines are often separated by a few metres. The Gallic notion that soil is an indispensable part of a wine's makeup – a crucial part of the microclimate, site and soil combination known in French as 'terroir' – is frequently undermined, however, when the most experienced palates mistake Californian wines for French ones that are grown on quite different soils. However, when the greatest wines of the world are lined up, some of the character of the soil – slate in Germany, gravel in Bordeaux, chalk in Chablis, for example – should be discernible, and it is not uncommon for experts to talk of a wine having a "mineral" quality.

## Aspect

Vines do best on slopes facing south in the northern hemisphere, and north on the other side of the world, because they get more sun and because they are at lower risk of sitting in pools of water after rainstorms and of frost caused by pockets of cold air. But there are more or less ideal parts of any slope, and the notion that steep hills are essential to great wine, though supported in the Rhine and Rhône, is undermined by the boringly flat Médoc.

# From grape to glass

**1** At the beginning of the growing season, vines are pruned according to the desired yield per plant and per hectare.
**2** During the growing season, the grower may remove leaves (leaf-plucking) to improve the ripening process.
**3** If the yields look over-generous, a 'green harvest' (the removal of bunches of unripe grapes) may take place.
**4** The harvest date is traditionally chosen by assessing whether the grapes have sufficient sugar. Modern winegrowers, however, tend to pick later than in the past, because they want the extra flavour that can develop as the grapes ripen further. This leads to wines with more alcohol and less acidity. In many regions, there is also the risk of bad weather spoiling the fruit before the harvesters get to it.
**5** Makers of top-quality-late harvest white wine, will generally not only wait until their grapes have enough sugar; they will also wait for a benevolent fungus called noble rot or *Botrytis cinerea* to cover the berries, concentrating their flavour and contributing a dried-apricot character of their own. Noble rot requires a combination of the right levels of humidity and warmth and, in Europe, does not appear every year. Some regions, like Neusiedlersee in Austria and Tokaj in Hungary get it more reliably than Sauternes, the Loire and Germany. In the New World, some winemakers guarantee that they will be able to make good sweet wine every year, by spraying noble rot spores onto the grapes.
**6** In Canada and Germany, and a few other regions, makers of a particular kind of sweet wine don't want noble rot; instead they hope that their ultra-ripe grapes will freeze.
**7** Another unusual winemaking method pioneered by the ancient Greeks involves leaving freshly picked grapes to dry on mats until they have become almost raisins before they are fermented. Wine made this way is known in France as Vin de Paille and in Italy as Recioto.
**8** Grapes can be picked by hand with secateurs or by machine using huge tractors with arms that cleverly shake the bunches off the vines. Machine picking has the advantage of being possible at night when temperatures are low, but it lacks the precision of harvesting manually.
**9** At high-quality wineries, grapes will pass along a conveyor belt (*table de tri*) to allow the removal of unripe and rotten grapes.
**10** White wine grapes can now be crushed in a press and the juice drawn off to be fermented. In this instance the skins are discarded, although for some relatively unexpressive grape varieties, the grapes may be crushed and the juice left in contact with the skins for 12 or 24 hours at a cool temperature, before fermentation begins. This technique is also used by some red wine producers, but in this case the grapes are left largely uncrushed.
**11** Fermentation of the white or black grapes may be kicked off by the natural or 'wild' yeasts found on their skins. The behaviour of these yeasts can be unpredictable, and most New World and many Old World winemakers prefer to kill them with a little sulphor dioxide and use cultured yeasts instead. These are not only more reliable, but can also bring out desirable flavours. Those who favour wild yeasts reasonably claim that they give more complex flavours to wines, to which comes the response that all Champagnes, even the most complex, are made with cultured yeasts.
**12** The essential difference between red and pink wine and white lies in the role of the grape skins in contributing colour, flavour and tannin. So, while the white grape skins are always discarded before fermentation, whatever the style of red or pink, they will always go into the vat.
**13** Temperature control is essential for red and white fermentation. Whites are fermented at 12-20°C; reds at 25-30°C. Beneath 10°C and at over 40-45°C the yeasts won't convert the sugar into alcohol and, at the higher figures, there is a danger of bacteria turning partly fermented wine into vinegar.
**14** White wine (especially Chardonnay) may be fermented in (possibly new) oak barrels; the process can take several weeks. Red wine is fermented in a tank a lot more rapidly. If the wine in question is Beaujolais or a wine that is intended to be fruity and for early drinking, the grapes may be left uncrushed and the process (known as carbonic maceration) will take place beneath a layer of carbon dioxide.
**15** When fermenting red wine grapes, it is essential to break up the 'cap' of skins that floats on top of the fermenting juice and to prevent it from drying out. There are various ways to do this, but 'pigeage' (breaking it up with a wooden paddle) is popular in regions like Burgundy.
**16** When making fortified wine like port, sherry or Muscat de Beaumes de Venise, neutral spirit is added to the partly fermented wine to stop the fermentation process.
**17** For other red wines, fermentation is allowed to continue until all of the sugar has been converted into alcohol. Usually, the new wine and skins are left for a further period of maceration to extract colour and tannin. In Australia, some producers skip this last stage and pass the still slightly-sweet wine into new oak barrels to finish the process there.
**18** All red and most white wine goes through a natural second fermentation, known as malolactic, which converts the natural appley acid in the wine into creamier yoghurty lactic acid. This may happen naturally or be helped along with special yeasts. Some wines will go through partial malolactic, to maintain their freshness. Wine going through malolactic fermentation is harder to taste, because of its odd, bruised apple flavour, than it is before or afterwards.

**19** Depending on the variety and the style of wine, it may be aged in stainless steel or concrete tanks or in small or larger barrels, which may be old or made from new oak. Aromatic whites, like Riesling, almost never go into new barrels because the flavour of oak is not considered desirable for them. Producers of cheaper reds and whites who do want an oaky character for their wine may put oak staves or chips into a vat, as a cheaper alternative to using new barrels which need to be replaced every couple of years.

**20** However the wine is stored, it will have to be racked: transferred from vat to vat or barrel to barrel to prevent it from becoming stale and 'reduced' with unpleasant, eggy sulphor dioxide (which has been used to protect the wine from bacteria) being transformed into hydrogen sulphide. Some producers replace the physical transfer of the wine with a process called micro-oxygenation which involves injecting it with tiny oxygen bubbles.

**21** Blending is another option – either between wines from the same grapes but different vineyards, or, as in Bordeaux, from different grape varieties.

**22** Before bottling, most wine will be fined (cleared of any suspended solids) by allowing egg white or powdered clay to sink through the liquid. Some producers prefer to omit this stage.

**23** When bottles of wine are subjected to low temperatures, crystals may naturally occur. To avoid this, producers of commercial wine usually chill the wine while it is still in the tank.

**24** Most wine is filtered before bottling to ensure that it is free of any bacteria that might subsequently spoil it. Some producers prefer not to filter their wine for fear of removing flavour.

**25** Wine will be bottled, with natural corks, stoppers made from granules of natural cork (possibly treated to prevent mould), synthetic corks or screwcaps. Alternatively, it might go into a bag-in-box.

## Yields

One of the major factors influencing the flavour and quality of any wine is the amount the producer has made from his or her plot of vines. This will vary from vintage to vintage, depending on the climate and rainfall or irrigation, but it fundamentally depends on the number of vines planted per hectare, their age (old vines have lower yields) and the way they are pruned. In the New World, the market is allowed to dictate which producers have overcropped their vines, but in Europe yields are dictated by law. French regulations ludicrously lay down limits per hectare, despite the fact that in a region like Bordeaux each hectare might have between 2000 and 8000 vines. In Italy, maximum yields are more sensibly dictated per vine (with a limit of 3 kg for example). Each kilo of grapes will yield between three quarters and a little less than a bottle of wine depending on how vigorously they are pressed, so your 3 kg vine might give you just under three bottles of wine. Elsewhere, vines might be much more heavily charged, while the frozen grapes used for Canadian Icewine, might produce less than a fifth as much wine as one might have got from the grapes if they had been harvested unfrozen a couple of months earlier.



## Grape growing and winemaking

The human touch is as important in wine as it is in a kitchen. This is where the French system of Appellation Contrôlée really falls down, because winegrowers with neighbouring vineyards can, through a combination of their innate skills, equipment, thoroughness, ambition, personal taste and luck, produce wines of quite different styles and qualities. This explains why, for a wine expert, the most important information to be found on any wine label, is not the region, the grape or the vintage, but the name of the man or woman who made it.

## New Latitude wines

Until the 1970s, the wine world was flat; its maps were skilfully charted and showed the edges over which one could not dream of sailing. The Pinot Noir grape, for instance, only produced good wine in the soil and climate of a small region called the Côte d'Or. Of course attempts had been made to grow it elsewhere – in Sancerre, Alsace and Champagne – but in none of these places did it produce red wine that was remotely comparable to the efforts of villages like Volnay and Vosne-Romanee. Much the same could be said for Chardonnay, while Sauvignon Blanc and Chenin Blanc only performed at their best in the Loire. Challenging these beliefs by trying to mimic Burgundy or Sancerre elsewhere was like sailing over the edge of the world.

Then, in 1970s, a Pinot Noir from Eyrie vineyards in Oregon (page 240) beat a set of red Burgundies, and Californian Cabernets and Chardonnays triumphed over their French counterparts in Steven Spurrier's famous 1976 Paris tasting (page 232). For a while, it seemed as though the Old World was going to have to acknowledge the curvature of the globe but, in fact, all that happened was that the flat map was redrawn. The new credo was that Pinot Noir and Chardonnay, for example, needed to be grown in places that were as

similar as possible to Burgundy. In fact, of course, there were huge differences between the soils of Puligny-Montrachet and Carneros in California but the followers of the amended faith were happy to gloss over these anomalies. What mattered above all, they said, was the climate. Experts charted the 'degree days' (average temperature during the growing season) of the classic regions of France and did their utmost to match these conditions when planting in the New World.

If you had asked any of these followers of the original or expanded flat earth beliefs (99.99% of the wine community), they would all have agreed on one absolute rule. Wine of any kind can only be produced between the latitudes of 30° and 50° in the northern or southern hemispheres. Anything closer to the North or South Pole is too cold, while grapevines simply don't do well in the tropics because they need to rest over a cold winter.

But then news began to leak out of vineyards in Thailand, between the 14th and 18th parallels. Conditions here are tropical and production methods are eccentric, to say the least. Indeed, in the **Siam Winery** (page 366), the grapes are grown on islands and harvested from boats and, in another hillside vineyard, workers sit astride elephants and irrigate the fruit with water from the beast's trunk. However, the budding Thai wine industry (there are six wineries at present and others due to open soon) was not launched on a whim; the King of Thailand commissioned a study in the late 1970s that took a dozen years to decide that the project would be worthwhile.

The obvious question is "how good are the Thai wines?" and the honest answer is that they are not currently likely to cause the owners of châteaux Margaux or Cheval Blanc any loss of sleep. Having said that, examples under the Monsoon Valley label are a much softer, more pleasant drink than most cheap Bordeaux. And, for those who judge by results, the Thais are planting vineyards, while the Bordelais are currently uprooting theirs – and sending the equivalent of 44,000,000 unsold bottles of their wine each year to be turned into industrial alcohol.

Thailand is only the most romantic example of a growing number

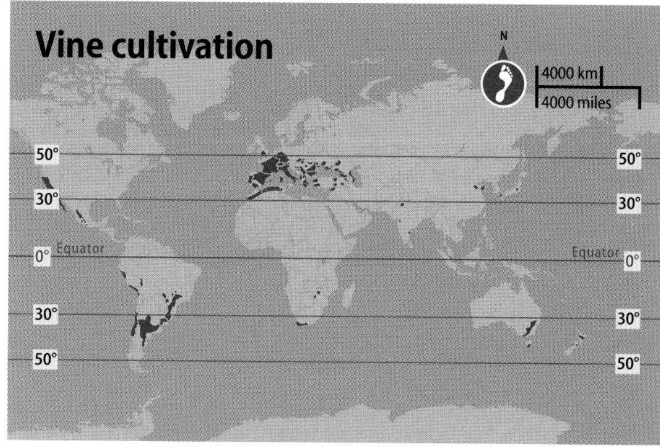


Village Farm Winery, Thailand



of wine regions that are situated beyond the pale of traditional vinegrowing. In 2005, *Decanter* magazine tasted a range of wines from the New World and gave their highest marks to the La Reserve Cabernet Shiraz from **Grover Vineyards** (page 362), near Bangalore in India. At the time, most of the news coverage focused on the fact that the wine was from the subcontinent and produced with the help of the ubiquitous Michel Rolland; no one pointed out that the vineyard is near to the 13th parallel, around 4000 km closer to the equator than it ought to be. This is, in fact, India's most southerly vineyard; most of the others are planted closer to Mumbai but, at the 18th parallel, they hardly conform to the old 30-50 degree rule either.

If India is going to be a country to watch – both in terms of production and consumption – then so is Brazil. This is where you'll find the most commercially intensive effort at what Thai-based wine writer Frank Norel calls "New Latitude" winemaking. In the warm, dry São Francisco Valley, between the ninth and 10th parallel, a carpet of vines is being unrolled. The region barely existed 20 years ago but it is already supplying 15% of Brazil's needs and is expected to triple production over the next four years, by which time it will be the source of one glass in every two that are drunk there. Yields per harvest are high in Brazil, by classical European standards, and the lack of a winter means that, as elsewhere in the New Latitude, vines can produce two vintages per year. They could produce more, but vineyard owners prefer not to wear the plants out completely. The early releases from São Francisco are perfectly acceptable and, again, considerably more drinkable than that unsaleable Bordeaux. So far, the Shiraz shows great promise (**Miolo's** Terranova is a good example, page 277), but there is no reason to suppose that other varieties will not thrive as well.

The idea of picking wine grapes more than once a year is not as novel as one might imagine. Way back in 1578, Don Juan de Pimentel, the governor of Venezuela, wrote a book in which he describes vineyards near Caracas being harvested three times a year. Today, the **Pomar** winery (page 279), which opened its doors in 1986, is the sole quality-conscious upholder of the Venezuelan vinous tradition. The wines it produces close to the 11th parallel have won medals in international competitions, such as the Challenge International du Vin in Bordeaux. By far the most surprising award-winner among the New Latitude wineries, however, has to be **Chaupi Estancia** Palomino in Ecuador (page 278), which won a Commendation (the equivalent of a mark of at least 14/20) at the 2004 Decanter Awards in London. This winery, established 15 years ago, makes its wines from vineyards at 2400 m above sea level and just 10 km from the equator.

All of these wines raise the essential question: how is it feasible to make wines in conditions that were once thought to be impossible. The simple answer is that we now know a lot more about plants and the way they grow than we used to. Like every other living thing, vines are programmed for survival and are a lot more adaptable than was previously imagined. And, vinegrowers are also a lot more sophisticated than they were. Precise use of irrigation and careful pruning will significantly affect the way the vines grow and the amount and ripeness of fruit they produce, but there is now a new piece of artillery in the grapegrower's arsenal. Crop-regulating hormones sound as though they could only have been produced by genetic manipulation but, in fact, they occur naturally in all living things. The trick today lies in extracting them from the plants and then using them to influence the way the vines grow. Those who favour absolutely natural winemaking will quite reasonably balk at this kind of procedure but they should be equally, if not more, concerned by the huge amounts of synthetic chemicals used by growers in Europe. Brazil and India, in particular, will both help to ensure that New Latitude wines are taken at least as seriously within the next decade as New World wines were in the 1980s. So far, of course, very little notice has been taken of them at all but if you believe that the world is flat, there is very little reason or temptation to go peering over the edge.

# Visiting wineries

## Wine tourism

Anyone who has ever compared wines from the New World (the Americas, Oceania and Africa) with those from Europe (the Old World) will almost certainly have been struck by their greater accessibility and comprehensibility. They have labels that usually clearly state the name of the grape from which the wine has been made, and 'fruit-driven' flavours that people across the globe increasingly find immediately enjoyable.

European wines expect the drinker to make a lot more effort. Labels often seem to be wilfully confusing if not downright incomprehensible: how many non-wine French buffs would know, for example, that white Rully is a Chardonnay from Burgundy and white Reuilly is a Sauvignon Blanc from the Loire? How many Italian wine drinkers would guess that a Spanna and a Barolo are made from the same grape variety? In the Old World, it is evidently up to the customer to do his or her homework before approaching the bottle.

There is a simple explanation for this difference. Most of Europe's wines were traditionally either drunk in the region where they were made (by locals who would know by experience how they were likely to taste) or by a relatively small number of wealthy people, most of whom lived in big cities, and who tended to drink, by modern standards, a very limited range of styles. Until the 1980s, it was a rare French wine producer who would have visited his counterparts in a different appellation a few miles down the road. Even today, few have travelled far beyond their own regions.

This attitude, which has helped sales of European wines to fall increasingly behind those of countries like Australia and the US, is just as apparent in the way the Old World approaches wine tourism. A visitor to a young region like Marlborough in New Zealand can choose between dozens of wineries that offer tasting rooms, picnic areas, cafés or restaurants. Bordeaux's winemakers, by contrast, with very few exceptions, almost seem to want tourists to go elsewhere. They prefer visits to be by appointment, by people who know about the region's wines, can discuss them in French and are seriously interested in filling at least a dozen holes in their wine rack.

This reveals another gulf that separates much of the Old World from the New: the realization that a first-time visitor to a winery nowadays is not necessarily looking to buy a bottle, let alone a case. He or she is more than likely treating the outing as an alternative to wandering around a museum or an amusement park. In short, they want to be entertained. The producers who have truly understood and exploited this most effectively are the bigger Champagne houses (who work in a region that has a very different philosophy to the rest of France) and wineries in California, many of which charge for tastings and tours of their cellars, and ensure that anyone buying a ticket feels that they have had value for money. According to the Napa Valley-based research firm MKF, nearly 15 million people visited California's vineyards and wineries in 2004, spending over US$40 each on wine, T-shirts, local arts and crafts, snacks and meals. Usefully, these visitors bought four out of every ten bottles produced by smaller wineries, making less than 60,000 bottles per year.

No one keeps these kinds of statistics for Bordeaux, but as a spokesperson for the region admitted, "we are only beginning to learn about tourism... You will still get a much worse reception at a Médoc chateau if you turn up on a Sunday than if you arrive during the week".

Of course it is dangerous to generalize. There are a growing number of European producers who can compete on level terms with the most tourist-oriented New World Winery. Georges Duboeuf's **Hameau du Vin** in Beaujolais (page 53), for example, the spa hotel at **Château Smith Haut Lafitte** (page 64) and The **Marqués de Riscal's** new Gehry-designed winery-and-hotel in Rioja (page 88), are all fine examples. There are plenty of small New Zealand, Australian and US wineries where your tasting will be hosted by the owner – and a fair few Argentine and Chilean wineries that have offered a poor welcome to tourists brave enough to make their way down the unmade road to their door. Even so, there is no denying that the Napa and Hunter Valley are now booming tourist regions; a description even the most generous critic could hardly use of Rioja or the Rhône.

The one advantage the Old World still has is its age-old ability to host wine festivals. In September and October, you only have to drive a few miles in any direction and you will almost certainly see signs advertizing some kind of get-together by the winegrowers of a village or appellation. Often these are combined with displays of traditional local foods and handicrafts that help to set the wines into an historic and regional context. Other European events include charity wine auctions, such as the annual event at the **Hospices de Beaune** in Burgundy and the **VdP** auctions in Germany (page 161), and even marathon races between wine communes. But the world's biggest charity auction is now the one held every year in the Napa Valley and the success of events like the **Marlborough Food & Wine Festival**, the **Barossa Valley Festival** and the **Food & Wine Festival** in Aspen all show that Europe has to fight increasingly hard to keep the attention of the modern wine lover.

## Planning a visit

The first decision to make is how many wineries you want to visit in a day. For most people, the ideal figure, depending on the distance between them is four or fewer. Professionals may manage six or eight, but they are used to tasting large numbers of wines quickly and efficiently. Bear in mind, too, that even if you spit out every drop you taste (which is advisable if you are driving), some of the alcohol still enters your bloodstream through the roof of your mouth. So, tasting a couple of dozen wines and drinking a glass or two with lunch might well push you over the legal limit.

Remember, you are under no obligation to buy, but if you haven't been asked to pay for the tour and tasting, it's bad manners to trespass for too long on a winegrower's time. He almost certainly has other work to do. However, be wary of any winery that refuses to let you taste before you buy. There will almost certainly be another winery close at hand that will be happy to pour you a sample.

Beware of flannel and hype. You will almost certainly be told that a wine was the favourite of a 16th-century monarch, or has won 95 points from a 20th-century US guru or a gold medal at a local competition. Just remember the occasions when your impressions of a film have differed with those of a newpaper critic or the Oscars jury, and make up your own mind.

As a rule, when asked what you think, it is best to be politely honest. Winegrowers have plenty of experience spotting bluffers and flatterers. If there is something you don't like or are uncertain about a wine, say so. It might be a poor vintage or a style you simply don't enjoy. Knowing your reaction will make it easier for the winemaker to show you something that might be more to your taste. It's also worth noting that in France and Italy, it is far from unknown for winegrowers to test visitors by watching their reaction to a wine of which they are less than proud. Intelligent and, still better, knowledgeable responses can act like hitting the required number of aliens on a computer game. You might just move up a level and be invited to taste something better.

If you are interested in buying some wine (and have worked out the logistics of getting the wine home; it is fiercely difficult to import wine into the US, for example), take advantage of the producer's expertise by asking him or her about how they like to serve it, the dishes it might accompany and the length of time it should be left in the cellar before opening.

One of the best reasons for buying at a winery is that it may enable you to get hold of wines that are unavailable elsewhere, or to save money. But in the latter case it's worth looking at **www.winesearcher.com** to check the difference in price. There are plenty of stories of people who have spent twice as much on excess luggage or import duty as they have saved. If you are travelling by car in a wine region, be sure to invest in an insulated coolbox or pack.

When choosing wineries to visit, the best way to find new ones – apart from this book and its associated website (www.worldwinetravelguide.com) and other guides you may pick up along the way – is to take note of the wines on offer in good restaurants and the advice of evidently knowledgeable sommeliers who should be keeping track of up-and-coming producers. In the US – and almost uniquely in the US – sommeliers expect to get a tip in addition to the huge percentage you are almost obliged to add to the cost of the meal. The excuse for this, as in all tip-related matters in America, is that if waiters, porters, bell boys don't get tips they die of hunger. Everyone has to make up their own mind over whether to give or not to give, and how much, but the sensible policy seems to be to reward exceptional service appropriately, and to punish the supercilious wine waiter who looked down his nose at your choice, or at your request to chill an overly warm red. However, whether or not you choose to give your sommelier some extra cash, it is a nice gesture when drinking a really good bottle, to leave a little wine in the bottle for him or her to taste.

When travelling in a wine region, you may well buy or be given a bottle that you'd like to enjoy with dinner in a local restaurant. In Australia and New Zealand, and in some US wine regions, you can simply turn up with your wine and negotiate a price for corkage. In Europe, 'bring-your-own' is less commonplace, at least among non-regulars, so it is advisable to call in advance to ask if it will be permitted. When discussing an acceptable price for corkage with a restaurant that is reluctant to let you drink your own wine, one option is to agree to pay the price of a bottle of house wine. This may be more than you'd like to pay but it may help to broker an otherwise impossible deal.

# Tasting wine





Wherever you are in the world, choosing and buying a wine can be a very daunting prospect. And, as the range on offer grows wider, life isn't getting any easier. The following section is intended to provide a little guidance through the wine jungle.

## The label

Wine labels should always reveal the country where the wine was produced and possibly the region and grape variety from which it was made. Both region and grape, however, offer only partial guidance as to what you are likely to find when you pull the cork. Bear in mind the following:

- Official terms such as Appellation Contrôlée, Grand or Premier Cru, Qualitätswein and Reserva are often as trustworthy as official statements by politicians.

- Unofficial terms such as Réserve Personnelle and Vintner's Selection are, likewise, as trustworthy as unofficial statements by the producer of any other commodity.

- Knowing where a wine comes from is often like knowing where a person was born; it provides no guarantee of how good the wine will be. Nor how it will have been made (though there are often local rules). There will be nothing to tell you, for instance, whether a Chablis is oaky, nor whether an Alsace or Vouvray is sweet.

- Big name regions don't always make better wine than supposedly lesser ones. Cheap Bordeaux is far worse than similarly priced wine from Bulgaria.

- Don't expect wines from the same grape variety to taste the same: a South African Chardonnay may taste drier than one from California. The flavour and style will depend on the climate, soil and producer.

- Just because a producer makes a good wine in one place, don't trust him, or her, to make other good wines, either there or elsewhere. The team at Lafite Rothschild produces less classy Los Vascos wines in Chile; the inexpensive Robert Mondavi Woodbridge wines bear no relation to the quality of the Mondavi Reserve wines from Napa.

- The fact that there is a château on a wine label has no bearing on the quality of the contents. Nor does the boast that the wine is bottled at that château.

- Nineteenth-century medals look pretty on a label but they say nothing about the quality of the 20th- or 21st-century stuff in the bottle.

- Price provides some guidance to a wine's quality: a very expensive bottle may be appalling, but it's unlikely that a very cheap one will be better than basic.

## Tasting

Wine tasting is surrounded by mystery and mystique, but it shouldn't be. All it really consists of is paying attention to the stuff in the glass, whether you're in the formal environment of a wine tasting or

drinking the house white in your local bar. The key questions are: do you like the wine? And is it a good example of what it claims to be? Champagne costs a lot more than basic Spanish Cava, so it should taste recognizably different. Some do, some don't.

**See** The look of a wine can tell you a lot. Assuming that it isn't cloudy (if it is, send it back), it will reveal its age and hint at the grape and origin. Some grapes, like Burgundy's Pinot Noir, make naturally paler wines than, say, Bordeaux's Cabernet Sauvignon; wines from warmer regions have deeper colours. Tilt the glass away from you over a piece of white paper and look at the rim of the liquid. The more watery and brown it is, the older the wine (Beaujolais Nouveau will be pure violet).

**Swirl** Vigorously swirl the wine around the glass for a moment or so to release any reluctant and characteristic smells.

**Sniff** You sniff a wine before tasting it for the same reason that you sniff a carton of milk before pouring its contents into coffee. The smell can tell you more about a wine than anything else. If you find this hard to believe, try tasting anything while holding your nose or while you've got a cold. When sniffing, take one long sniff or a few brief ones. Concentrate on whether the wine seems fresh and clean, and on any smells that indicate how it is likely to taste.

What are your first impressions? Is the wine fruity and, if so, which fruit does it remind you of? Does it have the vanilla smell of a wine that has been fermented and/or matured in new oak barrels? Is it spicy? Or herbaceous? Sweet or dry? Rich or lean?

**Sip** Take a small mouthful and – this takes practice – suck air between your teeth and through the liquid. Look in a mirror while you're doing this: if your mouth looks like a cat's bottom and sounds like a child trying to suck the last few drops of Coke through a straw, then you're doing it right. Hold the wine in your mouth for a little longer to release as much of its flavour as possible. Focus on the flavour. Ask yourself the same questions about whether it tastes sweet, dry, fruity, spicy, herbaceous. Is there just one flavour, or do several contribute to a 'complex' overall effect?

Now concentrate on the texture of the wine. Some – like Chardonnay – are mouth-coatingly buttery, while others – like Gewürztraminer – are almost oily. Muscadet is a good example of a wine with a texture that is closer to that of water.

Reds, too, vary in texture; some seem tough and tannic enough to make the inside of one cheek want to kiss the inside of the other. Traditionalists rightly claim tannin is necessary for a wine's longevity, but modern winemakers distinguish between the harsh tannin and the 'fine' (non-aggressive) tannin to be found in wine carefully made from ripe grapes. A modern Bordeaux often has as much tannin as old-fashioned examples – but is far easier to taste and drink.

**Spit** The only reason to spit a wine out – unless it is actively repellent – is simply to remain upright at the end of a lengthy tasting. If all you are interested in is the taste, not spitting is an indulgence; you should have had 90 per cent of the flavour while the wine was in your mouth. Pause for a moment or two after spitting the wine out. Is the flavour still there? How does what you are experiencing now compare with the taste you had in your mouth? Some wines have an unpleasant aftertaste; others have flavours that linger deliciously in the mouth.

## Should I send it back?

Wines are subject to all kinds of faults, though far less than they were even as recently as a decade ago.

**Acid** All wines, like all fruit and vegetables, contain a certain amount of acidity. Without it they would taste flabby and dull and go very stale very quickly. Wines made from unripe or overcropped grapes will, however, taste unpalatably 'green', like unripe apples or plums – or like chewing stalky leaves or grass.

**Bitter** Bitterness is quite different. On occasion, especially in Italy, a touch of bitterness may even be an integral part of a wine's char

## Tasting notes

### A way with words

Unfortunately, there's no alternative to returning to the thorny question of the language you are going to use to describe your impressions.

When Washington Irving visited Bordeaux 170 years ago, he noted that Château Margaux was "a wine of fine flavour – but not of equal body". Lafite on the other hand had "less flavour than the former but more body – an equality of flavour and body". Latour, well, that had "more body than flavour." Irving may have been a great writer, but he was evidently not the ideal person to describe the individual flavours of great Bordeaux.

Michelangelo was more poetic, writing that the wine of San Gimignano "kisses, licks, bites, thrusts, and stings...". Modern pundits say wines have "gobs of fruit" and taste of "kumquats and suede". Each country and generation comes up with its own vocabulary. Some descriptions, s uch as the likening to gooseberry of wines made from Sauvignon Blanc, can be justified by scientific analysis, which confirms that the same aromatic chemical compound is found in the fruit and wine.

Then there are straightforward descriptions. Wines can be 'fresh' or 'stale', 'clean' or 'dirty'. If they are acidic, or overly full of tannin, they will be 'hard'; a 'soft' wine, by contrast, might be easier to drink, but boring.

There are other less evocative terms. While a watery wine is 'dilute' or 'thin', a subtle one is 'elegant'. A red or white whose flavour is hard to discern is described as 'dumb'. Whatever the style of a wine, it should have 'balance'. A sweet white, for example, needs enough acidity to keep it from cloying. No one will enjoy a wine that is too fruity, too dry, too oaky, or too anything for long.

The flavour that lingers in your mouth long after you have swallowed or spat it out is known as the 'finish'. Wines whose flavour – pleasant or unpleasant – hangs around, are 'long'; those whose flavour disappears quickly are "short".

Finally, there is 'complex', the word that is used to justify why one wine costs 10 times more than another. A complex wine is like a well-scored symphony, while a simpler one could be compared to a melody picked out on a single instrument.

acter, as in the case of Amarone. Of course, it should be born in mind that the Italians like Campari, too.

⊗ **Brettanomyces (Brett)** The recent trend in making softer, richer wines and not filtering them before bottling to avoid removing flavour has provided ideal conditions for a bacterial infection to develop in red wines and to spread across the globe, though with varying degrees of severity. At its worst it makes wines smell of the floor of a stables; other descriptors include 'Band Aid' and 'mousey'. Wines with this condition, which can grow worse in the bottle, are beyond salvation but low-level Brett may add to a wine's interest.

⊗ **Cloudy** Wine should be transparent. The only excuse for cloudiness is in a wine like an old Burgundy whose deposit has been shaken up.

⊗ **Corked** Ignore any cork crumbs you may find floating on the surface of a wine. Genuinely corked wines have a musty smell and flavour that comes from mouldy corks. All corked wines become nastier with exposure to air. Around 5% of wines, irrespective of their price, are corked. Screwcaps are a better idea.

⊗ **Crystals** Not a fault, but people often think there is something wrong with a white wine if there is a layer of fine white crystals at the bottom of the bottle. These are just tartrates that precipitate naturally.

⊗ **Maderized/Oxidized** Madeira is fortified wine that has been intentionally exposed to the air and heated in a special oven. Maderized wine is stale, unfortified stuff that has been accidentally subjected to warmth and air. Oxidized is a broader term, referring to wine that has been exposed to the air or made from grapes that have cooked in the sun. The taste is reminiscent of poor sherry or vinegar. Anyone with experience of drinking wine in tropical countries will have encountered wines like this, because air-conditioned trucks and warehouses are far too rarely used for wine. However, it is also worth noting that cynical French producers have been known to send wine they cannot sell elsewhere to customers in Africa, Asia and the Caribbean, on the basis that no one will notice.

⊗ **Sulphur ($SO_2$/$H_2S$)** Sulphur dioxide is routinely used as a protection against bacteria that would oxidize (qv) a wine. In excess, sulphur dioxide may make you cough or sneeze. Worse, though, is hydrogen sulphide and mercaptans, its associated sulphur compounds, which are created when sulphur dioxide combines with wine. Wines with hydrogen sulphide smell of rotten eggs, while mercaptans may reek of rancid garlic or burning rubber. Aeration or popping a copper coin in your glass may clear up these characteristics.

⊗ **Vinegary/Volatile** Volatile acidity is present in all wines. In excess, however – usually the result of careless winemaking or bad shipping or storage – it tastes downright vinegary.

# Food and wine



One of the most daunting aspects of wine has always been the traditional obsession with serving precisely the right wine with any particular dish: of only ever drinking red with meat and white with fish or shellfish. Travelling to wine regions rapidly reveals how wrong these rules can be. In Portugal, for example, fishermen love to wash down their sardines and salt cod with a glass or two of harsh red wine. In Burgundy they even poach fish in their local red.

On the other hand, the idea that a platter of cheese needs a bottle of red wine can be trashed in an instant. Just take a mouthful of red Bordeaux immediately after eating a little goat's cheese or brie. The wine will taste metallic and unpleasant because the creaminess of the cheese reacts badly with the tannin – the toughness – in the wine. A dry white would be far more successful (its acidity would cut through the fat), while the Bordeaux would be shown at its best alongside a harder, stronger cheese. If you don't want to offer a range of wines, try sticking to one or two cheeses that really will complement the stuff in the glass.

Don't take anything for granted. Rare beef and red Bordeaux surprisingly fails the test of an objective tasting. The protein of the meat somehow makes all but the fruitiest wines taste tougher. If you're looking for a perfect partner for beef, uncork a Burgundy. If it's the Bordeaux that takes precedence, you'd be far better off with lamb.

The difference between an ideal and a passable food-and-wine combination can be very subtle. Most of us have after all happily quaffed red Bordeaux with our steak, but just as an avid cook will tinker with a recipe until it is just right, there's a lot to be said for making the occasional effort to find a pairing of dish and wine that really works. Some foods and wines simply seem to bring out the best in each other.

## A sense of balance

There is no real mystery about the business of matching food and wine. Some flavours and textures are compatible, and some are not. Strawberry mousse is not really delicious with chicken casserole, but apple sauce can do wonders for roast pork. The key to spotting which relationships are marriages made in heaven, and which have the fickleness of Hollywood romances, lies in identifying the dominant characteristics of the contents of both the plate and the glass. Then, learn by experience which are likely to complement each other, either through their similarities or through their differences.

## Likely combinations

It is not difficult to define particular types of food and wine, and to guess how they are likely to get along. A buttery sauce is happier with something tangily acidic, like a crisp Sauvignon Blanc, rather than a rich, buttery Chardonnay. A subtly poached fish won't appreciate a fruit-packed New World white, and you won't do pheasant pie any favours by ordering a delicate red.

## What to avoid

Some foods and their characteristics, though, make life difficult for almost any drink. Sweetness, for example, in a fruity sauce served with a savoury dish seems to strip some of the fruitier flavours out of a wine. This may not matter if the stuff in your glass is a blackcurranty New World Cabernet Sauvignon, but it's bad news if it is a bone-dry white or a tough red with little fruit to spare. Cream is tricky, too. Try fresh strawberries with Champagne – delicious; now add a little whipped cream to the equation and you'll spoil the flavour. Creamy and buttery sauces can have the same effect on a wine and call for a similarly creamy white – or, alternatively, a fresh, zippy one to cut through the fattiness.

Spices are very problematic for wine – largely due to the physical sensation of eating them rather than any particular flavour. A wine may not seem particularly nasty after a mouthful of chilli sauce; it will simply lose its fruity flavour and taste of nothing at all – which, in the case of a fine red seems a pity. The way a tannic red dries out the mouth will also accentuate the heat of the spice. The ideal wine for most Westerners to drink with any spicy dish would be a light, possibly slightly sweet white or a light, juicy red. Chinese palates often react differently to these combinations, however. They like the burning effect of the chilli and see no point in trying to put out the fire with white wine.

## Always worth a try

Some condiments actually bring out the best in wines. A little freshly ground pepper on your meat or pasta can accentuate the flavour of a wine, just as it can with a sauce. Squeezing fresh lemon onto your fish will reduce the apparent acidity of a white wine – a useful tip if you have inadvertently bought a tooth-strippingly dry Muscadet. And, just as lemon can help to liven up a dull sauce, it will do the same for a dull white wine, such as a basic Burgundy or a Soave, by neutralizing the acidity and allowing other flavours to make themselves apparent. Mustard performs a similar miracle when it is eaten with beef, somehow nullifying the effect of the meat protein on the wine.

## Marriage guidance

In the following pages, there are suggested wines to go with a wide range of dishes and ingredients, taking the dominant flavour as the key point. Don't treat any of this advice as gospel – use it instead as a launchpad for your own food and wine experiments.

And, if no wine seems to taste just right, don't be too surprised. Heretical as it may seem, some dishes are actually more enjoyable with other drinks. The vinegar that is a fundamental part of a good relish, for example, will do no wine a favour. Even avid wine lovers might well find beer a far more pleasurable accompaniment.

# Food list

## Beef and veal

**Beef stew** Pomerol or St. Emilion, good Northern Rhône like Crozes Hermitage, Shiraz or Pinot Noir from the New World.

**Beef stroganoff** Tough, beefy reds like Amarone, Brunello di Montalcino, Barolo, Côte Rôtie, or really ripe Zinfandel.

**Beef wellington** Top Burgundy, Châteauneuf-du-Pape.

**Blanquette de Veau** Aromatic, spicy whites from Alsace or from the Northern Rhône.

**Boeuf bourguignon** Australian Bordeaux-style Barolo, or other robust reds with sweet fruit

**Boiled beef and carrots** Bordeaux Rouge, Valpolicella Classico, Australian Shiraz.

**Bresaola (air-dried beef)** Beaujolais, Barbera, and tasty reds from the Languedoc.

**Calves' liver** Good Italian Cabernet, Merlot, or mature Chianti.

**Carpaccio of beef** Chardonnay, Champagne, Cabernet Franc and Pomerol.

**Corned beef** Loire reds from Gamay or Cabernet Franc.

**Creole-style beef** Cheap southern Rhône reds or Côtes du Rhône, Zinfandel.

**Hamburger** Zinfandel or country reds from Italy or France, eg, Corbières.

**Hungarian goulash** East European reds – Bulgarian Cabernet or Mavrud and Hungarian Kadarka – or Australian Shiraz.

**Meatballs** Spicy rich Rhône reds, Zinfandel, Pinotage and Portuguese reds.

**Oxtail** Australian Cabernet, good Bordeaux.

**Pastrami** Zinfandel, good Bardolino, light Côtes du Rhône.

**Rare chargrilled beef** Something sweetly ripe and flavoursome, but not too tannic. Try Chilean Merlot.

**Roast beef** Côte Rôtie, good Burgundy.

**Roast veal** Light, Italian whites, or fairly light reds – Spanish or Loire; St. Emilion.

**Steak** Pinot Noir and Merlot from the New World; Australian Shiraz; Châteauneuf-du-Pape; good, ripe Burgundy.

**Steak and kidney pie/pudding** Bordeaux, Australian Cabernet Sauvignon, southern Rhône reds or Rioja.

**Steak au poivre** Cabernet Sauvignon, Chianti, Rhône reds, Shiraz or Rioja.

**Steak tartare** Bourgogne Blanc; Beaujolais; Bardolino; or, traditionally, vodka.

**Steak with Dijon mustard** Bordeaux, Cabernet Sauvignon from the New World, or Australian Shiraz.

## Cheese

**Brie** Sancerre or New Zealand Sauvignon Blanc.

**Camembert** Dry Sauvignon Blanc or unoaked Chablis.

**Cream cheese, crème fraîche, mozzarella, mascarpone** Fresh light dry whites – Frascati, Pinot Grigio.

**Goat's cheese** Sancerre, New World Sauvignon, Pinot Blanc.

**Parmesan** Salice Salentino, Valpolicella.

**Roquefort** The classic match is Sauternes or Barsac, but almost any full-flavoured, botrytized sweet wine will be a good partner for strong, creamy, blue cheese.

**Stilton** Tawny port.

## Chicken and poultry

**Barbecued chicken** Rich and tasty white, Chardonnay.

**Chicken casserole** Mid-weight Rhône, such as Crozes-Hermitage or Lirac.

**Chicken chasseur** Off-dry Riesling.

**Chicken kiev** Chablis, Aligoté, or Italian dry white.

**Chicken liver pâté** Softly fruity, fairly light reds including Beaujolais, Italian Cabernet or Merlot plus Vouvray Moelleux, Monbazillac, or Amontillado sherry.

**Chicken pie** White Bordeaux, simple Chardonnay, or else a light Italian white.

**Chicken vol-au-vents** White Bordeaux.

**Chicken with ginger** White Rhône, Gewürztraminer.

**Confit de canard** Alsace Pinot Gris or a crisp red like Barbera.

**Cock-a-leekie** Dry New World white, simple red Rhône.

**Confit d'Oie** Best Sauternes, Monbazillac.

**Coq au vin** Shiraz-based New World reds, red Burgundy.

**Curried chicken** Gewürztraminer, dry white Loire, fresh Chinon.

**Devilled chicken** Australian Shiraz.

**Duck** Pinot Noir from Burgundy, California, or Oregon, or off-dry German Riesling.

**Duck pâté** Chianti or other juicy herby red, Amontillado sherry.

**Foie gras** Best Sauternes, Monbazillac.

**Foie gras de canard** Champagne, late harvest Gewürztraminer or Riesling, Sauternes.

**Fricassée** Unoaked Chardonnay.

**Goose** A good Rhône red like Hermitage, Côte Rôtie, or a crisp Barbera; Pinot Noir from

 Burgundy, New Zealand, Chile, California or Oregon; or even off-dry German Riesling.

**Lemon chicken** Muscadet, Chablis, or basic Bourgogne Blanc.

**Peking duck** Rice wine, Alsace Riesling, Pinot Gris.

**Roast duck** Fruity reds like Australian Cabernet, a ripe Nebbiolo, or Zinfandel.

**Roast duck with orange sauce** Loire red or a sweet white like Vouvray demi-sec.

**Smoked duck** California Chardonnay or Fumé Blanc.

**Roast/grilled chicken** Reds or whites, though nothing too heavy – Burgundy is good, as is Barbera, though Soave will do just as well.

**Roast/grilled chicken with garlic** Oaky Chardonnay or red Rioja.

**Roast/grilled chicken with tarragon** Dry Chenin Blanc, Vouvray, dry Chenin.

**Roast turkey** Beaujolais, light Burgundy, and rich or off-dry whites.

**Roast turkey with chestnut stuffing** Rhône, Merlot, or mature Burgundy.

**Saltimbocca (with mozzarella and ham)** Flavoursome, dry Italian whites – Lugana, Bianco di Custoza, Orvieto.

**Smoked chicken** Oaky Chardonnay, Australian Marsanne, or Fumé Blanc.

**Southern fried chicken** White Bordeaux, Muscadet, Barbera, light Zinfandel.

## Desserts

**Apple pie or strudel** Austrian off-dry white

**Apricot** Late harvest Sémillon or Riesling, Jurançon Moelleux.

**Baklava** Moscatel de Setúbal.

**Banoffee pie** Sweet Tokaji.

**Blackcurrant cheesecake** Sweet, grapey dessert wines.

**Blackcurrant mousse** Sweet sparkling wines.

**Black forest gâteau** Fortified Muscat, Schnapps, or Kirsch.

**Blueberry pie** Tokaji (6 Puttonyos), late harvest Semillon or Sauvignon.

**Bread and butter pudding** Barsac or Sauternes, Monbazillac, Jurançon. Muscat de Beaumes de Venise or Australian Orange Muscat.

**Caramelized oranges** Asti, Sauternes, or Muscat de Beaumes de Venise.

**Cherry** Valpolicella, Recioto della Valpolicella, Dolcetto.

**Christmas pudding** Australian Liqueur Muscat, tawny port, rich (sweet) Champagne, Tokaji.

**Chocolate** Orange Muscat, Moscatel de Valencia.

**Chocolate cake** Beaumes de Venise, Bual or Malmsey Madeira, Orange Muscat, sweet German, or fine Champagne.

**Chocolate profiteroles with cream** Muscat de Rivesaltes.

**Coffee cake** Asti.

**Coffee mousse** Asti, Liqueur Muscat.

**Crème brûlée** Jurançon Moelleux, Tokaji.

**Crème caramel** Muscat or Gewürztraminer Vendange Tardive.

**Crêpe suzette** Asti, Orange Muscat, Champagne cocktails.

**Dark chocolate mousse** Sweet Black Muscat or other Muscat-based wines.

**Fig** Liqueur Muscat.

**Fresh fruit salad** Moscato d'Asti, Riesling Beerenauslese, or Vouvray Moelleux.

**Goosberry fool** Quarts de Chaume.

**Gooseberry pie** Sweet Madeira, Austrian Trockenbeerenauslese.

**Grapefruit** Sweet Madeira or sherry.

**Ice cream (vanilla)** Try Marsala, Australian Liqueur Muscat, Muscadelle, or Pedro Ximénez sherry.

**Lemon cheesecake** Moscato d'Asti.

**Lemon sorbet** Late harvest Sémillon or sweet Tokaji.

**Lime** Australian Verdelho, Grüner Veltliner, Furmint.

**Milk chocolate mousse** Moscato d'Asti.

**Mango** Best eaten in the bathtub with a friend and a bottle of Champagne! Otherwise, go for Asti or Moscato.

**Melon** Despite its apparently innocent, juicy sweetness, melon can be very unfriendly to most wines. Try tawny port, sweet Madeira or sherry, Quarts de Chaume, late harvest Riesling.

**Nectarine** Sweet German Riesling.

**Orange sorbet** Moscato or sweet Tokaji.

**Orange zest** Dry Muscat, Amontillado sherry.

**Peach** Sweet German Riesling.

**Plum pie** Trockenbeerenauslese, Côteaux du Layon.

**Prunes** Australian, late harvest Semillon.

**Quince** Lugana.

**Raspberries** New World, late harvest Riesling; Champagne; Beaujolais; demi-sec Champagne.

**Rhubarb pie** Moscato d'Asti, Alsace, German or Austrian late harvest Riesling.

**Rice pudding** Monbazillac, sweet Muscat, Asti, or California Orange Muscat or Brown Brothers Orange Muscat & Flora

**Sorbet** Like ice cream, these can be too cold/sweet for most wines. Try Australian fortified Muscats.

**Summer pudding** Late harvest Riesling – German or Alsace.

**Strawberries (no cream)** Surprisingly, red Rioja, Burgundy (or other young Pinot Noir). More conventionally, sweet Muscats or fizzy Moscato.

**Strawberries and cream** Vouvray Moelleux, Monbazillac

**Strawberry mousse** Sweet or fortified Muscat.

**Tiramisu** Sweet fortified Muscat, Vin Santo, Torcolato.

**Toffee** Moscatel de Setúbal, Eiswein.

**Zabaglione** Rich sweet Marsala, Australian Liqueur Muscat, or a fortified French Muscat.

## Game

**Cold game** Fruity Northern Italian reds – Barbera or Dolcetto – good Beaujolais or light Burgundy.

**Game pie** Beefy reds, Southern French, Rhône, Australian Shiraz.

**Guinea fowl** Old Burgundy, Cornas, Gamay de Touraine, St. Emilion.

**Jugged hare** Argentinian Malbec Italians like Amarone, Barolo, and Barbaresco; inky reds from Bandol or the Rhône.

**Pheasant** Top-class, red Burgundy; good American Pinot Noir; mature Hermitage

**Pheasant casserole** Top class, red Burgundy; mature Hermitage.

**Pheasant pâté** Côtes du Rhône, Alsace Pinot Blanc.

**Quail** Light, red Burgundy; full-flavoured, white Spanish wines.

**Rabbit casserole** Red Burgundy, New World Pinot Noir, or mature Châteauneuf-du-Pape.

**Rabbit in cider** Muscadet, demi-sec Vouvray, cider, or Calvados.

**Roast game** Big reds, Brunello di Montalcino, old Barolo, good Burgundy.

**Roast grouse** Hermitage, Côte Rôtie, robust Burgundy, or good mature red Bordeaux.

**Roast partridge** Australian Shiraz, Gevrey-Chambertin, Pomerol, or St. Emilion.

**Roast rabbit** Tasty, simple, young Rhône – red, white, or rosé.

**Warm pigeon breasts on salad** Merlot-based Bordeaux or Cabernet Rosé.

**Well-hung game** Old Barolo or Barbaresco, mature Hermitage, Côte Rôtie or Châteauneuf-du-Pape, fine Burgundy.

**Venison** Pinotage; rich red Rhône; mature Burgundy; earthy, Italian reds.

## Lamb

**Casserole** Rich and warm Cabernet-based reds from France, Negroamaro or California Zinfandel.

**Cutlets or chops** Cru Bourgeois Bordeaux, Chilean Cabernet.

**Haggis** Beaujolais, Côtes du Rhône, Côtes du Roussillon, Spanish reds, malt whisky.

**Irish stew** A good simple South American or Eastern European Cabernet works best.

**Kabobs** Modern (fruity) Greek reds or sweetly ripe Australian Cabernet/Shiraz.

**Kleftiko (lamb shanks baked with thyme)** Greek red from Nemea, Beaujolais, light Cabernet Sauvignon.

**Lancashire hotpot** Robust country red – Cahors, Fitou.

**Moussaka** Brambly northern Italian reds (Barbera, Dolcetto, etc), Beaujolais, Pinotage, Zinfandel, or try some good Greek wine from a modern producer.

**Roast lamb with thyme** Try a New Zealand Cabernet Sauvignon or Bourgeuil.

**Shepherd's pie** Barbera, Cabernet Sauvignon, Minervois, Zinfandel, Beaujolais.

## Pork

**Bacon** Rich Pinot Gris or Alsace Riesling.

**Bacon with marinated scallops** Fino sherry or mature Riesling, Shiraz-based Australians, Zinfandel from the US, or a heavy Cape red.

**Boiled/roasted/grilled/fried ham** Beaujolais-Villages, Gamay de Touraine, slightly sweet German white, Tuscan red, lightish Cabernet (eg, Chilean), Alsace Pinot Gris, or Muscat.

**Braised ham with lentils** Light, fruity Beaujolais; Côtes du Rhône; Rioja or Navarra Crianza.

**Spare ribs with barbecue sauce** Fruity Australian Shiraz, Grenache, or Zinfandel; spicy Côtes du Rhône from a ripe vintage; or an off-dry white.

**Cassoulet** Serious white Rhône, Marsanne, or Roussanne; or reds including Grenache and Syrah from the Rhône, berryish, Italian reds, or Zinfandel.

**Honey-roast ham** Riesling.

**Liver and bacon** Côtes du Rhône, Zinfandel, Pinotage.

**Oak-smoked ham** Oaky Spanish reds.

**Pork and sage sausages** Barbera, Côtes du Rhône.

**Parma ham (prosciutto)** Try a dry Lambrusco, Tempranillo Joven, or Gamay de Touraine.

**Pork casserole** Mid-weight, earthy reds like Minervois, Navarra, or Montepulciano d'Abruzzo.

**Pork pie** Spicy reds, Shiraz, Grenache.

**Pork rillettes** Pinot Blanc d'Alsace, Menetou-Salon Rouge.

**Pork sausages** Spicy Rhône reds, Barbera.

**Pork spare ribs** Zinfandel, Australian Shiraz.

**Pork with prunes** Cahors, mature Chinon, or other Loire red, or rich, southern French wine such as Corbières, Minervois, or Faugères.

**Roast pork** Rioja reserva, New World Pinot Noir, dry Vouvray.

**Wienerschnitzel** Austrian Grüner Veltliner or Alsace or Hungarian Pinot Blanc.

## Seafood and fish

**Bouillabaisse** Red or white Côtes du Rhône, dry rosé or peppery dry white from Provence, California Fumé Blanc, Marsanne, or Verdicchio.

**Bream (freshwater)** Chablis or other unoaked Chardonnay.

**Bream (sea)** White Rhône, Sancerre.

**Carp** Franken Sylvaner, dry Jurançon, Hungarian Furmint.

**Carpaccio of salmon** Cabernet Franc, Chardonnay, Australian reds, red Loire, Portuguese reds, Puligny-Montrachet.

**Caviar** Champagne or chilled vodka.

**Clams** Chablis or Sauvignon Blanc.

**Cockles** Muscadet, Gros Plant, Aligoté, dry Vinho Verde.

**Cod** Unoaked Chardonnay; good, white Burgundy; dry Loire Chenin.

**Coquilles St Jacques** White Burgundy.

**Crab** Chablis, Sauvignon Blanc, New World Chardonnay.

**Dover sole** Sancerre, good Chablis, unoaked Chardonnay.

**Fish and chips** Most fairly simple, crisply acidic dry whites or maybe a rosé or Champagne (see cod). Go easy with the vinegar

**Fish cakes** White Bordeaux, Chilean Chardonnay.

**Fish pie** California Chardonnay, Alsace Pinot Gris, Sauvignon Blanc.

**Fish soup** Manzanilla, Chablis, Muscadet.

**Freshwater Crayfish** South African Sauvignon, Meursault.

**Fresh herrings** Sauvignon Blanc, Muscadet, Frascati, or cider.

**Grilled salmon** White Rhône (especially Viognier).

**Haddock** White Bordeaux, Chardonnay, Pinot Blanc, single-vineyard Soave, Australian unoaked Semillon.

**Hake** Soave, Sauvignon Blanc.

**Halibut** White Bordeaux, Muscadet.

**John dory** Good, white Burgundy or Australian Chardonnay.

**Kedgeree** Aligoté, crisp Sauvignon.

**Langoustine** Muscadet, Soave, South African Sauvignon.

**Lemon sole** Chardonnay.

**Lobster** Good white Burgundy.

**Mackerel** With Vinho Verde, Albariño, Sancerre, and New Zealand Sauvignon.

**Monkfish** A light, fruity red such as Bardolino, Valpolicella, La Mancha Joven, or most Chardonnays.

**Moules marinières** Bordeaux Blanc or Muscadet Sur Lie.

**New Zealand green-lipped mussels** New Zealand Sauvignon Blanc

**Octopus** Rueda white or a fresh, modern Greek white.

**Oysters** Champagne; Chablis; or other crisp, dry white.

**Pike** Eastern European white.

**Plaice** White Burgundy, South American Chardonnay, Sauvignon Blanc.

**Poached salmon** Chablis; good, white Burgundy; other Chardonnay; Alsace Muscat; white Bordeaux.

**Prawns** White Bordeaux; dry, Australian Riesling; Gavi.

**Red mullet** Dry rosé, California, Washington or Australian Chardonnay.

**Roll-mop herring** Savoie, dry Vinho Verde, Grüner Veltliner, Akvavit, cold lager.

**Salmon trout** Light Pinot Noir from the Loire, New Zealand; good, dry, unoaked Chardonnay, Chablis, etc.

**Salt cod (bacalhão de gomes)** Classically Portuguese red or white – Vinho Verde or Bairrada reds.

**Sardines** Muscadet, Vinho Verde, light and fruity reds such as Loire Gamay.

**Scallops** Chablis and other unoaked Chardonnay.

**Sea bass** Good white Burgundy.

**Seafood salad** Soave, Pinot Grigio, Muscadet, or a lightly oaked Chardonnay.

**Shrimps** Albariño, Sancerre, New World Sauvignon, Arnesis.

**Skate** Bordeaux white, Côtes de Gascogne, Pinot Bianco.

**Smoked eel** Pale, dry sherry; simple, fresh white Burgundy.

**Smoked haddock** Fino sherry or oaky Chardonnay.

**Smoked mackerel** Bourgogne Aligoté, Alsace Pinot Gris.

**Smoked salmon** Chablis, Alsace Pinot Gris, white Bordeaux, Hunter Semillon.

**Smoked trout** Bourgogne Aligoté, Gewürztraminer, Pinot Gris.

**Snapper** Australian or South African, dry white.

**Sprats** Muscadet, Vinho Verde.

**Squid** Gamay de Touraine; Greek, Spanish, or Italian white.

**Sushi** Saké.

**Tapenade** Dry sherry or Madeira.

**Thai Prawns** Gewürztraminer; dry, aromatic Riesling; or New Zealand Sauvignon Blanc.

**Trout** Pinot Blanc, Chablis.

**Tuna** Alsace Pinot Gris, Australian Chardonnay, Beaujolais.

**Turbot** Best white Burgundy, top California or Australian Chardonnay.

**Whitebait** Fino sherry, Spanish red/white (Albariño, Garnacha, Tempranillo), Soave.

## Spicy food

**Beef in peanut curry** New World Chardonnay; spicy, aromatic white Rhône.

**Cajun spices** Beaujolais Crus.

**Chilli** Cheap wine or cold beer.

**Chilli con carne** Robust fruity reds, Beaujolais Crus, Barbera or Valpolicella, spicy reds like Zinfandel or Pinotage.

**Chinese (general)** Aromatic white – Gewürztraminer, Pinot Gris, English.

**Chorizo (sausage)** Red or white Rioja, Navarra, Manzanilla sherry, Beaujolais, or Zinfandel.

**Coronation chicken** Gewürztraminer; dry, aromatic English wine; or a fresh Chinon.

**Goulash** Eastern European red like Bulgarian Cabernet or Mavrud, Hungarian Kadarka, or Australian Shiraz.

**Gumbo** Zinfandel or maybe beer.

**Indian (general)** Gewürztraminer (spicy dishes), New World Chardonnay (creamy/yogurt dishes), New Zealand Sauvignon Blanc (Tandoori).

**Tandoori chicken** White Bordeaux, New Zealand Sauvignon Blanc.

**Teriyaki** Spicy reds like Zinfandel or Portuguese reds.

**Thai green chicken curry** Big New World whites or dry Pinot Blanc from Alsace.

**Spring rolls** Pinot Gris, Gewürztraminer, or other aromatic whites.

**Sweet and sour dishes (general)** Gewürztraminer, Sauvignon Blanc (unoaked), or beer.

**Szechuan-style pork** Dry, aromatic whites; Alsace Pinot Gris; Riesling; Grenache rosé; beer.

## Vegetables

**Artichoke** White Rhône.

**Avocado vinaigrette** Unoaked Chardonnay, Chablis.

**Baked beans** Light Zinfandel, Beaujolais, dry rosé, or beer.

**Borscht** Rich, dry Alsace Pinot Gris; Pinot Blanc; or Italian Pinot Grigio.

**Broccoli and cheese soup** Slightly sweet sherry – Amontillado or Oloroso.

**Caramelized onions** Shiraz-based Australians, Priorat, Zinfandel or a good Pinotage.

**Carrot and coriander soup** Aromatic, dry Muscat; Argentinian Torrontes.

**Cauliflower cheese** Fresh crisp Côtes de Gascogne white; Pinot Grigio; softly plummy Chilean Merlot; or young, unoaked Rioja.

**Coconut (milk)** California Chardonnay.

**Corn on the cob** Light, fruity whites – German Riesling.

**Courgette gratin** Good dry Chenin from Vouvray or South Africa.

**Couscous** Spicy Shiraz, North African reds, or earthy Southern French Minervois.

**Fennel** Sauvignon Blanc.

**French onion soup** Sancerre or dry, unoaked Sauvignon Blanc; Aligoté; white Bordeaux.

**Houmous** French dry whites, Retsina, Vinho Verde.

**Lentils** Earthy country wines, Côtes du Rhône.

**Mushroom** Merlot-based reds, good Northern Rhône, top Piedmontese reds.

**Peppers (fresh green, red)** New Zealand Cabernet, Loire reds, crisp Sauvignon Blanc, Beaujolais, Tuscan red.

**Peppers (yellow)** Fruity, Italian reds – Valpolicella, etc.

**Pesto sauce** New Zealand Sauvignon Blanc, Valpolicella.

**Ratatouille** Bulgarian red, Chianti, simple Rhône or Provence red, Portuguese reds, New Zealand Sauvignon Blanc.

**Rocket** Lugana, Pinot Blanc.

**Roasted and grilled vegetables** Light, juicy reds; Beaujolais; Sancerre; and Sauvignon Blanc. Unoaked or lightly oaked Chardonnay.

**Spinach** Pinot Grigio, Lugana.

**Stuffed aubergines** Beefy spicy reds like Bandol, Zinfandel, a good Southern Rhône or a full-bodied Italian.

**Stuffed cabbage** East European Cabernet.

**Vichyssoise** Dry whites, Chablis, Bordeaux Blanc.

# France

**Burgundy vineyards.**

## Wineries

1 Champagne Launois Père et Fils p41, map p41
2 Champagne Mailly Grand Cru p42, map p41
3 Mumm p42, map p41
4 Pommery p43, map p41
5 Domaine Weinbach p44
6 Château d'Arlay p46
7 Alex Gambal p49, map p49
8 Château de Chorey-les-Beaune p50, map49
9 Château de Meursault p50, map p49
10 Domaine Comte Senard p50, map p49
11 Olivier Leflaive ★ p52, map p49
12 Château de Fuissé p53
13 Cave de Tain p55
14 Cave de Cairanne p56
15 Domaine Saint Benoît p56
16 Château de l'Aumérade Cru Classé p58
17 Château de Selle p59
18 Château Vignelaure p59
19 Domaine Comte Abbatucci p59
20 Château l'Hospitalet p60
21 Patrick Reverdy p61
22 Mas des Tourelles p61
23 Château Smith Haut Lafitte p64, map p64
24 Château Giscours p64, map p64
25 Château Lanessan p65, map p64
26 Château Mouton-Rothschild p65, map p64
27 Château Prieuré-Lichine p65, map p64
28 Château Carsin p66, map p64
29 Château de Monbazillac p68
30 Château de Tiregand p68
31 Domaine Cauhapé p68
32 Les Vignerons de Buzet p69
33 Plaimont p69
34 Alphonse Mellot p70
35 Château Moncontour p72, map p70
36 Domaine de la Charmoise p72
37 Domaine des Baumard p73, map p70

# Introduction



If you had to choose just one country to visit for its wine and food, it would have to be France. Other nations have a growing range of delights to offer, but nowhere else has the chalk caves of Champagne, the fairy-tale castles of the Loire, the vertiginous slopes of the Rhône, the gentle hills of Beaujolais, the golden slopes of Burgundy, the châteaux of Bordeaux. France is all about variety and about regional individuality. The restrictive wine laws that prevent producers from boldly experimenting in the same way as their counterparts in Italy and Spain, let alone the New World, have, with a little help from local chauvinism, ensured that little villages and huge regions continue to offer styles of wine that are still entirely their own. But this tapestry of small and large appellations (with new ones being created all the time) and the tens of thousands of producers, each of whom annually comes up with his or her own variations on the local theme, inevitably makes for a very confusing picture. To make matters more complicated still, those variations are becoming more pronounced. Some Chablis winemakers believe that their region's wine should be unmarked by new oak; others differ. There are now Bordeaux châteaux that produce delicious wines with 14.5% alcohol, next door to neighbours who never like to exceed 13%. The essential thing to remember is that, while the appellation will hopefully give you some idea of the kind of wine you are likely to get, the most important part of any wine label, here as everywhere else in the world, is the name of the producer.

# Travel essentials



### Planning your trip

**Roissy-Charles de Gaulle** (CDG, www.adp.fr, www.aeroport.fr) near Paris is likely to be your port of entry if you fly into France from outside Europe. However, within Europe, there are also scheduled flights (as well as Air France domestic flights) to Paris-Orly (ORY), Strasbourg (for Alsace), Lyon (for Burgundy and the Rhône), Marseille (for the south of France), Toulouse (for southwest France) and Bordeaux. In addition, charter and low-cost airlines serve regional airports. Driving to France from other European countries is straightforward. Car ferry services run from the UK to ports in northern France, including Calais, from where you could reach Champagne or Alsace in about 2½ or 5½ hours respectively. Toll highways (*autoroutes*) are the fastest way of covering large distances. Alternatively, there are efficient direct rail services to France from most European countries. **Eurostar** (www.eurostar.com) runs from London Waterloo via the Channel Tunnel to Lille and Paris, with onward connections on the French rail network, **SNCF** (T 08-92 35 35 35, www.sncf.com). High-speed TGV trains are quick and efficient, taking just three hours to reach Bordeaux from Paris, for example. A Railpass or Euro Domino Pass (purchased before you arrive) will save you money on multiple journeys.

France is the largest country in western Europe, so don't be over-ambitious when deciding what to see. Each region has retained its own distinctive character – especially evident in its food and wine – so it is better to base yourself in one area, rather than zooming along the *autoroutes*, ticking off as many sights as possible. A weekend in **Paris** could be followed by a tour of **Champagne**, say, the most visitor-friendly wine region in France. With more time, continue east to **Alsace** or even cross the Rhine into Germany. Alternatively, head southwest from Paris to visit the **Loire's** chateaux, vineyards and historic towns. **Burgundy** is also within reach of the capital but you may choose instead to base yourself in the gastronomic hub of **Lyon**, from where you can explore both southern Burgundy and the **Rhône**. In winter, head east to the **Alps** to enjoy skiing by day, followed by hearty Savoyarde cooking and local wines. The **south of France** offers the glamour and crowds of the Mediterranean coast but also beautiful historic towns, such as Aix, Arles, Nímes, Avignon and Carcassone, and the wildlife of the Camargue. **Corsica** is accessible from here by boat. To the west **Bordeaux** is not only France's most important wine region but is also close to the surf beaches of the Atlantic coast. To the south are the **Pyrenees**, while inland you can explore the caves and gastronomy of the **Dordogne**. For further information on visiting France, refer to the official website, www.franceguide.com.

**France country code** → +33. **IDD code** → 00 (France Telecom; other numbers available). **Internet ID** → .fr. **Emergencies** → T112 (European emergency number).

→ Fact file

| | |
|---|---|
| **International flights** | Air France and all major international airlines to Paris-Charles de Gaulle. European services to Paris-Orly, Strasbourg, Lyon, Marseille, Toulouse, Bordeaux and regional airports. |
| **Entry requirements** | No visa required for citizens of EU member states, the USA, Australia, Canada and Japan. Valid passport required for all accept citizens of EU states with a valid national ID card. |
| **Currency** | Euro (€) |
| **Time zone** | GMT/UTC +1 |
| **Electricity** | 230 volts (50Hz). European plug with two circular pins. |
| **Licensing hours** | Bars stay open and serve alcohol until at least 0200. |
| **Minimum age** | 16 for wine and beer, 18 for spirits; not strictly enforced. |
| **Drink-drive restrictions** | 50mg of alcohol per 100ml of blood. |

### When to visit

Paradoxically, perhaps, the very best time to visit France's wine regions is when they look their worst – between November and March. During these cold months, winemakers have less work to do in the vines and fewer other visitors to deal with (apart from professional buyers who tend to come at this time of the year). Avoid late March

Schlossberg, Domaine Weinbach, Alsace.

and early April in Bordeaux because this is when chateau owners are busy pouring their youngest wines for potential *en primeur* (futures) buyers. Harvest time – usually late September and early October – should also be avoided throughout France. Wine seasons aside, spring offers the best sightseeing weather, with beach tourism picking up in May. The French take their annual five-week vacation from mid-July to the end of August, so the coast and other holiday areas will be crowded, while shops and restaurants in the half-deserted cities may be closed. The same happens during February and March.

## Wine tourism

France's winemakers often make little effort to encourage people who would like to get to know their wines better. While their New World counterparts in the Napa Valley, Margaret River and Marlborough offer open-all-day tasting rooms, gift shops, picnic areas, cafés, restaurants and cottages, far too many French wine producers offer tastings exclusively by appointment and in French only. Visits at lunchtime are unwelcome and some cellars may be less than willing to open their doors at weekends. Wine labels tend to be wilfully uninformative when it comes to grape varieties and even (in regions like Alsace and the Loire) the level of sweetness you are likely to encounter. In simple terms, the French model places far more onus on the consumer, who is expected to do some homework in advance. All of which helps to explain why tourists who happily make their way around Chilean wine regions (where New World attitudes apply) often join organized tours in France.

Some French regions definitely do tourism, better than others. Alsace and Champagne would get the highest marks, while the Médoc in Bordeaux would be right at the bottom of the class. Almost all offer the chance to taste a wide range of their wines if your visit happens to coincide with a seasonal festival. Otherwise, it is well worth looking for a regional Maison de Vins, which may offer samples of local wine.

## Sleeping

Hotels are officially graded into six categories from no stars to four-star luxury. Rates are charged per room and do not usually include breakfast. France's high-end hotels range from belle époque beauties on the Riviera to famous Parisian landmarks, modern designer complexes and chi-chi boutique hotels. For a taste of true French luxury, however, stay at one of the country's châteaux, particularly in the Loire; refer to www.chateaux-hotels.com or www.relais chateaux.com. Lower-priced options in towns include independent hotels and standard chains but, if you're travelling between November and March, you should check out www.bon-week-end-en-villes.com, which offers two nights for the price of one in numerous urban hotels (excluding Paris). In more rural areas, look out for smaller, family-run Logis de France hotels (www.logis-de-france.com), which usually have their own restaurants, and B&Bs, known as *chambres d'hôte*. The most reliable *chambres d'hôte* are affiliated to and accredited by **Gîtes de France** (www.gîtes-de-france.fr) and are often located on farms or vineyards. Gîtes de France also offers popular self-catering cottages, houses and apartments, which are great if you want to base yourself in one region.

## Eating

One of the joys of visiting France is the close relationship that still exists between its regional foods and drinks. You never need to look far to find a restaurant serving dishes with a genuine historical link to the area in which they are going to be enjoyed. **Normandy** is the place to find seafood galore and dishes prepared with generous amounts of cream. Rouen is famous for its duck dishes and apples are widely used. This is not wine country – cider, calvados and beer are more appropriate – but Loire wines made from Chenin Blanc are great with those apples. Camembert, by the way – like brie and all other high-fat, creamy, runny cheeses – is a rotten partner for red wine. **Brittany** follows a similar pattern, though with more pancakes, lamb (good with Loire Cabernet Franc wines such as Chinon) and artichokes, which do no favours to any kind of wine.

The **Loire** is all about fish – both from the sea, close to the Muscadet vineyards – and from the river in Anjou, Vouvray, Sancerre and Pouilly Fumé. Freshness is the keynote of Loire wines, both red and white, and they go brilliantly with creamy dishes and the goat's cheeses of this region. Heading south, **Bordeaux** is meat-eating territory, although the local lamb goes far better with the region's red wines than beef, which is actually a more ideal match for Burgundy. There's also good seafood to enjoy with Sauvignon-dominant dry whites and foie gras to eat with Sauternes.

The classic dish of the **southwest** is cassoulet (or *ouillade* as it is known in Roussillon), while the Basques, whose most famous speciality is *piperade*, are masters at cooking with peppers and tomatoes. These are places to relish rustic wines like Cahors and Corbieres. The best Rhône reds call for game – or at least very flavoursome meat dishes – and the generous use of wild herbs that is customary here and in Provence. **Lyon**, the town that sits between the Rhône and Beaujolais boasts many of France's best classic cooks (page 54); this is the place to try dishes like *andouillette* (tripe sausage) in mustard and cream sauce, with good Beaujolais reds.

**Burgundy** is the place to break the rules. The tradition here is to poach eggs and trout in red wine – and to accompany the dishes with the wines used to cook them. Crayfish are popular here, too, as are *jambon persillé* and snails, all of which go brilliantly with white wines such as Meursault. Chablis, further north, is leaner and a better partner for oysters. To the northeast, the **Jura** and **Savoie** are great cheese regions, and the former area in particular has a great dish in the Poulet au Vin Jaune which is prepared with the local savoury white wine and morel mushrooms. In **Alsace**, the accent is Germanic, with lots of pork and cabbage, plus the local touch of egg and cheese tarts. Nothing matches these better than Riesling. Finally, there's **Champagne** which has a wide range of dishes to enjoy with various styles of the region's sparkling wine. But beware of Champenois who claim that their dry and demi-sec wines go well with pudding. As a rule, they don't.

# Wine essentials



## History

France's vinous history began in around 600 BC with the Greeks, who founded the city port of Massalia, which we now know as Marseilles, and planted vines nearby. From there, vines and the skills of grapegrowing and winemaking were carried northwards and westwards by the Celts and, more effectively, by the Romans, who planted extensive vineyards around Minervois (named after the Roman god). Bordeaux had to wait a little longer but Pliny describes wine being made there in AD 71. Seven centuries later, the Emperor Charlemagne made laws dictating how Burgundy should be made and stored, and gave vineyards to the church which would continue to make most of the region's wine for the next thousand years.

In the 12th century, the marriage of the French Queen Eleanor and English King Henry II brought Aquitaine (and Bordeaux) under the English crown, where it remained until 1438. This period was crucial to the development of Bordeaux as a port and as a winemaking region, thanks to the huge quantities of wine that were shipped to England.

Today, it is often forgotten how difficult it was to transport anything by land in the days before the widespread construction of roads and bridges. So, many of the most successful French wine regions tended to be either within easy reach of the Atlantic coast or in areas that were close to the cities of northern Europe. Some of these regions no longer feature on the wine map. In the 16th century, Parisians used to drink large quantities of wine from Orléans, for example, partly because of the quality of the road that led from there to the capital. The vineyards used for these wines have since disappeared, as have the huge swathes of vines that were planted to the south of Paris.

The advent of bridges, roads and canals all changed the fortunes of French regional wines, including Bergerac, which had been cut off by rivers and tariffs from the port of Bordeaux, and the Côte d'Or in Burgundy whose wines were hard to transport northwards until the Canal de Bourgogne was opened in the 19th century. Outsiders had their part to play, too, although this is not always recognized in France. It was Dutchmen who drained the Médoc and allowed vines to be grown in land that had previously been a swamp, and it was English and Irish merchants who created the international market for Bordeaux.

Finally, one of the defining moments in French wine history was the arrival of the phylloxera louse from America in the 1860s and its subsequent devastation of France's vineyards. The solution to this disaster was the grafting of traditional French vines on resistant American rootstock but in the aftermath of the phylloxera disaster, during the first decades of the 20th century, fraudulent winemaking was rife and huge volumes of wine were imported from the French colony of Algeria. The creation of Appellation Contrôlée in 1936 was a reaction to this situation; with it came the lack of flexibility that makes it so difficult for France's wines to compete internationally today.

## Understanding French wine

For its apologists, the French **Appellation Contrôlée** system is the envy of the world. Unlike any other system, it defines and regulates regions and styles precisely, enabling buyers to know whether they are buying a wine from the finest vineyard in a village or area. In fact, however, the system is now also widely recognised to be in severe need of reform because it has not adapted to the way wine is drunk today. The ban on the use of grape names on wine labels, for example, has been a handicap in an age when wines from other countries make no secret of their varietals. Another problem has been laws that prevent experimentation. Finally, there is the fact that, for historical reasons, no two regions follow the same rules. Grand Cru for example, changes its meaning depending on where it is used. Unfortunately, no one can agree on the nature of the reform, and French labels will probably be just as confusing in ten years time as they are today.

A winemaker may describe himself as a *vigneron*, a *viticulteur* or a *récoltant*; as opposed to a *négociant* (merchant), or a *cave cooperative* or a *union des producteurs*, both indicating a cooperative. A *château* or *domaine* is an individual estate, although its wine may be made, bottled and sold by a cooperative or merchant. The same can be said of a *clos* (a wine from a walled vineyard) or a *monopole* (a wine from a vineyard whose wines are only sold by one company). *Mis en bouteille par*... tells you who bottled the wine.

A **Vin de Table** (table wine) will, in theory at least, be the most basic of wines. Its label cannot legally mention a grape variety, region or vintage. Some high quality wines that fall outside stylistic rules are, however sold under this name. Higher in quality, should be, the 180 or so **Vins de Pays** (country wines). These come from small and large areas and allow producers a certain leeway of winemaking and labelling that is denied to wines with more elevated designations. Vins de Pays are allowed to name their grape varieties. Far rarer are the 30 or so **VDQS** (Vin Délimité de Qualité Superieure), a designation that is enjoying a half life, since being slated for abolition 30 years ago. The VDQS are supposedly on probation before being elevated to Appellation Contrôlée status. Today, this status is more questionable

A Premier Cru from Château de Meursault in Burgundy.

Grapevine

### A touch of class

Bordeaux has always been traded by brokers and merchants (page 63), who have set the prices for each château's wine in each vintage. In the 19 th century, when great vintages were rarer than they are now (thanks largely to greater winemaking expertise today), these men used to simplify this task by ranking the châteaux in a loose qualitative hierarchy in which the wines that were thought best, were priced at twice the level of the ones at the level beneath them, and so on.

In 1855, for the Great Exhibition in Paris, a *classement* (classification) was drawn up for the Médoc and Graves that ranked the former region's châteaux into five categories, descending in quality and prestige from the first growths, such as Latour and Lafite, to the fifth growths such as Lynch Bages and Pontet Canet. The classification has lasted ever since, with the slight change of Mouton Rothschild's promotion to first growth in 1973.

There are two flaws to the system. First, it was based on the name of the château rather than its vineyards, so it does not take account of the fact that some châteaux have sold good land they had in 1855, while others have improved their holdings. More importantly, the classification pays no attention to the skills of winemakers, so top fourth and fifth growths will sell for much higher prices than underperforming second growths.

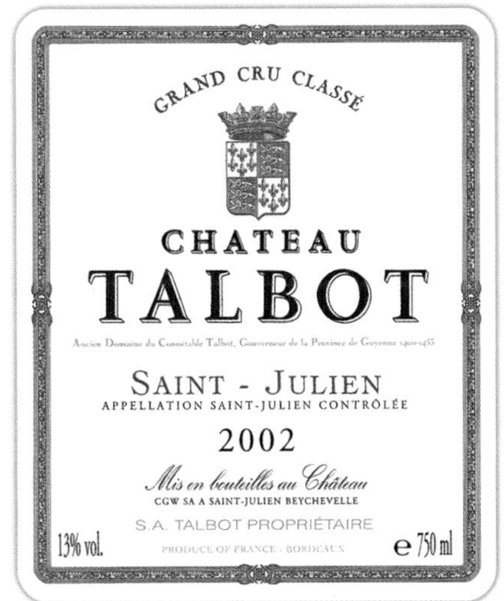


than in the past, because good Vins de Pays can sell for higher prices than basic Appellation Contrôlée wines.

In principle, Appellation Contrôlée provides no guarantee of quality but it is supposed to give an idea of the likely style in which a wine is made. Recent changes in winemaking in regions like Bordeaux, however, make even this last claim harder to uphold. Within Appellation Contrôlée regions there are areas with traditions of making better wine, indicated by the the word 'Villages', as in Beaujolais Villages. In Burgundy, better vineyards are designated as **Premiers Crus**, while the best plots are **Grands Crus**. Other regions have their own designations or none. So Provence has a number of Crus classes, as does the Médoc and Graves in Bordeaux. In the Médoc these are ranked in five levels, from first growth (such as Château Latour) to fifth (see A touch of class, above); in the Graves, there is no such ranking, apart from the one that recognizes Haut Brion as a first growth. The Médoc also has humbler Crus Bourgeois, Crus Bourgeois Superieur and Crus Bourgeois Exceptionnels – which were recently reclassified – and, lower than these, Crus Artisans. Red Bordeaux made from slightly riper grapes can call itself Bordeaux Supérieur, while any Bordeaux, however cheap and cheerful, can bear the words 'Grand Vin de Bordeaux' on its label, provided that the bottle is of the requisite height. St-Émilion has a totally different Grand Cru system to the Médoc and Graves. Or to be precise, it has two systems. On the one hand, there are hundreds of St-Émilion Grands Crus whose wines can be quite basic. Separate from these are 81 Grands Crus Classés, which will be of higher quality. Pomerol has no Grand Cru or Cru Classé system and does perfectly well without them. Alsace and Champagne have over-generously distributed Grands Crus vineyards (in Champagne the term is used to cover entire villages) but there are none in the Rhône.

"They are not long, the days of wine and roses..." Ernest Dowson.

Barrel-making at Smith Haut-Lafitte.

Other terms include *primeur* or *nouveau* for wine sold in the months after the harvest; *fûts de chene* for oak barrels that are probably, but not necessarily, new; and *vieilles vignes*, meaning old vines, which make better wine than young ones (no rules apply to the age at which they can be described old, however). *Vin doux naturel* or *vin de liqueur* are both fortified, while *mousseux, crémant, perlant, pétillant, méthode classique* and *méthode ancestrale* wines will all be sparkling. *Selection de vins nobles, vendanges tardives* (in Alsace), *moelleux* and *doux* are all sweet; *sec* and *brut* are dry. *Vin gris* will be pale pink, as might Blanc de Noirs sparkling wine, though it could be white. Blanc de Blancs, on the other hand will only have been made from white grapes. Wine bottled '*sur lie*', usually Muscadet, has been matured on its lees. A *cuvée*, like a *selection,* is simply a specific batch of wine; adding the word '*spéciale*' or '*personnelle*' to either of these suggests but does not guarantee higher quality. A *cuvée traditionelle* will tend to be less fruity and less oaky.

### White grapes

**Aligoté** The rarely-used, second-best grape variety of Burgundy that needs to be well handled and grown in the right areas. Not usually for keeping.

**Chardonnay** Best known for almost all white Burgundy, from unoaked Chablis and often featureless Mâcon Villages to oaky Meursault. Also used in Burgundian sparkling wine (Crémant de Bourgogne), in Champagne, in Anjou in the Loire, in Ardèche and in southern France (Vin de Pays and Limoux).

**Chenin Blanc** Honeyed, appley grape that is almost entirely restricted to the Loire, where it produces wines ranging from bone dry to richly sweet, plus large amounts of sparkling wine (Saumur, Vouvray, etc).

**Gewürztraminer** Only found in Alsace, this violet-and-lychee perfumed variety comes in styles ranging from dry to late-harvest sweet. Most examples are, or at least seem, slightly off dry, though labels often neglect to make this clear.

**Petit/Gros Manseng** Two related grapes (Petit is the finer of the pair) grown in the southwest for Jurançon and Vin de Pays des Côtes de Gascogne. Floral and dry or sweet.

**Marsanne** A rich lemony variety at home in the Rhône. At its best very young or after five years.

**Muscat** There are several strains of this variety, with the best being the Muscat Blanc à Petits Grains. Fine dry examples come from Alsace, while fortified sweet ones are made in the Rhône (Beaumes de Venise) and south.

**Pinot Blanc** The grape the Italians call Pinot Bianco produces the least aromatic whites in Alsace (like softer, unoaked Chablis) and is little used elsewhere, though it does appear anonymously in Burgundy (in some white Savigny-lès-Beaune).

**Pinot Gris/Tokay d'Alsace** Known as Pinot Grigio in Italy, but usually significantly more intensely flavoursome in Alsace, where it produces peary-spicy wines ranging in style from dry and off-dry to luscious late harvest. No relation to the Tokay of Hungary or Tocai Friulano.

**Riesling** Only grown in Alsace, but responsible for truly great dry and sweet wines there.

**Roussanne** The Marsanne's partner in the Rhône, used for wines including Côtes du Rhône and white Hermitage.

An *hotteur* unloads his hood during the harvest. When full, an *hotte* can weigh more than 50 kg.

**Sauvignon Blanc** At its best by itself in the Loire (Sancerre, Pouilly-Fumé) and (usually) in blends with Sémillon in sweet and dry white Bordeaux (though there are also some fine 100% Sauvignons, such as Ch. Couhins-Lurton).

**Savagnin** No relation to the Sauvignon, this is a variety used to make characterful wines in theJura.

### Red grapes

**Cabernet Franc** The more obviously berryish couisin of the Cabernet Sauvignon is used in Bordeaux blends (notably at Cheval Blanc and Vieux Château Certan). Flies solo with great success in Loire appellations such as Chinon and Bourgueuil.

**Cabernet Sauvignon** The cassis-flavoured mainstay of the finest wines of Médoc and Graves in Bordeaux, and of wines of widely varying quality in southern France.

**Carignan** When the vines are old and the yields are low, this variety can produce terrific richy, earthy wines in southern regions like Fitou, Corbières and Minervois. Lesser examples are very much lesser.

**Gamay** Juicy grape at home in Beaujolais, where it can/should make wines with fresh cherryish flavours. Also used in the Loire and in the Southwest but to less effect.

**Grenache** Peppery variety that can also have great strawberryish fruit. At its best in Côtes du Rhône, Châteauneuf-du-Pape and Gigondas.

**Malbec/Cot** Newly fashionable, thanks to the success of examples from Argentina. Once part of the Bordeaux blend, it is now best known in France for its role in Cahors. Unfortunately few Malbec wines from this region (and none from the Loire, where it is called Cot) have the soft appeal of the South American version. It may be that France was left with a weaker strain of Malbec, when it was replanted after the ravages of the phylloxera louse at the end of the 19th century.

**Merlot** The widest-planted red grape in Bordeaux, where it is usually blended with Cabernet Sauvignon and/or Cabernet Franc, although it is used by itself for some Pomerol and St-Émilion. Merlot is also now used to make rarely impressive Vin de Pays d'Oc.

**Pinot Noir** The grape behind almost all red Burgundy, red Sancerre and red wine in Alsace and Champagne, is now also producing good results in the Ardèche, Limoux and Corsica.

**Syrah** Known as Shiraz in Australia and some other countries, this spicy, peppery, brambly variety is at its finest in the northern Rhône in Hermitage or – with a little help from the Viognier – in Côte Rôtie. It also does well in various Languedoc wines, ranging from Vin de Pays d'Oc to Minervois.

**Tannat** The tough grape of Madiran has recently attracted attention from well-travelled wine lovers who have discovered good examples from Uruguay. Madiran, interestingly, seems to be combating its traditional toughness with greater success than Cahors.

Bottom: grapes at Château Vignelaure, Provence.

**One of the joys of visiting Paris lies in the quality of the wine lists at its best restaurants and wine bars. These have, if anything, improved in recent years, as a more open-minded approach has been applied to southern regions that were once overlooked or treated with disdain. Today, in another previously almost unthinkable development, you might even find wines from other countries – but don't bank on it.**

WINE BAR

## Juveniles

47 rue de Richelieu, 75001
T +33 (0)1-42 97 46 49
Mon 1600-2300; Tue-Sat 1200-2300.
$

People come from around the world to try proprietor Tim Johnston's latest vinous finds. These might include the unknown second wine of a well-known Loire producer, or a Portuguese stunner that few people outside Portugal knew existed. The food is just what wine bar fare should be: fresh, unpretentious, a good match for any wine, intelligently innovative and promptly served. Johnston, a transplanted Scot who has done virtually every job it is possible to do in the wine world, short of owning his own vineyard, is remarkable for attracting and maintaining a French clientele as well as a foreign one. The atmosphere is, thus, that of a neighbourhood local that welcomes strangers, although Johnston's direct manner has been known to surprise some more straitlaced newcomers. A Paris institution and a must for true wine lovers.

RESTAURANT

## L'Ami Louis

32 rue du Vertbois, 75003
T +33 (0)1-48 87 77 48
Wed-Sun 1200-1330 and 2000-2300.
$-$$

If I had to choose one bistro to be frozen for posterity in order to give later generations an idea of what this feature of Parisian life is all about, it would be L'Ami Louis, with its authentic decor and wood-fired stove. Tucked away from the more chic thoroughfares, it nonetheless attracts a well-heeled clientele, most of whom, unless they are regulars or celebrities, will have booked weeks in advance to secure their gingham-clothed table. Some Parisians scoff at the fact that it attracts Americans foodies undaunted by its hefty prices, but purists, Parisian or otherwise, admit that the fare is the real bistro deal, be it perfectly roast Challans chicken or succulent pâté de foie gras. A welcome point of difference from most bistros, though, is the wide selection of wine, including bottles rarely seen elsewhere.

View of Paris from Notre Dame.

In the 12th century, nuns in Montmartre used a wine press to make wine for their own consumption. The vineyard was part of a huge 42,000-ha region known as Vin de France, which included vines grown along the Seine to the west of Paris and extended as far as Ay in Champagne.

SHOP/RESTAURANT

## Lavinia

3-5 blvd de la Madeleine, 75001
T +33 (0)1-42 97 20 27
Mon-Fri 0900-2000; Sat 1000-2000.
$

Even if you are not planning to buy any wine while you're in Paris, you must make the pilgrimage to Lavinia, Europe's largest wine store. It's home to more than 6000 wines from around the world, including wines from such improbable regions as South Dakota. Like its sister establishments in Madrid (page 96) and Barcelona, it also has a restaurant in which you can drink any bottle sold in the store at no mark-up to accompany chef Régis Bruillon's fresh, light and seasonally changing dishes. There is, as one would expect, a terrific selection of wines by the glass. Thankfully, since the arrival of Lavinia, other wine shops in Paris have begun to take a more open attitude to non-French wines.

WINE BAR

## Le Baron Rouge

1 rue Théophile Roussel , 75012
T +33 (0)1-43 42 54 65
Tue-Fri 1000-1400 and 1700-2130; Sat 1000-2130; Sun 1000-1430.
$-$$

Welcome to neighbourhood Paris, in this case the gentrified Bastille area and the Marché d'Aligre, a daily street market that takes place on the doorstep of this wine bar. The Baron Rouge, a former wine cellar with untreated wooden floors and casks of plonk available to download into takeaway flasks, is a real locals' hangout. It does provide a warm welcome for non-Parisians, though, and is worth seeking out for the 30-odd, well-chosen wines that are regularly available by the glass (from €3), their names scrawled on a succession of blackboards. It also provides a respite from normal Parisian prices: plates of charcuterie start at €5.

RESTAURANT

## Le Comptoir

9 carrefour de l'Odéon, 75006
T +33 (0)1-44 22 07 97
www.comptoirparis.com
Mon-Sat 1200-0200; Sun 1200-2400.
$$

Yves Camdeborde (of the famous La Régalade restaurant) also has this small, funky restaurant in an annexe of the Relais Saint-Germain, right by the chaos of the carrefour de l'Odéon. The spirit is innovative and egalitarian: everybody gets the same menu, which changes every night. Typical offerings might include soup of green peas and mint with a couple of surprise pieces of foie gras, served with cumin wafers; zucchini purée with crab meat and caviar of herring; and Pyrenean lamb, served with fava beans, peas and carrots. The wine list offers lots of great-value French regional wines. A reservation, if you can get one, is a must.

### A flâneur in Paris

A day in Paris could start off with a morning visit to the beautiful **Musée Rodin** (77 rue de Varenne, 75007, T +33 (0)1-44 18 61 10, www.musee-rodin.fr). There are over 500 of Rodin's sculptures here, as well as works by Camille Claudel (his model and lover) and his own collection of paintings, including work by Van Gogh. Alternatively, head for the **Musée d'Orsay** (Quai Anatole-France, 75007, T +33 (0)1-40 49 48 48, www.musee-orsay.fr), an early 20th century train station-turned-art gallery that's worth visiting almost as much for the building as for the great Impressionist treasures it holds.

Afterwards head across to the Rive Droit to check out the wines at **Lavinia** (page 39). Take a pre-prandial stroll through the lovely **Jardin des Tuileries** – a popular spot with Parisians for centuries – before lunch and a well-earned glass of wine at **Juveniles** (page 38).

In the afternoon, cross the Seine via the **Pont Neuf**, the oldest and best-loved of all the city's 36 bridges, to île de la Cité, home to the indomitable **Notre Dame Cathedral**, France's most famous place of worship. Don't miss nearby **Sainte-Chapelle**, a glittering jewel of a chapel built by Louis IX to house his precious religious relics.

If you're still up for more sightseeing then cross to île St Louis – which is like stepping into a 17th-century film set – browsing its specialist olive oil shops and chocolatiers before joining the semi-permanent queue at **Berthillon** for one of their legendary sorbets. After all that, it's time to head back across to the Left Bank for an aperitif and dinner at **Le Comptoir** (page 39)

An even better alternative for dedicated flâneurs would be to take the Metro to the **Marais**, a favourite place for aimless wandering, thanks to its winding medieval streets, charming tea rooms and bars, and ultra-fashionable shops. The highlight is **Place des Vosges** a beautiful 17th-century square of arcaded buildings. The perfect end to the day would be dinner in **L'Ami Louis** (page 38), assuming you've booked of course.

Those wishing to spend more than a day in Paris could do a lot worse than the exquisitely furnished $$$ **Hôtel Bourg Tibourg** (19 rue du Bourg Tibourg, 75004, T +33 (0)1-42 78 47 39, www.hotelbourgtibourg.com). For something a little less ostentatious, there's $$ **Hôtel des Tuileries** (10 rue Saint-Hyacinthe, 75001, T +33 (0)1-42 61 04 17, www.hotel-des-tuileries.com).

Grapevine

**Paris wine – then and now**

Paris has a long history of wine production. The Romans built a temple dedicated to Bacchus, the god of wine, 2000 years ago and, in the 12th century, at a Benedictine abbey in what is now Montmartre, nuns apparently used a wine press to make wine for their own consumption. The winemaking abbey survived until the revolution when it was destroyed and the aged, deaf and blind abbess was guillotined. Today, it is commemorated by the Abbesses metro station. The Montmartre vineyard was part of a huge 42,000-ha region known as Vin de France, which included vines grown along the Seine to the west of Paris, but also extended as far as Ay in Champagne. No one can say how good these northern French wines might have been but high-quality grape varieties such as Pinot Noir, Pinot Gris and Chardonnay were certainly grown – at least until the intense frost of 1709, which killed most of the vines.

The region was largely replanted with the more productive but lower quality Gamay, whose large volumes of, almost certainly, very ordinary wine satisfied the Parisians for their daily drinking. However, in the mid 1800s the arrival of the railway brought competition from wine produced in the warmer southern region of Languedoc-Roussillon. Parisian wines went into terminal decline and the few that survived were not replanted after the phylloxera louse devastated vines throughout Europe at the end of the 19th century. However, a tiny strand of history survives in the shape of 150 tiny vineyards dotted around the city. Between them, they produce around 40,000 bottles of mostly white wine. The first of these vineyards, the Clos Montmartre, was planted in 1933 by a group of artists between rue St-Vincent and rue des Saules, about 400 m from the old abbey. The 2000 vines – a ragbag of over two dozen varieties, led by Gamay and Pinot Noir – cover some 1500 sq m and are harvested during a well-attended wild harvest festival, **Fête des Vendanges**, with parades and fireworks every October. Annual production is around 1700 half-litre bottles, most of which are auctioned off (for over €30 each) for charity.

Other Parisian vineyards include ones in the Parc de Bercy, close to the traditional centre of Parisian wine selling and warehousing, and in the Parc de Belleville. The **Clos des Morillons**, at the Parc Georges Brassens in the 11th arrondissement, boasts some particularly jolly harvest street-party activities, concluding at a wine bar called **Chez Mélac** (42 rue Léon Frot, T +33 (0)1-43 70 59 27, www.melac.fr). Unfortunately, reservations are not accepted here and anyone wanting to taste the Clos des Morillons should note that annual production is just 35 bottles.

To learn more about Paris's vineyards, visit www.vigneronsfranciliens.com (in French only), the website of the Association of Île de France winemakers.

RESTAURANT/WINE SHOP

## Le Verre Volé

67 rue de Lancry, 75010
T +33 (0)1-48 03 17 34
Mon-Sat 1100-2300.
$

Booking is a must at Cyril Bordarier's tiny six-table bistro by the charming Canal St Martin, which is perfect for a pre- or post-prandial walk. Some 200 wines are available, from Romanée-Conti to up-and-coming organic or artisan producers, at only a €5 mark-up. Alternatively, there are eight wines available by the glass. Either way, it will be hard to resist the various food offerings, which range from lighter *amuses bouches*, such as one of monkfish liver, to meals of robust traditional fare, such as *andouillettes* or *boudin* (both types of sausage). The shop is a great place to discover well chosen examples of wines from unfamiliar regions of France.

RESTAURANT

## Restaurant Astier

44 rue Jean-Pierre Timbaud , 75011
T +33 (0)1-43 57 16 35
www.restaurant-astier.com
Mon-Fri 1200-1400 and 2000-2200.
$$

A great juxtaposition of the traditional and rarified, this down-to-earth restaurant offers such classics as *blanquette de veau à l'ancienne* and rabbit with mustard, accompanied by a wine list offering such gems as Nicholas Joly's La Coulée de Serrant, 1995 at often ludicrously low prices. The set menu (€26 at dinner) offers one of the best deals in Paris, especially when you consider that it includes a celebrated cheeseboard, which is left on the table for customers to help themselves. The starters include an impressive range of terrines made, for example, from fish or leek and haddock, with a balsamic vinaigrette. There are only two drawbacks to this small slice of paradise. Tables are very very closely packed, so privacy is not an option and nor is the possibility of enjoying a meal here during a romantic weekend in Paris. Sadly, Astier is only open during the week.

## Champagne

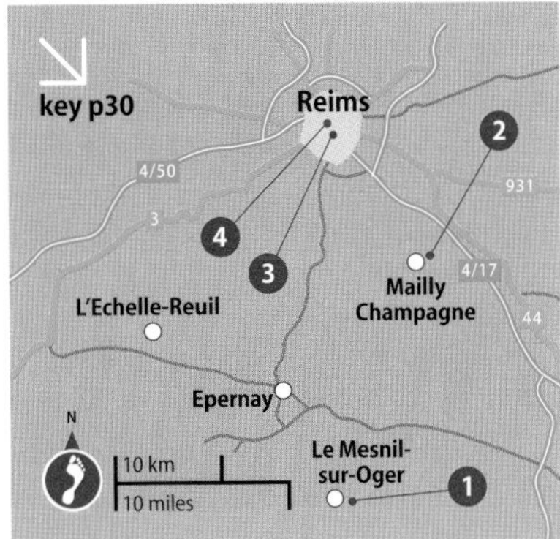


Long before this region became known for its bubbles, its wines were already recognized as being rather special. In the 15th century, *les vins d'Ay*, named after the Champagne village where Bollinger is situated today, were thought to be as fine as those of Burgundy. In the late 17th century, Dom Pérignon, the abbot of Hautvilliers, further raised the quality by mastering the art of making white wine from black grapes (by preventing the skins from dyeing the juice) but he almost certainly did not invent sparkling wine as is often thought. However, during the following century the wine did become *mousseux*, thanks to a process of refermentation in the bottle. This process, however, relied on the natural yeast in the wine, which meant that early Champagnes would have been cloudy and required decanting. In 1818, the cellarmaster working for the recently widowed Madame Clicquot devised a method of shaking the yeast down to the neck of the bottle in special racks – *pupitres* – freezing it and releasing it from the bottle in the form of a frozen plug. The same process is used today, in the same chalk caves, but now machines are often used to do the shaking rather than human beings.

Today, Champagne is, quite simply, the one French region that understands wine tourism in a way that might be recognizable to anyone who has travelled around New World regions like the Napa Valley or Margaret River. Several of the bigger producers, in particular, are used to welcoming thousands of visitors every day and, in many cases, to offering a tour and a tasting in return for an entrance ticket. At their best, these tours are as slickly planned as anything by Disney. Even so, most smaller Champagne houses and individual estates still prefer to welcome visitors 'by appointment'. When wandering around Champagne, bear in mind that while most big-name Champagnes are blends of two or three varieties (Pinot Noir, Chardonnay and Pinot Meunier) from possibly widely separated parts of the region, estates use grapes from their own vineyards. So, if you like pure Chardonnay Blanc de Blancs, it is worth going to a village like Le Mesnil, for example, where only Chardonnay is grown.

WINERY | LE MESNIL

### Champagne Launois Père et Fils

2 ave Eugène Guillaume, BP7,
51190 Le Mesnil-sur-Oger
T +33 (0)3-26 57 50 15
www.champagne-launois.fr
Visits by appointment only.
€6

To really understand the Champagne region, it is well worth getting out of the bigger towns and taking to the country roads to discover some of the smaller *maisons*. Champagne Launois, in the heart of the Côte des Blancs, has been making top-quality Champagne since 1872. The enchanting Renaissance château building is set in a park full of ducks, geese and other domestic animals, and there is also a mini-vineyard in which examples of France's principle grape varieties grow. The excellent two-hour tour, available by advance

Mumm office in Reims.

Exhibit at the Mumm museum in Reims.



booking only, takes in a delightful museum, which displays presses from the past three centuries, and a tasting of three Champagnes.

WINERY MAILLY

## Champagne Mailly Grand Cru

28 rue de la Libération, 51500 Mailly Champagne
T +33 (0)3-26 49 41 10
Visits by appointment only.

# Best producers

**Champagne**

Billecart-Salmon
Deutz
Gosset
Gratien, Alfred
Heidsieck, Charles
Jacquesson
Krug
Moet & Chandon (Dom Perignon)
Pol Roger
Roederer, Louis
Ruinart
Veuve Clicquot (Grande Dame)

To complete one's understanding of Champagne, a visit to a cooperative is in order. Champagne Mailly is the brand name of an excellent Grand Cru produced by a dynamic co-op of some 70 members. It is well worth booking ahead to arrange a tour here. You will gain an insight into Champagne from the ground up and see that it is the smaller winegrowers, who form the real backbone of the region, in their role as the main suppliers of increasingly valuable Champagne grapes. The impressive winery has a seven-storey gravity-fed installation that will delight wine anoraks.

HOTEL REIMS

## Les Crayères

64, bvd Henry Vasnier, 51100 Reims
T+33 (0)3-26 82 80 80
www.lescrayeres.com
Closed for Christmas and New Year.
$$$

This very grand château hotel truly fits the image of Champagne. It sits in an immaculately groomed 7-ha park right in the city of Reims, so you have the best of *rus en urbe*. The hotel offers several very well-organized tours of the region but you might prefer to hole up and let the Champagnes come to you, sipping them as you enjoy the luxury of the richly decorated rooms and suites. The restaurant is sumptuous, and sumptuously priced ($$$), with a seafood menu, accompanied by various vintage Louis Roederer Champagnes, including a glass of 1999 Cristal, priced at €305.

WINERY REIMS

## Mumm

34 rue du Champ du Mars, 51100 Reims
T +33 (0)3-26 49 59 70
Mar-Oct daily 0930-1050 and 1400-1640; Nov-Feb by appointment only.
€7.50-16

This distinctively labeled Champagne brand took over from Moët & Chandon as the Champagne of choice on the Grand Prix podium. The winery offers tours in French, German, English, Spanish and Italian, taking visitors around the cellars, housing 25 million bottles, and explaining the principal stages of the Champagne-making process. For an additional cost, there are also small tutored tastings of various Champagnes, including the chance to compare vintages. With advance notice, trips can also be organized to Mumm's vineyards, overlooked by the lovely Verzénay windmill, built in 1820; these are well worth doing, especially if you don't have a car.

Champagne Mailly Grand Cru.

MUSEUM L'ECHELLE-REUIL

## Musée du Vignoble en Miniature du Domaine Bacchus

4 rue Bacchus, 51480 L'Echelle-Reuil
T +33 (0)3-26 58 66 60
www.Domaine-Bacchus.com
Contact the venue for further details.

If only more French winemakers had the imagination and passion of Lydie et Arnaud Billard, I would feel far more optimistic for the future of France's wine industry. As well as making good Champagne, they have five *chambres d'hôte* ($), with fine views across the Marne Valley, and a restaurant ($). Much more unusual, though, is their charming 75 sq m model recreation of a winemaking village. It features 170 miniature figures wearing traditional costumes and engaged in all kinds of activities relating to winemaking and village life in general. Children will love it and adults will find it impossible to withhold a smile. An intimate insight into the region can be gained on organized vineyard visits in the area.

WINERY REIMS

## Pommery

5 pl du Général Gouraud, 51100 Reims
T +33 (0)3-26 61 62 63
www.pommery.com
Visits by appointment.
€7 per person

This exuberant, sprawling Elizabethan-style château, conceived by the maverick Louise Pommery, has anachronistic architecture, 30 m-deep cellars hewn from stone, tunnels (named after the principal cities to which the firm's Champagne was shipped a century ago) and artworks, including a 14th-century statue of the Madonna and Child. The tour takes in tastings of a variety of Champagnes, including the Cuvée Louise (subject to a higher fee). It is necessary to book in advance.

# Alsace

The Alsatians take pride in being neither French nor German but of combining the best of both nationalities. They have had plenty of chance to learn about these two cultures, since a succession of wars and treaties have bounced this region back and forth across the frontier; during the Second World War, for example, Alsace was under German rule. This mixed background has certainly influenced the wines (all that Riesling and Gewurztraminer), the architecture and the food.

The children's story-book beauty of Alsace's immaculate, flower-covered villages makes this a great place to visit irrespective of its wine. Fortunately, however, like their neighbours on the other side of the Rhine, the Alsatians take wine tourism seriously, so, apart from the numerous festivals, merchants, cooperatives (including some of France's best) and growers are often prepared for casual as well as prearranged visits. When tasting here, bear in mind that this is the only region of France that helpfully prints grape varieties on its labels. However, matters are confused by the fact that while very sweet and sweet late-harvest wines will be labelled 'Sélection de Grains Nobles' and 'Vendange Tardive' respectively, many wines bearing neither of these descriptions will also be slightly or even decidedly sweet because grapes are being harvested riper than in the past. The dryness or sweetness of a wine may depend on the stylistic preference of the producer, but there may also be variations between examples of the same grape variety in the same cellar. Also note that within a producer's range, a wine from a Grand Cru vineyard should be of higher quality. But, as elsewhere in France, a less skilled winemaker's Grand Cru may not be as good as a wine from his neighbour bearing a humbler label.

WINERY KAYSERSBERG

## Domaine Weinbach

25 rte du Vin, 68240 Kaysersberg
T +33 (0)3-89 47 13 21
www.domaineweinbach.com
Visits by appointment only

Domaine Weinbach provides a perfect introduction to what makes Alsace unique: the long history, the relatively small vineyard holdings and the movement towards biodynamic viticulture. It was founded in 1612 by Capuchin Monks at the foot of Schlossberg hill, on the site of a former monastery dating from at least the ninth century. Typical of Alsace, the winery offers a range of wines out of proportion to its size and offers visitors a chance to experience the quality of terroir in this region. A third of the 5-ha domaine has been biodynamic since 1998.

HOTEL OTTROTT-LE-HAUT

## L'Ami Fritz

8 rue des Châteaux, 67530 Ottrott-le-Haut
T +33 (0)3-88 95 80 81
$-$$

It is well worth opting for one of the accommodation and restaurant packages at this elegant, charming hotel. That way you can enjoy such dishes as warm salad of baby

Vineyard near Hunawihr on the Route du Vin Alsace.

Alsatian cuisine at Le Caveau d'Eguisheim.

pigeon with pan-fried duck foie gras or, for offal-lovers, brawn and pigs' tongues cooked in a traditional manner. Afterwards, recover in the beautiful garden or in your room. The hotel, an 18th-century stone structure, actually houses two restaurants ($-$$), one in the stone wine cellar.

RESTAURANT FAREBERSVILLIER

## La Table Alsacienne

9 av Saint-Jean, 57450 Farebersvillier
T +33 (0)3-87 89 12 01
Tue-Sat for dinner; Sun for lunch and dinner.
$

If you can plan ahead, give La Table Alsacienne 48 hours' advance notice to produce *baeckeofe* (for a minimum of two people): lamb marinated in white wine and cooked in an earthenware dish, or, for a larger group, stuffed suckling pig. Even without these delicacies, you will still enjoy a delightful meal featuring Lorraine and Alsace specialties and fairly priced local wines. Fabienne et Yves Freléchoux, Alsace natives, took over this local institution, in existence since 1919 and formerly called L'hôtel restaurant Karmann, and have maintained its excellent standards. There are ten rooms in the adjacent hotel ($).

RESTAURANT EGUISHEIM

## Le Caveau d'Eguisheim

3 pl du Château St Léon, 68420 Eguisheim
T +33 (0)3-89 41 08 89
Wed-Sun 1200-1400 and 1900-2130.
$-$$

Precisely what I want most of all after an Alsatian tasting marathon: a restaurant that is at once fine and unpretentious, offering good-value local fare and a range of mostly local wines at all price-points. People come for miles around for owner-chef Giles Vonderscher's *choucroute garni*, but you are also likely to see a fair number of local winemakers. Everything is excellent, including the *tarte a l'onion* and the *gugelhopf* (a bread or cake filled with fruit and nuts). The cheese tray is also a great introduction to Alsace's range of traditional cheeses – and the challenge they throw down for wine.

MUSEUM KIENTZHEIM

## Musée du vignoble et des vins d'Alsace

Château de la Confrérie Saint-Etienne, 68240 Kientzheim
T +33 (0)3-89 78 21 36
Jun-Oct daily 1000-1200 and 1400-1800. Closed Nov-May.
€4

Most wine museums are an acquired taste. This wine anorak's paradise is worth visiting for its collection of implements and tools relating to all aspects of viticulture and winemaking looking back almost three centuries. Highlights include a press dating from 1716 and a collection of filters and pumps, showing their evolution in form and function from the 19th century to the present day. Also of interest are the influences on the region's wines of its alternating occupation by the French and Germans.

# Best producers

**Alsace**

Becker, Jean
Beyer, Leon
Blanck, Paul
Bott-Geyl
Boxler, Albert
Deiss, Marcel
Faller/Weinbach » *page 44.*
Hugel (top wines)
Josmeyer
Kientzler, Andre
Mann, Albert
Meyer-Fonné
Muré, René
Ostertag
Rolly Gassmann
Trimbach
Zind Humbrecht

# Jura and Savoie

A forgotten pair of regions – at least for most outsiders. Arbois in Jura is the place where Louis Pasteur found out how wine was spoiled by bacteria; a discovery that had the same beneficial effect on wine as it did on the dairy industry. Pasteur's attention must have been caught by the benevolent bacteria that formed skins on the surface of his region's Vin Jaune, much as they do in the sherry bodegas of Jerez. The Juraciens still make this dry, nutty and sherry-like, but unfortified, gold-coloured wine, which has to be enjoyed with food to be properly appreciated. But they also produce more conventional whites, from Chardonnay and the local Savagnin grape and reds, from Pinot Noir and the similarly local Poulsard and Trousseau. Look out, too, for the great sweet white Vin de Paille, made from grapes that are laid out to dry on straw mats in a technique that was used by the ancient Greeks. Arbois itself is a charming town, while the hilltop village of Château-Chalon, where some of the best wines are made, is truly beautiful and quite unspoiled.

Savoie is perhaps a little better known, thanks to the proximity of its vineyards to the slopes of Val d'Isère. These light, refreshing wines are ideal for enjoying with a cheesey dish after an invigorating day's skiing. They are made from local grapes (Mondeuse for reds and Roussette for the whites) and need to be drunk young and in the region.



## Jura

WINERY — ARLAY

### Château d'Arlay

Rte de Saint-Germain, 39140 Arlay
T +33 (0)3-84 44 41 94/84 85 04 22
www.arlay.com
Castle and grounds Jun-Sep daily 1400-1800. Winery visits by appointment.
Castle and grounds €8.80

Even if you do not end up staying ($$) at this glorious monastery-turned-castle overlooking the Revermont, it is worth visiting the winery and the extensive gardens. The Côtes du Jura produced here is among the best in the appellation and visitors have the chance to taste such unusual varieties as Trousseau, Poulsard and Savagnin. The extensive 18th-century French gardens are full of surprise groves, and there's also an 'entertainment' garden, created in 1996, with a place to play boules and dominos. Bird lovers will find planty to keep them busy: Château d'Arlay houses the **Centre for the Reproduction of Wild Fauna Species** for the Jura, and most European birds of prey are represented. The château's owners can organize visits to other stately homes in the region for its guests.

HOTEL — PORT-LESNEY

### Château de Germigney

Rue Edgar Faure, 39600 Port-Lesney
T +33 (0)3-84 73 85 85
www.chateaudegermigney.com
$$$

Château de Germigney is a visual treat: a beautifully preserved 18th-century castle, sitting in 4 ha of beautifully groomed gardens full of trees from around the world that were brought back from the travels of a former owner. The garden also has a giant chessboard; an ecological swimming pool should soon be completed. Roland and Véréna Schön, Zurich-based interior designers, have meticulously decorated each of the 20-odd rooms in totally different, luxurious styles. (You may be very tempted to steal the silk curtains.) The restaurant ($$-$$$) offers great opportunities to match local wines to regional dishes or you can venture down the road to the Schön's Michelin-starred bistro, **Le Pontarlier** ($), where chef Pierre Basso-Moro offers cookery lessons and takes guests on early-morning mushroom hunts. The hotel can also arrange cycling tours and fishing weekends.

## Best producers

**Jura**

Bourdy
Château d' Arlay » *page 46.*
Rijckaert
Tissot, J

RESTAURANT — ARBOIS

### La Balance Mets et Vins

47 rue de Courcelles, 39600 Arbois
T +33 (0)3-84 37 45 00
Sep-Jun Mon, Thu-Sat 1200-1330 and 1900-2130; Tue 1200-1330.
Jul and Aug Mon-Sat 1200-1330 and 1900-2130.
$

Arbois native Thierry Moyne is mad about wine, especially the examples produced in the Jura, and his entire menu is structured around matching a full list of Jura wines with authentic local cooking. Call ahead to find out about special themed evenings, such as 'Litérature, Food and Wine' or 'The Garden of Spices'.

MUSEUM — ARBOIS

### Musée de la Vigne et du Vin

Château Pécauld, BP 41, 39600 Arbois
T +33 (0)3-84 66 40 45
www.juramusees.com/musee-vigne-vin/musee-vigne-vin.htm
Nov-Feb Wed-Mon 1400-1800; Jun, Aug-Oct Wed-Mon 1000-1200 and 1400-1800. Jul 1000-1230 and 1400-1800. Closed for Christmas and New Year.
€3.40

Aiguille du Dru in the French Alps.



The tour of this charming museum, which can be visited with a guide or independently, begins in the vineyards at the base of Château Pécauld. After examining the grape varieties and viticultural techniques indigenous to the region, the tour proceeds into the castle, parts of which date from the 13th to 18th centuries, where detailed exhibits demonstrate winemaking traditions in more general terms.

## Savoie

HOTEL | SAVOIE

### Hotel Ombremont

RN 504, 73370 Savoie
T + 33 (0)4-79 25 00 23
www.hotel-ombremont.com/
$$$

Josie et Jean-Pierre Jacob's elegant, 17-room hotel is dramatically situated on the edge of France's largest natural lake, Lac du Bourget. The hotel is a lovely retreat, with a large pool and a garden full of looming, century-old trees. In the delightful restaurant, **Le Bateau Ivre** ($-$$$), Jean-Pierre expresses his romantic bent through a choice of set menus, including two named after French poets Verlaine and Rimbaud; the latter is a 12-course extravaganza. Fish from Lac du Bourget and seafood dominate the menu, which includes such inventive offerings as oyster on a lettuce mousseline with peanut fondant. This is also a perfect place to sample Savoie wines at their best. And to discover how much more interesting they can be than the fare usually on offer in bars and restaurants in the region's ski resorts.

MUSEUM | MONTMELIAN

### Musée Régional de la Vigne et du Vin

46 rue Docteur Veyrat, 73800 Montmélian
T +33 (0)4-79 84 42 23
www.montmelian.com
Oct-Jun Wed-Fri 1400-1700; Jul-Sep Tue-Sat 1000-1200 and 1400-1830.
€4

A charming recreation of a traditional *vigneron*'s house is among the highlights of this museum in the heart of the old town of Montmélian. There is a detailed explanation of viticulture and winemaking, illustrated by a host of old tools and other artefacts, as well as an introduction to Savoie's unique viticultural traditions and grape varieties. Great for a day when there's no snow.

# Burgundy

Usually depicted as a single region on maps, Burgundy is in fact made up of five areas, beginning at Chablis, a clear 150 km northwest of the Côte d'Or at the heart of the region. Further south is the Côte Chalonnaise, which gives way to the Mâconnais and Beaujolais. Vines were introduced by the Romans throughout this area, as can be seen from names like Mercurey (site of a shrine to the god Mercury) and St-Amour (named after a centurion). The Romans had big plans for Burgundy; Autun, a town to the west of Beaune, was intended to become 'Rome in the West'. This never came to pass but, in the 14th century, the Duchy of Burgundy was effectively, if briefly, a powerful nation dealing on equal terms with the king of England (to whom the Burgundians handed Joan of Arc).

Burgundy's wines were enjoyed in the ninth century by the Emperor Charlemagne, who is commemorated in the name of one of the finest vineyards in Corton, in the Côte d'Or, but they subsequently enjoyed less prominence and prestige than those of Bordeaux. There were two reasons for this. First, the vines belonged to the church rather than the aristocracy or merchants, and secondly, until the building of canals, Burgundy's wine had to be transported overland at a time when roads were rudimentary.

In 1789, the French Revolution had less effect in Bordeaux than one might have expected; most estates survived, even if their owners sometimes did not. The redistribution of Burgundy's ecclesiastical vineyards to peasants did nothing to help the region to develop a coherent trade with other countries but matters grew still worse when the Napoleonic inheritance code, which gave all heirs equal shares, led to both the further division of the vineyards and to the alliance of families who intermarried with winemakers a few miles down the road. All of this helps to explain why so many Burgundian cellars are owned by families with double-barrelled names (such as Gagnard-Delagrange), why so many cellars produce small quantities of wines from small vineyard plots and why the region's merchants (*négociants*), who buy and blend wines from the small growers, have become so important.

When I lived in Burgundy in the late 1970s the region was a desert for tourists. Today, Beaune, once my home town, has a plethora of great restaurants and hotels.

## Chablis

Burgundy begins around an hour and a half's drive south of Paris along the Autoroute du Soleil. This is Chablis where, for some people, the Chardonnay grape is at its stony, unoaked best. The small town of Chablis is a sleepy place but well worth visiting for the quality of its restaurants and the opportunity to taste and learn about the subtle differences in character between the Grand Cru, Premier Cru, basic Chablis and Petit Chablis. La Chablisienne cooperative looks after visitors well and and the estate-owner and merchant Laroche (see below) does so brilliantly. Nearby, the village of St Bris makes Burgundy's only Sauvignon Blanc, while Irancy produces light Pinot Noir and the occasional eccentric example of another red grape, called the César, which is grown nowhere else in the world.

WINE BAR | CHABLIS

### Laroche Wine Bar & Restaurant

18 rue des Moulins, 89800 Chablis
T +33 (0)3-86 42 47 30
www.larochewines.com
Mon-Wed 1130-1700; Thu, Fri and Sat 1130-1700 and 1900-2200.
$-$$

Despite its location in a 10th-century water mill, this is the funky face of Chablis. The old machine room has been transformed into a stylish contemporary wine bar serving *tartines*, made with bread from Paris baker Poîlane (try the lamb kebab and a green salad laced with coriander) and more sizeable seasonal dishes. There are also Laroche wines by the glass, including Premiers and Grands Crus from Chablis, of course, as well as examples produced by this family firm in

Southwest France and Chile. Alternatively, you can buy a bottle from the adjoining shop and drink it with your meal at no extra cost. Tours of Laroche's impressive vaulted cellars can also be booked here.

## Côte d'Or

Another hour or so south of Chablis brings you to the north end of the Côte d'Or. This area – the heartland of 'great' red and white Burgundy – extends from the little-known village of Marsannay-la-Côte in a more or less straight line, known as the 'slope of gold', to the similarly obscure village of Cheilly-les-Maranges.

Between these two you will come across more familiar names, such as Gevrey-Chambertin, Morey-St-Denis, Chambolle-Musigny, Clos de Vougeot, Vosne-Romanée, Nuits-St-Georges, Pernand-Vergelesses, Savigny-les-Beaune, Aloxe- Corton, Beaune, Pommard, Volnay, Auxey- Duresses, Meursault, Chassagne-Montrachet, Puligny-Montrachet and Santenay. In each of these villages and their neighbours, you will find scores if not hundreds of small cellars, most of which produce small amounts of several different appellations. Here and there, especially in the towns of Beaune and Nuits-St-Georges, there are also *négociants*, merchants who buy wine or grapes from growers. Cooperatives are rarer here than in other parts of France but the **Cooperative des Hautes-Côtes** (Rte de Pommard, 21200 Beaune, T +33 (0)3-8025 0100), just to the south of Beaune, is worth a visit. Most cellars welcome visitors, although most will prefer it if you make an appointment, and English is not often spoken. Top class Burgundy is never cheap, but the prices in the cellars are far lower than you would pay elsewhere. Those seeking bargain Burgundies would do well to head to the west (into the hills) or the east (the plain), where humbler appellations command lower prices.

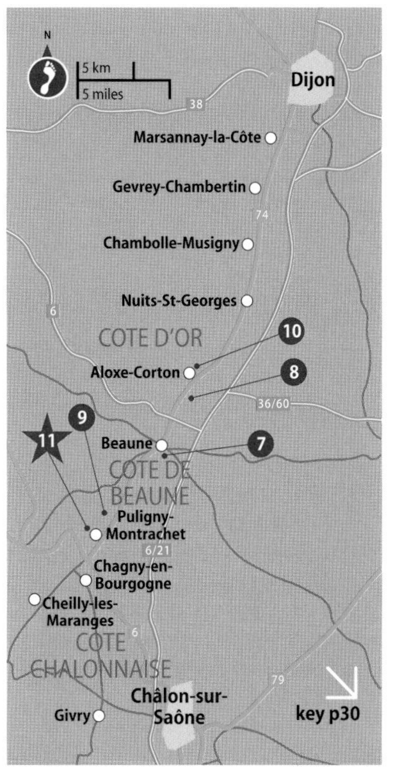

**Grapevine**

**The Burgundy name game**
Two individual qualities set Burgundy apart from most of the world's other wine regions. On the one hand there's the patchwork quilt of vineyards that catches the attention of every visitor to the region; on the other, there's the prevalence of double-barelled names, such as Gevrey-Chambertin and Chambolle-Musigny. The explanation for both is the region's long-held understanding of the way in which complex geological movements give individual vineyards very different soils and wines; a fact that is acknowledged by giving each individual plot a name. Le Chambertin, for example, one of the best plots in the region, was once '*le champ*' (field), owned by a man called Bertin. Unlike Bordeaux, which developed famous châteaux, the names that became well known in Burgundy were those of the vineyards and their villages, which were, in themselves, just collections of vineyards grown on similar soil. As the wines of some plots – le Chambertin in the village of Gevrey; le Musigny in Chambolle and St Georges in Nuits – grew in fame and reputation, so the villages simply tacked the name of the illustrious vineyard onto their own to create Gevrey-Chambertin; Chambolle-Musigny and Nuits-St-Georges. The vineyard of le Montrachet sat awkwardly on the border between the villages of Puligny and Chassagne, so they both adopted it. Villages without double-barreled names, such as Beaune, Volnay, Pommard and Meursault, thought that they were sufficiently famous to go it alone.

WINERY BEAUNE

### Alex Gambal

14 bvd Jules Ferry, 21200 Beaune
T +33 (0)3-80 22 75 81
www.alexgambal.com
Tours and tastings by appointment.

Burgundy may be challenging but it is not impenetrable. Case in point: Alex Gambal, the American who, in 1997, became a *négociant-éleveur* from scratch, and has gone onto garner plaudits and awards from around the world. E-mail ahead to make an appointment for a tour and tasting. With any luck Gambal himself will be on hand to explain a philosophy of qualitative winemaking that includes capping production at 60,000 bottles per year and a policy of not filtering or fining, except, very occasionally, for whites. Wines are produced across a number of Côte d'Or appellations, including Meursault, Chassagne-Montrachet, and Vosne-Romanée.

WINE MERCHANT BEANUE

## Camille Giroud

3 rue Pierre-Joigneaux, 21203 Beaune
T +33 (0)3-80 22 12 65
www.webstore.fr/giroud
Contact the venue directly for information.

Founded in the 19th century by Camille Giroud, this gem of a Burgundy *négociant* is still run by Giroud's grandsons Bernard and François, but under the ownership of a group led by Napa Valley superstar Ann Colgin and the guidance of Becky Wasserman, who may have been born in the USA but is credited as being more Burgundian than the locals. Standards are rigorous in every respect: the Giroud team doesn't buy vintages that are less than great, and doesn't go near a wine that in their opinion does not perfectly express its terroir. If you are able to arrange a visit, you will not only taste some of the best that Burgundy has to offer, but will also leave with an insight into the structure of this highly complex region.

WINERY COTE DE BEAUNE

## Château de Chorey-les-Beaune

Chorey-les-Beaune, 21200 Beaune
T +33 (0)3-80 22 06 05
www.chateau-de-chorey-les-beaune.fr
Visits by appointment only.

The Germain family will extend a warm welcome to visitors to their stunning moated château, whose towers date from the 13th century. On their 17 ha they produce a range of Beaune Premier Crus, as well as other wines, many of which are available for tasting, allowing you to note differences in terroir between, say, Les Teurons and Les Boucherottes. Even better, why not stay in one of the five rooms available for bed and breakfast ($$), and gain an even greater insight into the workings of a family-run Burgundy domaine.

Château de Meursault.

WINERY COTE DE BEAUNE

## Château de Meursault

21190 Meursault
T +33 (0)3-80 26 22 75
www.meursault.com
Sales daily 0930-1200 and 1430-1800.
Tours and tastings by appointment.
Tour and tasting €15.

The jewel in the crown of Patriarche, a big Burgundy merchant, and one of Burgundy's few vinous chateaux, the Château de Meursault heaves with a history that began in the 11th century. It is an excellent place to get an overview of how Burgundy's important place in French history intersects with its viticultural heritage. In a region of vineyard holdings barely larger than postage stamps, the Château de Meursault also groans with vines: some 60 ha in the Côte de Beaune, in and around Pommard, Volnay, Meursault and Puligny-Montrachet, among others. A visit provides the chance to taste several of the resulting wines and has become one of the most popular attractions in the region.

WINERY COTE DE BEAUNE

## Domaine Comte Senard

Clos des Meix, 21420 Aloxe-Corton
T +33 (0)3-80 26 41 65
www.domainesenard.com
Restaurant open for lunch only. Visits by appointment only.

Anyone wanting a quick snapshot of Burgundy should head out of Beaune towards Nuits-St-Georges and turn off to Aloxe-Corton, where in the shadow of the hill where the Emperor Charlemagne chose his vineyard 1200 years ago, you'll find the 13th-century Clos des Meix. At this estate, and at the Domaine des Terregelesses, nearby, Philippe Senard produces 17 wines including Grand Crus Corton and Corton Charlemagne. The best way to sample these (wines can also be tasted at the wine shop) is to have lunch at the restaurant, where, for €50, you can enjoy a meal and eight wines, including five red and white Grands Crus. (A €30 meal is also offered with four humbler wines, but there is little reason to skimp on the €20 difference.)

SHOP BEAUNE

## L'Atheneum

5 rue de l'Hôtel-Dieu, 21200 Beaune
T +33 (0)3-80 25 08 40
www.athenaeumfr.com
Daily 1000-1900.

As an author and passionate reader of wine books, I was bound to be impressed by this inspiring shop in the town where I once lived. Essentially devoted to books on wines and spirits in a wide range of languages, it stocks technical works, as well as others under categories such as Wine and Health, Wine and Literature, Essays on Wine and Wine Brotherhoods. There are also maps and wine-related items, including ties listing the various vineyards of Beaune, or splashed with Burgundy wine labels; candles scented with grapes varieties including Cabernet Sauvignon and Chardonnay; and a wide and funky array of corkscrews.

SCHOOL BEAUNE

## L'Ecole des Vins de Bourgogne

6 rue du 16ème Chasseurs, 21200 Beaune
T +33 (0)3-80 26 35 10
www.ecoledesvins-bourgogne.com

If you want to deepen your knowledge of this complex region but don't have much time, a stint at this school could impart years' worth of knowledge. Founded in 1974 as a joint venture between *négociants* and wine-growers, the emphasis is very much hands on. There are state-of-the-art tasting rooms, but also the opportunity to take to the vineyards for an al-fresco field study of wines and micro-terroirs. The exciting range of courses also includes a weekend at the Hospices des Beaunes auction, when students will be granted special access to many events that are usually only open to wine professionals, and will also have the opportunity to taste barrel-samples of cuvées auctioned on the Sunday.

HOTEL COTE DE BEAUNE

## Le Montrachet

Pl des Marronniers, 21190
Puligny-Montrachet
T +33 (0)3-80 21 30 06
www.le-montrachet.com
$

Thierry and Suzanne Gazagnes will welcome you to this converted early 19th century coach house, whose antique-filled bedrooms boast all mod cons, and will be delighted to help you plan your wine-tasting itineraries. The restaurant ($-$$) not only has a terrific wine list but also lets you buy wine to take away, allowing you to try examples from all those producers you haven't had time to visit or who aren't open to the public. When the weather permits, you can eat on a terrace overlooking the quiet village square. After which you could set off on foot to wander through the vineyards that begin as soon as the houses stop.

WINE BAR BEAUNE

## Le Bistrot Bourguignon

8 rue Monge, 21200 Beaune
T +33 (0)3-80 22 23 24
www.restaurant-lebistrotbourguignon.com
Tue-Sat 1030-1530 and 1830-late.

Since 1985 when Jean-Jacques Hegner turned his photographic studio and shop on a small pedestrian street in the heart of Beaune into a wine bar, this has been one of the most popular gathering points for local winegrowers and visiting wine professionals. There are 20 Burgundies by the glass and plenty of alternatives by the bottle. Food is simple and tasty, and includes local favourites such as *jambon persillé* (parsleyed ham). The bar – known to locals as Chez Jean-Jacques – is often busy on Saturdays when there are live jazz performances.

# Best producers

**Burgundy**

Ampeau, Robert
Barthod, Ghislaine
Bertagna
Carillon, Louis
Chandon de Briailles
Château de Meursault » *page 50.*
Château de la Tour
Château de Puligny-Montrachet
Clair, Bruno
Coche-Dury, J-F
Comtes Lafon
Dancer, Vincent
Dauvissat, René & Vincent
Domaine de l' Arlot
Domaine de la Vougeraie
Domaine de Montille
Domaine Leflaive
Drouhin, Joseph
Duboeuf, Georges
Dujac
Engel, Frédéric
Froujin-Laroze
Faiveley, Joseph
Gagnard, Jean-Noel
Girardin, Vincent
Giroud, Camille » *page 50.*
Gouges, Henri
Gros, Anne
Jadot, Louis
Jayer-Gilles, Robert
La Chablisienne
Lafarge, Michel
Laroche » *page 48.*
Leflaive, Olivier » *page 52.*
Leroy
Lignier, Hubert
Marquis d'Angervilles
Méo-Camuzet
Michelot, Alain
Mongeard-Mugneret
Mortet, Denis
Potel, Nicolas
Ramonet
Raveneau, Jean-Marie
Rodet, Antonin
Rollin Frères
Romanée-Conti
Roumier
Rousseau, Armand
Sauzet (top wines)
Senard, Daniel
Tollot-Beaut
Tremblay, Gerard
Verget
Vogue, Georges de

Checking the finished article at Olivier Leflaive.

MUSEUM BEAUNE

### Musée du Vin de Bourgogne

Hôtel des Ducs, Rue d'Enfer, 21200 Beaune
T +33 (0)3-80 22 08 19
musees@mairie-beaune.fr
Apr-Nov daily 0930-1800; Dec-Mar Wed-Mon 0930-1800
€5.40

This museum tucked away behind the cathedral, is as well worth visiting as the nearby tourist-packed Hôtel-Dieu (the home of the Hospices de Beaune). The museum, which was established almost 70 years ago, is well though-out and accessible, and offers thoughtful temporary exhibitions as well as an excellent permanent collection tracing the history of winemaking from antiquity to the present. Among the highlights is a 14th-century wine press.

WINERY COTE DE BEAUNE

### Olivier Leflaive

Pl du Monument, 21190 Puligny-Montrachet
T +33 (0)3-80 21 37 65
www.olivier-leflaive.com
1 Mar-31 Dec Mon-Sat 1230-1530. Winery experience by appointment only.
Winery experience €10.

Olivier Leflaive is one of my Burgundian heroes for the way that he has helped to make his complicated region enjoyably comprehensible. Under one roof, he offers not only rare access to his operating Burgundian winery but also the even rarer experience of spending a morning working in the winery yourself, doing whatever the season dictates, be it in the vines or the cellars. The tasting lunch (served from 1230, $$) is superb value: 15 wines matched to local dishes, with Leflaive often on hand to discourse on the various crus. It will be hard to tear yourself away, which is why it is such good news that a 12-room hotel has just opened ($$). This has to be one of the most integrated wine experiences in the world, certainly in terms of premium wines.

SHOP BEAUNE

### Perardel Grands Vins de France

Av de Gaulle, 21200 Beaune
T +33 (0)3-80 24 08 09
www.perardel.com/boutique
Mon-Sat 0830-1230 and 1400-1915.

This excellent shop offers wines from all over France but is especially strong in Burgundy. The Beaune shop, opened in 1991, followed on the heels of two Perardel outlets in the Champagne region, in Reims and Châlons-en-Champagne and so Champagne is also well represented. The staff will be happy to expound on the wines on offer in as much detail as you wish and it might be worth asking them for their views on how Pinot Noir and Chardonnay express themselves differently in the differing terroirs of Champagne and Burgundy.

## Côte Chalonnaise

The little town of Chagny (home of the great Lameloise restaurant) is effectively the gateway to the Côte Chalonnaise. As ancient as the Côte d'Or but not as celebrated, the villages of Mercurey, Rully and Givry can all offer wines that, by Burgundy standards, are relatively low-priced.

HOTEL CHAGNY-EN-BOURGOGNE

### Hôtel Restaurant Lameloise

36 pl d'Armes, 71150 Chagny-en-Bourgogne
T +33 (0)3-85 87 65 65
www.lameloise.fr
$$-$$$

Jacques Lameloise is the third generation to own and run this Burgundy institution in a 16th-century post station right on the main square of charming Chagny. Jacques was born in the hotel and so gives a new meaning to making guests feel at home. It is worth going for a package that includes a meal in order to experience the restaurant's ($$$) high-level cooking. Among other training, Jacques has done stints at the Savoy Hotel in London and worked under master *patissier* Gaston Lenôtre. Much thought has gone into choosing the wine list and in creating menus that allow for a broad sampling of the region's vinous offerings.

SHOP — CHALON-SUR-SAONE

### Maison des Vins de la Côte Chalonnaise

Promenade Sainte-Marie, 71100 Chalon-sur-Saône
T +33 (0)3-85 41 64 00
Mon-Sat 0900-1900

The staff at this inviting wine shop are more than eager to explain the 120 or so wines on offer, all sold at the same price as you'd pay at the producer's cellar door. You are welcome to taste some of the wines and to discover that, though less glamorous, some of the wines of the Côte Chalonnaise hold their own against those of neighbouring Mercurey, and at a much lower price. The shop is an easy walk from the centre of town.

## Beaujolais and Mâconnais

Supposedly two regions, Beaujolais and the Mâconnais overlap geographically and stylistically. Beaujolais is a large area whose reds are all made from the Gamay grape, at its best in the 38 communes that are allowed to label their wine as Beaujolais Villages and, more specifically, in the 10 'cru' villages of Brouilly, Chénas, Chiroubles, Côte de Brouilly, Fleurie, Juliénas, Morgon, Moulin à Vent, Régnié and St-Amour. Historically, Beaujolais was quintessential jug wine, served from pitchers in bars in Lyon and Paris. In recent times it has suffered from taking itself – and expecting to be taken – too seriously. Stated bluntly, most of the region's wine is perfectly nice, easy-drinking stuff sold at too high a price. The finest examples, however, can achieve true greatness.

Beaujolais Blanc exists but this Chardonnay is now often sold as St-Veran, which is, in turn, one of the more reliable white appellations within the Mâconnais. Historically, the best wines in this second region were the whites from Pouilly-Fuissé, Pouilly Vinzelles, St-Véran and Mâcon Clessé. Today investment from Côte d'Or producers, such as the Domaines des Comtes Lafon, and growing local ambitions have brought about huge improvements. Basic Mâcon Blanc is still often unremarkable but it is usually better than the vast majority of Mâcon Rouge, which merely shows how the Gamay performs on less-than-ideal soil with less-than-brilliant winemaking.

HOTEL — BAGNOLS

### Château de Bagnols

69620 Bagnols
T +33 (0)4-74 71 40 00
www.bagnols.com
$$$

This exquisite hotel, in a 13th-century castle boasts towers, a moat and a drawbridge, as well as stunning views across Beaujolais. This is château-living at its finest: no shabby gentility here. The building is a listed monument and its interiors have been painstakingly restored by wealthy British owners, a process that has uncovered Renaissance wall paintings from an era when nearby Lyon was one of Europe's most important cities. To complement the luxury of each of the 20 rooms, the Salle des Gardes restaurant ($$-$$$) offers delicious regional fare, as well as what has to be one of the best Beaujolais lists anywhere.

WINERY — POUILLY-FUISSE

### Château de Fuissé

71960 Fuisse
T +33 (0)3-85 35 61 44
www.chateau-fuisse.fr
Mon-Fri 0800-1200 and 1330-1730.

This family-owned estate provides proof that Pouilly-Fuissé in southern Burgundy can make white wines to compete with Meursault and Puligny Montrachet. Among the offerings here are three single-vineyard 'Climat' wines, none of which has been aged in new oak; their individual flavours reveal the influence of the soil. While the various Pouilly-Fuissés are from the estate's own vineyards, it is also worth tasting wines from the JJ Vincent selection of local whites and Beaujolais (single-vineyard Morgon and Juliénas), some of which are made from bought-in grapes.

MUSEUM — ROMANECHE

### Le Hameau en Beaujolais

La Gare, 71570 Romanèche-Thorins
T +33 (0)3-85 35 22 22
www.hameauenbeaujolais.com
Apr-Oct daily 0900-1900; Nov-Mar 1000-1800. Closed Jan.
€16

France has much to learn from California when it comes to wine tourism, but from the moment I first saw what Georges Duboeuf had done with the old railway station in Romanèche-Thorins, I could see that he could teach the most sophisticated Napa Valley winery a thing or two. This is an outing for the whole family, with the added attraction that children under 15 get in free. Start this voyage into viticulture and winemaking at the station, which has been restored in a late 19th-century style, complete with frescoes. Once you have your ticket, you board a small train to take you into the vineyards and other attractions. These are spread across 1 ha and include films, exhibitions on wine and art, and detailed explanations of every possible facet of winemaking, including bottle making and cork manufacturing. The visit includes a tasting of Beaujolais that reveals how much variation thre is between wines made from the same grape – the Gamay – in individual villages and vineyards

ATTRACTION MACON-VILLAGES

**Le Vigneroscope**

Domaine Saint-Philibert, Loché,
71100 Mâcon
T +33 (0)3-85 35 61 76
Berard.loche@wanadoo.fr
Jun-Sep Wed-Mon 1500-1830.

Even Philippe Bérard, the creator of the Vigneroscope, struggles to define it. It's not a museum exactly, more a sound-and-light meets puppet show. This highly stimulating, dynamic take on wine's history and production only takes 40 minutes. It's a big hit with children, so it is well worth making the trip into the vineyards surrounding Mâcon to seek it out. Certainly a candidate for 'world's most unusual wine museum'.



**The Lyon's share**

Lyon is the undisputed gastronomic capital of France, with more restaurants per head than anywhere else in the world. Its traditions are rooted in its surroundings; the region is rich in fowl, fresh fish and dairy cows, and surrounding it are the vineyards of Beaujolais and the Côtes du Rhône. This abundant natural larder is plundered by an army of celebrated chefs, who are the hot topics of conversation and speculation amongst locals. Visit the daily markets at **Les Halles de Lyon** and **quai St-Antoine** to witness famous chefs haggling over cured ham and goldleaf-dusted chocolates.

Top of the pile is legendary Paul Bocuse, with three Michelin stars, the inventor of nouvelle cuisine and today reigning supreme over five restaurants, one of which is the Mediterranean-style $$ **Le Sud** (11 pl Antonin-Poncet, T +33 (0)4-72 77 80 00, www.bocuse.com). Other kings of the kitchen include Pierre Orsi (the French swoon over his foie gras ravioli) and Jean-Paul Lacombe, although new chefs such as Nicolas le Bec are snapping at their heels. Sample his Michelin-starred food at $$$ **Restaurant Nicolas Le Bec** (14 rue Grolée, T +33 (0)4-78 42 15 00).

Some of the finest eating experiences in Lyon can be had in its simplest establishments. $ **Chabert et Fils** (11 rue des Marronniers, T +33 (0)4-78 37 01 94) is a typical Lyonnaise *bouchon*. Traditionally catering for silk workers, these serve the best of Lyon's specialities, such as *quenelles* (a poached pike mousse served with béchamel sauce) or kidneys with Madeira sauce and *andouillette* (chitterling) sausage.

To walk off all that food, France's second largest city has a delightful Renaissance quarter. Vieux Lyon feels somehow more Italian than French, with cobbled lanes lined with pastel-coloured Renaissance façades, a huge number of which are given over to bustling restaurants, cafés and boutiques. The city's wealth came from the silk industry and the fascinating **Musée des Tissus** (T +33 (0)4-78 38 42 00, www.musee-des- tissus.com) is an excellent introduction to this heritage. To the north, in the area of La Croix-Rousse, once home to silk weavers, is the **Musée des Beaux-Arts** (T04-72 10 17 40), which holds a vast fine arts collection, second in France only to the Louvre. Among the works on show are pieces by France's finest 19th-century painters, including Monet, Renoir and Gauguin.

**Established by the Romans as they moved north, the Rhône's vineyards have always quietly competed with Burgundy and Bordeaux. In the 18th century, Hermitage was famously added to Château Latour to give it more body but, along with its neighbour, Côte-Rôtie, Hermitage was also highly regarded by smart diners in Paris. At around the same time, the British Earl of Bristol was buying Vin d'Avignon, the early name for what we now call Châteauneuf-du-Pape. However, it was not until the late 20th century, thanks to the efforts of the dynamic Marcel Guigal in launching his single-vineyard Côte Rôties and to the enthusiasm of the top US critic Robert Parker for Châteauneuf, that this region's wines were finally taken seriously by a wider audience of wine drinkers.**

## Northern Rhône

The northern part of the Rhône begins just to the south of Lyon. Ampuis (Côte Rôtie), Cornas, Hermitage (and Crozes-Hermitage) and St Joseph are all Syrah country, while the white Viognier has its homeland in Condrieu and in the beautiful one-estate appellation of Château Grillet. In all these areas, the best-sited vines cling to steep slopes overlooking the river in much the same way as their counterparts in the Rhine, Mosel and Douro. Tourists are not particularly well catered for here, though all cellars will open their doors by appointment, so it is worth trying to time your visit to coincide with a festival. Keen walkers and motorists with four-wheel-drive should consider making their way up to the tiny chapel after which Hermitage is named. The route, though poorly marked, is quite straightforward and well worth trying at dusk in the company of a good bottle.

WINERY | HERMITAGE

### Cave de Tain

22 rte de Larnage, 26603 Tain-l'Hermitage
T +33 (0)4-75 08 20 87
www.cavedetain.fr
Sep-May daily 0900-1200 and 1400-1800; Jun-Aug Mon-Sat 0900-1230 and 1300 to 1900.

One of France's best cooperatives, this huge establishment, close to the river and at the foot of the Hermitage slopes, produces around half the wine in the northern Rhône and offers good examples of Hermitage, Crozes-Hermitage, Cornas, St-Joseph and St-Péray: everything, in fact, except Condrieu and Côte-Rôtie. It is worth coming here to taste the range and to pick up older vintages and the first-class single-vineyard Hermitage Gambert de Loché which is hard to find elsewhere.

HOTEL/RESTAURANT | COTE ROTIE

### Domaine de Clairefontaine

Chemin des Fontanettes, 38121 Chonas l'Amballan
T +33 (0)4-74 58 81 52
www.domaine-de-clairefontaine.fr
$

Set in delightful gardens, complete with resident peacocks, this is a peaceful base for exploring Côte-Rôtie and Condrieu. The hotel can help organize winery visits, as well as boat trips on the river, including cruises from Vienne to Lyon. In the kitchen ($$), award-winning chef-proprietor Philippe Girardon, a Meilleur Ouvrier de France, cooks in thrall to the seasons, amply helped by the hotel's kitchen garden and his visits to the local markets.

## Ardèche

Heading south, there is a hiatus to the southwest of Valence where the Rhône appellation vineyards give way to Vin de pays des Côteaux de l'Ardèche, which is where Louis Latour makes a good Chardonnay. To the southeast is the

Terraced vineyards in the southern Rhône.

appellation of Clairette de Die, where a good, grapey sparkling wine is made using the Muscat and the usually dull Clairette.

MUSEUM ROUMS

### Musée-découverte des Vins d'Ardèche

Pl de l'Eglise, 07120 Ruoms
T +33 (0)4-75 93 85 00
www.vinimage.tm.fr
Apr-Jun and Sep Tue-Sun 1000-1230, 1400-1830. Jul and Aug Sun-Fri 1000-1230, 1400-1830.
€4.60. Tours €20 per day.

Opened in 2002, this charming 10-room museum offers insights into all aspects of viticulture, winemaking and wine tasting, with special reference, not surprisingly, to the Ardèche. Displays are in both French and English, a welcome touch that one wishes was more widespread, but what really sets this museum apart is the terrific programme of tours to the surrounding area. The extremely good-value day-long visits include: 'Meet the wine growers of the Southern Ardèche', 'Countryside of the Midi', and 'Ruoms and its rich cultural heritage', which includes a visit to a silkworm nursery.

## Southern Rhône

Just beyond Montélimar you arrive in Côtes du Rhône territory where most wines are blends and the Grenache is more prominent. Unlike their northern counterparts, these southern Rhône vineyards are not on the banks of the river but are more widely spread, around a set of communes known as the Côtes du Rhône Villages (though there is a tendency to give them their own appellations). Syrah is grown here too, but blends are more customary, with Grenache often taking the main role. Villages like Rasteau and Cairanne are well worth visiting for their charm and for the efforts that are being made to welcome visitors. (Cairanne, for example now offers horse-driven tours of its vineyards.) In Châteauneuf-du-Pape, the ruins of Clement V's 14th-century Papal palace are well worth seeing but so too are the extraordinary pebbles in which most of the vines are grown.

WINERY COTES DU RHONE

### Cave de Cairanne

Rte de Bollène, 84290 Cairanne
T +33 (0)4-90 30 82 05
www.cave-cairanne.fr
Mon-Sat 1100-1600; Sun by appointment.
€6

This enterprising co-operative, in what is considered one of the best of the 16 villages in the Côtes du Rhône appellation, provides an interactive 'sensory' tour as part of its winery visit and tasting. The idea is that each of your five senses will be so stimulated – for example by a wall full of colourful pictures or a range of different isolated scents – that you will emerged with your faculties fully stretched. Vignerons are often on hand to give informal talks about the displays, a nice touch for those who might not have time to hit the vineyards.

WINERY CHATEAUNEUF-DU-PAPE

### Domaine Saint Benoît

Rte de Sorgues, BP 72, 84232 Châteauneuf-du-Pape
T +33 (0)4-90 83 51 36
www.saintbenoitvins.com
Visits by appointment only.

Founded in 1989, this family-run winery produces southern Rhône wines under its own label and also distributes those of other, smaller domaines. Both established appellations, such as Gigondas, and up-and-coming appellations, such as Côtes du Ventoux, are represented, providing a good opportunity to see a mid-sized southern Rhône winery up close as well as to taste a sampling of what this large region has to offer. The family's recent acquisitions include a producer of Clairette de Die and a sweet Muscat de Beaumes de Venise, further expanding the styles of wine available.

MUSEUM CHATEAUNEUF-DU-PAPE

### Musée du Vigneron

Domaine de Beaurenard, Rte de Roaix, 84110 Rasteau
T +33 (0)4-90 46 11 75/90 83 71 79
www.beaurenard.fr
Mon-Sat 0900-1200 and 1300-1730.

Emile Peynaud , the oenologist credited with dragging French wine out of the 19th century, extolled the excellence of this museum in an entry to the guest book in 1985. Founded by Paul Coulon, for many years the force behind top Châteauneuf-du-Pape producer Domaine de Beaurenard, it is clear that the museum has benefited from his attention to detail. There are more than 2500 tools and 2000 antique bottles on show, including some hand-blown examples from the late 19th century. Among the highlights are an exhibit tracing the evolution of pruning tools, which starts in the Stone Age; a film that explains, among other things, the Châteauneuf-du-Pape AOC regulations; and, of course, a tasting featuring Domaine de Beaurenard wines.

## Best producers

**Rhône**

Allemand, Thierry
Cave de St Désirat
Cave de Tain l'Hermitage » *page 55.*
Chapoutier
Château d' Ampuis
Château de Beaucastel
Château la Nerthe
Château Rayas
Chave, Jean-Louis
Clape, A
Clos des Papes
Colombo, Jean-Luc
Coursodon, Pierre
Cuilleron, Yves
Delas
Domaine de l' Oratoire St Martin
Domaine du Vieux Télégraphe
Domaine la Réméjeanne
Graillot, Alain
Guigal
Jaboulet Ainé
Jamet
Lionnet, Jean
Perret, André
Pochon, Etienne
Richaud, Marcel
Rocailles
Rostaing, Rene
Tardieu-Laurent
Vernay, Georges

HOTEL/RESTAURANT CHATEAUNEUF-DU-PAPE

### Restaurant Hôtel La Sommellerie

Rte de Roquemaure D17, 84230 Châteauneuf-du-Pape
T +33 (0)4-90 83 50 00
www.la-sommellerie.fr
$

Annie and Pierre Paumel provide a welcome as warm as the summer Provence sun at this charming 17th-century country house hotel. Annie is the talent behind the stylish Provençal decor of the 14 rooms and suites, while Pierre, a Maître Cuisinier de France, is the genius in the kitchen ($$), turning out such delights as velouté of baby artichokes, served with foie gras and truffles. La Sommellerie is an ideal base for exploring the vineyards and wineries of the southern Rhône, and the Paumels will be delighted to help guests plan their itineraries. Also recommended is a cooking lesson in Pierre's private kitchen, where you can refine not only your cooking but also your wine-and-food-matching skills.

Young vines at Guigal.

SHOP CHATEAUNEUF-DU-PAPE

### VINADEA – Maison des vins de Châteauneuf-du-Pape

8 rue Maréchal Foch, BP 68, 84232 Châteauneuf-du-Pape
T +33 (0)4-90 83 70 69
www.chateauneuf.com
Daily.

A perfect place to begin a visit to Châteauneuf-du-Pape, this shop provides the opportunity to sample and purchase at the cellar door price more than 90 wines from this appellation. There is no pressure to buy, however, as the purpose behind VINADEA, an initiative of the vignerons themselves, is to deepen visitors' understanding of a region that can be hard to penetrate. This is a great service, especially for those who have limited time and have not made prior appointments at domaines, and it is a special bonus that it is also open on Sundays. Hard-to-find vintages are also available, and there are regular informal exhibitions of wine-related art.

## Provence

One of the most beautiful of France's wine regions, this is also both a goldmine and a minefield for wine lovers, who have to negotiate a path between delicious and downright ordinary wines. There are 10 appellations here, the biggest of which is the huge Côtes de Provence, whose label appears on no less than half of France's, generally dull, pink wine. Côteaux d'Aix-en-Provence is also fairly large and very mixed, while Palette, Bellet and Cassis are all tiny. To confuse matters further, because of ongoing spats between local growers and the all-powerful INAO (Institut National des Appellations d'Origine Contrôlée) in Paris, many of the region's top wines are sold as Vins de Pays. Among these, the most famous is Domaine de Trévallon, which is situated in the appellation of Les Baux de Provence but bears a Vin de Pays des Bouches-du-Rhône label because its blend contains too much Cabernet Sauvignon. The hilltop medieval village of Les Baux is well worth visiting, partly for its views of the vineyards, as is the beautiful fishing port of Cassis whose white is one of the region's most distinctive wines. One word of warning: the closer you get to seaside resorts, the higher the prices wines command – irrespective of their quality.

WINERY PIERREFEU

### Château de l'Aumérade Cru Classé

83390 Pierrefeu
T +33 (0)4-94 28 20 31
www.aumerade.com
Mon-Sat 0800-1200 and 1330/1400-1730/1800

Henri and Charlotte Fabre rebuilt this estate, which has origins in the late 16th century, in the 1950s and, by 1955, it had become one of Provence's 17 *crus classés*. The winery, still run by the family, can arrange several types of visits and tastings and also houses Henri Fabre's collection of almost 2000 miniature figurines. Many are made in clay in Provence itself and date from the 17th century to the present day. The gardens are lovely and full of ancient trees, some more than 400 years old.

## Best producers

**Corsica**

Clos Nicrosi
Comte Peraldi

**Provence**

Château de Pibarnon
Château Vannières
Château Vignelaure » *page 59.*
Domaine de Trévallon
Domaine Richeaume

Château Vignelaure.

The tour offers an intimate look at a business that makes 2.5 million bottles of wine from 550 ha.

WINERY — COTES DE PROVENCE

### Château de Selle

Rte Départementale 73, 83460 Taradeau
T+33 (0)4-94 47 57 57
www.domaines-ott.com
Mon-Sat 1000-1200 and 1400-1800.

Housed in a stunning 18th-century chateau, the former home of the Counts of Provence, and surrounded by dramatic rocky landscape, this is a perfect place to understand the past and present of the often misunderstood and underrated, wines of Provence. The rosés are a revelation and the reds and whites are also excellent. The Ott family also own Clos Mireille (La Londe Les Maures) and Château Romassan (La Castellet).

WINERY — COTEAUX D'AIX-EN-PROVENCE

### Château Vignelaure

Rte de Jouques, 83560 Rians
T +33 (0)4-94 37 21 10
www.vignelaure.com
Sales Mon-Fri 0900-1800 (until 1730 in winter); Sat and Sun 1000-1800. Tours and tastings by appointment only

Château Vignelaure is Provence winemaking at its best, by former successful horse-trainer, David O'Brien with the help of his Australian-born wife Catherine. Dramatically situated at an altitude of 350-480 m in dramatic, savage countryside, this is an essential and easy trip from Aix. Among the attractions is a collection of modern art, including works by Miró and Henri Cartier-Bresson. Visits and tastings can be arranged for groups of up to 100 people, catering to all interests and levels of knowledge. The château can also help with booking meals in local restaurants.

Château Vignelaure.

## Corsica

Corsica is a glorious island to visit, irrespective of its wines, though these too are improving with every year. There is a confusing plethora of appellations, many of which have little real reason to exist, since some delicious wine is sold under the island-wide Vin de Corse.

WINERY — SARTENE

### Domaine Comte Abbatucci

20140 Casalabriva
T +33 (0)4-95 74 04 55
www.domaine-comte-abbatucci.com
Visits by appointment only.

On 24 ha of the wild and rugged landscape for which Corsica is famed, one of the island's oldest wineries makes prize-winning wines from such indigenous varieties as Sciacarello and Nielluccio, as well as from Barbarossa and Vermentino. Biodynamic since 2000, Domaine Comte Abbatucci is a prime example of the improving face of Corsican wines. Proprietor Jean-Charles Abbatucci is a major pioneer of biodynamic agriculture, and the remaining 70 ha of his estate are devoted to biodynamically produced fruit and olives, as well as cows and sheep. The results can all be sampled at the restaurant ($$). There are two gîtes for rent, as well as camping facilities on site. Tastings can be arranged at an old farmhouse on the estate.

# Languedoc-Roussillon

**A huge area – the largest single wine region in the world – Languedoc-Roussillon follows the coast west from Marseilles to the Spanish border. Originally developed by the Romans, for a long time this was the place to find France's most basic wine – the stuff that is most likely to end up in the European wine lake – but times are changing and outside investment is now pouring in from Bordeaux producers and others.**

**An ocean of varietal Vin de Pays d'Oc is made here, as well as a growing list of ambitious small appellations such as Limoux, Fitou, Faugères, St-Chinian and Collioure. There are also subsections of larger appellations, such as la Livinière in Minervois, Pic-St-Loup in Côteaux de Languedoc and Boutenac in Corbières. Styles and quality, even within the appellations, can vary widely. Cabardès, a young appellation, for example, can be made from 60% Cabernet Sauvignon and/or Cabernet Franc and/or Merlot and 40% Syrah and/or Grenache. Or vice versa.**



## Coteaux de Languedoc

SHOP — CLERMONT L'HERAULT

### Au Fil du Vin

Allées Roger Salengro, 34800 Clermont l'Hérault
T +33 (0)4-67 44 73 86
www.aufilduvin.com
Daily 0930-1400.

This the kind of wine shop you wish you could take home with you. Caviste Mokhsine Diouf, originally from Senegal, has painstakingly and lovingly scoured the surrounding countryside to find the best producers. He is full of advice about local wines and hosts informal tastings on market day (Wednesday), as well as other wine-related activities.

RESTAURANT — ST-GUIRAUD

### Le Mimosa

Grande Rue, 34725 St-Guiraud
T +33 (0)4-67 96 67 96
Mid Mar-early Nov Tue-Sat for dinner only; Sun for lunch only. Closed early Nov-mid Mar.
$

People make huge detours to come to this restaurant, run by Bridget and David Pugh, which offers extraordinarily fresh and innovative cuisine, masterminded by Bridget, and a chance to benefit from David's intimate knowledge of what the local *vignerons* have been up to. The Pughs have recently talked of retiring, so it is worth getting here sooner rather than later. The set menu offers four courses, plus cheeses aged by the Pughs themselves and dessert. A typical offering might be wild duck with preserved baby oranges, goat's cheese and cep tart or pot-au-feu of pigeon. The Pughs also own the nearby hotel, Ostalariá Cardabela ($$).

WINERY — NARBONNE

### Musée de la Vigne et du Vin

Château l'Hospitalet, Rte de Narbonne-Plage, 11100 Narbonne
T +33 (0)4-68 45 34 47
www.gerard-bertrand.com/hospitalet_musees.php
Museum daily 0930-1900. Tours and tastings by appointment only.

This is a one-stop-shop introduction to the region: a top producer, hotel ($$), restaurant ($$-$$$) and museum under one roof. The contrast between the ultra-modern winery and the massive underground cellars, hewn from the rock, is stunning, and sets the scene for the museum's insights into the huge progress that this region has made. Among the highlights are an account of the 1907 *vignerons* uprising and explanations of the unique flora and fauna, minerals and fossils particular to La Clape, which expands the context in which "terroir" is usually discussed in an interesting and welcome fashion.

# Best producers

**Languedoc-Roussillon**

Bertrand, Gerard
Château des Estanilles
Château l'Hospitalet » *page 60.*
Château la Voulte Gasparets
Clos Centeilles
Domaine Alquier
Domaine Auzieres
Domaine Cazes
Domaine de l'Hortus
Domaine Gauby
La Grange des Peres
Mas, Jean-Paul
Mas Bruguiere
Mas de Daumas Gassac
Mas Jullien
Prieuré de St Jean de Bébian
Sieur d'Arques

## Minervois

RESTAURANT — CAUNES

### Restaurant D'Alibert

Rue Saint Genes, 11160 Caunes-Minervois
T +33 (0)4-68 78 00 54
Contact the restaurant for opening hours.
$$

Tiny, hard to find but worth every effort and penny, this wine-mad provincial restaurant serves delightful local dishes from a refreshing, tourist-disappointingly slight menu. The only green thing you'll find will probably be snaking its way through some cheese. Wonderful and excellent value.

Eating in the evening in the titchy courtyard is something that you will never forget.

## Corbières

MUSEUM | LEZIGNAN-CORBIERES

### Musée de la Vigne et du Vin

3 rue Turgot, 11200 Lézignan-Corbières
T +33 (0)4-68 27 07 57
Museum daily 0930-1900. Tours and tastings by appointment only.

Two centuries' worth of the tools and machines used by Languedoc *vignerons* are on display in this large 19th-century structure, including a barrel-making display and a recreation of a 19th-century stable. One of the highlights is an explanation of all the key stages in the viticultural and winemaking calendar, including phylloxera-fighting measures (winter), treatment against mildew (spring) and bottling (autumn). There are also colourful displays of traditional Languedoc *vignerons* outfits.

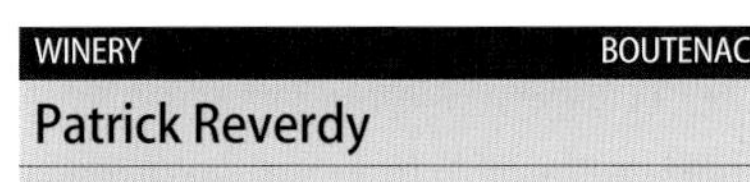

WINERY | BOUTENAC

### Patrick Reverdy

Chateau La Voulte-Gasparets,
11200 Boutenac
T +33 (0)4-68 27 07 86
chateaulavoulte@wanadoo.fr
Visits by appointment only.

Patrick Reverdy and his son Laurent continue the work of several generations before them that earned Patrick the title Vigneron of the Year by France's Gault-Millau guide in 1994. This is the place to come to get an insight into the passion and pride that characterizes the best producers of this region. It is an experience so authentic, in fact, that there is no guarantee that you will find an English speaker to guide you from the 17th-century chateau to the winery. No matter: the concentrated wines and surroundings can speak for themselves.

Corbières vineyards.

## Roussillon

HOTEL | COLLIOURE

### Hotel les Templiers

12 quai de l'Amirauté, 66190 Collioure
T +33 (0)4-68 98 31 10
www.hotel-templiers.com
$$

If you are an artist, you might just try to pay for your dinner or your stay in this classic hotel in the magical seaside town of Collioure, with a canvas or two. But you'd better be good, considering the company you'll be keeping. Picasso and Duffy were but two of the painters who frequented this bastion of Catalan culture and charm which was opened three generations ago by René and Pauline Pous. Pous' grandson still runs the hotel and restaurant, and extends a warm welcome to all guests. There are more than 2000 artworks displayed around the main hotel building, its three annexes and the restaurant, paintings given by various artists to René and Pauline in exchange for meals. The restaurant ($$) offers a host of delicious seafood recipes, many handed down from Pauline, including a Templiers bouillabaisse.

## Costières de Nimes

WINERY | BEAUCAIRE

### Mas des Tourelles

4294 Rte de Bellegarde, 30300 Beaucaire
T +33 (0)4-6659 1972
www.tourelles.com
Cellar door Mon-Fri 0900-1200 and 1400-1700. Tours Apr-Jun, Sep and Oct daily 1400-1800; Jul and Aug daily 1000-1200 and 1400-1900. Nov-Mar Sat 1400-1800.
€4.80

This is a must-visit if you are even remotely curious about the history of wine. The discovery of the remains of an old Roman winery beneath one of the vineyards here was the inspiration for not only reconstructing parts of it in a museum, complete with original amphorae, but also recreating the types of wines the Romans would have drunk. Of the three Roman wines, the most interesting is probably Turriculae, which is made using a recipe by Columella that describes the addition of seawater, fenugreek and grape juice syrup. This was a wine that starred in the recently published *Around the World in 6 Glasses* by Tom Standish, but is almost impossible to find outside the winery.

## Bordeaux

One name for a collection of regions, Bordeaux brings together the flat, aesthetically dull Médoc and Pomerol, the slopes and Roman caves of St-Émilion and the bucolic, gentle hills of Sauternes. The big name châteaux of Bordeaux often have no reason to open their doors to visitors, because they generally hope to have sold all their wine in barrel to local merchants (see How Bordeaux is sold, page 63). Smaller, less illustrious estates may have some stock to sell, but they are rarely as visitor-friendly as their counterparts in, say, Alsace. There are exceptions to these rules, however, such as Châteaux Mouton-Rothschild, Prieuré-Lichine and Pichon-Longueville Baron, but appointments are still generally advisable. One question that arises among people thinking of spending a few days in Bordeaux is where to stay. The city of Bordeaux itself has the advantage of being in the centre of the region as a whole and of boasting some great places to eat and drink. But it's worth remembering that a car here can be a liability, as it can take a long time to get in and out of town and to park. Staying in Pauillac in the north of the Médoc is not ideal if your visits are going to include St-Émilion but it is worth considering taking the ferry from Lamarque to Blaye to avoid the traffic of Bordeaux and its ring road.

### Bordeaux city

SHOP — BORDEAUX

**Badie**

62 Allées de Tourny, 33000 Bordeaux
T +33 (0)5-56 52 23 72
Mon-Sat 0900-1915.

Vladimir Protopopov manages this blue chip *caviste*, under whose roof is assembled one of the finest groups of the finest vintages of the finest Bordeaux. Come and drool, if not to buy. The spirit collection is also staggering.

MUSEUM — BORDEAUX

**Cellier des Chartrons**

41 rue de Borie, 33000 Bordeaux
T +33 (0)5-57 87 50 60
www.cellier-des-chartrons.com
Visits by appointment only.

For a concise history of Bordeaux's wine trade, make an effort to find the off-the-beaten-track Cellier des Chartrons. Located in the beautifully restored home of a former wine merchant, built in 1720, its tasting room is designed according to the strictures of celebrated Bordeaux oenologist Emile Peynaud. There are old bottles and tools throughout the museum: lovely tangible evocations of the Bordeaux wine trade of the past three centuries.

RESTAURANT — BORDEAUX

**La Tupina**

6 rue Porte de la Monnaie, 33800 Bordeaux
T +33 (0)5-56 91 56 37
www.latupina.com
Daily 1200-2300. Shop Mon-Sat 0900-1300 and 1700-2200.
$-$$

Jean-Pierre Xiradakis's life mission has been to seek out and make available to his friends and clients the best products that southwest France has to offer. His efforts have won him much recognition, including La Tupina being elected one of the world's best bistros by the *International Herald Tribune*. More significantly, perhaps, this is also the place to find on- and off-duty château owners and merchants. The restaurant has been going strong since 1968 and, since then, has bolted on a more informal wine bar and an *épicerie* selling La Tupina products and table-top snacks. Dishes are highly seasonal and dependent on what is available in the local markets, but might include boiled egg with foie gras, ham sautéed with shallots and asparagus omelette. It is well worth booking ahead to guarantee a table at this local institution. La Tupina provides a great insight into the city of Bordeaux and also an overview of the cuisine of southwest France.

WINE CENTRE BORDEAUX

## Maison du Vin de Bordeaux

1 cours du XXX juillet, 33075 Bordeaux
T +33 (0)5-56 00 22 66
www.ecole.vins-bordeaux.fr
Contact the venue for further details.

This one-stop shop in the heart of the city is run by the regional wine association and offers all of the information you could ever need to plan a day or a year of visits. But don't just drop in to pick up a few leaflets; wander into the newly-launched **Bar à Vin** to taste a few local examples, or sign up for the **École du Vin**, a wine school that offers a whole range of courses, lasting from two hours to several days. There is also the possibility of visiting châteaux, both well known and off the beaten track by car and on foot.

Grapevine

**How Bordeaux is sold**

One of the questions that's worth asking when visiting a top Bordeaux château is whether it is possible to buy a bottle or even a case. The notion would seem to be perfectly sensible; after all, it's common practice for wine producers elsewhere to happily sell their wine and every château would appear to have plenty of cases of freshly labelled young wine. But nothing is simple in Bordeaux. The wine sitting in the château has, if all has gone well, already been sold as futures 'en primeur' via brokers to local merchants (*négociants*), within a few months of the harvest. The wine is matured for 18 months or so, bottled and delivered to the *négociants*, who should have already sold it to merchants in other countries, who, in turn, have sold it to their customers.

In good and great vintages, such as 2000 and 2003, demand for the wine usually makes this process work very smoothly; in lesser years, such as 2002, it can be more fraught. Players at every stage of the game are 'encouraged' to buy what might well be unimpressive and overpriced wine by the threat that failure to do so may may mean they will miss the chance to purchase wines from the next great vintage when it comes along. While hundreds of châteaux try to sell their wine in this way, only the top 50 to 100 actually manage to dispose of all their stock by doing so.

MUSEUM BORDEAUX

## Vinorama de Bordeaux

10 Cours du Médoc, 33300 Bordeaux
T +33 (0)5-56 39 53 02
http://cugnac.perso.cegetel.net/vinorama/contact.html
Jul and Aug Tue-Sat 1400-1800; Sep-Jun Mon-Fri 1400-1800.
€5.40.

An unusual museum that is either fun or kitsch, depending on your point of view. Bacchus, the God of Wine, is the commentator on a guided tour through the history of wine that takes in 13 displays and some 75 life-size mannequins in traditional dress. Want to know how Charlemagne and Eleanor of Aquitaine influenced the wine trade? Bacchus will tell you. Highlights include the chance to sample an Ancient Roman-style wine, as well as a recreation of one made in 1850.

La Tupina.

## Entre-Deux-Mers

TASTING CENTRE — BEYCHAC ET CAILLAU

### Maison des Bordeaux

RN 89, Exit 5, 33750 Beychac et Caillau
T +33 (0)5-57 97 19 26
www.maisondesbordeaux.com
Jun-Sep Mon-Fri 0930-1730, Sat 1000-1800.
Oct-May Mon-Fri 0930-1200 and 1400-1730.
Tastings priced according to wines.

The centre is run by the association of producers of Bordeaux and Bordeaux Supérieur, much of which is sadly very ordinary, but can be very good value. In any case, apart from tastings, the Maison offers a good interactive insight into the region's soils, vinegrowing and winemaking.

## Graves

HOTEL — MARTILLAC

### Les Sources de Caudalie

Chemin de Smith Haut Lafitte, 33650 Bordeaux-Martillac
T +33 (0)5-57 83 83 83
www.sources-caudalie.com
$\$\$$

It's hard to think of what more you could want or need during a stay at Les Sources de Caudalie. Want to visit a top red and white wine-producing château? You are in the grounds of one: Smith Haut Lafitte. Want a meal? You have several top restaurants to choose from. Want a cigar? There is a clubroom dedicated to puffing Havanas, complete with a stunning view over the chateau and vines. What really sets Les Sources de Caudalie apart, however, is the spa, which uses a range of eponymous products based on extracts of grapes and vines. The spa and restaurants are open to non-guests but the winery itself may only be visited by guests. Wine tastings and cooking courses must be booked through the hotel.

## Haut-Médoc

HOTEL — PAUILLAC

### Château Cordeillan-Bages

Rte des Châteaux, BP 79, 33250 Pauillac
T +33 (0)5-56 59 24 24
www.cordeillanbages.com
$\$\$$

Whenever I am asked for advice on where to stay in the Médoc, this beautiful 17th-century building is the first place that comes to mind. Owned by the utterly unpretentious Cazes family of Château Lynch-Bages, this hotel's aged exterior belies the inside's incredibly modern take on Bordeaux glamour. It is both casual and luxurious, stylish yet fresh. In the restaurant ($$-$$$), Thierry Marx fuses Asian influences with the distinct culinary traditions of the Médoc, and is especially fascinated by the Gironde, so don't be surprised to find eel on the menu. The hotel can organize wine lessons and tours of neighbouring châteaux lasting from one to three days.

WINERY — LABARDE

### Château Giscours

33460 Labarde
T +33 (0)5-57 97 09 09/57 97 09 20
www.chateau-giscours.fr
Mon-Sat by appointment only.

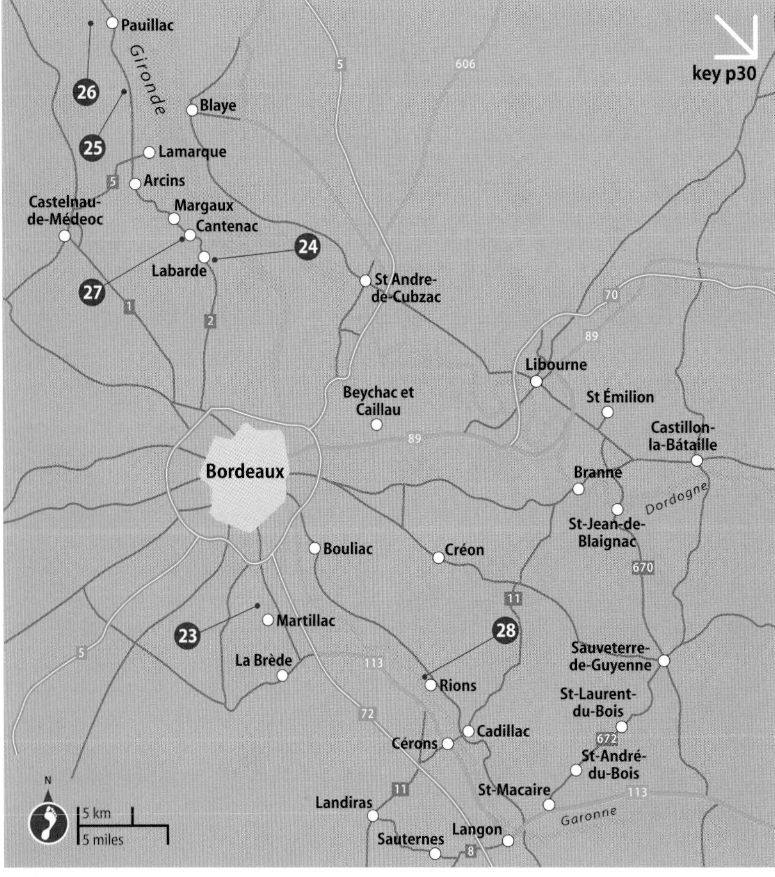

Winter and summer at Smith Haut Lafitte.

Château Giscours, a classed growth – for Bordeaux Crus classes, see page 35 – has a history going back to the 16th century. The previous owner was known for his love of polo and, although the horses are now gone, you can still see where the matches were played. Of greater interest to wine lovers, however, is the fact that the current proprietor, since 1995, is a Dutch businessmen with a keen interest in wine, who has not only raised the quality of the product, but also introduced the possibility of staying at the château in one of two very pretty rooms on a bed and breakfast basis ($). This should, needless to say, be booked as far in advance as possible.

WINERY — CUSSAC-FORT-MEDOC

### Château Lanessan

Cussac-Fort-Médoc
T +33 (0)5-56 58 94 80
www.lanessan.com
Daily 0915-1200 and 1400-1800.
€5.50

In the dull-looking no-man's land of the Haut-Médoc between Margaux and St-Julien, Château Lanessan has long been a stalwart of wine tourism. Most famous for a museum dedicated to horses and carriages, there are also nine themed tours, focusing on wine and the vine, wine and winemaking and wine and architecture. The château's own wine is never one of the showiest in the region but it is one of the most reliable.

WINERY — PAUILLAC

### Château Mouton-Rothschild

33250 Pauillac
T +33 (0)5-56 73 21 29
www.bpdr.com
Mon-Thu 0930-1100 and 1400-1600; Fri 0930-1100 and 1400-1500 by appointment only.
€5

Getting into four of the five first growths of Bordeaux is easy – provided you have written in advance, preferably providing a reference from a wine merchant indicating that you are the sort of person given to spending large amounts of money on wine. Mouton-Rothschild is the exception to this rule – as to so many others. The only château ever to see its ranking in the 1855 classification raised from second to first growth, this was the first Bordeaux estate to bottle all of its own wine, rather than sell it in barrels. It was also the first and only to introduce designer labels, using artists like Picasso and Andy Warhol; to launch a cheap branded wine associated with its name (Mouton Cadet); and to open a shop and visitor attraction in the shape of the **Museum of Wine in Art**. For an additional fee, it is possible to taste some of the wines; the 2005 vintage went on sale for £450 per bottle.

WINERY — MARGAUX

### Château Prieuré-Lichine

34 Av de la République, 33460 Cantenac
T +33 (0)5-57 88 36 28
contact@prieure-lichine.fr
Mon-Sat 0900-1200 and 1400-1700.

This former priory was the modern creation of a Russian-born American called Alexis Lichine, who bought it in 1951 for £8000. At the time it was known as Le Prieuré de Cantenac and, while boasting fourth-growth status, had just 11 ha of vines – all that was left after large areas had been sold to neighbouring estates. Lichine changed the name and embarked on a programme of purchases and vineyard-swaps with supposedly better second and third growth châteaux. When it was sold for £14 million in 1999, the estate had expanded to 71 ha of vines. From the outset, Lichine shocked the owners of other châteaux by putting up a 'Visitors Welcome' sign. That policy continues, providing an opportunity to sample some of the best wines produced in the commune of Margaux.

RESTAURANT | MARGAUX

### Le Lion d'Or

Pl de la République, 33460 Arcins
T +33 (0)5 56 58 96 79
Tue-Sat 1200-1400 and 1900-2200
$$

This restaurant, half way up the Médoc in the appellation of Margaux, is a real local's place, offering a seasonally changing menu of the freshest regional ingredients. Jean-Paul Barbier, the chef-pâtron, can be gruff, depending on the day, but that just adds to the Gallic atmosphere. And, when such delicious local treats as *tricandilles* (boiled then grilled pig intestine in Armagnac, garlic and parsley) are on the menu, who cares? There is a billiard table at which you can work off your meal, and one whole wall is devoted to bottles of wine from nearby chateaux. Locals are allowed to bring their own bottles; outsiders should phone ahead to ask if this will be allowed.

## Premières Côtes de Bordeaux

WINERY | RIONS

### Château Carsin

33410 Rions
T +33 (0)5-56 76 93 06
Visits by appointment.

While many of Bordeaux's smaller chateaux are having a hard time surviving, thanks partly to the fact that their wines are either insufficiently good or insufficiently fashionable, this is a happy exception to the rule. It was bought by a group of Finnish wine lovers in 1990 and, from the outset, aimed to combine the best New World expertise with classic Bordeaux soil. Thus, the winery was designed by Brian Croser of Petaluma in the Adelaide Hills. In blind tastings, Château Carsin wines regularly beat Bordeaux from more illustrious parts of the region. Of particular note are the white wines made from the rare Sauvignon Gris grape.

RESTAURANT | BOULIAC

### Restaurant Le Bistroy

Relais et Châteaux Hauterive St-James, 3 pl Camille Hostein, 33270 Bouliac
T +33 (0)5-57 97 06 00
www.saintjames-bouliac.com
Reservations must be made in advance.
Brasserie $-$$. Restaurant $$.

William Pencolé's passion is fish as he demonstrates by spinning a pretty terrific set menu around the catch of the day. His working rubric is 'quality, creativity and

### Exploring Bordeaux

**Langon**, on the banks of the Garonne, is known for its sweet dessert wines. It has a partly Romanesque church, with 12th-century frescoes, and 28 menhirs, said to be girls who were turned to stone for missing Mass. Leaving Langon on the N113, turn right towards **St-Macaire**, a medieval town, with an impressive church, named after the sixth-century bishop, St-Sauveur. Beyond St-Macaire, turn left onto the D672 towards St-André-du Bois and **Château de Malromé** (T+33 05-56 76 44 92, www.malrome.com). This castle was the final home of the artist Henri Toulouse-Lautrec (1864-1901), whose drawings are on display. Continue to St-Laurent-du-Bois and take a detour through the picturesque hamlet of Le Chantre before rejoining the D672 towards **Sauveterre-de-Guyenne**. This interesting, small *bastide* (fortified town) has four large gateways and a castle built by English King Edward I. From Sauveterre, follow the D670 north through Le Puch and St-Jean-de-Blaignac, where you cross the Dordogne. Follow signs for **St-Émilion**.

This medieval village and UNESCO World Heritage Site perches on a hilltop and is characterized by preserved ramparts and narrow, winding streets. Its most important sights are a monolithic church carved out of solid rock, the catacombs, the eighth-century Hermitage and the 13th-century Chapelle de la Trinité. Climb the medieval Tour du Roi for expansive views. After sightseeing, pause for lunch at **L'Envert du Décors** (page 67).

Heading south again, follow the D122 to Branne, before continuing to **Cadillac**. This fortified town on the Garonne has an impressive chateau, with vaulted basement rooms once used by tapestry weavers. On the other side of the river is **Cérons**, with its own *appellation* for dessert wines. From Cérons follow signs to Illats, Landiras and Budos. Cross the river on the D125 and continue through vines and forests to **Sauternes**. The **Maison de Vin** (T+33 05-56 76 69 83) offers wine tasting and **Château d'Yquem** produces one of France's most prestigious white wines. From Sauternes it's a short drive back to Langon.

Old bottles of Château Figeac, one of the best estates in St-Émilion.

rigour', all manifest in the meals in this modern, informal and affordable brasserie alongside the rather glitzier St-James hotel. This is a really terrific place to come to enjoy the region's often unsung white wines and to give the palate a break from the red wine and red meat marathon. But do take a look at the St-James as well. This is where the choosy US team from *Wine Spectator* magazine stay and taste the new vintage every year.

## St-Émilion

HOTEL ST-EMILION

### Le Logis des Remparts

18 rue Guadet, 33330 St-Émilion
logis-des-remparts@wanadoo.fr
T +33 (0)5-57 24 70 43/57 74 47 44
$-$$

A recently renovated boutique hotel with smallish yet comfortable and air-conditioned rooms, Le Logis des Remparts also has a lovely swimming pool and free parking – a great bonus in this small but highly desirable tourist destination. There is no restaurant but there are so many on its doorstep that it hardly matters.

WINE BAR ST-EMILION

### L'Envers du Décor

Rue du Clocher, 33000 St-Émilion
T +33 (0)5-57 74 48 31
Phone to confirm opening hours.
$-$$

The best wine bar and restaurant in St-Émilion – and the one in which you are likely to find many of the region's winemakers enjoying their time off – is on a small street, close to the church. In summer, the shady courtyard is a great place to pause and enjoy a good example of local wine and a plate of cheese or a bowl of gazpacho, while in winter it is friendly and cosy indoors, if a touch noisy and smoky.

# Best producers

**Bordeaux**

Château Angélus
Château Ausone
Château Belair
Château Bonnet
Château Branaire
Château Calon-Ségur
Château Canon
Château Canon la Gaffeliere
Château Carsin » *page 66.*
Château Cheval Blanc
Château Climens
Château de Pez
Château Cos d'Estournel
Château d'Issan
Château Ducru-Beaucaillou
Château Figeac
Château Gloria
Château Grand Puy Lacoste
Château Gruaud Larose
Château Haut Baillly
Château Haut Brion
Château Haut-Bages-Libéral
Château Labégorce-Zédé
Château Lafite
Château Lafleur
Château Lafon-Rochet
Château Lagrange
Château la Louvière
Château la Mission Haut-Brion
Château Langoa-Barton
Château Latour
Château le Bon Pasteur
Château Léoville Barton
Château Leoville Lascases
Château LéovillePoyferré
Château Lynch-Bages
Château Magdelaine
Château Margaux
Château Montrose
Château Mouton-Rothschild » *page 65.*
Château Palmer
Château Pape Clément
Château Petit-Village
Château Pétrus
Château Pontet-Canet
Château Potensac
Château Poujeaux
Château Prieuré-Lichine » *page 65.*
Château Rauzan-Ségla
Château Rayne Vigneau
Château Rieussec
Château Roc de Cambes
Château Smith Haut Lafitte » *page 64.*
Château St Pierre
Château Suduiraut
Château Talbot
Château Trotanoy
Château Vieux-Château-Certan
Château d'Yquem
Domaine de Chevalier

# Southwest France

A very mixed region, much of whose wine, like that of Bergerac, was historically prevented by tariffs and a lack of bridges across the Dordogne, from being sold through the port of Bordeaux. The most famous today is probably Cahors, a beautiful walled town, that is the source of often tough, unimpressive wines. Madiran is an increasingly impressive red and lovers of Basque cuisine should try the reds of Irouléguy. Buzet, Côtes de Duras and Côtes du Marmandais are all pleasant in their tannic, rustic way and Gaillac produces some attractive light sparkling whites. Jurançon and Pacherenc du Vic-Bilh are more interesting, thanks to the use of Petit and Gros Manseng, while Pécharmant, Montravel, Bergerac, Monbazillac and Saussignac are all very similar in style to – and often better than – wines made from the same grape varieties in nearby Bordeaux. Another success story here is Vin de Pays des Côtes de Gascogne, whose whites can be deliciously light and refreshing, although styles and quality vary widely.



## Bergerac

WINERY MONBAZILLAC

### Château de Monbazillac

24240 Monbazillac
T +33 (0)5-5363 6500/5361 5252
www.chateau-monbazillac.com
Nov-Mar daily 1000-1200 and 1400-1700; Jun-Sep 1000-1900; Apr, May and Oct 1000-1200 and 1400-1800.

Several strands of French history converge here. The imposingly photogenic Château de Monbazillac combines an intriguing blend of French medieval and Renaissance architecture on the outside, while inside there are rooms dedicated to such legendary local luminaries as Sem, an early 20th-century cartoonist. It is also furnished with a range of lovely antiques from many different periods. The château is owned by the Monbazillac cooperative, which produces about one-third of the wine in the Monbazillac appellation, and which offers a free tour and tasting. The excellent shop is a good place to stock up, not only on old bottles that you might not find elsewhere, but also Périgord delicacies, such as stuffed prunes and foie gras, and a wide range of wines and specialities from Bordeaux.

WINERY PECHARMANT

### Château de Tiregand

118 rte de Saint-Alvère , 24100 Creysse
T +33 (0)5-53 23 21 08
chateautiregand@club-internet.fr
High season Mon-Sat 0900-1100 and 1400-1700; low season 1000-1100 and 1400-1600. Closed public hols.

The de Saint-Exupéry family – relations of Antoine de Saint-Exupéry who wrote *The Little Prince* – are at the forefront of improvements in quality of the Pécharmant appellation to the northeast of Bergerac. Book ahead to make an appointment to visit the charming château, with its formal gardens, complete with an 18th-century summer house, and the stunning 17th-century *chai* , the typical local wine storage facility located above ground because the high water table prevented the digging of cellars.

SCHOOL GAGEAC-ET-ROUILLAC

### Château Gageac Monplaisir

24240 Gageac-et-Rouillac
T +33 (0)5-53 23 93 92
www.wineschoolbergerac.com

Helen Gillespie-Peck is well-placed to teach people about wine. This British woman is not only a fully accredited WSET (Wine & Spirit Education Trust) tutor, with first-hand knowledge of the wines of more than 30 countries, but also makes wine from the 23 ha of vines that surround the château she shares with her husband, David Baxter. Courses at Château Monplaisir thus offer hands-on vineyard experience as well as tastings and can last from half a day to five days or, by appointment, longer. You can get a flavour of this unique place by reading Gillespie-Peck's book, *Wine Woman @Bergerac.France*. Accommodation is not included but can be arranged; food is included on some courses.

## Jurançon

WINERY MONEIN

### Domaine Cauhapé

64360 Monein
T +33 (0)5-59 21 33 02
www.cauhape.com
Mon-Fri 0800-1800, Sat 1000-1800.

Henri Ramonteu is the star producer of Jurançon so it's essential that you visit this winery to sample the heights that Petit Manseng, and occasionally even Gros

Jurançon.

Manseng, can reach in both their sweet and dry incarnations. It is also a rare opportunity to experience wine stardom on an intimate scale, as, in a more prominent region, a high-flier such as Ramonteu might already have flown beyond the reach of visitors.

## Aveyron

HOTEL CONQUES

### Le Moulin de Cambelong

12320 Conques
T +33 (0)5-65 72 84 77
www.moulindecambelong.com
$$$

A perfect base for exploring the vineyards of Southwest France, this charming hotel is on the edge of the medieval town of Conques, a World Heritage site. But you don't need to leave the hotel to feel immersed in history, as it is located in a restored watermill perched on the river Dourdou, a tributary of the Lot. The region's gastronomic treats are also well represented. Award-winning chef, Hervé Busset, manages to temper the region's rich products with a welcome lighter touch, for example serving Aveyron roast suckling lamb with a chickpea emulsion and bulghur wheat suffused with hazelnuts ($$).

## Buzet

WINERY BUZET

### Les Vignerons de Buzet

BP 17, 47160 Buzet-sur-Baïze
T +33 (0)5-53 84 74 30
www.vignerons-buzet.fr
Sep-Jun Mon-Sat 0900-1200 and 1400-1800; Jul and Aug daily 0900-1200 and 1400-1800.

Wines have been made in Buzet for centuries, but it wasn't until 1973 that it was granted its own appellation. Most of Buzet wine is made in this cooperative on behalf of the area's myriad châteaux estates and the hugely popular free visit and tasting offers visitors the chance to gain an insight into the vital role that the better co-ops have played in France. If you are interested in seeing a bottling line, a co-op such as this is a great place to do so, offering both an impressive scale and a higher likelihood of seeing the clattering apparatus in action.

## Gascony

WINERY ST-MONT

### Plaimont

32400 St-Mont
T +33 (0)5-62 69 62 87
www.plaimont.com
Visits by appointment only.

This group of Gascony cooperatives has, with the similarly dynamic Yves Grassa (www.tariquet.com) at the Domaine du Tariquet, firmly put this once run-down region on the modern wine map. And, it has recently added another string to its bow by teaming up with both Logis de France and Gîtes de France to provide stays in *vignerons'* houses. The Logis offers a range of 'discovery' packages that include visits to wineries and restaurants featuring the best of the region's traditional fare. The co-op, which produces Madiran and Pacherenc du Vic-Bilh, among other appellations, is a good one-stop shop for getting an overview of the variety of wines that, fairly or not, tend to come under the catchall 'Southwest France' rubric.

# Best producers

**Southwest**

Château Bellevue la Forêt
Château Lagrezette
Château Masburel
Château Montus
Château Tirecul la Gravière
Château Tiregand » *page 68.*
Château Tour des Gendres
Clos d'Yvigne
Clos Uroulat
Domaine Cauhapé » *page* 68.
Domaine du Tariquet
Grande Maison
Les Verdots
Plaimont » *page 69.*
Plageoles, Robert
Vignerons de Buzet » *page 69.*

# Loire



More than any other wine-producing area in France, the Loire can be seen as a collection of sub-regions. To the west there's Muscadet, a region whose emphatically non-fruity, non-oaked whites are out of fashion at the moment but still - when good - offer the perfect partner for seafood. Following the river east, the next stop is Anjou, best known for dull, sweet rosé but now also a varied but potentially good appellation for rich Cabernet Sauvignon- and Cabernet Franc-based reds and Chardonnay-, Chenin Blanc- and Sauvignon Blanc-based whites. Nearby Saumur, famous for its sparkling wine, also produces rich Cabernet red under the Saumur-Champigny appellation. The Cabernet grapes are also used to make good reds in Chinon, Bourgeuil and St-Nicolas-de-Bourgeuil but, as with all Loire reds, warm vintages are the ones to go for if you don't want the flavour of green peppers in your glass. Haut Poitou and Touraine are Sauvignon Blanc country but, for most people, the top white grape of the region is the Chenin Blanc. At Savennières, this variety produces great, bone-dry wines, while in Côteaux du Layon and Quarts-de-Chaume the style is richly sweet, thanks to the grapes being picked when they are super-ripe and affected by 'noble rot'. Confusingly, there are several wines, including Vouvray, Montlouis and Jasnières, that are made in dry, medium and sweet styles and, in the case of Vouvray, sweetness is often not indicated on the label. Finally, at the eastern end of the river, Sancerre and Pouilly-Fumé (and less impressively Quincy and Menetou-Salon) produce Sauvignon Blanc that should be among the best in the world.

For a visitor, the Loire offers almost too many options but the ones that should not be missed are the Château de Chenonceaux, the troglodyte caves of Vouvray and the ruined castle of Chinon where, as was recounted in the film *The Lion in Winter*, the English king Henry II imprisoned his wife, Eleanor of Aquitaine.

## Sancerre

WINERY SANCERRE

### Alphonse Mellot

Domaine de la Moussière, 6 rue Porte César, 18300 Sancerre
T +33 (0)2-48 54 07 41
www.mellot.com
Apr-Oct daily 1000-1230 and 1430-1900; Nov-Mar Fri-Mon 1000-1230 and 1430-1900.

Confusingly, there are two Mellots in Sancerre. Joseph M's wines are actually very good and he has a worthwhile auberge in the heart of the town (see page 71), but Alphonse's individual cuvées are exceptional: textbook examples of this appellation's Sauvignon Blanc white and Pinot Noir red at their very best. The shop here is well worth a visit for bottles you might not find elsewhere.

With all Loire reds, warm vintages are the ones to go for if you don't want the flavour of green peppers in your glass.

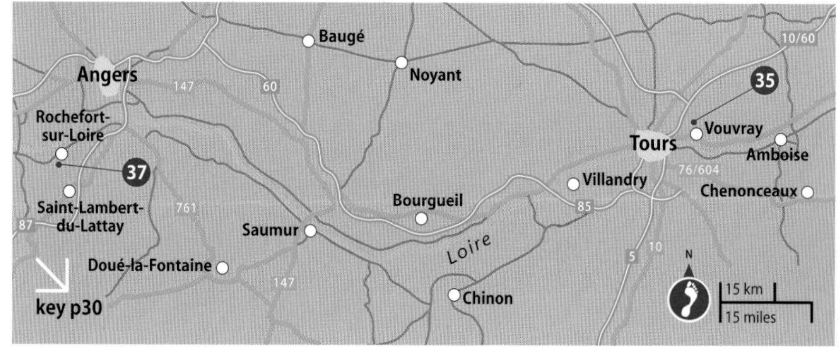

Château Villandry.

RESTAURANT SANCERRE

## Auberge Joseph Mellot

16 Nouvelle-pl, 18300 Sancerre
T +33 (0)2-48 54 20 53
www.joseph-mellot.fr
Mon, Thu-Sat for lunch and dinner; Tue and Sun dinner only. Closed mid Dec-mid Jan.
$

A true *auberge* with oak beams galore and plates of local goat's cheese, pâtés and salads for €10. The wines on offer by the glass and bottle are , unsurprisingly, made by Joseph Mellot and offer an interesting point of comparison with those produced by Alphonse (see page 70). This is also an opportunity to see how drinking Sancerre with food alters the experience.

HOTEL SANCERRE

## Le Panoramic

Rempart des Augustins, 18300 Sancerre
T +33(0)2-48 54 22 44
www.panoramicotel.com
$$

The name here says it all. The views from this recently upgraded, comfortable (rather than luxurious) hotel, are stupendous, especially if you happen to be here when mist floats across the vines beneath you. The pool is also a welcome option after a hard day wine tasting. There is no restaurant here but it does have a bar and there are plenty of good places to eat in the town.

# Touraine

MUSEUM BOURGUEIL

## Cave Touristique de la Dive Bouteille Chevrette

BP 68, 37140 Bourgueil
T +33 (0)2-47 97 72 01
Jul-Aug Wed-Mon 1400-1800; Apr-Jun and Sep-late Oct Sat and Sun 1400-1800.

This fun museum-cum-shop displays beautiful presses from the 14th and 15th centuries, as well as an opportunity to taste a wide range of Bourgueil wines and to get to know an often overlooked appellation.

ATTRACTION CHENONCEAUX

## Château de Chenonceau

37150 Chenonceaux
T +33 (0)2-47 23 90 07
www.chenonceau.com
Mar-Nov daily 0900-1900; Dec-Feb daily 0900-1800.
€8

Chenonceau is more often than not the favourite château of visitors to the Loire. Its dreamy situation across the Cher river is unforgettable and its architecture is among the prettiest and most elegant of any in the region. Among the château's many attractions are the Renaissance gardens (both formal and of the kitchen variety), a 16th-century farm, a maze and boat trips on the river. **L'Orangerie** restaurant ($$) is a very pleasant spot and features several generous set meals that include a bottle of either red or white AOC Touraine Château de Chenonceau. Among the dishes on offer are ragoût of pork cheeks with spices, salad of gizzards and duck breast and rib of beef roast in Chenonceau wine.

ATTRACTION VILLANDRY

## Château de Villandry

37510 Villandry
T +33 (0)2-47 50 02 09
www.chateauvillandry.com
Château Feb-early Nov daily 0930-1630 (longer hours in summer). Gardens daily 0900-1700 (longer hours in summer).
€5.50

Château de Villandry is part of the Loire's **Enfant Roy** scheme (www.piste-enfant-roy.com) to make tourist sites more interesting for seven- to 12-year-olds, so kids are given a leaflet to make their visit more fun and interactive. This is also a lovely place to appreciate why the Loire is called France's garden. The formal gardens are formidable, built in the 19th century in a similar style to

Chinon castle.

those in Parc Monceau in Paris, and there are wonderful vegetable gardens whose provender can be sampled in the simple yet charming restaurant ($-$$), which has a good wine list. The château, built in 1536, was the last of the great Loire Renaissance châteaux to be built, and is definitely worth a visit in its own right.

WINERY VOUVRAY

### Château Moncontour

37210 Vouvray
T +33 (0)2-47 52 60 77
www.moncontour.com
Mon-Sat 1000-1700. Sun and public holidays by appointment only.

A handsome, turreted château, dating in part from the late 15th century, Château Moncontour produces good Vouvray in various styles, from dry to sweet, still and sparkling. It is also worth visiting for its cellars, which are carved into the chalk, and for the old winemaking tools in its museum.

WINERY SOINGS-EN-SOLOGNE

### Domaine de la Charmoise, Henry Marionnet

41230 Soings-en-Sologne
T +33 (0)2-54 98 70 73
www.henry-marionnet.com
Tour and tasting by appointment.

Probably the best producer in Touraine, Henry Marionnet makes terrific Sauvignon but he is also worth visiting for examples of wines found nowhere else. He has, most notably, a small plot of Romorantin vines, a variety once grown in Burgundy but now almost extinct. More unusually still, Marionnet's were planted in

## Vintages

**2005** Great in Bordeaux and Southwest, Loire, Rhône and Alsace. Better white than red Burgundy. Mixed in storm-hit Languedoc.

**2004** Classic and very good in Bordeaux and for red Loires and white Burgundy.

**2003** Mixed red Bordeaux (top reds and sweet whites are great, lesser reds are ageing fast). Very good sweet whites from the Loire and the Southwest. Elsewhere, the heat and drought made for wide quality variations from short-lived and jammy to-great.

**2002** Very good dry white Bordeaux, Alsace, Loire, Jura and Southwest sweet whites. Burgundies and red Bordeaux were varied, with many green unripe wines at more modest levels.

**2001** Underrated. Very good in Bordeaux and the Southwest, Alsace, red Burgundy and northern Rhône, late harvest Loires and Provence.

**2000** Great in the Rhône, red and dry white Bordeaux and in the Southwest and Provence. Some very good red Burgundy (though with some failures) and Chablis.

1850, making them some of the oldest ungrafted vines in Europe. No one can say why the phylloxera louse has left them untouched but the ungrafted Gamay vines that went into the ground in 1989 are still going strong, too.

HOTEL | CHINON

### Hôtel Diderot

4 rue de buffon, 37500 Chinon
T +33 (0)2-47 93 18 87
www.hoteldiderot.com
$

Minutes from the centre of Chinon, this charming hotel is housed in a building that dates in part from the 14th century. It has a lovely terrace where, when it is warm enough, breakfast with home-made jams, is served under the olive trees. The perfect place to stay while in this part of the Loire.

RESTAURANT | TOURS

### Jean Bardet

Hôtel-Restaurant Château Belmont, 57 rue Groison, 37100 Tours
T +33 (0)2-47 41 41 11
www.jeanbardet.com
Apr-Oct Wed-Fri and Sun lunch and dinner; Mon, Tue and Sat dinner only. Nov-Mar Wed-Fri lunch and dinner; Tue and Sat dinner only; Sun lunch only. Reservations must be made in advance
$$-$$$

Jean Bardet is an extremely accomplished chef, who goes out of his way to create menus to match his fascinating wine list, which includes some amazing verticals of Loire wines, some with vintages from early last century. Among the creative dishes on the €125 tasting menu you might find foie gras poached in port, or chilled crayfish soup with candied cocoa beans and Aquitaine caviar. The charming hotel ($$) has lovely gardens, including a kitchen garden in which Bardet grows traditional and rare vegetables.

## Anjou-Saumur

WINERY | ROCHEFORT

### Domaine des Baumard

8 rue de l'Abbaye, BP 11, 49190 Rochefort-sur-Loire
T +33 (02)-41 78 70 03
www.baumard.fr
Mon-Sat 1000-1200 and 1400-1730.

Florent Baumard's ancestors first started making wine in 1634 and were going strong until the incursions of phylloxera, after which the family turned to raising vines in nurseries. In the mid-1950s, Florent's father Jean, widely respected for his dedication to quality, decided to go back to winemaking, eventually buying the plots in Quarts de Chaume and Savennières that are the pride of the estate. Jean also bought Logis de la Giraudière, the beautiful 17th-century building that houses the winery and boasts a stunning wall painting from the 18th century. Here, if you're lucky, Florent will explain both the traditions of these tiny appellations and also how he is contributing to their future innovation, by, among other things, bottling some of his production under screwcap.

## Best producers

**Loire**

Bourillon-Dorléans
Bouvet-Ladubay
Château de Fesles
Château de Tracy
Château du Hureau
Château de la Ragotiere
Château la Varière
Château Moncontour » *page 72.*
Château Pierre Bise
Clos de Coulée de Serrant
Domaine des Aubuisières
Domaine des Baumard » *page 73.*
Domaine des Forges
Domaine du Clos Naudin
Du Closel
Couly-Dutheil
Dagueneau, Didier
Druet, Pierre-Jacques
Filliatreau
Huët
Joguet, Charles
Marionnet, Henry » *page 72.*
Mellot, Alphonse » *page 70.*
Pinard, Vincent
Pithon, Jo
Prince Poniatowski
Ricard, Vincent
Soulez, Pierre & Yves
Vacheron

MUSEUM | ST-LAMBERT-DU-LATTAY

### Musée de la Vigne et du Vin d'Anjou

Les Celliers de La Coudraye, 49750 Saint-Lambert-du-Lattay
T +33 (0)2-41 78 42 75
www.mvvanjou.com
Mar-Jun and Sep-Oct Sat, Sun and hols 1430-1830; Jul-Aug daily 1100-1300 and 1500-1900.
€5 or more, depending on the exhibition

Thanks to its partnership with two scientific and agronomic institutions, this six-room museum features unusually detailed technical explanations of viticulture, as well as the expected presses and ancient winemaking paraphernalia that are on show in other wine museums. The barrel-making display is one of the highlights, and the museum contrives to strikes an unusual (for France) unchauvinistic balance between explaining the world of Anjou wine and the larger world of vinegrowing and winemaking in general. The museum also participates in the Enfant Roy scheme (page 71), so children will enjoy a visit here too.

# Spain

Miguel Merino winery, Briones.

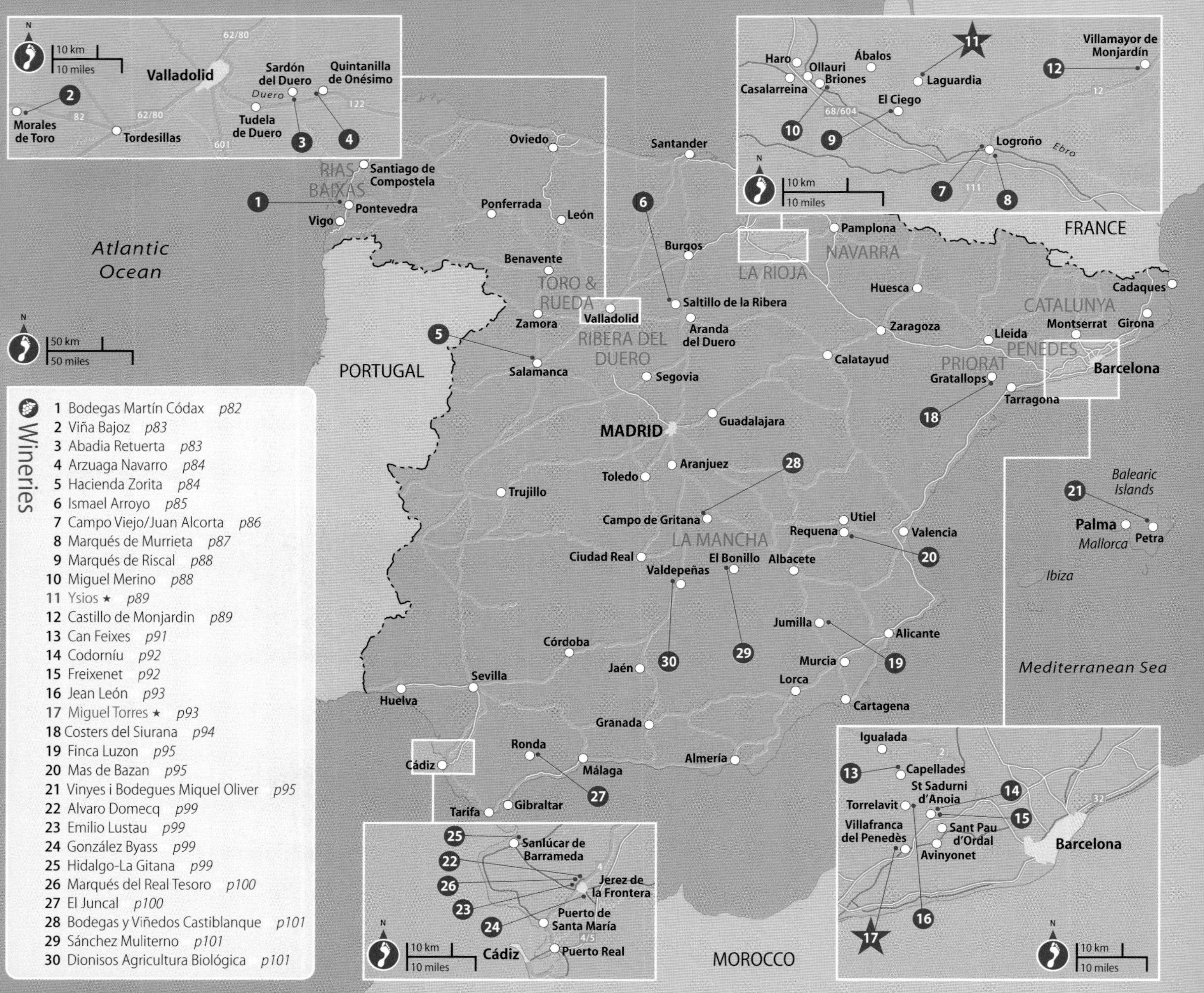


## Wineries

1 Bodegas Martín Códax p82
2 Viña Bajoz p83
3 Abadia Retuerta p83
4 Arzuaga Navarro p84
5 Hacienda Zorita p84
6 Ismael Arroyo p85
7 Campo Viejo/Juan Alcorta p86
8 Marqués de Murrieta p87
9 Marqués de Riscal p88
10 Miguel Merino p88
11 Ysios ★ p89
12 Castillo de Monjardin p89
13 Can Feixes p91
14 Codorníu p92
15 Freixenet p92
16 Jean León p93
17 Miguel Torres ★ p93
18 Costers del Siurana p94
19 Finca Luzon p95
20 Mas de Bazan p95
21 Vinyes i Bodegues Miquel Oliver p95
22 Alvaro Domecq p99
23 Emilio Lustau p99
24 González Byass p99
25 Hidalgo-La Gitana p99
26 Marqués del Real Tesoro p100
27 El Juncal p100
28 Bodegas y Viñedos Castiblanque p101
29 Sánchez Muliterno p101
30 Dionisos Agricultura Biológica p101

# Introduction



Compare the Spanish section of a wine book published 15 years or or so ago and one written today and you'll find a fascinating difference. Entire regions, like Priorat, La Mancha and Toro, and producers, like Pingus and Roda, have now leapt into the limelight, commanding critical acclaim and prices that were once almost unthinkable for this country. The UK has been relatively slow to notice these changes: for far too many British wine drinkers, Spanish wine is inexpensive, easily gluggable (usually red) stuff to be enjoyed in copious amounts on inexpensive summer holidays. But the loftier ambitions of Spain's wine producers have been rewarded by open-minded wine lovers in the smart restaurants of Madrid, Seville and Barcelona, and by the readiness of adventurous North Americans to spend as much on a bottle of critically praised Spanish wine from a previously unknown source as they would on a top-class Bordeaux.

Of course, Spain still produces plenty of cheap-and-cheerful wines, but in almost every region there are exciting efforts to be found, many of which are so untraditional in style that they come under a new collective description of '*alta expression*' – high expression.

There is an obvious parallel to be drawn with what has been happening to food, fashion and the arts in Spain. Just look at the waiting lists for tables at Fernan Adria's El Bulli – recently voted the world's finest restaurant by *Restaurant* magazine – and the nearly one million people who annually visit Frank Gehry's Guggenheim Museum in Bilbao.

# Travel essentials

### Planning a trip

There are international flights to **Madrid Barajas** (MAD, T +34 91-305 8346), **Barcelona International** (BCN, www.aena.es), **Bilbao** (BIL, T +34 944-869663), **Málaga** (AGP, T +34 952-048 844) and **Sevilla** (SVQ, T +34 954-449 000); Ryanair also flies to **Jerez** (XRY, T +34 956-150 083). Another option from the UK is to travel by P&O Ferries (www.poportsmouth.com) to Bilbao or by Brittany Ferries (www.brittanyferries.com) to Santander. Alternatively, rail and road links connect Spain to the rest of Europe, with a high-speed overnight train service from Paris to Madrid or Barcelona, for example. Public transport is generally good in Spain and it is possible to visit most parts of the country by bus or train, or a combination of both. The national rail network, RENFE (www.renfe.es) serves the main provincial towns and cities but buses are sometimes quicker and more efficient. For sheer convenience, though, it is advisable to hire a car. Petrol in Spain is considerably cheaper than in the UK and almost all major hire companies are represented, with offices at airports as well as in cities and provincial towns. Note, however, that Spain is a big country and getting around can take time.

If you're on a short break, the most convenient option is to centre your holiday around a city, particularly one which has an international airport. **Madrid** has a fabulous collection of western art and some of the best nightlife in Spain. From here you can reach beautiful **Toledo** and the Quixote plains of **La Mancha** or head north, via Segovia or Salamanca, to the upcoming wine regions of **Toro** and **Rueda**, where the Duero valley is studded with castles. Madrid's flamboyant Catalan rival **Barcelona** is one of Europe's hippest weekend destinations, thanks to its Modernista skyline, beaches and dedication to style. It also provides access to the sprawling Catalunya DOC, where Spain's best Cava is produced; the Costa Brava and the Pyrenees. Further west, **Bilbao** is home to the stunning Guggenheim museum and is the gateway to the Basque country. From here, explore the region's surf beaches and fishing villages, visit the gastronomic hub of **San Sebastián** (page 86) or head inland towards the **Rioja Álavesa** around La Guardia. Alternatively, combine wine with history and architecture by following the **Camino de Santiago** by car through Navarra, Rioja, Castilla y Leon and Galicia. The route takes in many of the finest cathedrals of the north at León, Burgos, Jaca and Santiago itself, as well as a superb series of Romanesque churches. You could celebrate the end of your journey with a glass of Albariño and some seafood in the **Rias Baixas**. Finally, in the south, Seville, Córdoba and Granada are the highlights of Andalucía. Málaga is the main transport hub for this region but there are also flights to **Jerez** (page 99).

**Spain country code** → +34. **IDD code** → 00. **Internet ID** → .es. **Emergency number** → T 112.

### Fact file

| | |
|---|---|
| **International flights** | There are multiple carriers (major and budget airlines) serving Spain's international airports. |
| **Entry requirements** | No visa required for EU passport holders and for US and Canadian citizens staying up to 90 days. |
| **Currency** | Euro €1. |
| **Time zone** | GMT +1 hour. |
| **Electricity** | 220V, 50Hz service is standard, although 110V service persists in some remote areas. The 2 round-pin plug is standard. |
| **Licensing hours** | Usual shop opening times are Mon-Fri 0930-1330 and 1630-2000; Sat 0930-1330. Pubs, bars and clubs until 0300, with some open 24 hrs. |
| **Minimum age** | 18. |
| **Drink-drive restrictions** | 25 mg of alcohol per 100 ml of blood (0.25 per cent BAC). |

Navaridas near La Guardia in La Rioja Álavesa.

For further information about visiting Spain, check out the national tourist board website, www.spain.info. Also refer to *Footprint Northern Spain* and *Footprint Andalucía*.

### When to visit

Spain has done such a good job of promoting its image as a country where the sun never stops shining that it is worth mentioning that the northern and central parts of the country can be decidedly chilly in winter. However, for many people who know and love Spain, spring and autumn are great times to visit. Harvest is usually in mid September and, as elsewhere, while amateur photographers will enjoy the chance to snap images of pickers, other visitors should note that smaller bodegas may not want to spend time with tourists.

### Wine tourism

Although there are still a number of old monasteries associated with winemaking, most bodegas date from the 19th and 20th centuries. Many of these, especially in Jerez and the Penedès, took huge architectural pride in their scale and their innovative use of materials such as poured concrete and steel. The tradition of employing top architects has never died. Today, wineries like **Raimat** in Lerida and **Domecq** in Jerez have an almost cathedral-like quality; the huge **Ysios** estate in Rioja brilliantly mimics the form of a row of barrels, while the **Marqués de Riscal**'s new winery-hotel reveals architect Frank Gehry at his wildest. Most of these wineries are increasingly equipped to welcome visitors but, outside the bigger bodegas of Rioja, the sparkling wine producers of the Penedès and the sherry houses of Jerez, wine tourism remains something of a novelty. An ability to speak Spanish will certainly come in handy in many places, as will the understanding that the time at which you'd like to visit may not always suit the local schedule.

### Sleeping

Places to stay (*alojamientos*) are divided into three main categories, based on regulations devised by the government. *Hoteles* (marked H or HR) are graded from one to five stars and usually occupy their own building, which distinguishes them from *hostales* (Hs or HsR), rated from one to three stars. *Pensiones* (P) are the standard budget option and are usually family-run flats. Less common are *fondas* (F), which are generally restaurants with cheap rooms available; a continuation of the old travellers' inn. Look out for the luxurious chain of state-owned hotels, the *paradors*. Often set in castles, convents and other historic buildings, they offer atmospheric accommodation and all kinds of special deals, which can make them surprisingly affordable. Another excellent option, if you've got your own transport, is the network of rural homes (*casas rurales* or *agroturismos*) which, although under a different classification system, are often as high in standard as any country hotel. Some are available to rent out whole, while others operate more or less as hotels. Each regional tourist office will have a list of properties in their area.

### Eating



Spanish cuisine can be divided into two categories: ancient and modern. On the one hand there are regional dishes that have barely changed in centuries; on the other, there is the growing number of new-wave innovative cooks, who have been inspired by Ferran Adria of **El Bulli** (Cala Montjoi, Ap 30, 17480 Girona, T +34 972-150457, www.elbulli.com). Adria is to food what Salvador Dali was to figurative painting and he admits that his eclectic dishes aren't always easy to pair with wine but his partner and front-of-house manager Juli Soler particularly recommends Manzanilla sherry and good Cava.

Traditional Spanish cuisine relies on meat, fish/seafood, beans and potatoes, which are given character by the chef's holy trinity: garlic, peppers, and, of course, olive oil. The influence of the Americas is evident, as is a lasting Moorish legacy, particularly in the south, where olives, saffron and almonds are cultivated. Local specialities range from the Michelin-starred *pintxos* of the **Basque** lands (page 86), ideally matched with the Txacoli wines made nearby, to **Catalonia**'s innovative combination of seafood from the Mediterranean, rice and vegetables from the plains and meat and game from the mountains. Here, the best bet is to explore some of the experimental wines from the Penedès, or a Torres Milmanda Chardonnay. **Valencia** is the birthplace of paella, a dish that is often made badly elsewhere in Spain. **Galicia** is seafood heaven, but even in areas far from the coast, good fish and seafood can be taken for granted. *Merluza* (hake) and *bacalao* (salt cod) are the staples, *gambas* (prawns) are another excellent choice and *pulpo* (octopus) is particularly good when served *a la gallega* (Galician style) and flavoured with paprika and olive oil. All of these go well with Albariño from **Rias Baixas**. *Pescadito frito*, fried fresh fish, is the specialitiy of **Cádiz**, and is perfectly combined with the region's sherry. Wherever you go, you'll find excellent cured ham (*jamón serrano*); look out for the pricey *ibérico*, taken from acorn-eating porkers in **Extremadura**. The Castilian plains specialize in roast sucking pig (*cochinillo* or *lechón*), which go well with mature Rioja – as does good Spanish lamb – while the innards of animals are popular around **Madrid**. Vegetable dishes tend to be based around beans, peppers and potatos, often served as a hearty stew, with bits of meat or seafood. Desserts focus on the sweet and milky, as in *flan* (crème caramel), *natillas* and *arroz con leche* (rice pudding), while cheeses tend to be eaten as a tapa or starter; try pungent Manchego, piquant Cabrales and Basque Idiázabal.

Lunch is the biggest meal of the day for most people in Spain, when just about all restaurants offer a *menú del día*, usually a set three course meal that includes wine or soft drink. Tapas has changed in meaning over the years, and now basically refers to all bar food. This includes free snacks given with drinks (increasingly rare, except in León and Granada), Basque *pintxos* and more substantial dishes, usually ordered as *raciónes*. Note that the Spanish eat late in the evening, particularly in the south and in Madrid, where it is not unusual to sit down to a meal at midnight.

# Wine essentials

## History

Spain's winemaking began with the Phoenicians, who established the port of Cádiz (close to the modern home of sherry) in 1100 BC, and the Celts, who were already making wine in Rioja when the Romans arrived a thousand years later. The Romans modernized production , introducing higher-quality, smaller, more transportable amphorae that kept wine fresher but, by the middle ages, Spain's winemakers were using huge amphorae called *tinajas*, upto 4 m high. As late as the 14th century, when thousands of oak barrels of Bordeaux were being shipped to England, Spanish wine was still being transported in bags made from animal skins. Wooden casks were introduced towards the end of the 15th century but the old tradition lives on in rural areas in the form of leather *botas*, small bags from which wine can be squirted directly into the mouth

In the 16th and 17th centuries, Spanish wines – Rioja in particular – were exported northwards to England (where they were mentioned by Shakespeare), Flanders and France, but they remained primitive and most would have been partly oxidized. In the late 18th century, a priest called Don Manuel Quintano revolutionized the wines of Rioja by importing new barrels and winemaking methods from Bordeaux, exporting nearly 10,000 litres of his 'modern' wine to Havana and Veracruz in 1795, where they were very well received.

Over the following century, the influence of Bordeaux became far stronger, thanks to the efforts of the Marqués de Murrieta and the Marqués de Riscal, who returned to Spain after periods of political exile in France. In 1858, Riscal, on behalf of the Diputación Foral de Álava (the local regional government), employed the Bordeaux winemaker Jean Pineau, cellarmaster at Château Lanessan, to improve Rioja's wines. Pineau's contract lasted for a decade but few Riojan winemakers chose to follow his advice, so, in 1868, he began full-time employment with Riscal, planting Cabernet Sauvignon to accompany the Tempranillo and Graciano that were traditionally planted in the region. Riscal's late 19th-century wines not only sold for high prices at the time, but also proved their longevity by surviving to be tasted over a century later.

Stubborn conservatism and Roman-style winemaking – treading grapes by foot in stone troughs and storing it in *tinajas* – remained commonplace in Spain until the mid 1900s. The Catalan, Miguel Torres Junior was considered a dangerous revolutionary when he introduced the stainless steel tanks he had seen in Bordeaux to his family winery in the Penedès. The success of Torres's wines in Spain and overseas – his 1970 Cabernet Sauvignon-based Mas la Plana beat Chateau Latour in a blind tasting in Paris – helped to raise aspirations and to open Spanish minds to the possibilities of making top-class wines in regions like Ribera del Duero, Rueda and Priorat.

Macabeo grapes at Can Feixes.

Until the 1990s, Spanish winemakers focused far more on how long a wine had been aged than on the year it was produced (see Beauty before age, page 83) and bodegas that wanted to sell wine under the official designations were required, by law, to hold a large number of barrels in stock. This, in turn, meant that Spain had almost no small estates of the kind that have been so important in Burgundy, Bordeaux and Barolo. One of the biggest and most welcome recent developments in Spanish wine has been the boom in dynamic smaller estates, known as *Pagos*. Another has been the readiness to question rules that are still set in stone in France. Irrigation, once illegal, is now allowing great wines to be produced in regions like La Mancha; Cabernet Sauvignon is being reintroduced to Rioja, and large regional denominations like Catalunya – and soon one covering the whole country – are enabling Spain to compete with the New World.

## Understanding Spanish wine

Spain's hideously complicated system of wine regions is, inevitably, hideously complicated in a different way to its European neighbours. And it's changing all the time. The newest trend is the official recognition of individual vineyards called **Pagos**, which may produce traditional or innovative wine and are, by definition, single estates. So far, there aren't many of these, but expect their number to grow apace. Next, there are Rioja and Priorat, regions with higher-quality wine, known as **DOCa** or, if you are Catalan, **DOQ**. (A *Pago* in a DOCa/DOQ can call itself a Vino da Pago Calificada, by the way.) A little lower down the ladder come the bewildering number of **DO** regions (Denominacion de Origen), some of which will be promoted to DOCa/DOQ eventually. Sizes vary widely. In 1999, the region of Catalonia (Catalunya), which included nearly a dozen DOs became a big inclusive DO in its own right. Sparkling wine bearing Spain's Cava DO mostly comes from Catalonia but can legally be produced elsewhere in Spain, although its exact provenance will never be clear from the label.

The more humble **VCIG** (Vinos de Calidad con Indicacion Geografica) come next, followed by **VdlT** (Vino de la Tierra), which, like Italy's Vino da Tavola and IGT has been used by vinous innovators. At the foot of the pyramid is **VdM** (Vino de Mesa), which, like France's Vin de Table, can be blends from across the country but may not mention grape varieties, regions or vintages on their labels. This restriction may soon be lifted, however, to allow Spanish producers to compete with the New World. Of all these designations, the most reliable is inevitably the Pago, because the quality of every wine bearing that name is the responsibility of a single producer.

### White grapes

**Albariño** The peachy variety of Rias Baixas, this is Spain's sexiest white grape at present. Usually unoaked and best drunk young.

**Chardonnay** Still a novelty but being used to great effect by Torres at Milmanda in Catalonia, and for fresher, fruitier examples of Cava.

**Godello** Gaining from the interest in its northwestern neighbour Albariño, this similarly aromatic, but naturally zingier Valdeorras variety might, in the right hands, prove even more exciting. Vina Godeval makes a good example.

**Verdejo** The grape most widely used in Rueda and obligatorily the principal player in Rueda Superior (where it has to be at least 85% of the blend). The quality of the wine made from Verdejo depends even more than usual on the skill of the winemaker. Handled poorly, the final result tends to be dull and flabby, but at its best, as in the efforts by the Marqués de Riscal, it can achieve real greatness.

**Viura/Macabéo** The principal grape of Rioja and Navarra and a major component of traditional Cava, this is a fairly non-aromatic variety whose wines depend for their flavour on the way they are made and/or aged. Old examples of Marqués de Murrieta Ygay show what it can do with age.

### Red grapes

**Bobal** A previously overlooked variety that is beginning to show promise in Valencia and Utiel Requena.

**Cabernet Sauvignon** A rarity, but well used by Torres (Mas de la Plana), Jean Léon and Raimat among others in Catalonia. Also used as a component in Priorat and now creeping usefully into Rioja blends and elsewhere in blends with Tempranillo.

**Cariñena/Mazuelo** As in France, where it is called Carignan, this variety is at its best when the vines are olds and yields low. Surprisingly little used in the region of Cariñena, it is a component of Rioja and is beginning to be used in rich Priorat blends.

**Garnacha** The grape the French and Australians call Grenache behaves in Spain as it does in those countries. With limited yields it can produce rich, dark blockbusters; grown more generously (as it often is in Rioja), the flavours are light and strawberryish. L'Ermita in Priorat makes a Châteauneuf du Pape-like version. Increasingly good examples are now coming out of Rioja and Navarra where it is used for rosé.

**Monastrell** Known as Mourvèdre in France, where it is grown in the Rhône, this is not an easy grape to get right; it can produce easy-going reds, and more serious wines with a bitter, leathery character but good producers like Casa de la Ermita in Jumilla are achieving impressive results.

**Tempranillo/Cencibel/Gotim Bru/Tinto de Toro/Tinto del País/Tinto** Known by all these names (and others) and as Tinta Roriz in Portugal, this is Spain's most widely grown red grape. Styles range from light and juicy to richly earthy, depending on the region, winemaking style and other grapes used in any blend (in Rioja, there is usually a quarter to a third of Grenache).

Sorting grapes at El Lagar de Isilla winery in La Vid.

Bodegas Juan Alcorta.

**The cool, green Atlantic coast of Spain was, for no good reason, traditionally overlooked by wine lovers focusing on more famous inland regions like Rioja, Navarra and Ribera del Duero. Wine lovers wanting dry white Spanish wine tended to opt for often-unimpressive dry Rioja when mouthwatering Albariño from Rias Baixas on the west coast would have been a far better choice. But, recently, as the world has rediscovered a taste for interesting whites, this coastal region has begun to attract international attention. The Basque region remains far less known to outsiders, thanks partly to a language and styles that are not immediately accessible. Inland, other up-and-coming regions include Ribeira Sacra, Ribeiro, Bierzo, and Valdeorras. All of these aspire to the fame that is now being attracted by the whites of Rueda and the reds of Toro, both areas that were historically known by few outsiders. The trio of classic northwestern regions, however, remains Ribera del Duero, Rioja and Navarra, each of which is now creating a quite distinct reputation for itself.**

## Rias Baixas

The *rias*, to which this northwestern region owes its name, are the broad, steeply sided inlets that serrate the Atlantic coast. The Albariño grape which has its home here, and on the other side of the Portuguese frontier, was once a little-known local speciality but, more recently, there has been a realization that the wines produced in this region are among Spain's best. New vineyards have been planted so that, between 1998 and 2004, the harvest doubled, rising to 14 million bottles.

WINERY — CAMBADOS

### Bodegas Martín Códax

Burgáns 91, Vilariño, Cambados (Pontevedra)
T +34 986-526 040
www.martincodax.com
Visits by appointment only; book via the website.

Martín Códax, founded in 1986 by co-operative of winemakers, including present chief winemaker, Luciano Amoedo, was a prime force in the founding of the Rias Baixas DOC. It is the perfect place to visit in order to understand Albariño, the aromatic, fragrant, tangy driver of this DOC.

## Toro and Rueda

The vineyards around the quiet town of Toro were famous in the 13th century, when this was a wealthy region, but its wines didn't live up to that early success, until very recently. Made from the Tempranillo (known as Tinto de Toro here) in vineyards at 600 m altitude, they have tended to be big, dark, alcoholic and rustic – not unlike those of Priorat. The parallel is appropriate because, today, Toro is happily riding on Priorat's coat tails, benefiting from investment by outsiders who are making reds that are still big and rich but far less rough-and-ready than the Toros of the past.

To the east of Toro lies **Rueda** which, following the example of the pioneering Marqués de Riscal, has used the local Verdejo and the Sauvignon to make generally reliable and sometimes exceptional wines. Since 2000, the Tempranillo has also been grown to make good wines, usually in blends with Garnacha, Cabernet Sauvignon and Merlot.

HOTEL — ZAMORA

### Hacienda Unamuno

Ctra Zamora–Fermoselle, Km 56, Fermoselle, Zamora
T +34 902-109 902
www.ruralgo.com/haciendaunamuno
Closed mid Dec-mid Jan.

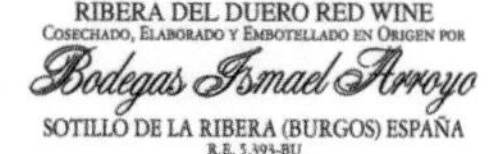

Grapevine

**Beauty before age**

The notion of vintage and the ideal age at which to enjoy a wine has gone through some interesting changes over the years. In the earlier part of the 20th century, the labels of even many of Spain's better wines used to refer to the number of years the wine had spent in barrel rather than the year in which the grapes were harvested. There was a simple logic to this; unsophisticated winemaking in a warm climate made for wines that seemed decidedly rough and tannic when young. As in Italy and Portugal, the preferred method of softening them was a prolonged sojourn in cask. And, since only the fullest-bodied wines survived this treatment without losing their flavour as well as their toughnesss, it was natural to associate age and barrel ageing with quality. This was given the official weight by wine laws that created a hierarchy of wine for any region. At the most basic level, there was Vino Joven – young wine sold almost as soon as it was fermented. Above this, there was Crianza (aged for at least two years, six months of which had to be in barrel), Reserva (three years ageing, one of which would have been in wood) and Gran Reserva (for which the rules required five years and two respectively). This tradition, combined with the strawberry fruit of the Tempranillo grapes (widely used for reds throughout Spain) and the sweet vanilla character that the wine picked up from the American oak barrels, gave Rioja a very recognisable style, and one that is still quite unique. Today, however, modern winemaking has enabled producers to make supple, intense reds that don't need long barrel ageing. Three-year-old bottles of modern Flor de Pingus from Ribera del Duero carry the same US$60 price tag in New York as a traditional 20-year-old Tondonia, Rioja Gran Reserva.

An exclusive rural hotel, ideally located for those looking for a relaxing holiday and/or those following the region's wine route. Set in a tranquil field of vines and olives, this four-room hotel is named after the writer and poet Don Miguel de Unamuno, who described the Los Arribes del Duero region as one of the most beautiful in Spain.

WINERY ZAMORA

### Viña Bajoz

Avda de los Comuneros 90, Morales de Toro, Zamora
T +34 980-698 023
www.vinabajoz.com
Mon-Sat 0800-2200; Sun 1100-1400 and 1600-1900.

One of Spain's growing list of top class cooperatives, this winery to the side of the main road into Toro, boasts a wine shop featuring the full range of Bajoz wines, including older vintages, many of which are available for tasting. Also well worth browsing through is an enticing a selection of locally produced gourmet items.

## Ribera del Duero

Of the world's four great wine rivers – the others are the Rhône, Rhine and Loire – the Duero (known in Portugal as the Douro) was the last to make its mark as the source of top red table wine. Curiously, both sides of the border boasted a wine that was thought of as the best in its country – Barca Velha in Portugal and Vega Sicilia in Spain but, until two decades ago, neither could field a team of other wines that were even half as good. In Spain, this was reflected by the fact that, despite the Vega Sicilia's high prices, it remained a *vino de mesa* until 1982 because the region had no DO. One of the producers who helped to earn the Ribera del Duero its denomination, was an agricultural engineer called Alejandro Fernandez, who began to make wine in 1972. In the late 1980s his wines caught the eye of the US critic Robert Parker. Others followed his lead and outsiders, such as Peter Sisseck (of the highly praised and priced Pingus)

Like Rioja, Ribera del Duero uses Tempranillo (known here as Tinto Fino and Tinto del Pais) but unlike that region, it uses it neat. Another difference lies in the high altitude (700-800 m) and the cool temperatures here, which make for more structured, long-lived wines.

WINERY SARDON DEL DUERO

### Abadia Retuerta

Abadia Retuerta, Santa Maria de Tetuerta, Sardón del Duero, Valladolid
T +34 983-680 314
www.abadia-retuerta.com
Tours Mon-Sat 1000 and 1200. Reserve as early as possible to ensure the desired date.
€10 per person

Founded in 1996, Abadia Retuerta's profile shot up when, in 2005, it won the prize for top red wine overall in the International Wine Challenge. Despite heading for cult status, the wines are still fairly priced, and the atmosphere is energetic and youthful, thanks to the influence of New Yorker Donald Cusimano who runs the winery on behalf of Swiss company, Novartis. The dramatic setting is anything but youthful, however: there is a 12th-century Romanesque monastery on the property, and wine tastings are held under the high vaults of the monks' former dining hall. Most of the wines in the range combine Tempranillo and Cabernet Sauvignon in varying proportions.

WINERY VALLADOLID

## Arzuaga Navarro

Ctra 122, Km 325, Quintanilla de Onésimo, Valladolid
T +34 983 681 146
www.arzuaganavarro.com
Restaurant daily 0900-2330. Tours by appointment only.

This would make a perfect base in the Ribera del Duero, combining one of the region's top wineries, a five-star hotel and a restaurant in one complex. The 24 rooms ($$$) are extremely comfortable and warm, and they all have a hydro-massager cabin and a jacuzzi. Wine tasting can be organized. Although it was built in the 1990s, the building evokes Spain's monasteries, and the atmosphere is classically serene yet luxuriously modern. Roam the 1400-ha park and you are likely to spot wild deer and boar. Wild game features on the restaurant menu, as does traditional roast lamb, all of which can be paired with Arzuaga Navarro wines.



RESTAURANT ARANDA DEL DUERO

## El Lagar de Isilla Restaurant & Cellar

C Isilla 18, Aranda de Duero
T +34 947-510 683
www.lagarisilla.es
Restaurant daily for lunch and dinner. Tours Mon-Fri from 1100; Sat and Sun 1330-1730.
$$

Aranda's speciality is roast baby lamb, and most restaurants in the town feature little else. As good as this dish is, one of the many things that make El Lagar de Isilla special is that it offers roast lamb and more. Among the highlights is a set Castilian menu, including traditional soup, *morcilla* (black pudding), *chorizo* (paprika sausage), piquillo peppers with tuna salad, and roasted lamb with green salad. The desserts showcase the restaurant's innovative side, with such offerings as cream- and cheese-stuffed peppers in custard. Visitors can watch their meat being cooked in the authentic Castilian 'mud oven', typically fuelled by dry wood and kept at 200ºC. Under these conditions, a quartered lamb will take only two hours to cook. The wine list is vast, featuring more than 400 wines, mostly from Ribera del Duero. Customers are invited to visit the extraordinary 12m-deep underground wine cellars, dating from the 13th century, which were often used in the past as an escape route to outside the city walls or to hide refugees.

El Lagar de Isilla.

WINERY SALAMANCA

## Hacienda Zorita

Ctra Salamanca–Ledesma, Km 12, Valverdón, Salamanca
T +34 902-109 902/923-129 400
www.haciendas-espana.com/www.vintagespain.com/zorita.htm
Bodega Sat and Sun 1200-1900; reserve in advance.
€6 per person

This is the perfect place to immerse yourself in northern Spanish history and architecture, as well as in wine. Founded in 1345 by Dominican monks, Hacienda Zorita also hosted Christopher Columbus in 1485 shortly before he set sail for the Americas. Restored in 2001 by Spanish architect Peridis, Hacienda Zorita combines the gravitas of its history with the comfort and luxury expected of a five-star hotel ($$). The same beguiling mixture of traditional and modern extends to the wine offerings of this working winery. The Durius range of eponymous Hacienda Zorita wines are aged in 1450 American oak casks in a former flour mill turned wine cellar, built in 1843. Here you can experience an audiovisual interactive wine tasting, and quiz the winemakers of the Durius Hacienda Zorita Crianza (Tempranillo 100%) and Durius Hacienda Zorita Blanco (Viura and Sauvignon Blanc). Hacienda Zorita has two restaurants ($$), one of which is for guests only. (The memorable breakfasts offer several kinds of local cheeses and as much wine as you feel like drinking along with your coffee.) They offer both traditional Castilian and more creative dishes, with many contributions from the vast kitchen gardens, and a range of Duero wines.

Ismael Arroyo.



WINERY SOTILLO DE LA RIBERA

## Ismael Arroyo

C Los Lagares 71, 09441 Sotillo de la Ribera
T +34 947-532 309
www.valsotillo.com
Visits by appointment only. Mon-Fri 1000-1400 and 1600-2000, Sat 1100-1400 and 1700-1900. Booking in advance is essential.

Located in the Sotilla de la Ribera region of Burgos, in the northeastern part of Ribera del Duero, Ismael Arroyo has been in the hands of the same family for 400 years. It was only in 1979, however, that the family, pioneers in the Ribero de Duero DOC, started bottling under their own name. The wines are more traditional than some, but are generally respected as some of the best in the area. The winery's fascinating tours can include visits to the 2000-sq-m network of rock- hewn, underground cellars, whose uniform temperatures of 11-12°C, no matter what the season, promote slow ageing and longevity.

MUSEUM VALLADOLID

## Museo del Vino de Valladolid

Castillo de Peñafiel, Peñafiel, Valladolid
T +34 983-881 199
www.museodelvinodevalladolid.es
Oct-mid Mar Tue-Sun 1130-1400, 1600-1900; late Mar-Sep Tue-Sun 1100-1430, 1630-1830.
€2.50

Not only does this museum provide terrific exhibits on all aspects of winemaking and tasting, but it is also a fascinating building in its own right. The museum is housed in an extraordinary elongated castle, built in 1456 by Henry IV, which curves, serpent-like, on a ridge overlooking the surrounding country. The central part is divided into two courtyards, the larger of which has been cleverly transformed by contemporary architect, Roberto Valle Rodriguez, using a stunning range of materials including wood, steel and glass, which collectively contrast dynamically with the Campassero stone of the original buiding.

## Rioja

This region, Spain's first holder of the superior DOC classification, ought, more sensibly, to be called Riebro. It owes its name to the Río Oja, a stream sufficiently inconsequential to rival the Californian trickle known as the Napa, but the river that really matters around here is the Ebro, which separates the northerly Rioja Álavesa from the Rioja Alta and the more southerly Rioja Baja.

Traditionally, it was thought that the best Rioja was a blend of grapes and regions, combining the lighter fruitiness and perfume of Tempranillo from the Álavesa with the structure of the same grape in the Alta, where it might also benefit from some Garnacha and Graciano. The warm Rioja Baja is Garnacha country: good for young, easy-drinking wine, although old vines here can deliver deeper, richer stuff. One of the characteristics for which the region is known is the sweet, oaky character that is given to the wine by the American oak barrels in which they are aged. Today, there is a move by some producers towards using French oak (which gives a more savoury character) and to introduce some Cabernet Sauvignon, as was done by the Marqués de Riscal a century ago (page 80). These producers are looking for more intensity of fruit and what is termed *alta expression* (high expression). Traditionalists disagree and continue to make wines the way they used to.

The old ways are still maintained for a very small number of white wines – most notably the deep-coloured, dry, nutty López de Heredia Tondonia Reservas – but most producers favour a light, modern style that seeks to extract all of the limited fruit that is on offer from the Viura grapes.

WINERY LOGROÑO

## Campo Viejo/Juan Alcorta

Camino de Lapuebla 50, Logroño
T +34 941-279 900
www.bodegasjuanalcorta.com
Tours Mon-Fri 1100, 1300 and 1600; Sat and Sun 1100 and 1300 (by appointment only).

Campo Viejo is not only the largest producer in Rioja, but also in recent years one of the most reliable. The Juan Alcorta winery building, named after its founder, is worth the visit alone. Situated at the highest point of this 110-ha estate, on a hill overlooking the Ebro Valley, it is an extraordinary example of modern winery architecture: a low-rise square building whose earth colours reflect those of the land it overlooks. Seven metres underground is a vast cellar housing 70,000 oak barrels and some million bottles in conditions that are free from air currents or temperature variations. This is a terrific introduction to both Rioja's traditions and the innovations that are being embraced by its top producers.

HOTEL BRIONES

## Casa Rural El Mesón

Travesía de la Estación 3, Briones
T +34 941-322 178
www.brioneslarioja.com
$

Located between Haro and Logroño in Briones, one of Rioja's most beautiful towns, El Mesón is the perfect base from which to explore Rioja Alta. The building, a historical wine inn, was fully restored in 2000 and its seven large rooms, decorated with local crafts, each has its own bathroom. Proprietor, Mari Cruz Díaz Matute, is a wine lover, and is pleased to organize visits to a range of local producers, artisanal as well as larger. She can also organize bike trips through the vines. The house is surrounded by a large garden and a small vineyard in which are planted locally grown grape varities. Though it serves breakfast, El Mesón has no restaurant.

MUSEUM BRIONES

## Dinastia Vivanco Wine Culture Museum

N-232, Km 442, Briones
T +34 902-320 001
www.dinastiavivanco.com
Museum Jun-Sep Tue-Sun 1000-2000; Oct-May Tue-Sun 1000-1800. Restaurant Tue-Sun 1330-1530, Fri and Sat 2030-2230. €6

### Cooking up a storm

Situated between Bilbao and Santander, the Basque region has one of the trickiest languages in Europe and produces almost exclusively white Chacoli or Txakoli (labels vary) wines, which, although pleasant, light and refreshing, are rarely worth buying outside the region. In its role as a magnet for cultural tourists, Bilbao has preferred to associate itself with Rioja rather than with these wines produced nearer to hand. For food lovers, however, this is one of Europe's great wine areas. Most of Spain grudgingly concedes that Basque cuisine is the peninsula's best: the San Sebastián twilight shimmers with Michelin stars and chummy all-male *txokos* (gastronomic societies) gather in private to swap recipes and cook up feasts in members-only kitchens. What strikes the visitor first are the *pintxos* (pronounced 'peenshos'), a stunning range of bartop snacks that range from the ubiquitous tortilla to elaborate miniature food sculptures which use esoteric ingredients and take many hours of painstaking work. In Bilbao the best place to sample *pintxos* is around Plaza Nueva in the Casco Viejo. In San Sebastián, the Parte Vieja is full of atmospheric old bars while across the river in Gros is **Garbola** ($), Paseo Colon 11, T+34 943-285019, something of a local legend.

One of the region's signature dishes is *bacalao al pil-pil*, salt cod in a spicy, gelatinous sauce. Others are *kokotxas* (fish cheeks) and *txangurro relleno*, spider crab blended with fish, tomato, onion, and spices and served in its shell. Beans also features on most menus. *Alubias de Tolosa*, the Rolls-Royce of beans, is best served with pickled cabbage and lumps of meat. *Idiazabal con membrillo*, a cheese made from sheep's milk, packs a punch and is superbly offset by the sweet quince jelly.

One of the very best places to try *bacalao al pil-pil* is in Bilbao at **Victor** ($$), Plaza Nueva 2, Casco Viejo, T+34 944-151678, a high-quality restaurant with an elegant but relaxed atmosphere and superb wine list. For a real gastronomic experience, head to **Zuberoa** ($$), Bº Iturriotz 8, in the hills south of San Sebastián near the town of Oiartzun/Oyarzun, T+34 943-491228, where chef Hilario Arbelaitz combines an essential Basqueness with a treatment inspired by the very best of French and Mediterranean cuisine.

Dinastia Vivanco Wine Culture Museum.

I honestly believe this to be one of the very best wine museums in the world; more than that, it is a celebration of wine the world over. Opened by King Juan Carlos in 2004, this huge modern complex houses exhibits about all facets of winemaking – from archeological artefacts to technical explanations to an intriguing collection of corkscrews. Outside, in the 'Bacchus Garden', there is one of the world's biggest collections of different grape varieties, assembled by the Vivanco family, who founded the museum. The museum café ($$) serves a range of appealing set menus, as well as à la carte dishes, many cooked on a wood fire that uses old wine casks and rootstock as fuel. Examples of the gastronomic offerings include *patorrillo*, a stew of lambs' shanks, pigs' trotters and tripe, and 'foie gras mi-cuit' with toasted corn and apple mousse.

HOTEL CASALARREINA

## Hospedería Señorío de Casalarreina

Plaza St Domingo de Guzmán 6, Casalarreina
T +34 941-324 730
www.hotelesconencanto.org
($)($)

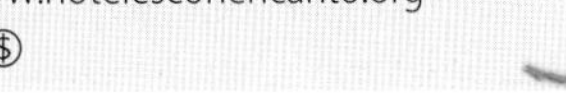

Staying in this hotel is a bit like sleeping in a museum. It is located in the Dominican monastery of Our Lady of Pity (Nuestra Señora de la Piedad), founded in 1509 by the Bishop of Calahorra. Restoration has preserved original decorative elements, such as precious stones set in forged metal, original washbasins, mirrors, curtains and trampantojos (traditional paintings on doors and walls). It offers an exciting menu of activities, including cooking classes, winery visits and meals, hot air balloon rides and, especially intriguing, stalking the more than 10,000 dinosaur tracks for which Rioja is known in archaeological circles.

HOTEL ALAVA

## Hotel Castillo El Collado

Paseo El Collado 1, Laguardia, Álava
T +34 945-621 200
www.euskalnet.net/hotelcollado
($)($)

This gem of a hotel, which has only eight rooms, took its owner Javier, an incurable romantic, 15 years to restore and convert. The rooms each have an original theme, such as 'Amor y Locura' (love and madness), which has a bath directly behind the headboard of a king-size bed. Right on the edge of the walled town of Castillo El Collado, the hotel has lovely views across the Rioja vineyards to the Catabrian mountains. Javier is delighted to organize visits to local bodegas, among other activities. The hotel has an excellent restaurant, divided into three elegant rooms, each quite different. The menu offers some 70 traditional and avant-garde dishes, from both Rioja and the Basque Country; Javier is especially proud of the desserts. There is also a more informal Taberna, open from Easter to October, serving tapas and lighter meals.

WINERY LOGRONO

## Marqués de Murrieta

Ctra de Zaragoza, Km 5, Logroño
T +34 941-271 370
www.marquesdemurrieta.com
Visits by appointment only.

This winery is worth visiting to learn about its extraordinary history, which officially began in 1852 when Luciano de Murrieta y García-Lemoine, born in Peru of a Basque father and a Bolivian Creole mother, first exported wine from the bodega to Cuba (another shipment to Mexico was dashed to pieces at sea). The wine, which benefited from Murrieta's self-imposed apprenticeship in Bordeaux, was an immediate success, and soon was being shipped to many other markets. Queen Isabel II named him Marqués de Murrieta, providing him with a catchy name for the winery that

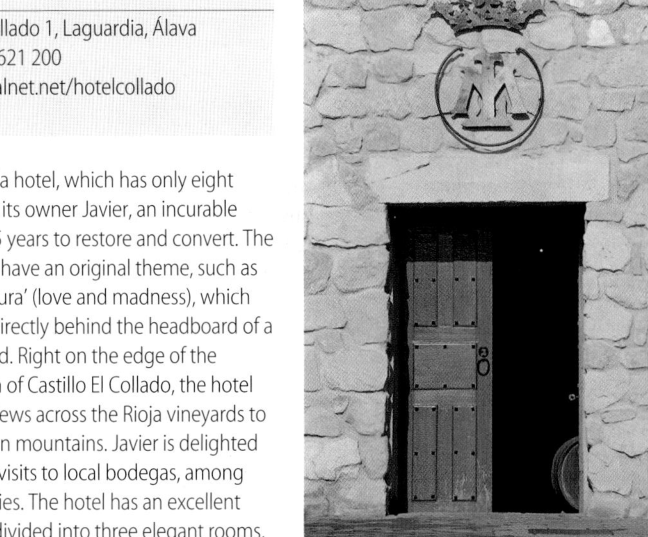

Marqués de Murrieta.

has endured, despite the fact that de Murrieta produced no heir and the winery passed into the ownership of another family.

WINERY ALAVA

### Marqués de Riscal

C Torrea 1, El Ciego, Álava
T +34 941-606 000
www.marquesderiscal.com
Visits by appointment only. Tue-Sat 1000, 1200 and 1600; Sun 1100 and 1300.
€6 including a glass of wine.



Since 1860, when it was one of the first Rioja wineries to introduce Bordeaux winemaking techniques to the region, Marqués de Riscal has been making waves. In 1972, for example, it was the first bodega to make a white wine under the Rueda appellation. Arguably the best is yet to come: Frank Gehry, architect of the Guggenheim Museum in Bilbao (among other iconic buildings) has designed a winery here. Making architectural references to the Guggenheim, the winery complex, opening in late 2006 houses a 14-room luxury hotel (www.starwoods hotels.com, $$$), a 120-seat restaurant ($$-$$$) and a health club.

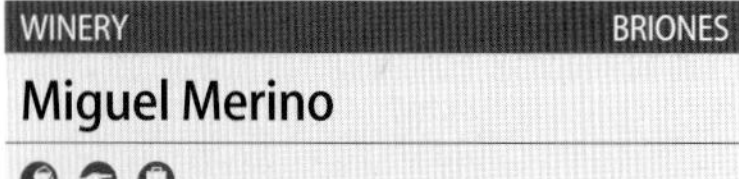

WINERY BRIONES

### Miguel Merino

Ctra de Logroño 16, Briones
T +34 941-322 263
www.miguelmerino.com
Visits by appointment only.

Appointments are essential at this award-winning family-owned winery, but it's well worth planning ahead. Miguel Merino's success belies the fact that the winery is not only small but a very recent, forward-looking venture in a very traditional part of viticultural Spain. Merino had long dreamt of owning his own bodega, a dream that he realized in the mid-1990s. The bodega makes only Rioja Reserva wines, made from Tempranillo with a pinch of Graciano, though in exceptional years they might select 3000 litres to be aged for longer as Gran Reservas. The vines are, on average, 40 years old and are hand picked. Fermentation starts naturally, using the natural yeasts on the skins, and lasts about three weeks at 30 degrees. Merino himself is the man to tell you what makes his wines such an intriguing celebration of the classical and modern, which he will do with passion. A visit to the bodega should also allow time to visit the striking medieval town of Briones and its Moorish castle.

Miguel Merino.

MUSEUM ALAVA

### Villa Lucia Wine Thematic Center

Ctra Logroño s/n, Laguardia, Álava
T +34 945-600 032
www.villa-lucia.com
Tue-Sun 1000-1400 and 1700-2000.
€4.50-14.50

This is a museum with a difference. Instead of a series of static exhibits, it offers visitors interactive displays, demonstrating all aspects of winemaking and. . .tasting! Using a range of colours, aromas and flavours, the 'virtual' wine tasting session will provide wine lovers with a new set of tasting skills. If and when you want to get back to the tangible world, step outside and explore the botanical gardens, in which grow more than 200 species of plants and trees.

HOTEL ABALOS

### Villa De Ábalos

Plaza Fermin Gurbindo 2, Ábalos
T +34 941-334 302
www.hotelvilladeabalos.com
$

Owners Merche and Jose Luis will make you feel so at home that you will not want to leave this special hotel. Opened in 2002, it is housed in a beautifully restored 17th-century nobleman's house and boasts 12 extremely comfortable rooms, all with en-suite bathrooms. Guests are free to use the solarium and the gardens where, weather permitting, breakfast is served. The restaurant is considered one of the best in the area, and ts wine list features all the wines produced in the town. Other highlights include jazz and wine evenings and a specially tailored 30 km bicycle tour of local wineries. In October, the hotel offers an 'Annual Cycle of Wine dedicated to the Harvest', in which guests can participate in such viticultural activities as pruning, bud removal, vine shoot trimming and harvesting. It is a unique and restful place to base oneself in Rioja.

The Calatrava-designed Ysios winery.

WINERY ALAVA

### Ysios

Camino de la Hoya s/n, Laguardia, Álava
T +34 945-600 640
www.bodegasysios.com
Mon-Fri 1100, 1300 and 1600; Sat and Sun 1100 and 1300 by appointment only.

Romantics won't like me saying this, but a winery is no more nor less than a wine factory and it is actually sometimes easier to produce beautiful wine in a building designed for efficiency rather than aesthetics. But when the same kind of thought has gone into the winery as the wine, I for one am very ready to applaud. The Ysios winery, designed by Santiago Calatrava to assimilate into the landscape at the base of the Sierra de Cantabria, is the winner of several architectural awards and is worth a detour. Inspired by a stack of barrels, the design is ultra modern but evokes such ancient monuments as the pyramids, both because of the simplicity of its lines and its stunning location. Owned by Pernod Ricard, Ysios is a classy example of how large-scale, intelligent investment can, in very short time, create modern wine classics. The Riojas it produces are good examples of the effects of well-managed oak.

## Navarra

To the east of Rioja, and slightly overlapping its territory, the old Kingdom of Navarra combines history – it has been on the pilgrim route to Santiago de Compostela for over 1000 years – with modern winemaking. This used to be the place to find large amounts of unexceptional Garnacha rosé, but now there is a wide range of good reds and whites produced from Tempranillo, Chardonnay, Cabernet Sauvignon and Merlot. While in the region, don't miss the Fuente de Irache at **Bodegas Irache** (www.irache.com), a steel and bronze fountain set into the wall, which offers free wine and water to thirsty pilgrims.

WINERY VILLAMAYOR DE MONJARDIN

### Castillo de Monjardin

Vina Rellanada s/n, Villamayor de Monjardin
T +34 948 537412/537589
www.monjardin.es
Mon-Fri 1100-1300 and 1530-1900; Sat 1100-1300.

This young winery focuses on making first-class modern Spanish wine from succh non-traditional – for Spain – varieties as Chardonnay (in particular), Pinot Noir, Cabernet Sauvignon and Merlot in impressive cellars. There is also a good restaurant ($$), in which there is the opportunity to see how well these wines age and how well matched they are to food.

## Best producers » *See also page 100.*

**Navarra**
Castillo de Monjardin » *page 89.*
Chivite
Palacio de la Vega
Bodegas Piedemonte

**Rias Baixas**
Lagar de Cevera
Martin Codax » *page 82.*
Pazo de Barrantes
Santiago Ruiz

**Ribera del Duero**
Abadia Retuerta » *page 83.*
Alíon
Ismael Arroyo » *page 85.*
Condado de Haza
Dominio de Pingus
Mauro
Pago de los Capellanes
Pagos del Rey
Pesquera
Vega Sicilia

**Rioja**
Baron de Ley
Ramon Bilbao
Bodegas Palacio
Campo Viejo » *page 86.*
Luis Canas
Contino
El Coto
Finca Allende
Marqués de Gríñon
Marqués de Murrieta » *page 87.*
Martinez Bujanda
Miguel Merino » *page 88.*
Palacio Redondo
Remelluri
Rioja Alta
Viña Tondonia
Viña Ijalba
Márques de Riscal » *page 89.*

**Toro**
Viña Bajoz » *page 83.*

## Catalunya

**The nearest wine region to the Costa Brava, Catalunya is now both a large DO (denominated region) in its own right and a collection of separate DOs, such as Penedès and Somontano, most of which are characterized by their innovative styles. Somontano is a wonderful region to visit for savage scenery, and tiny unspoiled villages and small towns. Like Campo de Borja, it is also an up-and-coming region for modern wine. Catalunya's winemaking was pioneered by the dynamic Miguel Torres (who also led the way in the sub-region of Penedès) and the region is now producing a wide range of wines. The area that is attracting the greatest interest (especially among US critics) at the moment is Priorato (or Priorat in Catalan) thanks to the intense flavours of its reds. Costers del Segre was more or less created as a region by Raimat, a subsidiary of the giant Codorniu sparkling wine company and remains one of Spain's most go-ahead areas. Conca de Barbera is another modern region that owes its reputation to Torres' Milmanda Chardonnay and his red Grans Muralles blend. Tarragona, by contrast, is still climbing out of a history that was focused on making thick old Garnachas for use in churches.**

### Barcelona

If you were to ask an older Madrileño about Barcelona, he might well generously describe it as the most vibrant of Spain's secondary cities. But talk to his counterpart in Barcelona and you will get a very different response: for him, this is the capital of the semi-autonomous region of Catalunya (Catalonia), the most vibrant, go-ahead region of the country. Barcelona is the place for great, innovative food, wine, fashion and nightlife. The only let-down for real wine lovers is that this is not a great place to find fresh zingy Fino sherry. Some bars treat Fino with (even) less respect than their counterparts in London and New York.

RESTAURANT — PLAÇA DEL OLLES

**Cal Pep**

Plaça del Olles 8
T +34 933-107 961
Mon 0830-2330; Tue-Sat 1300-1630 and 2030-2330.
$$

A real local's hangout, full of banter between Pep Manubens and his customers about food and wine. The front room is a bar with a counter at which you can eat, while the back room has only half a dozen tables. Recommended dishes include fried artichokes, a mixed medley of seafood that includes small sardines, clams in a spicy broth and tuna with sesame sauce, though whatever seafood Pep is cooking that day is bound to be as fresh and as delicious as could be imagined.

### Ampurdàn Costa Brava

RESTAURANT — CADAQUES

**Casa Nun**

Plaça de Port Dixtos 6, Cadaques
T +34 972-258 856
Mon-Sat lunch and dinner; Sun lunch only.
$$

An antique-filled restaurant, just over a couple of hours' drive from Barcelona, this intimate spot overlooks the sea and serves delicious fresh seafood dishes. It also offers a terrific wine list. Salvador Dalí, whose house is now a much-visited museum nearby, called Cadaques 'the most beautiful village in the world'. That's arguable, but it's certainly one of the most charming on the Costa Brava.

## 24 hours in Barcelona

Forget flamenco, sangría and other stock Spanish clichés, Barcelona is the proud capital of the ancient kingdom of Catalunya, with a distinct language and its own customs and traditions.

Get a feel for the city by strolling down the Ramblas, with a stop at **La Boquería** market on the way to take in the sights, sounds and smells. Alternatively, have a coffee at **Café de l'Òpera** and watch the world go by. Then dive into the chaotic maze of the **Barri Gòtic**, where you'll find the Gothic cathedral (take the lift to the roof for fantastic views) and plenty of great shops, bars and restaurants. Lovers of modern art should head across the Ramblas to El Raval, home to the excellent **MACBA** (Museum of Contemporary Art, Plaça dels Àngels, T +34 93-412 0810, www.macba.es), and lots of small galleries. Have lunch opposite MACBA on the terrace at **Pla dels Àngels** (C Ferlandia 23, T +34 93-329 4047).

Afterwards head to the Eixample area to explore **Passeig de Gràcia**. This elegant street is home to the city's most emblematic Modernista buildings, including Gaudí's **Casa Batlló** (www.casabatllo.es) and **La Pedrera** (C Providencia 261-265, T+34 902-400 973, www.caixacatalunya.es). Alternatively, pay a visit to the extraordinary **Sagrada Família** (C Mallorca 401, T +34 93-208 0414, www.sagradafamilia.org).

In the late afternoon head to the seafront for a stroll. A boardwalk runs from the foot of the Ramblas to the glittering Port Vell development. Beyond is the fishermen's district of Barceloneta, the city's beaches and the Port Olímpic. Enjoy an evening *aperitivo* at **Cal Pep** (page 90). You could stay here for dinner but for a real treat head instead to **Beltxenea** (C Mallorca 275, Eixample, T +34 93-215 3024), a grand restaurant with a romantic terrace overlooking an immaculately manicured garden.

Vines at Can Feixes.

## Penedès

This region – thanks mostly to Miguel Torres Junior and his father – introduced 20th-century winemaking to Spain. It includes high-altitude Riesling vineyards and warm areas close to the sea that are far better suited to rich reds, but the main focus here often appears to be the production of Cava sparkling wine.

WINERY | CABRERA DE IGUALADA

### Can Feixes

5 Finca Can Feixes, Cabrera de Igualada
T + 34 937-718 227
www.canfeixes.com
Visits by appointment only.

Santi doing the honours at Cal Xim.

Located some 400 m above sea-level on the slopes of the mountain that divides the comarcas of Penedès and Anoia, Can Feixes is a good place to visit to understand and sample the tempering affects of altitude and cooler weather on wine. The climate combines with a poor soil, containing little organic matter, to produce low yields of grapes that have a notable concentration. The Huguet family, which owns the winery, is dedicated to keeping their output limited but of high quality, and their concentrated, award-winning Cavas, Bordeaux-style blends and Chardonnays, among others, are good examples of how, with appropriate dedication, smaller wineries can punch above their weight.

RESTAURANT SANT PAU D'ORDAL

## Cal Xim

Plaça Subirats 5, Sant Pau d'Ordal
T +34 938-993 092
www.calxim.com
Mon-Thu lunch; Fri and Sat lunch and dinner.
$$-$$$

As soon as I discovered this restaurant, tucked away in a tiny wine country hamlet, an hour from Barcelona, I knew it was a wine lover's dream come true. Santi, the cheerful owner, has an unbelievable wine cellar, with a varied range that includes top international names, such as Grange and Opus One, and the best Spanish wines available today, from Vega Sicilia, Pingus, Roda, Clos Mogador to Finca Dofí. Apart from big names, Cal Xim's cellar also contains interesting, boutique wines such as our favorite sweetie, Albet I Noya's elixir, Dolç Adriá, and small batches of 'Garage Wines' from Priorat and Montsant, such as Mas Igneus, Clos Martinet and Clos de l'Obac.

The small stone villa-style restaurant has a huge woodburning stove right in the dining room, where they roast duck, rabbit, lamb and all colour and shape of Mediterranean vegetables. A sublime meal at Cal Xim would begin with Santi's great selection of Catalan cheeses, continue with fresh anchovies from the Cantabrian coast and the house salad (with a lovely almond-based sauce); next would come the most delicious roast artichokes on earth and the meal would culminate with roast lamb. To finish off, Santi's *crema catalan* (Catalan version of crème brûleé) is to die for.

WINERY SANT SADURNÍ D'ANOIA

## Codorníu

Av Codorníu s/n, Sant Sadurní d'Anoia
T +34 938-183 232
www.codorniu.com
Mon-Fri 0900-1700; Sat and Sun 0900-1300.

This is one of Spain's most important wineries and it produces some 27 million bottles of Cava a year but its sheer scale is not the only thing that is impressive. The winery, reminiscent of a series of cathedral naves, was designed by the modernista architect Josep Puig i Cadafalch and is classified as a national monument. It is a good place to come to understand the traditional method of making Cava, pioneered by Codorníu in 1872, and to put Cava in the context of winemaking in the area – Cordoníu has been making wine here for more than 450 years. To visit the Codorníu Cellars is to steep oneself in the history of Cava and its culture., and to taste examples of old-fashioned and more modern styles, including some that are made exclusively from Chardonnay, a grape disdained by traditionalists.

WINERY SANT SADURNÍ D'ANOIA

## Freixenet

Joan Sala 2, Sant Sadurní d'Anoia
T +34 938-917 000
Tours Mon-Thu 1100, 1200, 1300, 1600 and 1700; Fri 1000, 1100, 1200 and 1300; Sat and Sun 1000-1300. Shop Mon-Thu 1000-1430 and 1600-1900; Fri 1000-1430.

The second-largest Cava producer after Cordoníu, Freixenet is one of the more traditional. It is particularly worth visiting for its lovely19th-century winery, founded in 1889. The extensive tour includes a visit to the vast cellars, an informative overview of the Cava-making process, a tasting and an opportunity to purchase various examples of the bubble-maker's art.

Exterior and interior views of the Codorníu reception hall, designed by the Modernist architect Josep Puig I Cadalfach.

WINERY TORRELAVIT

## Jean León

Torrelavit
T +34 93 899 5512
www.jeanleon.com
Visits by appointment only. Tours Mon-Sat 0930-1730; Sun and hols 0930-1300.
€3

A native of Santander, the late Jean León went to the US to seek fame and fortune and found both when he opened the La Scala restaurant in Hollywood, which was frequented regularly by Natalie Wood, Grace Kelly, Lana Turner, Judy Garland, Marilyn Monroe and Humphrey Bogart, among others. A great wine lover, his second dream was fulfilled when he returned to Spain and founded the winery that still bears his name (though now it is a subsidiary of Torres), using grafts of Cabernet Sauvignon, Merlot and Chardonnay vines from the likes of Château Lafite-Rothschild and Corton Charlemagne. The one-hour tour provides a close-up of the Bordeaux-inspired procedures he poured his heart – and wallet – into implementing.

WINERY ILAFRANCA DEL PENEDES

## Miguel Torres

C Miguel Torres, Carbo s/n, Ilafranca del Penedès
T +34 938-177 487
www.torres.es
Mon-Fri 0900-1700, Sat 0900-1800, Sun and hols 0900-1300.

The Torres family, spearheaded by the dynamic and innovative Miguel, is one of Spain's – and the modern wine world's – great success stories. It is one of the best reference points for how Spanish winemaking traditions can be successfully fused with the most modern techniques. I have visited the winery over the years since 1984 and been dazzled by the spirit of innovation and curiosity I have always found there. Apart from the fascinating tasting of wines at various stages of maturation, the highlight of the free, hour-long visitor's tour of this Penedès institution is the 'Tunnel of Seasons', in which your senses will be exposed to the changes in climate and vine during the full year-long vineyard cycle.

It is impossible to overstate the positive influence Miguel Torres has had on the modern evolution of Spanish wine.

Castillo Milmanda at Miguel Torres.

## Priorat

Officially known as Priorato but described as Priorat on labels, this is now a place of pilgrimage for lovers of new wave Spanish wine. The story of the region is an interesting one, because it shows how solidarity among producers – a rarity in Europe – can achieve marvels.

Two decades ago, a group of winemakers, including Alvaro Palacios, Carles Pastrana and Rene Barbier Junior, collectively bought eight pieces of land high in the Siurana Valley and used the grapes to produce wine at a local cooperative. They believed that there was a magic in the schist soil here and the potential to make better wine than had been produced by the Cellers Scala Dei in the old priory from which the region as a whole takes its name. But they were also innovative in planting their vines in walled vineyards – 'clos', like the walled vineyards in Burgundy, and irrigating them. At first, their methods meant that the rich, dark, complex wines could not be sold as Priorat, but global success soon led to a change in the rules. Palacios's L'Ermita 2003 now sells in the US for US$500 per bottle. Priorat, including more modest efforts by Palacios, can be found for a 20th of that price, but this is no place to go looking for picnic wine. The heart of the region here is the town of Gratallops, but Falset and the village of Scala Dei are well worth visiting too.

WINERY GRATALLOPS

### Costers del Siurana

Camí Manyanetes s/n, Pol 11, Gratallops
T +34 977-839 276. Restaurant T +34 977-839 036.
www.costersdelsiurana.com
Mon-Fri 0830-1300 and 1500-1830.
Restaurant Tue-Sat 1200-1600; book in advance.

Miserere, Clos de L'Obac, Dolç de l'Obac and Kyrie, all of which are made by Carles Pastrana at Costers del Siurana, have been lauded the world over and have made their way onto wine lists of top restaurants in more than 40 countries. This kind of global reputation and the prices commanded by the wines are in direct contrast to the informality of **El Celler de Gratallops** ($$$), the winery restaurant, a five-minute walk away, which seats a mere 36 people at eight tables and offers a range of Mediterranean dishes to accompany these huge wines. The opportunity to taste these would be worth the pilgrimage in itself, but Costers del Siurana also offers rich insights into ancient and modern Spanish winemaking history. Pastrana and Mariona Jarque, the co-founder of Costers del Siurana, have also turned their hands to renovating Mas d'En Bruno, an imposing Priorat winery dating from 1273.

# Valencia, Murcia and the Balearics

**South of Catalunya, in the Mediterranean coastal region known as the Levant (because it is the place where the sun rises), the focus of attention is on Jumilla, where wineries like Casa de la Ermita and Finca Luzon have shown what can be done with the traditional Monastrell, as well as a range of international varieties. Yecla and Bullas, nearby, have some way to go to catch up but should eventually make it, as will Utiel-Requena, where the large Vicente Gandia winery makes commercial and estate wines.**

## Jumilla

Until the late 1980s, Jumilla produced rich red wine that was (illegally) used to improve wines from other more famous regions. Now, however, this is very up-and-coming area with several good bodegas that are now showing what can be done with the Monastrell grape both by itself and in blends with other varieties. A good wine route starts in the small town of Jumilla. Luzon and Casa de la Ermita and Casa Castillo are probably the best trio of estates in Jumilla.

WINERY MURCIA

### Finca Luzon

Ctra Jumilla–Ontur, Km 17, Apto 45, Jumilla
T +34 968-784 135
www.fincaluzon.com
Contact the winery for opening times. Tours and tastings must be booked in advanced.

The largest estate in the region, with 500 ha of vines, and also one of the oldest, this winery has converted an old farmhouse into a comfortable hotel ($$) whose rooms look out onto the organically-grown vineyards. The winery was undergoing reconstruction in 2006; contact the winery directly for further information.

## Utiel Requena

This region, which has made wine for 2000 years, takes its name from a pair of small towns. The tradition here – originally practised by householders who sold their wine to mariners – was to ferment red wine from the Bobal grape on grape skins from which wine has already been made. This made for darker, stronger, more tannic wine that was unusually long-lived but short on subtlety. Today, more modern styles are made and more Tempranillo is grown.

WINERY VALENCIA

### Mas de Bazan

Crta Villar de Olmos, Km 2, Requena, Valencia
T +34 962 -03 586
www.agrodebazansa.es
Visits by appointment only; book online.
€3-4

Housed in a modernist building dating from 1905, the Mas de Bazan bodega is one of the most striking wineries in the Spanish Levant. It produces a range of wines that reflect the nature of the land, climate and grape varieties. Well-equipped for visits, it offers a choice between a simple €3 tour with bottle tasting and a €4 tour that includes a barrel tasting. And, for anyone interested, there is even a chapel available for hire.

## The Balearics

The Balearics – and Mallorca in particular – are rebuilding their wine industry and exploiting the fact that, like many other islands, they have grape varieties that are not found elsewhere. Mallorca has long had a denominated region called Binissalem, but this fact has gone unnoticed by most tourists and, indeed, most expatriates who have

happily bought cheaper and generally better fare from the mainland. There were good wines to be found, including examples of traditional local grapes exclusive to the island, but the creation of a new DO in the shape of Pláy Llevant seems to have encouraged a new spirit of dynamism.

WINERY MALLORCA

### Vinyes i Bodegues Miquel Oliver

C Font 26, Petra
T +34 971-561 117
Sep-Jun Mon-Fri 1000-1400 and 1600-1830. Jul and Aug Mon-Fri 0800-1500. Visits by appointment only.

One of the New Wave of Mallorcan wineries, in the new DO of Pláy Llevant close to Petra, this family-owned firm grows a mixture of traditional local varieties – Callet, Fogoneu and Manto Negro – as well as ones that are associated with the mainland and other countries. Among the successes are the Aia Merlot and a dry Muscat. The equipment and winemaking methods are among the most modern on the island but there are vaulted cellars and wooden vats to satisfy the most romantic of visitors.

# Central & southern Spain



**The geographical centre of Spain includes the Meseta, the hot, dry, flat area surrounding and to the south of Madrid. The best known wine regions here are Valdepeñas and La Mancha, neither of which have any historic association with good wine. However, the challenge laid down by the quality of wines coming from similarly unprepossessing regions of the New World has forced producers here to raise their ambitions. It is no coincidence that it was here, in 2001, that nine producers, led by the Marqués de Griñón's Dominio de Valdepusa launched the association of Grandes Pagos de Castilla – great estates of Castilla. Watch out for more good things in these regions and in nearby Ribera del Júcar and in the Vinos de Madrid.**

**Further south in Andalucia, we are in the land of traditional fortified wines, like sherry and Malaga (a rich sweet wine), and of their unfortified neighbour, Montilla. Sherry, produced in and around Jerez, is one of the great wines of the world. In its various styles, it's a great partner for food and a firm favourite among wine professionals who regularly, though in vain, proclaim the dawning of renewed interest in this wine among wine drinkers. Málaga, meanwhile, has been reprieved from virtual extinction but there still are are less than a handful of producers here.**

## Madrid

The Spanish capital is often eclipsed nowadays by the Catalan flamboyance of Barcelona but Madrid has an appeal that is all of its own for anyone interested in food and drink. One of the essential and obvious differences between the two cities is the presence for one and the absence for the other of the ocean. Madrid has all of the characteristics of a continental city: the climate seesaws between very chilly winters and baking summers. Much of the food is very hearty – vegetables and salads are traditionally rarer than one might wish – but the tapas here are among the best in Spain, and restaurants and bars offer a broad range of wines from across the country; something that can not always be said of other cities that tend to favour their local area. Madrid actually has an officially denominated wine region of its own in the shape of Vinos de Madrid. Until quite recently, most of the wines sold under this name were of little interest but now quality is improving fast, and Jesús Díaz, Francisco Casas and Castejón all produce good reds, in several cases using Cabernet Sauvignon and Merlot as well as the ubiquitous Tempranillo and the local Malvar.

WINE SHOP — MADRID

### Lavinia

José Ortega y Gasset 16
T +34 91-426 0604
www.lavinia.es
Mon-Sat 1000-2100.

Lavinia is one of the most exciting of the new breed of wine emporia springing up around the world. A huge shop, offering thousands of wine from Spain and around the world, it also has an elegant, spacious restaurant ($) in which you can eat anything from a light selection of tapas to a full, innovative Mediterranean-inspired meal, accompanied by wine bought, without mark-up, from the shop. The wine selections range from tiny, artisanal producers that you would have to look hard for in their countries of origin, to local heavy-hitters, such as Vega Sicilia, represented in several vintages and formats. Barcelona and Paris (page 38) also have branches of Lavinia, but without a restaurant.

## Segovia

To the northwest of Madrid, the city of Segovia is a great place to enjoy local wines such as Rueda and Ribera del Duero.

### Understanding sherry

Sherry is made from three principal grape varieties, the Palomino (which is also known as the Listán), the Moscatel and Pedro Ximénez (usually referred to as PX). Palomino, which is also (rarely) used for flabbily unrefreshing white table wine, is perfectly suited to the chalky soil, hot, humid climate, the sea breezes and the particular technique involved in the making of sherry. The grapes are harvested and fermented to around 12-13% alcohol and left for around four months until January when their quality is judged. The finest batches are lightly fortified with neutral brandy to 14.5% and transferred to casks, where it is hoped that a layer of 'flor' yeast will develop on the surface of the liquid. The casks with the thickest and most active yeast are fortified by a further 1% and will become Fino. While all Finos start out in the same way, they vary in the way they evolve. Examples matured in Jerez tend to be nuttier and fuller-bodied, while those aged in the cooler, coastal towns of Sanlúcar de Barrameda or Puerto de Santa María (where they are called Manzanilla and Fino Puerto respectively) are fresher, saltier and tangier. All Fino is aged for at least five years.

Casks with little or no flor are fortified to 17.5% (a strength that will, in any case, kill off the yeast) and are destined to become Oloroso, which, at its intense, nutty, raisiny but dry finest (for example at Gonzalez Byass), can be aged for up to a century.

Whatever the style, however, sherry will almost all go through the 'solera' system. This is effectively a pyramid which permanently refreshes older wine with younger stock. At Domecq, there are soleras that originally began in 1792, 1830 and the beginning of the 20th century. The quality of the wine that is ultimately sold depends on the original wine and the management of the solera.

Sherry barrels at Emilio Lustau.

But sherry is not all about Fino and Oloroso. There are two styles of sherry that begin life as Finos but then go their own way. A Fino that loses its flor – after six years or so – will take on some of the nuttiness of an Oloroso and a deeper colour. It will be fortified to about 17.5% and renamed an Amontillado. Palo Cortado follows a similar evolution but is more of a rarity, ending up as a cross between a tangy Fino and a nutty Amontillado.

All these wines will be bone dry, though the raisiny character may make an Oloroso, in particular, smell as though it were sweet. There is a British tradition of sweetening Oloroso and Amontillado with PX to create styles such as cream sherry and Amoroso. The only sweet sherry that Spaniards countenance is the pure, treacly PX, which is brilliant poured over very good vanilla ice cream.

Recently, as part of the efforts to upgrade sherry's image, there has been a trend towards vintage dating non-solera-aged sherries (Gonzalez Byass launched a 1963 and 1966 in 1994) with an indication of age. VOS (Vinum Optimum Signatum, Very Old Sherry) has to be at least 20 years old, while VORS (Vinum Optimum Rare Signatum, Very Old Rare Sherry) will be at least 30 years old. Over 60 examples of these styles are now available.

RESTAURANT SEGOVIA

## Méson de Candido

Azoguejo 5
T +34 921-425 911/428 102
www.mesondecandido.es
Daily 1200-1630 and 2000-2400.
$$

This is a Segovia institution, famous especially for its speciality of roast suckling pig. The visitors' book, the 'Book of Gold', contains the signatures of heads of state, Nobel prizewinners and artists and writers of all descriptions, and the owner, A Candido, has been officially named, in pure Gilbert and Sullivan style, 'Highest Innkeeper of Castile'. The dining area consists of several salons decorated in an ornate traditional style, with artefacts, from antlers to hams and oil paintings, hanging from the walls and ceilings. The wine list is short but well chosen and the menu, in addition to roast pig, features such traditional local dishes as 15th-century Castilian soup, mushroom and pine nut soup, and butter beans with pig's ears and trotters.

Marqués del Real Tesoro.



### Things to do around Jerez

Once you've had your fill of sherry bodegas and marvelled at the balletic movements of the white Carthusian horses, it's time to sample the other delights of Andalucía. Only an hour and a quarter away by car is the city of **Sevilla**, Andalucía's magnificent capital. While the fortunes of this one-time mercantile powerhouse have waxed and waned, its allure has not; even within Spain its name is spoken like a mantra, a word laden with sensuality and promise.

Sevilla has an astonishingly rich architectural heritage within its old town, still girt by sections of what was once Europe' s longest city wall. The bristling Moorish tower of the **Torre del Oro**, the Baroque magnificence of numerous churches; the gigantic Gothic **cathedral** and the mudéjar splendours of the **Alcázar**; these and much more are ample reason to spend plenty of time here. Seville is also home to Spain's most famous **Semana Santa** (Holy Week) processions, when mesmeric lines of hooded figures and cross-carrying penitents make their way through the streets. Your best moments in the city, though, are likely to be spent eating. Tapas was invented here and it's the place in Spain where it is done best. Try the legendary **Bar Pepe Hillo** (C Adriano 24, T+34 954- 215390).

If it's summer, you might not want to spend too much time in the stifling inland heat, so consider the old-town streets of **Cádiz**, a mere 40 minutes from Jerez. With a proud and long maritime history stretching back to the Phoenicians, it comes as no surprise that Cádiz can seem less conservative and more outward-looking than many Andalucían cities; geographically it's not far off being an island, and culturally it's typified by its riotous **Carnaval**. Earthquakes and buccaneering have deprived it of a significant collection of monuments, but it's a very likeable place with the sea seemingly at the end of every narrow street. The architecture of the old town is a quiet and elegant blend of 18th- and 19th-century houses, while beyond the old city gates stretches the interminable Avenida de Andalucía, which runs parallel to the town's long beaches.

Running south from Cádiz is the **Costa de la Luz**, Andalucía's most enticing stretch of coastline. It has a range of vast sandy beaches, some calm, some with serious surf, and all happily free from much of the overdevelopment that has plagued the Mediterranean *costas*.

For further information on this area, consult Footprint's pocket guides to Seville and the Costa de la Luz.

Sherry in the cellar at González Byass.

## Jerez

Sherry may still be irredeemably unfashionable (despite frequent denials of this fact by those who produce and enjoy drinking it) but it's one of the world's great wines – especially as an accompaniment to food – and Jerez is one of the world's best towns to visit.

WINERY JEREZ DE LA FRONTERA

### Alvaro Domecq

C Madre de Dios s/n, Jerez de la Frontera
T +34 956-339 634
www.alvarodomecq.com
Visits by appointment only.

Not to be confused with the other, larger Domecq bodega on Calle San Idelfonso (which is also worth visiting), this family-owned business has been in operation since 1730. Its tours provide in-depth insights into the history, production and correct tasting of Sherry, and include an audio-visual presentation complete with footage of bullfighting and flamenco dancing. Tours are regularly available in Spanish, English and German and the 1400 tour includes an appetizer.

WINERY JEREZ DE LA FRONTERA

### Emilio Lustau

C Arcos 53, Jerez de la Frontera
T +34 956-341 597
www.emilio-lustau.com
Mon-Fri 0900-1400 by appointment.
€10

Founded in 1896, this small bodega's sherries have won awards and plaudits the world over. Unlike larger companies, Lustau specializes in sherries that are sourced from small family-run soleras known as '*almacenistas*'. The tasting here is arguably the most informative in the region. And once you've done it, you could join the 6500 people who have already become members of the Emilio Lustau Sherry Club. This in turn would enable you to obtain bottles of rare sherry at home – and the means to convert a few friends to the cause of sherry.

WINERY JEREZ DE LA FRONTERA

### González Byass

C Manuel María González 12, Jerez de la Frontera
T +34 902-440 077/956-357 016
www.bodegastiopepe.com
Tours Mon-Sat 1130, 1230, 1330, 1400, 1630, 1730 and 1830; Sun 1130, 1230, 1330 and 1400. Pre-booking is necessary.

The maker of Tio Pepe, arguably the best contemporary ambassador of sherry across the globe, Gonzalez Byass offers a range of tours, easily booked via the website, including special evening flamenco shows. The regular tour includes a train ride through the vineyards, a barrel-making demonstration, a video, a sherry tasting and, most remarkably of all, the chance to watch sherry-loving mice climb a tiny ladder up to get a mouse-sized sip of PX. Apparently, the little rodents used to gnaw at the barrels but now they have lost the desire to do so. (Whether this works on mice elsewhere is not certain.)

WINERY SANLUCAR DE BARRAMEDA

### Hidalgo-La Gitana

Banda de la Playa 42, Sanlúcar de Barrameda
T +34 956-385 304
www.vinicola-hidalgo.es
Visits by appointment only.

It is well worth making the trip to Sanlúcar de Barrameda in order to properly understand Manzanilla, of which Bodega La Gitana makes one of the best examples. The town's location between the sea and the marshlands to the north helps create a unique microclimate that allows a special, thicker type of 'flor', or yeast, to grow on the surface of the maturing wine that stays alive longer than the flor on other finos. The bodega is also running a campaign to save the Spanish imperial eagle.

WINERY JEREZ

### Marqués del Real Tesoro

Ctra Nacional IV – Km 640, CP 11408
T +34 956 321 004
www.grupoestevez.com
Mon-Fri 1000-1400 or by appointment.

This sherry bodega belonging to Valdespino offers an exhibition of prints by artists such as Picasso, Dali and Botero as well as an impressive range of 17th- and 18th-century antiques. Rare black Spanish horses are also bred here and 70 of the magnificent beasts live in the stables, close to an display of old carriages. The sherries available for tasting include Tio Mateo and Inocente and the bodega boasts areas dedicated both to great bullfighters (who have, of course, signed the barrels) and to Lola Flores, one of Spain's most famous flamenco singers.



## Málaga

Winemaking was introduced here by the Greeks in around 600 BC; a Roman fermentation vat discovered in the area proves that the tradition was maintained. Under the Moorish occupation, wine production was more difficult, since drunkenness was a capital offence but in the late 1700s the region's sweet wine, made from Pedro Ximenez grapes that had been partly dried by the sun after picking, was a favourite of the Russian court. In the 19th century, this wine was known as 'Mountain' because of the height of its vineyards, some of which are at 700 m, and had become as much of a staple of British dining rooms as Madeira and port. Fashions change, however, and, by the turn of the millennium, López Hermanos was the only Málaga producer left. The region's kiss of life came from Telmo Rodriguez, a dynamic producer who makes wine in several parts of Spain.

RESTAURANT RONDA

### Tragabuches

José Aparicio 1, Ronda
T +34 952-190 291
www.tragabuches.com
Mon-Sat 1330-1530 and 2030-2230;
Sun 1330-1530.
$$$

Tragabuches is the nickname of a bandit who used to roam the Serranía de Ronda mountains. Whether or not Daniel García's radical interpretations of Andalucian cuisine are to your taste will depend on how much of a purist you are, but the restaurant has raked in plaudits and boasts a Michelin star. The pleasant staff can help to navigate the vast wine list and, despite its emergence as a culinary pilgrimage site, the decor is funky and unassuming, with wood floors, brick walls and red-painted beams. It is owned by the same group that owns El Juncal (below), whose Pasos Largos wine is named after a fellow bandit of Tragabuches.

## Best producers » *See also page 89.*

**Castilla-la Mancha**
Dominio de Valdepusa

**Catalunya**
Can Feixes » *page 91.*
Marqués de Alella
Clos d'Agon

**Costers del Segre**
Raimat

**Jerez**
Barbadillo
Domecq » *page 99.*
González Byass » *page 99.*
Hidalgo » *page 99.*
Emilio Lustau » *page 99.*
Sanchez Romate
Valdespino » *page 100.*

**Jumilla**
Casa de la Ermita
Finca Luzon » *page 95.*

**La Mancha**
Bodegas y Viñedos Castiblanque » *page 101.*
El Vinculo

**Málaga**
Scholtz Hermanos

**Mallorca**
Miguel Oliver

**Penedès**
Rene Barbier fill (unrelated to Rene Barbier)
Can Rafols dels Caus
Codorníu » *page 92.*
Jean León » *page 93.*
Mas Rabassa
Massies d'Avinyó
Puig i Roca
Torres » *page 93.*

**Priorat**
Clos l'Ermita
Clos Mogador
Costers de Siurana (Clos de L'Obac, Dolç de l'Obac, Kyrie, Miserere) » *page 94.*
Finca Dofi
Mas Doix
Scala Dei

**Somontano**
Enate

**Utiel Requena**
Mas de Bazan » *page 95.*

WINERY RONDA

### El Juncal

Ctra de Roda el Burgo, Km 1, Ronda
T +34 952-161 170
www.eljuncal.com.
Tours and tastings by appointment.

This is a place to linger for several days. The hotel ($$) is elegant and sophisticated and its minimalist, modern interior contrasts strikingly with the 17th-century exterior of this Andalucian finca. The effect is soothing and enticing, and it will take willpower to leave the side of the large, gently sloping pool and gardens to get down to wine tasting. Luckily, you don't have to go far, as the winery is under the same roof. It released its first wine, Pasos Largos 2002, in spring 2006. There's also a restaurant ($$) serving modern Spanish cuisine. Wine-related activities can be organized and the stunning

# Vintages

2005 Often top class in Rioja and Priorat, but sometimes overripe.

2004 Very variable.

2003 A drought year with many unbalanced wines. Some Riojas were very good, however.

2002 Generally poor.

2001 Great.

2000 Some good wines from Catalunya but Rioja is poor.

hill town of Rondo is close by. The hotel is also an excellent base for visiting Seville, Córdoba and Granada.

## La Mancha

The vast sprawling plateau that is Don Quixote country has not traditionally been known for quality wine. But La Mancha, Europe's largest DO, has in the past decade or so benefited from permission to irrigate and from the increase of such varieties as Syrah, Chardonnay and Cabernet Sauvignon, as well as the banning of new plantings of the dull traditional Airén.

WINERY — CIUDAD REAL

### Bodegas y Viñedos Castiblanque

C Isaac Peral 19, Campo de Criptana, Ciudad Real
T +34 926-589 147
www.bodegascastiblanque.com
Visits by appointment only.
€3

Bodegas y Viñedos Castiblanque is a good place to witness the La Mancha wine revolution up close. After a €2 million restoration of the 19th-century winery, the result is not only the production of some of the best wine La Mancha has to offer, but also a wine school that offers a year-long in situ course (Vinademus), starting with an in-depth one-month tasting course, that exposes students to all the cycles of vine growing and winemaking. For those who do not have a year to spare, there are four seasonal 'Monographic Courses' and for more casual visitors, the bodegas' 'enotourism programme' offers several shorter courses and tours, such as a day-long guided visit to Campo de Criptana.

WINERY — ALBACETE

### Sánchez Muliterno

Ctra Bonillo–Ossa de Montiel, Km 11, El Bonillo, Albacete
T +34 967-370 749
www.muliterno.com
Visits by appointment only.

This winery was set up little more than a decade ago in the heart of El Guijoso, a 3000-ha property in the heart of Cervantes country. Its vineyards are located at 100 m above sea level and are now among Spain's best. Much investment and care has gone into the vineyard and cellar; it is a good example of the quality and concentration of which La Mancha is capable. The accommodation ($$$) is especially suited to larger groups. There are two- and five-bedroom houses for rent, as well as a hunting lodge. All kinds of activity can be arranged, from hunting to golf and wine tasting.

## Valdepeñas

Famed for its wines since the middle ages, this region enjoys a microclimate within the southern part of La Mancha that has enabled it to make finer, less sunbaked wine. However, until quite recently, far too much of the wine was made by blending Cencibel (the name for the local clone of Tempranillo) with the far more widely planted dull white Airen grapes. Now, however, a new spirit of ambition is evident and good modern wines are being produced.

WINERY — VALDEPEÑAS

### Dionisos Agricultura Biológica

C Unión 82, Valdepeñas
T +34 926-313 248
www.agrobio-dionisos.com
Mon-Fri 0900-1400 and 1600-1900; Sat and Sun by appointment.

Dionisos is one of the first ecological/organic producers in Spain. Although his father first grew organic grapes in 1984, since 1995 Dionisio de Nova Garcia has been a pioneer in Spain's organic movement, a tradition continued since 2000 by his son Carlos de Nova Torres. Besides their wine, the family also produces gourmet olive oil and vinegar. You can spend a rewarding day with the family, visiting the winery, having a tutored wine tasting and sharing a meal paired with the wines. Wine tasting courses can also be arranged.

MUSEUM — VALDEPEÑAS

### Museo del Vino de Valdepeñas

Antigua Bodega de Leocadio Morales, C Princesa 39, Valdepeñas
T +34 926-347 927
www.valdepenas.es
Winter Tue-Sat 1000-1400 and 1700-1900. Summer Tue-Sat 1030-1400 and 1700-2030; Sun 1200-1400.

Housed in what was previously the Leocadio Morales winery, this museum's six rooms, situated around a central courtyard cover the history, geography, culture and the wine trade of the Valdepeñas region. Of particular note are the audiovisual display and the huge *tinajas* (amphorae) that were used to ferment wine in the region until very recently. There is also a cafeteria and shop.

# Portugal

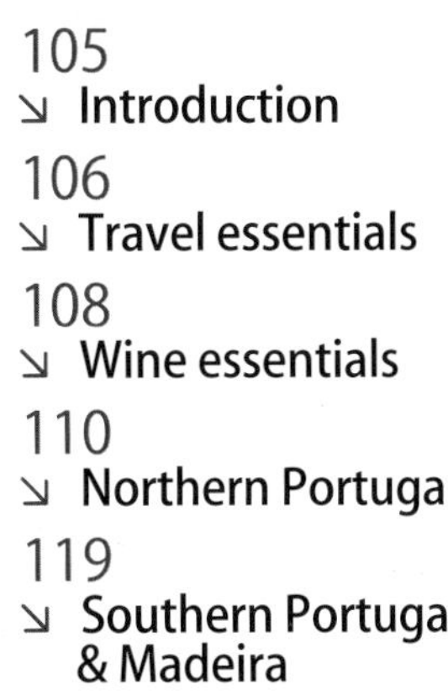

River Douro.

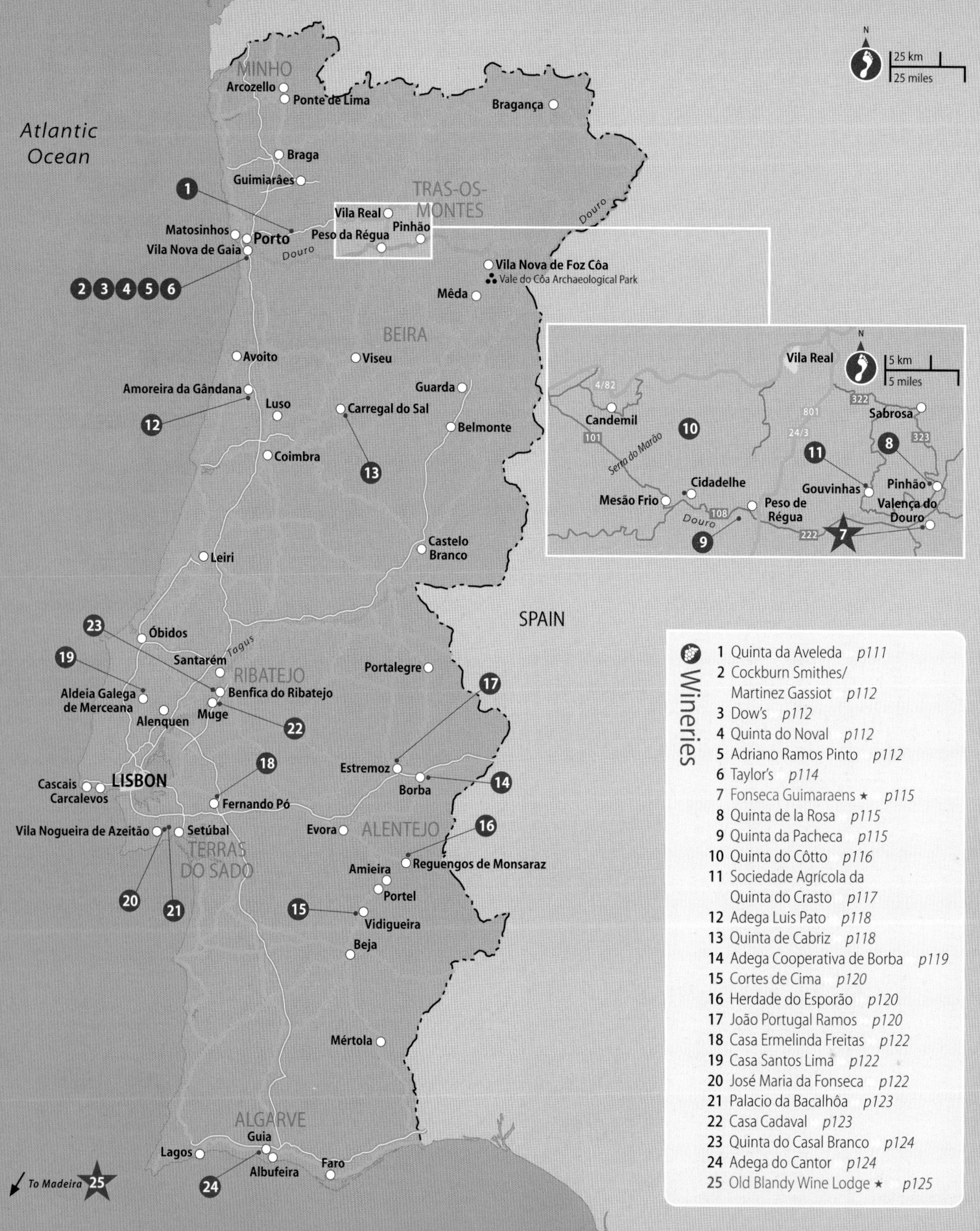

Atlantic Ocean
MINHO
Arcozello
Ponte de Lima
Bragança
Braga
Guimiarães
TRAS-OS-MONTES
Vila Real
Pinhão
Peso da Régua
Matosinhos
Porto
Vila Nova de Gaia
Douro
Vila Nova de Foz Côa
Vale do Côa Archaeological Park
Mêda
BEIRA
Avoito
Viseu
Guarda
Amoreira da Gândana
Luso
Carregal do Sal
Belmonte
Coimbra
Castelo Branco
Leiri
SPAIN
Óbidos
Tagus
Santarém
RIBATEJO
Benfica do Ribatejo
Portalegre
Aldeia Galega de Merceana
Alenquen
Muge
Estremoz
Borba
Cascais
LISBON
Carcalevos
Fernando Pó
Vila Nogueira de Azeitão
Setúbal
Evora
ALENTEJO
TERRAS DO SADO
Reguengos de Monsaraz
Amieira
Portel
Vidigueira
Beja
Mértola
ALGARVE
Guia
Lagos
Albufeira
Faro
To Madeira
25 km
25 miles
5 km
5 miles
Candemil
Serra do Marão
Sabrosa
Cidadelhe
Gouvinhas
Mesão Frio
Peso de Régua
Valença do Douro
Wineries
1 Quinta da Aveleda p111
2 Cockburn Smithes/ Martinez Gassiot p112
3 Dow's p112
4 Quinta do Noval p112
5 Adriano Ramos Pinto p112
6 Taylor's p114
7 Fonseca Guimaraens ★ p115
8 Quinta de la Rosa p115
9 Quinta da Pacheca p115
10 Quinta do Côtto p116
11 Sociedade Agrícola da Quinta do Crasto p117
12 Adega Luis Pato p118
13 Quinta de Cabriz p118
14 Adega Cooperativa de Borba p119
15 Cortes de Cima p120
16 Herdade do Esporão p120
17 João Portugal Ramos p120
18 Casa Ermelinda Freitas p122
19 Casa Santos Lima p122
20 José Maria da Fonseca p122
21 Palacio da Bacalhôa p123
22 Casa Cadaval p123
23 Quinta do Casal Branco p124
24 Adega do Cantor p124
25 Old Blandy Wine Lodge ★ p125

# Introduction



This country was the sleeping giant of European wine for so long that some people had begun to worry that it might be in a coma. Over the last decade, however, the eyes have opened and Portugal has joined the wine revolution. Unlike Spain and Italy, Portugal had no table wine region of any international renown. The Portuguese thought well of Dão and Bairrada but few foreigners shared their opinion. The tradition in Portugal was generally to produce white wines – known as *verde* (green) – that were light and acidic for immediate consumption by the jugful, and red wines – known as *maduro* (matured) – that began life tasting toughly tannic and were aged until they had softened sufficiently to be drinkable. Ageing wine can be beneficial, of course, but in Portugal the process often took place in huge concrete tanks that provided none of the benefits of the oak barrels used elsewhere.

In the early 1990s, membership of the European Union brought development grants and greater exposure to what was happening across the border in Spain. Just as the Spanish were openly acknowledging that new-wave wines from Priorat and Ribera del Duero might be better than old-wave Rioja, the Portuguese woke up to the potential of their own vineyards. The timing was ideal. Portugal's climate and its collection of grapes are perfect for the kind of full-bodied, fruity-spicy, rich wines that have become so popular across the globe. It is no coincidence that Peter Bright and David Baverstock, two young Australian winemakers, were right at the front of the Portuguese wine revolution. Nor that the owners of châteaux Lafite-Rothschild, Lynch-Bages and Cos d'Estournel have all decided to invest here.

# Travel essentials

## Planning your trip

European flights arrive into **Lisbon** (LIS; T+351 218-413500, www.ana-aerportos.pt), **Porto** (OPO; 228-432400) and **Faro** (FAO; T+351 289-800800). Direct flights from other continents are limited, so travellers are often routed through another European hub. Some visitors choose to fly to Spain and then take overland transport; there are regular rail services from Madrid, Seville and Santiago, as well as good road connections. **Madeira** has its own airport (FNC; www.anam.pt), although many flights are via Lisbon .

**Car hire** is very cheap in Portugal, with most international firms represented at airports and in towns, making this the most convenient means of exploring the country. Portugal's historically poor road network has benefitted from huge EU investment, which has provided new highways and faster access between towns and cities. However, in rural areas, road surfaces can still be very poor and travelling between remote wineries in a single region, let alone between regions, can take a very long time. Note, too, that Portugal has the highest rate of road traffic accidents in Europe! The **rail** network, run by Caminhos de Ferro Portugueses (www.cp.pt), covers much of the country and includes some scenic routes. It is often cheaper than travel by bus, with some good deals and special passes available, although local trains may be very slow. Intercity trains run between major centres and a high-speed, luxury service (*Alfa*) connects Lisbon and Porto.

The three airports usefully divide Portugal into thirds and may help to determine the scope of your trip. Lively **Porto** and its sister town, **Vila Nova de Gaia**, provide access not only to the port lodges and *quintas* of the magnificent Douro (page 113) but also to the **Minho** and **Trás os Montes** regions further north. Here you can explore long sandy beaches on the coast or the spectacular gorges of the **Peneda-Gerês** national park. Don't miss the market in **Barcelos** and the religious monuments in and around **Braga**. Heading south, the route from Porto to Lisbon passes close to the lagoon city of **Aveiro**, with its colourful fishing boats, and the ancient university town of **Coimbra**. Inland are the peaks of the **Serra da Estrela** and the **Dão** wine region. Closer to the capital, **Estremadura** and the **Ribatejo** are home to some of Portugal's most famous sights: the churches at **Batalha** and **Alcobaça**, the shrine of **Fátima**, and Tomar's impressive **Convento do Cristo**. **Lisbon** is an appealing city, with an atmospheric medieval quarter and unique nightlife in the Bairro Alto. There are some significant museums here too, headed by the **Museu Calouste Gulbenkian**, but you should also head out of the city to the coast or to visit the royal palaces at **Sintra**. Inland, the beautiful city of **Évora** is the main attraction of the Alentejo, although winelovers will want to uncover some of Portugal's most exciting new wines. In the far south, long sandy beaches and manicured golf courses are the hallmarks of the **Algarve**, Portugal's tourist honeypot. Bustling towns like **Faro**, Lagos, Albufeira and Portimão contrast with the untouched coast north of **Sagres** and with the quiet rural hinterland. For further information on visiting Portugal, consult www.portugalinsite.com.

**Portugal country code** → +351. **IDD Code** → 00.
**Internet ID** → .pt. **Emergencies** → T 112.

**Fact file**

| | |
|---|---|
| **International flights** | Major European airlines plus budget operators fly into Lisbon, Porto and Faro. Transatlantic flights use Lisbon only. Madeira has its own international airport. |
| **Entry requirements** | No visa required for citizens of the EU with a valid passport (UK citizens) or ID card. US, Canadian and Australian passport-holders do not require a visa for stays of up to 90 days. |
| **Currency** | Euro (€). |
| **Time zone** | GMT +1. |
| **Electricity** | 220 Volts, 50Hz. European plug with 2 circular metal pins. |
| **Licensing hours** | Bars and restaurants can serve alcohol until 0200 or later. Shops Mon-Fri 0900-1900; Sat 0900-1300. |
| **Minimum age** | 18. |
| **Drink-drive restrictions** | 50 mg per 100ml blood. |

## When to visit

Timing your visit depends on the region. The south has pleasant weather all year round, while the Douro tends to be very, very hot in the summer and very, very cold in the winter. Harvest time in September and October is a great time to be here, as is Easter.

Amarante, home of Vinho Verde.

Fishing boats in Aveira.

### Wine tourism

Wine tourism in Portugal has, surprisingly, developed rather more quickly than it has in Spain – and more rapidly than the Portuguese wine industry. The port houses have long histories of welcoming visitors to their lodges at Vila Nova de Gaia, just across the river from Oporto. Now, they're just as happy to see them at some of their *quintas* in the Douro Valley. A similar attitude is evident at bigger and smaller wineries in other regions, and there is a trend towards launching wine-related hotels like the **Vintage House** in Pinhão (page 117).

### Sleeping

Accommodation in Portugal is excellent value compared to many other western countries, although prices rise greatly in high season and you will always pay more in Lisbon and the Algarve. Hotels are graded from one to five stars, with comfort, facilities and service reflected in the price and rating. The official price includes IVA (VAT). *Pensões* and *residenciais* are a good budget choice and are classed from one to three stars. They are likely to have only basic facilities and will not serve meals other than breakfast. Privately owned country houses provide superb accommodation at excellent prices and are ideal if you are touring outside the cities. They range from simple *casas rústicas* to *quintas* (manors) and palaces. They are officially inspected by the tourist office and graded from A to C. Self-catering options are widely available, especially near the coast.

Grapevine

**Port and Madeira**

Both port and Madeira owe their existence to the British and to the difficulties they and others used to have in preventing wine from becoming vinegary when it was shipped or stored. No one knows precisely who decided to halt the fermentation of red wine in the Douro by dosing it with brandy. One story is that the process was developed to satisfy the sweet tooth of an abbot at a monastery at Pinhão, since stopping the fermentation leaves natural grape sugar in the wine. The more prosaic theory is that somebody noticed that, unlike wine, brandy whose high-alcoholic strength protects it from oxidation and bacteria, did not lose its flavour or go vinegary, and wondered about blending the two kinds of alcohol. From there, it only took a simple process of experimentation to discover that adding the brandy to the partly fermented grape juice not only produced a more stable product but also one that was attractively sweet. The British connection came in 1703, with the signing of the Methuen Treaty, which allowed cloth from Britain to be imported into Portugal free of duty, in return for a reduction by a third of the British duty on Portuguese wine.

Meanwhile, in Madeira (page 125), producers began to add brandy to fermenting wine to protect it during long ship voyages across the equator, in precisely the same way as their counterparts in the Douro. The ships' captains noticed that the fortified Madeira not only reached its destination in a far better condition than when it was unfortified but it actually seemed to have improved during the voyage. Madeira's British connection came in the form of a young soldier called John Blandy who, in 1807, was stationed in a garrison to protect Madeira from possible attack by Napoleon. A few years later, aged 27, Blandy started what would become the island's most successful producer and shipper and, in 1814, a case of Blandy's Madeira – of which a few bottles still survive – was ordered by Napoleon to drink on St Helena.

### Eating

The best word to describe authentic Portuguese food is 'hearty'. Big bowls of kale soup (*caldo verde*) are a staple in the countryside, as are plates of salt cod (*bacalhau*) and rice. A special treat in Portugal is suckling pig and the best region to eat it is definitely Bairrada, where it is known as *leitão à bairrada* and is widely available. In the same region, you could also try *cabidela*, which is made from the bits of the pig that are often neglected elsewhere: the liver, lungs and heart. For those with more modern tastes, there is also a move towards lighter, more innovative cooking, especially in the cities; try the **Bull & Bear** in Porto (page 111). The evolution in Portuguese cuisine is totally related to the evolution in wine: tough tannic Bairrada may have gone well with the suckling pig, but it's no match for lighter fare.

# Wine essentials



### History

Unlike Spain, Portugal did not develop as a wine-producing region under the Romans. Later, however, wine was made, particularly in the north of the country. The Portuguese wine that was shipped to England in the Middle Ages came from vines grown near Lisbon or from the Minho. Trade with Britain became much more important at the beginning of the 18th century when a cut in the duty charged on Portuguese wine happily coincided with a ban on the importation to Britain of wine from France. At the time, however, as contemporary records show, the wine, which was now coming from the Douro was "strong bodied... but not very palatable". One solution lay in shipping Bordeaux to Britain via Portugal and pretending that it was Portuguese. Another lay in improving the genuine article by fortifying it with brandy (page 107), while a third simply involved adding elderberries, sugar and alcohol.

The man who did his best to prevent this falsification was an Englishman called Baron Forrester who owned Quinta Boa Vista in the Douro and campaigned to ban the use of alcohol and elderberries in favour of making unfortified Douro wine better. If Forrester can see beyond the grave he must be taking a delight in the success of just such wines today.

In the 20th century, during Salazar's dictatorship, Portugal's wine industry stagnated. Unbelievably, in the Dão region, regulations obliged all wine to be made by cooperatives and, almost everywhere in the country, the wine business was in the hands of a few big companies. Most of the wines sold in Portugal were of a style and standard that would not be accepted overseas, while the Mateus and Lancers Rosés and sweet Vinho Verde that made up 60% of exports would have been unacceptable to anyone in Portugal. A few companies, such as Alianca, Sogrape and JM da Fonseca took a more modern approach but it was not until the 1980s that a need to modernize the industry was acknowledged. Today, the wine industry is still dominated by a group of big producers known as the G7 (Aliança, Aveleda, Bacalhôa, Esporão, JM da Fonseca, Messias and Sogrape) but the domination is benevolent and, for the first time, across the country the efforts of these companies is supplemented by dynamic small estates and rapidly improving cooperatives.

### Understanding Portuguese wine

Portugal has four main wine classifications. At the top (supposedly) are the regional **DOC**s (Denominação de Origem Controlada), which have to come from defined regions and have been made in a prescribed way from prescribed grape varieties. Next, there are the **IPR**s (Indicação de Proveniência Regulamentada), which, like Italy's IGTs, allow greater experimentation with foreign and non-traditional varieties. Beneath both of these (again, supposedly) is the **VR** (Vinho Regional), which is rather like France's Vin de Pays and allows blending across larger regions and greater freedom when it comes to the choice of grapes. Some of Portugal's smartest wines are VRs. Most basic of all is **Vinho da Mesa**: table wine. To all of these regional designations, there may soon be added a new all-embracing 'Wine of Portugal'.

An *adega* is a winery, although wine from an individual estate might bear the name of a *quinta* (farm) – or *herdade* or *monte* in the Alentejo. A *solar* is a manor house, which will be bigger than a *casa* or *casal* (large house), but smaller than a *paco* or a *palácio* (palace). A *vinha* is a vineyard, which becomes a *tapada* when it is enclosed by a wall. *Colheita* means vintage, especially when referring to tawny port. *Vinho tinto* is red; *branco* is white and *rosado*, pink. A dry wine is *seco*, while a sweet wine is *doce* and a fortified one, *generoso*. Wines that are both sweet and fortified are *licoroso*. *Reserva* is used for slightly superior wines, although, nowadays *grande escolha* (great selection) is increasingly used. *Garrafeira*, a traditional term for a wine from a good vintage that has been aged for at least three years before being sold, is less popular than it used to be.

### White grapes

**Alvarinho** The grape known as Albarino in Spain is used to make fresh Vinho Verde.

**Arinto** A widely grown, naturally acidic variety that is used in Bucelas and, more impressively, in Bairrada.

**Ferñao Pires/Maria Gomes** An aromatic grape that can produce some of Portugal's best whites.

**Loureiro** The Alvarinho's fuller-bodied partner in Vinho Verde

**Malvasia** The grape that produces Malmsey in Madeira is also used in the Douro, though rarely to great effect.

**Moscatel de Setúbal** Luscious sweet Muscat.

### Red grapes

**Alfrocheiro Preto** A quite widely planted grape that, when well handled, gives good blackberryish fruit character to Dão.

**Alicante Bouschet** Unloved outside Portugal, this is an unusual grape with black skin and dark flesh. It makes good, rich dark wines in the Alentejo.

**Aragonez/Tinta Roriz** The strawberryish grape that the Spanish know as Tempranillo.

**Castelão (Frances)/Joao de Santarem** Good in blends and by itself, this is a widely used grape in modern southern Portuguese reds. It is traditionally known as 'Periquita' (little parrot) in Portuguese.

**Touriga Nacional** The great grape of vintage port is now producing rich, spicy, berryish reds all over Portugal.

**Trincadeira** A widely-grown variety that is now competing with the Touriga Nacional for the role of Portugal's most interesting red wine grape.

Grapevine

**Types of port**

Port producers revel in the complexity of their labels and styles. Essentially there are two types of port, one of which is aged in the bottle while the other is aged in wooden barrels. The best examples of the former group are Vintage Port, which is bottled two years after the harvest; Late Bottled Vintage (LBV) which is bottled up to two years later, and Crusted – a blend of vintages, also bottled after no more than four years in cask. However, life is complicated by the fact that there are two kinds of Vintage Port. Most is made from grapes grown in more than one farm but, as its name suggests, Single Quinta Port comes from a single farm. British port houses traditionally decide which harvests are good enough to 'declare' as vintages and never, traditionally, declare two in a row, however good they are. The Portuguese-owned port houses and estates, by contrast, declare almost every vintage. In undeclared vintages, however, the Anglo Saxons may produce Single Quinta ports from their own farms. These will normally be of Vintage Port quality but a little lighter and for drinking earlier. Much the same can be said for LBV, but this too comes in a pair of styles. Most of it is filtered – the only bottle-aged port to undergo this process – and does not need to be decanted. Filtering, however, removes some of its character and ageing potential. LBV from producers like Warre's and Smith Woodhouse bearing the word "traditional" will not have been filtered.

The technical term for wood-aged port is tawny, however, as you'll have guessed, there are several types of tawny port. The finest is tawny with a vintage (here described as Colheita). Some of the Anglo Saxon houses decline to produce these for export (for fear of confusion with vintage port) but happily sell them in Portugal.

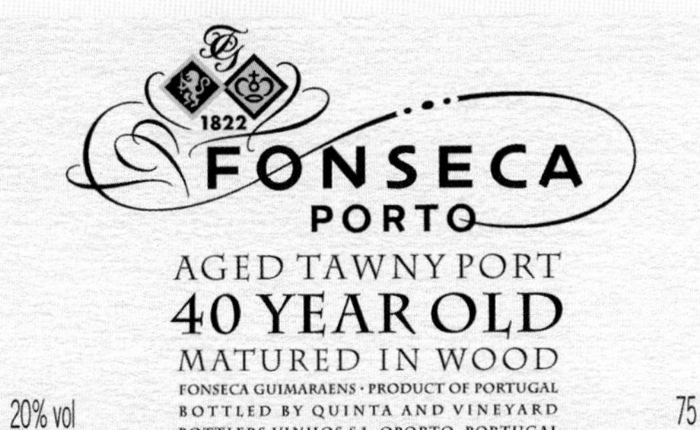

Another style you will find in Portugal but rarely elsewhere is tawny from a single quinta. What you will see everywhere is aged tawnies that have been in barrel for 10, 20, 30 or even 40 years. At their best, tawnies have a delicate woody, nutty character that some people prefer to the fruitier, more tannic and more powerful style of ports that have matured in the bottle. Tawny also has the advantage of being enjoyable after being open for a couple of days – and of being delicious when served chilled (which is how its producers drink it in the Douro in the hot summer). Beware, however of cheap tawny with no indication of age; it may be a blend of ruby and white (see below) that has never seen a barrel.

White port is generally very dull, ordinary stuff (revealingly served in the Douro with tonic water) but Churchill's and Ferreira make good examples. Finally, there's ruby, which is the most basic port of all, sold after little or no time in a barrel, and the misleadingly named Vintage Character which is essentially "reserve ruby": a bit better than basic and given a few years in a cask.

# Northern Portugal



**The top half of Portugal is effectively a book with three chapters. The Minho is still Vinho Verde country, home to one of the world's most distinctive white wines. Beiras brings together the often rustic wine-producing areas of Dão and Bairrada, the two areas that were once Portugal's answer to Bordeaux and Burgundy. It is, however, the Douro that today provides northern Portugal's sex appeal. For far too long the reluctance of port producers to commit themselves to table wine has delayed the arrival of the Douro onto the list of the world's great red wine regions, but a dynamic set of wine producers is now making up for lost time.**

## Minho

The Rios do Minho VR is the home of Vinho Verde, 'green' red and white wine produced from vines that are grown along the branches of trees at above head height to allow space beneath for other crops such as cabbages and kale. This is a perfect illustration of the way winemaking was regarded in most places a century ago: peasant activity carried on in tiny holdings by farmers who also grow other crops. The average Minho farm is still only 2.5 ha and produces just 1700 bottles of wine per year. The climate here is cool and damp, so the reds (70% of the total crop) and whites have traditionally had low-alcoholic strengths (8-10%) and have been marked by fierce acidity of a kind rarely encountered in other wine. This made sense when matched with oily sardines or fatty suckling pig, and was as palatable to Portuguese drinkers as warm English beer might be to someone brought up on it. Like the beer, however, Minho wines proved to be a tough taste to acquire for foreigners – which is why the red was

Grapevine •

**Tickled pink**

Portugal's most famous wine is still Mateus Rosé, despite the fact that recent research by its makers revealed that a remarkable number of people have no idea that it is Portuguese. One of the first successful global wine brands, Mateus shares with Penfolds Grange (page 302), the distinction of being a wine that was quite literally invented from scratch. Before its creator, Fernando Van Zeller Guedes, blended the off-dry, semi-sweet wine in 1942, nothing like it had been seen in Portugal, where wines are traditionally red or white and bone dry or very sweet. Guedes was clever enough to know that coming up with a commercial style of wine was only part of the story; its success would depend on the bottle and the label. Thinking laterally, he ignored anything that had been done in Portugal and copied the traditional pot-bellied *bocksbeutel* that was used in Franken in Germany. For the label, he decided to use the image of an old palace with which the wine had no connection. Its owner was famously offered the choice between a single payment for the use of the image or an ongoing royalty. Tasting the wine and believing it had no future, the aristocrat opted for the cheque.

By the late 1980s, Mateus's makers, SOGRAPE were selling nearly 40 million bottles of the rosé and a white every year; out of every five bottles of wine that left the country, two were Mateus. A couple of years after Guedes created Mateus, a rival company, JM da Fonseca, came up with a similar wine called Lancers, which it sold in mock pottery crocks, in huge quantities in North America.

QUINTA DO NOVAL
2003
VINTAGE
PORT
BOTTLED AND SHIPPED BY
QUINTA DO NOVAL - VINHOS, S.A.
PINHÃO
Produce of Portugal
BOTTLED IN 2005
19,5% vol
75 cl ℮

Oporto.

only exported to Portuguese-speaking countries and why the white that left the country tended to be sweetened. Until quite recently, little attention was paid to grape varieties, of which there is a long list, but now it is acknowledged that the best wines are made from Alvarinho and Loureiro. Today, there is a growing number of estates with higher aspirations, including Quinta da Aveleda (whose owner in the 1940s invented Mateus Rosé, page 110), Palácio da Brejoeira and Solar de Boucas.

RESTAURANT PONTE DE LIMA

### Carvalheira Restaurant

Arcozelo, Ponte de Lima
T +351 258 742 316
Mon-Sat for lunch and dinner.
$

This is one of the best places to eat around Ponte de Lima and it has a friendly, relaxed atmosphere. It's almost always busy, so it's best to call ahead and reserve a table. The menu has a bountiful range of delicious appetisers, plus excellent steak served in a variety of ways. Try the *bacalhau na broa*, a dish that combines two traditional ingredients of Portuguese food: cod and maize bread. There's a good range of local wines to accompany the food.

WINERY PENAFIEL

### Quinta da Aveleda

Apartado 77P, 4560-730 Penafiel
T +351 255 718 200
www.aveleda.pt
Mon-Fri 0900-1200, 1400-1700.
€4

You stroll through lush gardens to get to the 17th-century vine-covered mansion, where the Guedes family, owners of Quinta da Aveleda, have always lived. It was here, in 1860, that Dom Manuel Pedro Guedes da Silva da Fonseca laid the foundation of the company that is now the leading producer of Vinho Verde. Visitors are given a map of the estate and a brochure explaining the history of the Quinta and the region's wines. English-speaking guides are also on hand to take visitors on a tour of the old wine lodge built by Dom Manuel, with its huge handmade wooden storage vats, modern concrete vats and bottling and labelling lines. Each two-hour tour finishes with a stop at the old distillery, now converted into a wine shop. Visitors are always welcome, but it is better to call in advance to ensure that a tour guide will be available.

## Oporto and Vila Nova de Gaia

Oporto, or Porto as it is known in Portuguese, means port. It is a pleasant town with plentiful 19th century architecture and a growing number of good restaurants. Across an impressive iron bridge over the Douro is Vila Nova de Gaia, home to the 'lodges' where port has traditionally been matured after being shipped down the river from the vineyards where it was made.

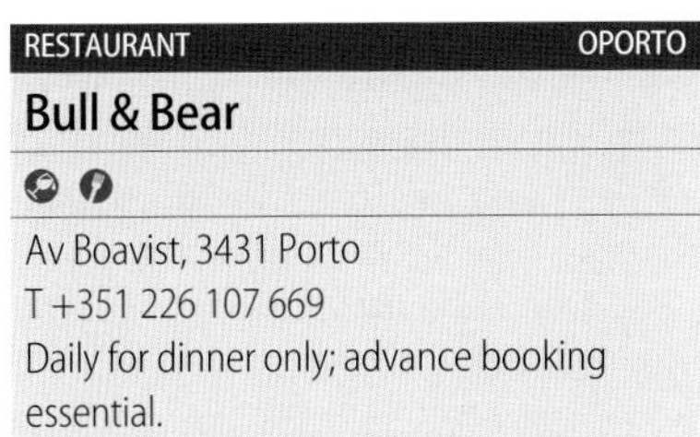

RESTAURANT OPORTO

### Bull & Bear

Av Boavist, 3431 Porto
T +351 226 107 669
Daily for dinner only; advance booking essential.
$$

Named for its location in the Portuguese stock market building, this restaurant is considered to be one of the best in Oporto. Innovative chef Miguel Castro e Silva, who has just published his first cookbook, is a champion of Portuguese cuisine and produces some of the country's best, concentrating particularly on fish. Here he serves up a menu of modern regional cuisine; typical dishes include carpaccio of sea bass, octopus risotto, cod cooked at 80°C, pigs' trotters with coriander, and melon soup with lime. Expect to pay around €40–50 per head for a world-class meal including a good bottle of wine – but be warned that the the wine list may tempt you to splash out a bit more.

RESTAURANT OPORTO

### Cafeina

Rua do Padrão 100, 150-557 Oporto
T +351 226 108 059 / 351 226 189 953
www.cafeina.pt
Daily 1230-1800 and 1930-0130.
$$

Located in a 19th-century villa close to the mouth of the river Douro, this fashionable restaurant, bar and café attracts a lively young crowd with its trendy, contemporary decor. The menu is predominantly Portuguese, with some French and Italian influences. Typical dishes include spit-roasted monkfish and scallops with rosemary and courgette risotto, lamb tenderloin with cassis sauce and baby onions, and a white and dark chocolate marquise with orange coulis. The 120-bin wine list focuses on Portuguese wines.

WINERY VILA NOVA DE GAIA

### Cockburn Smithes & Cia/ Martinez Gassiot

Rua D Leonor de Freitas, 4401-099 Vila Nova de Gaia
T +351 223 776 545
www.cockburns-usa.com, www.martinez.pt
Tours Mon-Fri 0930-1200 and 1430-1600.

This is one of the oldest port houses, established in 1815. The founder, Robert Cockburn, was the brother of a Scottish law lord and first came to Portugal to fight in the peninsular campaigns under Wellington. He later returned to Oporto and created his own firm. More recently, Cockburns, along with its associated company, Martinez Gassiot, has passed through the hands of various multi-national firms. Since 2006, the vineyards and winemaking have been handed over to the Symington family, who own Dow's, Graham's and Warres.

Visitors to the two port lodges which are in walking distance of ewach other are offered a free tour – often led by people involved in winemaking – which includes information on the history of the brands and winemaking in the Douro. There is also an on-site shop.

WINE BAR/RESTAURANT MATOSINHOS

### Degusto Ristorante

Rua de Sousa Aroso 540/544, Apartado 2087, Matosinhos, 4450-287
T +351 229 364 363
www.vinhoecoisas.pt
Wine bar daily 1230-1500 and 1800-0100.
Restaurant daily 1230-1500 and 1900-2300.
$$

Matosinhos, an industrial port and fishing village north of Oporto, was once a major centre for fish processing but the industry has slowed down considerably and many old buildings are now being converted to other uses. Degusto restaurant and wine bar is a good example; the interior design is quite dramatic, with wine bottles displayed all along a long, white corridor, which opens up into an impressive high-ceilinged dining room. The menu is international with a Mediterranean slant; typical dishes include a selection of innovative salads and grilled shrimps with mashed potatoes and leeks. For dessert try *la millefoglie alla crema* (layers of flaky dough with fruit and whipped cream), or lemon tart. The 2000 wines on offer are mainly from Portugal, Spain and France and include a great selection of dessert wines.

## Best port vintages

Note that British-owned port houses never 'declare' two vintages in a row, preferring to sell Single Quinta and LBV ports in other years. Also note that some producers make tawny port with a vintage year (*colheita*), while others don't.

2003, 2002 (Single Quinta), 2000, 1999 (Single Quinta), 1997, 1995, 1994, 1992, 1991, 1987, 1985, 1983, 1980, 1977, 1970, 1966, 1963, 1960

WINERY VILA NOVA DE GAIA

### Dow's

Travessa Barão de Forrester, Apartado 14, Vila Nova de Gaia 4401-997
T +351 223 776 300
www.dows-port.com
Visits by appointment only.

In 1890, port shipper George Warre, who held the unconventional view for his time that a shipper, or merchant, should take an interest in the production of port, purchased the Quinta do Bomfim (meaning 'good end') vineyard and farm in the Douro which will soon be open to the public. Warre joined forces with John Ramsey Dow and the firm became Dows. Plans are afoot to open Quinta do Bomfim to the public, but for now, the place to visit is the Dows lodge in Vila Nova da Gaia where you can taste a range of ports from of one of the two top producers. (The other is Taylor's, page 114.)

RESTAURANT OPORTO

### Peixes & Companhia

Rua do Ouro 133, 150-557 Porto
T +351 226 185 655
Daily 1230-1500 and 1900-2400.
$

A favourite with members of the port trade, this good-value fish restaurant does precisely what its name would lead you to expect: it offers some of the best fish and seafood in the city, with a menu that changes according to the daily catch. Wines include fine examples of Vinho Verde, with which to wash down all that fish.

WINERY VILA NOVA DE GAIA

### Quinta do Noval

Visitor centre Av Diogo Leite 26, 4400-111 Vila Nova de Gaia
T +351 223 770 270
www.quintadonoval.pt
Visitor centre Oct-May Mon-Fri 1000-1700; Jun-Sep Mon-Fri 1000-2000. Winery visits by appointment.

Following the relaxation of legislation governing port production in 1986, Quinta do Noval was the first port estate to move its wines from Vila Nova de Gaia to a new lodge close to the *quinta* itself for maturation. However, although winemaking is focused at the *quinta*, the company still has a visitor centre in Vila Nova de Gaia, where its offers free tastings. Visits to the *quinta* and the cellars on the Douro can be arranged by prior appointment.

Noval's flagship, Nacional, is probably the most concentrated and famous of all vintage ports. Made only in exceptional years (the first vintage was the legendary 1931) from a single vineyard of just 5000 ungrafted vines, it is available in only limited quantities (200-300

**Exploring the Douro**

This day trip takes in the spectacular scenery of the Douro Valley. From Vila Real take the IP4 towards Poro and Amarante, turning off this road after 24 km (15 miles) to join the N15 through the pine forests of the Ovelha Valley. Follow this road for 12 km (7 miles) to reach Candemil in the heart of the **Serra de Marão**. It's an extraordinary landscape, with the road descending through an enclosed gorge above the Ovelha river. After Candemil, turn left onto a steeply climbing road towards Bustelo. The road descends to join the N101, which recrosses the Serra do Marão, traversing a plateau with superb views of the mountains, before dropping down through vineyards to the small town of Mesão Frio on the River Teixera. Before you reach town, turn off northeast to visit the **Quinta do Côtto** (page 116). Beyond Mesão Frio you'll get your first view of the vine terraces and the river Douro far below. The steep valley sides have been terraced into one of Europe's most fertile grape-growing areas and the carefully tended terraces themselves are a work of art. At the intersection above the river turn left onto the N108. Follow this road to **Peso da Régua**, a thriving provincial town. Although Pinhão to the east is now the hub of the trade, all port still passes through here on its way to Oporto and you will see the traditional ornamental cargo boats (*barcos rabelos*) moored on the Douro. Contact **Quinta da Pacheca** (page 115) before you arrive for a chance to tour their wine lodge or visit the **Quinta de São Domingos** (Aptdo 130, T +351 254 320 100). Cross the river and follow the road to join the N222 to Pinhão. The 25-km (15-mile) drive takes you past terraced vineyards, olive groves and *quintas*, each with the name of the producer emblazoned on the hillside. **Pinhão** is a focus for port production and several of the leading houses have their *quintas* here, though few of the big names welcome tourists. Visit **Quinta de la Rosa**, which perches above the river just to the west of town (page 115) or stop for a drink or a meal at the **Vintage House** (page 117). On leaving Pinhão, take the N323 north towards **Sabrosa**, the birthplace of the explorer Ferdinand Magellan. Turn left onto the N322 to Vila Real. Just before town is the **Solar de Mateus** (5000 Vila Real, T +351 259 323 121), a perfect example of a baroque, 18th- century Portuguese manor house set in stunning formal gardens; it is renowned worldwide as the symbol of Mateus Rosé (page 110). Take a guided tour before driving back to Vila Real.

A more leisurely way to explore the region is on a day cruise from Porto to Régua with **Douro Azul** (Rua de San Francisco, 4-2º D, T +351 223 402 500, www.douroazul.pt, €7.50-€45), returning to Porto either by boat or steam train. There are also week-long cruises (from €585) from Vila Nova de Gaia, stopping at locations along the river such as Régua, Solar da Rede, Pinhão and Vega Terron in Spain. Guests of the **Vintage House Hotel** (page 117) can opt for a package that includes car rental and a cruise or train journey.

cases each vintage) and sold on allocation only. Noval was originally a Portuguese house, having been founded in 1813 by Antonio José da Silva, but the Dutch van Zeller family ran it for four generations until 1993, when it was bought by the French AXA-Millésimes insurance group.

WINERY/MUSEUM — VILA NOVA DE GAIA

### Adriano Ramos Pinto

Av Ramos Pinto 400, 4400-266 Vila Nova de Gaia
T +351 223 707 000
Jun-Sep Mon-Sat 1000-1800; Oct-May Mon-Fri 0900-1300 and 1400-1700; closed on public hols.

Stepping through the door of this port house is like stepping back in time. Dynamic brothers Ricardo and João Nicolau d'Almeida have been at the forefront of vineyard reorganization and recent research to find out which of Portugal's indigenous grape varieties are best suited to the Douro, but the cellars in Vila Nova de Gaia remain traditional in style and offer a great insight into the history of winemaking in the region. They include the original office of founder Adriano Ramos Pinto, preserved since the 1930s, and the company's archive and library, which can be visited by prior arrangement. Also worth a visit is the estate's Ervamoira museum (page 115), which is located in the Vale do Côa Archaeological Park and tells the story of the history of the company and winemaking in the region. Since 1990, when the 42 family members sold up, Champagne Louis Roederer has owned the controlling share in the estate.

Taylor's Chip Dry white Port.

WINERY — VILA NOVA DE GAIA

### Taylor's

Rua do Choupelo 250, 4400-088 Vila Nova de Gaia
T +351 223 742 800
www.taylor.pt
Tours and tastings by appointment only. Restaurant Mon-Sat for lunch and dinner; Sun lunch only.

Taylor's became the first port shipper to own property in the Douro when it purchased a vineyard at Salgueiral near Régua in 1744. The firm, now 300 years old, like Dows Warre's and Graham's its traditional rivals, remains family-owned and makes some of the region's finest wines. The jewel in the estate's crown is the famous 164-ha Quinta de Vargellas, purchased at the end of the 19th century, which has 41 ha of vines and produces much of the wine for Taylor's Vintage Port. In a remote position, high up in the Douro, it even has its own railway station. Taylor's also owns another outstanding 116-ha estate Quinta de Terra Feita, on the slopes of the Pinhão Valley.

Visitors are welcomed for a free tour of Taylor's lodge in Vila Nova de Gaia, which provides information (in several languages) on the company's history and the region. At the end of the tour, guests are invited to taste two port wines: the Chip Dry – Extra Dry White and Late Bottled Vintage (LBV) – in the elegant Library Room. The lodge's restaurant is also open for lunch and dinner ($), with outside dining in the summer months on a terrace offering views across to the town of Porto.

## Trás-os-Montes

The inland region 'behind the mountains' is a traditionally poor area that, until the roads improved, relied on the river for its access to Porto on the coast. Since the 17th century, the focus here has been on port, rather than table wine, a fact that has not helped the area's 25,000 winegrowers. Until recently, port production was, with a few exceptions, in the hands of a few big and mostly Anglo-Saxon producers; one family, the Symingtons, own Dow's, Warre's, Graham's, Smith Woodhouse and Gould Campbell, while the Fladgate Partnership has Taylor's, Fonseca Guimaraens, Croft and Delaforce. While companies like these have always made much of the need for good wine from which to make their port, they resisted the temptation to try to produce table wine. The man who helped to change their minds, and change the destiny of the region, was David Baverstock, who had learned to make wine in Australia before joining Symingtons. After being part of the team that produced Dow's, he helped a couple of small port estates – Quinta de la Rosa and Quinta do Crasto – to make award-winning reds based on the Touriga Nacional grape. Another pioneer table wine maker was Dirk Niepoort, whose Redoma Douro red is now one of Portugal's top wines. Today, the Douro has a long and growing list of producers and a very consistent range of wines, though Niepoort is rare in offering a top-class white.

HOTEL/RESTAURANT — PINHAO

### Casa do Visconde de Chanceleiros

Chanceleiros, 5085-2 Pinhão
T +351 254 730 190
www.chanceleiros.com
$$

Fonseca PDT Guimaraens vintage 1986.

Located at the heart of the Douro vineyards, close to the small wine village of Chanceleiros, this 18th-century former summer residence has been restored by the current owners and transformed into a luxury country house hotel. The 10 guest rooms are individually furnished and all have en suite bathrooms and private terraces. The extensive grounds include floodlit tennis courts and an outdoor swimming pool. There is also an indoor squash court, a bar and a restaurant ($$) for guests only.

WINERY — VALENCA DO DOURO

## Fonseca Guimaraens

Quinta do Panascal, 5120-496 Valença do Douro
T +351 254 732 321
www.fonseca.pt
Visits by appointment only; book through the website.

Of all the *quintas* that offer tours, this is the one that gets by far the highest praise from visitors. The Alto Douro (upper Douro) is a UNESCO World Heritage site and this majestic property on the banks of the river Távora is one of its finest buildings, offering a dazzling view down the valley. Bought by Fonseca in 1978, the estate offers an audio-guided tour (in a choice of nine languages), which provides information on the company's history, its wines and the estate, and also accompanies a walk through the vineyards. This is followed by the opportunity to taste some of the estate's wines. At harvest time, you can also enjoy the unique experience of watching the treading of the grapes in traditional granite *lagares*. The Guimaraens family has been making port since 1822 and, although Taylor's bought the firm in 1948, the family remains heavily involved, with the sixth generation, David Guimaraens, now making the wines.

MUSEUM — VILA NOVA DE FOZ COA

## Quinta da Ervamoira Museum

Vila Nova de Foz Côa
T +351 279 759 229
Jun-Sep Mon-Sat 1000-1800; Oct-May Mon-Fri 0900-1300 and 1400-1700; pre-booking required.

The Quinta da Ervamoira museum, which belongs to the port firm Ramos Pinto (see below), is situated heading towards the Spanish frontier in the **Côa Archaeological Park**, an area classified as a UNESCO World Heritage site. The museum is housed in an old schist-built dwelling that was restored in the 1970s as an example of the most traditional architecture of the region. It has rooms dedicated to the Roman, Visigoth and Medieval periods in the Douro region and the story of the evolution of port wine bottles. A visit to the museum ends with the tasting of wines at the bar and the possibility to enjoy a meal ($), while admiring the scenery of the Côa region from the vineyard terraces.

WINERY — PINHAO

## Quinta de la Rosa

Pinhão 5085-215
T +351 254 732 254
www.quintadelarosa.com
Mon-Sat 0900-1800.

This small, family-owned winery on the banks of the Douro river was one of the pioneers of making and selling Douro table wines alongside port. The Bergqvist family are originally from Germany but came to Portugal in the 18th century and have been shipping port since 1815. They purchased Quinta de la Rosa in 1905 and expanded it two years later by purchasing the neighbouring Quinta Amarela. Visitors are welcome at the winery to taste the wines. Lunch can also be arranged for groups with prior notice. The estate has six rooms of bed and breakfast accommodation ($-$$), all but one with river views, with access to a swimming pool on a nearby terrace. There is also a choice of two holiday villas for weekly rentals: Quinta Amarela, a few minutes' walk from the main house and Quinta das Lamelas, which is positioned high in the valley, with spectacular views down to the river.

WINERY — PESO DE REGUA

## Quinta da Pacheca

Apt 3, 5051 Péso de Régua
T +351 254 313 228
www.QuintaDaPacheca.com
Visits by appointment only; contact Catarina Serpa Pimentel.
Tour and tasting from €6.84.

This is a small property (37 ha) better known for its red wines than its ports, although its first Vintage Port (produced in 2000) demonstrates its potential. The family's connections with the Douro date from the 18th century but the business was founded in 1903 and is now run by fourth-generation

# Best port producers

Andresen (Tawny)
Barros (Tawny)
Burmester (Tawny)
Calem (Tawny, Quinta de Foz)
Churchill
Cockburn ›› *page 112.*
Croft
Delaforce (Quinta da Corte)
Dow's ›› *page 112.*
Ferreira
Fonseca/Guimaraens ›› *page 115.*
Gould Campbell
Graham's
Martinez
Niepoort
Offley (Boa Vista)
Poças (Tawny)
Quinta do Côtto ›› *page 116.*
Quinta do Crasto ›› *page 117.*
Quinta do Noval ›› *page 112.*
Quinta do Vesuvio
Quarles Harris
Ramos Pinto ›› *page 114.*
Sandeman (Tawny)
Smith Woodhouse
Taylor's ›› *page 114.*
Warre's



José Serpa Pimental and his sister Maria Serpa Pimental, who makes the wines. The estate uses the traditional Douro method of foot treading in stone *lagares* for all its wines, including its flagship Reserva, which is only made in the best years. The estate prefers visitors to call in advance to arrange a visit, so that a member of the family or someone from the winemaking team can be on hand to conduct the tour. There are plans afoot to refurbish the old wine cellar and convert it into a modern 14-bed rural hotel.

WINERY CIDADELHE

## Quinta do Côtto

Cidadelhe, 5040-154 Mesão Frio
T +351 254 899 269
www.quinta-do-cotto.pt
Visits by appointment only.

Quinta do Côtto is located far to the west of the big name port houses, but it can fairly claim to be in the heart of the oldest sector of the Douro. Its 50 ha of vineyards are mentioned in the documents by the Roman writer Strabo, referring to vineyards in the Douro Valley and the estate has a Royal Decree from 1757. The existing manor house is an elegant 18th-century building, although some parts date from the 15th and 16th centuries and there are ruins that were built before 1140. Only a portion of the grapes from the estate can be used for port production, according to current rules, which helped push the owner Miguel Champalimaud, who took responsibility for winemaking in 1976, into pioneering the production of high-quality Douro table wines.

GUESTHOUSE PINHAO

## Quinta do Passadouro

Vale de Mendiz, 5085-101 Pinhão
T +351 254 731 246
www.quintadopassadouro.com
$

Just two hours' drive from the city of Oporto, this house is set in 30 ha of vineyards at a tranquil spot close to Pinhão and makes a good base for visiting the local port houses. It's also well placed for outdoor activities, with opportunities for fishing, hiking and cycling close at hand. You can either rent one of the six rooms on a bed-and-breakfast basis or the whole house, which sleeps eight to 15 and is traditional in style, with a pretty flower-filled terrace for outdoor dining. There are special mid-week, weekend and full week deals or you can rent by the day. Wine is sourced from a vineyard whose grapes go into Dirk Niepoort's Redoma, one of Portugal's very best reds.

Vineyards along the Douro.

WINERY SABROSA

### Sociedade Agrícola da Quinta do Crasto

Gouvinhas, 5060-063 Sabrosa
T +351 254 920 020
www.quintadocrasto.pt
Visits by appointment only.

A very young producer by Douro standards, Quinta do Crasto produced its first vintage in 1994, but has already had success with both its port and its red table wines. It has around 60 ha of vines but is expanding rapidly, with the recent acquisition of a second property further up the river. The estate itself is more than four centuries old and has a spectacular setting, perched on top of a hill surrounded by steep vineyards. Guests here ($$) have use of an amazing infinity swimming pool, with uninterrupted views of the valley.

HOTEL/RESTAURANT PINHÃO

### The Vintage House

Pinhão
T +351 254 730 230
www.hotelvintagehouse.com
$$-$$$

This elegant luxury hotel, nestled among the vineyards on the banks of the Douro, is housed in a former port storage warehouse, dating from the 18th century. It has been refurbished to reflect the building's heritage and now manages to combine the character of a period property with modern comforts. The 37 bedrooms and six suites have individual decor and each has a private balcony overlooking the river. The magnificent outdoor pool has views of the steeply terraced vineyards, while the shaded riverside patio is an excellent spot to enjoy an early evening drink. The fine dining **Rabelo Restaurant** ($$-$$$) serves a sophisticated menu of local and international cuisine. The owners also run specialist wine-tasting courses for enthusiasts, and the bar is situated in the former Port wine lodge.

## Beiras

Most wine books published before 1990 would have focused their attention on Beiras's two most important DOCs: Dão, birthpace of Salazar, the Portuguese dictator from 1932 to 1968, and Bairrada, both of which have winemaking traditions going back to the Romans. Viewed in an international context, however, neither could field a team of great wines. The former was the source of dull, earthy reds and whites, while the latter turned out tough tannic reds and fresh but flavourless whites and sparkling wines. Of the two, Bairrada showed the greater promise, thanks to the efforts of Luis Pato who managed to tame the wildness of the Baga grape that is the region's red mainstay. More recently Pato has opted to sell his wines as Beiras; others have followed in his tracks – though not always adhering to the same traditions – and this regional designation is beginning to boast a growing range of flavoursome whites and rosés.

In Dão, the heroes have been SOGRAPE, Aliança and JM da Fonseca, who have performed Pato-style magic on the blend of grapes used here and have helped to shift the focus towards improving the region's whites. The success of these producers' wines and Dãos like Duque de Viseu and Quinta dos Rocques, is helping to rebuild its reputation but only time will tell whether Dão can build an identity for itself or whether it will end up being thought of as a sub-region of the more famous Beiras. An interesting recent move has been the decision by Filipa Pato, Luis's daughter to make a blend of Dão and Bairrada.

HOTEL/RESTAURANT LUSO

### Bussaco Palace Hotel

Mata do Bussaco, 3050-261 Luso
T +351 231 937 970
www.almeidahotels.com/bussaco
$$

I visited this former summer retreat of the Portuguese royal family on my very first trip to Portugal and, despite updating, it has hardly changed over the years. This former summer retreat of the Portuguese royal family is set in more than 100 ha of one of Portugal's most famous forests. There are more than 700 species of tree here, including rare local varieties and others from the Americans, Asia and Australia. Built on the site of a former monastery in 1907, only three years before the declaration of the Republic which brought the monarchy to an end, this hotel retains the original decor and furnishings but has all the modern conveniences in its 60 rooms and four suites. The hotel also boasts one of Portugal's finest restaurants ($$), which is open to non guests and housed in the palatial dining room. You can also eat on the terrace overlooking the gardens. The hotel's facilities include a helicopter and limousine service, and just 15 km away at the Curia Palace Hotel, guests can use the outdoor pool, mini golf and tennis courts.

HOTEL MEDA/MARIALVA

### Casa do Côro

Apartado 1, Marialva, 6430-081 Mêda
T +351 271 590 003
www.assec.pt/casa-do-coro
$$-$$$

This once derelict group of five traditional houses has been lovingly renovated and turned into charming little granite lodgings. The largest, Casa do Coro, has five air-conditioned rooms, which are perfect for couples; the Casa da Vila would suit a group of two or three couples and has a living room and kitchen. The rooms and apartments all have traditional furnishings, open fires and uninterrupted views of this unspoilt region. Marialva, the local village, is currently being classified as one of Portugal's 10 most historic villages. A great time to come is between the second week of February and the beginning of March when the almond trees are in full bloom. One of the highlights of a stay here is the breakfast of homemade bread, fresh from the oven. Carmen, the co-owner, is an excellent cook and offers either half or full board, including wine from the owner's vineyards.

WINERY AMOREIRA DA GÂNDARA

### Adega Luis Pato

Ribeiro da Gândara, 3780-017 Amoreira da Gândara
T +351 231 596 432
www.luispato.com
Daily 1000-1600. Tours by appointment.
Tours €10

Luis Pato has been called the king of Baga, the principal grape of the Bairrada region, because of his dedication to its full expression. (Pato believes that it is the only Portuguese variety that can be used unblended, but that its wines need time to soften). He began making his own wines in 1980 and, after inheriting 60 ha of vines from his father in 1984, left his job as a chemist to take on the role full-time. He quickly established himself as the region's most innovative and experimental winemaker, supported by his daughter Filipa Pato, who has since joined the company as assistant winemaker, while also producing wines under her own name. His modern tasting room often exhibits work by local artists and provides an inspirational setting for tasting. Guided tours are available by appointment and include a wine tasting and detailed explanation of the wine production process. Meals are also available by prior arrangement.

HOTEL/RESTAURANT BELMONTE

### Pousada Convento de Belmonte

6250-073 Belmonte
T +351 275 910 300
www.pousadasofportugal.com/portugal/belmonte.html
$$-$$$



# Best producers

**Bairrada**
Alianca
Casa de Saima
Caves Sao Joao
Luis and Filipa Pato » *page 118.*
Messias
Sidonia de Sousa
Sogrape

**Beiras**
Bela Fonte
Bucaco
Conde de Santar
Joao Pinto
Quinta d'Aguieira
Quinta de Foz de Arouce

**Dão**
Borges
Caves Sao João
Dado (blend of Dão and Douro)
Duque de Viseu
Pape
Quinta das Carvalhais
Quinta das Maias
Quinta de Cabriz » *page 118.*
Quinta de Garrida
Quinta dos Roques
Sogrape

**Douro**
Barca Velha
Casal de Loivos
Kolheita de Ideias
Lavradores de Feitoria
Pintas
Poeira
Quinta da Leda
Quinta da Portela
Quinta de Baldias
Quinta de la Rosa
Quinta de Nápoles
Quinta do Côtto » *page 116.*
Quinta do Crasto » *page 117.*
Quinta do Infantado
Quinta do Passadouro
Quinta do Portal
Quinta do Tedo
Quinta do Vale D Maria
Quinta do Vale da Raposa
Quinta do Vale Meão
Quinta do Vallado
Ramos Pinto » *page 114.*
Vale de Corça
Van Zeller/José Maria da Fonseca
Sogrape

**Minho**
Casa de Sezim
Palacio de Brejoeira
Quinta da Covela
Quinta de Aveleda » *page 111.*
Quinta de Azevedo
Soalheiro

The town of Belmonte is best known as the birthplace of the Portuguese explorer Pedro Álvares Cabral, who was the first European to discover Brazil in 1500. The Pousada Convento de Belmonte is situated on the slopes of the Serra da Esperança mountain range, just outside the town, and is housed in the former Convent of Nostra Senhora da Esperança. The original architecture of the convent has been preserved, including its 13th-century chapel and woodland amphitheatre. There are 25 elegantly decorated rooms, all with en suite bathrooms, and a delightful swimming pool. The restaurant ($$) serves delicious regional cuisine and a range of local wines. Outdoor activities in the area include fishing, hiking and horse riding.

WINERY CARREGAL DO SAL

### Quinta de Cabriz

Estrada N 234, Carregal do Sal
T +351 232 961 222
www.daosul.com
Daily 0900-2000. Restaurant daily until 2200.

This is the headquarters of one of Portugal's most dynamic young producers, Dão Sul. Founded in 1989, the company now makes wine in the Douro, Bairrada, Estramadura and Alentejo, too. Next door to the winery building is a cosy restaurant ($-$$) but it's often busy, so book your table in advance. Visitors can arrange a tour of the vineyards or a tasting in the specially designed tasting room and wine shop.

**Of the five regions of southern Portugal, two currently stand out for the dynamism of their wine producers. The Alentejo and Terras do Sado are both now home to some of the country's very best wines. But quality is rising in other areas too, with greater ambition being shown in the Ribatejo and, thanks to Sir Cliff Richard, even in the once-dire vineyards of the Algarve.**

**Madeira, like Jerez (but unlike the Douro) is still very firmly focused on its fortified wines. These are far from fashionable nowadays but the efforts of the owners fo the Madeira Wine company (including Blandy's) are beginning to pay off and there are signs that a growing number of people may be beginning to appreciate the unique style of these wines.**

## Alentejo

This huge VR has far fewer vines than its size might suggest; Estremadura, less than a quarter as large produces significantly more wine. In fact, Alentejo places rather greater emphasis on farming oak trees for corks. When the Romans were here, they erected a huge Temple of Diana in the heart of the region at Évora, which is now a UNESCO World Heritage site. The riches the Romans brought soon gave way to poverty; there were large landowners but little in the way of good wine, apart from the Cartuxa wine cellar whose 1776 press is still used today to produce wines like Fundação Eugénio de Almeida. As recently as the 1980s, wineries here were still making and ageing wines in the same huge kinds ofpottery amphorae that the Romans would have used.

Today, a long list of go-ahead producers can be found here, including Esporão, Pera Manca and Quinta do Carmo (which belongs to the owners of Château Lafite Rothschild). This is the region to find many of Portugal's most innovative wines.

WINERY BORBA

### Adega Cooperativa de Borba

Rossio de Cima, Apartado 20, 7150-999 Borba
T +351 268 891 665
www.adegaborba.pt
Shop Mon-Sat 0900-1900. Tours by appointment only.

The first co-operative to be established in the Alentejo is a shining example of its kind and one of the most modern, with gleaming new equipment installed thanks to financial help from the European Union. A huge range of wines is produced and incentives are offered to growers who produce the best quality grape varieties. A tour of the winery (in Portuguese, English or French) can be arranged by prior appointment, followed by a free tasting of the wines.

HOTEL MÉRTOLA

### Estalagem São Domingos

Mina de São Domingos, 7750-171 Mértola
T +351 286 640 000
www.hotelsaodomingos.com
$$

Until the mid-1960s, this part of the Alentejo boasted the largest copper mines in the Iberia peninsula. The São Domingos manor house was the headquarters of British mining company Mason & Barry but, following the closure of the last mines in 1965, the building fell into disrepair. Fortunately, in 2005, it re-opened as a five-star luxury country hotel, set in extensive grounds close to the town of Mértola. Guests can choose between one of the six spacious superior rooms in the manor house, which have retained many of the original furnishings, or from one of the 25 contemporary-styled standard rooms in the new building with views over the pool and gardens. They also have the opportunity to experience the full splendour of the Alentejo

night sky from the hotel's observatory, which is equipped with a GPS and computer-controlled 14 in Meade telescope. In the **Seppia** restaurant ($$), chef Michel serves up modern Alentejo cuisine using well-souced local ingredients and matched by a range of the region's wines.

WINERY — VIDIGUEIRA

### Cortes de Cima

7960-909 Vidigueira
T +351 284 460 060
www.cortesdecima.pt
Mon-Fri 0900-1200 and 1200-1700.

Founded in the late 1980s by Danish-American couple, Hans and Carrie Jørgensen, Cortes de Cima is one of the most dynamic estates in the Alentejo. Winegrower Hans Jørgensen made his money working as a technical engineer for a tropical plantation company in Malaysia and decided to spend it on this 365-ha property in Alentejo's southernmost demarcated winegrowing area. The land is planted with olive trees, cork trees and cereal crops, as well as 50 ha of vines. Carrie hails from California (although her great grandfather was Portuguese) and is responsible for marketing and administration. You can buy wine direct from the cellar door and the estate also holds a classical music concert in its vineyards each summer.

WINERY — REGUENGOS DE MONSARAZ

### Herdade do Esporão

7200-999 Reguengos de Monsaraz
T +351 266 509 280
www.esporao.com
Restaurant daily 1230-1530. Shop daily 1000-1830. Wine bar daily 1000-1800. Tours to the Esporão tower and archaeological museum daily 1100 and 1430; also 1800 in summer, by appointment. Wine tours daily 1200, 1530, and 1700, by appointment.

This is one of the largest wine estates in the Iberian peninsula, with 550 ha of vineyards, producing a wide range of wines from both indigenous and international grape varieties. It was founded in 1973 by agricultural holding company Finagra, although it was snatched back during the Revolution a year later and retained by the government for five years. On its return to private ownership it was in dire need of investment but new cellars were built in time for the 1987 vintage. The current winemaker, David Baverstock, is Australian, although he has worked in Portugal for more than 20 years, and his wines combine an accessible New World style with more typical Portuguese flavours. The winery and new visitor centre are an impressive sight, built to integrate with the surrounding landscape, facing a large dam and the estate's vineyards. Facilities include a wine bar, tasting room and a restaurant ($-$$) specializing in local and regional food. Lunch guests are offered a complimentary visit to the cellars and wine tasting. There's also an archaeological museum on the estate.

WINERY — ESTREMOZ

### João Portugal Ramos

Monte da Caldeira, 7100-149 Estremoz
T +351 268 339 910
www.jportugalramos.com
Reception/shop: Mon-Fri 0900-1830; Sat 1000-1800. Tastings Mon-Fri 1000-1200 and 1430-1630; Sat 1000-1700. Winery Mon-Fri 1000-1200 and 1430-1630; Sat 1000-1700.

João Ramos is one of Portugal's leading new-wave winemakers and, in 1990, after a long career as a consultant winemaker in all the major winegrowing regions of Portugal, he planted his own vines at Monte da Caldeira in the Alentejo. The original property, surrounded by vineyards, is a stunning example of traditional Portuguese architecture, while the new winery, built between 1997 and 2000, combines high-tech stainless steel tanks with traditional stone *lagares* for treading the grapes. Visitors can enjoy a wine tour, tasting or a lunch of traditional Alentajan cuisine, all of which must be pre-booked.

RESTAURANT — EVORA

### O Fialho

Travessa dos Mascarenhas 7, 7000-557 Évora
T +351 266 703 079
Tue-Sun 1230-1600 and 1900-2400; advance booking recommended.
$$

This unpretentious restaurant, hidden down a narrow backstreet in the centre of Alentejo's capital, has been described as a 'cathedral of Portuguese gastronomy' and regularly attracts gourmets from as far away as Lisbon. The restaurant was founded more than 40 years ago by Manuel Fialho and is now run by his children, Gabriel and Amore. They serve up a menu of traditional Alentejan dishes (including 'black pig') and modern local wines in a warm and friendly atmosphere.

HOTEL — MONTE DA FIGUEIRA

### Portel Hotel Rural

Monte da Figueira, 7220-134 Amieira
T +351 266 612 120
www.montedafigueira.pt
$$

This intimate hotel (with just 12 rooms) is on a 5000-ha hunting estate in the heart of the Baixo Alentejo region. It lies just east of Portel, close to the Alqueva Dam and the River Degebe, and makes a good base for visiting local wineries. It's at its busiest during the hunting season, which runs from winter through to June, and is a good base for outdoor activities. With a week's notice, staff can arrange mountain biking, horse riding, mountaineering, rafting, sailing, canoeing and even hot air ballooning. There is a pool and bikes are available for hire. The restaurant ($$) unsurprisingly, specialises in game, matched with the region's new-wave reds.

J Portugal Ramos's Vila Santa.

Harvest at the J Portugal Ramos vineyards in Vindima.

HOTEL — PORTEL

### Refúgio da Vila

Largo Dr Miguel Bombarda, 87220-369 Portel
T +351 266 619 010
www.refugiodavila.com
$

In the small Alentejo town of Portel, just outside Évora, this intimate country hotel and cooking school offers good-value rooms in a traditionally furnished former manor house, complete with an azure swimming pool and a cosy open fire in winter. Bikes are also available for hire should you wish to explore the surrounding countryside. The school teaches the art of preparing traditional Alentejo cuisine, with classes for all levels of ability. The on-site restaurant ($) serves up Mediterranean-style and traditional Alentejo cooking alongside the region's wines.

## Estremadura

Often referred to as the 'Oeste' (west), this region to the north of Lisbon is home to three DOCs that were once far better known than they are today. Colares is famous for having grown ungrafted vines in sandy trenches which protected them from the phylloxera louse that devastated most of the world's other vinifera vines – but that doesn't make its overly tannic, old-fashioned wines taste any better. Bucelas produces dull, old fashioned white, and only one producer – the Quinta dos Pesos – now makes the traditional sweet, fortified wine of Carcavelos. (This last village at the mouth of the Tagus is a great place to try body surfing on the Atlantic breakers however.) Elsewhere, this huge region produces generally easy-going wines, with a few more serious exceptions, such as Quinta de Pancas and Quinta do Monte d'Oiro.

HOTEL — OBIDOS

### Casa das Senhoras Rainhas

Rua Padre Nunes Tavares 6, 2510-999 Óbidos
T +351 262 955 360
www.senhorasrainhas.com
$$

This charming small hotel is located about 80 km north of Lisbon in the historic hill town of Óbidos. The town, which is dominated by its castle, was rebuilt in 1148 by Alfonso Henriques after he reclaimed it from the Moors and is one of the last remaining walled towns in Europe. The hotel has nine comfortable guest rooms, each with a balcony or terrace, and one deluxe tower room with views of the Santuário do Senhor Jesus da Pedra. The hotel dining room ($), **Cozinha das Rainhas**, serves regional cuisine alongside a well-chosen wine list. There is also a shared living room for guests, equipped with an honesty bar. Guests must leave their cars outside the city walls.

## Terras do Sado

This large Vinho Regional to the south of Lisbon includes the Setúbal DOC and Palmela IPR and is now used by wine companies JM Fonseca and Bacalhoa Vinhos as a designation for innovative wines, such as Quinta da Bacalhoa and Periquita that were once sold as Palmela. Setúbal is associated specifically with one wine, the deliciously luscious, long-lived fortified Moscatel de Setúbal, which is mostly produced by José Maria da Fonseca.

WINERY AGUAS DE MOURA

### Casa Ermelinda Freitas

Fernando Pó, 1695-621 Aguas de Moura
T +351 265 995 171
www.casaermelinda.com
Visits by appointment only.

The Freitas family has been producing grapes at Fernando Po, the best area of the Palmela region, for five generations. The Casa Ermelinda Freitas has 102 ha of vineyards: 94 ha planted with the Periquita grape variety (now called Castelão in Palmela) and 8 ha planted with the white Fernão Pires variety. Due to its location at Fernando Po, deep in the interior of Palmela district, these wines are some of the best in the region.

WINERY ALDEIA GALEGA DE MERCEANA

### Casa Santos Lima

Quinta da Boavista, 2580-081 Aldeia Galega de Merceana
T +351 263 760 621 / 263 769 093
www.casasantoslima.com
Visits by appointment only.

This family-owned company, set deep in the Portuguese countryside of Alenquer, is still only 45 minutes by car from Lisbon. Founded by Joaquim Santos Lima in the 19th century, it is now run by the dynamic José L Santos Lima Oliveira da Silva, who travels frequently overseas to promote his wines. The estate has more than 180 ha of vineyards (in addition to apple, pear and plum orchards), spread across not only Quinta da Boavista but also the gentle slopes of several neighbouring quintas. Around 90% of production is of indigenous Portuguese grape varieties but José also constantly experiments, most recently with Italian varieties such as Sangiovese. Although it only started making its own wines in 1996, the estate now exports to more than 30 countries.

WINERY AZEITÃO

### José Maria da Fonseca

Vila Nogueira de Azeitão, 2925-483 Azeitão
T +351 212 198 940
www.jmf.pt, www.azeitao.net
Daily 1000-1230, 1400-1730.

José Maria da Fonseca, the oldest wine company on the Setúbal Peninsula, was founded in 1834 and remains a family-owned and run firm. It is now Portugal's largest vine grower, with over 1800 acres of vineyards, and has a new state-of-the-art winery in which it produces its wines, mostly from indigenous Portuguese grape varieties. The company is famous as a producer of the sweet fortified Moscatel de Setúbal and has vintages that are more than a hundred years old in its cellar. The family home in the pretty village of Azeitão is now a museum and receives 25,000 visitors each year.

JM da Fonseca's Moscatel de Setúbal is one of the world's great undiscovered sweet wines

HOTEL CASCAIS

### Fortaleza Do Guincho

Cascais 2750-642
T +351 214 870 491
www.guinchotel.pt
$$$

Housed in a rather austere former fortress dating from the 17th century, this five-star Relais & Châteaux hotel has a superbly dramatic location, perched atop a rocky cliff at Europe's most westerly point. Just half an hour's drive from Lisbon airport, it is also close to the popular Guincho beach and the green hills of Sintra. Many of the 27 rooms and suites have terraces or balconies, overlooking either the beach to the south or the Cabo da Roca to the north. The Michelin-starred restaurant ($$$) has uninterrupted ocean views through its large, arched windows and is headed up by dynamic young chef Vincent Farges, who trained with Antoine Westermann of Buerehiesel restaurant in Strasbourg. He serves up a menu of traditional French cuisine with Portuguese influences, complemented by an extensive wine list focusing on Portuguese and French wines.

RESTAURANT LISBON

### Nariz do Vinho Tinto

Rua do Conde 75, 1200-636 Lisbon
T +351 213 953 035
narizdevinhotinto@hotmail.com
Tue-Fri 1300-1500 and 2000-2400; Sun 2000-2400.
$$

As a writer, I always keep an eye out for colleagues who are proving that they can do as well as criticize. Located in Lisbon's swanky Lapa district, this tiny restaurant (seating 40) is owned by the Portuguese editor of Spanish culinary magazine *Epicur*. José Cristovao prefers to call his eatery "an establishment where food is made" rather than a restaurant, and its name, which translates as 'red wine nose', gives an indication of the importance of the serious, yet well-priced wine list. The varied menu consists of traditional dishes prepared with carefully selected ingredients, including an appetiser of local cheeses and the meat of the free-ranging, black-hoofed pig. There is even a range of olive oils to choose from. Typical dishes include cod roasted with ham fat, served with sautéed onions, or chunks of *pata negra* ham, roasted and doused with piri-piri sauce.

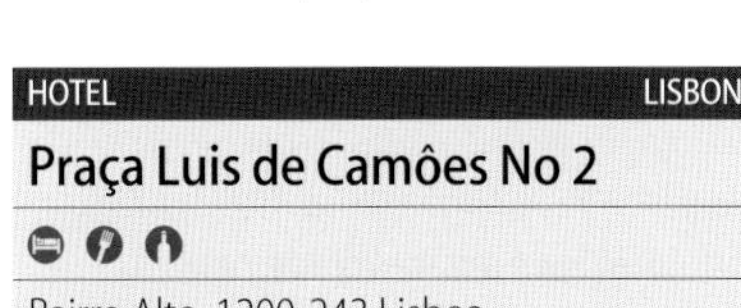

HOTEL LISBON

### Praça Luis de Camôes No 2

Bairro Alto, 1200-243 Lisboa
T +351 213 408 288
www.bairroaltohotel.com
$$$

Lisbon's and Portugal's first boutique hotel is hidden behind a yellow-painted 18th-century building in one of the city's coolest areas,

Lisbon rooftops in the sunshine.

overlooking the River Tagus and the historic Praça Luis de Camoes. The ground floor is minimally decorated with black and white art photographs, and the 55 bedrooms all have painted wooden panels and complimentary port. A roof terrace offers great views over the river. The **Flores** restaurant ($$-$$$) serves delicious Asian fusion food, prepared by a chef who learned some of his skills at Nobu in London and demonstrates his knowledgeable enthusiasm for wine in the range on offer.

WINERY AZEITAO

### Palacio da Bacalhôa

Bacalhôa Vinhos de Portugal, Vila Fresca de Azeitão, Estrada Nacional 10, 2925-483 Azeitão
www.bacalhoa.com
Tue-Sat 0900-1800.

Built in the late 15th century by the son of the great mariner and former viceroy of India, Afonso de Albuquerque, this fabulous palace has Moorish domed towers and is set in a classic renaissance park. Guided tours are available by appointment (in a variety of languages) and are limited to a maximum of 10 people. The wines, which can be tasted and bought here, are among Portugal's best

## Ribatejo

The second-largest wine region in Portugal covers both sides of the River Tagus. It is generally undeniably a fertile, warm part of a warm country and an easy place to produce large volumes of unambitious, inexpensive wine. But producers like Peter Bright, DFJ wines and Quinta do Lagoalva all show what can be done here onbetter sites when yields are kept in check.

WINERY MUGE

### Casa Cadaval

2125-317 Muge
T +351 243 588 040
www.casacadaval.pt
Mon-Fri 0900-1800; weekends by appointment.
€10 vineyard visit.

This 5000-ha estate, which is part of the Portuguese Wine Route, is a prize-winning stud farm as well as a winery. Visitors can arrange to see a horse demonstration or take a lesson in horse riding. A tasting of some of the estate's wines is available for €15 and a visit to the vineyards in a jeep or tractor can be booked for €10.

# Best producers

**Alentejo**
AC de Reguengos
Adega do Cantor
Cartuxa
Cortes de Cima » *page 120.*
Herdade do Esporão » *page 120.*
Herdade dos Colheiros
João Portugal Ramos » *page 120.*
Mouchao
Pera Manca
Quinta da Anfora
Quinta da Terrgem
Quinta do Carmo
Quinta do Mouro
Sogrape
Tinto da Anfora
Vinha d'Ervideira
Vinha do Monte

**Estremadura**
Quinta de Pancas
Quinta do Monte d'Oiro

**Ribatejo**
Fuiza
Quinta da Lagoalva

**Setúbal**
JM Fonseca » *page 122.*

**Terras do Sado**
Bright Brothers
Pegos Claros
Periquita
Quinta da Bacalhoa » *page 123.*
Quinta de Camarate

**Various**
Callabriga
Grand' Arte

WINERY — BENFICA DO RIBATEJO

## Quinta do Casal Branco

2080-362 Benfica do Ribatejo
T +351 243 592 412
www.casalbranco.com
Daily 1000-1800.

The estate's 140 ha of vineyards are planted on what was originally one of the largest royal falcon hunting grounds in Portugal. Founded in 1775, Quinta do Casal Branco has been owned by the same family for more than two centuries. The winery is housed in the original building, dating from the 18th century, complete with stone *lagares* as well as modern, high-tech winemaking equipment. The family also has a stud farm on the estate, where it breeds and trains pure Lusitaner horses. Visitors are welcome at the estate's wine shop for a tasting.

## Algarve

Thanks to local politics, this southern coastal region boasts no fewer than four DOCs. Unfortunately, until recently, it also had a total lack of interesting wine. The person who has begun to lead a move towards higher quality is British pop singer Sir Cliff Richard. With the help of David Baverstock, the Portuguese-based Australian winemaker, and a vine-owning friend and neighbour, Sir Cliff has produced the Algarve's first and only best-selling wine. Most of the sales were admittedly driven by affection for the singer, but the wine is palatable enough to warrant buying twice; the 2004 won a Bronze medal at the International Wine Challenge. Baverstock, who knows Portugal's wine regions intimately, has few illusions about the Algarve's potential: "it will never be famous for extremely high-quality wines, but it can make quite good wines. The Algarve's summer tourist market certainly makes it a good place for rosé".

Cliff Richard is the best thing ever to happen to the wines of the Algarve. The success of his wine – for whatever reason – has given the region ambitions it never had before.

WINERY — ALBUFEIRA/GUIA

## Adega do Cantor

Guia
T +351 968 776 971
www.adegadocantor.com
Mon-Fri 1000-1300, 1400-1700.
€7.50 for tour and tasting or €20-30, including transport.

The Adega do Cantor (winery of the singer) at Quinta do Miradouro was built by Nigel and Lesley Birch to produce Sir Cliff Richard's Vida Nova range of wines, made partly from grapes grown on the singer's Algarve property, Quinta do Moinho. There is a range of guided tours of the vineyards and winery on offer, plus tutored tastings and sales at the cellar door. Transport is available from various pick-up points at local hotels and resorts. Tours can be reserved by telephone or through the website.

# Madeira

George Washington, "a very regular, temperate, industrious" man, according to his friend Samuel Stearns, used to dine every day at three, drinking "half a pint to a pint of Madeira wine. This, with a small glass of punch, a draught of beer. And two dishes of tea". Washington would not have been unusual; in the 18th and 19th centuries Madeira was a staple of any self-respecting dinner table. It would have been enjoyed with tea, along with a slice of Madeira cake, and later in the evening by the fire. Fire and heat have, in fact, formed an essential part of the history of this eccentric drink.

The island of Madeira was accidentally discovered in 1418 by a Portuguese ship's captain whose surname, Zarco, means the 'Squinter'; the name may have referred to his pale blue eyes, known as *zarca* in Arabic. At the time it was covered in impenetrable forest (*madeira*), which Zarco cleared by setting light to it. The fire lasted seven years, after which this volcanic island was covered in fertile ash. In the 16th and 17th centuries, as trade developed with Africa, the Indies and the Americas, boats stopped here for provisions, including barrels of wine. The wine, initially of questionable quality, would have been made even worse by the heat in the hold of the ships as they crossed the equator, so producers began to add brandy to the fermenting wine to protect it. Soon, the fortified and much-improved wine was being used as ballast and customers were paying a premium price for 'vinhos da roda' – wines that had crossed the equator twice. What had been achieved over months in the ship was lengthily replicated in Madeira, beneath the uninsulated roofs of warehouses known as lodges and, more rapidly, in ovens or warm rooms for at least 90 days in a process called *estufagem*.

Madeira was initially often a blend of several grapes, though the single varietals known today – Sercial, Verdelho, Bual and Malmsey – were also produced, as well as the Bastardo which is no longer used. Today, there are various styles and qualities of Madeira. If no grape is mentioned, the wine will be made from a second-quality variety called the Tinta Negra Mole and will be semi-sweet stuff for use in the kitchen. Sercial is bone dry and refreshing while Verdelho is off-dry and lime-like. Bual is medium sweet, but with the tang of good marmalade, which can also be found in Malmsey, the sweetest, richest style. The best Madeiras carry vintages and will have been aged for 22 years after the *estufagem*. Otherwise look out for now-rare Solera Madeira (blended in the same way as sherry) and 15-year old or Extra Reserve examples.

WINE LODGE — FUNCHAL

## Old Blandy Wine Lodge

Avda Arriaga 32, Funchal
T +351 291 740 110
www.blandys.com
Mon-Fri 0930-1830, Sat 1000-1300; by appointment only.
Admission varies; check online.

I have always though that Madeira was caught in a time warp and that feeling is certainly bolstered when you walk into this 17th-century building that was once the annexe of a Franciscan monastery. This is one of the oldest working wine-ageing facilities – or 'lodges' – in Funchal and one of the only places in the world where you can sample wines dating from 1908. The main tasting bar features historic murals painted by the German artist Max Romer and in the vintage room, wines dating back a hundred years are available to purchase by the glass. There is also a gift centre and wine shop, selling a wide range of wines, spirits and liqueurs. Guided tours of the museum and ageing stores are held daily, as well as comprehensive tours of the winery itself a short walk away.

Traditional tiles at Old Blandy Wine Lodge.

HOTEL — FUNCHAL

## Casa Velha Do Palheiro

9060-415 Funchal
T +351 291 790 350
www.casa-velha.com
$$$

This five-star country house hotel offers a choice of 37 guest rooms with uninterrupted views over its gardens and 18-hole golf course. Built in the early 19th century as a hunting lodge, it was fully restored and transformed into a luxury hotel 10 years ago. It has an elegant fine dining restaurant ($$$), surrounded by beautiful gardens, and offers wines from all of Portugal's main wine regions, as well as a good range of Madeira. There is also a bistro-style restaurant ($$) and a terrace with breathtaking views.

# Best producers

**Madeira**

Barbeito
Blandy's » *page 125.*
Broadbent
Cossart
Henriques & Henriques
Rutherford & Miles

# Italy

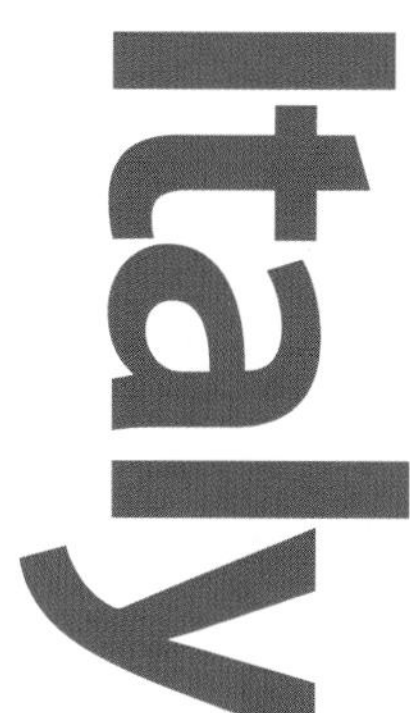

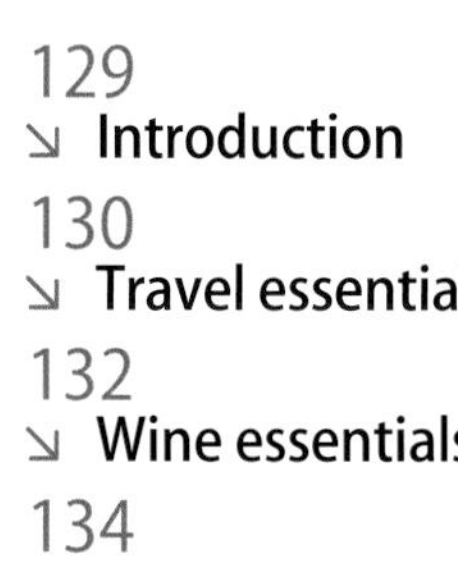

**View of Castello di Ama, Chianti.**

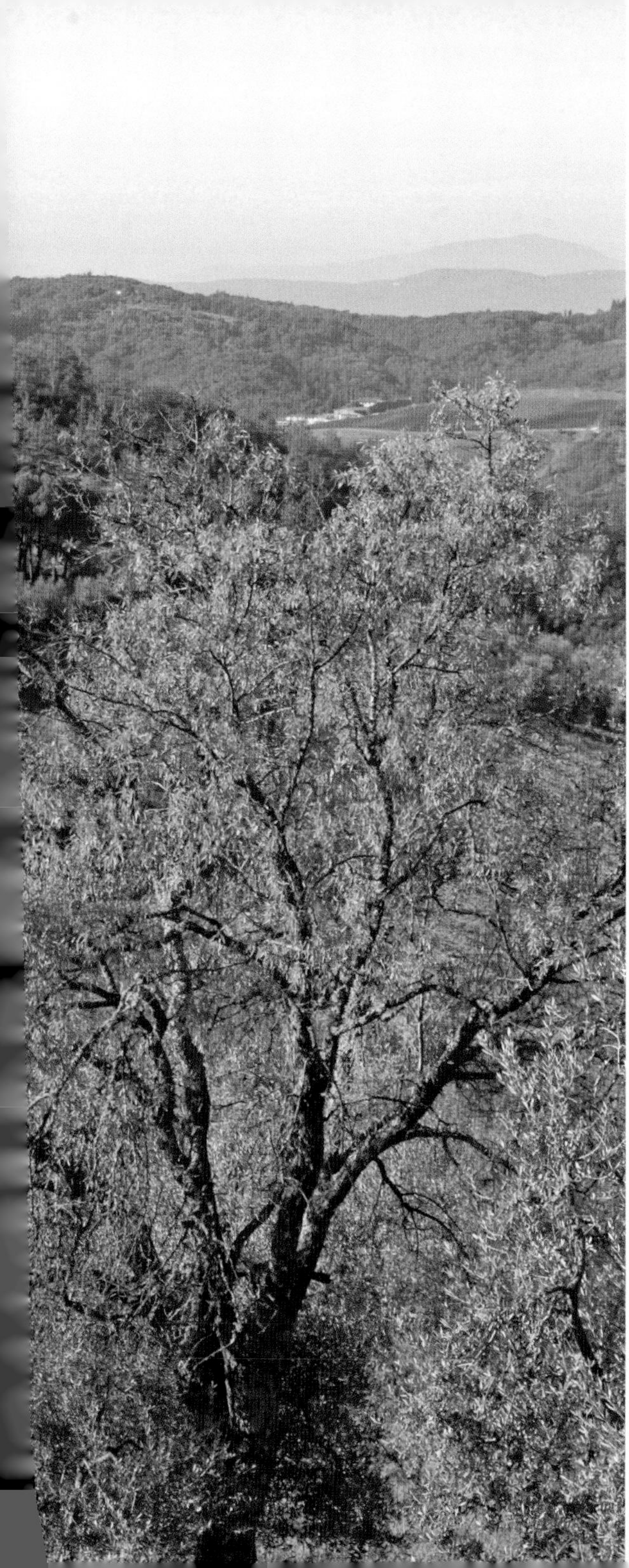

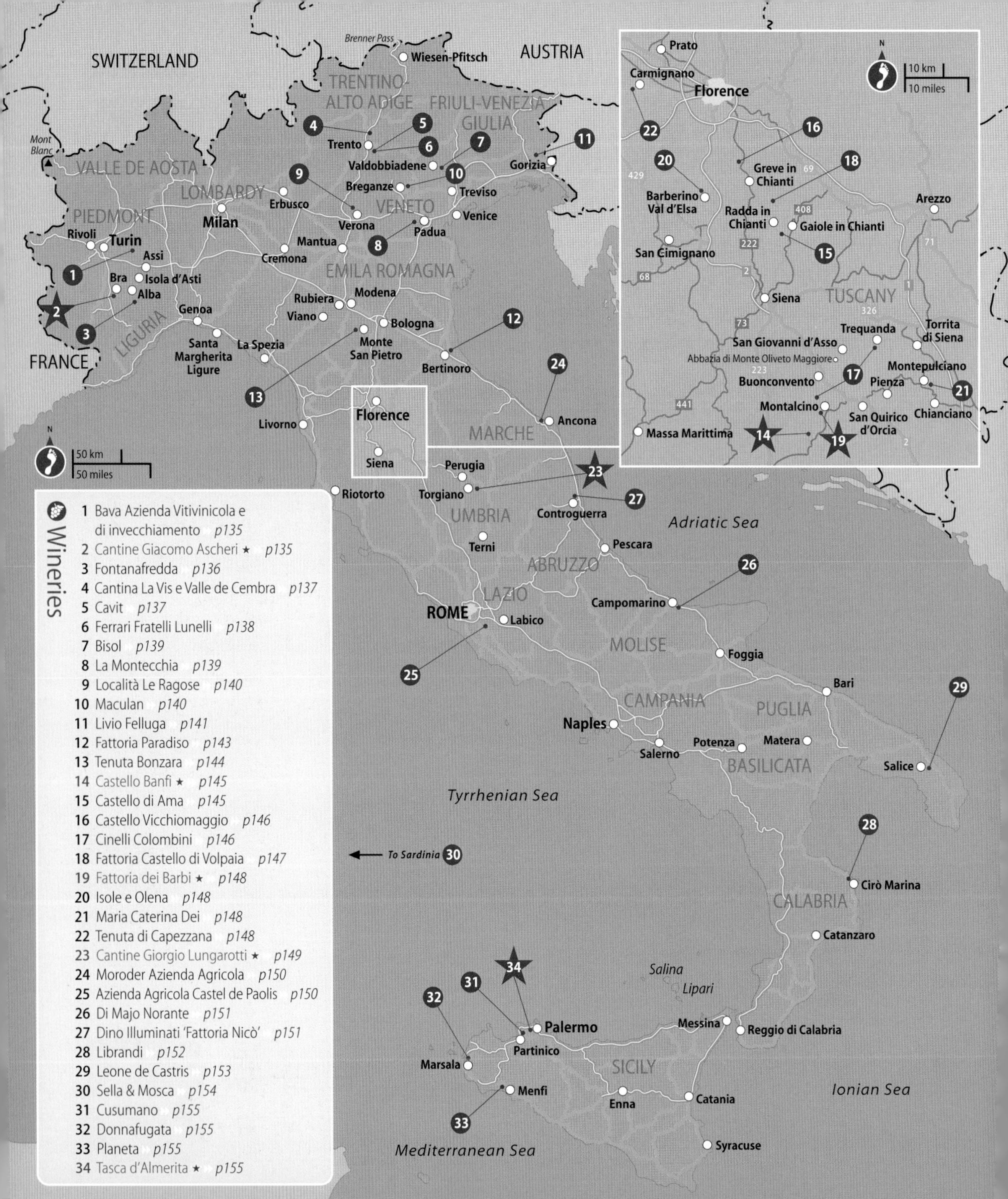


## Wineries

1 Bava Azienda Vitivinicola e di invecchiamento p135
2 Cantine Giacomo Ascheri ★ p135
3 Fontanafredda p136
4 Cantina La Vis e Valle de Cembra p137
5 Cavit p137
6 Ferrari Fratelli Lunelli p138
7 Bisol p139
8 La Montecchia p139
9 Località Le Ragose p140
10 Maculan p140
11 Livio Felluga p141
12 Fattoria Paradiso p143
13 Tenuta Bonzara p144
14 Castello Banfi ★ p145
15 Castello di Ama p145
16 Castello Vicchiomaggio p146
17 Cinelli Colombini p146
18 Fattoria Castello di Volpaia p147
19 Fattoria dei Barbi ★ p148
20 Isole e Olena p148
21 Maria Caterina Dei p148
22 Tenuta di Capezzana p148
23 Cantine Giorgio Lungarotti ★ p149
24 Moroder Azienda Agricola p150
25 Azienda Agricola Castel de Paolis p150
26 Di Majo Norante p151
27 Dino Illuminati 'Fattoria Nicò' p151
28 Librandi p152
29 Leone de Castris p153
30 Sella & Mosca p154
31 Cusumano p155
32 Donnafugata p155
33 Planeta p155
34 Tasca d'Almerita ★ p155

# Introduction



The most improved wine country in Europe, Italy, which produces a quarter of the world's wine, has quietly climbed from being the source of cheap basic red and white to the provider of some of the most sought-after bottles in the world. Two decades ago, how many people would have imagined paying top Bordeaux prices for wines from Barbaresco or from the Maremma, a region in western Tuscany that was a malaria-ridden swamp until it was drained in the 1930s? Things move fast here. Old regions are spawning new styles and new stars, while southern areas that were once the equivalent of vinous slums are being gentrified and producing wines that have a place on wine lists of Michelin-starred restaurants across the globe.

If the world of French wine is a little like Hollywood – with a set of established genres and famous big-name actors – Italy resembles European cinema. There are a few well-known stars – such as Barolo, Chianti and Soave – but you don't have to spend long in an Italian wine shop to feel completely lost. Unlike France, which has large areas without vines, Italy is carpeted with grapes, many varieties of which are unknown outside their region. There are over 500 officially recognized wine regions and styles, bound by rules that range from liberal to draconian. Attitudes towards these rules vary, of course, but it would be surprising if all the people licensed to produce and bottle wine, treated lists of official grape varieties and labelling regulations with greater reverence than they pay to no-entry signs and papal edicts on birth control. But if this anarchy has made Italy a confusing place for people seeking easy answers, it has also made for a greater spirit of experimentation than can be found anywhere in the New World.

# Travel essentials



## Planning your trip

International airports used by European carriers are spread throughout Italy but visitors from North America will arrive in either **Rome** (FCO), **Milan** (MXP) or, possibly, **Turin** (TRN). Within Europe, direct scheduled flights are supplemented by charter and low-cost airlines to smaller airports such as Ancona, Alghero, Brindisi, Cagliari, Catania, Pescara and Palermo among others.

Getting to Italy by train is also a viable option. There are direct services from major European centres to Turin, Milan, Venice, Rome and Naples. London to Paris (by Eurostar) and then on to Turin, for example, takes around 13 to 14 hours. Once in the country, getting around by train is the best alternative to driving. The network is run by **Trenitalia** and their website, www.trenitalia.com, has full details of times, fares and discount passes in English.

Another option is to drive. There are excellent road links to France via the Mont Blanc Tunnel, Switzerland via the Simplon Pass and Austria via the Brenner Pass. Note that all motorways are tolled and there are also charges at mountain passes and tunnels. Despite the reputation of Italians for overly aggressive driving, a car is the best means of getting around the country and those used to driving in big cities should have no problems. Most major hire car companies have offices in airports and city centres.

It would take a lifetime fully to explore all Italy has to offer in terms of culture, cuisine and beautiful landscapes. In the northwest, the **Valle D'Aosta** has stunning mountain scenery, fairytale castles and easy access to several top ski resorts. Heading south, don't miss **Alba's** famous truffles and red wine en route to the Ligurian coast and the tiny seafront villages of the **Cinque Terre**. Over in the northeast is, of course, **Venice**, about which nothing has gone unwritten, as well as the beautiful city of **Verona**, where you can conclude a night at the opera (page 140) with a glass of the local Prosecco, Valpolicella or Soave. North of here are the spectacular **Dolomites**, while to the south is the gastronomic heartland of Emilia-Romagna and its capital, **Bologna** (page 143). **Umbria** is Tuscany's less crowded neighbour and its medieval hilltowns offer a reprieve from the hordes of tourists in **Florence**, **Pisa**, **Siena** and in the picturesque wine-producing villages of **Tuscany**. All roads inevitably lead to **Rome**; the country's capital is home to many of its finest Renaissance treasures and Roman remains, not to mention some great restaurants. In the south is **Naples**, birthplace of the pizza and site of the world's most famous volcano, while the island of **Sicily**, only a few miles off the 'toe' of the Italian mainland, is a world away in terms of history and culture.

**Italy country code** → +39. **IDD code** → 00.
**Internet TLD** → .it. **Emergencies** → T 113.

→ Fact file

| | |
|---|---|
| **International flights** | Major European airlines fly to Rome, Milan, Venice, Verona, Turin, Bologna, Genoa, Florence, Pisa and Naples. North American carriers fly to Rome , Milan and Turin. |
| **Entry requirements** | No visa required by citizens of EU countries, US, Canada, Australia and NZ. Valid passport or identity card required. |
| **Currency** | Euro (€). |
| **Time zone** | GMT +1. Daylight saving end of Mar-end of Oct. |
| **Electricity** | 220 Volts, 50Hz. Plugs have 2 circular metal pins. |
| **Licensing hours** | No licensing hours. |
| **Minimum age** | 18 to drink and buy alcohol, unless under adult supervision. |
| **Drink-drive restrictions** | 80 mg per 100 ml blood. |

For further information, consult www.italiantourism.com and refer also to Footprint's pocket guides to Bologna, Siena, Turin and Verona. In the country, information is provided by a network of local tourists offices, identified by the letters **APT**.

Neptune's fountain, Bologna.

Foresteria Duca di Dolle guesthouse on the Bisol estate.

## When to visit

Italy has a surprisingly varied and extreme climate. Winter is cold in the north, with heavy snowfall in the mountains, and wet in the south. Summer is hot everywhere, so the best months for sightseeing are probably April to June and September/October. September and October are great times for anyone wanting to photograph the harvest, but bear in mind that smaller wineries are rarely geared up to give visitors lengthy welcomes during this period.

## Wine tourism

If Italy's wine industry is more dynamic than France's, this is also true of its attitude to wine tourism, which is part of what the Italians call *agriturismo*. The notion of blending agriculture with tourism is growing throughout Europe but nowhere does it better than Italy. Visitors to most Italian regions are likely to find far more places to eat, drink and sleep than visitors to similar areas in France, with signs, in many regions, helpfully informing you when you are entering a new DOC or DOCG appellation. Wineries, however, are not much better equipped to welcome visitors than their French counterparts, with very few of the tasting rooms that are so common in the New World. As a general rule you need to make an appointment in advance and, quite possibly, carry a phrase book. Be prepared for tasting to be a prolonged affair. Italians favour a vinous foreplay that involves using a fresh glass for every sample and rinsing it out with the wine it is about to receive. Most cellars provide spittoons nowadays but this is something of a novelty. Once you are in a winery, even if you think know a little about Italian wine, it is increasingly difficult to predict or get a handle on some of the styles of wine you are likely to encounter, unless you carry a comprehensive wine guide and speak Italian. Labels are gloriously uninformative or impenetrable, with the same words often referring to different things: Vino Nobile di Montepulciano is a Tuscan wine made from Sangiovese grapes, while Montepulciano d'Abruzzo is a red wine from much further south, produced from a quite different variety called Montepulciano. Grape varieties also change their names depending on the region or style – Nebbiolo becomes Spanna in Piedmont, for example. To add to the confusion, Italian winemakers everywhere are experimenting: making Chardonnay in Barolo country, for example, or a blend of Sauvignon and Gewürztraminer in the northeast, or a new twist on Chianti that includes a little Syrah. The best advice is always to ask about what you are tasting or drinking – in a winery or restaurant – and build up your knowledge as you go along.

## Sleeping

Hotels and *pensioni* make up the bulk of accommodation in Italy and there's a vast difference in quality between the top end and the many budget options. The gaping hole in between is now being filled by a growing range of B&Bs and *agriturismi* (farm stays). The latter is well organized, particularly in Tuscany, Umbria, Sicily and Sardinia. For a detailed list of *agriturismi* visit www.agriturismo.it. Italy is also slowly waking up to the boutique hotel revolution and the cramped medieval buildings of old are now supplemented by some stylish new alternatives to urban tourism. Prices are generally higher in major tourist destinations – especially Rome and Venice – and also tend to be higher in the north. Tourist offices have booklets listing all local accommodation.

## Eating

For far too many outsiders, Italian food exists as a caricature of itself: pizza, pasta, risotto, osso bucco and various kinds of tomato sauce. But Italian cuisine is, of course, about far more than that. Fine cooking here long pre-existed that of France, which didn't catch up until the late 16th century. Italian cookery has developed regionally, with Etruscan influences being apparent in **Tuscany** (where there's much reliance on olives) and Moorish, Greek and Spanish flavours being found in **Sicily**. Styles and amounts of pasta vary across the country; in **Lombardy**, until the late 19th century, it was rarely eaten due to the popularity of risotto and polenta. In northern Italy, cooks fry with butter, while olive oil is the order of the day in the south, and, between the two, lard is still favoured. Tuscans have a reputation as *mangiafagioli* (bean eaters) but although their cuisine is simple, it is a great foil for the region's best red wines. **Roman** cuisine favours offal, although its best-known dish is *saltimbocca alla romana* (veal with ham and sage, cooked in wine and butter). Fish and seafood feature prominently on both the Mediterranean and Adriatic coasts and on the islands, in dishes such as *zuppa di pesce* (fish soup, known as *brodetto* in Le Marche) and *pasta con le sarde* (pasta with fish sauce), although the port city of **Genoa** is more famous as the birthplace of *pesto*. **Naples** is the home of classic *napoletana* and *margherita* pizzas, while Sicily boasts the country's most famous desserts: *cassata* , *zabaglione* and *granita*. For details of Bolognese cuisine, see page 143.

# Wine essentials

## History

The Italians are as keen as the French to foster the impression that they were the first to produce wine. In fact, it was the Phoenicians who brought wine and vines on their trading trips to the south of the country around 3000 years ago, and the Greeks who truly introduced the culture of winemaking (and brought more vines). Also important were the obscure but sophisticated Etruscans, who lived in the area we now know as Tuscany from around 800 BC. Whoever laid the foundations, it was the Romans who developed a wine industry in Italy, known as 'Oenotria' (the country of wine), and in the lands they colonized.

Wine at this time was very different to the stuff we know today. It would often have been diluted with water or preserved with lead, salt or pine resin. Initially, it would have been stored in pottery amphorae sealed with a layer of olive oil and cork bungs that kept it alive for decades. Barrels were then introduced, which made transportation easier, but were less ideal for long-term storage. After the Dark Ages, wine developed regionally, with vineyards close to rich cities like Venice and Tuscany receiving the most investment and attention. Wines were rarely transported between regions and, outside Tuscany, were less favoured by aristocrats than they were in France.

Many of Italy's top wines have comparatively brief histories. Barolo and Brunello di Montalcino were first produced in something like their modern form in the late 19th century and, despite the 1716 laws governing its production, fine Chianti was usually a contradiction in terms until the late 20th century. The renaissance of Italian wine came in the 1970s and was undoubtedly influenced by the lateral thinking of successful winemakers in the New World.

## Understanding Italian wine.

As in France, Italy has a hierarchy of official designations but the one used here is unlike any other in the wine world. In 1963, the wine regions were divided between ones that produce basic table wine – **Vino da Tavola** – and the ones with greater potential, the **DOC**s (Denominazione di Origine Controllata). Very soon, however, it became clear that a DOC had more to do with geography and tradition than with quality. So, the label of the cheapest, nastiest Chianti or Soave could carry the three letters, provided it was made according to certain controversial rules. The introduction of a supposedly higher **DOCG** (Denominazione di Origine Controllata e Garantita) designation for a few regions, such as Barolo and Chianti, did not solve the problem, so a number of producers took a typically Italian approach: they simply sidestepped the DOC/DOCG system entirely and sold their wine as **Vino da Tavola**. The critical attention given to the top examples of these – such as Tignanello and Sassicai, which became widely known as the Supertuscans – led the establishment to introduce a new designation – **IGT** (Indicazione Geografica Tipica) – for non traditional but better than basic wines. Today there are 320 DOCs (under 600 different names), 30 DOCGs and some 200 IGTs (not to mention a few good wines that are still sold as Vino da Tavola). In all these cases, the designation is of far less importance when buying a bottle than the name of the producer.

Unlike France, Italy has no Premiers and Grands Crus designations for the finest vineyards in any region but the best part of many areas is referred to as 'Classico', as in Soave Classico. What's more, a producer – referred to on a label as a Tenuta, Azienda, Cascina or Fattoria (estate); a Casa Vinicola (commercial winery that buys in wine or grapes); or a Cantina Sociale (cooperative) might also indicate the name of a Vigneto, Vigna, Localita or Ronco (an individual vineyard).

Wine aged for longer in barrel (not always a good thing) is labelled 'Superiore', 'Riserva' or 'Riserva Speciale'. *Vino novello* is new wine, like Beaujolais Nouveau; *vecchio* and *stravecchio*, on the other hand, are old. Sweetness varies (for reds as well as whites). *Asciutto* and *secco* are dry, while *amaro* and *amarone* are dry and, ideally, pleasantly bitter. *Abboccato* is off-dry, while *amabile*, *pastoso* and *semi-secco* are medium sweet and *dolce*, decidedly so. Raisiny red and white wines made from partly dried grapes are *passito* or *recioto* (always sweet) and reds that have been refermented on the skins of *recioto* wines are called *ripasso*. Fortified sweet or dry wine is *liquoroso*, a term which does not refer to the sherry-like vin santo, which is supposed to be made from long-aged, intentionally oxidised *passito*. Like balsamic vinegar, cheap versions are made rapidly and fairly industrially.

## White grapes

**Albana/Greco** A soft, creamy central Italian and Emilia Romagnan variety that hit the headlines in 1987 when the unexceptional Albana di Romagna was made Italy's first white DOCG. That wine is much better made than it was then, but poor examples are still easy to find.

**Arneis** A light, floral and spicy Piedmont variety. At its best as Roero Arneis.

**Chardonnay** The ubiquitous variety is widely grown and, on occasion, capable of real greatness in the northeast, Tuscany and Piedmont. Also used in inventive blends.

Bottles of *spumante* at Ferrari Fratelli Lunelli.

Prosecco grapes at Bisol.

**Cortese** Best known for Gavi, the white from Piedmont. Can be both fresh and creamy with a hint of apple and yellow plums.
**Garganega** The grape responsible for dull, watery Soave and for the almondy examples of this wine at its best.
**Malvasia** Widely grown floral variety that comes in dry and sweet forms.
**Moscato** Grapey variety to be found throughout Italy but most famously in Asti Spumante and Moscato in Piedmont.
**Pinot Bianco** Known in Alsace as Pinot Blanc. Creamy, light and often featureless but occasionally well made in the northeast.
**Pinot Grigio** Newly fashionable in the USA, this variety (known as Pinot Gris in Alsace) is widely grown in northern Italy. It can be very good in the northeast, when in the right hands, otherwise, it's a light, easy-going alternative to beer. In 2005 Italy is said to have exported more Pinot Grigio than it actually produced.
**Prosecco** The grape used to make peary sparkling wine of the same name in the Veneto.
**Tocai Friulano** A light appley variety, unrelated to any kind of Tokay. Needs to be well made if it is to achieve more than easy drinkability.
**Trebbiano** Italy's most widely planted grape is a relatively flavourless variety that comes in subtly differing clones. In France, it is known as the Ugni Blanc and never used to make serious wine.
**Verdicchio** A limey, nutty variety used to make wine of the same name in the Marches.

### Red grapes

**Aglianico** A high-quality, smoky grape brought to southern Italy by the Phoenicians and now widely used. At its best in Aglianico del Vulture and Taurasi.
**Barbera** Grown all over Italy but at its best in Piedmont, where its wild berryish flavour shines in blends and by itself. Especially good in Barbera d'Asti and Barbera d'Alba and great with truffles.
**Cabernet Franc/Carmenère/Cabernet Sauvignon** 'Cabernet' is widely used for Cabernet Sauvignon, Cabernet Franc (especially in the north) and Carmenère, an obscure Bordeaux variety, which has been misidentified as Cabernet Franc. The finest Cabernet Sauvignons and Cabernet Sauvignon blends are probably the IGT Super Tuscans.
**Cannonau** The Sardinian name for the grape the French call Grenache. Rich and peppery.
**Dolcetto** A cherryish variety to be found in Piedmont. At its best when young.
**Lagrein** A typically Italian grape grown in the northeast, where it makes bitter-chocolatey wine with quite soft tannins.
**Lambrusco** A characterful grape that makes dry and off-dry refreshing, wild-berryish wines that are sealed with corks and are rarely seen overseas – and sugar-watery, screwcapped wines that are made for export.
**Montepulciano** Confusingly, unrelated to Vino Nobile de Montepulciano (a Tuscan wine made from Sangiovese), this is an earthy but potentially interesting grape when well handled in Montepulciano d'Abruzzo and Rosso Conero from the Marches.
**Nebbiolo** For many, this is the best red grape in Italy. At home in Piedmont (where it is also sold as Spanna), it is used by itself for Barolo and Barbaresco. Like Pinot Noir, it is acutely affected by the soil of the vineyard in which it is grown and is better by itself than in blends. Traditional versions tended to be tough when young, but modern ones are fresher and fruitier, with notes of smoke and roses.
**Negroamaro** Literally 'bitter black', this Apulian variety has flavours of bitter chocolate, cherries and violets.
**Nero d'Avola** 'Black' by name and black by colour, this Sicilian variety can produce delicious soft, herby-spicy wines.
**Primitivo** The spicy, dark southern grape known in the US as Zinfandel and in Croatia as Plavac Mali.
**Sagrantino** Umbrian grape with cherryish and plummy flavours. At its best in Montefalco.
**Sangiovese** The main grape of Chianti and, in different clones, of Vino Nobile de Montepulciano, Brunello di Montalcino, Morellino di Scansano and Super Tuscan IGTs in which it is used by itself and in blends with Cabernet Sauvignon and/or Merlot and/or Syrah. Herby, cherryish and quintessentially Italian.

Maculan winery in Breganze.

# Northwest Italy



The extraordinarily varied northwest of Italy includes Liguria on the Mediterranean coast between Genoa and la Spezia; the tiny Alpine valley of Aosta, where French or Provencal is spoken as widely as Italian; the sparkling wine-producing region of Lombardy and the glorious misty hills of Piedmont. Of these, Liguria and Valle d'Aosta are great places to visit – the former for the walks around the five villages of the Cinque Terre and the latter for its mountainous scenery (this is where you'll find the Mont Blanc tunnel) – but the wines are rarely special. Lombardy is far more interesting, thanks to its good sparkling Franciacorta wines and red Terre di Franciacorta and Valtellina reds. The jewel in the crown of the northwest, however, has to be Piedmont. This is home to the Nebbiolo – a grape many believe to be Italy's finest – which is used to make Barolo, Barbaresco and inexpensive Spanna.

## Liguria

WINE SHOP /BAR — LIGURE

### Sunflower Wine Shop

Via XXV Aprile 1, 16038 Santa Margherita Ligure
T +39 0185-285 602
sunflower@liguriaplanet.com
Mon-Sat 0900-1230 and 1530-1830.

A sophisticated hole in the wall, with smooth wooden floors and a groovily curved bar, Sunflower offers more than 200 Italian wines, as well as a vast selection of Champagne and spirits. There are a variety of snacks, but this is a place to concentrate on drinking and exploring labels that you might have never known existed.

## Lombardy

The grape varieties here are a mixed bunch, with Nebbiolo rubbing shoulders with Pinot Noir and Merlot. Look out for Sfursat which is made from partly dried grapes and is like Amarone di Valpolicella. The hilly region of Oltrepò Pavese allows you to choose between 11 different grape varieties, including Cabernet Sauvignon and Barbera; quality is just as varied.

RESTAURANT — ERBUSCO

### Ristorante Gualtiero Marchesi

Via Vittorio Emanuele II 23, 25030 Erbusco
T +39 0307-760 562
www.marchesi.it
Tue-Sat 1230-1400 and 1930-2200;
Sun 1230-1400.
$$-$$$

“”

If Bordeaux lovers feel drawn to the great estates of Tuscany, for Burgundy fans, the true Mecca of Italian wine has to be the tiny vineyards and cellars of Piedmont.

Podere di Sorano.

Italy is long on matriarchal home cooks but short on celebrity chefs. Gualtiero Marchesi, the first non-French person to win three Michelin stars, comes close but despite his status he is down to earth and has certainly earned his stripes. He no longer actively cooks in the restaurant he conceived but it still bears his mark, turning out stellar, nouvelle cuisine-inspired Italian dishes. The wine list is as exciting as you would expect and there is a huge range of grappas. The restaurant is located in a sumptuous hotel, **L'Albereta** ($$$), whose staff can organize visits to wineries.

# Best producers

**Lombardy**

Ca del Bosco
Nino Negri

**Piedmont**

Elio Altare
Ascheri » *page 135.*
Batasiolo
Bava » *page 135.*
Giacomo Bologna
Borgogno
Chiara Boschis
Ceretto
Michele Chiarlo
Domenico Clerico
Aldo Conterno
Giacomo Conterno
Luigi Einaudi
Fontanafredda » *page 136.*
Angelo Gaja
Bruno Giacosa
Elio Grasso
Marcarini (Dolcetto)
Marchesi di Gresy
Bartolo Mascarello
Giuseppe Mascarello
Prunotto
Renato Ratti
Luciano Sandrone
Vajra (Dolcetto)
Vietti (Barbera)
Roberto Voerzio

RESTAURANT — MILAN

## Il Luogo di Aimo e Nadia

Via Montecuccoli 6, 20147 Milan
T +39 024-16886
www.aimoenadia.com
Mon-Fri 1230-1415 and 2000-2215; Sat 2000-2215. Closed Aug.
$$$

This has risen from humble origins to become one of Italy's best contemporary restaurants. The owners, now joined by their daughter Stefania, arrived in Milan from Tuscany 40 years ago with barely a crust of bread between them. They opened a restaurant in the Milan suburbs and, by insisting on the finest ingredients and an iron focus in the kitchen, soon found that they were booked up weeks in advance. The wine list is excellent, with a generous number of labels offered by the glass. If you can't get a table, ask them to book one at their newer restaurant, **L'Altro Luogo di Aimo e Nadia**, in Piazza Repubblica.

## Piedmont

Nebbiolo reds used to be tough and impossible to drink for decades but modern winemaking brings out their extraordinary floral, smoky character within a few years of the harvest. The berryish red Barbera (at its best from Alba, also the place to buy white truffles) is also widely used here, both neat and in blends, while the cherryish Dolcetto is a traditional local star. The best known whites are the creamy (and often over-praised) Gavi and spicy-herby Arneis but the Favorita can also be freshly attractive. The most famous fizz here is Asti Spumante, the wonderful grapey sweet wine made from the Muscat, and Moscato, the less fizzy, less alcoholic version but its pale red counterpart, the Bracchetto, is also worth seeking out to enjoy with strawberries. The most interesting experimental wines in this region are sold under the Langhe DOC which covers most of the best regions.

WINERY — COCCONATO D'ASTI

## Bava Azienda Vitivinicola e di invecchiamento

Strada Monferrato 2, 14023 Cocconato d'Asti
T +39 0141-907 083
www.bava.com
Shop daily from 1000. Winery Mon-Fri from 1000; Sat and Sun by appointment only.

The Bava brothers, Roberto, Guilio and Paulo, are an enterprising, unusual lot. They have continued the innovations introduced by their father, Piero, which include ageing Barbera in oak, and have successfully experimented with wines that opt out of the Super Piedmontese DOC, such as blends of Chardonnay and Cortese. Firm believers in the affinity between music and wine, many of their winemaking insights have been reached while listening to concerts, and some of the wines, such as Stradivario, evoke this process. The winery frequently hosts concerts as well as seminars on subjects such as wine and religion. Roberto is, incidentally, also an expert on chocolate.

WINERY — BRA

## Cantine Giacomo Ascheri

Via G Piumati 19, 23 e 25, 12042 Bra
Winery T +39 0172-412394. Hotel 430312 Restaurant 431008.
www.ascherivini.it, www.ascherihotel.it
Restaurant Tue-Fri 1200-1400 and 1930-2300; Sat and Sun 1930-2300.
Tours by appointment.

For wine lovers so obsessed with wine that they wish they could sleep in a cellar, the enterprising Matteo Ascheri has, to my mind, provided the next best thing: a hotel ($$$) that sits on top of his winery, with a glass floor in the lobby through which you can see the vats below. Bra, in the Langhe and Roero, is the nerve centre of Italy's Slow Food movement and Ascheri embraces its tenets of artisanal food production and tradition in

Dining at Osteria Murivecchi, Ascheri: outside and in.



the vineyard and cellar. The movement is not averse to modernity in all its forms, however, and the hotel and winery are a very funky marriage of wood and chrome, brick and marble. The hotel makes a great base for visiting the surrounding area but whether or not you stay here, be sure to eat at the **Osteria Murivecchi** at No 19 ($$-$$$), which offers a menu of purely Piedmontese fare, along with suggested wines, that changes every week.

RESTAURANT — RIVOLI

## Combal Zero

Castello di Rivoli, Piazza Mafalda di Savoia, 10098 Rivoli
T +39 011-9565225
www.combal.org
Wed-Sun for dinner only.
$$-$$$

Stated simply, I had one of the most memorable meals of my life here, in this modern restaurant, next to the stunning royal palace in Rivoli, outside Turin. Davide Scabin's Combal Zero and the modern art gallery contained in that converted palace each contribute, in different ways, to deconstructing Italian heritage. Davide Scabin is often compared to Ferran Adrià of El Bulli in Spain, but he stresses that he is far more interested in presenting dishes in ways that strike the palate differently than in inventing new ways to cook them. As hard as it is to describe a painting, it is harder to describe Scabin's oeuvre, though his signature dish, the 'cyberegg' gives a gist of it. A mixture of egg yolk, vodka, caviar, shallots and black pepper is ensconced in a 'shell' of transparent film, which the diner is invited to crack open with a scalpel and to drink down. As a counterpoint to such an unusual dining experience, the traditional task of selecting a bottle of wine may well come as a relief. Mind you, there are 500 wines to choose from, so you may be grateful for some advice from Milena Pozzi who is responsible for them.

WINERY — SERRALUNGA D'ALBA

## Fontanafredda

Via Alba 15, 12050 Serralunga d'Alba
T +39 0173-626111
www.fontanafredda.it
Visits by appointment only.

In a region of discreet, small wineries, Fontanafredda, a sponsor of the 2006 Winter Olympics in Turin, stands out for its relative size and visibility. Fortunately, marketing energy does not compromise the drive towards quality, and its wide range of wines, including several stunning single vineyard Barolos and Barbarescos, goes from strength to strength. Currently owned by the Monte dei Paschi di Siena bank group, the impressive estate has intriguing origins, having belonged to the mistress of King Vittorio Emanuele II (1820-1878).

RESTAURANT — ISOLA D'ASTI

## Il Cascinale Nuovo

Strada Statale Asti Alba 15, 14057 Isola D'Asti
T +39 0141-958166
www.ilcascinalenuovo.it
Call ahead for bookings; closed Jan and Aug.

One of the exciting things about cooking in Italy is that the younger generation are not only taking over from mama and papa but are replacing the "rosso o bianco" fiasco-from-a-barrel offer with passionately conceived wine lists. Il Cascinale Nuovo is a case in point. A former truck stop founded by Armando and Silvana Ferretto in 1968, it is now in the hands of their sons, who have reduced the covers from 100 to 50, refined the Piedmontese menu and replaced the water-and-wine beakers with proper stemware. Walter's province is the kitchen, his wife Patrizia takes care of the hotel and Robert, with encouragement from top producers, Giacomo Bologna and Angelo Gaja, has built a cellar containing more than 20,000 bottles of the finest Piedmontese wine.

**The area that includes the Alto Adige (also known as the Südtirol), Friuli-Venezia Giulia, Trentino and the Veneto is another gloriously mixed region. The best wines have a freshness rarely found elsewhere; this is the place to go looking for great whites.**

## Alto Adige/Südtirol

The mountainous Alto Adige (aka Südtirol) is as Germanic as Valle d'Aosta is French and grapes are often known by their German names. So Pinot Grigio might be called Ruländer, while Pinot Noir is Blauburgunder. Freshness is the key here, thanks to the high altitude of many of the vineyards. Distinctive styles are Gewürztraminer; the soft juicy red Schiava; two kinds of Muscat – the red Rosenmuskateller and deeply hued Goldenmuskateller; and the wild-berryish Lagrein Dunkel which is found nowhere else. Similarly unusual are the wild white blend of Chardonnay, Sauvignon and Gewürztraminer made by Franz Haas.

RESTAURANT SÜDTIROL

### Pretzhof

Pretzhof Tulfer 259, 39040 Wiesen-Pfitsch, Südtirol
T +39 0472-764 455
www.pretzhof.com
Wed-Sun for lunch and dinner.
$

Karl and Ulli Mair offer visitors to their farm and restaurant the chance to glimpse back in time. The 'high house at the Tulfer' appears in records from the 13th century; Karl's ancestor, Hanns Mayr, bought it in the late 17th century. The Mairs' farm is dedicated to traditional agricultural practices and the resulting organic provender, including cheese and ham, is given the 'grandmother' treatment of traditional recipes that have been passed down the generations. Karl is passionate about wine and, although the restaurant is small, the wine list is large and excellent, with bottles that have benefited from storage in a beautiful stone cellar.

## Trentino

The wines of Trentino have little in common, except for their membership of a bewildering array of single-varietal grapes. Quality varies very widely too.

WINERY TRENTO

### Cantina La Vis e Valle di Cembra

Via Carmine 7, 38015 Lavis (Trento)
T +39 0461-246 325
www.la-vis.com
Visits by appointment only.
€2.50

To really understand vinous Italy in all its dimensions, and certainly to comprehend vinous Trento, add a cooperative to your itinerary. La Vis, which manages to produce several prizewinners across an enormous range and an output of several million bottles a year, demonstrates what the frequently maligned cooperative sector is capable of producing. It offers a tour, an excellent on-site museum and a restaurant, Maso Franch ($$), which serves authentic Trentino specialties.

WINERY TRENTO

### Cavit

Via del Ponte di Ravina 31, 38040 Trento
T +39 0461-381 711
www.cavit.it
Mon-Fri 0900-1230 and 1400-1830.

Another excellent cooperative, and one of the first Italian wineries to obtain ISO certification, Cavit's excellent marketing ability – not a skill for which Italian wineries are often known – has brought large quantities of its wines to markets worldwide. Forutnately, high volumes have not been at

the expense of devotion to Trentino's terroir, and a tour, for which you need to book ahead, will provide an insight into the range of diverse wines that the region can produce.

WINERY — TRENTO

### Ferrari Fratelli Lunelli

Via Ponte di Ravina 15, 38040 Trento
T +39 0461-972 311
www.cantineferrari.it
Mon-Fri 0930-1300 and 1430-1800.

The Ferrari winery bears no relation to the car manufacturer of the same name, but is, like its namesake, a leader in its field. The Lunelli family have gone from strength to strength in making prizewinning *spumanti* from Chardonnay and Pinot Noir grapes and have successfully expanded into still wines, bottled water, olive oil and coffee. The tour offers a study in contrasts: a gleaming winery building, a laboratory with eight full-time technicians dedicated to researching and improving upon Ferrari's winemaking, and endless rows of traditional *pupitres*, holding bottles that are rotated every day.



RESTAURANT — TRENTO

### Scrigno del Duomo

Piazza Duomo 29, 38100 Trento
T +39 0461-220 030
www.scrignodelduomo.com
Daily 1100-1430 and 1800-2400.
($)

You might never make it to this restaurant in the beautifully restored Casa Balduini, part of which dates from the Middle Ages. Leave Trento's cathedral square through a wrought-iron gate, go through a lovely courtyard, where you can eat outside in summer, and enter the ground-floor wine bar, and you might get so seduced by what's on offer that even the Michelin-starred restaurant below won't be able to lure you away. A huge list of wines from all over Italy and the world, many of them by the glass, is on offer, and the bar groans with tempting snacks. The restaurant is worth it too, though, so perhaps the solution is to spend a couple of days in Trento, enjoying its historical and artistic riches, and make a return visit or three.

Grape pickers and bottles at Ferrari Fratelli Lunelli.

## Veneto

The region close to Verona produces Prosecco fizz, Soave and Valpolicella. The last pair have deservedly mixed reputations. At their worst, they are dire but at their best, they can be glorious. Look out for single vineyard, creamy, almondy Soave from Pieropan, the top producer of this wine, and for serious Valpolicella from a producer like Allegrini, Tedeschi or Quintarelli. This wine comes in a range of styles: as a soft cherryish red (sold as Valpolicella), as sweetly rich Recioto della Valpolicella, made from dried grapes, and, most interesting of all, as Recioto della Valpolicella Amarone, which is reminiscent of fine bitter chocolate. Also worth seeking out are good Prosecco sparkling wines (particularly when made by Bisol) and the reds and whites of Breganze (especially Maculan).

Top: Village of Guia, near Valdobbiadene. Bottom: Bisol tasting room.

WINERY | TREVISO

## Bisol

Bisol Desiderio & Figli Azienda Agricola, 31040 Fol di Valdobbiadene, Treviso
T +39 0423-900138
www.bisol.it
Visits by appointment only.

The Bisols, among the leading producers of Prosecco, have been a prominent family in the Valdobbiadene for almost five centuries and have created several opportunities for visitors to immerse themselves in the history of their corner of the Veneto. They have reinstated a Veneto tradition, the *foresteria*, a dwelling on aristocratic estates in which foreign visitors were traditionally wined and dined, by restoring and converting a monastery on the estate as a guesthouse ($$$). The extremely comfortable **Foresteria Duca di Dolle** also houses a state-of-the-art kitchen, in which cookery classes are run by top local chefs. The family help to organize all sorts of wine-tourism activities, including mountain-biking through the vineyards, and also offers wine-tasting courses.

WINERY | PADUA

## La Montecchia

Via Montecchia 16, 35030 Selvazzano Dentro, Padua
T +39 049-637 294
www.lamontecchia.it
Tue-Sat 0900-1200 and 1430-1830.

Count Emo Capodilista's excellent winery is located on one of the Veneto's most lovely wine routes through the Colli Euganei, making it an excellent base, especially as

# Best producers

**Friuli**

Abbazia di Rosazzo
Enofriulia
Livio Felluga » *page 141.*
Marco de Felluga
Gravner
Jermann
Pierpaolo Percorari
Schiopetto
Steverjan
Venica

**Trentino-Alto Adige**

Ferrari » *page 138.*
J Hofstatter
Pojer & Sandri
Tiefenbrunner
Vigneto Scarzon
Zeni

**Veneto**

Allegrini
Anselmi
Bolla (single vineyard wines)
Boscaini
Romano Dal Forno
Maculan » *page 140.*
Masi
Pieropan
Quintarelli
Serego Alighieri
Fratelli Tedeschi

non-wine tourists in your party can find diversion in the contiguous golf club and massive swimming pool.The **Castello della Montecchia** promises an extremely stylish bed-and-breakfast experience ($$$) in a 70-sq-m suite of rooms that includes a dressing room and a massive fireplace. If this is unavailable, there are also three charming converted outbuildings that can be rented. Whether you stay or not, be sure to visit the **Villa Capodilista**, a huge, stately 16th-century hunting lodge on the estate that is filled with very fine frescoes.

WINERY — ARBIZZANO

## Località Le Ragose

37020 Arbizzano
T +39 045-751 3241
www.leragose.com
Visits by appointment only.

Arnaldo Galli, Marta Bortoletto and their sons, Paolo and Marco, turn out some extremely elegant Amarone della Valpolicella on this 40-acre estate in the Valpolicella hills. Valpolicella, whose name has been used and abused in recent years, is making a comeback, and smaller producers, such as the Gallis, who resurrected this abandoned estate only in 1969, have much to be thanked for. Ask to see the small old cellar.

WINERY — BREGANZE

## Maculan

Via Castelletto 3, 36042 Breganze
T +39 0445-873 733
www.maculan.net
Visits by appointment only.

Fausto Maculan's bijou winery was designed by the man himself. Here, you have the chance to see at close hand the production of one of Italy's delicious but sometimes elusive sweet wines made from dried grapes. Torcolato, of which Maculan is a leading producer, is made mostly from Vespaiola, an indigenous variety so named because wasps swarm around it, as well as from some Garganega and Tocai. Ask to see the attic in which bunches of the best grapes are hung to dry for at least five months, a process that causes them to develop noble rot and concentrates their flavours through dehydration. Other phases of production should also be on view, allowing for a glimpse into a process that has been a cottage industry in Italy for generations.

RESTAURANT — VERONA

## Ristorante Enoteca Bottega del Vino

Via Scudo di Francia 3, 37121 Verona
T +39 045-800 4535
www.bottegavini.com
Wed-Mon 1800-late.
$$

One of the highlights of my year is a visit to the annual Vinitaly Trade Fair in Verona. But just as important as walking around and tasting at the exhibition is a meal at this 116-year-old restaurant in the heart of the city. So popular with visiting Americans that New York City just had to have its very own version, Bottega del Vino still counts Italy's top wine producers as its customers. Whether you are a local or a tourist, you should expect to book and then still to wait for your table. The atmosphere is noisy, friendly and faintly chaotic: very Italian, in other words. There are 60 wines by the glass and the cellar, which

### Access all arias

Every summer, Verona's city walls resonate with the bel canto, arias and cadenzas of Verona's famous opera season. It seems entirely apt that opera's emotional drama and intensity reaches its apotheosis in this, the fictional home of Shakespeare's star-crossed lovers.

Events take place in the Arena, Verona's 20,000-seater Roman amphitheatre, the third largest in existence, after the Colisseum in Rome and the little-visited amphitheatre in Capua. The Arena was rediscovered as a performance space in 1913, when Verdi's *Aida* was first performed there, and the summer season is now a major event on the European calendar. Enormous, epic productions of the best-known operas are the Arena's stock in trade (Franco Zeffirelli directed the lavish 2003 productions of *Carmen*, *Aida*, *Rigoletto*, *Nabucco* and *Turandot*) and the tradition of spectators holding candles during the performance adds to the atmosphere.

Operas are alternated every night so that even those staying for a long weekend can see two or three operas if they want. Tickets can be bought over the phone (T+39 045-800 5151), via the website (www.arena.it) or in person from the Arena or from a number of outlets around the city. They range in price from around €20 for a seat on the Roman steps high above the stage, to over €150 for a central seat near the action. Renting a cushion is highly recommended in the cheap seats; buying a pair of ineffective binoculars less so. Librettos are widely (and cheaply) available in English from local bookshops if you want to check up on the storyline beforehand.

Most bars and restaurants around the Arena itself, especially those in piazza Bra, stay open late to catch the post-opera appetites, although, given the sudden influx of people, booking ahead is advisable if you want a table. Many restaurants also open earlier than usual on opera days to cater for pre-opera diners.

Grapevine

**Grappa**

If Italy has a bewildering array of wines, its spirits and liqueurs are just as diverse. The most famous and, on occasion, infamous of these is grappa, the clear spirit served at the end of a meal, or mixed with coffee as a *caffe corretto*. Likened by Italians to Cognac, a grape spirit that would also be colourless if it weren't aged in oak barrels, grappa is actually a different kind of product. Cognac, Armagnac and other famous grape brandies are made by distilling wine; grappa, like the *Marc* produced in Burgundy and Champagne, is what you get when you distill the skins and pips that are left over after you've fermented the juice. As any cook knows, delicious dishes can be made from left-overs, provided that the original ingredients were good and that they've been well stored. In the case of most grappa, both these rules were usually ignored. In the days when fine Italian wine was a rarity, the skins were often left to oxidize in the sun before being distilled. As winemaking improved, with more attention paid to the grapes and the way they were handled, so did the grappa. The man who revolutionized grappa was Benito Nonino, head of a family distillery, who, in 1973, created the first example made from a single grape variety and a single vineyard. Since then a large number of other producers have followed his lead, offering grappas made from almost every local and international grape, occasionally delicately ageing them in barrels to give them a bronze tint and almost always selling them in designer bottles. At its best from a producer like Nonino, Jacopo Poli, Zeni and Bertagnolli, grappa is a truly fascinating drink, packed with perfumed, grapey fragrances. But even the finest grappas have a woody note that some people never grow to love.

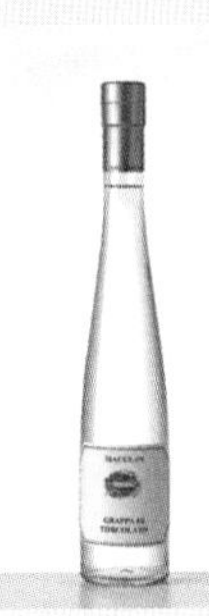

demands to be visited, holds almost 100,000 bottles. The obvious way to finish a meal here would be with grappa but you might be tempted to try one of the Armagnacs whose vintages stretch from 1900 to 1973.

WINE BAR/RESTAURANT VENICE

## Vini da Gigio

Cannaregio 3628, 30131 Venice
T +39 041-528 5140
Wed-Sun 1200-1430 and 1800-2300.
$$

Paolo Lazzari has built up a list of more than 1000 wines, many of them from small producers, and also offers simple but good carafe wine right from the barrel should you be suffering from palate fatigue. Wines from the Veneto, Friuli and Alto Adige are especially strong, and everything is reasonably priced. Popular with visiting Italians as well as Venetians for its food as well as its wine, Vini da Gigio has a wide selection of meat dishes and extremely fresh seafood dishes, all of which are as authentically Venetian as the atmosphere.

## Friuli

Most of the wines in Friuli-Venezia Giulia come from the hills of the Colli Orientali del Friuli. Bordeaux blends – including the Malbec – work well here, as do some wonderfully innovative blends from producers like the brilliant Silvio Jermann. Jerman is famous for a Chardonnay once quixotically called 'Where the Dreams Have No End' but now labeled as 'Were dreams, now it is just wine'. Another star here is Josko Gravner who brings together varieties such as Sauvignon, Ribolla, Malvasia, Picolit, Chardonnay, Pinot Grigio and Riesling Italico in ways that would send a shudder down the spines of traditionalists who believe this kind of behaviour to be utter heresy.

Look out also for the distinctive summer-puddingy Refosco reds. Picolit, the region's top sweet wine has been overgenerously likened to Château Yquem, presumably by Italian chauvinists who have never encountered that wine.

WINERY CORMONS-GORIZIA

## Livio Felluga

**Winery** Via Risorgimento 1, 34070 Cormons-Gorizia
Winery T +39 0481-602032. Osteria T +39 0481-60028.
www.liviofelluga.it, www.terraevini.it
Winery visits by appointment only. Osteria daily 1000-1500 and 1700-2200.

In the beautiful village of Brazzano di Cormons, in the middle of Friuli's Collio hills, whose white wines have been wowing the wine world in recent years, the commune's top producer Livio Felluga has created the **Osteria Terra e Vini** (Via XXIV Maggio), a traditional-style inn with rooms ($$), a restaurant ($$) and a wine bar. The osteria regularly hosts jazz evenings, art exhibitions and poetry readings, as well as offering a range of wine-tourism packages. The restaurant prepares meals ranging from lighter selections of Friulian cheeses to full-blown goulashes and tripe dishes for which the Friulian countryside is known. Livio Felluga also welcomes visitors to his cellar by appointment.

# Central Italy



**The heart of Italy brings together the Abruzzo, Emilia-Romagna, Lazio, Marche, Molise Umbria and, of course, Tuscany. It is this last region that is the magnet for most wine lovers. But the other areas have a growing range of exciting wines to offer.**

## Emilia-Romagna

Emilia-Romagna is home to DOC Lambrusco, the potentially wonderful, refreshing bitter-cherryish wine, as well as a torrent of sugar-watery fizz sold under this name overseas. Just as controversially, there's Albana di Romagna whose generally unexceptional dry and sweet wines were, against all possible logic, named as Italy's first white DOCG. But there are more interesting wines to be found in this area, including a variety of styles from the Colli Piacentini, including a Bonarda-Barbera blend called Gutturnio after an Ancient Roman silver goblet found nearby. This wine region was once among the most highly regarded in Italy, naming Pliny and Michelangelo among its fans. Go-ahead Emilia-Romagna producers include Fattoria Zerbina and Fattoria Paradiso.

RESTAURANT — BOLOGNA

### Al Cambio

Via Stalingrado 150, Bologna
T +39 051-328 118
Mon-Fri 1200-1430 and 1930-2200; Sat 1930-2200. Closed Aug.
$$$

Bologna claims to have the best food in Italy. However, as befits a town with one of the world's oldest universities, the Bolognese can be pretty conservative when it comes to the tradition of their cuisine. Massimo Poggi, one of Italy's most exciting young chefs, has the confidence to take on tradition and at Al Cambio, just outside the city walls, he's garnering increasing praise for his innovative interpretations of classic Emilia-Romagna dishes. The wines are good too.

Bologna.

RESTAURANT RUBIERA

## Arnaldo Clinica Gastronomica

Piazza XXIV Maggio 3, Rubiera
T +39 0522-626 124
www.clinicagastronomica.com
Tue-Sat for lunch and dinner.
$$

In Emilia-Romagna it pays to know your cold cuts, as there are endless permutations of ham, herb-scented lard and sausages to be had, with variations occurring from hamlet to hamlet, farm to farm. Arnaldo Clinica Gastronomica is an excellent place to get to grips with the meaty options, as well as pasta, which can also be a minefield of minute variations. A fun and much-loved local, close to Modena, one of Italy's most prosperous towns, and home of Ferrari, Maserati, De Tomaso, Bugatti, its walls are decorated with photographs from motor-racing history. The wine list provides a good introduction to the oft-misunderstood wines of this region.

AGRITURISMO VIANO

## Azienda Agricola e Agrituristica Cavazzone

Via Cavazzone 4, 42030 Viano
T +39 0522-858 100. Restaurant
T +39 0522-986 054
www.cavazzone.it
Restaurant Tue-Fri dinner only; Sat and Sun lunch and dinner. Tours by appointment. Tours €3

The *agriturismo* movement in Italy has opened up many of the country's small farms and agricultural estates to visitors, allowing them to see up close how everything from olive oil to sheep's milk cheese is made. Cavazzone offers several unusual variations on this theme. At the upmarket end of the *agriturismo* spectrum, it consists of 3000 ha of stunning countryside overlooking Reggio Emillia, which were bought in the 19th-century by Baron Raimondo Franchetti. Cavazzone specializes in producing DOP Traditional Balsamic Vinegar from grapes grown on the property. Balsamic vinegar comes in many fraudulent, sickly-sweet versions, so it is a delight to see how the genuine article is made and aged. In addition to accommodation ($), Cavazzone has a restaurant ($) offering wonderful, rich Emilian fare and an impressive selection of the region's wines, few of which ever travel outside Italy.

WINERY BERTINORO

## Fattoria Paradiso

Via Palmeggiana 285, 47032 Bertinoro
T +39 0543-445 044
www.fattoriaparadiso.it
Daily 1130-1500. Restaurant 1130-1500 and 1900-2200.

Romagna, the eastern part of Emilia-Romagna, is sometimes overlooked, as most of the region's best-known tourist sites are in Emilia. However Romagnan wines are going from strength to strength, especially the Sangioveses, and Fattoria Paradiso makes a



### Full fat Bologna

Bologna is to food what Milan is to fashion and the city strains with restaurants in the same way your belt might after you have spent a few days sampling the typically abundant and delicious food. Italy is a land full of deeply felt regional identities where local food specialities are the expression of a region's identity. It is not unusual to hear Italians from different areas claiming theirs to be the home of the best food in Italy. Rich, substantial and varied, *la cucina bolognese* has a better claim than most, something of which the *bolognesi* will lose no opportunity to remind you. Food here is taken (and eaten) seriously and copiously, and, as the city's nickname *la grassa* (the fat) suggests, you are unlikely to go home anything other than totally sated, and certainly no thinner.

The western part of the region, Emilia, is known for its cured meats and cheeses and has almost as many kinds of salami and prosciutto as there are towns. The world-famous prosciutto of Parma should not obscure other variants on the cold meat theme, such as *culatello* (also from Parma), *mortadella* from Bologna, *zampone* (stuffed pig's trotter) from Modena and the *pancetta* and *coppa* of Piacenza.

For the *primo piatto*, Bologna is the home of stuffed pastas, such as tortellini, tagliatelle and, of course, lasagne. Tortellini is said to have been inspired by the beauty of Venus' navel, while tagliatelle was created for the wedding feast of Lucrecia Borgia and the Duke of Ferrara and was reputedly inspired by the bride's long flowing tresses.

And on top of your pasta who could do without the cheese of Parma, *parmigiano*? This is also an essential ingredient in the many sauces and baked pasta dishes *alla parmigiana* which define the region's cooking. Parmesan is not the region's only cheese, however, and visitors should try the equally pungent *grana padano* and also the beautifully soft cow's milk *squacquerone*. On your side salad, drizzle a little *aceto balsamico* (balsamic vinegar) from Modena, and wash it all down with a glass of Sangiovese.

Among the best places in Bologna to sample these regional delights are **Antica Osteria Romagnola** (via Rialto13, T +39 051-263699), **Al Cambio** (see page 142) and **Dei Poeti** (via del Poeti 1, T +39 051-236166), an ancient *osteria* with an excellent selection of Italian wines.

perfect base from which to explore this up-and-coming region. There is so much on offer under one roof that it is difficult to know where to start: in the cellar, which contains 19th century bottles? At one of the three museums which celebrate, respectively, peasant culture, wine and motorcycles? In the winery itself? Or in the restaurant, named **Locanda Gradisca** after *Amarcord*, a film by former Fattoria Paradiso regular and Romagna native, Frederico Fellini? If indecision overwhelms you, the Pezzis, whose family has owned this 15th-century treasure for more than 100 years, should be able to help.

RESTAURANT RUBIERA

## Osteria del Viandante

Piazza XXIV Maggio 15, 42048 Rubiera
T +39 0522-260 638
www.osteriadelviandante.com
Tue-Fri for lunch and dinner; Sat dinner only.
$$$

The finest meat has been sourced from all over Italy to be served at this extremely elegant restaurant housed in a mansion with high, frescoed ceilings and chandeliers. Among the suppliers listed on the meat menu is 'Dario Cecchini' Panzano in Chianti, the Dante-spewing butcher made famous in Bill Buford's much publicized and celebrated book *Heat*. There are also choice cuts from regional butchers in the Marches, Piedmont and Tuscany, and elsewhere. The wine list has an impressive pan-Italian selection, with Piedmont and Tuscany especially strong.

WINERY MONTE SAN PIETRO

## Tenuta Bonzara

Via S Chierlo 37A, 40050 Monte San Pietro
T +39 051-676 8324
www.bonzara.com
Visits by appointment only.

Francesco Lambertini, whose Cabernets and Merlots have won him plenty of awards, has created a lovely *agriturismo* amidst his vineyards in the unspoilt Monte San Pietro in the hills overlooking Bologna. As well as providing accommodation ($$) that offers a perfect alternative to staying in the city, Tenuta Bonarza can help you organize trips and provides excellent restaurant recommendations in both the surrounding countryside and in Bologna itself.

## Tuscany

The historic wealth of Florence, in particular, and Tuscany, in general, and the efforts of a large number of small and large winemakers has ensured that this is the region that has monopolized the spotlight in recent years. It is, however, worth recalling that, as recently as the 1970s, with the exception of a few high-profile names like Frescobaldi, Antinori in Chianti and Biondi-Santi, Costanti and Barbi in Brunello di Montalcino, the wines from this region were either little known elsewhere or firmly in the category of cheap, daily drinking. In Chianti, in particular, this reputation was deserved. Until the law changed in 1967, nearly a third of every bottle of this red wine could legally be made from dull white grapes; on occasion the proportion was probably even higher. The success of a few high-profile producers in sidestepping the Chianti denomination and producing Vino da Tavola coincided with a serious review of the over-productive strains of Sangiovese planted here between the 1940s and 1970s. By the late 1980s, while plenty of basic Chianti could – and can – still be found, a growing number of Chianti producers had set their sights on being taken seriously. The region's finest wines are said to come from Chianti Classico (bottles are usually distinguished by a black cockerel) but Chianti Rufina and Chianti Colli Fiorentini can be just as good – everything depends on the producer.

Brunello di Montalcino is far more reliable and far more reliably expensive. Made, like Chianti, from Sangiovese, but from a different, better clone of this variety, Brunello di Montalcino can be gloriously rich, complex stuff that needs and rewards cellaring. In 1976, the Italian oenologist, Enzo Rivella, and the New York wine importer, John Mariani, were able to buy the 11th-century castle and nearly 3000 ha of undeveloped land that would become the Castello Banfi. Since then Montalcino has become a vinous mecca and the vineyards here are now among the most valuable in the world.

Another Sangiovese clone called Prugnolo Gentile is used to make Vino Nobile di Montepulciano which is never as fine as top Brunello but easily matches good Chianti Classico, while yet another, the Morellino, produces the often delicious wines of Morellino di Scansano in the southwest of the region.

The other trend in the region has been towards blending Sangiovese with Cabernet Sauvignon. Credit for introducing this French variety usually goes to Marchese Mario Incisa della Rocchetta, who produced his first commercial example of the Cabernet-based Sassicaia in 1968, and to Piero Antinori who added some Cabernet to Tignanello, his previously 100% Sangiovese Vino da Tavola, in 1975. The grape has been here since 1855, however, when it was planted at the Frescobaldi estate in Chianti Rufina and it has been (a small) part of the recipe for Carmignano since 1975.

One of the factors peculiar to Tuscany has been the revival of a complete winemaking area in the coastal west of the region. The Maremma, like the Médoc, is a natural swamp that depends on man-made drainage schemes if it is to serve any use at all. Unlike the Médoc, the Maremma was drained 2000 years ago by the Etruscans but the underground canals were not maintained and, by the 19th century, it was known as a place of poverty and malaria. It was Mussolini who re-established the area and, unknowingly, made it possible for the production of wines like Sassicaia (and the Bolgheri DOC where it is situated) and Morellino di Scansano.

Tuscany's whites are a less distinguished bunch but Vernacchia di San Gimignano can be pleasant. In any case, the small town – a UNESCO World Heritage Site – is well worth visiting for its extraordinary set of 14 medieval 'skyscrapers'.

WINERY MONTALCINO

## Castello Banfi

53024 Montalcino
T +39 0577-840 111
www.castellobanfi.com
Apr-Oct daily 1000-1900; Nov-Mar daily 1000-1800; tours daily by appointment.
**Il Ristorante** Tue-Sat 1930-2200; reservations required. **La Taverna** Mon-Sat 1300-1500; reservations required.

As a lover of Brunello di Montalcino, I am eternally grateful to the American owners of Castello Banfi for not only helping to drag this region into the 21st century, but also for demonstrating to their neighbours the benefits of opening their doors and their bottles for visitors. (The region's most famous old estate, Biondi Santi, used to take pride in refusing to allow even the most illustrious outsiders to taste its wines.) Today, Castello Banfi does wine tourism with consummate skill. There are two restaurants ($$-$$$), a fascinating wine glass museum and a cellar, complete with a solera system, devoted entirely to the production of balsamic vinegar. If your time is limited, visit the shop which, in addition to the estate's wines, offers olive oils, food and crafts from some of Tuscany's finest artisans. Castello Banfi regularly hosts courses and special events.

WINERY CHIANTI

## Castello di Ama

Loc Ama, 53013 Gaiole in Chianti
T +39 0577-746 031
www.castellodiama.com
Visits by appointment only.

Top: Castello di Ama vineyards. Bottom: *Revolution* by Kendell Geers, designed for the Ama wine cellar in 2003.

Marco Pallanti and Lorenza Sebasti are at the cutting edge of the revival of Chianti Classico, a region that only a few decades ago was veering towards mediocrity. In 2006 Pallanti was appointed as president of the newly revitalized Consorzio del Chianti Classico but this is just one of a long list of achievements for the former Italy canoeing champion. The tremendous energy he has put into Castello di Ama and its wines has resulted in prize after prize, most notably, in 2005, being named winery of the year by Italy's Gambero Rosso. Apart from the Chiantis, other internationally applauded wines here include a Pinot Noir (Il Chiuso), Merlot (L'Apparita) and a Chardonnay (Il Poggio), which is one of Italy's best examples of this grape. As keen enthusiasts of modern art, Pallanti and Sebasti each year commission a top artist, such as Anish Kapoor and Kendell Geers, to create an installation somewhere in or around the winery.

WINERY CHIANTI

## Castello Vicchiomaggio

Via Vicchiomaggio 4, 50022 Greve in Chianti
T +39 055-854 079
www.vicchiomaggio.it
Visits by appointment only.

Leonardo da Vinci is but one in a long series of distinguished visitors to this stunning castle, with origins in the fifth century, that overlooks the Greve Valley. Here British-born John Matta and his wife Paola, who were pioneers of quality Chianti, have now also created an integrated wine- and food-lovers' experience. The restaurant ($$) has resurrected a range of fascinating and tasty historic Tuscan dishes, which can also be taught in cooking courses of various lengths, and the couple, who also make the estate's wine, can explain and demonstrate all aspects of viticulture and winemaking.

There are several apartments for rent on and around the estate ($-$$), and guests can cool down in the large, sumptuous pool, which has been constructed so that it seems to disappear into the valley below.

WINERY TREQUANDA

## Cinelli Colombini

Fattoria del Colle, 53020 Trequanda
T +39 0577-662108
Casato Prime Donne, Montalcino
T +39 0577-849421
www.cinellicolombini.it

Donatella Cinelli Colombini, who has been instrumental in spearheading wine tourism in Italy, shows how it's done at her Fattoria del Colle and Casato Prime Donne estates. In addition to instructive tours at each estate,

### Tuscan treats

Southeast of Siena lies a quintessential Tuscan landscape of rolling hills, dotted with immaculately preserved hill towns, ancient abbeys and cypress trees that pierce the sky like dark green daggers. This area, once ravaged by power struggles between the Sienese and the Florentines, is now peaceful, the pace of life slow and the social fabric remarkably unruffled by the 21st century.

There are so many towns and villages worth seeing that you could easily spend several days exploring. One route might be to take the SR2 from Siena to **Buonconvento**, a low-lying town with a medieval heart and the little **Museo d'Arte Sacra** containing medieval painting and religious treasures. From there head northeast to the gloriously isolated **Abbazia di Monte Oliveto Maggiore** (T+39 0577-707611), a Benedictine abbey founded in 1313 by Sienese nobleman Bernardo Tolomei. The main draw are the cloisters, their walls smothered with 15th-century frescoes but it's also worth hearing the monks singing Mass in Gregorian chant. Get here early to beat the tour buses. Next stop is **San Giovanni d'Asso** famed for its white truffles. The new **Museo del Tartufo** (T+39 0577-803101) covers the history and folklore of the famed fungus.

From here minor roads snake through the countryside to Torrita di Siena. Stop off at Trequanda for a tour of **Cinelli Colombini**'s Fattoria del Colle (above) before bearing south for **Montepulciano**. The town dominates the flat Valdichiana, a once marshy area where high ground was of both strategic and economic importance. Wealthy Florentines would spend the summer here and there are plenty of Renaissance buildings to admire. If you've called ahead, you can do a tasting at **Maria Caterina Dei** (page 148); otherwise visit the church of **San Biagio**, one of the most important religious buildings in Italy.

Then follow the SS146 to **Pienza**, a remarkable Renaissance town transformed from the original medieval village by Florentine architect Bernardo Rossellino under the instructions of Pope Pius II. From here you can continue to **San Quirico d'Orcia**. Don't be put off by the dull modern outskirts, the centre of the village is charming, witha number of atmospheric medieval churches. Its origins are Etruscan but its heyday was in medieval times, when it was an important stopping place on the busy Via Francigena. A few kilometres further west is **Montalcino**, home of the lauded Brunello di Montalcino; visit **Castello Banfi** (page 145) or **Fattoria dei Barbi** (page 148) to gain an in-depth insight into this wine region before heading back on the S2 to Siena.

Cookery courses at Fattoria del Colle, Cinelli Colombini.

the former of which includes a visit to her 16th-century ancestral home, a large range of activities, from residential cookery classes to outdoor landscape painting classes to mountain bike tours, can be arranged, all run by top professionals in their fields. For more than 300 years these estates have been passed down through the female line, so it's no surprise that Colombini is a proud proponent of getting women into the vineyard and winery, making this a good place for women travelling on their own or in small groups. A range of rooms, apartments and villas are available across the two estates.

WINE BAR — FLORENCE

### Enoteca Fuori Puorta

Via Monte alle Croci 10/r, San Niccolò, Florence
T +39 055-234 2483
www.fuoriporta.it
Mon-Sat 1230-1530 and 1900-0100.

In an elevated residential area, just outside the city walls near the San Niccolò gate and the Belvedere, is a funky wine bar that's well worth the trek uphill. It has masses of wines from all of Italy's regions, many of them available by the glass, and plenty of local colour in the form of decadent Florentines to see you through several regions' worth of sampling. The great and the good of the deli counter are offered up as snacks in a wide range of toasted and open-faced sandwiches.

MUSEUM — SIENA

### Enoteca Italiana

Fortezza Medicea, Via Camollia 72, 53100 Siena
T +39 0577-228 811
www.enoteca-italiana.it
Mon 1200-2000; Tue-Sat 1200-0100.

In my opinion, this is one of the most exciting of Italy's wine attractions. Enoteca Italiana brings together wines from each of Italy's DOCs, making it possible to sample the length and breadth of vinous Italy without leaving the confines of this restored 16th-century fort. All of the 1200 wines are available for tasting by the glass or bottle, and there are regular wine events and classes held throughout the year. In the summer, enjoy the sun on a lovely terrace, though, if it is hot, you might be grateful for the subterranean cool of the old brick vaults.

WINERY — CHIANTI

### Fattoria Castello di Volpaia

Loc Volpaia, Piazza della Cisterna 1, 53017 Radda in Chianti
T +39 0577-738066 / 738619
www.volpaia.it
Shop Apr-Oct daily 1000-1900; Nov and Dec daily 1000-1800. Closed Jan-Mar.

Carlo and Giovannella Stianti-Mascheroni have injected vitality into Volpaia, the 12th-century village that she inherited from her father. The winery makes a range of seriously good Chiantis, with some help from super-consultant Riccardo Cotarella, and, in the restaurant ($$), Francesco Sabbadini turns out excellent, pure Tuscan fare. From March to December, it is also possible to arrange cookery classes, in a variety of languages, which can focus on any dishes from the pan-Italian repertoire – though, of course, when in Tuscany, it pays to eat as the Tuscans eat. Scattered in and around the village are several elegant villas and apartments that can be rented, some of them with beautiful pools. Staying here gives you the chance to immerse yourself not only in whatever phase of viticulture or winemaking might be taking place, but also in the village's various other agricultural enterprises, such as olive oil production.

WINERY MONTALCINO

## Fattoria dei Barbi

Loc Podernuovi 170, 53024 Montalcino
T +39 0577-841111. Restaurant 847117
www.fattoriadeibarbi.it
Mon-Fri 1000-1300 and 1430-1800; Sat and Sun 1430-1800. Tours Mon-Fri 1100-1700. Restaurant summer Thu-Tue lunch and dinner; winter Thu-Mon lunch and dinner, Tue lunch only.



The few days I spent in one of this estate's apartments were among the most perfect holiday moments. The estate is very much a family affair; its owners, the Colombinis, have had a presence in Montalcino since 1352 and have run the Fattoria dei Barbi since 1790. Stefano Cinelli's commitment to the area and its history is evident in the free daily tours and in the little museum he has opened here illustrating peasant life, including the way dressmakers or cobblers might have lived and records of Jews who settled in the region in the 13th century. It is also well worth paying for one of the special events they organize, such as 'An Evening at Barbi'. Thia starts with a tour of Montalcino and its museum and a survey of the Brunello DOC, before taking in a tasting of Barbi's first class wines, accompanied by cheese and salamis made by the estate and concluding with a meal of traditional Montalcino dishes, cooked in the estate's restaurant, **Taverna dei Barbi** ($$). The estate rents out several charming apartments that have been personally decorated by Francesca Colombini Cinelli using family heirlooms.

Taverna dei Barbi.

WINERY CHIANTI

## Isole e Olena

Loc Isole 1, 50021 Barberino Val d'Elsa
T +39 055-807 2763
Visits by appointment only.

Piedmont native Paolo De Marchi likes to shake things up – but with great style. A pioneer of growing Syrah in Italy, he also makes a terrific Chardonnay on his small estate. Especially exciting, though, is his Cepparello, a Sangiovese-only Supertuscan that is already one of the region's most sought after wines. There is no formal visiting programme but visitors have been rewarded by spontaneous visits to the winery, with its gorgeous new extraordinarily illuminated cellars. Calling ahead is advisable if you want to try and catch De Marchi himself, who is full of insights about the Chianti region's ever-changing politics.

WINE SHOP CHIANTI

## Le Cantine di Greve in Chianti

Galleria delle Cantine 2, 50022 Greve in Chianti
T +39 055-854 6404
www.lecantine.it
Daily 1000-1900.

The largest wine shop in Tuscany, and one of the most innovative wineshops anywhere, Le Cantine allows you to sample scores of its 1000-plus wines, as well as olive oils and even cheese and salamis by purchasing a 'tasting card'. Chianti is understandably the strong suit, but much of Tuscany is represented, and the shop will handle the shipping of any bottles you want to send home. There is a free permanent wine exhibition featuring ancient winemaking equipment, and the massive cellar in which Le Cantine is housed is alone worth a quick visit, though it will be hard to stop by without being tempted to taste or buy something.

WINERY MONTEPULCIANO

## Maria Caterina Dei

Villa Martiena, Via Martiena 35, 53045 Montepulciano
www.cantinedei.com
Visits by appointment only.

Montepulciano's wines have been getting better and better, offering Sangiovese lovers the opportunity to enjoy a different expression of this grape, often at lower prices than Brunello di Montalcino or other Tuscan wines. Maria Caterina Dei, who used to be a professional singer and actress, has dedicated herself to improving the wine on the family estate on which she used to spend summer holidays as a child, and she offers a great introduction to the area. Consider renting an apartment in the farmhouse, which has a restored 16th-century tower and sweeping views over the unspoilt surrounding countryside.

WINERY CARMIGNANO

## Tenuta di Capezzana

Via Capezzana 100, 59015 Carmignano
T +39 055-870 6005
www.capezzana.it
Visits by appointment only.

This estate was effectively the creator of Carmignano, a DOC that seceded from Chianti Classico in the 1970s out of the desire to exploit the potential shown by the Cabernet Sauvignon on Tuscan soil. Tenuta di Capezzana today offers so much to see and do, and in such style, that you might be tempted to make it your base in Tuscany. The Contini Bonacossi family, who have been making wine continuously for 12 centuries, have turned their estate into a gastro-tourist centre that, in addition to in-depth winery visits and tastings, also offers cooking courses at the **Wine and Culinary Centre**. There are tours of the state-of-the-art olive oil-making facility and of the cellar dedicated to vin santo, whose usually small-scale production is rarely seen by visitors. Accommodation is in a *fattoria* on the estate or in a separate 16th-century villa, a few kilometres away. There is a swimming pool and tennis courts for guests' use.

WINE SHOP/RESTAURANT MAREMMA

### Trattoria Cantina Il Tarlo

Piazza del Popolo, 17/18 Riotorto
T +39 0565-21058
www.trattoria-iltarlo.it
Fri-Wed for lunch and dinner. Cellar visits by appointment.
$$

Claudio Macelloni continues to source a terrific selection of local Maremma wines, offering them both in his *cantina* and to accompany his wife Liana's creative southern Tuscan cuisine. Liana is adamant about only cooking seasonally; she might produce home-made pasta with baby squid and tuna roe on the 'sea' menu, or pork with prunes on the 'land' menu. The Maremma is a relatively new and constantly changing region, with new wineries opening all the time; Il Tarlo is a good place to orientate yourself before striking into the field.

HOTEL MAREMMA

### Villa il Tesoro

Ristorante e Hotel di Fattoria Terrabianca, Loc Valpiana, 58024 Massa Marittima
T +39 0566-92971
www.villailtesoro.com
$$$

In the wilds of the Maremma, Villa il Tesoro offers a luxurious retreat, complete with a helicopter landing pad and a 140 sq m pool that seems to meander through the surrounding vineyards and olive groves. In the cigar bar you can puff a Havana and armchair travel, should you wish, to France by sampling the terrific selection of Cognac and Armagnac. For purists who like to drink local, however, there is a good wine list in the elegant restaurant ($$$). **Terrabianca**, the Chianti Classico winery that owns the hotel, also offers multi-vintage tastings in the on-site enoteca.

## Best producers

**Emilia-Romagna**
Fattoria Paradiso » *page 143.*
Ferrucci
Tenuta Zerbina

**Marche**
Boccadigabbia
Colonnara
Le Terrazze
Monte Schiavo
Umani Ronchi

**Tuscany**
Agiano
Alois Lageder
Antinori
Avignonesi
Banfi » *page 145.*
Barbi » *page 148.*
Biondi-Santi
Brancaia
Campo di Sasso
Casse Basse
Casse Basse
Castellare
Castello dei Rampolla
Castello di Ama » *page 145.*
Castello di Fonterutoli
Castello di Volpaia » *page 147.*
Col d'Orcia
Costanti
Dievole
Fattoria di Felsina
Fontodi
Frescobaldi
Il Cipressino
Il Due Cipressi
Il Palazzino
Il Poggione
Isole e Olena » *page 148.*
La Fortuna
La Serena
Marchese Incisa della Rocchetta (Sassicaia)
Monte Antico
Montevertine
Poggio Antico
Poliziano
Querciabella
Riecine
Rocca di Costagnoli
Ruffino
San Felice
San Quirico
Selvapiana
Tenute Ambrogio & Giovanni Folonari
Tenuta dell' Ornelaia
Teruzzi e Puthod
Tommaso Bussola
Villa Cafaggio
Villa de Cappezana

**Umbria**
Adanti
Lungarotti

## Umbria

Umbria has two memorable names: Orvieto, a sweet or dry white wine that varies from ordinary to tremendous depending on the maker, and Lungarotti, the producer who single-handedly created the Torgiano DOC and Torgiano Riserva DOCG. Also of interest is Montefalco Sagrantino, a rich berryish red made from the Sagrantino grape that deserves to be better known.

WINERY TORGIANO

### Cantine Giorgio Lungarotti

Via Mario Angeloni 16, 06089 Torgiano
T +39 075-988 661
www.lungarotti.it
Visits by appointment only.

I have always thought that Giorgio Lungarotti deserves greater recognition for the contribution he has made to Italy in general and Umbria in particular. As increasing numbers of wines from the region are coming to international attention, Lungarotti has also helped instigate a transformation in wine and food tourism. Maria Grazia Lungarotti has not only created two excellent museums – one dedicated to wine and one to food but also a hotel with a restaurant, **Le Tre Vaselle** (Via Garibaldi 48, T +39 0759-880447, www.3vaselle.it) in Torgiano, and a nearby *agriturismo*, **Poggio alle Vigne** (Loc Montespinello, T +39 075-982994, www.poggioallevigne.com), located in a 17th-century farmhouse in the middle of the vineyards. Both establishments can help design a itinerary for visiting the region's other wineries. The Lungarottis also own a shop, **La Spola** (Via Garabaldi 66), specializing in otherwise hard-to-find local handicrafts such as embroidery, lace and papier maché.



## Marche

The Adriatic region of Marche around Ancona is best known for Verdicchio, a white that has improved greatly since the 1970s, when it was sold in a curvy amphora-like bottle, nicknamed 'la Lollobrigida' after the well known actress. The rarer Falerio dei Colli Ascolani, which marries Verdicchio with Trebbiano, Malvasia and Pinot Bianco, can also be worth seeking out. The best Marche reds are the Montepulciano-based Rosso Conero and Rosso Piceno in which the Montepulciano is blended with Sangiovese.

WINERY ANCONA

### Moroder Azienda Agricola

Via Montacuto 112, 60029 Ancona
T +39 071-898232
www.moroder-vini.it
Contact the winery for opening times.

The farm has belonged to Alessandro Moroder's family since the 18th century but it was not until the 1980s that he and his wife Serenella started taking the vineyards seriously with a view to bottling wine under the estate name. In 1985 they qualified to join the Consorzio per la Tutela del Rosso Conero, a supervisory body of which Alessandro became the president in 2001. The Moroders firmly believe that wine is made for food, and their restaurant, **Aiòn** ($), housed in a beautifully restored 18th-century barn, offers traditional Marches dishes in which almost all the ingredients, from meat to vegetables, come from the farm.

## Lazio

If Lazio were not so close to Rome, the chances are that Frascati would be almost unknown. There are some interesting examples of this light, dry Trebbiano-Malvasia white, but these are the exceptions to the rule. At least Frascati doesn't take itself too seriously, unlike Est! Est!! Est!!! a usually dull white made from the same grapes that's said to owe its name to an abbreviated exclamation of enthusiasm ("vinum est bonum") by a 12th-century taster. The best wines are unconventional reds like Castel de Paolis's Syrah-based Campovecchio and Colacicchi's Cabernet-Merlot-Cesanese Torre Ercolana.

RESTAURANT LABICO

### Antonello Colonna

Via Roma 89, 00030 Labico
T +39 06-951 0032/951 0314
www.antonellocolonna.it
Contact the restaurant for opening times.
$$$

It is well worth making the 30 km journey south of Rome to Antonello Colonna's eponymous restaurant in which the maestro, who has cooked for Queen Elizabeth II, among other luminaries, spins such succulent variations on Roman cuisine as braised cheek of veal with pecorino mashed potatoes, salt-crusted squab, and salt-cod-filled ravioli. Like the food, the wine list is excellent and will take you by pleasant surprise, with plenty of scope for discovery. Ask to be taken down to the atmospheric cellar.

WINERY ROME

### Azienda Agricola Castel de Paolis

Via Val de Paolis, Grottaferrata, Roma
T+39 06-941 3648
www.casteldepaolis.it
Visits by appointment only.

The myth that Lazio equals Frascati, and insipid Frascati at that, dies hard, even among some wine connoisseurs. Myth debunkers should look no farther than Castel de Paolis, where, under the supervision of owner Adriana Croce Santarelli, world-class red blends, such as I Quattro Mori (Shiraz, Merlot, Cabernet Sauvignon, Petit Verdot) and, indeed, some excellent Frascatis, are putting Lazio back on the vinous map. Two great Italian consultants, Attilio Scienza and Franco Bernabei, have helped bring out the distinctive flavours of the vineyards.

RESTAURANT ROME

### Giuda Ballerino

Via Marco Valerio Corvo 135, 00174 Roma
T +39 06-7158 4807
www.giudaballerino.it
Fri-Tue lunch and dinner; Thu dinner only.
$

Light relief is provided here in the form of stacks of comic-books: chef-proprietor Andrea Fusco is crazy about the art form. Luckily he has more than enough zeal remaining to invest in the cooking. His largely organic and very creative take on Mediterranean cuisine includes dishes as broccoli cooked with Sicilian sardines and squid-ink cannelloni stuffed with buffalo mozzarella, as well as terrific pizzas. The wine list is excellent quality and value, as one would expect from a restaurant twinned with a wine shop.

International Wine Academy of Roma.

WINE SCHOOL — ROME

### International Wine Academy of Roma

Vicolo del Bottino 8, 00187 Roma
T +39 06-699 0878
www.wineacademyroma.com
For dates and times of classes, see the website.

From the moment it opened, this struck me as one of the most exciting and well-sited wine attractions in the world. You could stay at Rome's International Wine Academy for weeks and still want more. For starters, it is located in the 19th-century Il Palazzetto, overlooking the Spanish Steps and within walking distance of most of the city's spectacular sites. The hotel rooms are luxurious ($$-$$$) and the chef Antonio Martucci's take on his native Roman cuisine is fabulous. As for the classes and masterclasses, they offer something for everyone: from an introduction to tasting techniques to more in-depth coverage of specific world winemaking regions (Italy is understandably a strong suit) to seminars led by some of the wine industry's most important figures. The academy also organizes regular visits to Italy's wine regions, including newer ones such as Basilicata.

## Abruzzo and Molise

Like so many other regions in Italy, the Adriatic coastal region of the Abruzzo has changed its image in recent years, from being the source of basic wine for blending (legally or illegally) with more famous wine from further north, to gaining a reputation of its own. This change coincided with better handling of the Montepulciano grape which covers half the vineyards here and is used to make both the red Montepulciano d'Abruzzo and, in a marriage with Cabernet Sauvignon and Merlot, a young DOC called Controguerra. White Trebbiano d'Abruzzo is made from various strains of Trebbiano to which Chardonnay is added to produce white Controguerra.

Molise is tiny, mountainous and relatively poor region with a winemaking history that predates the Romans. Until 1963 it was lumped in with the Abruzzo, which made sense, given the dominance of the Montepulciano (it represents nearly two thirds of the vineyards) and Trebbiano. Now, however, ambitions are rising and other grapes are being exploited, thanks largely to the efforts of di Majo Norante in the village of Campomarino

WINERY — MOLISE

### Di Majo Norante

Fraz. Nuova Cliternia, Via Ramitelli 4, 86042 Campomarino, Molise
T +39 0875- 57208
www.dimajonorante.com
Visits by appointment only.

Tiny Molise, tucked in between Abruzzo and Puglia, often gets ignored in all the stakes, be they touristic or gastronomic. However Alessio Di Majo, like his father Luigi before him, is determined to reverse this phenomenon and put Di Majo Norante on the world's wine map. With the help of the consultant, Riccardo Cotarella, he is succeeding. His trump card has been indigenous, ancient varieties, such as Tintilia, used alone or in blends, but all the wines, which include an excellent Sangiovese, are exciting and good value.

WINERY — CONTROGUERRA

### Dino Illuminati 'Fattoria Nicò'

C da S Biagio 18, 64010 Controguerra
T +39 0861-808 008
www.illuminativini.com
Mon-Fri 0800-1200 and 1430-800;
Sat 0800-1200. Tours and tastings by appointment.

One of the best producers in the Abruzzo, this family-owned winery is also a leading pioneer of the recently created Controguerra DOC, which blends Montepulciano grapes with Cabernet Sauvignon and Merlot for the red, and adds Chardonnay to Trebbiano for the white. Established in 1890, Illuminati is both highly traditional and very modern in its approach, an ideal introduction to the way this region is evolving.

# Mezzogiorno



This region, known as the Mezziogiorno because of the heat of the noonday sun, is where some of the most exciting developments in Italian wine are to be found. Until the early 1980s, with the exception of a few star wineries, this historically poor region was thought of as a place to produce strong red wine to bolster feeble Chianti and Barolo, or as the basis of vermouth. But Basilicata, Calabria, Campania, Puglia, Sardinia and Sicily all have a longer vinous history than many regions further north: Homer wrote of the Cyclops becoming intoxicated after drinking the wine of Etna; Falernum – now known as Falerno del Massico – was the favourite wine of ancient Rome; Greco (Greek) and Uva da Troia grapes commemorate the role of the Ancient Greeks here, and the Etruscans introduced wine to Sardinia as early as the eighth century BC.

The revival of the region can be explained by several factors. First there was the example of the New World and of the Vino da Tavola producers in more northern Italian regions, such as Tuscany, who proved that good wine could be accepted even without a prestigious appellation. Modern technology also played a role, enabling the production of fresher, fruitier, less tannic reds. The south has also benefited from the arrival of foreign buyers (especially from the UK) in search of affordable wine that tastes as good as the now increasingly pricy efforts of Tuscany. A separate important element was the rediscovery of the region's traditional grapes. Puglia certainly profited from the realisation that its Primitivo was the same variety as the Zinfandel but the Negroamaro (bitter black) has also won a growing number of fans. Another rising star, the Aglianico of Campania and Basilicata, is actually one of the oldest varieties in the region and a favourite of the ancient Romans. Finally, there was the human factor. A mixture of dynamic locals and a few investors (such as the Tuscan Antinori) from outside the region accelerated the rate of change. Nowhere was this truer than in Sicily, where the example of a few dynamic estates and the results of a local government-funded study literally revolutionized the average quality of the island's wines. There is still much room for improvement, especially in Calabria, Basilicata and Campania, but progress is being made.

Today, the most interesting wines to look out for are Taurasi and Falerno di Massico from Campania; Aglianico del Vulture from Basilicata and Greco from good producers like Librandi in Calabria. In Puglia the emphasis has been on value-for-money rather than greatness but some of the Primitivos and Negroamaro compare easily to far pricier Californian Zinfandels. Sardinia, once only known for Marsala (little of which deserved a better fate than use in the kitchen) has good Grenache-based Cannonau and Carignan-based Carignano del Sulcis, as well as whites from the Muscat, Malvasia, Vermentino and Nurgaus. Most interesting of all these areas, though, is Sicily with its varied landscape and its array of international grapes: varieties, like the white Catarratto and red Nero d'Avola, that are grown nowhere else, and luscious sweet Malvasia from the island of Lipari.

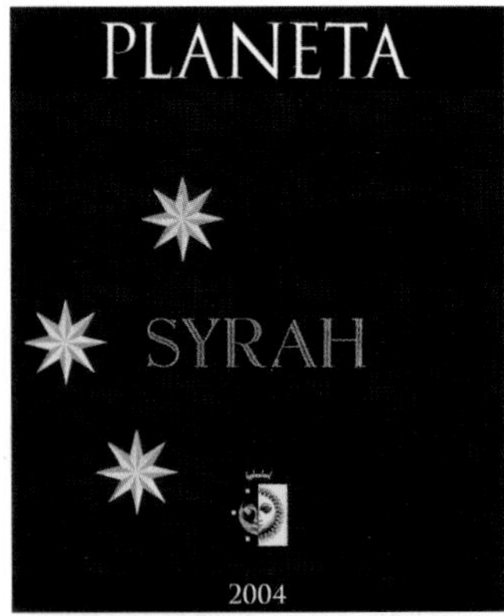

## Calabria

WINERY | CIRO MARINA

### Librandi

SS 106, C da S Gennaro, 88811 Cirò Marina
T +39 0962-31518
www.librandi.it
Visits by appointment only.

Nicodemo and Antonio Librandi are pioneers of southern Italian wine. They produce wines from vineyards close to the Ionian coast and use local grapes like Gaglioppo, Magliocco and Greco, as well as modern blends, including Cabernet Sauvignon for reds such as the masterful Gravello. Make an appointment here to see how fruitfully modern skills are being applied to a classic region.

View over the Bay of Naples.

The waterfront at Corricella on the island of Procida.



## Campania

The region close to Naples was once the source of the wines the Romans prized most highly, such as Falerno (whose name has now been taken by a wine from vineyards far closer to Rome). This hilly, indeed in some cases mountainous, region has, like its southern neighbours, produced frankly ordinary wines, with one brilliant exception in the shape of the Mastroberardino estate. However, also like its neighbours, Campania has recently seen huge improvements in its wines. The most interesting grape here is the Aglianico (from Taurasi and Aglianico del Taburno), which can rival the Piedmont's Nebbiolo for greatness, if properly handled. Also worth looking out for are good exmaples of the local Fiano di Avellino, Falanghina and Greco di Tufo whites.

RESTAURANT NAPLES

### George's

Grand Hotel Parker, Corso Vittorio Emanuele 135, 80121 Naples
T +39 0817-612 474
www.grandhotelparkers.com
Daily for breakfast, lunch and dinner.
$$$

George's, on the rooftop of one of Naples' finest hotels, enjoys a startling view over the Bay of Naples. Come here to escape the chaos of the city and enjoy your wine in peace: lovely sommelier Ylva Andersson has assembled a wine list with fancy as well as offbeat offerings, and is on hand to suggest interesting matches for Chef Baciòt's innovative Mediterranean-inspired cuisine.

# Best producers

**Calabria**
Umberto Ceratti
Ferdinando Messino

**Campania**
Mastroberardino

**Puglia**
Candido
Taurino
Vallone

**Sardinia**
Argiolas
Sella & Mosca » *page 154.*

**Sicily**
Marco de Bartoli
Donnafugata » *page 155.*
Carlo Hauner
Planeta » *page 155.*
Duca di Salaparuta (Duca Enrico)
Tasca d'Almerita (Regaleali) » *page 155.*

## Puglia

Introduced to wine by the Greeks, Puglia became the source, in more recent times, of huge quantities of dark, alcoholic, ordinary red wine. Destiny smiled on the region, however, when outsiders from further north began to exploit local grapes, such as the Primitivo (also known as Zinfandel), Negro Amaro and Uva di Troia. The most interesting DOCs are Salice Salentino, Copertino and Locorotondo, all of which are well made by Azienda dei Conti Leone de Castris.

WINERY SALENTINO

### Leone de Castris

Via Senatore d Castris 50, 73015 Salice Salentino
T +39 0832-731 112/ 0832- 731113/ 0832-733 608
www.leonedecastris.com
Tours and tastings Mon-Fri 0830-1230 and 1500-1800. Shop Mon-Wed, Fri and Sat 0900-1300 and 1630-2030; Thu 0900-1300.

Leone de Castris is among the leaders of Puglia's new-found reputation for premium wine. It is not a new winery, however, having been founded in the 17th century, as the first winery in the fertile Salentine Peninsula, near the remarkable baroque town of Lecce. This is a perfect place from which to explore Puglia, whose desolate-seeming, often-unmarked roads can make finding wineries challenging. Leone de Castris provides a strong introduction to the surprising range of wines that this baking hot, flat region is capable of producing. Book far ahead if you want to arrange a stay ($-$$).

## Sardinia

In 2004, Dutch and Italian archaeologists found grape pips and wine sediment dating from 1200 BC to the north of the island's capital, Cagliari. This discovery may call for a rewriting of history because it suggests that the Cannonau grape, the most widely planted in Sardinia, was brought here from Spain, where it is known as Garnacha. In 1392, Eleonara, governor of the part of the island known as Arborea issued an edict called the Carta de Logu which, among other things, required the inhabitants to plant vines on uncultivated land.

The grapes grown on Sardinia now are principally the red Cannonau and Monica and the white Vermentino and Nuragus, none of which are widely found on the mainland. Production here has dropped from 300 million bottles in the 1970s to around 90 million today but quality has risen. This is especially true of the peppery red Cannonau, the sweet red Monica, the fresh dry Nuragus and Vermentino and the sweet Moscato and Malvasia.

WINERY ALGHERO

### Sella & Mosca

I Piani, 07041 Alghero
T +39 079-997700
www.sellaemosca.com
Contact the winery for opening times.

Planeta's Menfi winery.

Sardinia is coming into its own as a producer of intriguing and excellent value wines. Just on the edge of Alghero, a beautiful medieval town, Sella & Mosca is one of the leading wineries. The winery, under the innovative eye of Mario Consorte, produces excellent Vermentino and blends, such as the Merlot and Cargignano Medeus as well as great liqueur wine. The tour includes the museum, which houses a collection of photographs of the island as well as the remains of a Neolithic settlement uncovered on the estate in 1903.

## Sicily

Colonized by the Greeks between the eighth and sixth centures BC, Sicily now has 130,000 ha of vines and an annual production of 850 million bottles,making it Italy's largest wine region. Despite the existence of 20 DOC regions, most wine was traditionally either distilled or used to beef up wine on the mainland. Even now that quality has improved, less than 2.5% of Sicilian wine is sold with a DOC.

Most of the best wine is Vino da Tavola following the precedent set by the Duca de Salaparuta's Corvo, which was created in 1824 and was, until recently, the island's best known wine. Today, producers like Tasca d'Almerita, Planeta and Donnafugata make great wines from local and international varieties, exploiting Sicily's varied altitudes and microclimates. Look out for examples of the local white Catarratto and Grillo, and the red Nero d'Avola. Marsala is by far the best known DOC but is usually disappointing. Far better are the sweet Moscato di Pantelleria and Malvasia delle Lipari from the small offshore islands.

WINERY PARTINICO

### Cusumano

Contrada San Carlo, 90047 Partinico
T +39 091-890 3456
www.cusumano.it
Visits by appointment only.

Is Sicily New World or Old World? Is this even a viable debate? Cusumano makes a good setting to consider this question. This relatively new winery was founded by two brothers, Alberto and Diego Cusumano, who have recently completed the construction of an extraordinary minimalist winery building made from wood, steel and leather. When it comes to the vineyard, however, the rhetoric is traditional and strictly terroiriste. The expressive potential of each plot is nurtured, a stance that also extends to the olive oil production.

WINERY MARSALA

### Donnafugata

Via S Lipari 18, 91025 Marsala
T +39 0923-724 200
www.donnafugata.it
Mon-Fri 0900-1300 and 1430-1830.

If you are traveling with a reluctant wine tourist, make this the first stop. The Rallo family, who founded this winery in 1983, bring a contagious joy to wine, most notably by combining it with their love of music. José Rallo, daughter of founders Giacomo and Gabriella, frequently participates with her husband in jam sessions both in Sicily and abroad, celebrating wine culture through jazz. If you are lucky enough to be in Marsala in July, you can hear José's amazing voice at the winery's jazz festival. There are other events throughout the year, such as an evening under the stars in August to mark the start of the nocturnal harvest, and if you run into José on your tour she might well honour you with an impromptu ballad.

WINERY MENFI

### Planeta

Contrada Dispensa, 92013 Menfi
T 39 091-612 4335
www.planeta.it
Tue-Sat 0900-1500 by appointment; closed public hols.

Cousins Alessio, Francesca and Santi Planeta have knocked a few clichés on the head, most notably the notion that it takes ages to claw through Sicily's bureaucracy and get anything done. In a matter of years, they have created a first-class winery whose products have zipped around the globe, trailing plaudits in their wake. Check out the excellent website, on which there are suggestions for characterful places to eat, drink and stay all over Sicily, along with contact details.

WINERY PALERMO

### Tasca d'Almerita

C da Regaleali, Loc Sclafani Bagni, 90020 Palermo
T +39 0921-544011
www.tascadalmerita.it
Visits by appointment only.

The noble Tasca D'Almerita family have been prominent on Sicily's social and winemaking scenes for more than a century and a half. Richard Wagner composed the third act of his opera *Parsifal* while wandering in the magical gardens of the family's Villa Tasca near Palermo, and the 500 ha of their Regaleali estate, under two hours away, have been at the forefront of the island's viticultural experimentation. As well as being a top wine destination, Regaleali is a pilgrimage for food lovers, as family member Anna Tasca Lanza, celebrated cook and author, offers wine lunches and residential cooking lessons at an old farmhouse on the estate.

Stained glass at Villa Tasca.

The family has recently added another gem to its empire: **Tenuta Capofaro** (Via Faro 3, 98050 Salina Isole Eolie, T +39 090-984 4330, www.capofaro.it), a 12-room hotel, in the middle of a vineyard on the sun-drenched Aeolian island of Salina. The vineyard is dedicated to the production of a stunning Malvasia di Lipari and, even if you don't stay at this romantic retreat, stop by for lunch, as it produces some of the best food on Salina. Salina, a UNESCO World Heritage Site, was the setting for the film *Il Postino*.

## Vintages

**2005** Very variable.
**2004** Generally very good to great.
**2003** Good but often over-ripe.
**2002** Better for whites than reds.
**2001** Great; possibly better than 2000.
**2000** Very good to great (sometimes over-ripe).

# Germany

Bacharach on the Rhine.

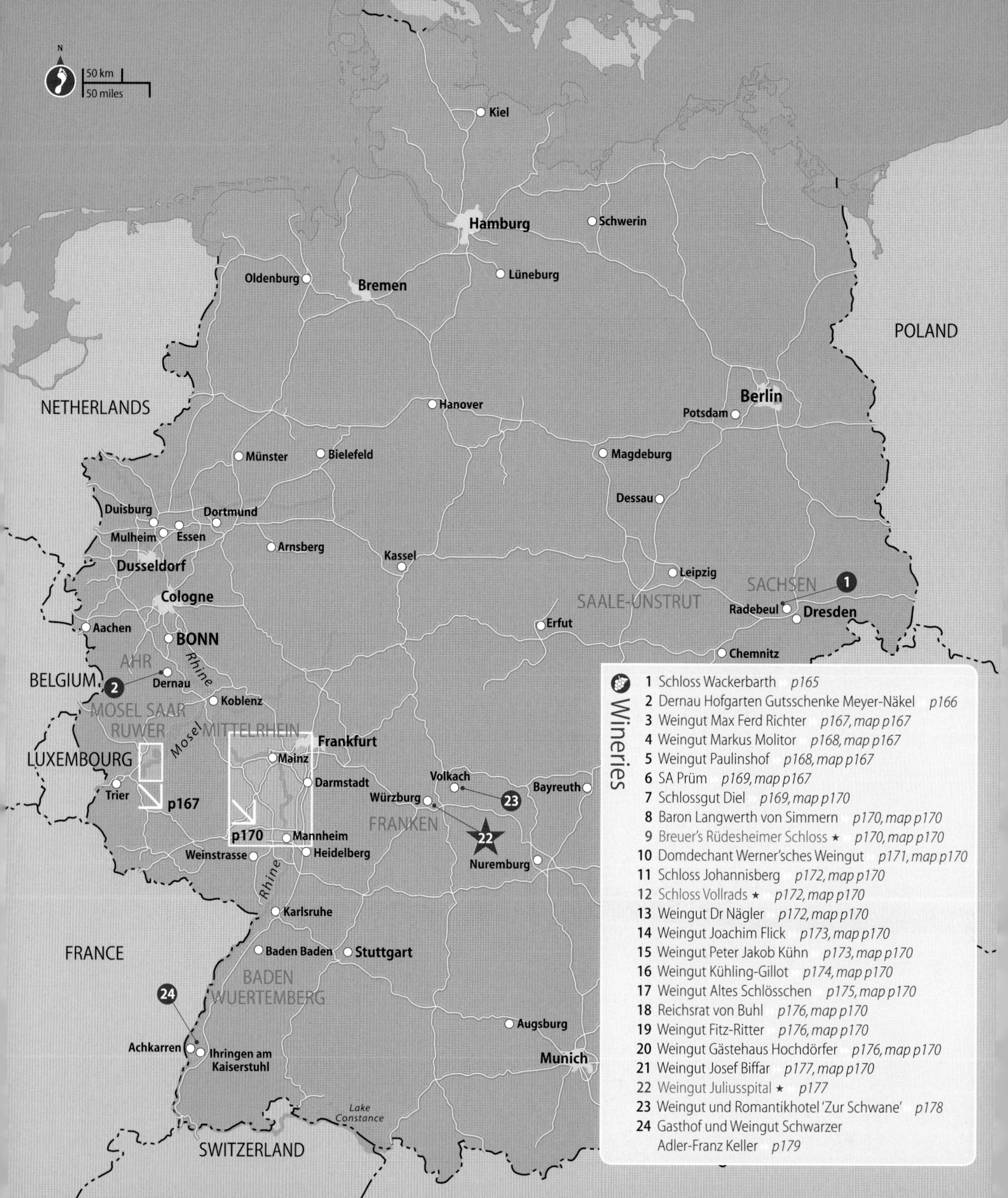
N
50 km
50 miles
Kiel
Hamburg
Schwerin
Oldenburg
Bremen
Lüneburg
POLAND
NETHERLANDS
Hanover
Berlin
Potsdam
Münster
Bielefeld
Magdeburg
Dessau
Duisburg
Dortmund
Mulheim
Essen
Arnsberg
Kassel
Dusseldorf
Leipzig
SACHSEN
Cologne
SAALE-UNSTRUT
Radebeul
Dresden
Aachen
Erfut
BONN
Chemnitz
AHR
Rhine
BELGIUM
Dernau
Koblenz
MOSEL SAAR RUWER
Mosel
MITTELRHEIN
Frankfurt
LUXEMBOURG
Mainz
Darmstadt
Volkach
Bayreuth
Trier
p167
Würzburg
p170
Mannheim
FRANKEN
Weinstrasse
Heidelberg
Nuremburg
Rhine
Karlsruhe
FRANCE
Baden Baden
Stuttgart
BADEN WUERTEMBERG
Augsburg
Achkarren
Ihringen am Kaiserstuhl
Munich
Lake Constance
SWITZERLAND
Wineries
1 Schloss Wackerbarth p165
2 Dernau Hofgarten Gutsschenke Meyer-Näkel p166
3 Weingut Max Ferd Richter p167, map p167
4 Weingut Markus Molitor p168, map p167
5 Weingut Paulinshof p168, map p167
6 SA Prüm p169, map p167
7 Schlossgut Diel p169, map p170
8 Baron Langwerth von Simmern p170, map p170
9 Breuer's Rüdesheimer Schloss ★ p170, map p170
10 Domdechant Werner'sches Weingut p171, map p170
11 Schloss Johannisberg p172, map p170
12 Schloss Vollrads ★ p172, map p170
13 Weingut Dr Nägler p172, map p170
14 Weingut Joachim Flick p173, map p170
15 Weingut Peter Jakob Kühn p173, map p170
16 Weingut Kühling-Gillot p174, map p170
17 Weingut Altes Schlösschen p175, map p170
18 Reichsrat von Buhl p176, map p170
19 Weingut Fitz-Ritter p176, map p170
20 Weingut Gästehaus Hochdörfer p176, map p170
21 Weingut Josef Biffar p177, map p170
22 Weingut Juliusspital ★ p177
23 Weingut und Romantikhotel 'Zur Schwane' p178
24 Gasthof und Weingut Schwarzer Adler-Franz Keller p179

# Introduction



Ask most wine experts around the world to name their favourite white grape and a substantial number will choose the Riesling. Then ask them where they'd look for the finest Riesling and, nearly without exception, they'd opt for Germany. Sadly, this enthusiasm is not so widely shared among wine drinkers, who all too often associate German wine with cheap sugary stuff by the name of Liebfraumilch or Hock. This lack of appreciation for German wine is actually a recent phenomenon. In 1896 the London merchant Berry Brothers and Co offered 1862 wines from Rüdesheim and Marcobrunn for 200 shillings per dozen; 56 shillings more than they were asking for their priciest red, the 1870 Lafite. Two world wars and a few decades when far too many producers focused on quantity rather than quality, wrought huge damage to the image of German wine. This was not helped by a brief period during the 1980s and early 1990s when supposedly quality-conscious producers misguidedly made large amounts of viciously acidic dry wines.

The renaissance of German wine began in the late 1990s, with the arrival of a new generation of winemakers, who took a fresh look at every aspect of the German wine industry. Today, this is quietly becoming one of the most exciting wine countries in the world. Famous regions like the Rheingau and Mosel are back on track and new domaines in areas like the Pfalz are producing dazzling wines. Previously overlooked areas like Baden, Franken and, to a lesser extent, Sachsen and Saale-Unstrut in what was once East Germany are all making impressive wines too. And it's not just Riesling. Look out too for Pinot Gris (known here as Grauburgunder) and Pinot Noir (known as Spätburgunder and Frühburgunder).

# Travel essentials

## Planning a trip

Germany's most important airport is **Frankfurt-Rhein-Main** (FRA, T +49 (0)1805-372 4636, www.frankfurt-airport.de) the hub for Lufthansa and for major international and domestic flights. Rheingau, Rheinhessen and Franken are all easily accessible from Frankfurt by either road or rail. Alternative points of entry include **Cologne** for the Mittelrhein, the Ahr and the Mosel, and **Stuttgart** for Baden-Württemberg. If you're focusing on the east of the country, you're likely to fly into **Berlin** or **Dresden**. As an alternative to flying, international trains run to Germany from most European cities; from the UK the Eurostar service connects with the high-speed route from Brussels to Cologne. The German rail network (run by Deutsche Bahn, www.bahn.de) is fully integrated and famously efficient. Standard fares are not cheap but a number of special tickets and passes make this an appealing way of exploring the country. Access to Germany by road is equally straightforward and the country's *Autobahn* network makes driving a quick means of travelling around. All major car hire firms are represented at airports and in the main towns. For details of river transport, see page 166.

Dedicated wine tourists are likely to focus their visit around the Rhine and the Mosel, where the vast majority of German wine is produced. Fortunately this area is rich in sights and scenery, many of which can be enjoyed by boat (page 166), and is easily accessible from both **Cologne** (Köln), with its awesome cathedral, and **Frankfurt**. **Mainz** is the unofficial capital of German wine and also boasts a church, St Stephan's, with Chagall windows. Further west, the Roman remains in **Trier**, the ancient cathedral at **Aachen** and the forested valleys of the **Eiffel** region are well worth a detour. South of Frankfurt, you can follow the **Deutsche Weinstraße** through the Pfalz, or visit the beautiful, historic towns of **Worms**, **Speyer** and **Heidelberg**. The spa town of **Baden Baden** is the gateway to the **Black Forest**, while, further east, **Lake Constance** (Bodensee) stretches along the Swiss border, backed by views of the Alps. There's more stunning mountain scenery in southern **Bavaria**, not to mention fairytale castles, built by Kaiser Ludwig II. **Munich** is one of the country's most appealing and culturally vibrant cities but you should take time out from the beer halls to visit Bavaria's well preserved medieval towns, many of which are linked by the '**Romantic Road**' from Würzburg to the Alps. In the northeast, **Berlin** warrants several visits to appreciate its complex past and dynamic present. And, with its baroque architecture and artistic legacy now restored, **Dresden** is a beautiful base from which to visit the wineries of **Sachsen**, not to mention the dramatic scenery of the Sächsische Schweiz and the watery landscape of the Spreewald.

**Germany country code** → +49. **IDD code** → 00.
**Internet ID** → .de. **Emergencies** → T 110 and T 112.

## → Fact file

| | |
|---|---|
| **International flights** | Lufthansa, Germany's national airline, and other international carriers fly into all of Germany's major cities. Budget airlines also operate services to smaller, regional airports. |
| **Entry requirements** | UK citizens require a valid passport to enter and stay in Germany for up to three months; no visa required. |
| **Currency** | Euro (€1). |
| **Time zone** | GMT +1. Daylight saving Mar/Apr-Sep/Oct. |
| **Electricity** | 230 volts (50Hz). Plugs have either 2 round or 2 flat pins. |
| **Licensing hours** | These vary throughout the country, with some bars in major cities staying open until 0500. |
| **Minimum age** | 16 for beer and wine; 18 for spirits. |
| **Drink-drive restrictions** | 30 mg of alcohol per 100 ml of blood. |

For further information about visiting Germany, refer to the official website, www.germany-info.org. Within the country, tourist information in English is provided by offices in almost every town.

Cochem on the Mosel.

Kabinett Riesling is Germany's most under-appreciated wine style and the world's best accompaniment to Asian food.

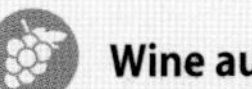

Grapevine

**Wine auctions**

Close to harvest time and well worth visiting if you are a German wine fan are the four wine auctions held on consecutive days in late September at which some of the best and lesser producers offer new and older vintages under the hammer. The pre-auction tastings, although very crowded, are fascinating experiences. Three of these – the Mosel, the Rheingau, and Ahr and Nahe – are run by the VdP (page 163), while the fourth, the Bernkasteler Ring, covers Mosel estates that are not members of the VdP. For details of the VdP events go to www.vdp.de. For the Bernkasteler Ring, go to www.bernkasteler-ring.com.



### When to visit

Summers in Germany are generally warm and quite humid, with temperatures averaging 25°C. Cold winters can see temperatures drop well below 0°C. At higher levels snow can start to fall in November. The ideal time to visit is from April until late summer and, again, in October after the harvest. Throughout the country, there are small and large wine and food festivals; the Rhine alone has 500, with a further 300 along the Mosel and at least another 200 along the Main and Neckar rivers and elsewhere. The **German Wine Institute** (www.deutschewein.de) in Mainz has details of these, but in any case, during the warmer months, you are unlikely to be far from one.

### Wine tourism

Compared to its neighbour across the Rhine, Germany does wine tourism pretty well. There are castles that really do deserve the adjective 'fairy-tale' as well as historical manor houses and, uniquely, numerous impeccably run Staatsweingüter (state wine estates). There are also many vineyards with restaurants. Visitors are welcome throughout the regions, though preferably by appointment, and, although each wine area has its own identity, the German Wine Institute is an invaluable information resource for the country as a whole.

### Sleeping

Accommodation in Germany ranges from luxury designer hotels with spa facilities to basic farm-stay rooms with clean sheets and hot water. Most hotels are rated from one to five stars and priced accordingly, although, at the lower end of the scale, stars aren't necessarily a guarantee of quality. Hotels tend to be better value than in the UK or USA, except in tourist areas, such as the Rhine and the Mosel, in peak season, and in cities during trade fairs. At other times it is quite possible to find a comfortable double with ensuite bathroom in the heart of a major city for as little as €85, including buffet breakfast. Visitors with more to spend will be spoiled for choice. No-frills pensions are a cheaper alternative, as are the ubiquitous hostels. Most tourist offices can advise on farm-stay or self-catering options and will also help visitors to find a room for a nominal fee; otherwise, consult the website www.germany-tourism.co.uk, which has a hotel finder.

### Eating

Beer (*Bier*) is a national institution in Germany, with literally hundreds , if not thousands, of breweries, beer halls and pubs producing their own. German beer tends to taste stronger than other European or American beers and is the usual accompaniment to much German food. Traditional German dishes tend to be wholesome, hearty and plentiful. Pork products, particularly sausages (*Wurst*), are the mainstay, often served with mashed potato (*Kartoffelpüree*), chips (*Pommes frites*) or potato salad (*Kartoffelsalat*). (Sausages are also eaten as a fast-food snack, bought from stalls on the street.) Other common accompaniments include *Sauerkraut* (pickled cabbage), *Knödel* (dumplings) and, in southern Germany, *Spätzle* (egg noodles). There are hundreds of different local dishes to try, many of which are only available in certain regions, but wherever you go, you'll find a variation of *Wienerschnitzel* (a thin slice of pork, covered in egg and breadcrumbs and then fried). In the Black Forest, look out for game-based dishes, such as *Rehrücken* (venison tenderloin). In this meat-dominated environment, vegetarian visitors need to beware seemingly innocuous dishes that have been prepared or spiced up with meat stock. Visitors who find most German food too heavy for their taste will not want to miss *Kaffee und Kuchen* (coffee and cakes), traditionally served in the mid afternoon and a chance to indulge in Germany's cakes and pastries. It is also worth noting that Germany's domestic cuisine is supplemented by foreign dishes. Flavours from all corners of the globe are available in the major cities, with Asian food providing a perfect match for the best Kabinett Riesling.

# Wine essentials

## History

The history of German wine can be traced back to the Romans, who produced wine here in the first century BC, if not before. A green-yellow glass amphora with handles in the shape of dolphins dating from AD 325 was found in a stone sarcophagus at Speyer in 1867. It contained sediment and the residue of what was probably the oil used to protect it from the air. The amphora is still to be seen at the Historisches Museum der Pfalz in Speyer (www.museum.speyer.de).

The eighth-century emperor Charlemagne, who also took an interest in winegrowing in Burgundy, is said to have ordered the planting of vines on the steeply sloping banks of the Rhine at Johannisberg or Rudesheim, after noticing that the snow melted here earlier than elsewhere. Over the following century, there was a boom in winemaking, with some 400 monastic vineyards along the Rhine. Large amounts of wine began to be sold across northern Europe and shipped to England. Towns like Strasbourg (Alsace was then part of Germany) and Cologne were the centre of wine trading and many of the monastic estates whose wines they sold, such as Kloster Eberbach and Schloss Johannisberg, still survive. This was, however, the heyday of German wine; in the 15th century, Germany had four times as many vines as it does today.

Curiously, for those who associate Germany with the Riesling grape, this variety does not seem to have been grown seriously until 1435. Before that, the duller Elbling was widely grown, along with the Trollinger, Silvaner, Spätburgunder, Muscat and Gewürztraminer. Even after the 15th century, evidence suggests that it wasn't until 1720, when a vineyard that consisted entirely of Riesling was planted at Schloss Johannisberg, that this grape was grown by itself.

In the 17th century, the overplanting of the previous years led to a wine glut and the uprooting of vineyards. It was then, too, that beer first began to gain the upper hand. Faced with the competition from the brewers, winemakers began to focus on improving quality. In 1712 Kloster Eberbach introduced the term Cabinet (which subsequently became Kabinett) to describe its best wine and 41 years later made wine from grapes that had been affected by noble rot. This, however, was merely a prelude to the achievement of Schloss Johannisberg in 1775, when an accidentally delayed harvest led to the first production of wine made from mostly nobly rotten grapes. Thus were Spätlese (late harvest) and Auslese born.

If the 15th century was the high point of German wine in quantity terms, the 19th century brought the apogee of its prestige. This was a time of technological improvements (partly driven by the French occupiers) and the development of a market for single estate wines that sold in London at higher prices than top Bordeaux. (These were, one should remember, also the days when the popular British queen was married to a German prince.) Unfortunately, while Germany's great wines basked in critical and commercial sunlight, German winemakers were beginning for the first time to sugar their poorest wines, a practice that would open the door to the floods of cheap Liebfraumilch and Hock that tarnished the image of German wine so much in the 20th century.

## Understanding German wine

There is no getting around it, German wine labels can be a nightmare, even when the words are not printed in indecipherable Gothic script. Almost all German wine should fit into one of three categories. The finest wine is **Qualitätswein mit Prädikat** (QmP), but this category, which is based on natural ripeness, can cover 10-75% of the annual crop. Within this category are the better known categories of, in ascending levels of ripeness, Kabinett, Spätlese, Auslese, Beerenauslese and Trockenbeerenauslese, with Eiswein as the ultra-sweet wild card. The last four of these will be sweet – lusciously so in the case of the Beerenauslese and Trockenbeerenauslese – while the first three might be sweet or dry. Dry wines may also bear the word '*Trocken*' and will certainly have higher alcohol levels (12%, for example, compared to 8% for a sweeter wine).

Beneath QmP, there is a secondary designation of **Qualitätswein bestimmter Anbaugebiete** (QbA), which covers wine whose alcohol has been boosted with grape concentrate (illegal for QmP) and supposedly refers to wines from specific regions. Unfortunately, this category covers everything from delicious efforts from good estates in less warm vintages to a torrent of the poorest-quality Liebfraumilch and Hock.

Lower still on the scale are **Landwein** and **Deutscher Tafelwein** but, given the generosity of the use of QbA, these are, sadly, quite rare. Occasionally, good producers use Deutscher Tafelwein for interesting non-traditional wines.

The worst part of the nightmare, though, is the wine name itself, such as Niersteiner Brudersberg or Niersteiner Gutes Domtal. People with intimate knowledge of German wine would know that Brudersberg is one of Germany's 2600 small vineyards (*Einzellage*),

Ralf Schafer wines.

close to the village of Nierstein (and thus potentially a source of good wine). Gutes Domtal on the other hand is a huge area (*Grosslage*), usually associated with stuff that is cheap and nasty and produced somewhere within driving diustance of Nierstein. Some of Germany's over 150 Grosslages are much smaller and associated with quality. One word of which you should always be wary when it appears on a label, however, is '*Bereich*', such as Bereich Bernkastel or Bereich Johannisberg. This indicates wine that has come from a huge area that could cover two or three thousand hectares.

Recently, if belatedly, attempts have been made to come up with Grand Cru-style designations for Germany's best Einzellage. Needless to say, this has been done inconsistently. In the Mosel-Saar-Ruwer the term is '*Erste Lage*', in the Rheingau it is '*Erstes Gewachs*', while other regions use '*Grosses Gewachs*'. In the Rheingau, over a third of the vineyards are now officially Grand Crus; elsewhere, the figure is, sensibly, lower. Fortunately, many producers are now beginning to simplify their labels and some are adopting the terms 'Classic' and 'Selection', which are supposed to describe good and very good dry wines.

There are a few additional signs that may indicate that a wine is better than others on the shelf. Gold-coloured capsules that conceal the cork are used by some producers for their best wine, with longer capsules going on the very best bottles. These, however, carry no legal weight. Of much greater value is the eagle symbol indicating membership of a quality-focused association, universally known as the **VdP** (Verband deutscher Prädikats- und Qualitätsweingüter).

### White grapes

**Gewürztraminer/Roter Traminer** Spicy, with a lychee and rose-petal character.

**Grauburgunder/Pinot Gris/Ruländer** A very successful grape in the Pfalz, Rheingau and Baden. Spicy, with a flavour that can put one in mind of pears. Sweeter versions are labelled as Ruländer.

**Huxelrebe** Slightly grapey and spicy but generally undistinguished.

**Kerner** A recently developed German grape made, unusually, by crossing a white Riesling with a black Trollinger grape. Often acidic and dull, but can display a leafy, floral character.

**Müller-Thurgau** The most widely planted modern grape variety in Germany but not responsible for any of Germany's best wines.

**Riesling** The finest white grape in Germany, or elsewhere, produces rich dry wines, light off-dry ones (Kabinett) and luscious late-harvest examples, as well as Germany's best Sekt (sparkling wine).

**Scheurebe** The most successful of the recently developed grapes, this one has an extraordinary grapefruit character.

**Silvaner** Traditionally dull and non-aromatic, but when well made (in Franken) it can be floral and attractive.

**Weissburgunder/Pinot Blanc** Popular for rich creamy wines.

### Red grapes

**Dornfelder** A recently developed variety with a character of wild mulberries.

Extremely ripe Riesling.

**Lemberger** Like the Dornfelder, but more cherry-like.

**Portugieser/Blauer Portugieser** A widely grown Austrian grape with no link to Portugal. Wines are light, easy drinking but rarely distinguished.

**Spätburgunder/Blauburgunder/Pinot Noir/Frühburgunder** The Pinot Noir is one of Germany's success stories, with world-class examples produced in several southern regions. Normally known as the Spätburgunder ('late Burgundy'), a separate strain called the Frühburgunder ('early Burgundy') shows real promise.

**Trollinger** Late-ripening grape (known as Schiava in Italy) that is only grown in Württemberg. Wines are light and fresh, not to say acidic in cooler years.

## Vintages

**2005** Great across the board.

**2004** Good, fresh wines, without the richness of 2003 and 2005.

**2003** Many wines are too big and rich but there were some great late-harvest examples. Reds are better than whites.

**2002** Generally very good to great whites, despite late-season storms.

**2001** Great red and white.

**2000** Poor.

**1999** Mixed.

# Germany



**Although the vineyards overlooking the Mosel produce some of Germany's finest Rieslings, the country's greatest wine river has to be the Rhine. Heading south, upstream, it passes through Mittelrhein, heads west along its tributary, the Nahe, and then sweeps to the east, with the Rheingau, its historic heartland, on the north bank sloping down to another tributary, the Main. The Rheinhessen covers a vast swathe of land within the bend of the river, much of it a long way from the water. Further south, are the warmer, riper Pfalz and ultimately, Baden.**

The vineyards overlooking the Mosel may produce some of Germany's finest Rieslings, but the country's greatest wine river has to be the Rhine.

## Hamburg

Too well known for its red light district, Hamburg, Germany's second biggest city, also boasts canals, parks and gardens and the trappings of its wealthy mercantile past.

RESTAURANT REIMERSTWIETE

### Weinrestaurant Shoppenhauer

M+K Gastronomie GmbH, Reimerstwiete 20-22
T +49 (0)40-371 510
www.weinrestaurant-schoppenhauer.de
Mon-Fri 1200-2300; Sat from 1800 or by appointment.
$

If you are looking to accompany traditional, rustic German cuisine with decent wine you should drop by this cosy wine tavern in the centre of Hamburg, which is housed in a 400-year old half-timbered repository with sturdy oak beams. In summer, you also have the choice of sitting outside in the leafy courtyard. The owners will arrange special sightseeing tours of the city for groups of more than 15 people.

## Berlin

Fifteen years after the wall came down, Berlin has regained much of its raffish pre-war spirit. It is now one of the coolest cities in Europe, with a wide range of culture and cuisine on offer, not to mention the continent's largest postwar reconstruction project around the Potsdamer Platz.

WINE BAR BERLIN MITTE

### Weinbar Rutz

Chausseestraße 8, Berlin Mitte
T +49 (0)30-2462 8760
www.rutz-weinbar.de
Mon-Sat 1700-2400
$$

There are never fewer than 1001 wines on sommelier Jürgen Hammer's list at this bustling, unpretentious restaurant just a short walk from Unter den Linden and the cool nightlife of the Hackescher Markt quarter. The restaurant also doubles as a wine shop so all the wines are available to either drink with your meal, subject to a corkage charge of €15, or to take home should you find something particularly enjoyable. Chef Marco Müller serves up an unusual international-style menu, featuring dishes that include an innovative take on crème brûlée using cream cheese and thyme, and leg of lamb with olive-potato purée and peppered figs. The small bar downstairs is a cosy spot, with a smattering of tables and walls lined with floor-to-ceiling wine racks.

## Saale-Unstrut and Sachsen

These two northern regions have only recently rejoined the mainstream of German wine. As elsewhere in the eastern block, quality was rarely a major consideration for the collectivist authorities and, while a few estates did their best to maintain standards, there was a shift towards producing ordinary Müller-Thurgau white, sparkling wine and reds for local consumption. Over the last decade and a

Away from the Rhine, Saale-Unstrut, southwest of Leipzig, is one of Germany's most promising wine regions.

half, there has been something of a renaissance in both regions, which, like the south of Britain, whose latitude they share, have benefited from some unusually warm summers. Whites, at their best, tend to be delicate, aromatic and fresh, while reds are often a little too light for most modern tastes. Saale Unstrut now claims to be the world's most northern fine wine region, but 'fine' may still be overstating it slightly. Gunter Born and Lutzkendorf are the producers to look out for here. Sachsen boast two starrier estates in the shape of Schloss Proschwitz (arguably the region's top producer) and Schloss Wackerbarth, both of which are well equipped to welcome visitors.

WINERY RADEBEUL

### Schloss Wackerbarth

Sächsisches Staatsweingut GmbH,
Wackerbarthstraße 1, Radebeul
T +49 (0)351-89550,
www.schloss-wackerbarth.de
Mon-Fri 1200-2200; Sat and Sun 1000-2200.

Tucked away in Radebeul, close to Dresden, this is one of Germany's largest estates. Beneath the vineyards, many of whose grapes are used to make the Schloss's Sekt sparkling wine, there is a belvedere which overlooks some of the world's most precisely trimmed box hedges. All of this provides a perfect setting for the concerts that are regularly held here. The tour is one of the most informative in Germany and the restaurant ($$) one of the most popular with Dresdeners in quest of a romantic evening.

## Cologne

The city that takes its name from the Roman town of Colonia is best known for its mighty Gothic cathedral and its carnival, but it is also one of Germany's most vibrant cultural centres. There's plenty to see here but most people miss out on one of Cologne's curiosities: the Schokoladenmuseum or the Imhoff- Stollwerck Museum of the Past and Present of Chocolate at Rheinauhafen 1a; it's well worth the detour.

RESTAURANT COLOGNE

### Vintage

Pfeilstraße 31-35, Köln
T +49 (0)221-920 710
www.weinseminare.de
Mon-Sat 11am-2400; Fri and Sat 1100-0100.
$$-$$$

To my mind, Vintage is the kind of place that every city should have. It's a novel combination of restaurant, wine bar and private dining room that also doubles as an upscale wine shop. Bottles are stored in floor-to-ceiling shelves, giving it the appearance of a wine library. Diners can choose from a selection of more than 900 wines, as all the shop's stock appears on the restaurant list at a modest markup. The menu includes traditional German dishes, such as roast suckling pig with honey-glazed cabbage and the southwest German speciality, *Badische Schupfnudln* (a type of home-made potato noodles). The Habana Room is the place to retire to after dinner if you wish to indulge in one of the selection of over 50 cigars from the Dominican Republic and Cuba.

Cologne's iconic cathedral.

## Rivers of wine

The Rhine valley is packed with sights and, although it's a bit of a tourist cliché, a Rhine cruise really does afford you the best view of them. The **KD Linie** (Frankenwerft 35, Cologne, T +49 (0)22-208 8318, www.k-d.com), which operates along the Rhine, Main and Mosel rivers, has 14 different boats, from a new super-catamaran, the MS *RheinEnergie*, to a range of more traditional paddle steamers. One of the best places to join the scheduled services is **Koblenz** at the confluence of the Rhine and the Mosel. From here, you can either travel south towards Rüdesheim or west on the Mosel towards Cochem.

South of Koblenz, the Rhine is at its most scenic. It is here that the notion of the 'Romantic Rhine', with its dramatic castles and steep vineyards, first flourished in the 18th century. You'll see numerous wine villages, the vineyards that follow the path of the river and the **Lorelei** rock, whose siren, legend has it, lured numerous fishermen to their deaths. On the other side of the river at St Goar are the ruins of the 13th-century **Burg Rheinfels** (T +49 (0)6771-599093, www.burg-rheinfels.com), once the biggest and most impressive castle on the Rhine. **Bacharach** is a small town that was once a prosperous centre of the wine trade, as is evident from its castles and half-timbered houses. Further south, as the Rhine swings east towards Mainz and enters the Rheingau wine region, is the little town of **Rüdesheim**, which has a good wine museum (T +49 (0)6722-2348, www.rheingauer-weinmuseum.de) and a wine festival in August. Enjoy a winetasting at **Weingut Dr Nägler** (page 172) before retiring to **Breuer's Rüdesheimer Schloss** (page 170) for a meal and a good night's sleep.

To properly explore the Mosel wine region, its probably best to take the boat as far as Cochem and then hire a car in order to visit the wineries of the Mittelmosel. En route from Koblenz, you'll pass **Burg Eltz** (Münstermaifeld, T +49 (0)2672-950500, www.burgeltz.de), perched high above the river. This is one of Germany's most romantic-looking castles, with sheer walls and tightly packed, slate-roofed towers. **Cochem** itself is also dominated by a hilltop castle and surrounded by vineyards. Take the chairlift from the centre of town for great views of the river below.

## Ahr

Paradoxically, despite appearing on the map as the most northerly of Germany's quality wine regions (a group to which Saale-Unstrut and Sachsen don't quite belong), the Ahr has a surprisingly warm climate in which the midday temperatures in August can actually be too hot to work in the vineyards. The explanation lies in fact that this deep, narrow valley acts as a sun-trap. This is savage, rocky country, good for walking and contemplation (Beethoven was a frequent visitor), where vines thrive on the steep river slopes. Over four out of every five bottles is red (Pinot Noir and Portugusier, generally), the quality of which has improved hugely in recent years thanks to the huge growth of demand in Germany for good German reds. Riesling is still the most widely planted white grape but fans of this variety will be disappointed to learn that it represents less than 8% of the vineyards, and seems unlikely to increase that proportion very significantly.

WINERY — DERNAU

### Dernau Hofgarten Gutsschenke Meyer-Näkel

Bachstraße 26, Dernau
T +49 (0)2643-1540
www.hofgarten-dernau.de
Restaurant daily 1100-2300.

Since taking over the 21-acre family estate in 1983, Werner Näkel has gone on to win numerous awards for his wines, including *Vinum* magazine's Best German Pinot Noir trophy and Gault Millau's Best German Red Wine award (for his '94 Meyer-Näkel 'S' Pinot Noir). He was also was the first Ahr Valley winegrower to be named German Winemaker of the Year by the Gault Millau wine guide. The estate produces wines mostly from Pinot Noir and was one of the first German wineries to start using French barriques to age its wines. The restaurant next door to the winery is a picturesque delight, set in the heart of this traditional German wine village. It has a cheerful outside eating area and serves hearty traditional German dishes, such as *Bratkartoffeln* (German-style sautéed potatoes) and *Blutwurst* (blood sausage), alongside a selection of the estate's wines.

## Mittelrhein

The Mittelrhein – the stretch of the river to the east of the Ahr between Bonn and Bingen – is a dying region. Today it has less than half of the 1200 ha of vines that it had in 1945. Riesling is king here and it can be good, but much of it is used to make sparkling wine. However, producers like Tony Jost in Bacharach show what can be done. The best way to see this region is from a boat, heading south from Koblenz (see above).

## Mosel-Saar-Ruwer

For many people, this is home to Germany's best Kabinett Riesling, the country's most under-appreciated style and the world's

The Mosel at Bernkastel.

Old crane on the Mosel near Trier.

best accompaniment to Asian food. The Mosel river twists and turns in such a snakelike manner that it takes nearly 250 km to cover a distance of little more than 110 km on a map. To say that the best slopes are steep is an understatement; in some parts the vines grow out of what looks like solid slate at an angle of 70 degrees. Tending these vines is a feat of mountaineering, as is the regular task of replacing soil that has been washed down by the rain.

The combination of the coolish climate in this northern area, the intensity of the sun on the steep slopes and the heat retention of the slate all contribute to a unique floral character that is the hallmark of the best wines. However, there is plenty of Mosel wine that does not come from these hills; avoid ordinary Mosel bearing the name Bereich Bernkastel, for example. The Mosel is in fact a tributary of the Rhine and its own pair of tributaries, the Saar and Ruwer, are too small to have their own separate identities. They do however boast some of Germany's top estates and vineyards. such as Egon Müller's Scharzhofberg in the Saar (which is shared with Von Kesselstatt; see below) and Maximin Grünhauser's Abstberg in Ruwer. Top Mosel producers include Theo Haart of **Weingut Reinhold Haart** (T +49 (0)6507-2015, www.haart.de), whose family has been making wine in Piesport for more than 650 years. Haart's winemaking style accentuates the purity of fruit and minerality of his Goldtröpfchen vineyards.

HOTEL TRABEN-TRARBACH

## Bellevue Hotel

Am Moselufer, Traben-Trarbach
T +49 (0)6541-7030
www.bellevue-hotel.de
$$

This fine building on the banks of the Mosel dates from the art nouveau period and is one of the best hotels to be found along the Mosel valley. Designed in 1903 by the noted architect Bruno Möhring, it features elaborate timberwork and a domed tower with a high-pitched roof, gables, and dormer windows. Many of the cosy rooms are furnished with antiques and the colour scheme throughout is dark wood furniture with royal blue carpets. The **Clauss-Feist Restaurant** ($$) is a popular local romantic spot for both breakfast and dinner, with stained-glass windows and an old-world ambience. There's also an ivy-covered terrace for dining outside.

WINERY MUELHEIM

## Weingut Max Ferd Richter

Hauptstraße 37/85, Mülheim
T +49 (0)6534-933 003
www.maxferdrichter.com
Mon-Fri 0900-1200, 1300-1800;
Sat by appointment only.

Founded over 300 years ago, this family estate has a traditional winery constructed from the local slate and a cellar that is stocked entirely with old oak casks. It is now in the hands of Dr Dirk Richter and winemaker

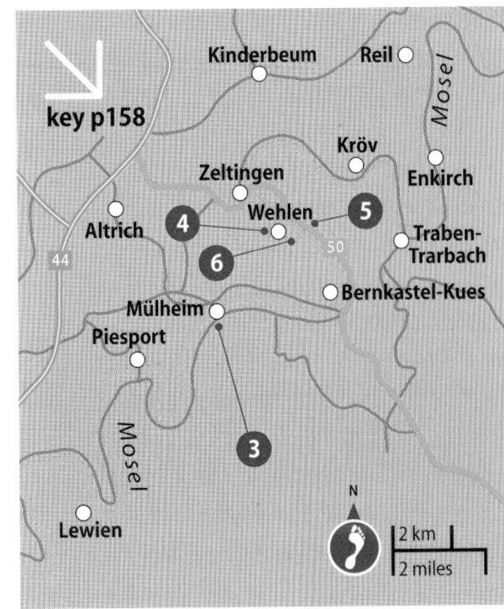


Germany Mosel-Saar-Ruwer

## Tasting notes

**Riesling**

Ask most wine professionals to name their favourite white grape and the chances are that the one they'll come up with will be Riesling. So what makes this variety so special, when compared to, say, Chardonnay or Sauvignon Blanc? The answer lies in a combination of qualities: the Riesling could be described as the naked grape: the variety that needs no help from oak barrels or other grapes. It is unique in its versatility, being able to produce a wide range of wines; from sweet examples with an alcoholic strength of as little as 9% to rich dry ones with 13%. Like the Pinot Noir (many of those same experts' top red) it brilliantly conveys the character of the soil in which it is grown. And nowhere does it do this better than on the slatey hillsides of Germany's best vineyards.

Walter Hauth, who is himself from a famous Mosel winegrowing family in Wehlen. The Baroque-style estate house and gardens dating from 1774 are unchanged and tourist landmarks in their own right. Eisweins from the Mülheimer Helenkloster vineyard are a speciality of the estate, which was the only one to produce a Mosel Eiswein in 1976. Should you wish to stay overnight, there are a couple of classy hotels close by, the **Richtershof** (four-star superior) and the **Weisser Bär** (five-star).

WINE MUSEUM — BERNKASTEL-KUES

### Mosel Weinmuseum & Vinothek

Weinkulturelles Zentrum Bernkastel-Kues, Cusanusstraße 2, Bernkastel-Kues
T +49 (0)6531-4141
www.bernkastel-vinothek.de
Museum mid Apr-end of Oct daily 1000-1700; winter daily 1400-1700. Vinothek daily 1400-1700 or by appointment.
Wine tasting €9.

On the banks of the river Mosel, at the foot of the bridge that joins the wine villages of Bernkastel and Kues on either side, sits the Mosel wine museum. It provides an opportunity to see how wine was made in days gone by, with displays of traditional vineyard tools and cellar equipment, including an extensive collection of wine glasses and bottles. You can also book a wine-tasting session in the neighbouring vinothek (wine shop).

WINERY — BERNKASTEL-WEHLEN

### Weingut Markus Molitor

Haus Klosterberg, Bernkastel-Wehlen
T +49 (0)6532-3939
www.markusmolitor.com
Mon-Fri 0900-1800; Sat and Sun by appointment.
Wine tasting €7 (including bread and cheese).

This is the largest estate in the Middle Mosel, with 38 ha of vineyards (4.5 of which are in the Saar region). Situated above a recently renovated baroque cloister, the winery has views across the river to the wine village of Zeltingen and the famous vineyards of Schlossberg, Himmelreich and Sonnenuhr. The winery dates from the 19th century; Markus Molitor took over the business in the mid-1980s, when he was just 21 years old. It has an old underground cellar stocked with large oak casks and a tasting room with space for up to 100 people. Tours of the cellar and vineyards are available by arrangement. The estate produces very fine Eiswein and one of its culinary specialities is homemade air-dried ham marinated in Riesling, which is made by Markus's father, Werner Molitor.

WINERY — KESTEN AN DER MOSEL

### Weingut Paulinshof

Paulinstraße 14, Kesten an der Mosel
T +49 (0)6535-544
www.paulinshof.homepage.t-online.de
Mon-Fri 0800-1800; Sat 0900-1600.

This winery was first mentioned in documents from 936 in its original incarnation as a monastery of the St Paulin order. The tasting room is housed in the former chapel and there is an old well in the ancient cellars, which, legend has it, forecasts the weather. The 8-ha estate moved into private hands at the start of the 19th century and, since the 1960s, has been owned by the Jüngling family. Klaus Jüngling is gradually handing over the reins to his son Oliver, who trained at Geisenheim and made his first vintage in 2000. Paulinshof is best known for its dry wines and the estate is the sole owner of the Brauneberger Kammer vineyard, which Thomas Jefferson described in his diary as, "without comparison".

Markus Molitor Riesling.

WINERY WEHLEN

### SA Prüm

Uferallee 25-26, Wehlen
T +49 (0)6531-3110
www.sapruem.com
Mon-Fri 1000-1200 and 1400-1600; Sat 1000-1600; Sun by appointment only.

Founded in 1911, when the Prüm estate was divided between seven family members (including the founder of neighbouring estate JJ Prüm), this estate in the middle Mosel is now in the hands of Sebastian Alois Prüm's grandson, Raimund Prüm, a tireless advocate of ecologically-correct winegrowing practices. Whereas JJ Prüm produces virtually no dry wines, SA Prüm has around 70 per cent dry and '*halbtrocken*' (off-dry) styles. In addition to Riesling, a sizeable proportion of the estate's plantings are Weissburgunder (Pinot Blanc). The winery guesthouse ($), which has seven well-appointed rooms and sits right next to the water's edge, is the domain of Raimund's wife Erika, who also looks after the business side of the winery.

HOTEL / WINERY NEUMAGEN-EHRON

### Gutshotel Reichsgraf von Kesselstatt

Gestade 2-3, Neumagen-Ehron, Bernkastel-Kues
T +49 (0)6507-2035
www.gutshotel-kesselstatt.de
$

This was the largest private family wine estate in the Mosel-Saar-Ruwer at one time, with around 100 ha of vineyards. In 1978 it was sold to the wine wholesaler, Günther Reh, and, five years later, he handed control to his daughter Annegret Reh. She has since leased some of the smaller or less distinguished sites and moved the winery headquarters from Trier to the Upper Ruwer. She also converted one of the estate houses into an intimate country house hotel, which overlooks the river from the right bank of the Mosel just outside the tiny hamlet of Neumagen-Ehron. It has a range of individually styled rooms, from singles to family size, and guests can make use of the hotel's swimming pool, sauna and solarium. The best room in the house is perhaps the converted attic, a large, airy space that takes up the hotel's entire top floor, with hardwood floors, a peaked ceiling and dormer windows on three sides. Bicycles can be rented from the hotel and just ten minutes' walk away is a small pier where day-trip riverboats stop for passengers.

## Nahe

This is the region that often flummoxes wine experts when they are asked to guess the origin of one of its wines 'blind', for the simple reason that the best Rieslings here can embody the floral freshness of the Mosel, the depth of the Rheingau and the spice of the Pfalz. The region has, in any case, only developed an identity of its own since the Second World War. Before that its wines were uninformatively sold as coming from the Rhine.

Today, this is a good place to visit, for the world's oldest radon spa at Bad Kreuznach and the extraordinary houses built on islands and bridges across the Nahe. Of these, the Mousetower at Bingerbruck is particularly worth a diversion. It is a 19th-century Gothic recreation of the store where a 14th-century local ruler is said to have hoarded the region's corn during a famine. The name refers to the mice which swam across to the tower and liberated the grain.

WINERY BURG LAYEN

### Schlossgut Diel

Burg Layen
T +49 (0)6721-96950
www.schlossgut-diel.com
Tastings by appointment.

Those who can't, become critics – or so they say. Armin Diel is the exception to that rule. One of Germany's leading wine and restaurant critics, he is also one of the three top producers in the Nahe, producing classic Riesling and new wave Burgundy-style reds and whites. Quite apart from the chance to taste the wines, the 12th-century Burg Layen castle is well worth visiting for its old cellars and the extraordinary artworks by Johannes Helle who, since 1987, has been painting the ends of the winery's steel tanks as well as creating wine-related sculptures from barrel staves.

HOTEL BAD SOBERNHEIM

### BollAnt's im Park

Bad Sobernheim
T +49 (0)6751-93390
www.bollants.de
$$

If you need to rejuvenate after a day of tasting, this art nouveau-style health spa and hotel is the place to come. Set in a large park with centuries-old lime trees, the hotel was built almost 100 years ago by Andres Dhonau. Today his descendants provide a healthy environment in which to unwind, including a wholefood vegetarian restaurant, Hermannshof ($-$$), with a wide-ranging local wine list, a nine-hole golf course and a health spa offering an array of beauty treatments.

## Rheingau

This is the classic heartland of German wine. In the ninth century, the Holy Roman Emperor Charlemagne (known for his contribution to the vinous history of Burgundy, page 48) is said to have ordered the planting of grapes here on slopes where he'd noticed the snow melting earlier than elsewhere. The parallels with Burgundy continue. The focal point of Burgundy's Côte d'Or is the walled vineyard of the Clos de Vougeot and a building that once belonged to monks. Likewise, in the Rheingau the 12th-century monastery of Kloster Eberbach planted its own walled vineyard, the Steinberg. The earliest record of the Riesling grape refers to it being grown close to the village of Hochheim in 1435 but the subsequent reputation of the grape and its wine was developed at Schloss Johannisberg, where the world's first late-harvest wines were accidentally produced in 1775. The Rheingau's supreme position was badly dented between the 1960s and late 1990s, when many of the most famous estates let standards drop as they became sidetracked by unsuccessful early efforts to make dry Riesling from grapes that were fundamentally unripe and overcropped. Today, the region is making a comeback, and estates like the historic Scholl Vollrads and Schloss Johannisberg domains have rejoined the region's top wines, alongside such supposedly less historically illustrious names as Franz Kunstler, Robert Weil, Domdechant Werner and the late Georg Breuer.

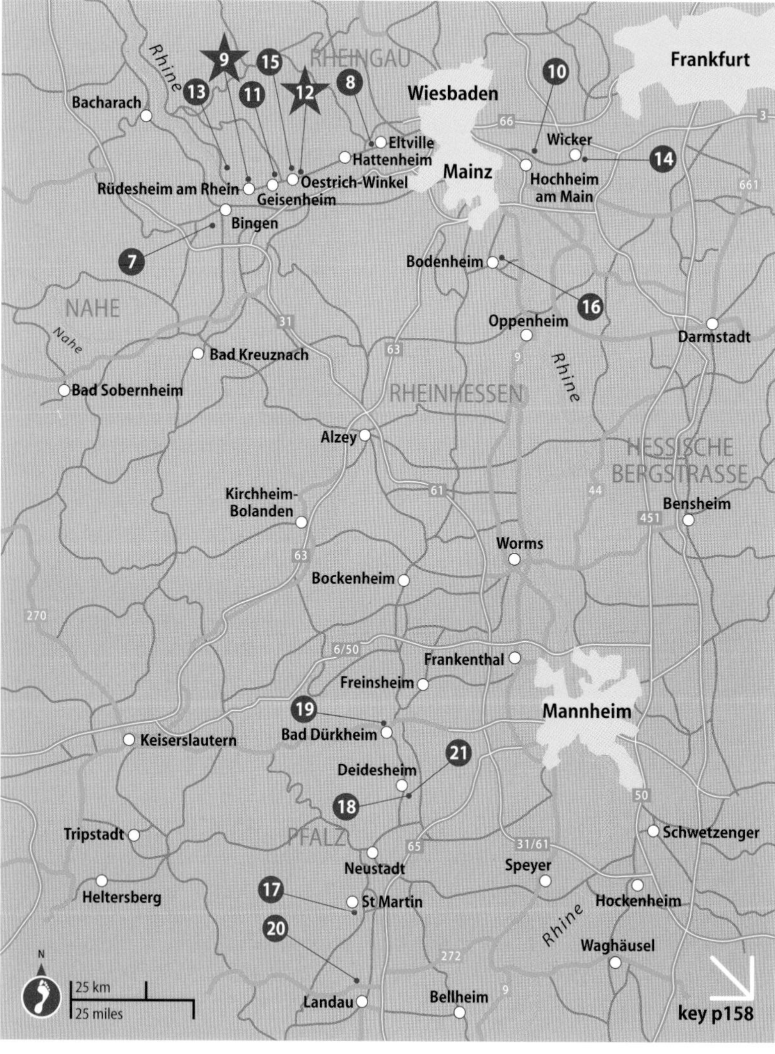


Germany Rheingau

WINERY ELTVILLE/RHEINGAU

## Baron Langwerth von Simmern

Kirchgasse 6, Eltville/Rheingau
T +49 (0)6123-92110
www.langwerth-von-simmern.de
Mon-Fri 0900-1200, 1300-1700 or by appointment. Wine shop Sat 1000-1700. Tastings and tours by appointment.

Located in the oldest part of the oldest village in the Rheingau, between the castle and the church, this estate is a charming assemblage of historic buildings surrounding an English-style garden. The Barons Langwerth von Simmern have been in the Rheingau since 1464 but first made their home in Eltville in 1711, after buying the Stockheimer Hof building. They added the Lichtenstern Hof to the estate in 1753 and now the estate has an impressive clutch of vineyards (Mannberg and Nussheim in Hattenheim, plus Erbacher Marcobrunn, Rauenthaler Baiken and Eltville Sonnenberg). A special tasting of the Auslese, Beerenauslese, Trockenbeerenauslese and Eiswein is available for groups.

WINERY HOTEL RUEDESHEIM AM RHEIN

## Breuer's Rüdesheimer Schloss

Steingasse 10, Rüdesheim am Rhein
T +49 (0)6722-90500
www.ruedesheimer-schloss.de
$-$$

Georg Breuer, who died recently at far too young an age, was one of my favourite German wine producers. A pioneer of good dry wine, he also understood wine tourism and was generally good company. His legacy today includes the estate and this hotel, both of which are run by his family. Housed in the former manor of the German prince elect, the hotel has a state-of-the-art interior that is a stark contrast to the traditional appeal of its façade, which dates from 1729. It showcases

Vines at Schloss Reinhartshausen in the Rheingau.

contemporary art and design but also gives visitors a taste of the rich Rheingau history. The hotel restaurant ($-$$) follows the 'slow food' philosophy, using high-quality local, seasonal ingredients, and has a wine list with over 300 of the region's wines, including some very old vintages. A programme of live music runs throughout the summer season and there is the option of sitting in the 'romantic' garden or cosy wine bar. Guests are invited to visit the nearby cellars and vineyards of the estate and taste the Breuer Rieslings, which are among the finest in the region.

WINERY HOCHHEIM AM MAIN

## Domdechant Werner'sches Weingut

Rathausstraße 30, Hochheim am Main
T +49 (0)6146-835 037
www.domdechantwerner.com
Mon-Sat 0900-1800 by appointment.
Wine tasting €20.

The present owner of this family estate, Dr Franz Werner Michel, is a former president of the German Wine Institute and the seventh generation of his family to run the property. The winery was founded in 1780 by the first Dr Franz Werner, Dean of the Cathedral of Mainz, who famously saved the cathedral from destruction during the French revolution. The winery's manor house was constructed in 1864 and is stylishly furnished from the period. Hochheim is liveliest during its annual Weinfest (wine festival), which takes place on the first weekend in July, but during the rest of the year it is possible to visit the old vaulted cellars, or book a tasting.

RESTAURANT MAINZ

## Haus des Deutschen Weins (HDW)

Gutenberg Platz, Mainz
T +49 (0)6131-221 300
Contact the restaurant for opening times.
$-$$

# Tasting notes

**Drying up**

For any but the keenest wine enthusiasts, the words 'German wine' will evoke something sweet and white. A visit to Germany, however, is likely to give those preconceptions a hefty jolt: nowadays, the chances are that the wine you'll be offered will be bone dry – and there's an ever-growing likelihood that it will be a red. So what has happened?

Well, in some respects, German winemakers have simply gone back to their roots. Until the 19th century, all but the latest-picked, super-ripe wines in rare great vintages would have been dry, because producers lacked the technique of stopping fermentation – by adding sulphur to kill the yeasts, or by filtering the yeasts out. In the mid- to late 20th century, these methods were used for QmP wines or, when the grapes weren't ripe enough, the wine was sweetened with grape juice. One of the drawbacks of this was that German wine was rarely thought of by sophisticates as an accompaniment to a main course. In the 1980s, a new generation of German producers in the Rheingau began to focus on making dry wine but unfortunately most of their efforts were made from fundamentally unripe grapes and were, to non-Germans at least, unpalatably acidic.

More recently, thanks in part to global warming, producers have been making increasing amounts of high-quality dry wine that competes with the best of Burgundy, the Loire and Alsace. Meanwhile, there has been a similarly recent drive towards making red wine rather than importing it. A generation ago, black grapes occupied less than 10% of the vineyards; today they cover over a third. Some of this red is modest, daily-drinking Dornfelder, but there are also increasing amounts of top class Pinot Noir – Spätburgunder – good enough to shame many a Burgundian.



A very popular restaurant in the Rheingau's capital, Mainz, which offers a wide selection of regional cooking alongside a highy impressive wines from every German winegrowing region. (Mainz is the city from which Germany's wine industry is effectively controlled.)

WINERY — GEISENHEIM

## Schloss Johannisberg

Geisenheim
T +49 (0)6722-700929
www.schloss-johannisberg.de
Wine shop Mar-Oct Mon-Fri 1000-1300 and 1400-1800; Sat, Sun and public hols 1100-1800; Nov-Feb Mon-Fri 1100-1700.
Tours and tastings by appointment.

Back in 1720, Schloss Johannisberg was the first German estate to adopt Riesling as its sole grape variety. This was originally a monastic estate, founded in the 12th-century, but the impressive buildings, a Romanesque basilica and Schloss (castle), date from the 20th century, as both were largely destroyed by Allied bombers in 1942. In 1992, it was bought by Henkell & Söhnlein, who also own the Mumm winery. Visitors are invited to descend beneath the Schloss to see the original cellars, lined with old oak casks and flickering candles. From the terrace above you'll find one of the most famous views of the German winelands, down the steep slope of the Schlossberg down to the Rhine. A substantial proportion of production is sweeter styles and about 60% of the estate's vineyards are classified as *'Erstes Gewächs'* (first growth).

WINERY — OESTRICH-WINKEL

## Schloss Vollrads

Oestrich-Winkel
T +49 (0)6723-660
www.schlossvollrads.de
Easter-end Oct Mon-Fri 0900-1800; Sat, Sun and public hols 1100-1900. Nov-Easter Mon-Fri 0900-1800; Sat, Sun and public hols 1200-1700.

Like Georg Breuer (page 170), Erwein Graf Matuschka-Greiffenclau was a pioneer maker of dry wines who died quite recently. In this case, however, I would have to say, that the wines of this 14th-century domaine are actually rather better than they were in his day. In fact, when Graf Matuschka died, the estate was facing financial ruin and had to be taken over by the Nassauische Sparkasse (savings bank). The appointment of Dr Rowald Hepp, one of Germany's top winemakers, as director in 1999, set the estate back on track and it is now once again among the best in the region. The tasting here is always an education, but it is also worth taking the time to enjoy a meal at the estate's restaurant, which is housed in the **Cavalier's House** ($) and food is also served in the Orangerie, overlooking the garden, or on the terrace.

WINERY — RUEDESHEIM AM RHEIN

## Weingut Dr Nägler

Friedrichstraße 22, Rüdesheim am Rhein
T +49 (0)6722-2835
www.weingut-dr-naegler.de
Visits by appointment only.
Wine tasting €9.50.

Tastings in the steeply terraced vineyards or on a riverboat cruise along the Middle Rhine (€15 per person) are on offer at this winery, now run by Tilbert Nägler. Or you can simply visit the cellars for a tasting of six of the estate's wines, including an Auslese. The winery dates from the end of the 19th

Joachim Flick 'castle'.

Vines at Weingut Peter Jakob Kühn.

century but the Näglers have been making wine in the area since 1826 and have an impressive collection of vineyards (14 ha) in some of the best sites in Rüdesheim, planted mostly with Riesling. The estate also has a wine shop in the centre of Rüdesheim at Bleichstraße 2a (Wed-Sun 1400-1800).

WINERY FRLUERSHEIM-WICKER

## Weingut Joachim Flick

Straßenmühle, Flörsheim-Wicker
T +49 (0)6145-7686
www.flick-wein.de
Tasting and sales Mon-Sat from 1500; Sun and public hols from 1100.

This is the place to soak up some local history as you taste your way through the estate's wines. Reiner and Kirsten Flick's winery is housed in a 700-year-old former mill, which in the 16th century, under the ownership of the Duke of Hesse, became a protestant enclave within the Catholic domain of the Bishop of Mainz. Passing into private ownership in the early 19th century, it was used as a liquor factory and then by local farmers. In 1994, following extensive renovations, it became the new home of Weingut Joachim Flick. The winery is a member of the Charta and the VDP associations.

WINERY OESTRICH-WINKEL

## Weingut Peter Jakob Kühn

Mühlstraße 70, Oestrich-Winkel
T +49 (0)6723-2299
www.weingutpjkuehn.de
May-Oct Mon-Fri 0900-1700; Sat and Sun 1100-1700. Tours by appointment only.

Peter Kühn, the 11th generation of his family to run this estate, has transformed the property into one of the best in the region since he took over in 1980. In 2004, his daughter Sandra, a graduate of the winegrowing course at Geisenheim, also joined the business. The estate's 15 ha of vineyards, mainly planted with Riesling, are cultivated without the use of chemical fertilizers and, since 2004, have been certified organic. About 80% of the estate's wines are dry and all are fermented in stainless steel, producing wines with an outstanding purity of fruit. A small proportion of the vineyards were planted to Pinot Noir in 1983 and these wines are aged in oak for 12 months. Every weekend during the summer the Wine Tasting Hut provides visitors with the opportunity to taste the estate's wine for free. Groups of up to 20 people can arrange a special wine tasting session by prior arrangement for €10 per person.

HOTEL ELTVILLE-HATTENHEIM

## Weinhaus und Hotel 'Zum Krug'

Hauptstraße 34, Eltville-Hattenheim
T +49 (0)6723-99680
www.hotel-zum-krug.de
$-$$

The pretty wine village of Hattenheim sits on the banks of the Rhine right at the heart of the Rheingau, and this charming traditional Fachwerk (half-timbered) hotel provides a great base for exploring the surrounding vineyards. Zum Krug is bedecked with hanging baskets of flowers in summer and has clean and simple, traditionally furnished rooms, but the real draw is its excellent restaurant ($$), which has a huge and impressive 600-bin wine list, featuring both young and older vintages from the Rheingau.

Nierstein, Rheinhessen.

Just follow the sign …



## Rheinhessen

Another region that is fighting to make a comeback, the Rheinhessen has been responsible for some of Germany's most ignoble vinous efforts, such as Liebfraumilch and Niersteiner Gutes Domtal, made from the easy-to-grow, productive Müller-Thurgau. Liebfraumilch owes its memorable name to the Church of Our Lady (Liebfrauenkirche) in Worms, though if you're searching for blue nuns you're likely to be disappointed. Great wines are made in this region, even in Nierstein, but you'll have to go looking for them; far too many of the grapes are grown on flat land a long way from the river.

WINE MUSEUM — OPPENHEIM AM RHEIN

### Deutsches Weinbaumuseum

Wormser Straße 49, Oppenheim am Rhein
T +49 (0)6133-2544
www.weinbaumuseum.com
Mon-Fri 1400-1700; Sat and Sun 1000-1700.
€3

Here you will find an authentic traditional cooper's workshop and an impressive collection of antique corkscrews. The German Wine Growing Museum, which is housed in a late Baroque building dating from 1731, takes visitors through more than two thousand years of German wine production. The impressive collection of exhibits from the 13 German wine-growing regions also includes antique drinking vessels from Celtic and Roman times.

WINERY — BODENHEIM

### Weingut Kühling-Gillot

Ölmühlstraße 25, Bodenheim
T +49 (0)6135-2333
www.kuehling-gillot.de
Mon-Fri 0900-1200, 1400-1700; Sat 0900-1200.

In 1970, two winegrowing families were joined in marriage, leading to the creation of this relatively young estate that combines over 200 years of winegrowing history. Cellar master Roland Gillot and his wife, Gabi, look after 10 ha of vines, spread across five villages (Oppenheim, Nierstein, Nackenheim, Bodenheim and Laubenheim), with the help of their winemaking daughter, Caroline. The *Erstes Gewächs* sites are Oppenheimer Kreutz and Bodeheimer Burweg, for Pinot Noir, and Oppenheimer Sackträger and Nackenheimer Rothenburg for Riesling, and the estate has released some fine TBAs.

## Pfalz

The driest, warmest region in Germany, the Pfalz, like Alsace to the southwest, benefits from the shelter of the mountain range the French call the Vosges and the Germans know as the Haardt. Although the Pfalz has never enjoyed the prestige of the Rheingau, this was the region that created Germany's first wine road, the **Deutsche Weinstraße** (www.deutsche-weinstrasse.de), which is well worth following on its leisurely way through vineyards and villages between Bockenheim and Schweigen-Rechtenbach on the French border. Until the late 1980s, the big names of the Pfalz were the three 'Bs' – Bassermann-Jordan, Von Buhl and Bürklin-Wolf – but these old estates now face strong competition from dynamic younger domains like Müller Cattoir, Kurt Darting and Knipser. Like the Rhône, its counterpart in France, the Pfalz has benefited from a combination of factors, including a new generation of ambitious winemakers, modernization of the cellars, and, perhaps most importantly, a growing international taste for spicy ripe flavours that grapes develop here more easily than anywhere else in Germany. The Riesling was not supplanted here as forcefully by the Müller-Thurgau as it was elsewhere but, ironically, this is the area where the most interesting efforts have been made with modern grape crosses such as the Rivaner and Scheurebe. In September every year, Bad Dürkheim hosts a vast wine festival, confusingly known as the **Wurstmarkt** (Sausage Fair), featuring music, fairground rides, wine tastings and fireworks. Also here is the Dürkheimer Fass, the largest wine barrel in the world. It could hold up to 1.7 million litres but in fact houses a restaurant.

HOTEL DEIDESHEIM

## Hotel Restaurant Deidesheimer Hof

Am Marktplatz, Deidesheim am Weinstraße
T +49 (0)6326-96870
www.deidesheimerhof.de
$$-$$$

Built by a local wine merchant in 1781 and owned by the Deidesheim wine-growers' cooperative from the 1920s until the Hahn family took over in 1970, this Relais & Chateaux hotel is steeped in wine heritage. In 2001 it became only the second hotel in the region to be awarded five stars. It boasts three restaurants: the upmarket **Schwarzer Hahn** ($$), with a French- influenced menu created by chef Stefan Neugebauer; the relaxed atmosphere of the country inn-style **St Urbanshof** ($), serving traditional regional cuisine, and the outdoor **Gallino** ($), which has a southern European-inspired menu. The cellar is filled with barrels of wine from the neighbouring Dienheimer Schloss estate.

RESTAURANT FREINSHEIM

## Luther Hotel und Restaurant

Hauptstraße 29, Freinsheim
T +49 (0)6353-93480
www.luther-freinsheim.de
Daily from 1800.
$$-$$$

Germany 's wine regions have some great old hotels and restaurants, but this is one of my absolute favourites. Located in one of the most beautiful buildings in the little town of Freinsheim on the Deutsche Weinstraße, it has continued to serve great food since I was first there in the early 1990s. When it opened, chef Dieter Luther was lured away from his own restaurant, the **Krone** at Munchweiler near Kaiserslautern, also with one Michelin star, to head up the kitchen. His light and original dishes include wild mushroom aspic with smoked goose liver, sauté of veal kidneys and sweetbreads with a lime-mustard sauce, and almond soufflé with raspberries. In late January, Perigord truffles turn up in a truffle soufflé with cepes and sweetbreads. The Luther's meticulously preserved baroque facade fronts onto Freinsheim's old main street, but the airy, casually elegant 40-seat restaurant faces a spacious and quiet courtyard, where an additional 20 to 25 people can be seated in the summer. Wines range from the best of the Rheinland-Pfalz to rare old Bordeaux and interesting Riojas. There are also 23 luxuriously appointed bedrooms.

RESTAURANT BAD DUERKHEIM-UNGSTEIN

## Spötzel's Honigsäckel

Weinstraße 82, Bad Dürkheim-Ungstein
T +49 (0)6322-8691
www.honigsaeckel.de/
Tue-Fri 1130-1400, 1700-2400; Sat, Sun and public hols 1100-2300.
$$

In the quiet wine village of Bad Dürkheim, on the Pfalz wine route, you'll find this traditional wine tavern, run by winegrower Helmut Wolf. The menu offers traditional Pfalz specialties and plenty of good, often lesser-known, Pfalz wines. There is a charming garden for outdoor dining in summer.

WINE BAR DEIDESHEIM

## Turmstübl

Turmstraße 3, Deidesheim
T +49 (0)6326-981081
www.turmstuebel.de
Tue-Sun from 1800; Sun and public hols from 1200.
$-$$

The previous owner of this idyllic little wine tavern (Heinz Rau) in the wine village of Deidesheim retired recently, but Volker Rau and his French partner, Véronique, have taken over and continue to serve up a simple menu of Pfalz specialities, alongside the best wines of the region. The interior is charming, with exposed stone walls and rustic wooden furniture, and there is a pleasant courtyard with outside seating in the summer.

WINERY ST MARTIN

## Weingut Altes Schlösschen

Maikammererstraße 7, St Martin
T +49 (0)6323-94300
www.altes-schloesschen.de
Mon-Fri 0800-1800; Sat 0800-1700; Sun and public hols 0915-1200.

This 400-year-old wine tavern is a picturesque delight of turrets, sandstone portals and half-timbering, situated right in the heart of the pretty Pfalz wine village of St Martin. Surrounding the village are the sloping vineyards at the foot of the Pfälzerwald mountain range and the Deutsche Weinstraße. Opposite is a hotel-cum-restaurant ($) also owned by the estate, where brothers Otto, Erich and

Reichsrat von Buhl.

Herbert Schneider work together to make the wines.

WINERY DEIDESHEIM

## Reichsrat von Buhl

Weinstraße 16, Deidesheim
T +49 (0)6326-96500
www.reichsrat-von-buhl.de
Mar-Dec Mon-Fri 0900-1800; Sat and Sun 1000-1700. Closed Sun in Jan.

Felix Mendelssohn famously admired this estate, which has vineyards in all the major villages of the Mittelhaardt, one of the warmest winegrowing areas in Germany. Founded in the mid 19th century by Franz Peter Buhl, a member of the Bavarian parliament, it remained in his family for almost 150 years. Now the current owner, Achim Niederberger, leases the estate to a Japanese consortium, which exports a third of the production to Japan. Since 1989, there has been considerable investment in the estate and the dynamic young winemaking team, headed by Stefan Weber, is once again producing some of the region's best wines.

WINERY BAD DUERKHEIM

## Weingut Fitz-Ritter

Weinstraße Nord 51, Bad Dürkheim
T +49 (0)6322-5389
www.fitz-ritter.de
Mon-Fri 0800-1200, 1300-1800; Sat 1000-1600. Tastings and tours by appointment only or during special events.

Green-fingered visitors will delight in the lush garden surrounding this 200-year-old estate mansion, a past winner of the award for the 'Most Beautiful Garden on the German Wine Route'. Konrad Fritz runs the estate with his American wife, Alice. It includes the nearby Fitz Sektkellerei, which produces the estate's sparkling wines. Konrad makes the wines with the help of oenologist Christian Klein and cellar master Bernd Henninger. There is a four-star cottage available for rent on the estate (€60-90 per night, seven-night minimum).

WINERY LANDAU-NUSSDORF

## Weingut Gästehaus Hochdörfer

Lindenbergstraße 79, Landau-Nußdorf
T +49 (0)6341-61598
www.weingut-h-m-hochdoerffer.de
Daily 0800-2000.

This winery has an eight-room Mediterranean-style guest chalet ($), set in wonderful gardens and overlooking the hills and vineyards, making it a great base for exploring the region. The winery itself was built in the late 18th century and the estate has remained in the same family ever since. Tastings in the vineyards are available, or you can book a food-and-wine-matching dinner, with traditional Pfalz cuisine provided by local caterers. Plans are also afoot for a winery restaurant.

Weingut Fitz-Ritter.

WINERY DEIDESHEIM

### Weingut Josef Biffar

Niederkirchener straße 13-15, Deidesheim
T +49 (0)6326-70130-0
www.biffar.com
Mon-Fri 0900-1200, 1300-1730; Sat 1000-1200, 1300-1600.

This family winery was founded in 1723 by Adam Biffar from the Rhône Valley, who introduced the tradition of candying fruits to the Pfalz. There is still a sister company (also family-run) next door, producing glacé fruits and chocolates. The winery was built 125 years ago, and you can still visit the original deep vaulted underground cellars. Small tastings before buying wine are free, or an educational tasting is available for €15-27 depending on the size of the group and the wines tasted.

## Hessische Bergstraße

Until the unification of Germany, Hessische Bergstraße was the smallest of the German wine regions. It lies in a narrow band to the east of the Rhine between Darmstadt and Heidelberg.

HOTEL BENSHEIM

### Hotel Bacchus

Rodensteinstraße 30, Bensheim
T +49 (0)6251-39091
www.hotel-bacchus.de
$

Conveniently located in the centre of the picturesque wine town of Bensheim, this wine-themed hotel is only three minutes from the train station and offers simple, modern accommodation, a restaurant and wine bar. Rooms also have wireless LAN and modem internet access. The hotel's 'Wine & Dine Weekend Special' offers you two nights in a double room including breakfast and a special 4-course dinner menu with wines on a Friday or Saturday night for €109 per person.

## Franken

One of the oldest, and once one of the largest wine regions in Germany, Franken has, until recently, been the place to find dry earthy wines made from the Silvaner grape, along with undistinguished examples of Müller-Thurgau. Franken wines have also been also set apart by the fact that, uniquely in Germany, they come in '*Bocksbeutel*' bottles that mimic the shape of leather wine sacks. (This bottle shape was adopted by the makers of Mateus rosé.) Today, as elsewhere, a combination of famous old estates and younger wolves are rapidly raising the reputation of the region. Among these, special note has to go to Horst Sauer whose wines have often beaten every other German offering at the International Wine Challenge. October is a good time to visit, during the Talavera wine festival.

WINERY WUERZBURG

### Weingut Juliusspital

Klinikstraße 1, Würzburg
T +49 (0)931-393 1400
www.juliusspital.de
Winery and shop Mon-Fri 0900-1800; Sat 0900-1600. Wine tavern daily 1000-2400.
Tour and tastings €5-23.

I am a late convert to Franken wines, which I used to find far too earthy. In my defence, I have to say that the winemaking in this area has improved hugely in recent years. Nowhere gives a better opportunity to learn about the region's past and present than this, the third-largest wine estate in Germany. Boasting some of Franken's best vineyard sites, it is part of a foundation set up in 1567 dedicated to the 'common good'. Revenue from the sale of its wines funds a hospice providing palliative care and accommodation for the elderly. You can take a tour of the historic wine vaults, lined with 230 huge wooden casks, which lie beneath the Fürstenbau, a palatial baroque-style building designed by the architect Antonio Petrini. The tour includes either a glass of wine, a tutored tasting of six wines or a little meal of cold meats and cheeses. You can also visit the Juliusspital wine tavern ($), which serves a fine selection of Franconian speciality dishes and has a terrace for outdoor dining.

Gasthof und Weingut Schwarzer Adler, above and below ground.



WINE BAR — VOLKACH

## Vitis Weinbar und Vinothek

Haupstraße 34, Volkach
T +49 (0)9381-71898
Thu-Tue 1100-2300.

This welcoming young little wine bar in picturesque Volkach is unusual in only serving wines from estates owned by a woman or with a female winemaker. Tanja Flammersberger, the owner is herself a winegrower and is happy to guide you through the selection of wines on offer. There is a seasonal menu of light meals and snacks, and, when the weather allows, there is the possibility of sitting outside

WINERY — VOLKACH

## Weingut und Romantikhotel 'Zur Schwane'

Familie Pfaff und Düker, Hauptstraße 12, Volkach
T +49 (0)9381-80660
www.schwane.de
Mon-Fri 0800-1700; Sat, Sun and public hols by apppointment only.

In 1934, when winegrower Josepf Pfaff and his wife Maria took over the traditional Franconian hotel and wine tavern 'Zur Schwane' (named after the Schwane family who founded it in 1404), all the wines came from their own little ½-ha vineyard. Since then wine production has been expanded by their son Michael, and now Michael's daughter Eva and son-in-law Ralph cultivate 15 ha in some of the best locations in Volkach, Eschendorf and Obereisenheim, making the wines in a bright, modern new winery, built six years ago. The hotel ($-$$) has four individually decorated bedrooms, varying in size and style, and the restaurant ($-$$) offers a selection of dégustation menus.

## Baden Württemberg

The southernmost and probably oldest wine region in Germany, Baden had both benefited from, and been handicapped by, the size and strength of Europe's biggest cooperative, the Badischer Winzerkeller, whose tanks hold the equivalent of a staggering 200 million bottles. The co-op is actually one of Germany's most reliable, but it has distracted attention from the efforts of a growing band of small estates here, many of whom are achieving impressive results with Pinot Noir (Spätburgunder) and Pinot Gris (Grauburgunder) grown on the slopes of the volcanic Kaiserstuhl (literally 'emperor's chair'). The region's main wine festival is held in September, in Achkarren, close to the Kaiserstuhl.

Württemberg is less interesting, unless you happen to find yourself with time to kill in Stuttgart. Around half the wine produced here is red, much of it from the Trollinger grape. This, like the Müller-Thurgau and Kerner whites, is best drunk in the region. There are wine festivals in Feuerbach , Obertürkheim, Uhlbach and Untertürkheim.

HOTEL — IHRINGEN AM KAISERSTUHL

## Bräutigam Hotel Restaurant und Weinstube

Bahnhofstraße 1, Ihringen am Kaiserstuhl
T +49 (0)7668-90350
www.braeutigam-hotel.de

Located in the town with the highest average temperature in Germany, this rustic four-star hotel with restaurant and wine bar makes a perfect base from which to explore the vineyards around the small group of volcanic hills known as the Kaiserstuhl. The hotel has 36 rooms and one apartment, all of which come with the usual mod-cons, and a restaurant ($$), where chef Joachim Bräutigam prepares traditional regional dishes using local produce, such as rabbit stewed in Grauburgunder (Pinot Gris) and line-caught fish in Riesling. On Tuesdays, a rustic Winzerbuffet (winegrower's buffet) is available for €22. The wine list features a wide range of German and imported wine to go with the French-influenced cuisine.

WINERY KAISERSTUHL

### Gasthof und Weingut Schwarzer Adler-Franz Keller

Badbergstr 22, Vogtsburg-Oberbergen, Kaiserstuhl
T +49 (0)7662-93300
www.franz-keller.de
Winery Mon-Fri 0800-1800; Sat 0800-1300.
Restaurant Fri-Tue 1200-1500 and 1830-2400.

Famed for its unique mountain cellar, which is dug deep into the basalt rock in the style of an Alpine tunnel, and its restaurant ($$) that has held a Michelin star since 1969, this winery and hotel is set in the heart of the Kaiserstuhl, overlooking the vineyards. The winery itself dates from around 1600 and is owned by Franz Keller senior, the third generation of this winegrowing family. He has been a fierce opponent of large-scale land consolidation and vineyard plot realignment, and also pioneered the introduction of Grauburgunder (Pinot Gris) to the area. His son, Fritz Keller, now runs the estate and shares his father's preference for French-inspired winemaking and the use of small, oak barriques. There's a winery shop on site and visitors are welcome to taste the wines and take a look at the 112-m deep cellar. Accommodation is available next door in the comfortable boutique **Hotel Schwarzer Adler** ($), part of the Small Luxury Hotels of the World group.

# Best producers

**Ahr**

Deutzerhof
Meyer-Näkel » *page 166.*

**Baden**

Bercher
Bernhard Huber
Dr Heger
Huber
Karl-Heinz Johner

**Franken**

Am Stein-Ludwig Knoll
Burgerspital Würzburg
Fürst Lowenstein
Juliusspital » *page 177.*
Hans Wirsching
Horst Sauer

**Hessische Bergstrasse**

Staatsweingut Bergstrasse

**Mittelrhein**

Toni Jost
Jochen Ratzenberger
Adolf Weingart

**Mosel**

Ernst Clüsserath
Grans-Fassian
Fritz Haag
Rheinhold Haart
Heymann-Lowenstein
Karlsmuhle
Dr Loosen
Maximin Grünhaus
Alfred Merkelbach
Markus Molitor » *page 168.*
Egon Müller
Peter Nicolay
Paulinshof » *page 168.*
Pauly Bergweiler
JJ Prüm
SA Prüm » *page 169.*
Reichsgraf von Kesselstatt » *page 169.*
Max Ferd Richter » *page 167.*
Willi Schaefer
Schloss Lieser
Schloss Saarstein
Selbach-Oster
St Urbannshof
Von Hövel

**Nahe**

Dr Crusius
Schlossgut Diel » *page 169.*
Hermann Donnhof
Emrich-Schönleber
Kruger-Rumpf
Prinz zu Salm
Tesch

**Pfalz**

Bassermann-Jordan
Josef Biffar » *page 177.*
Bürklin-Wolf
A Christmann
Kurt Darting
Dr Deinhard
Koehler-Ruprecht
Rainer Lingenfelder
Eugen Müller
Müller Cattoir
Reichsrat von Buhl » *page 176.*
JL Wolf

**Rheingau**

JB Becker
Georg Breuer » *page 170.*
Domdechant Werner'sches » *page 171.*
August Eser
Jakob Jung
August Kesseler
Peter Jakob Kuehn » *page 173.*
Franz Kunstler
Langwerth von Simmern
Josef Leitz
Prinz von Hessen
Schloss Johannisberg » *page 172.*
Schloss Rheinhartshausen
Schloss Schönborn
Schloss Vollrads » *page 172.*
Robert Weil

**Rheinhessen**

Bruder Dr Becker
Gebrüder Grimm
Gunderloch
Louis Guntrum
Gerhard Gutzler
Heyl zu Herrnsheim
Keller
Kuhling-Gillot » *page 174.*
St Antony
J & HA Strub
Wittmann

**Württemberg**

Graf Adelmann
Schwegler

# Rest of Europe



**Vineyards near Badacsonytomaj, Hungary.**

## Wineries

1 Wijnkasteel » p185
2 Caves St Martin » p185
3 Domaine Alice Hartmann » p185
4 Domaine d'Heerstaayen » p185
5 Breaky Bottom Vineyard » p191
6 Denbies Wine Estate ★ » p191
7 La Mare Vineyards & Distillery » p192
8 Willi Opitz » p196, map p194
9 Winzerkeller Neckenmarkt » p196, map p194
10 LOISIUM ★ » p196, map p194
11 Freie Weingärtner Wachau » p197, map p194
12 Weingut FX Pichler » p197, map p194
13 Weingut Prager » p197, map p194
14 Tanzberg Mikulov » p198, map p194
15 Château Belá » p198, map p194
16 Masaryk » p198, map p194
17 Figula Winery » p200, map p194
18 Szeremley » p201, map p194
19 Takler Pince » p201, map p194
20 Disznoko » p201, map p194
21 Royal Tokaji Co » p201, map p194
22 Attila Gere » p201, map p194
23 József Bock » p202, map p194
24 Guido Brivio » p203
25 Provins Valais » p203
26 Jean-René Germanier » p204
27 Cave Simon Maye et Fils » p204
28 Hofkellerei des Fürsten von Liechtenstein » p204
29 Bastijana » p205
30 Grgič Vina » p205
31 Chateau Kamnik » p205
32 Protnerjeva hiša Joannes » p206, map p194
33 Vino Kupljen » p206, map p194
34 Bessa Valley Winery » p206
35 Damianitza Winery Sandanski » p206
36 Cricova Oenotec » p207
37 Château le Grand Vostock » p208
38 Massandra » p208
39 Domaine Gerovassiliou » p211, map p211
40 Mount Athos Vineyards » p211, map p211
41 Domaine Helios » p212, map p211
42 Evharis ★ » p212, map p211
43 Katogi-Strofilia » p212, map p211
44 Semeli - Domaine George Kokotos » p212, map p211
45 Constantine Lazaridi » p212, map p211
46 Boutari Winery » p212, map p211
47 SC Cramele Recas » p213
48 Prahova Valley » p213

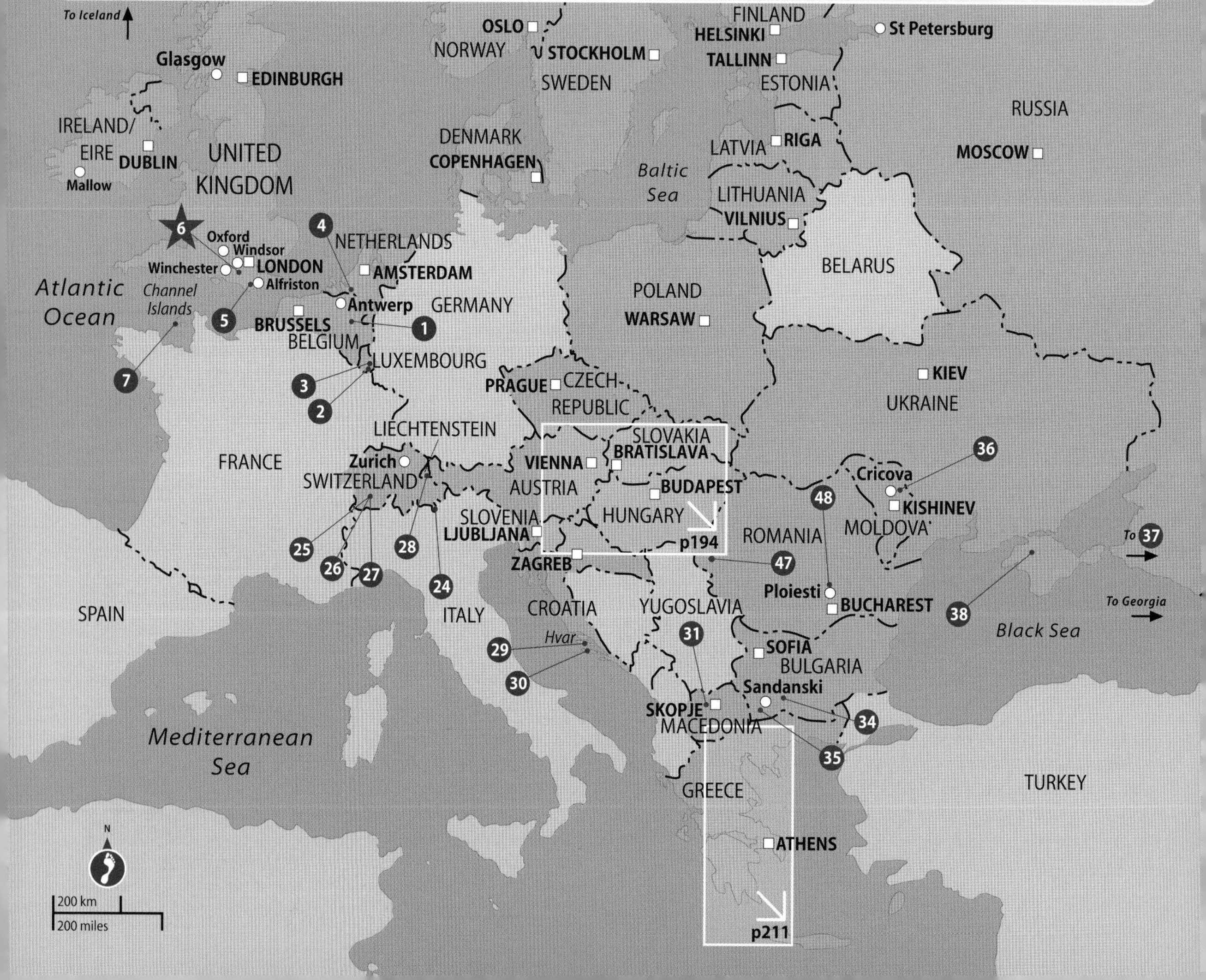

To Iceland
OSLO
NORWAY
STOCKHOLM
SWEDEN
FINLAND
HELSINKI
St Petersburg
TALLINN
ESTONIA
RUSSIA
Glasgow
EDINBURGH
IRELAND/ EIRE
DUBLIN
Mallow
UNITED KINGDOM
DENMARK
COPENHAGEN
Baltic Sea
LATVIA
RIGA
MOSCOW
LITHUANIA
VILNIUS
BELARUS
Oxford
Windsor
Winchester
LONDON
Alfriston
NETHERLANDS
AMSTERDAM
Atlantic Ocean
Channel Islands
Antwerp
GERMANY
POLAND
WARSAW
BRUSSELS
BELGIUM
LUXEMBOURG
KIEV
PRAGUE
CZECH REPUBLIC
UKRAINE
LIECHTENSTEIN
SLOVAKIA
BRATISLAVA
FRANCE
Zurich
SWITZERLAND
VIENNA
AUSTRIA
BUDAPEST
Cricova
KISHINEV
MOLDOVA
HUNGARY
SLOVENIA
LJUBLJANA
p194
ROMANIA
To 37
ZAGREB
Ploiesti
BUCHAREST
To Georgia
SPAIN
ITALY
CROATIA
YUGOSLAVIA
Black Sea
Hvar
SOFIA
BULGARIA
Sandanski
SKOPJE
MACEDONIA
Mediterranean Sea
GREECE
TURKEY
ATHENS
p211
N
200 km
200 miles

# Introduction

This chapter of the guide is the place to find suggestions for wineries in traditional European wine-producing countries, such as Austria, Switzerland, Hungary and Romania, whose wines are often known about, rather than actually known. At the other end of the scale, there are recommendations of restaurants and bars in countries that are too chilly to grow vines, such as Sweden, Iceland and Estonia.

Between these, however, there are several other countries in this section that have long vinous histories but very little international recognition. Most notable among these is the former Soviet republic of Georgia, where it is claimed that man first turned grapes into wine 5000 years ago. Vines have been grown throughout Eastern Europe for as long as they have in France, often to the surprise of people who take the recent vinous success of places like Australia and Canada for granted. The tiny countries of Liechtenstein and Luxembourg also take their winegrowing traditions seriously and boast museums that illustrate the fact.

Perhaps most unexpected, however, are the more northern countries, such as the United Kingdom, Ireland, Belgium and the Netherlands, which, partly thanks to the effects of global warming, have all recently spawned increasingly credible wine industries. England, in particular, is now producing sparkling wine of international standard. For the truly curious wine explorer and for those who relish discovering unexpected treasures, this is one of the most valuable sections of the guide.

# Baltic states

**Despite the cool temperatures of these Baltic states, efforts are made to produce wines in Latvia, where amateur winemakers are experimenting with local exotically named varieties such as Alpha, Zigla and Skukins-675. On a more commercial basis, the large Latvijas Balsams makes various styles of sparkling wine under the Rigas Sampanietis label (though it is not quite so clear where the grapes for this wine were grown). In Estonia, a huge food and drink manufacturer called Põltsamaa Felix produces a range of fruit wines but nothing made from grapes. All three countries are developing a taste for imported grape wines, however, and the quality of restaurant wine lists in the main towns is improving rapidly.**

## Estonia

RESTAURANT TALLINN

### Gloria

Müürivahe 2, Old City, Tallinn
T +372 644 6950
www.gloria.ee
Mon-Sat 1200-2400.
$$-$$$

Restaurateur Dmitri Demjanov has shot back in time, through the years of drab Communist architecture, and brought back gems from the art nouveau period to decorate what has fast become a Tallinn institution. The location is terrific, with a dramatic entrance in the Old City Walls. This bastion of pre-war Baltic style offers food that amply matches the surroundings, such as Estonian beef and foie gras in a Champagne-based sauce. The stellar wine list could hold its own in any world capital. There is one Communist product you might be grateful for, however: Cuban cigars are available to round off your meal.

## Latvia

RESTAURANT RIGA

### Talavera: Kugu 24

Ku u 24 (Radisson SAS), Riga
T +706-1111
Tue-Sat 1800-2300.
$$

Situated in the Radisson SAS Daugava Hotel, overlooking the River Daugava, this restaurant offers good Mediterranean cuisine and one of the best wine lists in town. Surprisingly for a hotel restaurant, it is closed on Sunday and Monday.

## Lithuania

RESTAURANT VILNIUS

### Vilnius Restaurant

Žemaiciu Smukle, (J-2) Vokieèiø 24, Vilnius
T +261 6573
Daily 1100-2300.
$$

Visitors to Lithuania should sample the local cuisine, if only once. Among the delicacies on offer are *cepelinai*, boiled sausage-like items made from grated potato, ground beef or cottage cheese; boiled pig's ears and the – hopefully – ironically named 'zeppelins' which have the same shape as the airships, but none of the lightness. Duck soup and the game dishes are a better option. A superb selection of Lithuanian specialties, including Samogitian dishes (originally from the lowland region, and using ingredients such as allspice, poppy seed, garlic, and mint). You can eat at the bar or in the cellar, and choose between local beer by the jugful and a good selection of wine. There will be tourists here, but it's none the worse for that.

## Best producers

**Benelux**
De Apostelhoeve
Domaine Alice Hartmann » *page 185.*
Domaine d'Heerstaayen » *page 185.*
József Bock
Kluisberg
Wijnkasteel bvba » *page 185.*

**Denmark**
Clos d'Opleeuw

**England**
Astley
Bothy
Breaky Bottom » *page 191.*
Camel Valley
Chapel Down
The Curious Grape
Davenport
Denbies » *page 191.*
Nyetimber
Ridgeview
Sedlescombe
Sharpham
Shawsgate
Three Choirs
Valley Vineyards
Wickham

# Benelux

In 2001, the 440,000 men, women and children in Luxembourg managed to consume 59 litres of wine each: two more than the French and over 30 more than their neighbours in Belgium and Holland. Curiously, despite their apparent thirst for wine, the Luxembourgers have always exported more of their wine than they have drunk themselves. Traditionally, the still and sparkling wine was fairly ordinary and made from the dull Elbling grape and the Müller-Thurgau, known here as the Rivaner). Recently, however, a new wave of producers are switching to Riesling, Pinot Gris and even Pinot Noir and using the steep slopes to produce some genuinely classy wines.

Luxembourg's neighbours are less illustrious producers. However, according to Dutch wine enthusiast Gerard Koning, Belgium has 20 commercial wineries, while the Netherlands can now boast 90 ha of vines and 135 wineries, of which 45 are commercial. These produce 540,000 bottles of what Koning possibly generously describes as "wonderful Dutch wine". He predicts the number of commercial vineyards in the Netherlands will more than double by 2010. To learn more visit www.dewijnhoek.com.

Luxembourg.

## Belgium

WINERY RIEMST

### Wijnkasteel

Kasteelstraat 9, 3770 Riemst
T +32 (0)12-391349
www.wijnkasteel.com
Visits by appointment only.

Joyce Kékkö-van Rennes, who trained in France, brought back Pinot Noir and Chardonnay cuttings to plant in her family's 16-ha vineyard at Belgium's only wine castle, near the Belgian-Dutch border. The region has a long history of winemaking but this estate was the first in the country to receive the Appellation d'Originie Contrôlée (AOC). It seems to be on track to revive Belgium's wine tradition and give beer a run for its money. As well as wines, the estate also produces a grappa. The magnificent grounds contain a rose garden and a small vineyard (separate from the main vineyard) with examples of 20 different vine varieties.

## Luxembourg

WINERY REMICH

### Caves St Martin

53 Rte de Stadtbredimus, 5570 Remich
T +352 2369 9774
vinumveritas@vo.lu
Apr-Oct daily 1000-1200, 1330-1800. Nov, Dec, Feb and Mar groups by appointment only. Closed Jan.
€2.55

The giant, rock-hewn cellars alone are worth seeing at this Moselle institution. A regular visit will include a glass of the sparkling wine but with advance notice a more extensive tasting can be arranged. Perhaps the best option, though, is to join the tour, with lunch or dinner in the adjoining restaurant ($$), where you can enjoy the wines along with traditional Luxembourg fare.

WINERY WORMELDANGE

### Domaine Alice Hartmann

rue Principale 72-74, 5480 Wormeldange
T +352 760 002
www.alice-hartmann.lu
Visits by appointment only

If you can't visit on a Friday afternoon, when this historic Luxemburg winery opens its doors for an informal tasting of its range of still and sparkling wines, then call ahead and they will be able to accommodate you on another day. This is a special treat for Riesling fans. Perched on the edge of the Moselle, the famous Terrasses de la Koeppchen are on a 55-degree slope and yield a range of fine Rieslings from vines that are up to 70 years old.

## Netherlands

WINERY STRIJBEEK

### Domaine d'Heerstaayen

Wijngaard, Markweg 6, 4856 AC Strijbeek
T +31 76-565 2262
www.heerstaayen.com
Visits by appointment only

Peter de Wit is a pioneer of Dutch winemaking, with 30 years under his belt. Every year – frost permitting – he makes 2000 bottles of Riesling, Cabernet Sauvignon, Merlot, Chardonnay, Tokay Pinot Gris, Gamay and Pinot Noir. Quality, flavour and colour (in the case of the reds) varies depending on the summer conditions (global warming has helped recently), but all are well made.

# Ireland/Eire

**The Irish differ from their neighbours in the United Kingdom in one specific regard: they are much readier to splash out on a bottle of wine (and probably a meal). Duty rates and VAT are actually higher than in the UK, which might be expected to drive Irish wine merchants to seek out cheaper wine than their British counterparts when they are on their buying trips. But they don't. Stated simply, the Irish drink better wine. Much of it is still French, but more is Chilean.**

WINE BAR | DUBLIN

## Ely Wine Bar & Ely CHQ

22 Ely Place, Dublin 2
T +353 (0)1-676 8986
IFSC, Docklands, Custom House Quay
T +353 (0)1-672 0010
www.elywinebar.ie
Daily for lunch and dinner.
$$

Ely's pair of wine bars are the best places in Dublin, by several country miles, to enjoy good food (ranging from carpaccio of tuna to Irish stew) and 90 wines by the glass. The original is situated on Ely Place, while a second is located in the Irish Financial Services Centre (IFSC) in a converted warehouse by the river. A third bar is scheduled for late 2006 in a city centre apartment complex called Hanover Quay. The food and wine is the same at Ely Place and CHQ, but the atmosphere is very different. Ely Place is a converted Georgian townhouse just off St Stephen's Green, while CHQ is vast and airy, with space for 350 people.

HOTEL | CO CORK

## Longueville House

Mallow, Co Cork
T +353 (0)22-47156 / 800 323 5463 (toll-free from the USA) / 1-800 006 359 (toll-free from Australia)
www.longuevillehouse.ie
$$$

The O'Callaghans will make you feel right at home in this beautiful Georgian country house in the Blackwater Valley, which has been in their family for almost 80 years. Everywhere you turn there is something to entrance you, be it the superb views, the antique-filled rooms or the grounds. The latter include a vineyard, a 2.5-acre walled garden, from where most of the hotel's produce is grown; a formation of oak trees, planted in 1815, representing the battle of Waterloo; and a one-hour circular walking route along an old canal. If you need more activity, the hotel can arrange, in season, shooting, fishing, and hunting. Having worked up an appetite, head for dinner in the **Presidents' Restaurant** ($$$) or in the conservatory, designed in 1866 by celebrated Victorian ironmaster Richard Turner. Chef and proprietor William O'Callaghan will regale you with such dishes as wild wood pigeon pâté with foie gras and garden cabbage in a beetroot vinaigrette, and you will have plenty of international wines to choose from on the extensive list. Before you choose, however, ask for a glass of Coisreal Longueville, the light white produced in small quantities and warm years from the hotel's own vines.

Longueville House.

Longueville House.

# Russia

Russia today is once again filling the role it held a century ago – as a market where a small number of ultra-wealthy people enjoy some of the most expensive wines on earth. Before the revolution, the people drinking Roederer Cristal were the Tsar (for whom the Champagne was created) and his entourage. Their place has been taken by men and women who have, in one way or another, made their fortunes since the collapse of the Iron Curtain. In Moscow, you can now telephone an order at 0200 for immediate delivery of 1982 Château Pétrus. If you want to know what kind of Russian drinks great Bordeaux at that hour, the answer is simple: the kind of Russian with the money to pay for it.

Russians looking for more affordable fare have traditionally bought wines from the Ukraine and, until the borders to both countries were recently closed, Moldova and Georgia. Most wine from these countries is red, much is sweet and quality has not generally been high. On the other hand it is higher than that of most "Russian" wine, which is usually made from imported grape concentrate. The famou s "Champagnski", known to visitors to the Soviet Union, still exists and is a little more reliable than before, when the same label was used on a wide variety of fizzes. For details of Russia's wine growing, see Black Sea states, page 207.

Peter and Paul Fortress, St Petersburg.

## Moscow

RESTAURANT MOSCOW

### La Grande Cave

30/1 Rublevskoye Shosse, Moscow
T +7 095 413 5656
Call ahead for opening times.
$$

This small, recently opened restaurant boasts good modern cooking, a genuine wine cellar and a list that offers a few hundred different wines and spirits.

RESTAURANT MOSCOW

### Nostalgie

12a Chistoprudny Bulvar, Moscow
T +7 095 925 7625
www.nostalgie.ru
Daily 1200-2400.
$$$

Less showily Belle époque than the recently opened Pushkin restaurant but similarly pricey, this is the place in Moscow to find great French cooking (including several ways of preparing foie gras). The restaurant and its sommelier school (which offers courses to the public but only in Russian) are associated with the successful glossy wine magazine *Vinomania*, so the quality of the award-winning wine list should come as no surprise. For an inexpensive chance to sample Nostalgie, check out the weekend jazz brunches that kick off at noon.

WINE SHOP MOSCOW

### Le Sommelier

5 Ul Smolenskaya, Moscow
T +7 095 783 8366
www.lesommelier.ru
Daily 1100-2400

"Buy Pétrus," screams the parrot in this upmarket wine shop, run in association with a sommelier school (which runs public courses but only in Russian). The staff are well-trained and aware that not all budgets permit such extravagance, especially after import and other duties are added. In addition to a wide range of wines on offer in the shop, Le Sommelier also offers a 24-hour dial-a-sommelier advice line, for those times when you need help navigating a restaurant wine list.

## St Petersburg

RESTAURANT ST PETERSBURG

### Moskva

Petrogradskaya nab 18, St Petersburg
T +7 812 332 0200
Mon-Fri 1200-0100, Sat 1500-0100,
Sun 1500-0100
$$

St Petersburg may seem glamorous to culture-hungry foreigners but those who live in this beautiful city feel short-changed when it comes to swanky restaurants and great wine lists. The capital, they feel, is where it all happens. This explains why the man behind this modern establishment on top of an office building overlooking the river, chose to call it 'Moskva' – enabling himself to coin the phrase 'The Capital of St Petersburg is Moscow'. The Italian-influenced cooking is good and the wine list wide-ranging. Both are – by Moscow standards – very fairly priced and they are evidently much appreciated by the great and good of the city, who are to be seen strutting their stuff on the dance floor.

# Scandinavia

## Denmark

The odd man out in Scandinavia, Denmark no longer has a state alcohol monopoly and has dropped the taxes it charges on wine. This has helped make this one of the most vibrant wine markets in the world, with a wine consumption of 35 litres per adult, the highest of any non-producing country. 'Non-producing' is not absolutely true, however, because a few brave Danes are making some wine in tiny quantities.

RESTAURANT COPENHAGEN

### Peder Oxe's Restaurant & Vinkælder Wine Bar

Gråbrødretorv 11, 1154 Copenhagen
T+45 3311 0077
Daily 1130-2400.
$$

This is a funky gathering place for locals and visitors. The upstairs dining room offers a perfectly executed selection of simple dishes, such as grilled meat, lobster bisque and prawns, and has an excellent salad bar that can be a meal in itself. Downstairs, in the cellar, you can enjoy a good range of wines and cocktails, surrounded by visible catacombs dating from the 16th century.

## Finland

Wine can only be bought in the 327 outlets of the Alko state monopoly, which has been in existence since 1932 and employs some 2500 people. The organization has evolved over the years. Initially, bottles were stacked in such a way that their labels could not be seen and customers had to ask specifically for the wine they wanted. In the 1980s, the stores were the last in Finland to switch to self-service, and the range and quality of wine offered has expanded radically, with Chile currently the favourite producing country, followed by France. Laws still, however, forbid the displaying of any wine in the shop windows, so all a browser will see is wine glasses and catalogues.

RESTAURANT HELSINKI

### Ravintola Carelia

Mannerheimintie 56, 00260 Helsinki
T+358 (0)9 2709 0976
www.carelia.info
Mon-Fri 1100-0100, Sat 1600-0100.
$$-$$$

Here is a rare opportunity to step back in time to pre-war Finland. Ravintola Carelia is located in a 1930s pharmacy, which has been left intact; the modern lighting fixtures are one of the few clues that almost a century has passed. The food is a contemporary take on European and the wine list is small but serious, listing some of the world's top (and top price) producers. Half of the Australia offering, for instance, consists of 1994 to 1997 Penfolds Grange; they've also managed to get a 2001 Torbreck RunRig.

## Iceland

Like the Scandinavian countries to the east, Iceland has a state monopoly over the sale of alcohol. In this instance, it consists of a chain of 46 Vínbúð stores. Prices are high.

WINE BAR REYKJAVIK

### Vínbarinn

Kirkjutorg 4, Reykjavík
T+354 552 4120
Mon-Fri 1600-0100; Sat and Sun 1600-0300.
$

Popular with Icelanders of all ages, including those working in the nearby Parliament building, Vínbarinn has possibly Iceland's best list of wines from all corners of the world. It can get quite crowded later at night, so those who want to focus on what's in their glass, rather than be forced to people watch, should go earlier in the evening or on a weekday.

## Norway

The state monopoly here is the Vinmonopolet (usually referred to as '*polet*'), which was founded in 1922 and has around 200 outlets. Advertising any alcohol to consumers is illegal and duty rates are high. However, wine has become increasingly popular in recent years at the expense of beers and spirits. Most of the wine on offer comes from France, Italy, Spain, Chile, Australia and Germany.

RESTAURANT OSLO

### Mares Brasseri

Frognerveien 12 B, Oslo 0263
T+47 2254 8980
www.mares.no
Mon-Sat 1700-1230.
$$

A comfortably sleek modern restaurant, Mares Brasseri is one of Oslo's finest restaurants. This is the place to come for fish and seafood, which arrives extremely fresh and is approached in an inventive manner, with some reference to French and Italian cuisine. You might, for example, be offered lobster and orange soup, a challenge that the varied wine list will certainly be able to match.

## Sweden

Since 1870, there has been a state monopoly on the sale of alcohol in Sweden. Between the First World War and 1955, it was rationed and neither unmarried women nor the unemployed were permitted to buy it. Today, the state-run Systembolaget (usually known as either '*systemet*' or '*bolaget*') is the largest wine retailer in the world. Run by the wife of the current prime minister, it enjoys total control over the sale of alcohol to the country's nine million inhabitants through its 400 shops, restaurants and caterers. The wine range on offer is capped at 2000, so, every time the monopoly's buyers choose a new wine, they have to drop another from the existing list. Although choice is limited and taxes are high, the prices of top wines are surprisingly low because of the fixed 17% profit margin. Wine-loving Danes and Germans, therefore, sometimes find it worth their while to stock up in Swedish outlets in the south of the country. Shopping in a Systembolaget store is, however, a joyless experience, due to the rules that require every product to be treated equally; either all Champagnes are displayed in the chiller cabinet or none of them are. Visitors may be surprised to see that around 70% of the wine being bought to drink at home is either in Tetrapak cartons or bag-in-box. Equally curious is the fact that the Systembolaget owns Absolut Vodka and the award-winning Domaine Rabiega wine estate in Provence (though the latter is currently for sale).

RESTAURANT STOCKHOLM

### Sturehof AB

Sturegallerian 42, Stureplan 2 , 114 46 Stockholm
T+46 (0)8 440 5730
www.sturehof.com/en/
Mon-Fri 1100-0200, Sat 1200-0200, Sun 1300-0200.
$$

A Stockholm institution since 1897, Sturehof has moved with the times and, in addition to the restaurant, now has two funky bars and a terrific wine list with blockbusters and interesting unknowns from around the world. Don't miss the food, though, as here is a great opportunity to try authentic *husmanskost* (homecooking) and endless permutations of herring.

# United Kingdom & the Channel Islands

**Britain can reasonably boast that it is home to the world's most respected wine writers, the two most famous wine auction houses – Christie's and Sotheby's – a long wine-drinking tradition, wine merchants with centuries of experience and shops that offer wines from a bewildering assortment of countries. When wine lovers move to London from the US, however, they often feel short-changed. It is startlingly difficult to find great and interesting wine by the bottle. There are some good shops – though nothing to compete with Lavinia in Paris, say, or any of the best stores in New York – but most people buy cheap wine in supermarkets, where 80% of wine is bought, or from Thresher, a discount-offering chain. Those few people looking for something better, order it by the case from a merchant. Restaurants are often similarly disappointing, as too many buy the same wines from the same wholesalers, but there are great exceptions. In recent years, the biggest trend has been away from French and German wine to the New World. Australia is the big seller, with a good range on offer (although you won't find some of the big name, big reds that go straight to the US), along with large-volume, heavily promoted Californian brands.**

**Winemaking has had a patchy history in this cool northern country. The Romans brought vines and wine for their own consumption and, by the time the Normans compiled the Domesday book in 1086, there were 46, mostly monastic, vineyards scattered across southern England. By 1509, when Henry VIII became king and owner of 11 vineyards, this number had tripled, with the church owning 52 and the remainder being in the hands of the nobles. This was the high point of English winemaking. There are various explanations for the subsequent decline. Among the most convincing is the 'Little Ice Age' in the 17th century, which caused temperatures to drop low enough for the Thames to freeze in winter. In a climate as marginal as that of the British Isles, any cooling would have jeopardized winemaking. The revival began in the 1950s, leading to the existence of around 400 supposedly commercial wineries today, although most of these make more of the little income they get from tourism than from the wine itself.**

Denbies.

**While there are some good dry whites, it is generally agreed that the best examples of English wine today are the sparkling efforts from producers like Camel Valley, Nyetimber and Ridgeway, all of which have done well in blind tastings against Champagne. Note that English wine is never referred to as 'British wine', a name that was, paradoxically, once used for stuff made with imported grape concentrate.**

## London

RESTAURANT LONDON

### Andrew Edmunds

46 Lexington St, Soho, London W1F 0LW
T 0871-223 8022 / +44 (0)20-7437 5708
Daily 1230-1500, 1800-1045.
$$

Not a place that you'll find on most tourist itineraries, but a favourite among British wine lovers who want to drink great wine at fair prices. Edmunds buys wine, lays it down and applies a low mark-up, allowing him to sell top wines on occasion for lower prices than they fetch at auction. The atmosphere is cosily reminiscent of a French bistro but the food is more modern European. With the money you save here, you might be tempted by the 18th- and 19th-century prints Edmunds sells in the shop next door.

WINE BAR/SHOP LONDON

### Bedales

5 Bedale St, London Bridge, London SE1 9AL
T +44 (0)20-7403 8853
www.bedalestreet.com
Mon-Fri 1100-2100, Sat 0900-1830.

In the heart of the foodie playground of Borough Market and familiar as the setting of a memorable scene in *Bridget Jones's Diary*, this is a great hybrid of deli and wine bar, with a range of bottles that aren't available elsewhere, including some great older bottles. Check out the website for specialist tastings, such as six vintages of Domaine de Trévallon.

MUSEUM LONDON

### Vinopolis

1 Bank End, London SE1 9BU
T 0870-241 4040
www.vinopolis.co.uk
Mon, Fri and Sat 1200-2100; Tue-Thu and Sun 1200-1800. Restaurants Mon-Sat 1200-1500, 1800-2230. Bar Blue Mon-Sat 1100-2300, Sun 1200-1600.
From £15

London's revitalized Bankside has become a food and culture centre: within spitting distance of each other are Shakespeare's Globe, the Tate Modern, Borough Market, and Vinopolis. London's own expansive (though much reduced from its initial size) wine attraction offers a large menu of tours, self-guided-tastings and masterclasses, as well as two excellent restaurants. Wine regions across the world are well represented, though the examples on offer are not always the finest of their kind, and there are spirits and whiskies and the Brew Wharf microbrewery for those who want to look beyond the grape. Watch out for special events, such as tastings with wine celebrities such as Oz Clarke and in-depth wine and cheese-matching workshops. Also of interest is the Majestic Wine Warehouse, the only example of this chain's shops that sells by the bottle rather than by the dozen.

RESTAURANT LONDON

### Vinoteca

7 St John St, London EC1M 4AA
T +44 (0)20-7253 8786
Daily Mon-Sat 1200-2300. Meals served Mon-Fri 1200-1445 and 1830-2200; Sat 1830-2200.
$-$$

Whenever I am asked for advice on where to go for a glass of wine or a meal in London, I heartily recommend this recently opened establishment close to Smithfield market. The Mediterranean-meets-modern-British food is great and comparable with the fare on offer nearby at the more famous St John. Wines can be bought to drink at home for £5 to over £100 but enjoying them here costs little more, as Vinoteca has the lowest mark-ups in the city.

Vinoteca.

Bedales.

## Southeast England

WINERY SUSSEX

### Breaky Bottom Vineyard

Rodmell, Lewes, East Sussex, BN7 3EX
T +44 (0)1273-476427
www.breakybottom.co.uk
Visits by appointment only.

Consider borrowing a 4WD if you are coming here in inclement weather, as the final approach is via a farm track. It is well worth the trip, however, as Breaky Bottom is located in a stunning, seemingly isolated valley in what is otherwise a highly populated part of the country. Peter Hall, a pioneer winemaker whose reputation has been built on Loire-style Seyval Blancs, promises a free tasting for those who make the journey.

WINERY SURREY

### Denbies Wine Estate

London Rd, Dorking, Surrey, RH5 6AA
T +44 (0)1306-876616. Restaurant T +44 (0)1306-734661.
www.denbiesvineyard.co.uk
Mon-Fri 1000-1700; Sat 1000-1730; Sun 1130-1730. Closed Christmas and New Year.
£7.25, £3.50 for children.

In an ideal world, I would bring coachloads of French wine producers to the south of England, where they would find a winery/tourist centre better than anything on offer in most of their wine regions. With 107 ha under vine, Denbies is by far the largest winery in the UK, comprising some 10% of the country's vineyards. Its distinguished history includes such players as celebrated Victorian architect Thomas Cubitt, who, after building London's Belgravia, bought Denbies Estate in 1850, and Prince Albert, who planted several rare conifers here in 1851.

The estate has glided into modernity with a skill that would have done Cubitt proud, although he might have winced at the supermarket-superstore exterior design. The excellent winery tour includes a terrific surround-sound film on a 360-degree screen, a tour of the winery and, in season, an outdoor train tour of the vineyard; kids will enjoy it as much as adults. The winery has two excellent restaurants ($$-$$$) and a seven-room guesthouse ($$), which makes a perfect base for walking in the stunning North Downs without having to rent a car.

SHOP SUSSEX

### The English Wine Centre

Alfriston, East Sussex, BN26 5QS
T +44 (0)1323-870164
www.englishwine.co.uk
Daily 1000-1700.
Tour and lunch with tasting £27.50.

Host of the annual English Wine & Regional Food Festival in early September, the English Wine Centre remains a celebration of the best of English wine and food all year round. The shop stocks a large range of English wine, but, especially for skeptical newcomers to these wines, the best place to start is with the tasting lunch of regional cheeses and local sausages, matched with an informal tutored tasting. Included in the price is a tour of the premises' 17th-century barn, as well as the museum. For visitors wanting to make a

Denbies.

## Vintages

- **2005** Very good.
- **2004** Very good.
- **2003** Great.
- **2002** Very good.
- **2001** Mixed with some very good wines.
- **2000** Mixed.

longer day of it, the Centre can also organize several excellent- value tour packages, including a visit to nearby Michelham Priory and the picturesque village of Alfriston. As we go to print, we have just learned that the Centre is for sale, so we hope that this will not jeopardise its future.

HOTEL HAMPSHIRE

### Hotel du Vin & Bistro

Southgate St, Winchester, Hampshire
SO23 9EF
T +44 (0)1962-841414
www.hotelduvin.com
$$$

This funky but classy chain of hotels and bistros is a godsend to anyone travelling in the British provinces. Each hotel has a personality which is particularly appropriate to the architecturally interesting building in which it is situated, so the Birmingham Hotel du Vin, for example, is a converted Victorian hospital, while in Bristol the transformation was from an old sugar warehouse. All of the rooms also have their own designs and are sponsored by particular wines.

The Bistros offer good modern Mediterranean food and international wines, with a tempting selection by the glass and unusually well-trained staff. Wine classes, dinners and tastings are also arranged, helping to make each Hotel du Vin a local focal point for wine lovers.

The chain was taken over recently by the Malmaison hotel group, another funky up-and-coming company so more new openings are to be expected.

WINE BAR OXFORDSHIRE

### Summertown Wine Café

38 South Pde, Summertown, Oxford
OX2 7JN
T +44 (0)1865-558800
www.summertownwinecafe.co.uk
Mon-Sat 0830-2330; Sun 1000-2200.
Tastings £2.

This quirky, elegant winebar-cum-café-cum-wine shop near Oxford is totally unique in the way that it is run. Many of the wines on sale in the shop are chosen by the café's customers: members of the curiously-named Nude Bottle Society. These enthusiasts are rewarded for their efforts by a policy of allowing anyone to drink a bottle bought from the shop in the café for only £5 corkage. Another appealing feature is the monthly selection of boutique wines from across the globe that can be tasted for a paltry £2 a glass.

MUSEUM BERKSHIRE

### Windsor Castle

Windsor, Berkshire SL4 1NJ
T +44 (0)20-7766 7304
Mar-Oct daily 0945-1715 (last admission 1600); Nov-Feb daily 0945-1615 (last admission 1500).
£13.50

Perhaps the favourite item on display at Windsor Castle, the Queen's country residence, is Queen Mary's Doll House. Designed by Sir Edwin Lutyens in 1924, this extraordinary feat of mini-engineering includes running hot and cold water and every possible item a house of the period could require. Of special interest is the wine cellar, which comes complete with inch-high bottles of vintage wine and spirits, which were filled with the genuine item (from Berry Bros & Rudd) using an eyedropper.

## Scotland

RESTAURANT GLASGOW

### The Ubiquitous Chip

12 Ashton Ln, Glasgow G12 8SJ
T +44 (0)141-334 5007
www.ubiquitouschip.co.uk
Restaurant Mon-Sat noon-1430 and 1730-2300; Sun 1230-1500 and 1800-2300.
Brasserie daily until 2300.
$$-$$$

This has been a Glaswegian and, indeed, a Scottish institution since 1971, when Ronnie Clydesdale decided to open a restaurant not only dedicated to preserving Scottish cooking but also to promoting Scottish producers, by listing the provenance of the ingredients on the menu. The same preoccupations extend to the massive wine and whisky lists; the latter includes 150 malts. Regular wine events, include producer visits and special tasting dinners. Under the same roof are a restaurant, a brasserie and a pub, offering eating and drinking opportunities at every price point.

## Channel Islands

WINERY JERSEY

### La Mare Vineyards & Distillery

St Mary, Jersey JE3 3BA
T +44 (0)1534-481178
Apr-Oct Mon-Sat 1000-1700. Shop Apr-Dec Mon-Sat 1000-1700.

The availability of cheap, duty-free wine may explain why, despite the friendly climate of the Channel Islands, winemaking has yet to take off here. La Mare, however, has been in business since 1972, producing three acceptable wines, as well as apple brandy, chocolates, jams and mustards. The set-up is child-friendly, with an adventure playground, chocolate workshops and the chance to get close to Shetland ponies and Jersey calves.

# Central Europe

"Grüner Veltliner from the Wachau in Austria is the only Old World wine style that genuinely competes with the great whites of France and Germany."

# Austria

## Fact file

| | |
|---|---|
| **International flights** | Major international airlines fly into Vienna. European and budget flights also serve Salzburg, Graz, Klagenfurt, Linz and Innsbruck. |
| **Entry requirements** | Passport but no visa required for citizens of the EU, US, Canada, Australia and New Zealand. |
| **Currency** | Euro (€). |
| **Time zone** | GMT +1. |
| **Electricity** | 230V, 50Hz. Plugs have 2 round pins. |
| **Licensing hours** | Vary across the country according to local police laws. |
| **Minimum age** | 16 for wine and beer; 18 for spirits. |
| **Drink-drive restrictions** | 50 mg of alcohol per 100 ml of blood or 10 mg for new drivers. |

### Planning your trip

The major international airport is **Vienna Schwechat** (VIE; www.viennaairport.com), although there are European budget flights to other cities. Vienna is the most useful entry point for exploring Niederösterreich, but Graz is more convenient for the Steiermark wine region in the southeast. During the summer, it's possible to catch a boat along the Danube from Vienna to Budapest. Österreichische Bundesbahnen (OBB; www.oebb.at) run the efficient and comfortable rail service, which includes some very scenic routes. Renting a car is relatively expensive (although cheaper if you book in advance from home) but may be the easiest way to reach some wineries; major hire firms have outlets at airports and in most towns.

At the centre of Europe, **Vienna's** imperial past is very much evident in its grandiose architecture, excellent museums, genteel cafés and musical heritage. To the west, the slopes of the Danube are carpeted in vines and dotted with historic old towns, romantic castle ruins (the region's hallmark) and baroque churches; don't miss the picturesque town of **Dürnstein** in the Wachau. South of the capital, **Burgenland** is characterized by Magyar steppe. The flat terrain around **Neusiedler See** is tailor-made for cyclists and birdwatchers. To the west, **Graz** is a lively university with one of the best preserved old centres in Europe. Venturing further afield, highlights of central and western Austria include **Salzburg**, **Hallstatt**, the **Hohe Tauern National Park** , **Innsbruck** and the Alpine scenery of the **Tirol**. For further information, see www.austria.info/uk.

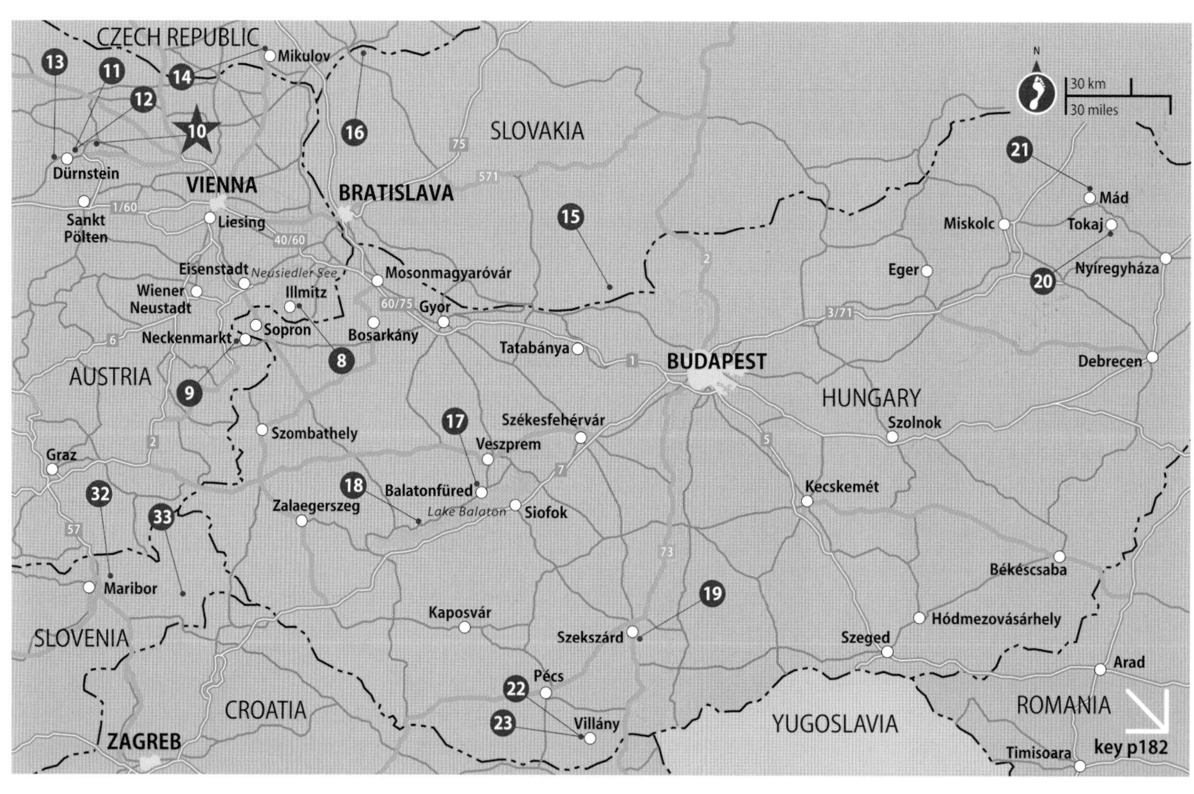

Imperial Palace, Vienna.

# Vintages

## Austria

- **2005** Mixed, but with some very good late-harvest wines.
- **2004** Mixed; better in Burgenland than in the Wachau.
- **2003** Great reds but some whites are overripe.
- **2002** Very good to great.
- **2001** Great.
- **2000** Generally great for both red and white, though some wines taste overripe.

### Wine tourism

While vines are grown across large areas of eastern Austria, the area that is most attractive for tourism are the eight regions of Niederösterreich, surrounding Vienna: Carnuntum, Donauland, Kamptal, Kremstal, Thermenregion, Traisental, Wachau and Weinviertel. There is a good wine route (www.wineroute.at), whose website includes 150 villages, 1500 wineries, hotels and bed-and-breakfasts, plus details of how to get the most out of visiting this area on foot. While English is not always spoken, wineries are increasingly equipped to welcome visitors. It is, however, generally worth telephoning in advance. The spring and autumn are the best times to visit, especially in Kamptal and the Wachau where there are village wine festivals throughout September.

### History

The history of winemaking here can be traced back to roughly 700 BC when vinifera grape pips were buried in a grave near Eisenstadt. The Romans made wine at Carnuntum, an amphora of which was said to be worth the value of a young slave. While a number of specific vineyards and estates, such as Gumpoldskirchen and Klosterneuburg made a name for themselves as early as the 16th century, Austrian wine remained almost unknown beyond its frontiers. Then, just over two decades ago, a small group of Austrian winemakers unintentionally did their neighbours and their country a huge favour. They also caused a great deal of short-term grief but everybody knows the relationship between broken eggs and omelettes. If the Austrians in question had not been caught adulterating their wine with a chemical loosely related to anti-freeze, it is quite possible that Austria might still be making cheap versions of German wine. Instead, this country is now making highly regarded and unmistakably Austrian wine.

### Understanding Austrian wine

Austria's wine labels follow similar rules to Germany's with categories such as **Tafelwein**, **Kabinett** and **Beerenauslese**. However, behind the apparent similarities lie some important differences. In Austria grapes have to be substantially riper to attain the same quality level. A German Qualitätswein has to have an *oechsle* (sweetness) level of 50-72, while in Austria the figure is 73. Austria also has a sweet style all of its own in **Ausbruch**. Almost as sweet as Trockenbeerenauslese, this wine is made from nobly rotten grapes that have been allowed to dry on the vines, so the style is slightly reminiscent of Tokaji. Other terms that may be used include *trocken* (dry), *halbtrocken* (medium-dry), *lieblich* (medium-sweet) and *süss* (sweet). A recently introduced appellation system allows dry, unoaked wines of sufficient quality and specified grapes – Grüner Veltliner in the Weinviertel, for example – to carry the letters DAC (Districtus Austria Controllatus) on their labels. In the Wachau, there is also a special *Smaragd* term for ripe, full-bodied wines. Finally, look out for *Heurigen* – wine bars that serve the newest vintage a few weeks after the harvest.

### White grapes

- **Bouvier** Often used for sweet, late harvest wines. Lacks intrinsic character.
- **Grüner Veltliner** Austria's ace card: peppery and limey and rich. Ages surprisingly well.
- **Morillon / Feinburgunder** Two Austrian names for Chardonnay, some examples of which can be good here.
- **Riesling** Austria's great white grape can rival Germany and Alsace.
- **Welschriesling** Nondescript grape that can make good sweet wine.

### Red grapes

- **Blaufränkisch** Styles of this grape depend on the winemaker. Some are rich and morello cherryish; others are light and not unlike Beaujolais. Widely grown in Mittleburgenland.
- **Blauer Portuguiser** This really does have a soft juiciness that is reminiscent of Beaujolais.
- **St Laurent** Easily confused with Pinot Noir – and sometimes better than many examples of that grape.
- **Blauer Zweigelt / Zweigelt** Widely grown; spicy and rich.

**Country code** → +43. **IDD code** → 00. **Internet ID** → .at.
**Emergency numbers** → T 112. Ambulance: T 122. Police: T 133. Fire: T 144.

## Burgenland

The warmest part of the country, this is the place to come looking for good reds, made from St Laurent, Zweigelt and Blaufränkisch.

WINERY NEUSIEDLERSEE

### Willi Opitz

St Bartholomäusgasse 18, 7142 Illmitz
T+43 (0)2175-2084 0
www.willi-opitz.at
Daily 1000-1700.

Former petfood executive and part-time winemaker, Willi Opitz is one of the stars of the modern Austrian firmament, with an extraordinary range of award-winning, limited production, late-harvest white and, more surprisingly, red wines that is regularly on offer to those flying first class on British Airways. But Opitz has also enterprisingly launched wine weekends that include a stay at the winery, dinners and tastings, a boat ride on the Neusiedlersee and a visit to the nearby Esterházy Castle on the other side of the Hungarian border.

WINERY NECKENMARKT

### Winzerkeller Neckenmarkt

Harkauer Weg 2, 7311 Neckenmarkt
T+43 (0)2610-42388
www.neckenmarkt.at
Vists by appointment only.

This Burgenland cooperative provides a good introduction to Austria's red wines, producing, as it does, about 5% of the country's total output, including some very good examples of Blaufränkisch and Zweigelt. It is also a great example of how a cooperative can be innovative. One of the enlightened practices here is providing an incentive to growers, who own vines that are at least 25 years old, to reduce yields. No English spoken.

## Kamptal

WINE CENTRE LANGENLOIS

### LOISIUM

Loisiumallee 1, A-3550 Langenlois
T +43 (0)2734-32240-0. Hotel 77100-0.
www.loisium.at, www.loisiumhotel.at
Feb-Dec daily 1000-1700.

My first impression of this extraordinary wine centre was that it was the wine world's answer to Gehry's Guggenheim museum in Bilbao. An aluminium cube set among vines, it stands above a kilometre of vaulted cellars that are almost 900 years old. As you wander from the vineyard into the cube and along the cellars you have the chance to experience the evolution of Austrian wine, from its primitive origins to its modern embodiment today. Within the cube there is a café, and alongside it is a spa hotel ($$) with a restaurant ($$) that offers great wine-focused dinners and wine-and-jazz evenings. Another unique experience are the moon- and torch-lit walking tours of the vineyards.

## Vienna

SHOP VIENNA

### Julius Meinl am Graben

Am Graben 19, 1010 Vienna
T+43 (0)1-532 3334 ext. 6100
www.meinlamgraben.at
Shop and café Mon-Wed 0830-1930; Thu-Fri 0800-1600; Sat 0900-1800. Restaurant Mon-Fri until 2400; Sat 0900-1800. Wine bar Mon-Sat 1100-2400. Sushi bar Mon-Wed 1100-1930; Thu and Fri 1100-2000; Sat 1100-1800.

For almost 150 years, Julius Meinl am Graben has been supplying Vienna with the best coffee, not a mean feat in a city that takes this drink so seriously. It has certainly kept up with the times, and, in addition to a café, bar, restaurant and world-class delicatessen, now also offers a sushi bar. The wine bar is of the caliber you would expect, given these credentials. Thirty wines are available by the glass, and, if you are lucky, your visit will coincide with one of the monthly wine tastings, presented by a top winemaker,

The cube at LOISIUM, designed by Steven Holl.

often Austrian but occasionally from elsewhere. There is a small corkage fee for bottles consumed in the bar, which can be accompanied by a delicious range of light meals and snacks.

SHOP | VIENNA

### Wein & Co

Jasomirgottstraße 3-5, 1010 Vienna
T +43 (0)1-535 0916
www.weinco.at
Mon-Sat 1000-2400, Sun 1100-2400.

Sometimes I wish I lived in Austria, a country where wine lovers are lucky to be able to do their shopping in the impressive Wein & Co chain of supermarket-style emporia. The Jasomirgottstraße branch (the chain's flagship) not only offers a phenomenally wide range of Austrian and imported wines, but also has a hip wine bar. There's chillout music, 100 wines by the glass, the chance to drink wines from the shop list at a small premium, and dishes that are chosen to complement the liquid in your glass.

RESTAURANT | VIENNA

### Zum Schwarzen Kameel

Bognergasse 5, Innere Stadt, 1010 Vienna
T+43 (0)1-533 8125
www.kameel.at
Mon-Sat 0830-1500, 1800-2230.
$$

A Vienna institution since 1618, Zum Schwarzen Kameel was a regular haunt of Beethoven. It houses both a café, whose counters groan with open-faced sandwiches, and a marvellously intact Art Deco restaurant, specializing in fish; the latter has only 11 tables so it is wise to book in advance. An excellent selection of Austrian wines is available, as are many opportunities for people-watching in what is still very much a local Viennese haunt.

## Wachau

Grüner Veltliner country par excellence, this is the region with the greatest buzz at the moment for dry white wines, thanks in part to its critical mass of top class winemakers.

WINERY | DUERNSTEIN

### Freie Weingärtner Wachau

3601 Dürnstein
T+43 (0)2711 371
www.fww.at
May-Sep Mon-Sat 0900-1800; Oct-Apr Mon-Sat 1000-1600.
€10 for tasting and tour.

One of the best cooperatives in Europe, and one of the best producers in Austria, FWW, as it is known locally, makes nearly half the wine in the Wachau. A tasting here is a great way to learn about Austrian wine today.

## Best producers

**Austria**

Alois Kracher
Alzinger
Bründlmayer
Emmerich Knoll
Erich Polz
Feiler-Artinger
Franz Hirtzberger
Franz Xavier Pichler » *page 197.*
Freie Weingärtner Wachau » *page 197.*
Gross
Kollwentz
Krutzler
Nikolaihof
Prager » *page 197.*
Tement
Umathum
Velich
Wieninger
Willi Opitz » *page 196.*



WINERY | DUERNSTEIN

### Weingut FX Pichler

Oberloiben 27, 3601 Dürnstein
T+43 (0)2732-85375
www.fx-pichler.at
Visits by appointment only.

Set in the stunning Wachau, a UNESCO World Heritage site, Franz Xavier Pichler's 13-ha estate is a magnet for fans of modern Austrian wine, as indeed is the man himself. Pichler's brilliant single vineyard Grüner Veltliners and Rieslings are hard to find outside Austria, as their popularity makes allocations far smaller than importers would wish, so a visit to the winery might be the best chance of sampling them. Pichler is a perfectionist, and so loyal to each parcel of vineyard that he gives new meaning to 'capturing terroir'. Not just an Austrian wine star, he is increasingly considered one of the world's top producers of white wine.

WINERY | WACHAU

### Weingut Prager

Weissenkirchen 48, 3610
T+43 (0)2715-2248
www.weingutprager.at
Visits by appointment only.

The Prager family has been making wine in the vineyards that make up this estate since the early 18th century. Toni Bodenstein, who took over from his father-in-law Franz Prager, has dedicated himself to studying the geology of each of terroir, down to the last tiny rock; an attention to detail that is evident in the complexity of his wines. Rieslings and Grüner Veltliners dominate, though there are some parcels of Chardonnay and Sauvignon Blanc. One of Wachau's pioneers, he was instrumental in the formation of **Vinea Wachau**, an association of around 200 Wachau winemakers "sustaining the support of quality and the worldwide reputation of their wines".

# Czech Republic and Slovakia

**In the days after the fall of the Iron Curtain, there were high hopes for wines from both of the countries of former Czechoslovakia. There are vineyard slopes that would not look out of place in the best parts of Burgundy and a winemaking history in Slovakia that may date back 3000 years. These days, though, beer has taken precedence over wine, with the average wine consumption under eight litres per person, less than a third of what it is in neighbouring Hungary. The interesting local white grape varieties in Slovakia are Grüner Veltliner and the Muscat-like Irsay Oliver, while the St Laurent and Frankovka can both produce good reds. Some of the vineyards are close to Tokaj in Hungary and produce similar wine, although, sadly, the quality is not as high. In the Czech Republic, where most of the wine is made in Moravia, the grape mix is similar, with rather more Riesling.**

## Czech Republic

RESTAURANT PRAGUE

### La Scene Restaurant

U Milosrdnych 6, Old Town, 11000 Prague 1
T+42 (0)222 312 677
www.lascene.cz
Restaurant daily 1900-2400. Wine bar 1100-0200; food served 1200-1600. Champagne Club 1900-0200.
$$-$$$

Located in the heart of the Old Town, La Scene is the face of new Prague. It exudes understated style and offers a range of special touches. At lunch, for example, natural light is allowed to flood the restaurant through an intricate system of sliding ceiling panels, while at night the live entertainment might feature a jazz band or a spot of Cuban music. Georges-André Rognard's food is exquisite; the shortish menu features such treats as foie gras or tiger prawns in tempura with mango and pineapple salsa, but if you prefer to drink rather than eat, there are two separate bars: a Champagne and cigar club, and a café and lounge bar that also does breakfast. The international wine list is good, if not long, though occasionally you may have to ask for producers' names.

WINERY MIKULOV

### Tanzberg Mikulov

Bavory 132, 69201 Mikulov
T+42 (0)519 500040 9
www.tanzberg.cz
May-Sep daily 0900-1700; Oct-Apr Mon-Fri 0700-1700. Tours by appointment.

Founded in 1999, this winery, located in a nature reserve, has a history that begins in the 17th century. The 68 ha of vineyards are located next to the Pálava Hills in the warmest part of the country and are planted to Welschriesling, Grüner Veltliner, Pinot Blanc and Pinot Gris, with an emphasis on low yields and limited chemicals. The winery is beautifully kept, with stunning, impressively lit stone cellars. It is worth contacting the winery ahead, as they are happy to help you plan your visit to this historic viticultural area.

## Slovakia

WINERY JU NOSLOVENSKÁ

### Château Belá

Kastiel Belá, 94353 Belá Posta Luba
T+421 903 201 780
www.scharzhof.de
Visits by appointment only.

Aerial view of old town Prague.

Château Belá, which first produced the Riesling in which it specialises in 2001, is a collaboration between top German producer Egon Müller and Baron Ullmann, who recently reclaimed his family's beautiful ancestral home near Stûrovo, close to Hungary's royal city of Esztergom. Tastings are by appointment only, but highly recommended.

WINERY MALOKARPATSKÁ

### Masaryk

Sasinkova 18A, 909 01 Skalica,
T+421 (0)34 664 6960
www.vino-masaryk.sk
Shop Mon-Fri 0700-1600. Tours and tastings by appointment only.

Aloiz Mazaryk's father made wine before the vineyards were taken over by the state and Aloiz continued to do so under the Communist regime until, in 1996, he relaunched his estate with the help of a local and a Swiss investor. Today his wines, which include a fine St-Laurent (Svatovařinečké) red, are some of the best in the region, and his old cellar is a great place to taste them.

# Hungary

### Wine tourism

Wine tourism is relatively embryonic in Hungary, as it is elsewhere in the countries that were once behind the Iron Curtain, but the areas of Eger in the northeast, Balaton and Tokaj-Hegyalja are all now keenly embracing the notion of welcoming visitors.

**Eger**, home of Bull's Blood (see below), is a lovely baroque town and the 140 km of labrynthine wine cellars in nearby Szepasszony-Volgy are well worth the detour. The name is helpfully translated in English on the sign as 'Nice Lady Valley', which may refer to a beautiful, long-haired female demon in a white dress who comes out in rain storms and seduces young men. Szilvásvárad, home of the Lippizzaner stallions, is also worth a visit.

The shallow lake **Balaton** was a favourite holiday spot during the Communist years, when travel to other countries was not an option. Today, however, the vineyards on the north side of the water are beginning to attract wine tourists with a yen to taste some of the local grapes that are grown here. English is, however, far from universally spoken in the cellars.

**Tokaj-Hegyalja** is far better set up for tourists, thanks to the efforts of the many outside investors who have helped breathe new life into this region. Wineries like Royal Tokay and Disznoko are not unlike their counterparts in France, but what sets the region apart is the plethora of individual cellars that are carved into the hillsides.

Hungary's climate is typically continental – baking hot in mid summer and very chilly in winter – but the spring and early summer (March to June) and autumn are great times to be here. October is a particularly good time to visit because it will provide the opportunity to see how Tokaji is made. In September, every year, the **Hungarian Viniculture Foundation** runs a wine festival in Budapest; for details go to www.winefestival.hu.94

### History

Hungary's winemaking began with the Romans and has continued ever since – even during the 150 years of Turkish occupation. Attila the Hun is said to have been a fan and, in the late ninth century AD, another ruler, Arpád, rewarded nobles with vines in the area we now call Tokaj.

Hungary's best known red wine, **Bikaver** or **Bull's Blood**, got its name in 1552, when the town of Eger repelled a besieging Turkish army. The man responsible for this feat was the local hero Istvan Dobo, who dragooned the womenfolk into bombarding the attackers with rocks and fueled the men's ardour with large quantities of red wine. When the teetotal Turks saw the stains on the Hungarians' shirts, they imagined it to be bull's blood, decided that it was giving the defenders extra strength and ran away. Ever since, the wine of Eger Bikaver has been known as Bull's Blood. It may say something about Hungarian preoccupations but **Tokaji**, the country's best known white, also has a reputation for providing strength, but in this case its effect is more Viagra-like.

The years of communism were not kind to Hungary's wine industry, with lovingly made Tokaji bartered for Russian petrol on a litre-for-litre basis. It is only now beginning to recover. However, outside investors have breathed new life into Tokaji and a new generation of winemakers is reviving the reputation of Eger Bikaver.

### Understanding Hungarian wine

*Bor* is wine, and a winemaker is a *Borász*, his or her winery is a *borászat*, a wine region is a *borvidék* and a wine merchant is a *borkereskedõ*. The official quality of wine rises from *Asztali*, *Folyóbor* and *Kimert* (basic) to *Tajbor* and *Kötnyéki* (country wine) and *minõségi* (quality wine); each of these terms precedes 'Bor'. If the wine is red, it is *vörös* , if white, *fehér*. If it is dry it is *száraz*, if semi-sweet *félédes* or *félszáraz* and if sweet it's *édes*. Sparkling wine is *pezsgõ* and a vintage is *évjárat*.

### Grapes

Hungary has large plantations of international varieties such as Cabernet Sauvignon, Chardonnay, Merlot and Sauvignon Blanc. The following varieties are the most interesting local grapes.

### White grapes

**Furmint** A perfumed grape principally used for Tokaji – and increasingly for dry wines there.

**Hárslevelü** An intensely spicy-floral grape that is used with the Furmint in Tokaji.

**Irsai Olivér** An interesting, grapey, Muscat-like grape that produces attractive dry wines.

### Red grapes

**Kadarka** The most widely planted grape in Hungary, but not the most interesting. The wines it makes are, at best, soft, easy and juicy.

**Kékfrankos** Limberger.

**Kékportó** Portugieser.

## Vintages

| | |
|---|---|
| **2005** | Very good to great. |
| **2004** | Good in Tokaj and generally good elsewhere but high acidity was often a problem. |
| **2003** | Good to very good in Tokaj and elsewhere but the drought caused overripening in many areas, particularly of white. |
| **2002** | Mixed everywhere. |
| **2001** | Mixed everywhere. |
| **2000** | Great in Tokaj and in other parts of the region. |

Grapevine

**Tokay /Tokaj/Tokaji**

One of the more confusing names of the wine world has to be Tokay. Until recent efforts were made to clear matters up, there were four different wines with very similar names. In Alsace, wine made from the Pinot Gris was known as Tokay d'Alsace; a sweet, fortified wine from northeast Victoria in Australia was also called Tokay, despite being made from a Bordeaux white grape called the Muscadelle. Italy still has the soon-to-be-phased-out Tocai Friulani, which is actually the name of yet another grape; and finally there is Hungary's Tokaji (the wine from Tokaj), which also used to be called Tokay. No one is certain why all these regions came to use the same term, although it is said that, in 1560, an Alsatian called Lazzarus Schwendi asked his vineyard manager to order some Tokaji vines from Hungary. When they didn't arrive, the manager simply substituted the Pinot Gris.

## Budapest

WINE BAR — BUDAPEST

### 1894 Borvendéglõ

Állatkerti út 2, 1146 Budapest
T+36 1 468 4044
www.gundel.hu
Daily 1200-1600 and 1830-2400.
$$$

Budapest institution Gundel, a restaurant that has dominated the city's culinary life for more than a century, now has a superb wine bar, 1894 Borvendéglõ, located in the cellar below. The list of wines by the glass is positively daunting: around 100 are offered at a time and the selection changes every month. Every possible corner of viticultural Hungary is represented, making it a good place to orientate yourself before striking out into the field. Delicious snacks are available or, if you prefer more ample refreshment, the chef can design a meal around your chosen bottle of wine. There are also some excellent set meals, such as a Hungarian wine and cheese menu. You can buy wine to take away and, if you book ahead, in-depth courses in Hungarian wine are also available.

DINNER CRUISE — BUDAPEST

### Mahart Passnave

Belgrád rakpart Nemzetközi-Hajóállomás, 1056 Budapest
T+36 1 20310 6685 / 484 4000
ext 145 or 156
www.mahartpassnave.hu
Jun-Aug daily 1900; Apr, May, Sep, Oct Fri, Sat, Sun only.
$$

Mahart Passnave's fleet of ships has recently added a new evening cruise to its many sightseeing options. Approximately one evening a month, you can turn up at the appointed pier on Vigadó Square and be spirited away for a few hours down the Danube for a tutored wine tasting followed by dinner. Each event is hosted by a different Hungarian winemaker, who might be an established Tokaji producer or an up-and-coming Villány one.

WINE BAR — BUDAPEST

### Vörös és Fehét

Andrássy út 41, Pest VI
T 413 1545
T +36 1 413 1545
Daily 1200-2400.
$

Figula winery.

A true local's haunt, Vörös és Fehét offers more than 100 wines, with a good selection by the glass. Once a month, a region or producer's wine is highlighted at a special dinner. Both snacks and meals are available.

## Balaton

WINERY — BALATONFURED

### Figula Winery

Siske u 44/b, 8230 Balatonfüred
T+36 8734 3557 / +36 87 481 661
www.figula.hu
Visits by appointment only.

Founded in 1993 by Mihály Figula, a passionate, welcoming man with an enormous shock of white curly hair, this Balaton winery has swiftly garnered awards in international competitions for its various varietal wines, which include Chardonnays, Pinot Gris and both Cabernets. The winery has a double-bedded apartment that can be rented, and is happy to arrange for visitors and guests to eat regional specialties at the local **Tölgyfa Csárda** restaurant ($).

## Badascony

**WINERY** BADASCONY

### Szeremley

Elsõ Magyar Borház Kft (First Hungarian Wine House), Fö út 51-53, 8258 Badacsonytomaj
T+36 87 571 210
www.szeremley.com
Shop Mon-Thu 0800-1530; Fri 0800-1300. Tastings Jul-Sep daily 1200-2000. Tours by appointment.

Huba Szeremley is a major figure on the Hungarian wine scene. As well as founding the Hungarian Winemaster Guild, he also spearheaded the annual Wine Village event (www.borfalu.hu), a festival of Hungarian wine that takes place in Budapest. His large holdings include the 19th-century Helvácia Estate, with views across Lake Balaton, and he produces a range of exciting wines from both international and indigenous grape varieties. Not content to stop here, he has also opened the nearby **Szánt Orban Restaurant** (Szegedy Róza utca 22, T +36 87-431382), which offers free-range beef and freshwater fish. Most recently, Szeremley has apparently become friends with Gérard Dépardieu and there is talk of a joint winemaking venture...

## Szekszárd

**WINERY** SZEKSZARD

### Takler Pince

Bem ut 13 7100 Szekszárd
T+36 74 315187 / 30 9293042
Tastings by appointment

The reputation of Hungary's red wines suffered badly during the years behind the Iron Curtain, but tighter regulations and dedicated producers are revitalising a region that inspired Liszt to write his Szekszárd Mass. Ferenc Takler and his sons, Ferenc and András, who make some of the best red wine in the region from Kékfrankos, Cabernet Sauvignon, Cabernet Franc, and Merlot are working their 75 ha hard in order to recapture the former glory of their area.

**Tasting notes**

**Understanding Tokaji**

Tokaji is a wholly unique wine that combines traditional techniques of making wine from partly dried grapes and from grapes affected by noble rot. Twenty-five-kilogram batches of nobly rotten Furmint and Hárlevelü grapes (called *aszú*) are left in wooden hods called *puttonyos* for a week, during which a thick, ultra-sweet syrup known as *esszencia* is drained from them. The remaining *aszú* is then worked into a paste and added to a 136 litre vat of dry wine made from the same grape varieties. The sweetness of a Tokaji is indicated by the number of *puttonyos* that have been added to the vat. Most are four to six *puttonyos* – similar to German Trockenbeerenauslese in sweetness – while *Aszúesszencia* is the equivalent of seven or eight *puttonyos*. This is the sweetest, most intense style, apart from pure *Esszencia* which, at 3-5% alcohol is barely describable as wine. Traditionally, *Esszencia* was the preserve of royalty and thought to have similar qualities to Viagra.

## Tokaj-Hegyalja

**WINERY** TOKAJ

### Disznoko

PF 10, 3910 Tokaj
T+36 47 569 410
www.disznoko.hu
Vists by appointment only.

An emblem of a revitalized Hungary, Disznoko was for centuries a celebrated producer of Tokaji, but was largely abandoned during the Socialist era. Since the 1990s, with the backing of French insurance group AXA (owners of Château Pichon Longueville in Bordeaux), it is back on its feet again and producing award-winning sweet wines. The impressive new winery features a long tunnel lined on either side, from floor to ceiling, with Tokaji 5 and 6 Puttonyos bottles. You will receive a warm welcome here and, if you book ahead, the winery can help arrange meals and accommodation.

**WINERY** MAD

### Royal Tokaji Co

Rakoczi Ut 35, 3909 Mád
T+36 47 548500
www.royal-tokaji.com
Visits by appointment only.

A must on any visit to the region, this winery is another Tokaji rags-to-riches story. With the help of foreign investment, input from celebrated wine writer Hugh Johnson and savvy marketing, Royal Tokaji has in the past couple of decades risen to garner top international awards and can be seen as an ambassador for both the region and Hungary itself. The stunning cellars will take you back centuries.

## Villány

**WINERY** VILLANY

### Attila Gere

Erkel Ferenc u 2/A, 7773 Villány
T+36 72 492 839
www.gere.hu
Wine shop and tasting room daily; call ahead to confirm times. Tours by appointment.

Attila Gere, a star of Villány, Hungary's southernmost winemaking district, produces premium wines, such as Solus Merlot, that give icon wines from other countries a run for their money. He is extremely passionate about both his region and what he has achieved. A tour here starts in the new visitor centre, with a view of the surrounding hills, and provides an excellent introduction to qualitative modern winemaking and also into working with such Hungarian specialities as Kékoportó and Kékfrankos. The winery also owns a 14-room guesthouse ($) in the heart of Villány (Diófás tér 4, T +36 72 492 195), which features a sauna and jacuzzi, a lovely terrace and a traditional cellar, perfect for tastings. With advance notice, meals can be provided ($) and a range of activities can be arranged.

WINERY VILLANY

### József Bock

Batthyány u 15, 7773 Villány
T+36 72 492 919
www.bock.hu
Cellar daily 0900-1800.
Restaurant Mon-Thu and Sun 1100-2000; Fri and Sat 1100-2200.

József Bock, another Villány star, has reinvigorated his family's vineyards and pursued his passion for making Bordeaux-style blends. The winery owns an inn ($) and a Villány restaurant ($), specializing in local dishes, and can provide various packages for wine tourists.

## Poland

**According to Polish wine and music critic, Wojciech Bonkowski, medieval Poland made enough wine to export to Germany and Italy. At one time, there were some 4000 vineyards, most based around Zielona Góra in the west and Warka in the east of the country, but it soon made more sense to import grapes and, subsequently, wine from warmer vineyards in neighbouring Hungary. The name Számorodni, now used for light Tokaji, is a Polish term meaning 'self-generating' and referred to the way the Hungarian grapes began to ferment on the journey to the winery in Poland. During the 19th century, as elsewhere in Eastern Europe, Poland had an aristocracy that enjoyed and could afford good French wine. This tradition has been revived since the fall of the Berlin Wall and there is now a flourishing wine market. Consumption is still low, however, at just six litres per head, and tastes still often run to wine that is sweet and red. Wine erroneously describing itself as 'Polish' is sold in the country, but small amounts of the genuine article are also being produced, by a retired chemist and nurseryman called Roman Mysliwiec from cold-resistant hybrid varieties like Seyval Blanc at the Winnica Golesz winery (www.winnica.golesz.pl), close to the Slovakian border at Jaslo.**

WINE BAR WARSAW

### Winiarnia 'Pod Pretextem'

ul Powstancow Slaskich 104, Warsaw
T+48 (0)22 436 4508
www.podpretextem.pl
Daily for lunch and dinner.
($)

Jolanta Gajewska and her son run this intimate wine bar, whose cosiness coolly contrasts with the impersonality of the high rise building in which it is located. The bar is owned by Grand Cru, a company that imports premium wine into Poland and is known for the diversity of its range as well as for the care with which it handles and stores the wines. Pod Pretextem offers a large selection of fairly priced wines by the glass and bottles to drink in situ along with light snacks, such as quiches and tarts.

Zamkowy Square, Warsaw.

# Best producers

**Hungary**

Bock, József » *page 202.*
Château Pajzos
Domaine de Disznoko
Figula Winery » *page 200.*
Attila Gere » *page 201.*
Hetszolo
Kamocsay, Akos
Királyudvar
Kúria, Malatinszky
Royal Tokaji » *page 201.*
Szepsy, Istvan
Szeremley » *page 201.*
Takler Pince » *page 201.*
Thummerer, Vilmos
Tokaj-Oremus
Weninger

# Switzerland

The line uttered by Orson Welles as Harry Lime in *The Third Man* is worth repeating: "In Italy, for 30 years under the Borgias, they had warfare, terror, murder, bloodshed, but they produced Michelangelo, Leonardo da Vinci and the Renaissance. In Switzerland they had brotherly love; they had 500 years of democracy and peace. And what did that produce? The cuckoo clock." Most people would concede that the Swiss have also given us some pretty good chocolate but few would mention wine. Switzerland is usually thought to be too cold to grow grapes and, besides, who has ever encountered a Swiss wine outside Switzerland? There are some simple explanations for the invisibility of these wines. First, export quantities are low. The Swiss get through around 50 litres per head – making them among the thirstiest wine drinkers in the world – of which two bottles in five are from their own vineyards, so exporting wine is not a priority. Even if it were, too many of the wines are made from the 'wrong' grapes: the widely grown non-aromatic Chasselas, known here as Fendant. What's more, when compared to offerings from other countries, Swiss wines seem to be expensive. Big wineries are quite rare too; the average landholding is just half a hectare and many producers tend their vines as a hobby.

For anyone approaching Swiss wines with an open mind, however, there are plenty of fascinating delights to be found. The country is divided into three linguistic zones: the small French-speaking area to the west, where over three quarters of the vineyards are to be found (including the Valais and Vaud regions); the huge German-speaking north and centre of the country where little wine is made and less that is good; and the Italian-speaking south where, in Ticino, some truly delicious red and, believe it or not, white Merlots are produced. Switzerland also does well with Pinot Noir (used in wine called Dôle, sometimes in blends with Gamay), Marsanne (known in Switzerland as Ermitage) and Syrah (the Rhône is closer than one might imagine). Other indigenous Swiss varieties of interest include the spicy white Petite Arvine, creamy white Amigne, rich red Cornalin and earthy red Humagne Rouge. The Chasselas, which usually makes flavourless, short-lived whites in France, can make delicately floral, creamy wines here, on the right soil and with limited yields. It also benefits from the sensible Swiss practice of using screwcaps on most of their wines.

Ticino, Switzerland.

## Ticino

WINERY — MENDRISIO

### Guido Brivio

Via Vignoo 8, 6850 Mendrisio
T +41 (0)91 646 0757-58
www.brivio.ch
Visits by appointment only.

President of the Ticino Wine Association (and a good person to ask for directions to other producers), Guido Brivio is also one of the region's biggest producers. He also invented the white Merlot, one of the most fascinating wines in the world and great stuff to serve to a wine buff friend who thinks he/she is good at blind tasting.

## Valais

WINERY — SION

### Provins Valais

Industrie 22, Sion
T+41 (0)840 666 112
www.provins.ch
Tue-Fri 1000-1200 and 1600-1800.

If you want to learn about Swiss wine at its best – or at least the wines of the Valais – there is no better place to go than the Espace Millésime shop at this cooperative's Sion winery. Provins actually has five wineries and produces a huge range of wines under the Maître de Chais, Charte d'Excellence, Le Pichet and Domaines & Découvertes labels, covering all the grape varieties grown here, including Sauvignon Blanc, Marsanne and Syrah as well as the local Humagne, Cornallin and Amigne. There are also some interesting blends and single domaine wines as well as the opportunity to try and buy the official wine of the Vatican Guard. The quality across the board is impeccable.

WINERY VETROZ

### Jean-René Germanier

Balavaud, 1963 Vétroz
T+41 (0)27 346 1216
www.jrgermanier.ch
Mon-Fri 1700-2300; Sat 1000-2000.

For more than a century the Germanier family has been making some of Switzerland's best wines. Jean-René Germanier and his nephew, Gilles Besses, are continuing the tradition and can give you an insightful introduction to some of the wonderful varieties that are mostly unknown outside Switzerland, which has traditionally kept its excellent wines to itself. These include the earthy Humagne Rouge and the aromatic Petite Arvigne, as well as the oft-maligned Chasselas, stuff of the plonkiest plonk, which, in the right hands, can become surprisingly complex and distinguished.

# Best producers

**Liechtenstein**

Hofkellerei des Fürsten » *page 204.*

**Switzerland**

Guido Brivio » *page 203.*
Jean-René (Bon Père) Germanier » *page 204.*
Robert Gilliard
Daniel Huber
Adriano Kaumann
Simon Maye » *page 204.*
E de Montmollin
Les Perrieres
Provins » *page* .
Rouvinez
Werner Stucky
Luigi Zanini

WINERY ST-PIERRE-DE-CLAGES

### Cave Simon Maye et Fils

Collombey 3, 1955 St-Pierre-de-Clages
T +41 (0)27 306 4181
www.simonmaye.ch
Visits by appointment only.

Like many Swiss producers, the Maye family make many wines, from many grapes, across many vineyard parcels. This is a particularly welcoming winery and it is worth calling ahead to see if Antoinette Maye can arrange a guided walk through some of the vineyards to explain the effect of the many intriguing soil-types and underlying rock beds created by Switzerland's unique geology.

## Zurich

WINE BAR ZURICH

### Caduff's Wine Loft

Kanzleistraße 126, 8004 Zurich
T+41 (0)44 240 2255
www.wineloft.ch
Mon-Fri 1130-1400 and 1700-2400; Sat 1700-2400.

I was taken to this unique wine bar by Alois Kracher, one of Austria's top producers, and I fell in love with it immediately. It operates on delightfully democratic principles. The menu changes each day, according to what is available in Zurich's market, and dishes are offered on a first-come, first-served basis until, inevitably, there is nothing left, so popular is the food. Half-portions are also available, a blessing for omnivores who want to try everything. If the food has run out, there are 60 cheeses to console you and that is even before you get a glimpse of the wine offer. Beat Caduff has put together more than 2000 wines, 20 or so of which are offered by the glass, rotating every other week. The setting is almost stark, but the ambience is so lively and the wines so good, that you won't notice.

## Liechtenstein

The Principality of Liechtenstein has a wine history stretching back at least as far as the Emperor Charlemagne in the ninth century. Wedged between Switzerland and the western tip of Austria, it is tiny enough for Prince Hans-Adam II to be able to invite all of his subjects to an annual garden party in his castle. The Prince has his own vineyard, as do some 99 other producers, including Harry Zech, captain of the national soccer team, whose wines are worth looking out for. The most widely-planted grape is Pinot Noir but other varieties include Gewürztraminer and even Shiraz. In a recent move, Liechtenstein has introduced an Appellation Contrôlée system, which requires growers to farm organically. Better wines are labelled 'Selection Liechtenstein' while there is a Grand Cru designation for wines scoring more than 85 out of 100 in a blind tasting. A great place to stay and enjoy the wines here is the luxury Park-Hotel Sonnenhof (www.Sonnenhof.li)

WINERY VADUZ

### Hofkellerei des Fürsten von Liechtenstein

Fürstliche Domäne, Feldstraße 4, 9490 Vaduz
T+423 (0)232 1018
www.hofkellerei.li, www.fuerstenhaus.li
Mon-Fri 0800-1200, 1330-1830;, Sat 0900-1300.
CHF22-25.

Ten minutes' walk from the heart of Liechtenstein, these royal cellars are in the heart of the equally royal vineyards and offer great views of the royal castle at Schloss Vaduz. The Hofkellerei's Vaduzer Pinot Noir 'Bocker' is a particular star. Admission includes a free tasting.

# The Balkans

**Before the country that was once Yugoslavia fell apart, it was known for cheap, off-dry white wine – Lazki Rizling – and for an unrealised potential to produce good red. Today three of the independent Balkan states are beginning to make a vinous name for themselves. Of these, Slovenia, the wealthiest of the trio has by far the best wines. It was the source of a red wine made in Istria called Pucinum that was said by Pliny to have been responsible for the Roman Empress Livia's longevity. Today, Slovenia's whites tend to be more impressive, which is also true of Croatia, but the discovery that this was the original home of the Zinfandel (known here as the Crljenak Kastelanski) has encouraged efforts to exploit it more than in the past. Macedonia – which confusingly shares its name with a winemaking province of Greece – is more focused on reds, using the local Kratosija and Vranac grapes. Mike Grgich, the Californian winery owner, has returned to his European roots; how long will it be before his example is followed by some of the many New Zealand winemakers with Croatian forebears?**

## Croatia

WINERY | HVAR

### Bastijana

21465 Jelsa, Hvar
T/F+385 (0)21 768160
www.bastijana.hr
Visits by appointment

The island of Hvar, which boasts a winegrowing history dating from Ancient Greek times, has been called the Madeira of the Adriatic. After years of making wine elsewhere, island native Andro Tomiæ has returned home to produce a range of premium wines, using mainly indigenous Dalmatian grape varieties, in styles ranging from young rosé to port. Of especial pride to Tomiæ is his Prošek, a traditional Croatian dessert wine made using dried grapes.

WINERY | TRSTENIK

### Grgič Vina

78, 20245 Trstenik
T+385 (0)20 748090
Visits by appointment only.

Grgič Vina is a lovely, if quirky, example of the reverse migrations that are increasingly taking place in the wine world as New World and Old World exchange talent and dynastic titles. It was founded in 1996 by Miljenko 'Mike' Grgich, a Napa Valley legend who had fled his native Croatia in 1954 and eventually found his way to California. Among many other career highlights, he was responsible for the 1976 Chateau Montelena Chardonnay that stumped the competition at the famous 1976 Judgment of Paris blind tasting. The winery specializes in Pošip and the red Plavać Mali.

## Macedonia

WINERY | SKOPJE

### Chateau Kamnik

Kamnik bb, 1000 Skopje
T +389 (0)2 252 3522
www.kamnik.com.mk
Contact the winery for opening times.

Chateau Kamnik's new winery is still being built as we go to press, but the **Hunter's Lodge** next door already offers 10 rooms ($-$$), a restaurant ($-$$), specializing in game and a wine bar offering 50 local and 100 non-Macedonian wines. All of this is between the airport and Skopje, making it an ideal alternative to the hotels in the city.

## Slovenia

WINERY | MARIBOR

### Protnerjeva hiša Joannes

Vodole 34, 2000 Maribor
T+386 (0)2 473 2100
www.slovino.com/joannes
Visits by appointment only.

The wood-fired oven in the restaurant ($) attached to this winery turns out wonderful bread and local delicacies. It's a perfect opportunity to continue to sample the wide range of wines produced after the tour.

WINERY | IVANJKOVCI

### Vino Kupljen

Jeruzalem-Svetinje, 2259 Ivanjkovci
Winery T+386 (0)2 719 4001.
Restaurant T+386 (0)2 719 4015
www.taverna-mn.si
Daily 1100-2300.

This enterprising winery offers not only a restaurant ($) and shop but also a wine academy where you can take lessons in wine-tasting leading to a certificate. It also boasts Slovenia's first 'national wine bank', whereby you can buy wine for laying down in the winery's own cellar. Family-owned since 1836, the winery and its surroundings are charming.

Wines from Thrace were praised by Homer in *The Iliad*.

## Bulgaria

**The recent discovery, near Assenovgrad, of a temple to Dionysus, the god of wine, and some 6000-year-old vinous artefacts support Bulgaria's claim to be one of the earliest wine-producing nations. Much of ancient Bulgaria was part of the kingdom of Thrace, home to Spartacus, the slave who led a rebellion against the Roman Empire, and the source of wines praised by Homer in *The Iliad*. The Romans took Bulgarian wine seriously and, in the second century AD, the Emperor Antonius Pius issued an edict to protect vineyards in the region of Lower Mizia. There are ideal conditions for winemaking here, as well as some interesting local grapes. Sadly, the wine industry is looking a lot feebler than it did 25 years ago, when Bulgarian Cabernet Sauvignon was synonymous with good value modern red. Bulgaria's recent heyday came in the 1970s when Pepsi Cola accepted wine from Bulgaria in exchange for the soft drinks it sold there. To make the wine more acceptable to American (and other non-Bulgarian) consumers, Pepsi helped to modernize the industry, with the help of Californian expertise. Sadly for Bulgaria, however, it has failed to build on those foundations and the privatized, post-Iron Curtain industry is struggling to find a role for itself. Recent investment may help.**

WINERY | PAZARDJIK

### Bessa Valley Winery

Zad baira, Pazardjik, Ognianovo 4417
T+359 (0)88 949 9992
www.bessavalley.com
Mon-Fri 0900-1200 and 1200-1700.

Count Stephan von Neipperg, of Canon La Gaffelière in St-Émilion, and Dr Karl-Heinz Hauptmann teamed up in 2001 to buy 266 ha of land from more than 800 people in Ognianovo, in the Bessa Valley. Although the winery is in its infancy, the millions of Euros that have been invested in planting new vines and building a modern winery are already paying off, with orders from around the world and plaudits from wine critics. This winery is clearly going places and is worth a detour not just for the wines themselves, but also to see just how fast, with the right know-how and resources, a winery can emerge from the dust. In future it may be a coup to be able to tell your grandchildren or great-grandchildren that you were one of the winery's earliest visitors.

WINERY | DAMIANITZA

### Damianitza Winery Sandanski

Damianitza 2813, Sandanski
T+359 (0)746 30090
www.damianitza.bg
Visits by appointment only.

Quality not quantity is key here, making Damianitza rather unusual in the recent history of Bulgarian winemaking for which the reverse has mostly been true. This small winery specializes in Melnik, an indigenous Bulgarian grape variety particular to this region, but also makes wines from Cabernet Sauvignon, Merlot and Cabernet Franc, as well as Rubin, a crossing of Nebbiolo-Syrah. As well as an illuminating one-hour tour of the winery, Damianitza also offers several tours to the nearby village of Melnik, which boasts examples of Bulgarian vernacular architecture from the Middle Ages onwards. A meal can be arranged in a villager's house, offering a chance to taste these traditional-style wines with traditional Bulgarian peasant food.

# Black Sea states

## Georgia

Rivalling Turkey and Armenia for the role of oldest wine-producing nation on earth, Georgia has archeological evidence of a winemaking history stretching back over 5000 years. During the Soviet era, Georgia, one of the most beautiful and most climatically blessed regions of the old Bloc, also benefited from being Stalin's homeland. People here lived rather easier lives than elsewhere and the wine industry continued to enjoy a much better reputation in the region than Moldova or the Ukraine. In particular, the area was known for red wines made from the Saperavi grape and whites from the Rkatsateli. Until the wall came down, as elsewhere in the area, most of the wine was badly made by cooperatives, with some being produced by farms where it was fermented and stored in huge amphorae of the kind used by the Greeks and Romans. One speciality for which few outsiders ever developed a taste was deeply golden white wine that looked 20 years older than it was and had the tannic dryness of a tough old French red. Recently, the proud Georgian wine industry was rocked by the announcement – by an official of the Food and Agriculture Organization of the United Nations (FAO) – that up to 80% of its wine was at least partly faked (made with alcohol and colouring). This news gave President Putin an excuse to ban all Georgian wine from its main market, Russia. For the moment, within and outside Georgia, the reliable brands to look out for are Tamada and Old Tblisi, both of which are made by GWS (Georgian Wine Services), a joint venture involving Pernod Ricard. One word of warning: any lunch or dinner with Georgians usually involves a 'head-of-table' whose task is to instigate a very large number of bottoms-up toasts.

RESTAURANT TBLISI

**Le Sans Souci**

13 Shavteli St, Tblisi
T+995 32 986594
Call ahead to confirm opening times.

This wooden restaurant, on a corner near the Anchiskati church, is run by Rezo Gabriadze, a puppeteer who has a theatre next door. This is a good place to taste *khatchapuri* (traditional pizza-like parcels filled with cheese), *Khinkali* dumplings filled with juicy mince meat and Georgian wine.

## Moldova

This former Soviet republic next to Romania has been producing wine for 3000 years – and exporting it to neighbouring countries, especially Russia. The Romanov Tsar Alexander I built a winery here – and gave his name to the region of Romanesti. During the Soviet era, while Stalin preferred wine from his native Georgia, he and his successors oversaw the importation of 80% of Moldova's annual crop. After the fall of the Soviet Union, there was a brief spate of European and Australian investment fuelled by a belief in the potential of the climate and soil of a region called Hincesti. (For a brief moment a German company actually thought an amenable government official might have sold them the monopoly of the entire country's vineyards). Today Moldova's wine producers have high hopes of winning over the world with whites made from the local Rkatsateli and a red blends using the local Saperavi and Cabernet Sauvignon. So far the world has yet to be convinced. Among the wines you are most likely to see are reds from the region of Purcari. Of these the greatest pride is taken in a rustic Saperavi-Cabernet Sauvignon called Negru de Purcari. The Rosu de Purcari is often an easier-going wine – thanks to its smaller dose of Saperavi.

During the Soviet era, Georgia, one of the most beautiful and most climatically blessed regions of the old Bloc, also benefited from being Stalin's homeland.

WINERY CRICOVA

**Cricova Oenotec**

Bookings: Vasile Alecsandri 111/7 St, Chisinau
T+373 22 27 73 78
www.cricova.md
Contact Cricova Tourism for further details.

Joseph Stalin had a very specific wine-related interest in a former limestone mine, buried 80 m beneath the ground at Cricova. This extraordinary place was converted in 1952 into an underground town with 120 km of roads (complete with traffic lights) and a population of over 7500. Cricova's supposed role today is as a winery, producing and storing fairly basic sparkling wine but it is also a vinous Bluebeard's castle. It was here, near the palatial dining rooms, that Stalin stashed Goering's confiscated wine cellar. The thousands of bottles date back to 1902 and include all of the greatest names of the wine world before 1945. The British wine writer Tom Stevenson is not the only person to have conjectured that this is where the Politburo would have relocated to in an emergency; at least they would not have gone thirsty. Recent visitors have noticed that the best vintages seem to be of the most modest wines, and vice versa; a cynic might imagine that the finest bottles of Romanée-Conti and Latour have found other homes.

## Russia

WINERY SADOVY

### Château le Grand Vostock

Krasnodarsky region, Krymsky area, Sadovy Village, 60 let Oktyabrya str., 7
T/F+7 86131 62 718
www.grandvostock.com
Visits by appointment only.

Russia's first and still only premium winery offers the opportunity not only to see top-notch French-inspired winemaking up close – everything, from grapes to barrels to the resident services of Frank Dusseigneur has been imported – but also to get a sense of what pre-revolution country life must have been like. The hotel ($) offers comfortable rooms with all mod cons, and the chance to sample traditional rural fare in the restaurant. Outdoor pursuits include fishing, shooting and horse-riding. Lovers of indigenous and unusual varieties will be able to add several names to their tasting notes. As well as a range of international varieties, the winery also produces wines from local grapes: Krasnostop, Sukholimansky, Golubo, Pkatsiteli and Saperavi.

## Ukraine

WINERY ODESSA

### Massandra

Ekaterinenskaya Sq, Odessa Crimea
T+380 (0)652-232662
www.massandra.crimea.com
Visits by appointment only.

# Best producers

**Bulgaria**

Bessa Valley » *page 206.*
Boyar
Damianitza » *page 206.*
Domaine Menada
Maxxima
Oriachovitza
Domaine Sakar
Santa Saarah
Stork Nest
Suhindol

**Croatia**

Bastijana » *page 205.*
Enjingi, Ivan
Grgič Vina » *page 205.*
Matosevic
Milos, Fran

**Georgia**

GWS

**Greece**

Aidirinis
Ktima Alpha
Antonopoulos
Argyros
Boutari (top wines) » *page 212.*
Evharis » *page 212.*
Gaia Estate
Gentilini
Gerovassilou, Ktima » *page 211.*
Hatzidakis
Hatzimichali
Johannou, Pape
Katogi-Strofilia » *page 212.*
D Kourtakis (top wines)
Kyr Yanni
Lazaridi, Costa
Manousakis
Mercouri, Ktima
Oenoforos
Papaiounnou
Samos Cooperative
Semeli Nemea
Sigalas
Spiropoulos
Tsantali
Tselopos

**Moldova**

Cricova-Acorex » *page 207.*

**Romania**

Halewood Prahova
Murfatlar
Prahova
Recas, Cramele
Reh, Carl
SERVE

**Russia**

Château le Grand Vostock » *page 208.*

**Slovenia**

Èurin-Prapotnik
Kupljen » *page 206.*
Simcic, Edi
Simcic, Marjan
Sutor

**Ukraine**

Massandra » *page 208.*

One of the most important and symbolic wineries in Eastern Europe, Massandra was founded by Tsar Nicholas II in 1894 as a purveyor of fine wines to the Russian royal family. In 1986, after many prior upheavals, it fell on hard times when Mikhail Gorbachev ripped up hundreds of hectares of vineyards in an anti-alcohol campaign. Back on its feet, the winery is now affiliated to the Crimean Research Institute and produces a wide range of wine in many styles, including some rather ordinary dry wines and the far more impressive sweet ones for which it is famous. The tour includes a generous tasting, though it is unlikely to include the older vintages that sometimes fetch high prices at auction.

# Greece

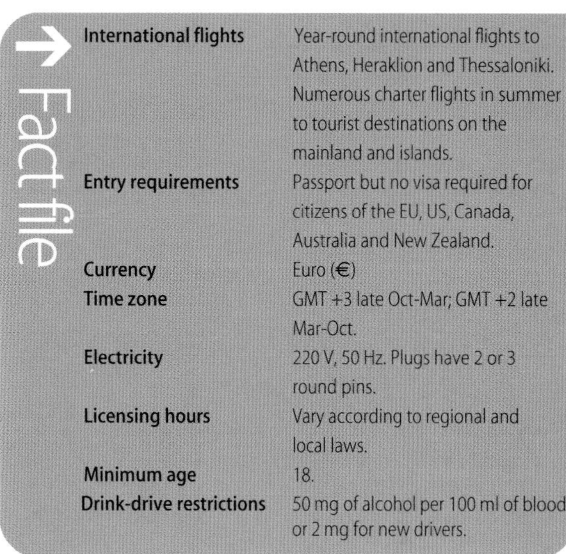

Fact file

| | |
|---|---|
| **International flights** | Year-round international flights to Athens, Heraklion and Thessaloniki. Numerous charter flights in summer to tourist destinations on the mainland and islands. |
| **Entry requirements** | Passport but no visa required for citizens of the EU, US, Canada, Australia and New Zealand. |
| **Currency** | Euro (€) |
| **Time zone** | GMT +3 late Oct-Mar; GMT +2 late Mar-Oct. |
| **Electricity** | 220 V, 50 Hz. Plugs have 2 or 3 round pins. |
| **Licensing hours** | Vary according to regional and local laws. |
| **Minimum age** | 18. |
| **Drink-drive restrictions** | 50 mg of alcohol per 100 ml of blood or 2 mg for new drivers. |

## Planning your trip

Most international airlines serve **Athens' Elefthérios Venizélos** (ATH; www.aia.gr) . This is the country's main hub, with numerous domestic flights serving the rest of the country, including the islands. Many visitors, however, opt to travel to the Greek islands by ferry from the ports at Piréas or Rafina (both near Athens). Tickets are available from domestic travel agents and the tourist office in Athens has up-to-date schedules. Intercity buses are a popular alternative on the mailand and serve almost the entire country, including routes to islands near the mainland, with the ferry crossing included in the price of the ticket. The system is efficient, reliable and relatively inexpensive. The rail network, in contrast, is extremely limited. Greek highways have undergone a massive improvement and expansion programme in recent years, which makes driving around the country much easier that it once was. It is worth noting, however, that the topography presents challenges in some areas and traffic accidents are very common. Car hire rates increase greatly in high season.

**Athens** benefited enormously from the investment and rebuilding programme associated with the 2004 Olympics so it's worth spending at least a few days in the city before you venture further afield. There are a number of wineries within easy reach of Athens, in Attica and on the **Peloponnese** peninsula. The latter also has numerous ancient sites, including **Mycenae**, **Epidaurus** and **Olympia**, the original home of the games. If you're in this area, don't miss the charming Venetian town of **Nafplio** or the train ride through the **Vouraïkos Gorge**. Northwest of Athens is **Mount Parnassos** and the spectacular ruins at **Delphi**. Between Athens and Thessaloniki are the cliff-top monasteries of the **Meteora**, accessed by a series of steps carved into the rocks. Another steep climb is required to reach the summit of **Mount Olympus**, Greece's highest peak at 2917 m. **Thessaloniki** is the dynamic capital of northern Greece. From here you could visit **Vergina**, site of the royal tombs of ancient Macedonia, or head east to **Mount Athos** to taste the spiritual calm – and the wine – of this semi-autonomous monastic region. Offshore, the myriad Greek Islands each have their own character and appeal. The closest to Athens are the **Saronic Gulf Islands** but the other groups are also easily accessible by boat or plane. For further information, consult www.gnto.gr.

## Wine tourism

Wine tourism is a relatively novel concept in Greece, but the new generation of Greek winegrowers is working hard to encourage visitors to explore vineyards throughout the country. Consult their excellent website, www.greekwinemakers.com. Most usefully, they have created nine wine routes (www.wineroads.gr), which bring together wineries, restaurants and hotels, as well as archaeological sites and other places of interest. Greek wineries are open throughout the year and are especially worth visiting during the spring and winter, when there are fewer tourists and distractions for the winemakers.

## History

Yannis Boutaris, one of the most visionary members of the Greek wine fraternity lamented in the 1980s that the trouble with his country's wine industry was that no one in Greece had ever sent a bottle of wine back because it was faulty. He was exaggerating, of course, but standards and expectations were generally woefully low. Given this country's history, as the place that introduced the Italians to wine, it is extraordinary how far Greece's wines had fallen from grace. The simple explanation was that they were not traded internationally and not subject to comparison with the best of France and Italy. One of the problems was that most people outside Greece thought Greek wine and retsina were synonymous and that retsina was a synonym for an unpleasant drink, neither of which is true (page 210).

The modern Greek renaissance began in 1972 when a Greek shipping millionaire, John Carras, employed Bordeaux's top expert Professor Émile Peynaud to help him make a Greek wine that would rival the best of France. Chateau Porto Carras never quite achieved that objective but it was undoubtedly Greece's best wine, until a raft of other small estates (including **Domaine Gerovassiliou**, page 211, produced by the former Carras winemaker) began to offer their modern wines, and until the **Boutari winery** (page 212) raised its game. Today, there is no shortage of top-quality, characterful Greek reds and whites, made from local and international grapes and blends between the two.

**Country code →** +30. **IDD code →** 00. **Internet ID →** .gr.
**Emergency numbers →** T 112. Police: T 166. Fire: T 199.

## Understanding Greek wine

The first barrier to understanding Greek wine labels is, of course, the use of script that non-classicists are ill-equipped to decipher. Nowadays, however, a growing number of producers are beginning to include information in a form that can be read by outsiders. This trend reveals that, while some wines fit into a French-style appellation system, there are also New World-style varietals and proprietary blends. Good and bad wines can be found in all three categories. Basic reds and whites (possibly blends of different grapes from a variety of regions) are **Epitrapezios Oenos** (EO). Examples bearing the word 'Kava' or 'Cava' (spellings vary) on their label are, in theory, of higher quality. Under Greek law, **Kava** wines have to be aged in barrel for at least six months and aged for two years for whites and three for reds. **Topikos Oenos** (TO) are more like French Vins de Pays, while **OPAP** (Onomasía Proeléfseos Anotéras Piótitos), of which there are two dozen, and the higher quality **OPE** (Onomasía Proeléfseos Eleghoméni), of which there are seven, are the equivalent of France's VDQS and Appellations Contrôlées. As in France, grape varieties and winemaking methods are prescribed, but there are also Italian- and Spanish-style rules that dictate how, and for how long, wines are aged before they can be sold. Reserve and Grand Reserve reds have to be barrel-aged for six months and two years respectively. They also have to remain at the winery until three and four years after the harvest. Similarly, Grand Reserva whites have to be aged for three years, of which a year has to be in barrel.

Perhaps unsurprisingly, producers wishing to sell wines with fresher fruit flavours opt for 'lower' official quality designations and rely on their own reputations and on those of local and international grape varieties. A wine from an estate will include the word 'Ktima' on its label and, if there is a grand building, it might mention an 'Archondiko' (chateau). Labels of wines made by monks – at Mount Athos (page 211), for example – will refer to the 'Monastiri' (monastery). Wines are made throughout the country and its islands. Quality often has more to do with the skills of its winemakers than the soil or the climate. Regions to look out for, with several good producers, include Nemea in the Peleponnese and Naoussa Drama in Macedonia.

Gerovassiliou Vineyard.

### Tasting notes

**Retsina**

When the ancient Greeks transported wine in amphora they found that the ones that were sealed with pine bungs and plaster kept their contents fresher. Putting two and two together, in the days before there was any understanding of the way wine oxidises, they reasoned that it was the presence of the pine rather than the absence of oxygen that was protecting the wine. So they began to add pine resin to fermenting wine. The recipe survived and was commercially revived in the 1960s.

Good retsina, although an acquired taste, can be delicious. It should be young, fresh and tangily aromatic, with only a hint of pine; ideally it should also come from Attica, source of the best Aleppo pine. Unfortunately, far too often, retsina is stale white wine that smells of bathroom cleaner. (One essential rule: never buy retsina without a vintage.)

### Greek grapes

- **Assyrtiko** Dry, minerally white; good in blends with Chardonnay.
- **Muscat** Widely grown but at its best in the luscious, sweet golden wines of Samos.
- **Roditis/Rhoditis** Interesting white grape with pink skin. Can produce pleasantly aromatic whites.
- **Robola/Ribolla** Minerally white at its best in Cephalonia.
- **Agiorgitiko (St George)/Mavro Nemeas** Plummy red wine grape at home in Nemea that does well by itself or in blends.
- **Limnio** Widely grown grape that makes herby red wine and contributes to Chateau Carras.
- **Mandelaria** Widely used grape that needs careful handling (or blending) to avoid its reds being too tannic.
- **Mavrodaphne** Berryish grape used to make sweet, port-like red on the island of Patras.
- **Xynomavro** Italy's Negroamaro can be translated as acidic black. Good in blends and in wines for long cellaring.

# Vintages

- **2005** Very good.
- **2004** Variable.
- **2003** Very good to great.
- **2002** Variable.
- **2001** Very good to great.
- **2000** Very good to great.

## Macedonia

WINERY THESSALONIKI

### Domaine Gerovassiliou

PO Box 16, Epanomi, 57500 Thessaloniki
T+30 23920-44567
www.gerovassilou.gr
Mon-Fri 0800-1530; weekends by appointment. Tastings and tours by appointment only.

Evangelos Gerovassiliou and his family produce award-winning wines such as a Viognier and Syrah that are recognized as being among the best wines in the world. The 45-hectare estate first produced wine in 1987 but only after Gerovassiliou reintroduced viticulture to his hometown of Epanomi, which had suffered badly with phylloxera. He studied in Greece and Bordeaux before becoming chief oenologist at Château Carras from 1976-1999. The family produce a range of wines, using Greek and international varieties such as Assyrtiko, Malagousia, Limnio, Mavroudi, Mavrotragano, Sauvignon Blanc, Chardonnay, Viognier, Syrah, and Merlot. Malagousia is an ancient indigenous Greek variety, which was almost extinct, but was revived thanks to Gerovassiliou's care and attention. Also of interest is Gerovassiliou's world-class collection of corkscrews.

Cellar at Domaine Gerovassiliou.

WINERY HALKIDIKI

### Mount Athos Vineyards

E Tsantali Wines, Agios Pavlos, 63080 Halkidiki
T+30 23 990 76100
www.tsantali.gr
Male visitors only, by appointment.

Mount Athos is an independent monastic community, with no fewer than 20 monasteries, and the area has had strong links with wine for many centuries. In 1971, during a storm, Evangelos Tsantalis found refuge with the monks in this area and then stayed to help cultivate the vineyards. Today, Tsantalis farms 80 hectares of organic vineyards. Low yields, long ripening, and perfect terroir all add to the complexity of the wines. The award-winning red and whites are made from local and international varieties including Limnio and Cabernet Sauvignon, Assyrtiko, Athiri, and Chardonnay.

## Peloponnese and Attica

RESTAURANT ATHENS

### Aristera Dexia

Andronikou 3, Rouf, Athens 11854
T+30 21 03 42 23 80, F+30 22 91 04 16 50,
info@aristeradexia.gr
Mon-Sat 2100-0115; reservations essential.
$$

In one of my occasional imaginings of a vinous utopia, wine makers, wine merchants and restaurateurs would regularly combine forces to demonstrate precisely what food and wine can do for each other. Well, here's one place where that's happened to great effect. Dimitris Litinos, a wine merchant, and Chrysanthos Karamolengos, a first-class che,f have come together to open Aristera Dexia (which means left-right) in a large industrial space. The name is reflected in the decor, with partitions dividing the restaurant and a glass floor offering a sneaky look into the magnificent wine cellar. It is possible to simply visit the bar for a taste of the extensive wine list, but the menu should be tried, if only for the outstanding fish dishes, such as salmon, shrimp and sushi. Other popular offerings include pheasant and pork and, in the summer, outside tables offer a simpler (and cheaper) taverna menu.

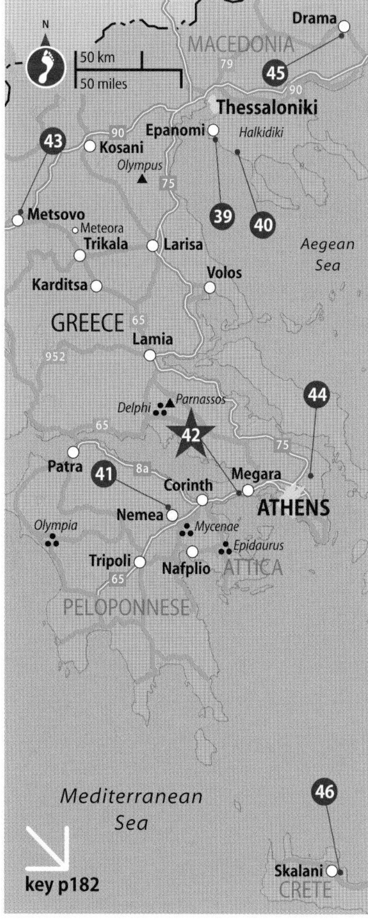

WINERY PELOPONNESE

### Domaine Helios

Koutsi, Nemea
T+30 27 4602 0360
www.semeliwines.com
Visits by appointment only.

George Kokotos' second winery is located in the Peloponnese region of Nemea, in stunning countryside, at an altitude of 600 m; the winery design uses the gravity to its full advantage. The wines produced include Orinos Helios white and red, with an appellation Nemea bottling and, at the top of the range, the Domaine Helios Nemea Reserve. There are eight rooms available for bed and breakfast accommodation ($$) and, as the estate is only five minutes from the ancient temple of Nemea, 30 minutes from Corinth and 40 minutes from Mycaenae, it makes a great base for sightseeing around the Peloponnese peninsula.

WINERY MEGARA

### Evharis

Pefkeneas, 19100 Megara
T+30 22 96 09 03 46
www.evharis.gr
Tasting and tours by appointment only.
Gallery and restaurant daily 1000-1600.

I've often been struck by the role outsiders have played in revealing the potential of some truly great wine regions, and that is precisely what Eva Boehme and Haris Antoniou have done at this 30 ha estate. Stated simply, they have breathed life into an region with absolutely no recent history of making good wine. But that's not all. There's an art gallery here and a good restaurant serving dishes that go brilliantly with the award-winning Evharis Syrah red and Asyrtiko, Savatiano and Roditis whites. If you are around when the harvest is due to begin in September, the estate holds an open-door at which you might get the chance to stomp on some grapes.

WINERY METSOVO

### Katogi-Strofilia

Metsovo 442 00, Epirus
T +30 26560 41010 / 26 5604 1684
Mon-Fri 0800-1430; Sat and Sun by appointment.

Evangelos Averoff-Tossizza was the first winemaker to bring Cabernet Sauvignon to Greece in 1950 and the first to blend it with native Greek varieties. His vision kick-started the beginning of a revolution in the Greek wine industry, and in 2001, his wine company, Katogi-Averoff SA, joined forces with Strofilia SA to create Katogi-Strofilia, one of Greece's leading wine producers. The name Strofilia became synonymous with white wine made from the indigenous Savvatiano and Roditis varieties. Today Katogi-Strofilia makes wine in three areas (Metsovo, Anavisso, Nemea) of which Metsovo is the most geared up to receive visitors.

WINERY ATTICA

### Semeli – Domaine George Kokotos

1 Semeli, Stamata, 14575 Attica
T+30 210 621 8119 / 621 6811
www.semeliwines.com
Mon-Fri 1100-1500 or by appointment.

George Kokotos named his first winery Semeli after the mother of Dionysus, the mythological god of wine, and planted the first vines at Stamata at the end of the 1970s. Semeli is a family boutique estate and has become internationally regarded for its traditional winemaking techniques and recognition of terroir. Kokotos was one of the first winemakers in Greece to plant French grape varieties (Cabernet Sauvignon, Merlot and Chardonnay) and all the vineyards fall under the EC Control System for Organic Farming. The wines include Chateau Semeli, a Cabernet Sauvignon-Merlot blend; Ktima Semeli, a Chardonnay; and Semeli White, a Savatiano. The estate offers book presentations, poetry evenings, cookery courses and exhibitions by local artists.

WINERY DRAMA

### Constantine Lazaridi

Adriani, Drama,66100
T+30 25 2108 2348
www.domaine-lazaridi.gr
Mon-Fri 1000-1500.

There are two recommendable winemaking Lazardidis in Drama: Constantine and his brother Nico (www.chateau-lazaridi.gr). Both are worth a visit but we've included Constantine here for his range of local and international grapes and for the combination of ancient cellars and modern equipment at his winery.

## Crete

WINERY IRAKLION

### Boutari Winery

Fantaxometocho, Skalani, Iraklion 70100
T+30 2810-731617
www.boutari.gr
Daily 1000-1800.

The name of this estate 'Fantaxometocho' translates as 'Haunted Cottage' and was adopted in the 1880s. A 300-year-old cottage located on the estate has been preserved in excellent condition but the winery itself is a spanking new building, completed in 2004. The 7 ha of vineyard were planted between 1990 and 1994 and sit at 168 to 213 m above sea level. Visitors may have guided tour of both the winery itself and the rest of the estate by appointment. Make sure to stay for the multi-media presentation and then taste the Fantaxometocho white and Skalani red.

# Romania

**Archaeological discoveries suggest that Romania may have as much as 5000 years of winemaking history. Plato described the vineyards of Transylvania as producing the finest wine in the world; this reputation subsequently slipped somewhat. Seven centuries or so ago, English wine drinkers would have been familiar with sweet Romanian wine which was sold as Rumney; the term denoted a second-class product (not necessarily from Romania) that was less good than Spanish Sack (sherry) and Malmsey from Crete but finer than the cheaper and more basic Bastardo. More recently, even before the fall of Ceausescu, Romania attracted interest for its good-value Pinot Noir; capitalism has since attracted a number of overseas investors. The classic regions are Dealu Mare in the foothills of the Carpathians in the central south of the country, where Cabernet Sauvignon, Merlot and Pinot Noir do well; Cotnari in the northeast and Murfatlar near the Black Sea coast, both of which are good at sweet wine. However, the vineyards – still a quarter state-owned – are a mess, infrastructure is poor and investment is in short supply, so it will take time before we see a broad range of top-quality Romanian wines. In the meantime, a decent range, cleverly labelled Vamp, is doing well in the US. The same company also produces a soft drink called Dracola.**

## Banat

WINERY — BANAT

### SC Cramele Recas

Complex de Vinificatie CP 1, Recas 307340
T+40 (0)256-330296
www.recaswine.ro
Visits by appointment only.

Located in the Banat, the westernmost region of Romania, which borders Hungary and Serbia, this impressive winery offers a chance to discover not only a very exciting Romanian-British joint venture, but also some of the wildest and least-known parts of Europe. Travelling Romania's back-country roads, you might well believe that the Middle Ages never ended; the horse and cart is still the most common means of transport and the countryside is barely populated and largely unspoilt. Arriving at Recas will pull you back into modern times, with an excellent tour and tasting that gives an idea of what Romania, once lauded for her wines, could once again achieve.

## Bucharest

WINE BAR — BUCHAREST

### Caffe & Latte Wine Bar Ristorante

B-dul Schitu Magureanu 35,
Bucarest Settore 1
T+40 (0)21-314 3800 www.caffelatte.ro
Tue-Sun 1200-1500, 1900-2300.
$

Bucharest citizens have been delighted to welcome this wine bar, especially as it comes courtesy of one of their long-time favourite cafés, of the same name, which is next door. Funky and laid-back, you can sit on the terrace and enjoy the views of the lovely Cismigiu Gardens as you tuck into modern Italian cooking and sip your Sangiovese.

RESTAURANT — BUCHAREST

### Casa Doina

Sos Kiseleff 4, Bucharest 1
T+40 (0)21-222 6717
www.casadoina.ro
Daily 1100-1300.
$

A Bucharest institution, Casa Doina offers continental and Romanian cooking and live gypsy music in a lovely 19th-century villa on a majestic boulevard, decorated in a colourful, peasant style. Standards of continental cooking are high in Bucharest, but opt for the Romanian food, which is authentic and delicious, as it can be surprisingly hard to find. There are many kinds of Romanian cheese on offer, from mature to the freshest soft ewe's milk cheeses, and, for the adventurous diner, there is usually a wide selection of offal dishes. There is a good choice of export-quality Romanian wine to accompany the food.

## Mutenia

WINERY — DEALUL MARE

### Prahova Valley

Gageni 92, Ploiesti 100137
T+40 (0)244-530955/530975/
www.prahova-wine.ro
Visits by appointment only; book through the website for tours and tastings.

An easy day trip from Bucharest along a good, recently built highway, this charming and beautifully restored Urlateanu winery and cellars have benefited from British investment. It makes an impressive range of wines from grapes grown in the Dealul Mare region under the Prahova label. For an intriguing insight into how palates can differ from country to country, ask to taste not only these wines, most of which are destined for western export markets, but also the wines made for the local market and other Eastern European countries. If you have time, book a traditional lunch cooked by a local woman which offers a rare taste of authentic, home-cooked fare, complete with meat roasted over the fire.

16

# North America

Oregon vineyard.

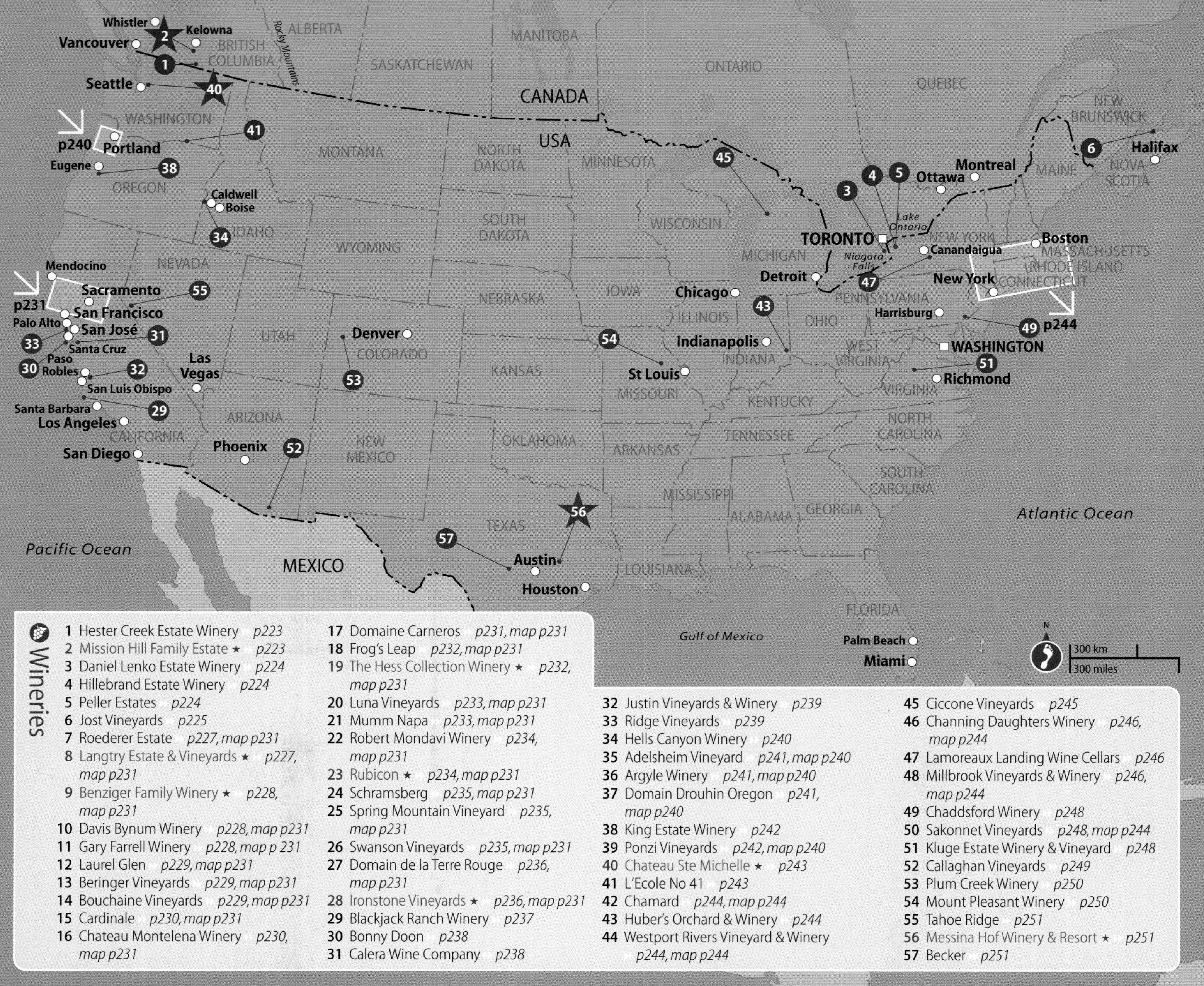

Wineries
1 Hester Creek Estate Winery p223
2 Mission Hill Family Estate ★ p223
3 Daniel Lenko Estate Winery p224
4 Hillebrand Estate Winery p224
5 Peller Estates p224
6 Jost Vineyards p225
7 Roederer Estate p227, map p231
8 Langtry Estate & Vineyards ★ p227, map p231
9 Benziger Family Winery ★ p228, map p231
10 Davis Bynum Winery p228, map p231
11 Gary Farrell Winery p228, map p 231
12 Laurel Glen p229, map p231
13 Beringer Vineyards p229, map p231
14 Bouchaine Vineyards p229, map p231
15 Cardinale p230, map p231
16 Chateau Montelena Winery p230, map p231
17 Domaine Carneros p231, map p231
18 Frog's Leap p232, map p231
19 The Hess Collection Winery ★ p232, map p231
20 Luna Vineyards p233, map p231
21 Mumm Napa p233, map p231
22 Robert Mondavi Winery p234, map p231
23 Rubicon ★ p234, map p231
24 Schramsberg p235, map p231
25 Spring Mountain Vineyard p235, map p231
26 Swanson Vineyards p235, map p231
27 Domain de la Terre Rouge p236, map p231
28 Ironstone Vineyards ★ p236, map p231
29 Blackjack Ranch Winery p237
30 Bonny Doon p238
31 Calera Wine Company p238
32 Justin Vineyards & Winery p239
33 Ridge Vineyards p239
34 Hells Canyon Winery p240
35 Adelsheim Vineyard p241, map p240
36 Argyle Winery p241, map p240
37 Domain Drouhin Oregon p241, map p240
38 King Estate Winery p242
39 Ponzi Vineyards p242, map p240
40 Chateau Ste Michelle ★ p243
41 L'Ecole No 41 p243
42 Chamard p244, map p244
43 Huber's Orchard & Winery p244
44 Westport Rivers Vineyard & Winery p244, map p244
45 Ciccone Vineyards p245
46 Channing Daughters Winery p246, map p244
47 Lamoreaux Landing Wine Cellars p246
48 Millbrook Vineyards & Winery p246, map p244
49 Chaddsford Winery p248
50 Sakonnet Vineyards p248, map p244
51 Kluge Estate Winery & Vineyard p248
52 Callaghan Vineyards p249
53 Plum Creek Winery p250
54 Mount Pleasant Winery p250
55 Tahoe Ridge p251
56 Messina Hof Winery & Resort ★ p251
57 Becker p251
N
300 km
300 miles
CANADA
USA
MEXICO
Pacific Ocean
Atlantic Ocean
Gulf of Mexico
Rocky Mountains
ALBERTA
BRITISH COLUMBIA
SASKATCHEWAN
MANITOBA
ONTARIO
QUEBEC
NEW BRUNSWICK
NOVA SCOTIA
WASHINGTON
OREGON
IDAHO
NEVADA
CALIFORNIA
MONTANA
WYOMING
UTAH
ARIZONA
COLORADO
NEW MEXICO
NORTH DAKOTA
SOUTH DAKOTA
NEBRASKA
KANSAS
OKLAHOMA
TEXAS
MINNESOTA
IOWA
MISSOURI
ARKANSAS
LOUISIANA
WISCONSIN
ILLINOIS
MICHIGAN
INDIANA
OHIO
KENTUCKY
TENNESSEE
MISSISSIPPI
ALABAMA
GEORGIA
FLORIDA
SOUTH CAROLINA
NORTH CAROLINA
VIRGINIA
WEST VIRGINIA
PENNSYLVANIA
NEW YORK
MAINE
MASSACHUSETTS
RHODE ISLAND
CONNECTICUT
Whistler
Kelowna
Vancouver
Seattle
p240
Portland
Eugene
Caldwell
Boise
Mendocino
Sacramento
p231
San Francisco
Palo Alto
San José
Santa Cruz
Paso Robles
San Luis Obispo
Santa Barbara
Los Angeles
San Diego
Las Vegas
Phoenix
Denver
Austin
Houston
St Louis
Chicago
Indianapolis
Detroit
TORONTO
Niagara Falls
Lake Ontario
Ottawa
Montreal
Canandaigua
Harrisburg
New York
Boston
Halifax
WASHINGTON
Richmond
p244
Palm Beach
Miami

# Introduction



North America is an extraordinary bundle of contradictions for the wine lover. On the one hand, this is the ultimate home of the 'can-do' culture, where everyone is encouraged to believe that no obstacle can stop them if they really want to do something. This is the spirit that has not only helped to create the dynamic wine industries of California, Oregon, Washington State, Ontario and British Columbia, but also an explosion of vinous activity throughout both countries. There are now wineries in all 50 states of the Union and in all the provinces and territories of Canada, although some are, admittedly, forced by the climate to make their wine from fruit, or from grapes grown elsewhere. Then again, these two countries are constrained by the world's biggest tangle of rules, restrictions and regulations when it comes to buying and selling wine. Stated simply, in some places it can be easier to obtain a car or a gun than a bottle of Chardonnay.

If individual effort is celebrated here, then so is the cult of celebrity. Being within driving distance of Hollywood has rubbed off on California's winemakers in particular: wineries 'release' new vintages as though they were albums or movies; critically acclaimed 'hot' new names and heavily marketed large-volume efforts tend to overshadow producers who, in many cases, are offering better quality and consistency. And if this is true within California, it is even more so when you look at the USA as a whole. It is immeasurably more difficult for a winery in, say, Virginia or New York State to catch the public eye than one in the Napa Valley. Which is great news for anyone who is more interested in the contents of their glass than the hype that surrounds it.

# Travel essentials

### Planning your trip

**San Francisco** (SFO, T +1-650 821 8211, www.sfo.com) provides the easiest access to most Californian wine regions, except perhaps the South Central Coast, for which **Los Angeles** is more convenient. Hubs in the northwest include **Seattle** and **Vancouver**, from which the wineries of both Washington State and British Columbia are accessible. In the east, all major international airlines serve **New York** (JFK or Newark), although flights to Chicago, Washington DC, Cleveland, Toronto, Montreal and other major centres will provide more direct access to individual wine regions. Internal flights are the easiest way to cover the vast distances that characterize both Canada and the United States, with a multitude of airlines serving the popular routes, including frequent flights between the two countries; good discounts are usually available. Once you've reached a particular region, a car is indispensable. Rail travel is limited, although enthusiasts should check out **Amtrak**'s *Coast Starlight* service (T 1-800 872 7245, www.amtrak.com), which runs close to many Californian wine regions en route from Los Angeles to Seattle.

Those arriving in San Francisco will want to spend some time soaking up the city's singular atmosphere before heading north into the Napa and Sonoma valleys, the heart of the US wine industry. Aside from the country's finest wines, you can also enjoy some of California's most beautiful scenery. From Sonoma it's a mere day trip to the more relaxed and low-key wineries of **Russian River Valley** and a short drive north to the artsy seaside town of **Mendocino**. A detour inland brings you to the heritage towns of the Gold Country (page 236) and the natural splendour of Yosemite National Park. Highways 1 and 101 follow the Pacific Coast south to Los Angeles and San Diego, with the desert stretching inland.

The northwestern states are accessed via **Seattle**, spiritual home of the coffee house and one of the great West Coast cities. Another of Seattle's attractions is its proximity to the spectacular wilderness of **Olympic National Park**. Oregon's capital, **Portland**, makes an ideal base for exploring the surrounding coast and mountains and the wineries of the **Williamette Valley**. Across the border in Canada, **Vancouver** is worth at least a few days of anyone's time. Further east, the sun-baked **Okanagan**'s so-called 'Golden Mile' is a must (page 225). It would be a sin to come all this way and not see the majestic **Rocky Mountains**, accessed via Calgary. You could then continue to Toronto and tour the **Niagara** wine region, Canada's largest, making sure you leave enough time to peek at the falls. Higher still are **Taughannock Falls**, one of many spectacular natural attractions in the Finger Lakes Region, the centre of New York State's wine production.

**USA country code** → +1. **IDD code** → +011. **Internet ID** → .us. **Emergencies** → T 911.

## → USA fact file

| | |
|---|---|
| **International flights** | International airlines from Europe and the rest of the world fly into the major cities, including Atlanta, Boston, Miami, New York, Washington, DC in the east, and Los Angeles, San Francisco and Seattle in the west. |
| **Entry requirements** | Passport plus valid visa. Visas not required for those travelling under US Visa Waiver Program (UK included). |
| **Currency** | United States dollar ($). |
| **Time zone** | From GMT –5 (Eastern Standard Time) to GMT –8 (Pacific Standard Time). Daylight saving Apr-Oct. |
| **Electricity** | 110 volts (60 Hz) Plugs have 2 flat pins. |
| **Licensing hours** | vary between states. Alcohol sold Mon-Sat 0600-0200, Sun 1000-0200. Few states allow 24-hr liquor sales. |
| **Minimum age** | 21. |
| **Drink-drive restrictions** | 80 mg alcohol per 100 ml blood. |

Okanagan valley, British Columbia.

## When to visit

California, in particular, is famously good to visit at any time of the year, but it is worth trying to be here during the harvest in August or September or in mid winter when there are fewer people crowding the tasting rooms. The northern states and Canada can be a less welcoming prospect in mid winter but it is interesting to be around between mid December and mid January when Canada's grapes are being harvested for Icewine.

## Wine tourism

North America, in general, and California, in particular, is very sophisticated when it comes to wine tourism. Regions have easy-to-use websites, with links to equally informative winery sites. It is rare for a winery not to have a tasting room and shop and many also offer tours and tastings led by well-informed guides. The reverse of the coin is that this very professionalism can make for a less personal experience than you might find in France, Italy or even Australia. Visitors to the **Robert Mondavi** winery (page 234), for example, have likened it to a winery run by Disney. It is also now usual to pay for tastings in California, something that is only beginning to be the case elsewhere. It is worth noting that the relationship between price and wine quality is often quite loose here. Wineries that have cost a lot of money to design and build tend to charge more for their wines than ones that have been converted from sheds. Napa commands a premium over other Californian regions, although their wine can be just as good. There is also a questionable link between prices and critics' scores; wines that cost US$100 with 90+ scores (see Points mean prizes, page 238) don't always taste better than ones costing US$20+, but they sell more quickly.

## Sleeping

There is no official grading for hotels in either Canada or the USA, although numerous organizations provide their own ratings. Hotel standards are at their highest in major cities and tourist areas, although amenities can still vary widely from basic rooms to full-service accommodation and prices will depend on the location and on the services provided by the hotel. Most mid-range hotels will have bars, restaurants, room service and laundry; all-inclusive resort hotels will have a multitude of additional services, including sports facilities and shopping, and will pride themselves on their high level of customer service and their location. Motels are the most basic type of accommodation in North America and have limited facilities but are very handy if you are on a self-drive itinerary. As an alternative, look out for lodges in Canada, which are usually in beautiful locations and may offer outdoor activities as well as accommodation. Bed and breakfast in the USA is generally more upmarket and luxurious then guesthouses in other parts of the world, including Canada. It is likely to be more expensive than a room in a standard chain hotel but you are guaranteed a much more intimate ambience. Self-catering is a great option for groups or families but may only be practical if you are basing yourself exclusively in one area for several days.

**Canada country code** → +1. **IDD code** → 001. **Internet ID** → .ca. **Emergencies** → T 911.

## → Canada fact file

| | |
|---|---|
| **International flights** | Major airlines fly to Montreal, Toronto or Vancouver; limited services to other airports. |
| **Entry requirements** | Citizens of the UK, EU and the British Commonwealth need a valid passport but not a visa. US citizens only require proof of citizenship and identity. |
| **Currency** | Canadian Dollar (CAN$). |
| **Time zone** | From GMT –3.5 (Newfoundland Standard Time) to GMT –8 (Pacific Standard Time). Daylight saving Apr-Oct. |
| **Electricity** | 110 volts (60 Hz) Plugs have either 2 or 3 flat pins. |
| **Licensing hours** | Restaurants, bars and clubs can serve liquor 0900-2400 or until 0400 with local government approval. Drinking alcohol in public is prohibited. |
| **Minimum age** | 19 in British Columbia; 18 in all other provinces and territories. |
| **Drink-drive restrictions** | 80 mg alcohol per 100 ml blood. |

## Eating

The range of food on offer in North America is probably as wide as can be found anywhere on earth. This is, after all, a continent, whose inhabitants almost all have roots somewhere else. There are, of course, regional cuisines – Texans like their steaks bigger and their chilli sauce hotter than Bostonians, who are probably happier tucking into crabs – but there's still a high chance that the best restaurant in town serves dishes based on French, Italian or Japanese cuisine. California cuisine relies on fresh local ingredients to create innovative, light fusion dishes that blend American, Mediterranean, Asian and Latin influences. Similar elements characterize the West Coast cuisine of Vancouver, with the addition of Native American techniques and game produce. Seafood is popular and prevalent along both the Atlantic and Pacific coasts, while the Southwest is heavily influenced by Mexican flavours.

Unlike in Europe, the food and wine industries have grown up quite separately here. Many of California's big, buttery Chardonnays and rich, alcoholic Cabernets may taste wonderful when sampled by themselves but will swamp the flavours of delicately conceived dishes. It is worth bearing this in mind when eating out; don't be surprised if a bright sommelier recommends a French or Italian wine – or a local effort you have never heard of – to accompany your meal.

# Wine essentials

### Understanding North American wine

California has nearly 200 **AVA**s (Approved Viticultural Areas), which range from the huge Central Coast to the tiny North Yuba. These provide no guarantee of quality or style but they should give some idea of the climate in which the grapes were grown. Labels bearing European wine names such as Burgundy, Chablis, Port and Champagne still abound in California – though not in Oregon where they have long been banned – but they are being phased out as part of a deal with the EU. Wine labelled as coming from California or Texas must be made from 100% and 85% respectively of grapes from that state. Elsewhere, the requirement is only 75%, a point worth recalling when you taste a surprisingly good wine from a state where grapes have trouble ripening. Another area of confusion concerns alcoholic strength. Under US law, winemakers are allowed leeway of 1.5%, in the case of wines containing 14% alcohol or less, and a tolerance of 1%, in the case of wines containing more than 14%. In other words, a wine claiming 15% could actually have 16%, while one claiming 14% could have 15.5%. California, Oregon and Washington State all grow *vinifera vitis* grapes exclusively. Other states tend to have all three, with higher proportions of labrusca and hybrids in the coldest regions. (For an explanation of these terms, see Essentials, page 9.)

Before 1990, there was no way of knowing whether any or all of the grapes used to produce a bottle of 'Canadian' wine were actually grown in Canada, or that the wine had not had water or sugar added during the winemaking process. In that year, producers in Ontario and British Columbia came up with a Vintners Quality Alliance appellation or **VQA** (see www.vqaontario.com and www.winebc.com /vqadefined.php) and a seal that serves as a guarantee of both the wine's provenance and the way that it was made. When buying Icewine, take the trouble to look for the grape variety; Riesling, which is a relative rarity in Canada, makes much better wine than the more frequently used Vidal vinifera.

### White grapes

**Chardonnay** Grown almost everywhere, but nowhere bigger, butterier and oakier than in California.

**Colombard** Widely planted variety used to make pretty basic wine in California.

**Pinot Gris** Peary Alsace variety that is on a roll at the moment in California but more established in Oregon.

**Riesling** At its best dry or late-harvest sweet in Washington State, Oregon, New York State and Canada, where it makes the best Icewine.

**Sauvignon Blanc** Grown in California to make bigger, richer, less zingy wine than in France, New Zealand or South Africa (sometimes oaked and sold as 'Fumé Blanc'). Does rather better in Washington State.

**Seyval Blanc** Hybrid that can produce Chardonnay-like whites.

**Vidal** Hybrid used for Canadian Icewine.

**Viognier** A niche player in California, where it is often over-alcoholic and over-oaked, this variety is now being grown successfully in Virginia.

### Red grapes

**Baco Noir** A smoky-tastng hybrid.

**Barbera** Once popular in California, this Italian variety is now making a comeback as part of the fashion for 'Cal-Ital' reds.

**Cabernet Franc** More widely grown than is usually imagined, this berryish variety does well in California and warmer regions of Canada.

**Cabernet Sauvignon** At its best in the Napa Valley but grown everywhere. It can ripen and is often blended with Merlot as 'Meritage'.

**Carignane** The grape the French call Carignan produces rich reds in California – in the right hands.

**Catawba** Foxy-tasting, pale-skinned labrusca widely grown in the northeastern United States.

**Charbono** A quirky, cherryish grape that probably began life in Italy.

**Concord** Foxy labrusca grape that is better used for jam or grape juice than for wine.

**Delaware** Popular hybrid, much grown in New York State.

Syrah grapes on the vine at Mission Hill.

Grapevine

**Icewine**

The process of picking grapes once they have been frozen on the vines began in the 1800s in the Rheingau in Germany, following its accidental discovery in Franken in 1794, when a cold snap hit the vineyards just before the harvest was due to begin. Stated simply, when the frozen berries are crushed, the concentrated extracts, sugars and acids are released, while the water content remains in the press as icy bullets. Juice from frozen grapes is then fermented to create an intensely sweet, flavoursome wine. Making wine in this way reduces yields to around a fifth of what they might have been. (This figure can be even lower if birds and – in Canada – bears get to the grapes before the human pickers.) Eiswein (as it is known in Germany) enjoys extra rarity because the unpredictability of the German winter means that it can only be made every three or four years. Canada's first commercial Icewine was made in 1978 by the German-born owner of Hainle Vineyards, who discovered that it can be produced here reliably every year. Since then, Icewine (including red and sparkling examples that would never have been imagined in Germany) has become a major part of the Canadian wine industry, in terms of value if not volume. In 2004, nearly 320,000 half-bottles, with price tags of US$50 or more, were exported, of which over a quarter went to Taiwan. Fake ice wine, is however a growing problem and hitting sales of the real thing.

Picking grapes for Icewine at Inniskillen, Ontario, Canada.

**Gamay / Gamay Beaujolais / Napa Gamay/ Valdiguie** There is almost no real Gamay in California. Napa Gamay and Valdiguie, by which it is also known, is a lesser variety that is no longer grown in France, while Gamay Beaujolais is a lesser clone of Pinot Noir.

**Grenache** Underexploited in California, but still quite widely planted and making something of a comeback.

**Lemberger** The German grape also known as Blaufrankisch produces light, easy-going reds in Washington State.

**Marechal Foch** Popular hybrid in Canada and New York State.

**Merlot** Far more widely grown than it should be (because of the ease of pronunciation and the association with Château Petrus), the Merlot produces some of its very best wines in California and Washington State, as well as large amounts of very ordinary red.

**Petite Sirah** Unrelated to the Syrah with which it is often confused, this variety produces rich, dark spicy wines in California.

**Pinot Noir** Flying high in Oregon, Carneros, Russian River and Santa Barbara and, to a lesser extent, Monterey.

**Sangiovese** The Tuscan grape is increasingly popular with Californian winemakers but there are few exciting examples.

**Syrah** Up and coming, the grape the Australians call Shiraz is rapidly winning friends in California and Washington State.

**Zinfandel** See page 235.

# Vintages

**2005** Great in California (especially Pinot Noir), British Columbia and Washington State, but variable in Oregon and on the East Coast.

**2004** Some great California Chardonnay, Pinot Noir and Merlot, but varied Cabernet Sauvignon and Zinfandel. Oregon and Washington State both made top class reds and the east coast produced terrific wines. In Canada, British Columbia made good reds and whites, while Ontario fared better with whites.

**2003** Great in California and really good wines in both Washington State and Oregon. There were also good East Coast whites. A great year in British Columbia and for Ontario whites.

**2002** Great in California, if slightly overripe. Varied in Oregon, but great in Washington and on the East Coast. Also good for British Columbia and for Ontario reds.

**2001** Terrific in California; great in Washington and varied in Oregon. Good on the East Coast. Very good for British Columbia whites.

**2000** A varied but sometimes great vintage in California and a terrific vintage for both Oregon and Washington. There were also some really good British Columbia whites.

# Canada



Leif Ericsson, "a big strapping fellow... temperate in all things", according to the contemporary chronicler Adam of Bremen, is said to have sailed from Norway in AD 1001, accompanied by 35 crewmen and provisions of beer and mead. After landing on Baffin Island and Labrador, he came ashore at a place he called "Winland, for the reason that vines yielding the best of wines grow there wild". Other sources suggest that the vines were actually discovered by Ericsson's foster father, and there are similar differences over the precise location of Winland – or Vinland as it was more usually described. Most experts believe it to have been at a spot called l'Anse aux Meadows in northern Newfoundland but there are suggestions that it might have been further south. In any case, it is believed that the native tribes made Canadian wine before the Norsemen. They are thought to have poured fermented grape juice into the river beneath Niagara Falls as a tribute to a god they called Wischgimi.

Wine was made from native grapes in the 16th and 17th centuries by French churchmen but it was a German called Johann Schiller who, in the 1800s, first introduced European production methods to his 4-ha vineyard at Cooksville in Ontario. In 1867 a wine made by the subsequent owner of this plot was tasted in Paris and likened to Beaujolais. At around the same time vines were being planted in British Columbia, south of Kelowna, by a priest and a couple of his neighbours. Within a few years, winemaking had really taken off and, in 1900, Ontario had some 2700 ha of vines and 35 of Canada's 41 wineries. Unfortunately none of this wine would have been good by modern standards; it was made from two grapes, the Concord and Cassady, that were chosen for their resistance to the cold rather than for their quality. Prohibition arrived in 1917 and turned the Canadians into a nation of home winemakers and people who needed to dose themselves with large quantities of alcoholic 'Dandy Bracer – Liver and Kidney Cure'. When Prohibition was repealed, it was replaced by rationing and by the state monopolies that survive today.

## British Columbia

British Columbia's vineyards have expanded from a mere 400 ha in 1989 to 2200 ha today. Eighty of the 132 wineries are in the Okanagan and Similkameen Valleys, which, given the fact that they share a latitude with the Mosel in Germany, enjoy surprisingly warm, semi-desert conditions. This is thanks to the same rain shadow created by the Cascade mountains that is responsible for the climate in Washington State's best vineyards. A wide range of grapes are grown here, including Cabernet Sauvignon, Cabernet Franc, Merlot and Pinot Noir, but whites such as Chardonnay, Riesling and Gewürztraminer also do well. British Columbia may have been a late starter but there are plenty of signs that its wines could soon eclipse those of Ontario.

RESTAURANT — WHISTLER

### Bearfoot Bistro

4121 Village Green, Whistler Village, V0N 1B4
T +1 604-932 3433
www.bearfootbistro.com
Book in advance.
$$

One of Canada's best restaurants, this also has to be one of the best ski resort restaurants anywhere. The menu is inventive without being taxing, just what you want after a bracing day on the slopes, and the wine list offers much scope for discovery. If you prefer a lighter meal, try the Champagne Bar, with its elegant pewter counter, and fare such as grilled lobster sandwiches, veal cheek pie and pork belly glazed with honey and chilli.

Mission Hill Family Estate.

RESTAURANT VANCOUVER

## Brix

1138 Homer St, Vancouver, V6B 2X6
T +1 604-915 9463
www.brixvancouver.com
Daily for lunch and dinner. Bar open until 0200.
$-$$

David Hannay has put together one of the most comprehensive and interesting lists of British Columbia wines, as well as providing rich offerings from the rest of North America and the world. The restaurant's name refers to the scale measuring the concentration of sugars in grape must, and the wine list, structured as it is into styles such as "medium, full-bodied red" and "full-bodied structured red", reflects a preoccupation with precision that in no way sabotages the fun of choosing. Sixty wines are available by the glass, with instructive tasting notes to accompany them. Hannay is rarely absent and is always willing to share a tip or impart advice on choosing a match for chef Jason Wilson's excellent fare.

This is the kind of place in which everyone will learn something they didn't know before, and have a great deal of fun doing so.



WINERY OKANAGAN

## Hester Creek Estate Winery

13163 Av 326, Box 1605, Oliver, V0H 1T0
T +1 250-498 4435
www.hestercreek.com
Daily 1000-1700.

South Okanagan's 'Golden Mile' is a concentrated stretch, south of Oliver, on which some of Canada's finest wineries are located. Hester Creek is a highlight of this area and offers visitors the chance to sample the effect of British Columbia's baking summer days and cool nights on vinifera varieties, including Merlot, Trebbiano and Chardonnay. Sample the delicious Pinot Blanc Icewine, if it is available, and ask veteran Canadian winemaker, Robert Summers, for his insights into his country's increasingly dynamic wine industry.

WINERY OKANAGAN

## Mission Hill Family Estate

1730 Mission Hill Rd, Westbank, Okanagan Valley, V4T 2E4
T +1 250-768 6448
www.missionhillwinery.com
Sep daily 1000-1800; Oct-Dec daily 1000-1700. Restaurant May-Oct daily for lunch and dinner.

As a lover of winery architecture, I particularly appreciate what Seattle architect Tom Kundig has achieved here at a sprawling yet ordered complex that's full of special touches. The 12-storey bell tower, complete with lightning rod, for instance, was made by the same foundry, Paccard, that cast the bells in New York's St Patrick's Cathedral and Paris's Sacré Coeur, while the keystone at the entrance was hand carved from a five-tonne block of

Indiana limestone by a British master stone mason. The prizewinning wines benefit from the same attention to detail under the ministrations of New Zealander John Simes. There are a range of possible tour and tasting packages, including the top option of a meal at the 'Chef's Table', during which winery chef and television personality Michael Allemeier offers seven courses paired with wine. Allemeier also regularly offers cooking classes but these need to be booked far in advance.

## Ontario

According to the provincial wine association (www.winesofontario.org), there are 65 wineries in Ontario. Winemakers here can boast that Niagara, the province's main wine-producing area, is on the same latitude as Provence, Chianti Classico and Rioja, and has summers that are warm enough to produce good Bordeaux-style reds (especially Cabernet Franc), Chardonnays and Rieslings, with the occasional successful Pinot Noir; even so, Labrusca and hybrids are still widely used. Icewine, which represents around one bottle in 20, remains the speciality.

# Best producers

**British Columbia**

Burrowing Owl
Gehringer
Hester Creek ›› *page 223.*
Mission Hill ›› *page 223.*
Quail's Gate
Sumac Ridge

**Nova Scotia**

Jost ›› *page 225.*

**Ontario**

Cave Spring
Château des Charmes
Henry of Pelham
Hillebrand ›› *page 224.*
Konzelmann
David Lenko
Peller Estates ›› *page 224.*
Thirty Bench

WINERY — BEAMSVILLE

### Daniel Lenko Estate Winery

5246 Regional Rd 81, Beamsville, L0R 1B3
T +1 905- 563 7756
www.daniellenko.com
Visits by appointment only.

After several decades as suppliers of vinifera grapes to other prizewinning producers, the Lenko family has decided to bottle its own production of Riesling, Chardonnay and Cabernet Franc, among other varieties. Several of the vineyards have old vines and it is clear that Lenko's star will rise and rise, making this a good place to add to your list of "I was there when they were just getting started..." wineries. Due to limited production, the wines are only available for purchase at the winery.

WINERY — NIAGARA

### Hillebrand Estate Winery

1249 Niagara Stone Rd, Niagara on the Lake, L0S 1J0
T +1 905-468 3201
www.hillebrand.com
Tastings and sales daily 1200-1800. Tours 1100-1700. Restaurant daily from 1200 for lunch and from 1700 for dinner.
Tours CAN$5.

Hillebrand has put a great deal of thought into its range of tours. As well as a general tour of the vineyards and winery, visitors can opt for a blending tour, in which you can blend and bring home a bottle of red wine; a tour focused on the detailed processes behind winemaking, such as barrel-ageing; and in-depth Icewine and sparkling wine tours. If you are able to visit at the weekend, you will also be able to take in afternoon performances by top Canadian jazz bands. There is an excellent restaurant ($$-$) with outdoor terrace seating, as well as a wine garden offering simpler meals and stunning views of the Niagara escarpment.

WINERY — NIAGARA

### Peller Estates

290 John St East, Niagara-on-the-Lake, L0S 1J0
T +1 905-468 4678/888-673 5537
www.peller.com
Daily 1200-1800. Restaurant daily from 1200 for lunch and from 1700 for dinner.
Tasting samples CAN$1-5.

Three successive generations of the Peller family, starting with Hungarian immigrant Andrew, have worked to put not only this winery but also Canada as a whole on the world wine map. The Peller family has a strong interest in the connection between wine and dining, which is reflected in themed tours such as 'The Art of Wine and Food', which matches a selection of wines with small dishes prepared by winery chef Jason Parsons, and 'Secrets of Stemware', in which various wines are paired with appropriate glasses. Among the other tours is one in which you will be invited to taste barrel samples at various stages of the ageing process, a fascinating and unusual opportunity. Lunch and dinner are available at the restaurant ($$).

WINE BAR — TORONTO

### Crush Wine Bar

455 King St, Toronto, M5V 1K4
T +1 416-977 1234
www.crushwinebar.com
Mon-Fri 1130-2230, Sat 1700-2230.
$$

Housed in an old warehouse on Toronto's principle food street, Crush features a different wine region each month, offering flights of four reds and four whites, each in

2-fl oz servings. If your wanderlust is such that you don't want to confine yourself to one region, huge selections of wine are also available in 3- and 5-fl oz servings. The restaurant menu is modern and unpretentious, but the bar food is so tempting – rabbit sausage with apricot chutney and scallop with salmon roe are typical offerings – that you might find yourself sticking to these.

## Canada's other provinces

While Ontario and British Columbia have the lion's share of Canada's vineyards, there are wineries in the remaining provinces, including Quebec, which used to be famous for shamelessly selling wine made from imported grapes under 'local' labels. Many of the wines are inevitably made from fruit, labrusca or hybrids.

WINE BAR MONTREAL

### BU Wine Bar

5245 St-Laurent, Montreal, H2T 1S4
T +1 514- 276 0249
www.bu-mtl.com
Tue-Fri 1200-0200, Mon and Sat 1700-0200.

Several excellent themed flights of three 2-fl oz glasses are the highlight of this delightful Montreal haven for wine lovers. The Champagne flight, for instance, might include such producers as Egly-Ouriet, Larmandier-Bernier and Bruno Paillard, while another flight might feature three wines from Chassagne-Montrachet producer Vincent Dancer. If you want to go solo, 30 wines are available in a choice of 3- and 4-fl oz glasses, and a further 300 by the bottle. The food, cooked by two Italian chefs, is refreshingly simple, delicious and worth the trip in itself.

WINERY NOVA SCOTIA

### Jost Vineyards

48 Vintage Ln, Malagash, Nova Scotia, B0K 1E0
T +1 902-257 2636/800-565 4567 toll free
www.jostwine.com
Tours daily 1200 and 1500. Wine store daily summer 0900-1800, winter 0900-1700.

This prizewinning producer is a good place to brush up on your French and Russian hybrids (Marechal Foch, L'Acadie Blanc, Mischurnitz and Severnyi) but the star attraction is the luscious Icewine, which is made in Muscat and Vidal versions. It is unlikely that this rare nectar will be proffered at the free tasting but you should get an insight into the fascinating process on the tour, especially if you visit in winter. As well as selling wines, the shop sells an excellent selection of high-quality local crafts ranging from jewellery to rugs.

### British Columbia in four seasons

British Columbia's capital, **Vancouver**, is a great place to visit but summer is undoubtedly the time to see it at its best. The compact Downtown peninsula contains most of the city's sights, but the real pleasure lies in discovering its many neighbourhoods and diverse architecture. Yaletown, Gastown and Chinatown (the third largest in North America) are particularly worth exploring. Beyond Downtown, at Point Gray, is the remarkable **UBC Museum of Anthropology** (T +1 604-822 5087, www.moa.ubc.ca), the one tourist attraction in Vancouver that absolutely must be seen. For more information on Vancouver's sights visit www.tourismvancouver.com.

A great scenic loop from Vancouver would be to take the **Sea to Sky Highway** north through the gloriously scenic Coast Mountains to **Whistler**, the biggest and best winter sports resort in North America and venue for the 2010 Winter Olympics. Between December and late April you can enjoy the abundant light powder for which Whistler is famous and an excellent lunch in the **Bearfoot Bistro** (page 222). Next door to Whistler is **Garibaldi Provincial Park**, a summer hiking haven of pristine lakes and rivers, alpine meadows, soaring peaks and huge glaciers. Beyond Whistler, the road gets rougher as it passes through the small villages of Pemberton and Lillooet. This section is best avoided in winter as snow chains are often required and road closures are common. From Lillooet, Highway 12 meets the TransCanada Highway, which squeezes its way through the spectacular **Fraser Canyon** then continues south through Yale to the town of Hope, where it heads west back to Vancouver.

Wine lovers will of course make a beeline for the **Okanagan Valley**. Canada's driest and sunniest region is best enjoyed in spring (mid-April to mid-May) and autumn (mid-September to end of October), not only to coincide with the seasonal wine festivals but also to avoid the summer hordes. Those who value peace and quiet should base themselves in **Naramata**, a sleepy little village about 16 km north of Penticton on the east side of Okanagan Lake, but for a taste of the real Okanagan and even fewer people, try the soporific shores of the west bank of the lake. Here, in Summerland, you can board the historic **Kettle Valley Steam Railway** (www.kettlevalley railway.org). This 10-mile stretch (16 km) is all that remains of the original 500 km that was built in 1910-15 to transport the silver struck in the Kootenays. More energetic souls may wish to hike or cycle the KVR. The best sections are between Penticton and Kelowna, especially Myra Canyon Trestles.

For further information consult the tourist website, www.hellobc.com and Footprint's *Discover Western Canada*.

# California

California is, to the rest of North America, what Bordeaux, Burgundy, Champagne, Alsace, the Loire and Rhône are collectively to France. In other words, as far as most Americans, and certainly most Californians, are concerned, this state produces almost all of the quality wine in the US. Of course, this is far from the mark but it is true that it is responsible for around 95% of all American wine.

California's wine history began in 1789 when a Franciscan friar is said to have planted a vineyard at the new Mission at San Diego de Alcala, using native Criolla vines he had brought with him by mule from Mexico. There are some doubts whether the plants could have survived this journey but, by the early 1870s, the grape that became known as the 'Mission' was certainly being grown in the south of the state. The Franciscans had 21 missions in this area and made wine at them all. In the early 1830s, a Frenchman, appropriately named Jean-Louis Vignes, produced wine and brandy from vinifera grapes on the site of the present Los Angeles Union Railway Station. The real vinifera pioneer, however, was a Hungarian, the eccentric self-styled 'Count' and 'Colonel' Agoston Haraszthy, who was commissioned by the state governor, a vinegrower called General Mariano Vallejo, to find and bring back 100,000 cuttings of 300 European grape varieties. Having planted them in vineyards, at what is now the Buena Vista winery in Sonoma, and effectively launched the Californian wine industry, Haraszthy then – after failing financially as a winemaker – disappeared to Nicaragua where he was reportedly eaten by alligators. Winemaking in Napa began, in a smaller way, at around the same time, when George Yount planted some Mission grapes, close to the village now called Yountville.

Whatever wine you drink, anywhere in the world, its style and quality today almost certainly owe something to the questions that were raised by California's wine pioneers.

The second half of the 19th century saw the launch of a succession of wineries, including such now-familiar names as Paul Masson, Chateau Montelena, Almaden, Charles Krug, Korbel, Wente and Christian Brothers, which was founded by a Catholic lay order in 1882. Germans called Jacob Schram and Jacob Beringer founded Schramsberg and Beringer Vineyards; Captain Gustave Niebaum, a Finnish fur trader, opened Inglenook, which now belongs to Francis Ford Coppola, next to which Georges de Latour, who had made money producing Cream of Tartar, started Beaulieu, using vines he had imported from his native France.

Prohibition closed nearly all of these wineries, with the exception of Christian Brothers, which continued to produce 'sacramental' wine. Repeal in 1933 (coincidentally a big vintage) brought the opening of some 800 new ones, including E&J Gallo and Louis Martini. Most of the early wine would, as elsewhere in the New World, have been labelled, 'Burgundy', 'claret' or 'Champagne' (a tradition that has only just begun to fade in California) but in 1939 an importer of European wine called Frank Schoonmaker realized that he could not sell both Californian 'Chablis' and the real thing, so he asked the producers to print the grape variety on the label. He could not have known it at the time, but Schoonmaker was the creator of the modern notion of varietal wines.

Although quality wines were produced in the 1940s and 1950s, it was during the following decade that modern Californian wine came into being, with the opening of the Ridge, Heitz, Chalone and Robert Mondavi wineries. In 1976, wines from the first three of these, and from Château Montelena (founded in 1883) and Stag's Leap (1971) were pitched against a set of wines from Bordeaux and Burgundy – and beat them. This event, which was replicated with the same wines and similar results in 2006, boosted the Californians' confidence and traumatized France to such an extent that it has yet fully to recover; see page 232.

**Today, many of the grand old names of California wine belong to multi-nationals and the pioneering spirit of the early days is far less apparent. Napa vineyard land that cost US$75,000-150,000 per hectare in 1997 now sells for nearly half a million dollars. Pricey land also makes for pricey bottles; with top Napa Cabernet commanding prices of around US$200 per bottle. Vineyard land in Mendocino might cost a quarter as much as land in Napa but it produces wine that is just as good, so it pays to look beyond the big name wineries.**

## Mendocino

According to local myth, marijuana is a major crop in this northerly region, and the *Easy Rider* bikes parked outside the Hopland Brewery certainly add to the 1970s feel. The vinous magnet here, until its visitor facilities were closed recently, was the Fetzer winery. But Mendocino's strongest card, in any case is its sparkling wines.

WINERY — ANDERSON VALLEY

### Roederer Estate

4501 Hwy 128, Philo, CA 95466
T +1 707-895 2288
www.roedererestate.net
Daily 1100-1700.
US$3

Unlike Taittinger, whose Domaine Carneros is a Disneyfied slice of Champagne, Roederer's US winery is hidden discreetly among its vines. The wines here are arguably California's best sparklers and well worth the US$3 tasting fee.

## Lake County

WINERY — MIDDLETOWN

### Langtry Estate & Vineyards

21000 Butts Canyon Rd, Middletown, CA 95461
T +1 707-987 2385/987 9127
www.langtryestate.com
Daily 1000-1700.

Celebrity-linked wineries are increasingly commonplace these days, but they are not a new phenomenon, as I discovered when I visited this estate, which belonged to the acress Lillie Langtry between 1888 to 1906. Formerly called Guenoc Valley winery, it still excels at producing top-notch Petite Sirah and Sauvignon Blanc. As well as the chance to taste the wines and visit the ultra-modern winery, you should consider bringing a picnic and making a day of it, as the winery is located on 35 sq miles of the Lake County's beautiful Guenoc Valley. The winery is next to the Detert Reservoir, which attracts a wide variety of birds and waterfowl, such as blue heron and snowy egrets; bears, cougars, and wild boar have also been spotted in the further reaches of the estate.

## Sonoma

Very different in mood to Napa on the other side of the ridge, this is a place where it's easy to get lost among the hills, vales and widely spread vineyards. The wines on offer are more varied and sometimes more modestly priced too, with Russian River and Carneros Pinot Noirs, Chalk Hill Chardonnay, Alexander Valley Italian varieties, Knights Valley Cabernet and Dry Creek Zinfandel all being of particular interest.

WINE BAR — HEALDSBURG

### Barndiva

231 Center St, Healdsburg, CA 95448
T +1 707-431 0100
www.barndiva.com
Wed-Thu 1200-2300, Fri-Sat 1200-2400, Sun 1100-2400.
$$-$

Housed in a huge red barn surrounded by lovely gardens, this Sonoma hangout for the hip specializes in organic cocktails that could fool you into thinking they are health drinks. It also offers a list of more than 200 Sonoma wines, including many hard-to-find producers and vintages. The food is light, simple and very good: long on fresh vegetables and short on heavy sauces.

Roederer Estate.

WINERY GLEN ELLEN

## Benziger Family Winery

1883 London Ranch Rd, Glen Ellen, CA 95442
T +1 888- 490 2739
www.benziger.com
Daily 1000-1700.
Tram tickets US$10

The *Wine Specator* magazine called the tour here, the "most comprehensive in the wine industry" and I'd agree. Benziger actually offers two tours: one on which you guide yourself, and one for which you board the tram, pulled by a huge Massey tractor, for an instructive lumber into the vineyards and surrounding wildlife sanctuaries. Back at the ranch – it was a working ranch when it was discovered by the first wave of Benzigers, Mike and Mary – the excellent staff in the shop will talk you through an informal tasting of whichever of the many wines you want to try. There are often Benzigers around, of one generation or another, to supplement this with first-hand winery history. The views from Sonoma Mountain are worth the trip in themselves.

WINERY RUSSIAN RIVER

## Davis Bynum Winery

8075 Westside Rd, Healdsburg, CA 95448
T +1 800-826 1073/707-433 2611
www.davisbynum.com
Daily 1000-1700.

Russian River's Davis Bynum Winery will give you a taste of the pioneer spirit that built the American West. Davis Bynum and his late wife, Dorothy, met at the house of photographer Ansel Adams, whose black and white photographs provide one of the greatest chronicles of America's natural landscapes. The couple decided, rather spontaneously, to start making wine, specializing in Pinot Noir. The vineyards have always been organic, and winemaking, with the aid of gravity, is made with as little interference as possible. There is always an informal exhibition of paintings by Californian artists hanging on the winery walls, which are available for sale. There are no tours, but picnic grounds are open to the public. Another nice local touch is that the website has links to several restaurants and hotels in the area.

WINERY RUSSIAN RIVER

## Gary Farrell Winery

10701 Westside Rd, Healdsburg, CA 95448
T +1 707-473 2900/473 2909
www.garyfarrellwines.com
Daily 1000-1700.
Tastings from US$5; tours (which include a tasting) US$10.

Russian River wines have become so popular in the past ten years that vineyard prices have increased fourfold as more winemakers pursue the magical effect of its climate on a range of grapes from Pinot Noir to Zinfandel. Gary Farrell's winery is an established producer of several sought-after single vineyards wines, as well as of Appellation Designate blends. It's an excellent place to learn about Russian River's geography and minute microclimates and to taste the great range of expression that is possible within less than an acre. The tasting room is managed by Gary's wife Debbie and visits have an intimate, close-up feel. Even if you haven't been able to book ahead for a tour, stop by for a tasting and to take in the superb views of the valley and the surrounding redwood trees.

Sonoma Valley.

Napa vineyards.

WINERY — GLEN ELLEN

### Laurel Glen

Box 1419, Glen Ellen, CA 95442
T +1 707-526 3914
www.laurelglen.com
Tasting room Wed-Mon1100-1800.

Patrick Campbell has since bought vineyards in Lodi and Argentina, but this is where he first began, in the late 1970s, to make the intense Cabernets on which he built his reputation. The winery is a place to learn about the impact of altitude, low yields, volcanic soils and organic agriculture on one variety in this unique corner of Sonoma.

Patrick Campbell also provides a chance to put the specificity he offers into context. Along with a handful of other 'nouveau hicks', he has opened the **Locals Tasting Room** (T +1 707-857 4900, www.tastelocal wines.com), in nearby Geyserville, in which more than 60 wines made by Laurel Glen and seven other wineries are offered in fun, variety-themed flights.

## Napa

This is the most famous and glitziest part of California – and the place most crowded by tourists. Go with the flow and enjoy what is on offer, particularly the delicious blackcurranty Cabernets. The best Napa Chardonnays and Pinot Noirs come from Carneros, the cool southern area that is shared with Sonoma.

WINERY — ST HELENA

### Beringer Vineyards

2000 Main St, St Helena, CA 94574
T +1 707-963 7115
www.beringer.com
Jun-Oct daily 1000-1800; Nov-May daily 1000-1700.
Tours and tastings from US$10.

Beringer is practically a household name in America, where its White Zinfandel is one of the best-selling wines. It's the oldest continuously operating winery in Napa and was the first in the region to offer a public tour. It has had years to perfect both its top wines and its tours, and now offers a profusion of both. Any of the wines in the many ranges can be tasted in the shop, while the tours are of various lengths and levels of depth about the winery's history. There are also two seminars – one on wine and artisanal cheese pairing and one on choosing the right wine to match with salty, sour, sweet, savoury and spicy foods – that make an interesting addition to a tour.

WINERY — CARNEROS

### Bouchaine Vineyards

1075 Buchli Station Rd, Napa, CA 94559
T +1 800 -654 9463
www.bouchaine.com
Daily 1030-1600. Tours by appointment only.

Bouchaine Vineyards, which specialize in Burgundy-inspired Chardonnays and Pinot Noirs, has implicit Burgundy credentials. One of Carneros' oldest wineries, it has had several owners, including Beringer, but its most recent owner, Gerret Copeland, is a member of the Confrérie des Chevaliers du Tastevin, of which his mother was the first female member. Copeland and his wife, Tatiana, have invested energy and passion into Bouchaine, most notably in restoring the winery building, which has won many awards, and in hiring veteran winemaker Mike Richmond, who, among many other credentials, founded the Steamboat Pinot Noir Conference. The winery is possibly the most dog-friendly in Napa, hosting regular dog-and-owner events. It offers a picnic service, whereby you call ahead and find a luxurious basket waiting for you to enjoy in the vineyards.

WINERY OAKVILLE

## Cardinale

7600 St Helena Hwy, Oakville, CA 94562
T +1 707-948 2643/800-588 0279
www.cardinale.com
Daily 1030-1700. Tours by appointment only.

The offer here at Kendall Jackson's top winery is simple but very, very good. Winemaker Christopher Carpenter makes only one wine per year based on Cabernet, but this deceptively simple formula involves a Bordeaux-like alchemy of separate-parcel vinifying. Variety is thus provided by vintage variations, nuances that can be sampled and discussed in the mini verticals that are offered at the tasting. The vineyards are certified organic, and this is a great, intimate setting in which to observe focused, qualitative winemaking up close.

# Best producers

**California**

Alban
Araujo
Au Bon Climat
Beaulieu Vineyard (top wines)
Benziger ›› *page 228.*
Beringer (top wines) ›› *page 229.*
Bonny Doon ›› *page 238.*
Bouchaine ›› *page 229.*
Byron
Cain Five
Cakebread
Calera ›› *page 238.*
Cardinale ›› *page 230.*
Carneros Creek
Caymus
Chalk Hill
Chateau Montelena ›› *page 230.*
Château Potelle
Chimney Rock
Cuvaison
Davis Bynum ›› *page 228.*
Diamond Creek
Domaine Carneros ›› *page 231.*
Domaine Chandon
Domaine de la Terre Rouge ›› *page 236.*
Dominus
Dry Creek
Duckhorn
Duxoup
E&J Gallo (Sonoma Estate)
Etude
Fetzer
Flora Springs
Frog's Leap ›› *page 232.*
Gary Farrell ›› *page 228.*
Geyser Peak
Gloria Ferrer
Grace Family
Grgich Hills
Groth
Guenoc
Halone
Hanzell
Harlan Estate
Hartwell
Hess Collection ›› *page 232.*
Iron Horse
Joseph Swan
Justin ›› *page 239.*
Kistler
Kunde
Laurel Glen ›› *page 229.*
Littorai
Lolonis
Long Vineyards
Louis Martini
Luna ›› *page 233.*
Marimar Torres
Matazas Creek
Mayacamas
McDowell
Morgan
Mumm Napa ›› *page 233.*
Murrieta's Well
Navarro
Newton
Niebaum Coppola
Opus One
Patz & Hall
Peter Michael
Phelps
Quivira
A Rafanelli
Ridge ›› *page 239.*
Robert Mondavi (top wines) ›› *page 234.*
J Rochioli
Roederer Estate ›› *page 227.*
Saintsbury
Schramsberg ›› *page 235.*
Selene
Shafer
Silver Oak
Spottswoode
Spring Mountain ›› *page 235.*
Stags Leap Wine Cellars
Stags Leap Winery
Steele
Stony Hill
Swanson ›› *page 235.*
Terre Rouge
Williams-Selyem

HOTEL MAYACAMAS HILLS

## The Carneros Inn

4048 Sonoma Hwy, Napa, CA 94559
T +1 707 -299 4900
www.thecarnerosinn.com
$$$

Halfway between Napa and Sonoma, in the heart of the Mayacamas hills, this resort is close to everything that might be on your winery itinerary but so comfortable that you might prefer to stay put; content to armchair travel throughout the region via the restaurant's terrific wine list. The dynamic PlumpJack group are behind the Carneros Inn and no expense has been spared by its partners, who include San Francisco mayor Gavin Newsom and oil heir Gordon Getty, in making this one of America's top wine-destination hotels. The rooms are in individual cottages which look minimalist on the outside but are, in fact, full of the trappings of luxury: heated slate bathroom floors, baths built for two, fireplaces, French windows leading to decks, outdoor showers, flat-screen televisions, fireplaces – you name it. The excellent **Hilltop Restaurant** ($$$) is open to guests only, but if you aren't staying you can still enjoy the wine selection at the more informal **Boon Fly** ($$$-$$).

WINERY CALISTOGA

## Chateau Montelena Winery

1429 Tubbs Ln, Calistoga, CA 94515
T +1 707-942 5105
www.montelena.com
Daily 0930-1600. Tours 1400, must be booked in advance.
Tastings from US$10.

Chateau Montelena sprang to the world's attention when its 1973 Chardonnay came top in the 1976 blind tasting, known as the Judgement of Paris, in which California generally trumped some of France's top wines. Thirty years later it is still going strong, and it offers one of the best tours available at a winery of this calibre: instructive for visitors of every level of knowledge, unpretentious and fun. Vertical tastings of three Cabernet Sauvignons are also available, a terrific chance to taste wines that are hard to come by and expensive.

RESTAURANT — ST HELENA

## Cindy's Backstreet Kitchen

1327 Railroad Av, St Helena
T +1707-963 1200
www.cindysbackstreetkitchen.com
Nov-Apr Sun-Thu 1130-2100, Fri and Sat 1130-2200; May-Oct daily 1130-2200.
$$

A glamorized hole-in-the-wall restaurant, this is the place to relax after a hard day hitting the wineries. The food at this informal locals' haunt might be simple but it is hardly pedestrian. You might find duck burger with shiitake mushroom ketchup on offer, or a perfectly cooked and juicy steak and fries, accompanied by a garlic-ginger dip. The Cindy in question is none other than Cindy Pawlcyn, a chef and restaurateur who seems to spin gold out of dishwater; in fact, the chef here, Pablo Jacinto, began work washing up at one of her other restaurants. The wine list offers an excellent array of Napa wines by the bottle and half bottle, as well as some carefully chosen selections from around the world.

ATTRACTION — NAPA

## COPIA: the American Center for Wine, Food & the Arts

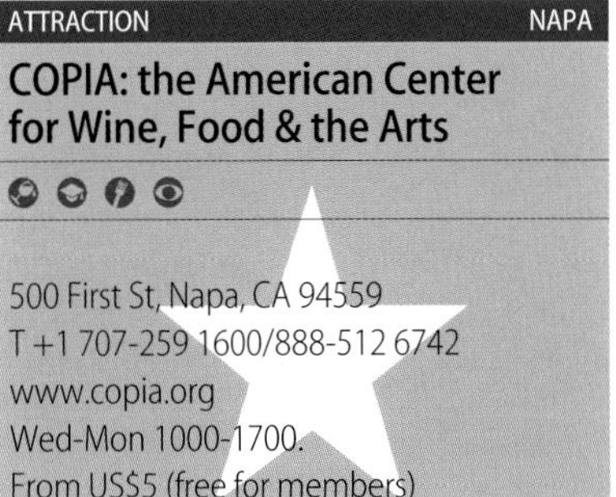

500 First St, Napa, CA 94559
T +1 707-259 1600/888-512 6742
www.copia.org
Wed-Mon 1000-1700.
From US$5 (free for members)

In my opinion, COPIA does for wine and food what the Metropolitan museum in New York does for art. A not-for-profit organization that has been conceived with great depth and care, the centre is devoted to studying and celebrating wine, food and the arts in all their dimensions. The range of offerings is staggering: you can take a half-hour introduction to wine tasting, view exhibitions on functional ceramics or photographs of American diners, learn how to make genuine baked beans or pesto, and meet a visiting winemaker, all in the space of a couple of hours. There are two excellent restaurants ($$) on the premises as well, so it is worth devoting at least half a day, if not more, to your visit.

WINERY — CARNEROS

## Domaine Carneros

1240 Duhig Rd, Napa, CA 94559
T +1 707 -257 0101
www.domainecarneros.com
Daily 1000-1800. Tours daily 1100, 1300 and 1500.

Owned by Taittinger, Domaine Carneros brings Champagne-style glamour and savvy

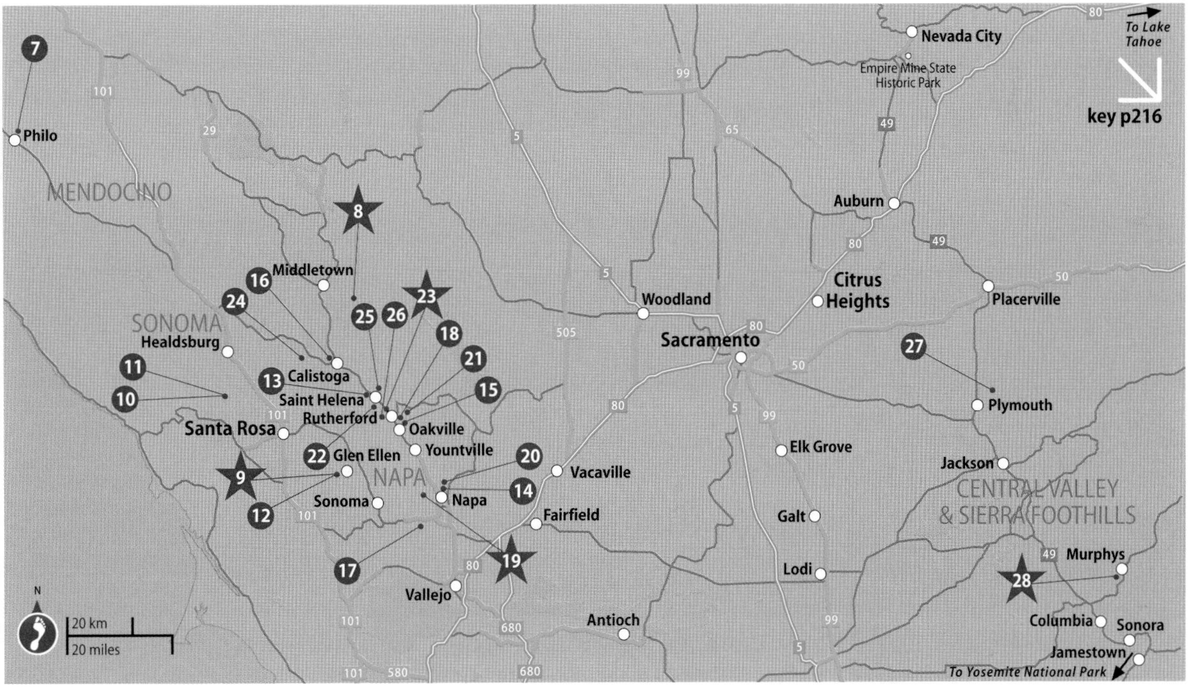

key p216

Grapevine

**The Judgment of Paris**

The quality of Californian wine is now routinely acknowledged. In the early 1970s, however, even the pioneering winery owners of the Napa Valley lacked real confidence that their efforts were comparable to the classic offerings of France. This situation changed dramatically in 1976, when Steven Spurrier, a young Englishman with a wine shop in Paris, decided to hold a tasting in which Cabernet Sauvignons from California were pitched against top Bordeaux, and white Burgundies competed with Californian Chardonnays. The identities of all the wines were hidden from the nine tasters who included eight of France's most highly respected palates. The results could not have been more shocking. The US Chardonnays took first (Chateau Montelena 1973), third (Chalone Vineyard 1974) and fourth (Spring Mountain Vineyard 1973) places and none of the tasters gave a white Burgundy their highest mark. The home team fared better when it came to the reds, taking four of the five top places, with Château Mouton-Rothschild 1970, Château Haut-Brion 1970 and Château Montrose 1970. Unfortunately for Gallic morale, however, the winner of this part of the competition was Stag's Leap Wine Cellars 1973.

In France, the immediate reaction was initially to ignore that the tasting had taken place and then, three months later in *le Figaro* and after a further three months in *le Monde*, to dismiss it as laughable. In contrast, the Californians and their colleagues in other parts of the New World gained huge confidence from the result and were given another boost by the decision of illustrious Bordeaux producers Baron Philippe de Rothschild of Château Mouton-Rothschild and Christian Moueix of Château Petrus to invest in Californian vineyards.

French apologists who were prepared to talk about the 1976 tasting took comfort from the notion that, however well the Californian wines might have shown in their youth, Bordeaux from a great vintage like 1970 (the year of three of the four winning clarets) would show its mettle over time. In 2006, this belief was put to the test when the original Judgment of Paris, as it was now known, was recreated for red wines only, with panels of tasters in California and London. The US producers all provided samples, despite doubting their chances of doing as well as they had 30 years earlier; the château-owners, by contrast, refused to take part, so the Bordeaux had to be bought. This time, the results were even better for the Californians than in 1976: the top five spots were taken by Ridge Vineyards Monte Bello 1971, Stag's Leap Wine Cellars 1973, Mayacamas Vineyards 1971, Heitz Wine Cellars 'Martha's Vineyard' 1970 and Clos Du Val Winery 1972.

Ironically, in 2006, there was also a taste-off by the same tasters of young wines from the same producers. This time France won but, since the French refused to allow this part of the tasting to be done blind, it was understandably more or less unpublicized.



to Carneros. Free tours of the grand *château* are offered in many languages, including Japanese, and include detailed insights into both the traditional method of making sparkling wines, in which Domaine Carneros specializes, as well as into the Carneros appellation.

Claude Taittinger visited Carneros in his youth and was taken with its excellent conditions for making sparkling wine, most notably the relatively cool growing season. He fulfilled his dream of realizing this potential in the late 1980s. Unique among sparkling wine producers in Carneros, the winery uses only Carneros grapes.

WINERY — RUTHERFORD

### Frog's Leap

PO Box 189, 8815 Conn Creek Rd, Rutherford, CA 95573
T +1 800- 959 4704
www.frogsleap.com
Garden and orchard daily 1000-1600; tours and tastings by appointment only.

Frog's Leap is housed in a charming red barn that was purpose-built as a winery in 1884. Although John Williams is not the original owner, much has been left unchanged for the past century. Chemicals have never made an appearance, and the vineyards are thus completely organic. There is an orchard with rare trees, a large kitchen and herb garden, and the frog pond that spawned the winery's name. Visits, which are informal and best planned ahead, provide an insight into life on one of California's ruggedly individualistic smaller estates.

WINERY — NAPA

### The Hess Collection Winery

4411 Redwood Rd, Napa, CA 94558
T +1 877-707 4377
www.hesscollection.com
Daily 1000-1600. Guided tastings by appointment only.
Tastings US$10.

Though it is slightly out of the way and up a long drive that keeps winding on, don't let this discourage you from visiting this very

Hess Collection.

special place. Swiss millionaire Donald Hess has used his beautifully designed and lit winery to house a rotating exhibition of works from his important collection of American and European contemporary art, which includes pieces by Francis Bacon and Franz Gertsch, among many others. Informal tastings of four wines of your choice are available, but it is better to book ahead for the regular small tutored tastings of the sought-after top reserve wines, held in the barrel cellar. A self-guided tour of the house and gallery is also available.

WINERY NAPA

## Luna Vineyards

2921 Silverado Trail, Napa, CA 94558
T +1 707- 255 2474
www.lunavineyards.com
Daily 1000-1700. Tours and special tastings by appointment only.

As well as talent for impersonating Elvis, winemaker Mike Drash excels at creating wines from Italian varieties such as Sangiovese, Pinot Grigio and Teroldego. The winery is friendly and low key, and can tailor a tour or tasting to suit your interests, as well as provide suggestions for places to stay and eat in the area. They can also organize special tastings matching their reserve wines with artisan-produced cheese, charcuterie and chocolates.

WINERY RUTHERFORD

## Mumm Napa

8445 Silverado Trail, PO Box 500, Rutherford, CA 94573
T +1 800-686 6272/707-967 7700
www.mummnapa.com
Daily 1000-1700. Tours 1000-1500.
Tastings from US$5 (free for members; join online).

Widely acknowledged to be one of the best tours in the Napa Valley, Mumm Napa offers not only an excellent introduction to the Napa Valley's unique and varied growing conditions but also an in-depth insight into traditional-method sparkling wine production. As one would expect from a winery of this kind, everything about the experience is rich and highly professional, from the sparklers themselves to the stunning views and immaculate winery.

The winery also boasts a world-class photography gallery, which displays a collection of work by Ansel Adams, on loan from the photographer's son, as well as hosting temporary photography exhibitions. There are regular special events, such as Bocce ball tournaments, and the excellent website's 'concierge' facility is full of suggestions and contact details to help you plan your trip to Napa.

MUSEUM YOUNTVILLE

## Napa Valley Museum

55 Presidents Circle, Yountville, CA 94599
T +1 707-944 0500
www.napavalleymuseum.org
Wed-Mon 1000-1700.
US$4.50

Mumm Napa.

Besides being rich in winemaking legend, Napa's history involves myriad cultures and peoples, including the Wappo tribe, who once made Napa their home, and Chinese labourers, who did much of the manual work involved in building up the valley. One excellent permanent exhibition tells Napa's many stories, while another interactive exhibition explains the technical aspects of making wine. There are also frequent temporary art exhibitions and events such as open-mike poetry readings.



ATTRACTION NAPA

## Napa Valley Wine Train

1275 McKinstry St, Napa, CA 94559
T +1 800 -427 4124
www.winetrain.com
Check-in Mon-Fri 1030 and 1730; Sat and Sun 1130 and 1730.
Tickets from US$49.50

This is one visit for which you can't be late. The wine train departs promptly for lunch, dinner and, occasionally, brunch trips through the Napa Valley. While you take in the lovely vistas, many of which can't be had from the road, you will be served several courses and have the choice of around 100 wines. There are several dining cars, most with original turn-of-the-century fixtures and fittings, such as etched glass windows, each offering a slightly different menu. Depending on the package, the train might make stops at either Grgich Hills Winery or Domaine Chandon.

SHOP OAKVILLE

## Oakville Grocery

7856 St Helena Hwy, Oakville, CA 94562
T +1 707-944 8802
www.oakvillegrocery.com
Shop daily 0900-1800. Espressso bar daily 0700-1800.

As much of a local landmark as the Robert Mondavi Winery, this roadside delicatessen, wine shop and, yes, grocery was built in 1881 and still boasts an old Coca Cola sign on one of its wooden walls. It's the place to mingle with locals and tourists and with horse riders who stop here to pick up provisions for the trail.

WINERY OAKVILLE

## Robert Mondavi Winery

Hwy 29, Oakville, CA 94562
T +1-888 766 6328
www.robertmondavi.com
Daily 1000-1700.
Tours from US$15.

The winery may have been sold to the world's biggest wine company, Constellation, and the younger generation of the Mondavi family may have moved away to start wineries of their own, but this is still an iconic place. The first modern winery in California, it set the pattern in the 1960s for many hundreds that followed, both here and in other countries. The shop, art museum, concerts and tours were all part of the experience almost from the outset and now, every day, large numbers of visitors set out on activities, ranging from the To Kalon Tour, which takes you from vineyard to winery and tasting room, to the three-hour Essence Tour that explores the smells and flavours associated with wine. All of the tours are best booked in advance.

WINERY RUTHERFORD

## Rubicon

1991 St Helena Hwy, Rutherford, CA 94573
T +1 707- 968 1100
www.rubiconestate.com
Daily 1000-1700.
Tours and tastings from US$25.

As someone who loves movies and gothic architecture almost as much as I love wine, I've always had a particularly soft spot for this winery. Owned by film director Francis Ford Coppola, Rubicon has been lavished with all the care and attention one would expect from this cinematic master. The wine tour is on the expensive side, but includes a visit to the **Centennial Museum**, where there is plenty of Coppola memorabilia as well as information about Gustave Niebaum, the winery's original founder. It also takes in the lovely **Inglenook Chateau**, built by Niebaum in 1886, and includes a tasting of five wines, including the flagship wine Rubicon, a Cabernet Sauvignon made from organic grapes. There is a very pleasant and child-friendly wine bar, **Mammarella**, named after Coppola's mother, where children can borrow boats to push around a fountain.

WINERY | CALISTOGA

### Schramsberg

1400 Schramsberg Rd, Calistoga, CA 94515
T +1 707-942 2414/800-877 3623
www.schramsberg.com
Visits by appointment only.

The fact that Robert Louis Stevenson visited Schramsberg and wrote about it in *The Silverado Squatters* is just one of the many historical higlights of this winery. Others are the listed late-19th-century winery building and the miles of underground caves, dug by immigrant Chinese labourers as cool storage for the wine. Schramsberg was also the first winery in the country to make traditional-method sparkling wines, and is an excellent place to learn about the process.

Schramsberg.

## Tasting notes

**California's grape**

If California has a single grape of its own, it has to be the Zinfandel. According to *Zinfandel: A History of the Grape & Its Wine* by Charles Sullivan (University of California Press, 2003), this variety which is now grown on some 20,000 ha by over 300 wineries, started out as a native Croatian grape called Crljenak Kastelanski. It was brought to England, where it was dubbed Black St Peters, and thence to a nursery on Long Island in the 1820s. In New York State, the Zinfandel was grown for eating rather than wine but, by the late 1800s, it was carried to California by gold miners and widely planted in the Sonoma Valley and Amador County. No one knows how it got its name but, curiously, unlike other varieties, the spicy wine it produced was never sold as 'Burgundy' or 'Claret'.

Zinfandel never developed a reputation for fine wine but it survived Prohibition because the grapes were sold for home winemaking. After Repeal, however, the growing focus on Cabernet Sauvignon led to Zinfandel being sidelined until, in the 1970s, it seemed as though most of the vineyards might have to be uprooted. In 1975, rescue came at the Sutter Home winery which began to sell pink, semi-sweet wine that was paradoxically labeled as 'White Zinfandel'. Brisk sales of this new style created a demand for the grape and helped to safeguard the venerable vineyards that supplied old-vine red 'Zin'. Today, Zinfandel is the fourth most widely planted variety in California, producing wines ranging from the great reds of Ridge Vineyards to the flood of White Zinfandel that is perfectly matched to a Big Mac.

WINERY | ST HELENA

### Spring Mountain Vineyard

2805 Spring Mountain Rd, St Helena, CA 94574
T +1 877-769 4637/707-967 4188
www.springmtn.com
Visits by appointment only.
US$25

Napa is a valley, but a valley can't exist without mountains. Napa's Spring Mountain District, in the Mayacamas hills, offers a chance to see what effect altitudes of 400 ft up to more than 2000 ft above sea-level have on wine production. When you want to head for the hills, make Spring Mountain Vineyard your first stop. It has more than 1000 acres, spread across many different mountain microclimates, and produces a fascinating range of wines from Cabernet Sauvignon, Syrah and Pinot Noir, among others. The one-and-a-half hour tour, which should be booked in advance, includes a walk through the vineyards, gardens and the late 19th-century mansion, one of the loveliest properties in Napa.

WINERY | RUTHERFORD

### Swanson Vineyards

1271 Manley Ln, Rutherford, CA 94573
T +1 707-967 3500
www.swansonvineyards.com
Visits by appointment only.

Swanson Vineyards offers perhaps the most glamorous tasting experience in California. Events take place in the Salon, a recreation of a 19th-century Parisian private sitting room, complete with 30-ft ceilings, a chandelier and huge, specially commissioned oil tableaux by artist Ira Yeager. No more than eight people will be seated around the grand table, set, as if for a dinner party, with the finest Riedel crystal glasses. You will be talked through a selection of the estate's wines, including the luscious Merlot, a variety they helped pioneer in the area, which will be paired with delicious morsels of cheese and chocolate. Despite the formal surroundings, the emphasis is on fun as well as on instruction.

## Central Valley and Sierra Foothills

The engine room of California wine, this warm region is where most of the affordable wines are made, as well as a growing number of ambitious, rich, pricier reds.

WINERY SIERRA NEVADA

### Domain de la Terre Rouge

10801 Dickson Rd, Plymouth, CA 95669
T +1209- 245 3117
www.terrerougewines.com
Fri-Mon 1100-1600.

One of the original Rhône Rangers (a nickname given to Californian Rhône-style winemakers), William Easton went a step further by using only French oak barrels for ageing his Syrahs. A maverick in many other respects, he makes a range of 20-odd wines, many in lots of no more than 600 cases, in a solar-powered winery. It is well worth making the trip to the beautiful Sierra Nevada foothills in the Shenandoah Valley to witness this branch of California winemaking. The winery hosts regular events and festivals, such as group tastings with neighbouring wineries, and there's a *pétanque* court that serves as a litmus test to identify genuine Francophiles.

WINERY MURPHYS

### Ironstone Vineyards

1894 Six Mile Rd, Murphys, CA 95247
T +1 209 -728 1251
www.ironstonevineyards.com
Daily summer 1000-1800, winter 1000-1700.

Precisely my idea of a fun and integrated wine destination, this is also a tribute to California's Gold Rush. The **Heritage Museum** has some wonderful photographs of life in the gold mining towns, as well as an evocative collection of miners' personal belongings that evokes the poignant slow-burning dramas behind the get-rich-quick dreams. It also claims to have the largest specimen of crystalline gold leaf in the world. Other highlights include the **Culinary Centre**, in which there are baking, cooking and wine-and-food pairing demonstrations; the underground wine

#### After the Gold Rush

Around the same time that the seeds of California's wine industry were being planted, many thousands were flocking to the 'Golden State' for an entirely different reason. The discovery of gold in the Sierra foothills east of Sacramento in 1848 changed the face of California and the legacy of those wild years can be explored in the former mining towns of the region. The appropriately named Highway 49 links most of the sights of the Gold Country and you'll need a car to explore this area properly. For further information, see www.visit-eldorado.com.

**Sacramento**, the state capital, is the starting point and though it is a fairly sterile town, it does possess some interesting museums, particularly the **California State Railroad Museum** (125 I St, T +1 916-445 6645, www.californiastate railroadmuseum.rig). Interstate 80 leads east to **Placerville**, known as Hangtown during the Gold Rush for its preferred method of dispensing justice. You won't find any bodies dangling from trees but the town is home to the excellent **El Dorado Country Historical Museum** (104 Placerville Dr, www.co.el-dorado.ca.us/museum) and the **Gold Bug Mine Park** (www.goldbugpark.org), which provides an insight into mining conditions.

Heading south from Placerville, visit the heritage museum at **Ironstone Vineyards** (page 236) en route to **Columbia**. This town is entirely preserved as a State Historic Park, complete with Wild West saloons, a Wells Fargo express office and many other buildings from the late 1850s. Six miles south, past Sonora, is **Jamestown**, used as a location for many Westerns, such as Clint Eastwood's *Unforgiven*. Here you'll find the excellent **Railtown 1897 State Historic Park**, one of the real highlights of the Gold Country. From here you can head east into unmissable **Yosemite National Park** (T+ 1 209 372 0200, www.www.nps.gov/yose/) or west towards San Francisco and the coast.

Alternatively, north of Placerville, Hwy-49 runs through the northern mining towns and some of the most beautiful scenery in California. Grass Valley's incredibly evocative **Empire Mine State Historic Park** is an undoubted highlight, as is **Nevada City**, 4 miles north, perhaps the most authentic of all the Gold Country towns. Continue on Hwy-49 to explore the mine towns further north or head east and join I-80 to beautiful **Lake Tahoe**, stopping for lunch at the **Plumpjack Squaw Valley Inn** (page 237) and, in winter, enjoying some of the best skiing in California at the **Squaw Valley Resort** (www.squaw.com).

Ironstone Vineyards.

caverns hewn from limestone and schist; and the 1920s pipe organ that is still used for silent film screenings and other special events. The tasting room doubles as an excellent delicatessen, where you can buy a picnic to eat on the grounds.

HOTEL LAKE TAHOE

### PlumpJack Squaw Valley Inn

1920 Squaw Valley Rd, PO Box 2407, Olympic Valley, CA 96146
T +1 530-583 1576/800-323 7666
www.plumpjack.com
$$$

Prior to becoming a politician, Gavin Newsom, the handsome boy-wonder mayor of San Francisco, spearheaded a mini wine empire that includes the PlumpJack winery in Napa, the PlumpJack Café and wine shop in San Francisco and this delightful inn near Lake Tahoe, housed in a remodelled Olympic ski resort. The name comes from Queen Elizabeth I's name for Falstaff and, like the other PlumpJack enterprises, the point here is to have a lot of fun, living it up without taking anything, least of all the wine, too seriously. Having said that, the wine list is impressive, offering a terrific worldwide selection by the glass, at very reasonable prices. The delicious food ($$$) veers on the rich side – think long-braised ox tail in red wine and buttery risotto – but you can always ski or hike it off the next day.

## San Francisco Bay

RESTAURANT SAN FRANCISCO

### Bacar Restaurant & Wine Salon

448 Brannan St, San Francisco, CA 94107
T +1 415-904 4100
www.bacarsf.com
Mon-Thu 1730-2300, Fri 1130-2400, Sat 1730-2400, Sun 1730-2200
$$$-$$

Debbie Zachareas runs one of my favourite wine bars and restaurants anywhere. In this warehouse than can seat up to 250 people in three different areas, she has created a superb wine programme that more than does justice to the upmarket French-bistro-meets-California-burger-joint creations of chef Arnold Eric Wong. From a list of more than 1000 wines, Zachareas offers around 80 by the glass at any one time, in either 2-fl oz glasses or decanters holding 250 ml or 500 ml. Another fun feature is the option to assemble flights of 2-fl oz glasses from the various geographically themed sections. There is a live jazz band most nights, as well as regular wine events, and the three-storey 'wall of wine' further sets the scene for informal entertainment and new variations on wine themes you thought you were familiar with.

## South Central Coast

This varied area encorporates Santa Barbara (made famous by the film *Sideways*), Monterey, San Luis Obispo and Santa Cruz, as well as inaccessible but worthwhile vineyards like Calera in Mount Harlan and Ridge in Cupertino.

WINERY SANTA BARBARA

### Blackjack Ranch Winery

2205 Alamo Pintado Rd, Solvang, CA 93463
T +1 805-686 9922
www.blackjackranch.com
Fri-Sun 1100-1700.

Grapevine

**Points mean prizes**

Wine critics around the world have traditionally marked wines out of five, ten or 20, depending on personal preference or where they got their vinous education. Since the early 1980s, however, all of these scales have been eclipsed by the so-called 100-point system introduced by the US critic Robert Parker. This scale, which Parker borrowed from the US education system, actually marks wines out of 50, because nothing gets less than 50 points. Parker's global influence rapidly ensured that the scale was adopted by *Wine Spectator* magazine and other critics and is now the global industry standard, though many Europeans would prefer that it were not. Stated simply: wines with more than 90 points sell easily, while those with less than 87 tend to stick to the shelves, unless they are keenly priced, and any wine with a mark under 80 might as well stay at home. Many major US retailers refuse to consider stocking a wine with insufficient scores, so the difference between an 89 and a 90 can be crucial.

This might suggest that there is some science involved in the allocation of these numbers, but they simply represent the taster's subjective impressions. So the same wine may earn a wide range of marks or different marks at various stages of its evolution. The numbers that really count among professionals and enthusiasts are the ones given by Robert Parker and his colleagues (in the *Wine Advocate* newsletter) and *Wine Spectator* magazine but US retailers know that many of their customers are less well informed, so often promote wines using high marks from a wide range of other critics and publications.

Roger Wisted began making wine at the tender age of 17 in his parents' grocery store (in a country where wine drinking is illegal for anyone under 21). He funded his own winery by inventing California Blackjack, a card game that successfully sidestepped the century-old ban on the '21' blackjack played elsewhere. The tasting room is made of recycled materials; the bar was once a lane in a bowling alley in nearby Solvang – and the wines are impressive Bordeaux varietals, Syrahs and Chardonnays.

WINERY — SANTA CRUZ

**Bonny Doon**

10 Pine Flat Rd, Santa Cruz, CA 95060
T +1 831-425 4518
www.bonnydoonvineyard.com
Daily 1100-1700.
Tastings US$3

Randall Grahm, founder of this ground-breaking winery, was the original Rhône Ranger and pioneer of Cal-Ital wine. He has recently sold several of his labels and is focusing on smaller quantities of screwcap-sealed, biodynamic wine. You can be sure that there will be plenty of wacky and experimental wines on offer at the winery.

WINERY — MOUNT HARLAN

**Calera Wine Company**

11300 Cienega Rd, Hollister, CA 95023
T +1 831- 637 9170
www.calerawine.com
Daily 1000-1600.

Josh Jensen, a renaissance man from an early age, followed undergraduate studies at Yale

**A day in the Bay**

Start the day with a ride on one of San Francisco's iconic cable cars. Climb aboard the **Powell-Hyde line** at the Market and Powell streets and enjoy the amazing city vistas as the car slowly drags itself uphill and then lunges downhill towards the end of the line at Hyde and Beach streets. Walk the short distance to **Fisherman's Wharf**, tourist honeypot and departure point for the 15-minute ferry ride to **Alcatraz Island** (http://alcatrazcruises.com). The boat trip is a highlight in itself but the tour of the famous prison is genuinely fascinating. Back at Fisherman's Wharf, you can lunch at one of the many seafood stands on **Pier 39** or instead head into North Beach where you can enjoy a meal at one of the Italian restaurants on **Columbus Avenue.** Afterwards head for **Vesuvio** (255 Columbus Av, T 1-415 362 3370), erstwhile hangout of Jack Kerouac and fellow Beat writers, for a coffee and a spot of people-watching. Just a block away is **Chinatown**, home to the second largest immigrant Chinese population in the US after NewYork City. Only a few blocks away from here is **Jackson Square**'s historic district, the only part of the city to survive the 1906 earthquake, towered over by the Transameric Pyramid. After exploring this neighbourhood of restored redbrick buildings, head south to the **SoMa** district for a well-earned rest and a glass of wine at **Bacar Restaurant & Wine Salon** (page 237).

with a graduate anthropology degree at Oxford, where he rowed for three years in the annual Oxford and Cambridge boat race. He then spent several years in Burgundy, hatching a plan that would eventually prove that world-class Pinot Noir could be produced in his native California. The rest, as they say, is winemaking history. If you want to add a bit more adventure to your visit, ask the winery to give you directions from King City via the back roads.

WINERY — PASO ROBLES

### Justin Vineyards & Winery

11680 Chimney Rock Rd, Paso Robles, CA 93446
T +1 805-238 6932/800-726 0049
www.justinwine.com
Tours and tastings daily 1030-1430 by appointment.
Tours US$10.

A leading light of the Central Coast, Justin and Deborah Baldwin's winery offers a romantic four-bedroom inn ($$$), award-winning wines, a delightful country restaurant and terrific views. There are several well thought-out tour options, including rare opportunities to see vineyard work up close and to delve into barrel samples in the cellar. The restaurant, **Deborah's Room** ($$$-$$), has a generously broad wine list, considering it is attached to a winery, and includes an impressive selection of Champagnes. The inventive menu offers celeriac ravioli and goat's cheese ice cream.

WINERY — SANTA CLARA

### Ridge Vineyards

17100 Monte Bello Rd, Cupertino, CA 95014
T +1 408- 867 3233
www.ridgewine.com
Sat and Sun 1100-1600.

Located high on the San Andreas fault in an old wooden building, this pioneering winery produces Cabernet and Zinfandel that are second to none. Getting to it, however, calls for a lot more effort than is required to visit any of the big names of Napa, which is why we are printing the winery's instructions:

Take Highway 280 to the Foothill Expressway exit. Proceed south on Foothill Boulevard (which becomes Stevens Canyon Road) approximately three miles to Monte Bello Road. Immediately after the rock quarry, turn right onto Monte Bello Road and continue for 4.4 miles to 17100. (Drive carefully, the road is twisting and narrow.)

WINE BAR — SAN LUIS OBISPO

### Taste

1003 Osos St, San Luis Obispo, CA 93401
T +1 805-2698 2783
www.taste-slo.com
Mon-Wed 1000-2100, Tue-Sat 1000-2200, Sun 1000-1800.

In an admirable feat of group organization and vision, the San Luis Obispo Vintners Association has created a fun, hip wine bar and tasting room in downtown San Luis Obispo. Some 70 of the area's wines are available to buy and more than 40 wines are regularly available for tasting through the Enomatic, a self-service wine-pouring machine. The shop also acts as the first stop on the area's new wine route, so is the perfect place to orient oneself.

WINE SHOP — PALO ALTO

### Vin, Vino, Wine

437 California Av, Palo Alto, CA 94306
T +1 650-324 4903
www.vinvinowine.com
Sat-Thu 1100-1900, Fri 1100-2000.

This thoughtful, well-conceived independent wine shop offers visitors a chance to put California's wine into a wider context. Specializing in the artisan wines of France, Italy and California, with a well-selected sprinkling from a few other regions, it regularly offers a wide range by the glass at its tasting bar. The exciting wine flights on offer might include a horizontal of six or seven Rosso di Montalcinos by seven different producers, or a similar assemblage of Chinons. Then again it might be six or seven white Burgundies by a pair of producers such as Jean-Marc Boillot and Bernard Morey.

## Los Angeles

RESTAURANT — LOS ANGELES

### Lucques Restaurant & Bar

8474 Melrose Av, Los Angeles, CA 90069
T +1 323-655 6277
www.lucques.com
Mon 1800-2200; Tue 1200-1430 and 1800-2200; Wed-Sat 1200-1430 and 1800-2300; Sun 1700-2200.
$$$-$$

My first experience of great California cuisine was provided by Alice Waters at Chez Panisse, in San Francisco. Today, her protégée, Susanne Goin, has taken Los Angeles by storm. Like Waters, who pioneered simple country cooking in California, Goin is dedicated to the idea of environmentally responsible gastronomy. This comes at no compromise to quality and taste, and the eclectic menu offers an excellent range of regional European dishes, with a California twist and, unusually for La-La Land, no alterations of fat content nor omissions of ingredients in the name of health. Goin's co-owner Caroline Styne is the sommelier, and has put together an exciting list, with many offerings by the glass. The duo have also recently opened **AOC** (8022 West 3rd St, Los Angeles, CA 90048, T +1-323-655 6277, www.aocwinebar.com), a nearby wine bar with more than 50 wines by the glass. Go to Lucques on Sunday for a terrific-value set-menu supper.

# Pacific northwest

## Idaho

Way back in 1898, Robert Schleisler's Idaho wine won a prize at the Chicago World Fair. Nearly 90 years later, the Ste-Chapelle winery, which looks like a Disney Chapel, was enjoying a similar reputation when it was revealed that 'grape-laundering' had been taking place, using grapes from California. According to the local wine association (www.idahowine.org) today there are over 50 wineries in the state, producing good sparkling wines and Chardonnays (which benefit from the high altitude) and, in the right sites, Cabernets and Syrahs.

WINERY | CALDWELL

### Hells Canyon Winery

18835 Symms Rd, Caldwell, ID 83605
T +1 208-454 3300/800 318 7873
www.hellscanyonwinery.org
Visits by appointment only.

Steve and Leslie Robertson make a fabulous Chardonnay, as well Cabernet Sauvignon, Merlot, Cabernet Franc and Syrah, from a simple winery on the edge of the Snake River Valley. As only 3000 cases are produced each year, a visit might be your only chance to try these wines, which are quickly snapped up. If you are in the area over the Thanksgiving weekend in late November, swing by for the annual open house.

## Oregon

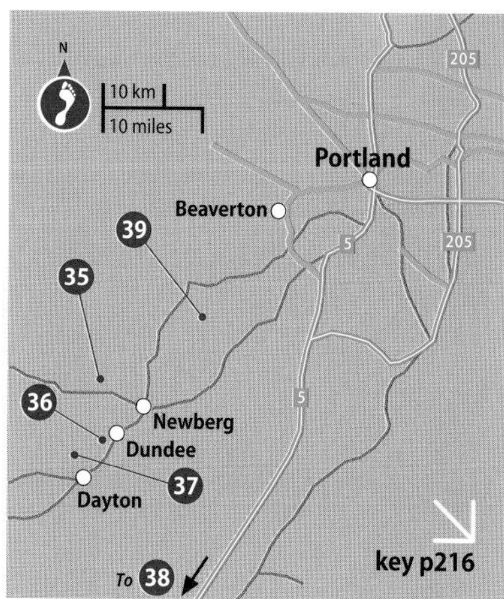


In the mid 1800s, German immigrants made wine in the Willamette and Umpqua Valleys, and made it well enough to win prizes. Following Prohibition, however, there was little wine of note until, in 1963, Richard Sommer opened a winery specializing in Riesling in the Umpqua, followed two years later by David Lett who decided to make Pinot Noir in the Willamette. Both men were graduates of the famous UC Davis wine school and both were well aware that the experts believed the climate in Oregon to be too cold for vinfera grapes. In 1979, David Lett entered a 1975 Pinot Noir from his Eyrie Vineyards into a blind tasting in Paris as a rank outsider; it came second to a 1959 Joseph Drouhin Chambolle Musigny. The impact of Eyrie's success had a similar effect on Oregon as California had enjoyed after its famous victory in Steven Spurrier's tasting of 1976 (page 232). The earlier event helped to persuade Baron Philippe de Rothschild of Mouton Rothschild to invest in the Napa Valley; the 1979 success gave Robert Drouhin the confidence to launch Domaine Drouhin.

Today, according to the Oregon Wine Board (www.oregonwine.org) there are over 300 wineries and 6000 ha of vines. Richard Sommer's bet on Riesling has not really paid off; the variety only makes up 200 ha and Chardonnay has done scarcely better, with 340 ha. In fact, well over half the vineyards are Pinot Noir, with Pinot Gris coming in second at 13%. From the outset, Oregon has been Pinot Noir country, with soil and a climate that is as close to that of Burgundy as anywhere else in the world; every summer the Pinot Noir Celebration in McMinville brings together pinotphiles and Pinot Noir makers from across the globe. The event was first held in the 1980s, when Oregon's place as the only real alternative to Burgundy seemed assured. Today, there is much stronger competition from California, New Zealand and Chile. This, and the high prices commanded by Oregon

Oregon vines.

# Best producers

**Idaho**

Hells Canyon » *page 240.*

**Oregon**

Adelsheim » *page 241.*
Amity
Archery Summit
Argyle » *page 241.*
Beaux Freres
Bethel Heights
Chehalem
Christom
Domaine Drouhin » *page 241.*
Eyrie
King Estate » *page 242.*
Ponzi » *page 242.*
Rex Hill
Willakenzie
Ken Wright
Yamhill Valley

**Washington State**

Andrew Will
Canoe Ridge
Chateau Ste Michelle (inc. Eroica) » *page 243.*
Chinook
Columbia Crest (top wines)
Covey Run
Delille
Hedges
Hohue Cellars
Kiona
L' Ecole no 41 » *page 243.*
Leonetti
McCrea Cellars
Quilceda Creek
Snoqualmie
Spring Valley
Woodward Canyon

Pinot Noirs, may help to explain why so few bottles are seen overseas. All the more reason to taste them here.

Domaine Drouhin.

WINERY NEWBERG

## Adelsheim Vineyard

16800 NE Calkins Ln, Newberg, OR 97132
T +1 503-538 3652
www.adelsheim.com
Jun-Sep and Christmas daily 1100-1600; Oct-Dec and Mar-May Wed, Thu and Sun 1100-1600. Tours by appointment only. Tasting US$10. Tour US$20 (includes tasting).

Inspired by a trip to Europe, David and Ginny Adelsheim started making wine in their basement in the early 1970s. Fast forward just a decade and the Adelsheims were already building a gravity-operated 6000-sq-ft winery to meet the production needs of their Pinot Noir, Chardonnay and Riesling. Adelsheim Vineyard has continued to expand and innovate, but not at the expense of its hands-off winemaking policy. It is an excellent, welcoming place to learn about cool-climate viticulture and to compare Burgundian and Oregonian approaches to handling Chardonnay and Pinot Noir.

WINERY DUNDEE

## Argyle Winery

691 Hwy 99W, Dundee, OR 97115
T +1 503-538 8520
www.argylewinery.com
Daily 1100-1700.

Argyle Winery was created in 1987 by Rollin Soles, the top Texan winemaker, and Brian Croser, the man behind both the Petaluma Winery in Australia and Croser, one of that country's best sparkling wines. This is the place to find Oregon's answer to Champagne, as well as good Willamette Pinot Noir, Chardonnay and Riesling.

WINERY DAYTON

## Domain Drouhin Oregon

6750 Breyman Orchards Rd, Dayton, OR 97114
T +1 503-864 2700
www.domainedrouhin.com
Wed-Sun 1100-1600. Tours by appointment only.
Tasting US$5. Tour US$20.

Harvest time in Oregon.

It is easy to see why Burgundy fans fall in love with Oregon; both regions share the same intimacy of scale and the same kind of nooks and crannies.

Many skeptics about Oregon's potential as a producer of serious wine put their doubts to rest when the Drouhin family of Burgundy decided to stake a claim in the Willamette Valley. Under the skilled supervision of Véronique Drouhin, the domaine has produced stellar Pinot Noir and Chardonnays since 1988, and is one of the most exciting examples of Old-meets-New World in contemporary wine lore.

The tour takes in the four-storey gravity-propelled winery and ends with an instructive comparative tasting of the Drouhins' Oregon and Burgundy wines.

WINERY EUGENE

## King Estate Winery

80854 Territorial Rd, Eugene, OR 97405
T +1 800-884 4441/541-942 9874
www.kingestate.com
Daily 1100-1700.

Kansas natives Ed King Jr and his son Ed King II have, in less than two decades, created a remarkable winery in the beautiful mountains southwest of Eugene. The 110,000-sq-ft winery, a clean-lined modern take on a French château, dominates more than 1000 acres, a third of which are dedicated to vineyards and the rest to varied farm land. There's also an impressive vine propagation centre here, which allows King Estate's vineyards to display incredible clonal diversity; the variety of trellising methods on show make this a great spot for anoraks. The visitor centre offers food made from organic farm produce ($$-$) and, at weekends there is a market in which flowers, vegetables and locally produced cheese and bread can be bought. The winery regularly hosts events ranging from car shows to antique fairs to salsa competitions.

WINERY BEAVERTON

## Ponzi Vineyards

14665 SW Winery Ln, Beaverton, OR 97007
T +1 503-628 1227
www.ponziwines.com
Daily 1100-1700. Tours by appointment only.

Willamette Valley pioneers Dick and Nancy Ponzi, who have been making stunning wines for almost 40 years, have been joined by their children Michel, Anna-Maria and Beaune-trained oenologist Luisa. Ever generous in promoting their region as a whole, they also own the excellent **Ponzi Wine Bar** (T +1 503-554 1500) and the **Dundee Bistro** (T +1 503-554 1650, www.dundeebistro.com) both at 100 SW Seventh St, in nearby Dundee. These venues showcase more than 70 Oregon wines, many by the glass, as well as wide selection of microbrews. The winery itself is also a tribute to the wider region, being entirely made of materials from the Pacific Northwest, such as recycled first-growth timber.

## Washington State

In 1872, Lambert Evans, a Civil War veteran, planted grapes on Stretch Island on Puget Sound and became Washington's first known winemaker. Thirty years later, a teacher-turned-lawyer-turned-farmer called William Bridgman decided that the Yakima Valley had more promise, thanks to the availability of irrigation water from the Columbia River, and planted vinifera such as Cabernet Sauvignon and Riesling. There is no evidence that the wine he produced from these tasted good but Bridgman had the right idea. He had realized that, while regions on the coast like Stretch Island could be cool and rainy (Seattle's unofficial mascot is a slug), the area to the east of the Cascade mountains was in a rain shadow and offered perfect conditions for grapes. Following Prohibition, Washington found itself with a state liquor board that more or less restricted the sale of wine to bars. It was not until 1969 that you could buy a bottle in a shop and, even then, the range on offer was limited. Frustrated by these restrictions, a group of academics got together in 1962 to produce some home-made wine from Yakima Valley grapes. The cooperative they founded began life as Associated Vintners but then became Columbia Winery, one of the state's biggest wineries. Meanwhile Chateau Ste Michelle, a winery that had started out making fruit wine after Repeal in 1934, also switched to vinifera, making its first varietal wines in 1967.

In 1981 there were still only 19 wineries here, but since then Washington has rapidly become a serious winemaking state with, according to the regional wine association (www.washingtonwine.org), a current tally of over 400 wineries and 12,000ha of vinifera grapes. As in California, there are huge producers – under the ownership of US Tobacco, Chateau Ste Michelle and its subsidiaries sell nearly four million cases of wine per year – and boutiques like Andrew Will and Cayuse. Most grapes do well here in the right hands, but Syrah, Merlot, Sauvignon Blanc and Riesling have all shown particular promise.

WINERY — WOODINVILLE

### Chateau Ste Michelle

14111 NE 145th, Woodinville, WA 98072
T +1 425-488 1133/800-267 6793
www.ste-michelle.com
Daily 1000-1700. Tours 1030 and 1630.

This was the first winery I ever visited in Washington State and it remains one of the most go-ahead in the US, both in its winemaking and the welcome it offers to visitors. Chateau Ste Michelle excels at producing both reds and whites – unusually, each has its separate winery – and fans of Italian and German wine should take note that winemaker Bob Bertheau has collaborated fruitfully with Ernst Loosen and Marchesi Antinori. The winery also offers meticulously taught wine-appreciation classes, culinary seminars and special dinners cooked by top chefs. There are several tours, culminating in the 'ultimate wine tasting', in which the estate tops wines are paired with specially conceived dishes. Get your timing right and you might get the chance to attend a concert here: Elvis Costello and Lyle Lovett are among the stars who have sung for their vinous supper.

WINERY — LOWDEN

### L'Ecole Nº 41

PO Box 111, Lowden, WA 99360
T +1 509-525 0940
www.lecole.com
Daily 1000-1700.

Megan and Martin Clubb have kept up the high standards of Merlot and Semillon production, among other varieties, set by her parents, Jean and Baker Ferguson, in this small winery located in an old French schoolhouse. Martin is president of the Walla Walla Valley Wine Alliance, a coalition of likeminded wineries in the area, and the penchant to educate people not only about their own

wines but about winemaking in general is part of the family philosophy. Interested visitors will get a chance to see the vineyard and gravity-operated winery up close, as well as to taste a selection of wines for free.

WINE BAR — SEATTLE

### Purple Café & Wine Bar

1225 4th Av, Seattle, WA 98101
T +1 206-829 2280
www.thepurplecafe.com
Mon-Thu 1100-2300, Fri 1100-2400, Sat 1200-2400, Sun 1200-2400.
$$-$

Each of the three branches of the Purple Café & Wine Bar have slightly different menus but they all share a funky informality that makes them comfortable places to hang out, even if you are on your own. There are meals or snacks to suit all moods and more than 70 wines from around the world by the glass. Each branch also offers specials, such as wines not usually on the list or unusual wine flights, most nights of the week. The other branches are in Kirkland (323 Park Pl, T 1-425 828 3772) and Woodinville (14459 Woodinville-Redmond Rd NE, T 1-425 483 7129).

# Atlantic northeast

## Connecticut

The wine industry here began in 1978 when the State Legislature passed a Farm Winery Act. Today the Wine Association (www.ctwine.com) has 16 members, but many of these make their wine from fruit or hybrid vines. The climate here is generally too cold for European varieties but well-sited vineyards like Chamard and Hopkins (www.hopkinsvineyard.com) benefit from warmer microclimates that allow grapes like Chardonnay to ripen well.

WINERY | CLINTON

### Chamard

115 Cow Hill Rd, Clinton, CT 06413
T +1 860-664 0299
www.chamard.com
Tue-Sun 1100-1700.

This pioneering venture was founded in the late 1980s by the then-CEO of Tiffany & Co with 20 acres of European varieties including Pinot Noir, Gewürztraminer and Cabernet Franc. The winery has recently been bought by Dr Jonathan M Rothberg, who plans to continue to support the work of long-time winemaker Larry McCulloch and to make Chamard into a major attraction.

## Indiana

In 1989, Indiana had nine wineries; today the Indiana Wine Grape Council (www.indianawines.org) boasts 30 members. Most make wine from fruit as well as hybrids. Vinifera wines are the exception to the rule and any kind of grapegrowing can be challenging in a region when, as happened in the winter of 1988, the temperature can drop to -29°C.

WINERY | STARLIGHT

### Huber's Orchard & Winery

19816 Huber Rd, Starlight, IN 47106
T +1 800-345 9463/812-923 9463
www.huberwinery.com
Tours and tastings by appointment only.

From blackberries to brandy, there is little that this 550-acre farm does not produce. Founded in 1843 by Baden-Baden native Simon Huber, who brought grapes with him when he left Germany, the farm has remained in the family for seven generations, continuously expanding its wine production. Its huge range includes Icewine and port-style wines, as well as still wines from 18 varieties, including Cabernet Sauvignon and Chambourcin. There are several types of tours and tastings on offer, including barrel tastings, and the winery has joined forces with five other Indiana wineries to form the state's first wine trail. There is plenty to keep children occupied, too, including an ice cream shop offering 17 flavours made on the farm.

## Massachusetts

In 1602, the English lawyer, explorer and privateer, Bartholomew Gosnold, discovered an island he called Martha's Vineyard. Four centuries later, in 1971, George and Catherine Mathiesen planted a range of European grapes here in their pioneering **Chicama Vineyard** (www.chicama vineyards.com). Thirty years' ago the Californian winemaker Joe Heitz went to court to prevent the Mathiesens from using the name Martha's Vineyard because, he claimed, it would cause confusion with his famous Martha's Vineyard Cabernet Sauvignon. Heitz failed, which was poetic justice because at the time, he was quite happily selling Californian Chablis. Today, Martha's Vineyard is an AVA.

There are now a dozen Massachussetts wineries, many of which make their wine from fruit or from grapes imported from other states. Wineries like **Westport Rivers** and **Chicama**, however, prove that it is possible to make good wine here from locally grown European varieties.

WINERY | WESTPORT

### Westport Rivers Vineyard & Winery

417 Hix Bridge Rd, Westport, MA 02790
T +1 800-993 9695/508- 636 3423
Www.westportrivers.com
May -Aug daily 1100-1700; Sep-Dec Tue-Sat 1100-1700, Sun and Mon 1300-1700; Jan-Apr Sat 1100-1700, Sun 1300-1700.
Tastings US$5.

A highlight of southeastern New England's Coastal Wine Trail, which crosses both Massachusetts and Rhode Island, the Russell family's winery specializes in excellent sparkling wines made from Chardonnay, Pinot Noir and Johannisberg Riesling, many of which are only available in situ. The winery is part of the family's 140-acre Long Acre Farm, on which they have also created a Wine and Food Centre, complete with a resident chef, dedicated to educating visitors about the important role that wine plays with food (although there is no restaurant), and an art gallery in which there are regular exhibitions of regional oil painters and water-colourists.

## Michigan

Michigan is the fourth-largest grape-growing state and 13th biggest wine producer in the USA. The gap between these statistics is easily explained, since 89% of the grapes are eaten or used for juice. The first wine vineyards were planted here in the 1850s but ,until the 1970s, the focus was on labrusca and hybrids. Proof that vinifera could work successfully was provided by Doug Welsch of **Fenn Valley** (www.fennvalley.com) and a Canadian brewery millionaire called Ed O'Keefe of the **Chateau Grand Traverse Winery** (www.cgtwines.com) and **The Inn at Chateau Grand Traverse.** Now a growing number of producers are following in Welsch's and O'Keefe's footsteps and the Wine Association (www.michiganwines.com) includes some 45 wineries.

WINERY — SUTTONS BAY

### Ciccone Vineyards

10343 East Hilltop Rd, Suttons Bay, MI 49682
T +1231- 271 5551
www.cicconevineyards.com
Jun-Oct daily 1200-1800; Nov Thu-Sat 1200-1700; Dec-Mar Sat 1200-1700; Apr and May Thu-Sun 1200-1700.

Silvio and Joan Ciccone insist that everything be done by hand at their stunning winery, which sits on the edge of the Grand Traverse Bay and has a terrific view of the Leelanau Peninsula. This means that all the grapes, which include Pinot Grigio, Gewürztraminer, Cabernet Franc and Dolcetto, are carefully picked and transported to the winery without mechanical interference, an attention to detail that is reflected in the concentration of the wines. Because of its beautiful backdrop, the winery is a favourite location for weddings, so your tour may coincide with an outdoor ceremony. In addition to being a winemaker and a retired physicist and engineer, Silvio is also the father of the pop icon, Madonna.

## New York State

Winemaking in New York is thought to have begun on Long Island in the mid 17th century with the planting of a vineyard by Moses 'the Frenchman' Fournier. At around the same time, the governor of New Netherland, Peter Stuyvesant, authorized the planting of a vineyard on Manhattan and decreed that sailors be given a daily ration. In the early 1670s, Stuyvesant's English successor, Richard Nicolls, wrote to the Lords of Trade in London that New York had the potential to supply all the wine needs of the Crown dominions.

Vines were also planted in the Hudson River Valley by French Protestants in 1677, while vineyards in the state's third main wine region, the Finger Lakes, were first established in the 19th century. In 1867, following the success of an award-winning Finger Lakes sparkling wine in Paris, the winery's post office was given the name of a famous French town to allow bottles of 'Champagne' to be labelled as coming from 'Rheims, New York'.

Wines from the Finger Lakes and the Hudson River Valley were made almost exclusively from labrusca grapes, such as Catawba, Dutchess, Isabella and Delaware, and from hybrids like Marechal Foch, Baco Noir and de Chaunac. These were the only types of vine thought able to survive the harsh winters. In the 1950s, however, a stubborn Russian immigrant called Konstantin Frank proved that the trick to growing vinifera lay in grafting the vines onto appropriate rootstock, which he found in Quebec. Since then, a growing number of winemakers here have produced good Chardonnay and, more particularly, Riesling.

Vines grown on Long Island, warmed as it is by the gulf stream, did not suffer from frosty winters, but no one noticed because, throughout the 19th and most of the 20th century, wine grapes weren't grown here.

## Best producers

**Connecticut**
Chamard » *page 244.*
Plum Creek

**Massachusetts**
Westport Rivers » *page 244.*

**Michigan**
Fenn Valley
Grand Traverse
Mawby L

**New York State**
Bedell
Channing Daughters » *page 246.*
Dr Konstantin Frank
Gristina
Heron Hill
Lamoreaux Landing » *page 246.*
Lenz
Millbrook » *page 246.*
Palmer
Pellegrini
Standing Stone

**Pennsylvania**
Chaddsford » *page 248.*

**Rhode Island**
Sakonnet » *page 248.*

**Virginia**
Barboursville
Linden
Prince Michel de Virginia
Williamsburg Winery

Winemaking on the island was only revived in 1973 when Alex and Louisa Thomas Hargrave planted a vineyard on the North Fork. The almost instant success of their Chardonnay and Merlot inspired a long list of others to follow in their wake. Among them were Prince Marco and Princess Ann Marie Borghese, who bought the Hargrave winery and renamed it **Castello di Borghese** (www.castellodiborghese.com).

Today, the **New York Wine & Grape Foundation** (www.newyorkwines.org) lists 36 Long Island wineries, all but three of which are on the North Fork, with the remainder competing for space with holiday homes in the Hamptons. The Finger Lakes region has 103 wineries, half of which are around Seneca Lake and there are 38 in the Hudson River and Catskills.

WINERY — BRIDGEHAMPTON

### Channing Daughters Winery

1927 Scuttlehole Rd, PO Box 2202, Bridgehampton, NY 11932
T +1 631-537 7224
www.channingdaughters.com
Summer daily 1100-1700; winter Thu-Mon 1100-1700.
Tasting US$5

A working definition of an artisanal winery, Channing Daughters produces 7000 cases of 26 different wines from grapes including Malvasia, Teroldego, Refosco and Lagrein. All grapes are picked by hand and even the tiniest plot is vinified separately. There is, not surprisingly, a wonderful maverick behind all this. Owner Walter Channing, a venture capitalist, is also a sculptor of sorts, having rescued much of the wood, destined for demolition, from the Hudson River piers and refashioned it into works of art, which are on display all over the winery and vineyards. The winery also organizes regular tastings of wines from around the world.

WINE BAR — NEW YORK CITY

### Flûte Gramercy

40 E 20th St, New York , NY 10003
T +1 212-529 7870
www.Flutebar.com
Sun-Wed 1700-0200; Thu 1700-0300; Fri-Sun 1700-0400.

With over a dozen Champagnes and sparkling wines by the glass and 100 different bottles to choose from, along with Petrossian caviar and offerings from La Maison du Chocolat, this is the perfect place for a spot of indulgence. From Thursday to Saturday, there's a DJ in the evenings and, on Sundays, there's live jazz.

RESTAURANT — NEW YORK CITY

### French Culinary Institute

462 Broadway, New York
T +1 888-324 2433
www.frenchculinary.com/lecole.htm
Restaurant Mon-Fri 1230-1430. Contact the venue directly for times and prices of courses.

This is one of the best-kept secrets of New York. If you want to eat really good Gallic cuisine and enjoy attentive service at a budget price, there is little to beat the restaurant at the French Culinary Institute. Of course, the fact that everything is being done by students may occasionally make for longer delays between courses and less than absolute consistency but its fans reckon that the food here is more reliable than in many a big name restaurant. The wine list which changes regularly is well chosen and runs to 200 French and Californian wines (priced at similar levels to other establishments). More Italian wines are likely to appear following the launch of the school's Italian cookery courses. Amateur cookery or food and wine classes are open to the general public.

RESTAURANT — NEW YORK CITY

### Jadis

42 Rivington St, between Forsyth and Eldridge, New York, NY 10002
T +1 212-254 1675
Mon-Thu 1700-2400; Fri and Sat 1700-0200.
$$

If you fantasise or reminisce about an ideal notion of a Parisian restaurant – brick walls, Miles Davis in the background, plates of rustic artisan cheeses and pâtés on the table and all those French wines that don't feature in most wine shops or other restaurants – then this is the place for you. And, to continue the Gallic theme, there's a patio for smokers...

WINERY — FINGER LAKES

### Lamoreaux Landing Wine Cellars

9224 Rte 414, Lodi, NY 14860
T +1 607-582 6011
www.lamoreauxwine.com
Mon-Sat 1000-1700, Sun 1200-1700. Tours by appointment.

The striking modern winery on the east side of Seneca Lake was named "one of the most notable buildings built in New York State in the 20th century" by the American Institute of Architects, which, given the competition from Manhattan, is something of an achievement. But if the winery and the views are worth a visit, so are the Merlot, Cabernet Franc and Chardonnay.

WINERY — HUDSON VALLEY

### Millbrook Vineyards & Winery

26 Wing Rd, Millbrook, NY 12545
T +1 845- 677 8383/800-662 9463
www.millbrookwine.com
Summer daily 1100-1800; rest of the year daily 1200-1700.
Tour and tasting US$6.

New York.

In Millbrook, one of New York State's most exclusive and secretive towns, John Dyson has created a very welcoming winery, offering visitors not only the chance to taste the effect of New York's unique climate on such different varieties as Tocai Friulano, Zinfandel and Pinot Noir, but also to take in the spectacular Hudson River Valley up close. Dyson is a fascinating man, who was a deputy to New York mayor Rudolph Giuliani during the aftermath of 9/11. He knows vast amounts about winemaking the world over, as he also owns an estate in Tuscany.

WINE BAR NEW YORK CITY

## Morrell Wine Bar & Café

1 Rockefeller Plz, New York, NY 10020-2003
T +1 212-262 7700
www.morrellwinebar.com
Mon-Sat 1130-2300 (bar closes 2400);
Sun 1200-1600 (bar closes 1800).
$$

Every time I go to Manhattan, I make a pilgrimage to two places: the Metropolitan Museum of Art and the Morrell & Co café and wine shop. Overlooking the skating rink that has appeared in so many New York-based movies, this is a paradise for wine lovers. There are over 2000 wines on offer by the bottle (including 100 big-name examples that feature in several vintages) and 150 by the glass. The menu has wine suggestions for every dish but one of the resident 'wine geeks' Nikos Antonakeas, Peter Morrell or Roberta Morrell will hopefully be on hand to give advice. A great place for a glass of wine before a Broadway show or for a serious vinous meal.

SCHOOL CANANDAIGUA

## New York Wine & Culinary Center

800 South Main St, Canandaigua, NY 14424
T +1 585-394 7070
www.nywcc.com
Mon-Sat 1000-1900, Sun 1200-1900.
Courses must be booked in advance.
Courses from around US$55.

I've always relished the chance to get out of Manhattan and to see what is happening in other parts of the State, so I was delighted by the opening of this celebration of New York's wine and food. The centre offers a rich selection of wine courses, from how to become a backyard winemaker to how to make cherry wine to understanding New York's Riesling revolution. Among the many first-rate facilities are a tasting room in which a massive selection of New York wines are available for informal tutored tastings, and a professional kitchen in which cooking and wine-and-food-matching classes are held.

RESTAURANT NEW YORK CITY

## Petrarca Vino E Cucina

34 White St, New York, NY 10013
T +1 212-625 2800
www.vinovino.net
Mon-Fri 1130-0100; Sat and Sun 1000-0100.
$$

If you have difficulty finding this recently-opened Tribeca hangout, simply ask for directions to the Baby Doll Strip Club which was its previous incarnation. The designers have done a fine minimalist job of removing all traces of Petrarca's raunchy past; this is now a stylish hangout for Italophiles who are into good parmesan, prosciutto and pasta as well as Prosecco, Puglian and Piedmonese reds, which are also on offer in the shop next door.

WINE BAR NEW YORKCITY

## Vin Noir

228 Mott St, New York, NY 10012
T +1 212-925 6647
www.vinnoir.com
Daily from 1700.
$$

Style, friendliness and value for money form an unusual ménage a trois but the three seem to coexist very happily in this young wine bar in

Nolita (North of Little Italy). In the skinny confines of Vin Noir – a former apartment – you'll find comfortable armchairs that glow in the dark, old black- and-white movies playing on the walls and an eclectic range of wines including hard-to-find offerings from Austria and Italy. There are also chic snacks – duck prosciuto and tuna tartare – to work up your appetite for a fuller meal at two top restaurants, within wine-spitting distance: **Rice** (227 Mott St, T +1 212-226 5775, www.riceny.com) or **In-Tent** (231 Mott St, T +1 212-966 6310, www.intentny.com), which also has one of the city's great wine lists.

## Pennsylvania

The state where William Penn failed to grow vines in 1683 is now the eighth biggest wine producer in the US. This might strike some people as curious, given the fact that Pennsylvania has a state alcohol monopoly but, as in Washington, this may, in fact, have helped to promote winemaking here. Pennsylvania wineries are allowed to run up to five retail outlets, to sell direct to the public at festivals and to sell wholesale to restaurants – all activities that are otherwise the preserve of the state liquor board. Over 90 wineries are members of the Pennsylvania Wine Association (www.pennsylvaniawine.com) and they grow a wide range of grapes, ranging from labruscas, such as Catawba, to Seyval Blanc and Chambourcin hybrids to Pinot Gris, Chardonnay and Cabernet Sauvignon vinifera. In a laudable effort to promote the latter, a Pennsylvania Quality Assurance (www.pqawines.com) scheme has recently been launched which will award seals to Pennsylvania wines produced from vinifera that pass a blind tasting.

WINERY CHADDSFORD

### Chaddsford Winery

632 Baltimore Pike, Chaddsford, PA 19317
T +1 610- 388 6221
www.chaddsford.com
Daily 1200-1800.

Lee and Eric Miller's small Brandywine Valley winery, located in a beautifully restored 17th-century colonial barn, punches way above its weight. Not only does it produce very good Pinot Grigio and a Sangiovese /Barbera blend, among other wines, but the winery also runs an excellent series of tasting dinners and classes, covering such topics as 'Zinfandel: from Croatia to California' and 'The New Spain'. It hosts several concerts and festivals throughout the year, including a blues festival on Memorial Day weekend and a jazz festival on Labour Day Weekend.

## Rhode Island

Wine was first made here by Huguenots in the 1820s and production continued until Prohibition. Today, there are four active wineries growing a range of grapes, among them the hybrid Vidal Blanc and a wide range of vinifera, including Burgundian clones of Chardonnay at Newport Vineyards (www.newportvineyards.com).

WINERY LITTLE COMPTON

### Sakonnet Vineyards

162 West Main Rd, Little Compton, RI 02837
T +1 800-919 4637
www.sakonnetwine.com
Summer daily 1000-1800; winter daily 1100-1700.

In the heart of coastal New England, in a town that has been devoted to fishing and farming since it was incorporated as part of Plymouth Colony in 1682, winemaking has found a successful new outpost. Sakonnet Vineyards produce a distinguished range of wines, including a traditional method sparkling wine from Chardonnay and Pinot Noir, a port-style wine made from Chancellor and an Icewine made from Vidal Blanc. The tour includes a well-produced video and a tasting of six wines. There is also a regular programme of cooking classes, led by top local chefs. The charming B&B ($$), open during the tourist season, is in a classic New England clapboard farmhouse.

## Virginia

In the days when California was a wine-free zone, Virginians were doing their darndest to start a wine industry. Their first unsuccessful vintage was made, probably from native Scuppernong grapes, in 1608. French vines and winemakers were imported but the plants were killed off by the humidity and pests. In 1618, the House of Commons ordered each male Virginian to plant and tend 20 vines; for every one that died or failed to bear grapes, a fine of a barrel of corn had to be paid. This approach proved to be no more fruitful and the settlers, who blamed the French for their plight, banned them from the far more reliable business of farming tobacco. Other hopeless efforts included offering a prize of 10,000 lbs of tobacco to the first person to produce two tons of wine. In 1770, Thomas Jefferson, keen to convert his countrymen from beer to wine, planted a vineyard at Monticello and gave 800 ha of land to an Italian called Mazzei to experiment with 200 varieties. In 1780, all these vines were trampled on and destroyed by the cavalry during the Revolutionary War.

More recently, in 2004, Mark Warner, the state governor, copied the successful Australian 2025 wine strategy plan with his own Vision 2015, which is intended to put Virginia on the national and international wine map. Warner is often touted as a possible presidential candidate, so could become the second Virginian wine fan to occupy the White House. The **Virginia Wineries Association** (www.vintagevirginia.com) now lists over 100 wineries and over 300 wine festivals and events. A wide variety of vinifera and hybrids are grown but Viognier is showing particular promise.

WINERY CHARLOTTESVILLE

### Kluge Estate Winery & Vineyard

100 Grand Cru Dr, Charlottesville, VA 22902
T +1 434-977 3895
www.klugeestateonline.com
Tue-Sun 1000-1700.

Overlooking Monticello, where Thomas Jefferson planted his own vineyards, British-born Patricia Kluge has created a corner of top-cru France. With input from consultant Michel Rolland and resident Italian and French winemakers, Kluge Estate makes excellent Bordeaux- and Champagne-style wines in a distinguished winery in which no expense has been spared.

Meanwhile, in a restored gas station in downtown Charlottesville, Kluge has also created a funky wine bar and restaurant, **Fuel Co** (901 East Market St, T +1 434-220 3700, www.fuel-co.com, $$), which regularly offers around 30 American wines by the glass and, on Sunday, offers brunch accompanied by live Gospel music.

## Washington DC

RESTAURANT WASHINGTON DC

### Sonoma

223 Pennsylvania Av SE, Washington DC 20003
T +1 202-544 8088
www.sonomadc.com
Mon-Sat 1130-1430 and 1730-2200; Sun 1130-1430 and 1730-2100.
$$

Drew Trautmann has scoured Pennsylvania, Virginia and Maryland for the finest fish, meat and vegetables to fill an exciting menu divided into charcuterie, pizza/pasta, wood-grilled meat and fish, and vegetable sections. For the wine list, which is even more exciting, he has scoured Italy and California to assemble a boutique-winery-focused selection of more than 200 wines, 40 of which are regularly available by the glass. This is a buzzy, fun locals' joint, though it is welcoming to all, and you might well spot an off-duty politician as you enjoy a discovery from Fresno or Friuli.

# Other states

## Arizona

Arizona has an active Wine Growers' Association (www.arizonawine.org) that boasts 22 members and a website offering an Arizona Wine Adventure Trail Map. The modern wine industry began in 1973 but has only really taken off in the last decade. The vines are grown in various parts of the state, in cooler microclimates.

WINERY ELGIN

### Callaghan Vineyards

336 Elgin Rd, Elgin, AZ 85611
T +1 520-455 5322
www.callaghanvineyards.com
Fri-Sun 1100-1500.

Since Kent Callaghan picked the first grapes from the Buena Suerte vineyard he had planted in 1990, this has not only become Arizona's best winery but also one of the most interesting in the USA. Callaghan is disarmingly frank about the learning curve he has been following, admitting that he is ripping up grapes that have won him critical plaudits because he does not think they are ideal for the conditions here. So Merlot and some of the Cabernet Sauvignon (for which he finds the region too warm) are being replaced by Petite Sirah and Tempranillo. Callaghan only makes 2000 cases, most of which are sold here, so it is well worth the detour. While you're in the area also visit the nearby **Village of Elgin** (T +1520-455 9309, www.elginwines.com), which is housed in a former bordello and produces eccentric Italian-style wines and Arizona's answer to port.

# Best producers

**Arizona**
Callaghan » *page 249.*

**Missouri**
Mount Pleasant » *page 250.*

**Nevada**
Tahoe Ridge » *page 251.*

**New Mexico**
Gruet

**Texas**
Becker » *page 251.*
Cap Rock
Fall Creek
Kluge
Llano Estacado
Messina Hof » *page 251.*
Pheasant Ridge
Ste Genevieve

RESTAURANT PHOENIX

### Tarbell's

3213 East Camelback Rd, Phoenix, AZ 85018
T +1 602-955 8100
www.tarbells.com
Mon-Sat 1700-2200, Sun 1700-2100.
$$

Mark Tarbell, who has cooked for Clint Eastwood, Andre Agassi and the Dalai Lama, is one of America's brightest young chefs, as well as being wine columnist for the Arizona *Republic* newspaper. The style here is chic bistro, with great 'designer' pizzas and a really good, well-priced wine list. If you are in Colorado, you should also check out Mark's new restaurant in Denver, **Oven Pizza e Vino** (www.theovenpizzaevino.com).

## Colorado

The first efforts at winemaking here were in the late 1800s, before Prohibition. The industry was rekindled in the 1970s but, in 1990, there were just five wineries; today there are over 60 as well as an active wine association (www.coloradowine.com). Vines are grown at 1300-2300 m, making these some of the highest-altitude vineyards in the world. The most widely planted grapes are Merlot, Cabernet Sauvignon and Chardonnay but Syrah, Riesling and Pinot Noir are all being grown in significant quantities.

WINERY — PALISADE

**Plum Creek Winery**

3708 G Rd, Palisade, CO 81526
T +1 970-464 7586
www.plumcreekwinery.com
Apr-Oct daily 0930-1800; Nov-Mar daily 1000-1700. Tours by appointment only.

Doug and Sue Phillips admit that in the early 1980s, when they first decided to open their winery, they were operating slightly in the dark. Trusting their instincts to plant Cabernet Franc, Riesling and Gewürztraminer, they have gone from strength to strength and now offer a wide range of varieties and styles, including a port-style Sangiovese dessert wine and a semi-sweet rosé made from Merlot. If you can't make it to the winery, you can taste Plum Creek wines and those of other Colorado wineries at the **Plum Creek Winery Tasting Room** at Tewksbury and Co (www.TewksburyCompany.com) in downtown Denver.

## Florida

RESTAURANT — PALM BEACH

**Bistro Chez Jean-Pierre**

132 N County Rd, Palm Beach, Fl 33480
T +1 561- 833 1171
www.bistrochezjeanpierre.com
Mon-Sat for dinner.
$$$

Jean-Pierre Leverrier has brought a bit of his native France to Florida, where, along with his wife Nicole and sons David and Guillaume, he serves perfect versions of pâté de foie gras, sole meunière and crème brûlée. Leverrier, who has spent most of his life in the US, has incorporated some American touches into both the menu and the decor, and the results, from the surrealist art-filled walls to the daily offering of short ribs in a Bourguignon sauce with a side of mashed potatoes, is a very successful Franco-US fusion. The wine list is similarly open-minded, while remaining deeply French in focus.

## Illinois

SHOP — CHICAGO

**Randolph Wine Cellars & The Tasting Room**

1415 W Randolph, Chicago, IL 60607
T +1 312-942 1212
www.tlcwine.com
Wine cellars Mon-Fri 1100-2000, Sat 1000-2000, Sun 1300-1800. Tasting room Mon-Thu 1600-0100, Fri and Sat 1600-0200.

Try and come on a Monday, when each of the 115 wines, champagnes and dessert wines are half price. If you are lucky, the next day will be the third Tuesday of the month, when the staff lay out 30 regionally themed wines, along with snacks, and, for US$30, you can partake of as much of this vinous feast as you want. As if this were not generous enough, every Saturday there is a free, informal themed tasting in the 1208 sq m shop. The upstairs lounge has a terrific view over Chicago's downtown.

## Missouri

WINERY — AUGUSTA

**Mount Pleasant Winery**

5634 High St, Augusta, Missouri 63332
T +1 636-482 9463/800-467 9463
www.mountpleasant.co
Daily 1100-1730

Mount Pleasant Winery has witnessed first-hand many of the vicissitudes of America's winemaking history. It was founded in 1859 by German immigrants, George and Frederick Munch, as a way of remembering the vineyard-covered landscape of their native land. The Missouri river valley might not have been a dead ringer for the Rhine but the brothers did manage to make some excellent wine there until Prohibition closed them down 40 years later. In 1966 the winery reopened and, in 1980, Augusta beat Napa to become the first recognized American Viticultural Area. The winery produces a range of prizewinning wines inspired by the great wines of Europe, including claret and port styles.

## Nevada

The only two things most people know about Nevada is that it's home to Las Vegas, and that it's basically a desert. The same spirit that helped to build a city in the middle of nowhere is now going into the planting of grapes and making of wine. Unlike California which, as Rick and Kathy Halbardier of Tahoe Ridge (page 251) point out, has 22 different climates, Nevada has four: extreme cold; cold; extreme hot and hot. Of these, only the latter suits vinifera grapes. The 'hot' region, where most of Nevada's grapes are grown, is the Amargosa Valley, 140 km north of Las Vegas. Not that these details will be of much interest to most of the high rollers; they are probably more interested in the rather fancier fare available from California and Europe.

RESTAURANT — LAS VEGAS

**Aureole**

Mandalay Bay, 3950 Las Vegas Blvd South, Las Vegas, NV 89119
T +1 877- 632 1766
www.aureolelv.com
Daily 1730-2200.
$$$

Only in America; only in Las Vegas. The antithesis of the kind of quiet winebar you might in a backstreet of a provincial European city, Aureole is a wonderfully over-the-top tribute to wine, built around a four-storey steel and glass 'wine tower', inspired by the film *Mission Impossible*. The tower contains almost 10,000 bottles of wine, arranged in plexi-glass racks. You can choose your wine from a hand-held computer at your table, which will oblige you with suggestions based on your food choices from the three-course set meal. One you have chosen, a cat-suited 'wine angel' will be dispatched to 'fly' up the tower, via a sophisticated pulley, to fetch your bottle. This is all very entertaining but make sure you leave some attention for Charlie Palmer's excellent modern American cuisine: try wood-grilled fillet mignon with Cabernet sauce.

WINERY GENOA

### Tahoe Ridge

2285 Main St, Genoa, NV 89411
T +1 775- 783 1566
www.tahoeridge.com
Jan-Mar Fri-Sun 1100-1700; Apr-Dec Tue-Sun 1100-1700.

Rick and Kathy Halbardier planted Nevada's first vineyard in 1990 and, 11 years later, produced its first commercial wines: Chardonnay, Cabernet Sauvignon and Syrah. Although the winery is a commercial operation, the Halbardiers have also worked with Cornell University and the University of Minnesota on a wide range of experimental plantings of various varieties. There are plans to expand the range of local vinifera wines, but, for the moment, many of the bottles on sale are made from Californian grapes and local hybrids.

## Texas

Franciscan monks made wine here in the 1660s and Spanish settlers may have done so in the previous century. In the 1880s, it was a Texan called Thomas Volney Munson who earned a Légion d'Honneur for providing the rootstock on which French growers grafted their vines following the devastation of phylloxera. In 1974, A&M University commissioned research into the best places to grow grapes in this generally hot, humid region, but more work still needs to be done if the general quality is to rise. Even so, according to the Texas Department of Agriculture (www.gotexanwine.org), Texas has around 100 wineries, twice as many as it had just two years ago.

WINERY BRYAN

### Messina Hof Winery & Resort

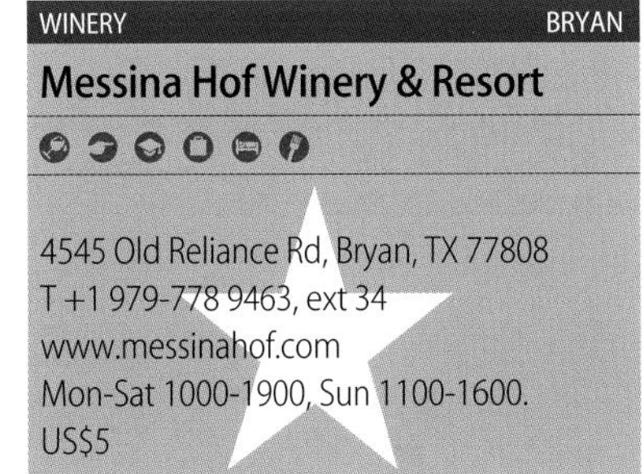

4545 Old Reliance Rd, Bryan, TX 77808
T +1 979-778 9463, ext 34
www.messinahof.com
Mon-Sat 1000-1900, Sun 1100-1600.
US$5

I'm delighted to see three winemaking, culinary and hospitality traditions converging in such great style here: those of Sicily, Germany and Texas. Winemaker Paul Bonarrigo's ancestors have been winemakers in Messina, Sicily, for almost two centuries, while his wife Merrill's family originally hails from Hof in Germany. The range of activities is almost as long as the list of wines produced. There are introductory cooking classes, cooking classes focusing only on mushrooms, wine-tasting courses and harvest dinners with murder mystery themes, all washed down with wines such as Cabin Noir (a Lenoir/Cabernet Sauvignon blend), Tex Zin (Zinfandel/Merlot) or varietal wines, including Gewürztraminer, Chardonnay, Semillon and Syrah. Most of the rooms in the hotel have patios and rocking chairs, in true Western fashion, and the restaurant serves such classic Texan fair as gulf shrimp and 12-oz rib-eye steaks. In Paul Bonarrigo's other life he is a physiotherapist, so excellent massages, including ones designed for couples, are available for resort guests.

It was a Texan called Thomas Volney Munson who earned a Légion d'Honneur for providing the rootstock on which French growers grafted their vines following the devastation of phylloxera.

WINERY GILLESPIE COUNTY

### Becker

464 Becker Farms Rd, Stonewall, TX 78671
Winery T +1 830-644 2681. Homestead T +1 830-997 5612.
www.beckervineyards.com
Mon-Thu 1000-1700, Fri and Sat 1000-1800, Sun 1200-1800.
Tours US$3 (if there are 20 people or more).

Dr Richard Becker grows good grapes – Cabernet Sauvignon, Viognier and Chardonnay – and produces some of Texas's best wine in a stone-built winery that is a replica of a German barn. He also grows lavender for his annual lavender festival. The romantic, log-cabin-style Texan homestead sleeps two in its cosy loft ($$).

# Latin America

Cool-climate vineyards, near the Andes in Chile.

UNITED STATES OF AMERICA
Tijuana
Caborca
Bahía Kino
Hermosillo
Monterrey
BAJA CALIFORNIA
MEXICO
MEXICO CITY
Gulf of Mexico
HAVANA
CUBA
NASSAU
BAHAMAS
Atlantic Ocean
Pacific Ocean
GUATEMALA
GUATEMALA CITY
HONDURAS
NICARAGUA
Caribbean Sea
BARBADOS
COSTA RICA
PANAMA CITY
PANAMA
CARACAS
VENEZUELA
GUYANA
SURI-NAME
GUYANE
La Unión
BOGOTA
COLOMBIA
QUITO
ECUADOR
Belém
Manaus
PERU
BRAZIL
Recife
LIMA
Ica
Nazca
Lake Titicaca
LA PAZ
BOLIVIA
BRASILIA
Salvador
Tarija
PARAGUAY
ASUNCION
São Paulo
Rio de Janeiro
Iguazú Falls
Curitiba
Salta
Tucumán
CHILE
Bento Gonçalves
Porto Alegre
ARGENTINA
Mendoza
URUGUAY
SANTIAGO
BUENOS AIRES
MONTEVIDEO
Neuquén
Trelew
Atlantic Ocean
Parque Nacional Los Glaciares
Río Gallegos
Falkland Islands
Tierra del Fuego
500 km
500 miles
Zapallar
Aconcagua
Mendoza
Godoy Cruz
Maipú
Viña del Mar
Valparaíso
Luján de Cuyo
Casablanca
SANTIAGO
San Antonio
Rancagua
ARGENTINA
CHILE
San Rafael
Santa Cruz
San Fernando
Curicó
50 km
50 miles
Wineries
1 Casa Madero p257
2 LA Cetto p257
3 Monte Xanic p257
4 Bodegas San Cristóbal p258
5 Bodega y Estancia Colomé ★ p262
6 El Esteco ★ p262
7 Bodega & Club Tapiz p264
8 Bodega Catena Zapata p264
9 Bodegas Salentein p264
10 Bodega Weinert p264
11 Carlos Pulenta p264
12 Familia Zuccardi Winery, Restaurant & Visitor Centre ★ p265
13 La Rural p265
14 Terrazas de los Andes p266
15 Familia Schroeder p266
16 NQN p267
17 Viña Errázuriz p272
18 Cousiño Macul p272
19 Viña Indómita p272
20 Clos Apalta/Casa Lapostolle p273
21 Viña Casa Silva p273
22 Viña Montes p273
23 Viñedos Orgánicos Emiliana p273
24 Viña Miguel Torres p273
25 Concha y Toro ★ p274
26 Santa Rita p275
27 Undurraga p275
28 Matetic Vineyards ★ p276
29 Bodegas y Viñedos de La Concepción (BVC) p276
30 Aurora Winery p277
31 Miolo p277
32 Vinícola Salton p277
33 Tacama p278
34 Bodega Bouza p279
35 Bodegas Carrau p279
36 Juanicó p279
37 Bodegas Pomar ★ p279

# Introduction



As soon as the Spanish *conquistadores* arrived in the New World, they needed wine for the Mass so, having tried to make wine from wild grapes he found in Mexico, Hernán Cortés asked his father to send vines from Europe. In 1522, an ordinance was issued requiring the settlers to plant 1000 vines "of the best quality available". Among the early efforts, one has survived to this day: the Casa Madero winery in Mexico (page 256), which made its first wine in 1597. Throughout the 16th century, winegrowing spread across the continent, but the revolution in quality has only taken place over the last 25 years. For this we have to thank a new generation of winemakers and investment from overseas.

Today, Chile leads the pack, but Argentina is snapping at its heels and increasingly impressive wines are also being produced in Uruguay and Mexico. Central and South America are challenging beliefs on which the rest of world's wine industry has been founded. In the São Francisco Valley in Brazil, innovative winemakers are exploiting the tropical conditions by bringing in two generous harvests a year. The implications for Europe of New World regions producing huge volumes of wine twice a year are clear, although, so far, these wines seem only to be of basic quality. This is not the case, however, for the high-altitude wines being made in Argentina (page 265), where vines are being grown at heights four times those of their supposedly high-altitude counterparts in Europe. There are convincing theories that the extra sunlight enjoyed by these vines contributes to flavour and may even give the wines extra health benefits.

# Mexico, Central America & the Caribbean



**Until very recently, Central America and the Caribbean had little if any relevance to quality wine. With the exception of Mexico, whose vinous history stretches back for over 400 years, all of these countries were thought to be too close to the equator to have anything to do with wine. Today, that picture is changing, as the quality of wines produced at high altitudes in some of these countries is taking the world by surprise**

## Mexico

Despite the efforts of the early settlers to introduce wine, Mexico's favourite alcoholic drinks are still *pulque* (fermented cactus juice), tequila (distilled *pulque*) and beer. Even today, Mexicans consume less than three bottles of wine per year each but tastes are changing. Mexico's earliest vines were planted by Spanish settlers in the 16th century and it has been Spanish investors, such as Domecq and Freixenet, who have helped to mould its modern wine industry. Admittedly, most of the initial efforts were

Most of Mexico's wine grapes are grown in the northern part of Baja California.

focused on producing wine and, more specifically, brandy of adequate rather than great quality for local consumption, but ambitions have been driven upwards, particularly by LA Cetto (see below), founded by an immigrant from Piedmont in the 1930s. Today, this family-owned firm has nearly 3000 ha of vines, exporting well over a quarter of the wine it produces and winning medals at international competitions. Together with Domecq, LA Cetto produces nearly 80% of Mexico's wine; most of the rest is made by eight other firms, but smaller boutique wineries are also sprouting up.

Most of Mexico's wine-producing vineyards are in the northern part of Baja California, where there is a 'ruta del vino', with a dozen wineries in the rugged Valle de Guadalupe but wine is also produced in Hermosillo, Caborca and Bahia Kino, which are on a similar latitude. Other, more southerly vineyards are devoted to brandy.

WINERY — MONTERREY

### Casa Madero

PO Box 244, Monterrey
T +52 (01)81-8390 0305
www.madero.com.mx
Daily 0900-1700.

Dating back to 1597, this is the oldest winery in the Americas. It's in Parras, where a wine harvest festival is held every August. As well as a tasting room, the winery also encompasses **La Casa Grande**. This isn't a hotel but an ornate 24 double-bedroomed house available for private hire. It's located in a large enclosed garden with swimming pool and has its own airstrip. Those preferring to travel in more sedate fashion can enjoy a horse-drawn carriage tour of the grounds and vineyards.

WINERY — BAJA CALIFORNIA

### L A Cetto

**Tijuana Winery** Av Cañón Johnson 2108, Col Hidalgo, Zona Centro, Tijuana
T +52 (01)664-685 3031
**Ensenada Winery** Km 108 Ctra Tijuana-Ensenada 2788, Fraccionamiento El Morro
T +52 (01)646-175 2363
**Valle de Guadalupe Winery** Km 73.5 Ctra Tecate El Sauzal , Valle de Guadalupe
T +52 (01)646-155 2179
**Mexicali Winery** C de la Induatria 692, Col Industrial, Mexicali
T +52 (01)686-557 3710
www.cettowine.com
Daily 1000-1700.
MXN$2

The largest wine producer in Mexico is also the largest producer of Nebbiolo in the world outside Piedmont in Italy, even if the Petite Sirah is the pick of the range. There are four tasting rooms worth visiting – in Tijuana, Mexicali and the Valle de Guadalupe – and the company also organizes concerts, dinners and other special events throughout the year.

WINERY — MÉXICO DF

### Monte Xanic

Lago Tangañica 18, 2do piso, Col Granada, 11520 México DF
T +52 (01)55-5545 1111/01-800 717 4633 (toll-free)
www.montexanic.com
Mon-Fri 0930-1600.

A candidate for Mexico's top winery, thanks to its remarkably refined red wines. The cellar is open for guided visits during the week, but it is advisable to book in advance.

## Guatemala

Guatemala is home to the wine-throated hummingbird (Selasphorus Ellioti) and plenty of good rum and decent beer. Wine is produced – often for home consumption by Italian immigrants – but anyone in search of something good to drink is best advised to order something from Chile.

RESTAURANT — GUATEMALA CITY

### Tamarindos Restaurant & Sushi Bar

11 Calle 2-19A, Guatemala City
T +502 2360 2815
Daily for lunch and dinner.
$$

This eccentric restaurant brings together local ingredients with influences from Thailand, Italy and Japan in an ambience that is at once romantic and offbeat. A truly great restaurant with a really good international wine list.

## Panama

In the place where you can watch the sun rise over the Pacific and set over the Caribbean, it is said that you can get anything you want. Wine is produced here at nine degrees north of the equator – but not from grapes. The Viños Don Coba winery run by 72-year old Don Coba

Mexico's earliest vines were planted by Spanish settlers in the 16th century. Casa Madero winery, which made its first wine in 1597, is still in operation today.

successfully produces and, in some cases barrel-ages, a range of serious wines made from tropical fruit and, most successfully, blackberries. There are rumours of plans by a foreign investor to produce grape wines, but nothing has been achieved yet.

WINE BAR | PANAMA CITY

### Wine Bar Amador

Cl Eusebio A Morales, Panama City
T +507 (0)265 4701
www.1985.com/wine-bar-amador.html
Phone ahead for opening hours.

Chef Willy Diggelmann has a number of eateries in Panama City and wine plays a major part in them all. His top operation is the French restaurant, 1985, which has won awards for both its food and wine. The Amador Wine Bar is more modest but its menu is strong on pizzas and has a great selection of cheese, and its 200-strong wine list (all available by the glass) deserves special attention. Live music adds to the convivial atmosphere.

## Bahamas

HOTEL | BAHAMAS

### Graycliff Hotel

Nassau, Bahamas
T +1 242 (1)-302 9150
www.graycliff.com
$$$

This high-class hotel is based at an old colonial estate overlooking Government House in the middle of Nassau. Seafood features prominently in the Graycliff restaurant and the wine cellar runs to more than 200,000 bottles. This is one of those lists that tends to dazzle label-hunters and people who think several vintages of the same wine indicates a quality selection; there are vintages – especially of white wines – that should by now have been pensioned off. That said, it is still among the very best wine lists in the region. Graycliff is also a paradise for cigar lovers, as the hotel has its own on-site cigar factory.

## Barbados

RESTAURANT | BARBADOS

### The Cliff

Hwy 1, Derricks, St James
T +1 246 (1)-432 1922
Daily 1800-2400.
$$$

One of the West Indies' finest restaurants is located in a spectacular setting overlooking a Caribbean bay that could make most almost anything taste special. Chef Paul Owens displays a deft hand in the kitchen, with the local seafood not surprisingly featuring prominently on a menu that blends elements of Caribbean cuisine with traditional European flavours, and includes several sumptuous puddings. A good rather than great wine list covers most bases efficiently but don't be surprised if you find yourself drinking Champagne throughout the meal; all the tables are candelit and have a bay view, making this one of the most romantic restaurants in this book. Reservations are recommended, especially in the winter.

## Vintages

**2006** Good throughout.

**2005** Very good in Chile and Argentina.

**2004** Great throughout.

**2003** Very good in Chile, Argentina and Mexico; mixed in Uruguay and Brazil.

**2002** Excellent in Argentina, Uruguay, Mexico and Brazil but mixed in Chile.

**2001** Very good in Chile; less so in Argentina.

**2000** Mixed in Chile and Argentina; very good in Uruguay.

## Cuba

Most visitors to Cuba sensibly stick to Mojito and Daiquiri cocktails or beer, but drinkable wine is being, at least partially, produced on the island.

WINERY | HAVANA

### Bodegas San Cristóbal

Calle 44, 305, esq 3ra y 5ta, Playa, Havana
T +53 (0)7-204 2566
www.fantinel.com
Visits by appointment only.

Bodegas San Cristobal has been producing wine from imported grape must for several years but, in 1998, it formed a joint venture with Vigneti Fantinel of Friuli in Italy to plant a vineyard on the island. Special clones of Merlot, Cabernet Sauvignon, Chardonnay and Tempranillo developed to cope with the humidity were planted and the first wines are now available. Cynics question whether Cuban wine might still have a significant Italian component but the vines do exist. The winery is not set up for visitors but will offer tastings to anyone who has made an appointment.

RESTAURANT | HAVANA

### El Ajibe

Ave 7ma, esq 24 y 26, Havana
T +53 (0)7-204 1584/204 1583
Daily 1200-2400.
$-$$

For those who really have to have a range of imported wines, this the place to come in Havana. El Ajibe's range of wines and cool cellar might be the envy of many a glitzier Caribbean restaurant. (The chicken dish is brilliant too.)

Opposite page: Central Valley, Chile.

# South America

Chile and Argentina are the Garden of Eden for grapes and winegrowers.

# Argentina

Fact file

| | |
|---|---|
| **International flights** | Aerolíneas Argentinas, British Airways, American, United, Delta, LanChile, Canadian Air International and Qantas all serve Buenos Aires. |
| **Entry requirements** | Visas are not required by EU or US passport-holders (among others), who will be issued a 90-day tourist card on arrival. |
| **Currency** | Argentine peso ($). US$ also widely accepted. |
| **Time zone** | GMT -3 hrs. |
| **Electricity** | 220 volts AC; Plugs have either 2 round or 3 flat pins. |
| **Licensing hours** | Bars serve until 0200 or later. |
| **Minimum age** | 18. |
| **Drink-drive restrictions** | 50 mg of alcohol per 100 ml of blood. |

## Planning your trip

All international flights from outside South America arrive into **Ezeiza International Airport** (EZE, T +54 (0)11-5480 6111) near **Buenos Aires**. From Buenos Aires, onward internal flights, plus some flights from neighbouring countries, are handled by **Jorge Newbery Airport** (aka Aeroparque, T +54 (0)11-4576 5111), with regular services to Mendoza, Salta and Neuquén, as well as many other destinations around the country. An 'Airpass Visit Argentina', bought in your own country, will get you better deals on domestic flights. There are also frequent flights to Santiago, Chile. Argentina has an extensive network of long-distance buses, which are efficient and cost-effective – just don't underestimate the time it will take to cover this enormous country overland. You might want to hire a car to visit out-of-the-way wineries and other sights. Bear in mind, however, that roads vary widely in quality and, even on good tarmac, journeys can take much longer than you expect. In some areas it is wise to hire a guide to accompany you or to sign up for an organized tour.

Even if it's not the main focus of your visit, you should spend some time in **Buenos Aires** at the beginning or end of your trip to enjoy the city's European-style architecture and vibrant culture. In order to experience archetypal Argentina, head southwest from the capital to the vast grasslands of the **Pampas**, home of the *gaucho* (cowboy) and large *estancias* (page 262). Alternatively, fly from Buenos Aires to **Mendoza**, a stylish, modern city that's a great base for visiting the surrounding vineyards (page 263) and the mountains to the west, including Aconcagua, the highest peak in the Americas, and Las Leñas ski resort. Further north a string of cities line the Andean foothills; follow the beautiful route from **Tucumán**, via the wine-growing area of **Cafayate** (page 262), to reach **Salta**. This colonial city is the departure point for the 'Train to the Clouds', which climbs to 4475 m. In the northeast are the wetlands of **Mesopotamia**, the ruined Jesuit missions in **Misiones** and, of course, the magnificent **Iguazú Falls**, so huge they make Niagara look like a dripping tap.

In the south, Patagonia is equally rich in attractions. **Neuquén** (page 266) lies on the northern edge of the **Lake District**, Argentina's best loved tourist area, where you should spend a few days in Bariloche enjoying the beautiful lakes, rivers, forests and snow-capped mountains. Then head east to **Trelew** to witness the bountiful wildlife on **Península Valdés**, or south to El Calafate to explore the peaks and glaciers of **Parque Nacional Los Glaciares**. A connecting flight will take you right down to Ushuaia on **Tierra del Fuego**.

For more information on visiting Argentina, consult the official website www.turismo.gov.ar. Also check out *Footprint Argentina*.

**Country code** → +54. **IDD** → 00. **Internet TLD** → ar.
**Emergencies** → Ambulance T107. Fire T100. Police T101.

## Wine tourism

The climate makes this a good place to visit at any time, but wine tourism in Argentina is a very schizophrenic affair. On the one hand, there are some of the most sophisticated, visitor-friendly wineries in the world (several of which are recommended in these pages) and on the other, there are countless old establishments that are entirely unequipped to welcome anyone. You should also not be surprised if the winery you are going to visit does not have a visible sign on the road, so take a mobile phone, a good map and possibly a guide. The busy seasons in Argentina are 7 December to 15 January and 10 July to 10 September, when you should book as far ahead as possible.

## Sleeping and eating

Accommodation in Argentina is excellent value for visitors from western countreis. In cities and tourist areas, such as the Lake District, there is usually a good range of hotels and *hosterías*. The latter are smaller than hotels rather than being lower quality and may offer a more personalized atmosphere. For details of *estancia* acommodation, see Home on the range, page 262. Self-catering *cabañas* are another popular option for groups.

Argentine steaks are legendary and are perfectly matched by good examples of local Malbec. The classic Argentine meal is the *asado*: beef or lamb cooked expertly over an open fire and served in *parrilla* restaurants throughout the country. Also look out for *puchero* (meat stew), *carbonado* (onions, tomatoes and minced beef) and *arroz con pollo* (a chicken and rice dish). When the Argentines aren't eating meat, they're eating pizza, a legacy of Italian immigration; pasta is also widely available. Regional specialities include *empanadas*, *humitas* and *tamales* in Salta; excellent seafood along the Atlantic coast, and trout and wild boar in the Lake District.

## History

Argentina and Chile are all too often treated as though they were siblings; in fact, while these two countries share a language, they are as different as Spain and Italy. The comparison is not as gratuitous as it might seem. Chile's wine industry is driven by big wineries, reminiscent of Spain's bodegas; its people tend to be conservative and good at following a coherent line. Argentina is more like Italy for a very good reason: between 1876 and 1925, no fewer than two million Italians arrived in Argentina. In 1881, a Buenos Aires newspaper declared that "no European population has had a greater influence on the Argentine Republic's destiny than the Italian with its huge number of immigrants, the energy they pour into their endeavours and the splendour of their contributions to culture and intellect." Another of their 'contributions' was the creation of small family-owned wineries; today, the region of Mendoza alone has no fewer than 30,000. Inevitably, as in Italy, this has made for a vibrant wine industry but one that has had little real sense of direction.

Argentina once did a great job of hiding this aimlessness – and the fact that it was the fifth-largest wine-producing country in the world – by drinking most of what it produced and exporting the rest as grape concentrate to be diluted and fermented in countries like Canada and Japan to become Canadian or Japanese wine. Most of what was drunk in Argentina was of poor quality, thanks in part to governments that, as in South Africa, were dedicated to supporting grape growers irrespective of what they produced. This picture has changed radically however. Wine consumption halved between 1980 and 2000, from a scarcely credible 76 litres per person to a still-impressive 38 litres. Just as significantly, as the Argentines slashed the volume of wine they drank, they increased the amount of better wine. By the end of the 20th century, they were pulling the cork on seven and a half bottles each of 'fine' wine; three times as much as in 1980.

Colomé vineyard.

Grapes at NQN.

Today, Argentina is intent on competing with Chile as a wine exporter and, since the 1990s, it has been helped to achieve this objective by a growing torrent of overseas (and over-the-mountains Chilean) investment, attracted by the low costs of production, the benevolent climate, the range of soils and of grape varieties. For many outsiders, while Chile and Argentina share the potential to produce huge amounts of good, attractively priced wines, it will be Argentina that eventually wins the highest numbers of trophies, thanks in part to its high-altitude vineyards (page 265). It is worth noting that Michel Rolland, the Gallic guru who is a consultant in Chile, Uruguay and Argentina, seems to be especially proud of the the Argentine efforts he is producing under his Clos de Siete label.

Unlike Chile, Argentina has yet to explore much of its vinous potential. Two thirds of its wine and over 90% all of the best examples are made in the region of Mendoza, just across the mountains from Santiago. This is admittedly a large area, with a range of varying altitudes and microclimates, but there is no question that regions like Neuquén in the south also have much to offer.

### Understanding Argentine wine

The principal wine regions of interest are Mendoza, Rio Negro, Salta and la Rioja, though volumes of good wine from the latter two areas are small. Among the most interesting grapes are the peppery **Malbec**, both by itself and in blends, the **Tempranillo** and a quartet of Italian varieties: the **Sangiovese**, **Barbera**, **Nebbiolo** and the **Bonarda**. This last variety, while almost certainly Italian in origin, confusingly, has nothing to do with the varieties bearing this name in Italy. Among Argentina's white wines, the unique player has to be the **Torrontes**, a variety that produces dry wines that smell enticingly grapey and as though they are going to be sweet.

## Buenos Aires

WINE BAR | BUENOS AIRES

### Gran Bar Danzon

Libertad y Santa F, Capital Federal, Buenos Aires
T +54 (0)11-4811 1108
www.granbardanzon.com.ar
Phone ahead for opening times.

This is a small intimate bar/restaurant where the good and the great of Buenos Aires gather to enjoy some of the city's best cocktails, a wide-ranging list of Argentinian wines by the glass, plus a short menu that includes both traditional Argentine beef and sushi. Expect low sofas, low lighting but no low life. Sucre (Sucre 676) and Bar Uriarte (Uriarte 1572) are similarly-styled sister venues in the city.

## Salta

Up in the northwest, this region produces less than 2% of Argentina's total wine output but a large proportion of its Torrontes whites, which are made from grapes grown in over three quarters of the vines here. There are vineyards at altitudes of 2000 m, 400 m above the tourist-friendly town of Cafayate. Historically, this has been big winery country, where Etchart and Michel Torino are kings, but other smaller investors are now moving in.

WINERY | MOLINOS

### Bodega y Estancia Colomé

Ruta Provincial, Molinos, 4419 Salta
T +54 (0)3868-494044/494043
www.bodegacolome.com
Visitor centre daily 1000-1700.

I'm a great fan of this, Argentina's highest and most remote winery. It produces wonderfully intense Malbec- and Cabernet-based reds, as well as some of the country's best Torrontes. Now owned by California's Hess Collection (page 232), it's also home to the nine-roomed **Estancia Colomé**, a luxury hideaway ($$-$$$) hotel that has various objects of art from the Hess Collection in California on display. There is a meditation room and massage facilities for those who wish to chill out, and a swimming pool, tennis court and jogging track for the more active.

WINERY | CAFAYATE

### El Esteco

Ruta Nacional 40 y Ruta Nacional 68, Cafayate, 4427 Salta
T +54 (0)3868-421747
www.micheltorino.com.ar
Tastings by appointment.

When I'm asked to recommend a hotel in Argentina's wine country, this is always right at the top of my list, partly for its quality and partly for the fact that it encourages people to

#### Home on the range

*Estancias* (ranches) are found all over Argentina. These great homes belonging to some of the country's wealthiest landowners have recently opened their doors to paying guests and offer wonderful places to stay. There's a whole spectrum of *estancias* from a simple dwelling on the edge of a pristine lake in the Patagonian wilderness to a Loire-style chateau in the Pampas. They might offer incredible luxury and the chance to be completely pampered, such as at **Bodega y Estancia Colomé** in Salta (page 262) or, more typically, a rare opportunity to spend a few days in the middle of otherwise inaccessible natural beauty and enjoy activities such as walking, horseriding, birdwatching and fishing. Often there's the chance to learn about the traditional *gaucho* (rancher) way of life and about how the farm is run. You'll certainly be treated to the traditional *asado*, meat cooked over an open fire, and most impressively, *asado al palo*, where the animal is speared on a cross-shaped stick and roasted to perfection.

In the province of Buenos Aires you will find *estancias* covering thousands of hectares of flat grassland, with large herds of cattle and windpumps to extract water; horseriding will certainly be offered and, perhaps, cattle-mustering. In Patagonia there are giant sheep *estancias* overlooking glaciers, mountains and lakes and, on Tierra del Fuego, there are *estancias* that are full of the history of the early pioneers who built them. In Salta, look out for colonial-style *fincas*, whose land includes jungly cloudforest with marvellous horseriding. In Mendoza's wine region, try **Posada Salentein** (page 264) or **Chateau D'Ancon** (RP 89, San José, Tupungato, T +54 (0)2622- 488245, www.estanciancon.com, Oct-Apr only), a French-style rural mansion at the heart of a traditional *estancia* and winery owned by the Bombal family. As well as horseriding and other activities you can taste the estancia's own wines and visit other local wineries.

Rates per night vary between US$50 for two in the most humble places, up to US$150 per person with all meals drinks, transfers and activities included. Reservations should be made about two weeks in advance. For more information see the national tourist website (www.turismo.gov.ar), which has all *estancias* listed in English.

discover regions beyond Mendoza. The estate is home to Michel Torino's best winery and vineyards but it is also the location of the top-notch **Patios de Cafayate Hotel** (part of the Starwood group; $$$), which has a restaurant and Argentina's first wine spa. The 30 deluxe rooms, including three suites, are housed in traditional colonial buildings, and there's a heated outdoor swimming pool in the peaceful gardens. As well as being an ideal location from which to visit the Cafayate wine museum and the local wineries (Etchart and Lavaque are the other major producers in the region), this is also a superb base from which to explore the amazing Salta Gorge, Argentina's version of the Grand Canyon.

## Mendoza

In 1556, a Chilean friar carried vine cuttings across the Andes which contributed to the creation in the province of Mendoza, still Argentina's major wine region. For most drinkers of Argentine wine, this is probably the only region they will have heard of.

The city was colonized from Chile in 1561 and played an important part in the South American independence movement since the 'Liberator', José de San Martín, set out to cross the Andes to Chile from here. In 1861 the city was completely destroyed by an earthquake which killed 10,000 of the 12,000 inhabitants and severely injured 1500 more. When the town was rebuilt, it was with low earthquake-proof buildings and wide streets, which helps to make it an attractive, airy town, with parks and museums and several wineries.

Mendoza has five sub-regions, North Mendoza (**Norte Mendocino**), Upper Mendoza River (**Alta del Río**), East Mendoza (**Este Mendocino**), Uco Valley (**Valle de Uco**) and South Mendoza (**Sur Mendocino**). The best regions within these are Lújan de Cuyo and Maipú in Upper Mendoza, where top reds are produced. Tupungato in Uco Valley, site of some of the highest- altitude vineyards (page 265) and much foreign investment, is another region to look out for. San Rafael in the south is home to the Valentin Bianchi winery. For information, consult www.vinesofmendoza.com.

Bodega Catena Zapata.

RESTAURANT — MENDOZA

### 1884 at Bodega Escorihuela

Belgrano 118, Godoy Cruz, Mendoza
T+54 (0) 261 424-2698
www.escorihuela.com.ar
Daily 0630-1100, 1230-1530, 2000-2400.
$$

Francis Mallmann is Argentina's celebrity chef, with a number of restaurants dotted around the country. His Mendoza outpost is located in the grounds of the Catena-owned Escorihuela winery and is named after the year in which the winery was founded. High-ceilinged and cool in the Mendoza heat, with a delightful courtyard, it's Mendoza's finest eatery. The food is a stylish take on traditional Argentine cuisine, with meat in plentiful supply, sometimes done on the grill, sometimes in the wood-fired ovens. 1884 is also excellent for pizza, risotto and pasta, making this one of very few places in Mendoza where vegetarians won't feel left out. The excellent wine list is strong on Catena, but also features wines from several other bodegas. The winery itself is only open to visitors accompanied by a specialist guide.

RESTAURANT — MENDOZA

### Azafrán Restaurant

Av Sarmiento 765, Mendoza
T+54 (0)261-429 4200
Daily 1000-1400 and 1600-1900.
$

Azafrán – meaning saffron – is an upmarket deli in a sympathetically restored old house on one of Mendoza's main eating streets. The selection of wines runs to more than 300 and an added bonus is that you can drink anything from the shop for a small corkage fee in the adjoining wine bar. The wooden tables and tiled floors give the impression of dining in a homely kitchen and, in summer, it's possible to eat at one of the tables on the pavement outside.

WINERY ALTA DEL RIO

## Bodega & Club Tapiz

Ruta 60 s/n, 5517 Maipú-Luján de Cuyo
T +54 (0)261-496 3433
www.tapiz.com/www.newage-hotels.com

Formerly the property of Californian wine giant Kendall Jackson, Bodega Tapiz is thriving under new ownership. Visitors can stay in one of the seven rooms at **Club Tapiz** ($$), housed in a recently refurbished 1890 dwelling that was declared a building of 'Historical, Architectural and Tourist Heritage' in June 2006. Surrounded by vineyards and with great Andean views, it has a swimming pool and gym, as well as the renowned **Terruño** restaurant ($$), where guests are offered wine tastings each evening before dinner. Chef Max Casa's menus usually involve the local Malbec (this area is a Malbec hot-spot) and large slabs of Argentinian beef.

WINERY ALTA DEL RIO

## Bodega Catena Zapata

Luján de Cuyo
T +54 (0)261-490 0214/15/16
www.catenazapata.com
Tours Mon-Fri 1100 and 1500; Sat 1100.
Advance booking required.

Argentina's most internationally minded producer is also among the country's finest. The striking Luján de Cuyo winery, in the form of a Mayan-inspired pyramid, is one of the most impressive in Mendoza, and offers tours in Spanish, English and Portuguese, as well as tastings of selected highlights from the generally excellent range. The on-site boutique sells wine and wine-related products.

Bodegas Salentein.

WINERY VALLE DE UCO

## Bodegas Salentein

Emilio Civil 778, Mendoza
T +54 (0)261-441 1000
www.bodegasalentein.com
Tue-Sat 1000-1300 and 1400-1600.

Bodegas Salentein is an ambitious venture in the Valle de Uco, roughly an hour and a half out of Mendoza City. Its winery is built in the shape of a cross and is known by locals as the 'Cathedral of Wine'. The basic 45-minute guided tour in English and Spanish is free or a more in-depth visit with a winemaker can be arranged. For those wishing to stay a little longer, there's **Posada Salentein**, a simple but attractive eight-bedroom lodge with swimming pool on the estate.

WINERY ALTA DEL RIO

## Bodega Weinert

Av San Martin, 5923 Luján de Cuyo
T +54 (0)261-496 0409
www.bodegaweinert.com
Mon-Sat 0930-1630.

Wine lovers who have read Robert Parker's description of this as the finest winery in South America might be surprised by what they discover at Weinert. Rather than the big, richly oaky and alcoholic wines that the US guru usually singles out for high praise, these Malbec-Cabernet Sauvignon blends are some of the most elegant, long-lived wines in the region. Founded in 1975 – in a striking Spanish colonial building from 1890 – Weinert was a pioneer in the introduction of modern winemaking equipment into Argentina.

WINERY ALTA DEL RIO

## Carlos Pulenta

Roque Saenz Pena 3531, 5509 Vistalba, Luján de Cuyo
T +54 (0)261-489 9400
www.carlospulentawines.com
Call ahead for opening times.

This branch of the Pulenta family is not to be confused with Pulenta Estate in Alto Agrelo, Mendoza which is run by Hugo and Eduardo Pulenta, brothers of Carlos. It has its base at Vistalba in the heart of Luján de Cuyo, where winemaking is overseen by the talented Italian, Alberto Antonini. There's a gift shop on site, offering various pieces of local art as well as

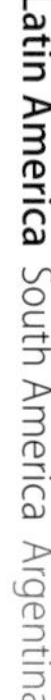

## Grapevine

### Hitting the high notes

Every winemaking country – especially in the New World – has to have a point of difference that sets it apart from the herd. Chile makes much of its proximity of the Andes, the absence of phylloxera and the uniqueness of the Carmenère grape. Argentina also has the Andes, though its vineyards are not as close to the mountains, and it has also been spared the attentions of phylloxera. Argentina's grape is the Malbec, a variety that is widely grown here and far more successfully than in France, its supposed European homeland. But Argentina has another unique bullet in its armory. Nowhere in the world has anything like the number of high-altitude vineyards.

In Europe, winegrowers boast loudly if they have vines at 450 m above sea level. In Argentina, grapes happily grow at nearly seven times this height.. There are several advantages to high-altitude vineyards. The cool nights allow the production in warm regions of wines with lower alcoholic strengths and they broaden the range of grapes that can be grown. Beyond this simple factor, however, there are some more mysterious qualities associated with the skyscraping vines. The greater exposure to ultraviolet rays seems to intensify flavour and, perhaps most interestingly of all, it may actually make the wines healthier to drink.

Research by Professor Roger Corder of the William Harvey Research Institute in London suggests that the UV contributes to the creation of polyphenols in the grapes that may help to prevent heart disease. When Professor Corder compared the effects of a selection of red wines, an Argentine red was particularly rich in polyphenols.

wine, and a 40-seat restaurant ($$) a sister establishment of La Bourgogne restaurant in the Alvear Palace Hotel, Buenos Aires) that also offers cookery lessons. For privileged guests, a two-bedroomed lodge called **La Posada** is available ($$).

HOTEL — MENDOZA

### Cavas Wine Lodge

Costaflores s/n, Alto Agrelo, 5507 Mendoza
T +54 (0)261-410 9627
www.cavaswinelodge.com
$$$

Just 20 minutes from the centre of Mendoza is this Spanish colonial-style luxury hotel surrounded by 14 separate adobe apartments set among the vines. Each apartment has a view of the Andes, an al fresco shower and its own plunge pool. The on-site vinotherapy spa offers a crushed Malbec scrub, while gourmets are catered for by food from chef Sebastian Flores ($$-$$$). The well-stocked cellar houses several top local wines. Special two-, three- and four-night packages are available, which can be tailored to include activities such as winery visits, golf, horse riding and rafting. Children under 12 are not permitted.

## Best producers

**Argentina**
Domaine Vistalba
Familia Zuccardi » *page 265.*
Pascual Toso
Trapiche (top wines)
Weinert » *page 264.*

WINERY — ALTA DEL RIO

### Familia Zuccardi Winery, Restaurant & Visitor Centre

Ruta Provincial 33, km 7.5, Fray Luis Beltran, 5531 Maipú
T +54 (0)261-441 0000
www.familiazuccardi.com
Mon-Sat 0900-1700 and Sun 1000-1600.

To my mind, Familia Zuccardi is the most innovative winery in South America, and a model for other Argentine producers to follow. The country's first commercial Viognier and Zinfandel came from here, and there are experimental plantings of several other grapes, including Gamay, Grenache and Mourvèdre. The visitor facilities are also spot on, with a shop where people can find as-yet-unreleased experimental wines, as well as current releases, an art museum and a restaurant ($-$$) set among the vines. Guided tours and tastings are available throughout the year. Look out, too, for the range of single-variety olive oils.

WINERY — ALTA DEL RIO

### La Rural

Montecaseros 2625, Coquimbito, 5513 Maipú
T +54 (0)261-497 2013
www.bodegalarural.com.ar
Mon-Sat 0930-1700; Sun 0930-1300.

Founded in 1885, and thus one of the oldest wineries in the region, La Rural also boasts the biggest wine museum in South America, with over 4500 painstakingly collected items, including vineyard and winery tools galore. This is not the most dynamic winery in Argentina, but its tours and tastings are not to be missed.

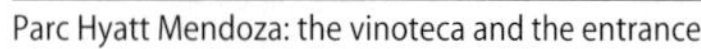

Parc Hyatt Mendoza: the vinoteca and the entrance.



HOTEL MENDOZA

## Parc Hyatt Hotel Mendoza

Chile 1124, Mendoza
T +54 (0)261-441 1234
www.mendoza.park.hyatt.com
$$$

Behind a beautifully restored 19th-century Spanish colonial façade in Mendoza's business district is this generally well-appointed, if slightly impersonal, international-style hotel. It has a casino and a series of restaurants and bars: **Bistro 'M'** is the pick for food; head to **Uvas** for a classy selection of Mendoza wines, international cocktails and live jazz. The outdoor pool and spa are ideal for relaxing at the end of a day touring vineyards. The hotel plays host to the annual 'Hyatt Wine Awards' every July.

WINERY ALTA DEL RIO

## Terrazas de los Andes

Thames y Cochabamba, Perdriel, Luján de Cuyo
T +54 (0)261-488 0058
www.terrazasdelosandes.com
Tastings Mon-Fri by appointment.

Champagne giant Moët & Chandon has had a presence in Argentina for several years. Bodegas Chandon is aimed at the domestic market (although some of the fizz does leave the country), while Terrazas is for export. Cheval des Andes is a super-premium wine made in conjunction with the team from Château Cheval Blanc in St-Emilion. **Terrazas Village** has six luxury suites ($$$) and a restaurant serving lunch and dinner menus ($$) designed by Fernando Trocca, one of Argentina's top chefs.

## Neuquén

This coolish new area in Patagonia has just three young wineries but between them, they have 1000 ha of vines, which are producing good wine, and offering a warm welcome to visitors.

WINERY SAN PATRICIO DEL CHAÑAR

## Familia Schroeder

Calle 7 Norte, San Patricio del Chañar, Neuquén
T +54 (0)299-588 0359
www.familiaschroeder.com
Tastings by appointment.

Competing head to head with its fellow Neuquén pioneers, Fin del Mundo and NQN, Familia Schroeder offers good wines and a restaurant. The two differences here are that the winery is built on five descending levels, allowing the grapes, juice and wine to be moved by gravity rather than by pumps (which are believed to reduce quality). Check out the display of fossilised dinosaur bones, unearthed during the building of the winery, which are commemorated on the labels of the Saurus range.

WINERY SAN PATRICIO DEL CHAÑAR

## NQN

Ruta Provincial 7, Picada 15, San Patricio del Chañar
T +54 (0)299-155 810 000
www.bodeganqn.com.ar
Restaurant and wine bar Mon-Fri 0900-1700; Sat and Sun 1030-1700. Winery Mon-Fri 1000-1200 and 1400-1600; Sat and Sun 1000-1200 and 1400-1700.

Close to Familia Schroeder and also opened in 2003, this glittering Neuquén winery sells its wines in Argentina under the Malma label. The wines, made by the former winemaker at Salentein (page 264), are first class, with Malbec and Pinot Noir among the stars. The restaurant ($) is a good choice, if you have time for a full meal, or there's a worthwhile tasting bar that pairs NQN wines with cheeses and a variety of dishes. (NQN is the abbreviation for Neuquén airport by the way.)

NQN winery and vineyards.

# Chile

## Planning your trip

International flights arrive in Santiago at **Aeropuerto Arturo Merino Benitez** (SCL; T +56 (0)2-690 1900). There are no direct flights from the UK but connections can be made in Buenos Aires, Paris or Madrid. From Santiago **LanChile** (Lanexpress; www.lanchile.cl) runs domestic flights to major Chilean cities. Its 'Visit Chile Airpass' may be worth buying if you're planning several internal flights; alternatively, the budget airline **Sky** offers cheap deals. Chile's long-distance bus network is efficient and fairly comprehensive, with additional services to Buenos Aires, Bariloche and other Argentine destinations. Hiring a car is more expensive than in Argentina. If you're basing yourself in the capital, beware the city's commuting traffic, which can be horrendous. Major routes tend to be in good condition but other roads, especially away from the towns, may be *ripio* or even earth; check your vehicle is suitable for these surfaces and that your rental agreement will cover you in the event of a breakdown. Signposting is also a frequent problem so you may want to consider joining an organized tour.

**Santiago** enjoys a dramatic setting, surrounded by Andean peaks. Although it's not the most appealing South American capital, it offers easy access to many of the country's highlights. Visitors here have the unusual opportunity of being able to ski within an hour's drive of the city – at **Valle Nevado** – and then visiting a winery on the same day. To the west, the appealing port city of **Valparaíso** and the Pacific beach resorts are only a couple of hours away or you could even hop on a plane to mysterious **Easter Island**. North of the capital, you can star-gaze around **La Serena**, or head into the **Atacama desert** to experience the lunar landscapes, hot geysers and salt flats around San Pedro de Atacama. In the far north is **Arica**, from where the road to Bolivia passes through the magnificent **Parque Nacional Lauca**, with its wealth of Andean wildlife, high lakes and remote volcanoes.

South of the capital, flanked by surf beaches to the west and the Andes to the east, stretches the fertile **Central Valley**, location of many of Chile's finest vineyards. Beyond is the popular **Lake District**, where lakes are backed by striking volcanoes. You could cross into Argentina here or continue south to Puerto Montt for access to the island of **Chiloé**. A flight will take you to Punta Arenas and the iconic **Parque Nacional Torres del Paine** or you could make your own way into the deep south on the remote Carretera Austral, with a detour to the **San Rafael glacier** on the way.

For further information on visiting Chile, refer to www.visit-chile.org and www.sernatur.cl. Also consult *Footprint Chile*.

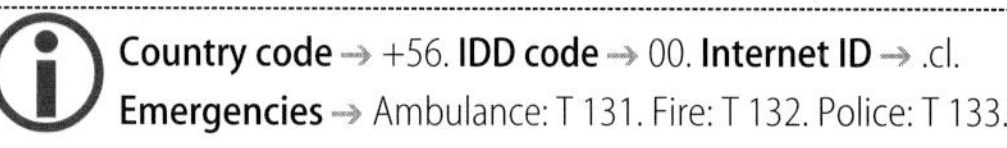
**Country code** → +56. **IDD code** → 00. **Internet ID** → .cl.
**Emergencies** → Ambulance: T 131. Fire: T 132. Police: T 133.

Fact file

| | |
|---|---|
| **International flights** | American Airlines, Delta and LanChile direct to Santiago from USA; Aerolíneas Argentinas, British Airways, Air France, Iberia, Lufthansa, LanChile to Santiago via Buenos Aires and European hubs. |
| **Entry requirements** | Visas are not required by EU or US passport-holders (among others), who will be issued a 90-day tourist card on arrival. |
| **Currency** | Chilean peso (CLP$). |
| **Time zone** | GMT –4 hrs (Mar-Sep); –3hrs (Sep-Mar) |
| **Electricity** | 220 volts AC; 2- or 3-pin plug |
| **Licensing hours** | Bars serve until 0200 or later. |
| **Minimum age** | No minimum drinking age; 18 to purchase alcohol. |
| **Drink-drive restrictions** | Less than 50 mg of alcohol per 100 ml of blood. |

## Wine tourism

Wine tourism is a relatively new concept in Chile. The big old wineries of the Central Valley, close to Santiago, are often well equipped to receive visitors and boast grand old buildings, impressive gardens and guides who speak a wide range of languages. In the further-flung regions, however, and even sometimes near to the capital, wineries are often much more focused on production. When visiting almost anywhere, a map and a mobile phone are essential and a knowledge of Spanish, or at least a phrase book, is almost as important. The **Chile Information Project** (www.chipsites.com) runs tours to all the main regions.

## Sleeping and eating

Accommodation in Chile is nearly double the price of Argentina. Prices tend to be even higher in Santiago and the further south you go from Puerto Montt. Hotels are readily available in major cities and tourist areas but smaller *hosterías* may be more prevalent elsewhere.

Chile's cuisine used to compete with Australia's for its lack of finesse. Big slabs of meat and fish were the order of the day, with the additional joy of *erizos* (sea urchins) for those who had acquired the taste. Today, outside influences have brought a growing focus on lighter, fresher dishes that make the most of Chile's high-quality local ingredients. The most outstanding element of Chilean cuisine is the seafood. The most popular fish are *merluza* (hake), *congrio* (ling), *corvina* (sea bass – often served as ceviche), *reineta* (bream), *lenguado* (sole) and *albacora* (swordfish). There is also a bewildering array of unique shellfish – look out for *machas*, *picorocos*, *locos* and *centolla* (king crab). Away from the coast, meat stews in various forms are common, accompanied by a rich assortment of vegetables. *Empañadas* (pasties) and *completos* (hot dogs) are popular snacks.

Montes vineyards, Colchagua.

Cellar at Matetic Winery.

### History

Five hundred years' ago, when parts of Bordeaux were still a swamp, the *conquistadores* introduced winemaking to the country we now know as Chile. The reference to Bordeaux is not gratuitous, as both wine regions are influenced by the proximity of the ocean; Chile's narrow geography means that no vineyard is more than 70 km from the coast. But there the similarities end. The French region has to struggle with an uncertain climate and a long list of pests and diseases; its South American counterpart has quite reasonably been described as heaven for grapevines. The climates (there are several) are constantly ideal and the twin threats in Europe of drought and untimely rain are almost unknown. Most vineyards in Chile get their water from irrigation trenches or pipes which are, in turn, filled with melted snow from the Andes. Crucially, the phylloxera louse has never made it to Chile, thanks to the *cordon sanitaire* formed by the ocean and the mountains. Whether or not making wine from vines grown on their own roots (as is also done in South Australia) has an impact on quality, it certainly has advantages for grape growers. Ungrafted vineyards are cheaper to plant and deliver a crop a couple of years before their grafted counterparts.

The absence of phylloxera has also turned Chile into a living repository of the strains of vine that were being used in Europe in the 19th century, when they were first brought here from France. However, like South Africa, Chile suffered from a long period of isolation and a lack of knowledge of developments elsewhere. Between 1938 and 1974, it was illegal to plant a new vineyard. When the Spaniard Miguel Torres arrived in 1979, the stainless steel tanks that had been used in Europe for a couple of decades were unknown here and, in 1995, there were a scant dozen significant wineries, mostly in the regions of Maipo, Rapel and Maule. Today the figure is closer to 100 and growing by the month.

Torres may have introduced stainless steel and modern cooling equipment but it was other European visitors who revealed to the Chileans that the grape they were using for Sauvignon Blanc was, in fact, an inferior, unrelated variety called the Sauvignonasse. More happily, they also uncovered the fact that many of Chile's 'Merlot' vines are actually Carmènere, a variety that is traditional and legal in Bordeaux but almost unknown there since the end of the 19th century.

Foreign investment has helped to boost Chile's wine industry, but so has the Chileans' readiness to develop new regions. Between 1994 and 2004, the acreage of vineyards across the country has doubled, much of it in areas that had to be added to the wine map. In 1989, the Casablanca Valley, for example, had just 90 ha of vines, the oldest of which were seven years old; a decade later, there were 3000. And, while the focus of international attention has been on the potential of this new region, an even newer one has been developed nearby at San Antonia that shows just as much promise – and possibly even more. Planting ungrafted vines in these new regions is cheap, so it is not uncommon to see investments like the 1000 ha vineyard recently planted by the family-owned Errazuriz winery in Chilhué, a dozen kilometres from the Pacific in Concón.

### Understanding Chilean wine

It is still too early to discern many clear regional styles, because too many wineries place too much of a personal, stylistic imprint on their wines. Most buyers are happy to choose a brand and a grape, without worrying whether the wine comes from an area like Colchagua or Curicó or from the umbrella area of the Central Valley. But Chile's most successful regions will soon be as well known as many of their older counterparts in Europe. For further information consult the **Wines of Chile** website, www.winesofchile.org.

# Chile

## A land overflowing with diversity and producing some of the most exciting, naturally organic wines in the world

Four hundred-fifty years ago Spanish settlers found Chile to be a winemaker's paradise. This long, thin country has diverse geography: the Atacama Desert, the Andes Mountains, the Pacific Ocean and Patagonia. In the centre, more than 112,00 hectares of

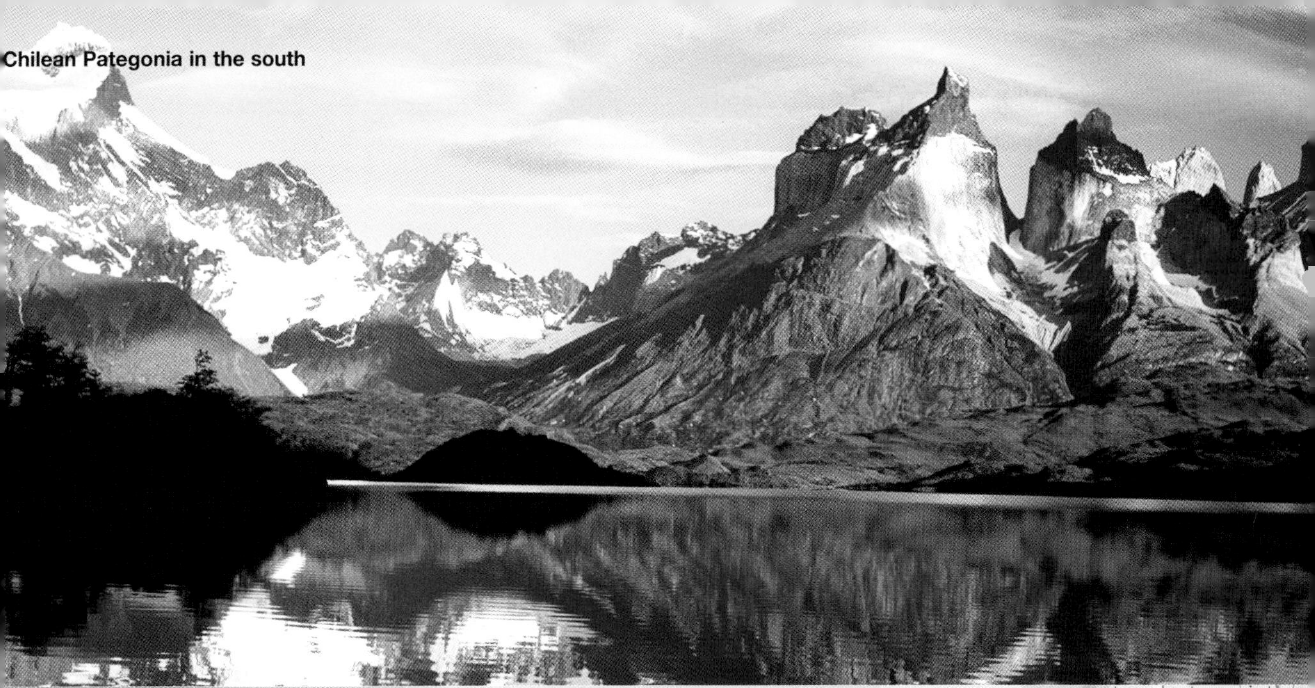

Chilean Pategonia in the south

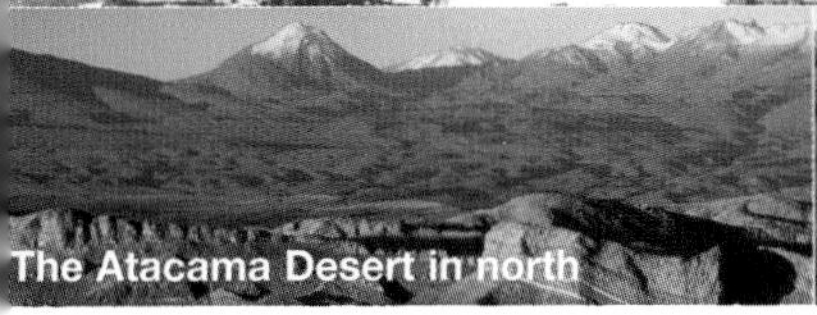

The Atacama Desert in north

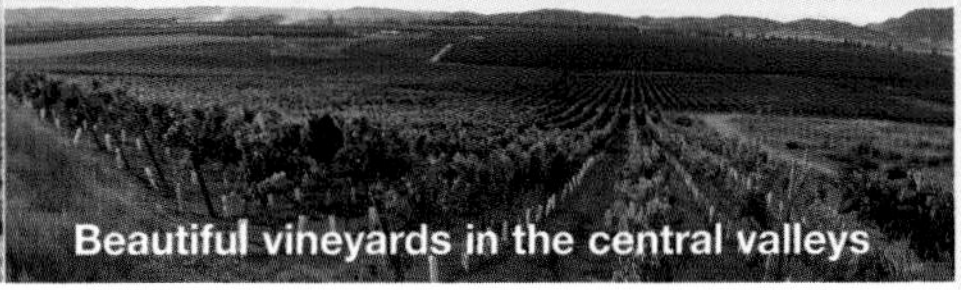

Beautiful vineyards in the central valleys

high-quality wine grapes benefit from sunny days, cool nights, a Mediterranean climate, a variety of soil types and talented winemakers: everything needed to produce a wide range of excellent wines.

The traditional home of Chilean wine is the large expanse of fertile flatland in the centre of the country known as the "Central Valley," where grapes grow well and ripen easily. Today's search for *terroir* has led winemakers to experiment with new varieties and seek out new and generally cooler places to plant them. Central Valley growers climb into the Andean foothills, and others move west toward the Pacific, north to the semi-arid mountainous regions and southward towards Chile's beautiful Lake district. The result is greater diversity and a large selection of exciting wines from Chile.

www.winesofchile.org
for more information about the wines from Chile please contact
info@winesofchile.org.uk

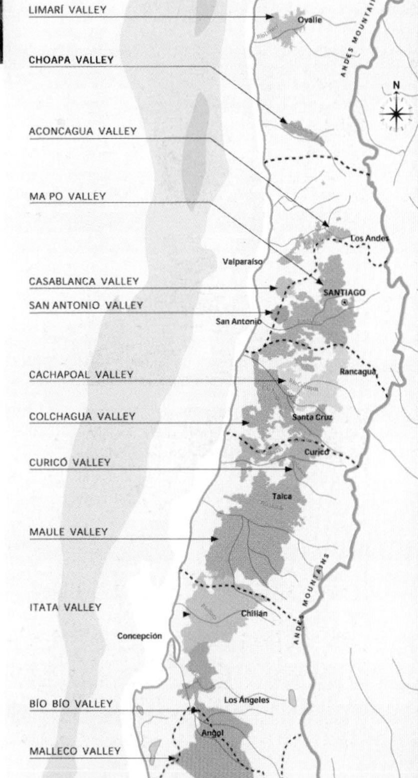

## Aconcagua

Only the keenest wine tourists are likely to find their way to this northern region but anyone making the recommended drive over the Andes to Mendoza in Argentina will pass through here. The area owes its vinous reputation to the efforts of one old but dynamic company, the family-owned Errazuriz (see below).

WINERY PANQUEHUE

### Viña Errázuriz

Lo Errázuriz, C Antofagasta, Panquehue
T +56 (0)2-203 6688
www.errazuriz.com
Tastings by appointment

Established in 1870, this beautifully situated winery surrounded by a bowl of vineyards, produces wines under its own label and under those of Sena (a joint venture with Mondavi, page 234) and Chadwick. Cabernet Sauvignons and Syrahs are the high points, along with some good Carmènere. Errazuriz's best wines regularly do well against top Bordeaux in blind tastings.

## Casablanca

WINERY CASABLANCA

### Cousiño Macul

Quilin 7100, Peñalolén, Casablanca
T +56 (0)23- 514175
www.cousinomacul.cl
Tours by appointment Mon-Fri 1100 and 1500.
CLP$10

This historic producer has very successfully mixed ancient and modern. The bulk of winemaking activity has recently moved from Macul in the suburbs of Santiago southwards to Buin. However, visitors are still received at the original Macul winery, with its underground cellar dating back to 1870, and there are daily tours (reservations necessary) in both Spanish and English. Wine quality has never been higher, and there's also an air of innovation about the company – how many other Chilean wineries boast a Sauvignon Gris?

WINERY CASABLANCA

### Viña Indómita

Ruta 68, Km 63, Casablanca
T +56 32 754400
Visits by appointment.

Come through the tunnel from Santiago on the way to Viña del Mar and Valparaiso and it's hard to miss Indómita, proudly standing up on the hill to the left. The wines, made from Casablanca and Maipo grapes, are good, but the main reason to pay a visit is the restaurant ($$), where chef Oscar Tapia offers modern dishes with a Chilean accent, such as rabbit dumplings with mango and ginger chutney, and smoked wild boar leg with celery mash and white truffle ratatouille.

## Colchagua

Gradually usurping Maipo's crown as Chile's top area for red wines, Colchagua is one of the country's older wine regions. There are some great steep slopes here, a factor that certainly attracted the attention of the Bordeaux guru Michel Rolland, who has been involved from the outset at the French-financed **Casa Lapostolle** winery. Colchagua's **Ruta del Vino** (www.rutadelvino.cl) was founded in 1996 and now extends to 14 wineries in the valley. Tourists are free to make up their own itinerary but the office in Santa Cruz (Plaza de Armas 298, T + 56 (0)72-823 199) can arrange day tours to a number of wineries in the valley and lunch if required, with options to visit a museum.

Chilean winemaking.

WINERY SANTA CRUZ

## Clos Apalta/Casa Lapostolle

Camino San Fernando a Pichilemu, km 36, Cunaco, Santa Cruz
T+ 56 (0)72-321803
www.casalapostolle.com
Tours Mon-Fri 1000 and 1130 by appointment.

Since the first vintage in 1997, Casa Lapostolle's Clos Apalta has been one of Chile's very best (and priciest) wines. 2005 saw the opening of a stunning new winery built just for this one wine in a dramatic setting on a hill overlooking the Apalta vineyard. Adjacent to the space-age, gravity-fed winery are four houses or *casitas*, each named after a Bordeaux grape variety. A two-night package including a winery tour and tasting, cocktails and meals, massage, hiking, swimming and other activities costs US$1500 per *casita*.

HOTEL SANTA CRUZ

## Hotel Santa Cruz Plaza

Plaza de Armas 286, Santa Cruz
T +56 (0)72-821010
$$

For those who don't fancy the three-hour trip from Santiago to Colchagua, this is the ideal base for a leisurely exploration of the region's wineries. The 85-roomed Santa Cruz Plaza in the main square of Santa Cruz, close to the Colchagua museum, has all the amenities of a modern hotel, from business facilities to a delightful outdoor pool, but still manages to retain a homely appeal. Various artworks and antiques, including a collection of vintage cars, are dotted around the old four-storey building, and there are four different restaurants and bars on the premises, including the acclaimed Los Varietales. The hotel offers special wine packages including tours to local vineyards.

WINERY SAN FERNANDO

## Viña Casa Silva

Hijuela Norte, Casilla 97, San Fernando
T+ 56 (0)72-716519
www.casasilva.cl
Daily 1000-1700.

How many wineries boast their own rodeo arena? As well as a standard winery tour and a wine tasting (including the Doña Dominga range), visitors to this Colchagua winery might find themselves treated to polo and rodeo demonstrations. For those wishing to extend the visit, the estate's original farmhouse has now been converted into a small hotel ($$), complete with a restaurant ($) that overlooks the rows of barrels.

WINERY SANTA CRUZ

## Viña Montes

Valle de Apalta, Santa Cruz
T +56 (0)72-825417
www.monteswines.com
Visits by appointment only.

Viña Montes is a spirited company, headed by the dynamic Aurelio Montes. It excels with high-class reds, both Bordeaux-style and Syrah, and its new Purple Angel shows just what the Carmenère grape is capable of. The Apalta winery, designed along feng shui principles, welcomes visitors to its tasting room and shop, which offers wines as well as books and wine accessories.

WINERY COLCHAGUA

## Viñedos Orgánicos Emiliana

Bodega Los Robles, Camino Lo Moscoso, Colchagua
T +56 (0)9- 7993641
www.voe.cl
Tours Wed-Sat 1030-1200 and 1500-1630. CLP$8.40

The first winery in South America to use exclusively organic grapes can also stake a very convincing claim to having the world's largest biodynamic vineyard. The wine's good, too, thanks to the deft hand of maestro Alvaro Espinoza, with the top cuvée Coyam being one of the world's best-value reds. The Colchagua winery, made from stone, copper, adobe and wood, welcomes visitors for a guided tour (in English or Spanish) through the vineyards (complete with geese, llamas and ladybirds), plus an insight into how the various biodynamic preparations are made and a tasting. More comprehensive visits with meals are also offered to those who book in advance.

# Curicó

This broad valley is less aesthetically striking than its neighbours, but there's a long winemaking tradition here at wineries like **San Pedro** (which opened its doors in 1830) and dynamic younger companies like **Valdivieso** and **Miguel Torres**. Many of Curico's grapes end up in blends with those of other regions.

WINERY CURICO

## Viña Miguel Torres

Ruta 5 Panamericana, km 195, Curicó
T +56 (0)75-564100
www.torres.es
Summer daily 1000-1900; winter daily 1000-1700. Shop summer daily 0830-2000; winter daily 0830-1830.

Miguel Torres was the first European producer to invest in the Chilean wine industry back in 1979. The setting for his winery on the edge of the Pan American highway may not be the most picturesque, but this is definitely a candidate for the country's most tourist-savvy enterprise. There's a visitor centre with a shop and tasting facilities, regular tours and a restaurant (lunchtime only; $-$$), all of which are open throughout the year. And, of course, there's the chance to try Torres wines from other parts of the world.

## Santiago and Maipo/Pirque

The city of Santiago has developed over the last decade or so from what looked like a sleepy Spanish colonial town to a dynamic global city, where the fruits of investment are to be seen at almost every turn. The backdrop of the Andes gives Santiago a particular appeal but also prevents a near-permanent layer of smog from dissipating. (Chilean engineers have seriously discussed trying to blow a hole in the range).

Many of the oldest vineyards in Chile are in the hills overlooking Santiago, but these vines now compete with housing. **Cousiño Macul**, one of Chile's longest-established wineries, recently sold off vineyards for huge sums and relocated, and Bruno Prats, co-owner of **Vina Aquitania**, freely admits that his vineyards would be worth far more to a property developer than they are to him as a winemaker. However Maipo remains a major region, with old wineries like Santa Carolina, Undurraga and Santa Rita, and new ones such as Aquitania, William Fevre and Haras de Pirque. Other grapes can do well here, but this is usually thought of as Cabernet Sauvignon country.

RESTAURANT SANTIAGO

### Akarana

Reyes Lavalle 3310, Las Condes
T + 56 (0)2-231 9667
Daily 1200-2400.

Not the grandest of Santiago eateries but Akarana, run by a New Zealander, gets it right where more pretentious restaurants fail. Service is crisp rather than fawning, and the food, a Chilean take on Pacific Rim cuisine, with plenty of seafood, is refreshingly devoid of the gloopy sauces found elsewhere. Kiwi wines feature on the efficient wine list. Arrive early for an outside table.

RESTAURANT SANTIAGO

### Astrid & Gaston

Antonio Bellet 201, Providencia
T + 56 (0)2-650 9125
Mon-Sat 1300-1530 and 2000-2400.
\$\$

He's Peruvian, she's German, and their restaurants – there are sister establishments in Lima and Bogotá – offer upmarket South American food with twists from other cuisines – foie gras, for example, certainly isn't a staple of the Chilean diet. Seafood, often with an Oriental influence, is first class, as are desserts, while the wine list, though pricey, includes all the big names of Chilean wine.

RESTAURANT SANTIAGO

### Camino Real/Enoteca

Parque Metropolitano, Cerro San Cristóbal, Providencia
T +56 (0)2-232 1758
Daily 1230-1600 and 2000-2300.
\$\$

It's a wine bar, it's a restaurant and it's a wine museum. From its elevated position on Cerro San Cristóbal, Camino Real (aka Enoteca) offers sweeping views of Santiago and the Andes (providing the smog isn't too heavy) and serves some of the city's most accomplished food – international Chilean, for want of a better term – with an equally impressive wine list. Expect to be serenaded by guitars in the evening.

# Best producers

**Chile**

Aguire, Francisco de
Almaviva » *page 275.*
Anakena
Antiyal
Aquitania
Calina
Calitera
Canepa
Casa del Bosque
Casa Lapostolle » *page 273.*
Casa Marín
Chadwick
Château Los Boldos
Concha y Toro (top wines) » *page 274.*
Cono Sur
Cousiño Macul » *page 272.*
De Martino
Domus Aurea
Edwards, Luis Felipe
Errázuriz » *page 272.*
Garces Silva
Haras de Pirque
La Rosa
Luca
Matetic » *page 276.*
Mont Gras
Montes » *page 273.*
Morandé
San Pedro
San Pedro de Yacochuya
Santa Carolilna
Santa Ines
Santa Rita » *page 275.*
Tarapacá
Terranoble
Tikal
Torres, Miguel » *page 273.*
Valdivieso
Ventisquero
Veramonte
Villard
Viña Batalcura
Viña Carmen
Viña Leyda
Viñedos Orgánicos Emiliana » *page 273.*

WINERY SANTIAGO

### Concha y Toro

Virginia Subercaseaux 210, Pirque
T+56 (0)2-476 5269
www.conchaytoro.com
Mon-Sat 1030-1600; closed public hols.
CLP$6

I was very impressed by Concha y Toro when I first visited in the 1980s but I never suspected that it would become as successful as it is today. Chile largest winery is also one of the best-equipped for visitors, with several guided tours in Spanish and English. The visit starts with a trip round the **Casona de Pirque**,

Grapevine

**Pisco sour?**

If you want to start an argument between a Chilean and a Peruvian, try raising the subject of pisco, the clear grape brandy that both countries claim as their own. The name of the drink reveals its Peruvian origins: it's called after the ceramic amphorae in which it was stored which, in turn, are named in the language of the Peruvian Quechua tribe after the little birds (*pisq*) that were common in the Ica Valley. It was the Peruvians who first began to make pisco in the 17th century, when the King of Spain banned them from drinking wine. While the two countries squabble over their right to sell their brandy as pisco, the Bolivians produce a very similar spirit they happily call singani (page 276). The quality of all these brandies varies widely, depending on the grapes used and the distillation equipment. Chile's pisco is mostly produced by large companies in continuous stills, using a blend of Moscatel and other local grapes. Singani is also produced from Moscatel, but like Peru's pisco – which is produced from the local Quebranta grape – goes into the more labour intensive pot still that has to be reloaded after every batch but gives more individual flavours. Top class examples of pisco and singani are good enough to sip with pleasure; the worst are as fiery as any rustic brandy in the world. In any case most pisco will end up in pisco sour cocktails which combine the brandy, lime, egg white and sugar. To add a note of spice to the inter-regional arguments, it is widely believed that the cocktail was invented in Chile by an English ship's steward called Elliot Stubb in his bar in Iquique.

built in 1875 as a summer residence for Don Melchor Concha y Toro and his family, and a walk through the tranquil 23-ha park that surrounds the house. Then it's on to the Pirque Viejo vineyard, the company's oldest, and the winery, before finishing with a tasting in the wine bar. Those who prefer to do their own thing can simply relax in the bar and sample some wines with a selection of savoury appetizers based on typical Chilean ingredients. There's also a new wine shop, which offers hard-to-find older vintages, as well as an extensive choice of wine accessories, books and magazines.

Nearby is the astonishing **Almaviva** winery (T +56 (0)2-852 9300, www.almavivawinery.com), Concha y Toro's joint venture with the Mouton-Rothschild of Bordeaux. Visitors are also welcome here, although booking is essential.

WINERY — CAMINO PADRE HURTADO

## Santa Rita

Camino Padre Hurtado 0695
T+ 56 (0)2-821 9966
Tue-Fri 1030, 1130, 1215, 1500 and 1600; Sat, Sun and public hols 1200 and 1530.

There are several reasons to visit this first-class estate. The 40-ha park is dotted with statues and has a variety of trees, including chestnut, cedar, olive, almond, orange and lemon, as well as the largest bougainvillea in the Americas. The sympathetically restored **Casa Real Hotel** ($$$) has 10 luxury bedrooms, six suites and a games room with a full-size billiards table. Nearby, another colonial building houses the **Doña Paula** restaurant ($$) and wine shop. There are tours of the estate in Spanish and English. Oh, and the wines are very good, too, especially the sumptuous Casa Real Cabernet Sauvignon.

Matetic winery.

WINERY — MELIPILLA

## Undurraga

Km 34 Camino Antiguo a Melipilla, Talagante
T +56 (0)2-372 2800
www.undurraga.cl
Tours Mon-Fri 1000, 1130, 140 and 1530; Sat and Sun 1000, 1100 and 1300.

Undurraga is a long-established Maipo winery with spectacular gardens designed by the renowned Frenchman Pierre Dubois. Tours of the gardens and the winery, plus a tasting in the wine shop, are offered.

## San Antonio

WINERY LAGUNILLAS

### Matetic Vineyards

Fundo Rosario, Lagunillas, Casablanca
T +56 (0)2-583 8660
www.mateticvineyards.com
Tue-Sun 1100 and 1530.
CLP$7

Most visitors miss out on seeing this fast up-and-coming region, but I reckon that this winery provides the perfect reason for going there. The wines are among the most refined in the country, especially the Syrah, and there are a number of different tours and tastings offered to visitors. There's also a restaurant ($$) and a recently revamped guesthouse ($$), dating from the early 1900s. Cycling and horse-riding are offered throughout the year and, depending on the season, guests can pick blueberries or take part in the grape harvest. Milk the goats if you're up to it; the resulting *queso rosario* is a cracker.

## Zapallar

RESTAURANT CALETA DE ZAPALLAR

### El Chiringuito

Caleta de Zapallar (south end of town)
T+ 56 (0)32-741024
Daily for lunch and dinner.
($)

With such an extensive coastline, Chile should boast dozens of decent seaside restaurants. This is one of the best, superbly situated with a massive view over the Pacific and the calmer waters of the Zapallar bay. The adjacent beach is perfect for dozing after an extensive lunch of *corvina* (a type of bass), razor clams, crayfish, oysters, calamari, albacora, congrio, and good local wine.

# Rest of South America

## Bolivia

The most popular drink in Bolivia is a characterfully aromatic spirit called *singani*, which is made by distilling wine made from Muscat grapes. As the production of *singani* has become more sophisticated, similar improvements have been apparent in the wine industry, though volumes are still small, and serious wineries few. Most wine (and *singani*) is produced in the Central Valley of Tarija, close to the borders with Paraguay and Argentina. There are around a dozen wineries and some 3700 ha of vines grown on the valley floor at an altitude of around 1750 m. Grapes are, however, grown at 1000 m higher than that (as compared to a maximum height of 1187 m for Europe's highest vineyard, in the Valais in Switzerland). The average temperature of 18°C might seem high but the difference of up to 21°C between the warmth of noon and the chill at night helps to mitigate the effects of this. According to a report from the Bolivian Ministry of Industry and Commerce "the climate of Tarija's Central Valley is optimal for the cultivation of wine grapes… [and] ...European varieties introduced in Bolivia have adapted exceptionally well". However, the report continues, "the level of quality of these products is not sufficient to compete in international markets against countries such as Chile". These comments, though generally true, overlook the efforts of Bodegas La Concepción (see below).

WINERY TARIJA

### Bodegas y Viñedos de La Concepción (BVC)

Calle Colon 585, Tarija
T +591 (0)24-6 63 2 250
www.bodegaslaconcepcion.com
Tastings by appointment

With vines planted at altitudes of 1600 to 2800 m, this producer claims to own the highest vineyards in the world. It is also far, far closer to the equator than is usually recommended for vineyards. However, Don Francisco and Sergio Prudencio, the owners and winemakers here are nothing if not ambitious. They annually sell some 350,000 bottles and their long-lived, subtle Cepas de Altura Cabernet Sauvignon has earned marks similar to those of high-profile efforts from Argentina and Chile. Bolivia's wine industry is tiny – BVC has nearly 10% of it – and wine tourism is almost non-existent. There are plans to open up a hotel and restaurant here, and those visiting nearby Tarija should be able to organize a visit with local travel agents. Anyone wanting to stay in comfort near the vineyards should consider the **Los Parrales Hotel** (www.losparraleshotel.com) in Tarija. www.boliviacontact.com offers vineyard tours.

## Brazil

Ask any well-informed international businessman today to name the countries in which the greatest fortunes are soon to be made and there's a high chance that his reply will refer to the acronym BRIC – Brazil, Russia, India, China – four giant countries with rapidly growing middle classes. Of these, Brazil has by far the strongest wine culture. Like the Spaniards, Portuguese settlers were early winemakers, producing their first vintage in Brazil at Tatuape, close to São Paulo in 1551. Little survives from Brazil's early wine history but the dynamism of the modern industry is clear from the giant concrete, barrel-shaped gateway that greets visitors to the town of Bento Gonçalves, an hour and a half's drive northeast of Porto Alegre. This is the capital of the Rio das Antes region, (aka Serra Gaucha), where the vast majority of Brazil's wine is produced. There are five separate areas here, all of which were founded by Italian settlers from the Veneto, as reflected in the name of towns like

Garibaldi (which produces sparkling wine). The inhabitants of this region each drink nearly 40 bottles of wine per year, compared to the average national consumption of just a couple of glasses per head.

The Serra Gaucha is a lush, fertile, relatively wealthy region, and a good place to visit but, like the Hunter Valley in Australia, it is less than ideal as a place to make wine. The problem is that torrential rain (and the rot and vine diseases that come with it) is a constant threat at harvest time. This is why there is such interest in developing vineyards elsewhere in Brazil. At present the São Francisco Valley, where tropical conditions allow for two harvests per year, has eight wineries and produces 6,000,000 litres of wine or 15% of Brazil's domestic consumption; this figure could rise to nearly 50% as early as 2008.

WINERY — BENTO GONCALVES

### Aurora Winery

Rua Olavo Bilac 500, Bento Gonçalves
T +55 (0XX)54-455 2000
www.vinicolaaurora.com.br
Tours daily; call for visiting hours.

Brazil's largest winery was founded 70 years' ago as a cooperative by Italian immigrants and was the first to open its doors to visitors for tours and tastings in the 1980s. Over 100,000 people now visit the winery each year to buy wines at the shop and to take the (free) 90-minute guided tour.

WINERY RESTAURANT — LEMOS

### Dal Pizzol

Rodovia RS 431, Km 5, Distrito de Faria Lemos
T +55 (0XX)54-3452 2055
www.dalpizzol.com.br
Mon-Fri 0900-1140 and 1330-1700; Sat, Sun and public hol 1000-1630.

This 32-year-old award-winning winery and restaurant is situated by the side of a lake and a park in which there are various items of winemaking paraphernalia. The wines are better than the food but the setting is delightful.

ATTRACTION — BENTO GONCALVES

### Maria Fumaca

Tickets from: Giordani Turismo, Rua 13 de Maio 581, Loja 109, Bento Gonçalves
T +55 (0XX)54-455 2788
www.mfumaca.com.br
Departures Jan-Jun and Aug-Nov Wed and Sat 0900 and 1400; Jul and Dec 0900 and 1400 daily.
Return trips BRL$21 (US$9.50)

The journey on this 19th century 'Smoky Mary' steam train through the Valley of the Vineyards from São João del Rei to Tiradentes is fantastic. The train which makes the trip twice per day in each direction takes half an hour, which might be quite long enough for those sitting on the old wooden seats, if it weren't for the spectaucular views of vineyards and waterfalls. There is also a railway museum and a giftshop at Tiradentes.

WINERY — BENTO GONCALVES

### Miolo

RS 444, Km 21, Vale dos Vinhedos, Bento Gonçalves
T +55 (0XX)54-459 1500/0800-541 4165 (toll free)
www.miolo.com.br
Tastings by appointment

One of the best and most dynamic producers in Brazil, Miolo has its headquarters (like most Brazilian wineries) in the state of Rio Grande do Sul but owns wineries in several other regions, including the São Francisco Valley. Miolo runs its own wine courses at the winery and in several Brazilian cities (T 0800-904165 /+55 (0XX)54-2102 1500), and also welcomes visitors to its premises for tours, tastings and meals at the **Osteria Mamma Miolo** ($$). The **Villa Europa** hotel ($$) is set to open in autumn 2006 and will have a Caudalie wine spa of the kind found at Château Smith Haut Lafitte in Bordeaux (page 64).

WINERY — BENTO GONCALVES

### Vinícola Salton

Rua Mário Salton 300, Distrito de Tuiuty, CEP 95700-000, Bento Gonçalves
T +55 (0XX)54-2105 1005
BRL$70

The Salton family, Italian immigrants who began to make wine in 1910, still preside over one of the best wineries in the country. Located 12 km outside Bento Goncalves, it is a splendid white colonial building with cellars full of new oak barrels that would not look out of place in Bordeaux. The winery offers tasting courses but these are still only available in Portuguese.

## Colombia

Colombia has vines; 1500 ha of them to be precise. Indeed, anyone with US$750,000 to spare in October 2005 could have bought the Tierra Prometida winery in the village of Villa de Leyva, 150 km northwest of Bogotá, including 3.5 ha of vineyards (at an altitude of 2225 m), an inn and restaurant. Most of Colombia's vines are grown close to the town of La Unión in Valle del Cauca province but quality is poor. As one wine-loving expatriate commented, most people begin the evening with a decent Chilean red and then move onto the local semi-sweet pink or red Grajales which, at US$2.50 in the shops, costs half as much as a Chilean bottle.

## Ecuador

Ecuador's vineyards cover an area of only around 250 ha, making it one of the smallest wine-producing countries on earth. Until recently, its greatest offering for wine

Juanicó cellar and tasting room.

drinkers was a palatable (when well chilled) sparkling effort called Champagne Grand Duval. However, in 2004 a white wine from the Chaupi Estancia winery won a commendation at the Decanter Wine Awards in London. This was doubly surprising; first, there was the fact that the vineyard is 10 km south of the equator (wine traditionally comes from regions between 30° to 50° latitudes). Secondly, there was the grape variety: the usually reliably dull Palomino whose only claim to fame is as the grape from which dry sherry is made. Chaupi Estancia's secret seems to lie in the location of the vines, which are grown at 2400 m in the Andean Yaruqui Valley, and in the skill of Chilean winemakers. Other wines produced here include a Chardonnay and a red Bordeaux-style blend.

## Paraguay

In Paraguay however, politics, corruption and difficulties in obtaining such basics as bottles, corks and labels have reduced what, in the 1980s, was 3,000 ha of vineyards by over 95%. These vines were almost all in the Colonia Indepencia region in the south of the country at an altitude of 500m. Most of the modern wine industry was run by German immigrants who arrived in the early part of the 20th century, and the one winery worth knowing about today is Vista Alegre, where a German called Gerhard Buhler makes good Riesling and acceptable Cabernet Sauvignon.

## Peru

Peru has around 10,000 ha of vines, roughly the same as Uruguay, but 90% of these grow grapes that are used for *pisco* brandy. There is a winemaking and drinking tradition here, and a winery (Tacama) whose vineyards impressed French experts in the 1960s, long before most outsiders had noticed Chile or Argentina. An attempt at agrarian reform by the military government in 1968, however, led to the handing over of vineyards to peasants and cooperatives. These ventures failed commercially and large areas of high quality winegrowing vines were uprooted, leaving only 1000 ha today. Other handicaps to winemaking have included terrorism and a semi civil war. Vines rely on irrigation and today there are three coastal wine regions to the south of Lima where water is available: Canete, Chincha and the Ica Valley. Of these, the best wine comes from the latter area which is also of interest to tourists because two pre-Inca civilisations, the Nazca and Paracas were based here. The former, were skilled engineers, building aqueducts and canals in 300 BC, as well as producing an extraordinary set of drawings of animals and humans spread over 350 sq km of land that can only be appreciated from the sky (Enjoy Peru, T+51 (0)1 445-2550 www.enjoyperu.com offers tours and flights). Ica's dunes are also one of the best places in the world for sand boarding.

RESTAURANT — LIMA

### Huaca Pucllana

Gral Borgona cuadra 8 s/n, alt cuadra, 45
Av Arequipa, Lima
T +51 (0)1-445 4042
Daily 1200-1600 and 1900-2400.
$-$$

Any restaurant facing the ruins of a 1500-year-old pyramid deserves attention. When the stunning situation is partnered by equally impressive cooking courtesy of chef Marilú Madueño Martinez, the combination is a winner. Peruvian *criollo* cooking is given a fusion edge in dishes such as as prawn ceviche, *ausitas pucllana* (mashed potato croquettes with shrimp and avocado) and lamb ribs with pumpkin stew. There's a notable wine list and, of course, various creations based on *pisco*. Go easy on the latter, however, if you want to wander over the ruins by moonlight after your meal.

WINERY — VALLE DE ICA

### Tacama

Valle de Ica
T +51 (0)34-218 3017/218 3019
www.tacama.com
Daily 0900-1630.

Peru's most famous winery owes much of its reputation and the quality of its wines to a series of luminaries from the University of Bordeaux (Jean Ribéreau-Gayon, Émile Peynaud, Max Rives, Alain Carbonneau, and Pascal Ribéreau-Gayon) who have acted as consultants since a French winemaker was first employed here in 1962. The operation is large by any standards, with 180 ha of vines, including Chardonnay, Sauvignon Blanc, Semillon, Tannat, Malbec and Petit Verdot. Pisco is also produced.

## Uruguay

This small country has several vineyard regions and some 300 wineries, most of which are close to Montevideo in the area known as San Jose Canelones. The climate and soil vary but in broad terms, conditions are ideal for vines, with sufficient rainfall for irrigation not to be necessary. Interestingly, the average summer temperature here is a little lower than it is in Madiran in southwest France, home of the Tannat grape with which Uruguay is having increasing success. Until 1990, this country focused on producing enough ordinary wine from around 11,000 ha of vines (a tenth of the area of Chile) to satisfy its own consumption. The removal of trade barriers with its neighbours led to competition from Chile and Argentina; quality has been raised as a result and there is now a focus on exports. The best wineries are now well equipped and the recently replanted and upgraded vineyards are some of the most impressive in the world. It is worth noting that wines that are labelled as Tannat for overseas customers are often called Harrigue in Uruguay, after the Frenchman who imported the grape. Another variety that is doing well here is the Sauvignon Blanc.

WINERY MONTEVIDEO

### Bodega Bouza

Cno de la Rendencion 7658 bis, Montevideo
T +598 (0)2-323 7491
www.bodegabouza.com
Visits by appointment only.

Visitors are welcome at this small, family-run winery. There's a tasting room and restaurant ($), with a hotel planned for the near future, and there are also several vintage cars in various states of restoration around the premises. The wines are good too, with Albariño and Tempranillo featuring alongside the more expected Merlot and Tannat. Phone in advance if you'd like a guided tour with a sommelier.

WINERY MONTEVIDEO

### Bodegas Carrau

Ruta Cesar Mayo Gutierrez 2556, Montevideo
T +598 (0)2-320 0238
www.bodegascarrau.com/
www.castelpujol.com
Visits by appointment only.

The Carrau family, who arrived in Uruguay in 1930 after 180 years of winemaking in Catalonia, has two wineries in Uruguay: Cerro Chapeu in the north of the country (location of the country's highest vineyards) and Castel Pujol close to Montevideo. Both welcome any visitors who contact them in advance. As for the company speciality, type www.tannat.com into your browser and see what comes up. Sauvignon Blanc is successful here, too.

WINERY CANELONES

### Juanicó

s/n, 90400 Juanicó, Canelones
T +598 (0)32-335 9725
www.juanico.com
Visits by appointment only.

Uruguay's second oldest winery was founded over 160 years ago and is now one of South America's most dynamic winemaking operations. Recently contracted consultants include Michel Rolland, who has helped to produce Preludio, the country's priciest red, and Australian-born, Portuguese-based flying winemaker Peter Bright. Tours here include walks through the vineyards as well as visits to the winery and cellars.

## Venezuela

Venezuela, with a total of 1,000 ha of vines, also boasts a decidedly serious winery in the shape of Bodegas Pomar, a US$22 million venture jointly launched by Cognac Martell (who are no longer involved) and the huge local Polar brewery. The 125 ha of vines are in the northwest of the country, in the foothills of the Sierra de Baragua, at an altitude of 500 m. The most successful varieties so far seem to be Syrah, Tempranillo and Petit Verdot. Other producers' wines should be treated with circumspection. Collectors of vinous trivia might wonder if Venezuela's controversial leader Hugo Chavez is related to Cesar Chavez, the founder of the United Farm Workers of America, whose members were involved in fierce struggles over wages and rights against some of California's biggest wineries.

WINERY CARACAS

### Bodegas Pomar

Ctra Lara-Zulia, km 1, Apartado 33, Carora, 3040 Estado Lara, Caracas
T +58 (0)212-202 8907
www.bodegaspomar.com.ve
Mon-Fri 0800-1200 and 1400-1800; also Sat during harvest.

I have to admit that Venezuela's best winery is also its only serious winery, the northernmost in South America. Bodegas Pomar is highly recommended as a place to visit in its own right. Sparkling wine is a speciality but the still wines also merit attention. The winery offers an extensive programme of tours and events, ranging from a three-hour trip around the vineyards and winery to entire weekends involving grape-treading, hot-air balloon trips, horse-drawn carriages and gourmet dinners. Maybe a few wineries in France should take the trouble to visit Venezuela; they could pick up quite a few wine tourism tips.

# Australia



Grapes on the Fleurieu Peninsula.

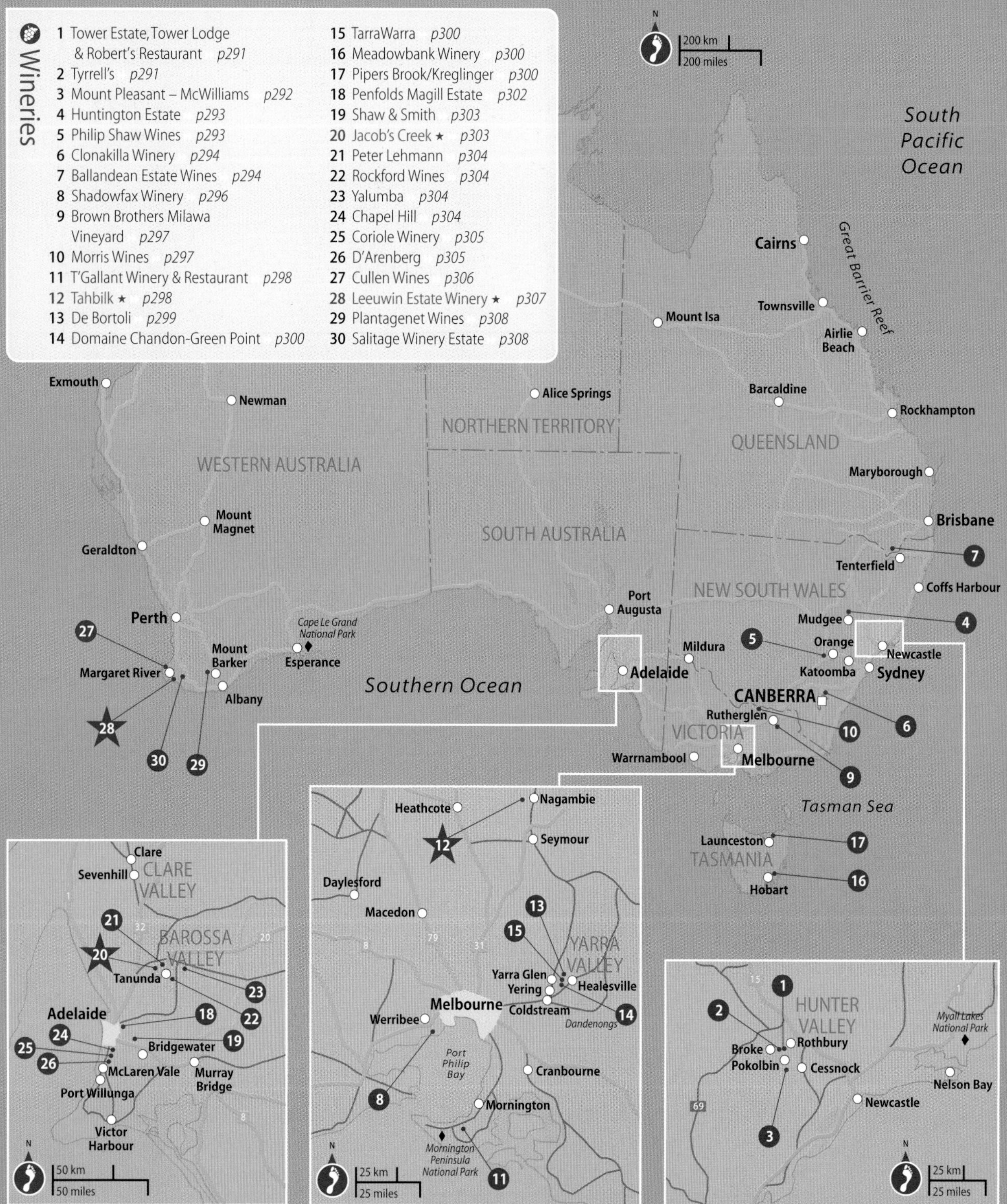

Wineries
1 Tower Estate, Tower Lodge & Robert's Restaurant p291
2 Tyrrell's p291
3 Mount Pleasant – McWilliams p292
4 Huntington Estate p293
5 Philip Shaw Wines p293
6 Clonakilla Winery p294
7 Ballandean Estate Wines p294
8 Shadowfax Winery p296
9 Brown Brothers Milawa Vineyard p297
10 Morris Wines p297
11 T'Gallant Winery & Restaurant p298
12 Tahbilk ★ p298
13 De Bortoli p299
14 Domaine Chandon-Green Point p300
15 TarraWarra p300
16 Meadowbank Winery p300
17 Pipers Brook/Kreglinger p300
18 Penfolds Magill Estate p302
19 Shaw & Smith p303
20 Jacob's Creek ★ p303
21 Peter Lehmann p304
22 Rockford Wines p304
23 Yalumba p304
24 Chapel Hill p304
25 Coriole Winery p305
26 D'Arenberg p305
27 Cullen Wines p306
28 Leeuwin Estate Winery ★ p307
29 Plantagenet Wines p308
30 Salitage Winery Estate p308
200 km
200 miles
South Pacific Ocean
Great Barrier Reef
Cairns
Townsville
Mount Isa
Airlie Beach
Exmouth
Newman
Alice Springs
Barcaldine
Rockhampton
NORTHERN TERRITORY
QUEENSLAND
WESTERN AUSTRALIA
Maryborough
Mount Magnet
Brisbane
SOUTH AUSTRALIA
Geraldton
Tenterfield
Coffs Harbour
Port Augusta
NEW SOUTH WALES
Perth
Mudgee
Cape Le Grand National Park
Mount Barker
Esperance
Mildura
Orange
Newcastle
Margaret River
Albany
Adelaide
Katoomba
Sydney
Southern Ocean
CANBERRA
Rutherglen
VICTORIA
Warrnambool
Melbourne
Tasman Sea
Launceston
TASMANIA
Hobart
Clare
Sevenhill
CLARE VALLEY
BAROSSA VALLEY
Tanunda
Adelaide
Bridgewater
McLaren Vale
Murray Bridge
Port Willunga
Victor Harbour
50 km
50 miles
Heathcote
Nagambie
Seymour
Daylesford
Macedon
YARRA VALLEY
Yarra Glen
Yering
Healesville
Melbourne
Coldstream
Dandenongs
Werribee
Port Philip Bay
Cranbourne
Mornington
Mornington Peninsula National Park
25 km
25 miles
HUNTER VALLEY
Myall Lakes National Park
Broke
Rothbury
Pokolbin
Cessnock
Nelson Bay
Newcastle
25 km
25 miles

# Introduction

In the 1970s the Monty Python team treated the very idea of Australian wine as hilarious. In a memorable 1972 sketch, a voiceover intoned that a lot of British people "pooh-pooh Australian table wines". This, it continued, is a pity, as many fine Australian wines "appeal not only to the Australian palate, but also to the cognoscenti of Great Britain". The irony was made clear by the descriptions that followed of wines with "lingering afterburn" and "a kick… like a mule". They were, in short, wines "for laying down and avoiding".

Three decades later, the Australians are, of course, enjoying the last laugh. Wine drinkers in both Britain and the USA now consume more Australian wine at home than French, and at a higher average price per bottle. And that gap is growing.

Popular Australian wine is actually less of a novelty than this sea-change might suggest. Wine grapes were introduced by the very first settlers who tried to grow them in Sydney on the site of the modern Intercontinental Hotel. The climate here was too humid, so the early winemakers headed north to the Hunter Valley. Vineyards were subsequently planted close to Melbourne, Perth and Adelaide and, then, further inland and along the coasts. No other country has developed so many wine regions so quickly and so successfully across such a wide area of land. And, as a comparison of Australian wine maps of the 1990s with those of today shows, that expansion is still continuing.

# Travel essentials



### Planning your trip

**Sydney** (SYD, T +61 (0)2-9667 6065, www.sydneyairport.com.au), **Melbourne-Tullamarine** (MEL, T +61 (0)3 9297 1600, www.melair.com.au) and **Perth** (PER, T +61 (0)8 9478 8888, www.perthairport.com) are served by most international airlines and are linked to most of the state capitals, large provisional towns, tourist destinations and wine regions by **Qantas** (www.qantas.com.au), **Jetstar** (www.jetstar.com.au), **Regional Express** (www.regional express.com.au) and **Virgin Blue** (www.virgin blue.com.au), supplemented by regional services. Domestic fares have dropped dramatically in recent years, making internal flights an attractive option if you're on a tight schedule. Otherwise, state and interstate bus services usually offer the most cost-effective way of constructing an interstate itinerary; see www.buslines.com.au. **Trainways** (T 1-800 888480, www.gsr.com.au) runs the *Indian Pacific* rail service from Sydney to Perth (three nights, via Port Augusta). To evoke nostalgia for a bygone era of travel, the 'Gold Kangaroo' ticket offers a sleeping cabin and all meals in the dining car. For maximum flexibility, however, there is no substitute for having your own transport. Cars, campervans and motorbikes can all be hired or bought easily, with international car hire firms represented in all major towns and cities.

Whichever form of transport you choose, remember that distances in Australia are vast. Tour operators often laugh at requests from foreigners who want to visit the Hunter and Barossa Valleys on the same day. These two regions are separated by well over 1000 km. In fact, it often isn't even practicable to visit regions in the same state on the same day, such as Barossa and Clare in South Australia or the Hunter and Mudgee in New South Wales. On a short visit, perhaps the best idea is to pick a city as a base and check out its hinterland. The **Blue Mountains**, **Hunter Valley** and the **NSW coast** can all be easily reached from **Sydney**; from **Melbourne** you can access the rest of Victoria, the **Great Ocean Road** and even **Tasmania**; and from **Perth** the obvious choice is to head south to the Cape-to-Cape region around **Margaret River**. You could also take a flight from Sydney or Melbourne to **Adelaide** to visit the **Clare** and **Barossa** valleys, or north to **Brisbane** to explore Queensland and the **Great Barrier Reef**. Alternatively, try a classic Aussie road trip, from Sydney to Melbourne, say, stopping off at wineries along the way.

Further information is available from the **Australian Tourist Commission** (www.atcaustralia.com). Also check out Footprint's *Discover East Coast Australia*. Tourist offices, or Visitor Information Centres (**VICs**), can be found in all but the smallest Australian towns.

**Australia country code** → +61. **IDD code** → 0011. **Internet ID** → .au. **Emergencies** → T000.

## → Fact file

| | |
|---|---|
| **International flights** | American, BA, Cathay, Emirates, Malaysian, New Zealand, Qantas, Singapore and others to Brisbane, Sydney, Melbourne and Perth. |
| **Entry requirements** | All visitors, other than NZ citizens, must obtain a valid visa in advance from the Australian Embassy or High Commission, or in electronic format. |
| **Currency** | Australian dollar (AUS$). |
| **Time zone** | GMT+8 hrs (WA); GMT+9½ hrs (SA, NT); GMT+10 hrs (QUE, NSW, ACT, VIC, TAS). Daylight saving Oct-Mar. |
| **Electricity** | 230/240 volts (50 Hz). Plugs have 2- or 3-blade pins. |
| **Licensing hours** | Public bars Mon-Sat 1000-2200 or 2400; Sun hours vary. Restaurants and clubs have more flexible hours. |
| **Minimum age** | 18. |
| **Drink-drive restrictions** | 50 mg per 100 ml of blood or 0 mg for drivers under 25. |

### When to visit

Australia's wine regions are good to visit almost throughout the year, thanks to the climate and the permanent welcome on offer at most of the wineries. The peak season, broadly speaking, in the southern third of the country is mid-December through to the end of January, when prices increase and accommodation gets booked up weeks in advance. Conversely, some hotels and tourist sites in Tasmania and coastal parts of Victoria may close in winter (May-July). Harvest begins in January and can last until late April, depending on the climate of each region, with cooler areas like Tasmania and Orange starting last.

### Wine tourism

The Australians are second to none when considering the needs of wine tourists. It is a rare winery that is not set up to welcome visitors with a keenly staffed 'Cellar Door' tasting room, as well, quite possibly, as a picnic and/or barbecue area outside and, in a growing number of cases, a café or restaurant. Plenty of wineries host major concerts and most regions have at least one annual food, wine and music festival. Some areas, however, are definitely ahead of their peers. Nowhere beats the Hunter Valley, which benefits from its proximity to the tourist-magnet that is Sydney, but the Margaret River, a four-hour drive south from Perth is, in its smaller scale, almost as impressive.

Several operators offer dedicated wine-tasting tours, including **Venture Winetours Australia**, www.venturewinetours.com.au, **Wine Tours Australia/NZ**, www.winetoursaustralia-nz.com, and **Avalon Wine Tours**, www.avalon-tours.com.

### Sleeping

Australia presents one of the most diverse and attractive range of accommodation options in the world, from cheap national park campsites alive with wildlife to exclusive and luxurious island retreats. Local VICs can supply full accommodation listings. At the top end of the scale in the biggest cities or prime tourist areas are impressive international-standard hotels and resorts ($$$), offering luxurious surroundings and facilities, attentive service and often outstanding locations. B&Bs ($$) offer comfortable and often upmarket accommodation that is rarely budget priced. Self-contained accommodation can be found in the national parks in the form of cattle and sheep stations. For the tighter budget, try Australia's large network of hostels ($).

### Eating

Although the quintessential image of Australian cooking may be of throwing some meat on the barbie, the truth is that Australia has developed a dynamic and vibrant cuisine all of its own. As the society has became increasingly multicultural, so the food of the Chinese, Thai, Vietnamese, Italian, Greek and Lebanese immigrants has found its way onto the Australian menu. Australia has a fusion cuisine that takes elements from many cultures and mixes them into something new and original. The more Asian the flavours, the better Riesling or Verdelho will go with them, although there is also scope here for Shiraz, provided that it is not too tannic or oaky. Recent versions of Chardonnay are less oaky than they were, which makes them a better match for a wide range of dishes.

Another striking quality is the super freshness of Australian food, achieved by using produce from the local area and cooking it in a way that preserves the food's intrinsic flavour. Native produce ensures that the ingredients are distinctive, with tasty examples including kangaroo, emu and crocodile, not to mention the native plants that Aboriginal people have been eating for thousands of years, such as quandong, wattle seed or lemon myrtle leaf.

While you are rubbing your hands with anticipation – a word of warning. While Australis a rapidly becoming a foodie nations and bad old-fashioned cooking is rarely encountered in major cities or areas popular with tourists, bad old habits of overcooking meat and overboiling vegetables have yet to be eradicated in rural areas.

> The 'Great Southern Land' offers beauty and diversity in spades, the world's oldest living culture and the very last word in weird wildlife.
>
> Andrew Swaffer
> *Footprint Australia*

Wok-fried free range egg with lap chong sausage and asparagus at D'Arenberg.

# Wine essentials



### History

The history of Australian wine differs from that of the USA in several very significant ways. It never went through Prohibition, although, like New Zealand, it certainly came close to doing so. Some of the best vineyards have, so far, never suffered from phylloxera, which means that no other country makes so many wines from vines that are over 100 years old. Very importantly, there has been the Australians' greater geographical fragmentation; no state has the predominance of California and no region the overriding prestige of Napa. New areas are, in fact, being developed all the time often in very unexpected places. The Australians have been far less interested in emulating the classics of Europe than in producing wines that satisfy local and overseas tastes. This helps to explain why there is far less Merlot grown here and far more Shiraz and Shiraz-Cabernet (a blend almost unknown in France and California). Given its small population, Australia has, in recent years, always relied on exports, whereas the US has to import wine to satisfy the demands of American wine drinkers. This has made the Australians unusually receptive to the tastes of other countries. To all of these factors must be added the peculiar phenomenon that 75% of Australia's wine, including many of the very best bottles, are produced by three huge companies: Fosters Wine Group; Constellation/BRL Hardy, the world's largest wine company, and Orlando Wyndham, which belongs to Pernod Ricard. While those who believe that 'small is beautiful' may regret this level of consolidation, there is no question that it has helped Australia become the world's most successful wine exporter.

### Understanding Australian wine

One of the reasons Australian wine has been so successful has been that it is so easy to understand; compared to the complexities of Europe, what you see is what you get. Australia's equivalent of an appellation system is a list of **Geographical Indications** (GIs) which are part of the fiercely policed Label Integrity Program. Regions range from the absurdly huge South East Australia (page 288), which includes New South Wales, Victoria, South Australia, Tasmania and Queensland – in other words, 95% of the country's vineyards – to the tiny Whitlands, a vineyard in Victoria. There is no official quality stamp to denote a finer region, like Italy's DOCG or France's Grand Cru, but great weight is placed on stickers that refer to the success of the specific wine and vintage in regional wine competitions. Most wine labels name the grape variety or varieties that have been used, though it is worth bearing in mind that winemakers are allowed to use 15% of a different variety and/or region and/or vintage. When Australian wines are sold in Europe, there is a 5% leeway allowed above or below the stated alcohol level. This is due to be increased to 8% but in Australia, the local allowance is 1.5%. In other words, a wine with a genuine strength of 14% could claim up to 15.5% or as little as 12.5%.

### White grapes

**Chardonnay** Australian Chardonnay has become almost a synonym for either attractively reliable, pineapply white wine – among its fans – or big oak, overly-flavoursome alcoholic white wine – among those who are less keen. What both camps tend to miss is that there are delicious Australian Chardonnays that are not hugely woody. In fact, wines like Giaconda, Tiers and Leeuwin Estate can easily be mistaken for top-class Burgundy. Styles depend on the region (cooler makes for finer) and the producer.

**Marsanne** A speciality in the Nagambie lakes in Victoria, this Rhône grape produces great, distinctive, long-lived lemony-limey wines that develop well over time.

**Muscat** While Brown Brothers has been successful with its light, sweet Orange Muscat & Flora, the best examples of this grape are the extraordinary liqueur Muscats of northeast Victoria, the best of which are like liquid Christmas pudding. The similar but spicier liqueur Muscadelles from the same region are made from an entirely different variety, the Muscadelle, which is only really used elsewhere as a small component in white Bordeaux.

**Riesling** Along with Shiraz and Semillon, this is the grape from which most of Australia's greatest wines have been made. Unoaked, dry and combining lime, lemon, grape and apple flavours, the best of these, from the Clare and Eden Valleys and from Great Southern in Western Australia, can develop over decades.

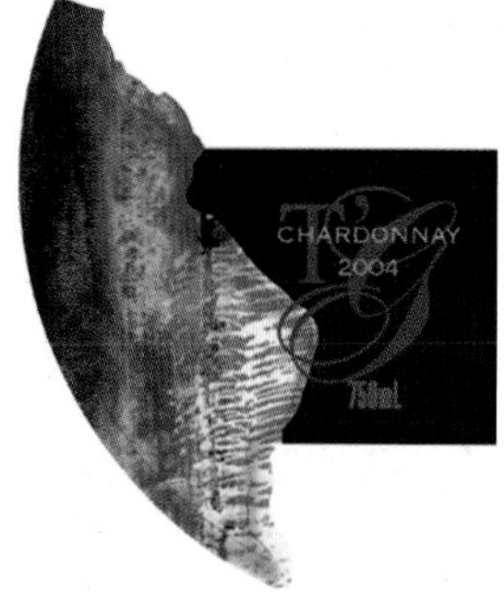


## Vintages

- **2006** Good to very good.
- **2004** Generally better for reds than whites, but good for Clare Riesling.
- **2003** Good to great.
- **2002** Great.
- **2001** Best in cooler regions such as Adelaide Hills and Tasmania.
- **2000** Mixed but great in Coonawarra.

Vineyards in the Adelaide Hills.

Winemaking at Tanunda, Barossa.

**Sauvignon Blanc** Not generally a great solo performer in Australia, but fine examples have been made in the Adelaide Hills (Shaw & Smith) and in the Riverland by Yalumba for its Oxford Landing label. Good in blends with Semillon in Margaret River (see below).

**Semillon** In the Hunter Valley, in particular, this Bordeaux variety produces extraordinary, long-lived, unoaked, low alcohol (12% or less), bone-dry wines that begin life with lemony zip and develop a combination of strawy, nutty (misleadingly oak-like) and honeyed flavours after a decade or so. Also impressive in the Barossa Valley (though often oaked and usually more alcoholic) and, in Bordeaux-like blends with the Sauvignon Blanc, in Margaret River. It is blended with Chardonnay for inexpensive wines.

**Verdelho** Used for fortified wines in Madeira but in the Hunter Valley and Western Australia it produces a refreshing, dry limey wine that has a character all of its own.

**Viognier** A spicy, white Rhône grape, pioneered in South Australia by Yalumba who have made world-class examples at several price levels. Now, as in the Rhone, it is being blended with Shiraz. A variety to watch.

## Red grapes

**Cabernet Sauvignon** Source of rich, intensely blackcurranty wines that tend to have an added note of mint in Coonawarra. Other places that excel with Cabernet Sauvignon include Margaret River, McLaren Vale and the Yarra Valley. The Hunter and Barossa Valleys are not usually ideal for Cabernet but there are exceptions, such as Lake's Folly in the former region.

**Grenache** At its peppery best in the Barossa Valley, this variety can make intense dark reds to suit lovers of modern Châteauneuf du Pape.

**Merlot** Increasingly widely grown but with few really world-class successes, although some US-based, Merlot-loving critics may take a different view.

**Pinot Noir** A relatively recent arrival (though longer established here than in New Zealand), this variety does best in cooler regions such as the Yarra Valley, Mornington Peninsula, Adelaide Hills, Tasmania, Tumburumba and Pemberton.

**Shiraz/Syrah** Australia's success story. While Californian producers were obsessively planting Merlot (largely because of its associations with Bordeaux), the Australians focused on this Rhône grape that has been part of the Aussie scene since some of the earliest vines were planted. Its secret lies in making truly great wines such as Grange and Henschke Hill of Grace as well as delicious inexpensive fare. It also blends well with other grapes. Styles vary according to climate and soil, with the most 'European' efforts coming from cooler parts of Victoria and the Hunter Valley.

Freshly picked Shiraz grapes from the Barossa Valley.

On 5 March, 1803, just over five years after the first shipful of convicts had landed in Sydney, the very first edition of the *Sydney Gazette & New South Wales Advertiser* included an article on vinegrowing and winemaking. The publication was full of official notices and it is easy to see the hand of the first governor Arthur Phillip behind the article, given the example he had set by planting a vineyard in his own garden almost as soon as he arrived. Sadly, the humid climate in Sydney and its attendant pests and diseases prevented the vines that had been imported from the Cape of Good Hope from flourishing. The first successful vineyard was planted in 1805, 60 km further south, by John Macarthur, paymaster of the Rum Corps. The true father of New South Wales' and Australian wine was, however, a young man called James Busby, who had studied winemaking briefly in France and Spain. On arrival in Australia in 1824, he planted the first vineyard in the Hunter Valley, 100 km north of Sydney, using vines he had imported from Europe.

## Sydney

An fabulous city that combines the qualities of Seattle, San Francisco and New York, Sydney retains a character that is uniquely its own. Among its other qualities, the city has developed one of the world's most extraordinary café and restaurant cultures, with great places to eat and drink that range from breakfast bars to Michelin-starred establishments with longer lists of Burgundies than you might expect to find in London. Add to that the existence of some great wine shops and plenty of restaurants that allow you to bring your own bottle, and you are in a wine drinker's paradise.

WINE SHOP SYDNEY

### Australian Wine Centre

Shop 3, Goldfields House, 1 Alfred St, Circular Quay
T +61 (0)2-9247 2755
www.australianwinecentre.com
Daily from 1000.

Visitors to Sydney inevitably end up at Circular Quay sooner or later. The Australian Wine Centre is conveniently located near the ferry terminal and is a good spot for anyone looking to buy top-notch Australian and New Zealand wines. The shop can arrange for your purchases to be shipped to you direct anywhere in the world.

Grapevine

**BYO**
The tradition of Australia's BYO ('bring your own') wine restaurants stems from the days when liquor licences were hard to get. Today, this is no longer the case but the habit lingers on, even in restaurants with really good wine lists, such as **Claude's** and **Atelier** in Sydney. **Tetsuya's** (page 290) began life as a BYO-only in a modest Sydney suburb. Today, it is in the heart of the city, you have to book months in advance and the degustation menu costs AUS$180. But you can still bring your own wine for a corkage fee of AUS$20, a figure that's hardly likely to deter wine lovers with old bottles of Grange or Bordeaux. The survival of the BYO culture has helped to turn Australia into a wine-drinking, restaurant-going nation, and prevented Australian restaurants from adding the outrageous mark-ups to wine that are seen elsewhere. Some Australian restaurants don't allow BYO, but it's always worth asking when you phone to make your booking.

## A weekend in Sydney

**Day one** For sunrise get yourself (and your camera) in position at **Macquarie Point**, which offers one of the best views of the Opera House and the harbour bridge. Then walk to the **Opera House** (Macquarie St, T +61 (0)2-9250 7777, www.sydneyoperahouse.com) via the waterfront, making a diversion in to the **Royal Botanical Gardens** (Mrs Macquarie's Rd, T +61 (0)2-9231 8111, www.rbgsyd.gov.au) to see the resident bat colony. From the Opera House, take your time negotiating Opera and Circular Quays, perhaps stopping for a leisurely breakfast at the **MCA Café** (Museum of Contemporary Arts, 140 George St, T +61 (0)2-9241 4253). Peruse the vintages at the **Australian Wine Centre** (page 288), thenmake your way to **The Rocks** via **Campbell's Cove**, where the replica of *HMS Bounty* is moored. Continue round to **Dawes Point Park** and marvel at the sheer size of the **Harbour Bridge**. There are great views from the southeast pylon (Cumberland St, T +61 (0)2-9240 1100, www.pylonlookout.com.au) or you could book yourself a **Bridge Climb** (www.bridgeclimb.com) for the following day. From there, head back towards George Street, which hosts the bustling **Rocks Market** at the weekend, as well as numerous clothing and jewellery boutiques. For lunch, try a croc or roo steak at the **Australian Hotel** (100 Cumberland St, T +61 (0)2-9247 2229) or enjoy the view from the top of the Customs House at **Café Sydney** (31 Alfred St, T +61 (0)2-9251 8683). In the afternoon, catch a ferry (T131500, www.sydney transport.com.au) from Circular Quay to **Taronga Zoo** (T1-900 920218, www.zoo.nsw.gov.au) and **Balmoral Beach**. In the evening, splash out on an unforgettable meal at **Tetsuya's** (page 290) or crawl the bars around The Rocks .

**Day two** Again, start early with a fascinating tour of **Sydney Fish Market** (Pyrmont, T +61 (0)2-9004 1143, www.sydney fishmarket.com.au) followed by an exploration of the city's seafaring history at the **National Maritime Museum** (2 Murray St, T +61 (0)2-9298 3777, www.anmm.gov.au). Then cross Pyrmont Bridge to the **Sydney Aquarium** (Aquarium Pier, T +61 (0)2-8251 7800, www.sydneyaquarium.com.au). Head back to Circular Quay to catch the ferry to **Watson's Bay**, where you should indulge in a seafood lunch at **Doyle's on the Beach** (11 Marine Pde, T +61 (0)2-9337 2007, book ahead), followed by a leisurely walk to South Head. Alternatively, from Circular Quay, take a ferry to **Manly**, where you can eat and drink at the **Manly Wharf Hotel** (Manly Wharf, T +61 (0)2-9977 1266) before spending the afternoon on the beach. Surf lessons are available from **Manly Surf School** (T +61 (0)2-9977 6977, www.manlysurfschool.com) or you could stroll along the **Manly Scenic Walkway** to Spit Bridge with lingering views of the harbour. In the evening, see if you can secure a last-minute booking for a performance at the Opera House, followed by a late dinner at **Quay** (Overseas Passenger Terminal, Circular Quay West, T+61 (0)2-9251 5600). Alternatively, have dinner in Chinatown and enjoy a quiet evening around Darling Harbour.

Grapevine

**Where on earth?**

The world of wine is governed by a body called the OIV, the International Organisation of the Vine and Wine (the initials are a hangover from the days when the French name was used), which does its best to impose some kind of order. Part of this involves an insistence that countries wishing to sell their wine overseas do so with labels bearing internationally recognized regional appellations. When Australia was confronted with the task of defining its wine-producing areas, it applied for and received official recognition for a vast region called South East Australia (see also page 286). It seems likely that the European bureaucrat responsible for rubber-stamping these applications must have passed this one across his desk in a matter of minutes, on a Friday evening before the summer holidays.



RESTAURANT SYDNEY

### Tetsuya's Restaurant

529 Kent St
T +61 (0)2-9267 2900
www.tetsuyas.com
Tue-Fri from 1830; Sat from noon.
$$$

Japanese-born Tetsuya Wakuda's Sydney restaurant seems to find its way onto lists of the top ten eating establishments in the world with monotonous regularity – and for good reason. The degustation menu (AUS$180 per head, plus wine) runs for anything between eight and 14 courses but always features his signature dish of slow-cooked confit of ocean trout along with a host of other delights that combine elements of classical French and Japanese cuisine. The quality of the wines on the encyclopaedic list is on a par with Tetsuya's cooking – and you can opt for the sommelier to make a selection of wines by the glass to accompany your meal. The setting for these gastronomic fireworks takes a bit of finding – it's on the ground floor of an anonymous-looking building on a street full of commercial blocks in Sydney's business district – but the experience of a meal here richly rewards the trouble taken to track Tetsuya's down.

Vineyards around Peppers Guesthouse in the Hunter Valley.

## Hunter Valley

The oldest and still, probably, the most famous wine region in Australia is also the most tourist-friendly and most frequently visited. An easy couple of hours' drive north from Sydney gets you to a place where, apart from choosing between a bewildering array of wineries and restaurants, you can decide whether to take in a view of the vineyards at dawn from a hot air balloon or play a round of golf at the Greg Norman course (before enjoying a glass or two of Greg Norman Estates Chardonnay). Alternatively, you could even get married in a chapel among the vines at the Hunter Valley Gardens.

Ironically, given the international resonance of its name, the Hunter Valley is actually something of a sideshow when it comes to the main business of Australian wine. The first commercial Chardonnay on this continent may have been produced here (by Tyrrell's) and Rosemount may have built a global reputation in the 1980s on its 'Show Reserve' Hunter Valley Chardonnay, but today most examples of this variety are produced elsewhere. The one bearing Greg Norman's name, for example, comes from the Yarra Valley in Victoria.

Winemakers are understandably slow to mention to visitors that while the Hunter Valley may be a far better place to grow wine grapes than the tropical conditions of Sydney where the first attempts were made, it is actually far from ideal. Perversely, the region suffers from both drought and untimely rainstorms that can drench the grapes and bring risks of rot during the harvest. Despite these handicaps, the Hunter Valley does produce some of the finest wines in Australia; they're just not the styles many people have been led to expect. The supreme achievement here is white wine made from the Semillon grape that could be described as the antithesis of traditional Aussie Chardonnay. With a strength of as little as 11% (compared to the Chardonnay's 13.5 or 14%) and not a trace of oak, these are wines that are made for the long haul. The best examples, from producers like Tyrrell's,

Nowhere does wine tourism better than the Hunter Valley.

Chez Pok restaurant and Homestead at Peppers Guesthouse.

McWilliams and Rothbury live for 20 or 30 years and are quite unique. The only other place to make great wines from Semillon is Bordeaux where it is blended with Sauvignon Blanc and aged in oak barrels. Confusingly, the Semillon here was once known as Hunter River Riesling or, even more erroneously, as Chablis, while the almost-as-impressive Shiraz were labelled as Burgundy. While it is nothing like the Pinot Noir of that French region, Hunter Valley Shiraz really is far more European in style – lighter and less overtly fruity and alcoholic – than its counterparts from other Australian regions, such as the Barossa Valley.

HOTEL POKOLBIN

## Peppers

**Peppers Convent**, Halls Rd, Pokolbin
T +61 (0)2-4998 7764. Reservations T +61 (0)2-4993 8999
**Pepper's Guest House**, Ekerts Rd, Pokolbin
T +61 (0)2-4993 8999
www.peppers.com.au
$$$

The Hunter Valley has a brilliant range of places to stay but, to my mind, one name stands out from the herd: Peppers, a very dynamic set of hotels dotted across Australia. Peppers has its roots at Pokolbin in the Hunter Valley, where it has two places to stay – the **Guest House** and the **Convent** – and a pair of restaurants. The Convent began life 600 km away in Coonamble as a home for the nuns of the Brigidine Order, before being transported here and converted into a very luxurious hotel that is a favourite among Sydney honeymooners. The Guest House is a little less romantic but has beautiful gardens, a spa and the excellent **Chez Pok** restaurant ($$), which, as its name suggests, adds Asian notes to French-modern-Aussie foundations and offers a terrific range of mature local wines.

WINERY POKOLBIN

## Tower Estate, Tower Lodge & Robert's Restaurant

Halls Rd, Pokolbin
T +61 (0)2-4998 7330
www.towerlodge.com.au,
www.robertsrestaurant.com
Tastings daily 1000-1700.
Robert's Restaurant daily 1200-1700 and 1900-0000.

Tower Estate and Lodge are the more recent creations of the late Len Evans, who could justifiably claim to have been the godfather, midwife, trainer and head of the modern Australian wine industry. Evans was the man behind both Rothbury Cellars in the Hunter Valley and Petaluma in South Australia, and is also the driving force behind the extraordinary network of national and regional wine 'shows' that have helped to build and grow the standard of Australian wine. Tower Estate is a recent development, offering small batches of wines from individual vineyards across Australia, while the **Lodge** ($$$) has a dozen rooms and a short 18-hole golf course. Rates of around AUS$600 per night for two are high by Australian standards but the hotel lives up to its slightly curious slogan as 'a compound of luxury'. Don't miss French-born Robert Molines's Provence-meets-modern Australia **Robert's Restaurant** ($$), a Hunter Valley landmark with a great selection of Hunter wines.

WINERY POKOLBIN

## Tyrrell's

Broke Rd, Pokolbin
T +61 (0)2-4993 7000
www.tyrrells.com.au
Cellar Door Mon-Fri 0830-1700; Sat 0830-1630. Tour Mon-Sat 1330.

One of the stalwarts of the Hunter Valley, this family-owned winery has been in business since the first vintage in 1864. The Tyrrells were pioneers of Chardonnay – the first release of the now-famous Vat 47 was in 1971, which is relatively prehistoric by Aussie standards – and, eight years later, its decidedly non-Burgundian Vat 6 Pinot

Noir was declared best in the world at a Gault Millau tasting in Paris. Today, while the Vat 47 is still a star, the really exciting wines here are the Vat 1 Hunter Semillons. This winery is particularly worth visiting at 1330 daily when the informative tour sets out.

WINERY POKOLBIN

### Mount Pleasant – McWilliams

Marrowbone Road, Pokolbin
T +61 (0)2-4998 7505
www.mcwilliams.com.au/
www.mountpleasantwines.com.au
Daily 1000-1630.

Although the Mount Pleasant vineyards were first established in the 1880s, it took the arrival of iconic winemaker Maurice O'Shea, who bought the property in 1921, for the winery to come into its own. When the McWilliam family bought Mount Pleasant in 1941, Maurice O'Shea stayed on as chief winemaker and went on to make some of Australia's most highly regarded wines. His legacy has been kept alive by his two successors, Brian Walsh (1956-1978) and Phil Ryan (1978 onwards) – a fact that has enabled the property to maintain an almost unparalleled degree of consistency. Mount Pleasant has its own restaurant, **Elizabeth's** ($$), which offers modern Australian cuisine, based on seasonal produce, and wines from the estate's cellar, including back vintages of both reds and whites.

## Mudgee

One of the oldest towns in Australia and one of the best preserved, Mudgee, whose name in aborigine means 'nest in the hills' was founded in 1838. Its early fortunes lay in wool-farming and, after the 1850s, in gold mining. Today it is famous among Australians as the birthplace of the poet Henry Lawson and as a source of some increasingly interesting wines. The best wines from the region are Rosemount's



**Around Sydney**

One of the wonderful things about Sydney is that you are never too far away from beaches or national parks. Heading out of the city on the Great Western Highway towards Orange (page 293) or by train towards Mudgee (page 292), a mere 70 km delivers you to the fringes of the Greater Blue Mountains (pictured). The 'Blues' encompass five national parks (www.npws.nsw.gov.au), eroded valleys, gorges, bluffs and caves.

Considered the capital of the Blue Mountains, Katoomba is an erstwhile mining town that offers a great range of amenities. Tourists come here to see the picture-postcard view from the famous Three Sisters lookout, which is built precariously 170 m above the valley floor. Take the **Scenic Railway** (T +64 (0)2-4782 2699, www.scenic world.com.au) for an exhilarating descent on one of the world's steepest inclined funicular railways. For further information and hotel reservations visit **Katoomba VIC** (Echo Point, T1-300-653408, www.bluemountainstourism.org.au).

North of Sydney, the Hunter Valley (page 290) conjures up images of mist-covered valleys and rolling hills, networked by patchworks of grape-laden vines. This is one of the best venues in the country to learn something of the winemaking process and to enjoy fine wine, food and accommodation. The nearest airport is at Newcastle and there are plenty of tours from Sydney, Newcastle and Port Stephens. The vast majority of the vineyards (over 80) are in the lower valley, near Cessnock. This town is decidedly drab and disappointing but the wine communities of Pokolbin, Broke and Rothbury to the north and west are more appealing. Though the vineyards are all comprehensively signposted, you are strongly advised to pick up the free detailed maps from **Hunter Valley VIC** (455 Wine Country Drive, north of Newcastle, T+61 (0)2-4990 4477, www.winecountry.com.au) or join one of the many organized tours. Try **Vineyard Shuttle Service** (T +61 (0)2-4991 3655, www.vineyardshuttle.com.au) or **Pokolbin Horse Coaches** (T+61 (0)2-4998 7305).

From Newcastle it's an easy hop to **Nelson Bay** and the **Tomaree National Park**, where you can laze about on glorious beaches and enjoy the views from Tomaree Head. Further north, **Myall Lakes National Park** combines beautiful coastal scenery with a patchwork of inland lakes, waterways and forest to create one of the best-loved eco-playgrounds in NSW.

Hill of Gold and the reds produced by Huntington Estate, one of the area's oldest wineries and home to the annual Huntington Music Festival. While you're in the region, drive along Hill End Road to Hargraves and invest in a gold-panning kit to use at Tambaroora 20 km further along the road. Once home to thousands of gold prospectors, this is now a ghost town, where the occasional speck of gold might still be found.

Tasting notes

**Blend it like Bordeaux**

Shiraz-Cabernet, one of the classic Australian red wine styles, bears some resemblance to a type of wine that was once highly prized in France. Until the 19th century, it was not uncommon to 'improve' red Bordeaux with a dollop of Syrah from the vineyards of Hermitage in the Rhône. Wine treated in this way was described as 'Hermitagé' and commanded a premium price. Today, such practices are strictly illegal but the blend lives on in Australian wines, like the best-selling example from Jacob's Creek. Interestingly, there is no evidence that the Australians were copying the French; they discovered the affinity between these grapes for themselves. The Shiraz was originally added to soften what can be hard tannins and to fill out what can also be the hollow character of some pure Cabernet Sauvignon. But the Aussie blend has an appeal of its own, bringing together the blackberry and spice of the Shiraz and the more straightforward Cabernet blackcurrant.

WINERY — MUDGEE

### Huntington Estate

Cassilis Road, Mudgee
T +61 (0)2-6373 3825
www.huntingtonestate.com.au
Mon-Fri 0900-1700; Sat 1000-1700; Sun 1000-1500.

Bob and Wendy Roberts planted their first vines in the up-and-coming region of Mudgee in 1969, under the guidance of Len Evans. Their first vintage was 1973 and, since then, Huntington Estate has gone on to win all kinds of awards for its wines, which include Cabernets, wooded and unwooded Chardonnays, a Pinot Noir, a Shiraz, a Semillon and a rosé. The winery itself is set amid splendid gardens and visitors are more than welcome to bring along a picnic to enjoy on the estate's lawns.

## Orange

Visitors to the Blue Mountains – the spectacular eucalypt-covered hills inland from Sydney (page 292) – should drive a little further to this recently developed region, three hours west of the city, which is now producing some of Australia's most interesting cool-climate wines. The area is rather paranoid about its name: in the key export market of the US, people apparently won't take Orange Wine seriously. Instead, the sensible answer for the winemakers might be to use the name of Mount Canobolas, the hill on whose slopes the grapes are grown, which, at 4600 ft, is one of Australia's highest peaks.

WINERY — AROUND ORANGE

### Philip Shaw Wines

Koomooloo Vineyard, Caldwell Lane, 8 miles outside Orange on Forbes Rd
T +61 (0)2-63 64 2556
www.philipshaw.com.au
Daily from 1000.

Philip Shaw was head winemaker at corporate giants Rosemount and Southcorp before jumping ship to make his own wines in Orange. His vineyards – where he grows Sauvignon Blanc, Pinot, Chardonnay and a range of other grapes – lie on the slopes of Mt Canobolas. Although Shaw's cellar door is less slick than those of more established labels, when tasting his wines you get the feeling you might be in at the start of something big.

## Canberra

Australia's capital rarely features on most tourist itineraries and there is little reason why it should. If there hadn't been such fierce rivalry between Melbourne and Sydney, this compromise city would never have been built. But it does boast the parliament and the National Art Gallery, which has an impressive collection of Aboriginal works and pieces of modern art by masters ranging from Monet to Warhol.

Canberra's wine district, which is actually in New South Wales, saw its first commercial vineyardin 1971 – but there are now some 30 wineries and an annual production of over two million bottles. The secret of the region lies in its high altitude, which creates some of the coolest vineyards in Australia. Riesling is a beneficiary of these lower temperatures, while the warmer vineyards produce some great Shiraz and Viognier.

WINE BAR — CIVIC

### Caffe della Piazza

19 Garema Place, Civic
T + 61 (0)2-6248 9711
Daily 1030-2300.
$

A wine bar disguised as an excellent café. The award-winning wine list is certainly the main attraction here, and many wines are available by the glass, but you can also bring your own bottle (corkage AUS$3.50) if you wish. The Italian food is also good, and the service is just as it should be: well-informed and speedy.

Grapevine

**The US factor**
American wine drinkers were rather slower to discover Australian wine than their UK counterparts, possibly thanks to a lack of enthusiasm by the leading US and global critic, Robert Parker who wrote – as recently as 2000 – that "Australia's overall wine quality is barely average, with oceans of mediocre and poorly made wines". California wine quality, in contrast, was "surging to greater and greater heights". The verdict would have surprised any open-minded observer who had done extensive tastings of both countries' commercial wines and encountered the plentiful mediocrity and poor winemaking on offer in the US. Even in 2000, however, Parker had happily made an exception to his own rule, by falling in love with a number of intensely flavoured limited-production reds from producers like Torbreck and Clarendon Hills. With his backing, many of these wines achieved cult status in the USA and, very soon, there were examples that were so difficult to find in Australia that they were said to have been produced specifically for the American market. Meanwhile, at the more affordable end of the market, where critical comment carries much less weight, bigger Californian producers openly winced at Australian wines such as Yellow Tail, which, less than five years after first hitting the streets, beat the hometeam to become the biggest-selling brand in the US.

WINERY MURRUMBATEMAN

### Clonakilla Winery

Crisp Lane, Murrumbateman
T +61 (02)-6227 5877
www.clonakilla.com.au
Daily 1100-1700.

This small family-run Canberra winery was established in 1971 by John Kirk, a scientist who came to Australia in the late 1960s to work for the Australian government science research organization, the CSIRO. He soon realized that, although the cool southern tablelands of New South Wales were the ideal location for vineyards, there was no wine industry in the region. In 1971, he bought a 44-acre farm near the village of Murrumbateman, some 40 km north of Canberra, and set about making Riesling and Cabernet Sauvignon. By the late 1990s, Kirk was joined in the vineyards by his son Tim, who bought a neighbouring 50-acre plot and planted it with the northern Rhône varieties, Shiraz and Viognier. Clonakilla's flagship wine, a Shiraz Viognier blend, was one of the first of its kind in Australia and can arguably be said to have set a trend – it's certainly won its fair share of awards. Clonakilla has no restaurant but it is close to **Shaw Estate** (www.shawvineyards.com.au), which offers fine Semillon and good Italian food ($-$$) as well as Sunday brunch overlooking the vineyards.

## Queensland

**Queensland, which boasts a 'granite belt' that is said to add character to its wines, has grown into a recognizable wine region over the last seven years, with over 70 wineries. The most famous is Ballandean, which recently celebrated its 75th birthday.**

WINERY BALLANDEAN

### Ballandean Estate Wines

354 Sundown Road, Ballandean
T+61 (0)7-4684 1226
www.ballandeanestate.com
Tours daily 1100, 1300 and 1500.

Ballandean, in Queensland's granite belt, is the state's oldest and largest winery. It is owned by the Puglisi family, descendants of Salvatore Cardillo, an Italian immigrant who bought the land and planted its first vines in the 1930s. In the early days, the focus was on bulk wines made from table grapes but now the emphasis is on quality, with a range of 18 wines made on the estate, from crisp Sauvignon Blanc to *méthode Champenoise* sparklies, Shiraz and fortified wines.

The tourist facilities and events calendar run by Ballandean are of almost as much interest as the wines . Visitors can rent a cottage ($) less than a kilometre away from the winery; enjoy a bite to eat at the **Barrel Room Café** ($), or indulge in the handmade chocolates and fudges sold at the cellar door. In addition, Ballandean hosts an annual winemakers' dinner, jazz and opera evenings, a spring wine festival among other events.

WINE BAR BRISBANE

### Cru Bar & Cellar

22 James Street, Fortitude Valley, Brisbane
T +61 (0)7-3252 2400
www.crubar.com
Mon-Fri 1130-2200; Sat and Sun 0830-2200.

Crubar isn't sure whether it's a wine bar with a wine shop attached or the other way around. Either way, it's probably your best bet in Brisbane when it comes to tracking down a cracking selection of Aussie and international wines by the bottle or by the glass (in the wine bar only). The food's not bad either ($-$$); chef Paul Hoffman makes the most of the neighbouring James Street Markets when doing his daily shopping, which ensures the ingredients are seasonal and fresh

**Australians make jokes about Tasmania – or simply forget to include it on maps. In fact, however, this small, spectacularly unspoiled island played a crucial part in the history of the Australian wine industry. It was here in the 1820s that a nursery produced the first-ever vines to be planted in Victoria and South Australia. Victoria's winemaking history began in the 1840s, on the eve of the gold rush, and, within four decades, the state had become the most important wine region in Australia. It was shipping enough wine to Britain in 1886 for Hubert de Castella, a Swiss-born historian and author of *Notes d'un Vigneron Australien*, to coin the term *John Bull's Vineyard* as the title of his third book. Much of that wine, sold in the UK under labels such as 'Australian Burgundy' or 'port', came from the warm region of northeast Victoria around Rutherglen and Glenrowan. By this time, Chateau Tahbilk in Goulburn had also planted vines, some of which are extraordinarily still producing grapes and wine today, and the Yarra Valley and Geelong had been established by Swiss winemakers. Other important regions today include Great Western, source of wonderful, eccentric sparkling Shiraz, and Bendigo, where the variety also flourishes but without bubbles. Today, Victoria offers delicate Pinot Noir and hefty fortified reds – and everything between the two.**

## Melbourne

In the early 1980s, the description 'Victorian' seemed to apply to Melbourne's starchy attitude as much as to its geographical location. Extraordinarily, it was illegal to serve food and drink out of doors and the whole city seemed to close down every evening at 1730. Today, this is a buzzing, cosmopolitan state capital with everything Sydney has to offer – except an opera house and a bridge. Some of the best restaurants in Australia are here – look out for great Asian and Italian cuisine – and some of the best cafés. And, for those with a little time to spare, the vineyards of the Yarra Valley and Mornington Peninsula are near at hand.

WINE BAR — ST KILDA

### Melbourne Wine Room

The George, 125 Fitzroy St, St Kilda
T +61 (0)3-9525 5599
Bar and bistro Sun-Wed 1200-0100;
Thu-Sat 1200-0200. Restaurant 1830-2300.
$$

Since my first visit to stuffy Melbourne, two decades ago, the city has lightened up and I have got to know it better. The Melbourne Wine Bar in the decidedly hip suburb of St Kilda is one of my favourite spots. It's huge, with loads of room for drinking and meeting people, which is handy, as the whole of Melbourne seems to hang out here. There are also a few chairs and tables outside for watching trendy Melburnians stroll past in the evening.

Don't go to the Wine Room looking for a quiet, romantic evening – the volume levels here prevent any hope of holding a quiet conversation – instead make the most of the good, honest food and a great wine list.

In the 1820s, a nursery in Tasmania produced the first-ever vines to be planted in Victoria and South Australia.

WINERY WERRIBEE

## Shadowfax Winery

Werribee Park, K Rd, Werribee
T +61 (0)3-9731 4000
www.mansionhotel.com.au
Daily 1100-1600.

A short 30-km drive from Melbourne, Shadowfax (named after the horse in the *Lord of the Rings*) is a winning combination of designer winery, café, gourmet foodstore, hotel and restaurant. Shadowfax's funky, contemporary winery turns out a range of wines, including some rare single-vineyard Chardonnay and Pinot Noir. Tours through the barrel hall and winery are offered to visitors as a complement to tastings in the cellar door building. The on-site café ($) offers a range of grazing plates that can be enjoyed outdoors, while the 'serious restaurant', **Joseph's** ($$), offers modern European cuisine and an extensive wine list. The **Mansion Hotel** ($$) is surrounded by splendid gardens, and its luxurious interior is the perfect setting for indulgence in the spa.



### Victoria

The state of Victoria revolves around **Melbourne**, the most European of Australia's cities. Theatres, bookshops and galleries all vibrate with the chatter of cosmopolitan urbanites, and its famously damp, grey weather lends the city an air of introspection lacking in other state capitals. Ultra-modern **Federation Square** has become the main focus for visitors. It is an intriguing combination of angular steel girders and plate glass, housing restaurants, cafés and performance spaces. **Melbourne VIC** (T +61 (0)3-9658 9658, www.visitmelbourne .com.au) is here, as is the Ian Potter Centre (T+61 (0)3-8620 2222, www.ngv.vic.gov.au). Part of the **National Gallery of Victoria**, it houses the largest collection of Australian art in the world. (The international collection is across the river at 180 St Kilda Rd.) North of Fed Square is the vast and high-tech **Melbourne Museum** (Carlton Gardens, T131102, www.melbourne. museum.vic.gov.au).

Melbourne is foodie heaven, with roughly 110 ethnic groups, who have enriched the city's cuisine. The best option is to head for an 'eat street', such as **Brunswick Street** in Fitzroy (north of the centre) or the Vietnamese restaurants of **Richmond** to the southeast. **Chinatown** (Little Bourke Street) and the **Southbank** are also busy dinner spots. One of the most treasured places on Southbank is **Walter's Wine Bar** (Upper level Southgate, T+61 (0)3-9690 9211, www.walters winebar.com.au), a relaxed spot with fantastic views of the river and the 'best wine list in the land'.

Just to the east of the city is the beautiful **Yarra Valley** wine region (page 299), which has some of the most sophisticated cellar doors and restaurants in Australia. Also here is the wonderful **Healesville Sanctuary** (Badger Creek Rd, Healsville, T +61 (0)3-5957 2800, www.zoo.org.au), devoted to the conservation of Australian wildlife, including Tasmanian Devils and platypus. Heading south, the **Dandenongs** is an area of mountain ash forests, with great views of Melbourne.

The **Mornington Peninsula**, often just called 'the bay', is Melbourne's beach playground, where you can swim with dolphins, dive and sail. The pristine south coast is protected

by the **Mornington Peninsula National Park**, and there are beaches and cafés at Sorrento and Portsea. Nearby Phillip island has surfing breaks in the south and sunny beaches around Cowes. Head to the far west of the island to see Australia's largest fur seal colony and the parade of fairy penguins at dusk.

West of Melbourne, the **Great Ocean Road** (www.greatoceanrd.org.au), runs from Anglesea, round the treacherous Cape Otway, to Warrnamboo. It is, truly, one of the world's great coastal routes with everything from stylish villages, such as Lorne and Apollo Bay, to **Port Campbell National Park**, with its famous golden rock stacks. The most famous group, the **Twelve Apostles**, was dramatically reduced to 11 when one collapsed into the sea in June 2005.

## Macedon, Pyrenees, Bendigo and Heathcote

These three cool(ish) regions to the northwest of Melbourne produce some of Victoria's most distinctive wines. Macedon is famous for Virgin Hills' restrained Bordeaux-like reds and, more recently, for Bindi, while the Pyrenees is home to Dalwhinnie and Taltarni. Heathcote, previously part of Bendigo, has recently taken on its own identity as a great source of European-style Shiraz. Producers to look for from these last two regions include Jasper Hill and Passing Clouds.

HOTEL — MACEDON RANGES

### Lake House Hotel

King St, Daylesford, Macedon Ranges
T +61 (0)3-5348 3329
www.lakehouse.com.au
$

Daylesford is a popular weekend escape for Melburnians and the Lake House Hotel is the best place for food and wine lovers to stay. The dining room overlooks Lake Daylesford itself, making it the perfect setting from which to enjoy the food ($-$$), which is turned out under the supervision of executive chef, Alla Wolf Tasker. The wine list is no slouch, either: it has won *Wine Spectator*'s Award for Excellence six years on the trot. Once you've eaten and drunk to your heart's content, you can retire to one of the spacious rooms, some of which have lake views, in the property's original homestead.

## Rutherglen, Glenrowan, Milawa and Beechworth

This great old gold-mining area has been well conserved – Rutherglen main street could be used in any Western – as have many of the traditional ports, Muscats and Muscadelles that are entirely unique to Australia. But, while many of these areas are warm enough for fortified wines, there are other places in this part of Victoria that are far cooler. Brown Brothers King Valley vineyards and Giaconda (T +61 (0)3-5727 0246, www.giaconda.com.au) in Beechworth are at higher altitudes and produce really good table wines. In fact, Rick Kinzbrunner at Giaconda makes some of Australia's most respected wines, including a Chardonnay many believe to be Australia's finest.

WINERY — MILAWA

### Brown Brothers Milawa Vineyard

239 Milawa Bobinawarrah Rd, Milawa
T +61 (0)3-5720 5547
www.brown-brothers.com.au
Cellar door daily 0900-1700. Epicurean Centre daily 1100-1600; à la carte daily 1200-1500.

The Brown Brothers vineyards, located throughout Victoria, are as varied as the wines made by the company. Within a 50-km radius of Milawa, climatic conditions range from cool alpine areas to lush temperate valleys and sun-drenched plains. Varietal diversity provides another point of difference and can be sampled at the cellar door: simply taste your way through as many wines as you want or opt for a full guided tour. Alternatively, you can book yourself a table at the **Milawa Epicurean Centre** ($-$$). The menu is changed each season to reflect the availability of fresh produce and to allow for new wine releases to be showcased.

WINERY — RUTHERGLEN

### Morris Wines

Mia Mia Rd, Rutherglen
No phone.
www.morriswines.com.au
Daily from 1000.

In 1859, George Francis Morris planted a trial 10-acre vineyard in the Rutherglen region of northeastern Victoria and, by 1885, plantings had expanded to cover over 200 acres, making the winery the largest producer of the era. Nowadays, Morris Wines is run by a member of the fifth generation of the family to oversee the estate. Although table wines are made by the estate, its strength lies in the production of Rutherglen's iconic liqueur Muscats. The cellar door is located in the heart of the old winery and visitors are encouraged to enjoy a picnic or barbecue in the grounds of the estate after a morning's tasting.

Brown Brothers' Epicurean Centre.

## Mildura

Few outsiders have any reason to come to Mildura, though drinkers of modestly priced Aussie wine will be interested to know that this is where many of the grapes for those reds and whites are grown. We've included it here, because Stefano Pieri is a great cook (a television celebrity chef in Australia) and the restaurant he runs in the recently refurbished art deco hotel has a truly terrific range of Australian and imported wines.

RESTAURANT MILDURA

## Stefano's at the Mildura Grand Hotel

Seventh St, Mildura
T +61 (0)3-5023 0511
www.milduragrandhotel.com.au
Mon-Sat for dinner; also Sun before bank hols.
$$-$$$



Mildura's Grand Hotel began life in 1891 as the Mildura Coffee Palace and has gone on to become one of Victoria's most iconic hotels ($-$$). One of the most enticing reasons to stay there, however, is for a chance to eat at the multi-award winning Stefano's Restaurant in the hotel's old cellars. Chef Stefano Pieri's food is based on the cuisine of northern Italy, and the five- or six-course banquet focuses on whatever seasonal ingredients Pieri happens to feel like cooking on the night you visit. Wines, naturally, are almost as much of a draw as the food itself

## Mornington Peninsula

Almost on the outskirts of Melbourne, this coastal wine region is under constant threat from housing developers but producers like Stoniers and T'Gallant regularly prove that wines made here can compete with the best on the planet.

WINERY MAIN RIDGE

## T'Gallant Winery & Restaurant

1385 Mornington-Flinders Rd, Main Ridge
T +61 (0)3-5989 6565
www.tgallant.com.au
Daily 1000-1700. La Baracca Trattoria daily for lunch.

Just a short drive from the Melbourne CBD, T'Gallant is perched on Victoria's Mornington Peninsula, a spit of land that juts out into Port Philip Bay. The relatively cool climate and encroaching housing development makes this an interesting place in which to grow grapes. Kathleen Quealy and Kevin McCarthy make a range of wines that include Chardonnay, Pinot Noir and their hallmark grape, Pinot Gris. In fact, they make two examples of Pinot Gris and two of Pinot Grigio, highlighting the difference between French and Italian methods of treating the grape, as well as a botrytised dessert version. The staff on hand at the cellar door are more than happy to educate visitors about the grapes and wines, which, incidentally, have some of the funkiest packaging in the business. There's also a laidback Italian-style trattoria ($) on site.

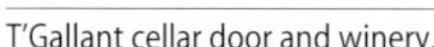
T'Gallant cellar door and winery.

## Nagambie Lakes

The Nagambie Lakes region of central Victoria lies around 120 km north of Melbourne and is a premium viticultural area. Once known as Goulburn, it is one of the great heartlands of classic Aussie wine and boasts some of the world's oldest productive vines (some are nearly 140 years old). The Marsanne and Shiraz here are among Australia's more old-fashioned wines and, as such, regularly surprise and delight Europeans with prejudices about how Australian wines taste.

WINERY NAGAMBIE

## Tahbilk

Nagambie
T +61 (0)3-5794 2555
www.tahbilk.com.au
Cellar door Mon-Fri 0900-1700; Sat, Sun and public hols 1000-1700.
Wetlands & Wildlife Reserve Mon-Fri 1100-1600; Sat, Sun and public hols 1030-1630.
Cruises Sat and Sun 1300 and 1430.
AUS$5 (accompanied children free).
Cruise and walk AUS$10.

One of Australia's most historic wineries, Tahbilk is laid out over 1214 ha of rich river flats. In 1860, a group of Melbourne businessmen formed a company, with the grand aim of planting a million vines around the Goulburn River. (This achievement is yet to be realized, with about 360,000 vines currently planted.) The site chosen was called 'tabilk-tabilk', meaning 'place of many waterholes', by local Aboriginals. The winery's speciality is the white varieties of the Rhône valley – Viognier, Marsanne and Roussanne – but the vineyards also include more conventional varieties such as Semillon, Cabernet Franc and Riesling. Visitors can make the most of the on-site café, where simple meals are served ($) or explore the estate's **Wetlands & Wildlife Reserve** on foot or by boat, and marvel at native species of reptiles, insects, birds and mammals.

Tahbilk cellar from 1875 (above).
Tahbilk Wetlands & Wildlife Reserve (below).

## Yarra Valley

This pretty, hilly and (for Australia) surprisingly green area close to Melbourne was said to have reminded early Swiss settlers of home. More recently it has been the focus for a wide range of wine styles, led by Pinot Noir and Chardonnay but also including good Shiraz (Yarra Yering, Yering Station) and Cabernet/Merlot (Coldstream Hills). It's a great place to visit for a bucolic afternoon away from the increasingly bustling city of Melbourne.

HOTEL — YERING

### Chateau Yering Historic House Hotel

Melba Highway, Yering
T 1-800 237 333 (toll free)
T + 61 (0)3-9237 3333.
www.chateauyering.com.au
$$$

This beautiful homestead was built in 1854, nine years after Victoria's first wine grapes were harvested from vineyards here. Today, it is an impeccable Relais & Chateau hotel, packed with Australian antiques. Enjoy a wine tasting laid on by the hotel before eating in one of the restaurants and heading off to sleep in a four-poster bed.

WINERY — DIXONS CREEK

### De Bortoli

Pinnacle Lane, Dixons Creek
T +61 (0)3-5965 2271
www.debortoli.com.au
Cellar door daily 1000-1700. Tours daily 1100 and 1500 (weather and vintage permitting). Restaurant daily from 1200; also Sat from 1900 (bookings recommended).

De Bortoli's Victorian operation (the company also owns wineries and vineyards in NSW) enjoys a worldwide reputation. You can opt to just turn up and taste the range of reds, rosés and whites, of course, but there's far more on offer. For instance, you could attend the **Yarra Valley Wine School**, held on the first Saturday of every month. If you do, you'll visit a couple of the winery's premium vineyards, then enjoy a meal matched with wines from the de Bortoli cellars and a visit to the winery itself. Discussions on tasting techniques, food-and-wine matching, cellaring and viticulture are woven into the day's activities. If you'd rather just enjoy a good meal with a bottle of wine, the winery's restaurant ($$) has won awards for its northern Italian cuisine. Alternatively, you could visit the cheese room, where cheeses from Australia and further afield are matured and sold.

WINERY — COLDSTREAM

### Domaine Chandon-Green Point

Maroondah Hwy, Coldstream
T +61 (0)3-9738 9200
www.chandon.com.au
Daily 1030-1630. Tours daily 1100, 1300 and 1500.

In the mid-1980s, Moët et Chandon invested in land in Victoria's Yarra Valley. Under the guidance of head winemaker Dr Tony Jordan, Domaine Chandon at Green Point has become one of the most respected producers of sparkling wines in Australia. The Domaine's 44 ha of vineyards produce Chardonnay, Pinot Noir, Pinot Meunier and Shiraz; the sparklies range in style from the bone-dry ZD (zero dosage) to a pretty pink rosé and a botrytised Extra-Riche. There are also vintage wines and a sparkling Shiraz. The visitor centre, known as the **Green Point Room**, is set amid the vineyards and has spectacular views across the valley; it's a great place to taste the Domaine's wines, then settle down to a lunch platter ($$) based on local Yarra produce and a glass, or two, of fizz.



WINERY — YARRA GLEN

### TarraWarra

311 Healesville-Yarra Glen Rd, Yarra Glen
T +61 (0)3-5962 3311
www.tarrawarra.com.au
Daily 1100-1700.

They make some pretty nice wines at TarraWarra, but the big draw isn't just the tastings at the cellar door. There's also the delicious food served at the estate's wine bar ($): wintery lunches can be enjoyed by the cosy fireside indoors and the outdoor terrace is the perfect place from which to admire the views of the valley in summer. The real tourist magnet, however, is the **TarraWarra Museum of Art**, a stunning contemporary gallery, designed to display works of Australian art from the 1950s to the present day.

## Tasmania

The antithesis of what Europeans think of as typical sun-baked Australia, this glorious green island has been declared a World Heritage Wilderness zone. People come here to walk, climb, fish or tour around. Tasmania's climate is cooler and windier than on the mainland and, in recent years, it has done best with Pinot Noir, aromatic whites and, most particularly,sparkling wine which is undeniably the area's major strength. Cooking used, by contrast, to be a decidedly weak point, but the success of the wine industry and the growth in tourism have encouraged some first-class cooks to apply their skills to the high-quality raw ingredients. Grapes are grown on the north, east and southeast coasts of the island.

WINERY — CAMBRIDGE

### Meadowbank Winery

699 Richmond Rd, Cambridge
T +61 (0)3-6248 4484
www.meadowbankwines.com.au
Cellar Door and shop daily 1000-1700. Restaurant daily 1200-1500 (bookings recommended); snacks served until 1700. Standard tasting free; premium tasting AUS$5 (refundable on any wine purchase).

Meadowbank's vineyards were originally grazing pasture but, in 1974, the land was planted with some hobby vines. The wines they produced exceeded all expectations and, within a few short years, Meadowbank's reputation was made. Visitors to the winery can eat at its award-winning restaurant ($), where Victoria-born chef Simon West weaves magic from the very best of local ingredients. The winery also runs a programme of events, including classical and jazz concerts, as well as art exhibitions featuring work by artists from near and far.

WINERY — PIPERS BROOK

### Pipers Brook / Kreglinger

1216 Pipers Brook Rd (Hwy C818), Pipers Brook
T +61(0)3-6382 7527
www.kreglingerwineestates.com
Daily from 1000.

Of all Tasmania's wineries, Pipers Brook is probably the best known. You can visit the winery via a scenic drive from Launceston, which takes in the beautiful Tamar River Valley and views out over the ocean. Once there, make the most of a tasting at the cellar door or take a tour of the winery. There's a café too, where you can enjoy a simple meal ($). Also worth tasting here are the Kreglinger sparkling wines which are among Australia's best. Not far from Pipers Brook, but on the other side of the Tamar river, you could also stop off at its sister vineyard, **Ninth Island**, where the restaurant ($-$$), run by chef Daniel Alps, is one of the most highly regarded on the island.

Meadowbank Winery restaurant by Peter Whyte.

Memorably once described as the engine-room of Australian wine, this is where huge quantities of many of Australia's more affordable wines are made – although often with a little help from grapes grown in other states – as well as some of the smallest batches of cult-status red. The first vines were planted between 1838 and 1870 by men whose names all live on today. Among these pioneers were John Reynell of Chateau Reynella in McLaren Vale (founded in 1838-40); Dr Christopher Rawson Penfold (1844); William Jacob of Jacob's Creek (1847); JE Seppelt (1850); Samuel Smith of Hill-Smith/Yalumba (1863); and Johann Christian Henschke (1868). As these names suggest, the early winemakers were a mixture of English colonists and German religious dissidents from Silesia. This last group mostly settled in the Barossa Valley, where their influence can still be felt to this day.

## Adelaide

Adelaidians won't like to hear this but their state capital doesn't really bear comparison with its southeastern neighbours, Sydney, Melbourne and Brisbane. All three of these have a raciness and a vibrancy that Adelaide lacks. However, it has more restaurants per head of population than any other city in the country and most of them are good and fairly priced. Also of note here is the **Central Market**, which brings together an extraordinary array of food, and the **National Wine Centre**, which offers a good insight into Australian wine and its history.

RESTAURANT ADELAIDE

### Grange

Hilton Adelaide, 233 Victoria Sq
T +61 (0)8-8217 2000
www.hilton.com/en/hi/hotels/dining
Wed and Thu 1830-2230; Fri and Sat 1830-2300.
$$-$$$

The multi-award-winning Grange (located in Adelaide's **Hilton Hotel**) has long been regarded as one of Australia's very best restaurants, thanks to the innovative approach of its chef, Cheong Liew. Liew, one of the first to mix French and Asian techniques and ingredients, was also one of the first to describe his culinary style as 'East meets West'. The wine list features a representative selection of South Australia's best bottles.

ATTRACTION ADELAIDE

### National Wine Centre

Botanic and Hackney roads, Adelaide 5000
T +61 (0)8- 8222 9444
www.wineaustralia.com.au
Daily 1000-1800.

Opened with great fanfares as a showcase for the Australian wine industry, this winner of several architectural awards attracted far fewer visitors than was projected and briefly seemed doomed to close. Fortunately it was handed over to the University and still offers a great experience for anyone interested in New or Old World wine. Among the exhibits are holograms of Australian vinous gurus and a working winery and vineyard that leads directly into the Botanic Gardens. The centre also offers wine courses and has a pleasant on-site café-restaurant.

## Adelaide Hills

By far the most chic of South Australia's wine regions, this area to the north of the city is where many of Adelaide's better-heeled inhabitants have built houses and planted hobby vineyards. But beautiful views and easy commuting are not the only reasons to be up here. The region has a long history of really top class winemaking from people like Brian Croser of Petaluma, whose Piccadilly Valley Chardonnay is one of the country's best.

## Tasting notes

### The story of Grange

Until the early 1980s, in the days when Australian wine was rarely seen overseas, reds, whatever the grape from which they were made, were often labelled as 'claret' or 'Burgundy' (with the former name being used for more tannic examples). One exception to this rule was Penfolds Grange, which was originally called Grange 'Hermitage'. This was, of course, as geographically inaccurate as the other European terms but it made more sense stylistically because Grange was at least made from the same grape variety, the Shiraz or, as it is known in France, the Syrah.

Penfolds Grange Hermitage was invented in 1951 by a very clever winemaker called Max Schubert. At the end of a trip to Spain and Portugal, where he was supposed to learn about sherry and port production (fortified wines being the focus of Australian attention for wine makers and drinkers), Schubert made an unscheduled stop in Bordeaux where he watched the undistinguished 1950 vintage being made. He took careful notes and resolved to replicate what he had seen once he was back in Australia. The wine he made was, however, very different from Bordeaux, and not only because of the difference in the climate and soil of the two regions. In Bordeaux the wine was made from Cabernet Sauvignon and Merlot; in Australia, Schubert opted for the more readily available Shiraz. In France, he'd seen lots of new barrels being used, so again he did the same, but went for American oak rather than French. The Bordeaux came from small sets of neighbouring vineyards; his grapes were sourced from a wide range of regions. When the first vintage was released it was greeted with derision in Australia and Schubert was ordered to halt production. But he continued in secret and, a few years later, the quality of the wines was recognized. Today, Grange is one of the most highly prized and priced wines in the world. It is quite unlike any other wine in its combination of peppery, spicy, plumy, cedary flavours. It has a richness that is somehow reminiscent of great Christmas pudding, but without a hint of sweetness.

RESTAURANT BRIDGEWATER

### Bridgewater Mill Restaurant

Mt Barker Rd, Bridgewater
T +61 (0)8-8339 9200/9222
www.bridgewatermill.com.au
Cellar door daily 1000-1700. Restaurant Thu-Mon 1200-1430, dinner by appointment.
$-$$

The pretty, historic Bridgewater Mill (built in 1860) nestles in the heart of the Adelaide Hills and serves as both a tasting room for wines from Petaluma, Croser, Bridgewater Mill and Tim Knappstein and as home to the award-winning Bridgewater Mill restaurant.

All the current releases of the wines can be sampled in the tasting room, along with a frequently changing list of cellar door exclusives that might feature magnums or older vintages. Visits to the sparkling wine cellars can be arranged by appointment.

Chef Le Lu Thai's cuisine is designed to match the bottles on the restaurant's list to perfection, and staff are trained to advise on the best matches between food and wine.

WINERY MAGILL

### Penfolds Magill Estate

78 Penfold Rd, Magill
T +61 (0)8-8301 5551
www.penfolds.com.au
Daily 1030-1630. Restaurant Tue-Sat for dinner.
Tastings and tours AUS$15-AUS$150

Penfolds' Magill Estate lies just 15 minutes' drive from the centre of Adelaide. The winery was established in 1845 by Dr Christopher Rawson Penfold, making it one of Australia's oldest wine estates. In 1951, winemaker Max Schubert began experimenting with a Shiraz-based wine called Grange Hermitage that went on to become Australia's most iconic wine (see box above).

View over the vineyards at Shaw & Smith in the Adelaide Hills.

Visitors to the Magill cellars can choose to taste a flight of Penfolds' premium wines, including Grange, by appointment, or they can sample some of the estate's other wines simply by turning up at the cellar door. There are guided tours of the original Penfold family home, Grange Cottage, on offer as well as visits to the working winery.

The **Magill Estate Restaurant** ($$-$$$) is one of South Australia's top restaurants and has glorious views out over the estate's vineyards. The menu is inspired by French and Italian cuisines, while the wine list features a wide selection of Penfolds' wines.

WINERY BALHANNAH

## Shaw & Smith

Lot 4, Jones Rd, Balhannah
T +61 (0)8-8398 0500
www.shawandsmith.com
Sat and Sun 1100-1600.

Shaw & Smith's contemporary winery, which was built in time for the 2000 vintage, is as sleek and elegant as the wines produced there. The winery doesn't produce a vast array of styles; the emphasis is on Shiraz, Chardonnay and Sauvignon Blanc, although there's a Merlot, a Pinot and a Riesling in the range as well. Wines can be bought by the flight or by the bottle, and you can sample them alongside a plate of locally produced cheeses. The view from the terrace over the Mount Lofty Ranges is stunning.

## Barossa

For many people in Australia and overseas the words 'Barossa' and 'Shiraz' are almost synonymous. And it's true that there is a rich intensity of flavour that the warm days and cool nights here give to this grape that is found nowhere else. There are great examples of Grenache too and, as you climb into the cooler hills of the Eden Valley, you find Cabernet Sauvignon and Riesling. For a visitor, the enduring impact that German settlers have had on Barossa is particularly striking. A roll call of modern winemakers reveals names like Henschke, Lehmann, Gramp and Seppelt, descendants of the Lutherans who fled persecution in Europe. Even today, there are Lutheran schools and churches, and German bakeries in the area.

Jacob's Creek.

WINERY ROWLAND FLAT

## Jacob's Creek

Barossa Valley Way, Rowland Flat
T + 61 (0)8-8521 3000
www.jacobscreek.com
Visitor centre daily 1000-1700.
Restaurant daily 1130-1430.

When German immigrant Johann Gramp planted his vines on the banks of Jacob's Creek in 1847, he can hardly have imagined that those vineyards – and the wines named after them – would become one of the most recognized brand names in the 21st-century world of wine. Now there's an award-winning state-of-the-art visitors' centre, where you can taste through the range (including the trophy-winning Reserves) or take a look at the interactive display that tells the Jacob's Creek story in full. It is also possible to book a special appointment to taste wines from the VIP cellar. Afterwards, repair to the on-site restaurant ($-$$), where you can wash down contemporary Australian dishes with Jacob's Creek wines. There's even a native animal enclosure where the kids can get a close-up look at some of Australia's famous fauna.

SHOP BAROSSA

## Maggie Beer's Farm Shop

Pheasant Farm Rd, off Seppeltsfield and Samuel Rds
T +61 (0)8-8562 4477
www.maggiebeer.com.au
Daily 1030-1700. Cooking demos 1400.

Foodies in Australia have long revered culinary icon Maggie Beer, who has run the gamut of the culinary industry, from owning restaurants to writing cookbooks. These days she's semi-retired, but still takes time out to run verjus-making workshops from her Barossa-based food shop. Even if you don't have the time to take a class, you can still stop by for a cup of coffee and a bite to eat. It's a fair bet, however, that you won't be able to walk out of the place without succumbing to the temptation to buy some of the mouthwatering local produce, including Maggie's renowned quince paste (delicious with cheese).

WINERY TANUNDA

### Peter Lehmann

Para Rd, Tanunda
T +61 (0)8-8563 2100
Mon-Fri 0930-1700; Sat, Sun and public hols 1030-1630.

One of the most consistent Australian producers, Peter Lehmann makes wines for all price points, from entry level right up to his iconic Stonewell and Eight Songs Shiraz. You can taste them all at the winery's stone-built cellar door building, set among green lawns and shady gum trees – or book yourself in for a private VIP session, where the focus will be on the premium end of the range. Take your own picnic along to enjoy after the tasting, or buy a platter of locally produced charcuterie, cheeses and pickles from the cellar door staff.

WINERY TANUNDA

### Rockford Wines

Krondorf Rd, Tanunda
T +61 (0)8-8563 2720
www.rockfordwines.com.au
Daily 1100-1700, except for public holidays.

Rocky Callaghan is one of the Barossa's real characters and his Rockford Wines operation is so small-scale and hands-on that there's a good chance that the man himself will be pouring tasting samples from behind his cellar's wooden counter (he's the one who looks like the Old Man of the Sea). Even if you don't get a chance to chat with Rocky himself, there's much to admire about his back-to-basics, purist's approach to winemaking, from the winery's antique, but still-used equipment to the characterful wines it produces.

WINERY ANGASTON

### Yalumba

Eden Valley Rd, Angaston
T +61 (0)8 8561 3200
www.yalumba.com
Daily 1000-1700.

Yalumba is one of the few remaining wineries in the Barossa still to be owned by the family that planted its original vineyards back in the 19th century. These days its interests have expanded well beyond the original 30-acre plot, but visitors can still taste wines from the company's ranges in one of the original stone buildings. Along with big brands, such as Oxford Landing, Yalumba makes a range of hand-crafted wines and is well known for its work with the Viognier grape, as well as some stunning old-vine Shiraz. It's also gaining a reputation for innovation, with its nursery working hard to introduce some unusual varieties to the Barossa. Visitors to the cellar door can enjoy the fruits of their labours well before outsiders get a chance to taste the wines themselves.

## Clare Valley

Clare is named after a region in Ireland that it doesn't in the least resemble. The tan-coloured rolling hills of this bucolic warm valley manage to achieve the seemingly impossible: to produce fine dry wine from the Riesling – a grape associated with cool regions – and rich reds from the Shiraz.

HOTEL SEVENHILL

### Thorn Park

College Road, Sevenhill
T +61 (0)8-8843 4304
www.thornpark.com.au
$$

An impeccably maintained 145-year-old homestead in the heart of the Clare Valley, with 20 ha of hills and gums, Thorn Park offers bed and breakfast and brilliant home cooking, as well as great local wines, in case you haven't brought any back from your own explorations.

## McLaren Vale

This old, yet up-and-coming region is close to the sea and to the city of Adelaide. If you visit in spring, you will be treated to a spectacular view of what looks like lavender punctuating the vineyards that stand between you and the ocean. Sadly, the spectacular crop, known as Blueweed, Patterson's Curse and Salvation Jane, is actually an invasive weed that was introduced as an ornamental plant in the 1880s. McLaren wines are (somewhat) lighter in style than those of Barossa but styles vary within the region.

WINERY MACLAREN VALE

### Chapel Hill

Corner Chapel Hill and Chaffey's Rd, McLaren Vale
T +61 (0)8-8323 8429
www.chapelhillwine.com.au
Daily 1200-1700.

Chapel Hill's cellar door is set within the 19th-century stone church from which the winery derives its name. There you can sample the estate's production: whites, pinks, reds and fortifieds. If you're feeling self-indulgent, you can book yourself in for a stay at the estate's beautifully designed guesthouse ($ per night; minimum three nights) or take a cookery course as part of a gourmet retreat under the watchful eye of former restaurateur, Pip Forrester. She's the woman behind the region's renowned Salopian Inn and is the estate's chef. The professionally equipped kitchen, where lessons are held, is as slick and modern as the rest of the estate's facilities, but the food cooked is good and honest, firmly rooted in the wonderful produce of the Fleurieu Peninsula.

D'Arenberg red wines.

WINERY — MCLAREN VALE

## Coriole Winery

PO Box 9, McLaren Vale
T +61 8 8323 8305
www.coriole.com
Mon-Fri 1000-1700; Sat, Sun and public hols 1100-1700. Lunch available Sat and Sun.

Coriole has made a name for itself as one of the prime movers in terms of introducing Italian varietals to the Aussie vineyards. In addition to the usual line up of Australianized French varietals (including, unusually, a Chenin), you can taste Sangiovese, Barbera and Nebbiolo. Coriole is currently working on a Fiano, which isn't yet in commercial production but may well be within the next year or two. As well as wine, Coriole is renowned for its olive oils, olives, vinegars and cheeses. You can get a chance to sample them all by stopping in on a Saturday or Sunday for a relaxed lunch in the courtyard ($-$$) or under the shade of the spreading branches of a Moreton Bay tree.

WINERY — MCLAREN VALE

## D'Arenberg

Osborn Rd, McLaren Vale
T +61 (08)-8323 8206
www.darenberg.com.au
Cellar door daily 1000-1700

D'Arenberg is one of the most significant wineries in McLaren Vale. In 1912 Joseph Osborn, a teetotaller and director of Thomas Hardy and Sons, bought the well-established Milton Vineyards. The winery was passed on to his son, Francis Ernest ('Frank'), then to his grandson, Francis d'Arenberg, universally known as 'D'Arry'. D'Arenberg is still a family-run winery, with D'Arry's son Chester in charge of winemaking these days. Chester oversees production of an eclectic range of wines, from Sauvignon Blanc to Roussanne whites, and reds based on Rhône Valley grapes, as well as Cabernet and Tempranillo. There's also a couple of fortifieds you could try, as well as a sublimely sticky late-harvest Riesling.

While you're visiting d'Arenberg, make sure you leave time for a meal at **D'Arry's Verandah** ($), the estate restaurant. It not only offers great views out over the Fleurieu Peninsula, but the food's pretty good too.

RESTAURANT — PORT WILLUNGA

## Star of Greece

The Esplanade, Port Willunga 5173
T+61 (0)8-8557 7420
Wed-Sun 1200-1500 (daily in summer),
Fri-Sat 1800-2100 (daily in summer)
$$

If you want to find a McLaren Vale – or a Clare, Adelaide Hills or Barossa – winemaker, one place to go looking for them is this converted beach café overlooking the ocean at Port Willunga. The food here is simply but brilliantly cooked, and served with some terrific local wines. The only problem is that a time warp seems to take over, making for long lunches that seem to merge seemlessly into dinner.

Dishes at the Star of Greece.

# Western Australia



**A country apart in many ways, Western Australia often seems to be closer spiritually to Singapore and the UK than to the rest of Australia. Its wine industry has developed separately and much of the wine is either drunk locally or shipped overseas rather than being sold elsewhere in Australia. One consequence of this, coupled with the smaller scale of many of the wineries, is that prices tend to be higher here. Often, this is reflected in the quality in the bottle; but not always. The earliest vineyards were planted close to Perth in the Swan Valley but, since the early 1980s, the focus has moved south, initially to Margaret River and then to Great Southern.**

## Perth

Perth has good restaurants and wine bars but not to the overall standard of Adelaide, Melbourne or Sydney. Some far better fare is on offer nearby in Fremantle.

WINE BAR HIGHGATE

### Must Wine Bar

519 Beaufort St, Highgate
T +61 (0)8-9328 8255
www.must.com.au
Daily 1200-0000
$-$$

When visiting Perth, the Must Wine Bar is a must-visit. The wine list features 500 bins, chosen from some of the very best bottles made in Australia and around the world. Forty of these are available by the glass, encouraging diners to explore some of the wine world's least trodden paths. The food is described by executive chef Russell Blaikie as "food you'd expect to see in the provincial French housewife's kitchen"; the ever-changing menu might feature charcuterie prepared in the restaurant, freshly shucked oysters, hearty stews in winter and lighter salads and pastas in summer.

## Margaret River

If Australia has a region that competes with Bordeaux, it has to be Margaret River. Despite the fact that the Mediterranean climate here is quite different to that of the Medoc or St-Émilion, this region of Western Australia is similarly maritime, making for great surfing and Cabernet country. The area is unusual in having had its vinous destiny mapped out in advance by an agricultural and viticultural scientist called Dr John Gladstones. The early winemakers were often doctors who initially planted grapes as a hobby, but the success of wineries like Cullens, Moss Wood, Vasse Felix and Cape Mentelle soon caught the attention of outsiders, causing a recent investment boom, followed by something of a bust. Tourism is highly developed here, thanks to its popularity with Perth weekenders.

WINERY COWARAMUP

### Cullen Wines

Cullen Caves Rd, Cowaramup
T +61 (0)8-9755 5277
www.cullenwines.com.au
Cellar Door and restaurant daily 1000-1600.

The premise that Margaret River was ideal for viticulture was first tested in Wilyabrup in 1966, when Diana and Kevin Cullen planted a trial acre of vines. The encouraging results led to a further 18 acres of their sheep and cattle farm being turned over to viticulture in 1971. Cullen Wines is still owned by the Cullen family but has moved on from its humble origins to become one of the most acclaimed wineries in Australia. The biodynamically grown grapes are sourced exclusively from the Cullen Estate and Mangan vineyards, and the flagship wines of the Cullen stable are the Sauvignon Blanc or Semillon, Chardonnay Mangan and Diana Madeline Cabernet Sauvignon or Merlot.

Margaret River looks nothing like Bordeaux or Burgundy, but it's the one place in Australia that makes wines that could be mistaken for examples from both those regions.

Tasting spoons at Cullen Estate.

The food served in the restaurant ($$) overlooking the vineyard is prepared using fresh, biodynamic and organic produce sourced from the estate's own garden and a number of local producers.

WINERY MARAGARET RIVER

## Leeuwin Estate Winery

Stevens Rd, Margaret River
T +61 (0)8-9759 0000
www.leeuwinestate.com.au
Daily 1000-1630. Restaurant also Sat for dinner. Tours daily 1100, 1200 and 1500.

I visited Leeuwin Estate on my first trip to Australia, way back in 1985. At the time it stood out from almost every other winery in the country. There was a sense of style and ambition that came as an instant reminder of some of the things I had seen in California. And that was no accident. In 1972, following an extensive search for the area most suited to producing the best varietal wines in Australia, legendary American winemaker Robert Mondavi identified the future site of the Leeuwin vineyard in the Margaret River. The estate evolved under the direction of Denis and Tricia Horgan, with Mondavi for a long time acting as consultant. Leeuwin

Leeuwin Estate tasting bar display.

Estate was a pioneer in producing a Chardonnay good enough to compete with the best of Burgundy. The Art Series, of which that Chardonnay is part, is still at the top of Australia's game. Lesser – but still

### West is best

Most visitors to Western Australia arrive in the modern, spacious city of Perth, whose Visitor Centre (Forrest Place, T 1-300-361 351, www.westernaustralia.net) is the main VIC for the state. The city centre is somewhat soulless but the **Art Gallery of Western Australia** (T+61 (0)8-9492 6600, www.artgallery.wa .gov.au) and the **Western Australian Museum** (T+61 (0)8-9427 2700, www.museum.wa.gov.au) in the Cultural Centre are both worth a look. **Kings Park** is a large area of bush, bordered by the excellent **Botanic Gardens** (T9480 3600, www.kpbg.wa.gov.au) and offering great views of the city centre. Perth's most attractive suburb is **Cottesloe**, where blindingly white sand slopes into the warm water of the Indian Ocean, overlooked by informal cafés. Further afield is lively **Fremantle**, characterized by 19th-century buildings and a strong community of immigrants and artists. Italian cafés line the 'cappuccino strip' along South Terrace and the Fishing Boat Harbour is a hub of eating and entertainment.

**Rottnest Island** (www.rottnest.wa.gov.au), or 'Rotto', was once a penal settlement but is now Perth's playground. Lying just 20 km west of the city, its entire coast is one long stretch of sandy bays and clear aquamarine water, with offshore reefs and wrecks full of fish and corals. The island's most famous resident is the quokka, a small wallaby only 30 cm high.

Beyond Perth, the majority of visitors head for the state's southwest corner, where the Indian Ocean laps snowy surf beaches, with a hinterland of forest and wine regions. Between **Cape Naturaliste** and **Cape Leeuwin** you can explore caves, dive reefs and wrecks, watch humpback and southern right whales or swim with dolphins. The Cape-to- Cape Track follows the coastline for 140 km and is a superb way to see the scenery. The town of **Margaret River** is a convenient base for exploring the Capes region and is particularly famous for its wine (page 306) and surf. It also acts as a focus for local artists, with restaurants and galleries to equal any in the country.

East of Cape Leeuwin, the coast is weathered into islands and bays of fine, clean sand. Some of the most beautiful beaches in the country are in the **Cape Le Grand National Park**, although the water is very cold. The historic town of **Albany** is a whale-watching centre – contact **Silver Star** (T +61 (0)4-2893 6711, www.whales.com.au) for trips – while, inland, are the dramatic peaks of the **Stirling Range National Park**.

recommendable – wines come under the Prelude Vineyards and Siblings labels.

Other reasons to visit the estate include the award-winning **Leeuwin Restaurant** ($$), the annual vineyard concerts (past performers include Ray Charles, Dame Kiri Te Kanawa, KD Lang and Tom Jones) and the art gallery, which contains a stunning collection of works by Australia's most iconic artists, all of which have been commissioned for the Art Series labels.



RESTAURANT MARGARET RIVER

### Wino's

85 Bussell Hwy, Margaret River
T +61 (0)8-9758 7155
Mon-Sat 1200-2400; Sun 1200-2200.
$$

If you've decided to eat in town rather than at one of Margaret River's winery restaurants, you should make a beeline for Wino's. Despite the slightly naff name, there's a buzz about the place. It's generated, in part, by the simple, unfussy food. Given its location, it's hardly surprising to discover that there's a great international and Australian wine list; what's unusual, however, is the fact that many of the wines are offered by the mini carafe, making it easy to sample a range of wines over the course of a relaxed, laidback evening.

## Great Southern

The stunning Great Southern region has a sweeping coastline, whale-watching opportunities galore and a colourful carpet of wildflowers throughout its mild spring season – no wonder it's such a tourist draw. If Margaret River has become famous for its Bordeaux-style reds and whites and its Chardonnays, Great Southern has excelled with Shiraz (at Plantagenet), Pinot Noir (Salitage) and Riesling (Howard Park). One word of warning, though, for anyone driving here from Margaret River – and there aren't many other options – do respect the speed limits on the temptingly open roads. If the speed cops don't get you, there's a strong risk that a kangaroo will. By jumping out in front of you and coming through your windscreen.

WINERY MOUNT BARKER

### Plantagenet Wines

Lot 45, Albany Hwy, Mount Barker
T +61 (0)8-9851 3111
www.plantagenetwines.com
Daily 0900-1700.

Plantagenet Wines was the first winery in the region and planted its vineyards in the late 1960s. Some 30 years after its first vintage in 1974, it has received much critical acclaim, making it one of West Australia's most respected wineries. The relatively mild climate allows Plantagenet's winemakers to focus on cool-climate styles, so visitors to the cellar door can taste Riesling, Pinot Noir and Chenin as well as Cabernet Franc and Shiraz.

WINERY PEMBERTON

### Salitage Winery Estate

Vasse Hwy, Pemberton
T +61 (0)8-9776 1195
www.salitage.com.au
Visits by appointment only.

Salitage is based in the spectacular viticultural region of Pemberton, in the southwest of Western Australia, one of Australia's top cool-climate regions. The owners, John and Jenny Horgan, first made wine in Margaret River, as pioneers of the region back in the 1970s (John is brother to Denis Horgan, owner of Leeuwin), but moved to Pemberton a few years later to found Salitage, one of the state's most important wineries. The Horgans have experience outside Australia: they've got shares in the Côte d'Or's Domaine de la Pousse d'Or, and John worked and studied in California under Robert Mondavi. All of this international experience feeds back into their winemaking at Salitage, where the focus is on elegance and poise.

Visitors to the winery can stay at the **Salitage Suites** ($$-$$$), a luxury retreat situated in a secluded forest setting on the Salitage river.

Al fresco dining at Leeuwin's Estate.

# Best producers

**Canberra**
Clonakilla » *page 294.*

**Hunter Valley**
Brokenwood
Lakes Folly
McWilliams Mount Pleasant (Semillon, Shiraz)
Tyrrell's » *page 291.*

**Mudgee**
Huntington Estate
Lowe Family (Semillon, Zinfandel)

**Tumbarumba**
Hungerford Hill

**Adelaide Hills**
Ashton Hills
Chain of Ponds
Croser (sparkling)
Leland Estate (Sauvignon Blanc)
Longview
Petaluma
Shaw & Smith » *page 303.*

**Adelaide Plains**
Primo Estate (sparkling red and Moda Amerone)

**Barossa**
Burge, Grant (Meshach)
Domain Day
Duval, John
Henschke
Jones, Trevor
Kaesler
Langmeil
Lehmann, Peter » *page 304.*
Buring, Leo (Riesling)
Melton, Charles
Penfolds (top reds and Yattarna Chardonnay) » *page 302*
Rockford (sparkling red) » *page 304.*
Torbreck
Turkey Flat
Two Hands
Yalumba » *page 304.*

**Clare**
Adams, Tim
Grosset
Barry, Jim (Armagh, McCrae Wood)
Kilikanoon (Riesling, Shiraz)
Knappstein (Riesling)
Leasingham (Riesling, Shiraz)
Mount Horrocks
O'Leary Walker
Paulett
Pikes
Stringy Brae
Taylor's
Wendouree

**Coonawarra**
Majella
Orlando (Jacaranda Ridge, Steingarten)
Wynns (John Riddoch, Michael Shiraz)

**Eden Valley**
Heggies Vineyard
Irvine
Pewsey Vale

**McLaren Vale**
Battle of Bosworth
Coriole (Sangiovese-Shiraz) » *page 305.*
D'Arenberg » *page 305.*
Merrill, Geoff
Pirramimma
Wirra Wirra

**South Australia**
Wolf Blass (Platinum, Gold, Grey, Black Label)

**Tasmania**
Clover Hill
Dalrymple
Freycinet
Jansz
Lubiana, Stefano

**Beechworth**
Giaconda

**Geelong**
Bannockburn
By Farr
Scotchmans Hill
Shadowfax

**Gippsland**
Bass Phillip

**Glenrowan**
Baileys of Glenrowan
Delatite (Riesling)

**Grampians**
Best's
Seppelt (Sparkling, Drumbog Riesling, St Peters Shiraz)

**Henty**
Crawford River (Riesling)

**Milawa**
Brown Brothers (top wines, including Patricia) » *page 297.*

**Mornington**
Dromana Estate
Paringa Estate
Stonier
T'Gallant (Pinot Grigio, Unwooded Chardonnay)

**Nagambie Lakes**
Tahbilk » *page 298.*

**Pyrenees**
Dalwhinnie

**Rutherglen**
All Saints
Campbells
Chambers Rosewood
Morris (Liqueur Muscat and Muscadelle) » *page 297.*
Stanton & Killeen

**Yarra Valley**
Coldstream Hills
De Bortoli (top wines)
Diamond Valley (Pinot Noir)
Domaine Chandon
Dominique Portet
Fgiant Steps
Mount Mary (Pinot Noir and Cabernets)
Seville Estate
Tarrawarra » *page 300.*
Yarra Yering
Yering Station

**Denmark**
Howard Park

**Frankland River**
Alkoomi
Ferngrove

**Margaret River**
Ashbrook Estate
Brookland Valley
Cape Mentelle
Capel Vale
Cullen » *page 306.*
Devil's Lair
Leeuwin » *page 307.*
Pierro
Stella Bella
Suckfizzle
Vasse Felix
Wise

**Mount Barker**
Plantagenet » *page 308.*
Houghton (Jack Mann, Frankland Riesling)

# New Zealand

Brancott Fairhall Estate, Marlborough.

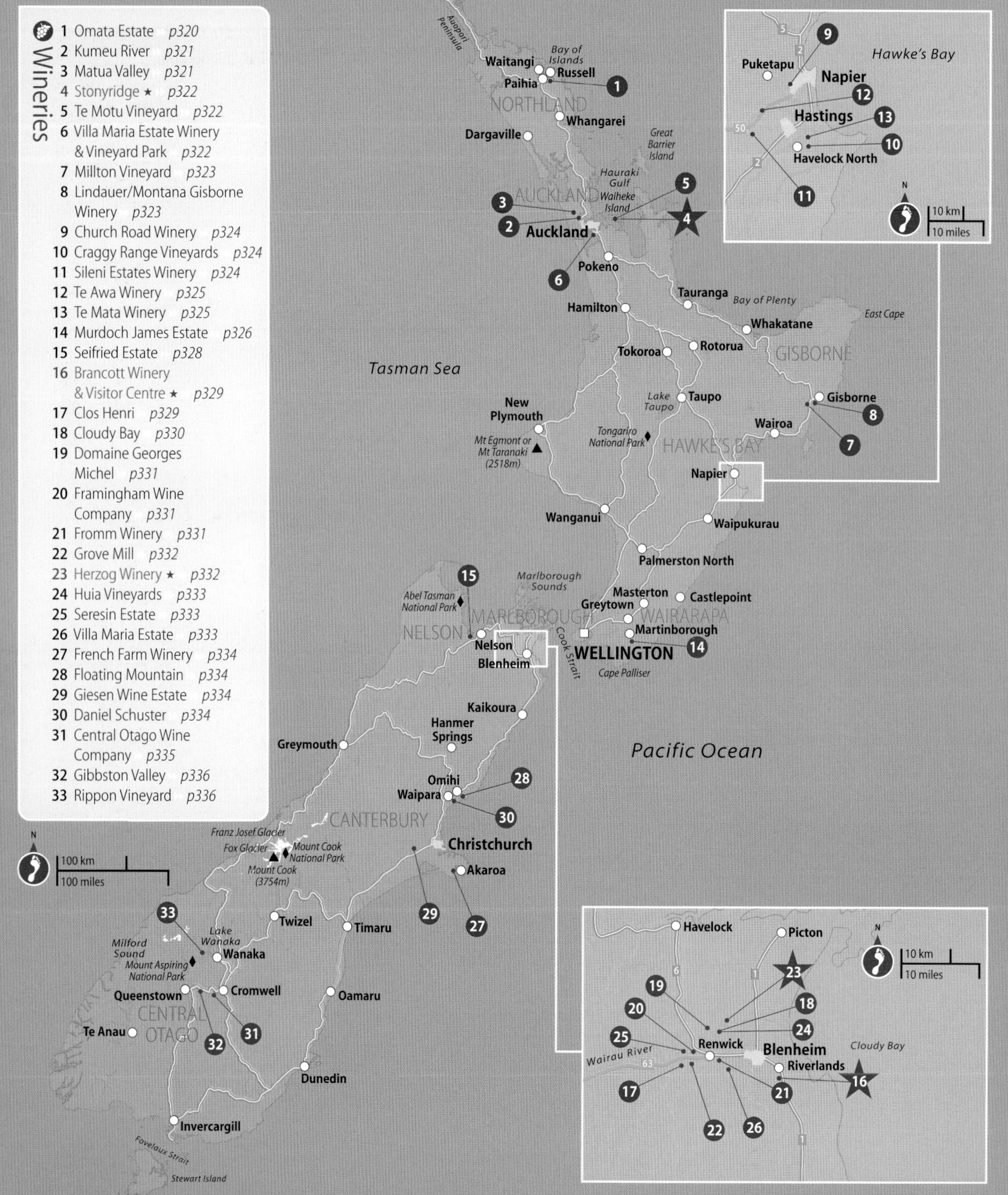

Wineries
1 Omata Estate p320
2 Kumeu River p321
3 Matua Valley p321
4 Stonyridge ★ p322
5 Te Motu Vineyard p322
6 Villa Maria Estate Winery & Vineyard Park p322
7 Millton Vineyard p323
8 Lindauer/Montana Gisborne Winery p323
9 Church Road Winery p324
10 Craggy Range Vineyards p324
11 Sileni Estates Winery p324
12 Te Awa Winery p325
13 Te Mata Winery p325
14 Murdoch James Estate p326
15 Seifried Estate p328
16 Brancott Winery & Visitor Centre ★ p329
17 Clos Henri p329
18 Cloudy Bay p330
19 Domaine Georges Michel p331
20 Framingham Wine Company p331
21 Fromm Winery p331
22 Grove Mill p332
23 Herzog Winery ★ p332
24 Huia Vineyards p333
25 Seresin Estate p333
26 Villa Maria Estate p333
27 French Farm Winery p334
28 Floating Mountain p334
29 Giesen Wine Estate p334
30 Daniel Schuster p334
31 Central Otago Wine Company p335
32 Gibbston Valley p336
33 Rippon Vineyard p336
Auopori Peninsula
Bay of Islands
Waitangi
Russell
Paihia
NORTHLAND
Whangarei
Dargaville
Great Barrier Island
Hauraki Gulf
Waiheke Island
AUCKLAND
Auckland
Pokeno
Tauranga
Bay of Plenty
Hamilton
Whakatane
East Cape
Tokoroa
Rotorua
GISBORNE
Tasman Sea
Lake Taupo
Taupo
Gisborne
New Plymouth
Mt Egmont or Mt Taranaki (2518m)
Tongariro National Park
Wairoa
HAWKE'S BAY
Napier
Wanganui
Waipukurau
Palmerston North
Marlborough Sounds
Abel Tasman National Park
Masterton
Castlepoint
Greytown
WAIRARAPA
MARLBOROUGH
NELSON
Nelson
Blenheim
Martinborough
Cook Strait
WELLINGTON
Cape Palliser
Kaikoura
Hanmer Springs
Greymouth
Pacific Ocean
Omihi
Waipara
CANTERBURY
Franz Josef Glacier
Fox Glacier
Mount Cook National Park
Mount Cook (3754m)
Christchurch
Akaroa
100 km
100 miles
Twizel
Timaru
Lake Wanaka
Milford Sound
Wanaka
Mount Aspiring National Park
Queenstown
Cromwell
Oamaru
CENTRAL OTAGO
Te Anau
Dunedin
Invercargill
Foveaux Strait
Stewart Island
Hawke's Bay
Puketapu
Napier
Hastings
Havelock North
10 km
10 miles
Havelock
Picton
Renwick
Blenheim
Cloudy Bay
Riverlands
Wairau River

# Introduction

Not so very long ago, New Zealanders had smilingly to put up with jibes from foreigners who claimed to have visited their beautiful country but to have found it closed. Other outsiders joked about airline captains advising passengers landing at Auckland to "turn your watch back 10 years". Harsh though these comments were, they certainly had the smack of truth when it came to tourism, cuisine and wine. The laws to permit the serving of wine in restaurants were only passed as recently as the 1960s and, even in the early 1980s, many of New Zealand's chefs were still taking some of the world's best raw ingredients and subjecting them to the worst kind of old-fashioned cooking. Now, however, Auckland, Wellington, Christchurch and Queenstown have all taken on a decidedly cosmopolitan style that, like the New Zealand climate, brings together elements of the Mediterranean and northern Europe. New wineries, speciality food shops and great places to eat and stay seem to open daily. In the 1980s there were around 100 wineries in New Zealand; at the last count the figure was closer to 550, many of which produce wines from various areas and under several labels. For all the noise that's being created, however, this remains a small country. It is no longer true that the Californian giant E&J could fit the entire New Zealand vintage into one of its vats, but annual production is still less than a 15th of that of Australia. The individual estates make limited amounts of wine and experimental cuvées are often only available at the cellar door, so if you find a wine you enjoy, it is worth enquiring where you might find it at home, or quite possibly buying a few bottles and shipping them yourself.

# Travel essentials



## Planning a trip

**Auckland International Airport** (AKL, T +61 (0)9-275 0789, www.auckland-airport.co.nz), is a relatively small, modern and friendly gateway to the nation. From here, all the main cities and provincial towns can be reached easily by air or by road. There are regular flights from Auckland to Gisborne, Napier (for Hawke's Bay) and Wellington (for Wairarapa), and from Wellington on to Blenheim (for Marlborough), Christchurch (for Canterbury) and Queenstown (for Central Otago). Standard fares can be expensive but special deals are available, especially if you book in advance. The two main bus companies are **Intercity** (www.intercitycoach.co.nz) and **Newmans** (www.newmans coach.co.nz); there are also many local operators. Inter-island ferries run from Wellington to Picton (near Nelson and Marlborough).

Although it is entirely possible to negotiate the country by public transport, for sheer convenience you are advised to get your own set of wheels. Almost all the major hire companies are represented, with offices at airports as well as in cities and provincial towns. Distances between regions are significant but not huge, though travelling between them by road takes longer than you might expect. Central Otago is some 600 km from Marlborough, for example, and Hawke's Bay is nearly 400 km from Martinborough. It is therefore not realistic to try to take in two major regions in the same day. While many of Marlborough's wineries are close to each other, those of Central Otago are far more widely scattered.

And, of course, you'll want to enjoy some of New Zealand's other attractions while you're here: **Rotorua**, the thermal and volcanic capital of New Zealand, with geysers and bubbling mud, can be visited en route from Auckland to Gisborne or Hawke's Bay. From Rotorua, you could head south to **Lake Taupo**, New Zealand's largest lake, backed by the volcanoes of the **Tongariro National Park**, or northeast around the isolated **East Cape**. For most visitors, however, it is the South Island that offers the true essence of New Zealand. From Nelson and Blenheim, make a detour to **Kaikoura** for whale watching or to the **Marlborough Sounds** and the **Abel Tasman National Park** for coastal walks and activities. Further south, don't miss the Fox and Franz Josef **glaciers**, en route to Wanaka and Queenstown. These towns are the jumping-off points for explorations of incomparable **Milford Sound** and offer a dizzying array of outdoor pursuits.

For further information about visiting New Zealand, refer to the New Zealand Tourism Board's website, www.purenz.com, and to *Footprint New Zealand*. Once in the country, information is provided by numerous visitor information centres, nationally known as **I-Sites**.

**New Zealand country code** → +64. **IDD code** → 00.
**Internet ID** → .nz. **Emergencies** T111.

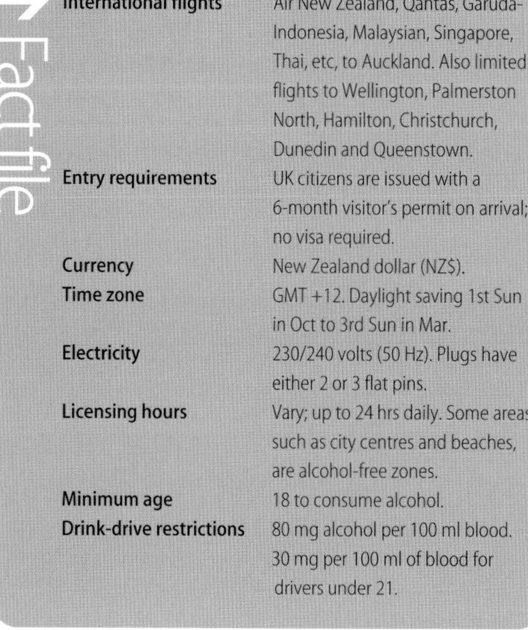

## → Fact file

| | |
|---|---|
| **International flights** | Air New Zealand, Qantas, Garuda-Indonesia, Malaysian, Singapore, Thai, etc, to Auckland. Also limited flights to Wellington, Palmerston North, Hamilton, Christchurch, Dunedin and Queenstown. |
| **Entry requirements** | UK citizens are issued with a 6-month visitor's permit on arrival; no visa required. |
| **Currency** | New Zealand dollar (NZ$). |
| **Time zone** | GMT +12. Daylight saving 1st Sun in Oct to 3rd Sun in Mar. |
| **Electricity** | 230/240 volts (50 Hz). Plugs have either 2 or 3 flat pins. |
| **Licensing hours** | Vary; up to 24 hrs daily. Some areas, such as city centres and beaches, are alcohol-free zones. |
| **Minimum age** | 18 to consume alcohol. |
| **Drink-drive restrictions** | 80 mg alcohol per 100 ml blood. 30 mg per 100 ml of blood for drivers under 21. |

The view of the Richmond Ranges from Cloudy Bay vineyard inspired the iconic label for Cloudy Bay wines by Kevin Judd ▸▸ *page 330*.

### When to visit

The New Zealand climate makes this a pleasant country to visit at any time. Harvest is generally in March and April, with varieties like Cabernet Sauvignon coming in last. Since most producers make wines from a number of varieties and many take in grapes from several regions, it is quite possible that their vintage will last for six weeks or longer. This is a great time to visit for anyone keen on seeing (and photographing) how wine is made but, as elsewhere, not the best time to turn up at smaller wineries where the focus will be on picking, crushing and fermenting grapes rather than welcoming visitors.

**January/February** At the beginning of the year, before harvest, there are several regional celebrations of particular wine styles. Among the longest established of these is the **Pinot Noir Celebration**, held every four years in Wellington. Central Otago now holds a similar event in years when there is no competition from the capital. Canterbury, Hawke's Bay and Marlborough all have wine and food festivals in February and Nelson hosts a festival of aromatic wines.

**August** At the beginning of the month, Auckland is home to the **Food Show**, which attracts over 30,000 food and wine lovers.

**October** The **Kaikoura Seafest** is a showcase for South Island food and wine from Kaikoura, Marlborough and Canterbury. A little later in the month Auckland attracts professionals to the annual **Wine New Zealand** trade show.

**November** The annual **Toast Martinborough Wine, Food & Music Festival** is held annually on the third Sunday in November and involves tours of numerous wineries in the region.

### Wine tourism

If one had to choose just one country in which to spend a day or a week visiting vineyards, New Zealand would have to be it. Wineries are widely spread across the two islands, making it easy to combine wine tasting with other activities. But most important of all is the way in which the entire industry has embraced the notion of wine tourism. If almost every winery boasts a cellar-door shop with helpful and usually informed staff, many also offer tours of the vineyards and cellars that often do not need to be booked in advance. Winery cafés and restaurants are common (with a few wineries also offering cookery courses), as are barbecue and picnic areas and even play areas for children.

All of the major wine regions have specialist operators offering tours to wineries. Some provide formal scheduled trips, while others can design a trip around your personal tastes or take in arts and crafts, restaurants and garden visits. The local I-Sites will also have information, leaflets and maps of the wineries in their area. For additional information about New Zealand wines refer to www.nzwine.com or www.winesnewzealand.co.nz.

My first thought on seeing the Marlborough Valley was how newly made New Zealand looks, and how unlike the ancient, weathered landscapes of Australia.

### Sleeping

Plenty of wineries offer accommodation, ranging from simple self-catering cottages to the kind of four-poster luxury that competes with the finest country hotels. You'll find large, modern and luxurious hotels ($$$) and more intimate boutique hotels ($$$-$$) in the major cities; standard chain hotels ($$) in all cities and large towns; traditional cheap wooden hotels in rural towns ($), plus motels ($) and hostels ($) of varying quality everywhere. Look out for luxury lodges ($$$) offering a classic 'bush setting' as well as sumptuous rooms, facilities and cuisine. B&Bs ($$-$) and homestays can also be attractive options, although they vary greatly in style, size and quality. If you hire a motorhome, you'll be spoilt for choice, with plentiful high-quality, well-equipped motorcamps and campsites. In the high season, especially from Christmas through to Easter, you are advised to book all forms of accommodation at least three days in advance.

### Eating

Although there are many types of cuisine in evidence in New Zealand, the principal style is 'Pacific Rim'. It dips into the culinary heritage of many of the cultures of the Oceania region, with influences from Thailand, Malaysia, Indonesia, Polynesia, Japan and Vietnam as well as others, such as Europe and the USA. For dishes that have a distinctly Kiwi edge look out for the lamb, pork, venison, freshwater fish such as salmon and eel, and fine seafood, especially warm-water fish, crayfish, oysters *paua* (abalone), scallops and green-lipped mussels. You should also try *kumara* (sweet potato), kiwi fruit, *feijoa* and *tamarillo*, and for a real feast try a traditional Maori *hangi*. In Europe, the wines of the region have developed over centuries to complement local dishes – and vice versa. New Zealand wine and cuisine are both far, far younger but the one quality that cooks and winemakers are both seeking is purity and freshness of flavour. Nothing exemplifies this better than a dish of Asian-influenced seafood with a cool Sauvignon Blanc or Riesling, or even a light, chilled Pinot Noir

# Wine essentials

### History

New Zealand's first grapes were planted by an English missionary called Samuel Marsden in 1819, but the first recorded wine was produced by James Busby 20 years later. Both men had high hopes for New Zealand wine but, over the following 150 years, their successors did little to turn these dreams into reality. The problems of vine diseases, pests and poor quality grapes (including hybrids in the early 20th century) were exacerbated by the limited skills of the English settlers. And progress was further hampered by the waxing and waning of a temperance movement that almost managed to introduce full-scale Prohibition in 1918. New Zealand's fledgling wine industry was only saved when the vote swung in its favour due to the last-minute return of a shipload of hard-drinking soldiers, who had been fighting in the trenches of northern Europe. Even so, wine did not become part of New Zealand life until the 1970s. And, when it did, it was generally in the form of light, semi-sweet wine that was, in effect, the local equivalent of Germany's cheap, basic Liebfraumilch – and made from the same Müller-Thurgau grape variety. There were, however, a few pioneers, like Tom McDonald and John Buck of Te Mata and Ivan Yukich of Montana Wines (producer of Brancott), who believed in the potential of higher quality grapes. It was men like these who finally dragged New Zealand's wine into the 20th century.

### Understanding New Zealand wine

One of the peculiarities of New Zealand's wine industry, especially when compared to that of the Old World, is the tendency of individual companies to produce reds and whites in a wide range of places, often in both the North and South Islands. There are parallels with Australia, where everyone seems to want a slice of Coonawarra, for example, but it's far more noticeable here, where it is increasingly common for a single brand name to appear on wines from, say, Hawke's Bay, Martinborough and Marlborough. Sometimes a company will have a winery of its own in each of these regions; sometimes it relies on a customized facility that makes the wine to its requirements. To an outsider – especially a European, used to Burgundians rarely straying outside Burgundy – this can smack of a jack-of-all-trades, trying to do too many things rather than focusing on a single speciality. But the frequent success of these multi-regional producers and their wines simply shows how well they have understood the decidedly Old World belief in choosing the appropriate soil and climate for each style of wine. Visitors, however, are sometimes surprised – not to say disappointed – to find that a producer whose Marlborough wine they have enjoyed does not actually have a winery in Marlborough.

Sauvignon Blanc on the vine.

### Wine styles

Until the recent success of its Pinot Noir, New Zealand was best known for its white wines. Sauvignon Blanc remains the country's trump card, thanks to a vibrant style that is found nowhere else in the world. There are also increasingly impressive examples of Chardonnay, Pinot Gris and the red Bordeaux varieties, as well as recent flourishes with Viognier and Montepulciano. However, among New Zealand's under-appreciated strengths are Riesling and Gewürztraminer: aromatic grapes that seem to thrive in the combination of relatively cool temperatures and intense unfiltered sunlight. These factors also suit sparkling wines such as Lindauer, Deutz Cuvée and Daniel le Brun's No1 Estate. As the wine industry evolves and new regions are developed it is certain that other grapes will come to the fore.

### White grapes

**Chardonnay** With a few key exceptions, such as Te Mata, Kumeu River and Felton Road, Chardonnay has not been as successful as Sauvignon Blanc, partly because of a frequently over-pronounced tropical character. However, recent efforts are improving fast and several New Zealand regions should be able to meet the growing demand for unoaked and lightly-oaked alternatives to Chablis.

**Gewürztraminer** Rarely remembered, Gewürztraminer was successfully produced by Matawhero in Gisborne before anyone noticed Sauvignon Blanc. The best examples combine the floral and spicy character of this grape with a zingy freshness.

**Pinot Gris** The rising star, here as elsewhere. The New Zealand style can be a delicious cross between the richness of Alsace and the bracing character of the best Italian Pinot Grigio. Beware, though, of examples with too much alcohol.

**Riesling** One of New Zealand's quiet successes from producers like Giesen, Rippon, Framingham and Villa Maria. New Zealand Riesling is made in a wide range of styles from dry to lusciously sweet and can easily match all but the finest efforts from Germany.

**Sauvignon Blanc** Most successful in Marlborough (where styles vary depending on sub-regions and producers), this remains New Zealand's calling card. Very rarely overtly oaked, it has an intense blackcurrant leaf and gooseberry flavour that is almost never found elsewhere, and certainly not in Europe where the grapes rarely ripen in the same way as they do here.

### Red grapes

**Cabernet Sauvignon** At its best in blends – Stonyridge's Larose is a great example – New Zealand Cabernet Sauvignon rarely performs well as a soloist. The Cabernet Franc may have a brighter future here, especially when mixed with Merlot.

**Merlot** More successful historically than Cabernet Sauvignon, which often fails to ripen properly, Merlot has great potential, especially in regions like Hawke's Bay, Kumeu and Waiheke Island.

**Pinot Noir** Initally associated with Martinborough but now excelling in Central Otago and Marlborough, the tricky Burgundy grape has found a home here, thanks to the coolish temperatures that prevent it from taking on the 'cooked', jammy flavours often encountered elsewhere in the New World. Freshness, perfume and the purity of raspberry and cherry fruit are the key notes.

Pinor Noir on the vine.

**Syrah/Shiraz** A rising star, though still rare. Watch out for intense peppery examples (Stonecroft does one) that lack both the jamminess of much of Australia and the earthiness of France.

Vineyards in Central Otago.

# Brancott wines

## from New Zealand's renowned winemaking regions

To craft some of the best New World wines, Brancott has based its premium vineyards in New Zealand's internationally renowned winemaking regions. Its superb wines hail from New Zealand's best known wine region, Marlborough, to the sunny and warm climes of the east coast regions of Gisborne and Hawke's Bay.

# The pinnacle of craftsmanship

## Brancott Letter Series

It takes a real boldness and thirst for adventure to create a range of superior quality wines which complement each other yet represent the intrinsic qualities of their different and unique regions. And that is what Brancott has achieved with the Letter Series. Named after Brancott's key vineyards – Brancott, Patutahi, Terrace and Ormond – these splendid wines represent the pinnacle of Brancott's winemaking craft.

# North Island

First a note of warning – and explanation. New Zealand's wine industry has developed, and is continuing to develop, at such a breakneck speed that there is much confusion about the names given to its wine regions. Look at any two books on the subject and there's a high chance that an area referred to as 'Wellington' in one is called 'Wairarapa' in another. To complicate matters further, some sub-regions, such as Matakana, are quietly becoming better known than the larger regions, such as Auckland, in which they have traditionally been said to be situated.

Until the late 1970s, however, there was one point on which all wine books agreed. New Zealand's wines almost all came from the North Island. This is where the first vines were planted – in 1819 in Northland – and where the Dalmatian settlers like Corban, Babich, Selak and Brajkovich (page 330) all subsequently began wine businesses that still, in one form or another, survive today. The larger population of the North Island and the importance of the cities of Wellington and Auckland also helped to ensure that, while vineyards in the South Island region of Marlborough have grown in importance, much of the wine industry is still run from Auckland and many of the bigger companies, like Brancott and Villa Maria, still have wineries and visitor centres there.

BRANCOTT
NEW ZEALAND

## Northland

The northernmost wine region in New Zealand, this is where Samuel Marsden planted the country's first vineyard at Kerikeri in 1819. His lead was followed by James Busby in 1835, who began to grow grapes at his home at Waitangi. The area did not, however, contribute much to the subsequent evolution of New Zealand wine until quite recently, when a new generation of winemakers was attracted by the warm climate. Watch this space.

WINERY — RUSSELL

### Omata Estate

Aucks Rd, RD 1, Russell
T +64 (0)9-403 8007
www.omata.co.nz
Visits by appointment only. Restaurant Wed-Sun 1200-1400 and from 1800; closed Jul.

One of the most spectacularly situated winery restaurants in New Zealand, Omata Estate offers glorious views of the Bay of Islands (page 321). The wines – including a commendable Syrah – are produced from a 5-ha vineyard and made at the nearby Marsden Estate, which also boasts a restaurant of its own. The latter, though, is not as memorable as the Omata Vineyard Restaurant ($$$), where the cook personally takes diners seated at the 'Chef's Bench' through the five-course degustation menu and the accompanying Omata wines. Eating here is not cheap and, despite the awards it has received, some customers have suggested that, for a similar price you could eat rather better in Auckland. But, then again, you wouldn't be enjoying those views. Book early in the summer, when restaurants in this area fill up quickly. Self-catering or suite accommodation ($$$) is provided in the Homestead, Boathouse and Loft.

## Auckland

Not the capital, as many outsiders suppose, Auckland is New Zealand's answer to Sydney, New York and San Francisco. Once a sleepy provincial town, it is now the increasingly sophisticated business and cultural centre of the country. The surrounding area was once the heart of the New Zealand wine industry, in much the same way that the Hunter Valley was the base of winemaking in Australia, but it has been unfairly pushed into the background by the recent successes of Hawke's Bay, Marlborough and Central Otago. Nevertheless, many of the big names in New Zealand wine still have their headquarters in this varied region. There are also some terrific small estates here, especially in Kumeu (including the world-beating Kumeu River) and on Waiheke Island, a short ferry ride from Auckland (Stonyridge, Goldwater and Te Motu). Business travellers arguably have better opportunities to enjoy high-quality wine tastings during a brief trip to Auckland than when visiting almost any other major city. The official *Wine Trail* and *Wineries of Auckland* leaflets can be found at I-Sites throughout the region.

HOTEL — POKENO

## Hotel du Vin

Lyons Rd, Mangatawhiri Valley, Pokeno
T +64 (0)9-233 6314
www.hotelduvin.co.nz
$$$

Despite being quite unrelated to the award-winning Hotel du Vin group in the UK (page 192), this Auckland establishment shares the modern, informal luxurious style associated with that chain. There are 48 chalets in the hotel's gardens and a restaurant ($$$) offering local dishes, such as carpaccio of ostrich, as well as one of New Zealand's best wine lists. The New Zealand Hotel du Vin holds two ace cards with which its British namesakes cannot compete, in the shape of a Balinese-style **Spa du Vin** and its own top-class Firstland wines from Hawke's Bay and Wairau Valley.

WINERY — KUMEU

## Kumeu River

550 State Highway 16, Kumeu
T +64 (0)9-412 8415
www.kumeuriver.co.nz
For opening times and other details, contact the winery directly.

Michael Brajkovich is one of the quiet influences behind New Zealand wine. With his brothers, Paul and Milan, he took over an already impressive operation from his father Maite, and made it into one of the country's top half dozen producers. The Chardonnay has taken the limelight but the Merlot is impressive too, benefiting, perhaps, from Michael's brief experience working at Chateau Petrus. This was also the place where the New Zealand screwcap revolution began, and no one who has blind-tasted mature examples of the Kumeu River from cork-sealed bottles and screwcaps has been able to deny that these already brilliant wines taste even better with alternative closures.

WINERY — WAIMAUKU

## Matua Valley

Waikoukou Rd, PO Box 100, Waimauku
T +64 (0)9-411 8301
www.matua.co.nz
Daily 1000-1700.

Now part of the giant Fosters Wine Group – along with Penfolds, Wolf Blass and Beringer – Matua Valley is still run very much as a family business by its founders Ross and Bill



### Visiting Auckland

Climb the 328-m futuristic **Sky Tower** (Victoria and Federal Sts, T0800-759 2489, www.skycityauckland.co.nz) for an all-encompassing view of the city. It's also worth visiting the **Auckland Museum** (Te Papa Whakahiku; T09-306 7067, www.akmuseum.org.nz), which houses the world's largest collection of Maori and Pacific artefacts. The waterfront is where Auckland truly becomes the 'City of Sails', centred around the **America's Cup Village**. (New Zealand held the cup from 1995 to 2003.) Harbour cruises are available from the **National Maritime Museum** (corner of Quay and Hobson Sts, T0800-725897, www.maritime.org), or you can have lunch in one of the many waterfront restaurants; **CinCin** in the Ferry Building, **Euro** on Princess Wharf and **Kermadec** overlooking the America's Cup Village are recommended. Across the harbour from the centre is the picturesque suburb of **Devonport**, where Victorian villas, craft shops, art galleries, pavement cafés and pleasant walks lie in wait, overlooked by Mount Victoria and North Head.

West of Auckland are the **Waitakere Ranges**, a mountainous area of wilderness with an extensive network of walking tracks. The 28-km **Scenic Drive** winds along the eastern fringes, offering stunning views across the city; visit the **Arataki Information Centre** (6 km from Titirangi, T09-817 0089) for details. Just to the north is the wine-growing area of **Kumeu**, while to the west are wild surf beaches.

**Waiheke** is the largest island in the Hauraki Gulf and is only 20 km from the city. It has plenty of beaches, activities and fine restaurants, as well as some notable wineries. Access is by air from Auckland airport or by ferry. The main village is **Oneroa**, where **Waiheke I-Site** (2 Korora Rd, T09-372 1234) can provide details of the island's vineyards. Other islands in the gulf include **Rangitoto**, the nature reserve of **Tiri Tiri Matangi** and isolated **Great Barrier Island**.

The **Bay of Islands** is also accessible from Auckland by air (40 mins) or road (4 hrs). It is one of the major tourist areas in the country, offering water-based activities and superb coastal scenery. It was here that the Treaty of Waitangi was signed in 1840, ceding sovereignty of New Zealand to the British. Although **Paihia** is the main resort town in the Bay, **Russell** is a more relaxed base and enjoys a village feel that eludes its frenetic, tourism-based neighbour.

Spence, who launched it in Auckland in the early 1970s. Today, wines are produced across the country under various labels (including Shingle Peak and Ararimu), examples of which can be tasted and bought at the cellar door in Kumeu. There's a pleasant park and garden, and Eileen Spence also offers accommodation in vineyard cottages (www.vineyard-cottages.co.nz).



RESTAURANT — AUCKLAND

## Otto's

40 Kitchener St, Metropolis Building, Auckland
T +64 (0)9-300 9595
www.ottos.co.nz
Mon-Sat 1800-2200.
$$

Once the haunt of lawyers and criminals, Auckland's high-ceilinged Old Magistrate's Court House is now the place to find New Zealand's winemakers and wine lovers when they are feeling like a big night out. Prices are among the highest in the city but the setting, the quality of dishes like apple-glazed duck, the service and the wine list all make cost a secondary consideration. And, when you've finished eating, you could work off some of the calories in the restaurant's **Sapphire Room** nightclub.

WINERY — WAIHEKE ISLAND

## Stonyridge

80 Onetangi Rd, Waiheke Island
T +64 (0)9-372 8822
www.stonyridge.co.nz
Café Jan-Apr daily; May-Dec Fri-Sun.
Tour and tasting Sat and Sun 1130.
Tour and tasting NZ$10.

Former Whitbread Round-the-World yachtsman, Stephen White, has built up a cult following for his wines over the last 25 years. A pioneer of Waiheke, he was the first New Zealand winemaker to produce red wine using all the classic Bordeaux varieties, including Malbec and Petit Verdot, and the first to adopt the Bordeaux technique of selling his top Larose wine 'en primeur', while still in the barrel. I knew all this before I took the ferry across to visit his Stonyridge vineyard and I'd already been dazzled by the super-Bordeaux quality of his Larose red. But I had no idea that I'd fall in love with the view of the beautifully tended vineyards from his wooden **Veranda Café** ($$). Or with the Mediterranean-meets-New Zealand food that's produced there by his chef Tony Moss, who gained some of his experience cooking at the Playboy Mansion for Hugh Heffner. This may have been useful training when catering for the Auckland glitterati who flock here in the summer. Book early and consider finding somewhere to stay as some evenings finish after the last ferry has left the island.

WINERY — WAIHEKE ISLAND

## Te Motu Vineyard

76 Onetangi Rd, Onetangi Valley, Waiheke Island
T +64 (0)9-372 6884
www.temotu.co.nz
Tastings and sales Thu-Sun from 1130.
Restaurant Thu-Sat only.

Terry Dunleavy shares the mantle of grand old(er) man of New Zealand wine with John Buck of Te Mata. However, while Buck has always been involved in his own winery, Dunleavy devoted his career to running the wine industry association in such an effective and feisty manner that no one seriously believed that he would ever retire. And sure enough, here he is, making great Cabernet-Merlot at one of the top wineries in an overgrown hut on Waiheke Island. As if that weren't enough, he also offers good simple food in **The Shed** ($$). But book in advance: space is limited and this is a favourite weekend spot for Aucklanders.

WINERY — AUCKLAND

## Villa Maria Estate Winery & Vineyard Park

118 Montgomerie Rd, Mangere, Auckland
T +64 (0)9-255 0660
www.villamaria.co.nz
Mon-Fri 0900-1800; Sat and Sun 1000-1700.
Tours 1100 and 1500.

The second biggest wine company in New Zealand, Villa Maria deserves credit for being one of the screwcap pioneers and for winning top trophies against tough local competition for long lists of wines, including some terrific Pinot Noirs sealed in this way. The Auckland 'winery and vineyard park' sits at the heart of a 40-ha estate within a dormant volcano, and includes lakes, ornamental trees (uprooted and replanted here) and a natural amphitheatre that is used for open-air concerts. Opened in 2004, it is

Gisborne vineyards.

a state-of-the-art establishment, which was designed to accommodate visitors as well as winemakers, so there are walkways throughout and special closed-circuit television coverage of every aspect of winemaking. A restaurant is also planned but, for the moment, this is a great place to enjoy a cheese platter from the winery café ($$) or a picnic of your own, with a bottle bought from the winery shop.

## Gisborne

On 31st December 1999, Gisborne briefly enjoyed a moment of global attention. Situated on the easternmost point of New Zealand, it was the first place on the planet to see in the new millennium. The region's other claim to fame is as the home of fine surfing beaches and some of the country's best Chardonnays and Gewürztraminers. Grapes have been grown on the wide open plains here for over a century and a half, but Gisborne's modern wine reputation was created by three producers. Initially, there was a maverick called Dennis Irwin, who first made a brilliant Gewürztraminer in Matawhero in the late 1970s. Recently, he sold that vineyard to the second of our Gisborne pioneers, Brancott, which now has over 400 ha of vines here. Third, there's James and Annie Millton who have led the way in the production of ultra-organic, bio-dynamic wines, including a world-class Chenin Blanc.

There are still relatively few wineries in Gisborne and this is an area that is often omitted from many tourists' itineraries, but, for anyone with a taste for swimming, surfing, ocean fishing... and good white wine, this is a great place to visit.

WINERY — MANUTUKE

### Millton Vineyard

119 Papatu Rd, Manutuke
T 0800-464558
www.millton.co.nz
Summer Mon-Sat 1000-1700; winter by appointment. Tours by appointment only.

If you are very lucky and you arrive in Gisborne at the right time of the year, James Millton will not only show you his wines but he'll also let you take a look at the huge piles of compost of which he is equally proud. As a bio-dynamic winemaker he is absolutely certain that the quality of his world-class Chenin Blanc Riesling and Chardonnay owe much to the painstaking natural treatments he gives the soil in which the vines are grown. Sceptics question the bio-dynamic practices, such as the use of manure that has been buried in a cow horn, but Millton is quietly making local converts.

WINERY — GISBORNE

### Lindauer/Brancott Gisborne Winery

Solander St, Lytton Rd, PO Box 1347, Gisborne
T +64 (0)6-867 9819
www.montanawines.co.nz
Daily 1000-1700. Tours 1030 and 1400. Restaurant from 1130.

Montana Wines (producer of Brancott), New Zealand's largest wine company, is also the biggest player in Gisborne, with some 400 ha of vines including the premium 'O' Ormond Chardonnay and 'P' Patutahi Gewürztraminer vineyards. The winery, which is also home to Lindauer sparkling wine, is only 400 m from the ocean and has a busy visitor centre, wine museum and a restaurant ($$-$), which offers food-and-wine-matching menus.

## Hawke's Bay

Before it gained a reputation for its wines, the gently rolling hills of Hawke's Bay were known as one of the best farming regions in the country. Even today, this is the place to find some of New Zealand's best fruit and vegetables at the weekly farmers' markets in Hastings and Havelock North. Napier boasts some very attractive art deco buildings, evidence of the area's popularity in the 1920s and 1930s. Modern tourism has grown with the wine industry and independent restaurants and cafés now have to compete with the quality of food being offered by many of the wineries.

While New Zealand owes most of its current international vinous fame to its Sauvignon Blanc and Pinot Noir, there

Grapevine

**Wine roads**

The world's most famous wine regions, vineyards and estates take their names from all sorts of sources but none outside New Zealand has developed such a propensity for referring to roads. (Burgundy has a Grand Cru vineyard called 'La Grande Rue' and Germany has the Hessische Bergstrasse but these are exceptions to the European rule and neither of them features among the finest of their respective country.)

The first New Zealand 'road winery' was Church Road in Hawke's Bay (below), which began life as the McDonald Winery. But this historic establishment now has to share its fame with the Hawke's Bay area of Gimblett Road, whose gravelly soil – the so-called Gimblett Gravels – is one of New Zealand's most respected red wine appellations. More recently, the Felton Road winery in Central Otago has gained an international following for its Pinot Noir.



have always been attempts to produce top class Bordeaux-style reds. And, despite the recent successes of Waiheke Island, nowhere does this better and more consistently than Hawke's Bay. Te Mata, the modern incarnation of New Zealand's oldest winery, which was launched in 1978, was the first producer to attract attention, with its Médoc-like Coleraine, but a long list of younger ventures, including Ngatarawa (1981), Church Road, Craggy Range, Te Awa, CJ Pask and Kingsley Estate all now compete with it on equal terms. Excitingly for those who believe in the traditional European notions of wines gaining flavour and quality from the soil, Hawke's Bay has several different soil types, the most famous of which, the Gimblett Gravels, seems to suit Cabernet Sauvignon better than almost any other soil in New Zealand.

WINERY NAPIER

### Church Road Winery

150 Church Rd, Taradale, Napier
T +64 (0)6-844 2053
www.churchroad.co.nz
Tours daily 1000, 1100, 1400 and 1500.
Tour and tasting NZ$10.

One of New Zealand's oldest wineries, Church Road was originally built at the end of the 19th century. Until the 1980s, it was known as the McDonald Winery after the pioneering winemaker Tom McDonald, who is also commemorated by the winery's top red 'Tom'. Today, visitors can learn how wines used to be made, by taking a tour around the winery museum, housed in the old fermentation vats. They can also watch today's reds and whites being produced here, with the aid of some of the most high-tech equipment in the country. **Church Road Winery Restaurant** is also a great place for a fairly priced lunch ($$).

WINERY HAVELOCK NORTH

### Craggy Range Vineyards

253 Waimarama Rd, Havelock North
T +64 (0)6-873 7126
www.craggyrange.com
Daily 1000-1700. Tours Sat and Sun 1100 or by appointment. Restaurant Tue-Sun from 1200 (lunch only Sun).
Tours NZ$20.

When Terry Peabody, an American-born, waste-management tycoon invested NZ$60 million in a state-of-the-art winery on the Gimblett Gravels, Hawke's Bay old-timers grumbled about flash newcomers. But, from the outset, manager Steve Smith, one of New Zealand's few Masters of Wine, has made this one of the region's stars. All of the wines – sourced from here and from Marlborough and Martinborough – are impressive but the recently launched Prestige range is especially worth looking out for. Also of interest is the lower-priced Capricorn Wine Estates range.

The **Terroir Restaurant** ($$) is one of the best in the region, serving French-influenced dishes cooked in a wood-fired oven, and Matthew Judd, New Zealand Sommelier of the Year in 2005, provides great guidance through the single-vineyard wines. Events here include harvest weekend meals and occasional open-air concerts, such as the one in 2003 that united Dame Kiri Te Kanawa, Tim Finn of Crowded House and the Auckland Philharmonic. There are also a couple of bedrooms in the **Cellarmaster's Cottage** ($$$) but you'll need to book early.

WINERY HASTINGS

### Sileni Estates Winery

Straford Lodge, 2016 Maraekakaho Rd, Hastings
T +64 (0)6-879 8768
www.sileni.co.nz
Tours daily 1100 and 1400. Restaurant daily from 1100 (lunch only Sun-Wed).
Tour and tasting NZ$12. Food and wine tasting from NZ$15.

Like Craggy Range, Sileni is another big investment by a newcomer to the region. And it's another success story, with wines like the 2005 Marlborough Sauvignon Blanc that won the 2005 International Wine Challenge prizes for top New Zealand white and for the best example of this variety in the competition. Among the Hawke's Bay wines, look out in particular for the EV (Exceptional Vintage) Merlot. Also of note here is the restaurant ($$), which matches local seasonal produce with the estate's wines, and the **Gourmet Store**, which stocks an enticing

Vineyards in the Dartmoor Valley near Puketapu, west of Napier.

range of local foods that might tempt you into signing up for a course at the **Sileni Culinary School**.

WINERY | HASTINGS

### Te Awa Winery

2375 Roys Hill Rd, State Highway 50,
Hastings, RD 5
T +64 (0)6-879 7602
www.teawafarm.co.nz
Daily 0900-1700. Tours by appointment.

There are a lot of influences at work here. On the one hand, the name is 100% New Zealand, coming from Maori, *te awa o te atua* (river of god), which is an oblique reference to the streams that flow beneath the vineyard. The winemaking gets a French touch from Jenny Dobson, who worked at Château Senejac in Bordeaux and Domaine Dujac in Burgundy, while the USA has a role to play in the shape of co-owner Julian Robertson from New York.

This international focus is also evident in the restaurant ($$), where Brent Cameron brings three decades of experience gained overseas to bear on local ingredients. Make sure to get an outdoor table overlooking the gardens if the weather is fine.

WINERY | HAVELOCK NORTH

### Te Mata Winery

349 Te Mata Rd, PO Box 8335,
Havelock North
T +64 (0)6-877 4399
www.temata.co.nz
Tasting Mon-Fri 0900-1700, Sat 1000-1700, Sun 1100-1600. Tours by appointment.

New Zealand's oldest winery was built here in the 1870s, on the outskirts of Havelock North and in the foothills of Te Mata Peak. Since the late 1970s, when the current smart white winery was built, John Buck and his

#### Hawke's Bay food and festivals

In hedonistic Napier, it seems, food, wine and all things convivial are the very core of the region's lifestyle. The love affair with food and wine ensures there is plenty of choice when it comes to eating out. In Napier there are essentially two main venues, the CBD (especially Marine Parade) and the suburb of Ahuriri, 2 km to the north. Besides that, you should try at least one meal at a winery. In addition to those reviewed above, wineries with recommended restaurants include: **Brookfields** (Brookfields Rd, Meeanee, Napier, T +64 (0)6-834 4615, www.brookfieldsvineyards.co.nz); **Crab Farm** (511 Main Rd, Bay View, Hawke's Bay, T +64 (0)6-836 6678, www.crabfarm winery.co.nz); **Mission Estate** (198 Church Road, Taradale, Napier, T +64 (0)6-845 9350, www.missionestate.co.nz) and **Vidal Estate** (913 St Aubyn St East, Hastings, T +64 (0)6-876 8105). For further details and a map ask at **Napier I-Site** (100 Marine Parade, T+64 (0)6-834 1911, www.hawkesbay.nz.com) for the 'Hawke's Bay Food Trail' leaflet. Bike tours of the vineyards, with stops for food and wine, can be arranged through www.onyerbikehb.co.nz.

The region also has a packed calendar of food-and-wine-related events. In February there's the **Hawke's Bay Wine & Food Festival**; the **International Mission Estate Concert**; the **Brebner Print Art Deco Weekend**, celebrating Napier's architectural heritage; and the **Weta Wine & Food Fest**, followed in March by the **Edible Arts Fest**. This event kicks off with the infamous 'Great Long Lunch', which attracts over 700 gourmands. The area celebrates the **Winter Arts** and **Winter Solstice Fire Festivals** in June, as well as **Matariki** (Maori New Year), accompanied by plenty of traditional *hangi* (feasts). Finishing off the festive year is the **Month of Wine & Roses** in November, a series of private garden tours with a little music and, naturally, lots (and lots) of food and wine.

partner, winemaker Peter Cowley, have been making Burgundian Chardonnay, Bordeaux-style reds and whites, and a Rhône-like Syrah called Bullnose that have all been almost synonymous with the region. Today, they face greater competition than in the past but these remain benchmarks of New Zealand wine. Three luxury accommodation units are available on site; contact the winery for details.

## Wairarapa

Not a name that will ring bells with many wine lovers outside New Zealand, Wairarapa (pronounced 'why-ra-rapa') is the area in the south of the North Island that surrounds and includes the far better known region of Martinborough. Until the recent meteoric success of Central Otago, Martinborough was unchallenged as the home of New Zealand Pinot Noir. But it now faces competition much closer at hand, from its Wairarapa neighbours Gladstone, East Taratahi, Masterton and, especially, Te Muna. This last is where one of Martinborough's most famous Pinot pioneers, Larry McKenna, has established his Escarpment vineyard. Although winegrowing is still something of a novelty in Wairarapa – Martinborough only began to attract attention in the late 1980s – the region has, by New Zealand standards, quite deep historic roots.

WINERY MARTINBOROUGH

### Murdoch James Estate

Dry River Rd, Martinborough
T +64 (0)6-306 9165
www.murdochjames.co.nz
Tastings daily 1100-1700. Café Nov-Mar Thu-Tue 1200-1530; Apr-Oct Fri-Sun only.
Tastings from NZ$5.

One of the more imaginative wineries in New Zealand, Murdoch James not only boasts the **Riverview Café** ($$-$) and self-catering accommodation in the restored **Winemaker's Cottage** ($$-$) but also offers a set of tours. These range from a personal 45-minute tour of the winery and vineyards with the winemaker or one of the owners to a five-hour odyssey, including lunch and hands-on experience in the vineyards and cellar. These are not cheap, particularly since some other wineries are happy to offer tours for nothing, but the experience will certainly be one to remember.

HOTEL MARTINBOROUGH

### Peppers Martinborough Hotel

The Square, Martinborough
T +64 (0)6-306 9350
www.martinboroughhotel.co.nz
$$

Part of the same group as the brilliant Peppers Guest House & Convent in the Hunter Valley (page 291), this grand old building, constructed in 1882 as "one of the finest hostelries ever erected in any inland town in New Zealand", shares their casually luxurious style. Order breakfast on your private veranda and you might find that you are in less of a hurry to rush out to explore the local vineyards, most of whose efforts are, in any case, on offer in the hotel's bistro and bar.

### Welcome to Wellington

Although Wellington is the nation's capital it enjoys a small-town atmosphere, with surrounding hills, a generally compact layout and well-preserved historical buildings.

The city's most famous visitor attraction is the multi-million dollar **'Te Papa' Museum of New Zealand** (south of Civic Sq, T +64 (0)4-381 7000, www.tepapa.govt.nz ), which attempts faithfully to represent the nation's heritage. Nearby is the revitalized **Museum of Wellington City & Sea** (Queens Wharf, T+64 (0)4-472 8904, www.museumofwellington.co.nz). Both museums are located on the revamped and buzzing waterfront, where anumber of charter boats are available.

For a view of the city, head to **Wellington's Botanic Gardens** (Glenmore St, Thorndon, T +64 (0)4-499 1400, www.wbg.co.nz). They're really quite magnificent but excruciatingly hilly, so take the cable car from 280 Lambton Quay, first built in 1902 and now a tourist attraction in its own right.

Wellington prides itself on its thriving café and restaurant scene. Head to Cuba Street for coffee, where **Fidels** (No 234), **Midnight Espresso** (No 178), **Olive** (No 170) and **Krazy Lounge** (No 132), all stand out. There are dozens of restaurants in the Courtenay Quarter (especially on Blair Street), offering mainly Pacific Rim cuisine. Queen's Wharf is also a favourite haunt.

Head north from the city to explore the scenic Kapiti coastline, with the nature reserve of **Kapiti Island** offshore. Alternatively, you can reach the beautiful region of the **Wairarapa**, beyond the natural barrier of the Ruahine and Tararua ranges. It has pleasant rural towns like Martinborough and Greytown, which is popular for antique hunting, and a number of quality vineyards (above). The new wine centre in the heart of Martinborough (T+64 (0)6-306 9040, www.martin boroughwinecentre.co.nz, is a good place to get a feel for what is available and ask about tours. The 'Martinborough Wairarapa Wine Trail' leaflet, available from the VIC, will also get your tour started. Further east is the coastal splendour of Castlepoint and Cape Palliser, the North Island's most southerly point.

For further information, visit the **Wellington I-Site** (Wakefield and Victoria sts, T +64 (0)4-802 4860, www.wellingtonnz.com).

# Showcase of Marlborough

## Brancott Reserve

A passion for creating wines that are dynamic, fresh and made from the best fruit available is the hallmark of Brancott Reserve wines. This internationally acclaimed range is superbly crafted to showcase the virtues of the now famous Marlborough wine region. Brancott Reserve wines are understatedly iconic and undeniably enjoyable.

# South Island



**Generally overlooked until the early 1980s, the South Island has now become the focus of New Zealand winemaking, with Marlborough Sauvignon Blanc and Central Otago Pinot Noir acting as joint flagships for this country's world-class wine. But these two regions and their respective speciality grape varieties are only part of the story. The South Island is proving to have a wider repertoire than many people expected: Marlborough Pinot Noirs sometimes beat Central Otago efforts and other regions throughout the South Island produce great Chardonnay, Pinot Gris and Riesling. And, while the inhabitants of the North Island would hate to admit it, visitors to New Zealand could enjoy the holiday of a lifetime down here without ever venturing north across the Cook Strait.**

## Nelson

Far too often overlooked by foreign visitors dazzled by the reputation of Marlborough to the east, the beautifully bucolic region of Nelson has developed a keen following amongst New Zealand holidaymakers who head to the Abel Tasman National Park (page 330) to hike and play around in canoes. Quite apart from its natural attractions, Nelson makes enormous efforts to attract visitors, ranging from arts and jazz festivals to the gloriously eclectic Montana World of Wearable Art (www.worldofwearableart.com), which elevates clothes into cultural objects, and attracts over 60,000 visitors every year.

Back in the 1980s, however, although they began winemaking at much the same time as Marlborough – Seifried and Neudorf opened their doors in 1974 and 1978, respectively – the handful of producers in this northwestern corner of the South Island were handicapped by a lack of recognition from wine experts and drinkers in Auckland. As Tim Finn said, "We can never get away with asking as much for our wine as our neighbours in Marlborough – however well we make it…". But that was then and this is now. Neudorf has won international recognition for the quality of its Pinot Noir, Pinot Gris and Chardonnay, but so have other more recent arrivals like Spencer Hill/Tasman Bay, whose Chardonnay is good enough to beat the best efforts of the rest of the country at the annual Gisborne Chardonnay Challenge.

RESTAURANT — NELSON

### Mapua Flax Restaurant & Bar

Mapua Wharf, Mapua, Nelson
T +64 (0)3-540 2028.
Tue-Sun lunch 1130-1530, dinner from 1730.

One of the best and busiest restaurants in Nelson is situated right on the wharf at Mapua. This recent arrival specializes in modern New Zealand versions of dishes such as skilfully cooked pork belly and home-made ice cream with pomegranate molasses. A good range of local wines is available.

WINERY — APPLEBY

### Seifried Estate

Corner of SH60 and Redwood Rd, Appleby
T +64 (0)3-544 5599
www.seifried.co.nz
Daily 1000-1700. Tours by appointment. Restaurant daily for lunch and dinner.

Austrian-born Hermann Seifried was one of the trail-blazers of Nelson wine, way back in 1974. Today, he and his family have the biggest winery in the region, the serious **Vineyard Restaurant** ($$) and a reputation for producing some of New Zealand's best Riesling, both dry and late-harvest. Confusingly, the Seifried name is hardly known overseas since, when the wines leave New Zealand, they are labelled Redwood Valley.

CLOUDY BAY

## Marlborough

The most famous wine region in New Zealand, Marlborough, in the northeast of the South Island, is also one of the most spectacular to look at, carpeted with vines and surrounded by hills that look like gently folded lengths of khaki carpet. While the small town of Blenheim has buildings that are over a century old, the wine industry here was created almost from scratch just 30 years ago. Today it produces over half of New Zealand's wine and is synonymous globally with an instantly recognizable style of vibrant, fruity Sauvignon Blanc.

The first vines were planted to the north of the region in the flat Wairau valley, close to Blenheim. More recently, vine-growing has expanded into a number of southern side valleys – Hawkesbury, Fairhall and Waihopai – and southeast into the cooler Awatere Valley. There are now 60 wineries in the Marlborough region and over 8000 ha of vines, a figure that will rise to 10,000 ha in 2007. Apart from boasting some of the world's most tourist-friendly wineries and a wealth of restaurants, Marlborough is a great place for outdoor activities (page 330). You can even book a hot-air balloon ride for a bird's-eye view of the vineyards.

Brancott vineyards.

Brancott Marlborough Sauvignon Blanc.

WINERY | RIVERLANDS

### Brancott Winery and Visitor Centre

Main Rd South, SH 1, Riverlands
T +64 (0)3-577 5777
www.montanawines.co.nz
Daily 0900-1700. Tours daily 1000-1500.
Restaurant 0900-1700.

When I first visited Brancott's winery in Marlborough in 1985, it was a purely functional establishment – for the simple reason that the region was too young to be of interest to wine-loving tourists. Today, the Marlborough home of New Zealand's biggest wine company has become one of the most popular attractions in the country and draws in no fewer than 100,000 visitors per year. Surrounded by vines against a backdrop of hills, the main building looks like a modern take on an early medieval church or manor house. Inside, the Wine Education Centre offers a dynamic audio-visual presentation and the opportunity to sniff the characteristic aromas of New Zealand's most widely planted grape varieties, before tasting in the cellar door beneath a 'cathedral ceiling' 8 m high. Another key attraction is the winery tours, which range from an hour-long educational visit to three-hour and full-day 'odysseys' priced at NZ$150 and NZ$250 respectively. These include forays into the vineyards, tutored tastings and wine-and-food-matching meals in the award-winning **Brancott Winery Restaurant** ($$). The restaurant, café and terrace are ideal places to enjoy lunch, especially for those travelling with children, who can be left to play safely in the playground.

WINERY | BLENHEIM

### Clos Henri

639 State Highway 63, West Coast Rd, Blenheim,
T +64 (0)3-572 7923
www.closhenri.com
Visits by appointment only.

When France's winemakers and critics first tasted New Zealand Sauvignon Blancs in the 1980s, they often dismissed them as 'exotic' or downright artificial. Today, one of the Loire's best-known and most highly respected producers, Henri Bourgeois of Sancerre, has paid Marlborough the compliment of investing in a vineyard of his own. The cellar door is beautifully situated in the restored wooden Sainte Solange chapel, set in the heart of the vineyard. The first vintage was produced in 2003 and made an impact as soon as it was released. Interestingly, Sancerre is one of the only places in the world apart from Marlborough to grow both Sauvignon Blanc and Pinot Noir. As to whether M Bourgeois' New Zealand Sauvignon beats the whites that he and his neighbours make in France, the jury is still out, but there are plenty who would say that his Kiwi Pinot Noir definitely eclipses most red Sancerre.

Grapevine

**101 Dalmatians**

While the early grapegrowers and winemakers in New Zealand were Britons, such as Samuel Marsden, James Busby, Bernard Chambers and Tom McDonald, many of the foundations of the modern New Zealand wine industry were laid by immigrants who arrived from the Croatian region of Dalmatia in the first three decades of the 20th century. Josip Babich (whose descendents still run the Babich winery), Mick Brajkovich (whose grandson is the star winemaker at Kumeu River), Andrew Fistonich (whose son founded Villa Maria) and Ivan Yukich (who began Montana Wines, producer of Brancott) all started out as market gardeners and gum tappers but they brought with them a tradition of family winemaking that was almost unknown in New Zealand. Decades later, their dynamism is still being felt: Michael Brajkovich has been named as one of the finest Chardonnay producers in the world; George Fistonich's Villa Maria was the first major wine company to switch almost entirely to screwcaps, and Frank Yukich, Ivan's son, not only created the wine region of Marlborough but also turned Brancott into what it remains today, New Zealand's biggest wine company.

WINERY BLENHEIM

## Cloudy Bay

Jacksons Rd, Blenheim
T +64 (0)3-520 9140
www.cloudybay.co.nz
Daily 1000-1700.

Named after an inlet at the east of the Wairau Valley that was, in turn, originally christened by Captain Cook in 1770, this world-famous winery produced its first Sauvignon Blanc as recently as 1985. Since then, it has been bought by Veuve Clicquot and has expanded greatly without losing its cult status. The winemaking, though, is still in the hands of Kevin Judd, the taciturn genius whose iconic black-and-white photograph has appeared on the label of every bottle of Cloudy Bay since he crushed the grapes for the very first vintage. Over the years Judd has become one of New Zealand's most respected landscape photographers.

One good reason for making a detour here is to taste and buy bottles that are not yet on sale elsewhere. The Riesling was first sold in this way, as was the first bottling of the Sauvignon Blanc in screwcaps and the

### The Marlborough Sounds and around

The Marlborough Sounds are the South Island's giant foyer. This vast, convoluted system of drowned river valleys, peninsulas and islets creates an astonishing 1500 km of coastline, where you can enjoy stunning scenery, cruising, tramping, kayaking, wildlife watching or just a few days' peaceful relaxation. The inter-island ferries from Wellington dock at the port of **Picton**, at the head of Queen Charlotte Sound, and water taxis are available from the enchanting village of **Havelock** at the head of Pelorus Sound. There are numerous other opportunities to get on the water, from scheduled cruises to fishing trips (try www.compass-charters.co.nz) and kayak expeditions. There are also two popular tramping tracks, the Queen Charlotte and the Nydia, details of which are available from **Picton I-Site** (T +64 (0)3-520 3113, www.destinationmarlborough.com).

From Picton it is only a short hop to **Blenheim**, the centre of New Zealand's most productive wine-growing region (page 329). The **Marlborough I-Site** (railway station, Grove Rd, T +64 (0)3-577 8080, www.destinationmarlborough.com) has details of the town and the wineries, most of which are located off SH6 around the small village of **Renwick**. South of Blenheim is the pretty coastal settlement of **Kaikoura**, famous for its whales, dolphins and seabirds. Contact **Whale Watch Kaikoura** (T +64 (0)3-3196767, www.whalewatch.co.nz) for specialist boat trips.

West of Havelock, meanwhile, is **Nelson** (page 328), a sunny, lively town surrounded by wineries. To the north, the **Abel Tasman National Park** encompasses some of New Zealand's best beaches, as well as tramping tracks and kayaking trips. For information on the region visit the **Nelson I-Site** (Trafalgar St and Halifax St, T +64 (0)3-548 2305, www.nelsonnz.com).

Te Koku 'Super Cuvée' of Cloudy Bay's Sauvignon. The Pinot Noir is also a great example of work in progress: a wine that was produced but not released outside the winery for several years, but is now acknowledged to be one of the best examples in the region. Don't miss the Chardonnay while you are here; it is too often overlooked.

WINERY BLENHEIM

### Domaine Georges Michel

56 Vintage Ln, Rapaura, Blenheim
T +64 (0)3-572 7230
www.georgesmichel.co.nz
Hortensia House Gardens & Craft Shed
Thu-Sat 1400-1730. Restaurant daily for lunch and dinner.

Georges Michel, who was born on the island of La Réunion, is owner of Château de Grandmont in Beaujolais. Since arriving in New Zealand in 1994, he and his wife, Huguette, have set out to create what they call a 'winery complex'. This is not, as some might imagine, a psychiatric condition but a great combination of winery, gourmet deli, gift shop and restaurant within a large Victorian villa, set in glorious gardens. The Domaine Georges Michel Chardonnay is one of the best in the region, and **La Veranda** restaurant ($$) is a perfect place to enjoy it with well-prepared local seafood.

WINERY WICK

### Framingham Wine Company

Conders Bend Rd, Renwick
T +64 (0)3-572 8884
www.framingham.co.nz
Daily 1000-1700.

The rose-filled courtyard, the luxuriant gardens and the tree-lined stream all reflect this winery's focus on fresh, aromatic wines, such as its range of signature Rieslings. The cellar door offers a good opportunity to discover wines like these and the similarly unusual Montepulciano – and to buy bottles that are not available elsewhere.

WINERY BLENHEIM

### Fromm Winery

Godfrey Rd, RD 2, Blenheim
T +64 (0)3-572 9355
www.frommwineries.com
Visits by appointment only.
NZ$10

One of New Zealand's several impressive Swiss-owned wineries, Fromm has, almost since it opened its doors in 1992, been a magnet for lovers of Pinot Noir. George and Ruth Fromm, and their compatriot winemaker Hatsch Kalberer, specialize in single vineyard wines, many of which are very hard to find outside the winery. Apart from La Strada Pinot Noir, look out for the Syrah and Merlot. Perversely, in the Sauvignon heartland that Marlborough has become, Fromm is almost unique in deciding not to make any wine from this variety. The cedar-clad winery is also well worth visiting for the clever way in which it combines aesthetic appeal, sympathy for the landscape that surrounds it and the efficiency required to make really good wine. Visits are well worth the NZ$10 fee.

Grape picking at Fromm Winery.

RESTAURANT BLENHEIM

### Gibbs Vineyard Restaurant

258 Jacksons Rd, Blenheim
T +64 (0)3-572 8048
www.gibbs-restaurant.co.nz
Oct-Apr daily from 1830; May-Sep Tue-Sat from 1800.
$$

After a day of tasting at Marlborough wineries, you might well recognize some of the faces at the other tables here because this is where many local winemakers like to meet, eat and enjoy each other's wines. The food is good, fresh and uncomplicated, with a definite Mediterranean accent, providing a perfect background for the wines. In October, however, the mood and the menu change, as the restaurant hosts a beer festival, complete with bratwurst and oompah music.

La Strada Pinot Noir.

WINERY RENWICK

## Grove Mill

Waihopai Valley Rd, Renwick
T +64 (0)3 572 8200
www.grovemill.co.nz
Daily 1100-1700.

If you want to learn a little more about wine and about New Zealand's native flora and fauna, this is the ideal place to come. One of the most visitor-friendly wineries in the region, Grove Mill has a highly unusual 'vine library' where you can compare and contrast 10 different vines (and, at harvest time in February or March, even taste the grapes), before sampling current and older examples of wines with appropriately chosen morsels of food. The flora and fauna are to be found in the **Native Gardens & Wetland Sanctuary**, where you can wander among local shrubs, grasses and trees, while keeping your eyes peeled for the rare southern bell frog, whose silhouette features on the Grove Mill label.

WINERY BLENHEIM

## Herzog Winery

81 Jeffries Rd, Blenheim
T +64 (0)3-572 8770
www.herzog.co.nz
Daily 1100-1500.

It was New Zealand's top wine writer Bob Campbell who first directed my attention to Herzog's Chardonnay soon after its first release, but what truly impressed me was the dedication of the winery's owners, Hans and Therese Herzog, in creating more than a wine estate. They came here with the declared aim of beating Europe's winemakers at their own game. Apart from planting Italian grape varieties, such as Montepulciano and Nebbiolo, rarely found elsewhere in New Zealand, and making top class Chardonnay and Pinot Gris, the Herzogs have also opened

> Marlborough Sauvignon Blanc achieves a razor-sharp clarity of varietal character, bitingly aromatic and flavoured: asparagus, herb, grass, mineral, citrus, gooseberry, passionfruit, and redcurrant.
>
> *James Halliday, Australian wine critic and writer*

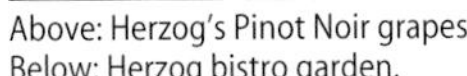

Above: Herzog's Pinot Noir grapes.
Below: Herzog bistro garden.

Herzog's Spirit Collection.

# Vintages

- 2006 Generally good to great.
- 2005 Generally good to great.
- 2004 Best in Central Otago.
- 2003 South Island, especially Marlborough.
- 2002 Best in Central Otago and Hawke's Bay.
- 2001 Very variable with some top Hawke's Bay wines.
- 2000 South Island, especially Marlborough.

Grapevine

**The birth of Marlborough Sauvignon Blanc**

Despite the existence of vineyards in this part of the South Island at the end of the 19th century, the story of one of the most iconic wine regions in the New World actually began on 24 August 1973. On that day, Frank Yukich, son of the founder of Montana Wines (producer of Brancott), dug a small hole and planted a vine along with a silver coin for luck. At the time, the journalists and farmers present at the ceremony had about as much faith in the superstitious gesture as in the development of what was, in effect, a wholly new wine region. History proved Yukich right, but not with the Müller-Thurgau and Cabernet Sauvignon vines that produced their first wine in 1976. Marlborough's global reputation was built by Sauvignon Blanc, the first example of which was produced by Montana Wines three years later. Other producers followed in the early 1980s, most notably Hunter's and Cloudy Bay, succeeded by much more recent arrivals, such as Henri Bourgeois from Sancerre. In the three decades since Frank Yukich planted that baby vine, Marlborough has grown to more than 8000 ha of vineyards, over half of which are Sauvignon Blanc. Today, the area turns out over half of all the wine in New Zealand and producers throughout the country include Marlborough wines in their portfolio, often trucking the grapes or juice to their wineries hundreds of kilometres away.

one of the region's best luxury restaurants ($$$), with a long list of wines from other producers, a comfortable **Vineyard Cottage** ($$) among the vines, and a cookery school at which visiting chefs turn their hands to local produce. A worthy New Zealand rival to some of Europe's classiest efforts.

WINERY — BLENHEIM

## Huia Vineyards

Boyces Rd, RD 3
T +64 (0)3-572 8326
www.huia.net.nz
Visits by appointment only.

Named after an extinct New Zealand bird, Huia was started in 1997 by Mike and Claire Allan who brought with them both the experience they had gained at Pelorus, Vavasour and Lawsons Dry Hills, and a desire to make aromatic white wines and Pinot Noir. Among their successes here, the most notable is probably the Pinot Noir. There's a picnic area, and parents with small children will appreciate the provision of a toy box.

WINERY — RENWICK

## Seresin Estate

Bedford Rd, PO Box 859, Blenheim
T +64 (0)3-577 9480
www.seresin.co.nz
Tours by appointment.

Michael Seresin has made his money as a top cinematographer on movies such as *Angela's Ashes* and *Harry Potter & the Prisoner of Azkaban*, but this winery is much more than a hobby. From the beginning, in 1992, Brian Bicknell (who helped to revolutionize wine-making in Chile) has produced wines that are as distinctive as Seresin's handprint logo. The wines benefit from differing soil types (gravel and clay), organic viticulture and the use of wild yeasts. Personal favourites include the Sauvignon and the Pinot Noir. The wooden winery is hard to find, so follow the standing stones bearing the image of that hand.

WINERY — BLENHEIM

## Villa Maria Estate

Paynters Rd and New Renwick Rd, PO Box 848, Blenheim
T +64 (0)3-577 9530
www.villamaria.co.nz
Tours by appointment.

One of the biggest producers in the region, Villa Maria has recently opened a striking new winery on the corner of Paynters and New Renwick Roads. Tours are by appointment only, but well worth taking if you want to learn how it is possible to make large quantities of wine that still maintain individual flavour. Look out for the Reserve Pinot Noir, an example of which surprised traditionalists by winning the top red trophy in an Air New Zealand wine competition, despite being sealed with a screwcap.

## Canterbury

The town of Christchurch (designed by Colonel Light employing the same grid as he used for Adelaide) sits astride the River Avon and has the feeling of a quiet English university town. It makes a great base from which to explore Canterbury, the large area that separates Marlborough from Central Otago and is one of the most picturesque regions in the country. When taking time off from exploring the hills, the gentle rivers and the French style of the little town of Akaroa, Canterbury is the place to sample local cheeses and unusually good Rieslings and Gewürztraminers.

The part of Canterbury that is exciting the greatest interest among wine lovers is the skiing area of Waipara to the north of Christchurch. This is still a young region but there is already plenty of evidence that its Pinot Noirs and Chardonnays could rival those of Central Otago further south. Top producers include Daniel Schuster (maker of New Zealand's first fine Pinot Noir), Waipara Springs, Pegasus Bay and Alan McCorkindale. There are some great lodges to stay in and thermal baths at Hanmer Springs.



WINERY AKAROA

### French Farm Winery

French Farm Valley Rd, RD 2, Akaroa
T +64 (0)3-304 5784
www.frenchfarm.co.nz
Daily 1000-1600.

Taking its name from the French settlers who made wine here nearly 200 years ago, this winery is as well known for its restaurant ($) and pizzeria ($) as for its wine. This is a quite perfect spot to enjoy Akaroa salmon and local vegetables and cheese, while soaking up the view of the boats on the Banks Peninsula below. Great in the summer when you can eat out of doors, it is also welcoming in the winter, when there is a log fire.

WINERY WAIPARA

### Floating Mountain

418 Omihi Rd, Waipara
T +64 (0)3-314 6710
www.floatingmountain.com
Tours by appointment only.

Floating Mountain is the English translation of 'Maukatere', the Maori name for Mount Grey, and refers to the way in which the winter mists often hide all but the summit. Previously part of Waipara Springs, this small organic vineyard produces just 1500 cases per year. It is run by Mark Rattray, who combines an understanding of the Burgundy varieties – he makes both Chardonnay and Pinot Noir – with experience gathered in the Rhine, which helps him with his Riesling and grapefruity Scheurebe, one of New Zealand's most unusual whites.

WINERY CHRISTCHURCH

### Giesen Wine Estate

Burnham School Rd, RD 5, Christchurch
T +64 (0)3-347 6729
www.giesen.co.nz
Daily 1000-1700. Tours by appointment.

Established way back in 1981 by Theo, Alex and Marcel, three brothers from Alsace, Giesen was one of the first wineries to show how well the Riesling grape can perform in New Zealand. Today, Giesen is just as well known for its Marlborough Sauvignon Blanc, of which it makes significantly larger quantities, but the winery in Burnham is still well worth a visit to explore a brilliant range of dry and sweet Rieslings with a uniquely fresh New Zealand style.

WINERY NORTH CANTERBURY

### Daniel Schuster

192 Reeces Rd, Omihi, North Canterbury
T +64 (0)3-314 5901
www.danielschusterwines.com
Tastings by appointment only.

One of the quiet heroes of New Zealand wine, Danny Schuster was among the first modern European winemakers to apply his skills in New Zealand. His first love remains Pinot Noir, which he pioneered at the Sainte Helena winery in the early 1980s and still produces here in several single-vineyard versions. Schuster is also one of the country's best-travelled winemakers, thanks to his commitments as a consultant to wineries such as Stags Leap in California and Solaia in Italy. Tastings are by appointment only but are often hosted by Danny or his similarly knowledgeable wife, Mari .

## Central Otago

If anyone were seeking to award a prize for the most beautiful and most tourist-friendly wine region in the world, Otago – or Central Otago, or simply 'Central' – would be among the frontrunners. Where else can you, depending on the time of year, visit a winery

Central Otago.

and then go waterskiing or snowboarding on the same day? Two centuries ago, like Rutherglen in Australia, this was gold-rush country. Then came tourism, including the kind of adventure tourism at which New Zealanders seem to excel: bungee jumping was invented here, over the Kawarau River. Tourists are arguably better catered for here than almost anywhere else in the country, with a plethora of luxury hotels, B&Bs, cafés and restaurants.

More recently and, for many people in the region, most excitingly, there has been wine. Among the pioneers were Rippon in Wanaka, whose vineyards run down nearly to the banks of Lake Wanaka and have featured in almost every photographic essay on wine in New Zealand, and the Gibbston Valley, which claims to attract the highest number of overseas visitors in the country. Other labels that have inevitably invited attention are Two Paddocks, which belongs to actor Sam Neill, and Sleeping Dogs, owned by the Australian film director, Roger Donaldson. The recent bout of Pinot-mania on the other side of the Pacific has attracted a number of Americans to invest in Central Otago. Among these have been landscape architect Richard Berridge of Berridge Vineyard and Garry Andrus of Pine Ridge in Napa and Archery Summit in Oregon, who produced his first Christine Lorraine Cellars Pinot Noir in 2003. New wineries open in this region almost by the month but the quality remains high.

The Big Picture.

ATTRACTION CROMWELL

### The Big Picture

State Highway 6 and Sandfly Flat Rd, Cromwell
T +64 (0)3-445 4052
www.wineadventure.co.nz
Daily from 0900.
WineAdventure is NZ$20.

If only the wine world had more people like Phil and Cath Parker, the couple behind this extraordinary enterprise. Situated among the vines, the Big Picture ambitiously sets out to offer a multi-sensorial experience of the region. So, there's an 18-minute film (made by Phil) that takes you on a helicopter tour of the region, including visits to and tastings with five winemakers; an Aroma Room that enables you to relate the smells of wine to 50 other aromas, a well-stocked wine shop and a good restaurant ($$-$) with local wines by the glass. The powers-that-be of Bordeaux and Burgundy ought to sign up the Parkers forthwith, but I suspect the couple's hearts are far too firmly attached to Central Otago to consider taking their talents elsewhere.

WINERY CROMWELL

### Central Otago Wine Company

Building 1, Lake Dunstan Estate, McNulty Rd, Cromwell
T +64 (0)3-445 3100
wine@cowine.co.nz
Summer Mon-Fri 1000-1700, Sat and Sun 1200-1700; winter Mon-Fri 1000-1700.

If you like your wine to be produced in picturesque chateaux then maybe you should give the COW – as it is known locally – a miss. If, on the other hand, you are interested in tasting a wide range of Central Otago wines and can accept that it is often far easier to make great wine in a purpose-built facility in an industrial park rather than in a fairytale castle, then you have

Tasting notes

**Against the odds: Central Otago Pinot Noir**
Central Otago would stand a high chance of walking away with the award for the place least likely to succeed at making a particular style of wine. Stated simply, this area of hills and lakes seems to be far too close to the South Pole and, for the most part, at far too high an altitude to ripen Pinot Noir grapes. The fact that Pinot Noir does well enough here to produce some of the New World's most sought-after examples is a tribute to an unusual combination of four factors. First and probably most crucially, there is the intensity of cloud-free sunlight which seems to compensate for the lower-than-ideal temperatures. If the sun helps to give the wines their intense fruit flavours, they also gain from the wide difference in temperature (up to 30°) between day and night. Warm nights contribute to 'cooked' flavours, while cool ones make for the kind of freshness that is a particularly desirable hallmark of Pinot Noir. The schistous-loess soil-over-gravel also suits the Pinot Noir well. Finally, rain comes more sparingly and more predictably here than in Burgundy, so grapes are less prone to rot and mildew.

 to include this in your itinerary. Apart from the winery's own Pinot Noir, Dean Jones also makes wines for over a dozen estates, including Sam Neill's Two Paddocks.

WINERY QUEENSTOWN

### Gibbston Valley

State Highway 6, Gibbston, RD1, Queenstown
T +64 (0)3-442 6910
www.gvwines.co.nz
Daily 1000-1700. Restaurant daily 1200-1500. Tours NZ$9.50.

Founded by one of this region's groundbreakers in the early 1980s, Gibbston Valley has been a flagship for Central Otago wine from the outset. Just as important as the multi-award-winning Reserve Pinot Noir and Chardonnay are the stone-built restaurant ($$) and cheesery. These have become such major tourist attractions that the current owner, Mike Stome, claims to get more visitors than at any other New Zealand winery.

WINERY LAKE WANAKA

### Rippon Vineyard

PO Box 175, Mt Aspiring Rd, 4 km from Lake Wanaka
T +64 (0)3 443 8084
www.rippon.co.nz
Dec-Apr daily 1100-1700. May and Jun by appointment only. Jul-Nov daily 1330-1630.

The view over Lake Wanaka from this pioneering (1974) vineyard would warrant the trip alone, even if the wines were mediocre. But they're not. Nick Mills, who runs the estate with his mother Lois, uses experience gained at the Domaine de la Romanée-Conti in Burgundy to make terrific bio-dynamic wines, including Pinot Noir, Gewürztraminer and Riesling.

Gibbston Valley winery.

## Best producers

**Auckland**
Kumeu River » page 321.

**Canterbury**
Giesen
Schuster Daniel

**Central Otago**
Akarua
Felton Road
Gibbston Valley » page 336.
Mount Difficulty
Olssens
Peregrine
Quartz Reef
Rippon » page 336.
Two Paddocks

**Gisbourne**
Lindauer » page 323.
Matua Valley
Millton

**Hawke's Bay**
Babich
CJ Pask
Craggy Range » page 324.
Delegat's Matariki
Matua Valley
Morton Estate
Ngatarawa
Sileni
Te Awa
Te Mata » page 325.
Trinity Hill
Villa Maria » page 322.

**Marlborough**
Babich
Brancott/Montana » page 329.
Church Road
Cloudy Bay » page 330.
Craggy Range
Dog Point
Forrest Estate
Framingham » page 331.
Fromm » page 331.
Giesen » page 334.
Grove Mill
Herzog
Hunter's
Jackson Estate
Matua Valley
Montana/Brancott » page 329.
No1 Family Estate
St Clair
Seresin » page 333.
Sileni
Vavasour
Villa Maria » page 333.
Wither Hills

**Martinborough**
Ata Rangi
Dry River
Martinborough Vineyards
Palliser

**Nelson**
Neudorf
Seifried
Spencer Hill/Tasman Bay

**Waiheke Island**
Goldwater Estate
Stonyridge

New Zealand South Island

## New Zealand's adventure capital

Queenstown is now the biggest tourist draw in New Zealand and considered one of the top (and almost certainly the most scenic) adventure venues in the world. Amidst the stunning setting of mountain and lake, over one million visitors a year partake in a staggering range of activities from a sedate steamboat cruise to the heart-stopping bungee jump. Add to that a superb range of accommodation, services, cafés and restaurants and you simply won't know where to turn. For non-biased advice head straight to the very efficient and busy **Queenstown Travel & Visitor Centre** (below the Clock Tower, Shotover and Camp sts, T +64 (0)3-442 4100, www.queenstown-nz.co.nz). The 'big four' activities in Queenstown are bungee jumping, jet boating, rafting and flightseeing although there are myriad others, including skiing in winter.

**Wanaka** is a quieter alternative base, with the lake of the same name lapping rhythmically at its heels and the peaks of the **Mount Aspiring National Park** as its backdrop. Both Wanaka and Queenstown are jumping off points for visiting **Milford Sound**, a fjord surrounded by towering peaks that is a highlight of New Zealand. The 12-hour day trip by road, via Te Anau, is one of the world's most spectacular bus journeys but there are also fly, fly-cruise-fly and bus-cruise-fly options. The majority of the day cruises explore the 15-km length of the sound, taking in the waterfalls, seal colonies, precipitous rock overhangs and **Milford Deep Underwater Observatory** (T0800-326969, www.milforddeep.co.nz). You can also explore the sound by kayak for an incredible sense of scale and serenity.

**Bungee jumping** The bungee made Queenstown famous. Sign up with **AJ Hackett** (The Station, corner of Shotover St and Camp St, T+64 (03)-442 7100, www.ajhackett.com).

**Jet boating** **Shotover Jet** (The Station, Shotover St, T+64 (03)-442 8570, T0800-746 86837, www.shotoverjet.com) offers the 'must-do' trip on the Shotover River (from NZ$95): an efficient, safe and thrilling 30-min, 70-kph 'blat' down the river, with superb 360-degree turns. Shotover Jet picks up from town several times a day for the 15-min ride to the riverside.

**Flightseeing** A scenic flight from Wanaka to Milford Sound is highly recommended, with the bonus of seeing Mount Aspiring National Park on the way (from NZ$370). Other options include Mount Cook and the glaciers and the Catlins Coast.

**Rafting and kayaking** There is a glut of rafting operators in Queenstown, all offering thrills and spills on the Kawarau and Shotover rivers. Some superb sea kayaking is also offered on Milford Sound.

**Skiing** Wanaka has two great ski fields within 50 km of the town, **Cardrona** to the south and **Treble Cone** to the northwest. For general information and snow reports check out www.snow.co.nz, www.nzski.com or www.skilakewanaka.com.

**Walking and tramping** Mount Aspiring National Park is a place of stunning and remote beauty, home to unusual wildlife like the New Zealand falcon, the kea and the giant weta. If you haven't the time or the energy for any of the major tramps, then the one-day Rob Roy Glacier walk is quite simply a 'must do'. The **Mount Aspiring Express** (T +64 (0)3-443 8422) can shuttle you from Wanaka to the start of the walk at Raspberry Creek for NZ$45 return. The bus departs 0900 and 1400, returning 1030 and 1530.

# Levant & Africa



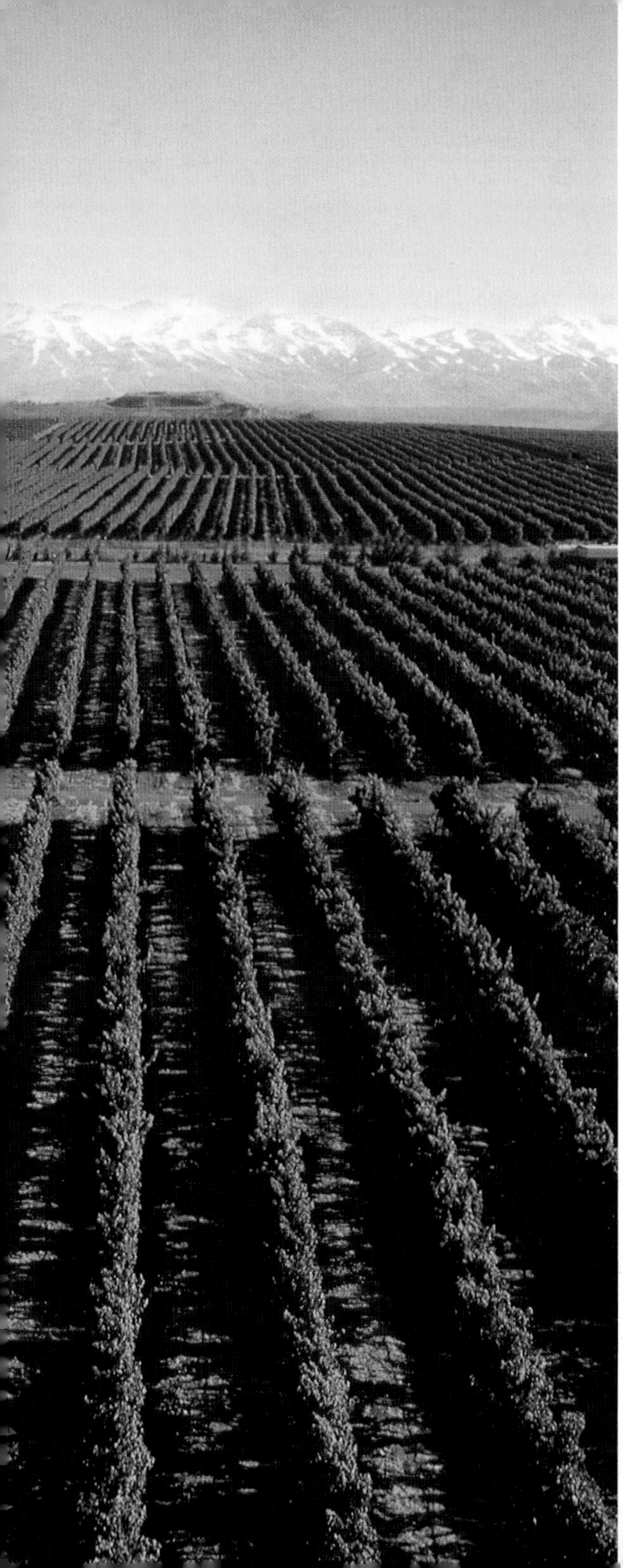

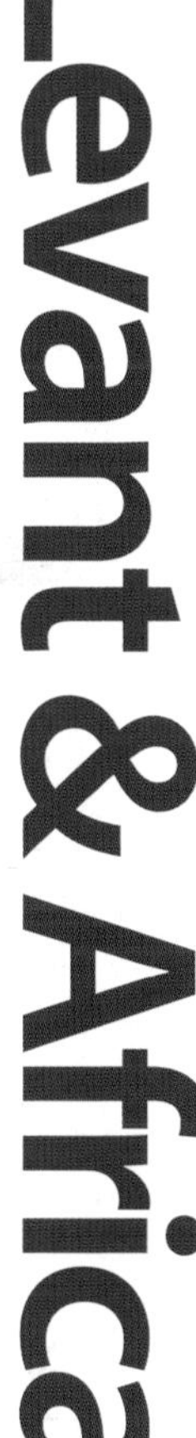

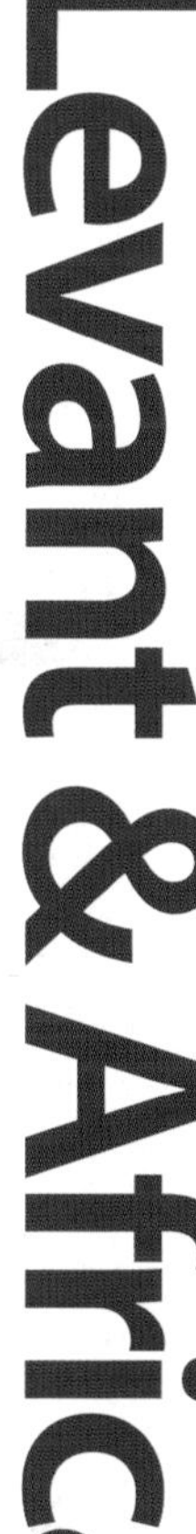

Vineyards on the Golan Heights.

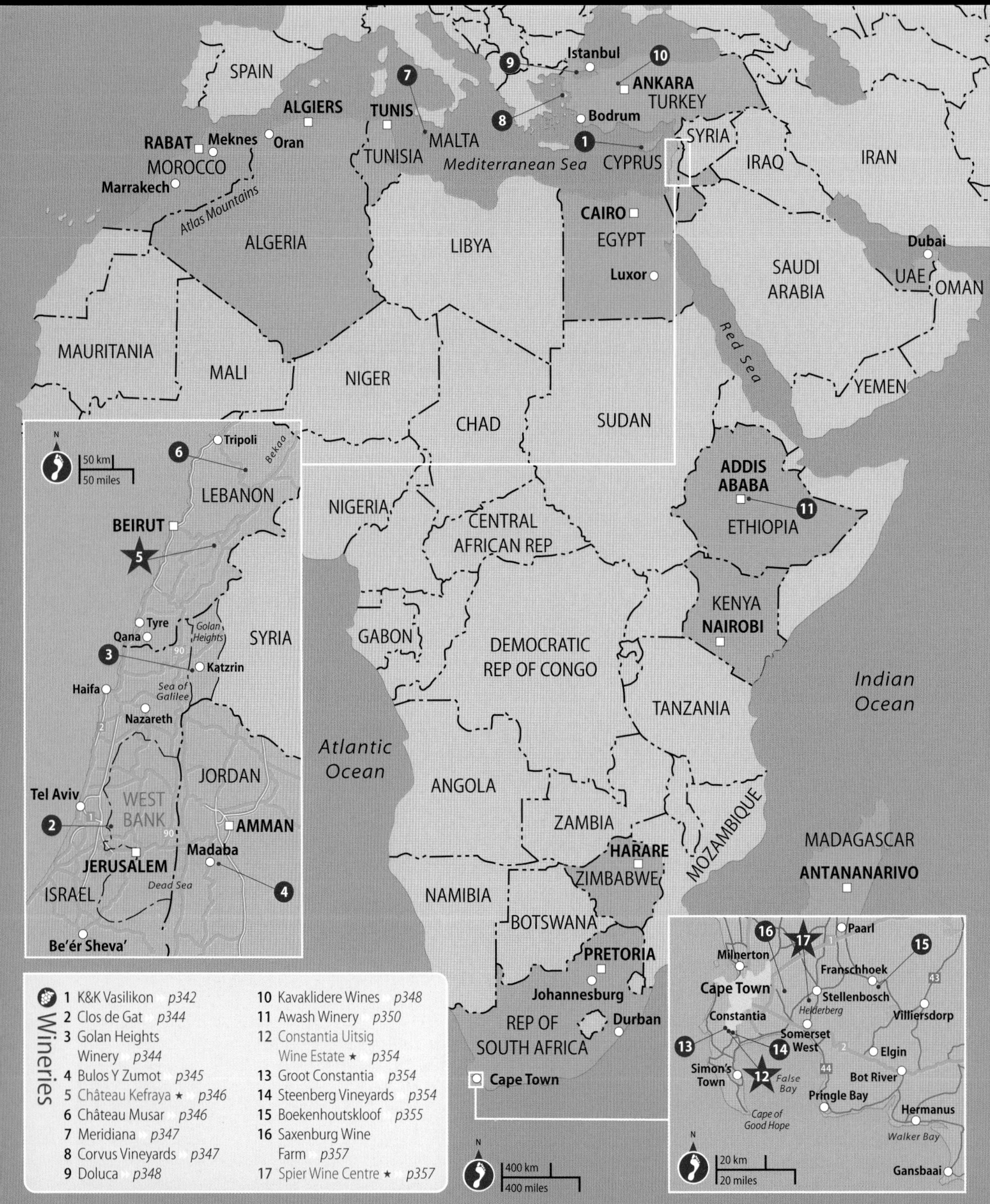
SPAIN
ALGIERS
TUNIS
Istanbul
ANKARA
TURKEY
Bodrum
RABAT
Meknes
Oran
MOROCCO
Marrakech
TUNISIA
MALTA
Mediterranean Sea
CYPRUS
SYRIA
IRAQ
IRAN
Atlas Mountains
ALGERIA
LIBYA
CAIRO
EGYPT
Luxor
Dubai
SAUDI ARABIA
UAE
OMAN
Red Sea
MAURITANIA
MALI
NIGER
CHAD
SUDAN
YEMEN
ADDIS ABABA
ETHIOPIA
NIGERIA
CENTRAL AFRICAN REP
GABON
DEMOCRATIC REP OF CONGO
KENYA
NAIROBI
TANZANIA
Indian Ocean
Atlantic Ocean
ANGOLA
ZAMBIA
MOZAMBIQUE
MADAGASCAR
ANTANANARIVO
HARARE
ZIMBABWE
NAMIBIA
BOTSWANA
PRETORIA
Johannesburg
Durban
REP OF SOUTH AFRICA
Cape Town
50 km
50 miles
Tripoli
Bekaa
LEBANON
BEIRUT
Tyre
Qana
Golan Heights
SYRIA
Katzrin
Haifa
Sea of Galilee
Nazareth
JORDAN
Tel Aviv
WEST BANK
AMMAN
Madaba
JERUSALEM
Dead Sea
ISRAEL
Be'ér Sheva'
Paarl
Milnerton
Franschhoek
Cape Town
Stellenbosch
Helderberg
Villiersdorp
Constantia
Somerset West
Elgin
Simon's Town
False Bay
Bot River
Pringle Bay
Cape of Good Hope
Hermanus
Walker Bay
Gansbaai
20 km
20 miles
400 km
400 miles
Wineries
1 K&K Vasilikon p342
2 Clos de Gat p344
3 Golan Heights Winery p344
4 Bulos Y Zumot p345
5 Château Kefraya ★ p346
6 Château Musar p346
7 Meridiana p347
8 Corvus Vineyards p347
9 Doluca p348
10 Kavaklidere Wines p348
11 Awash Winery p350
12 Constantia Uitsig Wine Estate ★ p354
13 Groot Constantia p354
14 Steenberg Vineyards p354
15 Boekenhoutskloof p355
16 Saxenburg Wine Farm p357
17 Spier Wine Centre ★ p357

# Introduction



Turkey, Cyprus, Algeria, Morocco and Tunisia are not countries that most people associate with good wine. Some adventurous or lucky wine drinkers may have come across good bottles from Israel and Lebanon, but these countries too, have hardly been part of the vinous mainstream. The only region on the continent of Africa to have gained a reputation for its wines is South Africa, one of the very oldest winemaking countries in the New World.

But that picture is changing. Throughout the area, a quality revolution is quietly taking place. French investors have brought the international winemaking guru to Algeria and Morocco. In Turkey, a new generation of winemakers are beginning to exploit the potential of grape varieties that are grown almost nowhere else on earth. Lebanon, which many people may have imagined to have only one winery, in the shape of Château Musar, has spawned an impressive set of other producers. In Israel, quality is rising rapidly too, thanks in part to a rapidly expanding number of small 'boutique' wineries, but also to the efforts made by big companies like Carmel. Other success stories, though smaller in scale, include Jordan and Malta, both of which can now boast wine producers that stand comparison with those of other countries.

And then, of course, there's South Africa which may have started at a higher quality level, but has still had to undergo a vineyard and winemaking revolution of its own since the 1990s in order to compete with the Americas and Oceania.

# Levant

**This is where the story of wine probably began. Despite the archaeological claims of the former Soviet republic of Georgia to be the 'cradle of wine', research by Patrick McGovern of the University of Pennsylvania suggests that wine grapes may have grown in Turkey's Taurus Mountains as long as 6000 years ago. The Levant was, in any case, crucial to the early development of wine and its introduction to northern Europe. The Egyptians were sophisticated winemakers, producing and drinking the stuff 5000 years ago. Wine jars from Tutankhamun's tomb prove that, as early as 1352 BC, distinctions were being made between different vintages and winemakers. The Phoenicians, who were keener on trading than farming, are believed to have carried the variety of vine used for wine – *vitis vinifera* – to southern Europe from their home in Lebanon, making it possible for the Greeks and then the Romans to take the vines further north.**

## Cyprus

Cyprus is enjoying a much-needed vinous renaissance. In the millennium before the Christian era, the island was colonised by the Phoenicians, Assyrians, Egyptians, Persians and Greeks and gained a wide range of winemaking expertise from all these cultures. Cyprus's most famous and historically best wine, the dark, sweet Commandaria, is made from grapes that are dried for two weeks before being pressed. Its ancient forebear was served at festivities honouring Aphrodite, who was said to have appeared from the ocean on the Cypriot coast at Paphos. It was also praised by the English king, Richard the Lionheart, who served it at his wedding at Limassol in 1191. Modern Commandaria, however, is less impressive than its ancestor must have been. Until recently, Cyprus's only claim to vinous fame was as the producer of cheap alternatives to sherry, and of grape concentrate that was rehydrated and fermented in the UK to be sold as 'British' wine and sherry. This last category no longer exists, happily, and Cyprus's winemakers, led by the giant KEO, have been busily improving their wines.

WINERY — PAPHOS

### K&K Vasilikon

8573 Kathikas, Paphos
T+357 26 63 32 37 / 99 46 69 60
www.cyprusvines.com
Daily 0900-1500 by appointment.

Yiannos Kyriakidis, his wife and two sons run this winery and vineyard situated in a village on the outskirts of Paphos. The vineyards are at 650 m above sea level and include some vines that are over 100 years old. This family's passion for winemaking shows in the consistently high quality of the small range of wines they produce year after year. These include Ayios Onoufrios Dry Red and Vasilikon Dry White from native Cypriot varieties. A new Cabernet Sauvignon has also been added to the range; it has 26 months ageing in barrel. There are currently plans for the construction of a new winery with tasting facilities on site, which will give tourists and wine-lovers the opportunity to visit this unique winery and taste the wines for themselves.

## Egypt

The nationalization of the wine industry by President Nasser in the 1960s caused less fuss than his seizure of the Suez Canal in 1956 but it was not good news for wine drinkers. During the first half of the 20th century, winemaking had enjoyed a revival in Egypt, thanks to the efforts of a Greek tobacco merchant called Nestor Gianaclis who, in 1903, planted 3000 ha of vines on irrigated desert land, close to Nubariya Canal. Gianaclis not only tried to make good modern wine but also to investigate the kind of wine the ancient Egyptians would have made.

Today, his name survives as the brand of one of Egypt's three privatised producers, but the quality is not great. However, given the US$100 price tag on imported bottles of wine, there is an attraction in local efforts costing a tenth of that price. Of several appealingly named, locally produced styles – Omar Khayyam, Rubis D' Egypte, Château Grand Marquis and Cru de Ptolemées – the Grand Marquis Cabernet Sauvignon is the most acceptable. Obelisk red is similarly decent, possibly because it is made from concentrated Italian grape juice, but by far the pick of the supposedly 'local' wines is Château des Rêves Cabernet Sauvignon, which is, in fact, produced from grapes grown in Lebanon. It is to be hoped that Egypt's wine industry will one day soon benefit from the kinds of skills that are now being so beneficial to Turkey. Its history deserves it.

Grapevine

**Wine, coffee and Islam**

The Islamic ban on alcohol is well known but few non-Muslims are aware of how it came to be introduced into a region where wine had been commonly drunk. According to Ghazal Omid (www.theislam101.com), an authority on Shiah Islam, the prophet Mohammed was passing through a particular district, when he saw some of his followers drinking. They invited him to join them and, although he declined the invitation, he wished them well, saying, "*Noosh, Noosh*" ("Enjoy, enjoy"). On his way back, he saw the same men, now quite drunk, touching each other in an inappropriate manner. The sight made him very angry and led him to declare that "From this moment on, I forbid my people, Muslims, to drink alcohol". As Ghazal Omid wonders, if that group of drinkers had been more moderate in their behaviour, perhaps the *fatwa* (prohibition) on alcohol would not have been issued.

Another alternative view of history raises the possibility that coffee might also have been subject to the same ban. In Arabic, *kahwah* means both wine and coffee and in the 16th century, an alcoholic drink was made by fermenting the pulp of coffee beans. In 1511, the Governor of Mecca saw some Muslims drinking (non-alcoholic) coffee in the mosque before a night of prayer and outlawed it. The edict was revoked the following year when the governor was executed for embezzlement but coffee-liquor remained a rarity.

ATTRACTION — LUXOR

### Tomb of Sennefer

Valley of the Nobles, Luxor
Information from the Egyptian Tourist Authority, Sh Cornich El-Nil, Luxor.
T +20 (0)95-382 215 / (0)95-372 215.
Visits only possible with a guide.
E£20

Sennefer made his impact in Egypt around 1439-1413 BC, when he became mayor of Thebes (now Luxor), an important Egyptian city at the time. He built his tomb on the west bank of the city in an area known as the Tomb of the Nobles. By the 19th century his burial chamber was known as the 'Tomb of the Vineyards' because of its extraordinary decorative theme.

Around 43 steps roughly cut into the rock lead down into the tomb, where a pergola of black grapes decorates the ceiling. Sennefer hoped that these images would impress Osiris the god of resurrection and of wine and lead Senefer smoothly into the afterlife. Other tombs in the area include the Tomb of Userhet, which has scenes of grape harvesting, feasting and wine storage; the Tomb of Rekhmire, which depicts people treading grapes; and the Tomb of Pabasa, which has scenes of viticulture.

The tombs of the nobles can easily be explored with a guide from Luxor. For a longer organized tour, contact Michael Ackroyd at Ancient World Tours in the UK (T +44 (0)20 7917 9494, www.ancient.co.uk), who can arrange special photography permits as well as visits to wineries and museums.

## Israel

Surprisingly, perhaps, Israel's modern wine industry has a much longer history than the state itself. Early settlers made sweet kosher wine in the 19th century, an example of which was sent, in 1875, to the British Prime Minister, Benjamin Disrael. His tasting note is worth recalling: "not so much like wine but more like what I expect to receive from my doctor as a remedy for a bad winter cough".

In 1882, Edmond de Rothschild, owner of Château Lafite in Bordeaux, decided to help the early Jewish settlers in Palestine by building a couple of wineries in Rishon Le Zion, south of Tel Aviv, and at Zichron Ya'acov, south of Haifa. He spent more on this investment than his father had on the purchase of Lafite. The wines were sold under the Carmel and Palwin brands and the firm became one of the most important in the young country. Two prime ministers – David Ben Gurion and Levi Eshkol – both worked for the company, which boasted

Golan Heights winery and vineyards.

Israel's first working telephone. In 1957, a later Rothschild turned the company into a cooperative and, for around 25 years, Carmel was almost synonymous with Israeli wine, despite the truly appalling quality of much of what it produced. In 1983 competition arrived in the form of the Golan Heights winery, which imported Californian methods and standards, and, in 1992, an Italian restaurateur made Israel's first 'boutique' wine, Domaine du Castel. The ensuing decade has seen a blossoming of around 150 boutiques which, between them, produce less than 10% of Israel's wine. The remainder is made by a dozen big companies, led by the much-improved Carmel, Golan Heights (under the Yarden label) and Barkan.

Israel's 4000 ha of vines are situated in five main regions: the Judean hills around Jerusalem; Shromrom to the south of Haifa (close to where Carmel was first established); the Negev (an irrigated semi-desert); the coastal region of Samson, and Galilee in the north. This last is where the Golan Heights is situated, a cooler region where it snows in winter and where many of the best wines have been produced. Students of modern politics may wonder at the long-term investment that has gone into this last area, given the existence of UN resolutions 242, 338 and 497, which effectively require Israel to give up all the land – including Golan – that it occupied in 1967.

WINERY — AYALON VALLEY

## Clos de Gat

Har'el Vineyards, Ayalon Valley 99740
T+972 (0)2- 999 3505
www.closdegat.com
Visits by appointment only.

The rolling countryside of the Ayalon Valley has been cultivated for thousands of years and has biblical associations as the location of Joshua's defeat of the five Kings. This 35-ha boutique winery is named after the low stone walls ('clos') surrounding some of the vineyards and after its historic wine press ('gat'), which predates Roman times. Eyal Rotem is the winemaker-owner. He produces varietal wines from international varieties – Cabernet Sauvignon, Merlot, Syrah and Chardonnay – using the broad experience he gained from working at Australian wineries. He enterprisingly chooses neither to fine nor filter his red wines with an aim to allowing the wines' true style to shine through. The estate has recently reached an agreement for international distribution by France's Maison Sichel.

WINERY — GALILEE

## Golan Heights Winery

PO Box 183, Katzrin 12900
T+972 (0)4- 696 8420
www.golanwines.co.il
Jul-Aug Sun-Thu 0830-1830, Fri 0830-1400; Sep-Jun Sun-Thu 0830-1700; Fri 0830-1330. Last tour 1 hr before closing; booking requested.

Despite its location in the politically controversial Golan Heights, this is considered Israel's leading winery when it comes to quality, technical innovation and variety development. It has also helped nurture the country's wine culture and has changed how Israel's wines are perceived worldwide. Since its founding in 1983, it has marketed three leading brands: Yarden, Gamla and Golan. It now supplies 20% of the domestic market and 40% of Israel's wine exports to 30 countries. Today, the company is owned by four kibbutzes and four moshavs, which manage the vineyards. The winery itself is state of the art and includes a microwinery for experimental winemaking, which focuses on scientific advances and new grape-growing techniques. There is also an impressive sister company, the Galil Mountain Winery in Upper Galilee.

RESTAURANT JERUSALEM

### Arcadia

10 Agrippas St, Jerusalem
T+972 (0)2- 624 9138
Mon-Fri 1230-1500, 1900-2230; Sat 1300-1500, 1900-2330; booking advised.
$$

Arcadia is to be found nestled discreetly down a quiet lane, off the beaten track of Jerusalem's nearby gastro-centre. Inside, the simple but contemporary decor does not detract from the quality of the food on offer. The restaurant offers French- and Mediterranean-influenced fare. Dishes range from liver to salmon to lamb, all prepared using local speciality ingredients such as home-pressed olive oil, and all treated with care, allowing the true flavours to prevail. The wine list has many interesting choices, from Israel's own boutique wineries to reliable and sought-after producers from other countries.

RESTAURANT JERUSALEM

### Mishkenot Sha'ananim

Yemin Moshe, Jerusalem
T +972 (0)2- 625 1042
Daily 1200-1500, 1830-2400.
$$

Located in the impressively restored 19th-century Yemin Moshe ('below the windmill') area, this popular restaurant boasts spectacular views of the Old City walls. It is a favourite with VIPs who visit the city and whose photographs greet you at the entrance; it is also the usual choice for those who are not kosher. Offering classic French-continental cuisine – ranging from duckling to foie gras to veal – and formal service, it also boasts a huge museum-like wine cellar that can be visited by special request.

## Jordan

Jordan's wine vineyards are shrinking fast, due to a lack of local demand. Only one producer, Bulos Y Zumot, produces wine of any quality, but there are hopes that others may soon follow its example.

WINERY AMMAN

### Bulos Y Zumot

Wadi Saqarah St, Amman
T+962 (0)6- 461 4125
www.zumotgroup.com
Visits Apr-Nov by appointment only.

Zumot Distilleries, part of the Bullos Zumot Group founded in 1954, began bottling spirits under licence in 1987. The first vineyards were planted in 1995 outside the 4000-year-old town of Madaba, not far from the Dead Sea. Advice was taken from French experts at the time of planting, and subsequent efforts by consultants have played a large part in maintaining the consistent quality of the wines. Marketed under the label Saint Georges Grand Vin de Jordanie, the red is an impressive if unconventional blend of Cabernet Sauvignon and Pinot Noir, while the white is a Chardonnay-Sauvignon Blanc. Present plans include increasing production to supply new markets and continuing the fight for high-quality Jordanian wines. It is hoped that growth in Jordanian tourism will help to spread the word.

## Lebanon

Grapes have been grown in Lebanon for 6000 years and, If the town of Qana is indeed the biblical Cana where Jesus is supposed to have turned water into wine, then this small, mountainous country has a unique place in the history of wine. The Lebanese – or the Phoenicians as they were then – certainly knew about wine; in another biblical reference, Melchizedek, an important Phoenician king and priest, offered it with bread to Abraham. If the Phoenicians produced wine, however, they were primarily merchants who built up trade routes across the region and were responsible for introducing wine and

## Best producers

**Cyprus**
KEO (top wines)
Loel
Sodap
K&K Vasilikon » *page 342.*

**Israel**
Barkan
Castel
Clos de Gat » *page 344.*
Elrom
Flam
Galil Mountain
Golan Heights » *page 344*
Tishbi

**Jordan**
Bulos Y Zumot » *page 345.*

**Lebanon**
Clos St Thomas
Château Kefraya » *page 346*
Château Ksara
Massaya
Château Musar » *page 346.*
Domaine Wardy

**Malta**
Meridiana » *page 347.*

winemaking to places such as Tunisia, Crete, Sardinia and Valdepeñas in Spain. In 1999, Dr Robert Ballard uncovered the wrecks of two Phoenician ships from 750 BC that were carrying ceramic amphorae full of wine to Tunisia or Egypt. The boats would almost certainly have taken their cargo aboard in Tyre, the Phoenician city that fell to Alexander the Great in 332 BC.

Tyre and Qana both hit the headlines during the 2006 conflict in Lebanon, as did the southern region of the Bekaa Valley, home of Lebanon's wine vineyards, which is tragically used to finding itself in the firing line. The best known winery, Château Musar, which was founded in 1930, was prevented by previous conflicts from even making wine in 1976 and 1984. Musar was the first quality-conscious Lebanese winery in recent times and it remains the best known. Its wines, however, stand apart from its younger neighbours in the way they are made and in their gloriously idiosyncratic, leathery, occasionally faintly vinegary but long-lived old-fashioned style.



WINERY — BEKAA VALLEY

## Château Kefraya

Bekaa Valley
T+961 (0)8-645 333 / (0)8-645 444
www.chateaukefraya.com
Tastings daily 1000-1800. Tours by appointment.

As a long time dedicated fan of Serge Hochar at Château Musar, though not always of his wines, I've been delighted to see others now playing a growing part in building Lebanon's wine reputation. And none do it better than Château Kefraya, which can be found spreading out over the Bekaa Valley, east of Beirut, as far as the foothills of impressive Mount Lebanon. This 300-ha estate is young in relation to its reputation, which has grown very quickly as the wines have won both numerous awards in international competitions, and recognition from critics such as Robert Parker. The terraced vineyards sit at an altitude of 950 to 1100 m and manage to weather the exceptional sun exposure and the (on average) six to seven months without rain.

Le Relais Dionysos restaurant, located inside the grounds of the estate, opened its doors in 1999. Its menu offers exclusive homemade dishes to be enjoyed with an array of Château Kefraya wines.

Château Kefraya.

WINERY — BEIRUT

## Château Musar

Sopenco Building, Baroudy St, BP281
Ashrafieh, Beirut
T+961 (0)1- 201 828 / (0)1-328 111 / (0)1-328 211
www.chateaumusar.com.lb
Visits by appointment only.

The Bekaa Valley was chosen by the Romans as the site for their largest temple to Dionysus and since the 1950s has been the location of Lebanon's best known winery. The Hochar family's interest in wine was inspired by Ronald Barton of Château Leoville Barton in Bordeaux, whom they met in Lebanon during the Second World War. Gaston Hochar then visited France and, on his return, created Château Musar in the cellars of the old Mzar castle in Ghazir. In 1959, his eldest son, Serge, began his winemaking career, joined in 1962 by his brother Ronald, who took over marketing and finance. The 180 ha of vineyard sit at an altitude of over 1000 m and produce the estate's red blend of Cabernet Sauvignon, Cinsault and Carignan, as well as the native Obeideh- and Merwah-based white. Tours of Lebanon can be arranged.

## Malta

An old joke told in Malta describes how, on his deathbed, an old winegrower finally reveals to his son the secret of winemaking: "what sets the best cuvées apart," he whispers, "is that for those wines, I actually use grapes".

Although grapes are, in fact, used for all Maltese wines, in many cases, they are either the wrong kinds of grapes – indigenous varieties such as the white Ghirghentina and the black Gellewza that are better for eating – or they are grown in Italy. Most Maltese wine also suffers from the addition of sugar, which on a sun-drenched island, merely illustrates the deficiency of the raw materials.

Winemaking began here under the Phoenicians and Romans and flourished under the Knights of St John. The recent industry only began, however, in the 1970s fuelled by the thirst of the local populace and growing number of tourists who have helped to push demand way beyond the limits of local supply. In recent years, Meridiana has spearheaded the establishment of legislation to govern Maltese vine-growing and to ban the traditional addition of sugar to Maltese wines.

Grapevine

**Wine in the dry zone: Saudi Arabia, Libya, Iran, Syria and Iraq**

The vinous history of these countries is quite varied. Two thousand years ago, the Greek geographer Strabo wrote that the country we now call Libya was "without good wine, since the wine jars receive more sea-water than wine; and this they call 'Libyan' wine". Syria, however had a thriving wine industry in the ninth century BC and a culture that associated food and wine. Syria still produces wine today, but nothing that most wine lovers would want to drink. Swedish consumers were, however, recently given the opportunity to buy very decent wine whose label declared its origin to be "Israel: from occupied Syrian territory." The wine in question was from the Golan Heights Winery (page 344), located in a region occupied by Israel in 1967 but still deemed by a United Nations resolution to be part of Syria.

Saudi Arabia, Iran and Libya are famously dry, though the use of home winemaking kits is not unknown among expatriates brave enough to risk the draconian penalties. Guests at embassy receptions also report that those wanting stronger liquor know that the orange juice being served by some waiters comes with a small dose of vodka.

Recently, wine-loving Iraqis were pleased and surprised to see the newly elected al Jaafari government remove the ban on the public consumption of alcohol that Sadaam Hussein had introduced in the 1990s. However, people selling wine and spirits are taking a big risk in modern Iraq; as we go to press, a number of, mostly Christian, liquor merchants have been killed by fundamentalist militia. It is also worth mentioning that in July 2005, Salam Maliki, the Transport Minister, who is a Shiite Muslim, forbade the sale of any alcohol at Baghdad International Airport (including the duty-free shop), describing it as "a holy and revered" piece of Iraq.

WINERY TA'QALI

### Meridiana

Ta' Qali, BZN09
T+356 (0)21- 41 3550
www.meridiana.com.mt
Visits by appointment Mon-Fri 1130-1530, Sat 0900-1300.

Meridiana was established in 1987 with the pioneering mission statement of producing 'world-class wines of Maltese character'. In 1994, in partnership with Italy's Marchese Piero Antinori, a 19-ha estate was planted in Ta' Qali, Malta's agricultural heartland. Meridiana's first vintage was released in 1996 and, since then, Meridiana has doubled its vineyard area. The estate follows sustainable farming techniques in soil management and vine husbandry; interestingly, its vineyards are irrigated and drained using a system laid out by the Royal Air Force in the Second World War. Its best-known wines are Isis Chardonnay, Mistral (Barrel-Fermented) Chardonnay, Melqart Cabernet Sauvignon and Merlot, Bel Syrah, Nexus Merlot, and Celsius Reserve Cabernet Sauvignon.

## Turkey

Turkey may be a Muslim nation, but wine drinking – though limited on a per capita basis – is far from uncommon and in recent times there have been great efforts to improve quality. Turkey's vinous renaissance is, however, a well-kept secret. Even well-informed wine professionals tend to have heard of a red called Buzbag, usually presumed to be oxidised and avoided, and nothing more. Two big firms, Doluca and Kvaklidere, have raised standards considerably and are making both good wines with indigenous grapes and blends with international varieties. Buzbag, too, is better than its reputation, following the privatisation of its production. There are also a growing number of small wineries worth watching.

WINERY BOZCAADA

### Corvus Vineyards

Bozcaada
T+90 (0)212- 444 2787
www.corvus.com.tr
Visits by appointment only.

The island of Bozcaada has been making wine for over 3000 years. Corvus Vineyards, however, were only established in 2002 and are already working hard to raise the quality and reputation of wines from the island. The company is keen to establish a national certified system that regulates vine-growing and winemaking. A mixture of international and local varieties are grown on the estate, such as Vasilaki, Cavus, Kuntra and Karalahna, and the winery equipment was shipped from Italy and France, as was the winemaking expertise. A wide range of wines is produced, including a frizzante and a passito-style red.

WINERY ISTANBUL

### Doluca

Istanbul
T+90 (0)212- 471 22 40 41/327 7777
www.doluca.com
Visits by appointment only.

This estate has been pioneering quality winemaking in Turkey since 1926, when Nihat Kutman retuned from the Geisenheim Wine Institute in Germany to set it up. Today, Doluca offers over 20 different wines, including the groundbreaking Sarafin brand with which the current company head, Ahmet Kutman, introduced Turkey's first varietal range. With around 250 acres of vineyard near Saroz Bay and a modern winery and bottling plant in Mürefte, Kutman aims to marry tradition with contemporary winemaking practices. Sarafin was launched in 1998 and since then the wine has won a number of international medals.

RESTAURANT BODRUM

### The Secret Garden

Eskiçeþme Mah, 20 Donaci Sokak, Bodrum
T+90 (0)252 -313 16 41
www.secretgardenbodrum.com
Tue-Sun 1930-2400.
$

The Secret Garden is one of the top restaurants in Bodrum. It has been serving its Mediterranean-style cuisine for six years, and sits in a a romantic location in a small street opposite the Karada. The British-born owner-chef, Helen Özer, sources all of the ingredients from one of the daily local markets to prepare dishes such as frogs' legs sea bass, duck, as well as top quality Turkish Delight. There is also an extensive wine list to ponder over before the meal, covering all price points. The wines are mainly from Turkey and made from native varieties, demonstrating the diversity of styles offered by this developing wine country.

WINERY ANKARA

### Kavaklidere Wines

Kav Kavaklidere Sarap Butigi Tunus Cad. No:88, Ankara
T+90 (312) 467 57 75
www.kavaklidere.com
Visits by appointment only.

Kavaklidere is Turkey's first and oldest private wine producer, established in Ankara in 1929 by Cenap And. The winery, located near Ankara International airport makes wines from 32 different grape varieties, sourced from the vast vineyards that stretch over 250 acres around Kalecik (Ankara), Nevsehir (Cappadocia) and Manisa Pendore (Aegea). For the moment, the best way to sample the wines – and those of other Turkish producers – is in the smart Kav shop in the heart of Ankara where, if your Turkish is up to it, you could also find a range of local-language wine books and *Karaf*, a glossy wine magazine published by Kavaklidere as part of its mission to increase wine appreciation in this country. Around 20% of the Kavaklidere wines are currently exported, but most of these are probably bought by ex-pat Turks. The next task lies in persuading foreigners to try them.

Kavaklidere labels, old and new.

## UAE / Dubai

In the countries that make up the United Arab Emirates, alcohol is freely available to non-Muslims. This, together with Dubai's booming expatriate and tourist-driven economy, has helped this state to become an increasingly welcoming place for wine lovers. Prices are high, but the range on offer is very impressive.

WINE BAR DUBAI

### The Agency

Emirates Tower, Sheikh Zayed Highway; also at Souq Madinat Jumeirah, Dubai
T+971 4330 0000/ 4366 6730
Daily 1200-0100.

Ask any expat where to go for a cocktail after work and ask any Dubai wine-lover where to get a decent glass or bottle of wine and you'll get the same answer. Or pair of answers, to be precise, because the original, minimalist but surprisingly cosy Agency in Emirate Towers has now been joined by a second outlet in the Souq Madinat Jumeirah. Both serve tapas and light snacks as well as 50 wines by the glass and 10 times that many by the bottle. Nowhere does wine better in Dubai and you'd even look hard to find a better wine bar in London.

# North Africa

**The Maghreb – which in Arabic means "place where the sun sets" or the west – actually describes the area to the west of the Nile and north of the Sahara. Or, more specifically, the countries of Algeria, Tunisia and Morocco. Despite its ancient history as a wine-producing region in the days of the Phoenicians, the Maghreb did not play a significant role in the history of quality wine in the 20th century – although Algeria certainly contributed plenty of quantity when it was a French colony (see below). Independence and the rise of fundamental Islamist governments with a penchant for state monopolies has not helped either, but over the last few years dramatic moves towards better wine are being made.**

## Algeria

The Romans made wine in this warm country and so did the French, who colonised Algeria in 1830 and spent the following century expanding its vineyards. By 1938 they covered 400,000 ha – over twice the area of Australia's vineyards today – and produced the equivalent of some 2750 million bottles per year. Vines were grown across the northwest of the country, around Algiers (notably Coteaux de Zaccar and Coteaux de Médéa) and Oran (Coteaux de Mascara and Coteaux de Tlemcen) on their own roots; the sandy soil here meant that the phylloxera louse that devastated Europe never arrived.

The departure of the French in the 1960s, the arrival of Appellation Contrôlée rules in France and the influence of Islam all helped to cut production to its current 6,250,000 bottles. Unfortunately, although an appellation system was introduced and the region of Coteaux de Mascara developed a small reputation for its full-bodied reds, quality was never the focus of attention. Wines were either used to bolster feebler efforts from regions like Bordeaux and Burgundy, or sold cheaply under their own name. Until recently, the only examples of modern Algerian winemaking seen overseas were Sidi Brahim (sold in France) and the better but still rustic Cuvée du Président.

Today there are producers with higher aspirations, most notably Bernard Magrez, owner of Château Pape Clement, who has joined forces with Gerard Dépardieu and Michel Rolland to launch two wines – Domaine de Saint-Augustin and Cuvée Monica from the Coteaux de Tlemcen – that have won high marks from Robert Parker and interest in the US. Watch out for a growing number of others.

## Morocco

Morocco only produces around five million bottles of wine per year, 90% of which is drunk locally (despite official figures suggesting that the Muslim population consumes no alcohol at all). The difference between Morocco and its neighbours, which all shared a similar Roman heritage, has been the efforts since 1964 of a single man, Brahim Zniber, who produces most of the country's wines from his big, modern Les Celliers de Meknes winery and from smaller facilities, such as the Château Roslane and Domaine des Ouled Thaleb in the foothills of the Atlas mountains. Since 1998, other improving wines have been made in Meknes under the Halana label by the French giant, Castel. French input has now increased in the shape of the dynamic triumverate of Bernard Magrez, Gerard Dépardieu and Michel Rolland, whose rich, jammy Grenache-Syrah Lumière d'Atlas from Meknes has won high praise from UK and US critics.

RESTAURANT MARRAKECH

### Yacout

79 rue Sidi Ahmed Soussi, nr Bab Doukkala, Marrakech
T+212 (0)44 -382 929 / 900
www.yacout-marrakech.com
Tue-Sun 1800-late; reservations essential.
$$$

This is Marrakech's most famous Moroccan restaurant and is well worth a visit. Found deep in the Marrakech Medina, Yacout is like a scene from an old *Arabian Nights* film. Pre-dinner drinks can be enjoyed on the roof-top terrace, while you decide where to dine: beside the pool, in a private alcove, or in the delightful main salon. Once this decision has been made, the choice of dishes is exceptional, with ingredients such as lamb, pigeon, veal or chicken cooked to perfection every time. The local Gnaouan music softly completes the atmosphere. A fixed-price menu includes unlimited drinks.

## Tunisia

Although the Phoenicians probably introduced winemaking to Carthage, northeast of modern Tunis, between 800 and 500 BC, little was produced in more recent times until Tunisia became a French colony in 1881. Following independence in 1956, the government took over the wine industry through L'Office de la Vigne and introduced a complex Gallic-style four-tier appellation system which could safely be ignored by wine lovers, who soon learned that the only wines worth trying were the sweet and dry Muscats.

The Office de la Vigne relaxed its hold in 1999, though the government still owns two thirds of Tunisia's two dozen wineries. Among the interesting newcomers is the partly German-owned Domaine Magon (named after a Phoenician agronomist), while the state-owned Domaine Hannon is also well worth knowing about. The latter began as a joint venture with a Sicilian firm called Calatresi but is now run by Dina Bel Ali, the President of Tunisia's niece, with the help of Australian winemaker, Linda Domas. Domaine Hannon wines are sold under the Thapsus label.

# East Africa

## Ethiopia

Far better known for coffee than wine, Ethiopia has a long history of growing grapes for the church. Land situated between 1800 and 2500 m is known locally as *'Wayna-dega'*, which can be translated as the "ideal height for grapes". During the Italian occupation, under Mussolini, Ethiopian Soave and Ethiopian Chiante [sic] were produced and indeed exported. Today, the country's most popular 'wine' is, in fact a mead (made from honey), called T'ej. The Awash winery, close to Addis Ababa also makes a range of grape wines, of which the best are reds called Dukem and Gouder (which comes from a specific vineyard). The quality of both these wines is surprising (though less than extraordinary) and, hopefully, is not explained by the use of imported grape concentrate, although this does happen here, as it does in Japan and Canada.

WINERY — ADDIS ABABA

### Awash Winery

PO Box 167, Addis Ababa
T+251 (0)1- 711010/202970
Visits by appointment only.

This 25-year-old winery is located in the Lideta district, close to Addis Abbaba, and is run by chairman Mohammed Ahmed. It recently closed while expansion work took place, with the installation of equipment from Germany and Italy. The Harar Brewery is also part of the business, producing around 15,000 barrels of beer annually for Ethiopia, the USA, Canada, and the Netherlands. The expansion will increase beer production by approximately 50%.

## Kenya

According to South African wine authorities and authors of *Africa Uncorked*, John and Erica Platter, the famous anthropologist and paleontologist, Richard Leakey (www.leakey.com), has planted Pinot Noir and Sauvignon Blanc at his farm in Ngong and has labelled it Ol Choro Onyore after the name of the vineyard. Quantities will be tiny but do ask for it if you are in Nairobi.

## Madagascar

Madagascar has been making wine for over 150 years. None is better than average but a visit to Frederic Chaix's shop, **La Cave á Vins** in Antananarivo (T +261 (0)22-48480) would make an interesting diversion if you are on the island.

“”

It takes real bravery to try to make wine seriously in these countries – but it's happening …

# Vintages

| | |
|---|---|
| **2006** | Early reports suggest a very good vintage in South Africa. |
| **2005** | Mixed in South Africa. |
| **2004** | A very good year in South Africa, but mixed in Lebanon. |
| **2003** | Great South African year, especially for reds. Very good in Lebanon. |
| **2002** | Mixed in South Africa but good in Lebanon. |
| **2001** | Good for South African reds. |
| **2000** | Mixed in South Africa. |

# South Africa

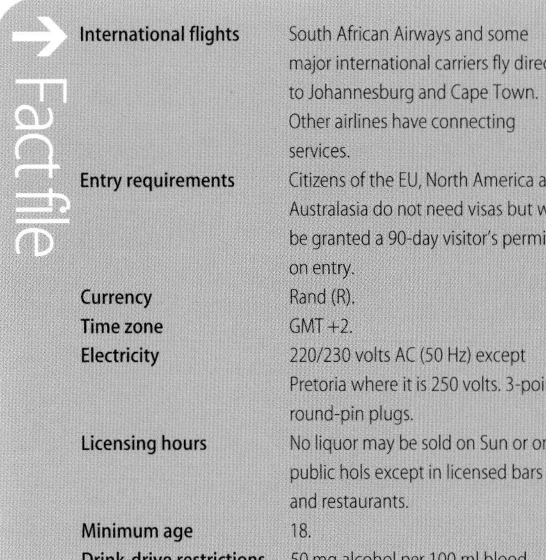

**Fact file**

| | |
|---|---|
| **International flights** | South African Airways and some major international carriers fly direct to Johannesburg and Cape Town. Other airlines have connecting services. |
| **Entry requirements** | Citizens of the EU, North America and Australasia do not need visas but will be granted a 90-day visitor's permit on entry. |
| **Currency** | Rand (R). |
| **Time zone** | GMT +2. |
| **Electricity** | 220/230 volts AC (50 Hz) except Pretoria where it is 250 volts. 3-point round-pin plugs. |
| **Licensing hours** | No liquor may be sold on Sun or on public hols except in licensed bars and restaurants. |
| **Minimum age** | 18. |
| **Drink-drive restrictions** | 50 mg alcohol per 100 ml blood. |

## Planning your trip

The three main international airports are Johannesburg, Durban and **Cape Town** (CPT, T +27 (0)21-937 1200, www.acsa.co.za), which is the main point of access for the Cape winelands. All of the major cities are linked by the national rail network **Spoornet** (T 0860-008888, www.spoornet.co.zarail) but this is a slow way to travel. However, if the journey is more important than the destination, then a trip on the *Blue Train* (www.bluetrain.co.za) is worth considering. This five-star hotel on wheels runs between Pretoria and Cape Town and offers 27 hours of uninterrupted indulgence. Otherwise, hiring a car for part, or all, of your journey is undoubtedly the best way to see the country. Tourist offices usually recommend large international organizations but there are also reliable local companies in most towns and cities, usually with a good fleet of cars and follow-up service.

**Cape Town** (page 352) is one of the world's great cities and is the perfect base from which to visit the Western Cape's historical wine estates but there's lots more to explore besides. North of the city, the west coast is characterized by rolling sand dunes, fishing communities and blankets of wild flowers in spring. South of Cape Town is the **Whale Coast**, a spectacular coastline where southern right whales can be spotted from the shore, especially at **Hermanus** from July to November. (Look out, too, for great white sharks.) Further east the beautiful **Garden Route** follows the coast from Heidelberg to the **Tsitsikamma National Park**, passing through seaside resorts and lush countryside that's great for hiking. For a sight of South Africa's big game, however, you'll have to go further afield. The **Greater Addo Elephant National Park** is easily accessible from Port Elizabeth, or, of course, there's **Kruger National Park**, with its top-flight facilities and the chance of spotting the 'big five'. Kruger can be visited from **Johannesburg** or **Pretoria**, both of which are worthwhile destinations in their own right, with informative township and city tours and some interesting museums, such as Pretoria's Voortrekker Monument or Johannesburg's excellent Apartheid Museum. Zulu culture has its heartland east of here in **Kwazulu Natal**, while the tropical seas around **Durban** provide a sharp contrast to the Atlantic coast of the Cape.

## Wine tourism

Almost all of South Africa's wines are produced, as they have always been, in the Cape, within a couple of hours' drive of Cape Town, although vineyards are now also being established in Kwazulu Natal. One of the most beautiful wine regions in the world, the Cape offers hills and valleys, covered with vines, Cape Dutch farms that have not changed in nearly 400 years, flowers and plants that are found nowhere else – and the chance to punctuate your wine tasting with a spot of whale watching or surfing. Wineries are mostly well-equipped to welcome visitors with a growing number, including **Groot Constantia** (page 354), the region's most famous 17th-century estate, now incorporating cafés or restaurants. Harvest time is February to March and is a fascinating time to visit. The small towns, particularly Stellenbosch, are gloriously photogenic, immaculately kept and very reminiscent of their counterparts in Alsace and Germany.

South Africa's food revolution began later than it did in Australia and California but, now, hefty, old-fashioned Dutch and British meat-and-two-veg cooking has given way to much more Mediterranean-style cuisine. Travellers will still come across biltong, however, a heavily salted and spiced sun-dried meat, made from beef or game such as ostrich, kudu or impala, and *Boerewors*, a strongly seasoned beef sausage usually grilled on a *braai* (barbecue). Seafood along the coast is excellent and usually very good value. In Cape Town, look out too for spicy Cape Malay dishes.

## History

The New World country with the longest consistent history of quality winemaking, South Africa boasts 17th-century wine farms that were in business before most of the chateaux of the Médoc. Vineyards were planted as soon as the Cape became a Dutch colony and, unlike the first settlers in Australia, New Zealand and the east coast of the US, the pioneering winemakers did not have to look far to find ideal sites. The areas they chose in Stellenbosch and Constantia are still growing vines today. In 2001, a bottle of sweet 1791 Vin de Constance was opened, tasted and enjoyed as one of the oldest wines still to be drinkable.

**South Africa country code** → +27 **IDD code** → 09 **Internet ID** → .za **Emergencies** → Police T10111; Ambulance T10177.

## A weekend in Cape Town

Cape Town is a city worth crossing the world for. First impressions simply don't get any better; the city is dominated by the stark splendour of **Table Mountain**, its steep slopes and flat top towering between the wild shores of the Atlantic. A cable car (T +27 (0)21-4248181, www.tablemountain.net) whisks visitors to the summit offering astounding views. From the foot of the mountain, take a taxi to **Government Avenue**, a delightful, oak-shaded pedestrian road flanked by Company's Garden and some of the city's finest museums and colonial buildings. To the west is the **Bo-Kaap**, Cape Town's brightly coloured Islamic district, while to the east is the superb **District Six Museum** (25a Buitenkant St, T +27 (0)21-461 8745, www.districtsix.co.za), which explores the devastating effects that apartheid had on local communities. Afterwards head to the **Victoria and Alfred Waterfront**, a tourist-friendly development, packed with shops, bars and restaurants, and an excellent **aquarium** (Dock Rd, T +27 (0)21-418 3823, www.aquarium.co.za). Nip into **Vaughan Johnson's** (page 355) for some tips on South African wine before enjoying an al fresco lunch at **Quay Four** (T +xx (0)21-419 2008), while watching the comings and goings of the working harbour.

The V&A Waterfront is the embarkation point for the ferry to notorious **Robben Island** (T +27 (0)21-4134200, www.robben-island.org.za), where Nelson Mandela was held prisoner for 18 years. Tours take three hours and provide an insight into the Machiavellian workings of the apartheid system. In the evening, dine at $$-$$$ **Aubergine** (39 Barnet St, Gardens, T +27 (0)21-465 4909, www.aubergine.co.za) for excellent modern European cuisine and an impressive wine list, or the $-$$ **Africa Café** (Heritage Sq, 108 Short Market St, Centre, T +27 (0)21-422 0221, www.africacafe.co.za) for a tourist-friendly introduction to the continent's cuisines.

Spend the following morning exploring the wineries of **Constantia**, Cape Town's most elegant suburb. As well as Constantia Uitsig, Groot Constantia and Steenberg (page 354), visit **Klein Constantia** (T +27 (0)21-794 5188), a beautifully hilly estate that's famed for its Vin de Constance dessert wine. Have lunch at **La Colombe**, before retreating to the Atlantic suburbs of **Clifton** or **Camps Bay** for a lazy afternoon on the beach. If you're feeling more energetic, drive along the Atlantic Seaboard to the **Cape of Good Hope Nature Reserve**, via spectacular **Chapman's Peak Drive**. The reserve is a beautifully wild area offering panoramic ocean views and good walks. Drive back along False Bay and stop off at **Boulders Beach**, a haven for a colony of Jackass penguins. Finally, if you're visiting in summer, enjoy a Sunday evening picnic and concert in **Kirstenbosch Botanical Gardens**. The gardens are amongst the finest in the world and enjoy a stunning setting on the slopes of Table Mountain.

Until the 1970s and 1980s, South Africa retained its lead over other New World countries; then the tide turned. At precisely the time when California and Australia were improving their wines, the Cape stood still, isolated from international evolution by sanctions and by the chauvinistic attitude of winemakers who thought they had nothing to learn. What they didn't know, however, was that 90% of their vineyards were infected by leaf-roll virus, which prevented the grapes from ripening properly. Moreover, the KWV, a semi-governmental organization that effectively ran the South African wine industry, was stifling innovation by preventing the launch of new wineries.

Paradoxically, before Nelson Mandela's release, South Africa benefited from a mixture of silence, on the part of writers who opted to ignore its wines on political grounds, and over-generous praise from those who were apolitical or sympathized with the regime. The advent of the Rainbow nation reversed the situation; suddenly critics flocked to flatter its wines in a collective effort to help the new country. Poor performance in blind tastings against other New and Old World countries, however, proved that South Africa's winemakers needed to raise their game. Some have done so dramatically but, more importantly, many more have been overtaken by newcomers. The list of top South African wineries now includes plenty of names that, a decade ago, had yet to produce their first vintage. Areas enjoying a revival include Franschhoek, plus Tulbagh and Swartland to the north (for red wines), while the new areas of Elgin/Walker Bay/Hermanus, Elim and Mossel Bay on the south coast are home to good whites and lighter reds such as Pinot Noir.

### Understanding South African wine

South African wines from specified regions will bear the initials **WO** – *Wyn van Oorsprong* (wine of origin) – within which are **Wine Districts** and, most precise of all, **Wine Wards**. A wine from a specific estate is a '*Landgoedwyn*'; if it is a sparkling wine it will be a '*Méthode Cap Classique*', while a red wine that combines Pinotage with other varieties will be known as a 'Cape Blend'. Sweet, late harvest wines are '*Edelkeur*' or '*Edel Laat-oes*', while sweet, fortified Moscadel is '*Jerepigo*'.

### White grapes

**Chardonnay** Good South African Chardonnay is a recent phenomenon but there are now several examples – such as Jordan and Mulderbosch – that are of world class.

**Chenin Blanc (Steen)** There's huge confusion over how this grape should be used, but as Cape producers develop their own style rather than apeing France, some delicious rich, buttery, appley wines are being made. Late-harvest examples can be very impressive too.

**Sauvignon Blanc** At their best, Cape Sauvignon Blancs are a happy medium between the gooseberry intensity of New Zealand and the minerality of the Loire Valley.

### Red grapes

**Cabernet Sauvignon** Widely grown and improving, though styles vary widely. Some are light and slightly unripe while others are big, rich and alcoholic.

**Cinsault** A Rhône grape used here by itself and in blends.

**Pinot Noir** At its impressive best in Walker Bay (at Bouchard Finlayson and Hamilton Russell), this variety cannot yet field a sizeable team of good Cape examples.
acquired taste because of its bitter, woodsmoke character. Definitely improves with age – and from dedicated producers such as Kanonkop, Beyerskloof; see page 355.

**Merlot** This Bordeaux variety shows real promise in South Africa, in the right hands. Plummy and not overdone.

**Pinotage** Controversial and an

**Ruby Cabernet** Undistinguished US cross between Cabernet Sauvignon and Carignan. Outside South Africa, this ugly, earthily bitter variety is used in cheap blends.

**Shiraz** Arguably South Africa's top red wine grape. Wines often have a berryish-smoky character that is purely South African.

**Tinta Baroca** A port variety that can produce good, rich dark wine.

**Touriga Nacional** Another port grape: there aren't many examples, but the good ones are deliciously plummy and mulberryish.

Cricket in the grounds of Constantia-Uitsig.

## The Cape

**While each of the wine regions of the Cape claims its own wine style, winemaking is currently playing a greater role than 'terroir', and the character of the regions is, in any case, changing as new vineyards are being planted.**

WINERY CONSTANTIA

### Constantia Uitsig Wine Estate

Spaanschemat River Rd, Constantia 7806
Hotel T+27 (0)21-794 6 500
Shop T+27 (0)21 7941 810
www.uitsig.co.za
Sales and tastings Mon-Fri 0900-1700, Sat 1000-1700. Restaurant daily 1230-1430, 1930-2130. River Café daily 0830-1700.

South Africa does wine tourism so well that choosing favourites is very, very difficult, but I think there really is something special about Constantia Uitsig. The winery, hotel and restaurants are situated only 20 minutes from Cape Town's city centre, but they could be in another world. In the shadow of the Table Mountain the estate offers a unique and exhilarating eating experience for travelling gourmets. Sixteen garden rooms have glorious views of the Constantia Valley, while a short walk through the gardens leads to the **Wine Shop**, where the estate's range of fine wines can be sampled. The luxuries of this hotel, its surroundings, wines, top restaurants – **Constantia Uitsig**, **La Colombe** (voted 28th Best Restaurant in the World by *Restaurant Magazine* 2006), and the less formal **Spaanschemat River Café** – make this the perfect destination for visitors with adventurous tastes. There is without doubt something for everyone, but reservations are highly advisable for those wishing to visit.

WINERY CONSTANTIA

### Groot Constantia

Constantia 7848
T +27 (0)21-794 5128
www.grootconstantia.co.za
Daily 0900-1700 (until 1800 in summer). Tours (by appointment only) summer daily 1000-1600; winter 1100, 1500, 1600.

The oldest working winery in the Cape was established in 1685 but, until recently, it was worth visiting for everything except its wine. The landmark building was undeniably interesting but the state-owned winery was underperforming woefully. A shift in philosophy and the arrival of a new winemaker have wrought huge changes, so that, today, the Gouverneur's Reserve Cabernet Sauvignon is one of the best, most subtle reds in the Cape. The **Manor House** contains a museum and the **Cloete Cellar** provides an idea of what winemaking was like here over two centuries ago. There are two restaurants: **Simons** ($-$$) and the more interesting **Jonkershuis** ($-$$), which offers good Cape Malay cooking and estate wines.

WINERY STEENBERG

### Steenberg Vineyards

PO Box 224, Steenberg 7947
T +27 (0)21-713 2211
Catharina Hotel T +27 (0)21-713 2222
www.steenberg-vineyards.co.za, www.steenberghotel.com
Mon-Fri 0900-1630, Sat and public hols 0930-1330. Tours Mon-Fri 1000-1500 by appointment only. Tastings by appointment only. Restaurant daily 0700-2230.

Garden guest rooms at Constantia Uitsig Wine Estate and al fresco dining at the estate's La Colombe restaurant.

The history of Steenberg stretches back to the 1600s, when the original name of this area was Swaaneweide, meaning 'the feeding place of swans'. Today, it is spur-winged geese that are to be found here. In the mid-1800s the estate was sold to the Louw family, who owned it until 1990, when it was purchased by Johannesburg Consolidated Investments, which re-developed it into the impressive vineyard that it is today. There are around 70 ha under vine; 60% is white – mostly Sauvignon Blanc, followed by Chardonnay, Sémillon and Muscat de Frontignan – and the rest is red: a mix of Cabernet Sauvignon, Merlot, Cabernet Franc, Pinot Noir, Shiraz, plus some Nebbiolo. The restaurant ($$-$$$) is in an old wine cellar and offers a classic menu in a cosy atmosphere. There is also a cigar lounge, as well as jazz on Sunday nights.

Tasting notes

**Pinotage**

One of the biggest controversies in South African wine concerns the Pinotage grape, a variety which is grown almost nowhere else in the world. For some winemakers and critics, this variety either used by itself or in blends, is uniquely South African and something to be treasured and promoted, like Australia's Shiraz and California's Zinfandel. Others retort that those two grapes have distinguished histories, while the Pinotage was created in South Africa in 1925 by crossing the Pinot Noir and the Cinsault. Fans like what they see as banana and earthy notes, while critics dislike what they call an earthy bitterness which they also find in the Cape Blends that have to contain 20 to 30% of this variety. The pro-Pinotage camp includes one of the Cape's top winemakers, Beyers Truter of Kanonkop, while the anti-brigade counts the similarly highly regarded André van Rensburg of Vergelegen among its number. It is perhaps revealing that a large number of the Cape's most internationally successful producers have chosen not to use the Pinotage and that, while the grape has been introduced into other countries, this has only been in very limited numbers and rarely to great critical applause.

WINE SHOP — CAPE TOWN

### Vaughan Johnson's

Dock Rd, Waterfront, Cape Town
T+27 (0)21-419 2121
www.vaughanjohnson.com
Daily 0930-1800.

Vaughan Johnson has over 30 years' experience in the South African wine industry as a winemaker, accountant and retailer. He now runs this shop, which stocks his recommendations of the top 100 wines from the 5000 or so produced across South Africa. His selection takes in a cross-section of styles and grape varieties, including Sauvignon Blanc, Chardonnay, Chenin Blanc, Riesling, Shiraz, Cabernet Sauvignon, Merlot, Pinotage, and Pinot Noir. He also includes a 'Best Value' selection of wines at affordable prices for everyday enjoyment and, conversely, does not stock well-known wines that he feels don't offer value for money. Johnson is very happy to advise keen wine-lovers and explorers which wineries to visit.

## Franschhoek

An old area, Franschhoek owes its name to the Huguenots who settled here. It is now a place to visit for its restaurants and landscapes as much as for its wine.

WINERY — FRANSCHHOEK

### Boekenhoutskloof

PO Box 433, Franschhoek 7690
T+27 (0)21-876 3320
www.boekenhoutskloof.co.za
Visits by appointment only.

Boekenhoutskloof was founded in 1776 in the Franschhoek foothills. Today, this cult estate produces four great-value brands: Boekenhoutskloof, Chocolate Block, Wolftrap (named after a trap that dates back 250 years to when settlers believed wolves roamed the area), and Porcupine Ridge, made from Sauvignon Blanc, Chardonnay, Chenin Blanc, Merlot, Syrah and Pinotage. Marc Kent is the mastermind, the winemaker, the cellarmaster and part-owner of the farm. His flagship range is made in only tiny quantities but is well worth finding and trying. Boekenhoutskloof is now rated one of the Cape's top producers.

RESTAURANT — FRANSCHHOEK

### Bread & Wine

Môreson Wine Farm, Happy Valley Rd,
La Motte, Franschhoek
Restaurant T+27 (0)21-876 3692
www.moreson.co.za
Restaurant Wed-Sun from 1200. Tastings summer only Wed-Sun 1100-1700.
$-$$

One of the best winery restaurants in the Cape, this is a surprisingly well-kept secret. Set among the lemon orchards and vineyards of the Môreson Wine Farm in Franschhoek, it focuses on modern South African country cooking, with plenty of rustic smoked meats and pâtés that can also be bought to take away at the Môreson Grocery. (Good news for anyone wanting to picnic in the hills.) The wine to look for on the Môreson list is probably the fresh, grassy Sauvignon Blanc.

Grapevine

**Zimbabwean wine**
Wine was produced in Zimbabwe in the 1950s from table grapes but, in 1966, when sanctions made it impossible to import any wine from overseas, wine grapes were planted in land previously used for tobacco. Twenty-five years later, the quality was good enough for whites to be exported and to win modest awards in blind tastings. Today, unfortunately, wine has been no more fortunate than any other form of agriculture in this beautiful, benighted country. Vineyards have been expropriated and the largely government-owned Mukuyu wine company has swallowed most of its competitors. Today, this company and African Distillers are all that remains of the industry, though the latter still makes good wine at its Worringham Farm. Cynics will be interested to know that in the days when the world was being urged to boycott goods produced under the apartheid regime in South Africa, the then well-regarded Robert Mugabe preferred drinking Cape wine to Zimbabwean.



HOTEL FRANSCHHOEK

### L'Auberge du Quartier Français

16 Hugenot Rd, Franschhoek 7690
T+27 (0)21 876 2151
www.lequartier.co.za
$$$

Every time I ask my friends in the Cape to recommend a new restaurant, they insist on adding an old one to the list of places I have to visit. L'Auberge du Quartier Français is a small, privately owned inn priding itself on contemporary and innovative cuisine, top-class service, the little touches that make every visitor feel special and great views. There are 15 elegant en-suite rooms that all look onto the courtyard and swimming pool. For true indulgence there are two suites with their own lounges, pools and bars. The restaurant was voted one of the top 50 in the world by *Restaurant Magazine* UK for two years running and was named Best Restaurant in the Middle East and Africa.

## Stellenbosch

Stellenbosch was one of the earliest heartlands of South African wine. Like neighbouring Paarl, it is a very varied region with diverse soils and altitudes. Today, the focus is shifting to the hills; some of Warwick Estate's valley floor land has now become a golf course and the hilly region of Helderberg in the centre of Stellenbosch is a major centre of attention for quality producers.

RESTAURANT HELDERVIEW

### 96 Winery Road: the Winelands Restaurant

Winery Rd, Helderview 7130
T+27 (0)21- 842 2020
www.96wineryroad.co.za
Mon-Sat 1200-1700 and 1900-2200; Sun 1900-2200.
$-$$

96 Winery Road celebrated its 10th birthday in May 2006. The restaurant uses only fresh, often organic and, where possible, local ingredients to prepare the dishes, and focuses on South African influences and

flavours. The menu changes four times a year, although new dishes feature on a daily basis. Many of the local winegrowers are regulars to the dining room, as wine plays an integral part here. The wine list features the work of Ken Forrester and Martin Meinert of Devon Valley, who part-own the estate. One of their many stated aims is to provide commitment to continuity and the local community.

WINERY STELLENBOSCH

## Saxenburg Wine Farm

Polkadraai Rd, Kuils River, 7580 Stellenbosch
Winery T+27 (0)21 903 6113. Restaurant T+27 (0)21-906 5232.
www.saxenburg.com
Sep-May Mon-Fri 0900-1700, Sat 1000-1700, Sun 1000-1600; Jun and Aug Mon and Wed-Fri 0900-1700, Sat 0900-1600; Jul Wed-Fri 0900-1700, Sat 0900-1600. Restaurant closed Jul.

The Bührer family of Switzerland took over Saxenburg in 1989 and dedicated their time to reviving the family tradition of the estate's historic past, ensuring its growth and development in future years. They also fulfilled their wish to have a sister vineyard in France, acquiring Château Capion, near Montpellier, in 1996. Saxenburg is situated on the hills above Kuils River, between the Atlantic and Indian Oceans, where the vineyards enjoy ideal conditions. There are around 90 ha of vines, growing predominantly Shiraz, Cabernet Sauvignon, Sauvignon Blanc, Merlot and Pinotage. The Guinea Fowl Restaurant ($$) opened in 1991 specialisig in fresh seafood, game and a variety of exclusive guinea fowl dishes. The wines are all Saxenburg, with plenty of older vintages . There is a vine-covered terrace giving a Mediterranean feel and wonderful views of the sunsets over Table Mountain.

WINERY STELLENBOSCH

## Spier Wine Centre

Annandale Road, Stellenbosch 7603
T+27 (0)21- 809 1100
www.spier.co.za
Wine centre Mon-Sat 0900-1700. Tastings daily 1000-1630.

I well remember when Spier opened its doors, as the first modern tourist-orientated estate in the Cape, combining a winery, hotel, restaurant and shop. Located in a beautifully restored 17th century barn on the main estate, the Spier Wine Centre stocks more than 200 wines. It is a haven for any wine-lover, with rare vintages, collector's labels, and the estate's own range of wines, including their award-winning Cabernet Sauvignon and Merlot. There is also a range of wine accessories available, a delivery service, and the knowledgeable staff are always keen to help. Tastings are run every day, with the emphasis on communicating the best way to truly appreciate wine. In its passion for growth and innovation, the estate also hopes to broaden the role of the Spier brand with its diverse Programs in Education for Wine, Food and the Arts.

# Best producers

**Algeria**
Coteaux de Mascara
Cuvée du President
Cuvée Monica
Domaine de Saint-Augustin

**Morocco**
Château Roslane
Domaine des Ouled Thaleb
Les Celliers de Mekne (top wines)
Lumière d'Atlas

**South Africa**
Alto
Avontuur
Backsberg
Bellingham
Beyerskloof
Boekenhoutskloof » *page 355.*
Bouchard Finlayson
Buitenverwachting
Clos Cabriere
Capaia
Cederberg
Clos Malverne
Cluver, Paul
Constantia Uitsig » *page 354.*
Darling Cellars
Ellis, Neil
Fairview
Flagstone
Fleur du Caop (unfiltered)
Forrester, Ken
The Foundry
Glen Carlou
Groot Constantia » *page 354.*
Groote Post
Hartenberg
Joostenberg
Jordan
Kaapzicht
Kanonkop
Klein Constantia
L'Avenir
Lourensford
Lynx
Meerlust (Merlot)
Moreson
Morgenhof
Morgenster
Mulderbosch
Nederburg (top wines)
Neethlingshof
Newton Johnson
The Observatory
Plaisir de Merle
Radford Dale (the Winery)
Russell, Hamilton
Rust en Vrede
Rustenberg
Sadie Family
Saxenburg » *page 357.*
Seidelberg
Simonsig
Spice Route
Spier » *page 357.*
Springfield
Steenberg » *page 354.*
Stellenzicht
Sterhuis
Thelema
Tokara
DE Toren
De Trafford
Vergelegen
Villafonté
Villiera
Warwick
Waterford
The Winery
Yonder Hill

**Tunisia**
Domaine Hannon/Thapsus
Domaine Magon

Opposite page: Steenberg vineyards.

# Asia

**Harvesting grapes on the Chao Praya river delta, Siam Winery, Thailand.**

KAZAKHSTAN
MONGOLIA
KYRGYZSTAN
TAJIKSTAN
PAKISTAN
Urumqi
Gobi Desert
CHINA
Qiqihar
Harbin
Changchun
Jilin
Fushun
Anshan
Baotou
Datong
BEIJING
Tianjin
Tangshan
Jinan
Lanzhou
Xi'an
Luoyang
Zhengzhou
Nanjing
Wuxi
Shanghai
Ningbo
Suizhou
Wuhan
Chengdu
Neijiang
Chongqing
Yueyang
Changsha
Nanchang
Guiyang
Kunming
Liuzhou
Fuzhou
Nanning
Guangzhou
Shantou
Macau
Hong Kong
TAIPEI
TAIWAN
Kaohsiung
Sapporo
NORTH KOREA
Sea of Japan
JAPAN
SEOUL
SOUTH KOREA
Pusan
Fukuoka
Osaka
TOKYO
Yokohama
East China Sea
Pacific Ocean
DELHI
Himalayas
NEPAL
Jaipur
Agra
Lucknow
Patna
BANGLADESH
Ahmadabad
Jabalpur
Kolkata
Vadodora
Bhopal
Surat
Nagpur
INDIA
Mumbai
Pune
Hyderabad
Vishakhapatnam
Vijayawada
Bay of Bengal
Bangalore
Chennai
Coimbatore
Madurai
Cochin
Trivandrum
SRI LANKA
MYANMAR
YANGON
LAOS
HANOI
THAILAND
BANGKOK
VIETNAM
CAMBODIA
PHNOM PENH
Dalat
Ho Chi Minh City
South China Sea
MANILA
PHILIPPINES
Davao
MALAYSIA
Medan
KUALA LUMPUR
SINGAPORE
Borneo
Sulawesi
Palembang
INDONESIA
JAKARTA
Bandung
Surabaya
Bali
PAPUA NEW GUINEA
AUSTRALIA
N
500 km
500 miles
Wineries
1 Grover Vineyards p362
2 Sula Vineyards ★ p363
3 Hatten Wines p363
4 Myanmar Vineyard p364
5 Granmonte Vineyard & Wines p366
6 Monsoon Valley (Siam Winery) p366
7 PB Valley Khao Yai Winery p366
8 Village Farm Winery ★ p367
9 Chateau Changyu-Castel p369
10 Great Wall Wine Company/Hua Xia Winery p369
11 Shanxi Grace Vineyards p369
12 Château Mercian p372
13 Coco Farm & Winery p372
14 Grace Winery p372
15 Comfe Winery p373

# Introduction



It is too early to say when or whether the American century will yield to the Chinese, Indian or Asian century but the wine world is already turning its attention eastwards. Until quite recently, the only parts of this region that offered any real prospect of a better-than-average glass of wine were Japan and the former British colonies of Singapore and Hong Kong. China, admittedly, had a recent history of producing large quantities of wine but none of it was of sufficient quality to interest anyone in Europe or the New World. Today, all that has changed. While Japan remains the country with the widest array of restaurants and wine bars with well-stocked cellars, wine lovers are increasingly well served in places like Taiwan, the Philippines, Korea and Vietnam. More surprising, perhaps, has been the recent explosion of quality winemaking in this area. The most striking successes are India and Thailand, where wines good enough to impress overseas judges in blind competitions have been produced. And, anybody who has followed Chinese wine over the last 20 years will have been struck by the improvements that have been made and by the number of top-class Western wines that are now being offered by restaurants in even out-of-the-way cities. The usual explanation for the Asian wine boom is that the region was heavily influenced by reports of wine's health-giving qualities – consumption in Thailand shot up after the King was advised to drink a glass of wine a day – but it is also likely that wine is being adopted because it is part of Western lifestyle. A word of warning, however. The region that brought us the fake Louis Vuitton bag and Rolex watch has been just as keen to produce knock-off examples of famous wines, which taste nothing like the real thing.

## India

Like China, India is a huge country that is now rediscovering a taste for wine after a gap of several centuries. And, like China, India is now both producing and importing increasing amounts of good and varied wine. But there are as many differences as there are similarities. If the Chinese only drink a third of a litre per head (compared to a global average of seven litres), the Indians are currently barely managing a teaspoon. The market is growing at 30% per year but still only amounts to around 3.5 m bottles, compared to China's 600 m. But if India's wine industry is tiny compared with China's, it has already hit higher points on the quality scale, with one wine beating a set of New World reds in a London blind tasting. Unlike China, which has a wide scattering of vineyards, in India the focus has, so far, with the single exception of Grover Vineyards near Bangalore, been on the regions of Pune, Narayangoan and Nashik in Maharashtra, close to Mumbai. This picture will change, however, if plans to grow wine grapes in the apple and apricot regions of Ilu and Manali in Himachal Pradesh come to fruition. In China, there is a long list of established wineries; India only has a trio of producers of any international standing – Chateau Indage, Grover and Sula– though this too is changing very rapidly as investment flows into new vineyards. Perhaps the most important difference for the moment, however, is the way wine is treated by local and national government. While Beijing has reduced duty rates across the country, allowing imported wine to be sold at the same price in Beijing as in Guangzhou and Shanghai, in India, federal excise duty was 'slashed' in 2003 – to quote a local newspaper – from 210% to 180%. There are also local taxes and restrictions. Until early in 2005, imported wines could not be bought from shops. Maharashtra still protects its own wine producers by levying an additional 28% on wines from other countries and Tamil Nadu simply bans them altogether. The good news for wine lovers is that pressure from other countries may help to reduce import duty which has, in any case, already been abolished for any wine bought in a hotel.

Winemaking is evolving so rapidly in these countries that vintage variation is less important than the skills of the producer.

WINERY BANGALORE

### Grover Vineyards

Raghunathapura Devanahalli,
Doddaballapur Rd, Doddaballapur,
Bangalore
T +91 (0)80-7622 123
www.groverwines.com
Visits by appointment only.

Spurning the table grapes that make up the bulk of India's domestic wine production, Grover Vineyards is one of the few wineries in India to use French varieties in its production. Having identified nine varieties that suit the hot climate, including Sauvignon Blanc, Cabernet Sauvigon and Shiraz, the winery has also looked to France for winemaking advice in the form of über-consultant Michel Rolland. This is a winery to watch: one of its earliest efforts, the Grover La Reserve Cabernet Sauvignon-Shiraz was the winner of a *Decanter* tasting of New World reds. Just as nearby Bangalore has spearheaded a computer and services revolution, so the chances are that Grover might spearhead a viticultural revolution in this region.

RESTAURANT MUMBAI

### Indigo

4 Mandlik Rd, Colaba, Mumbai 400001
T +91 (0)22-5636 8999
Daily 1230-1500 and 1930-2345.
Reservations essential.
$

# Best producers

**India**

Grover » *page 362.*
Indage (Sparkling)
Sula » *page 363.*

You'll have to book weeks ahead to get a table at Mumbai's coolest eatery, especially since it was voted one of the world's top 60 restaurants by Condé Nast. Restaurateur Rahul Akerkar wanted to bridge the gap between Bombay's typical dining options – over-the-top glitzy or hole-in-the-wall and he has succeeded, bringing minimalist splendour, delicious Asian fusion cuisine, stellar cocktails and a varied wine list to the city. There is a lovely terrace with frangipani trees, or you can observe the city's A-listers, including a regular complement of Bollywood stars, in the bar.

WINERY — NASHIK

### Sula Vineyards

Gat no 35/2, Govardhan,
Gangapur-Savargaon Rd, Nashik 422222
T +91 (0)253 -223 1663
/ +91 (0)253 -223 1720
www.sulawines.com
Mon-Thu 1230-2030; Fri-Sun 1220-2230.

When I first met Rajeev Samant, I knew that India's wine industry was likely to succeed beyond the imaginings of many Europeans. In 1993, Samant, a degree from Standford University in the US under his belt, gave up a plush job at Oracle in Silicon Valley and set about planting wine grapes in a family plot in Nashik, an area responsible for much of India's table-grape production. If Grover Vineyards is India's premium Old World-style winery, Samant's Sula Vineyards, 180 km north of Bombay, is its New World-style version, with imported Californian winemaking expertise and varieties, such as Zinfandel, Sauvignon Blanc and Chenin Blanc.

# Southeast Asia

**The tropical character of this part of Asia should, if the old theories apply, preclude it from producing drinkable wine. But the efforts of a growing set of wineries in Thailand is proving vines to be a lot more adaptable than was previously imagined. Elsewhere, wine drinking is also becoming far more commonplace, as is an appreciation of the need to store and transport wine in ways that protect it from the climate.**

## Cambodia

Cambodia's better tourist hotels (principally near Angkor Wat) increasingly offer reasonable ranges of wine, though the Sofitel in Siem Riep does this much better than its neighbours. Cambodia's only domestically produced wine is rather more rudimentary than Vietnam's. In 2000 Chan Thai Chhoeung planted 8000 Black Queen, Shiraz and Kyoho vines imported from France and Thailand at his farm at Phum Bot Sala in Battambang province. A self-taught non wine-drinker, Chan Thai Chhoeung admits that he is learning as he goes along and his wines could do with some improvement. But in this impoverished country, where an unreliable power supply has to be added to wine-unfriendly factors such as monsoon rains, one has to wish his US$10,000 investment well.

WINE BAR — PHNOM PENH

### Monsoon

17 Street 104, Phnom Penh
T +855 ( 0)16-35 5867 (mob)
Daily from 1800.
($)

There are monsoons in Cambodia, but this name also harks back to Pakistan, the country that inspires this funky yet cosy wine bar. Curry and Cabernet? Why not, when they're good and reasonably priced? Its location means that you can make Monsoon part of an evening of bar-hopping, as there are several other stylish watering holes on the same street, although this is the only place that offers a relatively wide selection of wine and for music that still allows for conversation.

## Indonesia

Despite its tropical conditions, Bali is one of the quirkiest success stories of the wine world. Vines destined for wine have been grown on the island for more than a century but it is only recently that Hatten Wines has been able to produce several vintages a year from its north Balinese vineyards.

WINERY — BALI

### Hatten Wines

Cellar door: Komplex Dewa Ruci 3,
Jl By-pass Ngurah Rai, Kuta Denpasar,
Simpang Siur, Bali
Winery: T +62 (0)36-128 6298.
Cellar door: T +62 (0)36-176 7422.
www.hattenwines.com
Cellar door Mon-Sat 1000-1830.

Hatten employs a resident French winemaker, Vincent Desplat, whose international experience includes a stint at Château Clarke in Bordeaux. His wines, made from evergreen Alphonse-Lavallée and Belgia grapes, are widely available in the island's hotels and restaurants. Even so, it's worth visiting the newly opened cellar door shop in Kuta, which offers the entire range and tastings. The winery itself is a model of environmental idealism, with a water-treatment plant and refusal to use chemical additives of any kind.

## Malaysia

Malaysia currently gets through nearly 4.75 million bottles of wine of which, since 2001 when France was pushed into second place, nearly half are Australian. Tastes here are less traditional than in Singapore and wine consumption is growing fast, but good wine lists are far from easy to find in Kuala Lumpur.

RESTAURANT | KUALA LUMPUR

### Shook!

Feast Floor, Starhill Gallery, 181 Jln Bukit Bintang, 55100 Kuala Lumpur
T +60 (0)3 2719 8535/ +60 (0)3 2719 8536
www.ytlcommunity.com/shook/
Daily 1200-2230; meals served 1200-1430 and 1830-2230.
$$$

Asia never ceases to amaze me, but to a Westerner, there are few more surprising sights than the shopping mall setting of this extraordinary restaurant in which you can find every vintage of Mouton Rothschild from 1945 to 1997. Ultra-cool and minimalist Shook! also offers 3000 other wines and four open kitchens, devoted respectively to Italian, Japanese, Chinese and Western grill cuisine. You can mix and match as you wish, starting, say, with a pizza marguerita and moving onto a spot of tempura and then Peking Duck. Though the decor is Zen and the wine list qualifies it for 'temple of wine' status, this is a place to have fun rather than meditate gravely upon what you are drinking. The atmosphere is lively and buzzy and attracts many shoppers from the plush mall in which it is located.

## Myanmar/Burma

Burma's only vineyard is situated in the hills of the Southern Shan States at 1300 m above sea level.

WINERY | SOUTHERN SHAN STATES

### Myanmar Vineyard

Aythaya Vineyard, Htone Bo, Aythaya
Taunggyi, Southern Shan States
T +95 (0)81 24536
www.myanmar-vineyard.com
Visits by appointment.

Myanmar Estate was launched in 1999, after an unsuccessful experience on less suitable land. German-born Bert Morsbach, whose experience includes mining engineering and organic rice farming has particularly high hopes for his Muscat – and for the prospects of the area to become a serious wine region.

## Philippines

This is not the place to go looking for locally produced wine, or at least not grape wine, but a former advertising man and snack food manufacturer has recently launched a palatable range of fruit wines under the Patubas label, produced in the Science and Technology Park of the University of the Philippines in Los Baños, Laguna. The long-term ambition is for the wines, which are made from pineapple, mango, guayabano and others, to be able to hold their own on restaurant wine lists.

RESTAURANT | MANILA

### Sala

610 J Nakpil St, Manila
T+63 (0)2-524 6770
Daily 1800-2300.
$

Colin Mackay has created an escape from the urban chaos at this delightfully simple restaurant. His food is modern and European rather than fusion, and features what is probably the freshest carpaccio, duck and lamb in the country. He has assembled a wine list that is especially strong on New Zealand, though offers scope for discovering other regions. The crowd is a fun combination of local wine lovers, expatriates and visiting celebrities.

## Singapore

Although wine was introduced to Singapore by the expatriate community, the vibrancy of the wine market here now is largely the achievement of a keen set of Singaporeans, such as Ch'ng Poh Tiong, the youthful editor of the locally published magazine, *The Wine Review*, and Dr NK Yong, a surgeon and internationally famous wine consultant who, in 1989 was made an Officier de l'Ordre du Mérite Agricole by the French government for services to wine. Raffles Hotel has a long history of running food and wine events and Singapore is a regular stop-off for producers visiting Asia on tours to promote their wines. Stated simply, this is one place in this region where you never need to be far from a good bottle of wine.

RESTAURANT | SINGAPORE

### Au Jardin Les Amis

EJH Corner House, Singapore Botanic Gardens Visitors Centre, 1 Cluny Rd, Singapore
T+65 6466 8812
www.lesamis.com.sg
$$$

Book as far in advance as possible to secure one of the 12 tables in this charming former colonial house in the Botanic Gardens. Gunter Hubrechsen's innovative cooking could hold its own among Paris's top restaurants and, although it's not strictly fusion, it does successfully incorporate a light, fresh touch reminiscent of Asian cuisine. The wine list has a retort to whatever Hubrechsen's oft-changing menu throws up, as it offers well over 1000 wines.

RESTAURANT SINGAPORE

## Zambuca Italian Restaurant & Bar

Pan Pacific Singapore, 7 Raffles Bvd 03-00, Singapore
T+65 6337 8086
www.zambuca.com.sg
Daily 1130-1400 and 1800-2230.
$$-$$$

Every time I go to Singapore I'm struck by the levels of wine knowledge and appreciation. Nowhere does wine in Singapore better, though, than Zambuca which offers more than 1600 labels at surprisingly fair prices. This is clearly a place created by wine lovers: a sleek, glassed-in cellar holds 8,000 bottles, and there are regular wine-tastings by top European producers. Australian-Italian Angelo Sanelli turns out cutting-edge, Asian-scented interpretations of Italian food, such as tofu, lemongrass, coriander, spring onion, garlic potato and polenta served on mixed arugula and lettuce, garnished with parma ham drizzled with a spicy plum sauce. There is plenty of advice on hand for matching such accomplishments to the wine, and the wine cellar doubles as a private dining room for 12 people, for those wishing to plan a special menu ahead of time.

## Thailand

The country that – indirectly – gave us Red Bull (it was launched by an Austrian called Dietrich Mateschitz and a Thai, called Chalerm Yoovidhya, and was loosely based on Krating Daeng, a popular local drink), Thailand now boasts no fewer than six wineries – a number that is growing fast. These wineries are situated between the 14th and 18th parallels, rather than in the traditional latitude for wine between the 30th and 50th parallels. The key to their success lies partly in their altitude; they are mostly between 300 and 600 m above sea level, although Siam, the largest, with 10,000 ha is only 5 m above the ocean.

Grape harvest at Siam Winery.

As elsewhere in what are being called 'New Latitude' vineyards across the world (page 14), the simple explanation seems to be that vines are actually more resilient than was ever previously thought. The recent flurry of activity was the result of a long period of research in the 1980s, commissioned by the king; government permission for winemaking to begin was given in 1992. Local and international grapes are used, with Syrah showing particular promise, and there are two harvests per year. For tours around the wine regions (including to a new vineyard where

Top: Sula Vineyard, India. Bottom: Village Farm Winery, Thailand.

the workers use elephants), contact Laurence Civil (laurence@csloxinfo.com).

WINERY NAKHON RATCHASIMA

## Granmonte Vineyard & Wines

52 Moo 9 Phayayen, Pakchong, Nakhon Ratchasima
T+66 (0)36 -227 334 5
www.granmonte.com
Shop daily 1000-1700. Tours Sat and Sun by appointment only.

Visooth and Sakuna Lohithnavy have created a mini-vinous paradise in a stunning valley next to the KhaoYai National Park, only an hour and half by car from Bangkok. The vineyards are immaculately tended and are at their peak for the harvesting of the Syrah and Chenin Blanc, celebrated at the winery's festival in February. The winery can be enjoyed at any time, however, and a tour can be combined with a meal at VinCotto ($), the Italian-inspired modern-cuisine restaurant on the estate.

WINERY BANGKOK

## Monsoon Valley (Siam Winery)

174/1-4 Moo 9, Viphavadee-Rangsit Rd, Sikun Donmuang, Bangkok
T +66 (0)2-533 5600
www.monsoonvalleywine.com
Visits by appointment only.

The creation of Chalerm Yoovidhya, co-owner of Red Bull, this winery 60 km southwest of Bangkok is not only Thailand's but also Southeast Asia's largest and most successful in overseas markets. Its wines are emphatically Thai, produced with a mandate that they match the spiciness and range of Thai food. Winemaker Laurent Metge-Toppin is French, but meets the challenge of finding a Thai sense of terroir in grapes from diverse vineyard locations, including the Chao Praya river delta, where the vines are planted on series of floating vineyards separated by canals, and the mountains near Pak Chong. The Monsoon Valley label includes wines made from Shiraz, Colombard, Malaga Blanc and Pokdum, and are beginning to receive worldwide critical attention; quite an achievement for a range started in 2003.

WINERY NAKHON RATCHASIMA

## PB Valley Khao Yai Winery

102 Moo 5, Phaya Yen, Pak Chong, Nakhorn Ratchasima
T +66 (0)3622 7328/29
www.khaoyaiwinery.com
Restaurant Mon-Sat from 1700; Sun from 1100.

In the late 1980s, Piya Bhirombhakdi, an entrepreneur with a love of wine, began to implement his dream of making premium wine in Thailand. Identifying the vicinity of the Khao Yai National Park as a suitable area, he called in German winemaking expertise, planting first Syrah and Chenin Blanc and, later, Tempranillo. The estate, one of the world's pioneers in making 'New Latitude'

Thailand has single handedly created a whole new category – tropical wines.

# Best producers

**Thailand**

Granmonte » *page 366.*

Château de Loei

PB Valley Khao Yai » *page 366.*

Siam » *page 366.*

wines, now has 80 of its 320 ha under vine. Visits are free, with a charge for tasting and various possible tour packages. Thai or Western meals are available in the Great Hornbill Grill and Restaurant ($). You could also stay at the stylish Juldis Khao Yai Resort & Spa Hotel on the estate ($-$$) and enjoy the terrific views from its 360 m vantage point.

WINERY | NAKHON RATCHASIMA

**Village Farm Winery**

103 Moo 7, Ban Pai Ngam, Tambon Thai Samakkee, Amphur Wang Nam Keow, Nakhon Ratchasima
T +66 (0)44-228 4078
www.villagefarm.co.th
Sun-Fri 0800-2100; Sat 0800-2200.

The Thai wine industry has fascinated me since I first tasted an example of a few years ago. At the Village Farm, local millionaire Viravat Cholvanich has created a corner of France, with many Thai twists, just three hours from Bangkok. His complex, in the stunning area between between the Tublan and Khao Yai national parks, includes a winery, a spa that includes grape-seed scrubs as well as Thai and Swedish massage, a French restaurant, a hotel and a working farm. All are immaculately conceived and maintained, and the Village Farm makes a good base for exploring the surrounding wineries and getting a sense of more traditional Thai rural life. The winery, **Château des Brumes**, is dedicated to the finest principles of French winemaking, and has convinced several skeptics that Thailand can not only make wine, but fine wine at that.

## Vietnam

Ask for 'wine' in Vietnam or Cambodia and there's a high chance you'll be pointed in the direction of a bottle containing yellow liquid and a snake, a lizard, starfish or even, in once case, a bird. These distilled rice wines, known in Vietnamese as *ruou*, have a medicinal role. One, enriched with the penis and testicles of a goat, is called 'One Night Five Times'; others, made with mushrooms and ginseng, are supposed to be good for the brain. The best place to try these in a congenial setting with food is the **Highway 4** bar in Hanoi (5 Hang Tre St., Hoan Kiem District. T +84 (0)4- 976 2647 www.highway4.com).

Real grape wine also exists. The UK-based multi-national Allied-Domecq was briefly – and prematurely – involved in launching Vietnam's first winery in 1995. That venture failed but at the hill-town of Dalat, nearly two million bottles of drinkable Vang Dalat are produced every year from table grapes and a blend of grapes and other fruit. Foreigners apparently tend to prefer the 16% Strong Red, which includes mulberries, to the 11% Superior Red, which doesn't. Most wine-loving locals and tourists, however, may prefer to seek out Vietnam's growing number of high-quality restaurants and wine shops which, thanks to increasing numbers of tourists and business travellers, and Vietnam's own expanding middle class, now offer a range of wines to equal those on offer in the UK and US. Interestingly, where France would once have benefited from its old colonial links here, the bottles now being sold are as likely to come from Italy, Australia or Chile.

WINE BAR | HANOI

**Vine Wine Boutique Bar & Café**

1A Xuan Dieu , Tay Ho, Hanoi
T +84 (0)4-719 8000
www.vine-group.com
Daily 0900-2300.
$

If I had to choose one style of cuisine it would have to be Vietnamese which – thanks only marginally, I suspect, to the influence of the French when Vietnam was their colony – is also one of the best in Asia to enjoy with wine. Hanoi and Ho Chi Minh have some great wine shops and restaurants, but the combination of the two run by Canadian-born Donald Berger is really something special. Berger with whom, to declare an interest, I have worked on the Vietnam International Wine Challenge and some charity dinners, has become nearest thing to 'Mr Wine' in this country. After stints as executive chef of the Hanoi Press Club and Hong Kong's Ritz-Carlton Hong Kong, he decided to go solo and started Vine Wine Boutique Bar & Café where he sells wines you might search to find in London, such as Beaux Freres Pinot Noir from Oregon. Regular tastings are also held at Bergers Wine Annex, where wine at reasonable prices can be bought to take away.

## China, Hong Kong and Macau

Watch this space. China is already the sixth- or seventh-biggest wine producer in the world, with a harvest that doubled between 2000 and 2005. Of crucial importance in China is the fact that the government is fully behind the development of the wine industry, believing as it does that a shift from drinks made from rice and grain to one produced from grapes will leave more food for poor people to eat. New plantings will almost certainly mean that, by 2012, China will not only be self-sufficient in wine, but it may actually need to export. Westerners who are now beginning to discover the delights of Chinese black truffles that were once thought to be the unique preserve of small corners of France and Italy, may soon find themselves enjoying a glass of Chinese red or white wine after driving home in their Chinese-manufactured MG car from a day working at a computer made by the Chinese-owned IBM.

Despite the popularity of Cognac, whisky and wine and brandy made from rice, there is, in fact, also a long history of grape wine in China. There is some doubt over whether the residue in a 3000 year-old, sealed copper container discovered in Henan province in 1980 was of grape wine, but there is no question that, in 138 BC the Han dynasty introduced grape growing and winemaking to Beijing after a messenger returned with details of how these were being done in the West Region.

Making wine from grapes may be easier than from rice – because there is no need to add yeast – but it is more seasonal and the quality, quantity and flavour vary more from year to year. Another problem in China is that, while native Chinese grapes have evolved to survive the frozen winters, they don't make good wine, so, in most regions, the strains of vinifera vine used to make quality wine have to be buried beneath small earth mounds during the cold months. In recent years, there have been moves to develop warmer areas, where this labour-intensive activity is unnecessary.

The first 'modern' Chinese winery was opened in Yantai in Shandong Province in 1892 by a Chinese businessman who had gained a taste for wine overseas. Eighteen years later a French priest started a winery in Beijing that would later become the Beijing Friendship Winery and, more recently, Dragon Seal, in a joint venture with Pernod Ricard. Other foreign investors have included Rémy Martin (who were involved in launching Dynasty) and Allied Domecq, who had a winery at Huadong. While all of these raised standards to a level of adequacy, the bar has been raised a lot higher over the last five years. Today, Changyu, one of the two biggest producers, has a joint venture with the French firm Castel that aims to sell its top Chinese wine for US$50 a bottle in the US. Great Wall – the other major player – has also raised its game significantly, and good wines are being made by Dragon Seal (Syrah) Grace vineyards (Cabernet Sauvignon and Chardonnay) and Suntime, a recent venture in the far west. None of the wines is as good as India's Grover Vineyards top reds (page 362) but progress is being made very, very rapidly. Quality will certainly be improved by the development of new regions and the planting of alternative grapes. So far, too much focus has been on Cabernet Sauvignon and a lesser variety wrongly described here as 'Riesling'. Syrah/Shiraz should do well, as does a grape called Cabernet Gernischt, similar to the Cabernet Franc, that was exported to China in the 19th century before becoming extinct in Europe.

Today, Hong Kong and the Chinese mainland boast a growing number of businessmen and officials who have taken to drinking wine in preference to Cognac. In some cases the wine has notoriously been mixed with Sprite (a blend which may be advisable for cheap Bordeaux, though less so for Mouton Rothschild and Pétrus) but sightings of this blend are becoming rarer.

China has created an export-driven truffle-growing industry from scratch. And what they can do with truffles, they can do with wine.

# China

WINE BAR — BEIJING

## Café Europa

1/F, 1113, Bldg 11, Jianwai SOHO, Chaoyang District, Beijing
T +86 (0)10- 5869 5663
Open 1000-2400
$-$$

A welcome addition to the capital's previously less than vibrant wine bar scene, this recently-opened establishment in the shiny SOHO development offers the opportunity to compare French Syrah with Australian Shiraz and German and New World Rieslings on the ground floor or to match the wines with food in the restaurant upstairs. It's minimally decorated but very comfortable and is already a favourite with Beijing wine professionals.

WINERY — SHANDONG PROVINCE

## Chateau Changyu-Castel

Yantai, Shandong Province
T +86 (0)535- 6632 892
www.changyu.com.cn
Contact winery for opening times.

Founded in 1892 by a retired Chinese diplomat who employed the Austrian consul to make the wine, Chateau Changyu is China's oldest and most established producer. The first Chinese winery to import and plant European varieties, it cemented the French connection by joining forces with the massive Castel group, France's largest wine producer and distributor (and owner of the Nicolas and Oddbins chains of shops). The vineyards, close to the edge of the Yellow Sea in Shandong Province, northeastern China, are on the same latitude as the Napa Valley, and produce a range of wines including Chardonnay, Cabernet Sauvignon and Cabernet Gernischt, a red variety that is now extinct in Europe.

WINERY — HEBEI PROVINCE

## Great Wall Wine Company/ Hua Xia Winery

Cofco Wines, ChangLi, Hebei Province
T +86 (0)335- 203 1837
www.huaxia-greatwall.com.cn
Contact winery for opening times.

Not far from China's Great Wall, this winery – part of the largest wine producer in China – was founded in 1983 and has mirrored China's extraordinary economic growth of the past couple of decades. From 75 ha of its own vines plus bought-in grapes, it produces a wide range of wines, for both export and national consumption, across myriad dry to sweet styles and varieties. Whether or not you are able to make the visit, it is worth trying the various wines, especially in local-style Chinese restaurants, to get a sense of the Chinese palate, which tends to favour lighter, sweeter wines than are found in the west. Beware, however, of various Great Wall lookalikes.

WINERY — SHANXI PROVINCE

## Shanxi Grace Vineyards

Dongjia, Ren Cun, Tai Gu, Shanxi Province
T +86 (0)354- 644 9188
www.grace-vineyard.com
May-Sep daily 1100-1700. Oct-Apr daily 1100-1600. Closed for Chinese hols.

Founded in 1997 by Hong Kong businessman, CK Chan, close to the foothills of the Tai Hang mountains, this boutique company is China's first premium winery. Dedicated to keeping production small, it is producing Cabernet Sauvignon and Chardonnay that have already received critical acclaim from some of the world's top wine writers. Some limited-production wines are only available at the winery.

RESTAURANTS — SHANGHAI

## Three on the Bund

3 Zhong Shan Dong Yi Rd, Shanghai
**Jean Georges** T +86 (0)21- 6321 7733. **Laris** T +86 (0)21-6321 9922. **New Heights** T +86 (0)21- 6321 0909. **Whampoa Club** T +86 (0)21- 6321 3737.
www.threeonthebund.com
Daily 1000-2230.
$$-$$$

In a beautifully restored building on Shanghai's riverfront, Three on the Bund brings together several of Shanghai's best restaurants, as well as a Giorgio Armani /Emporio Armani flagship store, an Evian Spa and the Shanghai Gallery of Art. At **Jean Georges Shanghai**, celebrated chef Jean-Georges Vongerichten has created a menu of light, delicate French dishes, most using organic ingredients, that play to the strengths of the restaurant's 5000-strong wine cellar and skilled sommelier. At **Whampoa Club**, Jereme Leung, author of *New Shanghai Cuisine*, brings an innovative hand to Shanghainese classics. Wine lovers can opt to stretch their palates in new directions by sampling the 50 rare teas on offer. Great fusion cooking is on offer at **Laris**, which was recently named the city's best and most fashionable restaurant, while **New Heights** has the most extraordinary views: sip a glass of something nice and take in a 180-degree panorama of the Bund, Pudong and the Huangpu river.

# Hong Kong

Like Singapore, Hong Kong developed a wine-drinking culture thanks to its expatriate population but, today, wine is increasingly being drunk by the local community, whether in the form of the cheap, basic fare on offer in Park 'n' Shop supermarkets, or the top Bordeaux on sale in smart restaurants and in the retail outlet of British wine merchants Berry Bros & Rudd.

RESTAURANT KOWLOON

## Prince

11/F, One Peking, Tsim Sha Tsui, Kowloon
T +852 2366 1308
www.prince-catering.com/en/Stra_HongKong2.php
Daily noon-1430 and 1830-2200.
$\$\$$

I love Hong Kong and its vibrancy, which seems to spawn new restaurants and wine bars almost every week. The first tip-off that you get that this is no ordinary dim sum restaurant is the wall of glassed-in wine bottles that greets you near the entrance. Dim sum is an adored culinary staple in this city, in which more than half of meals are eaten out, but few places offer much, if any, wine. The dim sum here is excellent and innovative, and the menu also includes authentic Japanese sushi and sashimi, as well as Western desserts, so there is plenty of scope for experimenting with interesting pan-menu matches. The views alone are worth the price of a meal.

RESTAURANT KOWLOON

## Spoon

InterContinental Hong Kong, 18 Salisbury Rd, Kowloon
T +852 2721 1211 (ext. 2323)
www.hongkong-ic.intercontinental.com
Daily 1800-2400.
$\$\$\$$

To a city obsessed by food, Alain Ducasse's ultra-hip Spoon brings both a highly innovative cuisine and hundreds of choices of wine. The dining room is built around a glassed-in wine cellar and the menu deconstructs the typical offering of three or four courses and, instead, allows you to build your own meal around a series of ingredients and Asian-inspired sauces. The Sexy Spoon set menu, consisting of six courses concocted spontaneously each night by the kitchen, is highly recommended: it removes the element of choice, allowing you to focus your full attention on the wine list.

Hong Kong panorama.

RESTAURANT CENTRAL

## Va Bene

58-62 D'Aguilar St, Lan Kwai Fong, Central
T +852 2845 5577
www.vabeneristorante.com
Mon-Thu 1200-1430 and 1800-2300; Fri 1200-1430 and 1900-2400; Sat 1900-2400; Sun 1800-2300.
$\$\$$-$\$\$\$$

Chefs from all corners of Italy are recruited to bring their respective regions' trattoria fare to this elegant, laid-back pan-Italian restaurant. In the middle of one of Hong Kong's original Western restaurant areas, Lan Kwai Fong, Va Bene offers not just authentic cuisine but also, in a city which is still finding its wine palate and confidence, a refreshingly focused, assured list of mostly Italian wines, veering away from a scattergun approach.

RESTAURANT CENTRAL

## Yung Kee

32-40 Wellington St, Central
T +852 2522 1624
www.yungkee.com.hk
Daily 1100-2300. Dim sum served Mon-Sat 1400-1730; Sun and public hols 1100-1730. Closed Chinese New Year.
$\$\$$

Founded more than 60 years ago by Kam Shui Fai, who started life as a near-penniless roast goose stall-holder, Yung Kee's development into a lucrative Hong Kong institution has mirrored Hong Kong's meteoric rise. It is loved by local Chinese, expatriates and tourists alike, who come here for the platters of succulent roast meat that are a speciality of southern China. Although roast meat is available in fast food joints all over the city, what's special about Yung Kee is that you can build a varied meal by selecting other Chinese delicacies, such as hotpots and bird's nest soup, and enjoy them with wine, which is not available at typical slap-it-on-the-table-with-a-scowl, hole-in-the-wall roast meat establishments. Yung Kee also, periodically, offers special Champagne and wine set meals.

## Macau

Macau is quite different to its neighbour, Hong Kong. Returned to China in 1999 by the Portuguese government with far less fanfare than accompanied the handover of the British colony two years earlier, it has gone through a whirlwind of development. From a sleepy island with a few modern hotels, it has, almost overnight, become the gambling centre of Asia. In 2001, the Beijing government put an end to a 40-year monopoly held by a local businessman and opened the way for Las Vegas operators like Sands and MGM. In 2006, Macau's casino revenue is predicted to overtake the US$9bn annually banked by Las Vegas and it is expected to grow a lot bigger, with at least 25 new hotels planned. So far, Macau's restaurants have yet to match the great, icon-packed wine lists of their Nevada counterparts but just give them time …

RESTAURANT MACAU

### Mezzaluna

Mandarin Oriental Hotel, 956-1110 Av da Amizade, PO Box 3016, Macau
T +853 793 3861
www.mandarinoriental.com
Tue-Sun 1200-1430 and 1830-2300.
$$$

Chef Igor Bocchia concocts innovative, Tuscan-inspired dishes in this elegant and romantic Italian outpost in one of the world's quirkiest cities. Typical offerings might include sea urchin risotto with fava beans and tomato comfit to start, followed by wild turbot in pistachio crust with steamed marron lobster. The Mandarin Oriental hotel group is expert at evoking Europe in Asia and, though you will doubtless be enjoying yourself with Chinese and Macanese food, this is the place to come to combine fine wine-ing with your fine dining.

# Asia-Pacific

## Japan

By far the most wine-sophisticated country in Asia, Japan enjoyed a wine boom in the mid 1990s, which has since slowed dramatically, along with other parts of the Japanese economy. This is still, however, the place to find the best wines and finest palates in Asia. Small restaurants tucked away in side streets sometimes offer great old Burgundies that would excite the passions of any Parisian wine enthusiast. There are several glossy wine magazines – notably *Wine Kingdom*, *Vinothèque* and *Wineart* – and frequent articles on wine in other publications but wine critics here have far less influence than Japan's sommeliers. The standing of this last group was hugely boosted in 1995 by the victory of Tasaki Shinya in the competition for the world's finest sommelier. The Japan Sommelier Association has over 6500 members – more than any country apart from Italy – and Japan is probably the only country in the world where standard bookshops stock works with titles like 'How to be a Sommelier'.

The Japanese taste in wine differs from that of many of their neighbours in much the same way as their cuisine. Chilli is not a major ingredient here and nor are strong flavours on the plate or in the glass. So subtler, less fruity, less oaky, less alcoholic wines have tended to be popular (this is a major market for Beaujolais), although younger drinkers are beginning to develop a taste for bolder, more New World styles.

Japan's whiskey is far better known than its wines but there is a small, dynamic wine industry, with some 200 wineries. Most are located in Yamanashi province, about 100 km south of Tokyo, but there are also some on the northern island of Hokkaido. Wine has been produced in Japan since at least the 16th century but it was not until 1875 that the first commercial winery opened its doors in Katsunuma in Yamanashi. This area is the ideal place for wine because the rain shadow caused by Mount Fuji makes it too dry for rice. A wide range of grapes is grown, including Merlot, Cabernet Sauvignon and Chardonnay, but the two best-established varieties are Koshu, a white thick-skinned vinifera that makes wines reminiscent of Muscadet, and Muscat Bailey, an American hybrid, which makes fairly basic reds. Up in Hokkaido, cooler temperatures favour Müller-Thurgau and Riesling.

While a number of smaller wineries are beginning to make waves, the Japanese wines with the highest local reputations come from two giant companies: Château Mercian's deservedly lauded Chardonnay and Merlot and Suntory's arguably overpraised Tomi.

# Best producers

### China

Changyu » *page 369.*
Dragon Seal
Dynasty
Great Wall » *page 369.*
Shanxi Grace Winery » *page 369.*
Suntime
Tung Hua

### Japan

Château Mercian (top Merlot and Chardonnay) » *page 372.*
Coco Farm » *page 372.*
Grace Winery » *page 372.*
Katsunuma
Manns
Okuizumo
Omar Khayam
Sapporo (Grande Polaire)
Suntory (Tomi red)
Takahata
Tsuno

RESTAURANT TOKYO

## Aux Amis Tokyo

35F Maru Biru, 2-4-1 Marunouchi, Chiyoda-ku
T +81 (0)3- 5220 4011
www.auxamis.com
Daily 1100-1530 and 1730-2400.
$$$

This is the most dramatic of a trio of restaurants of the same name, where great modern French cooking is matched with international wines. The sommeliers are younger and keener than most in Japan and the best fun to be had in any of these establishments is to leave yourself in their hands. If the food and wine are memorable, so is the view from the 35th floor of the Marunouchi Building, high above Tokyo station.

WINERY YAMANASHI

## Château Mercian

Mercian Katsunuma Winery, 5-8 Kyobashi 1-chome, Chuo-ku, Tokyo
T+81 (0)3- 3231 3910
www.chateaumercian.com
Visits by appointment only.

Grapes have been cultivated in Katsunuma for well over a millennium, but it was not until the late 19th century that wine began to be made from them. Mercian Katsunuma Winery, founded in 1877, led the way in both quality and scale, and today makes popular wines under the Château Mercian label specially to match Japanese food, including 'healthy' wines with a higher than average dose of polyphenols. Tours are free but you pay ¥1000 for a unique interactive feature: picking and eating as many grapes as you want.

WINERY TOCHIGI

## Coco Farm & Winery

611 Tajima-Cho, Ashikaga-City, Tochigi
T + 81 (0)284- 42 1194
www.cocowine.com
Daily 1000-1700. Café 1100-1700.
Tastings ¥500 for 5 wines.

Only an hour and a half by train from Tokyo, Coco Farm & Winery makes an easy and heartwarming day trip from the capital. It was founded in 1950 as a grape farm to give employment to underachieving Japanese youth by helping them to reconnect with nature and giving them a sense of purpose. The first wine was made in the 1980s and, today, quality has improved to such an extent that the sparkling wine, Novo, was served at the G-7 summit in Okinawa in 2000. Under the guidance of Bruce Gutlove, an Italian-American who arrived at Coco for six months and ended up staying for almost 10 years, around 90 disabled students from the nearby Coco Romi Gakuen school do most of the work in the vineyard and winery and on the farm. The shitake mushrooms and other produce can be tasted in the winery café. A huge harvest festival is held each year.

WINEBAR TOKYO

## El Vino

Roppongi 7-7-8, Minato-ku
T +81 (0)3-5771 2439
Mon-Sat 1800-0100; last order 2330.

On a small lane, tucked away off the busy, noisier parts of Roppongi, is one of Tokyo's best kept secrets. Jiro Kinsoshita has one of the best Australian wine bars in the world; although the range is not huge, it includes lots of really well-chosen wines that are not available elsewhere. (Some make their way into the country unofficially in bags carried back from Oz by J (as he is known) on his frequent visits there.) There is good simple food to go with the wines – and cigars aplenty when midnight approaches.

WINE SHOP TOKYO

## Ginza 6-9-5

Ginza Komatsu 1F, Tokyo
T +81 (0)3- 3571 1121
www.enoteca.co.jp
Call ahead for opening times.

This is the flagship of a very exciting chain of wine shops, with branches across Japan, many of which also have attached wine bars. Enoteca directly imports more than 1000 wines and is always adding new producers to its range. French wines are a speciality, with Jean-Claude Vrinat of Paris restaurant Taillevent specially selecting Enoteca's Burgundies, but all the world's wine regions are represented at reasonable prices, considering how far most have had to travel.

WINERY HIGASHIYAMANASHI-GUN

## Grace Winery

173 Todoroki katsunuma-cho, Higashiyamanashi-gun
T +81 (0)553- 44 1230
www.grace-wine.jp
Visits by appointment only.

Celebrated Bordeaux consultant Denis Dubourdieu has contributed his expertise to Grace wines made from international varieties but has had particular success with wines made from Koshu. This vinifera grape, with origins in Central Asia, has been grown in Japan for more than a millennium and is now considered as a indigenous Japanese variety. A challenging grape because of its extreme vigour, it reaches its full potential in the Katsunuma area. The 2004 Grace Koshu was hailed as the best wine made from a native variety by Robert Parker on a visit to Japan.

WINE BAR TOKYO

### Mr Stamp's Wine Garden

Roppongi 4-4-6, Chowa Bldg, Higashi-kan 1F, Tokyo
T +81 (0)334- 79 1390
Mon-Sat 1800-2230.
$$-$$$

The wine list at this informal, cosy French restaurant is good, but there are often unlisted surprises lurking in the cellar, so ask manager Sekimoto-san to tell you about any additional bottles. Founded in 1976 by expatriate American and wine expert, Albert Stamp, this is in an alley in Roppongi but feels miles away from the bustle of Tokyo. The food is excellent but you can also come later in the evening for a simple plate of cheese. It's the kind of place where you won't feel uncomfortable eating or drinking alone.

## Korea

Ask any internationally aware winemaker to name the countries that are attracting his or her interest and South Korea is almost bound to feature. Wine is still something of a novelty here. Out of every 100 litres of alcohol consumed, only one will be wine – whisky is still the alcoholic drink of choice and represents over 80% of all the alcohol imported into the country – but Western food is increasingly popular and people are becoming more interested in the health-giving properties of red wine. Korea now has a wine magazine and a sophisticated international wine competition. Anyone wanting to taste a local wine should ask for an Empery Cupid from the East of Eden winery in the hilly Pongwha County.

WINE BAR SEOUL

### Bar Bliss

72-32 Itaewon, Yongsan, Seoul
T+82 (0)749 -7738
Daily 1800-late.

Bar Bliss is a happy meeting ground for Seoul's increasingly open gay community and straight locals and wine lovers. Ted Park offers more than 70 wines by the bottle. You will likely discover new sounds as well as new wine, as there is always unusual music playing at a moderate volume. Some memorable paintings hang above the bar counter, which is a good, convivial place to meet new people or to catch up with old friends and, in summer, the terrace is a calm haven from the hectic streets of the capital.

WINERY SEOUL

### Comfe Winery

Anseong, Gyeonggi Province
T+82 (0)11 479 7843
www.kennethkimvineyards.com
Visits by appointment only.

Ken Kim is perhaps Korea's foremost wine ambassador. In 1987, after selling his computer business to Samsung, he decided to pursue his dual dreams of increasing wine knowledge and confidence in Korea, and proving that Korea could make good wine. The first he achieved by creating the **Wine Connoisseurs Club**, which gathers informally in Seoul, often around a feast of spicy Korean food, to sample and discuss wines from around the world. The second dream was realized on a trip to the area around Anseong, 80 km south of Seoul, where Antonione Combert, a French missionary from the Rhône, had planted Muscat grapes some 100 years before. Kim wasted no time in creating the Comfe winery and now offers fun day trips from Seoul that include tours of the winery, a Korean meal matched with Korean wines and a stop at the church in which Combert preached.

## Taiwan

Competing with Shanghai for the role of the busiest city in the Chinese-speaking world, Taiwan has more to offer visitors than many of them realize. This is not an aesthetically seductive city but it has an electric buzz, if you know where to look. Well-travelled wine professionals know it as the world's biggest market for Canadian ice wine but this is also an increasingly good place to find decent wine of every kind at surprisingly low prices. (People living in Hong Kong profit by doing their shopping here.) If there is one name to remember, it is **Eslite**, an extraordinary chain of shops which sell Chinese and foreign-language books, imported magazines, food, homeware and wine, including esoteric bottles like Leroy Aligoté that you might vainly search for in New York or London. There are coffee shops here too, but no restaurants as such. However, hunger (if not a thirst for wine) is well satisfied at the **Din Tai Fung** dim sum bar (194 Xin Yi Rd, Section 2, T 011 886 2 2391 7719).

WINE BAR TAIPEI

### Champagne 2 and Thr3e

www.champagnebar.com.tw

Champagne 2 169 AnHer Rd, Sec 2, Taipei
T+886 (0)2- 6638 1880
Mon-Fri 1900-0230; Sat and Sun 1900-0330.

Champagne Thr3e 171 SongDe Rd, B1
T+886 (0)2- 2728 5673
Sun, Tue, Thu 2100-0300; Wed, Fri, Sat 2100-0500.
Admission Fri and Sat US$15-17.

If you want to watch Taiwan's glitterati at play, you should check out these bars that, true to their name, offer over 50 Champagnes by the glass, as well as a range of other wines. Prices vary, with Moët & Chandon sold at Champagne 3 at a reasonable US$61 on Tuesday and Thursday when there is a chill-out mood. The rest of the week is rather wilder and there is a cover charge on Friday and Saturday. Food on offer includes Germany Style Sausage and Deep Fried Fish Finger with Thailand Dressing, so eating before you get here is a good option.

# Glossary

**Assemblage** French term for wine made from a blend of different grapes or for the action of blending.
**Barrique** Term used, often in Italy, on wines matured in new oak barrels.
**Baume** French system for measuring the sugar and potential alcohol in a grape. 1 degree baume will produce 1% alcohol. 1 baume is the equivalent of 1.8 Brix *qv*.
**Biodynamic** Far more fundamentalist than Organic *qv*, biodynamic producers follow rules laid down by Rudolf Steiner: they work according to the phases of the moon and treat their vines homeopathically with herbs and specially aged and hydrated cow dung. This all sounds flaky, but some of the best winemakers in the world are fully biodynamic.
**Blanc de blancs** White wine made from white grapes. Applies to 99.99% of still wines, but far fewer sparkling wines, many of which are made, at least in part, from black grapes whose skins are discarded before they can tint the wine. White wine made purely from black grapes is Blanc de noirs.
**Botrytis** Rot. Can refer to unwelcome grey rot that develops in warm temperatures after rain, but usually means Noble Rot *qv*.
**Brett(anomyces)** A widespread bacteria that can affect red wine in the barrel, giving it a smell that is reminiscent of stable floors or mouse cages or Band-Aids. Varies in intensity and offensiveness (as in beer, a small amount is said by some producers to add complexity), but is always incurable.
**Brix** US measure for the potential alcohol in grapes. See Baumé.
**Carbonic maceration** Fermenting black grapes in a way that keeps them away from oxygen, brings out more immediate boiled-fruit flavours. Particularly used for Beaujolais.
**Cask** Nice Australian and New Zealand term for what others call bag-in-box.
**Cepage** French term for grape variety. A Vin de Cepage is a varietal wine.
**Chai** Bordeaux term for the place where wine is matured in barrel. Elsewhere in France this would be a Cave *qv*, or cellar but the high water table in the region forces most producers to store their wine above ground.
**Château** Literally castle, but in France the term can refer to a building that is little bigger than a hut.
**Chips/Copeaux de bois** Small pieces of oak that are added to (inexpensive) wine to improve its flavour instead of the (costlier) use of new oak barrels. In France use of chips is frowned upon for wine (and currently illegal for Appellation Contrôlée wine) but strangely it is thought entirely acceptable for Appellation Contrôlée Cognac.
**Cleanskin** Australian term for wine sold without a label identifying its maker (a way of selling off excess stock). Illegal in Europe and the US.
**Clone** Within a single variety, such as Chardonnay or Pinot Noir, there are large numbers of individual clones, many of which are quite different in character. Most nurseries sell a range, offering buyers the choice of a melony or a pineappley version of Chardonnay, for example. Californian winemakers often make much of the fact that they have 'Dijon clones' of Chardonnay rather than ones isolated in California.
**Cold soak** The process of leaving red wine grapes in a vat for a period of hours or days before fermentation to increase and improve the flavour of the finished wine.
**Corked** A wine that has been spoiled by a mould called TCA that affects 3-5% of all natural corks.
**Crachoir** French term for spittoon.
**Critter brand** Recent term used in the US for the growing number of highly successful wines (such as Little Penguin, Yellow Tail and Fat Bastard) with animals (critters) on their labels.
**Cross** Some grape varietyes such as Pinotage, Muller Thurgau and Ruby Cabernet are crosses that have been created by marrying two strains of Vinifera *qv*. Often confused with Hybrids *qv*.
**Cult wine** Limited production wine that has developed a loyal following thanks, usually, to critical praise.
**Cultivar** South African synonym for grape variety; eg "Riesling is a noble cultivar".
**Cuvée** French term for a specific blend or vat.

**Decant** To transfer any wine from one container to another in order to separate it from its sediment and to aerate it.
**Dentelle** Lace. Used in France in expressions such as "tout en dentelle" to describe a very delicate wine. This kind of language is rarely used in English-speaking countries.
**Diam** A type of cork made from specially treated cork granules that genuinely seems to be free of TCA *qv* taint and Random Oxidation *qv* problems.
**En primeur** Wine sold while it is still in the barrel, as a future.
**Fining** Before bottling, wine is usually fined with a variety of inert substances ranging from powdered clay to egg whites in order to remove impurities. Some producers prefer not to fine their wines.
**Futs de chene** French expression for wines aged in oak barrels. May refer to new oak, but confusingly often does not.
**Futures** Wine sold while still in the barrel, also described as 'en primeur'.
**Garage wine** Named after a few cult Bordeaux (such as Valandraud and le Pin) launched in the 1980s and 1990s which were carefully made in tiny quantities in the producer's garages and sold for high prices. Now used globally.
**Grand Vin** Unofficial term used by Bordeaux chateaux to describe their top wine (as opposed to a lower quality 'second' wine). The term 'Grand Vin de Bordeaux', is totally meaningless however and appears on the most basic wine.
**Grassy** A term of approbation for fresh-tasting cool-climate whites - though not always in the US where such wines are not always popular - but usually negative when applied to reds.
**Green** Unripe.
**Hand picked** An increasing number of wines are now machine-harvested - picked by tractors that shake the bunches of grapes off the vines - because human harvesters are hard to find. Some wines are still hand-picked, however.
**Hectare** Unit of measurement equal to 2.47 acres.
**Hectolitre** Measurement (100 litres) used for wine in Europe, as in Yields *qv* per hectare.
**Hybrid** A cross between a Vinifera *qv* and a Labrusca vine. Widely grown in the cooler regions of N America and England.
**Icon wine** Highly priced, critically praised wine. Similar to 'cult wine'. See also Garage Wine.
**Industrial wine** Term used perjoritively (usually in Europe) to describe wine made in large volumes (usually in the New World).
**Jug Wine** US term for basic wine (often sold in 2 litre bottles/"jugs").
**Labrusca** The type of wild vine originally found on the east coast of the US but widely grown elsewhere. Resistant to cold, pests, funguses and Phylloxera *qv*, and good for eating, jams and juice, but makes poor wine when compared to Hybrids *qv* and, more particularly Vinifera *qv*.
**Late harvest** Vendange tardive in French, this refers to sweet wines made from grapes affected by Noble Rot *qv*.
**Leaf roll virus** A vineyard disease that affected 90% of South Africa's vines in the 1980s and 1990s, preventing the grapes from ripening properly. Now most producers hope to be growing virus-free Clones *qv*.
**Lees** The dead yeasts that drop out of wine in the winery and accumulate at the bottom of barrels or vats. Can add richness to Chardonnay - whose makers sometimes stir the lees with a stick to spread them around inside a barrel - and fresh zip and a slight fizz to Muscadet which is often aged on its lees (sur lie). But, in red wine, in particular lees can also produce stale Reduced *qv* characters. Hence the need to rack *qv*.
**Lutte raisonné** See Sustainable agriculture.
**Maderized** A wine that has been spoiled by heat, similar in effect to Oxidized *qv*.
**Malolactic fermentation** The secondary fermentation which converts the naturally occurring appley malic acid in wine into the creamier lactic acid. Usually occurs within months of the intial alcoholic fermentation. Wines before or during this tend to be difficult to taste.
**Mercaptan** A server case of Reduction *qv*.
**Méthode classique** Term used to describe sparkling wine made by the same method as Champagne.
**Micro (oxygenation)** Modern technique of injecting oxygen into wine in the form of tiny bubbles to soften tannins. Can cut down the need to Rack (qv) the wine.
**Nez / nose** Pretentious term for the smell of the wine.
**Noble harvest / Noble rot** A benevolent fungus, also known as botrytis that covers grapes in some areas in the late autumn, concentrating the flavour and providing a dried apricot flavour of its own.
**Oechsle** German measure of sweetness - and potential alcohol in a grape. Kabinett wine from the Rheingau has to made from grapes with an oechsle level of at least 73; less than half the 150 required for Trockenbeerenauslese. This is similar to the French Baumé *qv* and US Brix *qv*.
**Organic** Rules vary from country to country and some wines are fully organic, while others are made from organically grown grapes. Chemical use is restricted and wineries are subject to spot checks.
**Oxidized** Wine that has been spoiled by exposure to oxygen (or possibly just past it). May taste like sherry or may have very little flavour at all.
**Parker (points)** Robert Parker is the ultra-influential US-based guru who, through the Parker Points (marks out of 100) published in his Wine Advocate newsletter helps to dictate the style of wines that are made and the specific wines that are bought.
**Pétillant / Frizzante** Slightly sparkling.
**Phylloxera** The louse that, late in the 19th century, found its way from the east coast of the USA where vines had grown resistant to it, to Europe where they hadn't. In less than two decades, the louse devastated almost all of the vines in the world by eating through their roots. Lucky escapees included a few European vineyards, Chile and parts of Australia which have, so far, been protected by their geography. Phylloxera reappeared in California in the 1980s thanks to the widespread planting of a rootstock that

proved to be less resistant than was previously believed.

**Premium** Meaningless term that usually means 'pricy'. The same applies to 'Prestige'.

**Producteurs reunie** Term for French cooperative.

**Quintal** Measure of weight (100 kg) used in Italy.

**Rack** The process of transferring wine from barrel to barrel or vat to vat in order to separate it from any sediment (Lees *qv*) and to aerate it to prevent it developing stale Reduction *qv* odours.

**Random oxidation** Phenomenon increasingly recognized in Australia of the variation between bottles sealed with natural corks. For some, this is more of a problem than wines being corked *qv*.

**Reduced/reduction** A character that can be variously reminiscent of rotten eggs, stale dishcloth, manure and garlic. It is caused by the sulphor dioxide $SO_2$ used to protect the wine having run short of oxygen and become hydrogen sulphide $H_2S$. Can be removed in the barrel by Racking *qv* and in the bottle by decanting. Severe cases may require the addition of copper (a penny in a wine glass) and on occasion nothing can be done. Some grapes (Syrah/Shiraz, Tempranillo, Barbera, Merlot) are naturally more prone to it than others.

**Reserve** Apart from Spain and Portugal which have officially regulated 'Reserva' and 'Riserva' categories, this is a legally meaningless term in countries.

**Residual sugar (RS)** Any sweetness left in the wine after fermentation is known as residual sugar. Adding cane sugar to sweeten wine is illegal (though it has been widely allowed in cooler French regions to boost a wine's alcoholic strength), but commercial white (and red) wines are now often sweetened using grape concentrate.

**Rich** Mouthfilling, and possibly alcoholic.

**Riedel** The Austrian producer of specially shaped wine glasses for specific styles of wine which bring out their best characteristics.

**Rootstock** Apart from Chile and parts of Australia and a few other exceptions to the general rule, all vines have to be grafted onto Phylloxera *qv* resistant rootstock. Different strains of rootstock suit different soils and vine varieties.

**Selection** Meaningless term except in Germany where it refers to a particular quality of dry Riesling.

**Show reserve** Australian expression, originally for a wine that has done well in a wine 'show' or competition.

**Skin contact** Red and pink wines get their colour and some of their flavour from the grape skins. Some of this is extracted during fermentation, but usually there is a period of 'skin contact' after the sugar has been converted into alcohol. In some cases, winemakers also allow some skin contact before fermentation. White wine needs no skin contact (because no colour is derived from the skins), but some winemakers allow 12 or 24 hours to extract flavour from grape varieties that are not naturally aromatic.

**Staves** In the New World, and in some parts of Europe, wine is aged in stainless steel tanks containing oak staves that give their flavour to the wine. This is more cost-effective than using new barrels.

**Stelvin** The biggest brand of wine screwcaps.

**Sulfites** Sulphor Dioxide ($SO_2$) is routinely used in winemaking to protect wine from bacteria and oxidation. For this reason, legally, bottles sold in the US have to carry the words "Contains sulfites" (as should canned and dried fruit, jams etc, all of which also contain $SO_2$).

**Sustainable agriculture** A form of farming that is less rigorous than organic, and allows producers to apply non-organic products if absolutely necessary.

**Tannic** Tannin is the mouth-drying component of red wines that comes from the skins, stalks and pips. Well made wines from ripe vintages can be pleasantly tannic. Wines (from cool years) with hard, unripe tannins never lose them.

**TBA** Trockenbeerauslese or 'Totally Botrytis Affected'. Both refer to very sweet wine made from grapes affected by Noble Rot *qv*.

**Terroir** Hard-to-define French concept that combines soil, vineyard aspect and micro-climate that gives each vineyard its character. Inconveniently for Gallic chauvinists who thought that theirs was the only country with terroir, it is now clear that there are vineyards with individual character all over the world.

**Tradition** Expression sometimes used in France to describe wines that have not been aged in new oak barrels.

**Unfiltered** Filtering wine before bottling removes solids and bacteria that could spoil it later. It also removes flavour. Wine critics in particular like the idea of unfiltered wine.

**Ungrafted / own roots** Vines directly planted in the earth rather than being grafted onto Rootstock *qv*.

**Varietal** Term for a wine made from a single grape type: Chardonnay is a Varietal.

**Vieilles vignes / Old vines** Old Vines make better wine. However there is no legal definition of how old they have to be to qualify for this term on a label. 50 years old, would justify it.

**Vin de garde** French term for a wine made to be aged.

**Vinifera** The strain of vines that includes almost all of the quality wines that most of us drink. See also Hybrids *qv* and Labrusca *qv*.

**Volatile Acid (VA)** The technical term for the vinegary character of a wine.

**Vrac** French term for wine sold 'loose' or in bulk: ie you have to provide your own bottle.

**Yeast** Grapes carry natural wild yeasts on their skins that will usually kick off. fermentation. Many modern winemakers prefer to use cultured yeasts that are more reliable and can actually add desirable flavours. 'Wild yeast' wines tend to be less fruity and earthier.

**Yield** Winegrowers measure the productiveness in hectolitres per hectare (hl/ha) in Europe, or tons per acre in the US. (Australia uses both), 15 hl/ha is the equivalent of 1 ton/acre. Yields for a quality Bordeaux might be 60hl/ha or 4 tons/acre. Old vines give lower yields and sunnier regions can produce better wine at more generous yields. As a rule, however, higher yields make for thinner, less ripe, less flavoursome wine.

# Useful websites

**www.worldwinetravelguide.com** Updated site linked to this book.

## Wine competitions

**www.decanter.com** Organisers of the Decanter World Wine Awards.
**www.intwinechallenge.com** The results of the world's biggest wine competition.
**www.iwsc.net** Fast improving and expanding UK-based wine competition.
**www.top100wines.com** Results of the annual Sydney International Wine Competition.
**www.trinationswine.com** The results of the annual vinous tussle between Australia, New Zealand and South Africa.

## Wine courses

**www.masters-of-wine.org** The website of the leading UK-based educational institution.
**www.mastersommeliers.org** Home of the respected Court of Master Sommeliers.
**www.michaelschusterwine.com** UK-based wine lecturer is one of the best in the business.
**www.wset.co.uk** The UK-based Wine & Spirit Education Trust runs internationally respected courses.

## Wine tours

**www.abcwine.it** Carla Giomi runs great tours in Tuscany.
**www.amazingmendoza.com** Good tours in Argentina.
**www.bordeaux-wine-travel.com** Guided tours of Bordeaux.
**www.cellartours.com** Excellent tours in Spain and Portugal with local experts.
**www.intouchtravel.com** A range of locally-based wine tours.
**www.tastesa.com.au** Highly recommended personal tours of South Australia.
**www.wine-tours-france.com** First class tailor-made French wine tours.
**www.winetours.co.uk** Reliable UK-based operator Arblaster & Clarke offer tours almost everywhere.
**www.winetours.co.za** Specialist South African tour operators.
**www.uniworld.com** Specialists in river cruises. Good on the Rhine and Danube.

## Magazines and online publications

**http://www2.wbs.ne.jp** A useful Japanese-based but English-language portal full of links to other wine sites.
**www.bbr.com** UK and international merchants Berry Bros & Rudd offer news and information alongside the details of the wines they sell.
**www.bkwine.com** Scandinavian Britt Karlsson offers free wine and wine-and-travel information, wine courses and a photographic library.
**www.bordeaux-news.com** French site, clunkily translated and delivering less than it promises (eg "wine-television") at the moment, but worth keeping an eye on.
**www.burghound.com** Subscription-only site for Burgundy lovers run by Allen Meadows. Worth every penny.
**www.cecwine.co.uk** UK-based wine dinner-club.
**www.cellartasting.com** Free, independent US-based forum for wine enthusiasts.
**www.cellartastings.com** US-based site with information on events, and wine tourism, including tours.
**www.cephas.com** Great wine photography.
**www.decanter.com** Excellent free effort from the UK magazine. Useful for those seeking an alternative to the widely influential views of *The Wine Advocate* (Robert Parker) and the *Wine Spectator*. Good fine wine pricing information and news.
**www.drink-pink.com** UK-based site for rose lovers.
**www.erobertparker.com** US über-guru Robert Parker online - with over 80,000, wine reviews and their all-important mark out of 100. Very influential forum.
**www.finewinemag.com** Online effort from smart, thoughtful quarterly UK-based wine magazine.
**www.finewineonline.co.nz** New Zealand retailer site with good news coverage.
**www.finewinepress.com** Sophisticated site offering the best opportunity to get a Gallic view of the wine world in English - from

 Michel Bettane, France's top wine authority and Thierry Dessauve. Good podcasts.

**www.fortheloveofport.com** Informative free site from US-based port-enthusiast.

**www.grape.co.za** Tim James and others offer reliable and often controversial views on the South African wine scene.

**www.groups.msn.com/BordeauxCentral/** A great informative meeting point for Bordeaux-fans.

**www.harperswinespirit.com** Subscription-only site with useful archive material (and directory) covering the UK wine trade. Good archive features and international news.

**www.investdrinks.org** Check here before buying wine for investment. Site founder Jim Budd obsessively spotlights the ever-present fraudsters.

**www.jancisrobinson.com** Very classy, partly subscriber-only, site from the world's most respected (if not most powerful) wine writer. Good travel and food information from Ms Robinson's husband Nick Lander.

**www.just-drinks.com** Well respected UK-based subscription site for professionals.

**www.madeirawineguide.com** Free site offering independent and pretty comprehensive information on the wines of this island.

**www.natdecants.com** Award-winning opinionated but well-informed features and newsletters from one of North America's best wine writers, Canada-based Natalie MacLean.

**www.oenologie.fr** Very informative site on French wine. For French-speakers only, unfortunately.

**www.onwine.com.au** Subscription site from well-respected Australian writer Jeremy Oliver.

**www.platterwineguide.com** Subscription-based online version of the invaluable annual Platter Guide to South African Wine.

**www.slowfood.com** Good free information on Italian wine from the publishers of the annual wine guide which allocates very influential *tre bicchiere* ('three glass') awards

**www.verema.com/en/** A useful site dedicated to Spanish wine.

**www.stratsplace.com** Excellent free US-based site with international contributors, covering "wine, gardening and the arts".

**www.tablewine.com** US-based site, focusing on inexpensive wines.

**www.taste-in.com** Recently launched service offering tutored tastings by experts (including the author of this guide).

**www.thedrinksbusiness.com** Good online version of a UK trade-focused magazine. Good archive and statistics.

**www.thejosephreport.com** Information site by the author of this guide.

**www.thekeyreport.com.au** Subscription-based site covering the Australian wine industry. Fascinating - for professionals.

**www.thewinedoctor.com** One of the best free, independent sites, produced by UK-based Neonatalogist Chris Kissack.

**www.wineaccess.com / www.internationalwinecellar.com** Good subscription-based site with reviews from Steve Tanzer, the well respected rival to Robert Parker.

**www.winealchemy.com** Recommendable free site by UK-based biodynamic wine fan Paul Howard.

**www.wineanorak.com** Informative free site run by UK scientist and critic Jamie Goode.

**www.wineappreciation.com**

**www.wine-asia.com** Portal covering the fast-evolving wine market in this region.

**www.winebusiness.com** Useful US-based subscription site for anyone interested in the commercial aspects of the wine industry.

**www.winebusinessinternational.com** Recently launched site offering information on the global wine industry.

**www.wineenthusiast.com** Two separate US-based suppliers of corkscrews, racks, glasses and everything else you can imagine. Wineenthusiast.com is linked to the *Wine Enthusiast* magazine (www.winemag.com).

**www.wineindustryreport.com** Subscription-only, European-based coverage of the global wine industry.

**www.wine-intelligence.com** New site offering comparitive opinions on and profiles of a wide range of wines.

**www.wine-journal.com** UK-based, opinionated but informed site by the youthful Neal Martin.

**www.wineloverspage.com** Robin Garr's is the first independent wine information website and still one of the best. US-based but international in coverage. Good forum.

**www.winemag.co.za** Good offering from South Africa's *Wine Magazine*.

**www.winemag.com** Good online offering from the glossy US magazine that lingers in the shadow of the *Wine Spectator*. There's less here than on that publication's site, but this one's all free.

**www.wine-pages.com** Free site run by Scotsman Tom Canavan. Packed with features and recommendations.

**www.winepros.com** Australian guru James Halliday's brilliant information website.

**www.wineryexchange.com** *Free* wine news service for anyone wanting to keep up to date with events across the globe.

**www.wine-searcher.com** Essential, part subscription site for anyone interested in knowing where to find specific wines worldwide - and the market price.

**www.winespectator.com** Comprehensive, partly subscriber-only, site produced by the world's best selling wine magazine. Very good news coverage, features archive and plentiful wine ratings. Strikes some Europeans as too US-focused.

**www.wineterroirs.com** Excellent wine and photography site by Bertrand Celce. Lots of in-depth French winery visits.

**www.wineweb.com** US-based site with contact details of 34,000 wineries across the world and a wine-searcher facility.

**ARG** = Argentina; **AUS** = Australia; **BUL** = Bulgaria; **CAN** = Canada; **CHI** = Chile; **FRA** = France; **GER** = Germany; **HUN** = Hungary; **ITA** = Italy; **NZ** = New Zealand; **OES** = Austria; **POR** = Portugal; **SAF** = South Africa; **SPA** = Spain; **SWI** = Switzerland.

## D



## E



## F



## G

## N



## O



## P



## Q



## R



## S

## T



## U



## V



## W



## X



## Y



## Z

## Footprint credits

**Editor**: Sophie Blacksell
**Map editor:** Sarah Sorensen
**Layout and production:** Angus Dawson
**Proof reader:** Rosalind Cooper

**Publisher**: Patrick Dawson
**Editorial**: Alan Murphy,
Felicity Laughton, Nicola Jones
**Cartography**: Angus Dawson, Robert Lunn, Kevin Feeney
**Design**: Mytton Williams
**Sales and marketing**: Andy Riddle
**Advertising**: Debbie Wylde
**Finance and administration**: Elizabeth Taylor

## Print

Manufactured in Italy by EuroGrafica
Pulp from sustainable forests

## Footprint feedback

We try as hard as we can to make each Footprint guide as up to date as possible but, of course, things always change. If you want to let us know about your experiences – good, bad or ugly – then don't delay, go to www.footprintbooks.com and send in your comments.

Every effort has been made to ensure that the facts in this guidebook are accurate. However, travellers should still obtain advice from consulates, airlines etc about travel and visa requirements before travelling. The authors and publishers cannot accept responsibility for any loss, injury or inconvenience however caused.

## Publishing information

Footprint Wine Travel Guide to the World
1st edition

November 2006
Travel information and maps supplied by Footprint with additional text on Austria, California, France, Germany, Greece, Italy and Portugal supplied by AA Publishing who retain copyright of the original text.
Published in association with Montana Wine

ISBN 1 904777 85 6
CIP DATA: A catalogue record for this book is available from the British Library



## Published by Footprint

6 Riverside Court, Lower Bristol Road, Bath BA2 3DZ, UK
T +44 (0)1225 469141 F +44 (0)1225 469461
discover@footprintbooks.com www.footprintbooks.com

## Distributed in the USA by

Publishers Group West



## Photography credits

All images are supplied courtesy of the featured establishment, as captioned, except the following: **Essentials** pp1, 13, 18, 20, 24 Ralph Hodgson; p2 Wines of Chile; p7 Olivier Leflaive; pp8, 13, 14 NQN; p11 Stoneleigh Vineyard; p13 Golan Heights Winery; p13 Mission Hill, Ralf Schafer, Vinoteca; pp18, 25 Leeuwin Estate; p19 Weingut Joachim Flick; pp19, 27 International Wine Academy of Roma; p20 Bisol and and Dachota Renneau at communique-communication by design italian travel wine & food; p23 Brown Brothers; pp24, 26 Gloria Ferrer; p26 Mentzendorff via Hidalgo-La Gitana; p27 Francis Andrijich, Taylor's. **France** p28 GP Bowater/ALAMY; pp35, 37, 42 Ralph Hodgson; p36 Château Meursault; p38 Network Photographers/ALAMY; p41 Champagne Mailly Grand Cru; p44 David Noton Photography/ALAMY; p45 Gerald Weisl of WeinMax; p47 Chris Moran (www.hotshitpictures.com); pp54, 61, 69, 72 age fotostock/Superstock; pp56, 57 Guigal; p62 Domaine Clarence Dillon SA. **Spain** pp78, 81, 84 Ralph Hodgson; p89 Courtesy of the Domecq Bodegas collection; p91 Spanish Tourist Office; p92 Cellar Tours; pp98, 99 age fotostock/Superstock. **Portugal** pp102, 106, 107, 111, 113 Cortes de Cima; p109 Taylor's; p116 Ramos Pinto; p123 Pawel Wysocki/Monde/Hemisphere; p125 age fotostock/Superstock. Italy pp130 Jon Arnold Images/ALAMY; pp131, 133, 139 Bisol and Dachota Renneau at communique-communication by design italian travel wine & food; p134 Ascheri; p141 Maculan; pp142 CuboImages srl/ALAMY; pp146 John Mottershaw/ALAMY; p153 Julius Honnor. **Germany** pp156, 160, 165, 167 age fotostock/Superstock; pp163, 167 Weingut Markus Molitor; p174 Jacob Gerhardt. **Rest of Europe** p180 Cephas Picture Library/Alamy; pp185, 193, 202 age fotostock/Superstock; p187 Jon Bower/ALAMY; p195 Marvin Newman /TIPS; p196 LOISIUM/Robert Herbst; pp198 Czech Tourism; p203 Prisma/Superstock. **North America** pp215, 240, 242 Oregon Wine Board; p218 Mission Hill Family Estate; p227 Maisons Marques et Domaines Ltd; pp229, 234 Ralph Hodgson; p247 Julius Honnor, Susannah Sayler. **Latin America** pp252, 259, 269, 270, 275 Wines of Chile; p256 Tomás Castelazo; p261 Christabelle Dilks. **Australia** p280 Fleurieu Peninsula Tourism (South Australian Tourism Commission); pp284, 289, 292, Darroch Donald; pp285, 287, 302, 305 South Australia Tourism Commission; p286 T'Gallant; pp290, 291 www.peppers.com.au; p296 Prisma/Superstock; p303 Courtesy of the Jacobs Creek image collection; p307 Frances Andrijich. **New Zealand** pp310, 325 Cephas Picture Library/ALAMY; pp316, 329 Courtesy of the Montana/Brancott image collection; pp317, 323, 334, 336 Ralph Hodgson; p329 Colleen Tunnicliffe; p337 Darroch Donald. **Levant & Africa** p342 Golan Heights Winery; p350 Constantia Uitsig; p352 Francisca Kellett. **Asia** p370 Steve Vidler/Superstock.

# ISSUES AND PERSPECTIVES ON YOUNG OFFENDERS IN CANADA

SECOND EDITION

JOHN A. WINTERDYK

Harcourt Canada

Toronto Montreal Fort Worth New York Orlando
Philadelphia San Diego London Sydney Tokyo

**Canadian Cataloguing in Publication Data**

Main entry under title:
Issues and perspectives on young offenders in Canada

2nd ed.
Includes index.
ISBN 0-7747-3677-1

1. Juvenile delinquency – Canada. 2. Juvenile delinquents – Legal status, laws, etc. – Canada. I. Winterdyk, John.

HV9108.I8 2000 364.36'0971 C99-932325-3

Senior Acquisitions Editor: Heather McWhinney
Senior Developmental Editor: Martina van de Velde
Production Editor: Shana Hayes
Production Co-ordinator: Cheryl Tiongson

Copy Editor: Beverley Endersby
Cover and Interior Design: The Brookview Group Inc.
Typesetting and Assembly: Jansom (Janette Thompson)
Printing and Binding: Webcom Limited

Cover art: *Dark Angels* by Kathleen Vaughan (Detail.) Mixed media, 48" × 108".


Harcourt Canada
55 Horner Avenue, Toronto, ON, Canada M8Z 4X6
Customer Service
Toll-Free Tel.: 1-800-387-7278
Toll-Free Fax: 1-800-665-7307

This book was printed in Canada.
1 2 3 4 5 04 03 02 01 00

To

Dirk Winterdyk

… my grandfather and educator extraordinaire

# Preface

When I first began to study criminology in the early 1970s, the number of Canadian criminology resources on the subject of young offenders was quite limited. As we enter the new millennium, the array of Canadian textbooks that focus on young offenders has grown impressively. So, why yet another book on the subject when we are concerned about the preservation of our natural resources and when so many students have access to the Internet? Again, in this second edition, it is the general framework and content that set the book apart from most existing textbooks that deal with the subject of young offenders.

While this text does not profess to be the definitive work on the subject, it offers a number of unique features. All of the chapters are original contributions commissioned for this volume. The contributors have been carefully selected for their recognized expertise in the subject area. This rigour helps to ensure that the reader is provided with the most current interpretation of the subject, as well as a level of critical insight that may not be within the expertise of the volume editor.

The text is divided into three major sections. Part One comprises three chapters, covering such topics as the trends and patterns of youth crime in Canada; traditional as well as more recent theoretical perspectives on youth crime; and an insightful and informative look at young female offenders.

Part Two is made up of three chapters. Chapter 4 examines the history of juvenile justice legislation in Canada as well as providing a comprehensive and original overview of the major legal aspects of the Young Offenders Act and proposed Youth Criminal Justice Act. Chapter 5 examines the major amendments that have influenced the direction youth justice has taken since the early 1980s. Chapter 6 explores the role the media play in informing the public about youth crime issues.

Part Three comprises six chapters that focus on such topical issues as adolescent substance abuse (Chapter 7); runaways and homelessness (Chapter 8); youth gangs (Chapter 9); adolescent prostitution (Chapter 10); adolescent sex offenders (Chapter 11); aboriginal youth and the justice system (Chapter 12); and a Canadian examination of international juvenile justice (Chapter 13).

New to this edition are the helpful Web links at the end of each chapter, a glossary, and appendixes that contain the Juvenile Delinquents Act, Young Offenders Act, and newly proposed Youth Criminal Justice Act.

Finally, each chapter is pedagogically designed to facilitate understanding and comprehension of the subject matter.

## ACKNOWLEDGEMENTS

Although I did not know it at the time, the first edition of this book had its genesis back in 1978, when I agreed to run a wilderness adventure program in Ontario for an eager and creative probation officer by the name of Rick Mazur. My experience over those two years eventually drew me back to school, intent on learning more about young offenders. And while much has transpired since the days of ACTION (Accepting Challenge Through Interaction with Others and Nature), my interest in young offenders has only grown over the years.

In the preparation of this second edition, little has changed. Producing a collection of original articles requires considerable teamwork and dedication by all involved. Although challenging at times, it has also been a joyous experience to witness how well so many different ideas, agendas, and personalities can come together with dedication to a common cause. Therefore, I would like to express my appreciation to those involved directly and indirectly in the production of this edition.

First, I would like to thank all the contributors for their dedication to this project. Some of them are contributing for the second time; others, for the first time. Within reason, they all kept to the time lines set by the publisher (and myself). I am very appreciative of the "newcomers" (Don Fetherston, Fred Mathews, Tony Seskus, Marge Reitsma-Street, Sybille Artz, and Tracey Morris), for their task of writing completely new chapters was somewhat daunting. Again, I want to thank my students, who diplomatically endured being subjected to portions of the new material and who regularly offered constructive feedback.

I am grateful to Sandie McBrien and Rosemary Buck, fellow colleagues and dear friends, who have been invaluable in helping with the Computerized Test Bank and the Glossary, and who were also called upon to review some of my editorial comments. A special note of thanks goes to the department secretary, Brenda Laing. In addition to politely deflecting unwanted disturbances, she helped out when the computer "ate" pages of my work and she gently reminded me to get out to smell the roses and ride!

I would also like to thank Bill Rowberry, Lambton College, and Megan Way Nicholson, St. Lawrence College, who offered helpful suggestions for this edition.

To the gang at Harcourt—words cannot express my gratitude. Thanks to Heather McWhinney, Senior Acquisitions Editor, who adeptly helped to get this project on track; and to Martina van de Velde, Senior Developmental Editor, who skilfully helped to guide the project along and to keep me within the time constraints. A special thanks to Beverley Beetham Endersby who so skilfully provided invaluable copy editing.

I am indebted to Karen Jensen, who provided emotional support and displayed considerable patience during the early phases of this edition. Happy "unimoging"!

Finally, the caveat that so often appears at the end of acknowledgement sections: any shortcomings within this text remain mine alone. Just as we must learn to have compassion for each other rather than sympathy, I hope you will see the intent in this edition and provide feedback so that the book can continue to evolve to serve its readers even better.

John Winterdyk
Department of Criminology
Mount Royal College
Calgary, Alberta

## A NOTE FROM THE PUBLISHER

Thank you for selecting *Issues and Perspectives on Young Offenders in Canada*, Second Edition, by John A. Winterdyk. The author and publisher have devoted considerable time to the careful development of this book. We appreciate your recognition of this effort and accomplishment.

We want to hear what you think about *Issues and Perspectives on Young Offenders in Canada*. Please take a few minutes to fill out the stamped reader reply card at the back of the book. Your comments and suggestions will be valuable to us as we prepare new editions and other books.

# Contents

# Introduction

Although youth crime seems to be a growing contemporary social problem, it is, in fact, an age-old issue. It is not the number of delinquent children that has changed or grown, but rather the control techniques and intervention strategies that society employs to best handle these young persons.

Punishment that is imposed by law or social consensus reveals a great deal about a society. It tells us how a society views children, the roles children and youth play in the society, what constitutes "deviance" or "criminal activity," and the types of retribution that are socially acceptable. Punishment can therefore be a kind of social barometer that gauges the structure and moral standards of an era with remarkable precision.

Less humane times meant less humane treatment of children. For example, Item 195 of ancient Babylonia's Code of Hammurabi (c. 1750 B.C.) stated that if a son struck his father, the son's hand could be cut off. Up until the thirteenth century, England's King's Law decreed that persons as young as age 10 could be punished as adults. This punishment included beatings to the point of drawing blood.

Although such practices may seem unbelievably barbaric by today's standards, remember that we are looking at the evidence with early-21st-century eyes. All social behaviours, attitudes, and values are products of their time. All sorts of social, political, religious, and cultural factors shape a society's views of crime and punishment. Therefore, studying social history helps us to realize what is unique about our own modern society.

The exploitation of children and youth (e.g., slavery, abuse, pornography) is still very much evident in many parts of the world. In fact, history serves to illustrate that young people form a disadvantaged class, are powerless and alienated, and are economically and socially manipulated.

## CRIME AND PUNISHMENT IN CANADA: A HISTORICAL OVERVIEW[1]

In the sixteenth and seventeenth centuries, as Western society slowly changed from a rural, agrarian feudalism to the early stages of capitalism, poverty was rampant. As a result, delinquency became a growing problem, and a new class of young vagrants and beggars was created. Britain's response to the problem was direct: it introduced laws that effectively put children under the control of the British king. In 1555, as part of this plan, numerous correction houses for youth were built, referred to as "Bridewells." And, in 1576, British Parliament passed legislation authorizing every county to establish similar institutions.

One hundred years later, European pioneers in Canada were facing a similar dilemma. Although youth crime was not an acute problem in Canada's earliest settlements, some children were committing petty crimes such as theft and prostitution in order to survive. It was not until the 1800s, when official record-keeping became more reliable, that such delinquency became more evident.

In response, Canada began to set up correctional facilities to house orphaned children, runaways, and delinquents. During this period, the government also began to keep records of young offenders. As well, the state developed special services, programs, and facilities to "treat" young offenders. The very first treatment centre specifically for juveniles was opened in Penetanguishene, Ontario, in 1858, "to provide a better environment for youthful offenders" (Carrigan, 1991: 405).

With Confederation and the signing of the British North America Act in 1867, the juvenile justice system became more structured, with clearly delineated government responsibilities. The federal government was granted exclusive control over more serious crimes, such as murder, rape, and theft, while the provinces were given control over less serious offences, such as traffic violations and juvenile delinquency.

## THE JUVENILE DELINQUENTS ACT (1908)

By the turn of the twentieth century, social views were changing radically. There was a new empathy for young people that extended to young offenders. The Juvenile Delinquents Act (JDA) reflected a remarkable new compassion toward wayward youth. Rather than imprisoning, institutionalizing, or abandoning delinquents—thereby essentially giving up on their potential for good—the act reflected a desire to help youth through guidance and support (Winterdyk, 1997).

Although the JDA had been criticized by more than a few scholars because of its flexible enforcement and age variables, it nevertheless sparked more legislation directed toward keeping children away from crime, proving itself a worthy first step. And, as Bala, Hornick, and Vogl (1991) observed, the real growth in legislation directed at juveniles occurred only after the JDA was enacted. More treatment and reformative facilities opened as a result of the JDA, and new provincial child-welfare protection acts made basic education compulsory (also see Chapter 4).

## THE YOUNG OFFENDERS ACT (1984)

As is discussed in greater detail in Chapters 4 and 5, the second and perhaps more influential piece of legislation in the field of young offenders was the Young Offenders Act (YOA). The act not only marked a shift in terms of legal responsibility, but also reflected an attitudinal shift toward young people. However, throughout most of the 1990s, serious questions have been raised about whether the act remains our best **juvenile justice model**. Debate centred on whether the objective of the act was to respect individual rights or to respond to the special needs of youth. Several scholars went so far as to describe the act as the most complex and self-contradictory piece of young offender legislation in the world.

Under the act, the special needs of youth are officially dealt with through legal intervention and a wide variety of treatment programs. However, at the same time, the YOA reflects a return to more conservative and punitive measures for dealing with problem youth. This is especially evident with some of the amendments that were made to the act throughout the 1990s (see below). Without a doubt, young offenders under this jurisdiction were now much more accountable for their actions than they were under the JDA. Nevertheless, given some of the high-profile crimes involving young people in the 1990s, there was significant public outcry for even greater accountability and for greater protection for society.

## FACING THE NEW MILLENNIUM: THE YOUTH CRIMINAL JUSTICE ACT

By the end of the 1980s, it was clear to most observers that amendments to the YOA were necessary. In 1991 the transfer of young offenders to adult court was made easier under section 16 of the YOA. Legislators moved further in this direction with the 1994 proposal of **Bill C-37**, which would toughen penalties for murder convictions and make it more difficult for 16- and 17-year-olds to fight murder charges in youth court.

Then, in May 1998, the Youth Justice Strategy called for new actions on three complementary levels: *prevention*, *meaningful consequences*, and *harsher punishment for violent and repeat offenders*. This initiative culminated in the proposal for a new youth justice law called the Youth Criminal Justice Act. Although it was initially slated for late 1998, in January 1999 Justice minister Anne McLellan noted that the new act was being delayed because of frustration over cuts from Ottawa to contributions for dealing with offenders (Tibbetts, 1999). However, on 11 March 1999, the minister finally tabled the long-awaited **Bill C-68**, proposing the introduction of the new act, which she described as reflecting "a balanced, common sense and effective approach to youth justice." The Reform Party, among other critics, was quick to claim that the act does not go far enough in dealing with serious offenders ("New youth...," 1999) and that "the new legislation reflects, in its preamble and principles, the message Canadians want from their youth justice system; that it is there, first and foremost, to protect society, that it fosters values such as respect for others and their property" (Mofina, 1999). We discuss the new act and its elements in greater detail in Chapters 4 and 5.

Based on the outcome of the "Summit on Justice" meeting held in Calgary, Alberta, in January 1999, there appear to be a number of other issues at stake as well. For example, 58 major recommendations were made concerning youth justice. Some of the more notable recommendations include:

- a two-tiered system for dealing with violent and non-violent offenders;
- early-intervention strategies to facilitate prevention initiatives;
- lowering the age limit of responsibility;
- making parents more accountable;
- using incarceration as a last resort; and
- relying on alternative measures that make offenders more accountable to victims and their community (Slade, 1999).

Interestingly, most of these points have been included in the Youth Criminal Justice Act. It remains to be seen whether any of these changes will have a direct impact on youth crime.

While the public may think that the government is getting tougher on young offenders, current studies paint a less clear picture. For example, in Chapter 1 we will see that, while more youth are sentenced to custody, the average length of youth sentences has become shorter. Yet, Carrington's review of official youth crime data between 1977 and 1996 led him to suggest (1999: 25) that there is no basis for public concern about "the supposed failure of the YOA to control youth crime." In fact, property crime among youth declined by 23 percent between 1991 and 1997, and, since peaking in 1995, violent crime among youth has also decreased by 3.2 percent (*Fact Sheets*, 1999).

As we enter the new millennium, we continue to face the age-old problem of trying to control youth crime. One of Socrates' famous quotations still has the ring of truth: "our youths now love luxury, they have bad manners, they have disrespect for authority, disrespect for older people ..." In fact, according to several studies, we are witnessing disturbing new trends in youth crime. Certain types of violent crime, female delinquency, runaways, substance abuse, and violent gang activity are all on the increase. Many of these topics are addressed throughout this text.

As young people are the bearers of our future, such trends warrant concern and attention. In fact, a 1998 nationwide poll found that, among Canadians commenting on the criminal justice system, the number one priority was increasing the severity of sentences for violent youth (Environics Research Group, 1998). How do we account for these trends? What is being done to control their spread? What constitutes meaningful consequences? Will the multidisciplinary initiatives being supported by the Youth Justice Strategy work? It is hoped that, by the end of this book, you will have the information you need to form your own answers to these challenging questions.

## NOTE

1. For a more comprehensive history of juvenile justice and delinquency during the early days of Canada, see Winterdyk 2000, Chap. 14.

## WEB LINK

**The Great Young Offenders Act Debate**
<http://www.peelbarristers.com/~biss/pages/tgyad.htm>

Follow the ongoing debate on the Young Offenders Act and the Youth Criminal Justice Act. Created by a Toronto-based law firm, this site offers current observations about the act, as well as many useful links.

## REFERENCES

Bala, N., Hornick, J.P., and Vogl, R. (Eds.). (1991). *Canadian Child Welfare Law.* Toronto: Thompson Educational Publishing.

Carrigan, D.O. (1991). *Crime and Punishment in Canada: A History*. Toronto: McClelland and Stewart.

Carrington, P.J. (1999). "Trends in youth crime in Canada, 1977 – 1996." *Canadian Journal of Criminology*, 41(1): 1 – 32.

Environics Research Group. (1998). *The Focus Group Canada Report: 1998*. Toronto: Environics Research Group.

*Fact Sheets: Youth Criminal Justice Act*. (1999, March). Ottawa: Department of Justice Canada.

Mofina, R. (1999, 11 March). Personal communication from a reporter for the *Calgary Herald.*

"New youth justice system tougher on offenders." (1999, 11 March). *Toronto Star* (Online).

Slade, D. (1999, 30 January). "Albertans swamp minister with justice reform ideas." *Calgary Herald*, p. A12.

Tibbetts, J. (1999, 23 January). "Young offenders bill hinges on budget." *Calgary Herald*, p. A3.

Winterdyk, J.A. (Ed.). (1997). *Juvenile Justice Systems: An International Perspective.* Toronto: Canadian Scholars' Press.

———. (2000). "Young offenders." In D. MacAlister, P. McKenna, F. Schmallegee, and J. Winterdyk (Eds.), *Criminal Justice Today*. Scarborough, ON: Prentice-Hall.

# PART ONE

# Overview of Young Offenders in Canada

# Introduction

Part One provides an overview of young offenders in Canada and is intended to illustrate the complexity of the subject matter. Chapter 1 discusses past and present trends in Canadian youth crime to give readers a sense of perspective on the problem in today's world. The Young Offenders Act is described at length and contrasted with the Juvenile Delinquents Act of 1908, illuminating the unique characteristics of the current act. Interestingly, from this analysis we gain perspective on the young offender in the new millennium.

Chapter 2, "Explaining Delinquent Behaviour," offers some sociological, psychological, and biological explanations for delinquency. Its intent is to provide the reader with a solid understanding of the various perspectives and theories involved in the study of youth crime.

Chapter 3, "Girls and Crime," provides an insightful and informative look at young female offenders.

## SUGGESTED READINGS

Carrigan, D.O. (1991). *Crime and Punishment in Canada: A History.* Toronto: McClelland and Stewart.

An interesting historical overview of crime and punishment in Canada. Carrigan covers everything from crime in Canada's earliest settlements to contemporary white-collar crime, organized crime, and female offenders. Chapters 5 and 9 deal specifically with juvenile delinquents and, given their focus, relate well to Chapters 1 and 3 of this text.

DeMause, L. (Ed.). (1988). *The History of Childhood.* New York: Peter Bedrick Books.

DeMause's work has been overlooked by students and scholars interested in knowing more about child-rearing practices through the ages. Using a unique psychohistorical approach, DeMause solicited ten contributions covering the history of children, from antiquity to the nineteenth century. Collectively, these essays suggest that child-rearing practices are closely linked to societal developments; that is, as societies evolved, so did our child-care practices. Underlying any change has been the common denominator of parents' mistreatment of their children and projection of their own fears onto their children. A careful reading of this book should prompt the reader to think about the impact these ingrained attitudes have had on how we choose to respond to young offenders.

Platt, A.M. (1977). *The Child Savers*, 2nd ed. Chicago: University of Chicago Press.

This book is recognized as a classic work linking contemporary programs of delinquency control with the child-saving movement of the late nineteenth century. Platt presents a historical overview of the development of the juvenile court, the value of punishment, and civil liberties of youth. He also addresses the gap between the ideal and the actual implementation of social change as it affected juvenile offenders.

Smandych, R., Dodds, G., and Esau, A. (Eds.). (1991). *Dimensions of Childhood: Essays on the History of Children and Youth in Canada*. Winnipeg: Legal Research Institute of the University of Manitoba.

This book offers a comprehensive historical overview of the treatment of children and young people in Canada. The papers in this collection were selected from among those prepared for a multidisciplinary workshop celebrating the 75th anniversary of the University of Manitoba Law School. As the editors note in their introduction, this book focusses mainly "on attempting to understand historical developments that affected the lives of children" in Canada.

Williams III, F.P., and McShane, M.D. (1994). *Criminological Theory*, 2nd ed. Englewood Cliffs, NJ: Prentice-Hall.

Williams and McShane's little book (280 pages) provides students with a clear and concise overview of the main criminological theories. Each chapter includes a capsule history of a theory, a summary of its theoretical perspective, and a description of the classification schemes (e.g., classical versus positivist) of the theory. The final chapter discusses the future of criminological theory. The authors argue that, since no one theory takes in a complete view of the complexity of crime and delinquency, existing criminological theories should be merged and integrated to form new approaches. The result of such integration would lead not only to a better understanding of delinquent behaviour, but also to a body of knowledge that could be used by criminal justice officials to help them deal with crime and delinquency more effectively.

# Chapter 1

# Trends and Patterns in Youth Crime

JOHN A. WINTERDYK

## KEY OBJECTIVES

After reading this chapter, you should be able to:

- understand the importance of social and historical influences on the development of juvenile justice in Canada;
- describe juvenile delinquency trends and patterns prior to the passage of the Young Offenders Act (YOA) of 1984;
- describe some of the trends and patterns of youth crime after the passage of the YOA;
- identify some characteristics of young offenders;
- understand the strengths and weaknesses of official statistics versus self-report studies and victimization survey results, and what these tell us about young offenders in Canada;
- discuss possible future trends and patterns of delinquency in Canada.

## KEY TERMS

case filtration
dark figure
disposition
information distortion
official statistics
recidivism
self-report (SR) survey
status offence
telescoping
triangulation
victimization data
young person

## INTRODUCTION

As a criminologist who studies youth crime, I am regularly asked about the apparent increase in that type of crime. How serious is it? Is it getting worse? Who is committing these criminal acts and why do they do it? Unfortunately, we criminologists are seldom able to provide succinct answers to these questions. Our responses are usually couched in a variety of qualifiers that leave even the experts looking like fence-sitters. Nevertheless,

Brantingham and Brantingham (1984: 41) have pointed out the ongoing motivation for investigating youth crime: "Counting crime seems to satisfy some fundamental urge to know the dimensions of our misery, as if knowing by itself makes things better."

In order to better understand, explain, and eventually predict any social phenomenon such as youth crime, one needs to draw from a variety of sources, each of which has strengths and weaknesses. In this chapter, we begin by examining the major factors that have contributed to the emergence of juvenile delinquency and youth justice. Next, we draw on information and data from three sources: (1) official agencies of social control (e.g., police, courts, and corrections); (2) non-official sources, such as self-report studies and victimization surveys; and (3) observational reports (e.g., media sources). In addition to describing past and current trends and speculating about future ones as traced through these sources, we also examine trends and patterns of youth crime. Finally, we look at the amount, type, location, and gravity of youth crime, as well as how the young offender system has dealt with young persons in conflict with the law. To sensibly conduct this analysis, however, we must first appreciate the complexity of the term "delinquency."

## DEFINING "DELINQUENCY"

There are several different ways to define "juvenile delinquency." As Bartol (1995: 117) has noted, "juvenile delinquency is an imprecise, nebulous legal and social label for a wide variety of law- and norm-violating behaviour." To clarify the situation, we will summarize some of the more common definitions.

### LEGAL DEFINITION

Currently, we tend to focus on the legal rather than on the psychological or sociological definitions of delinquency. Section 291 of the 1972 revision to the Juvenile Delinquents Act (JDA) defined a juvenile delinquent as

> any child who violates any provision of the Criminal Code or any federal or provincial statute, or of any by-law or ordinance of any municipality, or who is guilty of sexual immorality or any similar form of vice, or who is liable by reason of any other act to be committed to an industrial school or juvenile reformatory under any federal or provincial statute. (Martin et al., 1974)

The JDA definition of delinquency was intended to support the concept of family, and to build an informal system of social control.

Under the 1984 Young Offenders Act, a juvenile delinquent or young person, as they are officially termed under the act, is defined as any person aged 12 to 17 who violates federal laws such as the Criminal Code, the Narcotic Control Act, or the Food and Drug Act. The YOA places greater legal responsibility for his or her actions on the young offender than did the JDA (see Chapter 4).

Although clearly restrictive, the legal definition focusses on predatory and aggressive behaviour that is deemed punishable by law. However, it ignores victimless crimes and **status offences** (punishable for youths but not for adults, such as being a runaway, truancy, and curfew violations), and, because of the vague meaning of delinquency, limits the scope of theoretical insight.

### SOCIOLOGICAL DEFINITION

From a sociological standpoint, juvenile delinquency can be defined as the actions of any young person that violate the norms or standards of proper behaviour set by the controlling group (Kratcoski and Kratcoski, 1990: 2). This suggests that delinquency somehow relates to social deviations or social diversions. Social deviation is behaviour that is not illegal, but rather socially unacceptable. Social diversion refers to frequent or faddish behaviours ranging from harmless acts, such as talking to plants, to dangerous activities, such as copycat murders.[1] Several sociological explanations of youth crime are discussed at length in Chapter 2.

### PSYCHOLOGICAL DEFINITION

Although there is no psychological definition of delinquency per se, some experts view the causes in, and hence define delinquency in, psychological terms. Numerous studies (see Chapter 2) have attempted to identify psychological factors, such as trauma at an early age, how young people learn, the urge to commit acts for pleasure or excitement,[2] or personality disorders that appear to correlate with delinquent behaviour.

## PROBLEMS IN ASSUMING A PURELY LEGAL DEFINITION

As noted above, while it is possible to define delinquency in a variety of ways, it is the legal definition that is generally relied upon to describe the problem. This approach raises a number of issues, however. Some of the more typical ones result from the following situations:

- **Case filtration and dismissal.** Depending on the nature of the **deviance**, cases of youth crime are often eliminated because they are perceived as lacking sufficient gravity, or are deemed unlikely to result in a conviction due to insufficient evidence. For these reasons, first offences are often dismissed.
- **Policy and administration variation.** How the Young Offenders Act is interpreted varies among, and even within, provinces. Similarly, the policies of police departments that report these crimes are likely to vary with the level of public pressure, police administration, and available personnel.

- **Gathering statistics.** The data used to track delinquency trends and patterns are derived from different administrative sources: police records, judicial records, and correctional records. Although these findings are published annually by Statistics Canada the resulting statistics are biased by social and political agendas. Nevertheless, the data are usually used to help practitioners make decisions about individual cases or to address administrative concerns.
- **Reporting rates.** The extent to which delinquency gets reported often depends on the public's willingness to report youth crimes. Reporting rates are intimately related to society's attitudes toward law enforcement, the perceived gravity of the offences, and society's level of punitiveness. Reporting rates are therefore connected to what Wheeler et al. (1968) refer to as the "cultural climate."
- **Public perception.** At any given time, society's perception of youth crime can profoundly affect the legal implementation of the YOA. Based on a 1982 survey of the general public, the British Columbia Corrections Branch (1982) reported the following:

  a) Sixty percent of those surveyed felt that juvenile delinquency was a serious problem in their community.
  b) Over 49 percent of those surveyed felt that, if a youth commits an offence of equal severity to that of an adult, the youth should receive the same punishment as the adult.
  c) Over 45 percent of those surveyed believe that young offenders are likely to become adult criminals.
  d) Approximately 25 percent of those surveyed felt that a youth should be considered old enough for transfer to adult court at 16 years of age.

These views, expressed while the JDA was still in effect, suggest that the public felt strongly that delinquency was a serious and growing problem. Nearly twenty years later, these views not only prevail but may have intensified (see Box 1.1). But is the public's growing concern supported by statistics? Given the observations noted above about the reliability of crime data, obtaining a realistic picture of the extent of youth crime is difficult. However, by drawing on a variety of data-collection techniques, as well as by reviewing historical trends and patterns, it is possible to present a reasonably accurate picture of youth crime.

As we will discuss later in this chapter, it appears that youth crime has, in fact, increased. But in order to trace this increase, we need to take a brief look at some early trends and patterns in youth crime.

## IS YOUTH CRIME ON THE INCREASE, OR IS IT A MATTER OF TIMING?

Juvenile delinquency is a social construction that has evolved over time and has created certain dilemmas for the youth justice system. Until recently, however, most interpretations of delinquency have lacked a sense of history.

**Box 1.1**

**IS YOUTH CRIME ON THE INCREASE OR IS IT A MATTER OF TIMING?**

### No End Seen to Spiral in Teenage Crime

Violent crime among Calgary's youth is soaring at a record pace—and there's no sign the trend is letting up, police say.

In the four years ending last December, violent crime among teens grew by 178 per cent, police statistics show. During the same time, city population increased about eight per cent....

Staff Sgt. Verne Fielder, head of the police youth unit ... sees no evidence suggesting youth violence might be subsiding. "I don't see anything significant that would bring about a change," including revisions to the Young Offenders Act....

**Source:** Ron Collins, *Calgary Herald*, 14 May 1992, p. B1.

### Young Criminals Taking a Holiday

Youth crime in Calgary—which has grown by leaps and bounds in recent years—took a sharp nosedive during the first half of 1992....

Fielder's statistics show a drop in almost all categories of youth crime. That includes:

- A 22-per-cent drop in violent crimes....
- A 31-per-cent decrease in car prowling....

In total, youth crime is down 16 per-cent over last year.

**Source:** Todd Kimberly, *Calgary Herald*, 13 July 1992, p. B1.

Yet, in order to understand the problems of juvenile delinquency today, we need to become familiar with how law-violating children and youth have been dealt with, both legally and socially, in the past. As the philosopher George Santayana (1905) has said, "those who cannot remember the past are condemned to repeat it."

The history of juvenile justice in Canada can be divided into three periods: pre-confederation, state intervention, and the twentieth century.

## DELINQUENCY TRENDS: PRE-CONFEDERATION TO THE NINETEENTH CENTURY[3]

Given the frontier spirit of Canadian pioneers during the early 1600s, children were likely allowed considerable freedom, resulting in crime and hooliganism. Carrigan (1998) notes that children were, indeed, involved in petty theft, brawling, and vandalism, and young girls in prostitution, as they were swept up in the violence that permeated the fur trade. J.G. Moylan, Inspector of Penitentiaries in New France at this time, claimed that immigrant children greatly added to the criminal ranks and that their immigration should be stopped (cited in Carrigan, pp. 82 – 83).

Youth crime in the 1600s was most likely caused by the uncontrolled growth of New France. Many young families were enticed to the New World with promises of land and prosperity. However, many of these families soon broke up due to extreme economic and physical hardships (Carrigan, 1991). This ultimately resulted in numerous young people being abandoned, neglected, or abused. It was this lack of supervision that led to crime (Carrigan, 1998).

Until **official statistics** in Canada began to be recorded in 1876 by the Dominion Bureau of Statistics (now Statistics Canada), accounts of juvenile delinquency were obtainable only through limited newspaper sources that were, in general, based on observational reports. As a result, the delinquency problem in pre-Confederation Canada cannot be accurately quantified. However, some information is available. Based on the *First Annual Report of the Board of Inspectors of Asylums and Prisons* in 1860, Carrigan notes that of 11 268 incarcerations, 6 percent were young offenders under the age of 16 and only 23.2 percent were female (p. 98, 86). Between 1869 and 1889, the rate of juvenile incarceration per 100 000 population fluctuated between 23.2 and 31.6 percent. As we will see shortly, the delinquency problem at the end of the 1800s in many ways resembles the trends we are experiencing at the end of the 1900s. Now, as then, boys continue to be disproportionately represented in the juvenile justice system, most crimes are property related, most delinquencies occur in urban centres, and familial problems are often associated with delinquency. Parental neglect is still seen as one of the more common characteristics among young offenders. Table 1.1 provides an overview of juvenile convictions for indictable offences between 1885 and 1889 in the existing provinces and territory. As noted above, during this time period significantly more young males than young females were convicted. Males accounted for over 90 percent of all convictions across the provinces. Although young males still represent a significant proportion of convictions today, the differences are narrowing, a change that is discussed in greater detail later in this chapter.

## STATE INTERVENTION: THE FIRST STEP IN TAKING RESPONSIBILITY

The American sociologist Anthony Platt (1977), in the postscript to his acclaimed book *The Child Savers*, suggests that the dramatic increase in delinquency and crime throughout the 1870s can be attributed, in large part, to a deterioration in economic conditions in North America. He notes that, at that time, more than a half-million young men and women were neither in school nor actively looking for jobs. By the late 1800s, the social-support networks that had typically characterized rural or agrarian communities were in the process of deteriorating. Urbanization and industrialization were

**Table 1.1**

**JUVENILE CONVICTIONS FOR INDICTABLE OFFENCES BY PROVINCE, 1885 – 1889**

| | Under 16 years | | | 16 – 20 years | | |
|---|---|---|---|---|---|---|
| **Provinces** | **Male** | **%Total** | **Female** | **Male** | **%Total** | **Female** |
| **Ontario** | 5687 | 96.0 | 242 | 6550 | 91.9 | 580 |
| **Quebec** | 2516 | 92.6 | 200 | 3095 | 92.3 | 256 |
| **Nova Scotia** | 367 | 96.3 | 14 | 446 | 91.4 | 42 |
| **New Brunswick** | 181 | 97.8 | 4 | 218 | 93.2 | 16 |
| **Manitoba** | 209 | 96.7 | 7 | 311 | 93.4 | 22 |
| **British Columbia** | 174 | 99.4 | 1 | 192 | 91.0 | 19 |
| **Prince Edward Island** | 81 | 98.7 | 1 | 57 | 86.3 | 9 |
| **Northwest Territories** | 21 | 100.0 | 0 | 94 | 95.9 | 4 |
| **Total/(Average)** | 9236 | (97.2) | 469 | 10963 | (91.8) | 948 |

**Source:** From *Juvenile Delinquency in Canada* by D.O. Carrigan, p. 93. Copyright © 1991 by D. Owen Carrigan. Reprinted by permission of Oxford University Press Canada.

changing the ways in which people lived. Children were less and less supervised, and, as a result, they became more criminally active, particularly in the growing cities.

As the problem of youth crime grew, it became increasingly evident, especially among the dominant middle and upper classes, that the problem could be solved by state intervention. In addition to mandatory education being instituted, several industrial schools for boys and girls were established across the country. The child savers believed that the root causes of delinquent behaviour rested in a child's environment, especially the family. In a paternalistic and romantic fashion, they advocated the implementation of a variety of welfare-based measures such as reform or industrial schools and foster care. Children during this era were treated less as children and more as adults in training. The psychohistorian Lloyd DeMause (1988) describes the mode of child-rearing during this time period as "intrusive." He characterizes the 1800s as a period when parents attempted to conquer their children's minds through strict discipline, threats of punishment, corporal punishment, and prayer.

The state intervention philosophy was also reflected in early-twentieth-century law. The JDA was intended to support the young offender within the context of the family as a social unit. The JDA sought to build an informal system of social control as opposed to a formal system. The social reformer John Joseph Kelso, who played a major role in the establishment of the Toronto Children's Aid Society in 1891, was instrumental in the establishment of the first North American juvenile court system. He argued that the most effective means of preventing and correcting juvenile delinquency was a positive family setting (Carrigan, 1998).

# DELINQUENCY TRENDS: THE TWENTIETH CENTURY

Right from the start, the early twentieth century marked a new era in youth crime. The rate of conviction in 1911 for youth between the ages 10 and 15 years was 172 per 100 000; it climbed to 300 by 1921, an increase of over 124 percent. This trend is in sharp contrast to the growth in population of youth aged 10 to 15 years, which was only about 28 percent.

The 1920s and early 1930s saw further growth in delinquency. In 1921, the delinquency rate for 10- to 15-year-olds rose to 300 per 100 000. Between 1921 and 1931, this percentage grew by over 67 percent, while the age-group population rose by only 19 percent. By 1931, the rate had risen to 423 per 100 000 (Carrigan, 1998). Although the increase is dramatic, most of the offences committed during the early 1900s were petty property-related offences. For example, between 1922 and 1945, the violent crime rate remained steady at 2 per 100 000, while property crimes without violence ranged from a high of 36 in 1930 to a low of 24 per 100 000 in 1945. It is generally suggested that these trends coincided with the changing social and demographic climate, and to some extent the increasing desire of the state to exercise social control. DeMause (1988) refers to this time period as the "socialization mode," during which youth were given extra attention by their parents and society. Parents spent more time training the minds of their children, rather than attempting to conquer them.

From 1940 to 1954, these numbers began to drop. From 1951 to 1955, the delinquency rate was just under 300 per 100 000. During this period, youth were given extra attention by their parents and society, and were thought to understand their own needs better than an adult would. DeMause (1988) refers to this stage as the "helping mode," during which there was an explosion of faddish techniques for child rearing and discipline.

This phase was short-lived, however, and soon delinquency rates began to climb again. The increase has been attributed, in part, to improved social and economic conditions as the country emerged from the hardships of World War II. By 1966, the delinquency rate had climbed to 459 per 100 000, as North American society experienced a social and cultural revolution. Families in which both parents worked had become more common, the influence of the mass media was everywhere, and there was a general erosion of values. Stephen Glenn (cited in Burns, 1989) notes that, in 1963, there was a dramatic increase in youth crime, teenage pregnancy, chemical use, and teen suicide. These social changes, among others, prompted calls for the revision of the JDA. A special committee report in 1965, entitled *Juvenile Delinquency in Canada*, stated that the increase in juvenile crime had become "alarming" and that it could be expect to continue to increase (Carrigan, 1998: 159).

Comparing these numbers to those of the 1980s and 1990s is eye-opening. By 1989, the delinquency rate was 2568 per 100 000. During the same year, young offenders between the ages of 12 and 17 represented 22 percent of all persons charged with Criminal Code offences (*Statistics Canada*, 1992). In 1991, the overall delinquency rate began to decline for the second time in the twentieth century. However, as we discuss below, this decline does not pertain to all offences.

Based on demographic trends which indicate that the number of young people has been increasing during the late 1990s, the implications for youth crime appear to be somewhat bleak. However, as we will learn, there is a great deal of room for change in how we address the problem of dealing with young offenders.

## FURTHER STATE INTERVENTION: SOLUTIONS FOR A CHANGING SOCIETY

By the early 1980s, it was becoming evident that new laws were needed to address the growing problem of youth crime. This resulted in the introduction of the Young Offenders Act of 1984. Although the YOA was designed to make children more accountable for their actions, it is based on the fundamental notion that young people have special needs and require special legal protection, and that they should not be held fully accountable for their crimes. To gauge the success of the YOA, we need to take a look at today's typical young offenders.

Before we begin, it should be pointed out that most of the information on youth crime is based on official data, collected primarily from the police and the courts. While these data are reliable, their quality can be affected by a variety of factors that do not necessarily lead to a precise picture of youth crime. Observations, therefore, should be viewed as suggestive rather than conclusive. Notwithstanding certain limitations, official data are the most consistent data available. Statistics Canada, through the Canadian Centre for Justice Statistics (CCJS), annually produces reports, commonly referred to as *Juristat Service Bulletin* reports (see the Web links at the end of this chapter), on a wide variety of criminological and criminal justice matters. In the next section, we draw on a variety of these reports to describe the characteristics of today's young offenders.

## CHARACTERISTICS OF TODAY'S YOUNG OFFENDERS

As was suggested at the outset of this chapter, the public tends to have a negative image, fuelled mostly by the mass media, of the extent and gravity of youth crime. In Western Canada, the federal Reform Party has used selected crime data to arouse public fear. In 1998, for example, Rob Anders, MP for Calgary West, distributed a pamphlet in which he states that "since 1986, violent crime by persons 12 – 17 has doubled." In the same year, Statistics Canada released data which reported that the rate of youths charged with violent crimes had declined by 3.2 percent since peaking in 1995. Who is telling the truth? They both are. The 1997 violent crime rate is double that of 1986, but has been in decline since 1995. Demographic variation is another factor that needs to be considered in trying to understand crime trends among youth. Both violent and property crime rates for young offenders tend to be slightly higher in the Western provinces than in the Atlantic provinces (CCJS, 1999, 19[2]).

Because the issue of problem youth is such a complex one, in the remainder of this section we examine the characteristics of youth crime and its correlates in more detail.

## GENDER

Ever since Canada started collecting data on young offenders, they have shown that young males tend to commit more crimes than do females. The percentage of young males involved in youth crime has remained consistent at around 80 percent. Furthermore, recent data show that male involvement in crime increases with age, while female involvement peaks at around 15 years of age (CCJS, 1999, 19[2]).

The data also reveal that young males tend to commit more violent crimes than do females. However, during the 1990s, the rate of violent crimes among females has been increasing (see Chapter 3): the rate of female youths charge with violent crimes has increased by 179 percent, while, for male youths, the increase was 85 percent. In fact, between 1992 – 93 and 1997 – 98, violent crime among males dropped 12 percent, while it increased 5 percent among females (CCJS, 1999, 19[2]). It is still unclear whether this increase can be attributed to changes in reporting patterns, media sensationalism, and the use of alternative measures to formal processing, or whether young females are becoming more like their male counterparts. Researchers have been paying more attention to crimes committed both by young males and young females, and they are relying on different sources of data to clarify the apparent trends.

## AGE

Next to gender, age is one of the most important determinants focussed on by researchers to explain youth crime trends and patterns. Data for 1997 – 98 show that about half of all youth court cases involve 16- and 17-year-olds, while 14- and 15-year-olds represent 37 percent, and 12- and 13-year-olds only 12 percent (of which 12-year-olds make up only 3 percent). This trend has remained stable throughout the 1990s.

While the data show that youths over 15 years of age are appearing in court, self-report data suggest that, throughout the 1990s, young people have been getting involved in delinquent activities at an earlier age than ever before. For example, 1997 – 98 data reveal that the proportion of caseloads dealing with 12- and 13-year-olds increased from 10 percent in 1992 – 93 to 12 percent for 1995 – 96, while, for 16- and 17-year-olds, the proportion declined from 52 percent to 49 percent during the same years (CCJS, 1998, 18[11]).

## GRAVITY

In 1986 – 87, the rate of youth charged with property and violent crime was around 4400 per 100 000 youths. This rate increased until 1991, after which it steadily declined through the remainder of the 1990s. By 1997, the rate had fallen to approximately 3400 per 100 000 youths (see Figure 1.1). However, we need to look at this trend more closely to determine what accounts for the declining rate.

**Figure 1.1**

**PROPERTY CRIMES WERE THE MOST COMMON CASES IN YOUTH COURT**

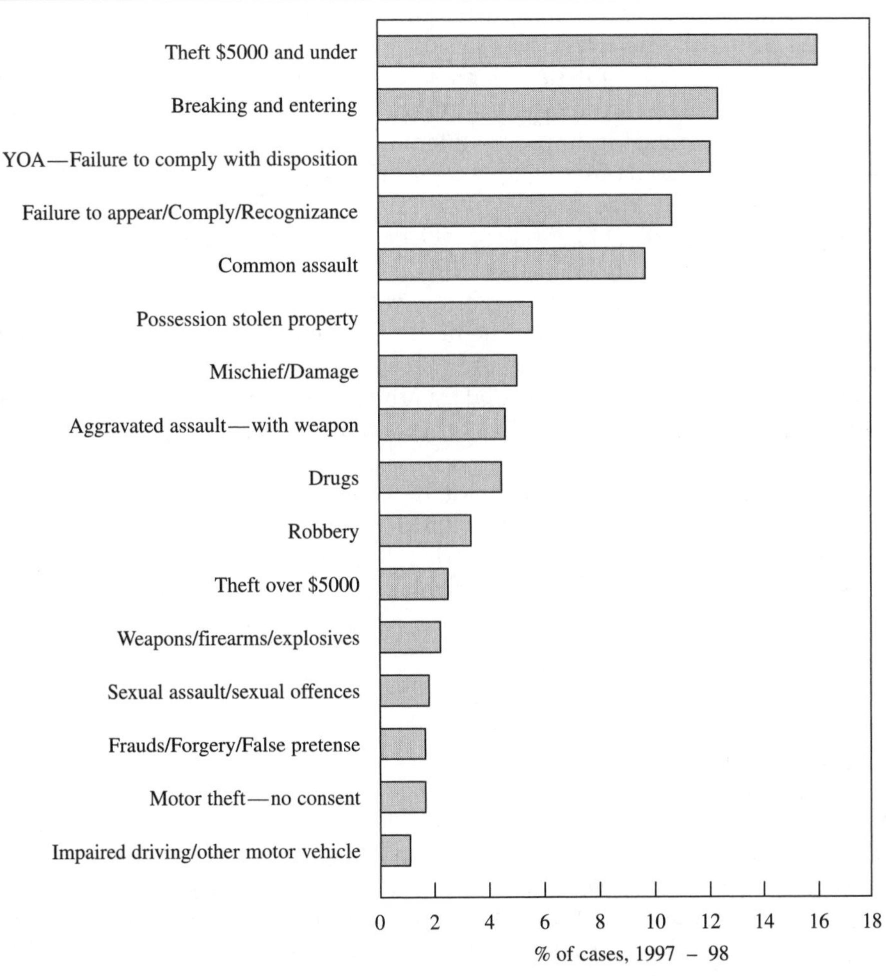


**Source:** Youth Court Survey, Canadian Centre for Justice Statistics. In CCJS, "Youth Court statistics, 1997 – 98 highlights," *Juristat Service Bulletin,* 19(2), p. 4: Figure 2, Catalogue no. 85-002 (Ottawa: Statistics Canada, 1999).

Since the enactment of the YOA, property crime has continued to make up a major part of youth crime (see Figure 1.1). Annually throughout the late 1990s, approximately 60 percent of youth charged with Criminal Code offences were involved in property-related crimes. This number is down from nearly 70 percent in the late 1980s.

Between 1992 – 93, when complete data from all youth court jurisdictions became available, and 1997 – 98, the property crime case rate declined nearly 23 percent. Theft under $5000 accounted for approximately 26 percent of all property-related offences, followed by break-and-enter, at 15 percent. The number of youths charged with property offences during the 1990s remained well above the proportion of adults charged with property offences (approximately 53 percent versus 38 percent in 1997 – 98). Persons charged with property crimes tend to be younger than those charged with violent crimes, and the age span for the former group is much wider.

Media coverage might leave you with the impression that youth crime consists primarily of violent offences (see Figure 1.1). However, according to official crime data, violent acts make up only 21 percent of charges filed against youths. This number is up from 9 percent in the late 1980s. While youths may be engaging in more violent crimes these days, the percentage of cases heard in court involving violent crimes is still relatively low. In the late 1990s, the rate was slightly under 1000 per 100 000, compared with nearly 3000 per 100 000 for property crimes. The proportion of violent crime cases declined in 1996 and 1997.

Regionally, Saskatchewan has the lowest proportion of violent crimes (11 percent), while Quebec has the highest proportion (22 percent).[4] In the majority of violent offence cases (63 percent), the principal charge is minor assault. Robbery is a distant second, at around 11 percent, while attempted murder and murder cases account for less than 1 percent of cases heard in court (CCJS, 1999, 19[2]).

It is interesting to note that, for more serious violent-offences cases, such as those involving attempted murder and manslaughter, the conviction rates were lower (at approximately 29 percent) than for the less serious violent-offences cases, such as robbery, assault, and sexual assault (at approximately 64 percent). Such differences might lead one to question either the leniency of the youth courts or the relevance in replacing the YOA with the tougher sanctions proposed in the YCJA toward violent crimes committed by young people.

## COURT DISPOSITIONS

Contrary to public opinion and such media headlines as "Teens 'laugh' at Young Offenders Act," data from the *Juristat Service Bulletin* throughout the 1990s suggest that there has been a shift toward harsher sentencing practices for young offenders (see Introduction, p.5 and Chapter 5). For example, from 1986 – 87 to 1997 – 98, the following trends were witnessed:

- In 1986 – 87, 63.3 percent of those youth found guilty of a crime were placed on probation. By 1995 – 96, this rate had risen to 66 percent, but, by 1997 – 98, the proportion had dropped to 48 percent.

- In 1986 – 87, 8 percent of young offenders were placed in open custody, while in 1997 – 98, the figure was 18 percent.
- In 1986 – 87, just over 6 percent of young offenders were placed in secure custody, while, in 1997 – 98, this proportion had jumped to 16 percent.
- Between 1992 – 93 and 1997 – 98, the number of youth court cases declined by 4.5 percent.

While there has been an apparent shift to greater accountability of young offenders, the 1995 – 96 data show that young offenders were given shorter sentences more often than in 1986 – 87. The percentage of youths in 1995 – 96 who received secure custody orders or sentences of less than one month increased over the comparable figure for 1986 – 87, from 6 percent to 30 percent. The highest median sentence length of 25 months was for murder/manslaughter cases, followed by attempted murder, at 5 months. In contrast, more common offences such as break-and-enter resulted in median sentence lengths of around 90 days.

For the fiscal year 1997 – 98, about 42 000 youths (nationally, excluding Saskatchewan) were placed in some type of custody. The admission rate equates to approximately 182 per every 10 000 youths. Manitoba had the highest rate (261), while Quebec had the lowest (82) (Youth Custody and Community Services, 1999).

Over 60 percent of all cases heard in youth courts resulted in a guilty verdict. Regional variations are evident, however. In 1995 – 96, Manitoba only had 54 percent of cases resulting in a guilty verdict, while the proportion of cases resulting in guilty verdicts in both New Brunswick and Prince Edward Island was 94 percent! Such variation reflects the degree of autonomy the provinces have in administering the YOA, yet it also raises questions about the consistency, flexibility, and complexity of the act.

According to data for 1997 – 98, 49 percent of young offenders were more likely to receive a term of probation, while 15 percent received sentences of 6 months or less (CCJS, 1999, 19[2]). For example, cases involving minor assaults regularly resulted in probation (65 percent), while 64 percent of all charges for motor vehicle theft resulted in a probation order. Given such variability, we might speculate that the courts lack clear sentencing guidelines because of ambiguity surrounding the interpretation of the YOA. It remains to be seen whether the amendments made during the late 1990s will have an observable influence on sentencing disposition patterns.

In the meantime, Kowalski and Caputo (1999) report that, while there may be much controversy around the alleged leniency of YOA dispositions, repeat offenders do tend to receive more severe dispositions than do first-time offenders. Furthermore, in keeping with previous research findings, they observed that the dispositions are influenced by the number of priors, by gender, and by the seriousness of the offence. Disposition rates and practices, although subject to federal legislation (i.e., the YOA), reveal that there is significant variation between the provinces.

## DELAYING JUSTICE

Increasingly, we hear about delays in our youth justice system. Between 1986 – 87 and 1997 – 98, youth-court cases were indeed taking longer to process. In 1989 – 90, youth-court cases took two additional days on average, from first appearance to decision (an average of 23 days) when compared with 1986 – 87 (CCJS, 1991, 11[4]).

Unfortunately, more recent data do not provide a similar breakdown. However, based on 1995 – 96 data, the median elapsed time for youth court cases was 68 days. Ontario averaged the longest time, at 88 days (CCJS, 1997, 17[4]). The fact that the volume of cases increased almost 10 percent from 1986 – 87 to 1995 – 96 may account for increased delays in processing cases, and for why the juvenile justice system is looking for ways to streamline the process.

## TRANSFERS TO ADULT COURT

In Chapter 5, Leonard and Morris note that the amendment in 1992 to section 16 of the YOA appears to reflect Parliament's concern about the public perception that the act is too lenient.

Between 1986 – 87 and 1989 – 90, the number of transfers to adult court dropped from around 80 to approximately 25. After the amendments were introduced, the number of transfers increased to 74 cases by 1995 – 96. Nearly half of these cases involved violent crime, while about one-third involved property crimes, and 7 in 10 transferred cases in 1997 – 98 involved 16- to 17-year-olds (CCJS, 1999, 19[2]). This trend is contrary to what some scholars predicted would happen after the passing of Bill C-37 (see Chapter 5).

Regionally, between 1994 and 1997, Manitoba had the highest number of transfers (1 per 2415) followed by Alberta (1 per 19 608), while New Brunswick, Nova Scotia, Prince Edward Island, and Newfoundland had no transfers in 1997 (Weber, 1998). Despite the modest increase throughout the 1990s, the overall trend and rate of transfer have remained fairly stable since the mid-1980s.

The amendments to the YOA do not appear to have affected the rate of transfers. However, as noted in the introduction to this text, it remains to be seen whether the Youth Criminal Justice Act and its provisions for facilitating the transfer of youths as young as 14 years of age will have any significant deterrent effect. A number of researchers have suggested that young offenders transferred to adult institutions tend to become repeat offenders.

## RECIDIVISM

It has been suggested that the success or failure of punishment can be measured by **recidivism**, or the rate at which convicted individuals reoffend. Recently, this definition has been extended in some instances to include youths who have dropped out of school or ended up on the street, or otherwise do not lead a socially acceptable lifestyle. Recidivism data on young offenders are not regularly recorded. Given the limitations of official information in such cases (many crimes go unreported or unrecorded by official agencies), official recidivism should perhaps be viewed as "a measure of political success ... how well (or poorly) our crime control policies are working" (Brantingham and Brantingham, 1984: 41).

Notwithstanding this cautionary comment, official data tell us that 19 percent of offenders who appeared in court from 1990 to 1991 have had five or more prior convictions (CCJS, 1992, 12[2]). The same report notes that 46 percent of those charged in youth court had one or more prior convictions since 1984. In 1996 – 98, nearly 43 percent of cases with convictions involved repeat offenders (CCJS, 1999, 19[2]).

Males are more likely to have had prior convictions than females (44 versus 33 percent) (CCJS, 1995, 15[16]). Furthermore, the older a youth gets, the more likely it becomes that he or she has had prior charges. Kowalski and Caputo (1999) found that young offenders between the ages of 14 and 15 are more likely (42 percent) to receive a custody disposition if they are repeat offenders than those between the ages of 12 and 13 (with a 39 percent likelihood), or those aged 16 to 17 (with a 36 percent likelihood).[5] An American study found that 28 percent of a birth cohort born between 1962 and 1965 were repeat offenders (35 percent of males and 15 percent of females). The study also found that the younger the youth was when first referred to youth court, the greater his or her risk of returning to youth court as a result of future law-violating behaviour (Snyder, 1988).

Before we examine the unofficial measures of delinquency, it should be reiterated that a number of real and artificial pitfalls affect the accuracy of these data. For example, since 1984, the data from various provinces (e.g., Ontario, Nova Scotia, and the Northwest Territories) has been excluded, since information was not always available. Furthermore, official data reflect the action (or inaction) of social-control agencies rather than the real numbers and features of delinquent behaviour. Nevertheless, if we view the data longitudinally, the trends remain relatively consistent, for the most part. As long as we remain sensitive to some of the pitfalls surrounding the use of official data, these data can provide insight into how official agencies have responded to youth crime over the years.

## UNOFFICIAL MEASURES OF DELINQUENCY

As we noted earlier, some other sources of information that can be used to gain insight into the extent of youth crime are self-report studies, victimization surveys, and observational data. These are referred to as "unofficial" sources of data because criminal justice agencies are not required by law to collect this information. Instead, it is usually compiled by academics and research centres.

## SELF-REPORT SURVEYS

West (1984: 86) suggests that **self-report (SR) surveys** and related scales were developed during the 1940s and 1950s because "police and court statistics were too hopelessly biased." While self-report studies have become more popular and are proving to be useful in helping to uncover the **dark figure** (unreported or unrecorded crimes) for certain offences, they are not without their limitations. Some of the more common limitations to conducting self-report studies with youths include their literacy level and ability to comprehend questions; their short-term versus long-term memory; the extent to which they are willing to give information voluntarily; and the fact that respondents may exaggerate their answers in order to conform, or may even telescope their answers by admitting to something that took place before the actual reference period.

Research methodology texts today are quick to point out that, despite the preceding problems with self-report surveys, a great deal of progress has been made in improving the validity and reliability of this method, to the point that SR surveys have gained acceptance as a valid measure of juvenile delinquency.

Although very few self-report studies for young offenders have been conducted in Canada (compared with the United States), we can summarize their findings as follows:

- Although the media may sometimes distort the "real" picture, the fact that they are reporting youths getting involved in delinquency at an earlier age has been supported by several SR studies (West, 1984).
- Various SR studies have shown that, when status offences (such as alcohol consumption and truancy) are included, youth crime appears to be a universal feature among young people (Huizinga and Elliott, 1987).
- As has already been witnessed in the United States and Europe, the onset of delinquency occurs early (age 10 to 12) and peaks at around age 16 to 18. Violent offences seem to peak later than property offences, a finding that is consistent with official statistics.
- Contrary to what has been implied by official statistics, West (1984) reported that there is little SR evidence to suggest that youth crime is on the increase. However, he also noted that there might be an increase in offences by young females.
- The findings of Canadian SR studies on delinquency conducted by Vaz (1965), West (1984), and Bartol (1995) consistently show that property offences far outnumber violent offences, and that the use of alcohol while committing an offence is very common.
- Early SR studies reveal that the difference between the amount of delinquent activity engaged in by males and females is not as dramatic as official data would lead us to believe. West (1984) reported the ratio to be about 1:5 and 3:1, whereas official statistics indicate that the ratio is between 5:0 and 10:1.
- An SR study by Keane, Gillis, and Hagan (1989) found support for the social-reaction theory, which asserts that attempts to deter young offenders by having police discourage youth from future delinquent behaviour actually increases the risk that those youths will become involved in illegal conduct.
- Several American studies had found that school failure and difficulties in school correlate with self-report delinquency. Canadian researchers

LeBlanc, Vallières, and McDuff (1993) found similar support for this observation in Canada.

With recent changes to the YOA and increased expressions of concern by the public, it would seem practical for Canadian criminologists to conduct more SR studies on young offenders. In addition to examining issues around reported delinquent behaviour, researchers could also begin to probe specific offence variations, compare demographic relationships, do comparative studies with other countries, and conduct follow-up surveys. Some of these concerns are already being addressed in an ongoing study involving researchers at the University of Southern California and the Dutch Research and Documentation Centre (see Junger-Tas, Terlouw, and Klein, 1994).

## VICTIMIZATION AND VICTIMIZATION SURVEYS

Although society and the media tend to focus on the offences committed by young people, it is important to remember that young people are also the recipients of a great deal of violence, not only from members of their own age group, but also from adults. Victim survey data indicate that young people are more likely to be victims of crimes than are adults. In fact, one recent international report observed that, even though 190 countries, including Canada, have signed the United Nations Convention on the Rights of the Child, victimization of children is on the rise (Chin, 1998). Data from the American national Crime Victimization Survey reveal that violent crimes against young people increased 25 percent between 1988 and 1992 (Snyder and Sickmund, 1995).

As a means of trying to uncover the dark figure of crime, or "hidden crime," researchers increasingly rely on various information-gathering techniques to tap the extent and nature of crime. This method is known as **triangulation**.

One of the most ambitious Canadian victimization studies, the Canadian Urban Victimization Survey (Solicitor General, 1983), involved seven major cities (Vancouver, Edmonton, Winnipeg, Toronto, Montreal, Halifax – Dartmouth, and St. John's) and included more than 61 000 interviews. However, because only youths 16 years of age and older where interviewed for this survey, the results were somewhat limited. When Sacco and Johnson (1990) compiled the results of another 1982 victimization survey, they found that:

- young offenders (they were grouped into the 15 – 24 age group) were the most victimized age group (37 percent versus 24 percent for all age groups);
- the group aged 15 – 24 had the highest incidence of repeat victimization (16 percent had been victimized two or more times) compared with all age groups;
- contrary to popular opinion, the difference between males and females in the percentage of victimization was not all that large (18 percent for males, and 14 percent for females, aged 15 – 24);

- the group aged 15 – 24 consistently had higher rates of victimization for personal theft, violent incidents, robbery, sexual assault, and common assault. This trend is consistent with Cohen and Felson's (1979) routine activities model, and Hindelang, Gottfredson, and Garafalo's (1978) lifestyle exposure theory, which indicate that the more your daily activities expose you to situations in which you lack "capable guardianship" (i.e., the more often you are alone), the greater your risk of becoming a victim.

## Teenage Victims of Violent Crime

In 1992, data on teenage victims of violent crime based on information from thirteen police departments across the country showed that nearly one-quarter of all violent-crime victims were teenagers. This number represents double the teens' representation in the 1990 Canadian population (CCJS, 1992, 12[6]). More recent data reveal that most of these victims are males, and that children under 12 years of age "were most often the victims of youths in common assault (43 percent) or sexual assault (34 percent)" (CCJS, 1999, 19[2]). Although adults were accused in the majority of these incidents, another 23 percent of those charged were between the ages of 12 and 15, and a further 23 percent between 16 and 19 years of age.

Table 1.2 shows that young females are more often the victims of violent crimes than young males. The main form of victimization is sexual assault, and the majority of these offences occur in the home, while a significantly smaller percentage occurs in schools. This trend sharply contrasts what one might be led to believe from most media reports. However, one media source reports that the system fails to help children who are being victimized by adults in society. For example, Mathews (1996) cites research which found that the first time many victimized teens receive attention is when they come in contact with the legal system because of an offence they have committed. This finding suggests that we need to look more carefully at the causes underlying delinquent acts, and at whether accountability and punishment are more important than treatment, counselling, or other forms of support. As we will see in Part Three, many of these victimized youths end up turning to a life of drugs, prostitution, crime, and general self-destruction.

Another area receiving considerable attention in the late 1990s is bullying and suicide among young people. A 1997 survey found that, among children in grades 1 to 8, 15 percent reported that they had been the victim of bullying in the past six weeks. The report found that a significant number of these young victims experience problems in school, as well as social and personal problems (Craig and Pepler, 1997).

As for suicides, in 1993, the suicide rate among Canadian youth aged 15 – 19 was the third-highest in the world (13.5 per 100 000), after New Zealand (15.7) and Finland (15). Dr. Antoon Leenaars, the author of the first comprehensive study of suicide among young people, questions why marriage and family do not offer a "protective factor" for Canadian youth in the way they do for American youth. According to Leenaars, part of the explanation lies in the conservative, melancholic, and passive mindset Canadians have about their culture. He points out that, unlike the case in the United States, the Canadian federal government does not provide an overall suicide-prevention strategy for young people (Bohuslawsky, 1998).[6]

Before concluding this section, we should briefly address the relationship between young offenders and young victims of crime. Some academics have argued that this distinction may not warrant separate categories (see Fagan, Piper, and Cheng, 1989), based on the general observation that victims of crime (e.g., youths who have been abused) are most likely to become offenders (abusers) themselves. These assertions, however, tend to rely on single disciplinary and theoretical perspectives, and do not acknowledge the complexity of human behaviour from an interdisciplinary perspective (discussed in greater detail in Chapter 2). For example, why don't all victims become offenders? Why do some non-victims become offenders? Supporters of victim – offender causality typically subscribe to the influence of the nurture assumption, which asserts that anything that goes wrong in our lives can be attributed to our upbringing (see Harris, 1998). Thanks to improved research strategies, we can explore the relationship between biological traits and a host of social and psychological factors, and how they might more accurately explain the similarities as well as differences between young offenders and young victims. As Ezzat Fattah, the Canadian pioneer of victimology has noted, this will require a new theoretical orientation.

**Table 1.2**

**CHILD VICTIMS OF ASSAULT, BY ACCUSED – VICTIM RELATIONSHIP AND GENDER OF VICTIM, 1996**

| Accused – Victim Relationship | | Total Assault[2] | Sexual Assault Victim Gender | | | Physical Assault Victim Gender | | |
|---|---|---|---|---|---|---|---|---|
| | | | Total | Female | Male | Total | Female | Male |
| **Total** | **Number** | 22 833 | 6 474 | 5 009 | 1 465 | 16 359 | 6 160 | 10 199 |
| | **Percent** | 100 | 100 | 100 | 100 | 100 | 100 | 100 |
| **Acquaintance[1]** | **Percent** | 52 | 49 | 48 | 52 | 53 | 52 | 53 |
| **Family** | **Percent** | 24 | 32 | 33 | 30 | 20 | 30 | 14 |
| **Stranger** | **Percent** | 19 | 13 | 13 | 11 | 22 | 14 | 27 |
| **Unknown** | **Percent** | 5 | 6 | 6 | 7 | 5 | 4 | 5 |

[1]"Acquaintance" includes any relationship in which the accused and victim are familiar with each other (on either a long-term or a short-term basis), but are not related, or in a legal-guardianship arrangement.
[2]Excludes cases for which the sex of the victim is unknown.
*Figures may not add to 100 percent due to rounding.

**Source:** Revised Uniform Crime Reporting Survey, Canadian Centre for Justice Statistics, 1996. In CCJS, "Assault against children and youth in the family," *Juristat Service Bulletin*, 17(11), p. 6: Table 3, Catalogue no. 85-002-XPE (Ottawa: Statistics Canada, 1997).

Although the quality of victimization and self-report studies have improved over the years, they are by no means perfect. The true nature of crime will always remain somewhat elusive. However, as we continue to examine the strengths and weaknesses of data collection, we will better be able to confirm or reject existing theoretical formulations and to develop new ones that have a more practical application in controlling and preventing youth crime.

## SUMMARY

In this chapter, we explored some of the trends and patterns in Canadian youth crime from the pre-Confederation era to the present day. A number of observations can be made about these trends. Since the pre-Confederation era, youth crime has increased, and it has become more serious and violent, although in the later 1990s there was a slight decline in this trend. What is perhaps more alarming is the fact that young persons are not only engaging in more serious delinquent acts, but are also becoming active criminals at an earlier age. Furthermore, even though the rate at which young offenders are sentenced has increased, the sentences have tended to be shorter in duration. As well, recidivism rates have steadily risen over the years, the courts have become backlogged, and the public has become increasingly dissatisfied with the judicial system's ability to control the problem. This explains why we have seen amendments to the YOA (see Chapter 5), as well as a move toward alternative solutions, such as wilderness camps and special outreach programs.

Although there are a limited number of studies, unofficial sources of data such as self-reports tend to support the general findings of official statistics. However, in some cases these unofficial reports show that the dark figure of youth crime is even larger than officially recognized. Future research needs to use both official and unofficial data-gathering techniques to better describe the trends and patterns of youth crime.

Finally, the fact that we seem less capable of controlling the growing youth problem does not bode well for our youth or our society. If we are going to make any inroads into the problem of youth crime in Canada, then we will need to look more carefully at why youth crime occurs and what it really means. The next chapter explains the various theories concerning causes of youth crime.

## NOTES

1. In 1996, 15-year-old Sandy Charles was found not criminally responsible for the killing of 7-year-old Johnathan Thimpson of La Ronge, Saskatchewan. At his trial, it was revealed that Charles had re-enacted a torture scene from the horror movie *Warlock*.
2. A French study in the early 1960s found that 30 percent of delinquents surveyed said they committed delinquent acts simply for pleasure or excitement (Cusson, 1983).

3. For a comprehensive review of how youth were treated during Canada's pioneer days, see D. Owen Carrigan, *Juvenile Delinquency in Canada: A History* (1998).
4. This is in sharp contrast to adult crime. In 1997, Saskatchewan had the second-highest violent crime rate (behind Manitoba), while Quebec had the lowest violent crime rate in Canada.
5. Kowalski and Caputo (1999: 78) concluded that "age, gender, and offence do not explain the relationship between the number of prior convictions and dispositions."
6. For additional insight into the plight and victimization of youth, see Fred Mathews, *The Invisible Boy* (1996). Mathews notes that Canada "lags far behind other western democracies in the study of male victims and their male and female abusers."

## WEB LINKS

**American Juvenile Justice**
<http://www.ncjrs.org/jjhome.htm>

A site by the National Criminal Justice Reference Study, which offers fact sheets, resources, and information on delinquency prevention, violence and victimization, and other issues related to youth crime, as well as a number of national and international links to related sites.

**British Columbia Ministry of the Attorney General—Youth Programs**
<http://www.youth.gov.bc.ca/>

This site features a number of British Columbia community programs that draw on the strengths and positive energy of youth and the community to help prevent youth crime, school violence, and criminal gang activity.

**Justice and Crime Statistics**
<http://www.statcan.ca/english/Pgdb/State/justic.htm>

A collection of statistics (in tabular format) on crime and justice in Canada, including youth crime and victimization.

## STUDY QUESTIONS

1. Identify some of the major factors that appear to have led to increased state intervention in the lives of young persons.
2. Identify several advantages and disadvantages of relying on official statistics to provide a picture of delinquency issues.
3. How can self-report studies and victimization surveys be used to better understand youth crime?
4. Review and discuss how violent crime has changed over the years. What explanations can you offer? Try to substantiate your explanations with evidence.
5. What types of delinquent activities appear to be most problematic for Canadians today? Explain your answer and offer a possible creative and constructive solution.
6. Why is it considered useful to practise triangulation when describing delinquency trends?
7. As a group or class exercise, draw up a comprehensive list of potential delinquent activities. Then conduct a survey to find out which crimes go largely unreported. What implications and problems might this lack of reporting pose for official criminal-justice response agencies?

8. What kinds of factors might help to explain the differences between delinquency rates at the turn of the century compared with the 1990s?
9. Throughout this chapter, we looked at how youth crime is getting worse in Canada. Based on the information presented, what do you predict for the future? What, if anything, should we as a society focus on in regard to youth crime? Are there particular problem-related areas that might require extra attention?

## REFERENCES

Anders, R. (1998, October). *Revolving Door: Cozy Prisons = Injustice.* Reform Party information pamphlet distributed to the public in Calgary West.

Bartol, C.R. (1995). *Criminal Behavior: A Psychological Approach*, 4th ed. Englewood Cliffs, NJ: Prentice-Hall.

Bohuslawsky, M. (1998, March 5). "Unity worries contribute to suicide rate." *Ottawa Citizen.* Online.

Brantingham, P.J., and Brantingham, P.L. (1984). *Patterns in Crime.* New York: Macmillan.

British Columbia Corrections Branch. (1982, August). *The Public Perception of BC Corrections.* Victoria: BC Corrections Branch.

Burns, T. (1989). *Anatomy of a Crisis: The Effects of Alcohol and Other Drugs on the Growing Brain.* New York: Ginn.

Canadian Centre for Justice Statistics. *Juristat Service Bulletin.* Ottawa: Statistics Canada.

———. (1990). "The changing workload in youth courts." Vol. 11, no. 10.

———. (1990). "Youth crime in Canada, 1986 – 1989." Vol. 10, no. 12.

———. (1991). "Processing time in youth courts, 1986 – 87 to 1989 – 90." Vol. 11, no. 4.

———. (1991). "Youth court statistics preliminary data, 1990 – 91 highlights." Vol. 11, no. 11.

———. (1991). "Violent offence cases heard in youth courts, 1990 – 91." Vol. 11, no. 16.

———. (1991). "Youth custody in Canada." Vol. 11, no. 18.

———. (1992). "Recidivism in youth courts, 1990 – 91." Vol. 12, no. 2.

———. (1992). "Teenage victims of violent crime." Vol. 12, no. 6.

———. (1992). "Sentencing in youth court, 1986 – 87 to 1990 – 91." Vol. 12, no. 16.

———. (1995). "Recidivism in youth courts, 1993 – 94." Vol. 15, no. 16.

———. (1997). "Adult Correctional Services in Canada, 1995 – 96." Vol. 17, no. 4.

———. (1997). "Youth court statistics 1995 – 96 highlights." Vol. 17, no. 10.

———. (1997). "Assault against children and youth in the family." Vol. 17, no. 11.

———. (1998). "Missing and abducted children." Vol. 18, no. 2.

———. (1998). "Canadian crime statistics, 1997." Vol. 18, no. 11.

———. (1999). "Youth court statistics 1997 – 98 highlights." Vol. 19, no. 2.

Carrigan, D.O. (1991). *Crime and Punishment in Canada: A History.* Toronto: McClelland and Stewart.

———. (1998). *Juvenile Delinquency in Canada: A History.* Toronto: McClelland and Stewart.

Chin, E. (1998, September). "Child victimization on the rise." *Crime and Justice International*, 13.

Cohen, L.E., and Felson, M. (1979). "Social change and crime rate trends." *American Sociological Review*, 44 (August): 588 – 607.

Collins, R. (1992, 14 May). "No end seen to spiral in teenage crime." *Calgary Herald*, B1.

Craig, W., and Pepler, D.J. (1997). "Naturalistic observations of bullying and victimization on the playground." Toronto: LeMarsh Centre for Research of Violence on Conflict Resolution, York University. Unpublished report.

Cusson, M. (1983). *Why Delinquency?* Toronto: University of Toronto Press.

DeMause, L. (Ed.). (1988). *The History of Childhood.* New York: Peter Bedrick.

Fagan, J., Piper, E., and Cheng, Y-T. (1989). "Contributions of victimization to delinquency in inner cities." *Journal of Criminal Law and Criminology*, 78: 586 – 613.

Harris, J.R. (1998). *The Nurture Assumption: Why Children Turn Out the Way They Do*. New York: Free Press.

Hindelang, M.J., Gottfredson, M., and Garafalo, J. (1978). *Victims of Personal Crime: An Empirical Foundation for a Theory of Personal Victimization*. Cambridge, MA: Ballinger.

Huizinga, D., and Elliott, D.S. (1987). "Juvenile offenders: Offender incidence, and arrest rates by race." *Crime and Delinquency*, 33: 208, 210.

Junger-Tas, J., Terlouw, G-J., and Klein, M.W. (Eds.). (1994). *Delinquent Behavior among Young People in the Western World: First Results of the International Self-Report Delinquent Study*. New York: Kugler.

Keane, C., Gillis, A.R., and Hagan, J. (1989). "Deterrence and amplification of juvenile delinquency by police contact: The importance of gender and risk orientation." *British Journal of Criminology*, 29: 336 – 53.

Kimberly, T. (1992, 13 July). *Calgary Herald*, B1.

Kowalski, M., and Caputo, T. (1999). "Recidivism in youth court: An examination of the impact of age, gender, and prior record." *Canadian Journal of Criminology*, 41(1): 57 – 84.

Kratcoski, P.C., and Kratcoski, L.D. (1990). *Juvenile Delinquency*, 3rd ed. Englewood Cliffs, NJ: Prentice-Hall.

LeBlanc, M., Vallières, E., and McDuff, P. (1993). "The prediction of males' adolescent and adult offending from school experience." *Canadian Journal of Criminology*, 35(4): 459 – 78.

Martin, J.C., et al. (1974). *Martin's Annual Criminal Code*. Agincourt, ON: Canada Law Book.

Mathews, F. (1996, March). *The Invisible Boy*. Ottawa: National Clearing House of Family Violence, Health Canada.

Platt, A.M. (1977). *The Child Savers*, 2nd ed. Chicago: University of Chicago Press.

Sacco, V.F., and Johnson, H. (1990, March). *Patterns of Criminal Victimization in Canada*. Cat. no. 11-612E, No. 2. Ottawa: Statistics Canada (Housing, Family & Social Statistics Division), Ministry of Supply and Services Canada.

Santayana, G. (1905). *The Life of Reason*. London: Constable.

Snyder, H.N. (1988). *Court Careers of Juvenile Offenders*. Washington, DC: US Department of Justice.

Snyder, H.N., and Sickmund, N. (1995). *Juvenile Offenders and Victims: A National Report*. Washington, DC: National Center for Juvenile Justice.

Solicitor General Canada. (1983). *Canadian Urban Victimization Survey*. Ottawa: Solicitor General.

Statistics Canada. (1992). *Canada Year Book 1992*. Ottawa: Ministry of Industry, Science and Technology.

Vaz, E. (1965). "Middle-class adolescents: Self-reported delinquency and youth culture activities." *Canadian Review of Sociology and Anthropology*, 2: 52 – 70.

Weber, B. (1998, 6 October). "Alberta, Manitoba toughest on young offenders." *Calgary Herald*, A13.

West, G. (1984). *Young Offenders and the State: A Canadian Perspective on Delinquency*. Toronto: Butterworths.

Wheeler, S., Bonacich, E., Cramer, R., and Zola, J.K. (1968). "Agents of delinquency control." In S. Wheeler (Ed.), *Controlling Delinquents*. New York: John Wiley and Sons.

Youth Custody and Community Services (1999, 9 June). <http://www.statcan.ca/daily/english/990607/d990607c.htm> (16 July 1999).

# Chapter 2

# Explaining Delinquent Behaviour

JOHN A. WINTERDYK

## KEY OBJECTIVES

After reading this chapter, you should be able to:

- describe major biological, psychological, and sociological explanations for delinquency;
- recognize the need for and merit of scientific inquiry and theory;
- describe the major contemporary integrated, or bridging, theories for delinquency.

## KEY TERMS

anomie
biosocial theory
born criminal
consensus/conflict perspective
deduction/induction
differential anticipation
dramatization of evil
economic/structural approaches
environmental criminology
epistemology
human ecology
integrated and interdisciplinary perspective
intrapsychic conflict
law of imitation
learning model
(left) realist
lobotomization of our youth
neutralization
post-Newtonian
primary/secondary deviance
psychodynamic
psychopharmacological factors
psychophysiological
routine activity theory
scientific inquiry
social adaptation
subjective/objective perspective

## INTRODUCTION

Perhaps one of the most perplexing issues we face in attempting to understand youth crime is that, strictly speaking, "young offender" is not a sociological or psychological term. Rather, this term was coined by the legal system to identify those young persons who, within the framework of our social values, engage in behaviour that is considered inappropriate or illegal. However, given the wide range of behaviour that our legal system must contend with, we need to examine the issue of causation in order to explain the frequency, perceived seriousness, and social impact of youth crime, and in order to deter, control, or prevent such behaviour.

Throughout the twentieth century, the causes of youth crime have been the target of a wide range of theorizing and informal explanatory models. Some of these theories have all but vanished, while others have evolved and flourished. For the purpose of this chapter, the theoretical orientations have been grouped into three major categories: sociological, psychological, and biological. This chapter also discusses integrated, or bridging, theories, which use aspects of the three main approaches to create interesting hybrid theories that are intended to reflect the complexity of human behaviour.

## ORDINARY WAYS OF KNOWING: LAY THEORIES

One of the first questions often asked of students taking a criminology course dealing with young offenders is: Why do you think young people commit delinquent acts? Inevitably, their answers reflect the full spectrum of explanations that are offered in this chapter. While the basic premise of the explanations offered by students will be correct, they usually exhibit limitations born of a constricted frame of reference and lack of objectivity. If we were to engage in a discussion about the **validity** and **reliability** of these opinions, not only would the debate likely become a heated one, but the integrity of our views might be compromised by a lack of evidence to substantiate them.

Generally, people rely on conventional ways of knowing. There are four typical ways in which we tend to explain our world, according to Kerlinger (1973), and these include:

- **Authority:** An authoritative individual (e.g., your teacher, an expert in the field) says that it is so, and you accept it as fact because the authority figure told you it was.
- **Intuition:** You use your internal capacity to make inferences and arrive at knowledge about underlying structures or dynamics. Intuition depends on immediate knowledge without the intervening steps and without logic or reasoning—for example, you just "know" that extraterrestrial beings exist.
- **Logic:** By following a set of systematic procedures or rules, you are able to draw a conclusion. This line of reasoning can take two basic forms. *Deductive* logic entails making a specific observation (e.g., good marks and good study habits), and then deducing that future good performance depends on good study habits. Hence, you move from a specific observation to a general observation. *Inductive* logic, on the other hand, involves the reverse process. For example, you observe that some

young people commit delinquent acts. You then find that all the youths on your block are involved in delinquent activity. Therefore, you might reason that all young persons are delinquent.
- **Observation:** You have seen it! For example, every time you worked at the local youth detention centre, you observed that the kids tended to be more aggressive toward each other when they were tired. Or, every time you did well on an exam, you had used the same pen and had worn the same shirt.

Although we regularly draw on these strategies for forming our understanding of issues, they often lack objectivity. Labovitz and Hagedorn (1981) identified a number of reasons why these ways of knowing are not always reliable. For example, conventional ways of knowing:

- rarely use representative samples;
- are frequently biased in their selection of samples and in their observations;
- sometimes naïvely assume that authority figures know it all; and
- can be clouded by our experiences and our frame of reference.

Therefore, if you want to know that something is "true," then you need to apply a technique that will minimize the limitations listed above. This procedure is generally referred to as scientific inquiry, the process by which theories are established. While this approach is not entirely fail-safe, it does allow researchers to minimize potential bias and to test the veracity of a theory. It is essential that we employ a scientific method of inquiry, if for no other reason than to avoid making decisions about young people based on feelings or observations that may turn out to be more harmful than beneficial because they have not been adequately substantiated. Bearing this in mind, then, we will now look at some sociological theories for human behaviour.

## SOCIOLOGICAL EXPLANATIONS FOR DELINQUENCY

Sociologists are primarily concerned with the effects on human behaviour of macro issues such as social organizations, norms, values, race, ethnicity, and social stratification. In general, sociology assumes that human nature is palpable and that we learn primarily by observing and participating in the ever-changing social environment.

There are two major sociological perspectives that have emerged to better explain social phenomena: consensus and conflict theories.

### CONSENSUS PERSPECTIVE VERSUS CONFLICT PERSPECTIVE

The **consensus perspective** is based on the assumption that there is agreement among people in society—that is, that people share common values, needs, and goals. This perspective stresses order and stability in society, and it depends on institutions such as the family, the school system, and the church to maintain social equilibrium. Delinquency is seen as dysfunctional, as is any potentially harmful part of the system.

In contrast, the **conflict perspective** assumes that there is, in fact, very little agreement in society, and that people and institutions hold conflicting social, political, or economic values or interests. Within the context of this perspective, deviance is any behaviour that violates the status quo's rules, norms, and attitudes. The general assumptions have given rise to several varieties of conflict theory that can be viewed as part of a continuum.

The theoretical principles of conflict theory can be traced back to the works of Karl Marx (1818 – 1883) and Friedrich Engels (1820 – 1895) during the late 1800s. This body of knowledge was later enriched by the work of William Bonger, Ralf Dahrendorf, and George Vold, as Marx and Engels were not directly concerned with crime and criminality.

It was not until the early 1960s, a time of considerable social unrest in North America (during which events such as the civil-rights movement, the Vietnam War, Watergate, and the FLQ crisis occurred) that conflict theory gained prominence. Throughout the 1970s and into the early 1980s, in particular, the conflict perspective tended to dominate criminological thought. This perspective, however, was being constantly adapted to the changing values and interests of the times. As a result, today there are several spinoffs of the New Criminology of the 1970s.

## The New Criminology and Beyond

The "New Criminology," as it was called by a group of British researchers, is based on a series of conflict-based assumptions, the most basic of which is that all capitalist societies are politically divided into ruling (bourgeoisie) and subservient (proletariat) classes. Although social class is a concept common to many sociological theories, for conflict theorists the primary ingredients of class conflict involve wealth, power, and social status. It is only the members of the ruling class who are able to obtain success and material gain. Young people in capitalist societies represent a subservient group that is not yet in a position to contribute economically to society. New Criminology views delinquency as a normal response by youth to the conditions created by a capitalist system. In other words, youth crime can be seen as a social reaction to a lack of opportunity, or different opportunity, as Richard Cloward and Lloyd Ohlin suggested with their popular theory of delinquency in the early 1960s. So, whether crime was seen as a reaction to strain and social disorganization, weakening the sense of attachment to social order, or some form of discrimination, under these conditions criminal behaviour seems almost logical.

Since the law embodies the values of those who control society (the status quo), it is more likely to criminalize those outside the controlling power group. Individuals who have turned to crime will now be caught. There is no end to this cycle; according to the New Criminologists, crime will persist as a social problem until society provides for the needs of all of its citizens.

One of the major strengths of the New Criminology and its more recent derivations, which include peacemaking, left realism, and deconstruction (Winterdyk, 2000), is that it demystifies law and legal practices. It defines crime and criminality along political lines by defining laws as social rules designed to protect the power holders. There are, however, several shortcomings to this general orientation. Mainly, its supporters have never been able to adequately verify their assertions about the purpose of criminal law. For example, is the Young Offenders Act (YOA) intended to address the needs of youth, or to punish them for their transgressions? Why has the act been relatively ineffective in accomplishing either objective?

One of the most revolutionary theoretical approaches to emerge in criminology as we enter the 21st century is the **post-Newtonian** paradigm. Physicist Sir Isaac Newton (1643 – 1727) provided us with a foundation for understanding the world in a mechanistic manner, and his ideas established the notion that our social world can also be understood in a logical, predetermined manner. On the other hand, post-Newtonian theorists, drawing on the field of quantum mechanics, feel that we cannot explain crime in a linear or cause – effect manner. Instead, proponents of this approach see human behaviour as fluid and open to constant change as new experiences occur. For example, a youth may have all the traditional social and psychological earmarks for becoming a delinquent, but his or her life-course could be changed instantaneously by a sudden, "unforeseen" experience. Within this framework, delinquency (for example, schoolyard bullying) is defined as a multidimensional construct that becomes a problem only when enough people behave as though it is one.

Whether the New Criminology or post-Newtonian paradigms can significantly contribute to our understanding of delinquent behaviour remains to be seen; however, they offer new, radical approaches that deserve our attention and scrutiny.

## HUMAN ECOLOGY THEORY

Among the first sociologically based explanations for delinquency to emerge were the ecologically oriented theories. Theodorson (1982) presents an array of early studies dating back to 1830 that attempted to link crime and delinquency. These early studies identified such factors as the weather, geography, urban and rural environments, population density and composition, economic stability, and social mobility as potential causes of social trends and behaviours. It was not until the early 1920s that Robert E. Park and Ernest W. Burgess used plant and animal ecological principles, borrowed from late-nineteenth-century biological writings, to develop a theoretical scheme that could be applied to the study of human communities.

Today, most of these early factors form the basis for tracking Canadian population demographics, as well as for predicting and explaining social trends such as crime and delinquency. Numerous contemporary researchers have found strong correlations between social and environmental factors, and delinquency, although such factors do not assume a causal relationship, nor are they capable of explaining all deviant behaviour.

## THE CHICAGO SCHOOL

A refinement of the early ecological work has been associated with the Chicago School. Established in 1892 at the University of Chicago, it is recognized as the first university sociology department in North America. The school also included studies of criminology, social psychology, and urban sociology.

The main principle of the school was that people are social creatures whose behaviour is the product of a social environment. In other words, our social environment provides the cultural values and definitions that govern our behaviour.

According to the Chicago School, increased urbanization and industrialization have created communities that contain a variety of competing cultures. It is these competing cultures, with their differing values and norms, that promote the breakdown of older, established value patterns. This culture conflict in turn causes the breakdown and impersonalization of our basic institutions, such as the family and social groups. Hence, deviance and criminal behaviour occur when the less dominant individual values and norms conflict with the more dominant cultural values and norms. Various supporters of the Chicago School believed that **social disorganization** and social pathology are most prevalent in the city-centre area, and decrease with distance from that area.

Based on a study conducted in the 1930s as part of the Chicago Area Project, Clifford Shaw and Henry McKay (1969) found that delinquency in Chicago decreased as one moved out from the central urban area to the peripheral suburban areas. High-delinquency areas were characterized by population decline, physical deterioration, and industrial zoning. Carrying on this line of study in 1964, Chilton compared Indianapolis, Baltimore, and Detroit on similar criteria. Despite the differences among the cities, he found that inner-city zones were characterized by a low-income population, an unskilled work force, and substandard housing. Similar findings in the United States have been reported by Bloom (1966) as well as by Tracy, Wolfgang, and Figho (1985). Social scientists in Canada and Europe have conducted similar studies that resulted in the same conclusions (Brantingham and Brantingham, 1984).

However, Brantingham and Brantingham note that while the Chicago School model worked reasonably well in predicting crime areas during the 1920s and the 1930s, multiple-nuclei models of urban areas with more than one high-density inner-city zone seem to be more appropriate models after World War II.

Today, interest in environmental and cultural influences on delinquency has evolved into more sophisticated models whose principles remain relatively intact. This is now commonly referred to as **environmental criminology** (see Box 2.1).

**Box 2.1**

**ENVIRONMENTAL CRIMINOLOGY**

The practical application of the principles of environmental criminology is often referred to as "Crime Prevention Through Environmental Design" (CPTED). The theory is premised on four assumptions:

1. *A Law*: Without law, there can be no crime.
2. *An Offender*: Without an offender, there can be no crime.
3. *A Target*: Without a target (an object or a victim), there can be no crime.
4. *A Place*: Without a time or place, there can be no crime.

Environmental criminologists focus on the fourth assumption by trying to address the notion of opportunity. Hence, *place* = *skill* + *motivation* + *opportunity*. Approaches that try to eliminate or control all the techniques that can be used to commit a crime, or to understand what motivates people to commit deviant acts has proven futile. Instead, environmental criminologists take a proactive approach by asking where and when crimes occur, what the physical and social characteristics of the scene are, and what the spatial patterns surrounding the scene are. These questions reflect environmental opportunity factors that can be environmentally addressed through improved surveillance, a higher risk of detection, and minimized attraction and accessibility. The environmental model has received wide support throughout Canada, the United States, and several European countries.

## ANOMIE THEORY

The term **anomie** was first used by the famous French sociologist Émile Durkheim (1858 – 1917) to describe social behaviour that discards traditional values and norms for a new value system that has not yet been embraced by the greater society. In short, for those individuals experiencing anomie, a collective social conscience no longer exists. When this occurs, individuals exist in a state of normlessness, lacking moral convictions, and failing or refusing to comply with the formal and informal means of social control. Based on his research at the turn of the century, Durkheim observed that, as the collective conscience weakened, higher rates of crime, suicide, and other social or behavioural aberrations occurred.

Robert Merton's refinement of Durkheim's theory in 1938 helped to broaden the framework of the anomie theory as well as to identify anomic conditions that could be linked with crime and other forms of deviance. Merton theorized that two elements in every culture interact to produce potentially anomic conditions: culturally defined goals and socially approved means for obtaining the goals.

Ordinarily, goals and means fit together within the confines of the law. For example, in Canada, we value the goal of attaining wealth and success, so we socially prescribe hard work, education, and saving money as acceptable means. However, we may not all have an equal opportunity to attain certain goals or an equal capability to follow the preferred means. These inequalities may produce what sociologists call "strain." When this occurs, legitimate means of obtaining success become limited, and anomic conditions may prevail.

Merton identified five different forms of individual adaptation that may or may not lead to delinquent behaviour:

- **Conformity.** This occurs when individuals adopt mainstream social goals and have the means with which to attain them.
- **Ritualism.** This occurs when goals become less important, but the means are still closely adhered to. For example, a young person might go to school despite the fact that he or she has no interest in education.
- **Innovation.** This occurs when individuals adopt social goals but reject or are unable to attain these goals through legitimate means. For example, a youth who wants but cannot afford a pair of in-line skates might obtain them by stealing.
- **Retreatism.** This occurs when individuals do not participate in society. People who are retreatists reject both the goals and the means of society. Merton described these individuals as being "in society but not of it." Drug addicts, alcoholics, vagabonds, and social outcasts can be described as retreatists.
- **Rebellion.** This occurs when individuals reject both the culturally defined goals and the institutionalized means to achieve these goals. Instead, they attempt to substantiate an alternative set of goals and means. Gang members can be described as being rebellious.

Yablonsky and Haskell (1988) suggest a sixth form of social adaptation—"dropping out." In addition to rejecting the goals and means of society, the dropout makes no effort to change anything. He or she "simply wait[s] for something to happen ... and ... to relieve boredom he [or she] engages in behaviour defined as criminal by society" (p. 376). The above points all imply that delinquent youths place an overemphasis on the goals themselves rather than on socially prescribed means of attaining them.

Robert Dubin (1959) has offered the most extensive critique of Merton's forms of adaptation. Dubin claims that Merton's adaptations should include people who accept cultural goals; reject the given institutionalized means; and substitute their own means, which are usually illegitimate in nature. Nevertheless, Dubin, and sociologists in general, have acknowledged that Merton's expansion of the anomie theory allows for a more adequate sociological theory of deviant behaviour.

## SOCIAL LEARNING THEORY AND DIFFERENTIAL ASSOCIATION

Social learning (SL) theory specifically isolates social factors from environmental factors that affect individuals. This theory claims that we learn by listening to people and witnessing events unfolding around us. The SL perspective maintains that behaviour is learned based on a system of positive and negative reinforcements. Note that while social learning is the *manner* in which the individual learns, the *process* by which the individual learns is given another name: differential association. Meanwhile, psychologists use such terms as observational learning and modelling or frustration induction to describe the learning process.

Differential association asserts that since human behaviour is flexible (i.e., it changes based on the situation), anyone can learn deviant and/or delinquent attitudes and behaviours, depending on who he or she associates with and the nature of that association. As an example of social learning, a young person who witnesses a role model or hero doing something illegal or socially inappropriate is very likely to copy or imitate the behaviour of the role model.

Gabriel Tarde (1843 – 1904) was among the first scholars to investigate social learning, in his 1890 book *Penal Philosophy*. In 1947, Edwin Sutherland (1883 – 1950) developed a broader theory that was more specifically aimed at explaining crime and delinquency. Some of Sutherland's key assumptions are as follows:

- Criminal behaviour is learned through interaction with intimate personal groups in a process of communication.
- Deviant behaviour occurs when favourable definitions of delinquent (and criminal) acts are given more credence than unfavourable ones.
- The specific direction of criminal motives and drives depends on the frequency, duration, priority, and intensity of contacts with deviant or criminal associates.
- Learning includes the skills required to commit the crime, the motives and/or rationalizations for the crime, and attitudes associated with the crime.

Whether or not learned behaviour becomes ingrained depends on the situation, Sutherland noted. Positive and negative reinforcement, over the long term, will determine whether the behaviour will become permanent. Positive reinforcement may take the form of praise from others, financial gain, or a sense of accomplishment, while negative reinforcement involves such unpleasant events or experiences as punishment or social rejection. In essence, differential association asserts that, since human behaviour is flexible, and changes based on the situation, anyone can learn criminal behaviour based on how he or she associates, and with whom.

Several sociologists have more thoroughly investigated the role of reinforcement in determining human behaviour. Ronald Akers (1985) developed the differential reinforcement theory, which stressed the importance of reinforcement. Akers believes that behaviour is the direct result of social interactions or exchanges in which the words, responses, presence, and behaviour of other persons make reinforcement available, and provide the setting for reinforcement. Other sociological theories that have been influenced by Sutherland's work include Sykes and Matza's neutralization theory (1957), and Glazer's differential anticipation/identification theory (1965). Each theory is based on social-learning principles but offers a slightly different interpretation of how the learning process occurs. It is important to recognize that no single view can adequately explain all the facts of a criminal or delinquent act.

Although the sociological variations of social learning theory remain popular because of their practicality in explaining how young people come to engage in crime, this perspective has also had its detractors. Some critics argue that social learning theory adds little to what is already well known and explainable. For example, key concepts such as frequency, duration, priority, and intensity are too broad to quantify and empirically test. Similarly, critics have pointed out that this theory does not adequately acknowledge internal or individual factors such as intelligence, different personality traits, or varying environmental conditions. Nevertheless, researchers continue to attempt a clearer definition of the time-and-order relationship between the effects of association and delinquency.

Meanwhile, the field of psychology takes a slightly different approach to social learning theory. In his famous bobo-doll studies, Bandura (1973) demonstrated that children who viewed violent television programs in a controlled setting displayed more aggression toward the dolls than children who had viewed less violent or non-violent programs. This form of observational learning or modelling accounts for how and why when young people witness violence as an acceptable means of resolving conflict, they are likely to imitate this behaviour in similar situations. It has often been said that prisons and youth detention centres are ideal settings for learning how to commit crimes and incorrectly resolve disputes. In a recent study, Singer and associates (1998) report that children who view six hours or more of television per day display higher levels of anxiety and violent behaviour than children who view less than six hours per day. According to Bandura and others who subscribe to the social learning model, whether or not a behaviour becomes ingrained depends on the situation and the expected potential gain. Such potential gains may come in the form of praise from others, as financial (external) rewards, or, from within, for example, as self-reinforcement for a job well done.

From a slightly different perspective Leonard Berkowitz (1962) adapted the social learning model to develop the frustration-induced theory to explain youth crime. According to this theory, when behaviour directed at a specific goal, such as academic success, is somehow blocked, a sense of anxiety is created that can increase tremendously, depending on the situation. When this happens, the individual experiences a strong drive to reduce the anxiety. In order to do so, he or she may turn to a number of solutions, including studying harder, dropping classes, or cheating on tests, for example. If the solution or response leads to reduced anxiety, this may serve to reinforce the adaptation method used.

In order to better determine what type of person would pursue deviant solutions, Berkowitz divided criminal personalities into two main classifications: the socialized offender and the individual offender. The socialized offender, similar to Bandura's and Aker's models, is primarily a product of learning, conditioning, and modelling. By contrast, the individual offender is the product of a long and generally intense series of frustrating experiences that are seldom, if ever, resolved.

A 1998 report on aboriginal youths in British Columbia found that they are increasingly turning to crime out of frustration. They are reacting to pervasive racism, unemployment, and long-standing land-claim disputes. The report showed that, between 1996 and 1998, the number of Native youth charged with shoplifting had doubled, serious crimes had almost tripled, and nearly 50 percent of these youths had broken their probation orders. One spokesperson pointed has out that society is now reaping the result of what has been done to Native people over the years (Moore, 1998).

Similar expressions of frustration-induced crime occurred in Brazil and Indonesia in 1998, when, during a time of political unrest and a general downturn in the economy, local residents turned to looting and theft from farms or supermarkets as a means of survival (CFRA, 1998).

## SOCIETAL REACTION PERSPECTIVES

How often have you thought that the reason some people behave the way they do is because someone else has branded or tagged them as given to that type of behaviour? For example, we have often been led to believe that men are superior to women in terms of intelligence. Testing this general notion, Beloff (1992) found that male students awarded themselves an average IQ of 127, while female students rated themselves, on average, as having an IQ of 120. This difference could be explained as being the result of a societal response to ideas about the differences between males and females.

Rather than investigating the root causes of crime, some sociologists have investigated the effects of a criminal lifestyle—criminals being in constant contact with some aspect of the criminal justice system. Franklin Tannenbaum (1979) is credited with developing the societal reaction theory in his book *Crime and the Community*. He believed that once a youth had been identified as having committed a delinquent act, "the person [then] becomes the thing he [or she] is described as being." In other words, once labelled as a criminal, an individual has a difficult time escaping criminal stereotypes. Worse, the individual begins to think of him- or herself as a criminal. Tannenbaum referred to this process as the "dramatization of evil." Deviance, therefore, does not describe the act committed by an offender, but rather is a consequence of applying rules, sanctions, and labels to the offender.

The societal-reaction perspective has provided some unique contributions to the study of delinquency. It drew attention to the detrimental effects of official labelling of young offenders. This perspective was instrumental in promoting more humane policies such as **alternative measures**, diversion programs, decriminalization of status offences, de-institutionalization practices, and, more recently, **reintegrative shaming**. It is believed that, by diverting them from the criminal justice system and by using minimal formal intervention, minor offenders will be helped to retain their normal identities. However, as many have noted, deviance is not entirely society's responsibility, and young offenders are not passive victims of their own criminal activities. Furthermore, this theory does not explain how labels are internalized or why society adopts specific labelling repertoires.

In summary to this section, sociological theorists have universally focussed on environmental and social factors to explain crime and delinquency.

However, in many cases these theories are difficult to empirically test and verify because of conceptual and operational problems. Since crime is a very complex phenomenon, however, members of other disciplines have preferred to study the subject from different perspectives. We will next look at some of the psychological theories used to explain crimes committed by young persons.

## PSYCHOLOGICAL EXPLANATIONS

Unlike classical sociological theories, psychological explanations follow what is referred to as a "positivistic" tradition and focus on micro, or individual, factors. That is, they concentrate on the mind of the offender in order to determine the cause of his or her criminal or delinquent actions.

### SIGMUND FREUD AND PSYCHOANALYTIC THEORY

Even though Sigmund Freud (1856 – 1939) did not write extensively about crime, his theories have often been used as a starting point for explaining delinquency. According to Freud's psychoanalytic theory, delinquency is the result of conflict among the three aspects of the unconscious mind: the id, which controls our biological and psychological drives and urges; the superego, which controls our unconscious sense of morality; and the ego, the conscious part of our personality that acts as a referee between the id and the superego. This psychodynamic approach has also been described as a theory that explains intrapsychic conflict within a person. According to Freud's theory, delinquency can be viewed as a personality disorder resulting from inner conflict.

The development of these three components is strongly influenced by our early childhood experiences, because during this time our personalities are most malleable. In particular, Freud stressed the importance of our psychosexual development during childhood. He believed that their delinquency was the result of an unconscious sense of guilt retained from a boy's *Oedipus complex* (or a girl's *Electra complex*). Guilt or conflict comes about when boys or girls are unable to identify with their same-sex parent. When this happens, they do not properly develop their social and life skills. These complexes are related to proper development in the first three phases of life: the oral phase (the first year, where the focus is on sucking and biting); the anal phase (the second and third years, where the focus is on eliminating body waste); and the phallic stage (the third year, where the focus is on the genitals). Freud believed that any difficulties experienced during any of these phases could trigger problems, and thus unacceptable or deviant behaviour in later life.

While his work has met with varying criticisms, Freud continues to have a strong following, and many of his followers have tested and modified psychoanalytic theory. For example, Alexander and Healy (1935) focussed on delinquents' inability to postpone gratification. Others have attempted to explain delinquency as a substitute means of obtaining affection and attention, or have used the theory to focus on such traits as neurosis and poorly formed superegos. Starting in 1989, Ontario psychologist E.T. Barker started to effectively use the traditional "ego-state therapy," which is derived from the psychoanalytic approach, with young offenders. More recently, he modified the theory to focus only on sharing current memories rather than past memories.[1] An extension of the psychoanalytic approach has been the developmental models, which are discussed in the next section.

## DEVELOPMENTAL MODELS: ERIKSON TO SULLIVAN, AND BEYOND

Working from the Freudian model, Erik Erikson (1959) identified the following stages of development (we summarize only those that relate to children and adolescents):

- *Infancy* (birth – 1st year of life): The struggle is between trust and mistrust. Development depends on basic needs being met.
- *Early Childhood* (1 – 3 years): The child wavers between autonomy and shame and doubt. The sense of self-reliance is often undermined by self-doubt.
- *Childhood* (3 – 6 years): Children attempt to act grown up and will try to accept responsibilities beyond their normal capacity, which at times may conflict with those of parents or other family members. This stage is characterized as one between taking initiative and resolving guilt.
- *School Age* (6 – 12 years): Industry is set against inferiority. In order for the child to continue to grow, he or she needs to be assigned basic tasks through which he or she achieves a sense of industry and learns to set and attain personal goals.
- *Adolescence* (12 – 18 years): The conflict is between identity and role confusion. Adolescence is a time for testing limits, for breaking dependency ties, and for establishing a new identity.

Erikson maintained that unless a person successfully progressed through each stage, the resulting trauma (what he termed an "identity crisis") would trigger a set of unacceptable behaviours later in life.

During the late 1950s, C. Sullivan and his colleagues took Erikson's ideas further to develop the Interpersonal Maturity Levels (I-Level) System, designed specifically to help classify delinquents. In theory, youths could be assisted according to their level of moral development as classified by this system. Sullivan's system entailed seven levels, ranging from level 1, in which a person can differentiate him- or herself from others only by comparison with others, to level 7, in which a person moves beyond self-absorption to a more altruistic attitude, seeking what is best for others (Sullivan, Grant, and Grant, 1957). Most young offenders fall between levels 2 and 4, and are characterized as being self-centred, overtly aggressive, and easily influence by peers, and as having a poor self-image.

Sullivan's system has never been adequately tested against non-delinquents, and as a result it has remained relatively obscure. However, another such test, the Jesness I-Level Inventory, which is also designed to assess delinquency, has received considerably more attention over the years, in part due to the California Youth Center Project. Youths involved in this project were classified as neurotic, power-oriented, or passive conformists. Based on the results of their classification, probation officers were able to provide more appropriate treatment in accordance with each youth's special needs and with respect to recidivism (Andrews, Bonta, and Hoge, 1990).

### THE FAMILY FACTOR

So far, the psychological theories we have discussed have emphasized individual factors, but as many psychologists have noted, family factors are also important. Some of the key factors that have been viewed as fundamental for healthy psychological development include parental consistency in providing love, as it has been proven that there is a strong relationship between parental rejection and delinquency; discipline and adequate supervision in the home; and positive stimulation in early childhood (Loeber and Stouthamer-Loeber, 1986). As well, numerous studies have linked violence within the family—especially abuse by one or both parents—to antisocial behaviour and delinquency (Finkelhor and Dzuiba-Leatherman, 1994). In fact, even witnessing family violence has been shown to have a marked effect on the socio-emotional development of children. However, since this relationship is still not clear, more research in this area is necessary (see Box 2.2).

In summary, this section has provided only a cursory overview of some of the main psychological perspectives that are currently being used to explain, describe, and predict youth crime.

You will notice that the psychological theories focus on individual traits or personality aberrations (a micro approach), while the sociological theories tend to focus on social factors such as poverty, education, and labelling (a macro approach). Biological explanations lot delinquency and youth crime offer another perspective.

## BIOLOGICAL EXPLANATIONS

### BIOLOGICAL DETERMINISM

One of the major contributors to biological theories of crime was Cesare Lombroso (1835 – 1909). Strongly influenced by the work of Charles Darwin, Lombroso adopted the idea of survival of the fittest, suggesting that humans can be categorized according to various levels of physical development. In his seminal work *The Criminal Man* (1876), Lombroso argued that criminals have "atavistic" traits (i.e., a "throwback" to an earlier stage of human evolution) that distinguish them from non-criminals.

Lombroso also coined the term "born criminal," which reflected his belief that some people will turn to crime because of their inherent physical traits.

Lombroso's theory included the following general principles:

- **Determinism.** The notion that behaviour is determined by forces that transcend individual choice or control. These forces include biology, economics, historical world spirit, and environment.

### Box 2.2

### DO PARENTS MATTER LESS THAN WE THOUGHT?

In her controversial and highly acclaimed book *The Nurture Assumption* (1998), Judith Harris attempts to debunk the traditional perception that who children become as adults is influenced by the type of parents and family upbringing they have. Drawing on a wide range of folklore; research literature from behavioural genetics, anthropology, evolutionary psychology; primate research; as well as her own experiences in raising both a biological and an adopted child, Harris argues that the role of parents is not as significant as we have been led to believe. Rather, she argues, our friends and peers play a much more pivotal role in forging who we become.

In the foreword to Harris's book, Steven Pinker describes the work as "revolutionary, insightful" and asserts that it "will come to be seen as a turning point in the history of psychology" (p. xiii). Harris herself admits that her views are not yet widely accepted by the old guard, but says "no matter ... they're not going to live forever" (Span, 1998).

Some key points that Harris raises in her book include the following:

- The nurturing we receive from our parents (e.g., interaction, guidance, love, and attention) is a "cherished cultural myth." Harris argues that, according to the work of other researchers, the evidence does not support the assertion of parental influence.
- Birth order plays, at best, "only a bit-part in the drama of sibling differences" (p. 42).
- The lifetime type of criminal behaviour espoused by some biologists and psychologists is quite rare. If anything, Harris suggests, some people are born with certain characteristics "that make them poor fits" (p. 229). When combined with poor peers, such individuals are more prone to commit delinquencies.
- As much as we might like to cling to the influence of our parents, it is the group of people we associate with that forges "our attitudes, our speech and behaviour to different social contexts" (p. 361).

However, Harris's ideas are not definitive. Drawing on interviews conducted over a 23-year period, some University of Michigan sociologists have concluded that family circumstances do matter. Axinn, Barber, and Thornton found that children born to mothers who did not want their children (approximately 9 percent) are more likely to suffer from low self-esteem and are at greater risk of becoming delinquent than those children who were wanted by their mothers. It is interesting to note that over 90 percent of the unwanted children were the fourth-born in their families (Boodman, 1999).

What do you think of Harris's observations? Do our peers play a more important role in our lives than do our parents? How effective might Harris's theory be for explaining familial sexual abuse or criminality? Conduct a class survey about the relative importance of birth order and the perceived level of "success" or perceived acceptance in the family.

- **Social protection.** Due to determinism, the state has a duty to protect itself and its citizens from dangerous criminal or deviant behaviours.
- **Power to prohibit.** The state has both a right and a duty to identify, prohibit, and repress certain behaviours.
- **The medical analogy.** Lombroso's theory considered crime as a disease, and criminals as sick people who must be cured or put under quarantine.

Many, if not all, of the biological or physical characteristics that Lombroso carefully logged and catalogued as criminal have since been discredited—characteristics such as telltale criminal handwriting or criminal ear shapes. Obviously, Lombroso's research techniques were primitive by today's standards, but, more importantly, he failed to recognize the importance of environment in the development of adolescent body structures. Nevertheless, his contribution was significant because he stressed the scientific method. Despite a resistance in some circles to research involving connections between crime and biology, those interested in this line of study have continued to improve their methodologies. As a result, today we are witnessing a resurgence of literature based on hereditary biological factors. A 1990 article by Diana Fishbein noted that research conducted in various disciplines such as behavioural genetics, physiological psychology, psychopharmacology, and endocrinology indicates that biological factors can indeed play an equally significant role in the development of antisocial behaviour and should be considered accordingly (see Box 2.3). A summary of some of the biologically based studies that have been conducted and that have met with varying degrees of acceptance is provided below.

## PHYSICAL FACTORS

During the late 1700s, convinced that the brain is literally the container of our personality, Franz Joseph Gall (1758 – 1828) attempted to map out the skull and relate the various lumps and bumps to 27 faculties, or personality traits. His work was expanded upon by one of his students, Johan K. Spurzheim (1776 – 1832), who identified 35 different traits (Vold, 1981). In early nineteenth-century North America, Charles Caldwell became one of the leading American supporters of this technique. However, due to poor methodology and questionable conclusions, this line of investigation has all but disappeared today.

Taking his cue from Lombroso, one of his contemporaries, Charles Goring, observed that criminals tended to be shorter and weighed less than non-criminals. Hence, Goring concluded that there must be an inferior hereditary factor at play. He documented these ideas in his 1913 book *The English Convict*. However, in his studies, Goring was unable to discriminate between the physical characteristics of prison inmates and those of students attending Oxford University (Goring, 1913)! Twenty-six years later, Ernest Hooton, a Harvard anthropologist, measured the physical traits of more than 17 000 people over a twelve-year period, and concluded that criminals were in some way "inferior" to non-criminals, in his work *Crime and the Man*.

German psychiatrist Ernest Kretschmer (1888 – 1964) identified three distinct body types, or somatypes, for weeding out criminals: the asthenic type, which is tall and thin; the athletic type, which is muscular; and the

**Box 2.3**

**NOBODY KNOWS WHY KIDS GO "BAD"**

To listen to the current round of public discourse, we're not only going to hell in a handbasket, but that vehicle of society's demise is being woven by an entire generation of slack-jawed, sneering youths whose purpose in life is to flout the system....

It is convenient to decry laxity in the judicial system, focusing on the Young Offenders Act, for looseness in society. It is comfortable for adults to look elsewhere to place the blame instead of inside themselves. But some of us aren't sucked in by rhetoric of retribution or the dubious value of punishment....

It isn't the Young Offenders Act that is at fault, if there are, indeed, all these criminal children; it is those of us who set the examples, and those of us who uphold the law.

If all a child sees from birth to the first car he steals is violence, disorder, hatred, chicanery and lies—and that's just politics and ice hockey—what lesson is he supposed to have learned? If all he knows is isolation—because of poverty, discrimination, bias or inequality of opportunity—why presume he understands community of responsibility? ...

Why does our solution focus somewhere between flogging the little devils and locking them up until they rot? The extremes of the "kids are hardened criminals" argument makes as much sense as the bloodlust over capital punishment did.

Those who want stiffer penalties for children, who are loudest in their demands, make two false assumptions.

First, they assume the world is full of children without any sense of morality who will do anything—no matter how abhorrent—because the Young Offenders Act protects them from public opprobrium and from a jail sentence longer than five years.... That a child so young could be so criminal and not be considered more sick than dangerous rarely enters the conversation. Neither, these days, does the call for reclamation and rehabilitation over retribution.

The second assumption is that the majority of people—children and adults—do not commit crimes because of the punishment involved. This is the more dangerous assumption of the two, because it posits the greater the punishment, the less likely the committal of the crime. It's a falsehood.... Legislation is merely the written expression of all the rules we live by....

There always were bad apples, and there always will be. Nobody knows what makes a kid go bad. Nobody can predict which child in a family will go wrong and which will come through the crucible of early life strengthened instead of defeated by adversity.

Suffice it to say that there are certain inalienable rules and rights: A child needs food, shelter, love, work, discipline and a sense of direction, not necessarily in that order.

All things being equal—which of course, they are not—that ensures a fairly normal member of adult society.

Take away any of those, and you increase the risk of failure, exponentially....

All of that means simply that no matter how unpopular the notion is today, it is true that society—and we are society—is to blame if its youngest citizens are criminal before they're old enough to drive a car....

Do you agree with the author's observation? Clarify your answer.

---

**Source:** Excerpts from "Opinion" column by Catherine Ford, *Calgary Herald*, 12 March 1992.

pyknic type, which is short and fat. In a 1955 publication, Kretschmer stated that asthenic types tended to be connected with theft or fraud, athletic types with crimes of violence, and pyknic types with crimes of deception. The American sociologist William H. Sheldon (1898 – 1977) was heavily influenced by Kretschmer's work and further refined the relationship between body types and delinquency. He also identified three body types—ectomorph, mesomorph, and endomorph, which correspond to those of Kretschmer. Today, these views have been all but discredited. However, the concepts continue to be applied in such areas as mental and physical health, as well as in athletics. Therefore, the importance of body type does not yet appear to have been resolved. Research into biological connections to crime has turned away from examining physical traits, as this line of investigation tended to use markedly racist or sexist stereotypes. Instead, researchers have started to examine the genetic and psychochemical make-up of criminals.

## GENETIC FACTORS

Since the work of Charles Darwin (1809 – 1882) and Gregor Mendel (1822 – 1884), who essentially revolutionized our understanding about humankind and the nature of human evolution, genetics has been the focus of much research. Darwin's famous work *The Origin of Species* (1859) suggested that species evolve through a reciprocal interaction between the environment and the genetic make-up of a plant or animal. Since Darwin's time, genetics has been the focus of much research. Countless studies have attempted to link criminality, delinquency, aggression, and antisocial behaviour to genetic abnormalities. While these studies have shown that there are no genes directly responsible for crime, they have also determined that some genes, in combination with certain hormonal conditions (e.g., the onset of puberty, or low serotonin levels) can be strongly associated with certain forms of delinquency. Recent studies demonstrate not only the importance of genetic traits but also the significance of maturational and environmental processes. The relationship between these factors may prove to be acutely important in explaining certain types of delinquency.

## PSYCHOPHYSIOLOGICAL FACTORS

A considerable number of studies have examined whether frontal brain dysfunction, traumatic head injury at an early age, reduced skin conductance, and/or lower resting heart rate might differentiate violent young offenders from non-violent offenders. For example, certain imbalances in neurotransmitters such as acetylcholine, norepinephrine, dopamine, and serotonin have been found to increase aggression levels (Moffit et al., 1998) and nervous system irregularities (Fishbein, 1990). For this reason, Raine (1993) and many others believe that this area may hold new insights into certain types of delinquent behaviour, but much more research needs to be done. Using PET scans to examine the brains of several impulsive murderers, Raine found that, when compared with those of non-criminals, the prefrontal areas of the murderers' brains were virtually inactive. In other words, the murderers' brains do not function in a normal manner. Another recent study where brain scans were used to measure brain-wave activity in the brains of both teenagers and adults found that emotional turbulence among young people may have a physiological basis. Doctor Yurgen-Todd found that teenagers process emotions more intensely and indiscriminately than do adults (cited in Hotz, 1998). This pioneering study will likely spawn further research in the area, as well as examine what role the environment plays in how young people respond to different environmental factors (e.g., family, television, school, peers).

## PSYCHOPHARMACOLOGICAL FACTORS

Since the mid-1970s, a number of studies have examined the effects of legal and illegal drugs on the brain. In the majority of these studies, drugs, including alcohol, have been found to affect individuals both at a psychological and at a behavioural level (see Raine, 1993). Moir and Jessel (1997) also note that certain drugs, particularly many illicit drugs, are reported to increase aggressive responses, although the actual expression of aggressive behaviour depends on the dose, the route of administration, genetic factors, and the type of aggression.

Drugs and alcohol are not the only mood-altering chemicals that relate to aggressive behaviour, particularly in young offenders. Surveys show that the majority of violent young offenders had consumed some form of mood-altering drug on the day they committed their crime. Of particular concern is the fact that the average age of onset for the use of mood-altering drugs has fallen since the 1980s, and there has been a shift toward more illicit drugs (Monitoring the Future, 1996). Seemingly harmless substances have also been linked to violence. In 1978, Leonard Hippchen was among the first theorists to suggest that dietary habits, vitamin and mineral imbalances, hypoglycemia, and even environmental toxins, are related to the development of crime and delinquency. Bennett and his colleagues (1998) found that by correcting food allergies in young offenders they were able to reduce antisocial tendencies. Similarly, one of the first studies undertaken to examine the effects of pesticides on children in Mexico found that children exposed to agricultural pesticides expressed significantly more aggressive and antisocial behaviour than children not living in the same agricultural region (Guilette et al., 1998).

As the scientific evidence involving the relationship between biology and delinquency grows, we must remember that correlations are not the same as causes. Before such conclusions can be drawn, more careful research is required. Ultimately, criminal justice policies must be based on well-founded theories and findings that survive scientific scrutiny.

In the final section of this chapter, we will take a brief look at some of the new integrated and interdisciplinary theories that reflect a growing awareness of the need to understand delinquency from several perspectives.

# INTEGRATED AND INTERDISCIPLINARY EXPLANATIONS

In the past, sociologists, psychologists, and biologists tended to formulate explanations for youth crime that relied on concepts unique to their particular disciplines. More recently, there have been attempts to bridge some of the disciplinary isolation. For example, in his 1998 Presidential Address to the American Association of Criminology, Zahn (1999: 2) observed that criminology needs "to incorporate other disciplines that affect human behaviour such as biology and biochemistry ... [and] ... make better use of historical studies." It is hoped that these new approaches will result in a better understanding of youth crime.

## BIOSOCIAL THEORY

The biosocial theory is an excellent example of a bridging theory, as it takes ideas from numerous fields of study. The American researcher Sarnoff Mednick and his associates have pioneered this orientation for explaining crime and delinquency. Some of the assumptions of the biosocial theory include the following:

- No two people are genetically alike. Each person's unique genetic makeup contributes significantly to his or her behaviour, but it should also be noted that behaviour patterns are a combination of genetic traits and the environment.
- Social behaviour is learned, and each individual learns according to varying brain functions and mental processing abilities. Learning is therefore fundamentally controlled by biochemistry (Raine et al., 1996), but individuals can learn to control their natural urges toward antisocial or delinquent tendencies.
- A wide range of biochemical factors can affect behaviour, from vitamin deficiency and vitamin dependency to hormonal influences, allergies, and even premenstrual syndrome.
- Biochemical factors, when combined with social environment, can play a significant role in determining whether young people develop antisocial or delinquent behaviours.

The major elements of the biosocial model can be summed up in the equation found in Figure 2.1.

Criticism of biosocial theory has focussed on its alleged tendency to medicalize political issues such as gender, race, and marginalized groups. In spite of these concerns, however, an increasing number of researchers are exploring how the biosocial approach could explain chronic delinquent behaviour. For example, Avshalom Caspi and colleagues (1995) conducted a longitudinal study in New Zealand and found a significant correlate of persistent antisocial behaviour among young persons that involved an interaction of social and psychological factors with neuropsychological dysfunctions. In terms of prevention, the biosocial perspective subscribes to a

**Figure 2.1**
**THE BIOSOCIAL EQUATION**

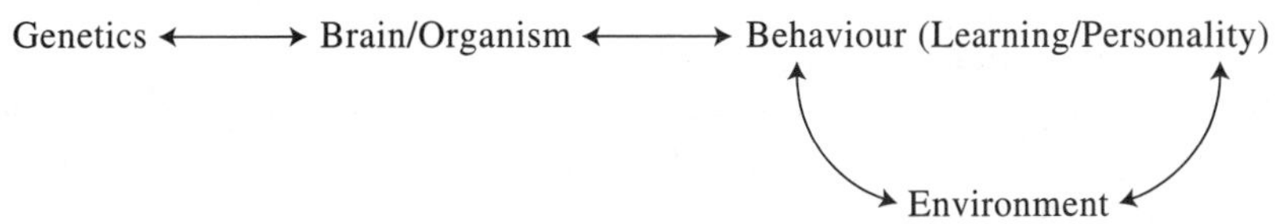


**Source:** Adapted from C.R. Jeffrey, "Biological and neuropsychiatric approaches to criminal behavior," in *Varieties of Criminology: Readings from a Dynamic Discipline* edited by G. Barak (Westport, CT: Praeger, 1994), p. 21. Reproduced with permission of Greenwood Publishing Group, Inc., Westport, CT.

proactive approach of detecting possible markers in individuals or their environment, and then targeting these markers through strategies such as public-health intervention.

## LIFESTYLE AND ROUTINE ACTIVITIES THEORY

During the 1990s the routine activities or opportunity theory became one of the most commonly tested theories in criminology. While the biosocial theory focusses on the interaction between the brain and the environment, the lifestyle theory focusses on the interaction between social and environmental opportunities and the individual's motivation to attain certain goals. Developed by Lawrence Cohen and Marcus Felson in the late 1970s, this theory claims that in every society there are people who are willing to commit a crime. Both the motivation to commit a crime and the availability of targets are constant. For a criminal act to occur, however, certain variables must be present. These variables include the availability of suitable targets, such as unattended cars or homes, or helpless individuals; the absence of capable guardians for the offender; and the presence of motivated offenders, such as unemployed, drug-addicted, bored, or homeless youth. If all of these factors are present, then a predatory crime will likely occur.

In testing this theory, Canadian researchers Leslie Kennedy and David Forde (1990) found that lower-class young males were at greater risk of being either offenders or crime victims, based on their lifestyle behaviour (e.g., going to bars; walking or driving at night). However, these lifestyle variables still need to be more clearly defined, and some critics suggest that even greater attention must be paid to the situational context that motivates individuals.

## INTEGRATING SOCIAL PROCESS AND STRUCTURAL CONDITIONS

Drawing on data from the National Youth Survey conducted in the late 1970s, Elliott, Huizinga, and Ageton (1985) developed a popular theory of delinquency that attempts to integrate social control, strain, and social learning theories. In their model, the socialization process is critical to establishing social control. As a young person ages, he or she must contend with a wide variety of social stresses that may reduce social-control bonds. Furthermore, life experiences (such as the youth's network of peers) may create a dysfunctional learning environment. Collectively, the interaction of these factors can weaken conventional social-control bonds and predispose a young person to delinquent behaviour.

Although this sophisticated model attempts to take into account a number of possible paths to delinquency, it has several methodological flaws. For instance, researchers have not been able to clearly measure the construction of social control and bonding, strain, or elements of learning.

The integrated theories hold promise because they attempt to offer a more comprehensive explanation of delinquency and crime, however, additional research needs to be conducted before we can determine whether they hold true promise for the future study and control of crime and delinquency. One of the more recent attempts to develop a sophisticated integrated explanatory model of delinquency is based on longitudinal data from the Dunedin Multidisciplinary Health and Development Study in New Zealand. An example of their findings focussed on the relationship between socio-economic status (SES) and delinquency. Using an integrated approach, they concluded that SES can have both negative and positive effects upon delinquency (Wright et al., 1999).

## FEMINIST THEORY

In the strictest sense, the feminist perspective is not an integrated theory, but it does represent an attempt to bridge male-dominated paradigms for explaining crime and delinquency. Radical-feminist theories emphasize the discriminatory treatment and oppression that women have experienced in the juvenile and adult justice system.

Since the pioneering works of Freda Adler in 1975 and Carol Smart in 1976, there have been numerous variations on feminist theory (see Chesney-Lind and Shelden, 1992), three of which we will summarize here. Liberal feminist theorists focus on different economic and social standards between males and females. Radical feminist theorists focus on the oppressive conditions that many girls and women face, such as sexual abuse, exploitation in the work force, and general dominance by the male status quo. Phenomenological feminist theories focus on the regulators of juvenile justice, and examine whether or not young females receive discriminatory treatment by the youth justice system, and how the YOA penalizes females.

Collectively, the feminist theories represent a comparatively new way of looking at the issue of youth crime, since, in the past, social issues were mainly studied from a male viewpoint. Current explanations of female delinquency can be divided into two main categories:

- **Developmental theories.** These theories stress the importance of psychological, developmental, and home-environment factors facing females, which differ from those facing males. For example, differences in hormonal traits and genetic make-up have successfully explained differences between male and female violence rates.

- **Socialization theories.** These theories examine the socialization process surrounding females, since young girls tend to be brought up with different role expectations than young boys. Female socialization theories focus on the behaviours of delinquent girls who were not raised in a nurturing environment (see Box 2.2 above).

The interdisciplinary approach of these new bridging theories marks the continuing evolution of a new burst of research into crime and delinquency. In the 1994 edition of their theory text, Williams and McShane note that "the field appears to be on the verge of a paradigm revolution." In their 1998 edition, they state that "contemporary criminology is now fermenting nicely," but that the direction new theories will take still remains in doubt.

## SUMMARY

This chapter has provided an overview of some of the theories used to explain youth crime. While none is perfect, each theory offers some insight. As we saw, sociologists offer insights on social organization, ethnicity, social stratification, and environmental conditions. These factors can create strain, thereby encouraging deviation, undermining social cohesion, and predisposing a young person to delinquency.

Psychological perspectives shift the focus from social factors to individual traits. These explanations of delinquency fall into two main theoretical camps: those that use the role of learning (e.g., committing copy-cat crimes or hanging around with the wrong crowd), and those that emphasize psychodynamic factors, such as family conflict, inappropriate discipline, and other developmental experiences that can prevent a young person's healthy emotional development.

Biological explanations similarly focus on specific individual traits. They stress the importance of genetic influences, hormonal imbalances, nutrition, drugs, and even physical traits. The biological theories also suggest a possible heredity link in the case of some young offenders.

Newer integrated and interdisciplinary theories reflect the fact that crime and delinquency are complex issues, and any attempt to deal with them must consider a wide variety of factors and interpretations. However, as we begin to accept the fact that crime is a complex phenomenon, we must acknowledge that there are no simple answers or solutions for understanding delinquency. Therefore, any attempt to deal with the issue must be open to a wide variety of interpretations and orientations.

Only through diligent testing, constant evaluation, and careful analysis can we begin to narrow the gap between simply describing the phenomenon of juvenile delinquency and explaining, predicting, and ultimately preventing youth crime.

# NOTE

1. Barker has a Web site where you can explore his ideas and findings. It can be found at: <http://www.bconnex.net/~cspcc/egostate>.

# WEB LINK

**Criminological Theory**
<http://www.criminology.fsu.edu/crimtheory>

Prepared by Cecil Greek, who teaches criminology at Florida State University, this site offers considerable information on a wide range of criminological theories. Click on "Lecture Notes" in the left-hand column to access extensive criminological-theory links.

# STUDY QUESTIONS

1. What is a theory and how does it differ from other forms of knowing?
2. What are the four major theoretical orientations used to classify delinquency in this chapter? Which do you favour? Why?
3. What constitutes a "good" theory? How should future criminologists pursue the "ideal" theory?
4. Explain the following forms of delinquency using all four perspectives:
   a) Running away from home
   b) Skipping school
   c) Committing assault
   d) Participating in a gang
5. Using first the conflict perspective and then the consensus perspective explain: a) gang delinquency, b) juvenile prostitution, and c) breaking and entering. Does one model appear to work better than the other? Why?
6. With so many possible ways to explain, predict, and understand delinquent behaviour, why does this type of behaviour persist?
7. Identify a number of ways in which theory and social policy might be brought together. What, if any, advantages would result?
8. How has the feminist perspective and realist perspective contributed to our understanding of young offenders?
9. How might an integrated and interdisciplinary approach hold promise in our quest to better understand delinquency?
10. Given that the concept of delinquency is both relative (time-specific) and evolving (changing), what kinds of criteria might we use in order to ensure that a particular theory is capable of accounting for these descriptive principles of delinquency?

# REFERENCES

Adler, F. (1975). *Sisters in Crime: The Rise of the New Female Criminal*. New York: McGraw-Hill.

Akers, R. (1985). *Deviant Behavior: A Social Learning Approach*, 3rd ed. Belmont, CA: Wadsworth.

Alexander, F., and Healy, W. (1935). *Roots of Crime*. New York: Knopf.

Andrews, D.A., Bonta, J., and Hoge, R.D. (1990). "Classification for effective rehabilitation: Rediscovering psychology." *Criminal Justice and Behavior*, 17: 19 – 52.

Bandura, W. (1973). *Aggression: A Social Learning Analysis.* Englewood Cliffs, NJ: Prentice-Hall.

Barker, E.T. (1998). "Ego-state therapy with juvenile delinquents." (Online: http://www.bconnex.net/~cspcc/egostate/)

Beloff, H. (1992, 16 April). "Men: Daft enough to think they're the brightest." *Calgary Herald*, p. A1.

Bennett, P.W., McEwan, L.M., McEwan, H.C., and Rose, E.L. (1998). "The Shipley project: Treating food allergy to prevent criminal behaviour in community settings." *Journal of Nutritional and Environmental Medicine*, 8:77 – 83.

Berkowitz, L. (1962). *Aggression: A Social-Psychological Analysis.* New York: McGraw-Hill.

Bloom, B.L. (1966). "A census tract analysis of socially deviant behaviors." *Multivariate Behavioral Research*, 1: 307 – 20.

Boodman, S. (1999, 16 January). "Unwanted children have no confidence." *Calgary Herald*, K24.

Brantingham, P.J. and Brantingham, P.L. (1981). *Environmental Criminology*. Beverly Hills, CA: Sage.

———. (1984). *Patterns in Crime.* New York: Macmillan.

Caspi, A., Henry, B., McGee, R., Moffitt, T., and Silva, P.A. (1995). "Temperamental origins of child and adolescent behavior problems: From ages 3 to age 15." *Child Development*, 65: 55 – 68.

CFRA. (1998). On line: http://interactive.cfra.com/1998/05/28/37195.html. News Talk Radio.

Chesney-Lind, M., and Shelden, R.G. (1992). *Girls, Delinquency, and Juvenile Justice.* Pacific Grove, CA: Brooks/Cole.

Dubin, R. (1959). "Deviant behavior and social structure: Continuities in social theory." *American Sociological Review*, 2(2): 147 – 64.

Elliott, D.S., Huizinga, D., and Ageton, S.S. (1985). *Explaining Delinquency and Drug Use.* Beverly Hills, CA: Sage.

Erikson, E.H. (1959). *Identity and the Life Cycle.* New York: International University Press.

Finkelhor, D., and Dzuiba-Leatherman, J. (1994). "Victimization of children." *American Psychologist*, 49: 173 – 83.

Fishbein, D.H. (1990). "Biological perspectives in criminology." *Criminology*, 28(1): 27 – 72.

Glazer, D. (1965). *Crime in Our Society*. New York: Holt, Rinehart & Winston.

Goring, C. (1913). *The English Convict.* London: His Majesty's Stationery Office.

Guillette, E.A., Maza, M.M., Aquilar, M.G., Soto, A.D., and Garcia, E. (1998). "An anthropological approach to the evaluation of preschool children exposed to pesticides in Mexico." *Environmental Health Perspectives*, 106(6): 347 – 53.

Harris, J.R. (1998). *The Nurture Assumption.* New York: Free Press.

Hotz, R.L. (1998, 11 July). "Brain scans reveal teenagers think differently." *Calgary Herald*, G13.

Jeffrey, C.R. (1994). "Biological and neuropsychiatric approaches to criminal behavior." In G. Barak (Ed.), *Varieties of Criminology: Readings from a Dynamic Discipline.* Westport, CT: Praeger.

Kennedy, L.W., and Forde, D.R. (1990). "Routine activities and crime: An analysis of victimization in Canada." *Criminology*, 28(1): 137 – 52.

Kerlinger, F.N. (1973). *Foundation of Behavioral Research* (2nd ed.). New York: Holt, Rinehart & Winston.

Labovitz, S., and Hagedorn, R. (1981). *Introduction to Social Research*, 3rd ed. New York: McGraw-Hill.

Loeber, R., and Stouthamer-Loeber, M. (1986). "Family factors as correlates and predictors of juvenile conduct problems and delinquency." In M. Tony and N. Morris

(Eds.), *Crime Justice: An Annual Review of Research*, 7th ed. Chicago: University of Chicago Press.

Lombroso, C. (1972 [1876]). "Criminal man." In S.F. Sylvester (Ed.), *The Heritage of Modern Criminology*, pp. 67 – 78. Cambridge, MA: Schenkman.

Moffit, T.E., Brammer, G.L., Caspi, A., Fawcett, J.P., Raleigh, M., Yuwiler, A., and Silva, P. (1998). "Whole blood serotonin relates to violence in an epidemiological study." *Biological Psychiatry*, 43(6): 446 – 57.

Moir, A., and Jessel, D. (1977). *A Mind to Crime*. New York: Signet.

*Monitoring the Future*. (1996, December). Survey conducted by the U.S. Department of Health and Human Services. Washington, D.C.

Moore, D. (1998, 7 May). "Violence on the rise among Native youth." On-line: http://interactive.cfra.com/1998/05/07/26149.html. CFRA, News Talk Radio.

Raine, A. (1993). *The Psychopathology of Crime*. New York: Academic Press.

Raine, A., Brennan, P.A., Farrington, D., and Mednick, S.A. (Eds.). (1996). *Biosocial Basis of Violence*. New York: Plenum.

Shaw, C.R., and McKay, H.D. (1969). *Juvenile Delinquency and Urban Areas*. Chicago: University of Chicago Press.

Singer, M.I., Slovak, K., Freirson, T., and York, P. (1998). "Viewing preferences, symptoms of psychological trauma, and violent behaviors among children who watch television." *Journal of American Academy of Child and Adolescent Psychiatry*, 37: 1041 – 48.

Smart, C. (1976). *Women, Crime and Criminology: A Feminist Critique*. London: Routledge & Kegan Paul.

Span, P. (1998, 25 November). "Nature vs. nurture: Brash author earns beefs, bouquets for discounting roles of parents." *Calgary Herald*, G4.

Sullivan, C., Grant, M.Q., and Grant, D. (1957). "The development of interpersonal maturity: Applications to delinquency." *Psychiatry*, 20(11): 373 – 85.

Sykes, G.M., and Matza, D. (1957). "Techniques of neutralization: A theory of delinquency." *American Sociological Review*, 22: 664 – 70.

Tannenbaum, F. (1979). "Dramatization of evil." Cited in J.E. Jacoby (Ed.), *Classics of Criminology*. Prospect Heights, IL: Waveland Press.

Theodorson, G.A. (Ed.). (1982). *Urban Patterns: Studies in Human Ecology*, Rev. ed. University Park: Pennsylvania University Press.

Tracy, P.E., Wolfgang, M.E., and Figho, R.M. (1985). *Delinquency in Two Birth Cohorts*. Washington, DC: U.S. Department of Justice.

Vold, G.B. (1981). *Theoretical Criminology*, 2nd ed. Prepared by T.J. Bernard. New York: Oxford University Press.

Winterdyk, J.A. (2000). *Canadian Criminology*. Scarborough, ON: Pearson.

Wright, B.R.E., Caspi, A., Moffitt, T.E., and Silva, P.A. (1999). "Low self-control, social bonds, and crime: Social causation, social selection, or both?" *Criminology*, 37(3): 479 – 514.

Yablonsky, L., and Haskell, M.R. (1988). *Juvenile Delinquency*, 4th ed. New York: Harper & Row.

Zahn, M.A. (1999). "Thoughts on the future of criminology: The American Society of Criminology 1998 Presidential Address." *Criminology*, 37(1): 1 – 16.

# Chapter 3

# Girls and Crime

MARGE REITSMA-STREET
AND SYBILLE ARTZ

## KEY OBJECTIVES

After reading this chapter, you should be able to:

- present an overview of the study of female youth and crime;
- examine offending patterns of Canadian female youth;
- review Canadian judicial responses to female youth crime;
- outline traditional explanations of female crime;
- identify promising directions in understanding and responding to female crime.

## KEY TERMS

administrative offences
differential association
differential intervention
dispositions
gender gap
gender role theory
masculinization
minor offences against the person
offending patterns
official statistics
prevention
self-report
social-control theory

## INTRODUCTION

Crimes by girls and boys are often everyday, banal behaviours, except that they are forbidden by law and can have serious implications. Shortly after the Young Offenders Act (YOA) was introduced and the public could sit in youth courts, we saw in 1986 a young girl charged in a Hamilton court with stealing two pairs of earrings, each worth $2.98. The shop detective used company policy to insist that the police charge her. Her parents took several days off work to go to youth court; they watched as their daughter pleaded guilty and was sentenced to 50 hours of **community service**. The next year, another girl from a small Ontario town had taken $50 from her mother's new boyfriend's wallet, and he laid a charge of theft against her. Both mother and daughter travelled long hours by bus to go to court several times; once they missed the bus, and the mother was charged with contempt of court for missing the court appearance. Charges against the mother and daughter were dismissed, and we heard the youth-court judge encourage them to go for family counselling.

A few crimes by girls, however, are terrifying for all those involved. In November 1997, seven girls and one boy attacked and beat up 14-year-old Reena Virk near Victoria, BC for allegedly showing interest in the boyfriend of one of the girls. As described in Chapter 6, the beating and eventual murder were brutal. The families and friends of both Reena and her attackers, along with the many human-services and justice-system workers involved, and the citizens of Victoria, are still caught up in the horror, costs, and consequences of this crime.

To understand and respond to girls and crime, it is necessary to examine patterns of crime and trends in juvenile justice. We begin this chapter looking at such patterns using self-report (SR) surveys and official statistics. Next, we present a brief history of theories that seek to explain female crime and delinquency and a critique of the ways in which female youth crime has thus far been conceptualized adequately. The chapter ends with a discussion of promising directions that can help to prevent and respond to crimes by girls.

In exploring promising directions, we raise questions about how and why we think about girls and crime as we do. Looking at the various ways female crime is understood and responded to can help reveal how social order is established, resisted, and changed by individuals and groups. We argue that crime is not just about illegal behaviours that threaten persons, property, or propriety. Rather, crime can be compared with "border crossings" or movements in the border zones between what is valued in a society as good and what is not valued. Border crossings by female youth invoke anxiety, harsh judgements, and sometimes official interventions, especially by those powerful adults, such as parents, police, or professionals, who decide and enforce the boundaries between what is legal and what is illegal, what is feminine and what is not, and what is productive and important and what is not valued in everyday life (Lees, 1997; Acland, 1995).

## PATTERNS OF CRIME AND TRENDS IN JUVENILE JUSTICE

Despite headlines that claim "crime rate falls again, except among teen girls" (Appleby, 1994: A1), girls, like boys, break the law sometimes, but not often. Whether we are looking at past or recent research studies, it is clear that girls in Canada and elsewhere commit serious crimes infrequently, engage sporadically in illegal behaviours, and rarely develop crime specialties (Chesney-Lind and Shelden, 1992; 1998; Biron and Gavreau, 1984; Reitsma-

Street, 1991). Since 1978, the number of murder, attempted-murder, and manslaughter charges laid in youth court against Canadian girls has been low and constant, rarely more than 10 per year, as seen in Box 3.1.

But sometimes girls do commit crimes. When girls are asked on anonymous surveys and in interviews whether they have committed illegal or antisocial acts in the last year or two, the majority report at least several acts per year, and a small minority report more frequent misbehaviours. Girls and boys admit to relatively similar rates of leaving home and school without permission, using drugs, and shoplifting, while boys report more frequent and serious behaviours that hurt people and property (Artz and Riecken, 1994; Figueira-McDonough, Barton, and Sarri, 1981; LeBlanc, 1983; Hagan and McCarthy, 1997). For example, in a 1998 study of 151 14-year-old girls and 181 boys, Artz and colleagues (1999), found nearly two-thirds of both groups reported they had "taken little things that don't belong to you" at least once in the last year, while 39.8 percent of the boys and only 10.4 percent of the girls reported they had "beaten up another kid" once in the last year.

## OFFICIAL CHARGES

An accurate summary of the crime rates by youth, or adults, of either sex is illusive. Most illegal activities are not reported, especially if minor or there

### Box 3.1

### ARE GIRLS BECOMING MORE VIOLENT?

Yes, according to headlines and some statistics.

No, according to 20 years of data on the total number of murder, attempt, and manslaughter charges by Canadian girls.

"Crime rate falls again, except among teen girls. They're committing more violent acts: Statscan."

| Year | Charges |
|---|---|
| 1978 | 10 |
| 1979 | 6 |
| 1980 | 9 |
| 1981 | 8 |
| 1982 | 5 |
| 1983 | 9 |
| ——* | |
| 1992 – 93 | 13 |
| 1993 – 94 | 9 |
| 1994 – 95 | 8 |
| 1995 – 96 | 6 |

* Charges against girls ages 7 to 16 before the YOA implemented in 1984, except up to 18 years in Quebec and Manitoba. After 1984, charges against girls ages 12 to 18 in all provinces. Data between 1984 and 1991 excluded Ontario, and hence omitted.

**Source:** Timothy Appleby, "Crime rate falls again, except among teen girls," *Globe and Mail*, 23 July 1994, pp. A1, A3; Canadian Centre for Justice Statistics, *Youth Court Statistics* [1978 through 1995 – 96] (Ottawa: Statistics Canada, various years).

is no victim. Of criminal incidents known to the police, it is estimated that less than 40 percent can be traced to an offender (Carrington, 1999). Before the YOA was introduced in 1984, and even today in some provinces, such as Quebec, police exercise significant discretion by cautioning, reprimanding, and letting go the majority of boys and girls apprehended for illegal activities, thereby avoiding court appearances and costs. By the 1990s, however, police in most provinces had reduced their use of discretion. They increased their charge rates so that nearly 60 percent of apprehended youth, male and female, are charged and brought to youth courts, even for minor crimes such as shoplifting (Carrington, 1999). As observed in Chapter 4, the proposed new Youth Criminal Justice Act (YCJA) includes provisions that will encourage, and at times oblige, police to increase their use of discretion and community alternatives, in order to decrease the charge rate and to ensure that courts are reserved for the most serious offenders.

Ultimately, official police or court statistics, published in reports, government documents, or on the Internet, are not measures of the true offending patterns of girls. Nevertheless, they are indicators of how the Canadian judicial system responds to some of the illegal behaviours of some girls. If various indicators are used, if the indicators are drawn from more than one source and from several years, and if the indicators are presented within a comparative context, then official statistics can give important clues to how Canadians react to girls and their crimes. These reactions vary by time and place, as suggested in the comments on official statistics that follow.

Based on the free Internet justice data provided by Statistics Canada, Figure 3.1 shows that only 5.2 percent of all Canadians charged in 1997 for breaking Criminal Code and related federal statutes are girls. It is not youth, but adults, especially adult men, who are much more likely to be charged for crimes, whether against persons, property, or the public order.

There are nearly equal numbers of girls as boys under the age of 18 in the Canadian population, and yet most of the charges laid in youth court are against boys. In the early 1980s, one in ten charges laid in youth courts were against girls. By the mid-1990s, the gender ratio changed to one in five. The absolute numbers of charges for both males and females increased from the 1980s in most, but not all, provinces, when the changes in upper age limits of the YOA were implemented, along with changes in police and court charging patterns (Leonard, Smandych, and Brickey, 1996; Doob and Sprott, 1996; Carrington, 1999).

Figure 3.2 does not suggest an explosion of female crime in the last five years. Whether there are increases or decreases, however, depends in part on what information is presented for what years and for which provinces. As indicated earlier in Box 3.1, the number of very serious violent crimes by girls has remained relatively constant since 1978. But some studies and data suggest an increase in the numbers and rates of violent crimes by girls (e.g., Artz, 1998; Corrado and Markwart, 1994; Doob and Sprott, 1998). One problem with the data is that the category of "violent" crime suggests horrifying acts of terror and hurt to the person. Yet very few of the "violent" crimes charged are like this. The data on violent crime can be misleading as

**Figure 3.1**

**CANADIANS CHARGED FOR CRIMINAL INCIDENTS, BY GENDER AND AGE, 1997**

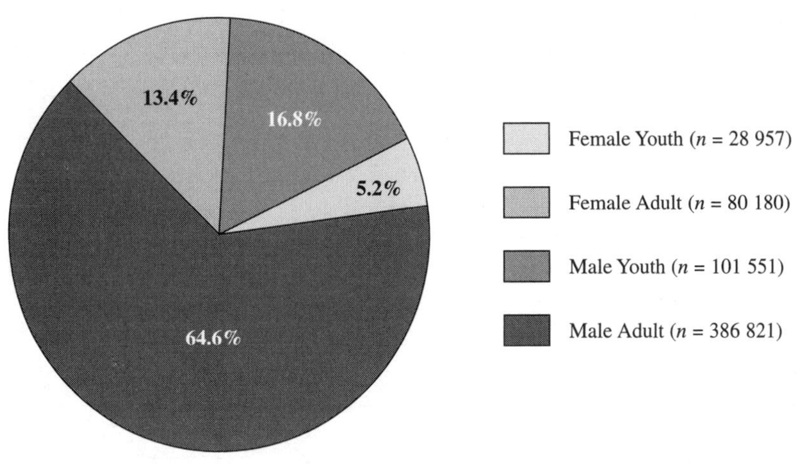


**Source:** Statistics Canada, "Youths and adults charged in criminal incidents, *Criminal Code* and federal statutes, by sex" <http://www.statcan.ca/english/Pgdb/State/Justice/legal14.htm> (19 August 1999).

they include minor **assault** charges for pushing and slaps, along with the major aggravated assaults with deadly weapons and murder. Looking at five years of data, Doob and Sprott (1998) found that there was a slight increase in the charge rates of minor "violent" crimes, and no changes in the charge rates for serious aggravated assaults or murder attempts, which remain at the annual low rate of 4 per 100 000 Canadian girls under age 18.

In contrast with the truly horrifying beating and drowning of Reena Virk, the story of Julie illustrates the more common types of "violent" behaviours of girls. Artz interviewed Julie, an aboriginal teen who went to school in a town close to Victoria, BC, in 1998. Julie spoke of racist taunts, and took action when peers and adults did not believe her: "Last year people started talking about my reserve and saying people were killing and all that stuff. And the teachers wouldn't believe me and it kept going on and on, and then I finally punched the kids." Scott (1989), Cain (1989), and Artz (1998) include many illustrations of such behaviour in their research on girls. Girls sometimes shout, shove, pull hair, and occasionally punch peers following alleged name-calling or slander. These authors put girls and their "violence" into a context of social interactions. These contexts form the basis for explanations and intervention strategies.

Returning to official statistics, Table 3.1 presents in some detail the types of crimes that girls and boys were charged with in youth courts in 1995 – 96. The information is listed in descending order of seriousness, starting with murder. Charges for theft under $5000 and possession of

**Figure 3.2**

**CHANGES IN CANADIAN YOUTHS CHARGED, BY YEAR AND GENDER, 1993 – 1997**

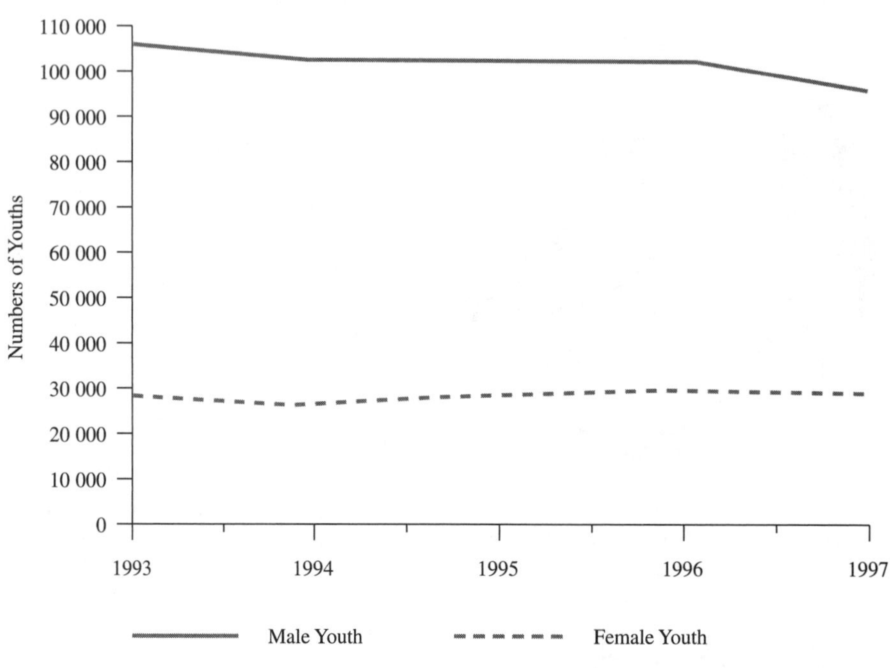


**Source:** Statistics Canada, "Youths and adults charged in criminal incidents, *Criminal Code* and federal statutes, by sex" <http://www.statcan.ca/english/Pgdb/State/Justice/legal14.htm> (19 August 1999).

stolen goods were the most common category for both sexes. Less frequent were major crimes against property, and minor crimes against the public order and people. Least frequent were major serious crimes against people.

## ADMINISTRATIVE OFFENCES

What is perhaps surprising is how often young people are charged with the kinds of **administrative offences** grouped as "failure to comply." These charges presently comprise 27.3 percent of total charges against girls. Administrative charges include mostly failure to appear in court, failure to comply with a condition of bail, or a probation order, committing an offence "against the YOA," or the infrequent escape from custody. A 1995 amendment to the YOA, section 26, gave more authority and discretion to justice officials to charge youth with failure to comply with any order issued under the YOA, possibly sparking a significant increase in charges, especially for girls. In 1985 – 86, fewer than 1000, or 5.1 percent, of total charges against girls were for failure to comply with administrative orders.

## Table 3.1

## SPECIFIC CHARGES, 1995 – 96, BY GENDER

| Principal Charge | Female n | Female % | Male n | Male % |
|---|---|---|---|---|
| **Murder Attempt** | 6 | .03 | 102 | 0.11 |
| **Robbery** | 369 | 1.69 | 2 261 | 2.53 |
| **Arson** | 53 | 0.24 | 409 | 0.46 |
| **Aggravated Assault; Assault with Weapon** | 701 | 3.20 | 3 473 | 3.90 |
| **Against Person** | 3 733 | 17.05 | 13 306 | 14.93 |
| **Theft Over/Auto** | 525 | 2.40 | 3 621 | 4.06 |
| **Break and Enter** | 1 087 | 4.96 | 12 045 | 13.51 |
| **Fraud** | 559 | 2.55 | 1 186 | 1.33 |
| **Theft Under/Possession Stolen Goods** | 6 820 | 31.15 | 20 860 | 23.40 |
| **Trafficking/Possession** | 573 | 2.62 | 4 324 | 4.85 |
| **Mischief** | 662 | 3.02 | 4 906 | 5.50 |
| **Nuisance/Disorderly** | 171 | 0.78 | 857 | 0.96 |
| **Immorality/Soliciting/Vice** | 198 | 0.09 | 84 | 0.09 |
| **Other** | 456 | 2.08 | 2 428 | 2.72 |
| **Failure to Comply** | 5 985 | 27.33 | 19 267 | 21.62 |
| **Total** | 21 898 | 100.00 | 89 129 | 100.00 |

**Source:** Canadian Centre for Justice Statistics, *Youth Court Statistics* (Ottawa: Statistics Canada, 1997), Table 3: "Charges laid in youth court against *Criminal Code* and federal statutes," pp. 7 – 12.

Since that time, there has been a rapid and sharp increase in these numbers, with the rate rising to 27.3 percent (5985) of total charges in 1995 – 96 (Reitsma-Street, 1993; in press). Rates for boys have increased during those years from 3.9 to 21.6 percent of total charges. These increases in administrative charges may help to account for the concern about total increases in both female and male youth crime.

The changes in administrative charges illustrate how difficult it is to get an accurate picture of girls and crime, and how attentive we need to be to changes in laws, regulations, and administrative practices that affect the perception of crime rates. Studies on the impact of the YOA and its 1985, 1991, and 1995 amendments (see Chapter 5) have clearly demonstrated that, although the true crime rate of youth is not known, far more girls and boys in all provinces but Quebec have been charged in youth courts since implementation of the YOA (Carrington, 1999; Doob, 1992; Reitsma-Street, 1993). More youth were drawn into the expensive juvenile justice system in the 1990s compared with the 1980s, mostly for minor, non-violent charges. Contrary to the minimal interference intent of the YOA and despite the *absence* of solid evidence for an increase in serious, violent, crime, more girls and their families were affected than expected or intended. The capacity of the youth justice system to intervene has increased with amendments that lengthened the maximum sentence from three to ten years, and with the substantial increase in judicial obligation and correctional discretion to use longer sentences, adult courts, and secure custody for serious offences. Most worrisome is that it appears that more girls (and boys) in the 1990s are sentenced to custody for failure-to-comply offences than for either minor or major violent or property offences (Conway, 1992; Doob, 1992; Gagnon and Doherty, 1993). Before another new law is passed, therefore, far more attention needs to be paid to the reasons why administrative non-compliance charges have increased so rapidly, and with such an impact. As the proposed new law requires that custody sentences are to be followed by conditional supervision, with the further proviso that a return to custody is possible if the conditions are not complied with, it is essential to attend to the unintended and costly impact of these regulatory changes, such as increases in charge rates, custody rates, and financial costs.

## COURT DECISIONS AND DISPOSITIONS FOR CONVICTED GIRLS

Not all girls charged in youth court are convicted and sentenced. In 1995 – 96 youth court, 60.4 percent of charged girls were found guilty and sentenced; of the rest, very few were transferred to adult court or found not guilty, while 39 percent had their charges dismissed or withdrawn. The remaining girls had their charges stayed. Only four girls in 1995 – 96 (0.02 percent of total charged) were transferred to adult court (Canadian Centre for Justice Statistics, 1997). The types of dispositions that girls received who were found guilty of crimes in 1995 – 96 are presented in Table 3.2.

The most common disposition for girls, like boys, is probation (see Chapter 1). One experience of probation is illustrated in Box 3.2. The length of custodial dispositions decreased from the 1980s to the early 1990s, but is

**Table 3.2**

**PERCENTAGE DISTRIBUTION OF DISPOSITIONS OF YOUTH FOUND GUILTY, BY GENDER, 1995 – 1996**

| Most Significant Disposition | Female (n = 13 229) | Male (n = 59 716) |
|---|---|---|
| **Secure Custody** | 8.9 | 16.2 |
| **Open Custody** | 14.5 | 19.3 |
| **Probation** | 55.8 | 47.6 |
| **Fine or Restitution** | 5.4 | 6.4 |
| **Community Service Order** | 9.1 | 6.4 |
| **Minimal Sanction** | 6.3 | 4.1 |
| **Total** | 100.0 | 100.0 |

**Source:** Canadian Centre for Justice Statistics, "Minimal sanction includes absolute discharge, apologies, essays, and counselling programs," *Youth Court Statistics* Catalogue No. 85-522 (Ottawa: Statistics Canada, 1997), p. 14.

now beginning to lengthen as maximum sentences stipulated in the YOA amendments have increased. The use of **fines** and minimal sanctions such as suspended sentence or absolute discharge has also decreased. Community service orders on their own are infrequent; but, as indicated in Chapter 4, they may be added to a **probation** order, with the unintended consequence, perhaps, of increasing the chance for youth to not comply, be charged with non-compliance, and be brought back to court as a recidivist. Contrary to what the YOA may have intended, however, custody rates for girls and boys have gone up, not down, since 1984 in all provinces except in Quebec. Before the YOA, **custody** included secure facilities and child welfare placements for girls. Rates ranged from a low of 7.8 percent of all dispositions to 17.4 percent between 1960 and 1984. By 1992 – 93, 18.9 percent of convicted girls were sentenced to either open or closed custody settings, increasing to 23.4 percent in 1995 – 96 (Reitsma-Street, 1991; in press).

Scholars and practitioners are wondering why there seems to be an increase in the use of custody. They are also asking what will the impact of the proposed new YCJA be on custody rates for girls (and boys), as there will be more offences for which the police and courts must apply for a transfer to adult court. Adult sentences for these "presumptive offences," such as attempted murder, or for habitual serious offenders will now also be considered for younger children, beginning at age 14, whereas the current age is 16 in Canada and in almost all European countries (see Winterdyk, 1997). If youth in general are being more harshly punished for more crimes, and girls in particular are affected by the sharp rise in admin-

### Box 3.2

### BEING ON PROBATION

I'm on probation right now and that was for breaking and entering. It's just did we have the guts to do it. Me and my friend, we're just a bad example for each other. And so we went into this house. Both of us. It's fun, so.

I've just been like this most of my life. My mom's just really yelling and screaming and stuff. I don't know. I used to get in trouble and they would ground me and stuff, and then they just stopped grounding me and I guess they just gave up.

And then I did this thing because I'm on probation right now. They're watching me way more closely. Once I show some responsibility, I'll be able to go over to my friend's house.

On probation, I'm not allowed to go to certain places and there's a time that I have to be home. I have to be good in school and everywhere, and I can't do anything wrong, like smoke or anything, for three months. If I do, like I got mug shots and fingerprinted, and if I do anything wrong they'll take me to court and those files will be on my record until I'm dead. It makes it really hard to get a good job, like with the government.

But if I'm good for three months, they'll rip them up and I won't have to go to court. If I'm bad then I'll have to do a hundred community hours. I really don't want to do community hours, it's just like raking leaves in the park and working at the women's shelter.

**Source:** Interview by Sybille Artz, 1998.

istrative charges, how, then, is girls' involvement in crime explained? An overview of theories of female crime follows.

## THEORIES OF FEMALE CRIME AND DELINQUENCY

Before the 1970s, few mainstream sociological theories concerned themselves with female crime and delinquency. Content with the assumption that crime and delinquency were masculine forms of behaviour, and bolstered in that assumption by statistical evidence of the overwhelming participation of males in such behaviour, the majority of theorists, who were themselves male, focussed on males. Those who did concern themselves with female participation in crime and delinquency still grounded most of their thinking in male experience, and in the notion that if females were delinquent, it was because they were likely sexually deviant and pathological. As well, when females were considered, the focus was generally on the **gender gap** and the proportionally low participation of females, rather than on either the conditions or the motivations that move females toward crime and delinquency (Artz, 1998; Chesney-Lind and Shelden, 1998; Tanner, 1996).

Three categories of theory emerged from the early literature: (1) those that explain the gender gap in crime and delinquency as given in the biological differences between the sexes and explain female deviance in terms of biologically based sexual problems; (2) those that explain the gender gap in crime and delinquency as derived from differences in gender-role socialization and explain the kinds of deviance females do participate in as based on their gender roles and changes in these roles; and (3) those focussing on increased female deviance relative to males and explain this rise in terms of a **masculinization** of women brought on by women's liberation and the feminist movement. All three categories of theory explain female crime and delinquency as a move away from the feminine toward the masculine. It was not until the mid-1980s and afterward that theorists called for a shift away from theories of delinquency that are uncritically grounded in male behaviour (Campbell, 1991; Chesney-Lind and Koroki, 1985; Morris, 1987; Reitsma-Street, 1991).

### BIOLOGICALLY BASED THEORIES OF FEMALE CRIME AND DELINQUENCY

Early theories of female crime, like early theories of male crime, were strongly affected by social Darwinism. Biology was destiny, and criminal behaviour was seen as the result of problems with evolution. Cesare Lombroso, working in 1895, explained all criminal elements in society as biological throwbacks resulting from an arrested evolutionary process. Lombroso believed that, because females were less evolved and less intelligent than males, and primarily destined to bear and care for children, they were not able to participate in challenging and independent activities like crime. Lombroso reasoned that, if females did become criminals, it was largely because they were degenerate, unwomanly, masculine throwbacks without maternal instinct.

The belief that biology is destiny, along with the notion that men and women had natural roles and true natures, outlived Lombroso, although his work has by now been, for the most part, discredited. Otto Pollack, working in the 1950s, and Cowie, Cowie, and Slater, working in the 1960s, wrote extensively about imbalances in physiology and sexuality as causative of female crime. For Pollack (1950) the explanation for the consistently low rates of female crime in relation to higher rates for males lay in the fact that he saw females as naturally more deceitful and concealing, and therefore able to get away with far more deviance than men can. He located this skill in deceit in female's sexual passivity and their ability to conceal or manufacture sexual arousal, something that males cannot do. Furthermore, Pollack suggested the various hormonal imbalances brought about by menstruation, menopause, and pregnancy predispose females toward criminality and, at the same time, provide them with the means to escape detection and responsibility for their actions.

For Cowie, Cowie, and Slater (1968), differences in male and female delinquency were largely explained by anatomy. In particular, two primary forces accounted for male/female differences in deviance: (1) biological, somatic, and hormonal differences derived from chromosomal differences between the two sexes; and (2) the natural timidity and lack of enterprise found in females. If females did get involved in criminal activity, Cowie and colleagues attributed this to an excess of male chromosomes.

The notion that biological factors exert a strong influence persists among some criminologists to the present day. Slade (1984), and Binder, Geis, and Bruce (1988) proposed pre-menstrual syndrome (PMS) as a cause for female criminality, although little evidence was brought to bear in support of this claim. Wilson and Herrnstein (1985) stated the case for the belief that biological factors are determinant of levels of aggression and differentials in male and female lawbreaking. Gisela Konopka (1983) broke new ground by being one of the first to go directly to adolescent females in order to formulate an understanding of their life-worlds. She broke further new ground by emphasizing the effects of psychosocial problems on identity formation, the changing cultural position of women, and the sexual double standard on female crime delinquency. Nonetheless, Konopka still assumed that, in the final analysis, girls and women were largely controlled by biology and sexuality. As Chesney-Lind and Shelden (1992) point out, Konopka, in noting that most girls come to the attention of the juvenile justice system because of sex-related behaviours, was convinced that "most female delinquency is either 'sexual' or 'relational' rather than 'criminal' in nature" (p. 61), and therefore requires help with sexual adjustment.

## GENDER-ROLE THEORIES OF FEMALE CRIME AND DELINQUENCY

In contrast to and in protest against biologically based theories of crime, **gender-role theories** of delinquency and crime emerged in the 1950s

(Grosser, 1951) and have grown in strength and number to the present day (Balkan and Berger, 1979; Hagan, Gillis and Simpson, 1985; Hoffman-Bustamente, 1973; R. Morris, 1965). Given that males are socialized to be more active, aggressive, and independent, and are rewarded for flouting conventional behaviour, while females are socialized to be more passive, caring, and dependent, and are rewarded for engaging in conventional behaviour (Berger, 1989; Gilligan, 1982; Hoffman-Bustamente, 1973), it is reasoned by gender-role theorists that the male/female differences in aggression and crime can be accounted for by differences in socialization.

The power of gender-role theories lies in the fact that an examination of delinquency and crime shows clear distinctions with regard to the kinds of crimes in which males and females engage. Berger (1989: 378) notes that "male juveniles have been consistently more likely than females to be arrested for every crime category (except running away and prostitution)." Chesney-Lind and Shelden (1998) tell a similar story using self-report data gathered in the United States by Cernkovich and Giordano (1979). Comparable data were reported by Figueira-McDonough, Barton, and Sarri (1981), who found significant gender differences in theft, vandalism, fraud, serious fighting, carrying weapons, and prostitution, with males reporting their involvement at ratios of between 3:1 and 6:1 over females. As Reitsma-Street (1991: 225) states,

> the overwhelming majority of girls conform to the law most of the time. This statement remains true even if a girl is officially charged for primarily non-violent property crimes. It still remains true when girls reveal [through self-report surveys] their frequent participation in delinquencies, especially those associated with adolescence such as truancy or use of drugs. For those few girls who report more than the average delinquencies or who are officially caught, continued participation is not likely.

Gender-role theorists often explain this difference in male and female participation as an outcome of the imposing of higher moral expectations and greater social controls on girls and women. As Berger (1989: 377) points out,

> family arrangements have kept females, in comparison to males, more cloistered, and females have been expected to provide support and nurturance to others ... As a result, girls have been more closely supervised by their parents than boys and have had less opportunity than boys to commit delinquent acts. They have been more likely to accept general moral standards, blame themselves for their problems, feel shame for their misconduct, taught to avoid risks, fear social disapproval and be deterred by legal sanctions.

Two mainstream approaches to crime and delinquency that fit with a gender-role analysis are differential association or learning theories, and social-control theories (also see Chapter 1). Noting that young offenders appear to gather in groups and **gangs**, and noting also that those who engage in crime appear to have more interaction with others who engage in crime than those who do not, Sutherland (1939), among others, argued that deviant behaviour, like other human behaviour, is learned. Thus, close association with others engaging in such behaviour provides learning opportunities in which the techniques, motives, and values that facilitate criminal behaviour are transmitted. According to Flowers (1990: 130), differential association theory suggests that "the probability of delinquent behaviour varies directly with the priority, frequency, duration, and intensity of a person's contacts with patterns of delinquent behaviour, and inversely with their non-deviant contacts ..."

Sutherland and his associates, while not confining themselves to a study of the lower classes in that they included white-collar crime and professional theft in their work, did, however, focus only on males. Despite this, differential association (or learning) theory holds some promise with regard to females, given the indications in more recent research that females who have frequent contact with deviant females appear to engage in deviant behaviour to a greater degree than those who do not. As was pointed out by Giordano, Cernkovich, and Pugh (1986: 1194), among others, females who become involved in deviance and delinquency, while still participating at lower rates than males, nevertheless "both adopt a set of attitudes in which they [see] delinquency as appropriate, possible, or desirable ... and a friendship style in which they ... encourage each other as a group to act on these orientations."

Social-control theories of crime and delinquency focus on the capacity of all human beings to engage in deviance and crimes, although most researchers who conceptualized them still select males as research subjects. For social-control theorists, crime and delinquency have less to do with motivation to deviate from the norm and more to do with the presence or absence of conditions favourable to breaking the law. Social-control theorists explore personal control or inner containment of deviant urges grounded in a positive self-concept, effective family and other external social controls of deviance grounded in a positive social structure, and the absence or presence of a social bond (see Reckless, 1961, and Nye, 1958, for a general review). Both Chesney-Lind and Shelden (1998) and Flowers (1990) select Hirschi as offering the most influential of the social-control theories. His hypothesis that individuals with strong bonds to social institutions like family and school are more likely to have lower rates of crime and delinquency has been, in part, borne out not only by Hirschi's own research, but also by that of others (see Chapter 1 for further details).

Hirschi's notions that social bonds, and the social controls exerted by these bonds, have a direct effect on the level of an individual's participation in delinquency and crime generated further research, including research on females. Jensen and Eve (1976), and others, have found that attachment to conventional others and a belief in the legitimacy of rules had predictive power for both male and female delinquency. Cernkovich and Giordano (1987), for example, also found that lower rates of female delinquency could be explained, in part, by higher levels of parental supervision and intimate communication between parents and daughters.

Hagan, Simpson, and Gillis (1987) and Hagan (1990) took up social-control theory and argued that social control or constraint varies across gender, with females experiencing more social control, especially in more traditional, patriarchal families. Hagan et al. (1987: 791) define the "ideal-type patriarchal family" as including "a husband who is employed in an authority position and a wife who is not employed outside the home." They define the "ideal-type egalitarian family" as including a mother and father who are both employed in authority positions outside the home (p. 792). They also define single-parent households headed by women as "a special kind of egalitarian family" that, like other egalitarian households, experiences "freedom from male domination" (p. 793).

It is their contention that, whenever males are dominant, as they most often are in the ideal-type patriarchal household, mothers are charged with the task of child rearing as a result of a division of labour along gender lines. This leaves fathers in control of production, that is, participation in the work force, and mothers in control of consumption and domestic labour and the "day-to-day control of their children, especially their daughters" (p. 792). According to Hagan et al., such families reproduce the gender divisions they model, and enforce and allow much less risk-taking behaviour in their daughters. As a result, these families produce lower deviance and delinquency rates for females than for males, while the ideal-type egalitarian families, which allow more risk taking in their female members, produce higher delinquency rates for females, rates that tend to move toward a closing of the gender gap. Therefore, according to Hagan et al., the more traditional the family, the lower the female delinquency rate.

Their argument rests upon two points: one suggesting that mothers working outside the home, especially in positions of authority, constitute a move away from patriarchy toward a more egalitarian system, and the second suggesting that such a move toward egalitarianism is linked with higher delinquency rates in girls. Therefore, for Hagen et al., the greater the control of men over women and girls in families, the lower the risk for female adolescent deviance. When this is not the case, and adult women in families take up more equal power with males, or find themselves in the position of being single heads of households, girls in these families become more like boys, and as a consequence also take more risks, including deviant risks.

In effect, Hagan and his associates appear to be suggesting that working mothers are contributing to higher delinquency in their daughters. However, Chesney-Lind and Shelden (1992: 96 – 97), among others, do not agree with Hagan's conclusions. There is no evidence to suggest that as

> women's labour force participation has increased, girl's delinquency has increased. Indeed, during the past decade, when women's labour force participation and the number of female-headed household soared, aggregate female delinquency measured both by self-report and official statistics either declined or remained stable.

Therefore, while Hagan and his associates may be correct in pointing out that gender and patriarchy are important with regard to the shaping of both male and female behaviour, their assumption that mothers working outside the home leads to increases in female delinquency does not appear to hold. This theory, like others that will be discussed below, is an example of the kinds of backlash theories that, in effect, suggest to women that it may be better to stay with traditional role configurations because, in the end, liberation, interpreted as a move toward the masculine, carries with it a price that may not be worth paying.

Given the consistency of the gender gap in both official crime rates and self-report data, especially for more serious crimes, an understanding of socialization patterns and gender expectations may indeed contribute to an understanding of male/female differences, but it does not explain either the motivations for females taking up crime and delinquency or the engagement of females in the so-called male crimes and delinquencies. Therefore, a reliance on socialization patterns and gender expectations "fails to explore motivation and intent as an integral part of female crime ... [W]hile significant in its contribution ... role theory still provides only a limited perspective on female crime and behaviour" (Chesney-Lind and Koroki, 1985: 7). Furthermore, while bringing into focus the need to understand the differences in social experiences and their effect on behaviour for males and females, gender-role theories also provide a basis for the feminist-backlash notion that a change in women's roles and the emancipation of women will ultimately lead to a greater participation of women in criminal activity.

## "MASCULINIZATION" THEORIES OF FEMALE CRIME AND DELINQUENCY

Freda Adler (1975) is generally credited with promoting the belief that a convergence of gender-role expectations brought about by feminism and the women's movement in the late 1960s and 1970s has contributed significantly to a rise in female crime. Adler claimed that "the phenomenon of female criminality is but one wave in ... [the] rising tide of female assertiveness—a wave which has not yet crested and may even be seeking its level uncomfortably close to the high-water mark set by male violence" (cited in Berger, 1989: 379). Basing her claims on largely unfounded notions that traditional attitudes toward women were rapidly changing and that women were indeed making substantial gains in all areas of the corporate world (Anderson, 1991), Adler contended that

> in the same way that women are demanding equal opportunity in the fields of legitimate endeavour, a similar number of determined women are forcing their way into the world of major crimes ... as the position of women approximates the position of men, so does the frequency and type of their criminal activity. (cited in Chesney-Lind and Koroki, 1985: 9)

Adler's claims supported those of Simon (1975), who noted a rise in women's arrest rates for white-collar crimes, such as embezzlement and fraud, and attributed this to women's greater participation in the work force.

Adler's claims created an ongoing debate because they appeared to be supported by official arrest statistics for the period between 1960 and 1975, which showed dramatic increases in female crime, especially in non-traditional offences for females. The primary objection to her thesis came from scholars who disputed her analysis of official crime statistics. Specifically they argued that, while percentage increases in non-traditional crimes for females including murder, aggravated assault, and robbery showed dramatic leaps, these increases were based on very small absolute numbers, where even a small change in number could create a large change in percentage (Chesney-Lind and Shelden, 1998).

Most increases in female crime were found in non-violent offences. Simon (1975) found the greatest increases in offences such as larceny, fraud, and cheque forgery, and argued that this was the direct result of the feminization of poverty brought on by the rise of single-family households headed by females. This finding was confirmed by Steffensmeir (1978) and Steffensmeir and Cobb (1981), who found major increases in female crime largely in shoplifting and cheque-forgery crimes that are consistent with traditional gender roles for women. And while they and others concurred that female violence for adults and juveniles had risen between 1960 and 1977, Steffensmeir and associates found that male violence had also increased at an equal rate, thus leaving the gender gap firmly in place. Steffensmeir's work itself sparked a further debate centring around interpretation of data and methods for calculating comparative changes in crime participation rates (see Berger, 1989).

This debate continues to the present. In the 1990s it does appear that both males and females are participating somewhat more in all forms of crime and delinquency than they were a decade ago (Carrington, 1999). Although Adler, Simon, and others hold the emancipation of women responsible for an apparent narrowing of the gender gap in crime rates, a number of researchers have found evidence to the contrary. For example, James and Thornton (1980) found that attitudes toward feminism had little to do with the extent and kind of female participation in delinquent behaviour. Cernkovich and Giordano (1979) found that positive attitudes toward feminism were not related to participation in delinquency, and that such positive attitudes may indeed inhibit delinquent behaviour, while more traditional attitudes toward the role of women were associated with increased delinquency. As Chesney-Lind and Shelden (1998: 77 – 78) point out,

> serious research efforts to locate the dark side of the women's movement have almost without exception been unsuccessful. Careful analysis of existing data fail to support the notion that girls have been committing nontraditional (i.e., "masculine") crimes. It seems peculiar ... that so many academics would be willing to consider a hypothesis that assumed improving girls' and women's economic conditions would lead to an increase in female crime when almost all the existing criminological literature stresses the role played by discrimination and poverty (and unemployment and underemployment) in the creation of crime.

Despite this, the notion that feminism is responsible for a rise in female delinquency and crime persists, especially in the popular press. Celeste McGovern (1995: 28) wrote in a weekly news magazine that, "prodded by feminism, today's teenage girls embrace antisocial behaviour." She suggested that most of the ills experienced by adolescent girls can be accounted for by "new masculinized attitudes [which] permeate girls' attitudes," and lamented that, because of feminism, "the rate of cultural degeneration seems to be accelerating."

Masculinization theories of female crime and delinquency have been shown to be inadequate, but this "persistent theme ... that masculinity, of one sort or another, is at the core of [female] delinquency" (Chesney-Lind and Shelden, 1998) nevertheless appears to be central to all sociological theories of crime. In every case, female experience is measured *against* that of males, and theories about female delinquency are constructed out of already-existing theories premised upon male experience. Reitsma-Street (1991: 272) offers the following summary statement:

> This pattern of seeing females as similar to, equal to, different from, less than, better than, the standard of male behaviours, thoughts, and theories is pervasive in all our sciences, laws and practices ... [To] contribute new ideas that may eventually transform existing practices with *both* males and females, I believe we need to consciously avoid filling our minds with the old tenacious comparisons.

## PROMISING DIRECTIONS

If we do not compare girls to boys, and if we do not adapt male-derived theories and interventions to females, where do we go? This section explores two possible directions. One is to develop theories and interventions that go beyond a limited focus on individual girls and their offending behaviours to include the context of their complex realities. The second direction is to look behind the scenes of these complex realities, and to ask who is creating the context in which girls live and commit crimes, and what are the benefits of creating certain ways of explaining, policing, helping, and preventing what crimes in which girls.

### CRITIQUE OF YOUTH-JUSTICE INTERVENTIONS FOCUSSED ON THE INDIVIDUAL GIRL

Too often judicial and correctional interventions for girls ignore the context, needs, aspirations, culture, families, victims, and associates of girls who have committed crimes. Interventions concentrate legal, professional, and financial attention on establishing individual guilt and on punishing specific deviant behaviour, and, in girl offenders, on treating their unfeminine behaviours (Royal Commission on Aboriginal Peoples, 1993; Adler and Baines, 1996; Lees, 1997). Exceptions to these trends include, for example, the Children's Hearings in Scotland that are premised on holistic and welfare assumptions, but, even here, after 25 years of experience, the participation of girls, their families, and friends are limited to answering questions from the professionals, while creative and effective interventions are restricted by resources (Hallett and Murray, 1998). When theoretical explanations for crimes, such as biological destiny, differential association, or social control, are incorporated into laws, regulations, and policies without attention to gender, the subsequent practices can be inappropriate, ineffective, and sometimes hurtful. Moreover, the "one size fits all" approach misses the complex varied situations in which girls live (Ackland, 1982; Sarri, 1976; Reitsma-Street, 1998).

The discriminatory justice practices of recent history, during which girls had been treated sometimes more benignly, sometimes more harshly than boys—even when severity of the offence and delinquency record were controlled—are no longer so obvious in Canada or elsewhere (Geller, 1987; De Como, 1998; Kowalski and Caputo, 1999; Parent, 1986). For example, under the Young Offenders Act, age differences by gender and provinces were eliminated as were status offences. Now girls and boys up to the age of 18 in all provinces and territories can be charged only with crimes against the Criminal Code and related federal statutes. Both sexes have equal rights to lawyers, open trials, and reviews of custodial sentences. In the proposed new Youth Criminal Justice Act (see Appendix C and Chapter 4), girls are acknowledged explicitly for the first time in the occasional use of the feminine pronoun (e.g., section 3 (1) (a) (ii)). Both girls and boys are eligible for the extrajudicial sanctions, if it is a first offence and if they are charged with a non-violent crime. Both also have equal "access" to long adult sentences if 14 years and older and convicted of a serious, violent crime (see section 61).

Reducing discrimination and increasing formal equality, however, can be illusory, even regressive. It appears that greater equality can mean both girls and boys become equally vulnerable to the increase in charges, convictions, and custody sentences in all provinces but Quebec, and both share equally in the loss of supportive interventions. Neither the YOA nor its amendments mandate attention or funding to understanding the context in which youth live or special circumstances, unless custody sentences are being considered. Mandatory funding has not increased support to female offenders (or males), their families, or those they have hurt.

Furthermore, discrimination may be creeping back into justice practices in new ways. As mentioned previously, amendments to the YOA have added to the discretionary powers of authorities to increase the use, level, and length of custody, and to lay more types of charges of non-compliance with administrative orders (see Chapter 5). These administrative "status-like" charges may be introducing another type of discrimination against girls. Over one-quarter of charges laid in youth court in 1996 against girls are for these "status-like" administrative charges. Section 56 of the proposed new act also includes similar offences, such as "contraventions of an order" and section 101, "breach of conditions" of custody. The new act proposes, however, that the youth-justice court must consider some of the context before laying non-compliance charges, including taking no further action or changing the conditions of the original sentence because of changes in the circumstances of the youth, the nature of the contravention, and the time served. Given the frequency and potentially discriminatory, harsh implications of convictions for administrative contraventions, including custody dispositions and the recidivist label, it is imperative that we attend closely to how authorities use non-compliance charges and how police and courts interpret the "circumstances of the youth."

## DIFFERENTIAL INTERVENTION

One promising direction to help attend to the circumstances of the young females who offend, and to prevent delinquency, is **differential intervention**. This draws, in part, on the older interactionist theories of Kurt Lewin, Jean Piaget, and Erik Erickson, in which behaviours, like crimes, are conceptualized as a function of the interaction between the personality and environment within an established social order that needs to be maintained. Differential intervention also draws from the newer conflict and feminist theories of Connell (1987), Lees (1997), and McRobbie (1991), who argue that acts, like crimes, are not just a function of interactions within an established order, but are part of active struggles within a changing social order in which privileges are unequally distributed and frequently contested. Thus, girls, their families, and judicial officials are not just struggling to become more functional. Rather, they are struggling to make sense of their lives and to take actions within a particular cultural, familial, geographic, economic, and historic place that is constrained by sets of acceptable ideas about what is a "good girl," "justice," and a "productive citizen," and the unequal distribution of resources to income, education, job opportunities, access to birth control, and child care.

Differential intervention directs policy-makers and practitioners to give equal attention to three aspects: (a) variations in the cognitive, emotional, and social capacities of youth; (b) variations in the resources, helpfulness, expectations, and messages of the familial, peer, educational, neighbourhood, and societal environments; and (c) interactions and struggles of girls (and boys) within the constraints and supports of their environments by which behaviours are reinforced or punished, and meanings and identities developed.

Differential intervention is most developed in the arena of correctional treatment for girls charged with and convicted of crimes. There is some research suggesting that sustained quality education, apprenticeship, and housing programs to reduce resource constraints of convicted girls are more effective in reducing recidivism and in increasing their health and income than are the general and short-term counselling for primarily emotional, cognitive, or family problems (Adler and Baines, 1996; Chesney-Lind and Shelden, 1998). Sophisticated differential-treatment systems, such as the Conceptual Level Matching Model and the Juvenile Interpersonal Maturity Level System, in which the female offenders, the correctional environments, and sometimes even the correctional or treatment staff, are differentiated into groups on dimensions such as complexity, maturity, structure, organization, emotional expressiveness, and autonomy have been designed and tested with youth. With such an approach, matches are hypothesized and mismatches are avoided to maximize treatment effectiveness. Thus far, results have been promising, but despite the cautious optimism of quasi-experimental and longitudinal research on the positive impact of differential treatment on recidivism (e.g., Reitsma-Street and Leschied, 1988; Stoppard and Henri, 1987), convicted girls, especially those of colour, remain vulnerable to poverty, ill health, lone parenting, substance misuse, and all types of abuse (Cain, 1989; Comack, 1996). Moreover, often missing are the political will and societal attention needed to sustain the high-quality, long-term, supportive combinations of programs for those convicted girls who suffer from serious mental illnesses, violence and violent behaviours, and dual substance dependencies (Artz, 1998; Palmer, 1995).

Differential intervention does not have to focus only on individual girls and their acts. Interventions can be directed to address the differential offending patterns associated with different times of the day or month, the different spaces and environments in neighbourhoods, schools, and families, and the different stages in the lives of youth and their peer groups. For example, Thurman and colleagues (1996) showed that providing youth at risk with attractive and safe alternative activities in their neighbourhoods, and, at times, particularly late at night, when they would normally be on the streets, helped to reduce crime considerably. As well, longitudinal studies of sustained family support and head start – type programs for children and families in poor neighbourhoods indicate delinquency rates are lower than in comparable neighbourhoods without these programs (Smith and Stern, 1997; Campbell, Muncer, and Bibel, 1998; Schwartz and Au Claire, 1995). Furthermore, Rutter (1980), in a study of eleven London schools, found that girls and boys with lower achievements and higher propensity for behaviour problems in Grade 9 did better on academic, social, and behaviour measures over four years in "good high schools," that is, schools with strong scholastic expectations, high relationship support, and cohesive, democratic governance structures, than did better students in schools with less positive environments. Overall, economic-social programs directed to disadvantaged communities decrease delinquencies; increase school attendance; and increase self-help, recreational, and social activities, especially for boys (Reitsma-Street, 1991).

## MOVING BEHIND OUR REACTIONS TO GIRLS AND CRIME

Differential intervention is a promising approach in that it invites the application of policies and practices premised on interactions between all participants in complex situations. The focus is not only on the girl and her accountability, but the accountability of all the participants in a situation before, during, and after crimes are committed. Research evidence that speaks to differential intervention is encouraging in that recidivism is reduced and life quality enhanced, provided the combinations of differential intervention programs are actually implemented and sustained. We must, however, note that differential intervention is not prevention. Nor are policies and practices premised on differential intervention necessarily focussed on issues of gender. It is conceivable that policy-makers and practitioners, in working with the principles of differential intervention, could resort to an "add girls and stir" approach without first paying serious attention to the dynamics that exist in a gendered world, and to such grave issues as, for example, females' vulnerability to poverty and the lack of recognition for the amount of unpaid familial and household work done mostly by women (Reitsma-Street and Offord, 1991; Reitsma-Street, 1998), and gender oppression and the objectification of girls and women (Artz, 1998; Campbell, Muncer, and Bibel, 1998). As an example of some early gendered prevention work, Box 3.3 speaks to research indicating that girls and boys respond very differently to violence-prevention programming. Girls accept the values and principles of prevention more readily and are more willing to change their behaviours than are boys.

Furthermore, differential intervention is problematic because it keeps the spotlight only on girls and their behaviours. Although the approach is directed toward the multifaceted interplay of the factors that contribute to

**Box 3.3**

**VIOLENCE PREVENTION PROGRAMS**

In a longitudinal study of a variety of violence-prevention programs involving more than 5000 students in a Vancouver Island school district, girls of all ages were found to be more receptive to violence-prevention programming, more willing to change their attitudes about violence, more proactive against violence, and more committed to behaviour change. Girls responded more positively than boys to peer helping/peer mediation, bully proofing, violence-awareness programming, and invitations to participate as youth leaders against violence.

Between 1993 and 1998, girls' self-reported rate of participation in physical fights dropped by 50 percent, while boys' self-reported rate of participation dropped by 22 percent. Girls also reported that they were significantly less involved in watching and encouraging fights, and significantly more willing to walk away from the possibility of a fight. Further, girls were more willing to accept that bullying victims should be reported to adult authority figures. Even girls who reported that they had themselves engaged in violence reported higher levels of social concern and endorsed interpersonal social values such as politeness, generosity, forgiveness, concern, and respect for others *at the same levels as non-violent girls* and *at significantly higher levels than all boys.*

**Source:** S. Artz and T. Riecken, "The survey of student life," in "A study of violence among adolescent female students in a suburban school district," unpublished report (Victoria, BC: British Columbia Ministry of Education, Education Research Unit, 1994); Sybille Artz, *Sex, Power and the Violent School Girl* (Toronto: Trifolium Books, 1998); S. Artz et al., "A community-based violence prevention project, seventh quarterly report," unpublished report (Vancouver, BC: British Columbia Health Research Foundation, 1999).

girls' crime, what needs more scrutiny are the behaviours and privileges of those behind the spotlights: those who construct the play in which the girls participate and commit crimes, and the people who gain from constructing and watching the spectacle of female crime.

We argue that crime and our responses to it need to be studied as a political project that can reveal how social order is established, by whom and how; and how it is resisted, by whom and how. For decades, there have been fears about youth and the increase in crime and violence. Law and order are often featured in debates on youth violence, popular culture, and political campaigns for elections. The crimes of youth do not just threaten people, property, or public order. They also threaten the apparent "natural order of things." This is especially true of crimes by girls, whose gender scripts do not include a "time to sow oats" or "to walk on the wild side." Girls stealing, breaking into homes, and hitting others scare us, even though the potential hurt and harm of these crimes is many times less than what can and does occur in automobile accidents, on worksites, or as a result of violence by adult family members. But girls acting is disconcerting, whether they are swearing, getting jobs, taking charge of birth control, calling boys, committing fraud, or punching. These types of activities, especially when committed in public and in our face, are challenges to the borders of what adults traditionally value as feminine, productive, or valuable. There is concern that girls are threatening the traditional nuclear family, and will not marry, will bear children outside of marriage, will take non-traditional jobs away from men, and will be less available to do parenting at home and housework or cooking (Lees, 1997: 36; Acland, 1995: 143).

Waves of public concern over youth crime and the violence of girls increase when there are economic downturns. When the future is uncertain, when markets expect people to take any job, and when family income is steadily eroding along with public service, we may well worry about who will perform the many relationship-building and daily tasks that keep families cohesive and communities healthy. If girls are not interested or less interested in this work, what will happen? What will happen if young females are less willing to do the placating, peacemaking, and little jobs that keep the lid on explosive, unhappy situations in peer groups, inside families, and in schools? If girls go on "strike" or "work to rule," there is a grave concern that there will be less social cement to keep youth focussed on preparing for the future, consuming goods, and helping out adults.

## SUMMARY

We have examined girls' patterns of crime and trends in juvenile justice and found that, although girls are involved in all manner of antisocial, deviant, and criminal behaviour, girls in Canada and elsewhere are far less likely than boys to commit serious crimes. We have noted, along with all other theorists, that young females' involvement in illegal behaviour is sporadic, and they rarely develop crime specialties. We have seen, in some ways, that this lack of involvement in crime has led to an approach to theorizing about female crime and delinquency that, until the 1970s, largely overlooked girls' experiences and simply attempted to explain girls' criminal behaviour as an aberration of femininity. With the rise of feminism in academia and a concomitant groundswell in gender studies, more attention is being paid to the need for differential explanations of deviance, delinquency, and crime, but, as yet, little that takes us away from an "add girls and stir" approach has been proposed. We note that we are still largely caught up in comparing girls to boys and in attempting to adapt male-derived theories to females.

Some promising work does exist. Theorists like Artz (1998), Chesney-Lind and Shelden (1998), and Reitsma-Street (1998), among others, remind us that crime is not just a function of interactions within an established order, but are part of active struggles within a changing social order in which power and privilege are unequally distributed and frequently contested. These theorists suggest that, if we want to make sense of girls' crime, we must first understand girls' lives, and the particular cultural, familial, geographic, economic, and historical conditions that prevail when girls become involved in crime. And we must certainly pay attention to law, its interpretation, and its application if we are to make sense of official crime statistics.

We suggest that the differential-intervention approach may be helpful in drawing together promising theory, in attending to the circumstances of girls who offend, and in preventing delinquency, although, where prevention is concerned, differential intervention needs further development. We have also suggested that girls' crime and our responses to it must be studied as a political project that reveals how social order is established, by whom and how, and who gains and loses from the process. In order to develop a fully delineated theory of girls' crime, we must resist applying the pervasive male standard to female behaviour and examine our expectations of girls, our fears and values in relation to them, our approach to constructing knowledge about them, and, most of all, we must be willing to include girls' voices in learning more about girls' crime.

## WEB LINKS

**Canadian Association of Elizabeth Fry Societies**
<http://www.elizabethfry.ca/caefs_e.htm>

The Elizabeth Fry Society of Canada is still the only organization dedicated to women and girls in conflict with the law. It has both a national location and provincial branches, so students can locate the one closest to them through regular Internet search engines.

**National Youth in Care Network**
<http://www.youthincare.ca/groups/index.htm>

This important site links youth across the country who have been under the care of protection or justice organizations.

# STUDY QUESTIONS

1. Do official crime statistics support the claim that female crime is increasing?
2. What impact has the 1984 YOA had on society's responses to girls' crime?
3. What are possible implications of the new YCJA?
4. What are the prevailing themes about girls in the theories of female crime and delinquency? What do the theories not explain?
5. What is the differential-intervention approach?
6. How would you describe and explain the context in which girls commit minor crimes? serious crimes? How is the context for girls different for boys?
7. Imagine yourself to be a member of the opposite sex. The police have caught you breaking into a neighbour's house. How would you explain yourself to your family? to your friends? How do you think the police would respond to you? What do you believe should happen to you?

# REFERENCES

Ackland, J.W. (1982). *Girls in Care: A Case Study of Residential Treatment.* Hampshire, UK: Gower.

Acland, C.R. (1995). *Youth, Murder, Spectacle: The Cultural Politics of "Youth in Crisis."* Boulder, CO: Westview.

Adler, C., and Baines, M. (1996). *... And When She Was Bad? Working with Young Women in Juvenile Justice and Related Areas.* Hobart, Tasmania: National Clearinghouse for Youth Studies.

Adler, F. (1975). *Sisters in Crime.* New York: McGraw-Hill.

Anderson, D. (1991). *The Unfinished Revolution: The Status of Women in Twelve Countries.* Toronto: Doubleday Canada.

Appleby, T. (1994, 23 July). "Crime rate falls again, except among teen girls." *Globe and Mail,* A1.

Artz, S. (1998). *Sex, Power and the Violent School Girl.* Toronto: Trifolium.

Artz, S., and Riecken, T. (1994). "The survey of student life." In "A study of violence among adolescent female students in a suburban school district." Unpublished report. Victoria, BC: British Columbia Ministry of Education, Education Research Unit.

Artz, S., Riecken, T., MacIntyre, B., Lam, E., and Maczewski, M. (1999). "A community based violence prevention project, seventh quarterly report." Unpublished. Vancouver, BC: British Columbia Health Research Foundation.

Balkan, S., and Berger, R. (1979). "The changing nature of female delinquency." In C. Knopp (Ed.), *Becoming Female: Perspectives on Development.* New York: Plenum.

Berger, R. (1989). "Female delinquency in the emancipation era: A review of the literature." *Sex Roles,* 21(5/6): 375 – 99.

Binder, A., Geis, G., and Bruce, D. (1988). *Juvenile Delinquency: Historical, Cultural, Legal Perspectives.* New York: Macmillan.

Biron, L., and Gavreau, D. (1984). *Portrait of Youth Crime.* Report no. A84.4. Ottawa: Secretary of State, Policy-Coordination Analysis and Management Systems Branch, Social Policy Trends Analysis Directorate.

Cain, M. (Ed.). (1989). *Growing Up Good: Policing the Behaviour of Girls in Europe.* London: Sage.

Campbell, A. (1991). *The Girls in the Gang* (2nd ed.). New York: Basil Blackwell.

Campbell, A., Muncer, S., and Bibel, D. (1998). "Female – female criminal assault: An evolutionary perspective." *Journal of Research in Crime and Delinquency,* 35(4): 413 – 28.

Canadian Centre for Justice Statistics, Statistics Canada (1981). *Juvenile Delinquents, 1980*. Ottawa: Ministry of Supply and Services.
———. (1983). *Juvenile Delinquents, 1982*. Ottawa: Ministry of Supply and Services.
———. (1987). *Youth Court Statistics, Preliminary 1985 – 86*. Ottawa: Youth Justice Program. Centre for Justice Statistics, Revised July.
———. (1989a). *Youth Court Statistics, Preliminary 1986 – 87*. Ottawa: Youth Justice Program. Centre for Justice Statistics, Revised April.
———. (1989b). *Youth Court Statistics, Preliminary 1987 – 88*. Ottawa: Youth Justice Program. Centre for Justice Statistics, Revised April.
———. (1989c). *Youth Court Statistics, Preliminary 1988 – 89*. Ottawa: Youth Justice Program. Centre for Justice Statistics, Revised August.
———. (1990). *Youth Court Statistics, Preliminary 1989 – 90*. Ottawa: Youth Justice Program, Centre for Justice Statistics, Revised September.
———. (1991). *Youth Court Statistics, Preliminary 1990 – 91*. Ottawa: Youth Justice Program. Centre for Justice Statistics, Revised September.
———. (1992). *Youth Court Statistics, Preliminary 1991 – 92*. Ottawa: Youth Justice Program. Centre for Justice Statistics, Revised September.
———. (1993). *Youth Court Statistics*, 1992 – 93. Ottawa: Youth Justice Program. Centre for Justice Statistics, December.
———. (1995). *Youth Court Statistics*, 1993 – 94. Ottawa: Minister for Statistics Canada and Industry, Science and Technology, January.
———. (1996). *Youth Court Statistics*, 1994 – 95. Ottawa: Minister for Statistics Canada and Industry, Science and Technology, March.
———. (1997). *Youth Court Statistics*, 1995 – 96. Ottawa: Minister for Statistics Canada and Industry, Science and Technology, October.
Carrington, P.J. (1999). "Trends in youth crime in Canada, 1977 – 1996." *Canadian Journal of Criminology*, 41(1): 1 – 32.
Cernkovich, S., and Giordano, P. (1979). "A comparative analysis of male and female delinquency." *Sociological Quarterly*, 20: 131 – 45.
———. (1987). "Family relationships and delinquency." *Criminology*, 25: 295 – 321.
Chesney-Lind, M., and Koroki, J. (1985). *Everything Just Going Down the Drain: Interviews with Female Delinquents in Hawaii*. Report. Hawaii: University of Hawaii Youth Development and Research Center.
Chesney-Lind, M., and Shelden, R. (1992). *Girls, Delinquency and Juvenile Justice*. Pacific Grove, CA: Brooks/Cole.
———. (1998). *Girls, Delinquency, and Juvenile Justice* (2nd ed.). Belmont, CA: West/Wadsworth.
Comack, E. (1996). *Women in Trouble*. Halifax: Fernwood.
Connell, R.W. (1987). *Gender and Power*. Cambridge, MA: Polity.
Conway, J. (1992). "Female young offenders, 1990 – 1991." *Juristat Service Bulletin*. Canadian Centre for Justice Statistics. 12(11).
Corrado, R.R., and Markwart, A. (1994). "The need to reform the YOA in response to violent young offenders: Confusion, reality or myth?" *Canadian Journal of Criminology*, 36(3): 343 – 78.
Cowie, J., Cowie, V., and Slater, E. (1968). *Delinquency in Girls*. London: Heinemann.
DeComo, R.E. (1998). "Estimating the prevalence of juvenile custody by race and gender." *Crime & Delinquency*, 44(4): 489 – 506.
Doob, A.N. (1992). "Trends in the use of custodial dispositions for young offenders." *Canadian Journal of Criminology*, 34(1): 75 – 84.
Doob, A.N., and Sprott, J.B. (1996). "Interprovincial variation in the use of the youth courts." *Canadian Journal of Criminology*, 38(4): 401 – 12.
———. (1998). "Is the 'quality' of youth violence becoming more serious?" *Canadian Journal of Criminology*, 40(2): 185 – 94.

Figueira-McDonough, J., Barton, W.H., and Sarri, R.C. (1981). "'Normal deviance': Gender similarities in adolescent subcultures." In M.Q. Warren (Ed.), *Comparing Female and Male Offenders*. Beverly Hills, CA: Sage.

Flowers, R. (1990). *The Adolescent Criminal: An Examination of Today's Juvenile Offender*. Jefferson, NC: McFarland & Company.

Gagnon, M., and Doherty, C. (1993). *Offences against the Administration of Youth Justice in Canada*. Ottawa: Canadian Centre for Justice Statistics.

Geller, G. (1987). "Young women in conflict with the law." In E. Adelberg and C. Curried (Eds.), *Too Few to Count: Canadian Women in Conflict with the Law*. Vancouver: Press Gang.

Gilligan, C. (1982). *In a Different Voice: Psychological Theory and Women's Development*. Cambridge, MA: Harvard University Press.

Giordano, P., Cernkovich, S., and Pugh, M. (1986). "Friendships and delinquency." *American Journal of Sociology*, 91: 1170 – 1202.

Grosser, G. (1951). "Juvenile delinquency and contemporary American sex roles." Unpublished doctoral dissertation. Cambridge, MA: Harvard University.

Hagan, J. (1990). "The structure of gender and deviance: A power-control theory of vulnerability to crime and the search for deviant role exits." *Canadian Review of Sociology and Anthropology*, 27(2): 137 – 56.

Hagan, J., Gillis, A., and Simpson, J. (1985). "The class structure of delinquency: Toward a power-control theory of common delinquent behaviour." *American Journal of Sociology*, 90: 1151 – 78.

Hagan, J., and McCarthy, B. with Patricia Parker and Jo-Anne Climenhage. (1997). *Mean Streets: Youth Crime and Homelessness*. Cambridge: Cambridge University Press.

Hagan, J., Simpson, J., and Gillis, A. (1987). "Class in the household: A power-control theory of gender and delinquency." *American Journal of Sociology*, 92: 788 – 816.

Hallett, C., and Murray, C. with J. Jamieson and B. Veitch. (1998). *The Evaluation of Children's Hearings in Scotland: Deciding in Children's Interests*, Vol. 1. Stirling: University of Stirling, Scottish Office Central Research Unit.

Hoffman-Bustamente, D. (1973). "The nature of female criminality." *Issues in Criminality*, 8 (Fall): 117 – 36.

James, J., and Thornton, W. (1980). "Women's liberation and the female delinquent." *Journal of Research in Crime and Delinquency*, 17: 230 – 44.

Jensen, G., and Eve, R. (1976). "Sex differences in delinquency." *Criminology*, 13: 427 – 48.

Konopka, G. (1983). *Young Girls: A Portrait of Adolescence*. New York: Hayworth Press.

Kowalski, M., and Caputo, T. (1999). "Recidivism in youth court: An examination of the impact of age, gender and prior record." *Canadian Journal of Criminology*, 41(1): 57 – 84.

LeBlanc, M. (1983). "Delinquency as an epiphenonmen of adolescence." In R.R. Corrado, M. LeBlanc, and J. Trépanier, (Eds.), *Current Issues in Juvenile Justice*. Toronto: Butterworths.

Lees, S. (1997). *Ruling Passions: Sexual Violence, Reputation and the Law*. Buckingham: Open University Press.

Leonard, T., Smandych, R., and Brickey, S. (1996). "Changes in the youth justice system." In J.A. Winterdyk (Ed.), *Issues and Perspectives on Young Offenders in Canada*. Toronto: Harcourt Brace.

McGovern, C. (1995). "You've come a long way baby." *Alberta Report*, 1(33): 24 – 7.

McRobbie, A. (1991). *Feminism and Youth Culture: From 'Jackie' to 'Just Seventeen'*. London: Macmillan Educational.

Morris, A. (1987). *Women, Crime and Criminal Justice*. New York: Basil Blackwell.

Morris, R. (1965). "Attitudes towards delinquency by delinquents, nondelinquents and their friends." *British Journal of Criminology*, 5: 249 – 65.

Nye, F. (1958) *Family Relationships and Delinquent Behavior*. New York: Wiley.
Palmer, T. (1995). "Programmatic and nonprogammatic aspects of successful intervention: New directions for research." *Crime and Delinquency*, 41(1): 100 – 31.
Parent, C. (1986). "Actualités et bibliographies: La protection chevalresque ou les réprésentations masculines du traitement des femmes dans la justice pénale." *Déviance et Société*, 10(2): 147 – 75.
Pollack, O. (1950). *The Criminality of Women*. New York: Barnes.
Reckless, W. (1961). *The Crime Problem*, 3rd. ed. New York: Appleton-Century-Crofts.
Reitsma-Street, M. (1991). "A review of female delinquency." In A. Leschied, P. Jaffe, and W. Willis (Eds.), *The Young Offenders Act: Revolution in Canadian Juvenile Justice*. Toronto: University of Toronto Press.
———. (1993). "Canadian youth court charges and dispositions for females before and after implementation of the *Young Offenders Act*." *Canadian Journal of Criminology*, 35(4): 437 – 58.
———. (1998). "Still girls learn to care; girls policed to care." In C. Baines, P. Evans, and S. Neysmith (Eds.), *Women's Caring: Social Policy in Canada*, Rev. ed. Toronto: Oxford University Press.
———. (in press) "Justice for Canadian girls: A 1990s update." *Canadian Journal of Criminology*.
Reitsma-Street, M., and Leschied, A. (1988). "The Conceptual Level Matching Model in corrections." *Criminal Justice and Behaviour*, 15(1): 92 – 108.
Reitsma-Street, M., and Offord, D.R. (1991). "Girl delinquents and their sisters." *Canadian Review of Social Work*, 8(1): 11 – 27.
Royal Commission on Aboriginal Peoples (1993). *Aboriginal Peoples and the Justice System*. Ottawa: Canada Communications Group.
Rutter, M. (1980). "School influences on children's behavior and development." *Pediatrics*, 65(2): 208 – 20.
Sarri, R. (1976). "Juvenile law: How it penalizes females." In I. Crites (Ed.), *The Female Offender*. Lexington, MA: Lexington Books.
Schwartz, I.M., and Au Claire, P. (1995). *Home-Based Services for Troubled Children*. Lincoln: University of Nebraska Press.
Scott, S.P. (1989). "The Young Offenders Act: Ideological models of disposition." Doctoral dissertation. Toronto: York University.
Simon, R. (1975). *Women and Crime*. Lexington, MA: Lexington Books.
Slade, P. (1984). "Premenstrual emotional changes in normal women: Fact or fiction?" *Journal of Psychosomatic Research*, 28: 1 – 7.
Smith, C.A., and Stern, S.B. (1997). "Delinquency and antisocial behavior: A review of family processes and intervention research." *Social Service Review*, 382 – 420.
Steffensmeir, D. (1978). "Crime and the contemporary American woman: an analysis of changing levels of female property crime, 1960 – 1975." *Social Forces*, 57: 566 – 84.
Steffensmeir, D., and Cobb, M. (1981). "Sex difference in urban patterns, 1934 – 1979." *Social Problems*, 29: 37 – 50.
Sutherland, E. (1939). *Principles of Criminology*. Philadelphia: Lippincott.
Stoppard, J.M., and Henri, G.S. (1987). "Conceptual level matching and effects of assertive training." *Journal of Counseling Psychology*, 43(1): 55 – 61.
Tanner, J. (1996). *Teenage Troubles: Youth and Deviance in Canada*. Toronto: Nelson Canada.
Thurman, Q.C., Giacomazzi, A.L., Reisig, M.D., and Mueller, D.G. (1996). "Community-based gang prevention and intervention: An evaluation of a neutral zone." *Crime and Delinquency*, 42(2): 279 – 95.
Wilson, J., and Herrnstein, R. (1985). *Crime and Human Nature*. New York: Simon & Schuster.
Winterdyk, J. (Ed.). (1997). *Juvenile Justice Systems: International Perspectives*. Toronto: Canadian Scholar's Press.

# PART TWO

# The Young Offenders Act

# Introduction

There are virtually no areas of our lives untouched by law today. Areas covered by civil, criminal, and tort law include legal stipulations designed to protect ownership by defining the parameters of private and public property; laws to regulate businesses; legal parameters regarding raising revenue; and laws to preserve order. Laws, in essence, represent a formal system of social control that tends to get exercised when informal measures, such as social ethics or mores, are no longer effective. However, as Part Two will make evident, the laws that we have put into place to control youth crime appear to have been relatively ineffectual. Why is this?

Much has been said and written about the laws that address Canada's youth crime. Part Two consists of three contributions, each of which examines the merits of these laws. These chapters also investigate how and why we continue to amend the laws to better address social concerns. Chapters 5 and 6 provide recent discussion on the Youth Criminal Justice Act. Also analyzed are the public perception of young offenders and the unique relationship among society, youth crime, and the mass media.

## SUGGESTED READINGS

Bala, N., Hornick, J.P., and Vogl, R. (Eds.). (1991). *Canadian Child Welfare Law*. Toronto: Thompson Educational Publishing.

Although this text focusses on how children are protected under the Child Welfare Act (CWA), it is also an excellent resource for readers who are interested in understanding the laws dealing with problem youth—those who need protection and support versus those who require criminal justice intervention. It is often argued that the YOA and the CWA are at odds with each other and that many young offenders are products of the CWA system.

*Canadian Journal of Criminology*. This is the only criminological journal published in Canada. The journal regularly features articles on the Young Offenders Act as well as many other issues pertaining to young offenders. The July 1994 issue entitled "The Young Offenders Act—Ten Years after Implementation" offers a series of articles that address different aspects of the act. For a more contemporary examination of the act and the new proposed Youth Criminal Justice Act, refer to the Web link in the Introduction on page 5.

Corrado, R.R., Bala, N., Linden, R., and LeBlanc, M. (Eds.). (1992). *Juvenile Justice in Canada.* Toronto: Butterworths.

This text offers a detailed assessment of the YOA and related issues, such as the effectiveness of juvenile justice, the challenging role of defence counsel, and treatment issues as defined under the act.

O'Reilly-Flemming, T., and Clark, B. (Eds.). (1993). *Youth Injustice.* Toronto: Canadian Scholars' Press.

This text consists mainly of articles previously published in the *Canadian Journal of Criminology*. Several chapters (specifically Chapters 3 through 8) explore a variety of issues as they pertain to the YOA.

Platt, P. (1991). *Police Guide to the Young Offenders Act.* Toronto: Butterworths.

Although the title suggests this book is for police use only, it is useful for readers who are interested in the implications of the act. This book carefully takes the reader through the act, explaining what the sections mean and how they can be enforced. For those who may question the leniency or the strictness of the act, Platt provides a clear and concise interpretation. Some of the topics covered in the eighteen chapters include fingerprinting and photographs, offences, alternative measures, transfers to ordinary court, and handling of court records.

# *Chapter 4*

# *The Law and Young Offenders*

DONALD W. FETHERSTON

## KEY OBJECTIVES

After reading this chapter, you should be able to:

- understand the evolution of juvenile-justice legislation in Canada;
- understand and develop skills in applying key provisions of the Young Offenders Act;
- examine the historical context of the Young Offenders Act and future trends within a framework of various legal-system models.

## KEY TERMS

absolute discharge
adversarial
alternative measures
Bill C-12
Bill C-37
Bill C-106
community service
conditional discharge
dangerous offence
extrajudicial dispositions
extrajudicial measures
fine-option program
judicial interim release
Juvenile Delinquents Act
modified justice model
*parens patriae*
presumptive offence
responsible person
restorative justice
status offence
surety

(Note: Many of the legal terms are also defined in the acts reproduced in Appendixes A, B, and C, at the end of this book.)

## INTRODUCTION

### A MODEL TO AID IN THE ANALYSIS OF LAW AND SOCIAL CHANGE

Although the primary objective of this chapter is to provide an overview of the key provisions of the Young Offenders Act (YOA) and the newly proposed Youth Criminal Justice Act (YCJA), as well as how their provisions relate to youth court, we will begin by offering a framework for consideration of those provisions. A useful summary of different juvenile justice models is provided by Reid and Reitsma-Street (1984) and Winterdyk (1997), and six different models are described on a continuum from the "far right" (conservative/Crime Control) to the "far left" (socialist/Community Change in Box 4.1, below). No legal system falls squarely within one type or another, but changes in law and society can be compared and analyzed using this framework. While studying this chapter, you are encouraged to use this model to more clearly understand changes in the youth justice system.

Next, we briefly trace the historical origins of the law regarding young offenders in Canada. This historical summary will give the reader a deeper appreciation and understanding for how and why such legislation is continually amended (see Chapter 5), as well as why, at different times, existing legislation may seem to be either appropriate or lacking in its mandate.

## HISTORICAL ORIGINS AND CHANGES IN THE LAW REGARDING YOUNG OFFENDERS

Concern with youthful problems has, in varying degrees, been a characteristic of all societies. It is also universal that societies strive for effective strategies for socializing their youth and for controlling problematic youth (see Chapter 1, and Winterdyk, 1997). Societies legitimize various institutions to teach, punish, and rehabilitate problematic youth.

Social change, be it culturally, economically, or politically based, causes every society to periodically re-examine the status quo. In the aftermath of broad social events, new attitudes and institutions tend to develop; for example, the development of a separate juvenile justice system for children followed similar patterns in a number of Western countries, reflecting general societal values and beliefs about children (see Ariès, 1962). As noted in the introduction to this book, over the past 150 years a number of major shifts have occurred in social attitudes toward the young, producing corresponding attempts to create new strategies and institutions for their socialization and control.

One of the first of such major shifts in North America occurred near the end of the nineteenth century. Beginning with the middle class and then becoming widespread, this perspective viewed children as being very different from adults. For the first time in Western history, childhood was recognized as a special state. The term "adolescence" was first coined in this period by the psychologist G. Stanley Hall. Special social-service institutions were established, and special laws for children were developed, including work laws, school laws, and special juvenile courts.

A second major shift began in the mid-twentieth century, when civil rights were fought for, and won, by diverse groups. This shift resulted in the legal rights enjoyed by adults being extended to children. We will examine how this played out in Canada.

During the 1800s, until the Canadian Parliament passed superseding statute law, the English common-law standard was applied to children in Canada, in that

- children under age 7 were considered to be *doli incapax*, or incapable of crime;

## Box 4.1

## MODELS OF YOUTH-JUSTICE SYSTEMS

**A. Crime Control Model:** This approach gives priority to due process and protecting the community from criminal activity. The major emphasis is on retribution and punishment in a model where "criminal activity" is broadly defined and offenders have fewer rights than in other models. Key players in this model are the police, courts, and penal agents.

*Country examples*: United States and Hungary

**B. Justice Model:** Like the crime control model, this model has as its dominant goal the protection of society. However, this approach goes further in protecting the rights of the accused and often has rules like "innocent until proven guilty" and the "right to a fair trial." The justice model is based on the classical school of criminology, which holds that crime prevention can best be achieved by ensuring that the punishment is sufficiently severe to outweigh any pleasure from committing the offence (Caputo, 1987). Lawyers play a key role in the adminstration of justice.

*Country examples*: Italy and Germany

**C. Modified Justice Model:** This model characterizes Canada's approach to youth justice. While emphasizing due process in the YOA, it also encourages an informal approach to the handling of young offenders. The model is divided in that minor offenders are dealt with less harshly than serious offenders. Sanctions are premised on the notion of trying to diagnose the youths' situation and devise the most appropriate sanction (Winterdyk, 1997).

*Country example*: Canada

**D. Welfare Model:** This model is based on the positivistic school of criminology, which became popular at the end of the nineteenth century and maintained that crime was a result of physiological, psychological, and environmental factors over which individuals had little control (Caputo, 1987: 130). Individuals should not be held completely responsible for their behaviour: society must be held at least partly responsible. The needs and best interests of the child are emphasized, and it is this approach that was most clearly expressed in the first establishment of a juvenile court.

*Country examples*: Australia and the Netherlands

**E. Participatory Model:** Characterized as an informal model that emphasizes minimal formal intervention; the key personnel under this model are educators and community agencies. The model encourages community and voluntary participation in the re-education of delinquent youth (Winterdyk, 1997).

*Country examples*: Japan and Fiji

**F. Community Change Model:** This model shares with the welfare model a concern for the welfare of delinquent youth and seeks to reduce youth crime by altering the fundamental environmental factors thought to cause criminal activity. Thus, social equality and citizen involvement are emphasized and the aim of social policy is "to change the processes that lead to inequality, poverty, and delinquency: youthful crime is prevented by promoting the welfare of all youth" (Reid and Reitsma-Street, 1984: 4).

*Country examples*: China and the former Soviet Union

- children between the ages of 7 and 13 were considered *prima facie* (presumptively) incapable of crime, but the presumption could be rebutted by the prosecution in order to allow for their prosecution in special cases (similar to current rules for transferring young persons to ordinary adult court); and
- children 14 years of age or older were considered to be fully responsible for their crimes. However, prior to the mid-1800s there is little evidence that law and practice differentiated among offenders on the basis of age.

In 1857, An Act for the Establishment of Prisons for Young Offenders was passed in Upper and Lower Canada, which provided for the construction of two reformatories for young offenders (Hylton, 1994). In the same year, An Act for the Speedy Trial and Punishment of Young Offenders was passed to institute special bail provisions and reduce pre-trial detention. This gave magistrates "the power to deal summarily with children, thereby protecting them from the full rigors of the criminal law, as the sentencing powers of the lower courts were less extreme" (Archambault, 1983: 1). In 1867, the British North America Act imposed a certain order on criminal-justice and child-welfare matters by clarifying the respective responsibility of the federal and provincial governments. In 1892, the Criminal Code (CC) was amended to ensure that children were tried separately from adults, and without publicity.

Some have suggested that the development of the youth-justice system must be understood in the context of the emergence of capitalism in late-nineteenth-century Canadian society. These analysts contend that "capitalism disrupted traditional social support systems, including the family and resulted in the marginalization of youth" (Hylton, 1994: 231). In turn, this resulted in higher levels of youth crime and heightened community pressure to "do something." Others contend that these legislative provisions occurred within a broader climate of concern for the welfare of children. Reform movements in the 1800s fought for public education and medical services, child-labour laws, and institutions to care for abandoned and neglected children (Archambault, 1983). Whatever the explanation, the justice system had some provisions for the separate treatment of children, but it failed to distinguish between neglected and delinquent children (Hudson, Hornick, and Burrows, 1993: 4).

The Juvenile Delinquents Act (JDA; see Appendix A), passed in 1908, embodied the **welfare model**. Delinquency was viewed as a product of social environment and amenability to treatment. The court acted in the best interests of the child as a stern but understanding parent (**parens patriae**) in an institution emphasizing treatment and minimizing accountability (see Introduction, p.2). The philosophy was explicitly set out in the act:

> This Act shall be liberally construed in order that its purposes may be carried out, namely, that the care and custody of a juvenile delinquent shall approximate as nearly as may be that which should be given by his parents, and that as far as practicable every juvenile delinquent shall

> be treated not as a criminal, but as a misdirected child, and one needing aid, encouragement, help, and assistance. (section 38)

The fact that proceedings were viewed as more civil than criminal was reflected in the failure to distinguish between neglected or delinquent children. *Informality* and *flexibility* were the key characteristics of the JDA. To mimic family process, proceedings were informal and held in private. Social workers and parents, rather than lawyers, were usually involved. The aim was to spare the strict application of the criminal justice system in such a way as to permit altruistic social intervention to save the child.

The JDA remained virtually unchanged (some minor amendments were made in 1929) until the enactment of the YOA in the early 1980s. The remarkable longevity of such significant public-policy legislation until the 1960s can be attributed to the widespread public, political, and stockholder support it had until that time.

As early as 1960, the JDA was widely criticized (Bala, 1986). The following were common criticisms:

- The court had too much discretionary power, which could lead to lack of due process.
- The all-inclusive crime of "delinquency" comprised all crimes plus general immorality. These were status offences (children because of their status as children and not adults could be charged and convicted).
- There was a great deal of variation across the country in the maximum age to which the act applied.
- The use of detention was indiscriminate, the length of custodial dispositions indeterminate.
- Judicial authority to utilize community resources for treatment was lacking.
- Being labelled a "juvenile delinquent" carried a stigma.
- Since there were few checks on those who exercised discretion under the JDA (police, court, and those who administered dispositions), great variability existed in the administration of the act.

In essence, the unintended results of the JDA were often

> arbitrariness, unfairness, and neglect of the interests of youth, consequences of the discontinuity between the ideals expressed in the JDA, and the actual delivery of services to juveniles. Moreover, juvenile delinquents were denied basic elements of due process: such things as clear right to counsel, right of appeal, and definite, as opposed to open-ended sentences. (Rosen, 1996: 1)

Many of these criticisms were motivated, at least in part, by the apparent dramatic increase in incidence of juvenile delinquency during the 1950s and 1960s (see Havemann, 1986). It should be noted, however, that adult crime apparently increased similarly during this period, and several analysts have concluded that the apparent increases can be attributed to more effective police surveillance and a greater determination to bring young people to justice. Carrigan (1998) points out that politicians during this period were seeking issues to divert attention away from the economy; capital punishment and juvenile crime waves proved to be fertile ground. In Canada, Fattah (1982) similarly concludes, politicians played on people's fears to gain, or increase, political power. For example, Robert Kaplan, then Solicitor General of Canada, played on popular public opinion by stating just before introducing the YOA that "kiddy-courts" had failed to stem crime and that the government was going to get tough and make child criminals more accountable (Caputo, 1987).

The "often tortuous process" of replacing the JDA with the YOA took nearly twenty years (Bala, 1986: 242; also see Hak, 1996). Hudson, Hornick, and Burrows (1993) describe the YOA as an attempt to achieve a compromise between the youth's needs, rights, and rehabilitation, and society's right to be protected from illegal behaviour. Subsequent amendments did not constitute a philosophical change, but rather a "fine-tuning" of the law.

The YOA adopted a **modified justice model** to deal with young offenders (see Box 4.1, and Winterdyk, 1997). While still recognizing the unique needs of young people, the YOA also emphasizes both the protection of society and the **due process** and constitutional rights of young persons. Where the JDA emphasized *social intervention*, the YOA emphasizes *rights and responsibilities*.

The trends toward a modified justice model, and even a crime-control model, show no sign of decreasing. As is reflected in Chapter 5, amendments to and recommendations for the YOA, since its coming into force, have generally increased punishment options. In the next section, we examine the major elements of the YOA and newly proposed YCJA.

## THE LAW OF YOUNG OFFENDERS TODAY: THE YOUNG OFFENDERS ACT IN PERSPECTIVE

This section focusses on the Young Offenders Act but frequently puts its provisions in perspective by comparing them to both the previous law, the Juvenile Delinquents Act, and the proposed new law, the Youth Criminal Justice Act.

### JURISDICTION

#### Conduct

In an effort to shield children from the stigma of a criminal charge, there was only one charge under the JDA: that of being a "juvenile delinquent." This charge applied not only to those who broke any federal, provincial, or municipal law, but, according to section 2, also to any child "who is guilty of sexual immorality or any similar form of vice, or who is liable by reason of any other act to be committed to an industrial school or juvenile reformatory under any federal or provincial statute."

The range of conduct that falls under the YOA is much narrower than that covered by the JDA. Section 2 of the YOA defines "offences" as those created by statute (federal, provincial, and municipal). The YOA is, on the whole, procedural (it doesn't create offences); it sets out procedures to be followed when charging young persons with offences. However, it was held in *R. v. Trimarchi* that offences under the YOA are different from those under the Criminal Code, as the potential legal and social impact of the consequences of a finding of guilt are quite different. The definition of "offence" under the YCJA is virtually the same as that under the YOA, but, as we shall see, in many cases sentences can be more severe under the proposed new act.

### Age

Age jurisdiction varied from province to province under the JDA. Section 2 of the YOA clearly sets out its definition of "young person," in that the act applies only to those persons 12 years of age or older but under 18 years of age. Section 2 of the YCJA retains the same age jurisdiction (see Appendix C).

### Court

"Young persons" are to be tried by "youth courts," designated by the government of a province (or, in the Territories, the Governor-in-Council) to deal with adolescents. Such courts have jurisdiction where an offence is committed by anyone while he or she was a "young person." Under the BNA Act, Parliament delegated this power to the provinces. In Alberta, the legislature designated the Provincial Court of Alberta as Youth Court (Provincial Court Act, RSA 1980, c. P-20). The provincial Young Offenders Act (see SA, 1984, c Y-1) also deals with provincial offences.

## PHILOSOPHY AND PRINCIPLES OF THE LEGISLATION

The philosophy of the JDA was singular and straightforward. A young person in trouble with the law was not to be treated as an offender but as one suffering from delinquency, a lawfully recognized form of social disease requiring parental-type help and supervision. In contrast, the philosophy and principles of the YOA (see section 3) are plural and manifold.

Some commentators argue that the principles enumerated in section 3 are inconsistent, and therefore offer no real guidance on how to apply the YOA (Bala, 1986). However, the courts disagree. Justice Lamer, former Chief Justice of the Supreme Court of Canada, commenting on what appear to be contradictions in section 3(1) in the case of *R. v. J.J.M.*, stated that the act reflects a courageous attempt to balance concepts and interests that are frequently conflicting. Carefully tailored dispositions should meet both the need to protect society and the need to reform the offender.[1]

An example of how the principles are put in action in determining guilt is evident in the case of *R.P.B. (No. 2)*, which involved a second-degree murder charge against a 12-year-old who killed his brutal father with a shotgun while protecting his 13-year-old sister from a physical attack by the father. Judge Lamarche decided that the proper test for second-degree murder committed by a young person under section 229(c) of the Criminal Code was different from the test that would be applied to an adult. Section 229 punishes "conduct, for an unlawful purpose, that an accused knows or ought to know is likely to cause death." The judge reasoned that, since the intellectual and emotional capabilities of a 12-year-old person are less developed than those of an adult, the objective criterion of the reasonable man must be modified and personalized. The specific knowledge of the surrounding circumstances possessed by the accused plus a 12-year-old's immature capacity to reason are to be considered in deciding what he "ought to know" (not how the judge relied on section 3).

The proposed YCJA adopts all of the principles of the YOA but adds several more principles, particularly the following:

- in section 3(1)(a), the principle that "the unequivocal and primary goal of the youth criminal justice system is to protect the public ...";
- the principle that young persons must be held accountable for their actions;
- the principle that victims have the right to be provided with information and to be given the opportunity to participate while also commanding respect for their dignity and privacy;
- the principle that measures taken against young persons should respect differences (cultural, linguistic, and special requirements); and
- the principles of **restorative justice**, including repair of harm done to the victim and the community, using meaningful rehabilitation and reintegration of the offender.

**Box 4.2**

**UNITED NATIONS CONVENTION ON THE RIGHTS OF THE CHILD**

Although Canada was a signatory member of the United Nations Convention on the Rights of the Child, its Young Offenders Act (YOA) did not refer to the principles set out at this convention.

The proposed Youth Criminal Justice Act (YCJA), however, explicitly recognizes these principles.

Some of the rights children are entitled to include:

- the right to be taken seriously;
- the right to good health;
- the right to a good education;
- the right to make mistakes; and
- the right to fair treatment.

For a more detailed look at children's rights, see <http://www.stemnet.nf.ca/nlhra/irchild.htm>.

## ALTERNATIVE MEASURES: EXTRAJUDICIAL MEASURES

The fourth principle in section 3 of the YOA, which states that non-judicial procedures should be considered in many circumstances, is given substance in section 4 of the act. The police have always had discretion in deciding whether to charge a young person, particularly a first-time offender. However, until the enactment of the YOA, the police had only two choices: to charge or not to charge. Section 4 authorizes the establishment, on a provincial basis, of alternative measures programs, thereby providing the police, the Crown, and the young person with a third alternative. The intention is to avoid formal, time-consuming, and often damaging effects of prosecution by diverting the young person to some form of extrajudicial educational or community-service program.

According to section 4, resorting to the program requires the consent of the young person, an acceptance of responsibility for the offence in question, and a determination by the Crown that there is sufficient evidence to support a prosecution. Furthermore, such a recommendation must be appropriate with regards to the needs of the young person and the interests of society. For example, in an alleged case of theft, if the Crown feels that any of the elements of theft may not be present, he or she should not recommend alternative measures.

Although alternative measures are now available across Canada, the Supreme Court ruled on 28 June 1990 that the provinces are not obliged to establish alternate measures (*R.* v. *Shelson, S.*). The parameters of the provincial programs vary. For example, in Alberta the program is limited to first-time offenders. Motivated, in part, by the need to reduce the growing backlog of cases in youth court, on 15 April 1991 the Alberta program was expanded to include all Criminal Code offences except those involving violence, or the threat of violence, perjury and giving of contradictory evidence, alcohol-related driving offences, and property offences where the value of the property exceeds $1000. Alternative measures programs usually offer a wide variety or responses ranging from notes of apology to 50 hours of community service (see Box 4.3).

Concern has been expressed about the fact that a youth must, in effect, admit guilt in order to take advantage of section 4. There is also concern that this legislated form of alternative measure excludes more informal types of diversion, such as those exercised by police at the arrest and apprehension stages (Rosen, 1996).

### Proposed Changes

The proposed YCJA greatly expands the role of extrajudicial measures beyond the alternative measures provisions of the YOA. The proposed YCJA begins with a comprehensive statement of principles and objectives for extrajudicial measures. Their use is highly encouraged. Section 4(a) states that "extra-judicial measures are often the most appropriate and

## Box 4.3
## LEGAL PROCESS EXERCISE

Nathan is 14 years old and has been charged with one count of being a party to theft (shop-lifting a pair of snowboarding pants worth $112 from SportCheck).

Assume that Nathan participates in the alternative-measures program and has been assigned to complete 40 hours of community service by doing janitorial work at the local swimming pool.

At Nathan's post-program court appearance, the Crown Attorney shows that Nathan did not complete the program and wants to proceed with the charges. The Defence thinks this is unfair, since Nathan did 25 of the hours required and then gave up after two failed attempts to contact the pool supervisor for times to complete the last 15 hours.

Identify, and then apply, the appropriate parts of section 4 to the above scenario. You are the judge. What would your decision be in this case? Would you need any further information before you could decide?

effective way of dealing with youth crime." Section 4(d) states that they "should be used if they are adequate to hold a young person accountable." Furthermore, they are deemed to be adequate to hold a young person accountable if the young person has committed a non-violent offence or is a first-time offender. They are also available even if the young person has a record or has been previously dealt with by **extrajudicial measures**.

Extrajudicial measures, under section 4, are divided into two types:

1. "Warnings, cautions, and referrals": If any province adopts a program allowing police officers to merely give warnings, or referrals to community-based programs, then every police officer must consider giving a warning, caution, or referral in every case involving a young person.
2. "Extrajudicial sanctions": This section covers everything that was previously covered by section 4, "Alternative Measures of the YOA." Before a young person is required to do anything as part of his or her extrajudicial treatment, it must be determined that he or she "cannot be adequately dealt with by a warning, caution or referral mentioned in sections 6, 7, or 8 because of the seriousness of the offences, the nature and number of previous offences committed by the young person or any other aggravating circumstances" (section 10(1), YCJA).

## PRE-TRIAL PROCEDURE

### Bail (Judicial Interim Release)

Section 51 of the YOA makes it clear that most of the arrest and bail (**judicial interim release**) provisions of the Criminal Code apply to the youth court, with necessary modifications. According to section 515(10) of the Criminal Code, the court considers whether continued detention is necessary to ensure attendance in court (primary grounds) or for the protection of society (secondary grounds), or whether the young person will be released conditionally or unconditionally. Traditionally, case law directs the judge to consider the following factors:

- the circumstances of the offence,
- previous record,
- existing bail or probation orders,
- likelihood of reoffending or interfering with the administration of justice,
- the age of the youth, and
- ties to the community.

## Proposed Changes under the YCJA

The JDA allowed pre-trial incarceration for child-welfare concerns, and the YOA does not forbid it. A child could be held in custody merely because his or her parents didn't want him or her at home or he or she had no place to go. However, the proposed YCJA specifically forbids incarceration for child-welfare reasons in section 29(1), which states that "a youth justice court judge or a justice shall not detain a young person in custody prior to being sentenced as a substitute for appropriate child protection, mental health, or other social reasons."

The proposed YCJA modifies the Criminal Code further by requiring the judge to presume that detention is not necessary on the secondary ground (section 515(10)(b)) of the Criminal Code: "if the young person could not, on conviction be committed to custody on the grounds set out in s. 38(1), unless there is a substantial likelihood that the young person will, if released from custody, commit a criminal offence or interfere with the administration of justice" (YCJA, section 29(2)). This requirement of section 29 in the YCJA would substantially decrease the number of young people subject to pre-trial incarceration.

## Detention Separate from Adults under the YOA

Until the passage of **Bill C-106** in June 1986 (see Chapter 5), the YOA contained a virtually absolute rule that young persons were to be detained separately from adults. In view of the logistical problems this was creating for law enforcement officials, section 7 was relaxed somewhat to permit mixed detention "under the supervision and control of a peace officer." The bill also relaxed the rule that justices could hear bail matters only if no youth-court judge was available. Justices can now hear bail applications anytime. These measures reflect aspects of the **crime control model** (see Box 4.1 above).

## Release to a Responsible Person under the YOA

The YOA provides for the possibility of releasing young offenders ordered detained under the Criminal Code. Under section 7(1) of the YOA, where the court is satisfied that a responsible person is willing and able to take care of and exercise control over the youth, and the youth agrees, he or she may be released. The application for release is made personally in court, usually with the responsible person giving evidence under oath and being subject to cross-examination by the prosecutor. However, since there is no official follow-up of the quality and quantity of supervision, there is probably great variability in how much supervision actually takes place. Only if the responsible person reoffends and appears before the court to be released from his or her duties do the courts become involved.

## Release Using a Surety

A further method of release unique to youth court is the use of a surety form of recognizance. A **surety** is a person who agrees to sign for the release of an offender and to forfeit money, or property, to the Crown if the offender violates the release conditions. The use of this device can result in transferring considerable power to parents who may otherwise be powerless to effect any control over the young person. Until the parent is prepared to sign the order, the youth remains in custody. This procedure has the potential to allow the courts to help strengthen families.

## Parents

In accordance with section 22(1) of the JDA, if a youth was found to be delinquent, and a fine or other financial penalty was imposed, the court could, if satisfied that the parent/guardian, contributed to the commission of the offence by failure to exercise due care, order the parent/guardian to pay the penalty. In addition, the court could order the parent/guardian to contribute to the financial support of the youth (section 20(2), JDA). These provisions were not incorporated into the YOA. The YOA and the YCJA both, generally, hold only the young person responsible for his or her illegal acts, but they do allow parental involvement; in particular, the proposed YCJA permits "the provinces to require young people or their parents to pay for legal counsel in cases where they are fully capable of paying" ("News Release," 1999).

Consistent with the principle of parental responsibility set down in section 3(1)(h) of the YOA, this legislation contains detailed provisions stipulating that the parent/guardian must be notified where a young person is arrested and charged. If the court is of the opinion that the attendance of the parent/guardian is necessary, or is in the best interests of the young person, the court can compel attendance at youth court, and hold the parent/guardian to be subject to a contempt conviction if he or she neglected, or refused, to attend. The detailed provisions of the YOA are virtually the same in the proposed YCJA.

## Medical and Psychological Reports

The JDA was largely silent on the subject of the preparation and use of medical and psychological reports with respect to accused young persons. This changed under the YOA (see Chapter 11), in which section 13 sets out detailed guidelines, including such things as when a report can be ordered;

the circumstances in which a young person can be detained for examination; restrictions on disclosure of the contents of the report, even to a young person in some circumstances; and the right to cross-examine the author of a report. Bill C-37 in 1995 amended section 13 to allow for such reports to be ordered in cases of serious personal-injury offences or repeated findings of guilt. The provisions of the YCJA are very similar to those in the YOA.

## THE TRIAL

### Procedure

Under the YOA, regardless of how the offence is expressed in the Criminal Code, all criminal proceedings involving a young person are summary in nature. This means no jury trial and no preliminary hearing is held for a young offender. The Charter of Rights and Freedoms guarantees a jury trial only where a person faces a possible punishment of five years' imprisonment or "a more severe punishment." Although challenges have been mounted, so far the courts have upheld the validity of the YOA.

Generally, procedures set out in the Criminal Code govern trial procedure at youth court. However, consistent with the principles as set out in section 3(1)(e) and (g) of the YOA requiring "special guarantees of their rights and freedoms" and the right to be informed thereof, there are several special requirements that apply to young persons facing trial, including the requirements that

- the court must read out the information to the accused (may be waived if young person is represented by counsel);
- if the accused is unrepresented, the court must inform the young person of his or her right to counsel; and
- the court may not accept a guilty plea without first inquiring as to whether there are facts that support the charges the YOA requires.

The YCJA retains these provisions, making several additions to give extra notice to the young person if he or she is facing transfer to ordinary court or there is an application for an adult sentence.

### The Right to Privacy

Since the enactment of the JDA, it is generally agreed that criminal proceedings against young persons should not be open to the public and that the identity of the accused, or convicted, youth should not be revealed to the public. This is consistent with the current philosophy of the YOA entitling youth to special consideration, and is further consistent with the findings of societal-reaction theories of crime discussed in Chapter 2, that youth should not be "labelled" or made to bear a stigma for acts they carried out at an immature age.

Under the JDA, all judicial proceedings were held in private (*in camera*). However, after the passage of the Charter of Rights and Freedoms, this requirement was deemed by the courts to be in contravention of guarantees of freedom of expression and freedom of the press (see Chapter 6).

When the YOA was first enacted, all proceedings were generally held in open court (public), except in special circumstances whereby the proceedings could be seriously "injurious" or "prejudicial" to a young person or child involved, or where exclusion of the public was in the interest of "public morals, the maintenance of order or the proper administration of justice" (see section 39). Furthermore, section 38 prohibits the publication of any report of an offence, hearing, disposition, or appeal (i.e., report of any judicial process) in which the name of the young person is disclosed. As a result, the public and the press may attend and report on youth-court proceedings, except where a court makes a specific order under section 39, but they may not identify any young person involved.

If we look at changes in the right of privacy from the JDA to the present, we see the right to privacy diminishing. Under the YOA, private proceedings are the exception, not the rule. Amendments to the YOA have eroded the privacy right further. Bill C-106, in 1986, amended section 38 to allow disclosure of the identity of dangerous indictable-offence offenders at large when necessary to assist in their apprehension; of a young offender if the young offender asks and it is not contrary to his or her interests; and disclosure of information within the justice system. Bill C-37, passed in 1995, made a number of changes to section 38 to allow access to information to persons involved in the care and supervision of young persons (see Chapter 5).

Under the proposed YCJA, publication of a young person's name will be permitted if an adult sentence is imposed; if a youth sentence is imposed for a "presumptive offence" (see "Transfer" below); or if a young person is dangerous and at large.

Records of investigations and proceedings are also relevant to privacy. The JDA was silent on the matter of records, whereas the YOA, as originally enacted, had strict rules regarding police, court, and government records. It was required that these be kept separately from adult records, and access was given to a limited number of persons and organizations. Furthermore, if the youth was acquitted, or if charges were withdrawn, records were to be destroyed without exception. All other records were to be automatically destroyed after the expiration of fixed times after conviction. Bill C-106 dramatically changed these record-keeping provisions. Exceptions were added, including allowing disclosure to victims; by the police, if necessary to conduct an investigation; and to insurance companies investigating claims arising out of an offence. Other agencies may keep their records, but the act restricts access to these records after the passage of certain periods of time. If a young person is acquitted by reason of insanity, records are not subject to restrictions.

## The Right to Counsel

The JDA did not give a young person a right to counsel. Informality was the procedure of choice, and many young offenders were not represented. Even if present, a lawyer did not always play a distinct role as the youth's advocate. The YOA made a fundamental change consistent with the justice model. Section 11 states that a young person has the right "to retain and instruct counsel without delay ... at any stage of the proceedings against him [*sic*]." In addition to this right, young persons also have rights adults don't have, including

- the right to be informed by the youth court of their right to a lawyer. If the young person wishes to be represented, the court must see that legal aid represents them or, if no legal aid is available, the court must direct that the youth be represented;
- the right to be assisted by an adult who is not a lawyer; and
- the right to have counsel independent of his or her parents where their interests are in conflict.

Generally, amendments have strengthened the right to counsel. Bill C-106 stipulates that a young person's right to counsel includes the right "to exercise that right personally," and Bill C-37, in 1995, amended section 11 to make it clear that young offenders have a right to counsel at hearings where their level of custody is reviewed (see Box 4.4).

The proposed YCJA leaves these provisions virtually unchanged (section 25). This appears to be the only due process right that has consistently increased since the JDA was enacted.

## Evidence: Statements of Young Persons

Section 56 of the YOA adopts the general common-law rule that statements made to persons in authority will be admissible as evidence only if they are "voluntary"; that is, there has been "no fear of prejudice nor hope of advantage held out by a 'person in authority'" (note: a parent or adult relative is not "a person in authority" without evidence to the contrary). Statements made to persons not in authority are admissible unless they were made under duress (YOA, section 56(5)).

Besides this general rule, section 56(2) of the YOA contains several additional requirements applicable only to statements given by young persons. Specifically, the person in authority must, before the statement is made, explain to the young person "in language appropriate to his/her age and understanding" that

- the young person does not have to make a statement;
- any statement given may be used as evidence against the youth; and
- the young person has a right to counsel, and the right to have a parent or other person present while giving the statement. This requirement can be waived if done so in writing.[2]

Section 145(6) of the proposed YCJA makes these requirements less absolute. It states that

> when there has been a failure to comply ... the youth justice court may, having regard to all the circumstances and principles and objectives of this Act, admit into evidence a statement ... if it is satisfied that admission of the statement would not bring the administration of justice into disrepute.

This would take away from current rights and makes admissibility of a youth's statements subject to virtually the same test as adult statements—namely, section 24(2) of the Charter of Rights and Freedoms.

## SENTENCING (DISPOSITIONS)

It has been written that the true magic of the youth court has always been in the dispositional stage—the stage of proceedings where the court can give concrete form to the principles underlying the legislation.

The treatment-oriented philosophy of the JDA provided a rationale that justified indefinite (open-ended) sentences for any type of delinquency, from first-degree murder to "sexual immorality or any similar form of vice." The implementation of this logic required the judge to focus on the "treatment" deemed necessary to discount a sentence proportionate to the crime or protection of society. This disparity in the name of treatment often resulted in injustices.

The YOA introduced a number of reforms that reflected a paradigm shift away from the *welfare model* with more of a focus on protection of society (*crime control*) and appropriate sentences proportional to the crime committed (*justice*) (see Box 4.1). Section 20(1) of the YOA details how custodial dispositions must be fixed and limited in duration. In addition, there is provision for a wider range of dispositions as well as periodic review to evaluate their usefulness. The dispositions in section 20(1) form a hierarchy, each being, in general, successively more severe than the previous one (see Chapter 1 for a statistical breakdown of dispositions). In accordance with section 3, the court is to choose the disposition that interferes least with a young person's freedom, taking into account the need for protection of society. The following is a descriptive breakdown of available dispositions.

### Absolute Discharge and Conditional Discharge

An **absolute discharge** is the most lenient disposition available. Once it is imposed, the disposition is completed, and, even though there is a finding

**Box 4.4**

**TREATMENT ORDERS**

When originally legislated, section 22 of the YOA allowed youth-court judges to order that a youth be detained in a treatment facility (e.g., a hospital) for the purpose of treatment. No consent was required. This option became very controversial, and in 1995 (Bill C-37) it was repealed. Since then, treatment dispositions are no longer allowed under the act.

What do you think about this amendment? Does it reflect the criteria of a modified justice model? Review section 34 of the YCJA and discuss how the proposed new section compares to the 1995 amendment.

of guilt, no sanctions follow. A **conditional discharge** comes into effect only after a specified time period and after specified conditions are met. The disposition was introduced with Bill C-37 in 1995. If the conditions are not met, the young person can be resentenced by the court. Typically these dispositions are given for minor first offences when they appear to be in the best interests of the young person. The conditions are similar to those defined in a probation order.

### Fines

Fines not exceeding $1000 may be imposed, although the court is required to consider the present and future ability of the young person to pay. In this regard, if available, the **fine-option program** allows the young person to work off the fine.

### Compensation for Victims' Losses

A young person may be ordered to compensate a victim of a break-in, theft, or mischief, but only if the amount of damage is easy to determine. Otherwise, the judge may inform the victim that he or she may sue the perpetrator civilly for the tort of assault, as these courts (Small Claims—now Civil Division or Queen's Bench) specialize in quantifying complicated damage claims. In addition, if the young person has possession of stolen property at the time of disposition, the judge can order that it be returned.

Other forms of compensation may also involve some personal services. In such situations, provided the court is satisfied that the young person is a suitable candidate, the court may order the young person to perform personal services for the victim of the offence. This disposition has the potential of benefiting both parties as it not only may compensate the victim and promote responsibility in the young person, but also may allow for *reconciliation* and *restoration* of amicable relations.

### Community-Service Order

Applying the criteria used for personal service orders, the court may order the youth to perform community service for a period not to exceed 240 hours. Such service can be ordered only when it is part of a designated program and when the potential beneficiary consents. Beneficiaries typically include parks and recreation departments, food banks, and charitable organizations.

### Probation

Probation orders are among the most common dispositions imposed on young offenders. They may be ordered as the only penalty or in conjunction with other penalties. A probation order has some conditions that must appear. These mandatory conditions are set out in section 23(1) of the YOA and require the youth to keep the peace, to be of good behaviour, and to appear in court, as required. Conditions that may or may not be put in the order include scheduled reporting to a probation officer; reporting changes in address, employment, or education; remaining in the territorial jurisdiction of the court; making efforts to find employment or attend school; and residing where directed (section 23(2)). A "miscellaneous" provision allows the court to impose conditions designed to secure the good conduct of the youth and may include abstention from alcohol and drugs, geographic limitations, curfews, non-association clauses, or prohibition orders as allowed by any federal legislation (e.g., guns).

## Custody

In any case where custody is considered, the court must have before it a "pre-disposition report" prepared by youth-court workers, or probation officer, as to the particular circumstances of the young person. Such a report is

### Box 4.5

### CRITICAL THINKING EXERCISE: UNDERSTANDING STATUTES

Find the appropriate sections and subsections of the YOA that set out the following restrictions on the use of custody:

a. No disposition may have a duration of more than two years, except for a prohibition, seizure, or forfeiture order, or a custodial disposition.
b. Where more than one disposition is made with respect to different offences, the continuous combined duration of these dispositions shall not exceed three years, except when one of the offences is murder, within the meaning of section 231 of the Criminal Code, in which case the continuous combined duration of those dispositions shall not exceed ten years in the case of first-degree murder, and seven years in the case of second-degree murder.
c. Dispositions for new offences can be added to a previous sentence even if it results in a total greater than three years (i.e., allows consecutive sentencing).
d. In the case of first-degree murder, a maximum of seven of the ten years maximum can be served in custody, with the remaining time to be served in the community, whereas the maximum in custody for second-degree murder is four years in custody, with the remainder to be served under community supervision.
e. No person under 14 years of age is to be committed to a secure custody unless the same offence committed by an adult would be punishable by imprisonment of five years or more and the youth has previously been convicted of such an offence; or the offence is prison breach or escape from custody.
f. A young person between 14 and 18 years of age can be committed to secure custody only if the offence is one for which an adult could be imprisoned for five years or more; the offence is prison breach or escape; or the young offender has previously been convicted of a serious offence or has been in secure custody.
g. A young person held in custody must be kept separate and apart from adult prisoners.
h. Although a disposition continues after the young person becomes an adult, no disposition can be longer than the maximum punishment that would be applicable to an adult who committed the same offence.

optional with respect to other dispositions. Custody may be "open" (e.g., community residential centre, group home, child-care institution, or forest or wilderness camp) or "secure" (essentially a jail)(see Box 4.5).

Case law generally supports the position that custody should be ordered when all else fails (*R.* v. *R.C.S.* and *R.* v. *G.K.*). However, the Supreme Court has held that "general deterrence" (making an example out of a convicted young person to stop others) as opposed to merely "specific deterrence" (just trying to stop the specific defendant from reoffending) is an appropriate consideration in youth-court dispositions (*R.* v. *J.J.M.*).

## Review of Disposition

**Parole**, which is available to adults, is not available to young persons. The closest the YOA gets to parole is "conditional supervision," available only for young persons convicted of murder, and available only for the part of their sentence that follows custody. Terms of release are set out in paragraphs 26.2(2) and (3) of the YOA.

In the place of a general parole provision, the YOA provides that every custodial disposition of more than one year must be reviewed annually. Also, the youth, the prosecutor, or the provincial director of probation may apply earlier for a review of custody. On review, the court, or a provincially constituted review board, may either confirm the disposition, change secure custody to open custody, or release the young person on probation.

The act also provides for a similar review of non-custodial dispositions and, as with custody reviews, the result cannot be an increase in sentence. The review is customarily used to reduce a sentence. But if a young person fails to obey his or her sentence, he or she can be charged under section 26 with a new offence—"willful failure or refusal to comply with a disposition."

## Appeals

Under the JDA, appeals were allowed, with permission (leave) of the court, only if they were considered to be "essential in the public interest, or for the due administration of justice." In contrast, under the YOA, any finding of guilt or innocence, or any disposition, can be appealed as a matter of right, such appeal going either to the Supreme Court of the province (Queen's Bench in Alberta) or to the provincial court of appeal. Section 36 of the YCJA proposed no major changes to the appeal process.

## Sentencing under the YCJA

The YOA has been criticized for having inconsistent and competing sentencing principles (Bala et al., 1994). The YCJA attempts to fine-tune sentencing in a number of ways. A comprehensive statement of sentencing principles heads the sentencing part of the new act (section 37). The YCJA retreats further from the treatment model of the JDA than did the YOA by requiring similar sentences for those convicted of similar offences; by requiring sentences proportionate to the seriousness of the crime; and by stating clearly that the purpose of sentencing is to protect the public. However, the offender is not totally ignored, as rehabilitation of the offender continues to be an important, although subordinate, purpose of sentencing.

The YCJA proposes new sentencing options, encouraging the use of non-custodial sentences (section 38). Custody is specifically prohibited, except for violent offenders; for those who have failed to comply with previous non-custodial sentences; for those who have committed an indictable offence that has more than a two-year maximum in the Criminal Code, and have a substantial criminal record; or where it would be inconsistent with sentencing factors to impose a non-custodial disposition. These exceptions are worded vaguely enough to allow custodial dispositions in many situations, and it remains to be seen how the courts will interpret and use these new provisions if they become law.

The number of possible dispositions has been increasing under the YCJA. It includes, as the most lenient disposition, a mere reprimand (cautions and warnings) by the judge. Furthermore, there are greater provisions for community programs than made in the YOA. Further, all periods of custody are to be followed by intensive periods of supervision (with conditions) in the community equal to half the period of time in custody. However, the total sentence cannot be longer than two years, except for crimes where life imprisonment is prescribed in the Criminal Code, where the maximum is three years total. For non-violent offences, the court may make a deferred custody and supervision order when consistent with sentencing principles set out in the act. Length of custody for murder remains the same as under the YOA. However, changes in "transfer" provisions (see below) under the YCJA, if approved, will most likely amount to tougher sentences for many more young offenders.

## TRANSFER TO ORDINARY (ADULT) COURT

### History of Transfer

As we enter the new millennium, the traditional concern of the youth justice system throughout Canada has shifted to a more punitive viewpoint, emphasizing community protection and retribution (i.e., *modified justice model*). For example, in July 1999, the 14-year-old youth responsible for the Taber, Alberta, high-school shooting death had his lawyers withdraw from the case and the Crown requested the youth be transferred to adult court ("Taber ...," 1999).[3] The selection of jurisdiction for adjudicating youth crime today is one of the most controversial topics in crime-control policy, reflecting differences in assumptions about the causes of crime and philosophies of jurisprudence and punishment. Changing views of the nature of childhood and adolescence may also be involved. Arguably, the most serious decision, with the greatest impact, that a youth-court judge can make is to transfer, or waive, proceedings against a young person to adult court. The choice between jurisdictions is a choice between the nominally rehabilitative dispositions of the youth court and the explicitly punitive dispositions of the criminal court.

Transfer provisions have been changed several times since the inception of the YOA, making it increasingly easier for transfers to occur. Specifically, prior to being amended through **Bill C-12** in May 1992, section 16 allowed the transfer to adult court if the court was of the opinion that this transfer was in the interests of society (*deterrence*), having regard to the needs of the young person (*due process*). The 1992 amendments changed the test. Section 16(1.1) states that, if the youth court in a transfer hearing cannot reconcile the objectives of protection of the public with rehabilitation of the youth, then the youth shall be transferred to ordinary court. Furthermore, prior to being amended, the Crown always had the burden of proof to show, on the balance of probabilities, that the youth should go to ordinary court. If the prosecution failed in its burden, the youth automatically stayed in youth court. This provision was amended to change the burden of proof for 16- and 17-year-olds who are charged with murder, attempted murder, manslaughter, or aggravated sexual. It is presumed that these individuals will go to adult court unless they bring an application for a transfer hearing and convince the court, on the balance of probabilities, that they should be dealt with in youth court. The factors that the court must consider are the same no matter who brings the application, and are set out in section 16(2) of the YOA. These factors must be considered in light of section 3. In *R. v. S.H.M.* the Supreme Court of Canada held that all factors in section 16(2) must be considered, but need not be given equal weight.[4]

The proposed YCJA makes many more young offenders liable for adult punishment (section 57) in many more situations than did the YOA. Basically, any young offender 14 years old or over who is convicted of either a "presumptive offence" or a "violent offence" can be sentenced as an adult. **Presumptive offences** are defined in section 2 to be: first- or second-degree murder or attempted murder; manslaughter; aggravated sexual assault; or a serious violent offence for which an adult could receive a sentence of more than two years, but only for young offenders with a record of at least two other serious violent offences. A "violent offence" includes any offence judicially determined under section 61 (also see section 2, "re Interpretations") to be a violent offence (requires an application by attorney general after finding of guilt and after giving both parties an opportunity to be heard). The burden of proof is on the young person if he or she has committed a presumptive offence and opposes being treated as an adult, while the burden is on the Crown if the young person committed a violent offence and the Crown wishes an adult sentence. Section 72 requires the judge to consider the general sentencing provisions of the act, but, in particular, whether or not the provisions of the YCJA are adequate to hold the young person "accountable," considering the following factors: the seriousness and circumstances of the offence; the degree of responsibility, age, maturity, character, background, and previous record of the young person;

and any other factors the court deems relevant. If the young person is to be sentenced like an adult, he or she is given an election to be tried at youth justice court without a jury, before a judge of adult court (in Alberta, Provincial Court Criminal Division) without a jury, or before a judge and jury (in Alberta, the Court of Queen's Bench).

There are procedural problems with transfer hearings. On the surface, transfer hearings are adversarial in nature, but they are not formal criminal trials. The rules of evidence are greatly relaxed; the court can receive hearsay evidence about the youth's background and the circumstances of the alleged offence. The court need not be satisfied beyond a reasonable doubt that an offence occurred, but rather determines what is the appropriate forum for the trial and disposition of the charge in question. Witnesses testify with regard to likely differences in fate—therefore, opinion evidence and significant discretion is the rule.

This situation leaves the door open to prosecutorial abuse. More serious charges than may ultimately be provable beyond a reasonable doubt can be laid in order to get the case out of youth court and into ordinary court. Judge Beaulieu (1994), meanwhile, sees the problem more as a conceptual one. The transfer hearing is handled more like a sentencing proceeding (as it focusses mainly on dispositional matters) and, as a result, the accused's right to be presumed innocent is compromised. During a transfer hearing, facts need not be proven, but only alleged, and the judge need be satisfied only that the alleged facts, if proven, would support a finding of guilt. Beaulieu concludes by stating:

> The testing of the prosecution's evidence, including cross-examination of key witnesses has historically provided examples of an apparently strong case ending up as a very weak case, or no case at all ... *All of which underlines the artificial nature of the proceedings, and the fundamental difficulty in reconciling such a process as a transfer hearing with the traditional principles of due process and judicial responsibility.* (Beaulieu 1994: 338 – 339; emphasis in original)

As pointed out by both judges, two of the most important mechanisms for testing the reliability of evidence are missing from transfer hearings; specifically, cross-examination and the prohibition of hearsay evidence (key elements in the **adversarial system**). Cross-examination is impossible concerning hearsay or second-hand evidence because the person whose senses experienced the evidence is not in court. Finally, the Sanding Committee on Justice and Legal Affairs, along with the federal – provincial – territorial task force "have recommended that the YOA be revised so that transfer provisions are imposed after the finding of guilt" (Cohen, 1997: 65).

It is evident from this overview that transfer issues are controversial and mirror the complexity of the youth justice system, and it remains to be seen whether the proposed YCJA could offer any resolution to the concerns.

# SUMMARY

Even though the YOA retained some provisions drawn from the welfare model, its main thrust has been toward a modified justice model and, in some ways, a crime control model. Evidence of further movement in this direction is found in the nature of the amendments to the YOA since it was enacted (see Chapter 5). Given the current predominance of the law-and-order lobby, fuelled, in part, by the sensationalist mass media (see Chapter 6), it is unlikely that justice policy in Canada and other Western nations will be dominated by a justice approach for the foreseeable future. Punishment is increasingly the focus under the proposed YCJA, both in the increased availability of adult sentences and in its required focus on youth accountability. The difficulty with this approach is that it does little to solve the problem of crime in so much as social-science research has been unable to endorse punishment as a deterrent.

However, the proposed YCJA is not unidirectional. It contains some provisions consistent with a **community change model**. Its principles speak of rehabilitation and reintegration into the community, respect for differences, and the involvement of victims in the legal process. The possibility of Youth Justice Committees created under the YOA to assist in the administration of justice is retained in the new act. Community involvement is potentially enhanced in the proposed new legislation as it makes it possible for a judge, provincial director, police officer, or any other person to convene a "conference" to give advice concerning appropriate extrajudicial measures, conditions for interim judicial release, sentences, and reintegration plans. The act also requires that sentencing be designed to promote community responsibility, among other things. It must be noted that many of these provisions provide for possible programs and actions, but do not require them. The proposed YCJA appears to be mainly a fine-tuning of the YOA, with some changes in the direction of crime control, but also with some potential in the direction of a community change model.

# NOTES

1. See also *R.* v. *T. (V)*. where Madame Justice L'Heureux-Dubé stated that section 3(1) attempts to balance the need to make young persons responsible for their crimes while recognizing their vulnerability and special needs. Section 3 should not be considered a mere preamble, but should be given the force normally attributed to substantive provisions.
2. An exception to most of the requirements is made with respect to "spontaneous statements"; however, such statements must still be voluntary. The courts have held consistently that any violation of this statutory protection renders a statement inadmissable *(R.* v. *J.T.J.)*, even if a young person has been transferred to adult court *(R.* v. *D.A.Z.)*.
3. Given the significance of the case and incident (it occurred about one month after the Littleton, Colorado, high-school shooting spree), you might want to follow the outcome in the media or via the Internet.

4. When Bill C-37 (C. 19) was passed in 1995, one of its amendments (see Chapter 5) allowed for lengthier sentence provisions. McGuire (1997) suggests that it will likely result in fewer transfers to the adult system. However, as indicated in Chapter 1, the number of transfers actually increased in 1995 – 96.

# WEB LINKS

**Alberta Legislation**
<http://www.gov.ab.ca/qp>

Scroll down and follow the link to "Alberta's legislation" for free access to full-text versions of Alberta statutes and regulations.

**Department of Justice, Canada**
<http://www.canada.justice.gc.ca/>

This site includes access to legislation such as the Criminal Code of Canada, the Young Offenders Act, the Youth Criminal Justice Act (Bill C-68). Click on "Legal Resources" for access to Supreme Court of Canada cases since 1993.

# STUDY QUESTIONS

1. The proposed YCJA greatly expands the potential for extrajudicial dispositions, including referrals to a "community-based program" (undefined in the YCJA, but apparently not considered sanctions). Since the procedures that result in these types of dispositions lack many of the due-process protections available in a trial—young persons are dealt with more administratively (being convinced to admit guilt or wanting to deal with a matter quickly is different than being found guilty beyond a reasonable doubt in court), discuss any potential for abuse that you see in relation to these measures.
2. With alternative measures and other options, there are more dispositional options under the YOA than under the JDA. This trend continues under the proposed YCJA, which creates even more options. Since there are more options, does this guarantee that imprisonment will be used less often? (Check statistics to see if imprisonment rates are increasing or decreasing). Can you offer any explanation?
3. Which group of people appears to be neglected under the YOA? What problems does this potentially create in trying to administer the act? Does the proposed new YCJA offer any solutions?
4. Since provinces are not obliged to set up programs for dealing with young offenders, and there are no rules standardizing programs, it seems inevitable that young offenders will be treated quite differently from province to province. Is this situation acceptable? Why or why not?
5. "Transfer proceedings" allow hearsay evidence and limit cross-examination. Explain, with examples, what these due-process requirements are and why they are so important.
6. The proposed YCJA promotes community corrections. Discuss the advantages and disadvantages of "net-widening" or more social control that can result from community-based corrections programs.
7. Using the summary of legal-system types provided at the beginning of the chapter as a model, analyze the changes in the legislation governing young offenders in Canada, from their beginnings to the present time. Summarize your findings on a time-line or chart.

8. Chambliss and Seidman (1982: 144) contend that every society, nation, economic system, and historical period contains within it certain contradictory elements that are the moving forces behind social change—including the creation of law. Contradictions lead to conflicts, which lead to dilemmas, which result in new laws. Overwhelmingly, these legal innovations are symbolic and, at best, partial solutions for dilemmas because they do not deal with underlying contradictions. Identify the contradictions and conflicts that led to the legislation for young offenders, and evaluate whether or not the resulting new law (either the JDA, the YOA, or the YCJA) dealt with the underlying societal contradictions. What dilemmas might alter the YCJA in the future?
9. How should politicians react to public pressure to amend/change a law they feel does not require change? Develop your argument, using examples.

## REFERENCES


Archambault, O. (1983). "Young Offenders Act: Philosophy and principles." *Provincial Judges Journal*, 7(2): 1 – 7, 20.

Ariès, P. (1962). *Centuries of Childhood.* New York: Knopf.

Bala, N. (1986). "The Young Offenders Act: A new era in juvenile justice?" In N. Bala (Ed.), *Children's Rights in the Practice of Family Law*. Toronto: Carswell.

Bala, N., Hornick, J., McCall, R., and Clarke, K.L. (1994). *State Responses to Youth Crime: A Consideration of Principles*. Ottawa: Department of Justice.

Beaulieu, L. (1994). "Youth offences—adult consequences." *Canadian Journal of Criminology*, 36(3): 329 – 41.

Caputo, T.C. (1987). "The Young Offenders Act: Children's rights, children's wrongs." *Canadian Public Policy*, 8: 125 – 43.

Carrigan, D.O. (1998). *Juvenile Delinquency: A History*. Toronto: Irwin.

Chambliss, J., and Seidman, R. (1982). *Law, Order, and Power*. Reading, MA: Addison-Wesley.

Cohen, S. (1997). *Renewing Youth Justice: Thirteenth Report of the Standing Committee on Justice and Legal Affairs*. Ottawa: Queen's Printer.

Fattah, E.A. (1982). "Public opposition to prison alternatives and community corrections: A strategy for action." *Canadian Journal of Criminology*, 24: 371 – 85.

Hak, J. (1996). "The Young Offenders Act." In J. Winterdyk (Ed.), *Issues and Perspectives on Young Offenders in Canada*. Toronto: Harcourt Brace.

Havemann, P. (1986). "From child saving to child blaming: The political economy of the Young Offenders Act, 1908 – 1984." In S. Brickey and E. Comack (Eds.), *The Social Basis of the Law*. Toronto: Garamond Press.

Hylton, J.H. (1994). "Get tough or get smart? Options for Canada's youth justice system in the twenty-first century." *Canadian Journal of Criminology*, 36(3): 229 – 46.

Hudson, J., Hornick, J.P., and Burrows, B.A. (Eds.). (1993). *Justice and the Young Offender in Canada*. Toronto: Thompson Educational.

McGuire, M. (1997). "C.19, An Act to amend the Young Offenders Act and control the Criminal Code—Getting tougher?" *Canadian Journal of Criminology*, 39(2): 185 – 214.

"News Release: Minister of Justice introduces new youth justice law." (1999). Ottawa: Department of Justice.

Reid, S.A., and Reitsma-Street, M. (1984). "Assumptions and implications of new Canadian legislation for young offenders." *Canadian Criminology Forum*, 7: 334 – 52.

Rosen, P. (1996). "The Young Offenders Act. Current issue review." Research Branch, Library of Parliament, No. 86-13E.

"Taber shooting suspect may face adult court." (1999, 6 July). *Calgary Herald*, A1 – A2.

Winterdyk, J.A. (Ed). (1997). *Juvenile Justice Systems: International Perspectives.* Toronto: Canadian Scholars' Press.

## Cases Cited

R. v. *Anderson* (1938) 3 D.L.R. 317 (Man. C.A.).
R. v. *D.A.Z.* (1992) 140 N.R. 327 (S.C.C.).
R. v. *G.K.* (1985) 21 C.C.C. (3d) 558 (Alta. C.A.).
R. v. *J.J.M.* (1993) 19 W.C.B. (2d) (S.C.C.).
R. v. *J.T.J.* (1990) 59 C.C.C. (3d) (S.C.C.).
R. v. *R.C.S.* (1986) 27 C.C.C. (3d) 239 (N.B. C.A.).
R. v. *Shelson, S.*, [1990] 2 S.C.R. 254.
R. v. *S.H.M.* (1989) 50 C.C.C. (3d)53.
R. v. *Trimarchi* (1987) 63 O.R. (2d) 515.
R. v. *T.(V)*, [1992] 1 S.C.R. 749.
*R.P.B.* (1998) No. 2, Ct. Que (Youth Court Division), YOS 59-684.

# Chapter 5

# Changes in the Young Offenders Act: Principled Reform?

CHRISTINE LEONARD AND TRACEY MORRIS

## KEY OBJECTIVES

After reading this chapter, you should be able to:

- understand the relationship between public fear of crime and the development of youth crime control strategies;
- examine the influence that the media has on the relationship noted above;
- understand the relationship between the Charter of Rights and Freedoms and the "Declaration of Principle" in the Young Offenders Act;
- examine why changes in the youth-justice system are needed in the use of incarceration and alternatives to the formal youth-justice process;
- describe the 1986, 1991, and 1995 amendments to the Young Offenders Act;
- describe the 1995 – 97 Phase II Review of the Young Offenders Act;
- describe the 1999 proposed Youth Criminal Justice Act.

## KEY TERMS

alternatives
Bill C-12
Bill C-37
Bill C-68
Bill C-106
crime prevention through social development (CPSD)
"Declaration of Principle"
social policy
YOA Phase II Review
Youth Criminal Justice Act

## INTRODUCTION

Crime policy must strike a delicate balance between social control and the protection of individual rights. Chapter 4 presented a comprehensive overview of youth-justice legislation. In this chapter, we look at the ongoing amendments to the Young Offenders Act (YOA) since its proclamation on 2 April 1984. The amendments are analyzed in terms of how they relate to the prevailing public mood and how they relate to section 3, the "Declaration of Principle" section of the act. The discussion thus examines the dilemma of crafting social policy that is both politically and programmatically correct. The chapter concludes by examining **Bill C-68**, given first reading in the House of Commons on 11 March 1999, calling for the repeal of the Young Offenders Act and passage of the Youth Criminal Justice Act (YCJA).

## LAW AND ORDER AS SOCIAL POLICY

The public demands that communities be made more safe, and obliging politicians respond with more laws (see Chapter 6). Problem solved. Or is it? If we are to believe the current catchy headlines that proclaim the failures of our criminal justice process and reinforce the call for even more punitive legislation, the problem is far from solved.

It is difficult to tell which comes first in the cycle of policy development: concern for the public or reaction to public outrage. It is commonly believed that crime and violence serve as targets of convenience for politicians hoping to deflect concern away from other pressing social issues. It is much easier to pass laws, build prisons, and talk tough than it is to solve the problems that contribute to crime, such as poverty, dropping out of school, and family violence.

Some have suggested that the calls to "get tough on crime" represent democracy at work. Throughout history, sensational crimes have raised public fear and resulted in demands for law reform (Schissel, 1997). Politicians respond to this concern in their drafting of policy and law. To do otherwise would give the appearance of being soft on crime and insensitive to public opinion. It is often said that, in order for justice to be done, it must be seen to be done. As Schissel (1997: 26) points out,

> although some politicians understand that panics are exaggerated—e.g., Liberal Minister Alan Rock's admission that the *Young Offenders Act* is not responsible for youth crime and that Canada is not suffering an epidemic of crimes by youth—they often choose to engage in moral panic debates to appeal to the electorate.

This theory that public opinion drives social policy can be easily challenged. First, if it were true, it would be fair to assume that there would be no GST, no North American Free Trade Agreement (NAFTA), and no legislated bilingualism. Second, the assumption that the public wants only a hard-line response to crime is not borne out by research; the public's sentencing expectations are more complex and reasonable than a simple "lock 'em up" approach (see, for example, Roberts, 1992). Third, as noted previously, politicians target crime in order to deflect concern away from other issues.[1] As Schissel (1997) points out, virtually all political platforms feature law and justice issues. Finally, the role of the media in discussions about crime and the justice process must be acknowledged (see Chapter 6). The media's love affair with crime news is well known and studies have shown that the media is the public's primary source of information about crime and the criminal justice system (e.g., Alberta Justice Corporate Support Services, 1999; Hartnagel and Baron, 1995; Canadian Sentencing Commission, 1987).

It is far from clear whether the media reflect or create public opinion. It is also unclear whether politicians lead or follow the sentiments of their constituents. What is clear is that this climate which stresses law and order is being reinforced by the words and deeds of our policy-makers. For example, an article written by Reform MP Chuck Cadman for the *Vancouver Sun* (1998, 9 June) states:

> McLellan [Minister of Justice] touts as one of her primary objectives the restoration of public confidence in the youth justice system. Canadians will never regain that confidence as long as:
>
> - 11-year-olds can commit rape with no consequence whatsoever;
> - a 17-year-old can commit murder and get 7 years;
> - convicted teenage pedophiles can live among young children with anonymity;
> - the consequence of a serious, violent offence depends on the prevailing corrections philosophy of the province in which it was committed; and
> - the participants in beating, torture and manslaughter can walk free after 3 years.

This example captures a number of elements of our discussion to this point: it speaks of public opinion, it calls for tighter controls, and it appeals somewhat to people's desire for revenge. This one-dimensional approach to crime fosters the acceptance of a one-dimensional response—to get tough. This, in turn, becomes reality for both government and the governed.

The interaction between public opinion and public policy comes as no real surprise, nor does the powerful effect that the media have on this interaction. What is surprising is how all of this has translated into crime-control strategies that almost entirely ignore warnings about their simplicity and lack of empirical foundation. As Schissel (1997: 14) points out,

> the existing public debates on youth crime, while largely uninformed, have the potency and the scientific legitimacy to direct public opinion and to effect social control policy that stigmatizes and controls those who are most disadvantaged and victimized.

## INFLUENCE OF THE CHARTER OF RIGHTS AND FREEDOMS

The Charter of Rights and Freedoms was enacted as part of the Constitution Act, 1982. The legal rights now guaranteed by the Charter include the right to be secure from unreasonable search and seizure, the right not to be arbitrarily detained or imprisoned, specific rights upon arrest or detention, specific rights relating to criminal and penal proceedings, witness rights against self-incrimination, and the right not to be subjected to cruel or unusual punishment. All criminal law in Canada is affected by these legal protections, including the Young Offenders Act (YOA) and the proposed Youth Criminal Justice Act (YCJA). Section 3 of the YOA, the **Declaration of Principle**, recognizes the Charter rights of young people, as does the "Declaration of Principle" section of the proposed YCJA.

# THE DECLARATION OF PRINCIPLE

## THE PURPOSE OF SECTION 3

Section 3 of the YOA, the "Declaration of Principle," can be seen as Canada's policy toward young offenders (also see Chapter 4). It reflects an evolution in values and attitudes toward criminal justice and, more specifically, juvenile justice. The declaration is based upon "extensive research and a more sophisticated knowledge of human behaviour generally, and the moral and psychological development of children in particular" (Archambault, 1983: 10). It is not simply a "'kiddies' Criminal Code" (Bala, 1992: 25) or a preamble; it is an integral part of the YOA that governs interpretation of the act (Platt, 1989). According to the Solicitor General of Canada (1979), the "Declaration of Principle" serves as a statement of the act's spirit and intent and provides a guide for its proper administration and the realization of its objectives.

## SECTION 3 IN PRACTICE

The "Declaration of Principle" recognizes legal rights, not "psychological rights," such as the right to an environment that facilitates the growth and development of a child (Awad, 1987). While it is acknowledged that these psychological rights cannot be clearly defined, some see the absence of any mention of them as reflecting their diminished importance.

Early criticism of the "Declaration of Principle" included the observation that, while the special needs of young people are recognized, each time they are mentioned in section 3, they are accompanied by a disclaimer that emphasizes responsibility or societal protection (Awad, 1987: 441). Changes to the "Declaration of Principle" in 1994 brought about through Bill C-37 (discussed in detail in the next section) partially rectified this problem by clarifying that the protection of society is best accomplished through the rehabilitation of young offenders. Bill C-37 also added a statement that crime prevention is an integral part of community safety.

According to Awad (1987: 441), another fundamental element of the "Declaration of Principle" is the suggestion that the act is a judicial act whose only goal is to provide justice under the due process of the law, and that other systems exist to deal with the clinical and educational needs of young people. However, as Bala (1992) observes, the difficulty is that there is no clear-cut division of functions and goals of the various institutions that deal with young people.

While the importance of the policies set out in section 3 is clear, the meaning of the policies is open to debate (Platt, 1989: 2 – 6), because they are neither consistent nor coherent. This lack of consistency and coherence has led to the current situation, in which the policies are used by both Crown and defence attorneys in arguing cases.

## CONCERNS ABOUT THE YOA

Many problems can arise when legislation is proclaimed, and intent must be translated into action. Despite the honest efforts of criminal justice professionals, there appears to be a widening gap between the YOA as designed and the YOA as practised. While many problems do exist, some of these fall into the category of technical or procedural ones. These types of problems are the subject of an extensive ongoing federal – provincial consultation. However, more substantive concerns have not been dealt with, such as the overuse of incarceration for young offenders and the underuse of alternative measures in place of the formal youth justice system. These concerns cannot be addressed through legislative tinkering; rather, they require major attitudinal shifts if they are to be dealt with in any meaningful way.

## THE OVERUSE OF INCARCERATION

The "Declaration of Principle" of the YOA directs that the disposition of incarceration be used as a last resort for young offenders. However, statistics indicate that, in practice, incarceration is overused as a disposition for young offenders. Fully one-third of convicted young offenders receive a sentence of custody (Canadian Centre for Justice Statistics, 1997). In fact, Canada has the highest youth incarceration rate of any Western democratic nation, including the United States (Schissel, 1997; see Chapter 1 for further details).

Given these statistics, it seems unlikely that detention is being used as a disposition of last resort for young offenders. Young offenders are not treated leniently by the justice system, as politicians and the media routinely suggest. For example, as noted in Chapter 1, nearly one-half of young offenders transferred to adult court have committed non-violent offences (Canadian Centre for Justice Statistics, 1999).

### UNDERUSE OF ALTERNATIVES TO FORMAL JUSTICE PROCESSING

The "Declaration of Principle" of the YOA calls for the use of alternatives to formal justice processing for young offenders when doing so is not inconsistent with the protection of society. Among the many alternatives to the youth justice system are police cautioning, youth-justice committees, family group conferencing, and circle sentencing.

In practice, however, such alternatives have been underutilized for youthful misbehaviour. In fact, the use of alternatives has been steadily declining since the implementation of the YOA (Schissel, 1997). Furthermore, in recent years we have seen a trend toward increased criminalization of behaviours previously dealt with informally, such as schoolyard scuffles (Schissel, 1997; John Howard Society of Ontario, 1998). For example, in the past, schoolyard scuffles were usually dealt with by school officials and parents; it is not uncommon for this behaviour to now result in an assault charge, particularly with the advent of "zero tolerance" policies.

## CALL FOR REFORM: MOVING TOWARD A CRIME CONTROL MODEL

### 1986 AMENDMENTS

Following a series of federal – provincial meetings, the federal government began a review of the YOA in the fall of 1985, a mere year after its enactment.[2] A news release issued by the office of the Solicitor General of Canada (1986) on 30 April 1986 outlined then solicitor general Perrin Beatty's proposals for amendments to seven aspects of the act: (1) non-compliance; (2) prohibition on publication; (3) records provisions; (4) adult contributions; (5) duration of dispositions; (6) custody; and (7) pre-trial detention.

The first area of amendment was in *non-compliance*, or *breach of a disposition* (section 26). The review process used when a young offender failed to comply with a non-custodial disposition was found to be inadequate. The amendment sought to "streamline the process and allow quick police and correctional intervention by way of arrest and detention where there has been a breach of a non-custodial disposition" (Solicitor General of Canada, 1986: 2).

Prohibition on publication (section 38(1)) was the second area of amendment. This was prompted by public dissatisfaction with the prohibition on publication of the identity of young offenders, particularly dangerous young offenders at large in the community. The proposed amendment (section 38(1.2)) would allow the youth court to reveal the identity of a young person who poses a danger to the public, when public assistance might aid in the youth's apprehension (Solicitor General of Canada, 1986).

Concerns were expressed that the record provisions of the act were too cumbersome and restrictive, thereby interfering with the efficient administration of justice. In addition, it was found that "the management of young offenders who were acquitted by reason of insanity" (section 13) was adversely affected by a lack of records (Solicitor General of Canada, 1986: 3). Thus, the Solicitor General of Canada proposed to change the records provisions of the act to address the specific concerns raised.

Another area of amendment dealt with adults contributing to offences committed by young offenders. The proposed amendment to the Criminal Code would address "individuals who counsel children under the age of twelve to commit crimes" (Solicitor General of Canada, 1986: 3). These individuals would be liable to criminal prosecution.

It was also felt that, under certain circumstances, the duration of dispositions under the act was inappropriate. The amendment sought to allow consecutive sentences to be imposed on a young offender who commits a criminal offence prior to completing a disposition for a different offence (section 20(4.1)). This would allow a possible aggregate sentence in excess of three years.

Custody (section 20(1)) was another area of concern. The amendments regarding custody sought to

> resolve difficulties in the custody provisions of the Act. Provisions for matters such as the transfer of young offenders from secure to open custody will be modified or clarified, while emphasizing that custody is a disposition of last resort intended to protect society. (Solicitor General of Canada, 1986: 4)

Amendments regarding pre-trial detention provided for accused young offenders to be kept in pre-trial custody for longer periods of time and made other procedural improvements. The amendments also sought to alter a variety of administrative, procedural, technical, and translation errors that did not affect the policy of the act (Solicitor General of Canada, 1986).

Bill C-106 was introduced in the House of Commons on 30 April 1986 and was subsequently assented to in the Senate on 26 June 1986.

## 1991 AMENDMENTS

The YOA was subject to further proposals for amendment in the ensuing years. It was felt that the act did not offer enough flexibility for dealing with serious youth crimes—judges were forced to choose between the extremes of a three-year sentence under the act or a possible life sentence in adult court (Bala, 1989). Not surprisingly, there was a judicial call for Parliament to create more flexible sentencing options for young offenders convicted of murder.

In response to the 1987 judicial call for further amendments, a meeting of the provincial attorneys general was held in Charlottetown in June 1989. They recommended the following amendments to the act (Bala, 1989: 174):

- that the sentence for a young person convicted of murder in youth court be a maximum disposition of three years' custody, to be followed by conditional release for a period of two years less one day;
- that the sentence for a young person convicted of murder in adult court be life imprisonment with eligibility for parole to be fixed by the trial judge at a period between five and ten years, inclusive; and
- that the test for transfer to adult court under section 16 of the act be amended so that protection of society is of paramount consideration.

A consultation meeting hosted by the Canadian Council on Children and Youth took place between representatives of 27 voluntary-sector organizations and federal Justice department members in October 1989. According to the Canadian Council on Children and Youth (1989: 1), "the participants pointed out that the proposed amendments did not focus on prevention or deal with the root causes of crime. It was suggested that the Department was attempting to deal with public outrage regarding violence in society without really addressing the causes of that violence." Participants at the conference were concerned that proposed amendments to transfer provisions in the YOA were being promoted in reaction to media coverage of several murder cases. Included in the concluding session of the conference was the following comment: "The Government should not rush into amending the Act when there is not enough research to make informed decisions on several of the issues discussed in the Consultation document" (Canadian Council on Children and Youth, 1989: 13).

Bill C-58 was drafted and given first reading in the House of Commons on 20 December 1989. Beuckart (1992) states that Bill C-58 was introduced in response to a wave of publicity about the murders committed by teenagers. According to the Minister of Justice and the Attorney General of Canada (Canadian Council, 1989: 1), the issue in Bill C-58 was how "to increase public safety while maintaining the principles of the *Young Offenders Act*." The proposed amendments under Bill C-58 were said to reflect extensive national consultation with various national and regional groups and organizations, ranging from the Canadian Bar Association and the John Howard Society, to the Church Council on Justice and Corrections.

Bill C-58 died on the order paper when the session of Parliament ended. However, it was later reintroduced as Bill C-12. Bill C-12 was introduced in the House of Commons on 25 November 1991 and passed by Parliament in December 1991. The Senate Standing Committee on Justice and Constitutional Affairs examined the bill further, and, in May 1992, Bill C-12 was proclaimed in force.

Bill C-12 clarified the meaning of the interests of society in a transfer decision (Clauses 16 and 17). The "interests of society" include both the protection of the public and the needs of the youth. In the event that the court decides that both of these objectives cannot be achieved if the youth remains in the young offender system, the protection of the public will be given priority and the youth will be transferred to adult court.

Bill C-12 extended the maximum disposition for a young offender under the Young Offenders Act to five years less a day. However, this five-year disposition is broken down into a maximum of three years to be served in custody, and the remainder of the five-year period to be served under community supervision. Bill C-12 included a "continuation of custody" provision in section 7. This section gives a youth court the power to order a young person to remain in custody for the full five years in the event that the court is satisfied that the youth is at risk for committing a criminal offence that would result in death or serious harm to another person prior to the expiration of the youth's disposition. In the event that a young offender charged with murder is transferred to adult court, he or she can be eligible for parole after serving five to ten years in custody under the Bill C-12 amendments. Parole eligibility is set by the judge during sentencing and authorized by the National Parole Board.

The federal Department of Justice issued a consultation document in July 1991 proposing further changes to the act. It is important to note that this document, proposing more amendments, was circulated before Bill C-12 was introduced. The three issues of concern in this round of proposed amendments were: (1) the legislative criteria for custody **dispositions**, (2) who decides on the level of custody and the criteria for review; and (3) the structure for release from custody. Changes were proposed to these three areas in response to a number of concerns raised by government and non-governmental organizations.

Regarding the criteria for custody dispositions, concerns were raised about the marked increase in committals to custody, and that custody may not always be desirable from a rehabilitative point of view, and in fact may be contrary to the "Declaration of Principle." Furthermore, high spending on custodial dispositions limits the resources available for other young offender programs (Department of Justice Canada, 1991: 12).

With regard to who decides on the level of custody, concerns with the current law included the suggestion that the court might lack the information necessary for it to make the most suitable placement, that the provisions may operate in opposition to the youth's needs; and that the provisions that restrict movement from one level of custody to another may cause delay and stand in the way of timely movement (Department of Justice Canada, 1991: 15).

While the first round of amendments to the YOA contained some "get tough" measures, the amendments dealt largely with technical and procedural changes.[3] In 1986, the YOA was still a new piece of legislation that required some fine-tuning. In addition, the debate about the need for changes involved mostly academics and those working in the system; there was little public involvement. The amendments focussed on court outcomes, including transfers and dispositions for young offenders charged with serious and violent offences. During this next round of amendments, the call for increased public safety was at the forefront of the debate, which now also involved the public and the politicians.

The amendments proposed in the 1991 consultation document received surprisingly little public attention. In the subsequent years, however, the public became increasingly vocal about the need for changes to the act. There were many public forums, petitions, and letter-writing campaigns in 1992 and 1993 that heightened and maintained the public tide of discontent with the YOA. The public called for increased penalties, publication of names of young offenders, changes to the age restrictions of the YOA, and automatic transfer of certain young offenders to adult court. The level of public involvement in the debate, the level of anger and hostility toward the legislation, and the specific nature of the calls for reform were difficult for the government to ignore.

## 1995 AMENDMENTS

Bill C-37 was introduced in the House of Commons on 2 June 1994 by then minister of justice Allan Rock. In the news release that announced the bill, the minister stated:

> With the introduction of this Bill, the Government is honouring its commitment to address the problems of violent youth crime by amending the *Young Offenders Act*. The amendments recognize the public's concern about youth violence, and demonstrate the government's determination that public protection must be our primary objective in dealing with violent young offenders. One of our goals must be to ensure that young people understand the consequences of their actions and take responsibility for them. (Department of Justice Canada, 1994: 1)

The bill was presented as the first step in a two-part strategy to reform the youth justice system; the next step was to be a parliamentary committee review (Department of Justice Canada, 1994: 1).

The changes proposed in Bill C-37 dealt with a few of the specific areas that most angered the public. The government implemented some of the tough changes requested by the public, while at the same time trying to remind the public that youth crime must be seen in a community context, related to issues of services for youth and the social and economic risk factors that relate to youth crime. Highlights of the bill included:

- increasing sentences for youth convicted of first- or second-degree murder in youth court to ten and seven years, respectively;
- transferring 16- and 17-year-olds charged with serious personal-injury offences to adult court unless they can show a judge that public protection and rehabilitation can both be achieved in youth court;
- extending the time that 16- and 17-year-old young offenders who have been convicted of murder in an adult court must serve before they can be considered for parole;
- improving measures for information sharing between professionals such as school officials and police and with selected members of the public when public safety is at risk;
- retaining the records of serious young offenders longer; and
- establishing provisions that will encourage rehabilitation and treatment of young offenders in the community when this is appropriate (Department of Justice Canada, 1994: 1 – 2).

Bill C-37 was proclaimed in force on 1 December 1995 (see Box 5.1).

## YOA PHASE II REVIEW

The comprehensive Phase II Review of the YOA was initiated by the House of Commons Standing Committee on Justice and Legal Affairs in July 1995. According to the letter of invitation issued to interested parties, the review was "to entail a comprehensive review of the youth justice system, youth

**Box 5.1**

**CHANGES TO THE YOUNG OFFENDERS ACT PROPOSED IN BILL C-37 COME UNDER FIRE**

Youth Rehabilitation Loses Priority: Ottawa Indicates Society Comes First as Harsher Justice Proposed.

Mr. Rock's proposals follow months of increased public and political debate on a perceived surge in youth crime fueled by a handful of recent sensational killings in several cities and a Liberal election promise to toughen the 10-year-old Young Offenders Act.... But despite Mr. Rock's tough-talking tone, the amendments presented in the House of Commons will not appease the Reform Party's demand for a more retributive justice.

Randy White, a spokesman for the Reform Party, called the proposals very disappointing for failing to lower the age brackets for young offenders to 10 and 15 years.

**Source:** Ross Howard, "Youth rehabilitation loses priority," *Globe and Mail*, 3 June 1994, p. A1.

Police Chiefs Tough on Teen Crime.

Older teenagers charged with serious crimes should be automatically tried in adult court without a chance to head back to youth court, says the Association of Chiefs of Police.

"Judges must have access to longer and more appropriate sentences where serious—especially violent—crime is involved," the association said ...

The association predicts most judges will send such teenagers back to youth court, defeating the purpose of the amendment and foisting a costly hearing on the justice system.

"If Parliament is really serious about addressing violent youth crime, then they can strengthen the section by providing simply for automatic transfer for serious offences ... without provision for return to youth court."

**Source:** The Canadian Press, "Police chiefs tough on teen crime," *Edmonton Journal*, 26 October 1994, p. A11.

offending and the operation and implementation of the YOA, as well as problems arising from the Act itself" (Dupuis, 1995: 1). The committee solicited input from all sectors of Canadian society, ranging from criminal justice professionals, children's services organizations, victims, parents, young offenders, and educators, to advocacy groups and social-policy analysts.

The committee examined a number of issues in relation to youth crime, including the direct and indirect community impacts and social costs of youth crime, youth-crime prevention measures, deterrents to youth crime, family responsibility for youth crime, and the risks and needs of young people under 12 years of age engaged in offending behaviours. In addition, the committee examined the following in relation to the youth justice system: the rationale for a youth justice system; police discretion and court diversion schemes; use of **alternative measures**; intermediate sanctions and mental-health treatment programs; pre-trial detention and custodial committals, and the relationship between responsibilities of the youth justice system and the child-welfare system. Finally, the committee examined the following issues in relation to the operation and implementation of the

YOA: the link between youthful criminality and the YOA; the appropriateness of the adversarial system to youth-justice proceedings; the impact of affording youth formal legal and procedural safeguards; the effectiveness of the act's "Declaration of Principle," the appropriateness of the minimum and maximum ages of criminal responsibility; the disparities in sentencing practices; and presumptive transfers to adult court (Dupuis, 1995).

As can be seen by the extent of these areas of inquiry, the review was intended to look beyond the limits of young offender laws for solutions to youth crime. The committee visited 23 facilities and youth programs and services across Canada, seeking input and met with 33 participants, as well as with interested parties, in a forum setting and received 123 briefs.

The Standing Committee submitted their final report, *Renewing Youth Justice*, to the House of Commons in April 1997. Their final report made fourteen recommendations:

1. Maintain a separate youth justice system.
2. Replace the "Declaration of Principle" with a statement of purpose and principles.
3. Foster public education programs about the YOA and youth crime.
4. Reallocate a percentage of the justice budget toward crime-prevention programs.
5. Discuss with the provinces options to shift resources away from custody into community-based programming.
6. Renegotiate cost sharing with the provinces to ensure that 80 percent of shareable costs are related to non-custodial programs and services.
7. Reform the system to accommodate alternatives to it.
8. Strengthen the section on the Youth Justice Committee in the act.
9. Allow 10- and 11-year-olds to be prosecuted in certain circumstances.
10. Retain the current maximum age in the act, at 17.
11. Allow transfer to adult court after conviction and before sentence.
12. Amend the act to require parental attendance in youth court.
13. Provide judicial discretion to publish names in certain circumstances.
14. Provide judicial discretion in whether statements made by young persons to a person in authority can be heard (Cohen, 1997).

Having taken a broad mandate in reviewing all issues related to youth crime, the Standing Committee demonstrated in its recommendations a fairly balanced approach to the issues. The committee made recommendations in the areas of change sought by the public, such as dealing with youth under age 12 who commit offences, and publishing names in certain circumstances. However, many groups felt that the recommendations did not go far enough. For example, Reform MP Jack Ramsay, a member of the parliamentary committee reviewing the act, said the majority Liberal committee turned a deaf ear to those who raised issues or problems with the act. According to Ramsay, "They'll quote all the witnesses that support the status quo and ignore all the witnesses that didn't" (Morris, 1997: A3).

Other groups, such as the John Howard Society of Alberta (1997), responded that, overall, they were pleased with most of the recommendations in the report. However, they pointed out that several recommendations conflicted with the overall flavour of the report. The John Howard Society felt that these contradictions appear to be in areas in which the standing committee fell prey to public pressures that were influenced by the varying misconceptions the committee observes in its report.

In late 1997, there was a meeting of federal – provincial – territorial ministers responsible for Justice. At that time, all provinces and territories were invited to tell the federal Minister of Justice, Anne McLellan, their views on the recent standing committee report on youth justice. They each put their views forward, ranging from supporting the status quo to specific amendments to the act (Minister of Justice and Attorney General of Canada, 1997). As summarized in Box 5.2, four provinces (Alberta, Ontario, Manitoba, and Prince Edward Island) brought forward for consideration a list of proposed amendments to the YOA.

The review of the YOA revealed widespread dissatisfaction with the handling of violent and repeat young offenders, as well as concern with the overuse of incarceration for less serious young offenders. These conclusions set the stage for a shift toward a **modified justice model** for dealing with young offenders in Canada.

### Box 5.2

### PROPOSED PROVINCIAL AMENDMENTS TO THE YOA

- Reduce the minimum age of criminal accountability in selected cases (at Crown discretion);
- Provide for easier transfer to ordinary court to address serious and chronic offending by youths rather than a general reduction to the maximum age;
- Amend the act to impose the presumption of adult court for youths 16 years of age and older who have committed serious violent offences not currently addressed in the act, and for those demonstrating a pattern of offending;
- Amend the act to require that youths transferred to adult court have the same parole-eligibility requirements as do adult offenders;
- Amend the act to allow, upon conviction, publication of the identity of chronic repeat offenders and those young offenders convicted of an offence involving serious violence;
- Amend the act to permit the admission into evidence of a voluntary statement given to a person in authority at the discretion of the youth court;
- Amend the act to provide for placement of a young offender, who has attained the age of 20 years, in a federal penitentiary, where the remainder of the youth-custody portion of the disposition is two years or more;
- Amend the act to apply the victim surcharge to young offenders;
- Amend the act to restrict court-appointed counsel to circumstances where youths or their guardians cannot afford to pay for legal services; and
- Amend the act to provide mandatory custody dispositions for youths convicted of an offence involving the use of weapons.

**Source:** Minister of Justice and Attorney General Canada, News Release: "Remarks by ministers at the conclusion of the federal – provincial – territorial ministers responsible for justice meeting." 4 – 5 December 1997, Montreal, Quebec, p. 6. Reproduced with the permission of the Minister of Public Works and Government Services, Canada.

# YOUTH JUSTICE STRATEGY

As noted in the Introduction to this text on page 3, in May 1998 the federal Minister of Justice, Anne McLellan, announced the government's proposed strategy for youth-justice renewal. In the minister's press release, she is quoted as saying:

> The current system is not working as it should in many significant areas. We need to do more to prevent youth crime in the first place, to develop meaningful responses to youth crime that emphasize responsibility and respect for the victim and the community, and to deal more firmly and effectively with violent and repeat young offenders. Canadians want a youth justice system that protects society and that helps youth avoid crime or turn their lives around if they do become involved in crime. The government's youth justice strategy will accomplish this. (Department of Justice Canada, 1998: 1)

According to the government, the strategy has three key elements that will work together to better protect the public: *prevention*, *meaningful consequences for youth crime*, and *intensified rehabilitation*. The prevention element is linked to other federal government initiatives aimed at children and youth, including a $32-million crime-prevention initiative, the National Children's Agenda, and the government's response to the Royal Commission on Aboriginal Peoples (Department of Justice Canada, 1998: 1). The other two features would be manifested in the new act that would replace the YOA.

The new youth-justice legislation will "put public protection first" and "command respect, foster values such as accountability and responsibility, and make it clear that criminal behaviour will lead to meaningful consequences" (Department of Justice Canada, 1998: 1). The legislation was also intended to foster the development of a full scope of community-based sentences and effective alternatives to justice-system processes for non-violent young offenders.

# PROPOSED LEGISLATION: YOUTH CRIMINAL JUSTICE ACT (YCJA)

The proposed YCJA (Bill C-68) was introduced in the House of Commons on 11 March 1999 by Justice Minister Anne McLellan (Department of Justice Canada, 1999a). Major features of the new legislation include the following:

- Youth will no longer be transferred to adult court for trial. Cases will be tried in youth justice court, and conviction would be followed by a hearing about whether the youth should receive an adult sentence.
- The option for youth receiving adult sentences will be available for youths aged 14 and older and for youths with patterns of repeat offending, in addition to the existing "transfer" offences.
- The test for whether a youth should receive an adult sentence is changed to whether or not there are sufficient sanctions available in youth-justice court to hold the youth accountable.

- For any custody disposition, the judge must set a period of the sentence that the youth must serve in the community under supervision. The norm will be one-half of the sentence.
- There will be a new intensive rehabilitative custody and supervision sentence available for youth convicted of presumptive offences, and youth with mental illness, psychological disorders, and emotional disturbances. It will allow youth-justice court judges to direct treatment and programming.
- Names will be published if an adult sentence is imposed or if the youth could have received an adult sentence, although the judge can deny the latter's publication.
- There will be strong measures around the use of community sentences. Use of diversion by the police and prosecution is built into the act.
- The act will allow a sentence of up to two years in jail for a parent who wilfully fails to supervise his or her children when that parent has such an undertaking with the court. (Department of Justice Canada, 1999b) (see Box 5.3).

## A QUESTION OF BALANCE

The YOA represents a balance between due process and special needs, public protection and offender rehabilitation, and child welfare and criminal justice (see Winterdyk, 1997). The act is not perfect: however, it represents a dramatic improvement, both in content and in application, over the JDA.

The most pressing problem facing the Canadian justice system today is the combined effect of an overreliance on incarceration as an answer to crime and the widespread acceptance of the lock-'em-up/get-tough philosophy on the part of the public. This is a particularly problematic feature of our response to youth crime: this approach is inefficient and ineffective; it provides a false sense of security; and it often prompts calls for more of the same when it fails. It is telling that the changes made to the YOA over the years repeatedly made the act tougher, yet did not quell the calls for more. It almost appears that changes made one year are forgotten the next, as a sensational incident involving a youth sparks calls for more reform. The government continues to promote the notion that "public confidence" in the justice system is tied to punitive measures for violent offenders. In doing so, they continue to reinforce the notion that punishment achieves public protection or that punishment promotes positive change in young people. Public safety becomes simply a matter of determining the perfect punishment.

As has been pointed out by Doob (1994), among others, crime levels among youth have little, if anything, to do with the laws that govern youth crime. Doob suggests that, if the public could be convinced that the youth justice system can do little for crime, then it not only might consider more productive ways of dealing with youth crime, but also improve the actual operation of the youth-justice system without the "baggage" of believing that youth crime can be solved by such a system (Doob, 1994: 4). The standing committee's review of the YOA attempted to look beyond the law to other solutions, as did the government-commissioned Youth Justice Strategy. Based on reactions to the strategy, however, it appears that the public is not yet prepared to look at the bigger picture of youth crime. Yet, while the government may understand the importance of the social context of youth crime, it has not invested much in trying to help the public understand it.

## Box 5.3

## YOUTH CRIME: A DEMOCRATIC DILEMMA

### YOA Changes Ripped

The new youth justice law was applauded in some quarters yesterday but blasted by Ontario's Attorney General as disappointing "cosmetic surgery."

The RCMP lauded the new act, while the victims' rights group CAVEAT said it was a landmark day because victims are finally getting a say.

Justice Minister Anne McLellan heralded the legislation as an important turning point for Canada's youth justice system.

But Ontario's Attorney General Charles Harnick says McLellan performed cosmetic surgery on a diseased YOA that needed an organ transplant.

---

**Source:** Mark Dunn and Jeff Harder, "YOA changes ripped," *Toronto Sun*, 12 March 1999, p. 7.

### Changes in New Youth Justice Act Not Enough, Provinces Complain.

"Changes to the youth justice system don't go far enough," says Alberta Justice Minister Jon Havelock.

He wanted to see the age of criminal accountability dropped to 10 years from 12. He also sought automatic transfer to adult court for trial rather than measures allowing a transfer for sentencing alone.

Alberta also supports tougher measures against chronic and repeat offenders involved in property and other less serious crimes.

They should have their names published and should face stiffer penalties, Havelock said. "The Act doesn't adequately address that area. That's one of our major disappointments because that's one of the key areas where Albertans have expressed some concerns."

---

**Source:** *Journal* Staff and The Canadian Press, "Changes in new youth justice act not enough, provinces complain," *Edmonton Journal*, 12 March 1999, p. A3.

### Call for Tougher Youth Law Assailed as "Vigilante Justice."

The parents of two slain Calgary youths told an audience of 50 on Monday night—including a retired judge—that a federal proposal to replace the controversial *Young Offenders Act* doesn't go far enough.

"In our opinion, the gist (of the proposed *Youth Criminal Justice Act*) doesn't deal with the new trend in youth violence: gangs," said Tim Reich, the organizer for a petition drive to toughen the youth justice system.

---

**Source:** Frank King, "Call for tougher youth law assailed as 'vigilante justice,'" *Calgary Herald*, 30 March 1999, p. B3.

There are a number of reasons why youth become involved in crime (see Chapter 2). This has always been so, and youth crime will no doubt continue to be a part of Canadian life. We must look beyond this simple reality toward the need for complex responses to a complex problem. Getting tough on youth crime is already a feature of what we do. In order to prevent crime, we must start paying attention to how we build communities. Ultimately legislation such as the YOA and the YCJA are only reactions to youth crime; they serve no purpose until a law has been broken.

We know the factors that contribute to the development of criminal behaviour—including poverty, dropping out of school, family violence, and substance abuse (see, for example, John Howard Society of Alberta, 1995a). It is only through social-development programs that address these crime risk factors that youth crime will be alleviated. **Crime prevention through social development (CPSD)** is now widely accepted as the most effective approach to preventing crime.

We live in a society that appears to be more willing to pay the costs of incarcerating youth than those of educating them: it costs more to lock up a youth for a year than it does to send him or her to college or university for a year. We need to put a stop to this short-sightedness and demand more thoughtful responses from our elected officials. To begin, we need to resolve just what it is we expect from government. Do we want a government that provides leadership, or one that responds to the loudest voices?

Youth-justice legislation could no doubt benefit from ongoing review. All legislation merits scrutiny and revision from time to time. However, the due-process and justice lobbyists that helped create the YOA continued to push for harsher amendments. This has led to the introduction of Bill C-68, calling for the repeal of the YOA and enactment of the YCJA. Our governments appear happy to implement simple solutions to social problems and claim to do this both in our best interests and at our request, but with limited consideration of what is in the best interest of young offenders.

Only after this dilemma is resolved in the minds of Canadians can our politicians properly get on with their jobs. Until then, we are destined to be encumbered with a muddled social policy that is somewhere between principle and platitude.

## SUMMARY

The 1986 amendments to the YOA dealt largely with technical and procedural changes to the act and were debated mainly by those involved in the system. The 1991 amendments, however, received considerable public attention and focussed on court outcomes for young offenders, including transfers to adult court and dispositions for young offenders charged with serious and **violent offences**. Following the 1991 amendments, public discontent with the YOA increased and further amendments to the act were implemented in 1995. The 1995 amendments addressed many of the tough changes to the YOA requested by the public, including increased sentences for murder, and automatic transfers to adult court for older youths convicted of serious personal-injury offences. Despite several rounds of amendments to the YOA, there were continued calls for further toughening of the act. In 1999, draft legislation was introduced in Parliament calling for the repeal of the YOA and introduction of the proposed YCJA.

The level of public involvement in the current debate will likely spur politicians to get tougher rather than to look at issues already identified as important, such as the overuse of incarceration. The government must be aware of and respond to the overreliance on incarceration as the answer to crime problems and the increasing acceptance of the "lock 'em up" philosophy. In addition, Canadians need to decide whether they want their politicians to provide leadership on solutions to crime, or simply to follow the loudest voices. Until this issue/dilemma is resolved, crime-control policy will continue to be only muddled, reactionary tinkering.

## NOTES

1. Also see Winterdyk 2000, Appendix 5, for a profile of the platform issues for Canada's federal parties.
2. The YOA represents a crime-control model of juvenile justice, emphasizing **due process of law** and the punishment of offending behaviours with determinate sentences. (See Box 4.1 in Chapter 4.)
3. Amendments to the YOA began to display a subtle shift away from a crime control model of juvenile justice toward a modified justice model. The modified justice model emphasizes punishment of serious and violent offenders and diversion of minor offenders.

## WEB LINKS

**John Howard Society of Alberta**
<http://www.johnhoward.ab.ca/res-pub.htm#yo>

The John Howard Society of Alberta offers a series of links to young-offenders issues, including reforms to the Young Offenders Act.

**The Young Offenders Debate**
<http://www.lawyers.ca/sbiss>

Formerly known as the Great Young Offenders Debate site, this page is maintained by Stephen Biss, a practising lawyer in Ontario. The site links to various Young Offenders Act issues and allows you read/offer comments on the latest amendments to the Young Offenders Act and/or the proposed Youth Criminal Justice Act.

## STUDY QUESTIONS

1. What is the relationship between the public fear of crime and the development of crime-control strategies?
2. Why do you think there is a widening gap between the YOA as designed and the YOA as practised?
3. Identify five key features of the 1986 amendments to the YOA.

4. Discuss Canada's youth incarceration rate, and contrast it with the use of alternative measures. What do you think the government could be doing to encourage greater use of alternatives?
5. List some of the alternatives to formal court processing that could be better used in Canada.
6. What do you think of the statement by the Minister of Justice that, as long as neither side is happy, the best thing has been done?
7. How has the Charter of Rights and Freedoms influenced the "Declaration of Principle" section of the YOA?
8. Describe the political climate preceding the 1995 amendments to the YOA.
9. Do you think politicians should provide leadership on justice issues or follow populist solutions to the problem of youth crime?
10. What are the major changes to youth justice proposed by the Youth Criminal Justice Act?
11. What main aspects of youth justice were examined by the standing committee in the Phase II Review?

# REFERENCES

Alberta Justice Corporate Support Services. (1999). "Summary of the Environics West poll of Albertans on the justice system." Edmonton: Alberta Justice Corporate Support Services.

Archambault, J.R.O. (1983). "Philosophy and principles of the Young Offenders Act. Notes for presentation to Young Offenders Act National Education Seminar," Ottawa, 10 – 12 January.

Awad, G.A. (1987). "A critique of the principles of the Young Offenders Act." *Canadian Journal of Psychiatry*, 32(6): 440 – 43.

Bala, N. (1989). "Transfer to adult court: Two views as to Parliament's best response." *Criminal Reports*, 69(3): 172 – 77.

———. (1992). "The Young Offenders Act: The legal structure." In R. Corrado, N. Bala, R. Linden, and M. LeBlanc (Eds.), *Juvenile Justice in Canada*. Toronto: Butterworths.

Beuckart, D. (1992, 22 August). "Youth property crimes soaring: Experts differ on what's causing the problem." *London Free Press*, p. 132.

Cadman, C. (1998, 9 June). "Official Ottawa refuses to denounce thuggery." *Vancouver Sun*, A15.

Canadian Centre for Justice Statistics. (1997). "The justice data factfinder." *Juristat Service Bulletin*, Vol. 17, no. 3.

———. (1999). "Youth court statistics, 1997 – 98." *Juristat Service Bulletin*, Vol. 19, no. 2.

Canadian Council on Children and Youth. (1989, 23 November). "Final minutes voluntary sector/government consultation on proposed amendments to the Young Offenders Act: October 13 – 14, 1989." Unpublished.

The Canadian Press. (1994, 26 October). "Police chiefs tough on teen crime." *Edmonton Journal*, A11.

Canadian Sentencing Commission. (1987). "Public knowledge of sentencing." In *Sentencing Reform: A Canadian Approach*. Ottawa: Canadian Sentencing Commission.

Cohen, S. (1997). *Renewing Youth Justice: Thirteenth Report of the Standing Committee on Justice and Legal Affairs*. Ottawa: Publishing, Public Works and Government Services Canada.

Department of Justice Canada. (1991). *Consultation Document on the Custody and Review Provisions of the Young Offenders Act*. Ottawa: Government of Canada.

———. (1994). "Minister of Justice tables YOA amendments." News release. Ottawa: Government of Canada.

———. (1998). "Minister of Justice announces Youth Justice Strategy." News release. Ottawa: Government of Canada.

———. (1999a, 11 March). "Minister of Justice introduces new youth justice law." News release. Ottawa: Government of Canada.

———. (1999b, 11 March). *Youth Criminal Justice Act: Backgrounder*. Ottawa: Government of Canada.

Doob, A. (1994). *Beyond the Red Book: A Workshop on Recommendations for Amendments to the Young Offenders Act*. Toronto: University of Toronto Press.

Dunn, M., and J. Harder. (1999, 12 March). "YOA changes ripped." *Toronto Sun*, 7.

Dupuis, R. (1995). "Subject: The Comprehensive Review of the Young Offenders Act (Phase II). Letter to the John Howard Society of Alberta, 24 July." Ottawa: House of Commons Standing Committee on Justice and Legal Affairs.

Hartnagel, T., and Baron, S. (1995). "'Lock 'em up': Attitudes towards punishing juvenile offenders." Unpublished manuscript. Edmonton: University of Alberta.

Howard, R. (1994, 3 June). "Youth rehabilitation loses priority." *Globe and Mail*, A1.

John Howard Society of Alberta. (1995a). *Crime Prevention through Social Development: A Literature Review*. Edmonton: John Howard Society of Alberta.

———. (1995b). *Crime Prevention through Social Development: A Resource Guide*. Edmonton: John Howard Society of Alberta.

———. (1997). *Response to Renewing Youth Justice: Thirteenth Report of the Standing Committee on Justice and Legal Affairs*. Edmonton: John Howard Society of Alberta.

———. (1998). *Youth Crime and Our Response: An Update*. Factsheet 11. Toronto: John Howard Society of Ontario.

*Journal* Staff and the Canadian Press. (1999, 12 March). "Changes in new youth justice act not enough, provinces complain." *Edmonton Journal*, A3.

King, F. (1999, 30 March). "Call for tougher youth law assailed as vigilante justice." *Calgary Herald*, B3.

Minister of Justice and Attorney General of Canada. (1997). News Release. Remarks by Ministers at the Conclusion of the Federal–Provincial–Territorial Ministers Responsible for Justice Meeting, 4 – 5 December 1997, Montreal, Quebec.

Morris, J. (1997, 17 March). "Review of Young Offender Act a joke—Reform." *Edmonton Journal*, A3.

Platt, P. (1989). *Young Offenders Law in Canada*. Toronto: Butterworths.

Roberts, J. (1992). "Public opinion, crime and criminal justice." In M. Tonry (Ed.), *Crime and Justice: A Review of Research*. Chicago: University of Chicago Press.

Schissel, B. (1997). *Blaming Children: Youth Crime, Moral Panics and the Politics of Hate*. Halifax: Fernwood.

Solicitor General of Canada. (1979). *Legislative Proposals to Replace the Juvenile Delinquents Act*. Ottawa: Solicitor General Canada.

———. (1986). News release. Ottawa: Solicitor General of Canada.

Winterdyk, J. (Ed.). (1997). "Introduction." In *Juvenile Justice Systems: International Perspectives*. Toronto: Canadian Scholars' Press.

# Chapter 6

# Young Offenders and the Press

TONY SESKUS AND RICK MOFINA

## KEY OBJECTIVES

After reading this chapter, you should be able to:

- illustrate how the news media report youth crime by studying specific cases;
- discuss the impact of the law on the news media's coverage of youth crime;
- show the role the news media play in the public's perception of youth crime;
- understand the evolution of youth-crime laws and how this has affected coverage by the press;
- review specific court challenges of publication restrictions that have been made by the press.

## KEY TERMS

Canadian Charter of Rights and Freedoms
*Canadian Press Stylebook*
freedom of the press
Section 38, YOA
Section 109, YCJA
Youth Criminal Justice Act (YCJA)

## INTRODUCTION

As noted in the introduction to this volume on page 3, on 11 March 1999, Canada's attorney general, Anne McLellan, unveiled a new set of laws that she said would revamp the country's youth-justice system. She said that Canadians want a system which protects society while instilling values such as accountability, responsibility, and respect. The newly proposed laws formed the Youth Criminal Justice Act (YCJA) and, for critics of the 15-year-old Young Offenders Act (YOA), the changes could not come soon enough.

Indeed, as noted elsewhere in this book, many Canadians believe youth crime, especially violent crime, has become an increasingly serious problem, and often blame a weak justice system for permitting it to happen (see Chapter 1). Still, of the more than 110 000 cases heard in youth court in 1996 – 97, murder and attempted murder accounted for less than 1 percent (Department of Justice Canada, 1998).[1] Assault charges, most of which were for common assault, made up just 12.9 percent. Canada even has a higher youth-incarceration rate than the United States. So what fuels public concern? It is, of course, a number of things, but perhaps none more important than the news media.

The public's most important and immediate source of information about youth crime is the press (see Box 6.1). The impact the justice system has had and will have on the media's reporting of youth crime is far-reaching, for it determines how information is obtained, presented, and ultimately interpreted by the public.

Beginning with a case study of a 14-year-old British Columbia girl who was beaten by a group of her peers and later drowned, this chapter focusses on how the media cover youth crime, the impact the law has on that coverage, and the role the media have had in shaping public opinion.

Though the stated principles of the YCJA emphasize the protection of society rather than the accused, the act still aims to guard youths from the glare of the media spotlight in order to protect them in their immaturity, ensuring their right to a fair trial and encouraging rehabilitation. But often these objectives come in direct conflict with those of a free press and the public's right to know.

## Box 6.1
## WHAT IS A NEWSPAPER?

Journalism is loosely defined by those in the industry as history's first draft. As the senior medium before radio and television, newspapers have for centuries been the primary source of information for everyone. It is a newspaper's function to offer a daily diary of events; opinions; and analysis of community; national and world events; however, a newspaper is never the *definitive* source of information on any subject.

A newspaper's allegiance is to the community it serves, reflecting the standards, values, and concerns of its readership. Understandably, the murder of a teenager in Charlottetown will be reported on the front page of the *Charlottetown Guardian and Patriot*, yet the same story likely won't be published in the *New York Times*.

News editors give their communities information that is immediately relevant to their readers, measuring stories on a descending scale of newsworthiness, beginning with local, regional, and national importance, and then categorizing the stories further.

The purely objective information provided by newspapers will always be interpreted differently by readers according to their personal beliefs and political agendas, as this chapter shows in respect to the YOA. But, to employ an adage, it is not the newspaper's job to tell people what to think, but rather to tell people what to think about. It is a reader's responsibility to use the information as a stepping stone to further participate in the democratic process.

In this chapter, we describe how the roles of the press and the criminal justice system for youth have evolved historically. We also look at how the courts have applied the laws to young offenders, and to the press when it has argued for more freedom of information.

## MEDIA ATTENTION ON YOUTH CRIME

The 1997 beating and drowning of 14-year-old Reena Virk not only shocked Canadians, but, thanks to media coverage, horrified people around the world. Police arrested eight teenage suspects in connection with the attack, including seven girls from a quiet bedroom community outside Victoria, BC. Police were besieged by media calls—some from as far away as Sweden. Dozens of reporters—including a crew from the American tabloid TV show "Hard Copy"—descended on the community, transforming the troubled, sometime runaway into the focus of a national debate on youth violence (Bailey, 1998).

The murder and subsequent trials also put the YOA under close scrutiny and became another rallying point for those Canadians who claimed the system was too weak to deter youths from participating in such crimes. For the media, the drama of the Virk case also highlighted the contrasting laws that govern coverage of youth and adult crime, and the unique challenges reporters face in dealing with those distinctions. Let's examine the media's coverage of this high-profile case and how the law governed that coverage.

### THE CRIME

On the evening of Friday, 14 November 1997, Reena Virk, 14, left her home in Saanich, BC, to meet some friends at a nearby store. Reena called two hours later to say she'd be back soon, but she never arrived. Later in the week, rumours surfaced at school that Reena had been attacked by a group of teenagers, and police began to investigate. Then, nine days after Reena went missing, police arrested eight teens on a Saturday morning and, by afternoon, found her partially clad body resting in a shallow inlet. Six girls were charged with aggravated assault, and a boy, 16, and a girl, 15, were charged with second-degree murder. Police sent the information to the media in a press release.

### THE COVERAGE

Reporters began flocking to Saanich the same day police reported they had found a girl's body and charged several teens. The police called it a "truly astronomical" investigation, refusing to rule out future arrests. News editors know that a particularly brutal or poignant crime—like the discovery of the body of a missing child—will seize the attention of the community for days or even weeks (Cumming and McKercher, 1994: 207). This crime attracted attention from media around the world and became fodder for radio call-in shows and newspaper columnists (see Box 6.2). Reena's death had media appeal for several reasons. First, the crime involved teenagers and played to the public's interest in—and, often, fear of—youth culture. Second, the alleged participation of young women challenged the public's notion that girls are less violent than boys. Third, the crime left many unanswered questions, including: "Could this have happened to me or my children?"

The manner in which the media set about answering these questions was largely dictated by the terms of YOA. Section 38 of the act states that, when it comes to crimes either committed or allegedly committed by youths aged 12 to 17, their names, or any information that might identify them, cannot be made public. Reporters, for example, may not be able to name the school a teenage suspect attended if that information could lead to him or her being identified. Therefore, the kind of detailed backgrounds the media provides on adult suspects are rarely possible in youth cases. Reporters covering the Virk case adhered to this provision of the YOA, and details of the suspects were generally left to court testimony. The office of the Attorney General of British Columbia had no complaints related to press coverage of the accused teens.

The rules, however, changed drastically when dealing with Reena herself. Though section 38 also forbid publication of the name of a young person or child who is aggrieved by or is a victim of the offence, a Quebec court decided in 1986 that the provision does not apply if the victim is dead. In the words of appeal court judge J.J.A. Tyndale, a young dead person is no longer a victim; that is, he or she has "no life, private or otherwise, to be protected." As a result, Reena and her family were fair game, and the media, eager to satisfy the curiosity of the public, rushed to uncover the details of her past. "We didn't even think about whether it was right or wrong," said one reporter who followed the Virk family for days after the discovery. "As soon as we saw her name in the paper, all bets were off. There's no time to sit in your car and weigh the moral implications of this or that."

**Box 6.2**

**WHO'S IN THE MEDIA**

In addition to newspapers, Canadians have access to a variety of news sources. At a local level, radio is the most immediate source, often broadcasting from the scene of a news event. Television has become increasingly instant, especially with the advent of 24-hour news stations that provide audiences with "up-to-the-minute" information and full coverage of breaking news events. Another conventional news source is the wire agency. These organizations don't produce news for one particular newspaper or broadcaster, but use their networks of writers to gather news reports for subscribers (e.g., Reuters, Bloomberg, and Knight Ridder). The Internet can also provide Canadians with news through digital radio or virtual newspapers. These sources, however, are still developing their own journalistic rules and, in some instances, are unreliable.

As with the case of Sylvain Leduc and Johnathan Thimpsen (see Box 6.3), Reena's name became known to the Canadian public within a few days of her body being discovered. Police did not release her identity initially, to give the victim's family members time to notify friends and relatives.[2] Reporters, however, rarely wait for the official release from the police, choosing instead to pursue the story and get an edge on their competitors. In this case, it was the *Victoria Times Colonist* who first named Reena as the victim by confirming the death with her grieving parents. From then on, the media focussed on two main themes: the details surrounding the girl's death and her life leading up to it. From court testimony, the public learned that Reena was called at home and asked to join some friends for a night

### Box 6.3

### WHEN THE NATION STOPS TO WATCH

Murders receive more media attention than any other crime, but they are not so rare they demand front-page attention. When youths commit murder, however, it's often a different story. These crimes can capture national, or even international, attention for weeks, months, or years. In addition to the Reena Virk case, several other recent murders have received exceptional media attention.

In July 1995, Sandy Charles, 14, shocked the country when he obeyed the voices in his head and imitated scenes from a horror movie. With the help of an 8-year-old boy identified only as "M," Charles stabbed, strangled, bludgeoned, and finally suffocated Johnathan Thimpsen, aged 7, in La Ronge, Saskatchewan. They cut strips of fat from the body for a potion they thought would make them fly. Charles was found not criminally responsible for the murder in 1996 and sentenced to treatment in a secure psychiatric facility. "M" will be kept in a therapeutic foster home until he is 18.

In October 1995, Sylvain Leduc, 17, and three other teens were kidnapped from his Ottawa home as a result of a street-gang vendetta. The group was taken to an apartment building where as many as eleven people—many of them teenagers—were waiting. Leduc was beaten and choked to death. His 16-year-old female cousin was sexually violated with a hot curling iron. Another youth, 17, was beaten unconscious. And a second girl, also 16, was shut in a storage closet, draped in black garbage bags, waiting to be executed. A suspicious tenant ended the attack when he called police.

The trial of three young offenders connected to the attack led to outrage. One of the young offenders had all his lawyers' bills paid for by legal aid—despite the fact his father is a wealthy doctor. Another of the young offenders was released on probation within two years of his conviction and, barely a month later, was arrested for holding up a cab driver. Three adults arrested for the crime were convicted of first-degree murder and 38 other charges, totalling individual charges of more than 73 years each.

In 1998, Clayton McGloan, 17, was attacked Hallowe'en night during a house party attended by more than 200 teenagers in Calgary. He died of multiple stab wounds two days later. Two brothers, aged 15 and 17, were charged with murder.

Each of these three cases illustrate how violent youths can be, but does it indicate that teenagers have become more violent or are "out of control"? No. These are rare cases that, if they weren't so infrequent, would not receive the kind of media coverage they do. These cases do, however, contribute to a growing concern about youth crime because they remain in the public conscience long after they occur.

out. At an isolated teen hangout near Victoria, Reena was the victim of two separate assaults. The first attack followed accusations that Reena was spreading rumours and having relations with the boyfriend of one of the teens. One girl stubbed out a cigarette on Reena's forehead before she was swarmed by a group of teens and beaten. After the attack was finished, Reena got up and tried to walk home, but two teens allegedly returned to beat her again. In the second attack, it's believed she was hit, likely with a heavy object, lost consciousness, and then drowned in the inlet. She suffered multiple injuries, including a broken neck.

The details reported on Reena's life prior to that fatal night are less violent than that of the attack, but certainly no less painful for her family. The press, through their own investigating, reported that Reena had accused her father of physical abuse, but dropped the charges. She had also told a social worker that she had been sexually abused by a relative five years earlier on a visit to India. She told the same social worker that she was unhappy at home and wanted to be placed in foster care. The media also reported that Reena had used drugs and had been a runaway. Months after her death, her family was still reeling from the glare of the media spotlight and spoke of how much more difficult it had made their lives. Several questions thus arise from the Virk case. Should the law allow the media to report more details on the alleged offenders, to put the emphasis on them? Is the media right in providing the public with such detailed accounts of Reena's life and death, or does it "re-victimize" the family? Why should the media be permitted to publish Reena's name at all?

## THE RIGHT TO KNOW

It is the inherent duty of the news media to provide the public with full and accurate information on local, national, and international issues and events (see Box 6.4). Such information is vital to a society that democratically makes decisions with respect to its mores, laws, policies, and governments. On an immediate level, publishing Reena Virk's name may not appear crucial to the maintenance of that democratic tenet. But imagine the alternative if the press were forbidden to publish the identity of the victims or the circumstances of their deaths. What kind of a society would we have if we allowed our citizens to, regardless of their age, to die anonymously and secretly, outside the realm of public scrutiny?

This is not to say that the news media should be allowed to publish everything and, indeed, it sometimes chooses not to. As Nick Russell, a professor of journalistic ethics, notes, "the freedom [of the press] continues to be earned or lost depending on performance. And it brings with it clear responsibilities of stewardship" (Russell, 1994: 195). When ethics, not the law, determines what can be published, it is the public that ultimately decides what is reported and what isn't. One can simply compare American tabloid television shows to Canadian news programs for evidence of societal influence. In the case of Reena Virk, then, the coverage provided by the press largely reflected the enormous public interest in the case.

Legally, however, there are other principles that must also be upheld. The public's right to know must be balanced with the right to a fair trial of anyone accused of a crime. And when events involve young people who are protected by the law because of their age, the news media must adhere to those rules that apply specifically to these young people.

Since the enactment of the YOA (see Chapter 4), press compliance with laws pertaining to youth crime has involved using the statement "The accused cannot be named under provisions of the Young Offenders Act." This statement has been automatically employed by news outlets and will continue to be used under the terms of the YCJA (though youth-court judges will have the option of permitting the publication of the names of young offenders sentenced for serious crimes, like murder, or who have a long history of violent crime). As mentioned earlier, the basis for not identifying anyone under age 18 accused of a crime is noted by the Quebec Court of Appeal in its 1986 decision in *R.* v. *Les Publications Photo-Police Inc.* In that case, Judge Tyndale ruled that the main object of the privacy section of Canada's youth laws is "to protect young persons in their immaturity from the stigma that tends to mark anyone involved in penal offences, so that their development and future success will not be jeopardized ..."

Still, given the constraints of the legal system, the press must deal with the task of supplying comprehensive information to its readers within the bounds of the law and in support of its underlying democratic principles and moral objectives. What does this entail in the daily gathering and reporting of news, a profession that requires crucial and immediate decisions to be made?

### Box 6.4

### HOW THE MEDIA HAS COVERED YOUTH CRIME

Except for a few sensational cases, which usually involved young people treated as adults by the law, up until the mid-1900s the press devoted little attention to juvenile crime, mainly because the reporting of such cases was banned.

Furthermore, national figures on youth and juvenile crime were seldom kept, making it difficult to measure the magnitude of the issue. By the mid-1980s, the YOA and the Canadian Charter of Rights and Freedoms had given the news media greater access to the judicial process for youths. While the system maintained the principle of privacy, news reporting of youth crime became common, with extensive coverage given to the most disturbing cases.

Following a general trend within crime reporting, stories on youth crime during the 1990s focussed heavily on the victims. This kind of reporting during particularly poignant cases can elicit the community's revulsion and action. In May 1999, hundreds of people turned out for a memorial service in the small southern Alberta community of Taber to mourn the shooting death of one student by another teenager. The service also commanded a national audience on the CBC. Coverage of youth crime is likely to continue to grow in Canada, fuelled by continued public interest and increased media competition. The popularity of tabloid television news—which focusses on crime and sex—would also indicate a continuing trend.

## DEADLINES, DECISIONS, AND THE LAW

The Criminal Code of Canada, various compendiums of media law, and news style guides are on the bookshelf of every senior editor in a newsroom across the country. Editors can also call the law firms retained by their companies for legal advice.

Such a call will entail a description of the questionable article, or photograph, and its circumstances. The lawyer typically outlines the paper's options and likely any possible consequences before making a suggestion to the editor. Ultimately, as a deadline ticks closer, the decision to follow expensive legal advice for the sake of prudence or to ignore it and risk court action in support of the principle of the freedom of the press rests with the editor.

Such high-stakes decision making may be the responsibility of a senior editor, but this does not lighten the burden of responsibility for reporters and photographers. Journalists are expected to be familiar with Canadian media law. Knowing the basic rules of daily journalism is crucial. Some of Canada's larger new groups produce their own policy and style guides, but the one guide that is almost universally regarded as the quick-reference bible is the **Canadian Press Stylebook** (Buckley, 1992) (see Box 6.5).

## THE CP STYLEBOOK

Canadian Press (CP) is a national news-wire co-operative. Nearly every Canadian daily newspaper is a CP member, and every Canadian journalist is familiar with the *Canadian Press Stylebook*, a guide for newspaper writers and editors. The legal section of the 1992 edition begins by firing off blunt, straight-to-the-point advice under this statement: "Engraved in the memory of every reporter and editor should be: Careless and bad judgment on legal questions can ruin people's lives. Every journalist must weigh this responsibility when working" (p. 95). The introduction's last point reads: "Juveniles involved with the law—accused witnesses or victims—must not be identified, even indirectly, without legal advice" (p. 95).

The section goes on to caution reporters that the *Stylebook* is not a substitute for legal advice, a warning that is echoed in the pages dealing specifically with the young persons and the law. The dangers pertaining to young offenders are highlighted and include naming young suspects, witnesses, and victims; providing identifying characteristics, such as the school they attend, sports teams they belong to, or a home location; naming relatives; quoting witnesses about youth crime; naming young persons in adult-court transfers; and not waiting 48 hours before reporting that a youth has been placed under a warrant. The *Stylebook* discourages use in news stories of the term "young offender" because the phrase automatically "convicts" a defendant. These warnings are discussed briefly in the section that concludes: "The entire issue of juveniles and the law is particularly treacherous because of the sweep of current law and uncertainties about its application. Whenever there is doubt

### Box 6.5
### TAKING IT TO THE STREETS

Having been crime reporters, the authors of this chapter have faced many challenges in covering youth crime. Often the greatest difficulty is providing the public with as much insight as possible while staying within the rules of Canada's youth laws. A quick glance at two high-profile crime stories illustrates the difficulty the media face in reporting on youth crime.

In January 1998, in Lethbridge, Alberta, a 41-year-old woman was beaten and stabbed to death in her own home. Her daughter, 13, and the girl's boyfriend, 15, were charged with murder (*Calgary Herald*, 1998). A reporter's first instinct is to gather as much information as possible, but the media had to decide first whether they would identify the victim or the suspects' relationship to her. Reporters could not choose both because that would identify the youths. Local radio stations, the first media to report the story, decided to identify the relationship rather than give the woman's name. The rest of the press were forced to follow suit so that they would not identify the youths. A local newspaper even delayed running the victim's obituary to avoid identifying the teens.

In April 1999, in Taber, a 14-year-old boy was charged with entering a high school with a shotgun and killing one student and injuring another. Media from across North America flocked to the small Alberta town as the crime occurred just days after two boys in Littleton, Colorado, killed 12 students, a teacher, and themselves. An eager press immediately identified the dead victim and then, in contravention of the YOA (i.e., section 38), named the injured teen. Several factors entered into that decision, but the two main reasons were: early reports indicated that the second victim would likely die, and in such a small community it would be unreasonable to think any of the people involved would remain anonymous. The media continued to name the second victim until the suspect's first appearance in court. The judge, at the request of the Crown, warned the press about section 38 of the act. The media immediately stopped naming the second victim.

about a certain case, consult a supervisor or legal counsel" (Buckley, 1992: 106). And when that is impossible, the rule of thumb is: *Leave it out!*

## THE YOUTH CRIMINAL JUSTICE ACT

When the YCJA was introduced in the House of Commons in March 1999, part of its intention was to renew the public's faith in the youth-justice system by providing a framework that promotes consequences for crime that are proportionate to the seriousness of the offence (see Chapters 4 and 5 for further details).

In doing so, the YCJA introduced programs such as community-based sentences for less serious crimes while adding tough new measures for those acts of violence least tolerated by society. For instance, the government expanded the list of offences for which a young offender could face adult sentences from murder, attempted murder, manslaughter, and aggravated sexual assault, to also include a pattern of serious **violent offences**. It also lowered the age limit for young offenders who are presumed to be liable to adult sentences from 16 years to 14 years of age. Media coverage has also been targeted by the changes in the YCJA and, though they could hardly be described as drastic, the new rules are significant.

Under the YOA, the media is permitted to report on youth-court proceedings only when the information does not lead to the identification of the youth. The court may make exceptions only if publication would assist in apprehending a youth who is a danger to others; or if the youth makes the request and a judge determines that it is not contrary to his or her best interests. A youth may also be named if—but only if—a case is raised to adult court and the defence has exhausted all of its appeals.

Under the YCJA, however, a judge may also choose to permit the publication of the names of teenagers aged 14 to 17 who receive a *youth sentence* for murder, attempted murder, manslaughter, or aggravated sexual assault, or who have a pattern of convictions for serious violent offences (section 109). The media will also be able to publish the names of all youths who receive an adult sentence, as was the case under the YOA.

The government did not enter into the changes lightly, weighing arguments for and against the new law before making a decision. Even so, there continues to be a great deal of debate about whether the identity of a young person accused, or found guilty, of an offence should be published by the media. The government acknowledged this general observation in its *Strategy for the Renewal of Youth Justice*, a discussion paper (Department of Justice Canada, 1998).

The government found, through consultation with the public, that people who supported the YOA's publication rules believed the changes would impede rehabilitation efforts and thereby compromise public safety in the long run (Department of Justice Canada, 1998: 31). It was also argued that the youth-justice system was sufficiently open; that publicity may unfairly taint parents and siblings of the offender; and that publication could prejudice the employment and educational prospects for youths. Supporters of the YOA also noted that some teens "seek notoriety and that publication may not only fail to act as a deterrent but instead reinforce behaviour" (Department of Justice Canada, 1998: 31).

But people who supported the changes argued that publication would be a deterrent in most circumstances, even encouraging parents to take greater responsibility for their children. They contend that the public, especially parents, have the right to know the identities of young offenders, pointing out that there is an intrinsic value in the public's right to know that is "abridged by the failure to release the names of young people, which in turn undermines confidence in the youth justice system" (Department of Justice Canada, 1998: 31).

In arriving at its decision, the government felt it had reached a compromise between two legitimate but competing values. They include the need to encourage rehabilitation by avoiding the negative effect of publicity on the youth *versus* the need for greater openness and transparency in the justice system, which contributes to public confidence in an open and accountable justice system.

As far as the media is concerned, it will take some time for it to determine if there are any legal pitfalls hidden within the legislation. As with any new law, those parties affected must learn the boundaries of the legislation. When the YOA was introduced in 1984, for example, a number of media outlets challenged the legislation in court (discussed under "Freedom of the Press," below). On surface, however, the YCJA appears to contain at least one ethical concern for journalists—namely, that the power to name teens convicted in youth court of particularly serious crimes belongs in the hands of a subjective judiciary. A teenager convicted of murder, for instance, may or may not be named, as determined by a judge. The question for the media is whether the decision to permit publication of the youth's name is being used as an additional punishment for the offender or as a service to the public. If it is interpreted as the former, the media may have to decide if they are comfortable with their power of publication being used as a punitive tool of the courts.

## THE YCJA AND REENA VIRK

The Reena Virk case was one of the most sensational cases of youth crime in Canada in recent memory. Reports of her death and related stories about the rise of violence among young women raised questions about the youth-justice system and whether it was an effective deterrent. While the case alone did not spur the government to change the system, it certainly contributed to the public concern that led Canadians, rightly or wrongly, to conclude that something must be done. Of course, the YCJA had no impact on the youths convicted in connection with the case, but how would it have changed the Virk trials from a media perspective? Let us first look at the trials under the YOA.

By April 1999, one girl who played a minor role in the beating was given a 60-day conditional sentence, to be served under her parents' supervision. Two others were sentenced to six months in jail and a year's probation. They were also sentenced to another three months for an unrelated assault that the court heard and that had "frightening parallels" to the Virk crime. Of the other five youths charged with the beating and murder of Virk, the two female ringleaders were sentenced to one year in jail and another year on parole. A 15-year-old girl who helped lure Virk to the scene, but later stopped the first assault, was sentenced to six months in jail and a year's probation. And the 16-year-old girl and 17-year-old boy charged with second-degree murder were still appealing rulings that raised their cases to adult court (Armstrong, 1999).

If the YCJA had been in effect, any of the teenage girls sentenced for aggravated assault could have had their names published if the assault was part of a long, violent history and if the judge believed publishing the names would best serve the public interest. As mentioned, two of the girls had participated in a similar crime, and another was involved with a previous assault on another teen, but how the judge would have decided is another matter. The fact that at least two of the teens had experienced violence at a young age might have convinced a judge to direct them to a diversion program rather than to jail.

As far as the media is concerned, the YCJA would probably have had the greatest impact on the two teens whose cases were moved to adult court. Under the YOA, they will be named only when they make an appearance in adult court, but, under the new act, they could be named even if sentenced in youth court. For example, at the trial, the female could only be referred to as "K.M.E." while the youth who was transferred to adult court had his name published—Warren Paul Glowatski—(Meissner, 1999).[3] This is in accordance with section 38 of the YOA. However, as the case unfolded, the young female was transferred to adult court and her name was subsequently published—Kelly Ellard.

## DOES THE MEDIA REFLECT REALITY ABOUT YOUNG OFFENDERS?

Because citizens tend to read, or hear, what they believe to be true, the news media often cater to public tastes. But is public perception realistic, and do the media provide representative coverage? There have been numerous studies analyzing the attention media pay to youth crime, and the impact that coverage has on public opinion.

One particular study by Sprott (1996: 272) found that "although the news media play a paramount role in constructing the reality of social phenomena for the public, the reality constructed by the news media ... may not necessarily reflect other images of reality."

In a two-month examination of three major Ontario newspapers—the *Globe and Mail*, the *Toronto Star*, and the *Toronto Sun*—Sprott found that 94 percent of the stories about youth crime involved violence, while youth court statistics showed that less than a quarter of Ontario youth-court cases involved violence. She also found that the articles focussed on the crime, the charges, and the impact of the crime on the victims, rather than on youth-court dispositions.

A survey of Toronto residents found that such reporting, if it did not distort reality, at least failed to enlighten readers as to the realities of the youth-court system. Sprott found that, "although readers of Toronto newspapers receive almost no information about youth court dispositions, a survey of Toronto residents demonstrated that most people believe youth court dispositions are too lenient" (1996: 271 – 72). When asked which cases they were thinking of, most of those people who thought the dispositions were too lenient cited the minority of cases (those involving serious, violent repeat offenders). Sprott also found that the respondents knew little of the youth-court system and underestimated the severity of dispositions that could be imposed.

Of course, the mainstream media do not set out to distort the news or present a biased view of the world. It is, after all, part of a journalist's early training to learn the importance of objectivity. But, as Sprott points out, the ultimate goal of the press is to sell newspapers and, because of that fact, journalists "interpret reality" and tell stories rather than reflecting reality or gathering facts (1996: 287). The same pressure also requires the press to choose stories that are "newsworthy" but are likely unrepresentative. As the old newspaper adage goes: "Dog Bites Man" is *not* news; "Man Bites Dog" *is* news.

The impact the media can have on public perception and the impact the public can have on government policy is demonstrated by the introduction of the YCJA itself.

In the Department of Justice's *Strategy for the Renewal of Youth Justice* (1998), the federal document that introduced many of the recommendations that make up the YCJA, the government notes that "Canadians see youth crime as an important issue—even at a time when youth crime rates seem to be falling." The government said that public-opinion surveys, media reports, and anecdotal accounts show widespread negative attitudes toward the YOA and youth courts:

> The criticism of sentencing practices seems widespread, even though most judges dealing with youth are the same as those who hear adult cases and despite the fact that Canadian youth incarceration rates are higher than those of other countries and higher than incarceration rates for adults. (Department of Justice Canada, 1998: 6)

After discussions with the public and consultation with youth-justice experts, the government decided that a key element of any new legislation would be to improve public access to the youth-court system, an acknowledgement of the important role the media play in shaping public attitudes.

> Fear of crime and growing concerns about the effectiveness of the Young Offenders Act are heightened, in part, by high-profile cases involving youth crime ... Steps need to be taken by all partners in the youth justice system to provide Canadians with better and more complete information about youth crime in their communities. (Department of Justice Canada, 1998: 9)

Whether the YCJA will achieve this goal remains yet to be seen. It is perhaps more important for the media to understand the importance of context when dealing with youth-crime coverage, and, indeed, many news outlets attempt to do this. Neil Hall of the *Vancouver Sun* points out that, during the Reena Virk case, his newspaper did its best to put the event in context by investigating the amount of violent crime committed by young women. Many other media outlets, magazines in particular, mimicked the approach. *Maclean's* went as far as to detail a list of recent violent crimes committed by young women (Chisholm and Harnett, 1997). But the press did more than collect anecdotal evidence, noting that a greater number of young women were, in fact, participating in youth crime. But that didn't stop members of the public from writing letters to the editor charging the press with sensationalizing the high-profile case. The accusations were largely based on the volume of stories written about Reena's death and not the content of the stories themselves. So what is sensationalism and what isn't?

## SENSATIONALISM OR "THE FACTS"?

How are laws, rules, and guidelines applied in the heat of reporting the daily news? If a murdered juvenile prostitute has a young son or daughter, should you name the child? Under the YOA and the YCJA, the law sees the child as a victim and protects her or his identity. If a young person claims to be a car thief and wants to tell a reporter how cars are stolen, how far can the press go in identifying him, the victims, and details of the crime?

All of the above examples are real cases. In the first, lawyers could have suggested that only the first name of the dead prostitute's child be given, or, depending on the circumstances of the murder and who was charged or suspected in the case, that the child not be mentioned at all. Most newspapers will choose not to name the child in such cases if there is no news value in doing so. In a case such as that of the car thief, he or she is usually given a fictitious name and not identified in photographs, to comply with federal laws. Also, when a young person is charged under the YOA, or, now, under the YCJA, with slaying his or her family, the youth cannot be identified. However, initial stories will state that "a 14-year-old" has been charged with murdering the "Jones family" and will report some of the circumstances.

The confidence needed to avoid the legal pitfalls of Canada's young offender laws and deliver accurate information comes with experience. Whenever dramatic events occur that involve potential young offenders, a news photographer should always take pictures of suspects at angles that protect their identities. But a photographer should always take pictures identifying the suspects, for something could develop that would later allow identification of the youth. The same rule applies to the reporter who is gathering information—how that information will be published is not a decision to be made on the spot. Clearly, reporting youth crime exposes the press to a myriad of legal challenges.

## FREEDOM OF THE PRESS

Great care must be taken to adhere to the law while reporting youth-related crime, because the courts do not suffer violators. The maximum penalty for contempt of court is a prison term not exceeding two years and/or a hefty fine.

The right to a fair trial and the right to privacy for youths accused of crimes are intrinsic principles of Canada's justice system, supported by the Canadian Charter of Rights and Freedoms, and entrenched in both the YOA and the YCJA. But where do the nation's news media stand when those rights conflict with the fundamental democratic principle of freedom of the press? Two cases involving challenges of the privacy provisions by the press will help to answer this question.

In the more recent case, Toronto-based Southam Inc. argued, in 1986, that section 39 of the YOA is an unconstitutional infringement upon the freedom of expression, including freedom of the press, as guaranteed under the Charter. In its ruling of February 1986, the Ontario Court of Appeal rejected the argument, stating that it is not necessary to show that the laws of the act are perfect, but rather that the limits they impose are reasonable in a democratic society. The court also ruled that banning the press from publishing identifying information about a young person involved in criminal proceedings is a reasonable restriction (*Southam Inc.* v. *R.*).

In a previous, similar case, the *Edmonton Journal* and its owner, Southam Inc., argued that the privacy sections of the JDA that prevented the press from publishing identifying information about an accused youth did not apply to any appeal proceeding. Such restrictions were inconsistent under the Charter and infringed upon the freedom of the press, the *Journal* and Southam argued. But the Alberta Court of Queen's Bench did not agree. In its January 1984 ruling, it called the limit placed upon the press reasonable: "The free and democratic character of our society is not imperiled by such a moderate limit on freedom of the press," stated the court, finding:

> There is a compelling State interest in the goal of attempting to rehabilitate wayward children without submitting them to the "harshness, stigma and harmful consequences of the criminal adjudicatory process" (43 C.J.S. 199, p. 520) and in the means chosen by Parliament to advance that goal: the preservation of anonymity as to protect the child from the reactive behaviour of others.

The court concluded: "The claim of Southam Inc., to a guaranteed freedom to publish identifying information 'is not tenable under the charter'" (*R.* v. *T.R.* [No. 1]).

## NEWS FOR PUBLIC CONSUMPTION

The Canadian attitude toward children and crime is reflected in the evolution of the nation's laws for and treatment of juvenile offenders. For the most part, Canada's press appears to have upheld the prevailing attitudes of the day.

As Canadian society became increasingly urban, it developed the problems associated with cities and youths (e.g., gang activity and vandalism). To better grapple with the issue of children and crime, Parliament implemented the Juvenile Delinquents Act in 1908 (see Chapter 4). The JDA proved to be a negative force, however, allowing for arbitrary and unfair treatment of young offenders, denial of their basic legal rights, including the right of appeal, and definite, as opposed to open-ended, sentences.

Using today's standards as a moral gauge, most Canadians would conclude that children were treated harshly in the formative years of Canada's criminal justice system. Although various groups called for reforms, it is apparent that the press of the day felt no duty to report and decry the heartbreaking cases. For example, although the details are sketchy, Anderson (1982) describes how up until the 1830s official records evoke images worthy of a Dickens novel:

- Eight-year-old Antoine Beauche was jailed in Kingston, Ontario, where he was whipped 47 times in the nine months he was there.

- Twelve-year-old Elizabeth Breen was flogged five times in four months, and 14-year-old Sara O'Conner "faced the lash" five times in three months. Both girls committed "insignificant crimes."
- Children were executed for theft and burglary.
- A 13-year-old Montreal boy was hanged in September 1803 for stealing a cow (Anderson, 1982: 9). However, his death did not warrant mention in the *Gazette*. As the press was almost exclusively the voice of the political hierarchy of the day, the crime and execution of a thieving waif were not considered newsworthy. In fact, it was not until around 1860 that records on juveniles were even collected (Carrigan, 1991).

Up until the 1860s, executions received little coverage by the press, except for some local newspapers. But as cities grew, communication technology improved, and literacy among the working class increased, the desire for more "human interest" stories grew. The press began paying more attention to crimes and reporting on the deeds of criminals, including youths.

## WHEN GIRLS LIVED AND BOYS WERE EXECUTED

The principle of protecting youths in their immaturity did evolve in the last days of the JDA, but the act allowed for unfairness and uneven application. This was chronicled closely by the press (see Carrigan, 1998). While under the JDA the minimum age for juveniles accused of crimes was set at 7 across the country, the provinces were allowed to set a maximum age, which varied from 14 to 17. In Quebec, British Columbia, and Alberta, the maximum age for girls was, during certain periods, higher than that for boys.

The historical inequality of the act is illustrated in a Calgary case. Seventeen-year-old Joseph deBarathay murdered his 14-year-old brother by shooting him with a rifle after a fight in October 1955 (*Calgary Herald*, 1955: 1). Joseph was sentenced to hang for the crime, a sentence later reduced to life improvement. At the time, Alberta's maximum age for juvenile delinquents was 17 for girls and 15 for boys. So, because of his age, deBarathay was regarded by the Alberta criminal justice system as an adult and was treated accordingly. If he had been a girl, he would have been dealt with under the JDA, which would have barred the press from publishing any identifying information and subjected him to a lesser maximum penalty. If the crime had occurred in Quebec, British Colombia, or Manitoba, deBarathay would again have been regarded as a juvenile and entitled to less severe punishment under the law.

The privacy provisions for dealing with young persons began to be enforced in the mid-1970s. This is evident in a case that resulted in a contempt-of-court charge for a Manitoba radio station. After a juvenile was charged with murder, the station interviewed his mother on an open-line program. An application to transfer the boy's case to adult court was ongoing at the time. The program never identified the boy or his mother, but it disclosed information about the boy's character and a confession he allegedly made. Despite precautions to protect the boy's privacy, the court ruled in 1976 that the action was contemptible, even though there was no intent to prejudice a fair trial for him (*A.G. Manitoba* v. *Radio OB Ltd.*).

## SUMMARY

The media has played an important role in the development of the youth-justice system and will continue to do so as the most popular source of information about youth crime. The introduction of the YCJA, brought on, in part, by public concern over reports of youth crime, stands as an example of how the press can influence policy.

Occasionally, the principles regarding freedom of the press clash with those principles guiding Canada's youth laws, but those laws are evolving. The press has more access to the justice system, which, in turn, provides the public with more information relating to criminal justice for youths. Still, the news media are bound by restrictions when it comes to informing the community about the criminal actions of young people. The media have challenged some laws as being in conflict with the principles of a democratic society that are enshrined in the Canadian Charter of Rights and Freedoms. For the most part, these challenges have been unsuccessful.

Nevertheless, through the news media, public awareness of Canada's youth laws and youth crime continues to be enhanced. It is the responsibility of the press to provide the public with detailed and accurate information about the treatment of Canada's young offenders. It is the public's responsibility to use that knowledge to make informed decisions about the future of Canada's youth laws.

## NOTES

1. To see how the Canadian magazine Maclean's covers (violent) youth crime, see the special report in the 5 April 1999 issue (pp. 16 – 21).
2. For an extensive discussion of the Ryan Garrioch case, see Mofina 1996.
3. On 19 June 1999, Warren Glowatski, then 18, was described by Justice Malcolm Macauley as an "'immature' teenager" and sentenced to five years in an adult prison for his role in the gang beating death of Ms. Virk. Glowatski's lawyer immediately filed an appeal after the sentencing. Kelly Ellard's case is scheduled to go to adult court in November 1999 (Girard, 1999).

## WEB LINKS

Virtually every major Canadian newspaper can be found on the Internet. Even a growing number of radio and television stations provide news information on the 'Net. Rather than limit our list, we encourage you to locate a local/regional media outlet as well as a national media source. The following are some links to get you started:

**Canadian Press**
<http://www.cp.org>

**CBC News**
<http://www.cbcnews.cbc.ca/>

***The Globe and Mail***
<http://www.theglobeandmail.com/>

***Maclean's***
<http://www.macleans.ca/index.stm>

***The National Post***
<http://www.nationalpost.com/>

## STUDY QUESTIONS

1. How does the press contribute to the democratic process?
2. What changes did the YCJA make to how the news media cover youth crime?
3. What competing values were identified by the federal government in introducing the YCJA's publication rules?
4. Historically, how has the press regarded child criminals? Why?
5. How does the press influence the public's perception of youth crime?
6. What risks do the news media face in reporting youth crime?
7. Locate two or more local or regional newspaper articles about a unique crime committed by young people. Do the sources provide the same kinds of details about the case? Are they both objective in their presentation of the story? How do they protect the identity of the offender(s) and/or victim(s)?
8. Analyze coverage of the April 1999 high-school shootings in Littleton, Colorado, and Taber, Alberta. Was there too much or too little coverage? Were the media responsible in their coverage? Should the public have the right to know more?

## REFERENCES


Anderson, F. (1982). *Hanging in Canada: Concise History of a Controversial Topic*. Surrey, BC: Heritage House.

Armstrong, J. (1999, 15 April). "Virk hit, kicked in head, trial told." *Globe and Mail*, A5.

Bailey, I. (1998, 9 February). "Doomed teen's last moments to unfold in court." *Canadian Press*. Vancouver.

Buckley, P. (Ed.). (1992). *The Canadian Press Stylebook: A Guide for Writers and Editors*. Toronto: Canadian Press.

*Calgary Herald*. (1955, 24 October). "Youth charged with murder of brother." A17.

*Calgary Herald*. (1998, 19 September). "Youth pleads guilty to first-degree murder." A17.

Carrigan, D.O. (1991). *Crime and Punishment in Canada: A History*. Toronto: McClelland and Stewart.

———. (1998). *Juvenile Delinquency in Canada: A History*. Toronto: Irwin.

Chisholm, P., and Harnett, C.E. (1997). "Stabbings, beatings: An unsettling record." *Maclean's*, 110: 12 – 16.

Cumming, C., and McKercher C. (1994). *The Canadian Reporter*. Toronto: Harcourt Brace.

Department of Justice Canada. (1998). *A Strategy for the Renewal of Youth Justice.* Ottawa, Department of Justice Canada.

Girard, D. (1999, 19 June). "Virk killer, 18, sentenced to adult prison." *Toronto Star.* (On-line service).

*Maclean's.* (1999, 5 April). "Canada Special Report on 'kids and crime'; 'project turn-around'; and 'nowhere to turn'," 16 – 21.

Meissner, P. (1999, 13 April). "Teen pleads not guilty to killing." *Calgary Herald,* A9.

Mofina, R. (1996). "Young offenders and the press." In John A. Winterdyk (Ed.), *Issues and Perspectives on Young Offenders in Canada.* Toronto: Harcourt Brace.

Russell, N. (1994). *Morals and the Media: Ethics in Canadian Journalism.* Vancouver: University of British Columbia Press.

Sprott, J.B. (1996). "Understanding public views of youth crime and the youth justice system." *Canadian Journal of Criminology,* 38(3): 271 – 90.

## CASES CITED

*A.G. Manitoba* v. *Radio OB Ltd.* (1976), 70 D.L.R. (3d) 311 (Man. Q.B.).

R. v. *Les Publications Photo-Police Inc.* (1986), 31 C.C.C. (3d) 93 (Que. C.A.).

R. v. T.R. (No. 1) (1984), 10 C.C.C. (3d) 481 (Alta. Q.B.).

*Southam Inc.* v. R. (1986), 25 C.C.C. (3s) 119 (Ont. C.A.).

# PART THREE

# Special Topics

# Introduction

When the subject of delinquency or young offenders comes up in a discussion, the conversation inevitably trails off on different tangents because delinquency encompasses a wide range of behaviours and touches upon a variety of disciplines. In this Special Topics section, we acknowledge the complexity of delinquency by focussing on different types of delinquent behaviour and phenomena. Collectively, the chapters in this section illustrate that we can no longer rely on blanket solutions, programs, or treatment techniques to solve youth crime.

The topics chosen for this section represent key issues in the area of young offenders: substance abuse, runaway and homeless youth, adolescent prostitution, and adolescent sex offenders. Chapter 12 presents a unique review of aboriginal delinquent youth. Like other minority groups around the world, Canadian Native youth are overrepresented in the criminal justice system. The final chapter in this section is an overview of the anglophone juvenile justice system that asks why Canada, England, the United States, and Australia are behind other developed countries in the area of juvenile justice.

## SUGGESTED READINGS

It is interesting to note that in Canada there are few books covering specific topics that pertain to young offenders. Most of the material appears in academic journals or special government reports, which are often not readily accessible. Therefore, most of the readings listed below are American. Nevertheless, they should provide the interested student with further insight into the various topics.

Chesney-Lind, M., and Shelden, R.G. (1996). *Girls, Delinquency, and Juvenile Justice* (2nd ed.). Pacific Grove, CA: Brooks/Cole.

This book was originally published in 1992; the second edition continues to focus exclusively on female delinquents. The text covers virtually every aspect of female delinquency, from its prevalence, to explanations for it, to effective programs.

Fowler, K. (1989). "Youth gangs: Criminals, thrillseekers or the new voice of anarchy?" *RCMP Gazette*, 51(7 & 8).

In this article, Fowler (a highly respected expert on gangs in Canada) outlines the phenomenon of youth gangs in Canada. The article presents a short historical overview of how youth gangs have evolved from images typified in the movie *West Side Story* to those portrayed in the movie *Colors*. Fowler points out that, in addition to becoming more sophisticated and generally more violent, some youth gangs are highly organized and dangerous. He notes that while most forms of youth gangs have originated elsewhere in the world, many of these forms are now appearing across Canada. Fowler suggests that intensive one-on-one communication with gang members is needed in order to curb the problem before it escalates.

Hagan, J., and McCarthy, B. (1998). *Mean Streets: Youth Crime and Homelessness*. Toronto: University of Toronto Press.

As James Short, Jr. notes in his foreword, this book "is the first study of its kind." As part of their study, the authors use new data from Toronto and Vancouver to explore and examine the growing problem of runaways and homelessness among Canadian youth. Methodologically very sound, this is a must-read for any student interested in learning more about this issue.

Heide, K.M. (1992). *Why Kids Kill Parents: Child Abuse and Adolescent Homicide*. Columbus, OH: Ohio University Press.

Heide examines the motivations and backgrounds of adolescents who kill their parents, drawing heavily on case studies to support her observations and recommendations. The author argues that adolescent murderers are almost always terrified victims of some kind of dysfunctional family who kill out of desperation. This book covers a topic that is a relatively new phenomenon in today's society.

Inciardi, J.A., Horowitz, R., and Pottieger, A.E. (1993). *Street Kids, Street Drugs, Street Crime: An Examination of Drug Use and Serious Delinquency in Miami*. Belmont, CA: Wadsworth.

Although this book is based on a case study of serious delinquent offenders in Miami, Florida, it provides a comprehensive look at serious offenders, many of whom are on the streets. The book explores in detail the risks, consequences, and legal complications of dealing with this special population, concluding with a discussion on how delinquency theory needs to better account for these youths, and the various policy implications that are involved.

Tower, C.C. (1989). *Understanding Child Abuse and Neglect*. Needham Heights, MA: Allyn and Bacon.

Although this book does not deal with delinquent offenders specifically, Tower offers a comprehensive overview of child abuse, many of whose victims become delinquent. The book is an excellent resource for understanding those young offenders who, because of their traumatic upbringing, turn to delinquent behaviour as a means of expressing their pain. The book serves as a balance to the view that all young offenders should be treated as criminals.

Winterdyk, J. (Ed.). (1997). *Juvenile Justice Systems: International Perspectives*. Toronto: Canadian Scholars' Press.

As reflected in its title, this reader comprises eleven foreign contributions on juvenile justice—one of which includes Canada. Each contributor examines a set of common elements: defining delinquency, describing the nature and extent of youth crime, and discussing issues confronting youth crime. The country selection will allow students to learn about six different juvenile justice systems and how they compare with other systems. The introduction provides a cogent summary and overview of the six models.

# Chapter 7

# Adolescent Substance Abuse and Delinquency

PHILIP PERRY AND JOHN A. WINTERDYK

## KEY OBJECTIVES

After reading this chapter, you should be able to:

- clarify the interrelationship between drugs and delinquency;
- highlight drug and delinquency trends and prevalence patterns;
- examine profiles of delinquent substance abusers with the aim of summarizing the most critical risk factors;
- point out the significant developmental considerations for substance-abusing delinquents;
- reflect on the effectiveness of community prevention and intervention approaches specific to substance-abusing delinquents.

## KEY TERMS

affective enhancement
aging-out process
atypical substance-abuse patterns
depathologizing approach
developmental factors
dual diagnosis
family dynamics
gateway drug
generalized progression
identity crisis
identity suicide
inhalants
joint occurrence
mood swing
peer culture
peer programs
poly-substance abuse
relapse
shotgun approaches
social pathologies
solvents
substance abuse

## INTRODUCTION

Booze, pot, crack, solvents, and, more recently, anabolic steroids and designer drugs—from the schoolyard to the streets, the world of the adolescent is permeated with mind- and mood-altering substances. The history of substance abuse dates back to ancient times and reveals that virtually no society has been immune to its lure (Schlaadt, 1992). However, in Canada, it was not until the late 1960s and early 1970s that adolescent substance use became more widely publicized, confusing its relationship with delinquency and youth crime. It was during this time that society went through a period of rapid change. Large numbers of young persons rebelled against society's standards by breaking its laws and by daring to experiment with a wide variety of drugs (Doweiko, 1993).

Since the mid-1980s, substance abuse has increasingly been perceived as treatable, and it has received much attention. Meanwhile, delinquency that involves substance abuse has taken a back seat. It is not always clear to the public or politicians whether all substance abuse is delinquency, and to what extent young persons engage in substance abuse. Further, adolescent substance abuse is being treated more and more as a behavioural illness according to the classification system outlined by the American Psychiatric Association in the *Diagnostic and Statistical Manual of Mental Disorders* (commonly known as *DSM IV* (American Psychiatric Association, 1994; see also Box 7.1). On the other hand, delinquency in the absence of substance abuse is widely perceived as a social problem needing correction (i.e., punishment), rather than as an illness needing treatment.

As West (1984) noted, we prefer to blame adolescent substance abuse on a wide range of loosely related negative causes. Some of the more common factors are peer influences, faulty and impotent legal systems, permissive and boring school environments, moral and spiritual erosion, fragmented families, cultural hedonism, and permissive parenting. Such diverse and vague concepts have made it difficult to implement effective treatment and/or intervention strategies (see below).

It can be argued that rapid social, cultural, and spiritual changes since the 1980s have resulted in a pronounced trend toward a breakdown in social values, an increasingly self-indulgent lifestyle, as well as a state of

## Box 7.1

## *DSM IV:* SUBSTANCE ABUSE

The *DSM-IV* (p. 112) defines substance abuse as "a maladaptive pattern of substance use leading to clinically significant impairment or distress" that can be characterized by a number of different indicators within a twelve-month period. The following are some of these indicators:

1. Usage may result in a failure to meet work and/or school obligations.
2. Usage may result in increased risks during the execution of physical activities such as driving or operating a machine while impaired.
3. Recurrent use may result in conflicts with the law.
4. Persistent use may impair social and interpersonal relations.

The manual also has a section on "substance dependence," which, in essence, refers to an inability to refrain from using drugs or alcohol.

learned helplessness for many youths. Faced with such challenges, more and more young people seek out ways to feel less insignificant by turning to mind- and mood-altering substances. In spite of supporting evidence, society tends to deny this trend, and views drugs and delinquency as nothing more than a part of teenage experimentation or a reflection of normal turmoil that young people will eventually grow out of.

In an attempt to shed light on the interrelated nature of drugs and delinquency, this chapter examines a number of important questions: How prevalent is adolescent substance abuse among Canadian youth? How is this abuse related to youth crime? What patterns of delinquent substance abuse exist? What do we know about the abusers? What are the significant prevention and intervention considerations? We begin by examining the question of prevalence of substance abuse and delinquency.

## PREVALENCE OF ADOLESCENT SUBSTANCE ABUSE

Adolescents, by nature, are experimental. As Newcomb and Bentler (1989) observe, a phase of drug experimentation and social rule-breaking has long been viewed as part of the ego development of adolescents. When this occurs, their personality development can be seriously impeded, affecting both their present and their future well-being. In response, research on adolescent substance abuse proliferates in search of the extent of this abuse and its causes.

To date, investigators are unclear about what actually constitutes drug abuse versus experimental use. For example, Zarek, Hawkins, and Rogers (1987) found that, of identified adolescent problem drinkers, 53 percent of the males and 70 percent of the females were not judged to be problem drinkers seven years later. As the Newfoundland Department of Health and Community Services notes, "using more does not, by itself, indicate dependency" (Government of Newfoundland and Labrador, 1999b). In fact, many users simply go through an aging-out process whereby they stop using drugs as they enter early adulthood. Yet, any youth who is found using drugs runs the risk of being stigmatized as being drug dependent (Schlaadt, 1992).

Measuring the overall adolescent substance-abuse problem is further complicated by the fact that many adolescents do not freely volunteer information about their use of substances (Kaminer, 1991). It is interesting to note that most adolescent drug-use surveys focus on those who are in school (see the Canadian Centre on Substance Abuse Web link). As a result, the data provided by these surveys may underestimate the severity of the substance-abuse problem, since adolescents who drop out or who skip school because of substance-abuse issues are not counted. Notwithstanding these limitations, several Canadian surveys conducted throughout the 1990s (in the Atlantic provinces, Manitoba, Ontario, and British Columbia) show that, while substance use declined in the early 1990s, it began to increase again in the mid- to later part of the decade. For example, Mumford, Dick, Kishimoto, and Cheng (1998: 3) found that 76 percent of males and 69 percent of females had used alcohol by age 11 and that the "overall age at onset of marijuana use also seems to be decreasing."

In addition to an apparent increase in drug use by adolescents, Mumford et al. (1998: 3) observed that, contrary to what they predicted, "a higher percentage of females than males use all of the drugs listed in the report." They also found that use of mood-altering drugs changed according to age. In the next sections, we examine the use of different substances such as alcohol, marijuana, cocaine, inhalants, and other drugs.

## ALCOHOL

As most people know, alcohol is the drug of choice among adolescents[1] (see Box 7.2). Although many parents worry about possible alcohol use by their children, whenever questioned they tend to underestimate how much their children actually drink (Rogers, Harris, and Jarmuskewicz, 1987). Gallup polls conducted by Health Canada in 1992 and again in 1994 that included Canadian youths aged 12 to 19 estimated the average age for the first use of alcohol at 12 years.

Smart and Jansen (1991) relate that most Canadian and American surveys report that anywhere between 60 and 90 percent of students have used alcohol in the past year. Alcohol use increases dramatically with age throughout adolescence, with prevalence rates reaching 93 percent among Canadian and American high-school seniors (Johnson et al., 1989; Smart and Adlaf, 1989). Alcohol use is somewhat heavier among youth from upper-middle-income and high-income white families (Weibel-Orlando, 1984). As reflected in Chapter 12, aboriginal youth are significantly more likely to be involved with alcohol than are their non-aboriginal counterparts.

Although a number of studies reported a reduction in adolescent drinking in the late 1970s and 1980s, more recent studies suggest that there has been an increase in alcohol consumption among young people in the 1990s (Erickson, 1997; Mumford et al., 1998). Interestingly, Mumford and colleagues observed that, while males are slightly more likely to have used alcohol than females (71 versus 68 percent), females are slightly more likely to use more alcohol on weekends than males (35 versus 32 percent).

## MARIJUANA

Marijuana, commonly called "dope," "grass," "pot," and a variety of other names, is the most widely used illegal drug among adolescents. Prior to the mid-1960s, there was almost no use of marijuana among Canadian youth. However, the late 1960s saw a wave of interest in marijuana that has continued to the present (Smart and Jansen, 1991). Prevalence rates ranged between 31.7 and 38.2 percent until the late 1970s, when use of the drug began to decline (Smart and Adlaf, 1989). A 1992 Health and Welfare Canada youth study indicated that 25 percent of 15-year-olds had used marijuana in the previous year. By contrast, in 1996 the Canadian Community Epidemiology Network on Drug Use (CCENDU) conducted a

### Box 7.2

### TOBACCO: THE SILENT KILLER

While society pays an inordinate amount of attention to the vices of alcohol, comparatively little attention or concern is directed toward tobacco use among young people. And while the government does set limits on how tobacco can be advertised and the age at which one can legally purchase cigarettes, out of fear of losing tax dollars and industry backlash the government does not appear to be prepared (or able) to ban tobacco use altogether. Boyd (1991) observes that next to drinking alcohol and coffee, tobacco is the third most common "social vice."

Various provincial surveys have found that about one in three high-school students has smoked in the past year. Girls are smoking more than boys in all grades (approximately 36 percent versus 31 percent across all grades). The 1996 Atlantic Student Drug Survey reported that peer pressure played a less significant role in smoking than it does for drinking (see the CCSA Web link at the end of this chapter). American research reports that the average age at which smokers try their first cigarette is 14.5 years. The survey also found that the three top brands used by young smokers were the three most heavily advertised brands (Marlboro, Camel, and Newport) ("On pump," 1999).

survey in six major cities across Canada and found that 48 percent of youth between the ages of 15 and 19 had used cannabis. Several individual provincial surveys reveal similar usage rates among high-school students (see Web Links, p. 186, for further details).

Marijuana is often called a gateway drug for most adolescents. That is, young people are more likely to experiment with marijuana before they try other illegal substances. However, marijuana is not physically addictive, and the effect of its long-term use is subject to much debate.[2] Nevertheless, Kandel (1982) found that only 1 percent of those not regularly using any drug and 4 percent of legal-drug users had experimented with opiates, cocaine, and hallucinogens, as compared with 26 percent of marijuana users. Other studies have shown that marijuana users receive more social support for their use, face fewer sanctions against it, and have parental models who favour use. A number of studies have found that marijuana use is highly correlated with adolescents who experience social and legal problems as well as feel alienated from society. But, as will be discussed later, any correlation between marijuana use and delinquency does not imply a causal relationship. Any relationship between the two factors is more complex.

## COCAINE

Cocaine, an alkaloid derivative of the coca plant, is the most powerful natural stimulant. It is also commonly called "acid," "rock," "gravel," or "crystal meth." Cocaine is a highly addictive drug. Although its use is not as prevalent among adolescents as it was in the mid-1980s, Canadian data estimate that between 1 and 3 percent of youths use cocaine (Smart and Adlaf, 1989; Mumford et al., 1998). However, Mumford and colleagues observed that nearly 40 percent of males and 45 percent of females had tried the drug at least once.

While the actual use of pure cocaine may have declined during the 1990s, deadly derivatives such as crack, which is made by mixing ammonia or baking soda with cocaine to remove the hydrochlorides and to create a crystalline substance that can be smoked, became more popular. Crack is also cheaper than pure cocaine. Another deadly derivative is "speedballs," a combination of cocaine and heroin.

Cocaine derivatives, as well as other new forms of man-made drugs, continue to represent a growing problem as they are cheaper to buy than natural drugs.

## INHALANTS

According to Newcomb and Bentler (1989), inhalants are likely to be the first chemicals used by children, especially Native children (see Chapter 12). Smart and Adlaf (1989) reported, in Ontario, 1.9 percent of students use glue while 3.3 percent use other solvents. This compares closely to figures from British Columbia, where 2.7 percent of students use glue and 3.8 percent use other solvents (Chamberlayne, Kierans, and Fletcher, 1988). Rates are higher in the United States, where 6.9 percent of students report having used inhalants (Johnson et al., 1989). Groves (1990) states that approximately two out of ten children experiment with solvents by the time they graduate from high school.

Solvents are popular among youthful abusers because of peer-group influences, cost effectiveness, universal availability, convenient packaging, and rapid mood elevation. Traditional treatment approaches do not appear to be effective with the inhalant abuser due to the mental impairment that results from the abuse.

## OTHER DRUGS

Prevalence estimates of the use of other illicit drugs are less accurate, as they are sometimes lumped together in one category. They include sedatives, tranquilizers, hallucinogens (e.g., magic mushrooms and LSD), barbiturates, and, more recently, designer drugs (e.g., ecstasy and budrenophine) and anabolic steroids (see Box 7.3). Also, prevalence surveys rely almost exclusively on self-reports, and underreporting, particularly of drugs other than alcohol, may be significant (Mumford et al., 1998). Estimates range from approximately 26 percent (Mumford et al., 1998) to 36 percent for senior high-school adolescents. Students in large urban areas are more likely to experiment with certain types of drugs.

## LINKS BETWEEN DRUGS AND DELINQUENCY

Different patterns of delinquency result from the use of different drugs. Nevertheless, the link between substance abuse and delinquency has been

### Box 7.3

### STEROIDS

Anabolic steroids are synthetic variations of the males sex hormone testosterone. They have two major effects on the body: (1) they build muscle (anabolic); and (2) they make you more masculine (androgenic). Although they have been used in veterinary medicine for a long time, more recently they have been used by physicians to treat youth who are slow to reach puberty, people with blood disorders, and patients with some types of breast cancer (Alberta Alcohol and Drug Abuse Commission, 1999).

Steroids affect males and females differently. Adolescents who use them may experience severe acne on their face and body and, in some cases, premature closure of the growth plates, leading to stunted growth. In addition to physical changes, users may also suffer from a host of psychological effects such as irritability, uncontrolled bursts of rage (known as "roid rage") that can lead to acts of violence, and severe mood swings. Long-term effects can include increased cholesterol levels; high blood pressure; heart, kidney, and liver damage; and the risk of contracting AIDS if users share needles (Government of Newfoundland and Labrador, 1999a).

While steroid users do not appear to develop a tolerance for the drug, they can develop a physical and psychological addiction because of the obsession with gaining muscle, strength, and bulk.

Because of a link to black-market sales, steroid use is not well documented these days. American surveys have estimated the sale of steroids at nearly US $1 billion. The 1996 Atlantic Student Drug Use Survey reports that approximately 2 percent of all high-school students surveyed had used steroids at least once in the past twelve months.

well documented (Fagan, Weis, and Cheng, 1990; Johnson et al., 1991; Winters, Weller, and Meland, 1993). One study reports that nearly 50 percent of serious young offenders (who admitted to committing three or more serious offences in the previous year) were also multiple-illicit-drug users. Eighty-two percent of these chronic serious offenders reported use, beyond experimentation, of at least one illicit drug. It was also reported that incidence rates of alcohol use among serious delinquents were 4 to 9 times those of non-offenders. Rates of marijuana use were 14 times those of non-offenders, and rates of use of other illicit drugs were 6 to 36 times those of non-offenders, depending on the drug (Hawkins, Jenson, and Catalano, 1988). A 1992 American survey found that, in some cities, more than 70 percent of all adolescent arrestees tested positively for an illicit drug (National Institute of Justice, 1992).

While some drugs are in fashion for certain periods of time, as are different forms of delinquency, both drugs and delinquency continue to persist as major social problems despite efforts to remedy them. As Wiel and Rosen (1983) state, "drugs are here to stay. History teaches that it is vain to hope that drugs will ever disappear and that any effort to eliminate them from society is doomed to failure." Much the same can be said for delinquency. The form it takes varies from community to community and from decade to decade. Yet the prevalence of delinquency continues in a predictable manner.

Since drug abuse correlates strongly with a wide variety of other delinquencies, these two issues are in many ways inseparable. Even though one can technically exist without the other, the two interrelate in ways that tear at the social, personal, and cultural well-being of young people during their important developmental years. The next section examines what we know about the patterns of each of these social issues.

# PATTERNS OF DRUG USE AND DELINQUENCY

## ADOLESCENT DRUG-USE PATTERNS

Adolescents are prone to atypical substance-abuse patterns. Unlike adults, they often mix drugs and they do not tend to follow a uniform pattern of use (Nowinski, 1990). Whereas adults often begin experimenting with alcohol, adolescents tend to experiment more freely with a variety of drugs, or poly-substance abuse (Holland and Griffin, 1984). Some studies have nevertheless shown a generalized progression from mild alcohol misuse, to marijuana use, to pronounced alcohol abuse, to hallucinogens, to cocaine, and then finally to heroin. If adolescents indeed move through the chain in a progressive way, rather than substitute one substance for another, they are more likely to add a drug to their use and abuse pattern.

Despite the fact that most adolescents do not follow predictable patterns of abuse, there appears to be a subtle yet progressive addictive stage of development that unfolds. According to Nowinski (1990), once more pronounced addiction to drugs becomes identifiable, several dimensions or stages of the addiction process retrospectively become evident. These dimensions might be best understood as four stages of progressive addiction:

- **Stage One.** Experimental
- **Stage Two.** Instrumental
- **Stage Three.** Habitual
- **Stage Four.** Compulsive

The experimental, or learning, stage is characterized by a heightened sense of curiosity and risk-taking behaviour. During this stage, the adolescent learns about the mood swings that drugs produce. The emotional impact of the use is secondary to the adventure involved in using drugs. Often related to the excitement of experimentation is a desire for peer acceptance.

The instrumental stage is characterized by a much more purposeful desire to manipulate emotions. This is when the adolescent seeks the mood swing for itself. Once acquainted with the mood swings that alcohol and different drugs produce, the adolescent begins to use substances with the intent of suppressing or enhancing certain feelings in order to seek pleasure or avoid pain. This stage is often marked by changes in friendship patterns, erratic school performance, unpredictable mood swings, and delinquent behaviours.

The habitual stage is characterized by drug-use binges. The use is, more and more, driven by the compensatory need to avoid pain and seek relief from unwanted or uncomfortable feelings of anguish, anger, anxiety, shame, guilt, loneliness, and boredom. If feelings are successfully suppressed, the adolescent may gradually acquire an addictive pattern. The habitual stage is characterized by drugs becoming a focal part of the adolescent's lifestyle. Both emotional and physical dependency become evident. Friends who do not use drugs are dropped, and family confrontations tend to develop (Jones, 1990). By now, the adolescent is likely using drugs on a daily basis.

In the final, compulsive stage, the adolescent becomes extraordinarily preoccupied with drug use, to the extent that getting high is nearly all that is important to him or her. As a result, the adolescent's life is now controlled by the drugs. At this point, the adolescent will experience physical complications, including memory loss and/or flashback experiences, pronounced paranoia, and uncontrollable anger.

## DRUG-RELATED DELINQUENCY PATTERNS

Delinquent behaviour generally comes before drug use. Among most youths, delinquent behaviour peaks between the ages of 15 and 17, while drug involvement increases during the later teenage years and peaks in the early 20s. However, for a small portion of the youth population, probably between 2 and 6 percent, both serious criminal behaviour and frequent drug use will persist into adulthood (Hawkins, Jenson, and Catalano, 1988).

Clouding our understanding of the relationship between delinquency and drug use is a social tendency to minimize the importance of minor delinquency and occasional use of alcohol. In a study by Fagan, Weis, and Cheng (1990), it was found that the frequency and seriousness of specific types of substance abuse increase with the severity of delinquent involvement. However, the frequency of use of all substances varies little with the severity or frequency of delinquency. It appears that there is a skewed relationship between substance abuse and delinquency. Explaining drug use from a knowledge of the severity of delinquency is much more valid than vice versa; knowing the frequency of drug use by adolescents adds little to explaining the severity of their delinquency. Drug use, then, is associated in a selective manner with serious delinquent behaviour.

Patterned use of substances that produce more intense highs may contribute to serious youth crime through their pharmacological effects. That is, it is the *intensity* of a drug high, rather than the *frequency* of getting high, that is more closely associated with serious delinquent behaviour. Social judgement is impaired and behavioural control is undermined when adolescents use pharmacologically powerful drugs.

The probability of more frequent and severe drug use increases with the frequency and severity of delinquent behaviour. As a result, a number of studies have assumed the relationship between drug abuse and crime to be linear, causal, and inextricably linked. As noted earlier, there is little evidence that consuming alcohol or other illicit substances directly causes crime. Yet, the joint occurrence explanation is based on the realization that delinquency often occurs before drug use. Longitudinal studies indicate that delinquency and drugs are linked to a similar set of social, psychological, and demographic variables (Brunnelle and Brochu, 1996; Fagan, Weis, and Cheng, 1990).

In summary, it is not conclusive that drugs and alcohol cause crime. It is also not conclusive that crime causes substance abuse. Further, it is not conclusive that some cause is common to both crime and drug abuse. Finally, research has not identified specific drug-produced motivations to commit crime. All of this suggests that patterns of substance abuse and delinquency are multidimensional and loosely interwoven. This has important implications for treating adolescent substance abusers, which will be reviewed in a later section. Prior to discussing prevention and intervention, it would be useful to examine the profiles and development of substance-abusing delinquents.

## PROFILES OF DELINQUENT DRUG ABUSERS

There are several key risk factors that underpin substance abuse. They are very similar to those factors linked to delinquency. Much has been said about the impact of such factors as family dynamics, peer culture, and social pathologies such as stress, child abuse, and self-harming behaviour. It is probably safe to say that the more pronounced and interactive these risk factors are, the more likely a pattern of delinquent substance abuse will develop (Farrell, 1993).

### FAMILY DYNAMICS

Research reveals that family composition alone is only weakly associated with adolescent substance abuse and delinquency (Bachman, Johnston, and O'Malley, 1981; Byram and Fly, 1984). However, families characterized by high levels of anxiety, tension between adolescents and parents, rejection of adolescents by parents, and a low degree of maternal control are more likely to produce delinquent substance abusers (Mayer, 1980). Kaminer (1991) finds that three different types of parental characteristics predict delinquent substance abuse:

- Parental substance use/abuse behaviours
- Parental attitudes toward delinquent substance abuse
- Parent – child interactions

Chemically dependent families are generally socially isolated from the community because of their need for secrecy and their fear of being rejected. These families are often less involved in recreational, social, religious, and cultural activities, and the parents demonstrate poor parenting skills (Kumpfer and Demarsh, 1986). As a result, the children in these families have fewer opportunities to interact with other children. Emotional neglect and characteristics of psychopathology have also been detected in substance-abusing parents. The emotional impact on the children results in their feeling resentment, embarrassment, anger, fear, loneliness, depression, and insecurity. Since behavioural and emotional disturbances often precede delinquent substance abuse, these children are at high risk of becoming abusers (Kumpfer and Demarsh, 1986).

## PEER CULTURE

The most consistent and reproducible finding in substance-abuse research is the strong relationship between an adolescent's substance behaviour and the concurrent substance use of his or her peers. Various studies have found that this relationship may result from socialization as well as from a process of interpersonal selection, in which adolescents with similar values and behaviours seek one another out as friends.

With regard to the values and attitudes of adolescent substance abusers, the abuse is correlated negatively with conventional behaviours and beliefs (e.g., church attendance, good scholastic performance, etc.). On the other hand, substance abuse is correlated positively with risk-taking behaviour, early sexual activity, higher value placed on independence, and greater involvement in delinquent behaviour (Jessor, 1987). Kaminer (1991: 331) states that "delinquency may reach a point at which adolescent gangs, groups, and cults engage in one or more of the following shared activities: using the same drug of choice, Satanism and related rituals, drug trafficking, and violence." These activities are deeply rooted in the identity-creating process of these groups and are inseparable components of their code of values.

## PATHOLOGICAL DYNAMICS

Behavioural problems are strongly correlated with delinquent adolescent substance abuse. It seems that many adolescents who undergo substance-abuse treatment also manifest affective disorders, conduct disorders, and anxiety disorders, among others (Kovach and Glickman, 1986). Many adolescents with eating disorders, especially bulimia nervosa, are also substance abusers. Friedman and Glickman (1986) reported in a National Youth Polydrug Study that 28 percent of the adolescents surveyed indicated that they had sought help for emotional and psychiatric problems. Schmidt (1991: 860) states that there is a danger that dual-diagnosis patients—those who have substance-abuse and behavioural problems—are likely to be "barred from treatment institutions because their multiple presenting problems do not conveniently fit into the diagnostic categories used by specialized alcohol and mental health programs." Although further research in this area is greatly needed, some possible relationships between co-existing substance abuse and psychopathology have been outlined by Kaminer (1991: 332):

- Substance abuse and behavioural problems may originate from a common cause.
- Psychiatric symptoms or disorders may develop or worsen as a consequence of use or abuse of substances.
- Substance abuse may develop as a consequence of psychiatric disorders when individuals use substances as self-medication.

- Psychiatric disorders may alter the course of substance abuse.
- Substance abuse may alter the course of psychiatric disorders.
- Psychiatric disorders and substance abuse may be mutually exclusive but coincidentally manifested.

## STRESS

Several studies have reported that a dysfunctional family and stressful life events correlate with increased substance abuse in adolescents (Farrell, 1993). Symptoms of negative as opposed to positive stress include nervousness and anxiety, irritability and agitation, insomnia, difficulty concentrating, sleep disturbances, appetite disorders, and compulsory substance abuse (Nowinski, 1990). One study by Pandina and Schuele (1983) reported that when self-report measures of anxiety, strain, and stress were administered to high-school students and a group of adolescents referred for treatment of alcohol and drug abuse, the findings revealed that the adolescents in treatment had higher levels of stress. Dependence on drugs, especially minor tranquillizers or alcohol, "helps" to ease the stress. However, these drugs are highly addictive and can pose long-term problems if the user develops a dependency.

## SEXUAL/PHYSICAL ABUSE

The relationship between sexual/physical abuse and substance abuse in adolescents has not yet been thoroughly explored. Pandina and Schuele's 1983 study found that 40 percent of the adolescents in treatment for substance abuse reported having been beaten or physically abused in their homes. Singer and Petchers (1989) report that the sexually abused group indicates more regular use of cocaine and stimulants, greater frequencies of alcohol and drug use, and more reported drunkenness and drug highs than their control-group partners. Studies focussing on substance abusers that did not use control groups have reported rates of childhood sexual abuse in the 30 – 44 percent range (Rohsenow, Corbett, and Devine, 1988).

## SUICIDAL AND SELF-HARMING BEHAVIOUR

Suicide is frequently associated with substance abuse among adolescents. Suicide rates for teenagers have almost tripled since the early 1970s. In 1998, Canada had the third-highest adolescent suicide rate in the world (*Teenage suicide*, 1998). On the basis of a year-long study completed in 1984, Rich and colleagues (1986) reported that substance abuse was strongly associated with 70 percent of suicides among victims under 30 years of age. Their findings, among others, support the view that drug use may be the most important factor in the increase in suicide among young people.

Downey (1990) relates that a significant number of today's youth are alienated from themselves, their families, and even their peers. For many adolescents, identity suicide begins at a young age, with drugs used as an outlet for denied, repressed, and misunderstood emotions such as loneliness, frustration, low self-esteem, and anger. Indeed, it may be that substance abuse is a form of slow suicide. However, drugs eventually do not meet the adolescent's needs for love, acceptance, and achievement, and suicide can then become the only perceived way out (Downey, 1990).

The factors that lead to mild delinquent substance abuse may be somewhat different from the factors that lead to serious and persistent delinquent substance abuse. Several researchers conclude that drug use is associated selectively with serious delinquent involvement, and that the type of drug use, as well as its frequency, may influence the severity of delinquent involvement (Kandel, Simcha-Fagan, and Davies, 1986; White, Pandina, and LaGrange, 1987). Moreover, the level of intensity of the pharmacological effects of drugs appear to be highly correlated with serious youth crime. In order to offer as clear a picture as possible of the risk factors associated with high-rate offending and adolescent drug abuse, Box 7.4 presents a summary of the relevant findings (Haggerty et al., 1989).

While the profiles of different substance-abusing delinquents are remarkably similar, dedicated solvent abusers are distinctive in that they are not commonly connected with other adolescent drug cultures (Groves, 1990). In fact, they tend to be ostracized and largely ignored as a substance-abusing population. Box 7.5 presents a profile of solvent abusers.

## DEVELOPMENTAL FACTORS

It goes without saying that both delinquency and substance abuse have a profound impact on a young person's personality development and future relationships. Instead of adolescence being a time to assert individualism, develop willpower and self-control, and adopt constructive values and ethics, delinquent drug abuse reinforces self-indulgence, the desire for immediate gratification, and relief from responsibility. Several major developmental factors are worth highlighting, as they have significant implications for treatment.

### ARRESTED SOCIAL LEARNING

The more pronounced the substance abuse, the more likely the adolescent will become further and further removed from the mainstream adolescent culture. His or her social learning becomes skewed toward a delinquent peer culture as the youth becomes ostracized by mainstream peers. The preoccupation with predominantly negative values and destructively competitive peer relationships generally leaves these adolescents without positive interpersonal skills. Thus, outside the delinquent culture, they tend to be confused and fearful. These adolescents also tend to lack adequate assertiveness and verbal communication skills. Often, they use drugs as a crutch to assist them in their struggle with relating to peers.

## Box 7.4

## CONTRIBUTING FACTORS TO GENERAL SUBSTANCE ABUSE AMONG DELINQUENTS

| | |
|---|---|
| Family | • Significant negative association between the quality of the parent – child relationship and substance use.<br>• Families characterized by high levels of anxiety, tension between parent and child, rejection by parent, and low degree of maternal control.<br>• Children sense a wide discrepancy between expectations of parents and expectations of peers.<br>• Parents tend to be substance abusers. |
| Cultural | • Users attach less importance to religion.<br>• Heavier use among youth from upper-middle-income and upper-income white males, as well as among Native youth.<br>• Experience of alienation and estrangement from mainstream cultural life.<br>• Increased use among older adolescents. |
| Social | • Low self-esteem, low achievement, under-socialized as to values and norms.<br>• General deviance and delinquency and increased risk-taking behaviour.<br>• First use occurs between 12 and 15 years of age.<br>• Develop circle of friends who drink or use other drugs.<br>• Are more tolerant of deviance/conduct disorders, and antisocial traits/beliefs prevalent.<br>• Users often have an extensive treatment history.<br>• More influenced by peers than family or society.<br>• Significant history of academic and behavioural problems in school from an early age. |
| Psychological | • Users often have a history of suicide attempts.<br>• History of hyperactivity and minimal brain dysfunction.<br>• Antisocial behaviour.<br>• Increased level of psychopathology and emotional disturbances.<br>• Affective disorders (e.g., depression). |
| Biological | • Users may have a deficiency or altered level of serotonin.<br>• Increased tolerance to alcohol.<br>• Genetic history of antisocial personality or parents with alcohol problems.<br>• Children of alcoholics run a biological risk of alcoholism that is four times greater than for children of nonalcoholics.<br>• Direct relation to cigarette smoking if users smoke a pack per day or more. Nicotine acts as a gateway drug. |

**Source:** Annis and Davis (1991), Doweiko (1993), Frances and Miller (1991), Novacer (1991).

## STAGNATED COGNITIVE GROWTH

As delinquent substance abusers take a holiday from thinking, they get caught up in survival tactics that are both adversarial and reactionary. This tends to make them dependent on rigid concrete responses for every situation. They can seldom depend on their abstract thinking, as it is all too often fragmented and based on inadequate knowledge. Basically, abstract thinking is painful for substance abusers because it reveals how they are avoiding moral and ethical values. For example, justice and social responsibility become black-and-white issues that are easily reinterpreted to defend ego-driven behaviour.

## ARRESTED MORAL DEVELOPMENT

Because they are preoccupied with the present and with immediate gratification, adolescent substance abusers' codes of morals and ethics are at best based on reciprocity or equity. Retribution and fairness become their main areas of concern. These young people tend to avoid issues such as social responsibility, future legal consequences of behaviour, respect for others, and acceptance of individual differences.

### Box 7.5

### CONTRIBUTING FACTORS TO SOLVENT-ABUSING DELINQUENTS

| | |
|---|---|
| Family | • Come from deprived or impoverished family background.<br>• Family members tend to be substance abusers.<br>• High incidence of sibling influence on initiating solvent-abuse experimentation.<br>• Significant absence of male father figure. |
| Cultural | • Predominantly culturally marginal male Native persons. |
| Social | • Antisocial and highly aggressive behaviour.<br>• Oblivious or uncaring about criminal or legal implications of delinquency.<br>• Alienated from community support systems.<br>• First occurrence between 6 and 10 years of age. |
| Psychological | • High levels of impulsivity and unpredictability.<br>• Easily labelled as having a conduct or personality disorder.<br>• Generally high risk of accidental suicide. |
| Biological | • Most solvent abusers are developmentally delayed.<br>• Prone to being cognitively impaired. |

## ARRESTED SELF-ESTEEM DEVELOPMENT

Self-esteem is a central factor in adolescent development and is formed through experiencing success versus failure in a wide range of physical, social, and intellectual situations. Achievement, skill acquisition, and interpersonal attractiveness form an important basis for self-esteem during adolescence. However, it is in the arena of peers that the adolescent forms his or her own self-perception. Being stigmatized, ostracized, or ridiculed by non-delinquent peers during adolescent years can have a severe arresting effect on self-concept and sense of well-being.

Since the delinquent peer culture tends to be based on defensiveness and survival, what self-esteem is gained from this association is largely undermined by the culture's predisposition to low self-esteem. At best, a temporary feeling of well-being is achieved during drug highs or as the aftermath to a delinquent adventure. It is important to point out, however, that almost all adolescents go through a roller-coaster ride with their self-esteem as part of their identity development. Research on this has shown that delinquent and non-delinquent self-esteem are not appreciably different (Siegal and Senna, 1994). The difference may well be that delinquent substance abusers have a prolonged identity crisis that results in arrested self-esteem development.

The earlier the substance abuse begins in an adolescent's life, the less likely his or her developmental stages will be met. Therefore, preventing and treating delinquent substance abuse is as much a matter of treating developmental deficits as it is a matter of intervening to stop the substance abuse and delinquency (see Box 7.6).

# TREATMENT CONSIDERATIONS

## PREVENTION POSSIBILITIES

Since the early 1980s, persistent efforts to prevent delinquent substance abuse have generally not fared well. There have been many outcome studies and articles on delinquent drug prevention and education programs. Tobler (1986) identified five types of prevention programs that either directly confronted drug problems or indirectly addressed drug use and were aimed at reducing the correlates of drug use. The indirect approaches included affective enhancement, which aims at interpersonal and social growth, and alternative programs, which focus on community and leisure activities and remedial skills. There were three general types of direct approaches: (1) the education approach, (2) peer programs focussed on refusal skills and social life skills, and (3) a combination of knowledge and affective approaches. Of these five approaches, Tobler found that the peer programs had the strongest outcomes for the average teenager, including enhanced social skills and assertiveness, reduced drug use, or prevention of the initiation of drug use by the teenager.

## Box 7.6

## TREATING SUBSTANCE ABUSE

### Toward a Model of Change

Whatever our new understanding of the change process, it must ... account for dramatic but unpredictable changes in addictive behaviour, for the fact is that most change occurs outside treatment, and that those changes that occur in a treatment context often occur in the non-specialist setting and for nonspecific reasons, and that people have been changing addictive behaviours for centuries and often in circumstances that seem to us very alien from our present perspectives.

### Three Things to Expect of a Theory of Change in Addictive Behaviours

An understanding of change in terms of decision making begins to do three general things that we should expect of a theory of addictive behaviour change, and which a disease model does not do.

1. It should unite different addictive behaviours on an equal footing. Disease models were always more comfortable with hard-drug addiction and severe drinking problems. It was clear that they were stretched to the breaking point when considering the full range of alcohol-related problems, the full range of forms of drug misuse, and certain forms of eating disorder. They were never serious contenders for embracing excessive gambling, most forms of excessive eating, excessive sexuality, and even tobacco smoking. On the other hand, all can be embraced within a model of decisional conflict.
2. Ideally, our theory should unite early and late choices or decisions. We can now begin to talk in the same terms about early decisions to take up a new form of potentially addictive behaviour that has become troublesome. In terms of practice, this is probably the single most important aspect of the shift from disease to psychological models of addictive behaviour.
3. Our theory should unite the clinical and the social-epidemiological fields. It was always unhelpful to use one language to describe a clinical change process (motivation to enter treatment, therapist, patient, relapse, etc.) and another to describe the more numerous changes that occur elsewhere (decision, spontaneous, unaided, etc.). A theory of conflict, decision, and action, with the help of influence based on social power of one kind or another, meets this criterion for a satisfactory theory much more adequately.

### Three Points That May Cause Trouble

1. We have given little attention to the possibility that change is most likely to occur at times of crisis. Is it the case that change is particularly likely to be initiated at one of a limited number of occasional choice points in a career of addictive behaviour? There is a saying that problem drinkers seek change only because of livers, lovers, livelihood, or the law. Are changes confined to those times when one of these factors plays up, when some humiliating event occurs, or perhaps when a person enters a new role position (e.g., as father, mother, manager, widow)?
2. The moral or spiritual aspects of the change process are largely missing. Whether an understanding of change in terms of a specific decision or action about an addictive behaviour can do justice to changes involving

*continued*

Box 7.6 *continued*

widespread modifications of attitudes and values remains to be seen.

3. We have given little attention to the possibility that some change may occur because the addictive behaviour loses its meaning or its functional significance, possibly without any direct contemplation or action, or even without the person being aware that the addictive behaviour was changing at all. This is presumably one of the ways in which "maturing out" works: as a person ages the formerly addictive behaviour simply ceases to perform the functions that the older person values.

Source: William R. Miller and Nick Heather, *Treating Addictive Behaviors: Processes of Change* (New York: Plenum, 1986), pp. 99, 103 – 5.

Other researchers have not been as optimistic as Tobler. For example, Erickson (1997) found that no approach to drug prevention or education had any appreciable effects, and that the methods to reduce demand among teenagers need to be re-examined. This may be due, in part, to the fact that traditional programs emphasize prevention/intervention by focussing on negative behaviour as opposed to reinforcing positive behaviours. When evaluating different approaches to treating substance abuse, numerous researchers consider relapse a part of the recovery process—especially with respect to young people, because of the developmental stages they are going through.

## INTERVENTION CONSIDERATIONS

The results of treating delinquents who are involved in serious drug abuse have not been well documented. Kaminer (1991: 337) states that the "paucity of reports from treatment services, scarce treatment quality assessments, and, above all, much disagreement about major treatment approaches account for the difficulty in suggesting optimal treatment strategies for substance abusing adolescents."

Kaminer relates that, frequently, adolescents are incorporated into mixed-patient populations or provided with adult services that are not suited to their specific needs. The most common treatment facilities are outpatient clinics (which serve 80 percent of adolescents who receive treatment), drop-in centres, therapeutic communities, residential programs, halfway houses, and inpatient units. An inpatient setting immediately interrupts the negative, self-destructive lifestyle by removing the adolescent to a substitute environment—a drug-free, highly structured therapeutic community (Newcomb and Bentler, 1989). Little evidence is available to argue whether inpatient or outpatient treatment is most useful, although lengthy and expensive residential treatment for adult alcohol abusers is apparently no more successful than shorter, less costly outpatient programs. It is also not clear whether the same conclusion can be drawn about treatment for adolescent substance abusers, however, and there are some indications that longer treatments may be more beneficial for this group (Friedman, Glickman, and Morrissey, 1986).

Kaminer (1991: 332) lists the types of patients who would be appropriately referred to an inpatient clinic:

- Patients who are severely physically dependent. Such patients need to be detoxified under medical supervision in order to prevent potentially life-threatening withdrawal symptoms.
- Delinquents who have failed in or do not qualify for outpatient treatment.
- Intravenous drug abusers and freebasers.
- Dual-diagnosis patients with moderate to severe psychiatric disorders requiring simultaneous treatment.
- Patients who need to be isolated from environmental factors that might promote a relapse of substance abuse.

The few attempts that have been made to treat substance abuse and delinquency together are perhaps best described as shotgun approaches. With drop-out and relapse rates tending to be alarmingly high, such treatments mix a variety of techniques, resulting in an individualized treatment approach. Examples of some commonly used forms of treatment for adolescents include individual treatment techniques such as individual counselling and cognitive and behavioural therapy. In addition, there are several commonly used group techniques: milieu therapy, which seeks to make sense of all aspects of a patient's environment as part of his or her treatment and which minimizes differences between staff and treatment personnel; positive peer culture, in which the group members themselves are the agents in changing behaviour; general social-skills training; and specialized anger-management training. Despite these efforts to treat delinquent substance abusers, no single strategy appears to stand out as superior in dealing with the drop-out and relapse problems (see Box 7.7).

One Canadian program, however, believes it has had some promising results with a more systematic approach to delinquent substance-abuse treatment. Operating in Calgary, Alberta, the program offers several interconnected, yet freestanding, stages of treatment (Canadiana Centre, 1991). Starting with a short detoxification component (three to five days), the program moves to engagement/assessment (up to three weeks), and ends with a more comprehensive discovery program (up to three months). The program recognizes the need for comprehensive treatment of adolescent substance abusers, yet it also offers several optional commitment points for treatment-resistant adolescents. Since adolescents can exercise choice in moving from one stage to another, they often quickly become attracted to this health-promoting, depathologizing approach to treatment.

## SUMMARY

In this chapter, we have seen that substance use among teenagers is widespread, and appears to be on the upswing once again. While certain drugs

## Box 7.7

## CHARACTERISTICS OF PROMISING DELINQUENCY TREATMENTS

### Systematic Assessment

Some characteristics of adolescent substance abusers are highly relevant to effective programming, while others are of less significance, which is why assessment and matching are important.

What should be assessed? Factors that are relevant to criminality should be assessed, as well as factors of general importance, such as suicidal intent, anxiety/worrying, and what is important to the client. Also assess on factors that are relevant to the choice of treatment.

In general, assessment should be done in order to

- Make treatment decisions.
- Classify clinical cases.
- Provide a management information system.
- Provide community information and advocacy.

### Therapeutic Integrity

Several indicators of integrity:

- The risk/need level of adolescent substance abusers is specified and needs are targeted for intervention.
- A detailed program manual outlines the specific steps involved in the intervention.
- Therapists receive at least two to six months of formal training in theory and practice.
- Therapists are assessed at the end of the training, and the therapeutic process is assessed at its midpoint in order to determine the level of adherence to principles and employment of techniques claimed to be employed.
- Assessment of changes in values and/or skills of substance abuser in relation to desired outcomes.
- The intervention period is tied reasonably to risk, need, and responsibility.

### Relapse Prevention

Transfer training must be built into residential programs as well as relapse prevention training. This training should address the following areas:

- The ability to monitor, recognize, and anticipate risky situations.
- Planning and rehearsing alternative responses.
- Practising new behaviours in increasingly difficult situations and rewarding improved competencies.
- Booster sessions.
- Training significant others to provide support.

### Appropriate Targeting

The following list suggests some promising targets of treatment programs:

- Changing antisocial attitudes.
- Changing antisocial feelings.
- Reducing antisocial peer associations.
- Promoting familial affection and communication.
- Promoting familial monitoring and supervision.
- Promoting identification and association with anticriminal role models.
- Increasing self-control, self-management, and problem-solving skills.
- Replacing the skills of lying, stealing, and aggression with more prosocial alternatives.
- Reducing chemical dependencies.
- Shifting the density of personal, interpersonal, and other rewards and costs for criminal and noncriminal activities in familial, academic, vocational, recreational, and other behavioural settings, so that the noncriminal alternatives are favoured.

*continued*

Box 7.7 *continued*

- Providing the chronically psychiatrically troubled teenager with low-pressure, sheltered living arrangements.
- Changing other attributes of adolescents and their circumstances that, through individualized assessments of risk and need, have been linked reasonably with criminal conduct.
- Ensuring that the adolescent is able to recognize risky situations and has a concrete and well-rehearsed plan for dealing with those situations.

Research also suggests a list of less promising targets:

- Increasing self-esteem without simultaneously reducing antisocial thinking, feeling, or peer associations.
- Focussing on vague emotional and personal complaints that have not been linked with criminal conduct.
- Increasing the cohesiveness of antisocial peer groups.
- Improving neighbourhood-wide living conditions, without touching the criminal needs of high-risk individuals.
- Showing respect for antisocial thinking on the grounds that the values of one culture are as equally valid as the values of another culture.
- Increasing conventional ambition in the areas of school and work without providing concrete assistance to realize these ambitions.
- Attempting to turn the client into a "better person," when the standards for being a "better person" are not linked with recidivism.

## Appropriate Styles of Services

Generally, the best styles of services are behavioural, in particular, cognitive-behavioural and social learning: modelling, graduated practice, role-playing, reinforcement, extinction, resource provision, concrete verbal suggestions (symbolic modelling, giving reasons, prompting), and cognitive restructuring. Five dimensions of effective correctional supervision and counselling are worthy of serious consideration:

- **Relationship factors.** Relating in open, enthusiastic, and caring ways.
- **Authority.** Being firm but fair, distinguishing between rules and requests, monitoring, and reinforcing compliance. *Not* using interpersonal domination or abuse.
- **Anticriminal modelling and reinforcement.** Demonstrating and reinforcing vivid alternatives to pro-criminal styles of thinking, feeling, and acting.
- **Concrete problem-solving.** Skill-building and removal of obstacles toward rewards for anticriminal behaviour in settings such as home, school, and work.
- **Advocacy and brokerage.** As long as the receiving agency offers appropriate correctional service.

**Source:** A. Leschied, P. Jaffe, D.A. Andrews, and P. Gendreau, 1992.

like alcohol remain common, we have also seen the introduction of new drugs such as steroids; date-rape drugs; more potent and deadlier derivatives of existing drugs, such as crack and LSD; and a host of new designer drugs. Although not as extreme as our American counterparts, we appear to be more willing to punish adolescent drug users than to rely on prevention and intervention programs, even though there has been a proliferation of these programs in the past few decades. Unfortunately, few attempts are being made to treat or prevent delinquency and substance abuse together. The attempts that have been made have not fared well, as drop-out rates have been high. The results of these efforts have not been well documented, but overall, the available research suggests that relatively few adolescents (less than 5 percent of all youths) should be targeted for identification and intervention strategies that recognize and deal with both their criminal behaviour and serious drug use. Nonetheless, it is this 5 percent that commits over 50 percent of recorded offences, resulting in huge social costs.

What are the community considerations for tackling adolescent delinquency and substance abuse? To begin with, the situation cries out for a coordinated network of services that is preferably community-based and -driven. Most importantly, this network should balance individual treatment needs with community needs. As a society, we need to focus on reconnecting disconnected or abandoned youth with a social-support network. Our community response needs to be firm as well as compassionate in its primary effort to interrupt unacceptable drug and delinquency patterns. Changing or replacing patterns of delinquency and substance abuse is possible. Getting rid of substance abuse and delinquency entirely is not. Therefore, our community efforts must focus more on helping young people to discover new, constructive, life enhancing behaviours rather than just helping them to recover from rebelliousness.

## NOTES

1. According to the 1993 General Social Survey, aspirin is the number one drug of choice among Canadians. In the past twelve months, over 70 percent of Canadians surveyed has used aspirin at least once.
2. There is research evidence that marijuana may lower sperm counts in male users and may cause pregnancy difficulties in female users (Schlaadt, 1992).

## WEB LINKS

**Against Drunk Driving**
<http://www.add.ca/>

This site features information on Operation Lookout; an index to Canadian, provincial, and international counter-measure activities; press releases and publications; and links to related sites that deal with impaired-driving issues.

**An Alcohol Awareness Web Site**
<http://www-personal.umd.umich.edu/~jobrown/justsayno.html>

This site, from the University of Michigan, offers an interesting perspective on how young people are informed about the vices of drug use. It also features a number of links to Alcohol Awareness Information sites.

**The Canadian Centre on Substance Abuse**
<http://www.ccsa.ca/>

Created in 1988, the Canadian Centre on Substance Abuse is a non-profit organization that works to minimize the harm associated with alcohol, tobacco, and drug use. This site features statistics on various types of drug use and abuse as well as drug-use survey results.

## STUDY QUESTIONS

1. Given that marijuana is considered a gateway drug for most adolescent substance abusers, do you think "get tough" laws against marijuana use should be adopted, or do you think marijuana should be legalized?
2. Discuss the similarities between profiles of substance abusers and delinquents. What factors seem most important for both groups?
3. What kind of treatment program would you implement for chronic delinquent substance abusers?
4. Alcohol is the drug of choice for most adolescents. Do you consider alcohol a drug? Explain. Since rebellious behaviour is universally viewed as part of adolescence, do you think it makes sense to preach abstinence through educational prevention programs?
5. Although not discussed specifically in this chapter, can an argument be made for the legalization or decriminalization of certain drugs? Explain.
6. How, if at all, does the media sensationalize the use of drugs among young people? Do antidrug campaigns work?

## REFERENCES

Alberta Alcohol and Drug Abuse Commission. (1999, 16 September). *Steroids*. On-line <http://www.gov.ab.ca/aadac/addictions/abc/steroids.htm>

American Psychiatric Association. (1994). *Diagnostic and Statistical Manual of Mental Disorders* (4th ed.). Washington, DC: American Psychiatric Association.

Annis, H.M., and Davis, C.S. (1991). *Drug Use by Adolescents: Identification, Assessment and Intervention*. Toronto: Addiction Research Foundation.

Bachman, J.G., Johnston, L.D., and O'Malley, P.M. (1981). "Smoking, drinking, and drug use among American high school students: Correlates and trends, 1975 – 1979." *American Journal of Public Health*, 71: 59 – 69.

Boyd, N. (1991). *High Society*. Toronto: Key Porter.

Brunnelle, N., and Brochu, S. (1996, 24 May). "La prediction de la delinquance et de la toxicomanie: Les risques, les facteurs de risque." Paper presented at the 63rd Congress of L'Association Canadienne-Française pour l'avancement des sciences, Quebec City.

Byram, W.O., and Fly, J.W. (1984). "Family structure, race, and adolescents' alcohol use: A research note." *American Journal of Drug and Alcohol Abuse*, 10: 467 – 78.

Canadiana Centre. (1991). "Executive report." Wood's Homes, Calgary, Alberta. Unpublished manuscript.

Chamberlayne, R., Kierans, W., and Fletcher, L. (1988). *British Columbia Alcohol and Drug Program Adolescent Survey: 1987. Technical Report*. Victoria, BC: British Columbia Ministry of Health.

Doweiko, H.E. (1993). *Concepts of Chemical Dependency*. Pacific Grove, CA: Brooks/Cole.

Downey, A.M. (1990). "The impact of drug abuse upon adolescent suicide." *OMEGA*, 22: 261 – 75.

Erickson, P. (1997). "Reducing the harm of adolescent substance use." *Canadian Medical Association Journal*, 156: 1397 – 99.

Fagan, J., Weis, J.G., and Cheng, Y. (1990). "Delinquency and substance use among inner-city students." *Journal of Drug Issues*, 20: 351 – 402.

Farrell, A.D. (1993). "Risk factors for drug use in urban adolescents: A three-wave longitudinal study." *Journal of Drug Issues*, 23: 443 – 62.

Frances, R.J., and Miller, S.I. (1991). *Clinical Textbook of Addictive Disorders*. New York: Guilford Press.

Friedman, A.S., and Glickman, N.W. (1986). "Program characteristics for successful treatment of adolescent substance abuse." *Journal of Nervous and Mental Disease*, 174: 669 – 79.

Friedman, A.S., Glickman, N.W., and Morrissey, M.R. (1986). "Prediction of successful treatment outcome by client characteristics and retention in treatment in adolescent drug treatment programs: A large-scale cross-validation." *Journal of Drug Education*, 16: 149 – 65.

Government of Newfoundland and Labrador. (1999a, 16 September). *Fast Facts: Anabolic Steroids*. On-line <http://www.gov.nf.ca/health/commhlth/factlist/ffstero.htm>

———. (1999b, 16 September). *Stages of Adolescent Substance Use*. On-line <http://www.gov.nf.ca/health/commhlth/factlist/adolesc.htm>

Groves, M. (1990). "The nature of inhalant-solvent abuse and American Indian youth: Implications for intervention and treatment." Paper presented at the 4th Annual National Native American Conference on Inhalant Abuse, Spokane, WA.

Haggerty, K.P., Wells, E.A., Jenson, J.M., Catalano, R.F., and Hawkins, J.D. (1989). "Delinquents and drug use: A model program for community reintegration." *Adolescence*, 94: 439 – 56.

Hawkins, J.D., Jenson, J.M., and Catalano, J.M. (1988). "Delinquency and drug abuse: Implications for social services." *Social Services Review*, 62(2): 258 – 84.

Health and Welfare Canada. (1992). *The Health of Canada's Youth*. Ottawa: Department of National Health and Welfare, Health Services and Promotion Branch.

Holland, S., and Griffin, A. (1984). "Adolescent and adult drug treatment clients: Patterns and consequences of use." *Journal of Psychiatric Drugs*, 16: 79 – 89.

Jessor, R. (1987). "Problem-behavior theory, psychosocial development and adolescent problem drinking." *British Journal of Addiction*, 82: 331 – 42.

Johnson, B.D., Wish, E.D., Schmeidler, J., and Huizinga, D. (1991). "Concentration of delinquent offending: Serious involvement and high delinquency rates." *Journal of Drug Issues*, 21: 205 – 29.

Johnson, L., Bachman, J.G., and O'Malley, P.M. (1989). "Details of annual survey." *University of Michigan News and Information Services*, 1: 1 – 5.

Jones, R.L. (1990). "Evaluation of drug use in the adolescent." In L.M. Haddad and J.F. Winchester (Eds.), *Clinical Management of Poisoning and Drug Overdoses*. Philadelphia: W.B. Saunders.

Kaminer, Y. (1991). "Adolescent substance abuse." In R.J. Frances and S.I. Miller (Eds.), *Clinical Textbook of Addictive Disorders*. New York: Guilford Press.

Kandel, D.B. (1982). "Epidemiological and psychosocial perspectives on adolescent drug use." *Journal of the American Academy of Child Psychiatry*, 20: 328 – 47.

Kandel, D.B., Simcha-Fagan, O., and Davies, M. (1986). "Risk factors for delinquency and illicit drug use from adolescence to young adulthood." *Journal of Drug Issues*, 16: 67 – 90.

Kovach, J.A., and Glickman, N.W. (1986). "Levels and psychosocial correlates of adolescent drug use." *Journal of Youth and Adolescence*, 15: 61 – 77.

Kumpfer, K.L., and Demarsh, J. (1986). "Future issues and promising directions in the prevention of substance abuse among youth." *Journal of Children in Contemporary Society*, 18: 49 – 91.

Leschied, A., Jaffe, P., Andrews, D.A., and Gendreau, P. (1992). "Treatment issues and young offenders: An empirically derived vision of juvenile justice policy." In R. Corrado, N. Bala, M. LeBlanc, and R. Linden (Eds.), *Juvenile Justice in Canada: A Theoretical and Analytic Assessment*. Vancouver: Butterworths.

Mayer, J.E. (1980). "Adolescent alcohol misuse: A family systems perspective." *Journal of Alcohol and Drug Education*, 26: 1 – 11.

Miller, W.R., and Heather, N. (1986). *Treating Addictive Behaviors: Processes of Change*. New York: Plenum.

Mumford, S., Dick, T., Kishimoto, K., and Cheng, H. (1998, 20 September). *Adolescent Substance Use Survey: Hope, British Columbia*. On-line <http://www.sfu.ca/criminology/860/98-3/adolescent/>

National Institute of Justice. (1992). *Drug Trends in Eleven Major Cities*. Washington, DC: U.S. Department of Justice.

Newcomb, M.G., and Bentler, P.M. (1989). "Substance use and abuse among children and teenagers." *American Psychologist*, 44: 242 – 48.

Novacer, J. (1991). "Why do adolescents use drugs? Age, sex and user differences." *Journal of Youth and Adolescence*, 20: 475 – 89.

Nowinski, J. (1990). *Substance Abuse in Adolescents and Young Adults*. New York: W.W. Norton.

"On pump." (1999, 16 September). *Cigarette Smoking: A Dangerous Addiction*. On-line <http://www.onpump.com/smoking.html>

Pandina, R., and Schuele, J.A. (1983). "Psychosocial correlates of alcohol and drug use of adolescent students and adolescents in treatment." *Journal of Studies on Alcohol*, 44: 950 – 73.

Rich, C.L., Young, P., and Fowler, B.C. (1986). "San Diego suicide study: Young vs. old subjects." *Archives of General Psychiatry*, 43: 577 – 82.

Rogers, P.D., Harris, J., and Jarmuskewicz, J. (1987). "Alcohol and adolescence." *Pediatric Clinics of North America*, 34: 289 – 303.

Rohsenow, D.J., Corbett, R., and Devine, D. (1988). "Molested as children: A hidden contribution to substance abuse?" *Journal of Substance Abuse Treatment*, 5: 13 – 18.

Schlaadt, R.G. (1992). *Alcohol Use and Abuse*. Guilford, CT: Duskin.

Schmidt, L. (1991). "Specialization in alcoholism and mental health residential treatment: The dual diagnosis problem." *Journal of Drug Issues*, 21: 859 – 74.

Siegal, L.J., and Senna, J.J. (1994). *Juvenile Delinquency: Theory, Practice and Law*, 5th ed. St. Paul, MN: West.

Singer, M.I., and Petchers, M.K. (1989). "The relationship between sexual abuse and substance abuse among psychiatrically hospitalized adolescents." *Child Abuse and Neglect*, 13: 319 – 25.

Smart, R.G., and Adlaf, E.M. (1989). *The Ontario Student Drug Use Survey: Trends between 1977 – 1989*. Toronto: Addiction Research Foundation.

Smart, R.G., and Jansen, V.A. (1991). "Youth substance abuse." In H.M. Annis and C.S. Davis (Eds.), *Drug Use by Adolescents: Identification, Assessment and Intervention*. Toronto: Addiction Research Foundation.

*Teenage Suicide*. (1998, 16 September). On-line <http://www.soenet.ca/starta/suicide/>

Tobler, N.S. (1986). "Meta-analysis of 143 adolescent drug prevention programs: Quantitative outcome results of program participants compared to a control or comparison group." *Journal of Drug Issues*, 16: 537 – 68.

Weibel-Orlando, J. (1984). "Substance abuse among American Indian youth: A continuing crisis." *Journal of Drug Issues*, 14: 313 – 35.

West, W.G. (1984). *Young Offenders and the State: A Canadian Perspective on Delinquency*. Toronto: Butterworths.

White, H.R., Pandina, R.J., and LaGrange, R. (1987). "Longitudinal predictors of serious drug abuse and delinquency." *Criminology*, 25: 715 – 40.

Wiel, A., and Rosen, W. (1983). "Chocolate to morphine." In J.B. Beasley and J.J. Swift (Eds.), *Institute of Health and Policy and Practice*. New York: Bard College Center, 1989.

Winterdyk, J. (2000). "Young offenders." In P. MacAlister, P. McKenna, F. Schmalleger, and J. Winterdyk (Eds.), *Canadian Criminal Justice*. Scarborough, ON: Pearson.

Winters, K.C., Weller, C.L., and Meland, J.A. (1993). "Extent of drug abuse among juvenile offenders." *Journal of Drug Issues*, 23: 515 – 24.

Zarek, D., Hawkins, D., and Rogers, P.D. (1987). "Risk factors for adolescent substance abuse." *Pediatric Clinics of North America*, 34: 481 – 93.

# Chapter 8

# Youth on the Street in Canada

BRUCE MACLAURIN

## KEY OBJECTIVES

After reading this chapter, you should be able to:

- examine the reasons for the increase in numbers of runaway and homeless youth in Canada;
- explore the risks youths living on the streets are exposed to;
- review the different typologies of runaway and homeless youth;
- develop an understanding of the types of services required by runaway and homeless youth.

## KEY TERMS

exiles
forsaken youth
homeless youth
in-and-outers
rebels
repeat runners
runarounds
runaways
runners
societal rejects
throwaways
true runaway/homeless

## INTRODUCTION

Most people are aware of the numbers of runaway and homeless youth living on the streets of most major Canadian urban centres. Runaway and homeless youth are not a recent phenomenon; nineteenth-century literature popularized Huckleberry Finn and Oliver Twist in stories of street children existing and surviving on their own. Street youth may be more visible today as the lives of young street teens described as panhandlers, **squeegee kids**, or teen parents have been highlighted in newspaper coverage during the past decade (Carmichael, 1997; Chase and Ketcham, 1997; MacDonald, 1997; Moyle, 1996). Despite this increase in recognition and awareness, the plight of street youth continues to grow in Canada.

Children living on the streets are typically described as **runaways** or **homeless youth**. These terms have been used interchangeably in some literature, but clear distinctions can be made between the two. One definition states that

> runaways are children and youth who are away from home at least overnight without parental or caretaker permission. Homeless are youth who have no parental, substitute, foster, or institutional home. Often these youth have left, or been urged to leave with the full knowledge or approval of legal guardians and have no alternative home. (National Network of Runaway and Youth Services, Inc., 1985: 1)

A variety of typologies, or classifications, of runaway and homeless youth have been developed to describe this population. This chapter will describe some of the typologies documented in current Canadian research to provide a comprehensive overview of runaway and homeless youth. These typologies are based on the intent or purpose of the running experience, the length of absence from home, the cause of the running behaviour, and whether there is a choice to return home. In spite of some limitations, such as being too simple or vague, typologies can assist us in understanding this population and the specific risks it faces on the street.

Street youth experience decreased rights, opportunities, and social supports. This situation increases their risk of developing mental health problems, some of which can lead to suicide; becoming involved in prostitution contracting sexually transmitted diseases; getting involved in criminal and delinquent activity; using and abusing drugs; and simply not meeting their basic needs for food, clothing, and shelter. A review of the literature will illustrate how these risk factors have a significant impact upon youth on the streets.

Insufficient attention has been given to the service needs of runaway and homeless youth. Services are needed that will support these youth while they are on the streets and while they try to leave the street life. This chapter explores the various forms of intervention available to runaway and homeless youth in Canada.

## UNDERSTANDING THE RUNAWAY PHENOMENON

Street children in Canada have been viewed in a number of ways during the twentieth century. Prior to the 1960s, running away from home was typically seen as a delinquent act resulting from a child's individual pathology. The early literature described runaways as deviant, antisocial, of low intelligence, and having little impulse control (Appathurai, 1988). This position changed dramatically during the 1960s, however, with the increased number of middle-class teens living on city streets, a part of the counter-cultural movement occurring in North America at that time. The focus shifted to examine structural and environmental influences that had an impact on running away from home. During the 1970s, research on runaway youth focussed on family and school factors within a larger environmental approach. A summary of research during this period identified that runaways were not strongly connected to their families, had problematic relationships with educators and school systems, and were highly alienated (Appathurai, 1988). Literature from the 1980s focussed primarily on the relationship between abuse and maltreatment of children and subsequent running away (Kufeldt and Nimmo, 1987; McCormack, Janus, and Burgess, 1986). Running away from chronic maltreatment in the home could be viewed as a logical response to a dangerous situation rather than a deviant act.

One final focus during the 1990s was on the structural factors that explain runaway behaviour. The impact of factors such as chronic poverty, inadequate housing, unemployment or underemployment, de-institutionalization, and the challenged and overworked system of child welfare continue to be explored in research (van der Ploeg and Scholte, 1997; Kufeldt and Burrows, 1994).

An ecological perspective has frequently be used as a theoretical framework for understanding the runaway and homeless phenomenon. The model described in this chapter was developed by Kufeldt and Burrows (1994), based on initial work by Bronfenbrenner (1979), and later expanded on by Garbarino (1982).

Bronfenbrenner's influence was acknowledged in the author's description of the ecological approach:

> that a child's development is influenced by a complex network of family, friends, school, community resources, and ultimately, by forces outside the child's immediate experience, such as government decisions and cultural or societal expectations. (Kufeldt and Burrows, 1994: 13)

This approach is useful to focus the reader or practitioner on the interaction of the individual within different systems (school, peers, child welfare), and within the predominant values, attitudes, and philosophies of society (see Figure 8.1).

## PREVALENCE OF RUNAWAY AND HOMELESS YOUTH

North America appears to be undergoing a vast increase in the recorded number of youths living on the street. Shane (1989) estimates the number of young runaways on the street in the United States at 1.5 million, and the total number of homeless youth at 500 000. Estimates of yearly runaway occurrences in the United States are at about 2 million adolescents (National Network of Runaway and Youth Services, Inc., 1991), and some reports suggest that up to 10 percent of these youths remain unaccounted for and at significant risk of exploitation (Regenery, 1986). It is estimated that between 11 and 12 percent of American youth have a history of being runaways before they turn 18 years of age (Rohr and James, 1994). The Division of Runaway and Homeless Youth of the U.S. Department of Health

## Figure 8.1
## AN ECOLOGICAL FRAMEWORK

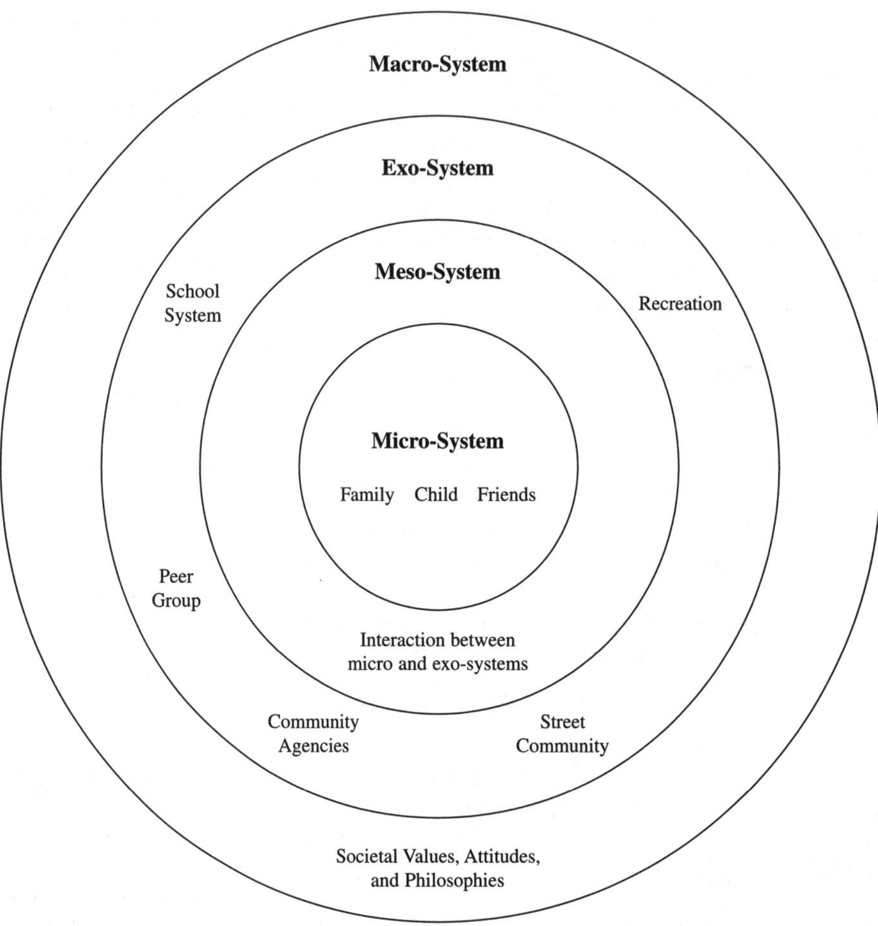


| | |
|---|---|
| Micro-system | This is the immediate setting in which a person resides. For the street population, it can include family, school, child-welfare placement, and the street culture itself. |
| Meso-system | Represents the connections between the child's micro-systems and exo-systems. Risk and opportunity relate to the quality of connections and relationships and the congruencies of values within the micro-systems. |
| Exo-system | Larger systems (school system, community agency) are exo-systems in which policies and operations can enhance or detract from opportunities for homeless youth. |
| Macro-system | Includes the culture and ideology of the society in which a person lives. The dilemma in leaving the street is the need to conform to predominant and straight culture without the means to incorporate and practise its values. |

**Source:** Kathleen Kufeldt and Barbara Burrows (Eds.), *Issues Affecting Public Policies and Services for Homeless Youth: Final Report* (Calgary: University of Calgary, 1994), p. 14. Adapted from U. Bronfenbrenner, *The Ecology of Human Development: Experiments by Nature and Design* (Cambridge, MA: Harvard University Press, 1979).

and Human Services has defined runaway and homeless activity as a virtual nationwide epidemic (Langdell, 1983).

The prevalence of street youth in Canada is equally alarming. The Coalition of Youth Work Professionals suggests there are 5000 homeless young people in Toronto, while the Evergreen Drop-in Centre estimates this number to be about 12 000 (McCullagh and Greco, 1990). The number of runners under 16 years of age has been estimated to be about 3 percent of the total population (Carey, 1976; Visano, 1983), while a Calgary study of teenagers indicated that 7 percent had run from home at some time (Wong and te Linde, 1986). Between 50 000 and 60 000 youth are reported missing each year in Canada, and estimates suggests that there were 10 000 youth on Toronto streets during 1987 (Appathurai, 1988). The Coalition of Social Service Agencies that services downtown Toronto indicates that there are more than 10 000 homeless young people between the ages of 16 and 24 on the streets of Toronto at any given time (O'Reilly-Fleming, 1993). Despite the broad range in the estimates of homeless youth, these numbers confirm that street youth present a significant concern in Canada, and are a population at high risk.

The range in the estimates of homeless youth in Canada and the United States raises several questions about the accuracy of estimates. This variety can be definitely attributed to the methodological challenges of developing an accurate count and estimate (Peressini, McDonald, and Hulchanski, 1995). Several critical issues to consider when planning an estimate of the number of homeless youth include the following:

- What criteria determine homelessness? Definitions of who should be considered runaway or homeless children need to be established. For example, if runaway children are included in homeless counts, should those who have run away but are staying with friends, and not on the streets, be included?
- How should homeless individuals be contacted? Some estimates on street youth have used street counts at random periods over the course of a year (Kufeldt and Nimmo, 1987), while other estimates were based on counts submitted by service providers. Different methods of contact will run the risk of missing different types of children on the streets.
- Should shelter numbers attempt to predict the uncounted street population who do not access street shelters or services? Estimates may be generated to include children who do not use traditional street resources; however, it is not known how accurate these estimates may be. This group would typically include youth involved in the sex trades, children who access adult services, or highly transient youth who do not access any services.

The difficulties in developing an accurate estimate of the number of Canadian street youth highlight the diversity and differences of runaway and homeless youth. Street youth do not make up a homogeneous group with respect to reasons for being on the street, presenting concerns, or needs for services.

## TYPOLOGIES OF RUNAWAY AND HOMELESS YOUTH

Due in large part to the complex backgrounds, behaviours, personal characteristics, and needs of runaway and homeless youth, a number of typologies were developed to describe them. These classification systems examine the pathways to the street, the frequency and duration of street episodes, the level of individual choice for being on the street, and options for leaving the street.

Based on a limited sample of twenty adolescent females, Homer (1973) developed one of the earliest dichotomous descriptions of runaways. The findings suggested that there were two classes of runaways: those who "ran away" from their homes, and those who "ran to" the streets.

Young people who were classified as running away from their families experienced family problems as well as intrapersonal conflicts. The running behaviour in this circumstance was thus seen as a means of relieving the pressure of the home situation.

Those young people who were described as running to the streets were searching for thrills or pleasure. These situations often included experimentation with drugs, sexual activity, truancy, and involvement with negative peer groups. The young women in this group described their family situations as being similar to other families, with minor complaints about rules and structure. This early research suggested that running to the streets can be a cry for freedom, in addition to a cry for help.

From a year-long study of 489 youths in Calgary, during 1984 – 85, Kufeldt and Nimmo (1987) distinguished two populations of runaway and homeless young people: "in-and-outers" and true "runaway/homeless." **In-and-outers** experimented with street life by running away from home several times a year, for less than two weeks at a time, before typically returning to their homes. This group was predominantly made up of younger females.

The young people described as true runaway/homeless were from single-parent homes and usually older; they also ran away fewer times but for longer periods of time (one month to three years). There were marked differences between the two groups in their identified reasons for running. The true runaway/homeless left home with the goal of never returning to their families, were away for longer periods, and often returned home against their will.

Adams, Gullotta, and Clancy (1985) developed a typology based on interviews with runaway and homeless youth with three classifications: runaways, throwaways, and societal rejects.

Under this system, runaways are those youths who leave home due to family conflict or alienation. They are likely to run after considering this option for some time. **Throwaways** are encouraged or asked to leave home by their parents, and they leave home following a short period of consideration (usually one week). Restrictive parenting was seen as the reason for leaving. **Societal rejects** are rejected by peers, family, and helping organizations, and may leave home to find acceptance, caring, and support on the streets.

In addition to youths who run to, who run from, and who are thrown out, Zilde and Cherry (1992) identify a significant proportion of youth who come from families who are no longer able to financially support their children. This family situation encourages children to leave home to seek an independent means of support. Zilde and Cherry referred to this group as "the forsaken." **Forsaken youth** come from large families with low incomes. They reported feeling unattached to the family, unloved, and unwanted. A higher level of victimization was common among this category of youths, as well as a higher level of risk of continued victimization on the streets. This group of youths can be related to the increased number of unemployed adults and homeless families in North America.

A final typology, offered by Kufeldt and Perry (1990), defines four groupings: throwaways, runaways, runners, and runarounds. Throwaways are the true homeless children who have been pushed out of their families or other living situations. Runaways are those youths who either run from their homes as an escape, or run to the streets in rejection of their families and communities. **Runners** have the largest representation in this total population. This group is similar to in-and-outers, and is made up of younger youth who engage in frequent runs for shorter periods of time. Since a percentage of this group comes from out-of-home placements (e.g., foster care, residential treatment centres, group homes), their behaviour is often a reaction to being moved repeatedly from child-welfare placements. The fourth category is that of **runarounds**: escapists who tend to be highly unrestrained by their families and very connected to their peer groups.

## PATHWAYS TO THE STREET

There has been significant research on why children run from their family home or out-of-home care placements. The reasons can include parent – adolescent conflict, family violence, child abuse and maltreatment, organizational dynamics, and peer-group dynamics. The next section focusses on two pathways: running from home and family, and running from out-of-home placements.

### RUNNING FROM HOME AND FAMILY

Farber et al. (1984) provide an overview of families of young people who run to the streets. Family disruptions play a key role in precipitating the adolescent crisis. These disruptions may include the death of a family member, divorce or separation of parents, blending of families, geographical moves, and abuse (Kufeldt and Perry, 1990). Jones (1988) found that children who moved to the street directly from home had either run away from their home or had been abandoned by their families. The author suggested that children typically run from home to escape a destructive home situation or family conflict, as a call for help, or because they have an acute personal crisis or problem (e.g., teen pregnancy or drug addiction). Youths who were abandoned by their families were edged out of the family as a result of divorce, the blending of two families, or scapegoating, or were forced out of the home because of their rebellious response to parental authority. These youths do not feel accepted or welcome in their families and lack strong connections with extended-family members (Jones, 1988).

Research completed with a sample of more than 3500 young people indicated that family problems were of high concern for the majority of young people (Kurtz, Jarvis, and Kurtz, 1991; see also Table 8.1). Emotional conflict within the home, problematic communication patterns, and parental neglect were issues frequently reported by the respondents.

Whitbeck, Hoyt, and Ackley (1997) compared the ways that runaways and their parents described their personal family situations. This is an important indicator of bias and potential overreporting. As shown in the ecological framework illustrated in Figure 8.1, children and their parents both identify interactions within the micro-system as being problematic. Parents/caretakers and youth consistently identified problematic parent–child relationships characterized by little parental monitoring, a lack of parental warmth and supportiveness, and high levels of parental rejection. Conduct problems were rated highly for runaways and caretakers/parents. Family violence was reported at a similar level by parents and by runaways, and both parties acknowledged critical levels of physical and sexual abuse occurring within the family.

The physical and sexual abuse of young people is seen as a primary factor contributing to children running away from home. The literature identifies that both sexual abuse (Rotheram-Borus et al., 1996) and physical abuse (Janus et al., 1995) are much more prevalent within families of runaway or homeless youth than for the general population.

Janus et al. (1995) completed research on a Canadian sample in Toronto and found that 40 percent identified physical abuse, and 12 percent identified sexual abuse, as the main reason for leaving their home on the initial run. These young people stated that additional family factors were important in prompting the initial running episode, and included drug and alcohol use by adults, and family conflict, among those factors.

Meanwhile, an American-based study by Powers, Eckenrode, and Jaklitsch (1990) examined the prevalence of maltreatment with a sample of adolescents seeking services from a runaway and homeless program. When compared to state and national comparison groups, this research indicated a higher level of maltreatment for the runaway and homeless sample. Thirteen percent reported sexual abuse, 42 percent reported physical abuse, and 43 percent cited parental neglect.

As part of a broader study, Rotheram-Borus et al., (1996) surveyed nearly 200 runaways. All of the youth were either homeless or currently on the run from home or out-of-home placements (e.g., detention, group homes, and foster homes). This research indicated that 37 percent of the sample had been sexually abused (25.8 percent abused before 13 years of age and the remaining 11.6 percent first abused after the age of 13). This

**Table 8.1**

**FAMILY PROBLEMS OF HOMELESS YOUTHS**

| Family Problem or Concern | Percentage |
|---|---|
| Neglect by Parent Figure | 35 |
| No Parent Figure | 14 |
| Not Wanted at Home | 21 |
| Emotional Conflict at Home | 62 |
| Poor Communication in Home | 59 |
| Parent Figure Too Strict | 8 |
| Parental Favoritism | 7 |
| Domestic Violence | 20 |
| Physically Abused by Parent | 17 |
| Sexually Abused by Parent | 6 |

**Source:** P. David Kurtz, Sara V. Jarvis, and Gail L. Kurtz, "Problems of homeless youths: Empirical findings and human services issues," *Social Work*, 36(4) (July 1991): 311. 

study found no significant difference between males and females, as 32 percent of males and 43 percent of females had been abused. This was a very high report level for the sexual abuse of males compared to previous research, as Kurtz et al. (1991) identified that sexual abuse was a factor of running for females more so than for males.

Family crisis and breakdown is a primary contributor to the increased numbers of young people on the streets of Canada. The increases in the number of single-parent families, divorce, and geographic relocation play a part in the instability of these young people (Kufeldt and Perry, 1989). The prevalence of child abuse and neglect for street youth is higher than the national incidence rates. Within this uncertain family context, running away from home might sometimes be seen as an adaptive response to a dangerous home life (Kufeldt and Burrows, 1994) (see Box 8.1).

## RUNNING FROM OUT-OF-HOME PLACEMENTS

A significant percentage of children on the street have previously lived in child-welfare settings (Wade et al., 1998). This was illustrated by research on a Calgary sample of street youth that examined where children ran from on their first and their final running episode (MacLaurin, 1991). Seventy-six percent of runaway youth ran away from their family home on their very first run. In contrast, 52 percent ran away from foster-care placements on the final time they ran away. This research was limited by a small sample ($n$ = 40); however, this trend would indicate that young people who run from home and continue to run from home may become involved with Child Welfare services and out-of-home placement (see Table 8.2).

## Box 8.1

## HOMELESS YOUTH FORMING "FAMILIES"

Homeless youth in Toronto are forming "street families" to compensate for the dysfunctional support they received at home, says a doctoral student of sociology.

Most homeless youths hook up with others to feel safer on the street, and to feel less alienated, said Jo-Anne Climenhage, while presenting a paper to the annual meeting of the American Sociological Association.

Peer pressure and the need for shelter, food, and money are also reasons they form "street families," said the University of Toronto student. Climenhage found they had parent – child relationships, or acted as siblings.

She quoted one youth who said, "We all just wanted family ... you know, like we just wanted love and support. Well we found what we wanted in each other." Climenhage interviewed 330 of Toronto's homeless youth in 1992, along with 152 in Vancouver, finding that 54.2 percent had been part of a street family since leaving home.

Her findings also showed 57 percent of the youth had experienced physical abuse from a family member while at home, and nearly 20 percent experienced sexual abuse. Repeated verbal abuse was experienced by nearly 60 percent of those interviewed.

"What becomes evident from the data is that, for some homeless youth, options are limited and, in some instances, the street family is their choice among those scarce options," Climenhage said. "The social support potentially provided is viewed as a resource which they can utilize to help them survive in a street environment."

But while the development of "pseudo-families" can provide emotional support for young people and an outlet for venting frustrations, they can also perpetuate violence that was present in their parents' homes.

Climenhage cited an incident where youths, with the good intention of trying to stop another youth from sniffing glue, beat her up. Violent behaviour may mirror their parents' interaction or violence directed toward them, she said.

They may also become "so dependent" on the emotional support that it may make it more difficult to re-enter mainstream society, she added.

"In some cases, it interferes with their ability to develop ties with those outside this narrow social realm, to maintain stable housing, to keep conventional jobs or to leave street jobs—like prostitution or drug selling—in the first place," Climenhage said.

**Source:** Tanya Ho, "Need to feel safer, less alienated, sociologist says," *Toronto Star,* 11 August 1997, p. A8.

Wade et al. (1998) agree that young people from out-of-home care are overrepresented on the streets and that there are some significant differences between runners from foster- and group-home placements and runners from home. In a review of the literature, it was seen that runners from care were more likely to be repeat runners, to run farther away from home, to stay away for longer periods of time, and to be picked up and returned to placement by the police (Rees, 1993).

Young people who are abandoned by or pushed out of their families often feel rejected, helpless, and worthless. As Moss and Moss (1984) note, these feelings are most often expressed through anger and rebellion, which

## Table 8.2

## WHERE YOUNG PEOPLE RAN FROM (FIRST AND LAST EPISODE)

| Where Child Ran From? | First Run | Final/Last Run |
|---|---|---|
| **Home** | 76% | 24% |
| **Foster home** | 8% | 52% |
| **Group home/treatment centre** | 12% | 16% |
| **Other site** | 4% | 8% |

**Source:** Bruce J. MacLaurin, *A Programme Evaluation of Exit: A Street Outreach Programme for Runaway and Homeless Youth in Calgary* (Calgary: University of Calgary, 1991), p. 26. Reprinted by permission of the author.

often culminates in continued running from out-of-home placements (see anomie theory in Chapter 2). Such young people frequently experience multiple placements in foster homes, group homes, and residential treatment centres as a result of their continued running behaviour. A high percentage of the total number of runaways reported to the authorities are repeat runners from institutional and community-based settings, as illustrated in research on Toronto street youth (Visano, 1983; Fisher, 1989).

Research by McNaught and McKamy (1978) suggests that children run from out-of-home placements for a wide range of reasons, including:

- discomfort brought about by growth or change;
- fear of intimacy or closeness with other people;
- rejection of treatment as a concept, or rejection of individuals responsible for treatment;
- anxiety about some lack of external control and a request for same;
- inability to undergo change while in a treatment setting;
- an overriding sense of responsibility for a situation outside of the setting;
- promotion of running away by other members of the group, by staff, or by other patients.

Later research suggests that young people run from out-of-home placements in reaction to peer pressures and organizational changes (Benalcazar, 1982; Miller, Eggertson-Tacon, and Quigg, 1990). Benalcazar (1982) suggests that running away was not primarily related to the therapeutic process of the treatment program, and that running seemed to improve the relationship between the young person and staff members.

Kashubeck, Pottebaum, and Read (1994) found that reasons for running from out-of-home care settings could be generally categorized under individual or program factors. Individual factors include having a history of adoption, a psychiatric diagnosis, a high level of distress, or a history of running; program characteristics include the type of staff – client relationships, level of staff turnover, level of program stability, and communication patterns between staff.

Youth often encounter and participate in a cycle of behaviours in out-of-home placements (Morrissette and McIntyre, 1989):

- placement
- adaptation
- experimentation
- escalation

During placement, the young person enters a group home, foster home, or treatment centre and is involved in reviewing the expectations and rules of the program. During adaptation, the young person develops relationships with peers and with staff, and adapts to his or her new home. During experimentation, the young person becomes more relaxed with his or her living environment and begins to test the limits and structure of the program. Power struggles begin to occur between staff members and the young person. Escalation occurs when consequences and further limits are placed on the young person in response to his or her previous oppositional behaviour, with the result being a higher level of opposition (aggression, property damage, etc.). Running is often a response to the high intensity at this point of the cycle, and the cycle is often repeated in subsequent placements if the child is removed from the conflict situation (see Figure 8.2).

There are significant numbers of "runners" from out-of-home care on the streets of most cities (Kufeldt and Nimmo, 1987; Fisher, 1989). Traditional means of treatment are not always successful, and alternative interventions need to be explored to reconnect with these children (Miller, Eggertson-Tacon, and Quigg, 1990) and reduce the risks of living on the street.

**Figure 8.2**

**CYCLES OF BEHAVIOUR IN OUT-OF-HOME CARE**

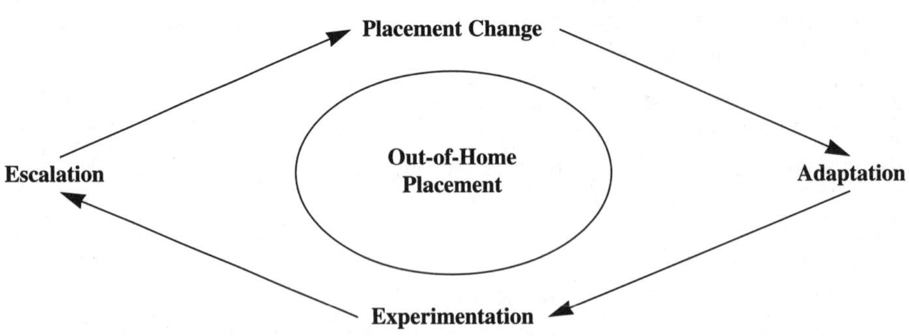


**Source:** Adapted from Patrick J. Morrissette and Sue McIntyre, "Homeless young people in residential care," *Social Casework: The Journal of Contemporary Social Work,* 70(10) (December, 1989): 604.

## RISKS ASSOCIATED WITH STREET LIFE

In running to the streets, or away from home, adolescents face a variety of significant risks. They have been described as adopting "illegal alien" status (Miller, Hoffman, and Duggan, 1980), in that they have the same basic needs as all Canadians, with none of the rights, opportunities, or social supports. Bassuk, Rubin, and Lauriat (1984) describe homeless youth as one of the most disenfranchised groups in our society. The subsequent sections explore some of the risks faced by this group.

### MENTAL-HEALTH ISSUES

Teenagers in supportive family situations face some typical developmental tasks, such as developing independence from their families, defining their individual roles and identities, and accepting their physical appearance. Homelessness, school failure, physical abuse, sexual abuse, parental conflict, and addictions complicate these normal developmental tasks (Cave, 1988). Street youth must deal with life transitions alone, with their newly adopted peer group, or with the assistance of outreach services for runaway and homeless children.

As reported by Kufeldt and Nimmo (1987), mental-health issues dominate any discussion of the causes of homelessness and runaway behaviour. Much of the recent literature reviewed by Kufeldt and Nimmo (1987) suggests that runaways are coming from multi-problem families characterized by economic disadvantages, addictions, and abuse. The mental-health resources for this population are limited, and those resources that are available have restrictive criteria for access. Thus, the crisis created by limited available resources promotes further mental-health risks for runaway and homeless youth.

While some researchers have argued that some young people opt to live on the street because they have problems adjusting to home life, Radford, King, and Warren (1989) suggest it is not clear whether the emotional problems cause or are caused by the runaway behaviour.

The incidence of thinking about suicide and attempting suicide is reportedly very high for all street children, especially for male drug abusers and children of both sexes who are involved in prostitution (Radford, King, and Warren, 1989). Research generated from self-report interviews with runaway and homeless youth at two shelters found that 30 percent of the population had attempted suicide a minimum of once, and over 50 percent had attempted suicide more than once (Staffman, 1989). Over half the total population had recently considered suicide.

Rotheram-Borus (1992) found that 37 percent of a large sample ($n$ = 576) of runaway children had previously attempted suicide. Children on the street who had been victims of sexual or physical abuse within their family home are at even more risk for suicide attempts. Meanwhile, Molnar et al. (1998) found that youth on the street who had been sexually abused were three times (female) to four times (male) more likely to attempt suicide than those street youth who were not sexually abused. This risk level is also strongly noted for street youth who were physically abused.

These findings were supported by Yoder, Hoyt, and Whitbeck (1998). In addition to previous sexual abuse by a family member, other predictors of suicidal ideation by street youth included knowing a friend who attempted suicide, drug abuse, and internalization (e.g., depression and low self-esteem). These findings are not for street-level services as there is a very high risk level for homeless children following a suicide attempt or death of one of their peers.

Street youth generally have high levels of depression. Smart and Walsh (1993) found that depression for street youth was related to three key variables in research completed in Toronto. The results illustrated that street youths' level of depression was clearly related to self-esteem, level of social support, and time spent in a youth hostel. Drug and alcohol use was not directly related to depression. The authors suggest it is possible that drug and alcohol use among street youth is so common that there is too little variation to be detected.

Other mental-health concerns for street youth include level of self-esteem and ratings on powerlessness and indecisiveness. The findings of Mundy et al. (1990) support previous research in that homeless youth who live alone reported high rates of depression, suicidal intent, and suicide attempts. In addition, these authors noted that the mental-health disturbances of these youth included symptoms of psychotic thought processes, which can involve thoughts of violence and "crazy" behaviour in addition to affective disorders (i.e., mood disorders, acute depression, elation, mania).

## PROSTITUTION

A percentage of runaway and homeless youth become involved in prostitution while living on the streets. The rate of involvement differs among cities, but prostitution is nevertheless a high-risk concern of street life (see Chapter 10).

The proportion of runaways receiving money for sex with adults is reported to range from 14 to 28 percent for males, and 7 to 31 percent for females (Rotheram-Borus and Bradley, 1991; Robertson, 1989). Brannigan (1996) highlights some of the previous research on runaway children in Canada who are involved in prostitution. Canadian research suggests that between 18 and 32 percent of children on the streets are engaged in prostitution (see Fisher, 1989; McCarthy, 1990). Brannigan cautions that significant research questions remain to be answered that are related to the age and sexual-abuse histories of teens involved in prostitution, links between running and prostitution, and links between a history of sexual abuse and running away.

However, it appears that the majority of young runaways do not leave home with the goal of taking up prostitution; rather, it seems that entering into prostitution occurs as a result of the street situation. A sample of street youth stated that they had known very little about the realities of street life and prostitution before landing on the streets, and what little they did know came from unrealistic and glamorous portrayals in the media (Michaud, 1988).

Michaud's work cites economic security as the primary motivation for entering prostitution. However, as noted in Chapter 10, Brannigan offers a range of theoretical rationales as to why young persons might enter into prostitution. He argues that the most prudent inference to draw is that understanding this conduct requires a perspective that views **adolescent prostitution** as a form of both delinquency and victimization.

Initiation into prostitution usually occurs quickly following a move to the street. The absence of social supports for street youth following their initial move to the streets lead them to accept increased support from new acquaintances, particularly pimps and others involved in prostitution (Weisberg, 1985). Silbert and Pines (1982) believe that the move to prostitution is a move to social supports, and a high percentage of new recruits are initiated by other teens in the business (see differential association theory in Chapter 2).

Much of the literature is in agreement on the issue of entrenchment. That is, the longer teenagers are involved in prostitution, the more difficult it becomes to leave street life. The most effective time to intervene with these young people is at their initial stage of involvement in prostitution, prior to a shift in loyalties to new street friends who share similar values and lifestyle.

A report prepared for the Canadian Child Welfare Association in 1987 made several statements regarding juvenile prostitution, including the following:

- Juvenile prostitution can be seen as society condoning the sexual abuse of children.
- Youth involved in prostitution are youth in need of protection.
- Juvenile prostitution is a social problem that all Canadians must take responsibility for.

In defining teen prostitution as a social issue, the report implied that Canadians must recognize the powerlessness of young people on the streets, the sexual abuse and family violence that most youth have suffered in the past and are currently experiencing, and their homelessness and poverty.

## HIV/AIDS

Pfeifer and Oliver (1997) have found that between 4 and 8 percent of runaway and homeless youth in the United States are infected with HIV. A 1989 study by Radford, King, and Warren revealed that Canadian street youth under the age of 20 are becoming one of the highest-risk groups for contracting the HIV virus. The purpose of the study was to provide information on AIDS and other sexually transmitted diseases to health-care policy-makers. This research was conducted in recognition of the fact that young street people are a difficult group to reach with social and health services as presently determined by mainstream society. Similar results were reported by Rekart et al. (1989), who explored the prevalence of HIV infection in Vancouver's street population during 1988 – 89.

Radford, King, and Warren state that the transmission of HIV among Canadian street youth is mainly a result of homosexual and bisexual activity, specifically anal intercourse. Intravenous drug use is responsible for a lower percentage of HIV transmission. This trend has shifted greatly over the past decade, however, as unprotected sexual activity with multiple partners has increased the risk level for both genders (Clatts et al., 1998). Less than 23 percent of a sample of street youth in the United States always used condoms during vaginal intercourse, and only 14 percent of females and 29 percent of males reported regular condom use (Clements et al., 1997).

Older street youth are at a much higher risk for contracting HIV due to continued unprotected sexual activity and increased drug use. At the same time, they are also less likely to receive street-level outreach and prevention services as they increase in age. Only 20 percent of an older homeless sample had any contact with a street outreach service during the 30 days previous to a contact with researchers (Clatts and Davis, 1996).

The results of Radford et al.'s research suggest that street youth know as much about AIDS as or more than other sample groups of high-school and university students, and drop-outs. Street youth seemed interested in obtaining further information about the risks from HIV and AIDS and about how to protect themselves from infection. This view is not supported by all research on runaway and homeless youth. Rotheram-Borus and Bradley (1991) support the claim of high risk of HIV infection for street youth, who are typically sexually active by the age of 13 and are involved with multiple partners. However, the authors reveal substantial gaps in street youths' knowledge about HIV/AIDS infection. This includes knowledge about the outcomes of HIV infection, how it is transmitted, how to prevent it, testing, and assessing the safety of sexual activity. These factors significantly increase the risk level for street youth to contract HIV.

## CRIMINAL INVOLVEMENT AND YOUTH CRIME

Runaway and homeless youth have considerable involvement with criminal activity while living on the streets (Nye, 1980). In Fisher's 1989 study of four Canadian cities, it was observed that 80 percent of the sample were reported to have been involved in criminal activities while away from home. Kufeldt and Nimmo (1987) reported that 71 percent of their sample of homeless youth were involved in delinquency, while McCarthy and Hagan (1992) found that more than three-quarters of a large sample ($n$ = 500) were involved in serious delinquent crimes, including shoplifting, theft, prostitution, vandalism, drug dealing, and break-and-enter. Non-violent crimes against property were the main crime category when compared with crimes against the person or crimes of vice.

The view of escalating involvement in criminal activity is supported by Hartman, Burgess, and McCormack (1987). However, it has been suggested that children on the streets do not prefer to be delinquent or elect to become involved in criminal activities, but, rather, become involved in response to the situational demands and challenges of living on the streets (Hagan and McCarthy, 1997).

The general consensus is that street youth are commonly involved in criminal activity as a form of survival. McCarthy and Hagan (1992) support the view that adverse situations contribute greatly to crime and delinquency. Situational delinquency suggests a shift in focus; to the impact of critical street events on the young runaway, rather than background or developmental factors of that young person. Therefore, youth who are hungry will steal, and young people without shelter will commit crimes to gain shelter (McCarthy and Hagan, 1992).

## DRUG USE AND ABUSE

Numerous studies have shown that drug use and drug trafficking are common among runaway and homeless children (Brennan, Huizinga, and Elliot, 1978). Fisher (1989) states that almost 70 percent of repeat runaways report using drugs that included alcohol, marijuana, hashish, cocaine, glue, and crack.

MacLaurin (1991) reported that 88 percent of respondents admitted to using drugs while living on the streets. Almost 60 percent of the sample group used drugs on a daily basis. In fact, runaway and homeless youth generally use alcohol and drugs at a rate three to four times higher than do samples of schoolchildren (see van der Ploeg and Scholte, 1997). Smart and Adlaf (1991) indicate that street youth report clinically significant alcohol concerns (50 percent) and drug concerns (24 percent); however, very few of these youth had ever been involved in treatment for those addictions. Finally, Hagan and McCarthy (1997) found that more than 45 percent of street youth regularly made drug sales as a way of making money.

Research that examined treatment compliance for drug and alcohol services for street youth in Toronto identified critical concerns for this population. Street youth in treatment were more likely to have significant drug problems, to be unemployed, to be on welfare, and to have legal problems than are non-street youth (Smart and Ogborne, 1994). They used drugs more frequently, and defined themselves as having an addiction problem. In spite of these significant concerns, street youth typically used interventions of a very brief nature, and frequently ended their involvement prematurely.

## RISKS RELATED TO BASIC NEEDS

The loss of family and community supports encourages street youth to identify more strongly with other street people. Acquaintance-based networks and relationships support the transition to a life on the streets. When such networks are absent, youth are at increased risk. They lack the required knowledge about how, when, and where to get the resources related to their basic survival needs, such as health care, food, and shelter.

Given the lifestyle of runaway and homeless youth, it is not surprising that Brannigan and Caputo (1992) observed that these youth are not receiving adequate health care. They are often unable to obtain this care because they lack current health-care coverage. Wright (1991) identified acute health concerns for runaway and homeless youth, including upper-respiratory-tract infections, skin disorders, gastro-intestinal disorders, and genito-urinary disorders. Chronic health concerns for runaway youth were seen to be twice as high as they were for a comparison group. Risk for chronic health concerns is higher for older than for younger street youth, and higher for males than females (Wright, 1991).

MacLaurin (1991) found that this population typically used a variety of street resources for food on a regular basis, because sometimes the funding for street outreach agencies temporarily dries up, so it is not wise to rely on only one resource. These meals were supplemented by eating with friends who were not homeless, sharing food with street friends, and "dine and dash" at local restaurants.

Meanwhile, Wright (1991) observed that shelter meals provided only one-third of daily nutritional requirements and did not promote good health.

In addition to nutritional issues, Kufeldt and Nimmo (1987) discuss the issues of availability and accessibility of services for street youth and stress that there is a need for emergency shelters, limited support services, and unrestricted criteria for access. Shelters that open their doors at 8:00 P.M. often have a line-up for beds that starts at 4:00 P.M. While this is an option for people who desperately need shelter, it does not address the specific needs of an adolescent population that is busy doing other things during the evening.

Hence, it is not surprising to read that some street youth stay with friends in downtown areas on a regular basis. These might be street friends who have cheap hotel accommodations, friends who have apartments, and adult friends who offer free shelter. A popular option during the winter is for a group of street youth to panhandle for a day to earn enough money for a single motel room for the entire group for one night (see Box 8.2).

## INTERVENTION APPROACHES

The identification of risk factors associated with runaway and homeless youth living on the streets encouraged the initial development of treatment programs for this population in the 1960s. Today, evaluations of the effectiveness of services offered to runaway and homeless youth often focus on whether these adolescents left street life or ended their involvement with prostitution or criminal activity. While these are end results that all professionals strive for, such an emphasis does not attend to the needs of the majority of young people currently living on the streets.

Services are needed that will support young people's existence and survival until they are able to make the decision and commitment to leave the streets. Unfortunately, such services are often lacking. In their 1987 study,

## Box 8.2

## ON THE STREETS

... Now that I have researched this article, I know getting off the streets is not that simple. Why these young people—some as young as 14—are out there is a complex and unpleasant story.

According to social workers, street youth usually have had an extremely unstable home life and problems with school, police, and the Children's Aid Society. If a young person has had dealings with the Children's Aid, as most street youth have, there is an 80 percent probability of some sort of abuse, according to youth counsellor Tracy Sheridan.

Some youth are kicked out of foster care or Children's Aid facilities and some have had enough of being treated like a case file in an institution. "The bottom line is that they turn to the streets as a last resort."

According to Sheridan, "These kids are running to (the streets), rather than away."

Initially, being homeless might seem okay.

For the younger kids (aged 14 to 16), there is a sort of "honeymoon phase," she says. "All of a sudden, they are part of a scene or counter-culture, and this may be the first niche they feel they fit into."

Sheridan says the youth acquire a family of friends, "street brothers and sisters" who look out for and support them. Their bond with these people may appear stronger than the bond with their own families.

They are also completely independent, often for the first time in their lives. They find people who care about them. They party and then trouble hits. There is not money for food and there are few options. They can squeegee, panhandle, steal, sell drugs, or prostitute themselves.

**Tabitha's Story**: I meet Tabitha, 20, while she is sitting on a heating grate outside a Toronto coffee house. After a difficult childhood, she is now a panhandler.

At a very young age, Tabitha was placed in a foster home after her father left the family. She was kicked out in her teens and came to Toronto, hoping to live with a friend. When that didn't work, she ended up sleeping briefly on the street before moving to a squat where she was again sexually molested. Then it was back to the streets.

"I had a rough life out here," she says. "There were people getting knocked out everyday. It was life living in hell."

Tabitha said it took years of people looking down their noses at her to motivate her to find a way to get her own place.

She is now living with James, her "street brother" and boyfriend. She receives money from the Children's Aid Society to cover her rent but still has to panhandle for food.

She spends the money she is given exclusively on necessities, and resents the stereotype that if you give street youth change they will run to the nearest liquor store or drug dealer. She has a Grade 3 education and few job prospects but refuses to give up.

**James's Story**: James, in his early 20s, is from Port Hope. When he was laid off, he came to Toronto where a temp agency had promised him work. It never materialized.

After recovering from a bad flu caught while staying at a Salvation Army shelter, he got involved in selling the *Outreach* newspaper. "It wasn't too bad," he says, "but paper sales have dropped. That's why I wash windows."

Now James has developed a regular clientele that pay him at various corners in Toronto as he washes car windows.

"Tabitha and me, we're trying to settle down. I only do this (squeegee work) part-time when I absolutely have to."

---

**Source:** Amy Carmichael, "On the streets," *Toronto Star,* 28 October 1997, pp. C1–2.

Kufeldt and Nimmo discovered that a lack of emergency shelters, limited resources for this group, restrictive criteria for accessing available resources, and a reluctance on the part of agencies to provide services as a result of perceived difficulties were not uncommon. This situation may be complicated by the fact that runaway and homeless youth are not the easiest population to work with, because they fluctuate in their commitment to change, often display troublesome behaviours, and rebel against extensive agency admission policies and criteria.

The range of typologies for runaway and homeless youth suggests the need for a variety of treatments to respond to their differences. The following discussion reviews the literature on general interventions.

Miller, Hoffman, and Duggan (1980) describe four categories of programs that serve runaway and homeless youth:

- Public agencies funded and operated by government social-service departments focus on the family as a whole. They investigate cases of child abuse, provide financial support, and co-ordinate medical services. The legal responsibility of these agencies to return youths to their homes is a barrier to the effectiveness of their services for runaway and homeless children.
- Private agencies include residential treatment centres, youth aid programs, and information and referral centres. Their focus is on youths who are agreeable to returning home or to alternative-care facilities, not specifically on runaway and homeless youth.
- Diversion agencies include residential and outpatient counselling programs that accept referrals for youth from probation services.
- Counter-cultural agencies run programs specifically designed for runaway children, including drop-in centres, outreach programs, formal and informal counselling, referral services, and family services. These services are usually voluntary, confidential, and not limited to youth who are agreeable to moving home.

Miller and colleagues found that different typologies of runaway and homeless youth used the four service groupings in different ways. For example, 42 percent of runaways described as **exiles** used free clinics, while only 13 percent of **rebels** used the same service.

"Exiles" were those young people who have some dependence on their parents and family, yet describe their move to the street in terms of parental abandonment or exile. This group has also been described as "pushouts," "throwaway children," or "kickouts." "Rebels" are young people who describe their running in terms of authority conflicts with parents or legal guardians that are intense, long-standing, and not easily resolved (Miller, Hoffman, and Duggan, 1980).

Treatments based on the duration of street life involve three levels of intervention for cyclical runaway behaviour (Hartman, Burgess, and McCormack, 1987). The authors developed three levels of interventions based on the length of time spent on the street:

- **Level 1** intervention focusses on those youth who have been on the street the least amount of time and who therefore have the greatest opportunity for success in leaving street life. This intervention involves a home assessment on the level of safety with respect to physical and sexual abuse, issues that prompted the initial or subsequent runs, stability of living environment, and the individual's understanding of his or her family.
- **Level 2** intervention is directed at those youth who have been on the street for longer than one month yet less than a year. This form of intervention assesses the level of the youth's safety with respect to physical and sexual health, drug and alcohol use, and involvement in criminal activity, in addition to all Level 1 interventions. This form of intervention addresses the risk factors that are inherent in continued street life.
- **Level 3** intervention includes levels 1 and 2 assessment, in addition to attempting to establish a stabilized living situation, activate the youth's vocational skills, initiate detoxification for drug and/or alcohol, and decrease the youth's anxiety about a radical change in lifestyle.

In a discussion of effective interventions, Appathurai (1988) provides a comprehensive outline of preventive, early intervention, and runaway treatment strategies. Runaway centres provide a combination of services, including emergency services, residential services, outpatient counselling, street outreach, transitional and after-care services, connection or attachment focus, and secure containment.

Silbert and Pines (1983) suggest that there are three logical intervention points in working with street youth: after the teen experiences difficulties in the home, following the first run from the home to the street, and after the adolescent experiences difficulties on the street. While the logical point of intervention seems to be after the initial difficulty at home, most youths do not become known to helping professionals until after they are on the streets. The greater the entrenchment in the street subculture, the more difficult the intervention becomes (Michaud, 1988). Therefore, a key to success is providing immediate and responsive services to youths before they have spent prolonged periods on the street. The goal of most outreach programs for runaway and homeless youth is also to approach and connect with them on their own turf and on their own terms. Many teenagers run away to gain some independence and control over their own lives, so the social-service agencies and outreach programs that are most successful are those that approach young people in a way that supports their demand for autonomy while providing for their social, medical, and physical safety.

Service delivery is not a simple prescription for filling the needs of runaway and homeless youth. Kufeldt and Perry (1990) describe a full continuum for resources that match the specific needs of the young person, and are located in convenient and appropriate locations for easy connection. For example, outreach services are best located in close proximity to the downtown area, while it is recommended that transition housing be established away from the downtown to establish distance from street life. The authors promote joint ventures involving multiple programs. Intervention strategies on the continuum can include outreach projects, storefront projects, safe-house projects, home support, outpatient support, and group homes.

A framework is offered to illustrate the service needs at the different stages of homelessness. Needs include shelter, food, health, and education, while the different stages of homelessness include life before the street, on the street, in transition from the street, and off the streets (Kufeldt and Burrows, 1994). This report provided a list of services offered to street youth in Calgary, based on the different stages of homelessness and a review of these services by street youth (see Table 8.3).

**Table 8.3**

**CONTINUUM OF SERVICES FOR HOMELESS YOUTH: STAGE OF HOMELESSNESS AND TYPE OF SERVICE REQUIRED**

| | Before the Street | On the Street | Transitional Services | Off the Street |
|---|---|---|---|---|
| **Accommodation** | • Affordable housing | • Emergency housing<br>• Place to go during the day | | • Affordable housing |
| **Protection** | • Community outreach<br>• Child welfare services | • Secure treatment<br>• Safe, protected accommodation<br>• Emergency child-welfare placements | | |
| **Food** | • Adequate family income | • Daily meals | | • Adequate income |
| **Clothing** | • Adequate family income | • Clothing<br>• Storage and laundry facilities | | • Adequate income |
| **Health and Hygiene** | • Accessible, affordable health care | • Walk-in or mobile medical services<br>• Showers | • Accessible, affordable health care | • Accessible, affordable health care |
| **Mental Health** | • Crisis-intervention counselling and/or mental-health services | • Crisis intervention | • Supportive counselling | • Informal social supports |
| **Substance Abuse** | • Information counselling and/or treatment | • Detoxification services | • Substance-abuse treatment and follow-up | • Informal social supports |

*continued*

Table 8.3 *continued*

| | Before the Street | On the Street | Transitional Services | Off the Street |
|---|---|---|---|---|
| **Education** | • Drop-out prevention<br>• Special-ed programs | • Walk-in schooling | • Transitional school programs | • Regular schools<br>• Adult upgrading |
| **Income** | • Adequate family income | | • Social assistance | • Job |
| **Employment** | • Job or school | | • Life-skills training<br>• Employment training<br>• Job-finding help | • Job |

**Source:** Kathleen Kufeldt and Barbara Burrows, *Issues Affecting Public Policies and Services for Homeless Youth: Final Report* (Calgary: University of Calgary, 1994), p. 65.

# SUMMARY

The number of runaway and homeless youth has been increasing during the past three decades and has reached critical levels in Canada. This increase has resulted in a significant level of research to gain further knowledge about this population and how they can best be served. Understanding the differences among different runaway and homeless youths provides for more effective service development and delivery. There are serious risks inherent in life on the streets for a short term or for extended periods. Services for street youth therefore also need to address their specific concerns and unique differences in a manner that increases accessibility and availability.

# WEB LINKS

**Covenant House**
<http://www.covenanthouse.org>

A North American organization dedicated to helping street kids get off the street. On this site, kids can find information about getting along with family and friends, answers about suicide and abuse; parents can find out about how to get along with teenagers, and how to locate a missing child.

**The Lost Child**
<http://www.gomcs.org/>

The Garden of Missing Children Society is a Canadian site with links to the R.C.M.P. missing children Web site and other sources.

**Missing Children Society of Canada**
<http://www.mcsc.ca>

This non-profit organization is dedicated to searching for runaway and abducted children. It provides a comprehensive investigative program to assist police and searching parents in the ongoing search for missing children.

**National Center for Missing and Exploited Children**
<http://www.missingkids.org>

This American organization spearheads efforts to locate and recover missing children, and raises public awareness about ways to prevent child abduction, molestation, and sexual exploitation. Explore the links to Education and Resources and Success Stories.

**National Runaway Switchboard**
<http://www.nrscrisisline.org/index.htm>

The National Runaway Switchboard is a not-for-profit volunteer organization that provides confidential crisis intervention and referrals to youth and their families, through telephone switchboards, advocacy, and educational services on behalf of youth.

**Street Teams**
<http://www.streetteams.com/info/about.htm>

This organization works specifically to contact and recover female youths between the ages of 10 and 17 who have become involved in prostitution or pornography, or are at risk for becoming involved.

## STUDY QUESTIONS

1. How would you propose getting an accurate count of the number of runaway and homeless youth currently living in a major Canadian city?
2. Identify and describe the factors that lead young people to run away from home.
3. What typology might you adopt or develop for working with runaway and homeless youth in Canada? Justify your answer.
4. What kinds of risks are runaway and homeless youth exposed to? Why?
5. What factors do you think would be important in developing a public awareness program for runaway and homeless youth?
6. How would you counter the debate that shelters and outreach services make it too easy for children to remain living on the streets, and that there is no incentive for them to get off the street?
7. Identify a group of street youth who are prominent in the public eye (e.g., youth involved in teen prostitution or squeegee kids). If you were designing a new program, what program components would be a priority for meeting their immediate and long-term needs?

## REFERENCES

Adams, G., Gullotta, T., and Clancy, M. (1985). "Homeless adolescents: A descriptive study of similarities and differences between runaways and throwaways." *Adolescence*, 20: 715 – 24.

Appathurai, C. (1988). *Runaway Behaviour: A Background Paper*. Toronto: Ministry of Community and Social Services.

Bassuk, E., Rubin, L., and Lauriat, A. (1984). "Is homelessness a mental health problem?" *American Journal of Psychiatry*, 141: 1546 – 50.

Benalcazar, B. (1982). "Study of 15 runaway patients," *Adolescence*, 17(67): 553 – 67.

Brannigan, A. (1996). "The adolescent prostitute." In John Winterdyk (Ed.), *Issues and Perspectives on Young Offenders in Canada*. Toronto: Harcourt.

Brannigan, A., and Caputo, T. (1992). *Runaways and Street Youth in Canada in the 90s: Revised Final Report*. Calgary: Social Science Consulting.

Brennan, T., Huizinga, D., and Elliot, S.D. (1978). *The Social Psychology of Family Issues*. Lexington, MA: Lexington Books.

Bronfenbrenner, U. (1979). *The Ecology of Human Development: Experiments by Nature and Design*. Cambridge, MA: Harvard University Press.

Canadian Child Welfare Association. (1987). *Proceedings of the National Consultation on Adolescent Prostitution*. Ottawa: Canadian Child Welfare Association.

Carey, A. (1976, 23 October). "The children who run away from home." *Toronto Star*, B1.

Carmichael, A. (1997, 28 October). "On the streets: Panhandling doesn't pay amid Bay Street towers." *Toronto Star*, C1 – C2.

Cave, C. (1988). "Street kids: A health care risk." In M.A. Michaud (Ed.), *Dead End: Homeless Teenagers—A Multi-service Approach*. Calgary: Detselig.

Chase, S., and Ketcham, B. (1997, 3 June). "Province to toughen prostitution penalties." *Calgary Herald*, B1.

Clatts, M.C., and Davis, W.R. (1996). "Correlates of homelessness among street youth in New York City: Implications for targeting AIDS prevention services." Paper Presented at the 11th International Conference on AIDS, Vancouver, BC.

Clatts, M.C., Rees Davis, W., Sotheran, J.L., and Atillasoy, A. (1998). "Correlates and distribution of HIV risk behaviours among homeless youths in New York City: Implications for prevention and policy." *Child Welfare*, 77(2): 195 – 207.

Clements, K., Gleghorn, A., Garcia, D., Kat, M., and Marx, R. (1997). "A risk profile of street youth in northern California: Implications for gender-specific HIV prevention." *Journal of Adolescent Health*, 20: 343 – 53.

Farber, E., Kinnst, C., McCord, J., and Falkner, D. (1984). "Violence in families of adolescent runaways." *Child Abuse and Neglect*, 8: 295 – 99.

Fisher, J. (1989). *Missing Children Research Project*. Vol. 1: *Findings of the Study: A Focus on Runaways*. Ottawa: Solicitor General Canada.

Garbarino, J. (1982). *Children and Families in the Social Environment*. New York: Aldine DeGruyter.

Hagan, J., and McCarthy, B. (1997). *Mean Streets: Youth Crime and Homelessness*. Cambridge: Cambridge University Press.

Hartman, C.R., Burgess, A.W., and McCormack, A. (1987). "Pathways and cycles of runaways: A model for understanding repetitive runaway behaviour." *Hospital and Community Psychiatry*, 38(3): 292 – 99.

Ho, T. (1997, 11 August). "Need to feel safer, less alienated, sociologist says." *Toronto Star*, A8.

Homer, L.E. (1973). "Community based resource for runaway girls." *Journal of Social Casework*, 54: 473 – 79.

Janus, M.D., Archambault, F.X., Brown, S.W., and Welsh, L.A. (1995). "Physical abuse in Canadian runaway adolescents." *Child Abuse and Neglect*, 19(4): 433 – 47.

Jones, L.P. (1988). "A typology of adolescent runaways." *Child and Adolescent Social Work*, 5(1): 16 – 29.

Kashubeck, S., Pottebaum, S.M., and Read, N.O., (1994). "Predicting elopement from residential treatment centers." *American Journal of Orthopsychiatry*, 64(1): 126 – 35.

Kufeldt, K., and Burrows, B. (1994). *Issues Affecting Public Policies and Services for Homeless Youth: Final report*. Calgary: University of Calgary Press.

Kufeldt, K., and Nimmo, M., (1987). "Youth on the street: Abuse and neglect in the eighties." *Child Abuse and Neglect*, 11: 531 – 43.

Kufeldt, K., and Perry, P.E. (1990). "Running around with runaways." *Community Alternatives: International Journal of Family Care*, 1(1): 53 – 61.

Kurtz, P.D., Jarvis, S.V., and Kurtz, G.L. (1991). "Problems of homeless youths: Empirical findings and human services issues." *Social Work*, 36(4): 309 – 14.

Langdell, J.I. (1983). "Teenagers who run away from home." *Medical Aspects of Human Sexuality*, 17(6): 28 – 56.

MacDonald, M. (1997, 19 September). "Pair fight child-sex business." *Toronto Sun*, 22.

MacLaurin, B.J. (1991). "A programme evaluation of Exit: A street outreach programme for runaway and homeless youth in Calgary." Unpublished paper. Calgary: University of Calgary.

McCarthy, W.D. (1990). "Life on the street: Serious theft, drug selling and prostitution among homeless youth." *Dissertation Abstracts International*, 51(4): 1397.

McCarthy, W.D., and Hagan, J. (1992). "Mean streets: The theoretical significance of situational delinquency among homeless youth." *American Journal of Sociology*, 98: 597 – 627.

McCormack, A., Janus, M.D., and Burgess, A., (1986), "Runaway youths and sexual victimization," *Child Abuse and Neglect*, 10(3): 387 – 5.

McCullagh, J., and Greco, M. (1990). *Servicing Street Youth: A Feasibility Study*. Toronto: Children's Aid Society.

McNaught, T.R., and McKamy, L.R. (1978). "Elopement of adolescents: Dynamics in the treatment process." *Hospital and Community Psychiatry*, 29: 303 – 5.

Michaud, M.A. (Ed.). (1988). *Dead End: Homeless Teenagers—A Multi-service Approach*. Calgary: Detselig.

Miller, A.T., Eggertson-Tacon, C., and Quigg, B. (1990). "Patterns of runaway behaviour within a larger systems context: The road to empowerment," *Adolescence*, 25(98): 271 – 89.

Miller, D., Hoffman, F., and Duggan, R. (1980). *Runaways—Illegal Aliens in Their Own Land: Implications for Service*. New York: Praeger.

Molnar, B.E., Shade, S.B., Kral, A.H., Booth, R.E., and Watters, J.K. (1998). "Suicidal behaviour and sexual/physical abuse among street youth." *Child Abuse and Neglect*, 22(3): 213 – 22.

Morrissette, P.J., and McIntyre, S. (1989). "Homeless young people in residential care." *Social Casework*, 70(10): 603 – 10.

Moss, S., and Moss, M. (1984). "The threat to place a child." *American Journal of Orthopsychiatry*, 54: 168 – 73.

Moyle, E. (1996, 25 October). "Kids having kids on the street." *Toronto Sun*, 96.

Mundy, P., Robertson, M., Robertson, J., and Greenblatt, M. (1990). "The prevalence of psychotic symptoms in homeless adolescents." *Journal of American Academy of Child and Adolescent Psychiatry*, 29(5): 724 – 31.

National Network of Runaway and Youth Services, Inc. (1985). *Meeting the Needs of Homeless Youth*. Albany, NY: New York Network of Runaway and Youth Services.

———. (1991). *To Whom Do They Belong: Runaways, Homeless and Other Youth in High-Risk Situations in the 1990s*. Washington, DC: NNRYS.

Nye, F.I. (1980). "A theoretical perspective on running away." *Journal of Family Issues*, 1: 274 – 90.

O'Reilly-Fleming, T. (1993). *Down and Out in Canada: Homeless Canadians*. Toronto: Canadian Scholars' Press.

Peressini, T., McDonald, L., and Hulchanski, D. (1995), *Estimating Homelessness: Towards a Methodology for Counting the Homeless in Canada. Background Report*. Toronto: Centre for Applied Social Research.

Pfeifer, R.W., and Oliver, J. (1997). "A study of HIV seroprevalence in a group of homeless youth in Hollywood, California." *Journal of Adolescent Health*, 20: 339 – 42.

Powers, J.L., Eckenrode, J., and Jaklitsch, B. (1990). "Maltreatment among runaway and homeless youth." *Child Abuse and Neglect*, 14: 87 – 98.

Radford, J.L., King, A., and Warren, W.K. (1989). *Street Youth and AIDS*. Kingston, ON: Queen's University Press.

Rees, G. (1993). *Hidden Truths: Young People's Experiences of Running Away*. London: The Children's Society.

Regenery, A.S. (1986). "A federal perspective on juvenile justice and reform." *Crime and Delinquency*, 32(1): 39 – 51.

Rekart, M.L., Chan, S., James, E., and Barnett, J. (1989). "HIV testing on the street." Abstract. Vancouver: STD Control, Ministry of Health.

Robertson, M.J. (1989). *Homeless Youth: Patterns of Alcohol Use. A Report to the National Institute on Alcohol Abuse and Alcoholism*. Berkeley, CA: Alcohol Research Group.

Rohr, M.E., and James, R.K. (1994). "Runaways: Some suggestions for prevention, coordinating services, and expediting the re-entry process." *The School Counselor*, 42(1): 40 – 47.

Rotheram-Borus, M.J. (1992). "Suicidal behavior and risk factors among runaway youth." *American Journal of Psychiatry*, 150: 103 – 7.

Rotheram-Borus, M.J., and Bradley, J. (1991). "Triage model for suicidal runaways." *American Journal of Orthopsychiatry*, 61(1): 122 – 27.

Rotheram-Borus, M.J., Mahler, K.A., Koopman, C. and Langabeer, K. (1996). "Sexual abuse history and associated multiple risk behaviour in adolescent runaways." *American Journal of Orthopsychiatry*, 66(3): 390 – 400.

Shane, P.G. (1989). "Changing patterns among homeless and runaway youth." *American Journal of Orthopsychiatry*, 59(2): 208 – 14.

Silbert, M.H., and Pines, A.M. (1982). "Entrance into prostitution." *Youth and Society*, 13: 471 – 500.

———. (1983). "Early sexual exploitation and influence in prostitution." *Social Work*, 28: 285 – 9.

Smart, R.G., and Adlaf, E.M. (1991). "Substance use and problems among Toronto street youth." *British Journal of Addiction*, 86: 999 – 1010.

Smart, R.G., and Ogborne, A.C. (1994). "Street youth in substance abuse treatment: Characteristics and treatment compliance." *Adolescence*, 29(115): 733 – 45.

Smart, R.G., and Walsh, G.W. (1993). "Predictors of depression in street youth." *Adolescence*, 28: 41 – 53.

Staffman, A.R. (1989). "Suicide attempts in runaway youths." *Suicide and Life Threatening Behaviour*, 19(2): 147 – 59.

van der Ploeg, J., and Scholte, E. (1997). *Homeless Youth*. London: Sage.

Visano, L.A. (1983). "Tramps, tricks, and troubles: Street transients and their controls." In T. Flemming and L.A. Visano (Eds.), *Deviant Designations: Crime, Law, and Deviance in Canada*. Toronto: Butterworths.

Wade, J., Biehal, N., Clayden, J., and Stein, M. (1998). *Going Missing: Young People Absent from Care*. Chicester: Wiley.

Weisberg, D.K. (1985). *Children of the Night: A Study of Adolescent Prostitution*. Lexington, MA: D.C. Heath.

Whitbeck, L.B., Hoyt, D.R., and Ackley, K.A. (1997). "Families of homeless and runaway adolescents: A comparison of parent/caretaker and adolescent perspectives on parenting, family violence and adolescent conduct." *Child Abuse and Neglect*, 21(6): 517 – 28.

Wong, L., and te Linde, J. (1986). "Youth in Calgary." *The Advocate*, 12(1): 3 – 4, 14 – 15.

Wright, J.D. (1991). "Health and the homeless teenager: Evidence from the national health care for the homeless program." *Journal of Health and Social Policy*, 2(4): 15 – 35.

Yoder, K.A., Hoyt, D.R., and Whitbeck, L.B. (1998). "Suicidal behaviour among homeless and runaway adolescents." *Journal of Youth and Adolescence*, 27(6): 753 – 71.

Zilde, M.R., and Cherry, A.L. (1992). "A typology of runaway youth: An empirically based definition." *Child and Adolescent Social Work Journal*, 9(2): 155 – 68.

# Chapter 9

# Youth Gangs

FRED MATHEWS

## KEY OBJECTIVES

After reading this chapter, you should be able to:

- provide a framework for understanding the phenomenon of youth gangs in Canada;
- provide an exploratory descriptive typology of youth gangs;
- explore the motivation to join a gang;
- present a variety of theoretical and research perspectives on gang formation and activities;
- discuss models for a comprehensive community-based strategy to respond to gangs.

## KEY TERMS

community development
gang suppression
social capital
social disorganization
youth gang

## INTRODUCTION

The phenomenon of youth gangs is not new to Canada or elsewhere (Tanner, 1996). Gangs can be found in Europe, Asia, Africa, South America, South East Asia, Australia, North and South America, that is, in capitalist and socialist countries alike (Korem, 1994). Despite the persistence of the gang phenomenon in Canada, surprisingly little research has been done on the subject. Few community-based intervention programs exist. No comprehensive, long-term strategy that focusses exclusively on gangs has been attempted. Generic outreach, recreation, or support programs for troubled youth have not been evaluated specifically for their efficacy in preventing gang formation in Canadian communities.

Fear and a desire to impose harsh legal sanctions characterize much public discussion pertaining to gangs, and youth involved in gang activity (Tanner, 1996; Mathews, 1993). However, this fear prevents adults from understanding that involvement with a group of friends—whether or not the group has adopted a name—is a normal, healthy part of growing up for children and adolescents. There is nothing developmentally or otherwise unusual about young people hanging out in groups that, in itself, should give adults concern; that is, unless they break the law or harm others or themselves through their activities.

Sometimes this line is crossed accidentally; sometimes, deliberately. Some young people in groups act with full knowledge of the law; some, with complete ignorance. Some group actions are the result of miscalculated pranks and lack of life experience or awareness of consequences; some are also serious transgressions of the law and require our attention as a community, as a society.

Concern about youth gangs appears to be cyclical. Interest can be sparked by a change in political beliefs and community values, economic conditions, intergenerational conflict, negative attitudes toward youth, public fear, political pressure on police to lay charges, and reactions to shifting employment or immigration patterns. These influences can shape how the "problem" of gangs is defined and which solutions are considered in response.

Public perceptions of gangs in contemporary Canadian society have likely been influenced by media stories of gang activity in the United States and sensational local gang-related incidents involving the most serious forms of crime or violence. Consequently, the media have helped create an impression in the public mind that gangs are a growing problem that is out of control, and that the situation in the United States and Canada is identical. While it is true that youth gangs present Canadian schools and communities with challenges that must be taken seriously, the problem is not as widespread as it is in large American cities. The youth-gang phenomena in Canada and the United States have a few similarities; however, substantial differences also exist.

Much of the difference between the Canadian and the American experience may be attributable, in part, to different philosophies of government and to the wider availability of social programs and stricter gun-control legislation in Canada. Social supports help reduce social marginalization and

### Box 9.1

### THE ROLE OF THE MEDIA: HELP OR HINDRANCE?

Sensationalized media stories obscure the complexity of the youth-gang phenomenon. Headlines such as "Teen Gangs Prey on Schools," "Schools Blackboard Jungles," "Fine Young Criminals," "Gang Woes Mirror L.A.," "Youth Gang Problem a Time Bomb," "Armed Gangs Fuel Violence in Schools," "Baby-faced Gangsters Major Threat to Toronto's Streets," and "Armed and Dangerous" can spark fear and lead to public pressure to "get tough" and resort to reactive criminal justice measures in response. Stories about exceptional incidents of gang violence become the stereotype in the public mind, and create a false impression that schools and communities are unsafe.

attenuate many of the effects of living in poverty and unsafe communities that can leave young people vulnerable to the lure of gangs. Gun control reduces the lethal force available to criminal youth gangs, and restricts or reduces the amount and types of crime and violence that might otherwise be perpetrated.

It should be noted that use of the term "youth gang" is not without controversy. One view is that "gang" is a judgmental and overly negative term applied too liberally and inaccurately by adults to adolescent peer associations ranging from a "group of friends," who hang out and occasionally get into trouble, to more serious organized criminal gangs. Second, the term can be misleading and fear-provoking because it evokes the stereotypes of violent adult gangs portrayed in sensational media stories. Third, gang members can range in age from under 12 to 21 years or older, so the term "youth" is not limited to a strictly legal definition of a 12- to 17-year-old "young offender." Fourth, some young people readily accept and identify with the term "gang," while others reject it (Mathews, 1993).

Also, gangs are not as tightly organized or clearly defined as the public often believes. For example, Cameron (1943) views gangs not as tightly organized entities, but as loosely configured "pseudo-communities." Likewise, Yablonsky (1973) challenges the notion of rigid hierarchies and stable membership, and believes that gangs are simply "near groups" characterized by diffuse role definitions, impermanence, loose group norms, limited group cohesion, often disturbed leaders, fluid membership, and limited definition of membership expectations.

For the purposes of this discussion, the term "gang" refers to a variety of adolescent peer associations whose common feature is lawbreaking, antisocial, or violent behaviour. A "gang," in this context, would generally consist of at least three or more youth whose membership, though often fluid, consists of at least a stable core of members who are recognized by themselves or others as a gang, and who band together for cultural, social, or other reasons and impulsively or intentionally plan and commit antisocial, violent, or illegal acts.

## PREVALENCE

It is difficult to determine the prevalence of gang activity in Canada, or the extent to which it might be increasing, decreasing, or becoming problematic. Studies are rare. No formal definition of "gang," "gang member," or "gang activity" exists. Statistics on gang activity are not gathered uniformly across police jurisdictions. No nationwide Uniform Crime Report data on gangs or gang activity are available.

In a study conducted in southern Ontario communities, including Toronto, there was consensus among youth-gang members, victims, parents, social workers, and police that gangs are a problem for schools and communities large and small, and that their activities are becoming more serious in nature (Mathews, 1993). Current estimates by police put the number of youth gangs operating in the amalgamated City of Toronto at 70 to 80, with 20 being identified as "hard core" (City of Toronto, 1999).

A Toronto based study of "multiple perpetrator" youth crime examined occurrence reports in just one of five police divisions in the city. All reports reviewed pertained to youth 12 to 17 years of age and covered the time period 1989 – 93. A total of 932 charges were laid in 310 separate incidents involving 483 individual youths (Banner, Ryan, and Mathews, 1994). However, it is impossible to determine from the occurrence reports how many of these incidents involved planned crime-focussed activity as opposed to impulsive or other types of group behaviour.

Regardless of how gang activities are defined or charging patterns interpreted, incidents of antisocial or negative peer-group behaviours in schools and communities are doubtless underreported. Unfortunately, school officials and others mistake low *rates* of reporting to mean low *actual* numbers of incidents, or an absence of problems. Confounding efforts to document prevalence is the fact that teen victims are extremely reluctant to report their victimization because of fear of retaliation; concern they may get friends or neighbourhood peers into trouble with the law; deference to peer norms against "ratting"; fear and mistrust of school officials, police, or adults in any position of authority; or a sense of hopelessness that anything will be done in response (Mathews, 1999).

Adults frequently underestimate the impact that gangs have on schools, a problem that cannot be easily quantified. High levels of fear can build in a school environment as a reaction to even a few incidents of what might appear to adults to be "minor assaults" or less visible forms of gang aggression such as extortion or intimidation. The presence of gangs has a negative impact on learning and compromises teachers' and school officials' abilities to maintain a safe environment. Schools also provide a readily available supply of victims.

Anecdotal evidence suggests, at a minimum, there has been an increase over the past few years in the *level* of violence used by youth in groups. Teachers and police report that: the age of youth involved in violent acts and gang activity is declining; the individual schoolyard bully has been largely replaced by a group of youths who commit assaults and thefts; there are more of these types of incidents; and intruders in hallways, on school grounds, and at sporting and other school events have become a serious problem. Students themselves, in remarkable numbers, report feeling unsafe in school (Mathews, 1993; Ryan, Mathews, and Banner, 1993) or fear being attacked by other youth in gangs (Smith et al., 1995).

## GANG CHARACTERISTICS

There is great **heterogeneity** both within and between youth gangs. Gangs exist in large urban centres and small towns alike. Some are ethnoculturally homogeneous, while others have mixed ethnocultural membership. Males appear to participate in greater numbers than females. There are all-male gangs and a few that have an all-female membership, though most are of mixed gender.

Females in gangs assume many roles. Their membership is often contingent upon having a boyfriend in the gang. Sometimes they are used as couriers to carry weapons or transport drugs. Even when accepted as full members, they are often in inferior status roles and deferential to male members. However, teachers, students, school administrators, and police report finding more all-female gangs, female-perpetrated crime in groups becoming more frequent, and female violent and antisocial behaviours being similar to those of males. Girls report that female perpetrators' victims tend primarily to be other girls. Girls are also reported to sometimes be the instigators of, but not direct participants in, intergang fights and conflict (Mathews, 1996; 1993).

It is important to note that Canada lags behind most Western democracies in the study of girls' use of violence and aggression, including their participation in gangs. Consequently, our understanding is limited, and much of what girls do to harm others remains invisible, underreported, and outside the discourse on violence and aggression. In part, the reason for this is our use of limiting research methods, narrow definitions of violence and aggression, and theories of delinquency based on male-centred patterns of offending (Mathews, 1999; also see Chapter 3 for further discussion on female offenders).

Youth gangs have, for the most part, a fluid membership. Names change frequently, and young people can be in several gangs/groups at the same time, sometimes in different parts of a city. Some gangs have mixed adult and youth members. Children under the age of 12 are sometimes used by youth gangs to carry out illegal activities because, if caught, they cannot be prosecuted under the Criminal Code of Canada (Mathews, 1993).

### Box 9.2
### GIRLS AND GANGS

In a national survey conducted in the United States, Miller (1982) found that 10 percent of gang members were female. A study conducted in the City of Toronto revealed that 15 percent of charges for incidents of multiple-perpetrator youth crime or violence were laid against girls. All-girl gangs accounted for approximately 7 percent of reported incidents studied (Banner, Ryan, and Mathews, 1994). The Denver Youth Survey (Esbensen and Huizinga, 1993) found that, between 1988 and 1992, 20 to 46 percent of self-reported gang members were female, the highest participation rate reported thus far. However, because most research on delinquency and gangs has focussed on males, it is difficult to draw any firm conclusions about female participation rates. Also, girls' participation rates and their roles are likely to vary according to the type of gang to which they belong. Girls may be less likely to join or be active or equal members in hard-core, crime-focussed gangs, but have higher participation rates in fashion/social gangs. The age of females in gangs spans from 9 to 30, and older (Goldstein and Glick, 1994).

Weapons use is a worrisome part of the youth-violence and youth-gang phenomenon, though the rate of seizure of weapons in schools remains low. Knives are the weapons most commonly seized by school authorities, followed by clubs, bats, sticks, and shop- or homemade weapons. The use of firearms by young people to commit crimes is still uncommon in Canada, even though guns can easily be obtained (Walker, 1994; Mathews, 1993).

# THEORETICAL AND RESEARCH PERSPECTIVES ON YOUTH GANGS

No single definition of "gang" fits all situations or historical periods. Miller's (1974) list of core gang characteristics—identifiable leadership, identifiable territory, continuous association, organization for a specific purpose, and involvement in illegal activities—is useful, but does not capture the breadth of all possible gang/group configurations, activities, and functions. Because of the emerging and constantly evolving nature of gangs, an inclusive definition of gang and a comprehensive analysis of the phenomenon remains to be formulated. Although theories of delinquency are presented in Chapter 2, in this section we will focus on some of the major sociological and psychological theories that have been used to explain youth gangs and gang members' activities.

# SOCIOLOGICAL THEORIES

## SOCIAL DISORGANIZATION

When the community or a macro-social level of analysis is used to account for the gang phenomenon, researchers often place emphasis on social disorganization or negative social forces, social relations, and characteristics of neighbourhoods to explain gang involvement. Examples of social disorganization include: poverty and class struggle (Shaw and McKay, 1931; Whyte, 1955; Curry and Spurgel, 1988; Edgerton 1988; Quinney, 1974); the existence of an underclass (Bursik and Grasmick, 1993; Hagedorn, 1988); the pre-existence of gangs in the community (Currey and Spurgel, 1992; Klein, 1995); easy access to guns and drugs (Currey and Spurgel, 1992; Hagedorn, 1988, 1994a, 1994b; Sanchez-Jankowski, 1991; Lizotte et al., 1994; Miller, 1982; Newton and Zimring, 1969); limited social and economic opportunities (Cloward and Ohlin, 1960; Cohen, 1955; Merton, 1957; Spergel, 1964; Fagan, 1990; Hagedorn, 1988, 1994a; Klein, 1995; Moore, 1990; Short and Strodbeck, 1965); distrust of police and discrimination (Wattenberg and Balistrieri, 1950); and local neighbourhood norms that encourage or promote gang behaviour (Miller, 1958; Short and Strodbeck, 1965).

Social-disorganization theorists who focus on socio-economic status believe that gangs grow out of frustration when youth fail to achieve the status and material goals of wider society by using sanctioned means.

Gangs become, in essence, a self-validating "subculture of delinquency" where lower-class youth rebel against middle-class norms and organize themselves into gangs as a legitimized structure for dealing with their thwarted material aspirations. Gangs also serve as "nonconformist alternatives" for alienated youth, where gang members support each other and help solve shared problems or frustrations.

### CONFLICT

Tannenbaum (1939) sees gang cohesion developing as members encounter disapproval and opposition from adults, police, or the community. He frames the problem of gangs as a value clash between young people who see their activities as interest, fun, and excitement, and adults who see it as crime in need of punishment and control. Tannenbaum also feels that gang involvement is appealing not in and of itself, but because the pressures and motivation toward more socially acceptable behaviour are less attractive or weak to young people.

Thrasher (1929) believes gangs form spontaneously, then become integrated through conflict. He views gang members as typical youth looking for ways to express developmentally appropriate needs for novelty and adventure. Landesco (1932) believes gang formation is rooted in conflict between new marginalized immigrants and the established society.

Jeffery (1959) views crime as resulting from the breakdown of social cohesion in small, interdependent communities and a product of urbanization where there is anomie, anonymity, and isolation. According to this view, young people become criminal when they have few or no satisfying interpersonal relationships with others.

## PSYCHOLOGICAL THEORIES

A psychologically oriented perspective on the gang phenomenon takes the individual youth as the starting point for the analysis. Emphasis is often placed on factors associated with individual learning and development, and on negative influences of peers, school, and families. Factors thought to contribute to gang involvement include doing poorly in school (Wattenberg and Balistrieri, 1950); thrill-seeking and a need to take risks (Mathews, 1993; Strodbeck and Short, 1964); the "addictiveness" of deviant youth subcultures and the influence of media-created youth consumer culture (Mathews, 1993; England, 1967); prior behaviour problems or early-onset antisocial behaviour (Bjerregaard and Smith, 1993; Curry and Spurgel, 1992; Esbensen and Huizinga, 1993); a need for status, identity, affiliation, and protection (Mathews, 1993; Fagan, 1990; Horowitz and Schwartz, 1974; Moore, 1978; 1991; Short and Strodbeck, 1965); attitudes supportive of deviance (Esbensen and Huizinga, 1993; Fagan, 1990); possessing a defiant character (Miller, 1958; Sanchez-Jankowski, 1991); aggression (Campbell, 1990; Horowitz, 1983; Sanchez-Jankowski, 1991); the existence of normlessness in the family, peer group, and school contexts (Esbensen, Huizinga, and Weiher, 1993); childhood maltreatment (Thompson and Braaten-Antrim, 1998); and alcohol and drug use (Bjerregaard and Smith, 1993; Curry and Spurgel, 1992; Esbensen et al., 1993; and Thornberry et al., 1993).

Hirschi (1969) believes individual human beings are antisocial by nature and that everyone is capable of committing delinquent acts. As discussed in Chapter 2, he feels that a youth's delinquency neither is learned nor follows from having insufficient means to achieve material gains, but emerges in the absence of values or beliefs discouraging it from arising and from poor social attachments to others. His *social-bond theory* suggests that, without these bonds and reinforcements, youth are more likely to commit deviant or delinquent acts, alone or in groups.

At the level of the *family*, factors such as ineffective parenting (Wattenberg and Balistrieri, 1950); chaotic communication patterns, disorganization, and parent drug/alcohol abuse (Bjerregaard and Smith, 1993; Esbensen et al., 1993; Vigil, 1988); incest and family violence (Moore, 1991); other gang members in the family (Curry and Spurgel, 1992; Moore, 1991); and ineffective parenting or lack of strong parental role models (Wattenberg and Balistrieri, 1950; Wang, 1995) are believed to exert influence on the decision to join a gang.

School-related factors such as behaviour problems or academic failure (Bjerregaard and Smith, 1993; Curry and Spurgel, 1992); limited interest in school (Bjerregaard and Smith, 1993); and negative labelling by teachers (Esbensen and Huizinga, 1993; Esbensen et al., 1993) are thought to push young people to join gangs.

Peer influences discussed in the literature include validation by peers of deviant values, attitudes, and beliefs (Mathews, 1993; Haskell, 1961; Bjerregaard and Smith, 1993; Esbensen and Huizinga, 1993; Vigil and Yun, 1990); the existence of other gang members in the school (Curry and Spurgel, 1992); and friends who use drugs (Curry and Spurgel, 1992). Sutherland and Cressey (1970) believe young people become delinquent and learn and develop their values, criminal behaviours, and beliefs from interaction with others in intimate small groups. Their *differential association* model suggests that the motivation to commit crimes does not come from the need to pursue status or material gain per se, but from the fact that the individual possesses more definitions of actions favourable to violation of the law than toward compliance with the law.

In terms of *self-perception* and *self-worth*, Tomson and Fielder (1975) believe that gangs give members an identity and provide social activity, friendships, material benefits, and a sense of belonging—all important developmental needs. They also feel that youth in gangs accept the dominant culture's material goals but use aggression to obtain these goals.

## LIMITS OF THE LITERATURE

The literature discussed above gives ample illustration of the difficulty of achieving a complete understanding of youth gangs in Canada. Much of the research focusses on gang characteristics and activities more reflective of earlier historical periods. Gangs in the 1990s differ in many aspects from gangs in the 1920s, 1930s, 1940s, or 1950s. The greater use of violence and weapons in gang conflicts; the availability of high-powered automatic weapons; the widespread existence and enormous profit potential of the drug trade and other organized crime; the involvement of younger children; an increasing number of female participants; the availability of high-tech communications equipment such as cell phones, pagers, and the Internet; the participation of suburban middle-class youth; and constantly shifting names and membership are examples of features of the present-day gang phenomenon, particularly in the United States, that were less common or did not exist in the past.

It is problematic that virtually all the research on gangs derives from the study of American society. Also, nothing published on gangs to date successfully integrates factors at the level of the individual youth, the local school or community context, the systems that serve young people, the larger social context, the views of youth themselves in all their diversity, or the influence of situational variables on behaviour into a comprehensive framework. And, there are other problems.

Much of the literature focusses on lower-class youth living in poverty. While valuable for its contribution to understanding particular types of gang formation, a reductionist view of gangs that focusses exclusively on poverty cannot account for the involvement of middle-class youth in gang activity or explain why *all* persons living in poverty do not become criminals or gang members. According to police, school officials, and social workers, a remarkable amount of gang activity in communities in Canada involves middle-class youth—as victims and as perpetrators (Mathews,

**Box 9.3**

**SITUATIONAL VARIABLES AND GANG BEHAVIOUR**

Studies in social psychology suggest that people in groups take their social cues for behaviour from others, and from the contexts and situations in which they find themselves. For example, gang/group members involved in a group assault continually read the faces and interpret the actions of others around them. If they see excitement and no obvious concern for the victim on others' faces, they initiate actions or continue in their present behaviour. Also, when a gang/group commits an offence, responsibility can be divided proportionally among the number of people present, significantly weakening one's sense of personal accountability (Latanne and Darley, 1968; Darley and Latanne, 1968).

Another study suggests that the anticipated ends of group activities may not be as strong a motivator as stimulus properties of the targets and cues to aggression in the environment, such as the presence of a weapon (Berkowitz and LePage, 1967). The presence and influence of peers can arouse some young people to become involved in behaviours they would not engage in alone. Peer pressure and the diffusion of responsibility may account for the worrisome number of group sexual assaults that occur in high schools (Mathews and Stermac, 1989).

1993). The majority of these gang members come from intact families, and have access to material comforts, career pathways, part-time jobs, and other supports. Also, writers (e.g., Cohen, 1955; Whyte, 1955; and Edgerton, 1988) who feel that class conflict and poverty are prime motivators driving gang activity would have difficulty justifying the paltry take of most swarmings—a single jacket, a pair of boots, or lunch money.

Much of the literature focusses on organized gangs with a definable membership and norms, or on groups that are fiercely territorial, strongly ethnic-, class-, or neighbourhood-based. These patterns of association and identification are thus far not as strongly evident in the youth-gang phenomenon in Canada (Mathews, 1993).

Little attention is paid in the literature to the wide developmental differences between young, middle, and older teens. The social pressures and motivation to join a gang and participate in illegal activity can vary according to a young person's level of maturity. For example, peer pressure typically has a greater influence on younger adolescents.

Most research on youth gangs/groups focusses on explanations of why young people get involved (vulnerability factors). A strong case could be made for shifting the research emphasis to why young people *do not* get involved (protective factors). Gang-proofing and other prevention strategies could benefit from the input of young people on both sides of the issue.

Finally, gangs are easily "pathologized" by adults who don't understand that they meet many developmental needs of adolescent members. Youth who are not part of a gang may feel vulnerable, and socially rejected. They provide a refuge from chaotic, dysfunctional families, and respite from the demands of adult authority figures to conform. Gangs provide peer associations and opportunities for socialization where personal identity and gender roles can be worked out. Gang activities also provide excitement, relieve boredom, and give young people means to take risks and test boundaries and limits (Mathews, 1992).

## RESPONDING TO YOUTH GANGS

Government response to gangs, like public interest, appears to be cyclical in nature. Response strategies typically follow economic trends and are often at the mercy of the fortunes of political parties. In times of economic expansion (1950s and 1960s), interventions consisted of outreach to marginalized youth and their communities, and prevention of gang involvement. Emphasis was placed on social services and supports. In times of economic downturn (1970s and 1980s), as funding for support services was reduced, interventions assumed a more "law and order" approach (U.S. Department of Justice, 1994). This pattern of policy mimicking expansion and contraction in the economy has also been identified in educational-policy development in Canada (Quarter and Mathews, 1987). When governments change, policy priorities and initiatives often shift. Any resulting loss of political will and consequential reduction in funding and support has

## Box 9.4

## AN EXPLANATORY TYPOLOGY OF YOUTH GANGS

If we are to obtain a more comprehensive understanding of lawbreaking groups of youth, including "youth gangs," it is important not to rely exclusively on police, legal, or academic definitions of the term. The following typology was drawn from interviews with youths aged 12 to 19 who were involved in a self-defined "gang." The categories in the typology are derived from the functions of the gang/group. Some youth were involved in more than one type of gang.

1. **Fashion or Social.** A loose configuration of middle-class youth, usually based at a school, community centre, neighbourhood mall, or strip plaza. Activities are largely social in nature, that is, "hanging out," though members do not participate intentionally or impulsively in group assaults or thefts. Members sometimes, though not always, wear common articles of styles of clothing that signify membership. Leadership is fluid and appears to be based on popularity.
2. **Ethnoculturally Homogeneous.** A slightly more stable configuration, though a small part of the overall gang phenomenon, usually centred around a community, public place, or school. Members are visible-minority youth who often feel cut off from or marginalized by mainstream society. Denied full and equal access to education and employment opportunities because of language barriers, assimilation problems, age, or other forms of discrimination and prejudice, many young people from these groups simply give up hope and turn to one another for support and a livelihood.
3. **Political, Pseudo-political.** The best example of this type of gang is the "Skinheads." There are various types of Skinhead groups, although the "Neo-Nazi" and "White Supremacist" individuals get the most attention in the media. Originally, the Skinhead movement was a British-based, pro – working class, and basically non-violent youth movement. In Canada, the regalia of the British Skins has been appropriated but evidently not a great deal of the political or class analysis. The Skinhead movement in Canada is small and marginal relative to other types of youth gang/group configurations.
4. **Violent (Sociopathic).** This group represents perhaps the smallest proportion of the youth gang/group phenomenon, but their activities present a threat to community safety. The violent behaviour of these youth is characterized by high egocentrism and limited feelings of guilt or remorse for destructive acts against others. The term "wilding" has been used to describe the activities of this gang/group. Membership consists of largely marginalized youth, some former or current psychiatric outpatients, and street "hangers-on." Group membership is unstable, and leadership is unstructured and shared. Their activities are almost always spontaneous and impulsive. Some of the activities of this type of group include common assault, sexual assault, vandalism, and theft.
5. **Crime-Focussed/Delinquent.** This gang/group can be both organized and relatively stable or loosely defined and "project specific." These youths organize themselves to carry out crimes or other antisocial behaviour. This type of gang/group is still a relatively small part of the phenomenon but evokes the most fear in adults and other youth, and the most concern for law enforcement officials. What distinguishes them from other groups is the fact that the members are wilfully criminal in their activities. This group can consist of three or more members who may otherwise have no other formal or informal association apart from being in a peer group of friends.

*continued*

Box 9.4 *continued*

6. **Street-Involved Youth.** Street-involved youth are not really a gang/group per se but an extremely fluid and unstable collection of marginalized youth, kids fleeing abusive home environments, and "weekend street kids" who are drawn to the romantic myth of life "on the street." These loosely associated groups can sometimes be involved in assaults, thefts, drug-trafficking, and vandalism. There appears to be no leadership or identifiable group structure. It should be noted that not all street youth participate in these gangs/ groups.
7. **Volatile Group.** This is more a situationally defined phenomenon of group/gang activity than anything organized or defined by members. In fact, there is no real membership per se, and such groups can consist of large numbers of strangers. Hooliganism or spontaneous acts of violence, thefts, and assaults that occur after rock concerts or sporting events are the typical behaviours perpetrated by this type of gang/group. They are a relatively small part of the phenomenon, though their actions receive a great deal of media attention.
8. **Vigilante.** The vigilante gang is usually made up of a group of familiar friends, relatives, or acquaintances, all or most of whom could be simultaneously in any of the above types of gangs/groups. What distinguishes this type of gang/group from the others is not the membership per se but the motivation for their actions. The vigilante gang/group is usually formed to get revenge or "settle scores" for acts of violence, thefts, or other perceived slights committed against their friends, brothers, sisters, or associates.

---

**Source:** Frederick Mathews, *Youth Gangs on Youth Gangs* (Ottawa: Solicitor General Canada, 1993), pp. 72 – 74. Reproduced with the permission of the Minister of Public Works and Government Services Canada, 1999.

harmful effects on long-term projects such as community development efforts to solve complex social problems like gangs.

Today there is growing recognition of the limitations of exclusive reliance on a law-and-order approach, and of the need for coalitions of diverse community partners to work together to respond to locally defined needs (see National Crime Prevention Council, 1997). Government, school officials, social services, parents, and police can all address specific issues, but no single group can solve the problem in isolation from the wider community.

## LESSONS FROM THE AMERICAN EXPERIENCE

Decades of effort in the United States to eradicate gangs has had mixed results. Much of the failure has been attributed to a lack of thorough understanding of the problem, the absence of a comprehensive response strategy, insufficient resources to accomplish the task, and failure to acknowledge the social context of the problem (U.S. Department of Justice, 1994).

According to U.S. Department of Justice research, communities that wish to be successful in their efforts to respond to youth-gang problems require:

1. early, clear, forthright recognition of the problem;

2. proactive leadership by representatives of criminal-justice and community-based agencies to mobilize political and community interests;
3. consensus on a definition of the problem;
4. clearly defined targets of agency and interagency efforts; and
5. concern for both community safety and the need to apply supports/resources that contribute to the personal development of present and potential gang members.

In a survey of 254 experts in 45 cities, the department found that the effectiveness of youth-gang response strategies was heavily dependent on the degree of community organization and opportunity provision in interaction, the proportion of local residents networking with one another, finding consensus on the definition of a gang incident, and the proportion of agencies with an external advisory group.

### Box 9.5

### A MULTI-LEVEL COMMUNITY GANG INTERVENTION STRATEGY

A review of best practices from communities in the United States indicates that a comprehensive solution must address three main issues: suppression, the development of community supports, and community mobilization.

#### Suppression

- target high-crime areas
- efforts to intervene sustained
- use officers familiar with the area
- gathering intelligence on youth gangs and members
- employing officers specifically trained to recognize/deal with gangs

#### Support Programs

- in-school education to teach students about the consequences of gang involvement
- encourage participation in positive alternative activities
- social-service agency crisis-intervention teams to mediate between gangs
- work closely with police or probation officers to identify trouble spots, prevent retaliations, resolve gang problems without violence
- alternative education programs
- vocational training and job placement
- pairing of gang members with local businesses
- parent-education classes and other programs that strengthen families, address resource issues for basic levels of care and sustenance
- instruction to school personnel, community residents, agency staff about gang activities, signs and symbols, community strategies to counter gang influence

#### Community Mobilization

- grass-roots participation
- interagency networking
- focus on individual youth behavioural and value change
- special focus on improved education, employment, job training
- criminal justice
- special gang units

**Source:** Office of Juvenile Justice and Delinquency Prevention, *Gang Suppression and Intervention: Problem and Response,* Research Summary (Washington, DC: U.S. Department of Justice, 1994), pp. 13 – 15.

## GANG SUPPRESSION

Communities in the United States with entrenched and serious gang crime and violence problems tend to rely on a control strategy known as **gang suppression**. Gang suppression targets law enforcement resources at high-gang-crime areas of cities or neighbourhoods. Gang suppression relies heavily on "gang units," or police officers specially trained to recognize gang activity, gather intelligence, communicate positively with gang members, and work hand in hand with district attorneys in gang-related case prosecutions. Currently, gang suppression is the dominant response to the youth-gang problem in the United States (U.S. Department of Justice, 1994).

## GANG RESISTANCE AND EDUCATION

Gang resistance and education programs typically target young people at risk for gang involvement and their parents or families. Resistance/education programs can be offered by local police officers, youth workers, teachers, or recreation workers. Brochures, newsletters, public-service announcements, and posters; and curriculum themes or information sessions in local schools or classrooms, community recreation centres, churches, or at gatherings of ethnic or cultural associations are just some of the ways resistance/education programs can inform young people or their parents and

### Box 9.6

### WINNIPEG STREET GANG PREVENTION PROJECT

In June 1997, the Street Gang Prevention Project was initiated by government departments at the federal, provincial, and municipal levels to address the street-gang problem in the city of Winnipeg, Manitoba. The two main goals of the project were: (1) reduce Winnipeg's street-gang membership by 25 percent, and (2) co-ordinate Winnipeg social-service strategies designed to impede gang recruitment and encourage current members to leave.

Glenn Cochrane, Project Co-ordinator, was hired to connect with young-gang members on their own turf. His vision for the work of the project was holistic, and he takes a realistic and positive message of hope and healing to the streets and communities where gang members hang out. He believes the attraction to gangs can be reduced, and that youth members will respond to efforts to provide assistance if they feel safe and see that their urgent survival, health, employment, educational, and other needs will be met by the community. He focusses on the strengths of young people, and works to build supportive webs of relationship that help them meet needs for affiliation, connection, and belonging. An evaluation of the first year of operation revealed that the project has begun to have an impact on meetings its goals.

**Source:** Michael Weinrath and Douglas Skoog, *Winnipeg Street Gang Prevention Project: First Year Evaluation.* Prepared for the Street Gang Advisory Committee, December 1998.

families about how to resist peer pressure to join gangs, the legal and personal consequences of gang involvement, and the warning signs of gang membership.

## A SOCIAL-CAPITAL RESPONSE TO YOUTH GANGS

A promising approach to prevention and intervention with respect to youth gangs and youth crime can be found in the development of a community's **social capital** (National Crime Prevention Council, 1997). Social capital differs from financial capital in that it is a measure of the quality of social relations and quantity of social supports, as opposed to being a money measure. Social capital is high in communities that build strong, protective support networks and nurturing relationships among children, parents, families, social institutions, and all community members. Communities with high levels of social capital are able to help meet the material, emotional, physical, mental, and spiritual needs of their members. Strong social capital enables people to create opportunities for themselves, reduce risk factors that lead to criminal involvement, decrease social isolation or marginalization of members, and significantly reduce vulnerability in children and families.

A social-capital approach to solving the problem of youth gangs involves several key issues:

1. Strengthening communities and the abilities of families to parent effectively and raise secure, healthy, and competent children and adolescents.
2. Eliminating the victimization of young people.
3. Reducing young peoples' involvement in antisocial behaviour.
4. Helping those young people who are already in trouble with the law to not become further involved in the criminal justice system.
5. Creating strong supportive networks of relationships and greater choices and opportunities for all young people.
6. Improving access and delivery of supports and services to children and families.
7. Removing bias and inequities in social systems that present barriers for youth and families, and
8. Building communities and stronger positive relationships among adults and youth.

## SCHOOL-BASED APPROACHES

Schools have an important role to play in teaching young people about the negative aspects of gang involvement and in reducing the motivation to join deviant peer groups (Lal, 1993). Keeping gang-prevention efforts in schools current means conducting annual safety audits and developing an ongoing process to tap student knowledge of problematic conditions in the school or surrounding community. It also means keeping abreast of changing population demographics, trends in youth crime, and the needs of exceptional students.

Students who become marginalized in the school community, or who fall through the cracks of the education system because of special needs, are vulnerable to the lure of gangs and to victimization. Teachers and administrators need to ensure that resources are available to provide support to "at risk" learners and students challenged by learning disabilities or suffering from social marginalization or emotional and behavioural problems. Schools who wish to be on the cutting edge of prevention should consider creating a student-wellness focus within guidance and counselling, linked to resources, supports, and other youth-serving organizations and agencies in the community. School officials who embrace this concept of an "open community school" with resources provided to students on-site will be in an optimal position to support and assist their vulnerable students (Dryfoos, 1994; Mathews, 1993).

Gang behaviour becomes difficult in school settings where interpersonal problem-solving skills are taught, and making friends is encouraged and facilitated by teachers. Alternative teaching methods such as group learning or co-op education; peer mentoring and tutoring; school peace gardens; self-help groups; across-the-curriculum themes pertaining to racism, sexism, and anti-violence—all contribute to a positive social ecology in the school. Outreach to isolated or marginalized parents of troubled students, breakfast programs, substance-abuse counselling and referral, paid or unpaid work-experience programs, flexible school hours, and no-fee extracurricular activities can also contribute substantially to student wellness, reduce isolation and marginalization, and reduce the appeal of gangs (National Crime Prevention Council, 1997).

Unprepared for the needs of young people from so many different cultures, many schools are struggling under a heavy burden. Given that so many of these new demands were unanticipated, change has been slow, and teachers often feel overwhelmed. Given the complexity of students' needs and the rapid social change that has become a part of life in Canada, ongoing professional development of educators is paramount. Faculties of education must also be conscientious in the preparation of new teachers. Teachers trained in multicultural sensitivity and possessing basic skills to identify abused, neglected, and vulnerable students will contribute significantly to the prevention of gang formation in schools.

## SUMMARY

While the problem in Canada is not comparable in scale to that in the United States, there is growing evidence to suggest that Canadian schools and communities, large and small, are experiencing problems with crime and violence on the part of young people in groups—some very serious. Most youth-gang configurations are not violent or crime-focussed, though all can and do break the law impulsively or in a planned manner.

The social phenomenon of youth gangs is complex and defies simple definition. There are no standard, one-size-fits-all solutions to the problem. Community needs differ, depending on geographic location, population demographics, and available resources. Solutions must be designed to match the situational demands of the local context to be most useful. Solutions must address root causes of problem behaviours.

Marginalization, or isolation, of communities from social influence and political power creates ideal conditions for gang formation. Once established they can become an entrenched part of a community. Social controls become less relevant and meaningful to gang members who feel excluded from full participation in society. Young people who are excluded from conventional career paths can become attracted to crime because it provides a means to earn a livelihood. Solutions must address social isolation of communities or groups to reduce or prevent the entrenchment of gangs. Solutions must also address the problem of drug use and selling because both are inextricably linked with organized crime-focussed gang activity.

Comprehensive community strategies must begin with a review or assessment of the community's problems and strengths. Strategies must address simultaneously issues related to law enforcement and to prevention and intervention. Lasting solutions will need to harness all community resources, focus on consensus building in defining the problem, involve broad-based community partnerships, include active local citizen mobilization and participation, and have sustained government support that is reflected in social policy and legislation directed toward building social capital. Community-based policing, alternative justice models in the form of community youth-justice councils or conferencing, restorative-justice programs, greater use of community-service orders, and pre- and post-charge diversion programs are all also promising approaches within the justice system.

Most important, communities that actively involve youth as equal partners in all efforts to define problems and solutions stand the best chance of being successful in their efforts. Young people provide experientially based knowledge and an everyday understanding of problems that can make intervention and prevention more relevant for youth in a school or community.

## WEB LINKS

**Canadian Council on Social Development**
<http://www.ccsd.ca/index.html>

The Canadian Council on Social Development promotes better social and economic security for all Canadians. Their Web site features links to resource materials concerning social development, health indicators, and wellness of children and youth, as well as some statistics.

**Department of Justice Canada**
<http://canada.justice.gc.ca/en/index.html>

This site provides access to federal government publications and resources pertaining to youth justice, with links to programs and services, conferences, and other Canadian legal resources.

**Department of the Solicitor General Canada**
<http://www.sgc.gc.ca/ehome.htm>

This site features federal government publications pertaining to police, crime, and community partnerships, with links to similar sites.

**Justice Information Center**
<http://www.ncjrs.org/>

This site from the U.S. Department of Justice features a wealth of information on youth crime, gangs, delinquency prevention, and community development. Click on "Juvenile Justice" for access to various informative links and listservs.

**National Crime Prevention Centre**
<http://www.crime-prevention.org/english/index.html>

This site contains information on resources and programs pertaining to the promotion of community safety and the prevention of crime, with links to similar national and international sites.

## STUDY QUESTIONS

1. What constitutes a "gang" and "gang activity"?
2. Identify and describe factors that motivate young people to join a gang.
3. In what ways does a community's definition of the term "gang" affect how it responds?
4. What are some key components of a comprehensive gang prevention/control strategy?
5. What issues should be highlighted in a public education program directed toward gang awareness?
6. What actions can schools take to be effective in preventing or confronting gang problems?
7. What issues do you believe should be a priority for government in preventing gang activity?

## REFERENCES


Banner, J., Ryan, C., and Mathews, F. (1994). *Multiple Perpetrator Youth Crime and Violence in Toronto: A Demographic Study*. Toronto: Central Toronto Youth Services.

Berkowitz, L., and LePage, A. (1967). "Weapons as aggression-eliciting stimuli." *Journal of Personality and Social Psychology*, 7: 202 – 7.

Bjerregaard, B., and Smith, C. (1993). "Gender differences in gang participation, delinquency, and substance use." *Journal of Quantitative Criminology*, 9: 329 – 55.

Bursik, R., and Grasmick, H. (1993). *Neighborhoods and Crime: The Dimension of Effective Community Control*. New York: Lexington Books.

Cameron, N. (1943). "The paranoid pseudo-community." *American Journal of Sociology*, 49: 32 – 38.

Campbell, A. (1990). *The Girls in the Gang*. (2nd ed.). New Brunswick, NJ: Rutgers University Press.

City of Toronto. (1999). *Action Plan on Youth Violence in Schools*. Toronto: Community and Neighbourhood Services Department.

Cloward, R., and Ohlin, L. (1960). *Delinquency and Opportunity*. Glencoe, IL: Free Press.

Cohen, A. (1955). *Delinquent Boys: The Culture of the Gang*. New York: Macmillan.

Curry, G., and Spurgel, I. (1988). "Gang homicide, delinquency, and community." *Criminology*, 26: 381 – 405.

———. (1992). "Gang involvement and delinquency among Hispanic and African American adolescent males." *Journal of Research in Crime and Delinquency*, 29: 273 – 91.

Darley, J.M., and Latanne, B. (1968). "Bystander intervention in emergencies: Diffusion of responsibility." *Journal of Personality and Social Psychology*, 8: 377 – 83.

Dryfoos, J.G. (1994). *Full Service Schools: A Revolution in Health and Social Services for Children, Youth, and Families*. San Francisco, CA: Jossey-Bass.

Edgerton, R. (1988). Foreword. In J.D. Vigil, *Barrio Gangs: Street Life and Identity in Southern California*. Austin: University of Texas Press.

England, R. (1967). "A theory of middle-class juvenile delinquency." In E.W. Vaz (Ed.), *Middle-Class Juvenile Delinquency*. New York: Harper & Row.

Esbensen, F., and Huizinga, D. (1993). "Gangs, drugs, and delinquency in a survey of urban youth." *Criminology*, 31: 565 – 89.

Esbensen, F., Huizinga, D., and Weiher, A. (1993). "Gang and non-gang youth: Differences in explanation variables." *Journal of Contemporary Criminal Justice*, 9: 94 – 116.

Fagan, J. (1990). "Treatment and reintegration of violent juvenile offenders: Experimental results." *Justice Quarterly*, 7: 233 – 63.

Goldstein, A., and Glick, B. (1994). *The Prosocial Gang*. Thousand Oaks, CA: Sage.

Hagedorn, J. (1988). *People and Folks: Gangs, Crime, and the Underclass in a Rustbelt City*. Chicago: Lakeview Press.

———. (1994a). "Homeboys, dope fiends, legits, and new jacks." *Criminology*, 31: 223 – 35.

———. (1994b). "Neighbourhoods, markets, and gang drug organization." *Journal of Research in Crime and Delinquency*, 32: 197 – 219.

Haskell, M.R. (1961). "Toward a reference group theory of juvenile delinquency." *Social Problems*, 8: 220 – 30.

Hirschi, T. (1969). *Causes of Delinquency*. Berkeley, CA: University of California Press.

Horowitz, R. (1983). *Honor and the American Dream: Culture and Identity in a Chicano Community*. New Brunswick, NJ: Rutgers University Press.

Horowitz, R., and Schwartz, G. (1974). "Honor, normative ambiguity, and gang violence." *American Sociological Review*, 39: 238 – 51.

Jeffery, C.R. (1959). "An integrated theory of Crime and Criminal Behavior." *Journal of Criminal Law, Criminology and Police Science*, 50: 533 – 52.

Klein, M. (1995). *The American Street Gang*. New York: Oxford University Press.

Korem, D. (1994). *Suburban Gangs: The Affluent Rebels*. Richardson, TX: International Focus Press.

Lal, S.R. (1993). *Handbook on Gangs in Schools: Strategies to Reduce Gang-Related Activities*. Newbury Park, CA: Corwin Press.

Landesco, J. (1932). "Crime and the failure of institutions in Chicago's immigrant areas." *Journal of Criminal Law and Criminology*, 23: 238 – 48.

Latanne, B., and Darley, J.M. (1968). "Group inhibition of bystander intervention." *Journal of Personality and Social Psychology*, 10: 215 – 21.

Lizotte, A., Tesoriero, J., Thornberry, T., and Krohn, M. (1994). "Patterns of adolescent firearms ownership and use." *Justice Quarterly*, 11: 51 – 73.

Mathews, F. (1992). "Reframing gang violence: a pro-youth strategy." *Journal of Emotional and Behavioural Problems*, 1(3): 24 – 28.

———. (1993). *Youth Gangs on Youth Gangs*. Ottawa: Solicitor General Canada.

———. (1996). *The Badge and the Book: Building Effective Police/School Partnerships to Combat Youth Violence*. Ottawa: Solicitor General Canada.

———. (1998). "Violent and aggressive girls." *Journal of Child and Youth Care*, 11(4): 1 – 23.

———. (1999). "Girls' use of violence and aggression." *Orbit*, 29(4): 10 – 15.

Mathews, F., and Stermac, L. (1989). *Adolescent Sex Offenders: A Tracking Study*. Toronto: Central Toronto Youth Services.

Merton, R.K. (1957). *Social Theory and Social Structure*. (2nd Ed.). New York: Free Press.

Miller, W. (1958). "Lower class culture as a generating milieu of gang delinquency." *Journal of Social Issues*, 14: 5 – 19.

———. (1974). "American youth gangs: past and present." In A. Blumberg (Ed.), *Current Perspectives on Criminal Behavior*. New York: Knopf.

———. (1982). *Crime by Youth Gangs and Groups in the US*. Washington, DC: U.S. Department of Justice, Office of Juvenile Justice and Delinquency Prevention.

Moore, J. (1978). *Homeboys*. Philadelphia: Temple University Press.

———. (1990). "Gangs, drugs, and violence." In M. De La Rosa, E.Y. Lambert, and B. Gropper (Eds.), *Drugs and Violence: Causes, Correlates, and Consequences*. Rockville, MD: National Institute for Drug Abuse.

———. (1991). *Going Down to the Barrio: Homeboys and Homegirls in Charge*. Philadelphia: Temple University Press.

National Crime Prevention Council. (1997). *Preventing Crime by Investing in Families and Communities. Promoting Positive Outcomes in Youth 12 – 18 Years Old*. Ottawa: NCPC.

Newton, G., and Zimring, F. (1969). *Firearms and Violence in American Life: A Staff Report to the National Commission on the Causes and Prevention of Violence*. Washington, DC: U.S. Government Printing Office.

Quarter, J., and Mathews, F. (1987). "Back to the basics." In D. Livingstone (Ed.), *Critical Pedagogy and Cultural Power*. South Hadley, MA: Bergin and Garvey.

Quinney, R. (1974). *Criminal Justice in America*. Boston: Little-Brown.

Ryan, C., Mathews, F., and Banner, J. (1993). *Student Perceptions of Violence*. Toronto: Central Toronto Youth Services.

Sanchez-Jankowski, M. (1991). *Islands in the Street: Gangs and American Urban Society*. Berkeley: University of California Press.

Shaw, C.R., and McKay, H.D. (1931). "Social factors in juvenile delinquency." In *Report on the Causes of Crime*. National Commission on Law Observance and Enforcement Report no. 13. Washington, DC: U.S. Government Printing Office.

Short, J., and Strodbeck, F. (1965). *Group Process and Gang Delinquency*. Chicago: University of Chicago Press.

Smith, R., Bertrand, L., Arnold, B., and Hornick, J. (1995). *A Study of the Level and Nature of Youth Crime and Violence in Calgary*. Ottawa: Solicitor General Canada.

Spergel, I. (1964). *Racketville, Slumtown, Haulberg: An Exploratory Study of Delinquent Subcultures*. Chicago: University of Chicago Press.

Strodbeck, F., and Short, J. (1964). "Aleatory risks versus short-run hedonism in explanation of gang behaviour." *Social Problems*, 12: 128 – 29.

Sutherland, E., and Cressey, D. (1970). *Criminology*. Philadelphia, PA: Lippincott.

Tannenbaum, F. (1939). *Crime and Community*. New York: Columbia University Press.

Tanner, J. (1996). *Teenage Troubles: Youth and Deviance in Canada*. Toronto: Nelson.

Thompson, K., and Braaten-Antrim, R. (1998). "Youth maltreatment and gang involvement." *Journal of Interpersonal Violence*, 13(3): 328 – 45.

Thornberry, T., Lizotte, A., Krohn, M., and Chard-Wierschem, D. (1993). "The role of juvenile gangs in facilitating delinquent behaviour." *Journal of Research in Crime and Delinquency*, 30: 55 – 87.

Thrasher, F.M. (1929). *The Gang*. Chicago: University of Chicago Press.

Tomson, B., and Fielder, E.R. (1975). "Gangs: a response to the urban world." In B. Tomson and E. Fielder (Eds.), *Gang Delinquency*. Monterey, CA: Brooks/Cole.

U.S. Department of Justice. (1994). *Gang Suppression and Intervention: Problem and Response*. Washington: Office of Juvenile Justice and Delinquency Prevention.

Vigil, J. (1988). *Barrio Gangs: Street Life and Identity in Southern California*. Austin: University of Texas Press.

Vigil, J., and Yun, S. (1990). "Vietnamese youth gangs in Southern California." In C.R. Huff (Ed.), *Gangs in America*. Newbury Park, CA: Sage.

Walker, S.G. (1994). *Weapons Use in Canadian Schools*. Ottawa: Solicitor General of Canada.

Wang, Z. (1995). "Gang affiliation among Asian-American high school students: A path analysis of a social development model." *Journal of Gang Research*, 2: 1 – 13.

Wattenberg, W., and Balistrieri, J. (1950). "Gang membership and juvenile misconduct." *American Sociological Review*, 15: 181 – 86.

Weinrath, M., and Skoog, D. (1998). *Winnipeg Street Gang Intervention Project. First Year Evaluation*. Unpublished report prepared for the Street Gang Advisory Project. Winnipeg: Author.

Whyte, W.F. (1955). *Street Corner Society*. Chicago: University of Chicago Press.

Yablonsky, L. (1973). *The Violent Gang*. New York: Penguin.

# Chapter 10

# The Adolescent Prostitute: Policing Delinquency or Preventing Victimization?

AUGUSTINE BRANNIGAN

## KEY OBJECTIVES

After reading this chapter, you should be able to:

- identify the conflicting agendas of Canadian legislation regarding prostitution—namely, suppressing delinquency versus preventing adolescent victimization;
- outline some of the problems in defining adolescent prostitutes and what adolescent prostitution consists of;
- describe the trends in arrests of young prostitutes in Canada since 1985;
- explore evidence of early physical and sexual abuse of adolescent prostitutes;
- examine the links among early abuse, runaway behaviour, and adolescent prostitution.

## KEY TERMS

anti-communication law
Badgley Report
communication
delinquency perspective
Fraser Report
prostitution
victimological perspective

## INTRODUCTION

The purpose of this chapter is to explore the subject of adolescent prostitution. First, we want to understand how public awareness of adolescent prostitution as a pressing problem has grown as a result of media reports over the past decade. Second, we want to examine two competing perspectives on adolescent prostitution: the **delinquency perspective**—the idea that prostitution is a form of misconduct like theft or narcotics use, and the **victimological perspective**—the idea that prostitution is a form of child sexual abuse. Third, we report some problems in defining what activities constitute adolescent prostitution and what ages are involved. Fourth, we examine some estimates of the magnitude of the problem in Canada. Fifth, we examine evidence on the backgrounds of adolescent prostitutes, and the role of earlier physical and sexual abuse in their careers. Sixth, we explore the link between early abuse, runaway behaviour, and prostitution among street youth. Finally, we draw some conclusions about what can be done about adolescent prostitution, especially in terms of the conflicting perspectives on this problem.

## THE MEDIA AND ADOLESCENT PROSTITUTION

The problem of street prostitution has received considerable attention in the popular press throughout the English-speaking world, and has resulted in a number of public inquiries and studies to determine its extent and what can be done about it (Badgley, 1984; Fraser, 1985).[1] In addition, new legislation against prostitution and dramatic changes in the enforcement of this legislation have occurred. For example, in England, the number of convictions for soliciting and loitering jumped from 4200 in 1981 to 5800 in 1982 to about 10 000 in 1983 (United Kingdom, 1984; 1985). In the state of Victoria, Australia, the number of persons charged with soliciting increased by three times between 1977 and 1980, and declined to previous levels by the mid-1980s (Neave, 1985).

In Canada, street activity is believed to have increased in a similar way, although the arrest figures for soliciting during this period were extremely low since the law was virtually unenforceable after the *Hutt* v. *R.* decision of 1978. *Hutt* v. *The Queen* gave a narrow meaning to soliciting, requiring the conduct to be pressing or persistent. However, the problem is not limited to unwanted solicitation. According to evidence given to the Fraser Committee at public hearings held across Canada in 1985, street prostitution is associated with noisy, intrusive traffic of "johns" circulating at all hours of the day, or night, harassing females for sexual attention. Frequently, this results in friction between the community residents and pimps, prostitutes, and their customers. Prostitutes often turn tricks in alleys, in vacant lots, behind buildings, and in residents' driveways. Residents must deal with discarded condoms and used needles from the intravenous-drug trade often associated with prostitution. Evidence suggests that, when an area is taken over by street prostitution, the quality of life and the values of property both decline. In the early 1980s, Canadian municipal politicians were so angered by the street-prostitution problem that by-laws were enacted in Calgary, Montreal, Vancouver, and Niagara Falls in an attempt to suppress the growing trade. In Calgary, over 500 tickets were issued to prostitutes before the Supreme Court declared these by-laws to be legally beyond the power of city regulation and an infringement of federal powers under Canada's constitutional framework in the *Westendorp* v. *R.* case (1983). In 1985, the federal Parliament passed a law making it a crime for anyone to communicate in public for the purpose of prostitution (see Box 10.1), thereby making it possible for communities to eradicate the nuisance of street prostitution.

Many researchers believe that most adult prostitutes begin their careers as adolescents. Studies show that while most prostitutes are females between the ages of 18 and 22, many began their careers as minors (Brannigan, Knafla, and Levy, 1989). Throughout the 1980s, Canadian newspapers painted a picture of an epidemic of juvenile prostitution. Rings of juveniles were said to be working in hundreds of escort agencies that were grossing

**Box 10.1**

**PROSTITUTION LAWS**

1. The Anti-Communication Law (section 213, Criminal Code of Canada)

Every person who in a public place or in any place open to public view

(a) stops or attempts to stop any motor vehicle
(b) impedes the free flow of pedestrian or vehicular traffic or ingress to or egress from the premises adjacent to that place, or
(c) stops or attempts to stop any person or in any manner communicates or attempts to communicate with any person

for the purpose of engaging in prostitution or of obtaining the sexual services of a prostitute is guilty of an offence punishable on summary conviction.

2a. Protection of Adolescents from "johns" (section 212(4), Criminal Code of Canada)

Every person who, in any place, obtains or attempts to obtain, for consideration, the sexual services of a person who is under the age of eighteen years or who that person believes is under the age of eighteen years is guilty of an indictable offence and liable to imprisonment for a period not exceeding five years.

2b. Protection of Adolescents from pimps (section 212(2.1), Criminal Code of Canada)

Every person who lives wholly or in part on the avails of prostitution of another person under the age of eighteen years, and who

(a) for the purpose of profit, aids, abets, counsels or compels the person under that age to engage in or carry on prostitution with any person or generally, and
(b) uses, threatens to use or attempts to use violence, intimidation or coercion in relation to the person under that age,

is guilty of an indictable offence and liable to imprisonment for a period not exceeding fourteen years but not less than five years.

*continued*

Box 10.1 *continued*

**3. The Alberta Protection of Children Involved in Prostitution Act (Child Welfare Act)**

s. 1(1)(a) "Child" means a person under the age of 18 years

s. 2 For the purpose of this Act a child is in need of protection if the child is engaging in prostitution or attempting to engage in prostitution

s. 2(1) If a police officer believes on reasonable and probable grounds that a person is a child and is in need of protection, the police officer may apply to a judge of the Court or to a justice of the peace for an order

(a) authorizing the police officer to apprehend and convey the child to the child's guardian or to an adult who in the opinion of the police officer is a responsible adult who has care and control of the child, or

(b) authorizing the police officer to apprehend and convey the child to a protective safe house and authorizing a director to confine the child for up to 72 hours to ensure the safety of the child and to assess the child.

millions of dollars annually (*Globe and Mail*, 28 September 1987: 1). The Children's Aid Society of Ottawa reported a secret ring of juvenile prostitutes circulating among various Canadian cities. In the early 1990s, a ring of juvenile prostitutes from Nova Scotia were being circulated through Toronto and Montreal by a group of Halifax pimps. Between the years 1994 and 1998, the *Globe and Mail* alone carried 38 stories, including a front-page, seven-part series on child prostitution (InfoGlobe Search, 1999).

Television carried similar reports. The CBC documentary "Twenty Four Hours a Runaway" (broadcast in September 1987) suggested strong links between running away from home, surviving on the streets, abusing drugs, and entering into prostitution (see Chapter 8). U.S. estimates of 1 million homeless teenagers involved in prostitution and making pornographic materials were readily transported to Canada, giving us a proportional epidemic (McCaghy and Berenbaum, 1983). The Defence for Children International reported that 60 000 children were involved in making kiddie porn in Canada (Buys, 1989). In 1981, one Montreal social worker estimated that there were 5000 adolescent prostitutes working in the city (*Globe and Mail*, 22 July 1981: 8). In the aftermath of the federally funded Fraser and Badgley reports on adult pornography and prostitution and sexual offences against young people, respectively, the federal Minister of Justice granted special funds to outreach services to provide support systems for adolescent prostitutes, and in 1985 the Solicitor General of Canada initiated a major study of missing children, some of whom were thought to be runaways working in the sex trade.

It is impossible to determine whether adolescent prostitution is on the rise. As we shall see in Table 10.1, arrests of young people for communication is declining, but such statistics are often a better measure of the behaviour of the police than of changes in the behaviour of the persons arrested. It is probably more accurate to say that awareness of the problem has increased, though we cannot conclude that the problem itself has become worse.

## VICTIMIZATION VERSUS DELINQUENCY

The rationale for suppressing adult street prostitution derives from considerations of public nuisance. This issue is overshadowed by an entirely different orientation where adolescents are concerned. Although there is an issue of diminished responsibility associated with adolescent misconduct generally, adolescent prostitution is regarded as a special case. Many regard prostitution as a form of pathological conduct most often caused by early sexual abuse, therefore calling for social-welfare intervention. From this victimological perspective, in contrast to a delinquency perspective, juvenile prostitution constitutes a form of continuing sexual victimization. Thus Bagley and Young (1987: 23) report that "the girl who finally tries prostitution is one who is already degraded and demoralized, in a state of psychological bondage, with grossly diminished self-confidence." A similar perspective is evident in the 1984 **Badgley Report**, which focussed on the involvement of adolescents in prostitution, the role of sexual abuse in the backgrounds of adolescent prostitutes (as well as of the general public), and the medical and psychological consequences of sexual abuse. The Badgley Committee found that the law was ill equipped to ensure the protection of adolescents, or to censure the conduct of their customers (pp. 1960 – 61). For the committee, prostitution was less a case of delinquency *by* young people than a case of sexual abuse *of* young people.

The victimological perspective was also strongly represented by the National Consultation on Adolescent Prostitution in September 1987 (Canadian Child Welfare Association, 1988). The consultation was sponsored by the federal Ministry of Health and Welfare and the Department of Justice and was hosted by the Canadian Child Welfare Association. Its mandate was "to develop a thorough understanding of the problem of juvenile prostitution ... to contribute to the improvement in the quality of response to juvenile prostitution by various helping professionals ... and to conceptualize a national framework for action to effectively prevent and treat the abuse and exploitation of young people involved in prostitution" (p. 12). The consultation recommended that juvenile prostitution be decriminalized, that the customers of juveniles be severely penalized, and that the effectiveness of provincial child-welfare protections be reviewed (p. 7). A second national consultation was sponsored by the Halifax Children's Aid Society in 1990, a third was hosted by the Federation of Canadian Municipalities in Calgary in 1993 and the most recent was held in Victoria in March 1998.

In response, the federal government passed the Child Exploitation Law, in 1987, which, among other changes, revised the age of consent to sexual acts in Canada, created relatively harsh penalties both for those living on the avails of adolescent prostitutes and for those procuring adolescents for prostitution, and made it a further offence for any person to purchase the sexual services of an adolescent (Rogers, 1990). Although the new law was greeted enthusiastically by social workers and children's rights advocates, between

1993 and 1999 the police have laid few charges for both ethical and procedural reasons. Using undercover adolescent decoys would risk public wrath, and the passive surveillance of real adolescent prostitutes involved with their customers might open the police to charges of abrogation of duty for failure to rescue the child at risk as required by provincial child-welfare legislation. A 1998 change to the Alberta Child Welfare Act defined sexual abuse to include purchase of the sexual services of a person under 18 years of age. It provided for a $25 000 fine and/or imprisonment for up to two years less a day for the "abuser." It also gave social workers the power to seize adolescent prostitutes and to hold them in a "safe house" for up to 72 hours. Five months after the proposed legislation, there have been 82 cases of young children and young prostitutes, as young as 12, locked up for their safety (Martin, 1999). Over the same period, nearly a dozen customers have been charged with sexual abuse relating to underage youth.

When we compare the focus on suppressing street soliciting with the concern for childhood sexual victimization, it appears that the victimological, or social-welfare, view has come to dominate our approach to adolescent prostitution. Comparing these two approaches suggests that adult prostitution should be controlled by virtue of its being a public nuisance, while adolescent prostitution should be controlled because it is a form of victimization. These competing social objectives appear to demand competing—and potentially incompatible—forms of state intervention.

## ESTIMATING THE NUMBERS OF ADOLESCENT PROSTITUTES

In 1987, the Department of justice undertook an evaluation of the federal anti-communication law. The communication law came about based on the findings in the **Fraser Report** (1985). Part of the evaluation entailed examining the issue of adolescent prostitutes to determine whether the law had had an impact on this population in major Canadian cities. Before examining the findings regarding numbers of adolescents, it is essential to discuss some of the problems of defining juvenile prostitution.

### DEFINITION PROBLEMS

Different authorities use different age criteria and hence define juvenile prostitution differently. The Badgley Committee defined juvenile prostitutes as those under 21 years of age, but 56 percent of the 229 "juvenile prostitutes" interviewed in the national survey were aged 18, 19, or 20 (Badgley, 1984: 967ff.). In other words, most of the "juveniles" had reached the age of majority. In its discussion of "Sexual Activity for Reward with Juveniles," the Fraser Committee identified a lower age: "We recommend the creation of a specific offence aimed at those who engage in sexual activity for money or other consideration or reward with persons under 18" (Fraser, 1985: 658). Others, such as youth case workers, police, and provincial social workers, confine the concept of juvenile prostitution to those under age 16, particularly in the context of provincial child-welfare legislation, which mandates control of children who may be seized and brought into custody for their own protection if they are a danger to themselves. Since at least half the Canadian prostitution population is under 21, the majority of prostitutes fall into the disputed age range. The argument over age is important if we assume that young people cannot be permitted to work as prostitutes because their lack of maturity makes their decision uninformed or meaningless and their immaturity causes them to minimize the long-term costs in terms of loss of social status, social alienation, risk of arrest, and physical and emotional health risks. The concern over sexual abuse raises the issue of capacity further by implying that the decision to prostitute is similarly meaningless since the capacity to rationally make such a decision has been corrupted. In particular, victims of childhood trauma are at greater risk of developing serious psychological problems (Ross et al., 1990; Brannigan and Van Brunschot, 1997; Goodman and Fallot, 1998; Van Brunschot and Brannigan, 1999).

A second definitional problem concerns the kinds of behaviour that are considered adolescent prostitution. Interviews conducted in five major cities as part of the evaluation of Bill C-49 indicated that, when social agencies and members of the media talk about adolescent prostitutes, they are often referring to a broad group of homeless or runaway youths (Fleischman, 1989). These young people are sometimes known to exchange sexual favours for food, lodging, gifts, affection, or just to experiment with their own sexuality (Mathews, 1988). Field research suggests that young male homosexuals frequently work on the street as a way of "coming out" and meeting other gays; indeed, over half the prostitutes in one study were gay (Visano, 1987). This group may leave home as a result of parents' hostility over their sexual orientation (Mathews, 1993; Visano, 1987: 103ff.). These young people often do not come to the attention of law-enforcers or appear in official statistics as prostitutes (see Chapter 8 for a comparison with young runaways). Obviously, the different age criteria, with their correspondingly different populations, may account for different explanations of what adolescent prostitution is and how prevalent it is, and the disparities in the estimates of its prevalence.

Linda Hancock (1985: 6) made a similar observation in her study of juvenile prostitutes in Melbourne, Australia. She argued that the social definition of prostitution extends beyond those persons working the streets and seeking money in exchange for sex and includes

> acts involving the provision of sexual services in return for goods or services such as drugs, food or accommodation and/or acts involving indiscriminate sexual promiscuity often motivated by desires for approval, attention or affection ...

By way of explanation, indiscriminate sexual promiscuity refers to young people who are not just

> sexually active (as this may include many young people) but who had engaged in indiscriminate sexual relations with a succession of partners, often not knowing them by name.

Hancock argued that the justification for such an inclusive definition by police and welfare authorities was to prevent "a slide into illegal prostitution," and to give a wider account for "the sexual exploitation of young people." Hancock identified 63 juveniles who appeared in Melbourne police reports in 1984 and, as a result of interviews with case workers and social-welfare authorities, estimated a total population of some 180 young people (contrast the figures of 5000 and 10 000 attributed to Canadian cities of similar size). Of the 63 who appeared in police reports, 34 were involved in street prostitution and 29 were involved in "indiscriminate promiscuity" apparently "motivated by the quest for attention or approval, rather than exchanged directly for money, drugs or accommodation." By contrast, there were an estimated 2000 – 3000 adult women working as prostitutes in Melbourne, although for an undetermined number the work was casual or part-time (Neave, 1985).

Canada's federal Department of Justice was advised repeatedly throughout the 1980s by members of the social-service sector that there were large numbers of juveniles working as prostitutes in their cities. As part of the review of the federal solicitation law (Bill C-49), researchers in the major Canadian field sites (Halifax, Toronto, Winnipeg, Calgary, and Vancouver) sought evidence to document the epidemic estimates, either through direct street observations and systematic counts of persons on view, or via police arrest data. The data gathered in the evaluation of Bill C-49 made it possible to estimate the proportion of persons charged in the various urban centres who were adolescents or juveniles. For our purposes, we will confine our attention to those persons aged 12 to 17 who were prosecuted under the Young Offenders Act. In fact, the police arrest data made it possible to describe quite accurately the age distribution of all persons charged with soliciting. Table 10.1 shows the numbers and percentages of persons arrested who were under 18. Although there were not as many as we expected, where arrest data were available in the major research sites, approximately 10 – 15 percent of those arrested for soliciting were female youth offenders; the majority of these were aged 16 and 17 (Fleischman, 1989). There were reports of 14- and 15-year-olds, but these cases were relatively rare and were more liable to involve adolescents who were provincial wards on the run from foster homes or group homes (Fleischman, 1984). It is instructive that no figures were reported for Montreal, since in that city police do not view adolescent prostitution as a problem of delinquency but rather as a child-welfare problem. As a consequence, all adolescent prostitution cases in Montreal are diverted by police to social-service agencies.

Table 10.1 lists the total prostitution charges for the period 1985 to 1997. The figures include procurement and bawdy-house offences. The table breaks out adult male and adult female charges that come under the Criminal Code and the total number of charges under the Young Offenders Act. A closer inspection of the annual trends from Canadian Centre for Justice Statistics data and major police forces suggests four things that make it easier to interpret these total charge trends. First, most prostitution charges are for street soliciting. Second, the overwhelming majority of males charged are "johns." Third, with few exceptions the female adults are sellers. Fourth, this means that the vast majority of young offenders charged are female prostitutes. As of 1992, it was possible to identify male and female young offenders separately. If these assumptions are sound, then it is possible to estimate the proportion of all female sellers who are adolescents. Table 10.1 shows that figures vary between 5.5 percent in 1996 and 18.5 percent in 1986. However, the total number of charges affecting adolescents since the bill was passed is very significant—nearly 5500. This suggests that, when we take a long-term view, there certainly is a major problem of adolescents at risk, even if the numbers at risk at any time represent only a small part of what turns out to be a large street trade. This evaluation makes sense of the dramatic media estimates of "thousands" of runaways in all the major cities dabbling in prostitution, drugs, and theft. Over the long term, the *actual* numbers of adolescents reflected in the arrest statistics who appear to be prematurely removed from family and school before they have acquired basic economic and educational skills represent a significant social problem.

## Table 10.1

### TRENDS IN PROSTITUTION CHARGES IN CANADA BY OFFENDER TYPE, 1985 – 1997 (UNDER 18 YEARS OLD)

| Year | Adult Male Charges | Adult Female Charges | Juvenile Male Charges | Juvenile Female Charges | Total Juvenile Charges | Young Offenders as % of all Female Charges | Juvenile Female as % of all Female Charges |
|---|---|---|---|---|---|---|---|
| **1985** | 385 | 566 | | | 78 | 12.0 | |
| **1986** | 2 939 | 3 863 | | | 880 | 18.5 | |
| **1987** | 5 340 | 4 938 | | | 548 | 10.0 | |
| **1988** | 5 179 | 5 445 | | | 548 | 9.0 | |
| **1989** | 4 411 | 5 277 | | | 1018 | 16.0 | |
| **1990** | 4 944 | 5 523 | | | 400 | 6.7 | |
| **1991** | 5 075 | 5 596 | | | 500 | 8.2 | |
| **1992*** | 5 182 | 5 572 | 44 | 312 | 356 | 6.1 | 5.3 |
| **1993** | 4 503 | 4 200 | 53 | 250 | 303 | 6.8 | 5.6 |
| **1994** | 2 603 | 3 000 | 22 | 160 | 182 | 5.8 | 5.1 |
| **1995** | 3 446 | 3 945 | 42 | 213 | 255 | 6.1 | 5.1 |
| **1996** | 2 742 | 3 197 | 20 | 165 | 185 | 5.5 | 4.9 |
| **1997** | 2 576 | 3 090 | 24 | 194 | 218 | 6.6 | 5.9 |
| **Totals** | 49 325 | 54 212 | 205 | 1294 | 5471 | | |

* Until 1992, young offenders were not differentiated by gender in the annual reports.

**Source:** Canadian Centre for Justice Statistics, *Canadian Crime Statistics* (Ottawa: Statistics Canada, various years).

## VICTIMIZATION LEVELS OF FEMALE PROSTITUTES

The literature on abuse of females is surprisingly inconsistent. Social-welfare agencies find epidemic levels of sexual, physical, and emotional abuse. National research projects in Canada and studies of practising prostitutes report either equivalent levels of abuse in the backgrounds of juvenile prostitutes and the population at large, or modest levels of abuse in the target population. The Fraser Report states:

> When we conclude ... that prostitutes do not appear to have higher levels of being sexually abused as children, it is not because they are unlikely to have been abused, but because it appears to be such a common phenomenon in our society ... What we do not know ... is the extent to which prostitutes, as children, may have been the victims of more serious sexual abuse ... [and] whether the levels of serious sexual abuse of prostitutes when they were children are different from the level of the general population. (1985: 373 – 74)

The Badgley Committee examined the early sexual experience of 84 juvenile prostitutes. The data suggested that, in comparison with the national population survey of 1002 persons, the young prostitutes were sexually precocious, although their first sexual encounters were "described as non-abusive adolescent or pre-adolescent sexual experimentation" (Badgley, 1984: 977), which is rather different from incest. Ritch and Michaud (1985) reported that 80 percent of females in a Vancouver hostel for prostitutes had been sexually abused as children. Bagley and Young (1987) reported a figure of 73 percent in a sample of 45 former prostitutes in therapeutic care in Alberta. Silbert and Pines (1982) reported that 60 percent of the 200 female prostitutes they interviewed had been sexually abused. In contrast, Mathews (1988) reported a figure of 10 percent, and Brannigan, Knafla, and Levy (1989) a figure of 12 percent. It is difficult to explain the dramatic variations among these different studies. Immediate issues that might contribute to these variations are differences in deciding which acts to count and at which ages, which populations to survey in order to reliably link background experiences and prostitution, and the social agendas of the estimators. All may be contributing factors.

Few of the estimates describe the extent of the sexual abuse. By way of illustration, Silbert and Pines suggested that, for 90 percent of their victims, the abuse led to the loss of virginity, and that in two-thirds of the cases the assailant was a natural, step-, or foster father. Here we have strong statements on the prevalence of incest. By contrast, Badgley examined the first unwanted sexual experiences of juvenile prostitutes and compared these with the first sexual acts committed against males and females in the general population, not the total *prevalence* of abuse (the percentage of people ever abused) nor the *incidence* of abuse (how often it occurred). In the majority of other reports—nearly all linked to social-service agencies—

virtually no details are given about the nature of the abuse, its prevalence versus its incidence, and the ages at which it occurred.

Two other concerns arise from agency-based reports. People contacted for interviews by social-service agencies may be using social services because they suffer from emotional disabilities arising from childhood trauma. Therefore, the link between trauma and prostitution may be artifactual (Bagley and Young, 1987). Conversely, agencies may have a vested interest in making liberal estimates of the numbers of children working as prostitutes and/or the earlier traumatic childhood events, since public support may depend on identifying high levels of pathology among the potential treatment population. This was suggested to Neave by the Inner City Street Kids Program in her 1985 study of prostitution in Melbourne. There were an estimated 2000 to 3000 women working as prostitutes in Melbourne, although, for an undetermined number, the work was casual or part-time. In another Australian study, Hancock (1985) made a similar observation when comparing official Melbourne police occurrence reports for 1984 with results of interviews with case workers and social-worker authorities. Hancock observed: "A number of welfare agencies may have incentives for exaggerating the number of young people involved in prostitution ... in order to seek public empathy and financial assistance" (1985: 17).

In reaction against using sexual abuse to explain entry into prostitution, the National Consultation on Adolescent Prostitution suggested that there is "a lack of understanding about the possible relationship between early sexual experience and/or sexual, physical and emotional abuse and subsequent engagement in prostitution. [This issue] was identified as a serious knowledge gap" (Canadian Child Welfare Association, 1988: 3).

Does abuse indeed make victims emotionally dysfunctional, does it promote promiscuity, and does it force kids to run away? Frederick Mathews, a well-known Toronto authority on adolescents and prostitution, cautions about jumping to conclusions. In reviewing the epidemic levels of early abuse described in the Badgley Report, Mathews observes:

> If these figures are to be believed, then there is a great potential for Canada to turn into a nation of prostitutes. The simple fact that there are not hundreds of thousands of prostitutes working should indicate that intra- or extra-familial sexual abuse, and/or early sexual experience are not, or may not be, the central issue in the decision to begin working in prostitution. (1988: 13 – 14)

In his work, Mathews found that only two out of nineteen adolescent prostitutes had been sexually victimized as children. For Mathews, the pathological approach mystifies prostitution and the reasons people take it up. Research conducted in Calgary in 1987 suggested that there were indeed very high levels of abuse—physical and sexual—among the city's prostitutes. However, this abuse occurred overwhelmingly after the respondents had started working as prostitutes, and the most important abusers were clients and pimps (Brannigan, Knafla, and Levy, 1989).

This does not mean that gravely dysfunctional families, personal problems, or pressures in the backgrounds of adolescents fail to influence their decision to become prostitutes. Rather, the attention mustered by the sexual-abuse problem has been at the expense of the other complex issues that push children out of the home, and the cultural and market factors that make prostitution attractive to certain young people. One fruitful line of inquiry linking problems in the family environment and entry into prostitution revolves around the conduct of runaways.

## LINKING RUNAWAYS, ABUSE, AND ADOLESCENT PROSTITUTION

There has been a great deal of speculation on the link between runaways, prior sexual abuse, and adolescent prostitution. Table 10.2 compares data from four studies of runaways in Canada that explore this link (also see Chapter 8). This comparison reinforces Mathews's caution about considering abuse to be the main determinant of prostitution. What is surprising is that the levels of prior sexual abuse do not appear to be nearly as serious as one would predict.

Fisher's 1989 study for the Solicitor General of Canada was based on a nationwide sample of 12 000 police reports of missing children in Canada in 1986. About 6000 different children accounted for 86 percent of the reported cases, and these were all runaways. In a second phase of the study, which focussed on a sample of 341 repeat runners, Fisher concluded:

> There was no evidence that either sexual or physical abuse was a major source of running away. However, the results indicated that a relationship did exist between repeat runaway cases and some combination of other problems.

**Table 10.2**

**PERCENTAGE OF RUNNERS REPORTING CHILD ABUSE**

| Source | Sample Data Source | Size | Sexual Locale | Physical Abuse | Abuse |
|---|---|---|---|---|---|
| **Fisher (1989)** | **National Survey Agency files** | 341 | Canada | 10.0% | 14.0% |
| **Kufeldt & Nimmo (1987)** | **Street interviews** | 474 | Calgary | 7.3% | 28.0% |
| **McCarthy (1990)** | **Street interviews** | 390 | Toronto | 14.0% (females) | 32.3% |
| **Hagan & McCarthy (1998)** | **Street interviews** | 872 | Toronto and Vancouver | 14% (females) | 60% |

Parental drinking, marital conflict, generational conflict, mental illness, spousal violence, and child abuse were cited as reasons for running away. Rather than a simple linkage, Fisher identified 21 separate patterns of mixed neglect, conflict, school problems, and abuse. Sexual abuse was common to 10 percent of the repeat runners, physical abuse to 14 percent. Kufeldt and Nimmo's 1987 work was based on interviews with 474 minors in Calgary, about a quarter of whom were repeat runners (or "in-and-outers"). Their findings are consistent with the national study particularly in the area of sexual abuse. McCarthy (1990) found that 14 percent of females and 2.4 percent of males had experienced sexual abuse, and about 32.3 percent experienced physical abuse "sometimes" or "often." In a follow-up study, Hagan and McCarthy interviewed a further 482 street youth in Vancouver and Toronto (for a total sample of 872). Sixty percent of the respondents reported that, on at least one occasion, they had been hit with enough force to cause bruising or bleeding. Fourteen percent of the females and 6 percent of the males reported being victims of sexual abuse (Hagan and McCarthy, 1998: 23 – 24), although their families were marked by numerous problems of substance abuse, criminality, and conflict.

What percentage of adolescents who run away from home enter into prostitution? The Canadian studies have tried to systematically link populations of runaways with prostitution. Fisher's study focussed on 341 repeat runners who were chosen because they appeared to present the most troubled populations. Approximately 18 percent of them became involved in prostitution. In the Kufeldt and Nimmo study, interviewers sought runaways from many locations, including the main Calgary prostitution stroll, and discovered that 25 percent of their respondents were engaged in prostitution. Methodologically, neither sample allows for a reliable identification of the proportions of total runaway populations who gravitate toward prostitution. McCarthy's study of runaways in Toronto was more systematic. He found that 32 percent of his respondents had engaged in prostitution, but his sample group was considerably older than Fisher's. Hagan and McCarthy (1998: 116) reported that about one quarter of their sample had engaged in prostitution. Priscilla Alexander (1982) reviewed police data on runaways in the United States in the early 1980s. Of the 164 000 children who were known by the police to be runaways, 3000 were working as prostitutes, or less than 2 percent. Other U.S. data from 1980 looked at 2637 children arrested for roaming the streets; 178 of these were detained on prostitution as well as immoral charges, or about 7 percent.

So where does all this leave us? We have more questions than answers regarding the prevalence of abuse in the background of adolescent prostitutes. Canadian research based on interviews with active prostitutes—as opposed to those associated with social-welfare agencies—fails to confirm the high levels of sexual abuse identified in Silbert and Pines's San Francisco study, in addition to the extremely youthful age distribution found there. Also, the link between abuse and the decision to run away, and the link between running and entry into prostitution are similarly open questions. Hagan and McCarthy (1998: 125ff.) report that physical abuse is critical in estimating the number of nights a runner spends away from home, and that this exposure puts runners into networks of other young persons already engaged in a range of illicit behaviour (theft, drugs, prostitution, and violence).

## IMPLICATIONS FOR STATE CONTROL

What lessons might we draw from the previous observations? Two alternative control strategies are possible here. First, we might treat the population of street prostitutes as a whole. In our view, persons engaged in street soliciting do not generally appear to be a pathological population requiring social-welfare consideration due to age or prior abuse, although this does not deny that prostitutes face conditions that generally contribute to delinquency. The suggestion that adolescent prostitutes are simply survivors of childhood sexual abuse who have learned that their only worth is sexual or who have developed no internal fortitude as a result of sexual trauma and so fall prey to prostitution is not, in our review of the evidence, convincing. As Roger Matthews (1986) writes:

> Prostitution and kerb-crawling may be far more "opportunistic" crimes than is generally imagined ... The continued prevalence of prostitution and kerb-crawling over some areas in recent years is probably less a function of the "intractable" nature of the problem than a consequence of the limited methods which have been employed to deal with it.

The second control strategy is to view the adolescent prostitute population as socially differentiated on the issue of vulnerability to abuse. Some adolescents might justifiably be thought to be endangering themselves through prostitution by virtue of their age or mental health. In these cases, the experience of the police has been that arrest is usually necessary to confine such youths to try to make them receptive to advice from social workers regarding the hazards of their circumstances. In some jurisdictions, agency workers employ the police to target juveniles before they become entrenched in street life, since juveniles are typically uninterested in voluntarily leaving the fast pace, easy money, late nights, and street camaraderie. From this perspective, limiting the adolescent prostitution trade through a general embargo would further the social-welfare objective. This would require deterring both sellers and their customers by making the risk of personal apprehension certain or predictable, and by making punishment meaningful in terms of personal costs. A regime of infrequent arrests penalized by small fines is viewed by the sex trade as an informal licence, a cost of doing business, and consequently an ineffectual intervention. Arresting johns appears to be a far more effective strategy.

There has been a move in Toronto, Ottawa, and Edmonton to divert individuals arrested for communication from the criminal courts to john "schools" (Duchesne, 1999: 251), where they are lectured on the risks of STDs (sexually transmitted disease) and the negative impact of prostitution on the "sellers" and on communities. The accused avoids a criminal conviction and is required to pay a "tuition" fee of several hundred dollars. Ironically, the very thing the "schools" are designed to eradicate—prostitution—is not actually forbidden in the Criminal Code. In addition, the gender neutrality of the communication law is superseded by a focus on men. Other cities have experimented with publishing the names of johns arrested for communication (Winnipeg), seizing the cars of johns (Winnipeg), and sending "dear john" letters to men observed "kerb crawling" on known strolls (Edmonton). The long-term effectiveness of such policies is unknown. The existing rate of recidivism for communication is already quite low.

## CRIMINALIZING COMMUNICATION BUT NOT PROSTITUTION?

This brings us to the first of two basic conundrums—the paradox of criminalizing **communication** as opposed to prostitution itself. Since we confine police control to the suppression of soliciting (and, until recently, have tended to target the sellers more than the customers), penalties can never in principle be very serious, since the charge is only a summary conviction matter (i.e., tried in lower court with minimal penalties). Communication consists of speech in public, and speech by itself has never been viewed as very harmful. In the aftermath of the 1982 Charter, which guarantees freedom of expression, including commercial expression, proscriptions against publicly contracting to conduct a lawful transaction (i.e., communication for money for personal services) appear something of a red herring—and just one of several in this area (see Box 10.2). However, the issue may be deeper. Prostitution may cause "nuisance" not through immodest soliciting, or noisome traffic from clients, but through its proximity to communities that reject the public acknowledgement that sex is recreation, that sex is entertainment, and that it can be had commercially, anonymously, and promiscuously. This appears to be part of the objection that the Fraser Committee described as the effect of prostitution on communities, families, and morals (Fraser, 1985: 348 – 50). Ostensibly, Canadian law criminalizes communication, not when it is indiscreet, but when it takes place on streets in an attempt to negotiate a contract for prostitution. Both in terms of the common law and in terms of the new constitutional framework, the law is not designed, and arguably *cannot be designed*, to deter prostitution effectively by limiting the nature of the advertising.

The Manitoba Court of Appeal suggests that the control of all activities except consummation of the contract is the preferable approach, since the latter would entail intrusion of police into the nation's bedrooms (and parked cars) in order to establish the requisite evidence (*Reference re Criminal Code Sections 193 and 195.1(1)(c)*, [1987] 6 W.W.R. 289). In this construction, the legality of prostitution is a legal fiction—since every avenue of its expression (save the transaction) contravenes other laws. Notably, the Supreme Court of Canada failed to strike down the communication law in the 1990 cases of *Skinner* and *Stagnitta*—a move that would have given some legal recognition to the right to communicate for the purposes of prostitution. In 1985, Parliament created powers by which the Crown could seize the assets of persons engaged in organized criminal activities (the proceeds of crime law).

## Box 10.2

## SOLUTIONS TO PROSTITUTION: RED HERRINGS OR VIABLE ANSWERS?

Red herrings are points that distract attention away from the main issue. When people talk about prostitution, a lot of conventional wisdom points to quick solutions. Are these solutions red herrings or do they go to the heart of the matter? In other words, do they colour the question of the social acceptability of prostitution with miscellaneous considerations? Consider the following examples:

- "Women only prostitute because they are forced to do so by pimps." This is a way of saying that prostitution is a form of white slavery, so that, presumably, there would be no prostitution without pimps (see McLaren, 1986). But it is possible to work as a prostitute without a pimp. And of course, if anyone is forced to do any kind of work under threat of physical intimidation and against his or her will, people would judge this unacceptable. Prostitution is no different. If coercion were eliminated, would that make a difference?
- "Legalizing prostitution just makes the government play the role of pimp." Since legalization appears to merely formalize coercion, this statement dismisses it. But doesn't just about everyone pay taxes to government? What does that make us? Pimping and state regulation are not equivalent.
- "Prostitution is the oldest profession—you'll never get rid of it." Sometimes this observation is called "impossibilism." It is reflected in a quotation from James Gray: "The best and most succinct definition I know of the world's oldest profession is 'promiscuous unchastity for gain'.... At the time of writing ... the Canadian Parliament is taking another run at eradicating, suppressing, controlling, containing—call it what you will—promiscuous unchastity for gain. This effort will fail, of course, regardless of how draconian the provisions of the new code happen to be, and for a very simple reason: such efforts have always failed" ("Introduction" to the Spectra Edition of *Red Lights on the Prairies*, 1986). The problem with this logic is that it is like saying that since we have always had murder and theft, we cannot do anything about them. Few people would find this line of reasoning compelling. Is prostitution different?
- "It is best to just bite the bullet and legalize it as a way of controlling it." If we accept that not everyone who might want to prostitute would be permitted to work in legal brothels—because of age, evidence of HIV infection, substance addiction, or coercion etc.—then it follows that the sex trade would continue to occupy an unregulated, illegal sector which would simply diversify the market. Escort services do not supersede the street trade. Why would brothels? Even in Melbourne, Australia, where brothels are legalized, street prostitution still occurs and is still contrary to the criminal law. Legalization does not preclude criminalization.
- "Prostitution must be regulated in order to protect adolescents from being sexually exploited." If there are grounds for thinking of prostitution as sexually abusive and exploitive because of the vulnerability of youth, why is this concern less pressing when young sex trade workers turn 18? A related question: for whom is it to say that the institution is exploitive?
- The point: Neither criminalization nor legalization offers easy solutions.

Among the specific areas enumerated by Section 462.3 in the Criminal Code were keeping a bawdy house and procurement—making it possible for the Crown to seize property or capital acquired by acts associated with prostitution. Neither the Supreme Court nor Parliament seems to be moving toward decriminalization or to a more permissive attitude toward the business of prostitution—in spite of the paradoxical legality of the activity, and in spite of such moves in other jurisdictions.

## MORAL ROOTS OF "NUISANCE"

Although the communication law was designed explicitly to eradicate the nuisance associated with street soliciting, there are grounds for thinking that that "nuisance" runs far deeper into moral areas than we sometimes admit. This is evident in discussions of land-use conflicts between people who would use the streets for communicating and those who would prefer to have their neighbourhoods free of the sex trade. Although couched in terms of land-use conflicts, these may actually represent competing values about the commercialization of sex. The ambiguity over nuisance is most explicitly evident, not in the Canadian sources, but in the British Criminal Law Revision Committee.

"According to police evidence heard by the Police Advisory Committee the nuisance to the public involved men being seen leaving the premises showing obvious signs of injury or distress, behaving indecently, vomiting in the vicinity and depositing offensive litter (such as soiled and blood stained linen) in nearby litter bins. The Police Advisory Committee heard details of a number of cases which make it plain that men who visit such places do so with the deliberate purpose of subjecting themselves to torture, humiliation and pain" (United Kingdom, 1985: 16). Here the "nuisance" of off-street prostitution was alarm over morally questionable conduct. The same ambiguity appears in the discussion of street soliciting: "What the law should be concerned with are offers, whether made by men or women, in circumstances which can cause a nuisance. We say 'can cause a nuisance' because an act of soliciting by a single prostitute or kerb-crawler does not necessarily amount to a nuisance; but when prostitutes and clients congregate in numbers, as commonly occurs, there is no doubt that this does amount to a nuisance. In this sense every act of soliciting has the potential for causing a nuisance" (United Kingdom, 1984: 4).

British thinking over nuisance is similar to the Canadian law on communication in this sense: although nuisance is the rationale for criminalizing the transaction, it is not an element of the offence. The crime occurs even if there is no evidence of harm to community peace and security. The discussion of nuisance is an indirect way of registering protest over conflicting values. A better remedy might be to make prostitution per se a summary offence—along with communicating—as is the case in most American jurisdictions, in order to clarify the heart of what we find objectionable.

One might argue in a contrary vein that the public should consider whether sex-trade workers who are *not* forced to work involuntarily, who are *not* working as a result of prior sexual abuse or mental incapacitation, who are *not* adolescents, who do *not* view the work as exploitative, and who are *not* a nuisance are entitled to have their services viewed in the manner of any personal-service industry, and to be freed from the array of criminal restrictions that surround the activities of prostitution. While common-law countries such as Canada have tended to resist the moves toward the legalization of prostitution that have been adopted in several European countries, two of the largest Australian states (New South Wales and Victoria, which share much of our common-law tradition) have moved in the direction of legalization. In 1984, Victoria removed the anti-brothel laws from the Criminal Code and permitted zoning for prostitution by local municipalities under a town-planning framework while controlling the exploitative aspects of the trade in the Prostitute Regulation Act, 1986 (Bryant, 1985; 1986; 1987). The provisions regarding prostitution in the Canadian Criminal Code appear to be directed at some of the negative aspects of the sex trade. Is it wiser to place the regulation of brothels under an urban planning framework and the exploitation of sex trade workers under a criminal law framework as has been done in Victoria? These matters are worth public discussion, particularly when we realize that prostitution already operates in many Canadian cities under the framework of municipal escort services that are duly advertised in the phone books and newspapers of virtually every city in Canada (see Box 10.3).

## TOLERANCE AND *DE FACTO* DECRIMINALIZATION

Although recent reforms to the communication laws have targeted purchasers—men in every case—there survives a permissive attitude toward prostitutes that holds them as victims. Certainly, the literature we have reviewed makes this point and emphasizes the need to decriminalize

### Box 10.3

### CALGARY OFF-STREET PROSTITUTION: ESCORT SERVICES

The Calgary By-Law Governing the Escort Industry By-Law Number 34M86

"Dating service or escort service means any business which offers to provide or does provide instructions, for a person or persons with another person or persons for a period of companionship of short duration for which said service or introduction a fee is charged, levied or otherwise imposed for each occasion the escort service is provided or each occasion an introduction is made."

A period of companionship of short duration?

**Source:** *City of Calgary By-law Handbook*, 1992.

offences by adolescent sellers. Penalties for sex-trade workers certainly have the potential to entrench them more deeply in the trade by incurring fines and stigma and by aggravating their marginality. In consequence, there is a recurrent attitude that suggests that prostitution ought to be viewed tolerantly. The conundrum is that, as a consequence of this attitude, men are permitted to continue to purchase the services of the sex-trade workers. The sympathy is ironically self-serving. Both the earlier paradox that targets advertising and the current one that encourages minimal intervention appear to *foster* prostitution (although in a legal and social twilight zone), giving it *de facto* recognition without providing those involved *de jure* protection. Prostitution continues to be one of the most dangerous activities in Canada (see Box 10.4). Social and legal progress is possible only by exposing these contradictions in order to deal with them more reflectively. Indeed, there has been a failure to mediate successfully the interests of all the key stakeholders: prostitute advocates who cherish the right of sex trade workers to legal recognition and protection (Pheterson, 1987); feminist critics who view the sex trade as degrading and exploitative and the workers as victims (Bell, 1987); and the wider community with its interest in the peace, security, and values of the affected urban neighbourhoods. The result is the contradictory tendencies we have noted in the laws and their enforcement. Even in feminist circles the conflicting perception of

## Box 10.4

## CARNAGE IN THE SEX TRADE

In Vancouver, twenty women involved in the street trade have disappeared since 1995, eleven of them in 1999 alone (Bailey, 1999). The local government is considering distributing several thousand free cell phones prewired to call 911 as a harm-reduction measure to increase the safety of street prostitutes.

In Calgary, from 1985 to 1994, some fifteen women involved in prostitution were murdered, seven of them adolescents. Two were murdered by pimps, three were killed in arguments about debts from narcotics, and the balance appear to have been abducted while working as prostitutes. During the same period, three prostitutes were murdered in Winnipeg. Most of these crimes remain unsolved (Brannigan, 1996b).

Between 1991 and 1995, 63 prostitutes were murdered in Canada (Duchesne, 1999: 249). In April 1999, Marcello Palma was indicted for the murders of 3 prostitutes in 1996 in Toronto (Mascoll, 1999).

Prostitutes are among the most vulnerable females in society. They are targeted frequently by male sexual predators, and are kept in line by beatings, threats, and murder by pimps. The underworld lifestyle and the illegal venues where they work make it difficult to clear their murders. Concerns for harm reduction have led community organizations to distribute condoms and free needles to limit the spread of HIV and other STDs. Harm reduction is behind the plan to distribute cell phones in Vancouver. These programs inadvertently support narcotics use and prostitution.

When we consider the extreme dangers of working as a prostitute, will harm-reduction policies force communities to consider fuller decriminalization policies, based not so much on worries about morality as on worries about the personal health and security of people working in the sex trade?

prostitution as work (Jenness, 1993) versus sexual slavery (Barry, 1979) continues to divide feminists (see Brannigan, 1996a for a review).

## SUMMARY

Public concern about adolescent prostitutes has resulted in a significant increase in media coverage since the 1980s and, as we saw earlier, a significant increase in the numbers of juveniles charged under the Young Offenders Act with soliciting for the purpose of prostitution. While adolescent prostitutes constitute only a minority of all YOA arrests, the absolute number of arrests suggests that adolescents represent a sizable proportion of the street trade. Evidence of high levels of pathology is found in the backgrounds of young people who leave home prematurely, but the link between prior abuse, personality disorganization, and the acquisition of a self-destructive lifestyle is far from being clear and far from being the only explanation for adolescent prostitution. Prostitution appears to be significantly linked to runaway behaviour and functions, along with other forms of delinquency, as a survival strategy, often of a transitional nature. In terms of the delinquency and victimological perspectives, the most prudent inference to draw is that understanding this conduct requires considering both perspectives. Adolescent prostitution is a delinquency engaged in by a very vulnerable population—vulnerable in terms of age and in terms of economic and educational status. To date, the major form of intervention in adolescent prostitution has been arrest by police, a solution that deals relatively swiftly with the delinquency aspect, but a solution that by itself can do little to meet the emotional, financial, and other needs of this population.

Part of the problem with the legal forms of intervention provided by the Criminal Code and social-service legislation is that they send mixed messages about prostitution. Prostitution per se does not attract arrest, but communication does—a peculiarity of the Canadian Criminal Code. The Code appears to be designed to curb the exploitative elements of prostitution, but society has very mixed feelings about the propriety of prostitution as a form of *work* even in the absence of such elements. Also, the social-welfare approach to sexual exploitation that lies behind the victimization outlook sets the age at which persons are considered to be at risk rather arbitrarily. As a result, *social-welfare protection* stops at *child welfare*—as though our obligations to vulnerable sectors of society ended at age 18. These legal ambiguities arise in part from the lack of social consensus regarding prostitution. The lack of a social consensus is an impediment to achieving an effective framework—criminal, welfare, or otherwise—that can maximize the needs and values of all the interested parties.

## NOTE

1. In North America, prostitution exists on the street in locations described informally as "strolls," which are frequented by customers, or "johns," typically driving cars. However, a thriving trade occurs off-street through escort agencies that adver-

tise as dating services in telephone directories and local papers. In addition, massage parlours are often fronts for brothels, and individual prostitutes often work in hotel bars. In Calgary, in the early 1990s, vice detectives discovered mobile "trick pads" in which parties were held and young prostitutes forced to service dozens of men. However, until recently public concern has been limited to only one part of the trade—street prostitution.

# WEB LINKS

**Male Youth Prostitution**
<http://www.virtualcity.com/youthsuicide/links6.htm#hustler>

This site offers a wide range of links to Canadian, American, and international studies on adolescent prostitution, with a focus on male youth.

**Prostitution Research Home Page**
<http://users.uniserve.com/~lowman/welcome.htm>

This is the home page of John Lowman, School of Criminology, Simon Fraser University. Although it does not discuss adolescent prostitution specifically, it does offer a rich list of reference and related material on prostitution.

**Street Kids**
<http://www.nfb.ca/FMT/E/MSN/17/17447.html>

This link provides a summary of the 1985 National Film Board documentary *Street Kids*, a 22-minute film that is well worth viewing. It deals, in part, with adolescent prostitution.

# STUDY QUESTIONS

1. Identify the two contradictory perspectives on adolescent prostitution. Develop a position that: (a) explains why this contradiction exists and (b) points to a way in which the contradiction can be resolved.
2. Describe some of the problems in defining what constitutes an adolescent prostitute.
3. In your opinion, what would be the pros and cons of decriminalizing adolescent prostitution?
4. In your view, what constitutes the "nuisance" of street soliciting?
5. Prostitution is often classified as a victimless crime. Do you think such crimes belong in the Criminal Code? Why or why not?
6. What are some of the problems in estimating the number of young prostitutes? Is adolescent prostitution getting worse? Explain your response.
7. What factors can be used to explain why certain youth drift into prostitution?
8. Quebec has traditionally viewed adolescent prostitution, not as a problem of delinquency, but as a child-welfare problem. Alberta is taking a similar approach in viewing adolescent prostitution as child abuse. What are the advantages and disadvantages of this approach?
9. What are the pros and cons of schools for johns? Should there be schools for prostitutes?

# REFERENCES

Alexander, P. (1982). *Working on Prostitution*. San Francisco: National Organization for Women.

Badgley, R. (Chair). (1984). *Committee on Sexual Offences against Children and Youths*. Ottawa: Supply and Services Canada.

Bagley, C., and Young, L. (1987). "Juvenile prostitution and child sexual abuse: A controlled study." *Canadian Journal of Community Mental Health*, 6(1): 5 – 26.

Bailey, I. (1999, 29 April). "A.B.C. Prostitutes urged to register," *Toronto Star*, A12.

Barry, K. (1979). *Female Sexual Slavery*. New York: Basic Books.

Bell, L. (1987). *Good Girls, Bad Girls: Sex Trade Workers and Feminists Face to Face*. Toronto: Women's Press.

Brannigan, A. (1996a). "The postmodern prostitute: A thematic review of recent research," *Criminal Justice History*, 15: 275 – 88.

———. (1996b). *Violence against Prostitutes in Calgary and Winnipeg*. Ottawa: Department of Justice, Technical Report No. TR1996-15E.

Brannigan, A., Knafla, L., and Levy, J.C. (1989). *Evaluation of Bill C-49 in Calgary, Regina and Winnipeg*. Ottawa: Department of Justice.

Brannigan, A., and Van Brunschot, E. (1997). "Youthful prostitution and child sexual trauma." *International Journal of Law and Mental Health*, 20 (3): 337 – 54.

Bryant, T.L. (1985). "Planning town and country brothels: Now red lights have the go-ahead." *Law Institute Journal*, March: 2020 – 205.

———. (1986). "Brothels revisited." *Law Institute Journal*, May: 442 – 46.

———. (1987). "Planning and social issues in the Prostitution Regulation Act." *Law Institute Journal*, September: 903 – 5.

Buys, H.W.J. (1989). *Report on the Sexual Exploitation of Children and Young Persons*. Strasbourg: Council of Europe, European Committee on Crime Problems.

Calgary. (1992). *City of Calgary By-Law Handbook*. Calgary, AB: City of Calgary.

Canadian Child Welfare Association. (1988). *Proceedings of the National Consultation on Adolescent Prostitution*. Ottawa: Canadian Child Welfare Association.

Duchesne, D. (1999). "Street prostitution in Canada." In *The Juristat Reader*, Ottawa: Thompson Educational.

Fisher, J. (1989). *Missing Children Research Project: Findings of the Study Executive Summary*. Ottawa: Solicitor General of Canada.

Fleischman, J. (1984). *Prostitution in Ontario: An Overview*. Ottawa: Federal Department of Justice.

———. (1989). *Street Prostitution, Assessing the Impact of the Law: Synthesis Report*. Ottawa: Department of Justice Canada.

Fraser, P. (Chair). (1985). Special Committee on Pornography and Prostitution. *Pornography and Prostitution in Canada*. Ottawa: Supply and Services Canada.

*The Globe and Mail*. (1981). "Montreal officials doubt 5000 figure of young prostitutes." 22 July.

———. (1987). "Crackdown on soliciting is boon for escort services." 28 September.

Goodman, L.A., and Fallot, R.D. (1998). "HIV risk-behavior in poor urban women with severe mental disorders: Association with childhood physical and sexual abuse." *American Journal of Orthopsychiatry*, 68(1): 73 – 83.

Hagan, J., and McCarthy, B. (1998). *Mean Streets: Youth Crime and Homelessness*. Cambridge: Cambridge University Press.

Hancock, L. (1985). *The Involvement of Young Persons in Prostitution*. Melbourne, Australia: Crown Law Office.

Infoglobe Search. (1999). Search tool. Available online at www.infoglobe.net/

Jenness, V. (1993). *Making It Work: The Prostitutes' Rights Movement in Perspective*. New York: de Gruyter.

Kufeldt, K., and Nimmo, M. (1987). "Youth on the street: Abuse and neglect in the eighties." *Child Abuse and Neglect*, 11: 531 – 43.

Martin, D. (1999, 16 June). "Three-day lock-up gives young hookers fresh start in life." *Calary Herald*, A23.

Mascoll, P. (1999, 29 April). "Accused man admits he killed prostitutes." *Toronto Star*, B1.

Mathews, F. (1988). *Familiar Strangers: A Critical Study of Adolescent Involvement in Prostitution*. Toronto: Central Toronto Youth Services.

———. (1993). "Adolescent (juvenile) prostitution." Speech to the National Meeting on Prostitution in Canada, 10 May. Calgary, AB, Federation of Canadian Municipalities.

Matthews, R. (1986). *Policing Prostitution: A Multi-Agency Approach*. London: Centre of Criminology Series, Middlesex Polytechnic.

McCaghy, C., and Berenbaum, T. (1983). "Child pornography: The rise of a social problem." American Society of Criminology, Annual Meetings, November, Denver, CO.

McCarthy, W. (1990). "Life on the street: Serious theft, drug selling and prostitution among homeless youth." PhD diss., University of Toronto.

McLaren, J.P.S. (1986). "Chasing the social evil: Moral fervour and the evolution of Canada's prostitution laws, 1867 – 1917." *Canadian Journal of Law and Society*, 1: 125 – 66.

Neave, M. (1985). *Inquiry into Prostitution Final Report*. 2 vols. Melbourne, Australia: Crown Law Office.

Pheterson, G. (Ed.). (1987). *A Vindication of the Rights of Whores*. Seattle: Seal Press.

Ritch, A., and Michaud, M. (1985). *Juvenile Prostitutes—A Profile*. Vancouver: West Coast Consultants.

Rogers, R. (1990). *Reaching for Solutions: The Summary Report of the Special Advisor to the Minister of National Health and Welfare on Child Sexual Abuse in Canada*. Ottawa: Supply and Services Canada.

Ross, C.A., Anderson, J., Heber, S., and Norton, R.G. (1990). "Dissociation and abuse among multiple-personality patients, prostitutes and exotic dancers." *Hospital Community Psychiatry*, 41(3): 328 – 30.

Silbert, M.H., and Pines, A. (1982). "Entrance into prostitution." *Youth and Society*, 13: 471 – 500.

United Kingdom. Criminal Law Revision Committee. (1984). *Sixteenth Report: Prostitution in the Street*. London: HMSO.

———. (1985). *Seventeenth Report: Off-Street Prostitution*. London: HMSO.

Van Brunschot, E., and Brannigan, A. (1999). "Childhood maltreatment and subsequent conduct disorders: The case of female prostitution." Annual Meetings of American Society of Criminology, Toronto, 16 – 29 November.

Visano, L. (1987). *This Idle Trade*. Concord, ON: VitaSano Books.

## CASES CITED

*Hutt* v. *R.* (1978), 38 C.C.C. (2d) 418 (S.C.C.).

*Westendorp* v. *R.* (1983), 2 C.C.C. (3d) 330 (S.C.C.).

# Chapter 11

# Adolescent Sexual Offenders

GARY BRAYTON

## KEY OBJECTIVES

After reading this chapter, you should be able to:

- define sexual assault;
- identify sexual **paraphilia** associated with adolescent sexual perpetrators;
- understand the psychological and sociological explanations for sexually assaultive behaviour;
- list characteristics of adolescent sexual perpetrators;
- summarize the available treatments and intervention strategies for adolescent sexual perpetrators.

## KEY TERMS

assault
cognitive-behavioural therapy (CBT)
disturbed impulsives
learning theory
naïve experimenters
paraphilia
peer group influenced
pro-social skills
Section 13
sexual aggressives
sexual assault
sexual compulsives
undersocialized child exploiters

## INTRODUCTION

Much has been written and said about young people who are victims of sexual abuse. In Canada, the gravity of such behaviour became public knowledge with the release of the Badgley Report in 1984. This study found that 53.5 percent of the women surveyed (one in two) and 30.6 percent of the men surveyed (one in three) had experienced unwanted sexual acts while under the age of 18. Since then, numerous other studies have reported similar findings. In response to these alarming statistics, researchers and various lobby groups were instrumental in having amendments made to the Criminal Code that are intended to protect young people from sexual assault.

While the concern with adult sexual victimization of young people has resulted in higher levels of social awareness, adolescent sexual offenders have been largely overlooked. For many years, adolescents who committed sexual assault were not regarded as serious offenders. Their behaviour was often dismissed as innocent sexual experimentation, so they were rarely held accountable from a legal or social perspective. Furthermore, the response from the community indirectly reinforced the continuation of undesirable and exploitative behaviour.

Nothing in the field of youth crime is more perplexing than the question of why an adolescent would sexually assault another child or an adult. What drives young people to use sex as a weapon against others?

For many years, the sexual behaviour of male youths was ignored or accepted as a rite of passage into manhood. Society did not take seriously the impact of sexually assaultive behaviour, let alone acts committed by young offenders. In turn, parents frequently denied or minimized their child's actions, further impeding intervention and management of the behaviour. Many parents today continue to deny the severity of these offences. Today, the youth courts no longer minimize the seriousness of sexual assault. This is evident in the increasing number of dispositions requiring young sexual offenders to undergo special counselling.

Ryan and Lane (1991) suggest that adolescents who commit sexual offences are caught in a cycle that perpetuates itself. These adolescents are frequently victims of emotional, psychological, and sexual abuse, and are simply repeating on others many of the acts inflicted upon themselves. A recent document from Health Canada (1999: 1) points out that adolescent sex offenders

**Box 11.1**

**ADOLESCENT SEX OFFENDER DECLARED DANGEROUS OFFENDER**

In 1999, a 17-year-old male from Quesnel, BC, was declared Canada's youngest dangerous offender. The youth had been charged with the brutal sexual assault of a 3-month-old infant. The infant was so badly injured that it required reconstructive surgery. When the offender, Adam Laboucan, was 11, he confessed to drowning a 3-year-old. Ironically, there were no services available for him at the time.

The case was raised to adult court in spite of testimony indicating that he had been the victim of poverty, abuse, neglect, and systematic discrimination against aboriginal people. In addition, Laboucan suffers from a variety of personality disorders, including limited intellectual functioning.

Laboucan was sentenced to 3 – 4 years to be followed by 10 years of close supervision.

**Source:** N. Horner, "Teenage sex offender locked up indefinitely," *Calgary Herald*, 19 June 1999, p. A6.

are not defined by their socio-economic, ethnocultural, or religious background, or by their intellectual functioning or motivation. In other words, trying to define an adolescent sex offender "can sometimes be difficult." Without intervention by the courts and social-service agencies, these young people are trapped in a cycle of compensatory behaviours and illogical distortions that result in sexually offending and reoffending behaviours. Should they be charged and ordered into treatment, or should they be diverted from the justice system, thereby reducing the effects of labelling? Brayton (1991b) supports the notion that external controls are often needed, both in order to hold the young person accountable, and to motivate him or her to begin and maintain treatment. This process is needed to counteract the rationalization, minimization, and denial patterns presented by many perpetrators.

This chapter examines the nature of sexually assaultive behaviour from a legal and clinical perspective. In addition, it differentiates adolescent offenders by the nature and compulsivity of their behaviour.

Holding young people responsible for their sexually offending behaviour is imperative if we are to begin to address this troubling phenomenon. Using the judicial process to obtain probation dispositions mandating treatment for sex offenders is essential to deal with the many treatment issues presented by such offenders. Understanding the nature of sexually offending behaviour from a legal, psychological, and sociological perspective enables us to realistically examine the role of the justice system in facilitating interventions designed to help the offender alter such behaviour.

In this chapter, we begin by defining the legal term "sexual assault" before examining the extent of this behaviour among young people. Then we explore the causes and origins, or mitigating factors, of sexually deviant behaviour. Finally, using O'Brien's typology (1984), we review the different types of adolescent sex offenders. The chapter concludes with a discussion of the generic treatment issues for all adolescent sexual offenders.

## WHAT IS SEXUAL ASSAULT?

### LEGAL DEFINITION

In general terms, assault implies the intentional use of force on another person against his or her will. This could include touching, slapping, kicking, punching, or pushing. A **sexual assault** occurs when a person forces another person to engage in sexual contact, or bribes, tricks, or coerces another person into participating in a sexual act.

In 1983, the term "rape" was replaced in the Criminal Code with the gender-neutral, multilevel offence of sexual assault (see Box 11.2). Even though the list of offences is directed toward adult offenders, they also apply to adolescent offenders.

On 1 January 1988, with the passing of Bill C-15, amendments to the Criminal Code and Canada Evidence Act, legal protection was given to children in the same manner afforded to adults.

## Box 11.2
## SEXUAL OFFENCES IN THE CRIMINAL CODE

### Section 151—Sexual Interference

This section deals with the touching, directly or indirectly, of any part of the body of a child under the age of 14, for a sexual purpose.

### Section 155—Incest

Having sexual intercourse or sexual contact with a blood relation.

### Section 173(1)—Indecent Acts

Exposing one's genitals in public and/or masturbating in public in the presence of one or more persons.

### Section 173(2)—Exposing Genitals to a Child

Any person who exposes their genitals to a child under the age of 14.

### Section 271—Sexual Assault

Applying force of a sexual nature.

### Section 272—Sexual Assault with a Weapon, Threats to a Third Party, or Causing Bodily Harm

The commission of a sexual assault while carrying, using, or implying use of a weapon.

Other relevant Criminal Code sections include Section 152—Invitation to Sexual Touching, Section 153—Sexual Exploitation (an extension of Sections 151 and 152), and Section 273—Aggravated Sexual Assault. In addition, Part V of the Criminal Code includes sexual offences considered to be relatively "victimless" (e.g., Section 174—Simple Nudity, and Section 175—Causing Disturbance, Indecent Exhibition).

## CONSENT

Sexual activity without consent is always a crime, regardless of the age of the individual. However, the Criminal Code now recognizes the need to protect young people and has categorized the concept of consent accordingly. For example:

- Children under 12 years of age are *never* considered able to consent to sexual activity.
- Children aged 12 or older, but under 14, are deemed unable to consent to sexual activity except under specific circumstances involving sexual activity with their peers.

- Young persons between the ages of 14 through 18 can be considered to have been sexually exploited if the offender is in a position of trust or authority (Wells, 1990: 15).

With these changes to the Criminal Code and Canada Evidence Act, children may enjoy the same protection that adults have before the law, but the changes do little to protect adolescents from becoming sex offenders. This area still requires considerable attention. Intervention, treatment, and prevention strategies are limited, and legal intervention may not be appropriate in all cases. Before we explore some of these elements, let us look at the prevalence of the behaviour.

## PREVALENCE OF ADOLESCENT SEXUAL OFFENDERS

In Canada, the Committee of Sexual Offenses Against Children and Youth (Badgley, 1984) reported that one in two females and one in three males would be the victim of unwanted sexual acts at some point in their lives. Specifically, three in four females and one in four males revealed being sexually abused before the age of 16 (Marymound Family Resource Centre, 1992).

More recently, Health Canada (1999: 2) reports that between 15 percent and 35 percent of all sex offences in Canada are committed by persons, predominately males, under 21 years of age. In the past few years, findings obtained from child-welfare agencies, hospitals, and various treatment facilities, across the country, indicate "that females comprise 3 percent – 10 percent of the adolescent sex offender population" (Health Canada, 1999: 3). Yet, trying to obtain an accurate account from such victims is difficult, as reporting is influenced by such factors as embarrassment, concern about bringing shame to the family, fear of parental reaction, and/or perceptions that such behaviour maybe harmless curiosity or simple experimentation.

The Badgley Report (1984) noted that 14.9 percent of convicted sexual offenders were under the age of 21. A National Police Survey also completed in 1984 indicated that one-third of all suspected sex offenders in Canada were under the age of 21 (cited in Badgley, 1984).

Becker et al. (1986), in a survey of centres treating child and adult victims of sexual assault, found that up to 56 percent of the perpetrators were under the age of 18. Similar results were reported by Abel and Rouleau (1990) who, in a study of 561 male offenders, found that 53.6 percent reported the onset of at least one deviant sexual interest prior to the age of 18. Of this percentage, each adult offender reported two different paraphilias, or deviations, and an average of 38 sex offences by the time they reached adulthood, while the adolescent perpetrators revealed 1.9 paraphilias and 7 sex offences, with child molesting and rape accounting for over 54 percent of the deviant acts.

In a study of 35 adolescent sexual perpetrators, the Marymound Family Resource Centre (1992) found the average age of onset of first deviant sexual interest was 12.6 years. However, nearly 3 percent were only 8 years of age, while 14-year-olds accounted for the greatest percentage (25.7 percent). The Health Canada report (1999: 2) reveals that most adolescent sex offenders are older than their victims and, like adult sex offenders, tend to use force and threat, trickery, bribery, or blackmail when victimizing those younger than themselves.

As Carnes (1984) observed, the addictive nature of sexually assaultive behaviour can lead to increased deviant activity. And as evidenced in the few studies conducted in the area of adolescent sexual perpetrators, sexually assaultive behaviour can begin at an early age. Without adequate legal and clinical intervention, the chances of this behaviour continuing into adulthood are quite high.

## SEXUAL BEHAVIOURS VERSUS SEXUAL DEVIANCE

When young people are exposed to sexually explicit scenes on television and in movies, in books and magazines, and, more recently, through the Internet, how are they to discern what is acceptable behaviour? Where do we draw the line between sexual experimentation and sexual exploitation?

While it is relatively easy to identify acts of sexual contact, it is more difficult to define inappropriate sex acts. Sexual contact can include behaviours or activities ranging from exposing genitals and/or breasts; to oral sex, vaginal and anal penetration; to watching others engage in sexual activity. While the issue of legal consent defines the appropriateness of the act, what other criteria can we use to differentiate between acceptable and unacceptable sexual behaviour? When and how do certain acts become defined as sexually deviant or, ultimately, criminal?

According to Sacco (1988), defining deviance has met and continues to meet with considerable disagreement. Holmes (1991) has identified four standards that can be used to define or determine "normalcy" (see Table 11.1).

It should be apparent that any sexual act must take into account both the behaviour itself and the process by which it becomes inappropriate in a

**Table 11.1**

**STANDARDS OF SEXUAL BEHAVIOUR**

| Standard | Description |
|---|---|
| **Statistical** | What most people do |
| **Religious** | What one's religion permits or prohibits |
| **Cultural** | What one's culture encourages or discourages |
| **Subjective** | Persons judge their own behaviour |

**Source:** R. Holmes, *Sex Crimes* (Newbury Park, CA: Sage Publications, 1991), p. 2. Reprinted by permission of Sage Publications, Inc.

particular society (Sacco, 1988). However, Holmes found that, while sexually deviant acts had four common elements, any sexually active person is likely to display the same elements. These include sexual fantasy and symbolism (e.g., using sex to sell cars, beer, and even household appliances), ritualism (couples can often sense when their partners are receptive by the words spoken, clothes worn, gestures made, or other behavioural expressions), and compulsion (individuals experience something and just have to tell their partners how much they care about them). The difference between normal and perverse sexual acts involves a combination of Holmes's standards. Ultimately, notwithstanding the most perverse acts, deviant sexual behaviour is relative and evolves over time, and should always be gauged against the values, norms, and needs of society. Table 11.2 illustrates the relative and evolutionary nature of "normal" sexual conduct.

In summary, definitions of sexual behaviours and sexual deviance have changed not only through the ages, but within society relative to social, cultural, religious, and personal beliefs and experiences. What is considered "normal" behaviour is subject to much debate; however, our values and norms dictate that certain forms of sexual conduct are not only socially inappropriate but criminal as well.

Next we examine whether sexual deviance is a paraphilia, and, if so, the ramifications for dealing with the adolescent perpetrator.

## PARAPHILIA

The American Psychiatric Association (APA, 1997: 493) defines paraphilia "as recurrent, intense sexual urges, fantasies, or behaviors that involve

**Table 11.2**

**SEX THROUGH THE AGES**

| Family Types | "Sexual Normalcy" |
|---|---|
| **Hebrew** | Before the time of Christ, sex was primarily reserved for procreation and the pleasure of the male. |
| **Greek** | Ancient Greece viewed sex as being recreational and procreational. Homosexuality, lesbianism, hedonism, polytheism, etc. were considered normal. |
| **Roman** | The ancient Romans were the first to allow equal status for males and females. Sex was not only viewed as procreational but also recreational and fun. Both genders could enjoy each other's intimacy. |
| **Christian** | In early Christian times, sex was considered utilitarian. Sex was not meant to be fun but solely procreational. |
| **Current times** | Both sexes are freer to express and enjoy themselves. Sex is often based on love and strong affection for one's partner. |

**Source:** R. Holmes, *Sex Crimes* (Newbury Park. CA: Sage Publications, 1991), pp. 9 – 15. Reprinted by permission of Sage Publications, Inc.

unusual objects, activities, or situations that cause clinically significant distress or impairment in social, occupational, or other important areas of functioning." It is not uncommon for sex offenders to engage in several aberrant behaviours or paraphilias. *DSM IV* (1994) defines paraphilia as follows:

- Exhibitionism: sexually arousing fantasies/thoughts, urges or behaviours associated with exposing one's genitals to strangers. This is not uncommon in adolescent sexual perpetrators who engage in child molestation.
- Fetishism: intense sexually arousing fantasies, sexual urges or behaviour involving non-living objects (e.g., female underwear).
- Frotteurism: intense sexually arousing fantasies, urges or behaviours associated with touching or rubbing against a non-consenting person.
- Pedophilia: intense sexual fantasies, urges or behaviour involving sexual activity with children (usually under the age of 13).
- Sexual masochism: intense sexually arousing fantasies, urges, behaviours involving the act of being humiliated, beaten, bound, or made to suffer.
- Sexual sadism: intense sexually arousing fantasies, urges, behaviours involving acts in which the suffering of the victim is sexually exciting.
- Transvestic fetishism: in a heterosexual male, intense sexual fantasies, urges, behaviours involving cross-dressing (female clothing).
- Voyeurism: intense sexually arousing fantasies, urges, behaviours involving the act of observing an unsuspecting stranger who is naked, disrobing, or engaged in a sexual act.

Given that sexual paraphilias are the domain (principally) of the adult mental health system, adolescent offenders under the age of 15 or 16 are rarely given the "paraphilia" label. This is not to say they do not engage in such behaviour.

In my fifteen years of working with adolescent sex offenders, I have noted that many undersocialized child exploiters engage in voyeurism in addition to molesting children. I have also noted that mentally challenged offenders who molest children often engage in exhibitionism. Non-contact offences such as exhibitionism and voyeurism were noted in 87 percent of adolescent sexual offenders prior to the commission of a contact offence such as child molestation or rape (Wieckowski et al., 1998). In order to determine the presence of a paraphilia, certain criteria are necessary. The APA guidelines suggest that a paraphilia exists if the behaviour, or intense sexual urges, are evident for a period of at least six months, or the person has acted upon these urges, or the person is distressed by the fantasies and sexual urges.

In applying these criteria to a sample of 50 adolescent sexual perpetrators (who committed offences ranging from fondling to anal penetration), Brayton (1991a) found that 67 percent presented sexual behaviours that could be defined as paraphilia. It is interesting to note that in 80 percent of these cases, none of these paraphilia were identified as a presenting problem, nor were the adolescents charged by the police for these behaviours.

This implies that if a behaviour is not identified and treated, it will continue. People with these disorders have, on average, three to four different paraphilia (APA, 1997).

Wieckowski et al. (1998), in a study of 30 sex offenders between the age of 13 and 15, note that 70 percent committed acts of frottage, 63 percent committed acts of voyeurism, and 40 percent committed acts of exhibitionism. As Brayton's findings (1991a) indicated, few of the youths were criminally charged with behaviours diagnosed as paraphilias. Carnes (1989) defines paraphilia as sexually addictive behaviours that, without intervention, will progress to more serious sexually assaultive behaviours. There is evidence to support Carnes, in that a recent study of 30 adolescent sex offenders reported that 87 percent had a history of non-contact offences (e.g., exhibitionism and voyeurism) prior to contact offences (e.g., sexual assault) (Wieckowski et al., 1998). Therefore, it is essential that criminal justice investigators and clinicians examine the existence of paraphilia in the adolescent perpetrator before the behaviour worsens.

Mental health professionals must use caution in the diagnosis of sexual paraphilia. For example, in order for a young person to be diagnosed as a pedophile, he or she must be at least 16 years of age and be five or more years older than his or her victim. One needs to be cognizant of the tendency toward a self-fulfilling prophecy, yet at the same time recognize the importance of a correct diagnosis, in order to develop appropriate interventions.

## CAUSES AND ORIGINS OF ADOLESCENT SEXUAL MISCONDUCT

### LEARNING THEORY

Sutherland (1937) was among the first to emphasize the role of learning in the acquisition of deviant behaviour. He noted that learning takes place in intimate groups whereby one learns certain attitudes that are predisposed to deviant acts. The techniques and skills associated with the deviance are also learned. In essence, a preponderance of attitudes and beliefs support deviant or criminal behaviour. The rewards for this behaviour are greater than the rewards for compliance to social norms. Sutherland's account encompasses social process, social structure, skills, and cognitions that are acquired behaviours just like any others and are not signs of some mysterious psychopathology.

Finkelhor (1984) suggests that one of the motivating factors for committing a sexual assault is sexual victimization in childhood. If the perpetrator was a family member, the victim may have assumed the behaviour to be appropriate. Kahn (1990: 41) suggests that, "if this early sexual experience was arousing and exciting, and you want to recreate that experience of satisfaction and reward, you may seek out sexual contact with other children." Furthermore, if the perpetrator is not punished for the sexual violations, the victim may further perceive that the behaviour is acceptable. The victim then engages in the same behaviours that were perpetrated upon her or him. From the standpoint of social learning theory, then, the acquisition of assaultive behaviours and the attitudes conducive to committing the offences can be traced to either modelling or imitation.

Goldstein and Huff (1993) suggest that the models for such behaviours can be found not only in the family, but also in the television, motion picture, and printed media. Not only is such behaviour learned, but the mental, or cognitive, process associated with the continuation of these behaviours is also a part of the modelling process. Lane (1991) describes cognitive distortions as thinking errors or irrational beliefs. According to Marshall, Laws, and Barbaree (1990: 243), there is also evidence to suggest "that sexual perpetrators are illogical and simplistic in their thinking." Typical examples of cognitive distortions include statements such as "The victim asked for it," "The victim consented," "I did not hurt him/her," "He/she seems O.K.," and "He/she will forget about it." These distortions are designed to minimize the offender's behaviour in his or her own mind, thereby enabling the offender to deny responsibility or project it onto the victim (Goldstein, 1990). If this pattern is maintained, the risk to sexually reoffend will increase (Brayton, 1987).

In order to learn and maintain aggressive behaviours, a process of acquiring, instigating, and maintaining such behaviours occurs (Goldstein, 1990) (see Box 11.3). Acquiring a normative base that supports inappropriate sexual behaviour can occur through family interactions. Family systems that support through their actions the victimization and exploitation of family members through physical, emotional, or sexual abuse provide the adolescent perpetrator with a living laboratory of behaviours to imitate. A number of studies show that if an individual observes another person—the model—behaving aggressively toward another person and not being punished, this experience can make the behaviour seem acceptable to the

## Box 11.3

## THE CASE OF RICHARD

Richard, age 15, was convicted for sexually assaulting his 10-year-old sister. He had vaginally penetrated her on many occasions. Upon his arrest, he disclosed that his father had been sexually abusing him since he was 6 years of age. Richard assumed that the behaviour was acceptable because his father had not been punished. Not only did Richard acquire this aggressive behaviour through family influences, but he instigated his actions based on the model before him (his father). Richard maintained this behaviour through a series of cognitive distortions (e.g., "Children can consent to sexual contact," "I wanted to know what it was like to have power over someone else"). These distortions enabled him to not only dehumanize his sister, but to displace responsibility elsewhere.

**Source:** Gary Brayton, case files.

observer (Goldstein, 1990; Lane, 1991; Perry and Orchard, 1992; Ryan and Lane, 1991; Wieckowski et al., 1998).

## PRE-CONDITIONS MODEL

Understanding learning theory enables us to understand the factors or conditions that lead to sexually assaultive behaviour. Finkelhor (1984) and Kahn (1990) describe a number of pre-conditions that must be present in order for a sexual offence to occur:

- **Motivation.** The motivation to sexually offend occurs as a result of three factors. First, the perpetrator must be able to identify with the emotional level of his or her victim in order to prepare the victim for the assault. Hence, emotional congruence is required (Finkelhor, 1984). Second, the perpetrator must be sexually aroused by children. Kahn (1990) suggests that the perpetrator may have had an early sexual experience that was arousing and exciting, and so he or she wants to recreate those feelings. Third, there must be a blockage to normal sexual urges. For example, masturbation may not be an acceptable sexual outlet for the perpetrator because of moral or religious beliefs, or he or she may avoid sexual contact with peers because of a lack of confidence or social skills.

  Both Finkelhor and Kahn believe that all three factors must exist in order for the perpetrator to be motivated to commit a sexual assault.
- **Disinhibited internal barriers.** Our moral beliefs help us to behave in socially appropriate ways. According to Hirschi's social-bonding theory (1969), when an individual does not feel connected or attached to conventional norms and belief systems, there is a reduction in internal control mechanisms, resulting in reduced compliance with social values (see Chapter 2 for further discussion of sociological theories of deviance). Hirschi suggests that social bonds grow from social controls and internal controls that develop mainly from a positive connection to our parents. According to Goldstein (1990: 18), the weaker the social bonding, "the greater the purported likelihood of delinquent behaviour."
- **Disinhibited external barriers.** Kahn (1990) describes reducing external boundaries as a process of selecting and preparing the victim. This is frequently done through offers to baby-sit, to supervise children at the playground, or to take children on outings, for example. According to Kahn, a majority of teenage sex offenders commit their sexual offences while baby-sitting, when they have the victims alone.
- **Overcoming victim's resistance.** In order to overcome the victim's resistance, the perpetrator may have to bribe or threaten the victim into participating in the sexual act. In reality, because of the emotional congruence of the perpetrator to children, the offender's victims are gradually introduced to sexual behaviour through playing games. In order for perpetrators to break their cycle of offending behaviour, they will need to understand those conditions that contributed to their

actions. Operationalization of the pre-conditions model is represented in the work of Lane (1991) who purports that adolescent sexual perpetrators present sequential patterns or steps in their assaultive behaviours.

## STEPS TO SEXUALLY ASSAULTIVE BEHAVIOUR

Lane (1991: 109) suggests that sexual offending behaviour is compensatory in nature, because "the sense of being in control or having some power reportedly serves to decrease anxiety and substitutes for distressing feelings or thoughts." A feeling of powerlessness may originate in unresolved issues from childhood. Typically, many offenders have experienced some form of abuse or rejection. Consequently, they may feel emotionally vulnerable and that they have little control over their situation. Offenders thus use sex in a destructive manner to meet their emotional needs (Ross, Loss, and Assoc., 1988; Health Canada, 1999). Lane outlines eight steps that may lead to sexually assaultive behaviour (see Box 11.4).

Research and clinical observations demonstrate that adolescent sexual perpetrators present an alarming risk to the community. For example, Perry and Orchard (1992) report that the average adolescent sexual perpetrator can be expected to victimize 380 individuals throughout his or her lifetime.

## TYPOLOGY OF OFFENDERS

What are the differences among adolescent sexual perpetrators? Are all at risk of reoffending? A typological review may help to answer these questions.

Typologies can provide useful criteria for examining and responding to adolescent sex offenders. O'Brien (1984) has developed one typology that can be helpful in diagnosing an offender's risk of reoffending (see Box 11.5). In turn, this diagnosis can be used to decide whether placement in an institution or a community-based setting would be more appropriate for the offender.

Using an adolescent sex offender typology can assist judicial and clinical officials in the planning and treatment process. Coupled with assessment data, we can derive generic treatment areas that are common to the adolescent perpetrator. Some of these areas are examined in the next section.

## TREATMENT AND INTERVENTION

### JUDICIAL INTERVENTIONS

Sexual offences committed by adolescents are dealt with under the Young Offenders Act (YOA). Once an adolescent offender is found guilty, the judge has a number of options to consider. He or she can request a psy-

### Box 11.4

### STEPS TO SEXUALLY ASSAULTIVE BEHAVIOUR

1. **Problems.** Associated with physical, emotional, psychological, and sexual abuse; dysfunctional families; and academic and behavioural difficulties at school. Absence of or difficulty with peer group.
2. **Thoughts.** Self-perception emanating from the problems associated with family, school, peers, or community. Examples include feeling like a failure, a bad person, or the one responsible for family problems.
3. **Feelings.** About self and the situation as a direct result of problems and self-perceptions. Examples include feeling sad, lonely, depressed, angry, and powerless.
4. **Revenge Thoughts.** Thoughts about actions designed to hurt the person(s) who have inflicted past pain. Examples include thinking "I hate you," "I want to hurt you," "I will get you back in some way," "You will pay."
5. **Control/Anger Behaviours.** Compensating for feelings of powerlessness and helplessness by, for example, putting others down, picking on less powerful people, hitting others, bullying others, running away, abusing drugs or alcohol, failing at school, and being noncompliant at home.
6. **Sexual Thoughts.** A "maladaptive, compensatory, power-based reaction style is developed to cope with feelings of helplessness and lack of control, and may eventually be expressed through sexual behaviours" (Lane, 1991: 118). Previous sexual victimization may trigger fantasies of increasing intensity until they result in acting out the fantasies on a real person. For example, a child in a blended family who resents the intrusion of the new parent and child may choose to sexually assault the child as a means of driving the step-parent out of the home. Such behaviour would be considered a maladaptive, compensatory, and power-based reaction.
7. **Planning.** Although many adolescent perpetrators will deny planning their assaults, it is evident that sexually assaultive behaviour involves a planning process, regardless of whether the planning took five minutes or two weeks.
8. **Sexual Behaviour.** The perpetrator carries out the sexual assault.

**Source:** S. Lane, "The sexual abuse cycle." In G. Ryan and S. Lane (Eds.), *Juvenile Sexual Offending, Causes, Consequences, and Corrections* (Lexington, MA: Lexington Books, 1991). Reprinted by permission of Jossey-Bass, Inc., a subsidiary of John Wiley & Sons, Inc.

chological assessment under Section 13 of the YOA. Data from such an assessment can assist the court in determining the risk of reoffending. If the risk is determined to be high, the young person can be detained in custody for a period of time (e.g., twelve months) and upon discharge serve another period of time on probation (such as twelve months). The judge may require the offender to attend counselling specifically for the sexually offending behaviour (see Bosco Homes Web link at the end of this chapter). In this way, the court not only holds the young person accountable for his or her behaviour, but also reduces the risk of him or her reoffending. If the young person does not comply with the counselling requirement, he or she can be brought before the court on a breach charge. In this manner, the offender must answer to the court for the non-compliant behaviour. For

## Box 11.5

## O'BRIEN'S TYPOLOGY OF ADOLESCENT SEX OFFENDERS

O'Brien and Bera (1986) developed a descriptive typology enabling practitioners to differentiate adolescent offenders by behaviours, characteristics, and family dynamics. The typology, although useful in ascertaining risk level and developing subsequent interventions, should not be the sole determinant in making clinical decisions. The typologies are described with case illustrations from the author's clinical practice (identifying data has been altered to protect client identity).

### Naïve Experimenter

The Naïve Experimenter is generally between the age of 11 and 13, with little history of acting-out behaviour. He generally possesses adequate social skills and achieves a degree of success both in school and in peer relationships. For the most part, he is from a functional and intact family system. His victims are younger children, and the abuse generally involves a single or several incidents of opportunistic sexual exploration. He often gains access to his victim(s) through babysitting or family activities involving young children. The sexually aggressive behaviour is often of the fondling nature and would not normally involve penetration. The primary motive is to explore and experiment with his new sexual feeling. Naïve Experimenters are generally responsive to intervention of an educational nature. They are low-risk offenders who can be treated safely in the community.

*The Case of Chris*

Chris, a 13-year-old, touched the penis of a 4-year-old boy while babysitting. Chris did not present a history of acting-out/pre-delinquent behaviour. Both school and peers were positive. His parents responded to the complaint appropriately and sought a risk assessment, and eventually a psychosexual educational program. The program focussed on human sexuality, relationship development, and victim empathy. He successfully completed the program.

### Undersocialized Child Exploiter

Undersocialized Child Exploiters gravitate to younger children (male or female) in search of acceptance, recognition, friendship and, in their own way, affection. They tend to come from less functional family systems, characterized by a distant or emotionally isolated father and a somewhat neurotic mother. Peer relationships are often conflictual or absent. They tend to feel isolated and alone. In addition, they may have experienced sexual victimization. Their abuse of children is compensatory in nature. They often exhibit a chronic pattern of sexual behaviours with younger children. Their offences are often planned, frequently involving manipulation, threats/bribes, and coercion to gain the participation and trust of their victims. Victims may be siblings or children they baby-sit. In fact, because they tend to get along well with younger children they are often sought after to baby-sit. Their sexual behaviour ranges from fondling to penetration. Depending on the number of victims, and range and length of offending behaviour, they may be treated safely in the community or they may require a specialized residential sex-offender treatment program.

*continued*

Box 11.5 *continued*

### Sexual Aggressive

Sexual Aggressive offenders are the product of a dysfunctional and abusive family system. They often present histories associated with child abuse, sexual victimization, and antisocial behaviour. They are frequently diagnosed with a Conduct Disorder and, to a lesser degree, Attention Deficit Hyperactive Disorder. They are often involved in substance abuse. They can be somewhat gregarious and display outward charm. They do not discriminate in victim selection; therefore, children, peers, and adults are all at risk. The sexual behaviour is often forceful, using threats and or overt aggression in order to control their victims. Sex is used to experience power and control as well as to displace aggression/anger. These individuals are difficult to engage in treatment and, for the protection of both the community and self, are probably best served in a specialized sex-offender residential centre.

*The Case of Jack*

Jack presented a long history of acting-out behaviour (e.g., fire setting, cruelty to animals, and school suspensions for fighting). He came from a home in which he was subjected to years of spousal and child abuse. He sexually abused his sister (e.g., fondling—multiple events) and raped a peer after physically assaulting her. He was incarcerated and, after his release, attended an out-patient sex-offender treatment program (group and individual therapy). He made minimal gains and reoffended sixteen months into his treatment program. The offence was of a violent nature, resulting in a period of incarceration in the adult system.

### The Sexual Compulsive

These individuals come from rigid and closed family systems. The parents are often emotionally and behaviourally repressed. They are motivated to commit their offences in response to anxiety and tension, and achieve the corresponding release while engaging in deviant sexual behaviour. They engage in sexually arousing behaviours of a compulsive or addictive nature (e.g., exhibitionism, voyeurism, obscene phone-calling, stealing female underwear). These individuals may be treated in the community; however, the nature, extent, and risk of escalation may require a residential sex-offender treatment program.

*The Case of Pete*

Pete came from a physically and sexually abusive family. He was removed at age 9 and placed in a number of foster homes. He began stealing female underwear at age 11. He has also engaged in peeping and calling the sex lines. He minimized his behaviour and does not see the need for therapy. In his mind there is no victim. He has been referred for a risk assessment.

### Pseudo-Socialized Child Exploiter

These are generally older adolescents (16 – 18) who possess good social skills and are comfortable but not intimate in peer settings. They present little history of acting-out behaviour. However, they are often victims of physical, emotional, and or sexual abuse. They are often bright students, but maybe underachievers. They typically view their sexual assaults as mutual and consensual despite their manipulation/coercion of victims. They feel little guilt and no remorse, and often maintain a mask of goodness and propriety for family and societies sake. Their sexual assaults range from fondling to penetration. They are difficult to motivate and are reluctant to engage in treatment. Depending on the nature and extent of their sexually abusive behaviour, they may be treated in the community or may require a specialized sex-offender residential program.

*continued*

Box 11.5 *continued*

### Disturbed Impulsive

These individuals often present a history of mental illness. Their sexual offending behaviour is frequently impulsive and often reflects an acute disturbance in reality testing. In addition, substance abuse and significant learning problems may be evident. Their offences may range from non-contact (e.g., exhibitionism and voyeurism) to acts of violence. Victims may be children, peers, and or adults. Because of their mental illness and or limited cognitive ability, the prognosis for control (without restrictive interventions) is poor. These individuals are best treated in a residential and/or psychiatric setting.

*The Case of David*

David was diagnosed as mentally retarded. He began to display sexually inappropriate behaviours (e.g., touching other children) by 10 years of age. At age 15, he was charged with the sexual assault of an 8-year-old boy (anal penetration), pleaded guilty, and was placed on probation. He received treatment on an out-patient basis (individual and group therapy) and was under psychiatric care for impulse and depression. He continued to struggle with impulse control, and finally was placed on medication to control his libido. He remains in psychiatric care, and, when in the community, is under constant adult supervision.

### Group-Influenced Offender

These individuals may lead others in the commission of a sexual assault or may assist in the assault (e.g., set the victim up). They have no history of antisocial acts and generally have a normal background. Victims are frequently peers (females). When caught, they tend to minimize their behaviour and or involvement in the assault. They often blame others or the victim. Generally they can be treated (safely) on an out-patient basis.

---

* Individual profiles are from Gary Brayton's case files.

**Source:** M.J. O'Brien and W.H. Bera, "Adolescent sexual offenders: A descriptive typology." *Preventing Sexual Abuse*, 1, pp. 1 – 4.

some adolescent perpetrators the external control of probation is required in order to motivate them to attend counselling. Therefore, intervention through the justice system is a critical component of the treatment process.

## CLINICAL INTERVENTIONS

In addition to a combination of individual, group, and family treatment, adolescent sexual perpetrators require a structured program that will, at minimum, address the issues directly associated with their sexually offending behaviour. Many clinicians working with these young people believe that cognitive-behavioural, action-oriented therapies and empathy training are more effective than insight-based models, such as individual or group psychotherapy or system-directed interventions (see, for example, Perry and Orchard, 1992; Barbaree, Marshall, and Hudson, 1993). The cognitive-behavioural approach has its theoretical roots in social learning theory (see Bandura, 1986) and cognitive development theory (see Kohlberg, 1973).

The term **cognitive-behavioural therapy (CBT)** has been applied to a variety of procedures that emphasize the importance of the role of both cognitive and behavioural processes in shaping and maintaining psychological disorders (Zarb, 1992). Cognitive-behavioural approaches assume that thinking processes mediate behaviour and that there is a relationship between these processes and arousal.

The CBT approach requires the therapist to take an active teaching, modelling, and challenging role. The therapist establishes a working relationship with the client, who is encouraged and challenged to practise new skills, some of which are listed in the next section (see Goldstein, 1990: 96 – 98 for a comprehensive list and review of the various cognitive approaches).

## COGNITIVE-BEHAVIOURAL TREATMENT AREAS

In order to effect CBT, the following generic treatment areas must be addressed with all adolescent perpetrators:

- Controlling deviant sexual fantasies.
- Altering cognitive distortions regarding victims.
- Identifying and understanding the physical, emotional, behavioural, and psychological consequences of sexual assault.
- Understanding how assaultive behaviour has affected the direct victim and the indirect victims (such as parents and siblings).
- Making amends to the victims through structured apology sessions, and making restitution.
- Dealing with their own victimization (e.g., unresolved feelings of anger, loss, or powerlessness).
- Identifying the steps involved in their sexually assaultive behaviour cycle.
- Developing strategies to break the cycle.
- Implementing and evaluating these strategies.
- Dealing with unresolved family issues.
- Developing pro-social skills (e.g., managing anger, building relationships, solving problems).
- Preventing relapse by developing strategies to deal with high-risk situations.

Patterns of denial and minimization of behaviour also need to be addressed throughout the treatment period. The length of time required to deal with treatment areas varies from person to person—twelve to eighteen months is not an unreasonable period of time.

Both individual and group therapies are desirable intervention modes. Using peer support and confrontation assists the achievement of goals. It is also important to build into the treatment program a follow-up component in order to solidify treatment gains and prevent any relapses of assaultive behaviour.

## SUMMARY

It is evident that the causes of adolescent sex offences are numerous and complex. A number of conditions need to be present in order to trigger offending behaviour. This chapter has presented a family- and learning-theory-based model as a clinical tool to understanding such behaviour and developing intervention strategies designed to control this behaviour. Recognizing that not all offenders are the same allows for individualized intervention. In addition, risk factors can be considered in terms of the need for treatment and the need for protection of society.

Identifying and treating adolescent sexual perpetrators is critical in order to break the cycle of sexual abuse. Using the youth justice system and appropriate dispositions under the Young Offenders Act enables society to hold young people accountable for their behaviour. Without court-ordered intervention, many offenders will continue to abuse and exploit vulnerable members of our society.

## WEB LINKS

**Adolescent Sexual Offenders**
<www.hc-sc.gc.ca/hppb/familyviolence/html/adosxofeng.html>

Health Canada offers some facts about adolescent sexual offenders from the National Clearinghouse on Family Violence, with additional information on intervention methods.

**Bosco Homes**
<www.bosco-homes.com/pages/paswinter991.htm>

Find out more about the treatment programs for adolescent sex offenders, offered by the Canadian-based Bosco Homes Web page.

**Central Toronto Youth Services Publications**
<www.ctys.org/twa/booksales/booksales.html

A comprehensive list of publications on adolescent sex offenders available from Central Toronto Youth Services.

## STUDY QUESTIONS

1. Identify three sections of the Criminal Code that deal specifically with sexual offences.
2. Define the term "paraphilia."
3. How does learning theory relate to sexual offenders?
4. What are the four pre-conditions to sexually assaultive behaviour?
5. Describe the steps in the cycle of sexual assault.

6. What are the differences between sexual aggressives and undersocialized child exploiters?
7. What role should the judicial system play in dealing with the adolescent sexual perpetrator?
8. What is cognitive-behavioural therapy?
9. What is the role of the counsellor in cognitive-behavioural therapy?
10. Identify five possible treatment areas for adolescent sexual offenders.
11. How might we explain the differences between gender prevalence?

# REFERENCES


Abel, G., and Rouleau, J. (1990). "The nature and extent of sexual assault." In W. Marshall, D. Laws, and H. Barbaree (Eds.), *The Handbook of Sexual Assault: Issues, Theories and Treatment of the Offender*. New York: Plenum.

American Psychiatric Association. (1994). *Diagnostic and Statistical Manual of Mental Disorders* (4th ed.). Washington, DC: American Psychiatric Association.

Badgley, R. (Chair). (1984). *Sexual Offences against Children, Vol. 1*. Ottawa: Government of Canada.

Bandura, A. (1986). "Learning and behavioral theories in aggression." In I.L. Katash, S.B. Katash, and L.B. Schleissinger (Eds.), *Violence: Perspectives on Murder and Aggression*. San Francisco: Jossey-Bass.

Barbaree, H., Marshall, W., and Hudson, S. (1993). *The Juvenile Sex Offender*. New York: Guilford.

Becker, J., Kaplan, M., Cunningham-Rather, J., and Kavoussi, R. (1986). "Characteristics of adolescent incest perpetrators: Preliminary findings." *Journal of Family Violence*, 1(1): 85 – 97.

Brayton, G. (1987). "Adolescent sexual offenders: A group treatment model." Unpublished PhD diss. Columbia Pacific University, San Rafael, CA.

———. (1991a). *The Adolescent Sex Offender: No Not My Child, A Guide for Parents and Caregivers*. Calgary, AB: G. Brayton.

———. (1991b). *Working Together: A Workbook for Adolescent Perpetrators* (3rd ed.). Calgary, AB: G. Brayton.

———. (1992). "Profile of adolescent sexual perpetrator offenses." Unpublished manuscript.

Carnes, P. (1984). *The Sexual Addiction*. Minneapolis, MN: CompCare.

———. (1989). *Contrary to Love, Helping Mental Disorders* (3rd ed.). Minneapolis, MN: CompCare.

Finkelhor, D. (1984). *Child Sexual Abuse, New Theory and Research*. New York: The Free Press.

Goldstein, A. (1990). *Delinquents on Delinquency*. Champaign, IL: Research Press.

Goldstein, A., and Huff, R. (Eds.). (1993). *The Gang Intervention Handbook*. Champaign, IL: Research Press.

Health Canada. (1999). "Adolescent Sex Offenders." Health Canada. (Online service <www.hc-sc.gc.ca/hppb/familyviolence/html/adosxofeng.html>)

Hirschi, T. (1969). *Causes of Delinquency*. Berkeley: University of California Press.

Holmes, R. (1991). *Sex Crimes*. Newbury Park, CA: Sage.

Horner, N. (1999, 19 June). "Teenage sex offender locked up indefinitely." *Calgary Herald*, A6.

Kahn, T. (1990). *Pathways: A Guided Workbook for Youth Beginning Treatment*. Orwell, VT: The Safer Society Press.

Kohlberg, L. (Ed.). (1973). *Collected Papers in Moral Development and Moral Education*. Cambridge, MA: Harvard University Press.

Lane, S. (1991). "The sexual abuse cycle." In G. Ryan and S. Lane (Eds.), *Juvenile Sexual Offending, Causes, Consequences, and Corrections*. Lexington, MA: Lexington Books.

Marshall, W., Laws, D., and Barbaree, H. (Eds.). (1990). *Handbook of Sexual Assault, Issues, Theories, and Treatment of the Offender*. New York and London: Plenum.

Marymound Family Resource Centre. (1992). *The Marymound Model: A Sequential Approach to the Treatment Of Adolescent Sexual Offenders and Sexual Abuse Victims*. Winnipeg: Marymound Family Resource Centre.

O'Brien, M. (1984). *Typology of Adolescent Sex Offenders*. Maplewood, MN: Program for Healthy Adolescent Sexual Expression.

O'Brien, M.J., and Bera, W.H. (1986). "Adolescent sexual offenders: A descriptive typology." *Preventing Sexual Abuse*, 1: 1 – 4.

Perry, G., and Orchard, J. (1992). *Assessment and Treatment of Adolescent Sex Offenders*. Sarasota, FL: Professional Resources Press.

Ross, J., Loss, P., and Associates. (1988). *Risk Assessment/Interviewing Protocol for Adolescent Sex Offenders*. Mystic, CT: Ross, Loss, and Associates.

Ryan, G., and Lane, S. (Eds.). (1991). *Juvenile Sexual Offending, Causes, Consequences, and Corrections*. Lexington, MA: Lexington Books.

Sacco, V.F. (Ed.). (1988). *Deviance*. Scarborough, ON: Prentice-Hall.

Sutherland, E. (1937). *Principles of Criminology* (3rd ed.). Philadelphia: Lippincott.

Wells, M. (1990). *Canada's Law on Child Sexual Abuse*. Ottawa: Minister of Justice and Attorney General of Canada.

Wieckowski, E., Hartsoe, P., Mayer, A., and Shortz, J. (1998). "Deviant sexual behaviour in children and young adolescents: Frequency and patterns." *Sexual Abuse: A Journal of Research and Treatment*, 10(4): 293 – 303.

Zarb, J. (1992). *Cognitive-Behavioural Assessment and Therapy with Adolescents*. New York: Brunner/Mazel.

# Chapter 12

# Aboriginal Youth and the Youth Justice System

LINDA FISHER AND HANNELE JANTTI

## KEY OBJECTIVES

After reading this chapter, you should be able to:

- outline the overrepresentation of aboriginal youths in the Canadian youth justice system;
- discuss the impact of history, colonization, and assimilation on the overrepresentation of aboriginal youth in the justice system;
- discuss the impact of the Young Offenders Act on aboriginal youth;
- discuss the implications of the Youth Criminal Justice Act for aboriginal youth;
- examine some of the programs aimed at preventing delinquency and crime among aboriginal youth;
- examine the need for cultural-awareness training for criminal justice personnel who are involved with aboriginal people.

## KEY TERMS

anomie
assimilation
colonization
cultural awareness
culture conflict
disintegration
institutionalization
Native Youth Justice Committees
overt discrimination
residential schools
restorative justice
social disorganization
systemic discrimination

## INTRODUCTION

Aboriginal justice issues have received an increasing amount of attention in recent years, as exemplified by the Donald Marshall Inquiry in Nova Scotia

(Harris, 1986) and the Public Inquiry into the Administration of Justice and Aboriginal Peoples in Manitoba (Hamilton and Sinclair, 1991) and the Royal Commission on Aboriginal Peoples (1993). Although there is a paucity of literature and data available on the extent and nature of crime involving aboriginal youth, the existing data paint a bleak picture. Statistics indicate that aboriginal youth in Canada are overrepresented at every stage of the youth justice system. For example, in the *Report of the Aboriginal Justice Inquiry of Manitoba*, aboriginal youth had more charges laid against them as compared with non-aboriginal youth, are more often detained before trial and for longer periods of time, are more likely to be sentenced to custody, and serve longer dispositions.

This chapter has several objectives. First, it presents the rates of involvement of aboriginal youth in the Canadian youth justice system. Second, it examines several factors that contribute to this overrepresentation, including the impact of past government assimilation policies, social disorganization and community breakdown, self-destructive behaviour, the youth justice system, the Young Offenders Act (YOA), and the Youth Criminal Justice Act (YCJA). Finally, this chapter examines the implications for intervention programs, which must take into account the cultural needs and backgrounds of aboriginal youth; in this discussion, examples of both preventive and treatment-oriented programs and services are examined.

## GENERAL POPULATION STATISTICS

According to Statistics Canada (1998), the 1996 census recorded that there are approximately 799 010 aboriginal people in Canada, (about 3 percent of the total population), the greatest proportion of them living in northern Canada and the Prairie provinces. As reported by Statistics Canada (1998), two-thirds of the aboriginal population were North American Indian, one quarter were Métis, and one-twentieth were Inuit. It is important to keep in mind, though, that these numbers are approximate only, and the actual figures could be higher.

It is interesting to note that the population of aboriginal youth in 1996 was ten years younger than the general population (Statistics Canada, 1998). The Canadian Medical Association (1994: 28) notes that the aboriginal population is, and will continue to be, younger than the Canadian population. In fact, in 1995, almost 50 percent of the registered Indian population in Canada was under 25 years of age (Department of Indian Affairs and Northern Development, 1997). Based on their assessment of aboriginal population statistics, the Department of Indian and Northern Affairs (1990b) projects that the number of status Indians age 0 – 17 will increase to 235 000 in 2011, compared with 172 000 in 1976 (a 37 percent increase) and the 14 – 17 age group will increase from 37 000 in 1986 to 52 000 in 2011. In 1996, there were about 144 000 in the 15 – 24 age group (Statistics Canada, 1998). By 2006, it is projected that this figure could increase by 26 percent. This change in population will inevitably have an impact on the criminal justice system, social services, and educational programs to aboriginal youth.

In addition to being younger than the general population, the aboriginal population has a life expectancy that is about ten years less than that of the average Canadian. The Canadian Medical Association (1994), in its submission to the Royal Commission on Aboriginal Peoples, noted that the rate of accidental deaths (injuries and poisonings) in many aboriginal communities is very high, as is violence, suicide, sexual abuse, and alcohol and other substance abuse.

It is also important to note that a substantial number of aboriginal people live in remote communities, accessible only by air (Yerbury and Griffiths, 1991; Canadian Medical Association, 1994). In addition, rural and remote communities may often have substandard housing and heating systems, inadequate health care, and inadequate firefighting equipment (Department of Indian and Northern Affairs, 1990a). As one can imagine, many houses fail to meet basic building-code standards, are overcrowded, and lack many or all basic amenities (Siggner, 1992). This includes what many take for granted, such as running water, indoor toilets, and baths or showers. Maslove and Hawkes (1994) report that, in 1986, the average number of persons per room in non-aboriginal homes was 0.54, compared with approximately 1 person per room in aboriginal homes.

There are a variety of other indicators that indicate that the life of aboriginal people in Canada is a disadvantaged one. As stated by the Canadian Medical Association (1994), aboriginal people in Canada are to be considered the most marginalized group in Canadian society. A very high proportion of aboriginal people live below the poverty line; they have higher unemployment rates, lower income levels, and, on average, larger families. These problems are exacerbated because, as Maslove and Hawkes (1994) point out, aboriginal people are much more dependent on government assistance than are non-aboriginal people.

These differences point not only to the disadvantages that aboriginal people face, but also possibly indirectly to their sense of hopelessness. Suicide is often recognized as an indicator of helplessness and hopelessness, a means used to escape life. The Royal Commission on Aboriginal Peoples (1994) reports that the rate of suicide for aboriginal people in Canada for all age groups is two to three times higher than the rate for non-aboriginal people. Even more alarming is the fact that the suicide rate among aboriginal youth is five to six times higher than that among their non-aboriginal peers. Furthermore, "statistical analysis predicts a growing increase in the number of suicides by Aboriginal youth as the 'population bulge' of children now under the age of 15 enters the vulnerable years of young adulthood" (Royal Commission on Aboriginal Peoples, 1994: 2).

While some improvements have been made, serious problems still exist. Poor economic conditions and the lack of available services have had a drastic impact on the lives of aboriginal people, including young people. As is discussed in this chapter, these conditions have had an effect on the level of crime and delinquency among aboriginal youth.

# ABORIGINAL YOUTH IN THE JUSTICE SYSTEM

## STATISTICS

The numbers of aboriginal youth, and aboriginal people in general, in the criminal justice system are of concern. Aboriginal youth are overrepresented at every stage of the criminal justice system: arrests, convictions, and populations in youth detention facilities (Department of Justice, 1991; LaPrairie, 1983; LaPrairie and Griffiths, 1984; Morin, 1990; Royal Commission on Aboriginal Peoples, 1993).

As pointed out in a discussion paper by the National Indian Brotherhood, Assembly of First Nations (Department of Justice, 1991: 2):

> A study entitled "Locking Up Indians in Saskatchewan" concluded that a treaty Indian boy turning 16 in 1976 had a 70% chance of at least one stay in prison by the age of 25. The corresponding figure for a non-Indian was 8%. Put into context, in Saskatchewan, prison for young treaty Indians had become the equivalent to the promise of a just society which high school and college represented to the rest of Canada.

One of the more influential indicators of this overrepresentation came out of a two-year study of a community of 20 000 in the Canadian North (LaPrairie, 1983: 343). The study indicated that

> Native juveniles are vastly over-represented in the juvenile justice system: that Native juveniles became involved with the system at an earlier age, and that the group was severely disadvantaged in comparison to their non-Native delinquent counterparts in terms of structural support.

The province of British Columbia provides an example of the overrepresentation of aboriginal youth in custody. Aboriginal people constituted 3.8 percent of the province's population according to the 1996 census; statistics are not available separately for those under the age of 18. The 1997 – 98 statistics for provincial corrections indicate that 20 percent of the provinces youth custody population was aboriginal (see Table 12.1). In the same year, aboriginal youth made up 17.2 percent of the bail supervision and probation caseloads (see Table 12.2). These figures demonstrate the overrepresentation of aboriginal youth in youth corrections, and underscore the concern over the current situation.

## CONTRIBUTING FACTORS

Why are aboriginal youth overrepresented in the justice system? Contributing factors include the role of history, economic and cultural disparities, and the present operation of the justice system (Hamilton and Sinclair, 1991). In addition, the YOA has contributed to the overrepresentation. The next section focusses on the general factors that help to explain the number of aboriginal youth in the justice system.

**Table 12.1**

**ABORIGINAL YOUTH IN BRITISH COLUMBIA: YOUTH CORRECTIONAL INSTITUTIONS, 1991 – 1998**

| Year | Number of Admissions | % of Total Admissions | Average Count | % of Total Count |
|---|---|---|---|---|
| **1991 – 92** | 501 | 20.6 | 70 | 23.3 |
| **1992 – 93** | 524 | 19.4 | 65 | 20.5 |
| **1993 – 94** | 609 | 18.1 | 64 | 17.8 |
| **1994 – 95** | 608 | 17.1 | 71 | 17.5 |
| **1995 – 96** | 696 | 18.5 | 72 | 18.0 |
| **1996 – 97** | 758 | 18.9 | 82 | 20.6 |
| **1997 – 98** | 843 | 20.0 | 86 | 21.8 |

Note: These numbers include both remanded and sentenced youths.

**Source:** Province of British Columbia, Ministry for Children and Families, 1999. Used with permission.

## The Role of History

In order to understand some of the present-day problems faced by aboriginal youth, it is helpful to have some knowledge of the historical context from which these problems have emerged. This includes the impact of colonization, forced assimilation, protectionism by a dominant society, and residential schools.

**Table 12.2**

**ABORIGINAL YOUTH IN BRITISH COLUMBIA: YOUTH COMMUNITY CORRECTIONS (BAIL AND PROBATION), 1991 – 1998**

| Year | Number of Admissions | % of Total Admissions | Average Count | % of Total Count |
|---|---|---|---|---|
| **1991 – 92** | 982 | 16.5 | 826 | 18.7 |
| **1992 – 93** | 940 | 16.4 | 727 | 16.4 |
| **1993 – 94** | 1057 | N/A* | N/A* | N/A* |
| **1994 – 95** | 1061 | 14.7 | 879 | 16.5 |
| **1995 – 96** | 1154 | 16.1 | 883 | 15.9 |
| **1996 – 97** | 1261 | 16.6 | 871 | 15.7 |
| **1997 – 98** | 1244 | 17.2 | 959 | 17.5 |

* = Not available.

**Source:** Province of British Columbia, Ministry for Children and Families, 1999. Used with permission.

**Colonization**, according to Yerbury and Griffiths, "has been an intentional, long-term process and has involved replacing the traditional, self-determinant lifestyle of indigenous people with a dependent and subordinate status" (1991: 321). In 1867, the federal government of Canada, through the British North America Act, consolidated existing laws directed toward aboriginal people in what is still known as the Indian Act, which gave the federal government extensive powers to control the lives of aboriginal people (Furniss, 1995). This included the development of the reserve system, through which federal Indian policy "explicitly sought to protect Native peoples in isolated reserve communities, where they would be sheltered from white encroachment and from the immoral influences of the rougher side of white frontier culture, and where Indians could be subject to government efforts to steer them into the process of cultural change" (Furniss, 1995: 22).

**Assimilation** was a formal policy of the Canadian government with respect to aboriginal people (Dosman, 1972). As stated by Pointing and Gibbons (1980: 17), a belief in assimilation as being in the best interests of aboriginal people was "the central pillar to Canadian Indian policy." The goals of this policy included the "civilization" of aboriginal peoples, specifically by introducing new values and beliefs as well as new skills such as farming and homemaking. Aboriginal peoples were to give up their traditional lifestyles, cultures, and belief systems in exchange for assimilation into the dominant European society that had settled Canada (Bull, 1991; Martens, Daily, and Hodgson, 1988). Aboriginal children were a prime target of this policy of assimilation.

The federal Indian Act required that aboriginal children attend **residential schools**, which were established by the government and operated by the churches from the early 1800s through the 1960s. In these schools, children were forbidden to speak their traditional language or practise their cultural and spiritual beliefs, and were severely punished if they engaged in these practices (Bull, 1991; Haig-Brown, 1988). As Haig-Brown found as a result of her research on the Kamloops Residential School in British Columbia, "Indian culture was never accepted by the school as a real, living culture. Rather it was seen as something archaic and undesirable, something to be annihilated" (1988: 53). In addition, Furniss (1995: 24) found in her study of the Williams Lake, British Columbia, residential school, that the "potlatch law was introduced in large part due to the lobbying of Christian missionaries in British Columbia, who realized the potlatch was a central cultural and political institution of Northwest Coastal societies, and thus stood as a barrier to the establishment of the missionary authority." This is yet another example of coercive legislation aimed at assimilation.

Separating the children from their families and communities had a devastating impact on many families. As stated by Martens, Daily, and Hodgson (1988: 110),

> the structure, cohesion and quality of family life suffered. Parenting skills diminished as succeeding generations became more and more

> institutionalized and experienced little nurturing. Low self-esteem and self-concept problems arose as children were taught that their own culture was inferior and uncivilized, even "savage."

The consequences of such segregation from families and of forced assimilation has been referred to as **culture conflict** (Martens, Daily, and Hodgson, 1988). Aboriginal youth became caught between two worlds—the world of Native communities and the world of non-Native society—with no solid footing in either world. Children who attended residential schools so completely internalized this institutionalization that they were unable to function as independent adults when they returned to their communities (Bull, 1991). As they grew older, they replaced the institutionalization of the residential schools with other forms of institutionalization, such as foster homes or imprisonment (Martens, Daily, and Hodgson, 1988). These experiences negatively affected aboriginal people's self-esteem, parenting skills, problem-solving abilities, and ability to trust others. The impact of these experiences has been summarized by Ing (1991: 114):

> The chaotic condition of the Native family is traced to the residential school education that caused this disintegration. There simply has not been adequate recognition that residential school education is a major contributing force to this disintegration. Consequently, the symptoms and social indicators of alcoholism, child and spouse abuse and neglect, prison incarceration, violence, and drug dependency are ineffectively dealt with.

The policy of facilitating assimilation via institutions such as residential schools has ultimately been devastating for generations of aboriginal families. Furniss (1995) provides an excellent account of how the focus on the Williams Lake residential school has led to a comprehensive police investigation into allegations of sexual abuse. This investigation, begun in the late 1980s, continued into the 1990s, with the Royal Canadian Mounted Police broadening it to include abuse at all BC Indian residential schools. The gradual disintegration of Native cultures has resulted in family and community breakdown; high rates of violent deaths, child abuse, alcoholism, and suicide; high rates of child apprehension by law enforcers; and poor social and economic opportunities both on and off reserves. The lives of aboriginal youths are particularly in jeopardy—they are the ones most susceptible to violent deaths, suicide, and alcohol and solvent abuse (Griffiths, Yerbury, and Weafer, 1987; Royal Commission on Aboriginal Peoples, 1994).

## Social Disorganization and Community Breakdown

A consequence of enforced assimilation has been social disorganization (Yerbury and Griffiths, 1991). Social disorganization is often the result of the breakdown of community social and leadership structures, including the internal social controls that help to maintain peace and harmony. Stressful conditions placed on a community may threaten the personal and social welfare of individuals—their lives, safety, social relationships, and mental health.

Social disorganization and community breakdown may also result in deviant and criminal behaviour. In her research on the community of Grassy Narrows, Ontario, and its forced relocation to a new reserve close to an urban centre, Shkilnyk (1985) found that crime was a means of escape for youth from the poor conditions of reserve life. As a result of the relocation and the loss of their traditional lifestyle, the youth of Grassy Narrows experienced anomie, or confusion about which norms of conduct to adhere to.

In his 1990 book *The Dispossessed: Life and Death in Native Canada*, York provides several accounts of how sociostructural deprivation affects the lives of aboriginal youth. York gives the example of bored teenagers on a remote northern Manitoba reserve who commit crimes in order to be sent to Winnipeg's Youth Detention Centre. He quotes an alcohol and drug counsellor who estimates that "30 percent of the reserve's teenagers are prepared to commit criminal offenses to escape the reserve" (p. 142). Youths turn themselves in or carve their names into walls of buildings they break into so the police will know whom to arrest. The result of these actions is that about 75 percent of the youths in Winnipeg's Youth Detention Centre are aboriginal.

## Self-Destructive Behaviour

Suicide, criminal behaviour, and substance abuse are often the means used to cope with stress and disintegration, and with the loss of self-worth and emotional well-being. Many youth turn to such abusive behaviour as a means of escapism. For aboriginal youth, additional stresses may come in the form of cultural problems, whereby they are caught between their traditional culture and mainstream society. As well as the inevitable boredom, there may be family pressures to remain on the reserve, uncertainty about the future, and a lack of opportunities for employment and education (LaPrairie, 1996).

As stated earlier, the suicide rates for aboriginal people, specifically aboriginal youths, are significantly higher. In an effort to understand such rates, the Royal Commission on Aboriginal Peoples (1994), in completing their report on suicide among aboriginal peoples, spoke to many aboriginal youth. They report that the precipitating causes of suicide are obvious and pervasive: "in the confusion they feel about their identity, in the absence of opportunity to make a good life, in the bleakness of daily existence where alcohol and drugs sometimes seem to offer the only relief" (Royal Commission on Aboriginal Peoples, 1994: 2). Furthermore, the commission found that aboriginal youth have to deal with a society that devalues their identity as aboriginal people and have few supports or role models in families and their communities to help them cope with the effects of colonialism.

With respect to crime among Native youth in Manitoba, Shkilnyk (1985: 30 – 31) states:

> Juvenile crime most often involves: wilful damage to property, break and enter, and theft. In 1977, young people were responsible for 96 percent of all the break and enter charges, 100 percent of the theft charges,

> 66 percent of the offensive weapons charges, 89 percent of the wilful damage charges, and 11 percent of the liquor offenses.

In explaining such patterns of crime, Shkilnyk concludes that youths who are repeatedly in trouble with the criminal justice system feel that no one cares about them, since they often lack guidance and love from others. In addition, the elaborate rituals surrounding puberty and the transition to adulthood that are a part of many traditional Native cultures have largely disappeared.

A vicious cycle often results among aboriginal youth, in which substance abuse and violence are used to relieve stress, and profits from crime provide the means to obtain alcohol, drugs, and solvents. The Canadian Medical Association (1994: 39) reports a survey of schoolchildren in 25 communities in northern Manitoba in which it was reported that 20 percent of the children had used solvents, and 4 percent were regular users. A similar survey in Quebec reported a rate of 15 percent for experience. The rates were two to three times higher than those reported for the general population in Ontario. Reasons cited for use of solvents included the ease of availability of gasoline and peer pressure.

In a compelling account, York discusses how gasoline-sniffing has taken control of the children of many aboriginal communities in Canada. The well-publicized case of Davis Inlet gave Canadians a glimpse of the despair these children face (see Box 12.1).

## The Youth Justice System

The youth justice system itself has contributed to the overrepresentation of aboriginal youth within the system through both overt and systemic discrimination (Department of Justice, 1991). Indeed, "a pressing concern among academics ... has been, and continues to be, the issue of disparity in the treatment of Native people in the criminal justice system" (LaPrairie, 1983: 337). The differential treatment of aboriginal people is reflected in their arrest and conviction rates, as well as the number of aboriginal offenders involved in the correctional system. A lack of understanding on the part of justice system personnel in regard to aboriginal customs, values, and traditions can translate into a dismissal of these cultural factors and of their role in the conduct of aboriginal people.

This lack of understanding of aboriginal ways and wisdom may be due to inadequate training in cultural awareness for those working in the youth justice system, or reluctance of justice personnel to undertake such training. Both of these reasons could be attributable to historical assimilation policies and the notion that the same process of justice should fit all. It is the lack of recognition of cultural differences and their importance that makes the youth justice system discriminatory toward aboriginal youth in conflict with the law.

A multitude of aboriginal cultures exist across Canada, so these cultural differences vary across the country, and from one First Nation to another. However, examples of such difference include willingness to provide a statement to persons in authority due to respect, and pleading guilty because it is interpreted "as acknowledgement of the facts rather than admission of

## Box 12.1

## ISLAND OF DESPAIR

*Even the children of two stranded Innu residents long for death in a place where "abnormalities have become normal."*

DAVIS INLET, NFLD. Charlie Rich points at the plastic bags lying on the floor of an abandoned waterfront shack. "Look," he says, tugging at the rope keeping his black Lab dog at bay. "Gas." Lying scattered about are a dozen corners of green garbage bags, cut wide at the top so kids can cover their faces and breathe in deadly gasoline fumes. Rich, 11, says he knows better.

"It kills," says the round-faced boy sporting an Irving tuque and a neon-green ski jacket. "They tell us in school."

About 42 of 340 kids regularly sniff gas in this remote Innu island off the coast of Labrador, where six teens high on fumes tried to kill themselves last month.

Youths have blown holes in their stomachs with shotguns. Some sniff gas until they're hallucinatory or brain-damaged.

Native leaders blame themselves and government policies over the past 25 years for such tragedy amongst their children, a generation that has limited knowledge of the traditional nomadic way of life.

"This is a place where abnormalities have become normal," says Peter Penashue, president of the Innu Nation. "You can't take a system that's already pre-packaged and apply it to Davis Inlet. It causes chaos. Kids are learning their culture is not important."

The lives here are filled with contradictions. Ramshackle, frigid houses with little furniture and no running water or toilets usually contain large television sets equipped with cable.

Parents remember living in tents as children, learning to hunt and trap. These kids watch Michael Jackson videos and ads for fancy toys, while they learn about confederation in school.

The Innu once hunted in the interior and visited the coast only to trade with Europeans.

They were moved to the north coast of Labrador just before Newfoundland joined confederation in 1949 as workers for the Inuit—a dismal experiment that ended in disease and death.

After two years they disappeared into the interior again but began frequenting a trading post at Davis Inlet. They became increasingly dependent on the community after the arrival of Roman Catholic missionaries who started a church in 1945.

"The priests were very much in control of their flock," says Penashue, who lives in another Innu settlement near Goose Bay.

"We gave up our spiritual beliefs. They started creating an elite back in the 1960s. We started believing they were radically superior to us. That's still the mentality in the church, the schools, the government and the RCMP."

By 1967, Davis Inlet consisted of 150 people living in four houses and 31 tents on the mainland. The community was moved several kilometres that year to the present island site, with promises of running water and a sewer system.

Those services never materialized and the community has grown to more than 500 people.

Since the move, the Innu say they've repeatedly been victims of bureaucratic struggles between the federal and provincial governments.

They've lodged a formal complaint with the Canadian Human Rights Commission over the issue.

Unlike some 9,000 Innu across the border in Quebec, Labrador Innu are not covered by the federal Indian Act. They want Ottawa to acknowledge they are entitled to the same programs and services as natives on reserves. Ottawa contributes about 90 per cent of funds that go to the village—more than $1 million a year—but the money is administered by the Newfoundland government.

*continued*

Box 12.1 *continued*

"We don't even know who we're supposed to call," says Penashue.

While Labrador's 1,500 Innu want to take control of their own affairs, they say they need direct help from Ottawa until self-government is in place and land-claim negotiations—currently stalled—have produced an agreement.

Most of all, the Innu want to move back to the mainland where there is room to expand and they will feel less isolated.

Government officials are studying a report that endorses the plan.

**Source:** Beth Gorham, *The Province,* 7 February 1993, p. A34.

culpability" (Mandarin et al., 1992: 16). These behaviours can result in differential treatment of aboriginal youth by the youth justice system.

Aboriginal people themselves perceive the justice system to be insensitive and discriminatory. Indeed, "aboriginal people believe they are dealt with more harshly by the justice system generally" (Department of Justice, 1991: 9). According to a federal Department of Justice report (1991: 11),

> clearly some aboriginal people have come to view the system as their enemy, a view too often derived from first hand experiences with the systems of child welfare, youth justice, family court and criminal justice. Thus, any approach to reform will have to address both overt and systemic discrimination.

The underrepresentation of aboriginal people as professionals in the youth justice system may further contribute to the sense of mistrust and alienation. For example, in British Columbia, in 1997, 2 percent of all adult and youth probation officers and correctional officers were of aboriginal ancestry (Province of British Columbia, 1997). In the province's youth custody centre, 26 out of 1500 officers in 1997 were of aboriginal origin (Province of British Columbia, 1997). The lack of aboriginal professionals in the justice system adds to the gap in understanding between aboriginal youth and the youth justice system.

It is clear that mutual misunderstandings and mistrust abound between aboriginal people and the justice system. The youth justice system does not understand or take into account cultural and socio-economic differences, and aboriginal people do not understand the workings of the system. These gaps in understanding must be addressed if we are to deal with the overrepresentation of aboriginal youth in the justice system.

## THE YOUNG OFFENDERS ACT

The Young Offenders Act (YOA) became law in 1984. While the newly proposed legislation, the Youth Criminal Justice Act (YCJA), was introduced in the House of Commons on 11 March 1999, it is worthwhile to note the impact of the YOA on aboriginal youth. The act emphasizes the *needs* of young offenders and the *protection* of society. It underscores youths' *responsibility* for their criminal actions. The YOA also protects accused youths' rights (section 3(e)). These goals are stated in section 3 of the act, the "Declaration of Principle" (see Chapters 4 and 5, and Appendix B).

The YOA also recognizes the importance of protecting accused youths legal rights (section 3(e)). While the provision of legal rights and safeguards is desirable, and while the public is supportive of holding youths accountable for their criminal behaviour, several concerns have been raised about the act's implications for aboriginal youth in conflict with the law.

First, focussing on individual responsibility and consequences can make it difficult to deal with crime and its impact in ways that include the community. Many aboriginal communities perceive community involvement as an integral part of both accountability and rehabilitation. Dealing with the aboriginal young offender as an individual, without encouraging community input and engaging the community in the sentencing of that youth, negates many aboriginal cultures' notions of justice, reparation, and healing.

Second, while the YOA emphasizes meeting the needs of young offenders through rehabilitation (section 3(c.1)) and through the use of alternative measures (section 4), and recognizes the right of youths to the "least possible interference with freedom" (section 3(f)), aboriginal communities often lack the resources to address the youths' rehabilitative needs. Consequently, aboriginal youths receive custodial dispositions that remove them from their communities (Morin, 1990; Hamilton and Sinclair, 1991). At the completion of the custodial disposition, youths return to their communities as outsiders, which may contribute to alienation from their culture and to a life of trouble with the law. Aboriginal communities require resources and the right to have input in sentencing so that young aboriginal offenders' needs can be meaningfully met.

Third, legal rights, specifically the right to counsel, may have little meaning for aboriginal youth due to a shortage of experienced legal counsel in many aboriginal communities (Department of Justice, 1991). In addition, as pointed out by LaPrairie (1983), non-aboriginal legal counsel lack sufficient understanding of the socio-economic and cultural factors that affect aboriginal youth; this brings the quality of the legal representation into question. The inability to appreciate and bring forth such factors throughout the judicial process can lead to both inappropriate and more severe dispositions for aboriginal young offenders (Doob, Marinos, and Varma, 1995).

In summary, while the Young Offenders Act recognizes the need to address youths' rehabilitative needs, in its application, it does not provide adequate and appropriate measures and resources to deal with the needs and legal protection of aboriginal young offenders.

## THE YOUTH CRIMINAL JUSTICE ACT

On 11 March 1999, Anne McLellan, Minister of Justice and Attorney General of Canada, announced the Youth Criminal Justice Act (see Appendix C), the newly proposed law that replaces the Young Offenders Act. The new act is an important part of the federal government's Youth Justice Strategy, announced in May 1998 (Department of Justice, 1999). The act addresses public concerns about youth crime by increasing the possible legal consequences for youths' criminal behaviour (Canadian Criminal Justice Association, 1998; Department of Justice, 1999).

Concurrently, the act acknowledges the continued importance of rehabilitation and the "use of effective, meaningful alternatives to custody for non-violent youth." As well, the act encourages involvement by victims and communities in the youth justice system (Department of Justice, 1999: 1). It is hoped that the commitment to meeting the rehabilitative needs of young offenders and to encouraging community input and involvement will translate into culturally appropriate programming for aboriginal young offenders. Commenting on the then anticipated new youth legislation, the Canadian Criminal Justice Association stated in November 1998 that "it is our hope that a greater number of programs for youth will be developed that incorporate the philosophy of restorative justice" (p. 5). Perhaps meaningful change for aboriginal young offenders in meeting their needs and in allowing for community involvement can be anticipated.

## RESPONSES TO YOUNG ABORIGINAL OFFENDERS

While the overall availability of programs and services for aboriginal youth may be limited, a variety of initiatives have been developed (Hamilton and Sinclair, 1991). These include role-model programs, youth-justice committees, rediscovery camps, Native youth court workers, and cultural-awareness training. Many of these programs directly involve aboriginal communities in developing and implementing community-based alternatives to the formal criminal justice system. Many of these programs also incorporate traditional Native methods of social control while increasing the cultural awareness and self-esteem of aboriginal youths (Henley, 1989).

As moved by the Aboriginal Justice Inquiry of Manitoba,

> we believe the answer to dealing with the problems of young offenders is to provide services that take into account the cultural background and needs of an aboriginal young person. These services must be supportive rather than punitive. Finally, they must be provided by aboriginal people and if that is not possible, by individuals educated to work with aboriginal people and to supply culturally appropriate situations. (Hamilton and Sinclair, 1991: 589)

Hamilton and Sinclair also stated that crime-prevention approaches for aboriginal people must take into account the culture of the community and the severe poverty, deprivation, and isolation faced by many aboriginal communities, and must endeavour to understand the causes of family dysfunction and the historical and contemporary situations facing aboriginal people. Building self-esteem, a cultural identity, and a positive association with being aboriginal are crucial steps to preventing aboriginal youths from committing acts of delinquency or engaging in crime.

The subsequent sections examine a number of initiatives developed by aboriginal communities and by the criminal justice system to deal more effectively with the unique problems faced by aboriginal youth.

## NATIONAL NATIVE ROLE-MODEL PROGRAM

This program, based in Kahnawake, Quebec, focusses on providing positive role models for aboriginal youths. As stated in the program's information pamphlet, the goals of this program are:

> 1. To provide inspirational and motivational materials to communities, organizations and Native people throughout the country.
> 2. To make Indian Role Models available to communities in order to:
>    a) Motivate and inspire young Native people.
>    b) Present lifestyles and achievements of Native Role Models as alternatives to drinking and other destructive lifestyles.
>    c) Provide young Native people with specific ideas for personal development and achievement.
>    d) Provide Native communities with the opportunity to help celebrate and enjoy the accomplishments of some of their more visible, accomplished young people. (Kahnawake Social Services, n.d.)

Former role models include actress Margo Kane, actor/dancer/weaver Evan Adams, symphony conductor John Kim Bell, and ex-NHL player Ted Nolan. Tiiu Lana Cli, an RCMP member, and Warren Winnipeg, Youth Chief of the Blackfoot First Nations Reserve, are examples of current role models.

## NATIVE YOUTH-JUSTICE COMMITTEES

In a report on aboriginal peacemaking, Price and Dunnigan (1995) discuss the importance of **Native Youth-Justice Committees** as a means of reconciliation and healing in aboriginal communities. Such committees are used by the courts for sentencing recommendations. In addition, they can operate as diversion committees for first-time offenders who are charged with relatively minor offences (Jackson, 1988).

Usually youth-justice committees comprise a group of elders and interested community members who meet and make recommendations to the court that focus on healing, restitution, and rehabilitation. It is important to note that this healing is for both the young offender and the community (Price and Dunnigan, 1995). Elders are able to share the history of their culture, and share with the young person how he or she is valued by the whole community (Jackson, 1988). Elders play a vital role in acting as a bridge between offenders and the community. Elders also serve as a liaison between the criminal justice system and aboriginal traditions. Such initiatives apply cultural and traditional approaches to dealing with present-day problems of aboriginal youth.

This kind of philosophy is found in the South Island Tribal Council program in British Columbia. It operates as a diversion program, typically for first-time offenders who have committed less serious offences (Jackson, 1988). The youth must accept responsibility for his or her actions and must be willing to participate in the program. Once referred to the program by Crown counsel, the youth meets with two members of the tribal court and the diversion co-ordinator, who conducts an interview with the youth and then reports to the tribal council. The tribal court then decides whether or not to accept the youth into the program. If accepted, a contract is drawn up outlining what is expected of the youth. An elder supervises and counsels the youth for the duration of the diversion contract (Jackson, 1988; Stevens, 1990). The South Island Tribal Council program is based on the customs, traditions, and history of their people. Similar to those elder committees who make sentencing recommendations to the courts, elders in this program play a vital role in the rehabilitation of the offender.

Price and Dunnigan (1995) have focussed on similar initiatives that operate in Alberta. Here, a number of different programs, which are referred to as "community sentencing panels," have been developed. Generally speaking, these programs are more likely than the contemporary justice system, "to be culturally appropriate because they consist of members of the offender's own community" (Price and Dunnigan, 1995: 25). The committee members will meet with the offender and his or her family, and recommend an appropriate sentence. Such sentences entail counselling for the youth, and a means for the young offender to make amends with the community. This way, the sentence meets not only the needs of the youth, but also the needs of the community. In essence, they "consider the feelings of the offender, the victim, their families, and other members of the community because the goal is healing for all" (Price and Dunnigan, 1995: 26). Such a response to crime, incorporating aboriginal values and traditions is a lesson for all communities to learn.

## REDISCOVERY CAMPS

Since 1978, rediscovery camps have been enriching the lives of aboriginal and non-aboriginal youth. These programs, which focus on outdoor education, teach traditional skills, dances, legends, and songs. Young people learn more about their culture, about one another, and about themselves. The rediscovery program is similar to that offered by Outward Bound, in that both promote self-discovery through outdoor activities (Orr, 1993). As Henley states, "In many respects rediscovery reverses the process of the Indian residential schools" (1989: 26).

In the wilderness, young people are brought back in touch with the land and with their cultural roots. The specific elements of the rediscovery model are outlined in Box 12.2. Programs are found in British Columbia and Alberta and are developing in the United States. Participants include both aboriginal and non-aboriginal youth who are referred by justice officials and by family and community members.

According to Henley (1989), there are a variety of reasons why rediscovery programs have been developed. For example, a community may

## Box 12.2
## THE REDISCOVERY MODEL

Fourteen key elements provide the model for a rediscovery program.

1. **Homeland heartland.** Contact with the land is crucial. Settings should be beaches, desert dunes, meadows, etc.
2. **Living from the land.** Conservation and stewardship are emphasized (e.g., eat what you catch).
3. **Extended family.** Groups are small to ensure family intimacy. Limit the number of participants.
4. **Elders.** Assume a respected position in programs. They share crafts, songs, stories, and skills.
5. **Cultural context.** Site should be located near place holding significance for local aboriginal people (e.g., near ancient village).
6. **Authenticity.** Camps should be based on Native North American cultures and organized by Native communities.
7. **Cross-cultural understanding.** Is promoted to emphasize interdependency and mutual understanding, and to erase stereotypes.
8. **Flexible schedule.** 10-day to 2-week sessions full of a variety of activities.
9. **Sharing, speaking out.** Activities include those that encourage children to share their feelings and problems.
10. **Personal achievement.** Receiving recognition for positive achievements.
11. **Healthy living.** Exercise, nutritious foods, no alcohol or drugs.
12. **Leadership skills.** Participants are encouraged to be leaders in future camps.
13. **Further education.** Environmental and cross-cultural learning is emphasized.
14. **Follow-up.** Programs need to include follow-up events and counselling and encourage youth conferences.

**Source:** T. Henley, *Rediscovery. Ancient Pathways—New Directions. A Guidebook to Outdoor Education* (Vancouver: Western Canada Wilderness Committee, 1989). Revised edition: Lone Pine Publishing, 1996.

wish to introduce its youth to traditional seasonal hunting and fishing camps, while another might want to challenge its youth with a wilderness experience. Other communities may wish to address some of the social problems that their young people are facing.

Program activities are numerous and varied. Youths take part in environmental education, outdoor theatre, and wilderness skills, as well as learn more about aboriginal cultures. In addition, participants spend a 24-hour period completely on their own, with the guidance of elders. The solo experience takes place at the end of the program, when each youth is placed in an isolated area and provided with minimal survival gear. An elder will visit the site one or more times per day, but often without the participant's awareness. The purpose of this exercise is to ensure the safety of the youth. The idea of the solo is to help youths to integrate all they have learned and to realize their own strengths. This is crucial for increasing self-awareness and connectedness with the natural world (Henley, 1989).

In response to the success and growth of these programs, the Rediscovery International Foundation was established in 1985 to assist aboriginal communities all over the world in developing their own programs (Henley, 1989).

## NATIVE YOUTH COURT WORKERS

Native youth court workers provide youths with information concerning legal rights and court procedures, arrange for legal counsel, and speak on behalf of their clients (Loucks, 1982). In addition, Native court workers provide youth and family counselling and legal education for the community as a whole.

Native court workers also ensure that aboriginal people have the opportunity to participate fully in the criminal justice system and develop programs that are suited to the needs of aboriginal youth. The court workers are thus vital resource persons for justice officials and aboriginal communities.

## CULTURAL AWARENESS TRAINING

It is apparent that personnel within the criminal justice system need to be more aware of and sensitive to the problems faced by aboriginal people. As stated by Jackson (1988: 104), "a space must be made for education for those who presently possess power within the criminal justice system and who, through the initiatives advanced by native people, are being asked to exercise it with greater respect and understanding for native values."

Cultural-awareness training can include a variety of topics, such as awareness of aboriginal values, traditions, and spirituality; the historical and present-day impact of colonization and assimilation policies and

**Box 12.3**

**THE ADVERSARIAL AND THE RESTORATIVE JUSTICE MODELS**

Key concepts of the adversarial and restorative justice models include:

| *Adversarial* | *Restorative* |
|---|---|
| • violation of state | • violation of victim, community |
| • accountability to state | • accountability to victim, community |
| • determination of legal guilt | • offender takes responsibility for act(s) |
| • focus on accused | • focus on victim, accused, community |
| • retribution | • healing, repair, reconciliation, reintegration |
| • conflict | • co-operation |

**Sources:** L. Elliot, "Restorative justice: A summary outline," unpublished, Simon Fraser University, School of Criminology, April 1999; Rick Linden and Don Clairmont, *Making It Work: Planning and Evaluating Community Corrections & Healing Projects in Aboriginal Communities* (Ottawa: Solicitor General Canada, 1998), APC-TS 3 CA: <http://www.sgc.gc.ca/epub/abocor/e199805b/e199805b.htm>.

processes; expectations of aboriginal youths, families, and communities; and community problems, needs, and resources. Such training needs to include an overview of the unique problems faced by aboriginal people and the services that have been developed to deal with these problems. Cross-cultural education of police, court personnel, and correctional staff is necessary to ensure fair and appropriate dealings with aboriginal youth.

### ABORIGINAL PROGRAMS IN YOUTH CUSTODY

Programs aimed at promoting self-identity and self-esteem in aboriginal youth in custody exemplify efforts within the youth justice system to address the issue of aboriginal overrepresentation. These programs consist of cultural awareness, spirituality, and the use of traditions. These programs, through this transfer of knowledge, encourage connection to aboriginal cultures, thereby aiding in the process of self-discovery. An example of such a program is the one at the Youth Secure Custody Centre, in Burnaby, BC. This program provides young offenders with "spiritual guidance and support through individual counselling, sweatlodges, and smudges" (Burnaby Youth Secure Custody Centre, 1997). The connection to culture and spirituality can be an important component of the rehabilitation process.

## RESTORATIVE JUSTICE

The term restorative justice occurs often in correctional dialogue today. A wide variety of terms exist to describe restorative justice, such as "community accountability," "transformative justice," and "peacemaking." Essentially, restorative justice promotes the involvement of communities and victims in the processing of the offender and in the determination and execution of the sentence (see Box 12.3). A central concept is the reparation for harm caused to the victim, and the restoration of harmony in the community (Solicitor General of Canada, 1999). The damage done by the crime is to be repaired through the co-operation and the active participation of the offender, the victim, and the community (Linden and Clairmont, 1998; Solicitor General of Canada, 1999). This approach is significantly different from the adversarial nature of the current youth-justice system, a process that promotes individual responsibility and inhibits the involvement of victims and communities. Restorative justice therefore

> seeks to prevent crime in the future by repairing past harms and by restoring relationships. Rather than relying on imprisonment and other forms of punishment, the focus of restorative justice approach is to reconcile offenders with those they have harmed and to help communities to reintegrate victims and offenders.
>
> The source of peace and order lies in a strong, active, and caring community, and proponents of restorative justice feel that a more humane and satisfying justice system can help to rebuild communities that may have been weakened by crime and other social ills. (Linden and Clairmont, 1998: 7)

Aboriginal communities traditionally have dealt with offenders in ways that have allowed for active victim and community input (Linden and Clairmont, 1998). In essence, recognizing restorative-justice measures allows aboriginal people to follow their cultures and traditions. Aboriginal communities have been leaders in the reintroduction of restorative-justice measures.

Allowing aboriginal communities to deal with young offenders in a restorative context promotes healing and rehabilitation of the youth, the victim, and of the community as a whole. An example of a type of a restorative-justice program is family group conferencing, originating in New Zealand and in use in several parts of Canada to deal with youth crime (Elliot, 1999). Family-group conferencing allows the victim and the offender to provide their stories about the crime, promotes their healing, and allows family and community members the opportunity to have input into how the harm resulting from the crime should be repaired (Elliot, 1999). Circle sentencing is another example of a restorative-justice measure. Similar in many ways to family group conferencing, circle-sentencing differs in that a judge and elders are part of the decision-making process (Elliot, 1999). An example of a restorative-justice program that is striving for implementation is that of the Haisla people of Kitamaat Village, British Columbia. This program seeks to heal and to reintegrate victims and offenders, including the youth, through the use of traditional justice processes. These processes include seeking the advice of elders, utilizing family healing rituals, and referring to traditional teachings (Robinson, 1999).

While concerns have been raised about restorative-justice programs, such as that they widen the scope of the justice system's net and place a heavy responsibility on communities, such programs potentially offer an avenue through which aboriginal communities can have a greater say in their youths' accountability. The concept of restorative justice allows for the recognition and implementation of aboriginal traditions and spirituality, and the right to self-determination for aboriginal communities.

## SUMMARY

This chapter has discussed the involvement of aboriginal youth in the Canadian youth justice system, including an examination of several factors that may account for their overrepresentation in this system: the historical impact of government assimilation policies; the consequences of social disorganization and community breakdown; the role of self-destructive behaviours, such as suicide, crime, and substance abuse; the role of the criminal justice system itself; the role of the Young Offenders Act and that of the Youth Criminal Justice Act. The programs developed to address the needs of aboriginal youth underline the importance of cultural awareness on the part of the young people themselves and on the part of the people who work with them.

Addressing the overrepresentation of aboriginal youth in the justice system requires a multidimensional approach that includes initiatives within the justice system and alternatives to that system. Above all, reducing the numbers of young aboriginal offenders requires that aboriginal communities be involved in developing, implementing, and controlling programs for their youth.

## WEB LINKS

**Aboriginal Justice Learning Network**
<http://www.usask.ca/nativelaw/jah_AJLN.html>

A component of the Aboriginal Justice Strategy approved by the Department of Justice in 1996, this site is intended to help communities set up alternative-justice systems. The site includes a summary of Native legal cases, as well as a link to the Native Law Centre of Canada.

**Aboriginal Links: Canada & U.S.**
<http://www.bloorstreet.com/300block/aborcan.htm>

A comprehensive list of links to various aboriginal sites, directories, festivals, associations, land treaties, and much more.

**Aboriginal Youth Network**
<http://www.ayn.ca/>

An on-line resource created by youth for youth, this forum for young people presents information on upcoming aboriginal events, chat groups, news, and much more.

**Developing and Evaluating Justice Projects in Aboriginal Communities: A Review**
<http://www.sgc.gc.ca/epub/Abocor/e199805b/e199805b.htm>

A review of literature pertaining to justice issues and projects in Canada's aboriginal communities.

**Native Youth and Alternative Justice in Lethbridge**
<http://www.usask.ca/nativelaw/jah_barsh2.html>

Background information and a discussion of the Native Youth and Alternative Justice project in Lethbridge, Alberta, with links to the *Justice as Healing* newsletter.

## STUDY QUESTIONS

1. How has the history of the relations between aboriginal people and government played a role in the problems faced by aboriginal youth today?
2. What is meant by the overrepresentation of aboriginal youths in the justice system? Try to give specific figures in your answer.
3. Why should efforts be spent on prevention when developing responses to the current overrepresentation of aboriginal youths in the justice system?
4. If you had to develop and implement a preventive program for young aboriginal offenders that was supportive of them and culturally appropriate, what kind of program would you develop? What factors would you consider in designing and implementing your program?
5. How can justice system personnel become part of the solution to the overrepresentation of aboriginal youths in the justice system?

6. Several prevention programs were reviewed in this chapter. What is their common theme, and how does this theme relate to addressing criminal justice issues that involve aboriginal youths?
7. How has the Young Offenders Act contributed to the overrepresentation of aboriginal youth in the youth-justice system?
8. What is restorative justice? How are the concepts of restorative justice compatible with aboriginal traditions? How will these concepts promote the rehabilitation of aboriginal young offenders?

# REFERENCES

Bull, L.R. (1991). "Indian residential school: The Native perspective." *Canadian Journal of Education*, 18: 1 – 65.

Burnaby Youth Secure Custody Centre. (1997). "Directory of programs and services at Burnaby Youth Secure Custody Centre." Unpublished.

Canadian Criminal Justice Association. (1998, 15 November). *Bulletin*. Ottawa.

Canadian Medical Association. (1994). *Bridging the Gap. Promoting Health and Healing for Aboriginal Peoples in Canada*. Ottawa: Canadian Medical Association.

Department of Indian Affairs and Northern Development. (1997). *Basic Departmental Data—1996*. Ottawa: Department of Indian Affairs and Northern Development.

Department of Indian and Northern Affairs. (1990a). *Highlights of Aboriginal Conditions, 1989 – 2001*. Part II: *Social Conditions*. Ottawa: Indian and Northern Affairs.

———. (1990b). *Population Projections of Registered Indians, 1986 – 2011*. Part II. *Social Conditions*. Ottawa: Indian and Northern Affairs.

Department of Justice. (1991). *Aboriginal People and Justice Administration: A Discussion Paper*. Ottawa: Department of Justice.

———. (1999). "Minister of Justice introduces new youth justice law." <http://canada.justice.gc.ca/News/Communiques/1999/yoa_en.html>

Doob, A., Marinos, V., and Varma, K. (1995). *Youth Crime and the Youth Justice System in Canada: A Research Perspective*. University of Toronto: Department of Justice Canada.

Dosman, E.J. (1972). *Indians: The Urban Dilemma*. Toronto: McClelland and Stewart.

Elliot, L. (1999). "Restorative Justice: A Summary Outline." Unpublished. Burnaby: Simon Fraser University.

Furniss, E. (1995). *Victims of Benevolence. The Dark Legacy of the Williams Lake Residential School*. Vancouver: Arsenal Pulp Press.

Gorham, B. (1993, 7 February). *The Province*, A34.

Griffiths, C.T., Yerbury, J.C., and Weafer, L.F. (1987). "Canadian Natives: Victims of socio-structural deprivation." *Human Organization*, 46: 277 – 82.

Haig-Brown, C. (1988). *Resistance and Renewal. Surviving the Indian Residential School*. Vancouver: Tillicum Library.

Hamilton, A.C., and Sinclair, C.M. (1991). *Report of the Aboriginal Justice Inquiry of Manitoba*. Vol. 1: *The System and Aboriginal People*. Winnipeg: Queen's Printer.

Harris, M. (1986). *Justice Denied: The Law Versus Donald Marshall*. Toronto: Macmillan.

Henley, T. (1989). *Rediscovery, Ancient Pathways, New Directions: A Guide to Outdoor Education*. Vancouver: Western Wilderness Committee.

Ing, R. (1991). "The effects of residential schools on Native child rearing practices." *Canadian Journal of Native Education*, 18: 65 – 118.

Jackson, M. (1988). *Locking Up Natives in Canada. A Report of the Committee of the Canadian Bar Association on Imprisonment in Canada and Release*. Ottawa: Canadian Bar Association.

Kahnawake Social Services Resource Centre. (n.d.) *National Native Role Model Program.* Pamphlet.

LaPrairie, C.P. (1983). "Native juveniles in court: Some preliminary observations." In T.V. Fleming (Ed.), *Deviant Designations.* Toronto: Butterworths.

———. (1996). *Examining aboriginal corrections in Canada.* Ottawa: Solicitor General of Canada. <http://www.sgc.ca/epnb/abocor/e199614/l199614.htm>

LaPrairie, C.P., and Griffiths, C.T. (1984). "Native juvenile delinquency: A review of recent findings." *Canadian Legal Aid Bulletin,* 5(1): 39 – 46.

Linden, R., and Clairmont, D. (1998). *Making It Work: Planning and Evaluating Community Corrections and Healing Projects in Aboriginal Communities.* Ottawa: Solicitor General Canada. <http://www.sgc.gc.ca/epub/abocor/e199805b/e199805b.htm>

Loucks, B. (1982). *Preliminary Response to the Ontario Consultation Paper on Implementing Bill C-61. The Young Offenders Act.* Toronto: Native Council on Justice.

Mandarin, L., Callihoo, D., Argus, A., and Buller, M. (1992). "The Criminal Code and aboriginal people." In M. Waskentin (Ed.), *University of British Columbia Law Review, Special Edition: Aboriginal Justice.* Victoria, BC: Morriss.

Martens, T., Daily, B., and Hodgson, M.(1988). *The Spirit Weeps. Characteristics and Dynamics of Incest and Child Sexual Abuse with a Native Perspective.* Edmonton: Nechi Institute.

Maslove, A., and Hawkes, D. (1994). "The northern population." *Canadian Social Trends* (2nd ed.). Toronto: Thompson.

Morin, B. (1990). "Native youth and the Young Offenders Act." *Legal Perspectives,* 14(4): 13 – 15.

Orr, A. Outward Bound director. (1993, 10 May). Interview with author. Vancouver, BC.

Pointing, J.R., and Gibbons, R. (1980). *Out of Irrelevance.* Toronto: Butterworths.

Price, R.T., and Dunnigan, C. (1995). *Toward and Understanding of Aboriginal Peacemaking.* Victoria: University of Victoria Institute of Dispute Resolution.

Province of British Columbia. (1997). "Employment Equity Analysis, 1997." Unpublished. Victoria, BC: Ministry of Attorney-General, Corrections Branch.

———. (1999). "Statistics on youth corrections, 1991 – 98." Unpublished. Victoria, BC: Ministry for Children and Families.

Robinson, R. (1999). "Goals and objectives of Aboriginal Justice Program." Unpublished. Kitamaat Village, BC: Haisla Resource Office.

Royal Commission on Aboriginal Peoples. (1993). *Aboriginal Peoples and the Criminal Justice System. Report of the National Round Table on Justice Issues.* Ottawa: Canada Communication Group.

Royal Commission on Aboriginal Peoples. (1994). *Choosing Life. Special Report on Suicide among Aboriginal People.* Ottawa: Canada Communication Group.

Shkilnyk, A.M. (1985). *A Poison Stronger than Love: The Destruction of an Ojibway Community.* New Haven, CT: Yale University Press.

Siggner, A. (1992). "The social demographic conditions of registered Indians." In R.A. Silverman and M.O. Nielsen (Eds.), *Aboriginal Peoples and Canadian Criminal Justice.* Toronto: Butterworths.

Solicitor General Canada. (1999). *Restorative Justice.* <http://www.sgc.gc.ca/EFact/erestjustice.htm>

Statistics Canada. (1996). *1996 Census, Aboriginal Data.* Ottawa: Statistics Canada.

Statistics Canada. (1998). "1996 Census: Aboriginal data." *The Daily.* 13 January. <http://www.statcan.ca/Daily/English/980113/d980113.htm>

Stevens, S. (1990). "An aboriginal view of the Canadian justice system." *Legal Perspectives,* May: 10 – 12.

Yerbury, J.C., and Griffiths, C.T. (1991). "Minorities, crime, and the law." In M.A. Jackson and C.T. Griffiths (Eds.), *Canadian Criminology. Perspectives on Crime and Criminality*. Toronto: Harcourt Brace.

York, G. (1990). *The Dispossessed: Life and Death in Native Canada*. London: Vintage.

# Chapter 13

# International Juvenile Justice: Why Anglophone Systems Are Inferior

JAMES HACKLER

## KEY OBJECTIVES

After reading this chapter, you should be able to:

- identify some of the assumptions, myths, and practices that make anglophone juvenile justice systems less effective than those of many other nations;
- give examples of systems in other countries that may be more effective;
- question whether those in authority in anglophone juvenile justice systems are really interested in reducing delinquency, or rather in perpetuating a system that rewards lawyers, other professionals, and people in power.

## KEY TERMS

adversarial system
due process
*foyers*
reintegrative shaming

## INTRODUCTION

### PEOPLE OF GOOD WILL CREATING A CLUMSY SYSTEM

Once, when I was finished a workout at the gym, I noticed that an acquaintance who had just departed had left his shoes and gym clothes on the bench without locking them in his locker. Or so I thought. I locked the clothes into my own locker and, when I got home, called to let him know that his shoes and sweaty clothes were safe. But they weren't his.

I rushed back to the gym, took the clothes to the towel room, and left notes taped to several lockers in the area. Two weeks later, the clothes were still unclaimed. I suspect that an annoyed person returned from his shower and cursed the thief who had stolen his shoes and clothing. My intentions were good, but did I end up doing harm?

In some respects, this may symbolize the juvenile justice system in North America. Many well-meaning people have tried to draft laws and build systems to deal with juveniles. Since the United States has more lawyers than the rest of the world combined, it is not surprising that much effort went into creating a legal process that would balance individual rights with the protection of society. However, it is my contention that despite the good will of many individuals, the United States and Canada have created juvenile justice systems that are inferior to the systems in Europe and other parts of the world. Fiji, for example, with fewer resources and supposedly less sophisticated legal and social-work systems, has created responses to youth crime that are more likely to be effective than the responses that have been developed in North America.

## THE SHIFT FROM A SOCIAL-SERVICE TO A LEGAL ORIENTATION

Why has North America fallen behind so many parts of the world? I suggest that the shift from a social-service orientation, often called a welfare model, to a legalistic orientation has been dysfunctional (see Chapter 4 for a general review of juvenile-justice models or Winterdyk [1997] for a more detailed review). Assumptions of superiority by a legal system that tends to ignore its own deficiencies, combined with an ethnocentrism about non-anglophone systems, makes it difficult for North Americans to appreciate the contributions of other countries. For example, North Americans know very little about the local political units known as the *barangays* that play an important part in the processing of juveniles in the Philippines (Shoemaker and Austin, 1996: 241 – 43). Similarly, the *panchayats* of India, local village units comprising prominent and respected leaders, carry out an unofficial judicial/correctional role with juveniles (Hartjen and Kethineni, 1996: 184 – 87). The dispositions of the *panchayats* do not have the force of law, but they have the backing of custom and community acceptance.

Such informal practices, especially those in "developing" countries, are readily dismissed by "developed" countries. The North American pattern in responding to youth crime is to pass laws, usually of a punitive nature, often contrary to evidence that is widely available. This was illustrated by the introduction in March 1999 of the Youth Criminal Justice Act in the Canadian House of Commons (see Chapters 4 and 5). The most publicized features of the act were that parents could be punished if they do not properly supervise their children, and adult sentences would be possible for 14-year-olds convicted of serious offences. Admittedly, the new act also encourages community-based alternatives, but such options were already available to local jurisdictions if they were willing to make the effort.

While many European countries have been utilizing widespread knowledge about children and families, North America has been shifting toward the "rule of law." The legal profession has taken over systems and excluded those with other orientations. Many others, and even some lawyers and judges, recognize that much damage is being done, but usually these concerns are swept away by political pressures and the pervasiveness of the legalistic perspective.

In the past, a probation officer or social worker with experience in youth court might become a judge. There is no evidence that they were less capable than those with law degrees. However, a government bureaucrat or minister with a law degree can become a youth-court judge with very little knowledge of juvenile or family matters. The law degree has a certain magical quality, even when completed many years ago. In reality, the legal profession has developed a monopoly based on unsupported assumptions.

My many interviews suggest that former bureaucrats and politicians usually learn to be good judges, but not because of their legal training. Many are perceptive, adaptable people who understand bureaucracies. Sometimes they begin their careers as family-court judges a bit innocent about family struggles. Many believe they can reduce delinquency by making the parents responsible, as proposed in the new legislation. However, they soon learn that parents are often struggling against severe odds. The single mother of four may find that her oldest boy is in trouble with the law. She has concerns about her other children. A new judge quickly learns that locking up, fining, or punishing a harassed mother with three small children is probably not going to prevent her son from being a delinquent. Help is needed, but, compared with those in many other countries, Canadian judges have little authority to help, even though they have the power to punish.

The same could be said for prosecutors. Some begin work in "kiddie" court with little enthusiasm. However, many of them develop a broader understanding of juvenile family issues and begin co-operating with others to find intelligent responses to complex problems. But is a juvenile justice system dominated by a legal orientation the best for society? In *Getting Away with Murder: The Canadian Criminal Justice System* (1999), David Paciocco argues that "our law is the collected wisdom of generations of people, working in pursuit of justice, fairness, and equality, working to find a way to protect the inherent dignity of human beings" (p. x). Others argue that the law is the product of powerful people who create legislation for their own interests and consider Paciocco's statement a reflection of naïvete, narrow vision, and self-interest. Paciocco's high opinion of the law is combined with a low opinion of social scientists. "We have to exercise inordinate caution about letting behavioural scientists into our courts. They know less about human behaviour than some of them claim, and even less about justice" (p. 14). For years, social scientists have tried to make court systems sensitive to cultural differences. In Canada, First Nations people are overrepresented in prisons, but Paciocco feels that "our" law, that is, law created largely by upper-class, white, elderly males, is sacred: "Considerations of culture cannot be allowed to compromise those standards of behaviour *ordained* by criminal law" (p. 320; emphasis added).

Naturally, those restorative-justice types such as Bazemore and Walgrave (1998) get short shrift. "Any effort to build a criminal justice system around 'reconciliation' for serious crime is a rose-coloured fantasy that expects more than humans can give" (p. 39). Michael Hadley (in press), writing about the spiritual roots of restorative justice, and who thinks that spirituality in aboriginal cultures might be useful in responding to deviant behaviour, would be, according to Paciocco, just a dreamer.

## COPING WITH LEGAL RIGIDITY

My goal is not to ridicule lawyers. However, since the social-service orientation to juvenile justice, which definitely had weaknesses, has been taken over by lawyers, there is a need to provide them with broader perspectives and an awareness of the practices that are used elsewhere. Thus, this chapter will argue that

- North American juvenile justice systems are now inferior to those in most of the developed world;
- the English-speaking world is hampered by inappropriate assumptions, myths, and practices as these relate to law and juvenile justice;
- North Americans confuse punishing juveniles with helping them;
- arrogance makes it difficult for wealthy nations to learn from poorer nations. Applying common sense instead of expensive legalistic rituals can help in developing an effective juvenile justice system;
- finally, those in authority may have a vested interest in perpetuating a system that rewards lawyers, other professionals, and people in power.

# COMPARING THE IMPACT OF JUVENILE JUSTICE SYSTEMS

We are increasingly aware that programs that have a meaningful impact on delinquency must begin in kindergarten and the early school grades (Tremblay, in press; Kellam et al., 1994). By the time juveniles appear in court, much of the damage has been done. However, the courts can, and often have, increased the damage. Assessing a juvenile justice system, especially from one country to another, is extremely difficult. Crime statistics do not permit more than a crude comparison among countries (Silverman, 1992) or even within a country (Hackler and Dagger, 1993; Hackler and Don, 1990). To complicate matters, juvenile justice statistics are more difficult to interpret than adult data (Cossins, 1991). At present, most official international juvenile statistics are simply not comparable (Hackler, 1986; Hackler, 1991b), so this chapter will not engage in the misleading statistics game. However, one could argue that societies that resist casting out juveniles respond to troubled and troublesome young people more effectively. While the courts cannot remedy economic disparities or make education more meaningful, they can make matters worse for certain individuals. In general, anglophone systems add to the suffering of marginal juveniles more than the systems found in many other countries.

The damage done in anglophone countries is not the product of nasty individuals. In Canada, judges, probation officers, lawyers, social workers, and police officers are often "good people in dirty systems" (Hackler, 1991a). Given the right conditions, innovative individuals sometimes make even our inefficient systems work reasonably well. In general, however, talented and well-meaning people work at a disadvantage in a system in which assumptions, myths, and practices nullify their sincerity and efforts. It is unrealistic to expect Canadians to adopt the ideas and practices of other cultures, but by looking at the juvenile justice systems of other countries we might question some of our own assumptions and practices.

## QUESTIONING SOME COMMON ASSUMPTIONS

One advantage of studying foreign courts and systems is that it encourages us to view the dynamics of our own system in a much different light. Let me illustrate this with an experience in Vienna, Austria, that led me to question the utility of our adversarial system. During the trial, the prosecutor presented evidence against the juvenile. The defence attorney then rose and did a poor job—he simply pleaded for mercy for his client without dealing with the facts of the case. The prosecutor rose again and this time called attention to facts and other information that supported the defence. Later, when I approached the prosecutor, he admitted that he had done both the prosecution and the defence because the defence lawyer had done such a poor job. The prosecutor felt that his obligation was not simply to present facts against the defendant, but to provide all the facts so the judge could make an intelligent decision. His goal was not to win the case, but to have it decided intelligently. His final comment was revealing: "I understand that you have an adversarial system in Canada where lawyers fight a battle and each one tries to win. Aren't you interested in justice?"

Now that defence attorneys are found routinely in juvenile courts in Canada, we should question the appropriateness of the adversarial system for dealing with juveniles. A number of myths have led us astray.

### Myth No. 1: We have an adversarial system that protects juveniles.

Naffine, Wundersitz, and Gale (1990) explain why this myth persists. Few juveniles go to trial and, when they do, very few avoid being found guilty (Corrado and Markwart, 1992: Table 10). Although lawyers often see themselves as adversaries and try to present this image to clients, in reality they play different roles in a system where co-operation is likely to be the norm. Like professional wrestlers, there is only a display of battle. Sometimes the defendants are convinced that defence lawyers are fighting strenuously on their behalf. Many lawyers even delude themselves into believing the adversarial myth, because that's what they learned in law school. Actually, the different players in juvenile justice usually have compatible goals, even in the short run.

*Playing roles with integrity is different from playing them in a truly adversarial manner.* Experienced and skilled prosecutors (not necessarily those from adult court grudgingly doing their stint in "kiddies court") have much in common and often help the defence work out an intelligent plan for the judge. Once freed from the adversarial pretence, these professionals co-operate to do something constructive.

## Myth No. 2: Due process protects and helps juveniles.

Belief in an adversarial system also means faith in due process. The *Gault* case in the United States in 1967 reflected the concern that, under the guise of helping them, juveniles were being incarcerated without due process. But is the *Gault* case particularly relevant to Canada today? or to most courts in the United States, for that matter? The abuse of the welfare model raised concerns in the 1960s and 1970s, but there were considerable changes in practices that, by the 1970s, avoided most of these abuses (Hackler, 1991a). In the 1960s, for instance, I observed a judge berate a juvenile for saying he was not guilty. By the 1970s, while still under the old Juvenile Delinquents Act, judges were very careful about taking pleas. The law had not changed, but practices had.

Railroading completely innocent juveniles is rare, but delaying their cases and locking them up while our inefficient system deals with red tape is common. Our unquestioning allegiance to due process blinds us to the reality that the real problem facing judges is with sentencing—what to do with juveniles in trouble—not with the question of guilt. Naffine, Wundersitz, and Gale write:

> The task of the court is simply to consider what to do with confessed offenders. Since there is very little adjudication in criminal justice, reforms designed to introduce formal processes of adjudication and thus strengthen the individual's legal rights are bound to have little effect. (1990: 200)

## Myth No. 3: Juveniles are "innocent until proven guilty."

The notion that the accused is innocent until proven guilty does not square with reality. In Australia (McDonald, 1989) and Canada (Ericson and Baranek, 1982), juveniles are treated by the police and prosecutors as though they are guilty. One would have to be naïve to think that arrested juveniles are treated as if they are innocent. While the law and the judges may try to operate under this assumption, the system does not. Lawyers who accept the fact that most of their clients have probably done some wrong are better able to enlist social workers and others in a plan that will lead to a constructive disposition. When they spot those few who are genuinely not guilty, lawyers who have not been playing games have greater credibility and defend clients more effectively. Clinging to the myth of innocence, when no one believes it, adds to the charade and is dysfunctional for the young person.

One consequence of hanging on to this pretence is that we detain juveniles for longer periods of time, adjourn their cases more frequently, and punish them and their parents in a variety of ways. As Feeley (1979) has argued, the *process* is the punishment. That is, after harassing young offenders and their families, we find a very high percentage of them guilty (Corrado and Markwart, 1992: 197).

### Myth No. 4: The courts are a good way to discover truth.

Truth is often a casualty of our juvenile justice system. Much important information is deliberately kept from the court. In addition, the presentations of prosecution and defence are not intended to be truthful—they are usually biased.

To summarize, the conceptual frameworks of our juvenile justice system are sometimes unrelated to actual practice. The rhetoric that pervades legal debates and courtroom rituals have little to do with changing juveniles. Lawmakers eulogize the idea of the Rule of Law, despite evidence that it does not fit with reality (McBarnet, 1981: 166 – 67; Paciocco, 1999: x).

## LEARNING FROM OTHER COUNTRIES: JUVENILE JUSTICE IN FRANCE

We can learn something from other countries even though it is unlikely that we can borrow their specific practices. Obviously, we cannot make dramatic changes to our juvenile justice system, but we can broaden our vision by realizing that some of our basic assumptions are worth questioning. Let us look at the French system as an example.

North Americans frequently view the French justice system as "inquisitorial" and hence inappropriate for effectively handling juveniles. This image has misled many anglophone scholars. The real action does not take place in court but in the *cabinet*, or office of the judge. In this setting, the judge is able to act in a much more constructive manner than his or her North American counterpart.[1] Witnessing a trial in a French juvenile or adult court can give North American observers the impression that the judges are very harsh. In one of the first trials I observed, I was shocked to hear a French judge begin a trial by listing the past offences of the defendant, berating the juvenile for not taking advantage of previous help. She had avoided sending him to trial, providing assistance instead. She was annoyed because she had given him many opportunities to avoid further criminal activities. How could this juvenile get a fair trial from such an angry judge who was so familiar with his past sins?

After the prosecutor (*procureur*) presented the case, the juvenile had to answer more questions. (Defence attorneys do not speak for the juvenile; they make their presentation at the end.) Again the judge was aggressive in cross-examining the boy, who could not remain silent. By the time the defence attorney stood to present his argument, I was convinced that the judge was determined to convict.

The defence had only one argument. There was some slight doubt about this particular offence, and thus the court was obliged to acquit. After returning from the adjournment, the judge acquitted the juvenile, who was immensely relieved. I was amazed. Only later did I come to appreciate the expectations that are inherent in the system. Judges, and others, play certain roles on different occasions. Being angry at the juvenile was the *expected* role for the parental figure who had been working to keep this boy out of trouble. Displaying her annoyance was appropriate and proper, but deciding on guilt for this specific offence was a separate task. Everything else had to be set aside, including the fact that the youth had admitted past crimes to the judge in her office. French judges are expected to display integrity in this second capacity. Canadian judges seem to think that the two roles are incompatible.

## THE PROCESSING OF JUVENILES IN FRANCE

The French police cannot lay charges against a juvenile, and can hold a juvenile for only one night in a cell. In fact, most cases are seen by the *procureur* and the judge the same day. The delays that characterize many North American juvenile courts are unnecessary. The *procureur* (prosecutor) can screen out the case or send it to the *juge des enfants* (juvenile-court judge). Complicated cases or serious crimes go to the *juge d'instruction* (magistrate), who conducts a more thorough investigation before the case is given to the juvenile-court judge. Few juveniles are detained, but, when they are, they stay in juvenile sections of adult prisons. Periods of detention are usually very short, and even sentences after conviction are typically no more than a few weeks. Detention is not confused with rehabilitation—this experience is meant to be punishment. Detention is also relatively rare. In Creteil, an industrial suburb of Paris of 1.2 million people, ten cases in 1985 resulted in periods of custody, including those held for trial (the city of Paris was holding about 40 in the same year). Alberta locks up juveniles at more than ten times this rate (Hackler et al., 1987).

The *juge des enfants* handles the vast majority of cases informally in her *cabinet*, the primary scene of activity for juvenile court judges. If the judge feels that the offence is serious, or if the youth continues to offend, the case is referred to trial. However, judges may be in court only once or twice a month. The judge cannot incarcerate a juvenile or use punitive sanctions without a trial (Syndicat de la magistrature, 1979). The juvenile can be assigned to supervision by a correctional social worker (*educateur*), but if the juvenile resists being supervised, being placed in a closed institution is not an alternative. Judges work out options, use persuasion with juveniles, and arrange for a variety of services. Judges have even been known to meet with a youth's family in the evening so as not to disrupt the parents' workday. (Our juvenile justice system rarely readjusts its hours for struggling parents.) In Canada, we must find juveniles guilty before we offer help. In France, helping comes first!

The French judge works with the *educateur*, who provides a variety of social-work services and contacts, including making arrangements for juveniles to stay in residential facilities (Martaguet, 1983). Being placed in a residential facility is a matter of negotiation—it is not a sentence. If a juvenile leaves a residential facility, the judge cannot punish him or her. The judge can, however, have the police bring the youth to his or her office, which can be an unpleasant experience. But, unless the juvenile wants to be helped, little can be accomplished. Most judges try to find solutions that have some degree of support from the juveniles. Thus, the courtroom role for a *juge des enfants* during a trial differs dramatically from the social-work role the judge adopts in his or her *cabinet*. This latter role is clearly the most important. I was surprised at the interaction I witnessed in the *cabinet*: juveniles were confessing to the judge almost immediately. They were telling the truth, which would have earned disapproval from Canadian lawyers. Clearly, the judge was more interested in stopping future crime than in punishing the juveniles for current offences. Thus, the vast majority of cases are resolved without a trial.

Some juveniles also view "their" judge in a personal way. One juvenile who had left a residence appeared at juvenile court asking to see "his" judge, who was away for a few days. The boy wanted to tell his story to his judge and no one else. Arrangements were made for the boy to stay in another residence until his judge returned. In Canada, it is unlikely that the system would respond to a runaway in such a tolerant manner (see Chapter 8).

When placements in residential care appear to be appropriate, they are negotiated, not decreed. This process is very different from assuming guardianship as we do in North America, leaving a juvenile somewhat helpless while adults take over his or her life. In France, one does not lock up a juvenile "for his own good."

## RESIDENTIAL FACILITIES FOR JUVENILES IN FRANCE

Non-custodial facilities in France vary from small group homes to the relatively rare larger facility of 80 or so beds. As in North America, a variety of private agencies and religious orders operate these *foyers*. There are two categories of *foyers*. *Centres d'accueils* are something like receiving centres in North America, where juveniles stay for relatively short periods of time, but they are definitely not for closed custody. Centres with *reorientation* in their title are usually longer-term centres. Some of these may be located in less-populated areas. They also do not confine youths. Juveniles who leave do not think of themselves as running away from the *foyer*, a perspective shared by social workers. *Foyers* cannot be used to hold juveniles to protect the public—their purpose is to help youngsters. On the other hand, prisons are for detention, punishment, and possibly public protection.

*Foyers* try to create normal living conditions. In one group home I visited, two girls over the age of 18 were still living there while working in the community. Since they were over the age limit, I was curious as to how they could stay at the *foyer*. A juvenile-court judge has the authority to continue help for juveniles for one year after the age of 18. In other words, one does not "release" a young person from a *foyer*; instead, the question is whether a juvenile will be allowed to stay. In 1985, there were 10 juveniles in actual custody in the Creteil district near Paris, but 140 young people over 18 had successfully petitioned the judge to let them stay in a group home while they completed an educational program. In Canada, I cannot imagine young people asking judges to let them stay in most facilities. French juveniles often view their residences as homes and judges as helping them to achieve normal lives.

Admittedly, there are similarities between French centres and non-custodial facilities in North America. Much staff interaction and relaxed internal atmospheres are common in both places. The major difference seems to be in the consequences for disobeying rules or leaving. In France, juveniles must follow certain rules to be allowed to stay. Leaving a facility is a nuisance, not a delinquent act. Judges fuss, complain, and act like disappointed parents, usually with good effect, but punishment can be used only for a new crime. Thus, disobeying rules has not been criminalized in France, as it has in North America.

## Housing Difficult Juveniles

Marseilles, the largest port and second-largest city in France, has a reputation for being tough, is well known for drug and Mafia activities, and is noted for violent crime. The district juvenile court serves about 1.8 million people, with more than 1 million in the city of Marseilles. Usually 25 to 40 boys are in custody at any one time. There is no separate institution for girls; such rare cases stay in a cell in the women's section of the prison. Only one girl, who had strangled her mother, was locked up at the time that I was there. Obviously, the French resist incarcerating girls.

There are *foyers* for "difficult" girls. In one I visited, 40 girls lived in the building, but 15 others lived in apartments nearby. All attended school or worked outside the *foyer*. Nurses, psychologists, athletic facilities, and so on are not found in these facilities because they prefer to use community services in order to create a normal atmosphere. Each girl had a key to the door of her room; the staff did not.

A bicycle trip organized by a staff member provided a useful insight. As the group left, no one took a formal count of the juveniles. With my Canadian concern for control, I asked why no one was counting noses. "They won't get lost," I was told. Of course, I had meant, "Aren't you worried that they will run away?" Obviously, no one was, because it is easy for juveniles to leave at any time.

Attempts to create the atmosphere of a normal boarding school appeared to be effective, and the emphasis on persuading rather than controlling was readily apparent. The conditions that lead to confrontation and conflict in many North American residential facilities were considerably reduced. For example, an angry argument with a staff member might lead to a juvenile storming out of the building and walking around for an hour or two. One soon believes what the *educateurs* say repeatedly: you can't get kids to act normally if they are locked up. Runaways are uncommon and inconvenient, a symptom of something not working well but not a problem that requires a dramatic response.

### *Foyers* for Short-Term Care

Most *foyers* are smaller than the one described above and are likely to be co-ed, with residents carrying on normal lives. The length of stay is usually not a major issue. If things work out at home, the young person goes home. In one case, a 14-year-old girl was in conflict with her mother. The stepfather was sympathetic toward the girl, but felt that he should not interfere. The girl ran away, stole food, and was soon before a judge, who quickly set aside the criminal aspects of the case and concentrated on the family conflict. The judge made arrangements for the girl to stay in the *foyer*, but encouraged a family reconciliation. Note that the judge did not decide how the case should be resolved. That was up to the family, but in the meantime the girl had food and shelter and continued to go to school.

Another *foyer* was preparing for its annual closure in August for the traditional French vacation period. Staff were busy finding places at summer camps for some youth, while other young persons were going home. The staff did not decide on specific camp placements. Instead, staff and juveniles looked at brochures together. Some of the camps were even in other countries. In other words, these juveniles were being treated as normal. In Canada, it would be hard to imagine emptying the entire population of a residence for difficult children and sending them off to summer camp.

## THE RELATIONSHIP BETWEEN AUTHORITIES AND JUVENILES IN FRANCE

In Canada, we put juveniles in places *we* think will be good for them. French juveniles are involved in decisions that affect them and have more influence over their fate. Since such youths are not "inmates" in a *foyer*, their relationship with *educateurs* is different. Judges cannot always incarcerate juveniles who do not obey; this can only be done if the youth commits another crime.

Our Young Offenders Act also makes it improper for a juvenile to face a judge, or someone else in authority, without having a parent, lawyer, or some other advocate present. By contrast, the French place considerable faith in the professionalism of judges and prosecutors and give them more discretion (King and Petit, 1985/86). Many juveniles prefer to talk to the judge without parents being present. Judges in France can certainly punish juveniles after a trial, but they are more often seen as a source of aid. The Canadian due-process mentality supposedly protects youth, but in reality takes control out of the hands of those who are most involved (Christie, 1977). We usually prevent young persons from telling their stories in their own way to someone who has the authority to make a difference. Increasingly, Canadian juveniles must speak through a legal "mouthpiece."

## FORCING JUVENILES TO RECEIVE HELP

The tendency to "lock them up in order to help them" is common in Canada. We punish children who do not follow our rules, even when they have no voice in deciding on the rules. Thus, when a young offender goes AWOL from an open facility, the next step may be a closed facility. North Americans criminalize disobedience while the French reject the possibility of effective treatment during confinement. They believe that abandoning criminal behaviour requires commitment from the juvenile.

The French realize that someone occasionally has to be harsh with young offenders. This nasty work is given to the police and the prisons. Confrontations with the French police tend to be unpleasant, giving juveniles an incentive to be receptive to judges and social workers. Some juveniles exceed the tolerance limit, but until that point is reached and the judge concedes failure, there is a flexibility that lessens some of the problems that exist in Canada.

# WEALTH: A REQUIREMENT FOR INEFFICIENCY?

While France has considerable resources, Fiji is comparatively poor. However, it responds to youth more effectively than Canada. Can wealth actually encourage inefficiency?

Consider these three hypotheses: (1) the larger the number of lawyers per capita, the worse the juvenile justice system; (2) the thicker the juvenile legal code, the worse the juvenile justice system; and (3) the greater the emphasis on due process, the worse the juvenile justice system. If these hypotheses are correct, Fiji would have a juvenile justice system superior to that of Canada. This may seem simplistic, but we must ask whether the institutions created by developed countries serve their stated functions—organizations often do not serve those they purport to serve.

Despite their good intentions, professionals can have a negative impact on the people they are supposed to serve. Complex legislation may interfere with intended goals. When Canada's Young Offenders Act (YOA), over 100 pages long, was passed in 1984, it kept many lawyers and other professionals busy. By contrast, Hong Kong's act, also passed in 1984, was 15 pages long and did not consume as many resources (see Traver, 1997). The proposed Youth Criminal Justice Act (YCJA) is over 100 pages and is in keeping with the legalistic shift which has increased job opportunities for lawyers (also see Chapters 4 and 5). There is no evidence that the YOA or the additional resources required have reduced delinquency or helped juveniles and families. We can expect the same from the YCJA of 1999. Fiji has fewer lawyers and other professionals, and this may be a distinct advantage.

## REINTEGRATING JUVENILES

John Braithwaite (1989) argues that reintegrative shaming is a superior means of reducing crime. He uses Japan as an example of a country that uses shame constructively. Reintegrative shaming creates conditions whereby the deviant accepts societal values and is reintegrated into the larger society. The Fijian system appears to be more compatible with this logic than the systems created in North America, England, and Australia. If North Americans have intellectual blinders when it comes to other developed countries like France, one can imagine the difficulty of conceding that a poor country like Fiji does a better job than we do. Not being able to afford our cumbersome, inefficient, and damaging institutions seems to promote a common-sense approach that is more effective than our supposedly more sophisticated systems.

## PROCESSING YOUNG OFFENDERS WHILE EMPHASIZING REINTEGRATION

Fiji has a population of about 700 000, with 70 000 people living in Suva, the capital, and another 30 000 in Lautoka, the second-largest city. With its port and commercial activity, Suva has the greatest concentration of juvenile crime. The juvenile justice system there serves about 100 000 people in the area. Suva also contains the only detention centre in Fiji for juvenile boys. There is no specialized juvenile court in Fiji, but the chief magistrate hears a major portion of the cases that involve young people. Compared with the situation in Canada, relatively few juvenile cases come to court. The vast majority are handled by police. In 1989, only twelve juveniles were charged and appeared in the Suva court; two of these were committed to the detention centre.

The tiny trickle of official juvenile cases going through the Suva courts is not a result of Fiji being relatively crime-free. Suva is a port city, with drugs and glaring gaps between the wealthy and the poor. It is also the site of many family disputes and other social problems. The reason that few cases get to court is because they are resolved earlier.

### Screening Prior to Court

Following a recommendation by a Royal Commission on Crime in 1975, the police screen extensively. In 1979, the Police Juvenile Bureau was established under the direction of Merewalesi Verebalavu, the only female commissioned officer in the Fijian police force. This program began in Suva and was then extended to Lautoka and other communities. Under the program, before a charge could be laid, the Police Juvenile Bureau investigated the background of the case. This might involve a visit to the victims and the family of the juvenile. Senior Inspector Verebalavu made the decision as to whether a charge would be laid against the juvenile. A large majority of juveniles were only cautioned. In addition, the bureau had close relations with social and government organizations that could provide support for families. Juveniles who were cautioned rarely got in trouble again.

In 1987, the government of Fiji was removed in a military coup, and supposedly for economic reasons the Police Juvenile Bureau was abolished. However, the communication links developed by the bureau still seem to operate. The police continue to lay relatively few charges, and still use the network that was established during the eight-year period the bureau was in operation.

### Contrasting Attitudes Toward Proving Guilt

In Canada, we separate the issue of finding guilt from that of sentencing. The Fijians, like the French, find this reasoning absolutely absurd for many juvenile cases. As one magistrate pointed out, the child who never gets breakfast and steals food may clearly be guilty. but there are extenuating circumstances that are not just mitigating factors for sentencing—they are related to the question of guilt.

While Canada spends thousands of dollars to find young offenders guilty (with a great deal of success, incidentally), the Fijian magistrate, like the juvenile court judges in France, is more inclined to go directly to the source of the problem (Hackler, 1988). As Qoriniasi Bale, a former attorney general and solicitor general of Fiji pointed out to me during my visit, "We expect our magistrates to use common sense as well as the law." Canadian lawyers would be horrified at the casual protections offered to juveniles in Fijian courts. In reality, cases involving any doubt at all are simply screened out of the system. In Canada, we mistakenly assume our slavish devotion to due process serves juveniles better than reliance on sensible judges.

## CONTRASTING FIJI WITH MORE WASTEFUL SYSTEMS

It may be inappropriate to compare Fiji with Canadian cities. Therefore, let us look at Kauai, one of the Hawaiian Islands. The island has a population about half that of Suva, most of it in the town of Lihue. Many of the residents are of Japanese origin, a group that has a tradition of low crime rates. One might assume that this relaxed tropical island would not require a highly developed juvenile justice system. However, Kauai is part of the United States, where expensive, inefficient criminal justice systems abound. While Suva handles the occasional juvenile once a week, tiny Kauai keeps two full-time and two part-time judges busy. A juvenile section in the police department is headed by a lieutenant and two sergeants. About 100 cases per month come through the intake system for probation. Seven probation officers handle about 200 juveniles who are on probation. There is a noncustodial treatment centre at Poipau called Hale'opio. Young offenders can also be detained on an informal basis at Hale'opio. With only one main road around the island, options are limited for someone wishing to flee the centre.

The few juveniles from Kauai deemed too dangerous to have roaming around are flown to the youth correction centre on the island of Oahu. This requires expensive airplane shuttle service. Fiji gets by with much less: the facility servicing the 35 most serious juvenile offenders is completely open, with the boys going to school or work daily. Kauai does not appear to be flooded with many more delinquents than Fiji, but it devotes vast resources to the processing of juveniles. This wastefulness characterizes most of Canada, the United States, and Australia. If expensive resources actually helped juveniles, they might represent an acceptable way for wealthy societies to spend their surplus money. If, instead, we are perpetuating legal myths, guaranteeing inefficiency in our courts, and alienating troubled youth even more, this is a poor investment. Societies that stigmatize people and cast them out of society only push them into deviant subcultures, creating more crime.

The contrast between Kauai and Fiji also calls attention to a larger issue. Traditionally, we view a juvenile justice system as a rational and reasonable response to young offenders, but this is naïve. Juvenile justice systems are the creation of legal and political climates. What these youths do has a minimal impact on these systems. The major differences among juvenile justice systems lie in the legal and political traditions that have evolved in each society and that generate institutions to meet the needs of the agencies of control, often at the expense of the needs of the juveniles. The detention centre in Fiji provides an illustration of a more sensible option.

## A Detention Centre without Walls

Before the military coup in Fiji, there was a more elaborate juvenile detention centre on the edge of Suva, but since this site was suitable for military purposes, the youths were relocated to a former leper colony where buildings had been condemned. The physical facilities for the current centre might be viewed as substandard, but its director, Aseri Rika, put them to intelligent use. Up to 35 serious offenders are placed in this former leper colony, where they are not locked up. Most attend school outside the centre. Some boys go back to the same school they attended before being placed in the centre. Sending a "convicted" boy back to his school is not typical in North America, but it makes sense in the context of reintegrative shaming. A few boys enrol in vocational training programs run by the Salvation Army. Others work as apprentices with an employer who has agreed to take up to six boys.

Although this centre is the end of the line for Fijian delinquents, neither fences nor other restrictive devices are employed. Not surprisingly, boys occasionally run away. At one time, staff chased runaways, but now the system is more relaxed. The director asks police to contact the centre, rather than apprehend a boy, if they know his location; then centre staff pick up the boy. Parents are told that the boys need a pass if they are on leave from the centre. When boys arrive home without a pass, about half the parents contact the centre. Running away is still a nuisance, but it has not been dramatized. When a group of four boys absconded recently, they put a letter under the door of the director's office saying that they were disappointed with one of the staff members. They were leaving for a few days but would be okay and would return. They added "we love you." These hardened criminals went off to the home of some relations and returned the next day.

The Fijian response is in marked contrast to an Australian incident of 1990. A runaway boy from a Sydney detention centre contacted the staff there and spent considerable time talking to one of them. The cabinet minister in charge of the corrections portfolio was highly critical of the staff members who were in touch with the boy, feeling that they should have immediately contacted the police to have him apprehended. She fired the director of the detention centre and had him charged with malfeasance. This reaction typified the conservative attitude of the New South Wales government at that time, but it also reflects the thinking of many North Americans.

In Edmonton, Alberta, which has a population about the same size as Fiji's, over 120 young offenders are locked up in one of the most costly, modern, electronically equipped prisons in Canada. A similar number are in a variety of noncustodial facilities, and others are on probation. We are constantly told that we do not have enough money to provide help for juveniles. In fact, our wealth enables us to have an inefficient legal system and seduces us into thinking that building prisons for juveniles is an intelligent alternative to more reintegrative strategies. In Fiji, common sense is a substitute for wealth.

There is no specific evidence that the detention centre in Fiji or the system in general has great rehabilitative potential. However, the mass of social-science evidence clearly favours the practices used in Fiji. It is difficult to see how these juveniles will be less successful at becoming law-abiding adults than those being processed in North America.

## SUMMARY

North American juvenile justice has been caught up in a legalism that serves professionals. Some of the assumptions underlying our legal system contribute to its ineffectiveness and inefficiency. For example, the focus on punishment casts troubled and troublesome juveniles out of mainstream society. Such rejection leads them to search for gangs and other deviant subcultures that nurture outcasts and reinforce criminal behaviour. In other words, we have created a system that fosters crime. In contrast, France and Fiji have recognized the dangers of such practices. Unfortunately, anglophone countries appear to resist learning from other countries, especially those that are "less developed."

Does North America really want to have an effective juvenile justice system? Perhaps Diana Gordon is correct when she argues that the symbolic politics of crime encourage the development of control mechanisms (1990). For the politician, it is important to appear to be doing something about crime. Incarcerating juveniles and administering clumsy legal systems fulfils this need. The fact that these activities do little to diminish delinquency may not be politically relevant.

Of course, within all of the anglophone countries we see pockets of innovation. For example, and RCMP officer and local lawyer in Sparwood, British Columbia, borrowed ideas from family group conferencing in New Zealand in a constructive manner. Australia provides numerous illustrations. Traditionally a leader on social issues, South Australia displayed more progressive thinking by introducing family group conferencing in the 1990s (Wundersitz, 1994). Like so many countries, it is difficult to generalize in Australia because practices differ from place to place. Being a penal colony influenced Sydney and the system in the state of New South Wales, but Adelaide and the state of South Australia did not import convicts and became known for progressive thinking. For example, this was the first place in the Commonwealth where women could vote. In 1890 juvenile court legislation led to juvenile courts in 1895 (Newman, 1991). This was four years before the Chicago Juvenile Court, which many American texts incorrectly claim to be the first. Clearly, we need to widen our horizons and counter some of the ethnocentrism that characterizes much of North American thinking on juvenile justice.

## NOTE

1. Many magistrates in France are women. In juvenile justice, they appear to be in the majority. Whether this helps the French system to be more progressive is left for the reader to decide.

## WEB LINKS

**International Principles of Juvenile Justice**
<http://www.amnesty.ca/library/1998/principles.htm>

Amnesty International Canada lists the International Principles of Juvenile Justice.

**Juvenile Justice Information Portfolio**
<http://www.unicef-icdc.org/information/portfolios/juvenile-justice/index.htm>

This UNICEF site offers a wealth of information on juvenile justice, including a review of major issues in the field, a selection of case studies, selected readings, and current and upcoming events.

**Trends in Juvenile Violence in European Countries**
<http://ncjrs.org/txtfiles/fs000202.txt>

This site features a research preview by Christian Pfeiffer, which discusses international issues and statistics pertaining to juvenile justice.

## STUDY QUESTIONS

1. Comment on the statement "Juveniles are innocent until proven guilty."
2. What are some of the myths perpetuated by North American juvenile justice systems?
3. Why is the French system apparently more attuned to the needs of juveniles?
4. Provide illustrations of the greater flexibility of the French system in responding to juveniles.
5. How does the relationship between juveniles and authorities differ in France and North America?
6. Why could wealthy juvenile justice systems hurt juveniles more than if they had fewer resources?

## REFERENCES

Bazemore, G., and Walgrave, L. (Eds.). 1998. *Restorative Juvenile Justice.* Monsey, NY: Criminal Justice Press.

Braithwaite, J. (1989). *Crime, Shame, and Reintegration.* Cambridge, UK: Cambridge University Press.

Christie, N. (1977). "Conflicts as property." *British Journal of Criminology*, 17: 1 – 26.

Corrado, R., and Markwart, A. (1992). "The evolution and implementation of a new era of juvenile justice in Canada." In R. Corrado, N. Bala, R. Linden, and M. LeBlanc (Eds.), *Juvenile Justice in Canada.* Toronto: Butterworths.

Cossins, D. (1991). "Canadian juvenile justice before and after the Young Offenders Act." Unpublished Master's thesis, University of Alberta.

Ericson, R., and Baranek, P. (1982). *The Ordering of Justice: A Study of Accused Persons as Dependents.* Toronto: University of Toronto Press.

Feeley, M. (1979). *The Process Is the Punishment.* New York: Russell Sage.

Gordon, D. (1990). *The Justice Juggernaut: Fighting Street Crime, Controlling Citizens.* New Brunswick, NJ: Rutgers University Press.

Hackler, J. (1986). "Juvenile justice in Canada: Comparisons with other systems." In H. Kerner, B. Galaway, and H. Janssen (Eds.), *European and North American Juvenile Justice Systems: Aspects and Tendencies.* Munich: Deutschen Vereinigung für Jugendgerichte und Jugendgerichtshilfen.

———. (1988). "Practicing in France what Americans have preached: The response of French judges to juveniles." *Crime and Delinquency*, 34: 467 – 85.

———. (1991a). "Good people, dirty system: The Young Offenders Act and organizational failure." In A. Leschied, P. Jaffe, and W. Willis (Eds.), *The Young Offenders Act: A Revolution in Canadian Juvenile Justice.* Toronto: University of Toronto Press.

———. (1991b). "A strategy for the cross-cultural study of juvenile justice." In J. Hackler (Ed.), *Official Responses to Problem Juveniles: Some International Reflections.* Oñati, Spain: Oñati International Institute for the Sociology of Law.

Hackler, J., and Dagger, D. (1993). "Improving crime statistics by "correcting" them for system characteristics." *Australian and New Zealand Journal of Criminology*, 26: 116 – 23.

Hackler, J., and Don, K. (1990). "Estimating system biases: Crime indices that permit comparison across provinces." *Canadian Journal of Criminology*, 32: 243 – 64.

Hackler, J., Garapon, A., Frigon, C., and Knight, K. (1987). "Locking up juveniles in Canada: Some comparisons with France." *Canadian Public Policy*, 13: 477 – 89.

Hadley, M.L. (Ed.). In Press. *Trial by Race: The Spiritual Roots of Restorative Justice.* Albany: State University of New York Press.

Hartjen, C.A., and S. Kethineni. (1996). "India." In D.J. Shoemaker (Ed.), *International Handbook on Juvenile Justice.* Westport, CT: Greenwood.

Kellam, S.G., Rebok, G.W., Ialongo, N., and Mayer, L.S. (1994). "The course and malleability of aggressive behavior from early first grade into middle school: Results of a developmental epidemiologically-based preventive trial." *Journal of Child Psychology and Psychiatry*, 35: 259 – 82.

King, M., and Petit, M. (1985/86). "Thin stick and fat carrot: The French juvenile justice system." *Youth and Policy*, 15: 26 – 31.

Martaguet, M. (1983). "Le nouveau droit pénale des mineurs." Report presented at the VI[e] Congrès de l'Association Française de Droit Pénal, November, Montpellier, France.

McBarnet, D. (1981). *Conviction: Law, the State and the Construction of Justice*. London: Macmillan.

McDonald, E. (1989). "Strategic action in situations of unfamiliarity: The case of juvenile defendants in the Children's Court system in Western Australia." PhD thesis, University of Western Australia.

Naffine, N., Wundersitz, J., and Gale, F. (1990). "Back to justice for juveniles: The rhetoric and reality of law reform." *Australian and New Zealand Journal of Criminology*, 23: 192 – 205.

Newman, K. (1991). "Juvenile justice in South Australia: In need of tune up or a complete overhaul?" In J. Hackler (Ed.), *Official Responses to Problem Juveniles: Some International Reflections*. Oñati, Spain: Oñati International Institute for the Sociology of Law.

Paciocco, D.M. (1999). *Getting Away with Murder: The Canadian Criminal Justice System*. Toronto: Irwin Law.

Shoemaker, D.J., and Austin, W.T. (1996). "The Republic of the Philippines." In D.J. Shoemaker (Ed.), *International Handbook on Juvenile Justice*. Westport, CT: Greenwood.

Silverman, R. (1992). "Crime rates." *Encyclopedia of Sociology*. New York: Macmillan.

Syndicat de la Magistrature. (1979). "Mineurs: l'art de la fugue." *Justice*, 69.

Traver, H. (1997). "Juvenile delinquency in Hong Kong." In J. Winterdyk (Ed.), *Juvenile Justice Systems: International Perspectives*. Toronto: Canadian Scholars' Press.

Tremblay, R.E. (in press). "When children's development fails." In D. Keating and C. Hertzman (Eds.), *Developmental Health: The Wealth of Nations in the Information Age*. The CIAR Human Development Program. New York: Guilford.

Winterdyk, J. (Ed.). (1997). "Introduction." In *Juvenile Justice Systems: International Perspectives*. Toronto: Canadian Scholars' Press.

Wundersitz, J. (1994). "Family conferencing in South Australia and juvenile justice reform." In C. Alder and J. Wundersitz (Eds.), *Family Conferencing and Juvenile Justice: The Way Forward or Misplaced Optimism?* Canberra, ACT: Australian Institute of Criminology.

# Appendix A
## Juvenile Delinquents Act

CHAPTER J-3
An Act respecting juvenile delinquents

**Short title**
1. This Act may be cited as the *Juvenile Delinquents Act*. R.S., c. 160, s. 1.

**Definitions**
2. (1) In this Act

**"child"**
"child" means any boy or girl apparently or actually under the age of sixteen years, or such other age as may be directed in any province pursuant to subsection (2);

**"court"**
**"juvenile court"**
"court" or "juvenile court" means any court duly established under any provincial statute for the purpose of dealing with juvenile delinquents, or specially authorized by provincial statute, the Governor in Council, or the lieutenant governor in council, to deal with juvenile delinquents;

**"court of appeal"**
"court of appeal" has the same meaning as it has in the *Criminal Code*;

**"guardian"**
"guardian" includes any person who has in law or in fact the custody or control of any child;

**"industrial school"**
"industrial school" means any industrial school or juvenile reformatory or other reformative institution or refuge for children duly approved by provincial statute or by the lieutenant governor in council in any province, and includes such an institution in a province other than that in which the committal is made, when such institution is otherwise available;

**"judge"**
"judge" means the judge of a juvenile court seized of the case, or the justice, specially authorized by federal or provincial authority to deal with juvenile delinquents, seized of the case;

**"justice"**
"justice" except in section 5 has the same meaning as it has in the *Criminal Code*;

**"juvenile delinquent"**
"juvenile delinquent" means any child who violates any provision of the *Criminal Code* or of any federal or provincial statute, or of any by-law or ordinance of any municipality, or who is guilty of sexual immorality or any similar form of vice, or who is liable by reason of any other act to be committed to an industrial school or juvenile reformatory under any federal or provincial statute;

**"magistrate"**
"magistrate", except in subsections 13(1) and (4), and except in section 14, means two or more justices of the peace and also a police magistrate, a stipendiary magistrate and any other person having the power or authority of two or more justices of the peace;

**"probation officer"**
"probation officer" means any probation officer for juvenile delinquents duly appointed under any provincial statute or this Act;

**"superintendent"**
"superintendent" means a superintendent of neglected children, or of neglected and delinquent children, or a superintendent or director of child welfare, or a commissioner of the Bureau of Child Protection, or, in general, any officer, whatever is his designation, who is appointed by any provincial government to have the general charge or supervision of work in the province dealing with delinquent children, and also the lawful deputy of such officer;

**"supreme court judge"**
"supreme court judge" means
(*a*) in the Province of Ontario, a judge of the Supreme Court of Ontario;
(*b*) in the Province of Quebec, a judge of the Superior Court;
(*c*) in the Province of Nova Scotia, a judge of the Supreme Court of Nova Scotia;
(*d*) in the Province of New Brunswick, a judge of the Supreme Court of New Brunswick;

(*e*) in the Province of British Columbia, a judge of the Supreme Court of British Columbia;
(*f*) in the Province of Prince Edward Island, a judge of the Supreme Court of Prince Edward Island;
(*g*) in the Province of Manitoba, a judge of the Court of Queen's Bench;
(*h*) in the Province of Saskatchewan, a judge of the Court of Queen's Bench;
(*i*) in the Province of Alberta, a judge of the Supreme Court of Alberta;
(*j*) in the Province of Newfoundland, a judge of the Supreme Court of Newfoundland; and
(*k*) in the Yukon Territory, a judge of the Territorial Court of the Yukon Territory.

**Alteration of definition "child"**
(2) The Governor in Council may from time to time by proclamation
(*a*) direct that in any province the expression "child" in this Act means any boy or girl apparently or actually under the age of eighteen years, and any such proclamation may apply either to boys only or to girls only or to both boys and girls, and
(*b*) revoke any direction made with respect to any province by a proclamation under this section, and thereupon the expression "child" in this Act in that province means any boy or girl apparently or actually under the age of sixteen years. R.S., c. 160, s. 2.

**Delinquency**
3. (1) The commission by a child of any of the acts enumerated in the definition "juvenile delinquent" in subsection 2(1), constitutes an offence to be known as a delinquency, and shall be dealt with as hereinafter provided.

**How child dealt with**
(2) Where a child is adjudged to have committed a delinquency he shall be dealt with, not as an offender, but as one in a condition of delinquency and therefore requiring help and guidance and proper supervision. R.S., c. 160, s. 3.

**Court's jurisdiction**
4. Except as provided in section 9, the juvenile court has exclusive jurisdiction in cases of delinquency including cases where, after the committing of the delinquency, the child has passed the age limit mentioned in the definition "child" in subsection 2(1). R.S., c. 160, s. 4.

**Summary trials**
5. (1) Except as hereinafter provided, prosecutions and trials under this Act shall be summary and shall, *mutatis mutandis*, be governed by the provisions of the *Criminal Code* relating to summary convictions in so far as such provisions are applicable, whether or not the act constituting the offence charged would be in the case of an adult triable summarily, except that
(*a*) the provisions relating to appeals do not apply to any proceeding in a juvenile court, and
(*b*) the provisions prescribing a time limit for making a complaint or laying an information in respect of offences punishable on summary conviction where no time is specially limited for making any complaint or laying any information in the Act or law relating to the particular case, do not apply to any such proceeding other than a proceeding against an adult, except when an adult is dealt with under section 4 of this Act.

**Time for commencement**
(2) The provisions of the *Criminal Code* prescribing a time limit for the commencement of prosecutions for offences against the *Criminal Code* apply, *mutatis mutandis*, to all proceedings in the juvenile court.

**"Justice"**
(3) Whenever in such provisions the expression "justice" occurs, it shall be taken in the application of such provisions to proceedings under this Act to mean "judge of the juvenile court, or justice specially authorized by federal or provincial authority to deal with juvenile delinquents". R.S., c. 160, s. 5.

**Powers of judge**
6. (1) Every judge of a juvenile court in the exercise of his jurisdiction as such has all the powers of a magistrate.

**Idem**
(2) In addition to those expressly mentioned in this Act, the juvenile court judge has all the powers and duties, with respect to juvenile offenders, vested in, or imposed on a judge, stipendiary magistrate, justice or justices, by or under the *Prisons and Reformatories Act*.

**Discretion of court**
(3) The discretion of the juvenile court judge as to the term for which a juvenile delinquent may be committed is not affected by this section. R.S., c. 160, s. 6.

**Appointment of deputy judge**
7. (1) The judge of a juvenile court may with the approval of the attorney general of the province in which such court is situated appoint a deputy judge, who has all the powers and authority of a judge of a juvenile court in case of the absence or illness or other disability of such judge.

**Tenure of office**
(2) A deputy judge so appointed holds office during pleasure and is removable at any time by the attorney general or by the judge, with the approval of the attorney general, without cause.

**Resignation**
(3) The resignation of a deputy judge may be accepted by either the judge by whom he was appointed, or the attorney general. R.S., c. 160, s. 7.

**All cases to go to juvenile court**
8. (1) When any child is arrested, with or without a warrant, such child shall, instead of being taken

before a justice, be taken before the juvenile court; and, if a child is taken before a justice, upon a summons or under a warrant or for any other reason, it is the duty of the justice to transfer the case to the juvenile court, and of the officer having the child in charge to take the child before that court, and in any such case the juvenile court shall hear and dispose of the case in the same manner as if the child had been brought before it upon information originally laid therein.

**Exception**
(2) Subsection (1) does not apply to any justice who is a judge of the juvenile court or who has power to act as such under any Act in force in the province. R.S., c. 160, s. 8.

**Exceptional procedure when offence is indictable**
**9.** (1) Where the act complained of is, under the provisions of the *Criminal Code* or otherwise, an indictable offence, and the accused child is apparently or actually over the age of fourteen years, the court may, in its discretion, order the child to be proceeded against by indictment in the ordinary courts in accordance with the provisions of the *Criminal Code* in that behalf; but such course shall in no case be followed unless the court is of the opinion that the good of the child and the interest of the community demand it.

**Order may be rescinded**
(2) The court may, in its discretion, at any time before any proceeding has been initiated against the child in the ordinary criminal courts, rescind an order so made. R.S., c. 160, s. 9.

**Notices to parents**
**10.** (1) Due notice of the hearing of any charge of delinquency shall be served on the parent or parents or the guardian of the child, or if there is neither parent nor guardian, or if the residence of the parent or parents or guardian is unknown, then on some near relative, if any, living in the city, town or county, whose whereabouts is known, and any person so served has the right to be present at the hearing.

**Service of notice**
(2) The judge may give directions as to the persons to be served under this section, and such directions are conclusive as to the sufficiency of any notice given in accordance therewith. R.S., c. 160, s. 10.

**Powers of clerk**
**11.** (1) The clerk of every juvenile court has power *ex officio* to administer oaths and also, in the absence of the judge and deputy judge, to adjourn any hearing for a definite period not to exceed ten days.

**Duties of clerk**
(2) It is the duty of the clerk of the juvenile court to notify the probation officer or the chief probation officer, in advance, when any child is to be brought before the court for trial. R.S., c. 160, s. 11.

**Private trials**
**12.** (1) The trials of children shall take place without publicity and separately and apart from the trials of other accused persons, and at suitable times to be designated and appointed for that purpose.

**Place of trials**
(2) Such trials may be held in the private office of the judge or in some other private room in the court house or municipal building, or in the detention home, or if no such room or place is available, then in the ordinary court room, but when held in the ordinary court room an interval of half an hour shall be allowed to elapse between the close of the trial or examination of any adult and the beginning of the trial of a child.

**Names not to be published or identity of child indicated**
(3) No report of a delinquency committed, or said to have been committed, by a child, or of the trial or other disposition of a charge against a child, or of a charge against an adult brought in the juvenile court under section 33 or under section 35, in which the name of the child or of the child's parent or guardian or of any school or institution that the child is alleged to have been attending or of which the child is alleged to have been an inmate is disclosed, or in which the identity of the child is otherwise indicated, shall without the special leave of the court, be published in any newspaper or other publication.

**Application to newspapers**
(4) Subsection (3) applies to all newspapers and other publications published anywhere in Canada, whether or not this Act is otherwise in force in the place of publication. R.S., c. 160, s. 12.

**Detention home**
**13.** (1) No child, pending a hearing under this Act, shall be held in confinement in any county or other gaol or other place in which adults are or may be imprisoned, but shall be detained at a detention home or shelter used exclusively for children or under other charge approved of by the judge or, in his absence, by the sheriff, or, in the absence of both the judge and the sheriff, by the mayor or other chief magistrate of the city, town, county or place.

**Penalty**
(2) Any officer or person violating subsection (1) is liable on summary conviction before a juvenile court or a magistrate to a fine not exceeding one hundred dollars, or to imprisonment not exceeding thirty days, or to both.

**Exception**
(3) This section does not apply to a child as to whom an order has been made pursuant to section 9.

**Idem**
(4) This section does not apply to a child apparently over the age of fourteen years who, in the

opinion of the judge, or, in his absence, of the sheriff, or, in the absence of both the judge and the sheriff, of the mayor or other chief magistrate of the city, town, county or place, cannot safely be confined in any place other than a gaol or lock-up. R.S., c. 160, s. 13.

**Where there is no detention home**
14. (1) Where a warrant has [been] issued for the arrest of a child, or where a child has been arrested without a warrant, in a county or district in which there is no detention home used exclusively for children, no incarceration of the child shall be made or had unless in the opinion of the judge of the court, or, in his absence, of the sheriff, or, in the absence of both the judge and the sheriff, of the mayor or other chief magistrate of the city, town, county or place, such course is necessary in order to insure the attendance of such child in court.

**Promise to attend may be accepted**
(2) In order to avoid, if possible, such incarceration, the verbal or written promise of the person served with notice of the proceedings as aforesaid, or of any other proper person, to be responsible for the presence of such child when required, may be accepted; and in case the child fails to appear, at such time or times as the court requires, the person or persons assuming responsibility as aforesaid, shall be deemed guilty of contempt of court, unless in the opinion of the court there is reasonable cause for such failure to appear. R.S., c. 160, s. 14.

**Bail may be accepted**
15. Pending the hearing of a charge of delinquency the court may accept bail for the appearance of the child charged at the trial as in the case of other accused persons. R.S., c. 160, s. 15.

**Court may adjourn or postpone hearing**
16. The court may postpone or adjourn the hearing of a charge of delinquency for such period or periods as the court may deem advisable, or may postpone or adjourn the hearing *sine die*. R.S., c. 160, s. 16.

**Proceedings may be informal**
17. (1) Proceedings under this Act with respect to a child, including the trial and disposition of the case, may be as informal as the circumstances will permit, consistent with a due regard for a proper administration of justice.

**Not affected by irregularities**
(2) No adjudication or other action of a juvenile court with respect to a child shall be quashed or set aside because of any informality or irregularity where it appears that the disposition of the case was in the best interests of the child.

**Service of process in another jurisdiction**
(3) Except as provided in subsection (5), if a person, whether a child or an adult, against whom any warrant has issued out of a juvenile court cannot be found within the jurisdiction of the juvenile court out of which the warrant was so issued, but is or is suspected to be in any other part of Canada, any judge or deputy judge of a juvenile court within whose jurisdiction such person is or is suspected to be, or if there is no juvenile court having jurisdiction in such place, then any justice within whose jurisdiction such person is or is suspected to be, upon proof being made on oath or affirmation of the handwriting of the juvenile court judge or other officer who issued the warrant, shall make an endorsement on the warrant, signed with his name, authorizing the execution thereof within his jurisdiction.

**Authority to arrest**
(4) Such endorsement is sufficient authority to the person bringing such warrant, and to all other persons to whom the warrant was originally directed, and also to all probation officers, constables and other peace officers of the juvenile court or of the territorial division where the warrant has been so endorsed, to execute the warrant therein and to carry the person against whom the warrant issued when apprehended, before the juvenile court out of which the warrant issued.

**Child outside of jurisdiction**
(5) Where a child who has been before a juvenile court and is still under the surveillance of such court has been caused by the court to be placed in a foster home outside of the jurisdiction of such court or has been committed by the court to the care or custody of a probation officer or other suitable person or to an industrial school, outside of the jurisdiction of such court, the court may take any action with respect to such child that it could take were the child within the jurisdiction of such court, and for any such purpose any warrant or other process issued with respect to such child may be executed or served in any place in Canada outside of the jurisdiction of such court without the necessity of complying with subsection (3). R.S., c. 160, s. 17.

**Seal not required**
18. It is not necessary to its validity that any seal should be attached or affixed to any information, summons, warrant, conviction, order or other process or document filed, issued or entered in any proceeding had or taken under this Act. R.S., c. 160, s. 18.

**Child's oath may be dispensed with**
19. (1) When in a proceeding before a juvenile court a child of tender years who is called as a witness does not, in the opinion of the judge, understand the nature of an oath, the evidence of such child may be received, though not given under oath, if in the opinion of the judge the child is possessed of sufficient intelligence to justify the reception of the evidence and understands the duty of speaking the truth.

**Corroborative evidence**
(2) No person shall be convicted upon the evidence of a child of tender years not under oath unless such evidence is corroborated in some material respect. R.S., c. 160, s. 19.

**Release on probation**

20. (1) In the case of a child adjudged to be a juvenile delinquent the court may, in its discretion, take either one or more of the several courses of action hereinafter in this section set out, as it may in its judgment deem proper in the circumstances of the case:

(*a*) suspend final disposition;

(*b*) adjourn the hearing or disposition of the case from time to time for any definite or indefinite period;

(*c*) impose a fine not exceeding twenty-five dollars, which may be paid in periodical amounts or otherwise;

(*d*) commit the child to the care or custody of a probation officer or of any other suitable person;

(*e*) allow the child to remain in its home, subject to the visitation of a probation officer, such child to report to the court or to the probation officer as often as may be required;

(*f*) cause the child to be placed in a suitable family home as a foster home, subject to the friendly supervision of a probation officer and the further order of the court;

(*g*) impose upon the delinquent such further or other conditions as may be deemed advisable;

(*h*) commit the child to the charge of any children's aid society, duly organized under an Act of the legislature of the province and approved by the lieutenant governor in council, or, in any municipality in which there is no children's aid society, to the charge of the superintendent, if there is one; or

(*i*) commit the child to an industrial school duly approved by the lieutenant governor in council.

**Support of child**

(2) In every such case it is within the power of the court to make an order upon the parent or parents of the child, or upon the municipality to which the child belongs, to contribute to the child's support such sum as the court may determine, and where such order is made upon the municipality, the municipality may from time to time recover from the parent or parents any sum or sums paid by it pursuant to such order.

**Return of juvenile delinquent to court**

(3) Where a child has been adjudged to be a juvenile delinquent and whether or not such child has been dealt with in any of the ways provided for in subsection (1), the court may at any time, before such juvenile delinquent has reached the age of twenty-one years and unless the court has otherwise ordered, cause by notice, summons, or warrant, the delinquent to be brought before the court, and the court may then take any action provided for in subsection (1), or may make an order with respect to such child under section 9, or may discharge the child on parole or release the child from detention, but in a province in which there is a superintendent, no child shall be released by the judge from an industrial school without a report from such superintendent recommending such release, and where an order is made by a court releasing a juvenile delinquent from an industrial school or transferring such delinquent from an industrial school to a foster home or from one foster home to another under this subsection, it is not necessary for such delinquent to be before the court at the time that such order is made.

**Evidence on hearing**

(4) When a child is returned to the court, as provided in subsection (3), the court may deal with the case on the report of the probation officer or other person in whose care such child has been placed, or of the secretary of a children's aid society, or of the superintendent, or of the superintendent of the industrial school to which the child has been committed, without the necessity of hearing any further or other evidence.

**Child's own good**

(5) The action taken shall, in every case, be that which the court is of opinion the child's own good and the best interests of the community require. R.S., c. 160, s. 20.

**May be dealt with under provincial law**

21. (1) Whenever an order has been made under section 20 committing a child to a children's aid society, or to a superintendent, or to an industrial school, if so ordered by the provincial secretary, the child may thereafter be dealt with under the laws of the province in the same manner in all respects as if an order had been lawfully made in respect of a proceeding instituted under authority of a statute of the province; and from and after the date of the issuing of such order except for new offences, the child shall not be further dealt with by the court under this Act.

**Order in advance**

(2) The order of the provincial secretary may be made in advance and to apply to all cases of commitment mentioned in this section. R.S., c. 160, s. 21.

**Parent or guardian may be ordered to pay fine, damages or costs**

22. (1) Where a child is adjudged to have been guilty of an offence and the court is of the opinion that the case would be best met by the imposition of a fine, damages or costs, whether with or without restitution or any other action, the court may, if satisfied that the parent or guardian has conduced to the commission of the offence by neglecting to exercise due care of the child or otherwise, order that the fine, damages or costs awarded be paid by the parent or guardian of the child, instead of by the child.

**Limit of amount**

(2) Where a fine is imposed and ordered to be paid by the parent or guardian, the limit of amount imposed by subsection 20(1) does not apply, but shall in no case exceed the amount fixed for a similar offence under the *Criminal Code*.

**Recovery of amount**

(3) Where, under the provisions of this section or of section 20, a sum of money is ordered to be

paid, the court may adjudge, either by the order respecting the payment of such sum or by an order made subsequently, that the money shall be recoverable by distress and sale of the goods and chattels of the party and in default of such distress by imprisonment, and the amount is so recoverable or is recoverable in the same manner as a fine imposed under any provision of the *Criminal Code* is recoverable, or is recoverable as provided in any Act of the legislature of the province making provision for the recovery of fines.

**Parent or guardian to be heard**
(4) No order shall be made under this section without giving the parent or guardian an opportunity of being heard; but a parent or guardian who has been duly served with notice of the hearing pursuant to section 10 shall be deemed to have had such opportunity, notwithstanding the fact that he has failed to attend the hearing.

**Appeal**
(5) A parent or guardian has the same right of appeal from an order made under this section as if the order had been made on the conviction of the parent or guardian.

**Additional action**
(6) Any action taken under this section may be additional to any action taken under section 20. R.S., c. 160, s. 22.

**Religion of child to be respected**
23. (1) No Protestant child dealt with under this Act shall be committed to the care of any Roman Catholic children's aid society or be placed in any Roman Catholic family as his foster home; nor shall any Roman Catholic child dealt with under this Act be committed to the care of any Protestant children's aid society, or be placed in any Protestant family as his foster home; but this section does not apply to the placing of children in a temporary home or shelter for children, established under the authority of a statute of the province, or, in a municipality where there is but one children's aid society, to such children's aid society.

**Order to enforce preceding provision**
(2) If a Protestant child is committed to the care of a Roman Catholic children's aid society or placed in a Roman Catholic family as his foster home or if a Roman Catholic child is committed to the care of a Protestant children's aid society or placed in a Protestant family as his foster home, contrary to this section, the court shall, on the application of any person in that behalf, make an order providing for the proper commitment or placing of the child pursuant to subsection (1).

**Children of religious faith other than Protestant or Roman Catholic**
(3) No child of a religious faith other than the Protestant or Roman Catholic shall be committed to the care of either a Protestant or Roman Catholic children's aid society or be placed in any Protestant or Roman Catholic family as his foster home unless there is within the municipality no children's aid society or no suitable family of the same religious faith as that professed by the child or by his family, and, if there is no children's aid society or suitable family of such faith to which the care of such child can properly be given, the disposition of such child is in the discretion of the court. R.S., c. 160, s. 23.

**Children not allowed to be in court**
24. (1) No child, other than an infant in arms, shall be permitted to be present in court during the trial of any person charged with an offence or during any proceedings preliminary thereto, and if so present the child shall be ordered to be removed unless he is the person charged with the alleged offence, or unless the child's presence is required, as a witness or otherwise, for the purposes of justice.

**Exception**
(2) This section does not apply to messengers, clerks and other persons required to attend at any court for the purposes connected with their employment. R.S., c. 160, s. 24.

**Children under twelve**
25. It is not lawful to commit a juvenile delinquent apparently under the age of twelve years to any industrial school, unless and until an attempt has been made to reform such child in his own home or in a foster home or in the charge of a children's aid society, or of a superintendent, and unless the court finds that the best interests of the child and the welfare of the community require such commitment. R.S., c. 160, s. 25.

**Children to be separated from adults**
26. (1) No juvenile delinquent shall, under any circumstances, upon or after conviction, be sentenced to or incarcerated in any penitentiary, or county or other gaol, or police station, or any other place in which adults are or may be imprisoned.

**Exception**
(2) This section does not apply to a child who has been proceeded against under section 9. R.S., c. 160, s. 26.

**Juvenile court committee**
27. (1) There shall be in connection with the juvenile court a committee of citizens, serving without remuneration, to be known as the "juvenile court committee".

**Juvenile court committee *ex officio***
(2) Where there is a children's aid society in a city or town in which this Act is in force, the committee of such society or a sub-committee thereof shall be the juvenile court committee; and where there is both a Protestant and a Roman Catholic children's aid society then the committee of the Protestant children's aid society or a sub-committee thereof shall be the juvenile court committee as regards Protestant children, and the committee of the Roman Catholic children's aid society or a sub-committee thereof shall be the juvenile court committee as regards Roman Catholic children.

**Appointment by court**
(3) Where there is no children's aid society in a city or town in which this Act is in force, the court may, and, upon a petition signed by fifty residents of the municipality in question, shall appoint three or more persons to be the juvenile court committee with respect to Protestant children, and three or more other persons to be the juvenile court committee with respect to Roman Catholic children; and the persons so appointed may in their discretion sit as one joint committee.

**When child of religious faith other than Protestant or Roman Catholic**
(4) In the case of a child of a religious faith other than Protestant or Roman Catholic, the court shall appoint three or more suitable persons to be the juvenile court committee as regards such child, such persons to be of the same religious faith as the child if there are such suitable persons resident within the municipality willing to act, and if in the opinion of the court they are desirable persons to be such committee. R.S., c. 160, s. 27.

**Duties of committee**
28. (1) It is the duty of the juvenile court committee to meet as often as may be necessary and consult with the probation officers with regard to juvenile delinquents, to offer, through the probation officers and otherwise, advice to the court as to the best mode of dealing with such delinquents, and, generally, to facilitate by every means in its power, the reformation of juvenile delinquents.

**Representatives may be present**
(2) Representatives of the juvenile court committee, who are members of that committee, may be present at any session of the juvenile court.

**Certain cases reserved for judge**
(3) No deputy judge shall hear and determine any case that a juvenile court committee desires should be reserved for hearing and determination by the judge of the juvenile court. R.S., c. 160, s. 28.

**Court may appoint probation officer**
29. Where no probation officer has been appointed under provincial authority and remuneration for a probation officer has been provided by municipal grant, public subscription or otherwise, the court shall, with the concurrence of the juvenile court committee, appoint one or more suitable persons as probation officers. R.S., c. 160, s. 29.

**Powers of a probation officer**
30. Every probation officer duly appointed under this Act or of any provincial statute has in the discharge of his or her duties as such probation officer all the powers of a constable, and shall be protected from civil actions for anything done in *bona fide* exercise of the powers conferred by this Act. R.S., c. 160, s. 30.

**Duties of probation officer**
31. It is the duty of a probation officer
(*a*) to make such investigation as may be required by the court;
(*b*) to be present in court in order to represent the interests of the child when the case is heard;
(*c*) to furnish to the court such information and assistance as may be required; and
(*d*) to take such charge of any child, before or after trial, as may be directed by the court. R.S., c. 160, s. 31.

**Probation officers under control of judge**
32. Every probation officer, however appointed, is under the control and subject to the directions of the judge of the court with which such probation officer is connected, for all purposes of this Act. R.S., c. 160, s. 32.

**Adults liable who contribute to delinquency**
33. (1) Any person, whether the parent or guardian of the child or not, who, knowingly or wilfully,
(*a*) aids, causes, abets or connives at the commission by a child of a delinquency, or
(*b*) does any act producing, promoting, or contributing to a child's being or becoming a juvenile delinquent or likely to make any child a juvenile delinquent, is liable on summary conviction before a juvenile court or a magistrate to a fine not exceeding five hundred dollars or to imprisonment for a period not exceeding two years, or to both.

**Liability of parents and guardians**
(2) Any person who, being the parent or guardian of the child and being able to do so, knowingly neglects to do that which would directly tend to prevent the child being or becoming a juvenile delinquent or to remove the conditions that render or are likely to render the child a juvenile delinquent is liable on summary conviction before a juvenile court or a magistrate to a fine not exceeding five hundred dollars or to imprisonment for a period not exceeding two years, or to both.

**Adjournment**
(3) The court or magistrate may postpone or adjourn the hearing of a charge under this section for such periods as the court may deem advisable or may postpone or adjourn the hearing *sine die* and may impose conditions upon any person found guilty under this section and suspend sentence subject to those conditions, and on proof at any time that those conditions have been violated may pass sentence on such person.

**No defence if child does not become delinquent**
(4) It is not a valid defence to a prosecution under this section either that the child is of too tender years to understand or appreciate the nature or effect of the conduct of the accused, or that notwithstanding the conduct of the accused the child did not in fact become a juvenile delinquent.

**Limitation**
(5) Notwithstanding anything to the contrary in section 5 or in the provisions of the *Criminal Code* referred to in paragraph 5(1)(b), any prosecution for an offence under this section may be commenced within one year from the time when

the offence is alleged to have been committed. R.S., c. 160, s. 33.

**Penalty for inducing, etc. child to leave home, etc.**

34. Any person who induces or attempts to induce any child to leave any detention home, industrial school, foster home or any other institution or place where such child has been placed under this Act or who removes or attempts to remove such child therefrom, without the authority of the court, or who, when a child has unlawfully left the custody of an institution or foster home knowingly harbours or conceals such child without notice of the child's whereabouts to the court or to the institution or the local police authorities, is guilty of an offence and is liable upon summary conviction before a juvenile court or before a magistrate to a fine not exceeding one hundred dollars or to imprisonment for a period not exceeding one year, or to both. R.S., c. 160, s. 34.

**No preliminary hearing**

35. (1) Prosecutions against adults for offences against any provisions of the *Criminal Code* in respect of a child may be brought in the juvenile court without the necessity of a preliminary hearing before a justice, and may be summarily disposed of where the offence is triable summarily, or otherwise dealt with as in the case of a preliminary hearing before a justice.

**Application of *Criminal Code***

(2) All provisions of the *Criminal Code* not inconsistent with this Act that would apply to similar proceedings if brought before a justice apply to prosecutions brought before the juvenile court under this section. R.S., c. 160, s. 35.

**Contempt of court**

36. (1) Every juvenile court has such and like powers and authority to preserve order in court during the sittings thereof and by the like ways and means as now by law are or may be exercised and used in like cases and for the like purposes by any court in Canada and by the judges thereof, during the sittings thereof.

**Enforcing of process**

(2) Every judge of a juvenile court, whenever any resistance is offered to the execution of any summons, warrant of execution or other process issued by him, may enforce the due execution of the process by the means provided by the law for enforcing the execution of the process of other courts in like cases. R.S., c. 160, s. 36.

**Appeals by special leave**

37. (1) A supreme court judge may, in his discretion, on special grounds, grant special leave to appeal from any decision of the juvenile court or a magistrate; in any case where such leave is granted the procedure upon appeal shall be such as is provided in the case of a conviction on indictment, and the provisions of the *Criminal Code* relating to appeals from conviction on indictment *mutatis mutandis* apply to such appeal, save that the appeal shall be to a supreme court judge instead of to the court of appeal, with a further right of appeal to the court of appeal by special leave of that court.

**When leave to appeal may be granted**

(2) No leave to appeal shall be granted under this section unless the judge or court granting such leave considers that in the particular circumstances of the case it is essential in the public interest or for the due administration of justice that such leave be granted.

**Application for leave to appeal**

(3) Application for leave to appeal under this section shall be made within ten days of the making of the conviction or order complained of, or within such further time, not exceeding an additional twenty days, as a supreme court judge may see fit to fix, either before or after the expiration of the said ten days. R.S., c. 160, s. 37.

**Act to be liberally construed**

38. This Act shall be liberally construed in order that its purpose may be carried out, namely, that the care and custody and discipline of a juvenile delinquent shall approximate as nearly as may be that which should be given by his parents, and that as far as practicable every juvenile delinquent shall be treated, not as criminal, but as a misdirected and misguided child, and one needing aid, encouragement, help and assistance. R.S., c. 160, s. 38.

**Not to affect provincial statutes**

39. Nothing in this Act shall be construed as having the effect of repealing or overriding any provision of any provincial statute intended for the protection or benefit of children; and when a juvenile delinquent, who has not been guilty of an act that is under the provisions of the *Criminal Code* an indictable offence, comes within the provisions of a provincial statute, he may be dealt with either under such statute or under this Act as may be deemed to be in the best interests of the child. R.S., c. 160, s. 39.

**Repeal of former law**

40. Whenever and so soon as this Act goes into force in any province, city, town, or other portion of a province, every provision of the *Criminal Code* or of any other Act of the Parliament of Canada inconsistent with the provisions of this Act, stands repealed as regards such province, city, town, or other portion of a province. R.S., c. 160, s. 40.

**Sections in force in Canada**

41. Subsections 12(4) and 17(3) and (5), and section 34 shall be in force in all parts of Canada, whether this Act is otherwise in force or not. R.S., c. 160, s. 41.

**When Act shall be enforced**

42. Subject to section 41, this Act may be put in force in any province, or in any portion of a province, by proclamation, after the passing of an Act by the legislature of any province providing for the establishment of juvenile courts, or designating

any existing courts as juvenile courts, and of detention homes for children. R.S., c. 160, s. 42.

**Any city or town may ask for this law**
**43.** (1) Subject to section 41, this Act may be put in force in any city, town, or other portion of a province, by proclamation, notwithstanding that the provincial legislature has not passed an Act such as referred to in section 42, if the Governor in Council is satisfied that proper facilities for the due carrying out of the provisions of this Act have been provided in such city, town, or other portion of a province, by the municipal council thereof or otherwise.

**Special appointment of judge**
(2) The Governor in Council may designate a superior court or county court judge or a justice, having jurisdiction in the city, town, or other portion of a province, in which the Act is so put in force, to act as juvenile court judge for such city, town, or other portion of a province, and the judge or justice so designated or appointed has and shall exercise in such city, town, or other portion of a province, all the powers by this Act conferred on the juvenile court. R.S., c. 160, s. 43.

**Enforcement of Act**
**44.** This Act shall go into force only when and as proclamations declaring it in force in any province, city, town or other portion of the province are issued and published in the *Canada Gazette*. R.S., c. 160, s. 44.

**Operation of Act**
**45.** Notwithstanding section 44, this Act shall be in force in every part of Canada in which the *Juvenile Delinquents Act*, chapter 108 of the Revised Statutes of Canada, 1927, was in force on the 14th day of June 1929. R.S., c. 160, s. 45.

# Appendix B
## Young Offenders Act

Note: This consolidation is not an official version of the law and therefore should not be used in case law. It was taken from the Department of Justice Web site and should be considered accurate for the purposes of this book.

CHAPTER Y-1
An Act respecting young offenders

SHORT TITLE

**Short title**
**1.** This Act may be cited as the *Young Offenders Act.*
1980-81-82-83, c. 110, s. 1.

INTERPRETATION

**Definitions**
**2.** (1) In this Act,

**"adult"**
"adult" means a person who is neither a young person nor a child;

**"alternative measures"**
"alternative measures" means measures other than judicial proceedings under this Act used to deal with a young person alleged to have committed an offence;

**"child"**
"child" means a person who is or, in the absence of evidence to the contrary, appears to be under the age of twelve years;

**"disposition"**
"disposition" means a disposition made under any of sections 20, 20.1 and 28 to 32 and includes a confirmation or a variation of a disposition;

**"offence"**
"offence" means an offence created by an Act of Parliament or by any regulation, rule, order, by-law or ordinance made thereunder, other than an ordinance of the Yukon Territory or the Northwest Territories or a law of the Legislature for Nunavut;

**"ordinary court"**
"ordinary court" means the court that would, but for this Act, have jurisdiction in respect of an offence alleged to have been committed;

**"parent"**
"parent" includes, in respect of another person, any person who is under a legal duty to provide for that other person or any person who has, in law or in fact, the custody or control of that other person, but does not include a person who has the custody or control of that other person by reason only of proceedings under this Act;

**"pre-disposition report"**
"pre-disposition report" means a report on the personal and family history and present environment of a young person made in accordance with section 14;

**"progress report"**
"progress report" means a report made in accordance with section 28 on the performance of a young person against whom a disposition has been made;

**"provincial director"**
"provincial director" means a person, a group or class of persons or a body appointed or designated by or pursuant to an Act of the legislature of a province or by the Lieutenant Governor in Council of a province or his delegate to perform in that province, either generally or in a specific case, any of the duties or functions of a provincial director under this Act;

**"review board"**
"review board" means a review board established or designated by a province for the purposes of section 30;

**"young person"**
"young person" means a person who is or, in the absence of evidence to the contrary, appears to be twelve years of age or more, but under eighteen years of age and, where the context requires, includes any person who is charged under this Act with having committed an offence while he was a young person or is found guilty of an offence under this Act;

**"youth court"**
"youth court" means a court established or designated by or under an Act of the legislature of a province, or designated by the Governor in Council or the Lieutenant Governor in Council of a province, as a youth court for the purposes of this Act;

**"youth court judge"**
"youth court judge" means a person appointed to be a judge of a youth court;

**"youth worker"**
"youth worker" means a person appointed or designated, whether by title of youth worker or probation officer or by any other title, by or pursuant to an Act of the legislature of a province or by the Lieutenant Governor in Council of a province or his delegate, to perform, either generally or in a specific case, in that province any of the duties or functions of a youth worker under this Act.

**Words and expressions**
(2) Unless otherwise provided, words and expressions used in this Act have the same meaning as in the *Criminal Code.*
R.S., 1985, c. Y-1, s. 2; R.S., 1985, c. 24 (2nd Supp.), s. 1; 1993, c. 28, s. 78; 1995, c. 39, s. 177; 1998, c. 15, s. 41.

**Powers, duties and functions of provincial directors**
2.1 Any power, duty or function of a provincial director under this Act may be exercised or performed by any person authorized by the provincial director to do so and, if so exercised or performed, shall be deemed to have been exercised or performed by the provincial director.
R.S., 1985, c. 24 (2nd Supp.), s. 2.

**DECLARATION OF PRINCIPLE**

**Policy for Canada with respect to young offenders**
3. (1) It is hereby recognized and declared that
(*a*) crime prevention is essential to the long-term protection of society and requires addressing the underlying causes of crime by young persons and developing multi-disciplinary approaches to identifying and effectively responding to children and young persons at risk of committing offending behaviour in the future;
(*a*.1) while young persons should not in all instances be held accountable in the same manner or suffer the same consequences for their behaviour as adults, young persons who commit offences should nonetheless bear responsibility for their contraventions;
(*b*) society must, although it has the responsibility to take reasonable measures to prevent criminal conduct by young persons, be afforded the necessary protection from illegal behaviour;
(*c*) young persons who commit offences require supervision, discipline and control, but, because of their state of dependency and level of development and maturity, they also have special needs and require guidance and assistance;
(*c*.1) the protection of society, which is a primary objective of the criminal law applicable to youth, is best served by rehabilitation, wherever possible, of young persons who commit offences, and rehabilitation is best achieved by addressing the needs and circumstances of a young person that are relevant to the young person's offending behaviour;
(*d*) where it is not inconsistent with the protection of society, taking no measures or taking measures other than judicial proceedings under this Act should be considered for dealing with young persons who have committed offences;
(*e*) young persons have rights and freedoms in their own right, including those stated in the *Canadian Charter of Rights and Freedoms* or in the *Canadian Bill of Rights*, and in particular a right to be heard in the course of, and to participate in, the processes that lead to decisions that affect them, and young persons should have special guarantees of their rights and freedoms;
(*f*) in the application of this Act, the rights and freedoms of young persons include a right to the least possible interference with freedom that is consistent with the protection of society, having regard to the needs of young persons and the interests of their families;
(*g*) young persons have the right, in every instance where they have rights or freedoms that may be affected by this Act, to be informed as to what those rights and freedoms are; and
(*h*) parents have responsibility for the care and supervision of their children, and, for that reason, young persons should be removed from parental supervision either partly or entirely only when measures that provide for continuing parental supervision are inappropriate.

**Act to be liberally construed**
(2) This Act shall be liberally construed to the end that young persons will be dealt with in accordance with the principles set out in subsection (1).
R.S., 1980-81-82-83, c. 110, s. 3; 1995, c. 19, s. 1.

**ALTERNATIVE MEASURES**

**Alternative measures**
4. (1) Alternative measures may be used to deal with a young person alleged to have committed an offence instead of judicial proceedings under this Act only if
(*a*) the measures are part of a program of alternative measures authorized by the Attorney General or his delegate or authorized by a person, or a person within a class of persons, designated by the Lieutenant Governor in Council of a province;
(*b*) the person who is considering whether to use such measures is satisfied that they would be appropriate, having regard to the needs of the young person and the interests of society;
(*c*) the young person, having been informed of

the alternative measures, fully and freely consents to participate therein;
- (*d*) the young person has, before consenting to participate in the alternative measures, been advised of his right to be represented by counsel and been given a reasonable opportunity to consult with counsel;
- (*e*) the young person accepts responsibility for the act or omission that forms the basis of the offence that he is alleged to have committed;
- (*f*) there is, in the opinion of the Attorney General or his agent, sufficient evidence to proceed with the prosecution of the offence; and
- (*g*) the prosecution of the offence is not in any way barred at law.

**Restriction on use**
(2) Alternative measures shall not be used to deal with a young person alleged to have committed an offence if the young person
- (*a*) denies his participation or involvement in the commission of the offence; or
- (*b*) expresses his wish to have any charge against him dealt with by the youth court.

**Admissions not admissible in evidence**
(3) No admission, confession or statement accepting responsibility for a given act or omission made by a young person alleged to have committed an offence as a condition of his being dealt with by alternative measures shall be admissible in evidence against him in any civil or criminal proceedings.

**No bar to proceedings**
(4) The use of alternative measures in respect of a young person alleged to have committed an offence is not a bar to proceedings against him under this Act, but
- (*a*) where the youth court is satisfied on a balance of probabilities that the young person has totally complied with the terms and conditions of the alternative measures, the youth court shall dismiss any charge against him; and
- (*b*) where the youth court is satisfied on a balance of probabilities that the young person has partially complied with the terms and conditions of the alternative measures, the youth court may dismiss any charge against him if, in the opinion of the court, the prosecution of the charge would, having regard to the circumstances, be unfair, and the youth court may consider the young person's performance with respect to the alternative measures before making a disposition under this Act.

**Laying of information, etc.**
(5) Subject to subsection (4), nothing in this section shall be construed to prevent any person from laying an information, obtaining the issue or confirmation of any process or proceeding with the prosecution of any offence in accordance with law.
1980-81-82-83, c. 110, s. 4.

## JURISDICTION

**Exclusive jurisdiction of youth court**
5. (1) Notwithstanding any other Act of Parliament but subject to the *National Defence Act* and section 16, a youth court has exclusive jurisdiction in respect of any offence alleged to have been committed by a person while he was a young person and any such person shall be dealt with as provided in this Act.

**Period of limitation**
(2) No proceedings in respect of an offence shall be commenced under this Act after the expiration of the time limit set out in any other Act of Parliament or any regulation made thereunder for the institution of proceedings in respect of that offence.

**Proceedings continued when adult**
(3) Proceedings commenced under this Act against a young person may be continued, after he becomes an adult, in all respects as if he remained a young person.

**Powers of youth court judge**
(4) A youth court judge, for the purpose of carrying out the provisions of this Act, is a justice and a provincial court judge and has the jurisdiction and powers of a summary conviction court under the *Criminal Code*.

**Court of record**
(5) A youth court is a court of record.
R.S., 1985, c. Y-1, s. 5; R.S., 1985, c. 24 (2nd Supp.), s. 3.

**Certain proceedings may be taken before justices**
6. Any proceeding that may be carried out before a justice under the *Criminal Code*, other than a plea, a trial or an adjudication, may be carried out before a justice in respect of an offence alleged to have been committed by a young person, and any process that may be issued by a justice under the *Criminal Code* may be issued by a justice in respect of an offence alleged to have been committed by a young person.
R.S., 1985, c. Y-1, s. 6; R.S., 1985, c. 24 (2nd Supp.), s. 4.

## DETENTION PRIOR TO DISPOSITION

**Designated place of temporary detention**
7. (1) A young person who is
- (*a*) arrested and detained prior to the making of a disposition in respect of the young person under section 20, or
- (*b*) detained pursuant to a warrant issued under subsection 32(6)

shall, subject to subsection (4), be detained in a place of temporary detention designated as such by the Lieutenant Governor in Council of the appropriate province or his delegate or in a place within a class of such places so designated.

**Exception**
(1.1) A young person who is detained in a place of temporary detention pursuant to subsection (1) may, in the course of being transferred from that place to the court or from the court to that place, be held under the supervision and control of a peace officer.

**Detention separate from adults**
(2) A young person referred to in subsection (1) shall be held separate and apart from any adult who is detained or held in custody unless a youth court judge or a justice is satisfied that
(*a*) the young person cannot, having regard to his own safety or the safety of others, be detained in a place of detention for young persons; or
(*b*) no place of detention for young persons is available within a reasonable distance.

**Transfer by provincial director**
(3) A young person who is detained in custody in accordance with subsection (1) may, during the period of detention, be transferred by the provincial director from one place of temporary detention to another.

**Exception relating to temporary detention**
(4) Subsections (1) and (2) do not apply in respect of any temporary restraint of a young person under the supervision and control of a peace officer after arrest, but a young person who is so restrained shall be transferred to a place of temporary detention referred to in subsection (1) as soon as is reasonably practicable, and in no case later than the first reasonable opportunity after the appearance of the young person before a youth court judge or a justice pursuant to section 503 of the *Criminal Code.*

**Authorization of provincial authority for detention**
(5) In any province for which the Lieutenant Governor in Council has designated a person or a group of persons whose authorization is required, either in all circumstances or in circumstances specified by the Lieutenant Governor in Council, before a young person who has been arrested may be detained in accordance with this section, no young person shall be so detained unless the authorization is obtained.

**Determination by provincial authority of place of detention**
(6) In any province for which the Lieutenant Governor in Council has designated a person or a group of persons who may determine the place where a young person who has been arrested may be detained in accordance with this section, no young person may be so detained in a place other than the one so determined.
R.S., 1985, c. Y-1, s. 7; R.S., 1985, c. 24 (2nd Supp.), s. 5.

**Placement of young person in care of responsible person**
**7.1** (1) Where a youth court judge or a justice is satisfied that
(*a*) a young person who has been arrested would, but for this subsection, be detained in custody,
(*b*) a responsible person is willing and able to take care of and exercise control over the young person, and
(*c*) the young person is willing to be placed in the care of that person,
the young person may be placed in the care of that person instead of being detained in custody.

**Condition of placement**
(2) A young person shall not be placed in the care of a person under subsection (1) unless
(*a*) that person undertakes in writing to take care of and to be responsible for the attendance of the young person in court when required and to comply with such other conditions as the youth court judge or justice may specify; and
(*b*) the young person undertakes in writing to comply with the arrangement and to comply with such other conditions as the youth court judge or justice may specify.

**Removing young person from care**
(3) Where a young person has been placed in the care of a person under subsection (1) and
(*a*) that person is no longer willing or able to take care of or exercise control over the young person, or
(*b*) it is, for any other reason, no longer appropriate that the young person be placed in the care of that person,
the young person, the person in whose care the young person has been placed or any other person may, by application in writing to a youth court judge or a justice, apply for an order under subsection (4).

**Order**
(4) Where a youth court judge or a justice is satisfied that a young person should not remain in the custody of the person in whose care he was placed under subsection (1), the youth court judge or justice shall
(*a*) make an order relieving the person and the young person of the obligations undertaken pursuant to subsection (2); and
(*b*) issue a warrant for the arrest of the young person.

**Effect of arrest**
(5) Where a young person is arrested pursuant to a warrant issued under paragraph (4)(b), the young person shall be taken before a youth court judge or justice forthwith and dealt with under section 515 of the *Criminal Code.*
R.S., 1985, c. 24 (2nd Supp.), s. 5.

**Offence and punishment**
**7.2** Any person who wilfully fails to comply with section 7, or with an undertaking entered into pursuant to subsection 7.1(2), is guilty of an offence punishable on summary conviction.
R.S., 1985, c. 24 (2nd Supp.), s. 5.

**8.** (1) [Repealed, R.S., 1985, c. 24 (2nd Supp.), s. 6]

**Application to youth court**
(2) Where an order is made under section 515 of the *Criminal Code* in respect of a young person by a justice who is not a youth court judge, an application may, at any time after the order is made, be made to a youth court for the release from or detention in custody of the young person, as the case may be, and the youth court shall hear the matter as an original application.

**Notice to prosecutor**
(3) An application under subsection (2) for release from custody shall not be heard unless the young person has given the prosecutor at least two clear days notice in writing of the application.

**Notice to young person**
(4) An application under subsection (2) for detention in custody shall not be heard unless the prosecutor has given the young person at least two clear days notice in writing of the application.

**Waiver of notice**
(5) The requirement for a notice under subsection (3) or (4) may be waived by the prosecutor or by the young person or his counsel, as the case may be.

**Application for review under section 520 or 521 of *Criminal Code***
(6) An application under section 520 or 521 of the *Criminal Code* for a review of an order made in respect of a young person by a youth court judge who is a judge of a superior, county or district court shall be made to a judge of the court of appeal.

**Nunavut**
(6.1) Despite subsection (6), an application under section 520 or 521 of the *Criminal Code* for a review of an order made in respect of a young person by a youth court judge who is a judge of the Nunavut Court of Justice shall be made to a judge of that court.

**Idem**
(7) No application may be made under section 520 or 521 of the *Criminal Code* for a review of an order made in respect of a young person by a justice who is not a youth court judge.

**Interim release by youth court judge only**
(8) Where a young person against whom proceedings have been taken under this Act is charged with an offence referred to in section 522 of the *Criminal Code*, a youth court judge, but no other court, judge or justice, may release the young person from custody under that section.

**Review by court of appeal**
(9) A decision made by a youth court judge under subsection (8) may be reviewed in accordance with section 680 of the *Criminal Code* and that section applies, with such modifications as the circumstances require, to any decision so made.
R.S., 1985, c. Y-1, s. 8; R.S., 1985, c. 24 (2nd Supp.), s. 6; 1999, c. 3, s. 86.

NOTICES TO PARENTS

**Notice to parent in case of arrest**
9. (1) Subject to subsections (3) and (4), where a young person is arrested and detained in custody pending his appearance in court, the officer in charge at the time the young person is detained shall, as soon as possible, give or cause to be given, orally or in writing, to a parent of the young person notice of the arrest stating the place of detention and the reason for the arrest.

**Notice to parent in case of summons or appearance notice**
(2) Subject to subsections (3) and (4), where a summons or an appearance notice is issued in respect of a young person, the person who issued the summons or appearance notice, or, where a young person is released on giving his promise to appear or entering into a recognizance, the officer in charge, shall, as soon as possible, give or cause to be given, in writing, to a parent of the young person notice of the summons, appearance notice, promise to appear or recognizance.

**Notice to relative or other adult**
(3) Where the whereabouts of the parents of a young person
(*a*) who is arrested and detained in custody,
(*b*) in respect of whom a summons or an appearance notice is issued, or
(*c*) who is released on giving his promise to appear or entering into a recognizance

are not known or it appears that no parent is available, a notice under this section may be given to an adult relative of the young person who is known to the young person and is likely to assist him or, if no such adult relative is available, to such other adult who is known to the young person and is likely to assist him as the person giving the notice considers appropriate.

**Notice to spouse**
(4) Where a young person described in paragraph (3)(*a*), (*b*) or (*c*) is married, a notice under this section may be given to the spouse of the young person instead of a parent.

**Notice on direction of youth court judge or justice**
(5) Where doubt exists as to the person to whom a notice under this section should be given, a youth court judge or, where a youth court judge is, having regard to the circumstances, not reasonably available, a justice may give directions as to the person to whom the notice should be given, and a notice given in accordance with those directions is sufficient notice for the purposes of this section.

**Contents of notice**
(6) Any notice under this section shall, in addition to any other requirements under this section, include
(*a*) the name of the young person in respect of whom it is given;
(*b*) the charge against the young person and the time and place of appearance; and

(*c*) a statement that the young person has the right to be represented by counsel.

**Service of notice**
(7) Subject to subsections (9) and (10), a notice under this section given in writing may be served personally or may be sent by mail.

**Proceedings not invalid**
(8) Subject to subsections (9) and (10), failure to give notice in accordance with this section does not affect the validity of proceedings under this Act.

**Exception**
(9) Failure to give notice under subsection (2) in accordance with this section in any case renders invalid any subsequent proceedings under this Act relating to the case unless
(*a*) a parent of the young person against whom proceedings are held attends court with the young person; or
(*b*) a youth court judge or a justice before whom proceedings are held against the young person
(i) adjourns the proceedings and orders that the notice be given in such manner and to such persons as the judge or justice directs, or
(ii) dispenses with the notice where the judge or justice is of the opinion that, having regard to the circumstances, the notice may be dispensed with.

**Where a notice not served**
(10) Where there has been a failure to give a notice under subsection (1) in accordance with this section and none of the persons to whom such notice may be given attends court with a young person, a youth court judge or a justice before whom proceedings are held against the young person may
(*a*) adjourn the proceedings and order that the notice be given in such manner and to such person as he directs; or
(*b*) dispense with the notice where, in his opinion, having regard to the circumstances, notice may be dispensed with.

(11) [Repealed, R.S., 1985, c. 24 (2nd Supp.), s. 7]
R.S., 1985, c. Y-1, s. 9; R.S., 1985, c. 24 (2nd Supp.), ss. 7, 44(F); 1991, c. 43, s. 31.

**Order requiring attendance of parent**
**10.** (1) Where a parent does not attend proceedings before a youth court in respect of a young person, the court may, if in its opinion the presence of the parent is necessary or in the best interest of the young person, by order in writing require the parent to attend at any stage of the proceedings.

**Service of order**
(2) A copy of any order made under subsection (1) shall be served by a peace officer or by a person designated by a youth court by delivering it personally to the parent to whom it is directed, unless the youth court authorizes service by registered mail.

**Failure to attend**
(3) A parent who is ordered to attend a youth court pursuant to subsection (1) and who fails without reasonable excuse, the proof of which lies on that parent, to comply with the order
(*a*) is guilty of contempt of court;
(*b*) may be dealt with summarily by the court; and
(*c*) is liable to the punishment provided for in the *Criminal Code* for a summary conviction offence.

**Appeal**
(4) Section 10 of the *Criminal Code* applies where a person is convicted of contempt of court under subsection (3).

**Warrant to arrest parent**
(5) If a parent who is ordered to attend a youth court pursuant to subsection (1) does not attend at the time and place named in the order or fails to remain in attendance as required and it is proved that a copy of the order was served on the parent, a youth court may issue a warrant to compel the attendance of the parent.

(6) [Repealed, R.S., 1985, c. 24 (2nd Supp.), s. 8]
R.S., 1985, c. Y-1, s. 10; R.S., 1985, c. 24 (2nd Supp.), ss. 8, 44(F).

## RIGHT TO COUNSEL

**Right to retain counsel**
**11.** (1) A young person has the right to retain and instruct counsel without delay, and to exercise that right personally, at any stage of proceedings against the young person and prior to and during any consideration of whether, instead of commencing or continuing judicial proceedings against the young person under this Act, to use alternative measures to deal with the young person.

**Arresting officer to advise young person of right to counsel**
(2) Every young person who is arrested or detained shall, forthwith on his arrest or detention, be advised by the arresting officer or the officer in charge, as the case may be, of his right to be represented by counsel and shall be given an opportunity to obtain counsel.

**Justice, youth court or review board to advise young person of right to counsel**
(3) Where a young person is not represented by counsel
(*a*) at a hearing at which it will be determined whether to release the young person or detain him in custody prior to disposition of his case,
(*b*) at a hearing held pursuant to section 16,
(*c*) at his trial,
(*c*.1) at any proceedings held pursuant to subsection 26.1(1), 26.2(1) or 26.6(1),
(*d*) at a review of a disposition held before a youth court or a review board under this Act, or
(*e*) at a review of the level of custody pursuant to subsection 28.1(1), the justice before whom, or the youth court or review board before which, the hearing, trial or review is held shall advise the young person of his right to be represented by counsel and shall give the young person a reasonable opportunity to obtain counsel.

**Trial, hearing or review before youth court or review board**

(4) Where a young person at his trial or at a hearing or review referred to in subsection (3) wishes to obtain counsel but is unable to do so, the youth court before which the hearing, trial or review is held or the review board before which the review is held

(*a*) shall, where there is a legal aid or an assistance program available in the province where the hearing, trial or review is held, refer the young person to that program for the appointment of counsel; or

(*b*) where no legal aid or assistance program is available or the young person is unable to obtain counsel through such a program, may, and on the request of the young person shall, direct that the young person be represented by counsel.

**Appointment of counsel**

(5) Where a direction is made under paragraph (4)(*b*) in respect of a young person, the Attorney General of the province in which the direction is made shall appoint counsel, or cause counsel to be appointed, to represent the young person.

**Release hearing before justice**

(6) Where a young person at a hearing before a justice who is not a youth court judge at which it will be determined whether to release the young person or detain him in custody prior to disposition of his case wishes to obtain counsel but is unable to do so, the justice shall

(*a*) where there is a legal aid or an assistance program available in the province where the hearing is held,

(i) refer the young person to that program for the appointment of counsel, or

(ii) refer the matter to a youth court to be dealt with in accordance with paragraph (4)(*a*) or (*b*); or

(*b*) where no legal aid or assistance program is available or the young person is unable to obtain counsel through such a program, refer the matter to a youth court to be dealt with in accordance with paragraph (4)(*b*).

**Young person may be assisted by adult**

(7) Where a young person is not represented by counsel at his trial or at a hearing or review referred to in subsection (3), the justice before whom or the youth court or review board before which the proceedings are held may, on the request of the young person, allow the young person to be assisted by an adult whom the justice, court or review board considers to be suitable.

**Counsel independent of parents**

(8) In any case where it appears to a youth court judge or a justice that the interests of a young person and his parents are in conflict or that it would be in the best interest of the young person to be represented by his own counsel, the judge or justice shall ensure that the young person is represented by counsel independent of his parents.

**Statement of right to counsel**

(9) A statement that a young person has the right to be represented by counsel shall be included in

(*a*) any appearance notice or summons issued to the young person;

(*b*) any warrant to arrest the young person;

(*c*) any promise to appear given by the young person;

(*d*) any recognizance entered into before an officer in charge by the young person;

(*e*) any notice given to the young person in relation to any proceedings held pursuant to subsection 26.1(1), 26.2(1) or 26.6(1); or

(*f*) any notice of a review of a disposition given to the young person.

R.S., 1985, c. Y-1, s. 11; R.S., 1985, c. 24 (2nd Supp.), s. 9; 1992, c. 11, s. 1; 1995, c. 19, s. 2.

## APPEARANCE

**Where young person appears**

12. (1) A young person against whom an information is laid must first appear before a youth court judge or a justice, and the judge or justice shall

(*a*) cause the information to be read to the young person;

(*b*) where the young person is not represented by counsel, inform the young person of the right to be so represented; and

(*c*) where the young person is a young person referred to in subsection 16(1.01), inform the young person that the young person will be proceeded against in ordinary court in accordance with the law ordinarily applicable to an adult charged with the offence unless an application is made to the youth court by the young person, the young person's counsel or the Attorney General or an agent of the Attorney General to have the young person proceeded against in the youth court and an order is made to that effect.

**Waiver**

(2) A young person may waive the requirement under paragraph (1)(*a*) where the young person is represented by counsel.

**Where young person not represented by counsel**

(3) Where a young person is not represented in youth court by counsel, the youth court shall, before accepting a plea,

(*a*) satisfy itself that the young person understands the charge against him; and

(*b*) explain to the young person that he may plead guilty or not guilty to the charge.

**Idem**

(3.1) Where a young person is a young person referred to in subsection 16(1.01) and is not represented in youth court by counsel, the youth court shall satisfy itself that the young person understands

(*a*) the charge against the young person;

(*b*) the consequences of being proceeded against in ordinary court; and

(*c*) the young person's right to apply to be proceeded against in youth court.

**Where youth court not satisfied**
(4) Where the youth court is not satisfied that a young person understands the charge against the young person, as required under paragraph (3)(*a*), the court shall enter a plea of not guilty on behalf of the young person and shall proceed with the trial in accordance with subsection 19(2) or, with respect to proceedings in Nunavut, subsection 19.1(2).

**Idem**
(5) Where the youth court is not satisfied that a young person understands the matters referred to in subsection (3.1), the court shall direct that the young person be represented by counsel.
R.S., 1980-81-82-83, c. 110, s. 12; 1995, c. 19, s. 13; 1999, c. 3, s. 87.

## MEDICAL AND PSYCHOLOGICAL REPORTS

**Medical or psychological assessment**
**13.** (1) A youth court may, at any stage of proceedings against a young person,
(*a*) with the consent of the young person and the prosecutor, or
(*b*) on its own motion or on application of the young person or the prosecutor, where
(i) the court has reasonable grounds to believe that the young person may be suffering from a physical or mental illness or disorder, a psychological disorder, an emotional disturbance, a learning disability or a mental disability,
(ii) the young person's history indicates a pattern of repeated findings of guilt under this Act, or
(iii) the young person is alleged to have committed an offence involving serious personal injury, and the court believes a medical, psychological or psychiatric report in respect of the young person is necessary for a purpose mentioned in paragraphs (2)(*a*) to(*f*),
by order require that the young person be assessed by a qualified person and require the person who conducts the examination to report the results thereof in writing to the court.

**Purpose of assessment**
(2) A youth court may make an order under subsection (1) in respect of a young person for the purpose of
(*a*) considering an application under section 16;
(*b*) making or reviewing a disposition under this Act, other than a disposition made under section 672.54 or 672.58 of the *Criminal Code*;
(*c*) considering an application under subsection 26.1(1);
(*d*) setting conditions under subsection 26.2(1);
(*e*) making an order under subsection 26.6(2); or
(*f*) authorizing disclosure under subsection 38(1.5).

**Custody for assessment**
(3) Subject to subsections (3.1) and (3.3), for the purpose of an assessment under this section, a youth court may remand a young person to such custody as it directs for a period not exceeding thirty days.

**Presumption against custodial remand**
(3.1) A young person shall not be remanded in custody pursuant to an order made by a youth court under subsection (1) unless
(*a*) the youth court is satisfied that on the evidence custody is necessary to conduct an assessment of the young person, or that on the evidence of a qualified person detention of the young person in custody is desirable to conduct the assessment of the young person and the young person consents to custody; or
(*b*) the young person is required to be detained in custody in respect of any other matter or by virtue of any provision of the *Criminal Code*.

**Report of qualified person in writing**
(3.2) For the purposes of paragraph (3.1)(*a*), when the prosecutor and the young person agree, evidence of a qualified person may be received in the form of a report in writing.

**Application to vary assessment order where circumstances change**
(3.3) A youth court may, at any time while an order in respect of a young person made by the court under subsection (1) is in force, on cause being shown, vary the terms and conditions specified in that order in such manner as the court considers appropriate in the circumstances.

**Disclosure of report**
(4) Where a youth court receives a report made in respect of a young person pursuant to subsection (1),
(*a*) the court shall, subject to subsection (6), cause a copy of the report to be given to
(i) the young person,
(ii) a parent of the young person, if the parent is in attendance at the proceedings against the young person,
(iii) counsel, if any, representing the young person, and
(iv) the prosecutor; and
(*b*) the court may cause a copy of the report to be given to a parent of the young person not in attendance at the proceedings against the young person if the parent is, in the opinion of the court, taking an active interest in the proceedings.

**Cross-examination**
(5) Where a report is made in respect of a young person pursuant to subsection (1), the young person, his counsel or the adult assisting him pursuant to subsection 11(7) and the prosecutor shall, subject to subsection (6), on application to the youth court, be given an opportunity to cross-examine the person who made the report.

**Report to be withheld where disclosure unnecessary or prejudicial**
(6) A youth court shall withhold all or part of a report made in respect of a young person pursuant to subsection (1) from a private prosecutor, where disclosure of the report or part, in the opinion of the court, is not necessary for the

prosecution of the case and might be prejudicial to the young person.

**Report to be withheld where disclosure dangerous to any person**

(7) A youth court shall withhold all or part of a report made in respect of a young person pursuant to subsection (1) from the young person, the young person's parents or a private prosecutor where the court is satisfied, on the basis of the report or evidence given in the absence of the young person, parents or private prosecutor by the person who made the report, that disclosure of all or part of the report would seriously impair the treatment or recovery of the young person, or would be likely to endanger the life or safety of, or result in serious psychological harm to, another person.

**Idem**

(8) Notwithstanding subsection (7), the youth court may release all or part of the report referred to in that subsection to the young person, the young person's parents or the private prosecutor where the interests of justice make disclosure essential in the court's opinion.

**Report to be part of record**

(9) A report made pursuant to subsection (1) shall form part of the record of the case in respect of which it was requested.

**Disclosure by qualified person**

(10) Notwithstanding any other provision of this Act, a qualified person who is of the opinion that a young person held in detention or committed to custody is likely to endanger his own life or safety or to endanger the life of, or cause bodily harm to, another person may immediately so advise any person who has the care and custody of the young person whether or not the same information is contained in a report made pursuant to subsection (1).

**Definition of "qualified person"**

(11) In this section, "qualified person" means a person duly qualified by provincial law to practice medicine or psychiatry or to carry out psychological examinations or assessments, as the circumstances require, or, where no such law exists, a person who is, in the opinion of the youth court, so qualified, and includes a person or a person within a class of persons designated by the Lieutenant Governor in Council of a province or his delegate.

(12) [Repealed, R.S., 1985, c. 24 (2nd Supp.), s. 10]
R.S., 1985, c. Y-1, s. 13; R.S., 1985, c. 24 (2nd Supp.), s. 10; 1991, c. 43, ss. 32, 35; 1995, c. 19, s. 4.

**Statements not admissible against young person**

**13.1** (1) Subject to subsection (2), where a young person is assessed pursuant to an order made under subsection 13(1), no statement or reference to a statement made by the young person during the course and for the purposes of the assessment to the person who conducts the assessment or to anyone acting under that person's direction is admissible in evidence, without the consent of the young person, in any proceeding before a court, tribunal, body or person with jurisdiction to compel the production of evidence.

**Exceptions**

(2) A statement referred to in subsection (1) is admissible in evidence for the purposes of

(*a*) considering an application under section 16 in respect of the young person;

(*b*) determining whether the young person is unfit to stand trial;

(*c*) determining whether the balance of the mind of the young person was disturbed at the time of commission of the alleged offence, where the young person is a female person charged with an offence arising out of the death of her newly-born child;

(*d*) making or reviewing a disposition in respect of the young person;

(*e*) determining whether the young person was, at the time of the commission of an alleged offence, suffering from automatism or a mental disorder so as to be exempt from criminal responsibility by virtue of subsection 16(1) of the *Criminal Code*, if the accused puts his or her mental capacity for criminal intent into issue, or if the prosecutor raises the issue after verdict;

(*f*) challenging the credibility of a young person in any proceeding where the testimony of the young person is inconsistent in a material particular with a statement referred to in subsection (1) that the young person made previously;

(*g*) establishing the perjury of a young person who is charged with perjury in respect of a statement made in any proceeding;

(*h*) deciding an application for an order under subsection 26.1(1);

(*i*) setting the conditions under subsection 26.2(1);

(*j*) conducting a review under subsection 26.6(1); or

(*k*) deciding an application for a disclosure order under subsection 38(1.5).

1991, c. 43, ss. 33, 35; 1994, c. 26, s. 76; 1995, c. 19, s. 5.

## APPLICATION OF PART XX.1 OF THE CRIMINAL CODE (MENTAL DISORDER)

**Sections of *Criminal Code* applicable**

**13.2** (1) Except to the extent that they are inconsistent with or excluded by this Act, section 16 and Part XX.1 of the *Criminal Code*, except sections 672.65 and 672.66, apply, with such modifications as the circumstances require, in respect of proceedings under this Act in relation to offences alleged to have been committed by young persons.

**Notice and copies to counsel and parents**

(2) For the purposes of subsection (1), wherever in Part XX.1 of the *Criminal Code* a reference is made to

(*a*) a copy to be sent or otherwise given to an accused or a party to the proceedings, the reference shall be read as including a reference to a copy to be sent or otherwise given to

(i) counsel, if any, representing the young person,

(ii) any parent of the young person who is in attendance at the proceedings against the young person, and

(iii) any parent of the young person who is, in the opinion of the youth court or Review Board, taking an active interest in the proceedings; and

(*b*) notice to be given to an accused or a party to proceedings, the reference shall be read as including a reference to notice to be given to counsel, if any, representing the young person and the parents of the young person.

**Proceedings not invalid**

(3) Subject to subsection (4), failure to give a notice referred to in paragraph (2)(*b*) to a parent of a young person does not affect the validity of proceedings under this Act.

**Exception**

(4) Failure to give a notice referred to in paragraph (2)(*b*) to a parent of a young person in any case renders invalid any subsequent proceedings under this Act relating to the case unless

(*a*) a parent of the young person attends at the court or Review Board with the young person; or

(*b*) a youth court judge or Review Board before whom proceedings are held against the young person

(i) adjourns the proceedings and orders that the notice be given in such manner and to such persons as the judge or Review Board directs, or

(ii) dispenses with the notice where the youth court or Review Board is of the opinion that, having regard to the circumstances, the notice may be dispensed with.

**No hospital order assessments**

(5) A youth court may not make an order under subsection 672.11 of the *Criminal Code* in respect of a young person for the purpose of assisting in the determination of an issue mentioned in paragraph 672.11(e) of that Act.

**Considerations of court or Review Board making a disposition**

(6) Before making or reviewing a disposition in respect of a young person under Part XX.1 of the *Criminal Code*, a youth court or Review Board shall consider the age and special needs of the young person and any representations or submissions made by the young person's parents.

**Cap applicable to young persons**

(7) Subject to subsection (9), for the purpose of applying subsection 672.64(3) of the *Criminal Code* to proceedings under this Act in relation to an offence alleged to have been committed by a young person, the applicable cap shall be the maximum period during which the young person would be subject to a disposition by the youth court if found guilty of the offence.

**Application to increase cap of unfit young person subject to transfer**

(8) Where an application is made under section 16 to proceed against a young person in ordinary court and the young person is found unfit to stand trial, the Attorney General or the agent of the Attorney General may, before the youth court makes or refuses to make an order under that section, apply to the court to increase the cap that shall apply to the young person.

**Consideration of youth court for increase in cap**

(9) The youth court, after giving the Attorney General and the counsel and parents of the young person in respect of whom an application is made under subsection (8) an opportunity to be heard, shall take into consideration

(*a*) the seriousness of the alleged offence and the circumstances in which it was allegedly committed,

(*b*) the age, maturity, character and background of the young person and any previous findings of guilt against the young person under any Act of Parliament,

(*c*) the likelihood that the young person will cause significant harm to any person if released on expiration of the cap that applies to the young person pursuant to subsection (7), and

(*d*) the respective caps that would apply to the young person under this Act and under the *Criminal Code*,

and the youth court shall, where satisfied that the application under section 16 would likely succeed if the young person were fit to stand trial, apply to the young person the cap that would apply to an adult for the same offence.

***Prima facie* case to be made every year**

(10) For the purpose of applying subsection 672.33(1) of the *Criminal Code* to proceedings under this Act in relation to an offence alleged to have been committed by a young person, wherever in that subsection a reference is made to two years, there shall be substituted a reference to one year.

**Designation of hospitals for young persons**

(11) A reference in Part XX.1 of the *Criminal Code* to a hospital in a province shall be construed as a reference to a hospital designated by the Minister of Health of the province for the custody, treatment or assessment of young persons. 1991, c. 43, s. 33.

## PRE-DISPOSITION REPORT

**Pre-disposition report**

14. (1) Where a youth court deems it advisable before making a disposition under section 20 in respect of a young person who is found guilty of an offence it may, and where a youth court is required under this Act to consider a pre-disposition report before making an order or a disposition in respect of a young person it shall, require the provincial director to cause to be prepared a pre-disposition report in respect of the young person and to submit the report to the court.

**Contents of report**
(2) A pre-disposition report made in respect of a young person shall, subject to subsection (3), be in writing and shall include
(*a*) the results of an interview with
(i) the young person,
(ii) where reasonably possible, the parents of the young person and,
(iii) where appropriate and reasonably possible, members of the young person's extended family;
(*b*) the results of an interview with the victim in the case, where applicable and where reasonably possible;
(*c*) such information as is applicable to the case including, where applicable,
(i) the age, maturity, character, behaviour and attitude of the young person and his willingness to make amends,
(ii) any plans put forward by the young person to change his conduct or to participate in activities or undertake measures to improve himself,
(iii) the history of previous findings of delinquency under the *Juvenile Delinquents Act*, chapter J-3 of the Revised Statutes of Canada, 1970, or previous findings of guilt under this or any other Act of Parliament or any regulation made thereunder or under an Act of the legislature of a province or any regulation made thereunder or a by-law or ordinance of a municipality, the history of community or other services rendered to the young person with respect to those findings and the response of the young person to previous sentences or dispositions and to services rendered to him,
(iv) the history of alternative measures used to deal with the young person and the response of the young person thereto,
(v) the availability and appropriateness of community services and facilities for young persons and the willingness of the young person to avail himself or herself of those services or facilities,
(vi) the relationship between the young person and the young person's parents and the degree of control and influence of the parents over the young person and, where appropriate and reasonably possible, the relationship between the young person and the young person's extended family and the degree of control and influence of the young person's extended family over the young person, and
(vii) the school attendance and performance record and the employment record of the young person; and
(*d*) such information as the provincial director considers relevant, including any recommendation that the provincial director considers appropriate.

**Oral report with leave**
(3) Where a pre-disposition report cannot reasonably be committed to writing, it may, with leave of the youth court, be submitted orally in court.

**Report to form part of record**
(4) A pre-disposition report shall form part of the record of the case in respect of which it was requested.

**Copies of pre-disposition report**
(5) Where a pre-disposition report made in respect of a young person is submitted to a youth court in writing, the court
(*a*) shall, subject to subsection (7), cause a copy of the report to be given to
(i) the young person,
(ii) a parent of the young person, if the parent is in attendance at the proceedings against the young person,
(iii) counsel, if any, representing the young person, and
(iv) the prosecutor; and
(*b*) may cause a copy of the report to be given to a parent of the young person not in attendance at the proceedings against the young person if the parent is, in the opinion of the court, taking an active interest in the proceedings.

**Cross-examination**
(6) Where a pre-disposition report made in respect of a young person is submitted to a youth court, the young person, his counsel or the adult assisting him pursuant to subsection 11(7) and the prosecutor shall, subject to subsection (7), on application to the youth court, be given the opportunity to cross-examine the person who made the report.

**Report may be withheld from private prosecutor**
(7) Where a pre-disposition report made in respect of a young person is submitted to a youth court, the court may, where the prosecutor is a private prosecutor and disclosure of the report or any part thereof to the prosecutor might, in the opinion of the court, be prejudicial to the young person and is not, in the opinion of the court, necessary for the prosecution of the case against the young person,
(*a*) withhold the report or part thereof from the prosecutor, if the report is submitted in writing; or
(*b*) exclude the prosecutor from the court during the submission of the report or part thereof, if the report is submitted orally in court.

**Report disclosed to other persons**
(8) Where a pre-disposition report made in respect of a young person is submitted to a youth court, the court
(*a*) shall, on request, cause a copy or a transcript of the report to be supplied to
(i) any court that is dealing with matters relating to the young person, and
(ii) any youth worker to whom the young person's case has been assigned; and
(*b*) may, on request, cause a copy or a transcript of the report, or a part thereof, to be supplied to any person not otherwise authorized under this section to receive a copy or a transcript of the report if, in the opinion of the court, the person has a valid interest in the proceedings.

**Disclosure by the provincial director**

(9) A provincial director who submits a pre-disposition report made in respect of a young person to a youth court may make the report, or any part thereof, available to any person in whose custody or under whose supervision the young person is placed or to any other person who is directly assisting in the care or treatment of the young person.

**Inadmissibility of statements**

(10) No statement made by a young person in the course of the preparation of a pre-disposition report in respect of the young person is admissible in evidence against him in any civil or criminal proceedings except in proceedings under section 16 or 20 or sections 28 to 32.

R.S., 1985, c. Y-1, s. 14; R.S., 1985, c. 24 (2nd Supp.), s. 11; 1995, c. 19, s. 6.

## DISQUALIFICATION OF JUDGE

**Disqualification of judge**

**15.** (1) Subject to subsection (2), a youth court judge who, prior to an adjudication in respect of a young person charged with an offence, examines a pre-disposition report made in respect of the young person, or hears an application under section 16 in respect of the young person, in connection with that offence shall not in any capacity conduct or continue the trial of the young person for the offence and shall transfer the case to another judge to be dealt with according to law.

**Exception**

(2) A youth court judge may, in the circumstances referred to in subsection (1), with the consent of the young person and the prosecutor, conduct or continue the trial of the young person if the judge is satisfied that he has not been predisposed by information contained in the pre-disposition report or by representations made in respect of the application under section 16.

1980-81-82-83, c. 110, s. 15.

## TRANSFER

**Transfer to ordinary court**

**16.** (1) Subject to subsection (1.01), at any time after an information is laid against a young person alleged to have, after attaining the age of fourteen years, committed an indictable offence other than an offence referred to in section 553 of the *Criminal Code* but prior to adjudication, a youth court shall, on application of the young person or the young person's counsel or the Attorney General or an agent of the Attorney General, determine, in accordance with subsection (1.1), whether the young person should be proceeded against in ordinary court.

**Trial in ordinary court for certain offences**

(1.01) Every young person against whom an information is laid who is alleged to have committed

(*a*) first degree murder or second degree murder within the meaning of section 231 of the *Criminal Code*,

(*b*) an offence under section 239 of the *Criminal Code* (attempt to commit murder),

(*c*) an offence under section 232 or 234 of the *Criminal Code* (manslaughter), or

(*d*) an offence under section 273 of the *Criminal Code* (aggravated sexual assault),

and who was sixteen or seventeen years of age at the time of the alleged commission of the offence shall be proceeded against in ordinary court in accordance with the law ordinarily applicable to an adult charged with the offence unless the youth court, on application by the young person, the young person's counsel or the Attorney General or an agent of the Attorney General, makes an order under subsection (1.04) or (1.05) or subparagraph (1.1)(*a*)(ii) that the young person should be proceeded against in youth court.

**Making of application**

(1.02) An application to the youth court under subsection (1.01) must be made orally, in the presence of the other party to the proceedings, or in writing, with a notice served on the other party to the proceedings.

**Where application is opposed**

(1.03) Where the other party to the proceedings referred to in subsection (1.02) files a notice of opposition to the application with the youth court within twenty-one days after the making of the oral application, or the service of the notice referred to in that subsection, as the case may be, the youth court shall, in accordance with subsection (1.1), determine whether the young person should be proceeded against in youth court.

**Where application is unopposed**

(1.04) Where the other party to the proceedings referred to in subsection (1.02) files a notice of non-opposition to the application with the youth court within the time referred to in subsection (1.03), the youth court shall order that the young person be proceeded against in youth court.

**Deeming**

(1.05) Where the other party to the proceedings referred to in subsection (1.02) does not file a notice referred to in subsection (1.03) or (1.04) within the time referred to in subsection (1.03), the youth court shall order that the young person be proceeded against in youth court.

**Time may be extended**

(1.06) The time referred to in subsections (1.03) to (1.05) may be extended by mutual agreement of the parties to the proceedings by filing a notice to that effect with the youth court.

**Order**

(1.1) In making the determination referred to in subsection (1) or (1.03), the youth court, after affording both parties and the parents of the young person an opportunity to be heard, shall consider the interest of society, which includes the objectives of affording protection to the public and rehabilitation of the young person, and determine whether those objectives can be reconciled by the youth being under the jurisdiction of the youth court, and

(*a*) if the court is of the opinion that those objectives can be so reconciled, the court shall
(i) in the case of an application under subsection (1), refuse to make an order that the young person be proceeded against in ordinary court, and
(ii) in the case of an application under subsection (1.01), order that the young person be proceeded against in youth court; or
(*b*) if the court is of the opinion that those objectives cannot be so reconciled, protection of the public shall be paramount and the court shall
(i) in the case of an application under subsection (1), order that the young person be proceeded against in ordinary court in accordance with the law ordinarily applicable to an adult charged with the offence, and
(ii) in the case of an application under subsection (1.01), refuse to make an order that the young person be proceeded against in youth court.

**Onus**
(1.11) Where an application is made under subsection (1) or (1.01), the onus of satisfying the youth court of the matters referred to in subsection (1.1) rests with the applicant.

**Considerations by youth court**
(2) In making the determination referred to in subsection (1) or (1.03) in respect of a young person, a youth court shall take into account
(*a*) the seriousness of the alleged offence and the circumstances in which it was allegedly committed;
(*b*) the age, maturity, character and background of the young person and any record or summary of previous findings of delinquency under the *Juvenile Delinquents Act*, chapter J-3 of the Revised Statutes of Canada, 1970, or previous findings of guilt under this Act or any other Act of Parliament or any regulation made thereunder;
(*c*) the adequacy of this Act, and the adequacy of the *Criminal Code* or any other Act of Parliament that would apply in respect of the young person if an order were made under this section, to meet the circumstances of the case;
(*d*) the availability of treatment or correctional resources;
(*e*) any representations made to the court by or on behalf of the young person or by the Attorney General or his agent; and
(*f*) any other factors that the court considers relevant.

**Pre-disposition reports**
(3) In making the determination referred to in subsection (1) or (1.03) in respect of a young person, a youth court shall consider a pre-disposition report.

**Where young person on transfer status**
(4) Notwithstanding subsections (1) and (3), where an application is made under subsection (1) by the Attorney General or the Attorney General's agent in respect of an offence alleged to have been committed by a young person while the young person was being proceeded against in ordinary court pursuant to an order previously made under this section or serving a sentence as a result of proceedings in ordinary court, the youth court may make a further order under this section without a hearing and without considering a pre-disposition report.

**Court to state reasons**
(5) Where a youth court makes an order or refuses to make an order under this section, it shall state the reasons for its decision and the reasons shall form part of the record of the proceedings in the youth court.

**No further applications for transfer**
(6) Where a youth court refuses to make an order under this section in respect of an alleged offence, no further application may be made under this section in respect of that offence.

**Effect of order**
(7) Where an order is made under this section pursuant to an application under subsection (1), proceedings under this Act shall be discontinued and the young person against whom the proceedings are taken shall be taken before the ordinary court.

**Idem**
(7.1) Where an order is made under this section pursuant to an application under subsection (1.01), the proceedings against the young person shall be in the youth court.

**Jurisdiction of ordinary court limited**
(8) Where a young person is proceeded against in ordinary court in respect of an offence by reason of
(*a*) subsection (1.01), where no application is made under that subsection,
(*b*) an order made under subparagraph (1.1)(*b*)(i), or
(*c*) the refusal under subparagraph (1.1)(*b*)(ii) to make an order,
that court has jurisdiction only in respect of that offence or an offence included therein.

**Review of youth court decision**
(9) An order made in respect of a young person under this section or a refusal to make such an order shall, on application of the young person or the young person's counsel or the Attorney General or the Attorney General's agent made within thirty days after the decision of the youth court, be reviewed by the court of appeal, and that court may, in its discretion, confirm or reverse the decision of the youth court.

**Extension of time to make application**
(10) The court of appeal may, at any time, extend the time within which an application under subsection (9) may be made.

**Notice of application**
(11) A person who proposes to apply for a review under subsection (9) shall give notice of the appli-

cation in such manner and within such period of time as may be directed by rules of court.

**Inadmissibility of statement**
(12) No statement made by a young person in the course of a hearing held under this section is admissible in evidence against the young person in any civil or criminal proceeding held subsequent to that hearing.

(13) [Repealed, 1992, c. 11, s. 2]

(14) [Repealed, R.S., 1985, c. 24 (2nd Supp.), s. 12] R.S., 1985, c. Y-1, s. 16; R.S., 1985, c. 24 (2nd Supp.), s. 12; 1992, c. 11, s. 2; 1995, c. 19, s. 8.

**Detention pending trial—young person under eighteen**
**16.1** (1) Notwithstanding anything in this or any other Act of Parliament, where a young person who is under the age of eighteen is to be proceeded against in ordinary court by reason of
(*a*) subsection 16(1.01), where no application is made under that subsection,
(*b*) an order under subparagraph 16(1.1)(*b*)(i), or
(*c*) the refusal under subparagraph 16(1.1)(*b*)(ii), to make an order,
and the young person is to be in custody pending the proceedings in that court, the young person shall be held separate and apart from any adult who is detained or held in custody unless the youth court is satisfied, on application, that the young person, having regard to the best interests of the young person and the safety of others, cannot be detained in a place of detention for young persons.

**Detention pending trial—young person over eighteen**
(2) Notwithstanding anything in this or any other Act of Parliament, where a young person who is over the age of eighteen is to be proceeded against in ordinary court by reason of
(*a*) subsection 16(1.01), where no application is made under that subsection,
(*b*) an order under subparagraph 16(1.1)(*b*)(i), or
(*c*) the refusal under subparagraph 16(1.1)(*b*)(ii), to make an order,
and the young person is to be in custody pending the proceedings in that court, the young person shall be held in a place of detention for adults unless the youth court is satisfied, on application, that the young person, having regard to the best interests of the young person and the safety of others, should be detained in a place of custody for young persons.

**Review**
(3) On application, the youth court shall review the placement of a young person in detention pursuant to this section and, if satisfied, having regard to the best interests of the young person and the safety of others, and after having afforded the young person, the provincial director and a representative of a provincial department responsible for adult correctional facilities an opportunity to be heard, that the young person should remain in detention where the young person is or be transferred to youth or adult detention, as the case may be, the court may so order.

**Who may make application**
(4) An application referred to in this section may be made by the young person, the young person's parents, the provincial director, the Attorney General or the Attorney General's agent.

**Notice**
(5) Where an application referred to in this section is made, the applicant shall cause a notice of the application to be given
(*a*) where the applicant is the young person or one of the young person's parents, to the provincial director and the Attorney General;
(*b*) where the applicant is the Attorney General or the Attorney General's agent, to the young person, the young person's parents and the provincial director; and
(*c*) where the applicant is the provincial director, to the young person, the parents of the young person and the Attorney General.

**Statement of rights**
(6) A notice given under subsection (5) by the Attorney General or the provincial director shall include a statement that the young person has the opportunity to be heard and the right to be represented by counsel.

**Limit—age 20**
(7) Notwithstanding anything in this section, no young person shall remain in custody in a place of detention for young persons under this section after the young person attains the age of twenty years. 1992, c. 11, s. 2; 1995, c. 19, s. 9.

**Placement on conviction by ordinary court**
**16.2** (1) Notwithstanding anything in this or any other Act of Parliament, where a young person who is proceeded against in ordinary court by reason of subsection 16(1.01), where no application is made under that subsection, or by reason of an order under subparagraph 16(1.1)(*b*)(i) or the refusal under subparagraph 16(1.1)(*b*)(ii) to make an order, is convicted and sentenced to imprisonment, the court shall, after affording the young person, the parents of the young person, the Attorney General, the provincial director and representatives of the provincial and federal correctional systems an opportunity to be heard, order that the young person serve any portion of the imprisonment in
(*a*) a place of custody for young persons separate and apart from any adult who is detained or held in custody;
(*b*) a provincial correctional facility for adults; or
(*c*) where the sentence is for two years or more, a penitentiary.

**Factors to be taken into account**
(2) In making an order under subsection (1), the court shall take into account
(*a*) the safety of the young person;
(*b*) the safety of the public;
(*c*) the young person's accessibility to family;
(*d*) the safety of other young persons if the

young person were to be held in custody in a place of custody for young persons;

(*e*) whether the young person would have a detrimental influence on other young persons if the young person were to be held in custody in a place of custody for young persons;

(*f*) the young person's level of maturity;

(*g*) the availability and suitability of treatment, educational and other resources that would be provided to the young person in a place of custody for young persons and in a place of custody for adults;

(*h*) the young person's prior experiences and behaviour while in detention or custody;

(*i*) the recommendations of the provincial director and representatives of the provincial and federal correctional facilities; and

(*j*) any other factor the court considers relevant.

**Report necessary**

(3) Prior to making an order under subsection (1), the court shall require that a report be prepared for the purpose of assisting the court.

**Review**

(4) On application, the court shall review the placement of a young person in detention pursuant to this section and, if satisfied that the circumstances that resulted in the initial order have changed materially, and after having afforded the young person, the provincial director and the representatives of the provincial and federal correctional systems an opportunity to be heard, the court may order that the young person be placed in

(*a*) a place of custody for young persons separate and apart from any adult who is detained or held in custody;

(*b*) a provincial correctional facility for adults; or

(*c*) where the sentence is for two years or more, a penitentiary.

**Who may make application**

(5) An application referred to in this section may be made by the young person, the young person's parents, the provincial director, a representative of the provincial and federal correctional systems and the Attorney General.

**Notice**

(6) Where an application referred to in this section is made, the applicant shall cause a notice of the application to be given

(*a*) where the applicant is the young person or one of the young person's parents, to the provincial director, to representatives of the provincial and federal correction systems and to the Attorney General;

(*b*) where the applicant is the Attorney General or the Attorney General's agent, to the young person, the young person's parents and the provincial director and representatives of the provincial and federal correction systems; and

(*c*) where an applicant is the provincial director, to the young person, the parents of the young person, the Attorney General and representatives of the provincial and federal correction systems.

1992, c. 11, s. 2; 1995, c. 19, s. 10.

**Order restricting publication of information presented at transfer hearing**

**17.** (1) Where a youth court hears an application for a transfer under section 16, it shall

(*a*) where the young person is not represented by counsel, or

(*b*) on application made by or on behalf of the young person or the prosecutor, where the young person is represented by counsel,

make an order directing that any information respecting the offence presented at the hearing shall not be published in any newspaper or broadcast before such time as

(*c*) an order for a transfer is refused or set aside on review and the time for all reviews against the decision has expired or all proceedings in respect of any such review have been completed; or

(*d*) the trial is ended, if the case is transferred to ordinary court.

**Offence**

(2) Every one who fails to comply with an order made pursuant to subsection (1) is guilty of an offence punishable on summary conviction.

**Definition of "newspaper"**

(3) In this section, "newspaper" has the meaning set out in section 297 of the *Criminal Code*.
R.S., 1980-81-82-83, c. 110, s. 17; 1995, c. 19, s. 11.

## TRANSFER OF JURISDICTION

**Transfer of jurisdiction**

**18.** Notwithstanding subsections 478(1) and (3) of the *Criminal Code*, where a young person is charged with an offence that is alleged to have been committed in one province, he may, if the Attorney General of the province where the offence is alleged to have been committed consents, appear before a youth court of any other province and,

(*a*) where the young person signifies his consent to plead guilty and pleads guilty to that offence, the court shall, if it is satisfied that the facts support the charge, find the young person guilty of the offence alleged in the information; and

(*b*) where the young person does not signify his consent to plead guilty and does not plead guilty, or where the court is not satisfied that the facts support the charge, the young person shall, if he was detained in custody prior to his appearance, be returned to custody and dealt with according to law.

1980-81-82-83, c. 110, s. 18.

## ADJUDICATION

**Where young person pleads guilty**

**19.** (1) Where a young person pleads guilty to an offence charged against him and the youth court is satisfied that the facts support the charge, the court shall find the young person guilty of the offence.

**Where young person pleads not guilty**

(2) Where a young person charged with an offence pleads not guilty to the offence or pleads

guilty but the youth court is not satisfied that the facts support the charge, the court shall, subject to subsection (4), proceed with the trial and shall, after considering the matter, find the young person guilty or not guilty or make an order dismissing the charge, as the case may be.

**Application for transfer to ordinary court**
(3) The court shall not make a finding under this section in respect of a young person in respect of whom an application may be made under section 16 for an order that the young person be proceeded against in ordinary court unless it has inquired as to whether any of the parties to the proceedings wishes to make such an application, and, if any party so wishes, has given that party an opportunity to do so.

**Election—offence of murder**
(4) Notwithstanding section 5, where a young person is charged with having committed first degree murder or second degree murder within the meaning of section 231 of the *Criminal Code*, the youth court, before proceeding with the trial, shall ask the young person to elect to be tried by a youth court judge alone or by a judge of a superior court of criminal jurisdiction with a jury, and where a young person elects to be tried by a judge of a superior court of criminal jurisdiction with a jury, the young person shall be dealt with as provided in this Act.

**Where no election made**
(5) Notwithstanding section 5, where an election is not made under subsection (4), the young person shall be deemed to have elected to be tried by a judge of a superior court of criminal jurisdiction with a jury and dealt with as provided for in this Act.

**Preliminary inquiry**
(5.1) Where a young person elects or is deemed to have elected to be tried by a judge of a superior court of criminal jurisdiction with a jury, the youth court shall conduct a preliminary inquiry and if, on its conclusion, the young person is ordered to stand trial, the proceedings shall be before a judge of the superior court of criminal jurisdiction with a jury.

**Preliminary inquiry provisions of *Criminal Code***
(5.2) A preliminary inquiry referred to in subsection (5.1) shall be conducted in accordance with the provisions of Part XVIII of the *Criminal Code*, except to the extent that they are inconsistent with this Act.

**Parts XIX and XX of the *Criminal Code***
(6) Proceedings under this Act before a judge of a superior court of criminal jurisdiction with a jury shall be conducted, with such modifications as the circumstances require, in accordance with the provisions of Parts XIX and XX of the *Criminal Code*, except that

(*a*) the provisions of this Act respecting the protection of privacy of young persons prevail over the provisions of the *Criminal Code*; and

(*b*) the young person is entitled to be represented in court by counsel if the young person is removed from court pursuant to subsection 650(2) of the *Criminal Code*.

R.S., 1985, c. Y-1, s. 19; R.S., 1985, c. 24 (2nd Supp.), s. 13; 1995, c. 19, s. 12.

**If young person pleads guilty—Nunavut**
**19.1** (1) If a young person pleads guilty to an offence charged against the young person and the youth court is satisfied that the facts support the charge, the court shall find the young person guilty of the offence.

**If young person pleads not guilty—Nunavut**
(2) If a young person charged with an offence pleads not guilty to the offence or pleads guilty but the youth court is not satisfied that the facts support the charge, the court shall, subject to subsection (4), proceed with the trial and shall, after considering the matter, find the young person guilty or not guilty or make an order dismissing the charge, as the case may be.

**Application for transfer to ordinary court—Nunavut**
(3) The court shall not make a finding under this section in respect of a young person in respect of whom an application may be made under section 16 for an order that the young person be proceeded against in ordinary court unless it has inquired as to whether any of the parties to the proceedings wishes to make such an application, and, if any party so wishes, has given that party an opportunity to do so.

**Election re offence of murder—Nunavut**
(4) If a young person is charged with having committed first degree murder or second degree murder within the meaning of section 231 of the *Criminal Code*, the youth court, before proceeding with the trial, shall ask the young person to elect

(*a*) to be tried by a judge of the Nunavut Court of Justice alone, acting as a youth court, or

(*b*) to have a preliminary inquiry and to be tried by a judge of the Nunavut Court of Justice, acting as a youth court, with a jury,

and if a young person elects under paragraph (*a*) or (*b*), the young person shall be dealt with as provided in this Act.

**If no election made—Nunavut**
(5) Despite section 5, if an election is not made under subsection (4), the young person shall be deemed to have elected under paragraph (4)(*b*).

**Preliminary inquiry—Nunavut**
(6) If a young person elects or is deemed too have elected under paragraph (4)(*b*), a preliminary inquiry shall be held in the youth court and if, on its conclusion, the young person is ordered to stand trial, the proceedings shall be before a judge of the Nunavut Court of Justice, acting as a youth court, with a jury.

**Preliminary inquiry provisions of *Criminal Code*—Nunavut**
(7) A preliminary inquiry referred to in subsection (6) shall be conducted in accordance with

the provisions of Part XVIII of the *Criminal Code*, except to the extent that they are inconsistent with this Act.

**Parts XIX and XX of the *Criminal Code*—Nunavut**
(8) Proceedings under this Act before a judge of the Nunavut Court of Justice, acting as a youth court, with a jury shall be conducted, with any modifications that the circumstances require, in accordance with the provisions of Parts XIX and XX of the *Criminal Code*, except that

(*a*) the provisions of this Act respecting the protection of privacy of young persons prevail over the provisions of the *Criminal Code*; and
(*b*) the young person is entitled to be represented in court by counsel if the young person is removed from court pursuant to subsection 650(2) of the *Criminal Code*.

**Application to Nunavut**
(9) This section, and not section 19, applies in respect of proceedings under this Act in Nunavut. 1999, c. 3, s. 88.

DISPOSITIONS

**Dispositions that may be made**
**20.** (1) Where a youth court finds a young person guilty of an offence, it shall consider any pre-disposition report required by the court, any representations made by the parties to the proceedings or their counsel or agents and by the parents of the young person and any other relevant information before the court, and the court shall then make any one of the following dispositions, other than the disposition referred to in paragraph (*k*.1), or any number thereof that are not inconsistent with each other, and where the offence is first degree murder or second degree murder within the meaning of section 231 of the *Criminal Code*, the court shall make the disposition referred to in paragraph (*k*.1) and may make such other disposition as the court considers appropriate:

(*a*) by order direct that the young person be discharged absolutely, if the court considers it to be in the best interests of the young person and not contrary to the public interest;
(*a*.1) by order direct that the young person be discharged on such conditions as the court considers appropriate;
(*b*) impose on the young person a fine not exceeding one thousand dollars to be paid at such time and on such terms as the court may fix;
(*c*) order the young person to pay to any other person at such time and on such terms as the court may fix an amount by way of compensation for loss of or damage to property, for loss of income or support or for special damages for personal injury arising from the commission of the offence where the value thereof is readily ascertainable, but no order shall be made for general damages;
(*d*) order the young person to make restitution to any other person of any property obtained by the young person as a result of the commission of the offence within such time as the court may fix, if the property is owned by that other person or was, at the time of the offence, in his lawful possession;
(*e*) if any property obtained as a result of the commission of the offence has been sold to an innocent purchaser, where restitution of the property to its owner or any other person has been made or ordered, order the young person to pay the purchaser, at such time and on such terms as the court may fix, an amount not exceeding the amount paid by the purchaser for the property;
(*f*) subject to section 21, order the young person to compensate any person in kind or by way of personal services at such time and on such terms as the court may fix for any loss, damage or injury suffered by that person in respect of which an order may be made under paragraph (*c*) or (*e*);
(*g*) subject to section 21, order the young person to perform a community service at such time and on such terms as the court may fix;
(*h*) subject to section 20.1, make any order of prohibition, seizure or forfeiture that may be imposed under any Act of Parliament or any regulation made thereunder where an accused is found guilty or convicted of that offence;
(*i*) [Repealed, 1995, c. 19, s. 13]
(*j*) place the young person on probation in accordance with section 23 for a specified period not exceeding two years;
(*k*) subject to sections 24 to 24.5, commit the young person to custody, to be served continuously or intermittently, for a specified period not exceeding
(i) two years from the date of committal, or
(ii) where the young person is found guilty of an offence for which the punishment provided by the *Criminal Code* or any other Act of Parliament is imprisonment for life, three years from the date of committal;
(*k*.1) order the young person to serve a disposition not to exceed
(i) in the case of first degree murder, ten years comprised of
(A) a committal to custody, to be served continuously, for a period that shall not, subject to subsection 26.1(1), exceed six years from the date of committal, and
(B) a placement under conditional supervision to be served in the community in accordance with section 26.2, and
(ii) in the case of second degree murder, seven years comprised of
(A) a committal to custody, to be served continuously, for a period that shall not, subject to subsection 26.1(1), exceed four years from the date of committal, and
(B) a placement under conditional supervision to be served in the community in accordance with section 26.2; and
(*l*) impose on the young person such other reasonable and ancillary conditions as it deems advisable and in the best interest of the young person and the public.

**Coming into force of disposition**
(2) A disposition made under this section shall come into force on the date on which it is made or on such later date as the youth court specifies therein.

**Duration of disposition**
(3) No disposition made under this section, other than an order made under paragraph (1)(*h*), (*k*) or (*k*.1), shall continue in force for more than two years and, where the youth court makes more than one disposition at the same time in respect of the same offence, the combined duration of the dispositions, except in respect of an order made under paragraph (1)(*h*), (*k*) or (*k*.1), shall not exceed two years.

**Combined duration of dispositions**
(4) Subject to subsection (4.1), where more than one disposition is made under this section in respect of a young person with respect to different offences, the continuous combined duration of those dispositions shall not exceed three years, except where one of those offences is first degree murder or second degree murder within the meaning of section 231 of the *Criminal Code*, in which case the continuous combined duration of those dispositions shall not exceed ten years in the case of first degree murder, or seven years in the case of second degree murder.

**Duration of dispositions made at different times**
(4.1) Where a disposition is made under this section in respect of an offence committed by a young person after the commencement of, but before the completion of, any dispositions made in respect of previous offences committed by the young person,
(*a*) the duration of the disposition made in respect of the subsequent offence shall be determined in accordance with subsections (3) and (4);
(*b*) the disposition may be served consecutively to the dispositions made in respect of the previous offences; and
(*c*) the combined duration of all the dispositions may exceed three years, except where the offence is, or one of the previous offences was,
(i) first degree murder within the meaning of section 231 of the *Criminal Code*, in which case the continuous combined duration of the dispositions may exceed ten years, or
(ii) second degree murder within the meaning of section 231 of the *Criminal Code*, in which case the continuous combined duration of the dispositions may exceed seven years.

**Custody first**
(4.2) Subject to subsection (4.3), where a young person who is serving a disposition made under paragraph (1)(*k*.1) is ordered to custody in respect of an offence committed after the commencement of, but before the completion of, that disposition, the custody in respect of that subsequent offence shall be served before the young person is placed under conditional supervision.

**Conditional supervision suspended**
(4.3) Where a young person referred to in subsection (4.2) is under conditional supervision at the time the young person is ordered to custody in respect of a subsequent offence, the conditional supervision shall be suspended until the young person is released from custody.

**Disposition continues when adult**
(5) Subject to section 743.5 of the *Criminal Code*, a disposition made under this section shall continue in effect in accordance with the terms thereof, after the young person against whom it is made becomes an adult.

**Reasons for the disposition**
(6) Where a youth court makes a disposition under this section, it shall state its reasons therefor in the record of the case and shall
(*a*) provide or cause to be provided a copy of the disposition, and
(*b*) on request, provide or cause to be provided a transcript or copy of the reasons for the disposition
to the young person in respect of whom the disposition was made, the young person's counsel and parents, the provincial director, where the provincial director has an interest in the disposition, the prosecutor and, in the case of a custodial disposition made under paragraph (1)(*k*) or (*k*.1), the review board, if a review board has been established or designated.

**Limitation on punishment**
(7) No disposition shall be made in respect of a young person under this section that results in a punishment that is greater than the maximum punishment that would be applicable to an adult who has committed the same offence.

**Application of Part XXIII of *Criminal Code***
(8) Part XXIII of the *Criminal Code* does not apply in respect of proceedings under this Act except for section 722, subsection 730(2) and sections 748, 748.1 and 749, which provisions apply with such modifications as the circumstances require.

**Section 787 of *Criminal Code* does not apply**
(9) Section 787 of the *Criminal Code* does not apply in respect of proceedings under this Act.

**Contents of probation order**
(10) The youth court shall specify in any probation order made under paragraph (1)(*j*) the period for which it is to remain in force.

**No orders under section 161 of *Criminal Code***
(11) Notwithstanding paragraph (1)(*h*), a youth court shall not make an order of prohibition under section 161 of the *Criminal Code* against a young person.
R.S., 1985, c. Y-1, s. 20; R.S., 1985, c. 27 (1st Supp.), s. 187, c. 24 (2nd Supp.), s. 14, c. 1 (4th Supp.), s. 38; 1992, c. 11, s. 3; 1993, c. 45, s. 15; 1995, c. 19, s. 13; 1995, c. 22, ss. 16, 17; 1995, c. 39, s. 178.

**Mandatory prohibition order**
**20.1** (1) Notwithstanding subsection 20(1), where a young person is found guilty of an offence referred to in any of paragraphs 109(1)(*a*) to (*d*) of the *Criminal Code*, the youth court shall, in addition to making any disposition referred to in subsection 20(1), make an order prohibiting the young person from possessing any firearm, cross-bow, prohibited weapon, restricted weapon, prohibited device, ammunition, prohibited ammunition and explosive substance during the period specified in the order as determined in accordance with subsection (2).

**Duration of prohibition order**
(2) An order made under subsection (1) begins on the day on which the order is made and ends not earlier than two years after the young person's release from custody after being found guilty of the offence or, if the young person is not then in custody or subject to custody, after the time the young person is found guilty of or discharged from the offence.

**Discretionary prohibition order**
(3) Notwithstanding subsection 20(1), where a young person is found guilty of an offence referred to in paragraph 110(1)(*a*) or (*b*) of the *Criminal Code*, the youth court shall, in addition to making any disposition referred to in subsection 20(1), consider whether it is desirable, in the interests of the safety of the person or of any other person, to make an order prohibiting the person from possessing any firearm, cross-bow, prohibited weapon, restricted weapon, prohibited device, ammunition, prohibited ammunition or explosive substance, or all such things, and where the court decides that it is so desirable, the court shall so order.

**Duration of prohibition order**
(4) An order made under subsection (3) against a young person begins on the day on which the order is made and ends not later than two years after the young person's release from custody or, if the young person is not then in custody or subject to custody, after the time the young person is found guilty of or discharged from the offence.

**Definition of "release from imprisonment"**
(5) In paragraph (2)(*a*) and subsection (4), "release from custody" means a release from custody in accordance with this Act, other than a release from custody under subsection 35(1), and includes the commencement of conditional supervision or probation.

**Reasons for the prohibition order**
(6) Where a youth court makes an order under this section, it shall state its reasons for making the order in the record of the case and shall

(*a*) provide or cause to be provided a copy of the order, and
(*b*) on request, provide or cause to be provided a transcript or copy of the reasons for making the order

to the young person against whom the order was made, the young person's counsel and parents and the provincial director.

**Reasons**
(7) Where the youth court does not make an order under subsection (3), or where the youth court does make such an order but does not prohibit the possession of everything referred to in that subsection, the youth court shall include in the record a statement of the youth court's reasons.

**Application of *Criminal Code***
(8) Sections 113 to 117 of the *Criminal Code* apply in respect of any order made under this section.

**Report**
(9) Before making any order referred to in section 113 of the *Criminal Code* in respect of a young person, the youth court may require the provincial director to cause to be prepared, and to submit to the youth court, a report on the young person. 1995, c. 39, s. 179.

**Where a fine or other payment is ordered**
**21.** (1) The youth court shall, in imposing a fine on a young person under paragraph 20(1)(*b*) or in making an order against a young person under paragraph 20(1)(*c*) or (*e*), have regard to the present and future means of the young person to pay.

**Fine option program**
(2) A young person against whom a fine is imposed under paragraph 20(1)(*b*) may discharge the fine in whole or in part by earning credits for work performed in a program established for that purpose

(*a*) by the Lieutenant Governor in Council of the province in which the fine was imposed; or
(*b*) by the Lieutenant Governor in Council of the province in which the young person resides, where an appropriate agreement is in effect between the government of that province and the government of the province in which the fine was imposed.

**Rates, crediting and other matters**
(3) A program referred to in subsection (2) shall determine the rate at which credits are earned and may provide for the manner of crediting any amounts earned against the fine and any other matters necessary for or incidental to carrying out the program.

**Representations respecting orders under paras. 20(1)(*c*) to (*f*)**
(4) In considering whether to make an order under paragraphs 20(1)(*c*) to (*f*), the youth court may consider any representations made by the person who would be compensated or to whom restitution or payment would be made.

**Notice of orders under paras. 20(1)(*c*) to (*f*)**
(5) Where the youth court makes an order under paragraphs 20(1)(*c*) to (*f*), it shall cause notice of the terms of the order to be given to the person who is to be compensated or to whom restitution or payment is to be made.

**Consent of person to be compensated**
(6) No order may be made under paragraph 20(1)(*f*) unless the youth court has secured the consent of the person to be compensated.

**Order for compensation or community service**
(7) No order may be made under paragraph 20(1)(*f*) or (*g*) unless the youth court
(*a*) is satisfied that the young person against whom the order is made is a suitable candidate for such an order; and
(*b*) is satisfied that the order does not interfere with the normal hours of work or education of the young person.

**Duration of order for service**
(8) No order may be made under paragraph 20(1)(*f*) or (*g*) to perform personal or community services unless those services can be completed in two hundred and forty hours or less and within twelve months of the date of the order.

**Community service order**
(9) No order may be made under paragraph 20(1)(*g*) unless
(*a*) the community service to be performed is part of a program that is approved by the provincial director; or
(*b*) the youth court is satisfied that the person or organization for whom the community service is to be performed has agreed to its performance.

**Application for further time to complete disposition**
(10) A youth court may, on application by or on behalf of the young person in respect of whom a disposition has been made under paragraphs 20(1)(*b*) to (*g*), allow further time for the completion of the disposition subject to any regulations made pursuant to paragraph 67(*b*) and to any rules made by the youth court pursuant to subsection 68(1).
R.S., 1985, c. Y-1, s. 21; R.S., 1985, c. 24 (2nd Supp.), s. 15.

**22.** [Repealed, 1995, c. 19, s. 14]

**Conditions that must appear in probation orders**
**23.** (1) The following conditions shall be included in a probation order made under paragraph 20(1)(*j*):
(*a*) that the young person bound by the probation order shall keep the peace and be of good behaviour; and
(*b*) that the young person appear before the youth court when required by the court to do so.
(*c*) [Repealed, R.S., 1985, c. 24 (2nd Supp.), s. 16]

**Conditions that may appear in probation orders**
(2) A probation order made under paragraph 20(1)(*j*) may include such of the following conditions as the youth court considers appropriate in the circumstances of the case:
(*a*) that the young person bound by the probation order report to and be under the supervision of the provincial director or a person designated by the youth court;
(*a*.1) that the young person notify the clerk of the youth court, the provincial director or the youth worker assigned to his case of any change of address or any change in his place of employment, education or training;
(*b*) that the young person remain within the territorial jurisdiction of one or more courts named in the order;
(*c*) that the young person make reasonable efforts to obtain and maintain suitable employment;
(*d*) that the young person attend school or such other place of learning, training or recreation as is appropriate, if the court is satisfied that a suitable program is available for the young person at that place;
(*e*) that the young person reside with a parent, or such other adult as the court considers appropriate, who is willing to provide for the care and maintenance of the young person;
(*f*) that the young person reside in such place as the provincial director may specify; and
(*g*) that the young person comply with such other reasonable conditions set out in the order as the court considers desirable, including conditions for securing the good conduct of the young person and for preventing the commission by the young person of other offences.

**Communication of probation order to young person and parent**
(3) Where the youth court makes a probation order under paragraph 20(1)(*j*), it shall
(*a*) cause the order to be read by or to the young person bound by the probation order;
(*b*) explain or cause to be explained to the young person the purpose and effect of the order and ascertain that the young person understands it; and
(*c*) cause a copy of the order to be given to the young person and to a parent of the young person, if the parent is in attendance at the proceedings against the young person.

**Copy of probation order to parent**
(4) Where the youth court makes a probation order under paragraph 20(1)(*j*), it may cause a copy of the report to be given to a parent of the young person not in attendance at the proceedings against the young person if the parent is, in the opinion of the court, taking an active interest in the proceedings.

**Endorsement of order by young person**
(5) After a probation order has been read by or to a young person and explained to him pursuant to subsection (3), the young person shall endorse the order acknowledging that he has received a copy of the order and acknowledging the fact that it has been explained to him.

**Validity of probation order**
(6) The failure of a young person to endorse a probation order pursuant to subsection (5) does not affect the validity of the order.

**Commencement of probation order**
(7) A probation order made under paragraph 20(1)(*j*) comes into force

(*a*) on the date on which the order is made; or
(*b*) where the young person in respect of whom the order is made is committed to continuous custody, on the expiration of the period of custody.

**Notice to appear**
(8) A young person may be given notice to appear before the youth court pursuant to paragraph (1)(*b*) orally or in writing.

**Warrant to arrest young person**
(9) If a young person to whom a notice is given in writing to appear before the youth court pursuant to paragraph (1)(*b*) does not appear at the time and place named in the notice and it is proved that a copy of the notice was served on him, a youth court may issue a warrant to compel the appearance of the young person.
R.S., 1985, c. Y-1, s. 23; R.S., 1985, c. 24 (2nd Supp.), s. 16, c. 1 (4th Supp.), s. 39.

**Conditions for custody**
**24.** (1) The youth court shall not commit a young person to custody under paragraph 20(1)(*k*) unless the court considers a committal to custody to be necessary for the protection of society having regard to the seriousness of the offence and the circumstances in which it was committed and having regard to the needs and circumstances of the young person.

**Factors**
(1.1) In making a determination under subsection (1), the youth court shall take the following into account:
(*a*) that an order of custody shall not be used as a substitute for appropriate child protection, health and other social measures;
(*b*) that a young person who commits an offence that does not involve serious personal injury should be held accountable to the victim and to society through non-custodial dispositions whenever appropriate; and
(*c*) that custody shall only be imposed when all available alternatives to custody that are reasonable in the circumstances have been considered.

**Pre-disposition report**
(2) Subject to subsection (3), before making an order of committal to custody, the youth court shall consider a pre-disposition report.

**Report dispensed with**
(3) The youth court may, with the consent of the prosecutor and the young person or his counsel, dispense with the pre-disposition report required under subsection (2) if the youth court is satisfied, having regard to the circumstances, that the report is unnecessary or that it would not be in the best interests of the young person to require one.

**Reasons**
(4) Where the youth court makes a disposition in respect of a young person under paragraph 20(1)(*k*), the youth court shall state the reasons why any other disposition or dispositions under subsection 20(1), without the disposition under paragraph 20(1)(*k*), would not have been adequate.
R.S., 1985, c. Y-1, s. 24; R.S., 1985, c. 24 (2nd Supp.), s. 17; 1995, c. 19, s. 15.

**Definitions**
**24.1** (1) In this section and sections 24.2, 24.3, 28 and 29,

**"open custody" «garde en milieu ouvert»**
"open custody" means custody in
(*a*) a community residential centre, group home, child care institution, or forest or wilderness camp, or
(*b*) any other like place or facility
designated by the Lieutenant Governor in Council of a province or his delegate as a place of open custody for the purposes of this Act, and includes a place or facility within a class of such places or facilities so designated;

**"secure custody" «garde en milieu fermé»**
"secure custody" means custody in a place or facility designated by the Lieutenant Governor in Council of a province for the secure containment or restraint of young persons, and includes a place or facility within a class of such places or facilities so designated.

**Youth court to specify type of custody**
(2) Subject to subsection (3), where the youth court commits a young person to custody under paragraph 20(1)(*k*) or (*k*.1) or makes an order under subsection 26.1(1) or paragraph 26.6(2)(*b*), it shall specify in the order whether the custody is to be open custody or secure custody.

**Provincial director to specify level of custody**
(3) In a province in which the Lieutenant Governor in Council has designated the provincial director to determine the level of custody, the provincial director shall, where a young person is committed to custody under paragraph 20(1)(*k*) or (*k*.1) or an order is made under subsection 26.1(1) or paragraph 26.6(2)(*b*), specify whether the young person shall be placed in open custody or secure custody.

**Factors**
(4) In deciding whether a young person shall be placed in open custody or secure custody, the youth court or the provincial director shall take into account the following factors:
(*a*) that a young person should be placed in a level of custody involving the least degree of containment and restraint, having regard to
(i) the seriousness of the offence in respect of which the young person was committed to custody and the circumstances in which that offence was committed,
(ii) the needs and circumstances of the young person, including proximity to family, school, employment and support services,
(iii) the safety of other young persons in custody, and

(iv) the interests of society;
(*b*) that the level of custody should allow for the best possible match of programs to the young person's needs and behaviour, having regard to the findings of any assessment in respect of the young person;
(*c*) the likelihood of escape if the young person is placed in open custody; and
(*d*) the recommendations, if any, of the youth court or the provincial director, as the case may be.

R.S., 1985, c. 24 (2nd Supp.), s. 17; 1992, c. 11, s. 4; 1995, c. 19, s. 16.

**Place of custody**
24.2 (1) Subject to this section and sections 24.3 and 24.5, a young person who is committed to custody shall be placed in open custody or secure custody, as specified pursuant to subsection 24.1(2) or (3), at such place or facility as the provincial director may specify.

**Warrant of committal**
(2) Where a young person is committed to custody, the youth court shall issue or cause to be issued a warrant of committal.

**Exception**
(3) A young person who is committed to custody may, in the course of being transferred from custody to the court or from the court to custody, be held under the supervision and control of a peace officer or in such place of temporary detention referred to in subsection 7(1) as the provincial director may specify.

**Young person to be held separate from adults**
(4) Subject to this section and section 24.5, a young person who is committed to custody shall be held separate and apart from any adult who is detained or held in custody.

**Subsection 7(2) applies**
(5) Subsection 7(2) applies, with such modifications as the circumstances require, in respect of a person held in a place of temporary detention pursuant to subsection (3).

**Transfer**
(6) A young person who is committed to custody may, during the period of custody, be transferred by the provincial director from one place or facility of open custody to another or from one place or facility of secure custody to another.

**Transfer to open custody—youth court**
(7) No young person who is committed to secure custody pursuant to subsection 24.1(2) may be transferred to a place or facility of open custody except in accordance with sections 28 to 31.

**No transfer to secure custody—youth court**
(8) Subject to subsection (9), no young person who is committed to open custody pursuant to subsection 24.1(2) may be transferred to a place or facility of secure custody.

**Exception—transfer to secure custody—youth court**
(9) Where a young person is placed in open custody pursuant to subsection 24.1(2), the provincial director may transfer the young person from a place or facility of open custody to a place or facility of secure custody for a period not exceeding fifteen days if
(*a*) the young person escapes or attempts to escape lawful custody; or
(*b*) the transfer is, in the opinion of the provincial director, necessary for the safety of the young person or the safety of others in the place or facility of open custody.

**Transfer to open custody—provincial director**
(10) The provincial director may transfer a young person from a place or facility of secure custody to a place or facility of open custody when the provincial director is satisfied that the needs of the young person and the interests of society would be better served thereby.

**Transfer to secure custody—provincial director**
(11) The provincial director may transfer a young person from a place or facility of open custody to a place or facility of secure custody when the provincial director is satisfied that the needs of the young person and the interests of society would be better served thereby
(*a*) having considered the factors set out in subsection 24.1(4); and
(*b*) having determined that there has been a material change in circumstances since the young person was placed in open custody.

**Notice**
(12) The provincial director shall cause a notice in writing of the decision to transfer a young person under subsection (11) to be given to the young person and the young person's parents and set out in that notice the reasons for the transfer.

**Where application for review is made**
(13) Where an application for review under section 28.1 of a transfer under subsection (11) is made to a youth court,
(*a*) the provincial director shall cause such notice as may be directed by rules of court applicable to the youth court or, in the absence of such direction, at least five clear days notice of the review to be given in writing to the young person and the young person's parents; and
(*b*) the youth court shall forthwith, after the notice required under paragraph (*a*) is given, review the transfer.

**Interim custody**
(14) Where an application for review under section 28.1 of a transfer under subsection (11) is made to a youth court, the young person shall remain in a place or facility of secure custody until the review is heard by the youth court unless the provincial director directs otherwise.

R.S., 1985, c. 24 (2nd Supp.), s. 17; 1995, c. 19, s. 17.

**Consecutive dispositions of custody**
24.3 (1) Where a young person is committed to open custody and secure custody pursuant to subsection 24.1(2), any portions of which dispositions are to be served consecutively, the disposition of secure custody shall be served first without regard to the order in which the dispositions were imposed.

**Concurrent dispositions of custody**
(2) Where a young person is committed to open custody and secure custody pursuant to subsection 24.1(2), any portions of which dispositions are to be served concurrently, the concurrent portions of the dispositions shall be served in secure custody.
R.S., 1985, c. 24 (2nd Supp.), s. 17; 1995, c. 19, s. 18.

**Committal to custody deemed continuous**
24.4 (1) A young person who is committed to custody under paragraph 20(1)(*k*) shall be deemed to be committed to continuous custody unless the youth court specifies otherwise.

**Availability of place of intermittent custody**
(2) Before making an order of committal to intermittent custody under paragraph 20(1)(*k*), the youth court shall require the prosecutor to make available to the court for its consideration a report of the provincial director as to the availability of a place of custody in which an order of intermittent custody can be enforced and, where the report discloses that no such place of custody is available, the court shall not make the order.
R.S., 1985, c. 24 (2nd Supp.), s. 17.

**Transfer to adult facility**
24.5 (1) Where a young person is committed to custody under paragraph 20(1)(*k*) or (*k*.1), the youth court may, on application of the provincial director made at any time after the young person attains the age of eighteen years, after affording the young person an opportunity to be heard, authorize the provincial director to direct that the young person serve the disposition or the remaining portion thereof in a provincial correctional facility for adults, if the court considers it to be in the best interests of the young person or in the public interest, but in that event, the provisions of this Act shall continue to apply in respect of that person.

**Where disposition and sentence concurrent**
(2) Where a young person is committed to custody under paragraph 20(1)(*k*) or (*k*.1) and is concurrently under sentence of imprisonment imposed in ordinary court, the young person may, in the discretion of the provincial director, serve the disposition and sentence, or any portion thereof, in a place of custody for young persons, in a provincial correctional facility for adults or, where the unexpired portion of the sentence is two years or more, in a penitentiary.
R.S., 1985, c. 24 (2nd Supp.), s. 17; 1992, c. 11, s. 5.

**Transfer of disposition**
25. (1) Where a disposition has been made under paragraphs 20(1)(*b*) to (*g*) or paragraph 20(1)(*j*) or (*l*) in respect of a young person and the young person or a parent with whom the young person resides is or becomes a resident of a territorial division outside the jurisdiction of the youth court that made the disposition, whether in the same or in another province, a youth court judge in the territorial division in which the disposition was made may, on the application of the Attorney General or an agent of the Attorney General or on the application of the young person or the young person's parent with the consent of the Attorney General or an agent of the Attorney General, transfer the disposition and such portion of the record of the case as is appropriate to a youth court in the other territorial division, and all subsequent proceedings relating to the case shall thereafter be carried out and enforced by that court.

**No transfer outside province before appeal completed**
(2) No disposition may be transferred from one province to another under this section until the time for an appeal against the disposition or the finding on which the disposition was based has expired or until all proceedings in respect of any such appeal have been completed.

**Transfer to a province where person is adult**
(3) Where an application is made under subsection (1) to transfer the disposition of a young person to a province in which the young person is an adult, a youth court judge may, with the consent of the Attorney General, transfer the disposition and the record of the case to the youth court in the province to which the transfer is sought, and the youth court to which the case is transferred shall have full jurisdiction in respect of the disposition as if that court had made the disposition, and the person shall be further dealt with in accordance with this Act.
R.S., 1985, c. Y-1, s. 25; R.S., 1985, c. 24 (2nd Supp.), s. 18; 1995, c. 19, s. 19.

**Interprovincial arrangements for probation or custody**
25.1 (1) Where a disposition has been made under paragraphs 20(1)(*j*) to (*k*.1) in respect of a young person, the disposition in one province may be dealt with in any other province pursuant to any agreement that may have been made between those provinces.

**Youth court retains jurisdiction**
(2) Subject to subsection (3), where a disposition made in respect of a young person is dealt with pursuant to this section in a province other than that in which the disposition was made, the youth court of the province in which the disposition was made shall, for all purposes of this Act, retain exclusive jurisdiction over the young person as if the disposition were dealt with within that province, and any warrant or process issued in respect of the young person may be executed or served in any place in Canada outside the province where the disposition was made as if it were executed or served in that province.

**Waiver of jurisdiction**
(3) Where a disposition made in respect of a young person is dealt with pursuant to this section in a province other than that in which the disposition was made, the youth court of the province in which the disposition was made may, with the consent in writing of the Attorney General of that province or his delegate and the young person, waive its jurisdiction, for the purpose of any proceeding under this Act, to the youth court of the province in which the disposition is dealt with, in which case the youth court in the province in which the disposition is so dealt with shall have full jurisdiction in respect of the disposition as if that court had made the disposition.
R.S., 1985, c. 24 (2nd Supp.), s. 19; 1992, c. 11, s. 6; 1995, c. 19, s. 20.

**Failure to comply with disposition**
**26.** A person who is subject to a disposition made under paragraphs 20(1)(*b*) to (*g*) or paragraph 20(1)(*j*) or (*l*) and who wilfully fails or refuses to comply with that order is guilty of an offence punishable on summary conviction.
R.S., 1985, c. Y-1, s. 26; R.S., 1985, c. 24 (2nd Supp.), s. 19.

**Continuation of custody**
**26.1** (1) Where a young person is held in custody pursuant to a disposition made under paragraph 20(1)(*k*.1) and an application is made to the youth court by the Attorney General, or the Attorney General's agent, within a reasonable time prior to the expiration of the period of custody, the provincial director of the province in which the young person is held in custody shall cause the young person to be brought before the youth court and the youth court may, after affording both parties and the parents of the young person an opportunity to be heard and if it is satisfied that there are reasonable grounds to believe that the young person is likely to commit an offence causing the death of or serious harm to another person prior to the expiration of the disposition the young person is then serving, order that the young person remain in custody for a period not exceeding the remainder of the disposition.

**Idem**
(1.1) Where the hearing for an application under subsection (1) cannot be completed before the expiration of the period of custody, the court may order that the young person remain in custody pending the determination of the application if the court is satisfied that the application was made in a reasonable time, having regard to all the circumstances, and that there are compelling reasons for keeping the young person in custody.

**Factors**
(2) For the purpose of determining an application under subsection (1), the youth court shall take into consideration any factor that is relevant to the case of the young person including, without limiting the generality of the foregoing,

(*a*) evidence of a pattern of persistent violent behaviour and, in particular,
  (i) the number of offences committed by the young person that caused physical or psychological harm to any other person,
  (ii) the young person's difficulties in controlling violent impulses to the point of endangering the safety of any other person,
  (iii) the use of weapons in the commission of any offence,
  (iv) explicit threats of violence,
  (v) behaviour of a brutal nature associated with the commission of any offence, and
  (vi) a substantial degree of indifference on the part of the young person as to the reasonably foreseeable consequences, to other persons, of the young person's behaviour;

(*b*) psychiatric or psychological evidence that a physical or mental illness or disorder of the young person is of such a nature that the young person is likely to commit, prior to the expiration of the disposition the young person is then serving, an offence causing the death of or serious harm to another person;

(*c*) reliable information that satisfies the youth court that the young person is planning to commit, prior to the expiration of the disposition the young person is then serving, an offence causing the death of or serious harm to another person; and

(*d*) the availability of supervision programs in the community that would offer adequate protection to the public from the risk that the young person might otherwise present until the expiration of the disposition the young person is then serving.

**Youth court to order appearance of young person**
(3) Where a provincial director fails to cause a young person to be brought before the youth court under subsection (1), the youth court shall order the provincial director to cause the young person to be brought before the youth court forthwith.

**Report**
(4) For the purpose of determining an application under subsection (1), the youth court shall require the provincial director to cause to be prepared, and to submit to the youth court, a report setting out any information of which the provincial director is aware with respect to the factors referred to in subsection (2) that may be of assistance to the court.

**Written or oral report**
(5) A report referred to in subsection (4) shall be in writing unless it cannot reasonably be committed to writing, in which case it may, with leave of the youth court, be submitted orally in court.

**Provisions apply**
(6) Subsections 14(4) to (10) apply, with such modifications as the circumstances require, in respect of a report referred to in subsection (4).

**Notice of hearing**
(7) Where an application is made under subsection (1) in respect of a young person, the

Attorney General or the Attorney General's agent shall cause such notice as may be directed by rules of court applicable to the youth court or, in the absence of such direction, at least five clear days notice of the hearing to be given in writing to the young person and the young person's parents and the provincial director.

**Statement of right to counsel**
(8) Any notice given to a parent under subsection (7) shall include a statement that the young person has the right to be represented by counsel.

**Service of notice**
(9) A notice under subsection (7) may be served personally or may be sent by registered mail.

**Where notice not given**
(10) Where notice under subsection (7) is not given in accordance with this section, the youth court may
(*a*) adjourn the hearing and order that the notice be given in such manner and to such person as it directs; or
(*b*) dispense with the giving of the notice where, in the opinion of the youth court, having regard to the circumstances, the giving of the notice may be dispensed with.

**Reasons**
(11) Where a youth court makes an order under subsection (1), it shall state its reasons for the order in the record of the case and shall
(*a*) provide or cause to be provided a copy of the order, and
(*b*) on request, provide or cause to be provided a transcript or copy of the reasons for the order

to the young person in respect of whom the order was made, the counsel and parents of the young person, the Attorney General or the Attorney General's agent, the provincial director and the review board, if any has been established or designated.

**Review provisions apply**
(12) Subsections 16(9) to (11) apply, with such modifications as the circumstances require, in respect of an order made, or the refusal to make an order, under subsection (1).

**Where application denied**
(13) Where an application under subsection (1) is denied, the court may, with the consent of the young person, the Attorney General and the provincial director, proceed as though the young person had been brought before the court as required under subsection 26.2(1).
1992, c. 11, s. 7.

**Conditional supervision**
**26.2** (1) The provincial director of the province in which a young person is held in custody pursuant to a disposition made under paragraph 20(1)(*k*.1) or, where applicable, an order made under subsection 26.1(1), shall cause the young person to be brought before the youth court at least one month prior to the expiration of the period of custody and the court shall, after affording the young person an opportunity to be heard, by order, set the conditions of the young person's conditional supervision.

**Conditions to be included in order**
(2) In setting conditions for the purposes of subsection (1), the youth court shall include in the order the following conditions, namely, that the young person
(*a*) keep the peace and be of good behaviour;
(*b*) appear before the youth court when required by the court to do so;
(*c*) report to the provincial director immediately on release, and thereafter be under the supervision of the provincial director or a person designated by the youth court;
(*d*) inform the provincial director immediately on being arrested or questioned by the police;
(*e*) report to the police, or any named individual, as instructed by the provincial director;
(*f*) advise the provincial director of the young person's address of residence on release and after release report immediately to the clerk of the youth court or the provincial director any change
(i) in that address,
(ii) in the young person's normal occupation, including employment, vocational or educational training and volunteer work,
(iii) in the young person's family or financial situation, and
(iv) that may reasonably be expected to affect the young person's ability to comply with the conditions of the order;
(*g*) not own, possess or have the control of any weapon, ammunition, prohibited ammunition, prohibited device or explosive substance, except as authorized by the order; and
(*h*) comply with such reasonable instructions as the provincial director considers necessary in respect of any condition of the conditional supervision in order to prevent a breach of that condition or to protect society.

**Other conditions**
(3) In setting conditions for the purposes of subsection (1), the youth court may include in the order the following conditions, namely, that the young person
(*a*) on release, travel directly to the young person's place of residence, or to such other place as is noted in the order;
(*b*) make reasonable efforts to obtain and maintain suitable employment;
(*c*) attend school or such other place of learning, training or recreation as is appropriate, if the court is satisfied that a suitable program is available for the young person at such a place;
(*d*) reside with a parent, or such other adult as the court considers appropriate, who is willing to provide for the care and maintenance of the young person;
(*e*) reside in such place as the provincial director may specify;

(*f*) remain within the territorial jurisdiction of one or more courts named in the order; and
(*g*) comply with such other reasonable conditions set out in the order as the court considers desirable, including conditions for securing the good conduct of the young person and for preventing the commission by the young person of other offences.

**Temporary conditions**
(4) Where a provincial director is required under subsection (1) to cause a young person to be brought before the youth court but cannot do so for reasons beyond the young person's control, the provincial director shall so advise the youth court and the court shall, by order, set such temporary conditions for the young person's conditional supervision as are appropriate in the circumstances.

**Conditions to be set at first opportunity**
(5) Where an order is made under subsection (4), the provincial director shall bring the young person before the youth court as soon thereafter as the circumstances permit and the court shall then set the conditions of the young person's conditional supervision.

**Report**
(6) For the purpose of setting conditions under this section, the youth court shall require the provincial director to cause to be prepared, and to submit to the youth court, a report setting out any information that may be of assistance to the court.

**Provisions apply**
(7) Subsections 26.1(3) and (5) to (10) apply, with such modifications as the circumstances require, in respect of any proceedings held pursuant to subsection (1).

**Idem**
(8) Subsections 16(9) to (11) and 23(3) to (9) apply, with such modifications as the circumstances require, in respect of an order made under subsection (1).
1992, c. 11, s. 7; 1995, c. 39, s. 180.

**Suspension of conditional supervision**
**26.3** Where the provincial director has reasonable grounds to believe that a young person has breached or is about to breach a condition of an order made under subsection 26.2(1), the provincial director may, in writing,
(*a*) suspend the conditional supervision; and
(*b*) order that the young person be remanded to such place of custody as the provincial director considers appropriate until a review is conducted under section 26.5 and, if applicable, section 26.6.
1992, c. 11, s. 7.

**Apprehension**
**26.4** (1) Where the conditional supervision of a young person is suspended under section 26.3, the provincial director may issue a warrant in writing, authorizing the apprehension of the young person and, until the young person is apprehended, the young person is deemed not to be continuing to serve the disposition the young person is then serving.

**Warrants**
(2) A warrant issued under subsection (1) shall be executed by any peace officer to whom it is given at any place in Canada and has the same force and effect in all parts of Canada as if it had been originally issued or subsequently endorsed by a provincial court judge or other lawful authority having jurisdiction in the place where it is executed.

**Peace officer may arrest**
(3) Where a peace officer believes on reasonable grounds that a warrant issued under subsection (1) is in force in respect of a young person, the peace officer may arrest the young person without the warrant at any place in Canada.

**Requirement to bring before provincial director**
(4) Where a young person is arrested pursuant to subsection (3) and detained, the peace officer making the arrest shall cause the young person to be brought before the provincial director or a person designated by the provincial director
(*a*) where the provincial director or the designated person is available within a period of twenty-four hours after the young person is arrested, without unreasonable delay and in any event within that period; and
(*b*) where the provincial director or the designated person is not available within the period referred to in paragraph (*a*), as soon as possible.

**Release or remand in custody**
(5) Where a young person is brought, pursuant to subsection (4), before the provincial director or a person designated by the provincial director, the provincial director or the designated person
(*a*) if not satisfied that there are reasonable grounds to believe that the young person is the young person in respect of whom the warrant referred to in subsection (1) was issued, shall release the young person; or
(*b*) if satisfied that there are reasonable grounds to believe that the young person is the young person in respect of whom the warrant referred to in subsection (1) was issued, may remand the young person in custody to await execution of the warrant, but if no warrant for the young person's arrest is executed within a period of six days after the time the young person is remanded in such custody, the person in whose custody the young person then is shall release the young person.
1992, c. 11, s. 7.

**Review by provincial director**
**26.5** Forthwith after the remand to custody of a young person whose conditional supervision has been suspended under section 26.3, or forthwith after being informed of the arrest of such a young person, the provincial director shall review the case and, within forty-eight hours, cancel the suspension of the conditional supervision or refer the case to the youth court for a review under section 26.6.
1992, c. 11, s. 7.

**Review by youth court**
26.6 (1) Where the case of a young person is referred to the youth court under section 26.5, the provincial director shall, as soon as is practicable, cause the young person to be brought before the youth court, and the youth court shall, after affording the young person an opportunity to be heard,
(*a*) if the court is not satisfied on reasonable grounds that the young person has breached or was about to breach a condition of the conditional supervision, cancel the suspension of the conditional supervision; or
(*b*) if the court is satisfied on reasonable grounds that the young person has breached or was about to breach a condition of the conditional supervision, review the decision of the provincial director to suspend the conditional supervision and make an order under subsection (2).

**Order**
(2) On completion of a review under subsection (1), the youth court shall order
(*a*) the cancellation of the suspension of the conditional supervision, and where the court does so, the court may vary the conditions of the conditional supervision or impose new conditions; or
(*b*) the continuation of the suspension of the conditional supervision for such period of time, not to exceed the remainder of the disposition the young person is then serving, as the court considers appropriate, and where the court does so, the court shall order that the young person remain in custody.

**Reasons**
(3) Where a youth court makes an order under subsection (2), it shall state its reasons for the order in the record of the case and shall
(*a*) provide or cause to be provided a copy of the order, and
(*b*) on request, provide or cause to be provided a transcript or copy of the reasons for the order

to the young person in respect of whom the order was made, the counsel and parents of the young person, the Attorney General or the Attorney General's agent, the provincial director and the review board, if any has been established or designated.

**Provisions apply**
(4) Subsections 26.1(3) and (5) to (10) and 26.2(6) apply, with such modifications as the circumstances require, in respect of a review under this section.

**Idem**
(5) Subsections 16(9) to (11) apply, with such modifications as the circumstances require, in respect of an order made under subsection (2). 1992, c. 11, s. 7.

APPEALS

**Appeals for indictable offences**
27. (1) An appeal lies under this Act in respect of an indictable offence or an offence that the Attorney General or his agent elects to proceed with as an indictable offence in accordance with Part XXI of the *Criminal Code*, which Part applies with such modifications as the circumstances require.

**Appeals for summary conviction offences**
(1.1) An appeal lies under this Act in respect of an offence punishable on summary conviction or an offence that the Attorney General or his agent elects to proceed with as an offence punishable on summary conviction in accordance with Part XXVII of the *Criminal Code*, which Part applies with such modifications as the circumstances require.

**Appeals where offences are tried jointly**
(1.2) An appeal involving one or more indictable offences and one or more summary conviction offences that are tried jointly or in respect of which dispositions are jointly made lies under this Act in accordance with Part XXI of the *Criminal Code*, which applies with such modifications as the circumstances require.

**Deemed election**
(2) For the purpose of appeals under this Act, where no election is made in respect of an offence that may be prosecuted by indictment or proceeded with by way of summary conviction, the Attorney General or his agent shall be deemed to have elected to proceed with the offence as an offence punishable on summary conviction.

**Where the youth court is a superior court**
(3) In any province where the youth court is a superior court, an appeal under subsection (1.1) shall be made to the court of appeal of the province.

**Nunavut**
(3.1) Despite subsection (3), if the Nunavut Court of Justice is acting as a youth court, an appeal under subsection (1.1) shall be made to a judge of the Court of Appeal of Nunavut, and an appeal of that judge's decision shall be made to the Court of Appeal of Nunavut in accordance with section 839 of the *Criminal Code*.

**Where the youth court is a county or district court**
(4) In any province where the youth court is a county or district court, an appeal under subsection (1.1) shall be made to the superior court of the province.

**Appeal to the Supreme Court of Canada**
(5) No appeal lies pursuant to subsection (1) from a judgment of the court of appeal in respect of a finding of guilt or an order dismissing an information to the Supreme Court of Canada unless leave to appeal is granted by the Supreme Court of Canada within twenty-one days after the judgment of the court of appeal is pronounced or within such extended time as the Supreme Court of Canada or a judge thereof may, for special reasons, allow.

**No appeal from disposition on review**
(6) No appeal lies from a disposition under sections 28 to 32.

R.S., 1985, c. Y-1, s. 27; R.S., 1985, c. 24 (2nd Supp.), s. 20; 1995, c. 19, s. 21; 1999, c. 3, s. 89.

## REVIEW OF DISPOSITIONS

**Automatic review of disposition involving custody**

**28.** (1) Where a young person is committed to custody pursuant to a disposition made in respect of an offence for a period exceeding one year, the provincial director of the province in which the young person is held in custody shall cause the young person to be brought before the youth court forthwith at the end of one year from the date of the most recent disposition made in respect of the offence, and the youth court shall review the disposition.

**Idem**

(2) Where a young person is committed to custody pursuant to dispositions made in respect of more than one offence for a total period exceeding one year, the provincial director of the province in which the young person is held in custody shall cause the young person to be brought before the youth court forthwith at the end of one year from the date of the earliest disposition made, and the youth court shall review the dispositions.

**Optional review of disposition involving custody**

(3) Where a young person is committed to custody pursuant to a disposition made under subsection 20(1) in respect of an offence, the provincial director may, on the provincial director's own initiative, and shall, on the request of the young person, the young person's parent or the Attorney General or an agent of the Attorney General, on any of the grounds set out in subsection (4), cause the young person to be brought before a youth court

(*a*) where the committal to custody is for a period not exceeding one year, once at any time after the expiration of the greater of

(i) thirty days after the date of the disposition made under subsection 20(1) in respect of the offence, and

(ii) one third of the period of the disposition made under subsection 20(1) in respect of the offence, and

(*b*) where the committal to custody is for a period exceeding one year, at any time after six months after the date of the most recent disposition made in respect of the offence,

or, with leave of a youth court judge, at any other time, and where a youth court is satisfied that there are grounds for the review under subsection (4), the court shall review the disposition.

**Grounds for review under subsection (3)**

(4) A disposition made in respect of a young person may be reviewed under subsection (3)

(*a*) on the ground that the young person has made sufficient progress to justify a change in disposition;

(*b*) on the ground that the circumstances that led to the committal to custody have changed materially;

(*c*) on the ground that new services or programs are available that were not available at the time of the disposition;

(*c*.1) on the ground that the opportunities for rehabilitation are now greater in the community; or

(*d*) on such other grounds as the youth court considers appropriate.

**No review where appeal pending**

(5) No review of a disposition in respect of which an appeal has been taken shall be made under this section until all proceedings in respect of any such appeal have been completed.

**Youth court may order appearance of young person for review**

(6) Where a provincial director is required under subsections (1) to (3) to cause a young person to be brought before the youth court and fails to do so, the youth court may, on application made by the young person, his parent or the Attorney General or his agent, or on its own motion, order the provincial director to cause the young person to be brought before the youth court.

**Progress report**

(7) The youth court shall, before reviewing under this section a disposition made in respect of a young person, require the provincial director to cause to be prepared, and to submit to the youth court, a progress report on the performance of the young person since the disposition took effect.

**Additional information in progress report**

(8) A person preparing a progress report in respect of a young person may include in the report such information relating to the personal and family history and present environment of the young person as he considers advisable.

**Written or oral report**

(9) A progress report shall be in writing unless it cannot reasonably be committed to writing, in which case it may, with leave of the youth court, be submitted orally in court.

**Provisions of subsections 14(4) to (10) to apply**

(10) The provisions of subsections 14(4) to (10) apply, with such modifications as the circumstances require, in respect of progress reports.

**Notice of review from provincial director**

(11) Where a disposition made in respect of a young person is to be reviewed under subsection (1) or (2), the provincial director shall cause such notice as may be directed by rules of court applicable to the youth court or, in the absence of such direction, at least five clear days notice of the review to be given in writing to the young person, his parents and the Attorney General or his agent.

**Notice of review from person requesting it**

(12) Where a review of a disposition made in respect of a young person is requested under subsection (3), the person requesting the review shall cause such notice as may be directed by rules of court applicable to the youth court or, in the

absence of such direction, at least five clear days notice of the review to be given in writing to the young person, his parents and the Attorney General or his agent.

**Statement of right to counsel**
(13) Any notice given to a parent under subsection (11) or (12) shall include a statement that the young person whose disposition is to be reviewed has the right to be represented by counsel.

**Service of notice**
(14) A notice under subsection (11) or (12) may be served personally or may be sent by registered mail.

**Notice may be waived**
(15) Any of the persons entitled to notice under subsection (11) or (12) may waive the right to that notice.

**Where notice not given**
(16) Where notice under subsection (11) or (12) is not given in accordance with this section, the youth court may

(*a*) adjourn the proceedings and order that the notice be given in such manner and to such person as it directs; or
(*b*) dispense with the notice where, in the opinion of the court, having regard to the circumstances, notice may be dispensed with.

**Decision of the youth court after review**
(17) Where a youth court reviews under this section a disposition made in respect of a young person, it may, after affording the young person, his parent, the Attorney General or his agent and the provincial director an opportunity to be heard, having regard to the needs of the young person and the interests of society,

(*a*) confirm the disposition;
(*b*) where the young person is in secure custody pursuant to subsection 24.1(2), by order direct that the young person be placed in open custody; or
(*c*) release the young person from custody and place the young person
(i) on probation in accordance with section 23 for a period not exceeding the remainder of the period for which the young person was committed to custody, or
(ii) under conditional supervision in accordance with the procedure set out in section 26.2, with such modifications as the circumstances require, for a period not exceeding the remainder of the disposition the young person is then serving.

(18) [Repealed, R.S., 1985, c. 24 (2nd Supp.), s. 21]
R.S., 1985, c. Y-1, s. 28; R.S., 1985, c. 24 (2nd Supp.), s. 21; 1992, c. 11, s. 8; 1995, c. 19, s. 22.

**Application to court for review of level of custody**
**28.1** (1) Where a young person is placed in secure custody pursuant to subsection 24.1(3) or transferred to secure custody pursuant to subsection 24.2(11), the youth court shall review the level of custody if an application therefor is made by the young person or the young person's parent.

**Report**
(2) The youth court shall, before conducting a review under this section, require the provincial director to cause to be prepared, and to submit to the youth court, a report setting out the reasons for the placement or transfer.

**Provisions apply**
(3) The provisions of subsections 14(4) to (10) apply, with such modifications as the circumstances require, in respect of the report referred to in subsection (2), and the provisions of subsections 28(11) to (16) apply, with such modifications as the circumstances require, to every review under this section.

**Decision of the youth court**
(4) Where the youth court conducts a review under this section, it may, after affording the young person, the young person's parents and the provincial director an opportunity to be heard, confirm or alter the level of custody, having regard to the needs of the young person and the interests of society.

**Decision is final**
(5) A decision of the youth court on a review under this section in respect of any particular placement or transfer is, subject to any subsequent order made pursuant to a review under section 28 or 29, final.
1995, c. 19, s. 23.

**Recommendation of provincial director for transfer to open custody or for probation**
**29.** (1) Where a young person is held in custody pursuant to a disposition, the provincial director may, if he is satisfied that the needs of the young person and the interests of society would be better served thereby, cause notice in writing to be given to the young person, his parent and the Attorney General or his agent that he recommends that the young person

(*a*) be transferred from a place or facility of secure custody to a place or facility of open custody, where the young person is held in a place or facility of secure custody pursuant to subsection 24.1(2), or
(*b*) be released from custody and placed on probation or, where the young person is in custody pursuant to a disposition made under paragraph 20(1)(*k*.1), placed under conditional supervision,

and give a copy of the notice to the youth court.

**Contents of notice**
(1.1) The provincial director shall include in any notice given under subsection (1) the reasons for the recommendation and

(*a*) in the case of a recommendation that the young person be placed on probation, the conditions that the provincial director would recommend be attached to a probation order; and
(*b*) in the case of a recommendation that the young person be placed under conditional supervision, the conditions that the provincial director would recommend be set pursuant to section 26.2.

**Application to court for review of recommendation**

(2) Where notice of a recommendation is made under subsection (1) with respect to a disposition made in respect of a young person, the youth court shall, if an application for review is made by the young person, his parent or the Attorney General or his agent within ten days after service of the notice, forthwith review the disposition.

**Subsections 28(5), (7) to (10) and (12) to (17) apply**

(3) Subject to subsection (4), subsections 28(5), (7) to (10) and (12) to (17) apply, with such modifications as the circumstances require, in respect of reviews made under this section and any notice required under subsection 28(12) shall be given to the provincial director.

**Where no application for review made under subsection (2)**

(4) A youth court that receives a notice under subsection (1) shall, if no application for a review is made under subsection (2),

(*a*) in the case of a recommendation that a young person be transferred from a place or facility of secure custody to a place or facility of open custody, order that the young person be so transferred;

(*b*) in the case of a recommendation that a young person be released from custody and placed on probation, release the young person and place him on probation in accordance with section 23;

(*b*.1) in the case of a recommendation that a young person be released from custody and placed under conditional supervision, release the young person and place the young person under conditional supervision in accordance with section 26.2, having regard to the recommendations of the provincial director; or

(*c*) where the court deems it advisable, make no direction under this subsection

and, for greater certainty, an order or direction under this subsection may be made without a hearing.

**Conditions in probation order**

(4.1) Where the youth court places a young person on probation pursuant to paragraph (4)(*b*), the court shall include in the probation order such conditions referred to in section 23 as it considers advisable, having regard to the recommendations of the provincial director.

**Notice where no direction made**

(4.2) Where a youth court, pursuant to paragraph (4)(*c*), makes no direction under subsection (4), it shall forthwith cause a notice of its decision to be given to the provincial director.

**Provincial director may request review**

(4.3) Where the provincial director is given a notice under subsection (4.2), he may request a review under this section.

**Where the provincial director requests a review**

(5) Where the provincial director requests a review pursuant to subsection (4.3),

(*a*) the provincial director shall cause such notice as may be directed by rules of court applicable to the youth court or, in the absence of such direction, at least five clear days notice of the review to be given in writing to the young person, his parents and the Attorney General or his agent; and

(*b*) the youth court shall forthwith, after the notice required under paragraph (*a*) is given, review the disposition.

(6) [Repealed, R.S., 1985, c. 24 (2nd Supp.), s. 22] R.S., 1985, c. Y-1, s. 29; R.S., 1985, c. 24 (2nd Supp.), s. 22, c. 1 (4th Supp.), s. 40; 1992, c. 11, s. 9; 1995, c. 19, s. 24.

**Review board**

**30.** (1) Where a review board is established or designated by a province for the purposes of this section, that board shall, subject to this section, carry out in that province the duties and functions of a youth court under sections 28 and 29, other than releasing a young person from custody and placing the young person on probation or under conditional supervision.

**Other duties of review board**

(2) Subject to this Act, a review board may carry out any duties or functions that are assigned to it by the province that established or designated it.

**Notice under section 29**

(3) Where a review board is established or designated by a province for the purposes of this section, the provincial director shall at the same time as any notice is given under subsection 29(1) cause a copy of the notice to be given to the review board.

**Notice of decision of review board**

(4) A review board shall cause notice of any decision made by it in respect of a young person pursuant to section 28 or 29 to be given forthwith in writing to the young person, his parents, the Attorney General or his agent and the provincial director, and a copy of the notice to be given to the youth court.

**Decision of review board to take effect where no review**

(5) Subject to subsection (6), any decision of a review board under this section shall take effect ten days after the decision is made unless an application for review is made under section 31.

**Decision respecting release from custody and probation**

(6) Where a review board decides that a young person should be released from custody and placed on probation, it shall so recommend to the youth court and, if no application for a review of the decision is made under section 31, the youth court shall forthwith on the expiration of the ten day period referred to in subsection (5) release the young person from custody and place him on probation in accordance with section 23, and shall include in the probation order such conditions referred to in that section as the court considers advisable having regard to the recommendations of the review board.

**Decision respecting release from custody and conditional supervision**

(7) Where a review board decides that a young person should be released from custody and placed under conditional supervision, it shall so recommend to the youth court and, if no application for a review of the decision is made under section 31, the youth court shall forthwith, on the expiration of the ten day period referred to in subsection (5), release the young person from custody and place the young person under conditional supervision in accordance with section 26.2, and shall include in the order under that section such conditions as the court considers advisable, having regard to the recommendations of the review board.

R.S., 1985, c. Y-1, s. 30; R.S., 1985, c. 24 (2nd Supp.), s. 23; 1992, c. 11, s. 10.

**Review by youth court**

**31.** (1) Where the review board reviews a disposition under section 30, the youth court shall, on the application of the young person in respect of whom the review was made, his parents, the Attorney General or his agent or the provincial director, made within ten days after the decision of the review board is made, forthwith review the decision.

**Subsections 28(5), (7) to (10) and (12) to (17) apply**

(2) Subsections 28(5), (7) to (10) and (12) to (17) apply, with such modifications as the circumstances require, in respect of reviews made under this section and any notice required under subsection 28(12) shall be given to the provincial director.

R.S., 1985, c. Y-1, s. 31; R.S., 1985, c. 1 (4th Supp.), s. 41.

**Review of other dispositions**

**32.** (1) Where a youth court has made a disposition in respect of a young person, other than a disposition under paragraph 20(1)(*k*) or (*k*.1) or section 20.1, the youth court shall, on the application of the young person, the young person's parents, the Attorney General or the Attorney General's agent or the provincial director, made at any time after six months from the date of the disposition or, with leave of a youth court judge, at any earlier time, review the disposition if the court is satisfied that there are grounds for a review under subsection (2).

**Grounds for review**

(2) A review of a disposition may be made under this section

(*a*) on the ground that the circumstances that led to the disposition have changed materially;

(*b*) on the ground that the young person in respect of whom the review is to be made is unable to comply with or is experiencing serious difficulty in complying with the terms of the disposition;

(*c*) on the ground that the terms of the disposition are adversely affecting the opportunities available to the young person to obtain services, education or employment; or

(*d*) on such other grounds as the youth court considers appropriate.

**Progress report**

(3) The youth court may, before reviewing under this section a disposition made in respect of a young person, require the provincial director to cause to be prepared, and to submit to the youth court, a progress report on the performance of the young person since the disposition took effect.

**Subsections 28(8) to (10) apply**

(4) Subsections 28(8) to (10) apply, with such modifications as the circumstances require, in respect of any progress report required under subsection (3).

**Subsections 28(5) and (12) to (16) apply**

(5) Subsections 28(5) and (12) to (16) apply, with such modifications as the circumstances require, in respect of reviews made under this section and any notice required under subsection 28(12) shall be given to the provincial director.

**Compelling appearance of young person**

(6) The youth court may, by summons or warrant, compel a young person in respect of whom a review is to be made under this section to appear before the youth court for the purposes of the review.

**Decision of the youth court after review**

(7) Where a youth court reviews under this section a disposition made in respect of a young person, it may, after affording the young person, his parent, the Attorney General or his agent and the provincial director an opportunity to be heard,

(*a*) confirm the disposition;

(*b*) terminate the disposition and discharge the young person from any further obligation of the disposition; or

(*c*) vary the disposition or make such new disposition listed in section 20, other than a committal to custody, for such period of time, not exceeding the remainder of the period of the earlier disposition, as the court deems appropriate in the circumstances of the case.

**New disposition not to be more onerous**

(8) Subject to subsection (9), where a disposition made in respect of a young person is reviewed under this section, no disposition made under subsection (7) shall, without the consent of the young person, be more onerous than the remaining portion of the disposition reviewed.

**Exception**

(9) A youth court may under this section extend the time within which a disposition made under paragraphs 20(1)(*b*) to (*g*) is to be complied with by a young person where the court is satisfied that the young person requires more time to comply with the disposition, but in no case shall the extension be for a period of time that expires more than twelve months after the date the disposition would otherwise have expired.

(10) and (11) [Repealed, R.S., 1985, c. 24 (2nd Supp.), s. 24]

R.S., 1985, c. Y-1, s. 32; R.S., 1985, c. 24 (2nd Supp.), s. 24; 1992, c. 11, s. 11; 1995, c. 39, s. 181.

**Review of order made under s. 20.1**
**33.** (1) A youth court or other court may, on application, review an order made under section 20.1 at any time after the circumstances set out in subsection 45(1) are realized in respect of any record in relation to the offence that resulted in the order being made.

**Grounds**
(2) In conducting a review under this section, the youth court or other court shall take into account
(*a*) the nature and circumstances of the offence in respect of which the order was made; and
(*b*) the safety of the young person and of other persons.

**Decision of review**
(3) Where a youth court or other court conducts a review under this section, it may, after affording the young person, one of the young person's parents, the Attorney General or an agent of the Attorney General and the provincial director an opportunity to be heard,
(*a*) confirm the order;
(*b*) revoke the order; or
(*c*) vary the order as it considers appropriate in the circumstances of the case.

**New order not to be more onerous**
(4) No variation of an order made under paragraph (3)(*c*) may be more onerous than the order being reviewed.

**Application of provisions**
(5) Subsections 32(3) to (5) apply, with such modifications as the circumstances require, in respect of a review under this section.
R.S., 1985, c. Y-1, s. 33; R.S., 1985, c. 24 (2nd Supp.), s. 25; 1995, c. 39, s. 182.

**Sections 20 to 26 apply to dispositions on review**
**34.** (1) Subject to sections 28 to 32, subsections 20(2) to (8) and sections 21 to 25.1 apply, with such modifications as the circumstances require, in respect of dispositions made under sections 28 to 32.

**Orders are dispositions**
(2) Orders under subsections 26.1(1) and 26.2(1) and paragraph 26.6(2)(*b*) are deemed to be dispositions for the purposes of section 28.
R.S., 1985, c. Y-1, s. 34; R.S., 1985, c. 24 (2nd Supp.), s. 25; 1992, c. 11, s. 12.

TEMPORARY RELEASE FROM CUSTODY

**Temporary absence or day release**
**35.** (1) The provincial director of a province may, subject to any terms or conditions that he considers desirable, authorize a young person committed to custody in the province pursuant to a disposition made under this Act
(*a*) to be temporarily released for a period not exceeding fifteen days where, in his opinion, it is necessary or desirable that the young person be absent, with or without escort, for medical, compassionate or humanitarian reasons or for the purpose of rehabilitating the young person or re-integrating him into the community; or
(*b*) to be released from custody on such days and during such hours as he specifies in order that the young person may
(i) attend school or any other educational or training institution,
(ii) obtain or continue employment or perform domestic or other duties required by the young person's family,
(iii) participate in a program specified by him that, in his opinion, will enable the young person to better carry out his employment or improve his education or training, or
(iv) attend an out-patient treatment program or other program that provides services that are suitable to addressing the young person's needs.

**Limitation**
(2) A young person who is released from custody pursuant to subsection (1) shall be released only for such periods of time as are necessary to attain the purpose for which the young person is released.

**Revocation of authorization for release**
(3) The provincial director of a province may, at any time, revoke an authorization made under subsection (1).

**Arrest and return to custody**
(4) Where the provincial director revokes an authorization for a young person to be released from custody under subsection (3) or where a young person fails to comply with any term or condition of release from custody under this section, the young person may be arrested without warrant and returned to custody.

**Prohibition**
(5) A young person who has been committed to custody under this Act shall not be released from custody before the expiration of the period of his custody except in accordance with subsection (1) unless the release is ordered under sections 28 to 31 or otherwise according to law by a court of competent jurisdiction.
R.S., 1985, c. Y-1, s. 35; R.S., 1985, c. 24 (2nd Supp.), s. 26, c. 1 (4th Supp.), s. 42; 1995, c. 19, s. 25.

EFFECT OF TERMINATION OF DISPOSITION

**Effect of absolute discharge or termination of dispositions**
**36.** (1) Subject to section 12 of the *Canada Evidence Act*, where a young person is found guilty of an offence, and
(*a*) a youth court directs under paragraph 20(1)(*a*) that the young person be discharged absolutely, or
(*b*) all the dispositions made under subsection

20(1) in respect of the offence, and all terms of those dispositions, have ceased to have effect,
the young person shall be deemed not to have been found guilty or convicted of the offence except that

(*c*) the young person may plead *autrefois convict* in respect of any subsequent charge relating to the offence,

(*d*) a youth court may consider the finding of guilt in considering an application for a transfer to ordinary court under section 16,

(*e*) any court or justice may consider the finding of guilt in considering an application for judicial interim release or in considering what dispositions to make or sentence to impose for any offence, and

(*f*) the National Parole Board or any provincial parole board may consider the finding of guilt in considering an application for parole or pardon.

**Disqualifications removed**
(2) For greater certainty and without restricting the generality of subsection (1), an absolute discharge under paragraph 20(1)(*a*) or the termination of all dispositions in respect of an offence for which a young person is found guilty removes any disqualification in respect of the offence to which the young person is subject pursuant to any Act of Parliament by reason of a conviction.

**Applications for employment**
(3) No application form for or relating to

(*a*) employment in any department, as defined in section 2 of the *Financial Administration Act*,

(*b*) employment by any Crown corporation, as defined in section 83 of the *Financial Administration Act*,

(*c*) enrolment in the Canadian Forces, or

(*d*) employment on or in connection with the operation of any work, undertaking or business that is within the legislative authority of Parliament,

shall contain any question that by its terms requires the applicant to disclose that the applicant has been charged with or found guilty of an offence in respect of which the applicant has, under this Act, been discharged absolutely or has completed all the dispositions made under subsection 20(1).

**Punishment**
(4) Any person who uses or authorizes the use of an application form in contravention of subsection (3) is guilty of an offence punishable on summary conviction.

**Finding of guilt not a previous conviction**
(5) A finding of guilt under this Act is not a previous conviction for the purposes of any offence under any Act of Parliament for which a greater punishment is prescribed by reason of previous convictions.
R.S., 1985, c. Y-1, s. 36; R.S., 1985, c. 24 (2nd Supp.), s. 27; 1995, c. 19, s. 26; 1995, c. 39, ss. 183(1), (2), 189(a).

## YOUTH WORKERS

**Duties of youth worker**
37. The duties and functions of a youth worker in respect of a young person whose case has been assigned to him by the provincial director include

(*a*) where the young person is bound by a probation order that requires him to be under supervision, supervising the young person in complying with the conditions of the probation order or in carrying out any other disposition made together with it;

(*a*.1) where the young person is placed under conditional supervision pursuant to an order made under section 26.2, supervising the young person in complying with the conditions of the order;

(*b*) where the young person is found guilty of any offence, giving such assistance to him as he considers appropriate up to the time the young person is discharged or the disposition of his case terminates;

(*c*) attending court when he considers it advisable or when required by the youth court to be present;

(*d*) preparing, at the request of the provincial director, a pre-disposition report or a progress report; and

(*e*) performing such other duties and functions as the provincial director requires.

R.S., 1985, c. Y-1, s. 37; R.S., 1985, c. 24 (2nd Supp.), s. 28; 1992, c. 11, s. 13.

## PROTECTION OF PRIVACY OF YOUNG PERSONS

**Identity not to be published**
38. (1) Subject to this section, no person shall publish by any means any report

(*a*) of an offence committed or alleged to have been committed by a young person, unless an order has been made under section 16 with respect thereto, or

(*b*) of any hearing, adjudication, disposition or appeal concerning a young person who committed or is alleged to have committed an offence

in which the name of the young person, a child or a young person who is a victim of the offence or a child or a young person who appeared as a witness in connection with the offence, or in which any information serving to identify such young person or child, is disclosed.

**Limitation**
(1.1) Subsection (1) does not apply in respect of the disclosure of information in the course of the administration of justice including, for greater certainty, the disclosure of information for the purposes of the *Firearms Act* and Part III of the *Criminal Code*, where it is not the purpose of the disclosure to make the information known in the community.

**Preparation of reports**
(1.11) Subsection (1) does not apply in respect of the disclosure of information by the provincial

director or a youth worker where the disclosure is necessary for procuring information that relates to the preparation of any report required by this Act.

**No subsequent disclosure**
(1.12) No person to whom information is disclosed pursuant to subsection (1.11) shall disclose that information to any other person unless the disclosure is necessary for the purpose of preparing the report for which the information was disclosed.

**Schools and others**
(1.13) Subsection (1) does not apply in respect of the disclosure of information to any professional or other person engaged in the supervision or care of a young person, including the representative of any school board or school or any other educational or training institution, by the provincial director, a youth worker, a peace officer or any other person engaged in the provision of services to young persons where the disclosure is necessary
(*a*) to ensure compliance by the young person with an authorization pursuant to section 35 or an order of any court concerning bail, probation or conditional supervision; or
(*b*) to ensure the safety of staff, students or other persons, as the case may be.

**No subsequent disclosure**
(1.14) No person to whom information is disclosed pursuant to subsection (1.13) shall disclose that information to any other person unless the disclosure is necessary for a purpose referred to in that subsection.

**Information to be kept separate**
(1.15) Any person to whom information is disclosed pursuant to subsections (1.13) and (1.14) shall
(*a*) keep the information separate from any other record of the young person to whom the information relates;
(*b*) subject to subsection (1.14), ensure that no other person has access to the information; and
(*c*) destroy the information when the information is no longer required for the purpose for which it was disclosed.

***Ex parte* application for leave to publish**
(1.2) A youth court judge shall, on the *ex parte* application of a peace officer, make an order permitting any person to publish a report described in subsection (1) that contains the name of a young person, or information serving to identify a young person, who has committed or is alleged to have committed an indictable offence, if the judge is satisfied that
(*a*) there is reason to believe that the young person is dangerous to others; and
(*b*) publication of the report is necessary to assist in apprehending the young person.

**Order ceases to have effect**
(1.3) An order made under subsection (1.2) shall cease to have effect two days after it is made.

**Application for leave to publish**
(1.4) The youth court may, on the application of any person referred to in subsection (1), make an order permitting any person to publish a report in which the name of that person, or information serving to identify that person, would be disclosed, if the court is satisfied that the publication of the report would not be contrary to the best interests of that person.

**Disclosure with court order**
(1.5) The youth court may, on the application of the provincial director, the Attorney General or an agent of the Attorney General or a peace officer, make an order permitting the applicant to disclose to such person or persons as are specified by the court such information about a young person as is specified if the court is satisfied that the disclosure is necessary, having regard to the following:
(*a*) the young person has been found guilty of an offence involving serious personal injury;
(*b*) the young person poses a risk of serious harm to persons; and
(*c*) the disclosure of the information is relevant to the avoidance of that risk.

**Opportunity to be heard**
(1.6) Subject to subsection (1.7), before making an order under subsection (1.5), the youth court shall afford the young person, the young person's parents, the Attorney General or an agent of the Attorney General an opportunity to be heard.

***Ex parte* application**
(1.7) An application under subsection (1.5) may be made *ex parte* by the Attorney General or an agent of the Attorney General where the youth court is satisfied that reasonable efforts have been made to locate the young person and that those efforts have not been successful.

**Time limit**
(1.8) No information may be disclosed pursuant to subsection (1.5) after the record to which the information relates ceases to be available for inspection under subsection 45(1).

**Contravention**
(2) Every one who contravenes subsection (1), (1.12), (1.14) or (1.15)
(*a*) is guilty of an indictable offence and liable to imprisonment for a term not exceeding two years; or
(*b*) is guilty of an offence punishable on summary conviction.

**Provincial court judge has absolute jurisdiction on indictment**
(3) Where an accused is charged with an offence under paragraph (2)(*a*), a provincial court judge has absolute jurisdiction to try the case and his jurisdiction does not depend on the consent of the accused.
R.S., 1985, c. Y-1, s. 38; R.S., 1985, c. 24 (2nd Supp.), s. 29; 1995, c. 19, s. 27; 1995, c. 39, s. 184.

**Exclusion from hearing**
39. (1) Subject to subsection (2), where a court or justice before whom proceedings are carried out under this Act is of the opinion
(*a*) that any evidence or information presented to the court or justice would be seriously injurious or seriously prejudicial to
(i) the young person who is being dealt with in the proceedings,
(ii) a child or young person who is a witness in the proceedings, or
(iii) a child or young person who is aggrieved by or the victim of the offence charged in the proceedings, or
(*b*) that it would be in the interest of public morals, the maintenance of order or the proper administration of justice to exclude any or all members of the public from the court room,
the court or justice may exclude any person from all or part of the proceedings if the court or justice deems that person's presence to be unnecessary to the conduct of the proceedings.

**Exception**
(2) Subject to section 650 of the *Criminal Code* and except where it is necessary for the purposes of subsection 13(6) of this Act, a court or justice may not, pursuant to subsection (1), exclude from proceedings under this Act
(*a*) the prosecutor;
(*b*) the young person who is being dealt with in the proceedings, his parent, his counsel or any adult assisting him pursuant to subsection 11(7);
(*c*) the provincial director or his agent; or
(*d*) the youth worker to whom the young person's case has been assigned.

**Exclusion after adjudication or during review**
(3) The youth court, after it has found a young person guilty of an offence, or the youth court or the review board, during a review of a disposition under sections 28 to 32, may, in its discretion, exclude from the court or from a hearing of the review board, as the case may be, any person other than
(*a*) the young person or his counsel,
(*b*) the provincial director or his agent,
(*c*) the youth worker to whom the young person's case has been assigned, and
(*d*) the Attorney General or his agent,
when any information is being presented to the court or the review board the knowledge of which might, in the opinion of the court or review board, be seriously injurious or seriously prejudicial to the young person.

**Exception**
(4) The exception set out in paragraph (3)(*a*) is subject to subsection 13(6) of this Act and section 650 of the *Criminal Code*.
R.S., 1985, c. Y-1, s. 39; R.S., 1985, c. 24 (2nd Supp.), s. 30.

## MAINTENANCE AND USE OF RECORDS

***Records that may be Kept***
**Youth court, review board and other courts**
40. (1) A youth court, review board or any court dealing with matters arising out of proceedings under this Act may keep a record of any case arising under this Act that comes before it.

**Exception**
(2) For greater certainty, this section does not apply in respect of proceedings held in ordinary court pursuant to an order under section 16.

**Records of offences that result in order under s. 20.1**
(3) Notwithstanding anything in this Act, where a young person is found guilty of an offence that results in an order under section 20.1 being made against the young person, the youth court may keep a record of the conviction and the order until the expiration of the order.

**Disclosure**
(4) Any record that is kept under subsection (3) may be disclosed only to establish the existence of the order in any offence involving a breach of the order.
R.S., 1985, c. Y-1, s. 40; R.S., 1985, c. 24 (2nd Supp.), s. 31; 1995, c. 39, s. 185.

**Records in central repository**
41. (1) A record of any offence that a young person has been charged with having committed may, where the offence is an offence in respect of which an adult may be subjected to any measurement, process or operation referred to in the *Identification of Criminals Act*, be kept in such central repository as the Commissioner of the Royal Canadian Mounted Police may, from time to time, designate for the purpose of keeping criminal history files or records on offenders or keeping records for the identification of offenders.

**Police force may provide record**
(2) Where a young person is charged with having committed an offence referred to in subsection (1), the police force responsible for the investigation of the offence may provide a record of the offence, including the original or a copy of any fingerprints, palmprints or photographs and any other measurement, process or operation referred to in the *Identification of Criminals Act* taken of, or applied in respect of, the young person by or on behalf of the police force, for inclusion in any central repository designated pursuant to subsection (1).

**Police force shall provide record**
(3) Where a young person is found guilty of an offence referred to in subsection (1), the police force responsible for the investigation of the offence shall provide a record of the offence, including the original or a copy of any fingerprints, palmprints or photographs and any other measurement, process or operation referred to in the *Identification of Criminals Act* taken of, or applied

in respect of, the young person by or on behalf of the police force, for inclusion in any central repository designated pursuant to subsection (1).
R.S., 1985, c. Y-1, s. 41; R.S., 1985, c. 24 (2nd Supp.), s. 31; 1995, c. 19, s. 28.

**Police records**
42. A record relating to any offence alleged to have been committed by a young person, including the original or a copy of any fingerprints or photographs of the young person, may be kept by any police force responsible for, or participating in, the investigation of the offence.
R.S., 1985, c. Y-1, s. 42; R.S., 1985, c. 24 (2nd Supp.), s. 31.

**Government records**
43. (1) A department or an agency of any government in Canada may keep records containing information obtained by the department or agency
(*a*) for the purposes of an investigation of an offence alleged to have been committed by a young person;
(*b*) for use in proceedings against a young person under this Act;
(*c*) for the purpose of administering a disposition;
(*d*) for the purpose of considering whether, instead of commencing or continuing judicial proceedings under this Act against a young person, to use alternative measures to deal with the young person; or
(*e*) as a result of the use of alternative measures to deal with a young person.

**Private records**
(2) Any person or organization may keep records containing information obtained by the person or organization
(*a*) as a result of the use of alternative measures to deal with a young person alleged to have committed an offence; or
(*b*) for the purpose of administering or participating in the administration of a disposition.

(3) and (4) [Repealed, R.S., 1985, c. 24 (2nd Supp.), s. 32]
R.S., 1985, c. Y-1, s. 43; R.S., 1985, c. 24 (2nd Supp.), s. 32.

***Fingerprints and Photographs***
***Identification of Criminals Act* applies**
44. (1) Subject to this section, the *Identification of Criminals Act* applies in respect of young persons.

**Limitation**
(2) No fingerprints, palmprints or photographs or any other measurement, process or operation referred to in the *Identification of Criminals Act* shall be taken of, or applied in respect of, a young person who is charged with having committed an offence except in the circumstances in which an adult may, under that Act, be subjected to the measurements, processes and operations referred to in that Act.

(3) to (5) [Repealed, R.S., 1985, c. 24 (2nd Supp.), s. 33]
R.S., 1985, c. Y-1, s. 44; R.S., 1985, c. 24 (2nd Supp.), s. 33; 1995, c. 19, s. 29.

***Disclosure of Records***
**Records made available**
44.1 (1) Subject to subsections (2) and (2.1), any record that is kept pursuant to section 40 shall, and any record that is kept pursuant to sections 41 to 43 may, on request, be made available for inspection to
(*a*) the young person to whom the record relates;
(*b*) counsel acting on behalf of the young person, or any representative of that counsel;
(*c*) the Attorney General or his agent;
(*d*) a parent of the young person or any adult assisting the young person pursuant to subsection 11(7), during the course of any proceedings relating to the offence or alleged offence to which the record relates or during the term of any disposition made in respect of the offence;
(*e*) any judge, court or review board, for any purpose relating to proceedings relating to the young person under this Act or to proceedings in ordinary court in respect of offences committed or alleged to have been committed by the young person, whether as a young person or an adult;
(*f*) any peace officer,
(i) for the purpose of investigating any offence that the young person is suspected on reasonable grounds of having committed, or in respect of which the young person has been arrested or charged, whether as a young person or an adult,
(ii) for any purpose related to the administration of the case to which the record relates during the course of proceedings against the young person or the term of any disposition,
(iii) for the purpose of investigating any offence that another person is suspected on reasonable grounds of having committed against the young person while the young person is, or was, serving a disposition, or
(iv) for any other law enforcement purpose;
(*g*) any member of a department or agency of a government in Canada, or any agent thereof, that is
(i) engaged in the administration of alternative measures in respect of the young person,
(ii) preparing a report in respect of the young person pursuant to this Act or for the purpose of assisting a court in sentencing the young person after he becomes an adult or is transferred to ordinary court pursuant to section 16,
(iii) engaged in the supervision or care of the young person, whether as a young person or an adult, or in the administration of a disposition or a sentence in respect of the young person, whether as a young person or an adult, or
(iv) considering an application for parole or pardon made by the young person after he becomes an adult;
(*h*) any person, or person within a class of persons, designated by the Governor in Council, or the Lieutenant Governor in Council of a province, for a purpose and to

the extent specified by the Governor in Council or the Lieutenant Governor in Council, as the case may be;

(*i*) any person, for the purpose of determining whether to grant security clearances required by the Government of Canada or the government of a province or a municipality for purposes of employment or the performance of services;

(*i*.1) any person for the purposes of the *Firearms Act*;

(*j*) any employee or agent of the Government of Canada, for statistical purposes pursuant to the *Statistics Act*; and

(*k*) any other person who is deemed, or any person within a class of persons that is deemed, by a youth court judge to have a valid interest in the record, to the extent directed by the judge, if the judge is satisfied that the disclosure is

(i) desirable in the public interest for research or statistical purposes, or

(ii) desirable in the interest of the proper administration of justice.

**Exception**

(2) Where a youth court has withheld the whole or a part of a report from any person pursuant to subsection 13(6) or 14(7), the report or part thereof shall not be made available to that person for inspection under subsection (1).

**Records of forensic DNA analysis of bodily substances**

(2.1) Notwithstanding subsections (1) and (5), any record that is kept pursuant to any of sections 40 to 43 and that is a record of the results of forensic DNA analysis of a bodily substance taken from a young person in execution of a warrant issued under section 487.05 of the *Criminal Code* may be made available for inspection under this section only under paragraph (1)(*a*), (*b*), (*c*), (*d*), (*e*), (*f*), (*h*) or subparagraph (1)(*k*)(ii).

**Introduction into evidence**

(3) Nothing in paragraph (1)(*e*) authorizes the introduction into evidence of any part of a record that would not otherwise be admissible in evidence.

**Disclosures for research or statistical purposes**

(4) Where a record is made available for inspection to any person under paragraph (1)(*j*) or subparagraph (1)(*k*)(i), that person may subsequently disclose information contained in the record, but may not disclose the information in any form that would reasonably be expected to identify the young person to whom it relates.

**Record made available to victim**

(5) Any record that is kept pursuant to sections 40 to 43 may, on request, be made available for inspection to the victim of the offence to which the record relates.

**Disclosure of information and copies of records**

(6) Any person to whom a record is required or authorized to be made available for inspection under this section may be given any information contained in the record and may be given a copy of any part of the record.

R.S., 1985, c. 24 (2nd Supp.), s. 34; 1992, c. 1, s. 143(E); 1995, c. 19, s. 30; 1995, c. 27, s. 2, c. 39, s. 186.

**Disclosure by peace officer during investigation**

**44.2** (1) A peace officer may disclose to any person any information in a record kept pursuant to section 42 that it is necessary to disclose in the conduct of the investigation of an offence.

**Disclosure to insurance company**

(2) A peace officer may disclose to an insurance company information in any record that is kept pursuant to section 42 for the purpose of investigating any claim arising out of an offence committed or alleged to have been committed by the young person to whom the record relates.

R.S., 1985, c. 24 (2nd Supp.), s. 34.

***Non-Disclosure and Destruction of Records***

**Non-disclosure**

**45.** (1) Subject to sections 45.01, 45.1 and 45.2, records kept pursuant to sections 40 to 43 may not be made available for inspection under section 44.1 or 44.2 in the following circumstances:

(*a*) where the young person to whom the record relates is charged with the offence to which the record relates and is acquitted otherwise than by reason of a verdict of not criminally responsible on account of mental disorder, on the expiration of two months after the expiration of the time allowed for the taking of an appeal or, where an appeal is taken, on the expiration of three months after all proceedings in respect of the appeal have been completed;

(*b*) where the charge against the young person is dismissed for any reason other than acquittal or withdrawn, on the expiration of one year after the dismissal or withdrawal;

(*c*) where the charge against the young person is stayed, with no proceedings being taken against the young person for a period of one year, on the expiration of the one year;

(*d*) where alternative measures are used to deal with the young person, on the expiration of two years after the young person consents to participate in the alternative measures in accordance with paragraph 4(1)(*c*);

(*d*.1) where the young person is found guilty of the offence and the disposition is an absolute discharge, on the expiration of one year after the young person is found guilty;

(*d*.2) where the young person is found guilty of the offence and the disposition is a conditional discharge, on the expiration of three years after the young person is found guilty;

(*e*) subject to paragraph (*g*), where the young person is found guilty of the offence and it is a summary conviction offence, on the expiration of three years after all dispositions made in respect of that offence;

(*f*) subject to paragraph (*g*), where the young person is found guilty of the offence and it is an indictable offence, on the expiration of five years after all dispositions made in respect of that offence; and

(*g*) where, before the expiration of the period referred to in paragraph (*e*) or (*f*), the young person is, as a young person, found guilty of

(i) a subsequent summary conviction offence, on the expiration of three years after all dispositions made in respect of that offence have been completed, and

(ii) a subsequent indictable offence, five years after all dispositions made in respect of that offence have been completed.

**Destruction of record**

(2) Subject to subsections (2.1) and (2.2), when the circumstances set out in subsection (1) are realized in respect of any record kept pursuant to section 41, the record shall be destroyed forthwith.

**Transfer of records relating to serious offences**

(2.1) Where a special records repository has been established pursuant to subsection 45.02(1), all records in the central repository referred to in subsection 41(1) that relate to

(*a*) a conviction for first degree murder or second degree murder within the meaning of section 231 of the *Criminal Code*,

(*b*) an offence referred to in the schedule, or

(*c*) an order made under section 20.1,

shall, when the circumstances set out in subsection (1) are realized in respect of the records, be transferred to that special records repository.

**Transfer of fingerprints**

(2.2) Where a special fingerprints repository has been established pursuant to subsection 45.03(1), all fingerprints and any information necessary to identify the person to whom the fingerprints belong that are in the central repository referred to in subsection 41(1) shall, when the circumstances set out in subsection (1) are realized in respect of the records, be transferred to that special fingerprints repository.

**Meaning of "destroy"**

(2.3) For the purposes of subsection (2), "destroy", in respect of a record, means

(*a*) to shred, burn or otherwise physically destroy the record, in the case of a record other than a record in electronic form; and

(*b*) to delete, write over or otherwise render the record inaccessible, in the case of a record in electronic form.

**Other records may be destroyed**

(3) Any record kept pursuant to sections 40 to 43 may, in the discretion of the person or body keeping the record, be destroyed at any time before or after the circumstances set out in subsection (1) are realized in respect of that record.

**Young person deemed not to have committed offence**

(4) A young person shall be deemed not to have committed any offence to which a record kept pursuant to sections 40 to 43 relates when the circumstances set out in paragraph (1)(*d*), (*e*) or (*f*) are realized in respect of that record.

**Deemed election**

(5) For the purposes of paragraphs (1)(*e*) and (*f*), where no election is made in respect of an offence that may be prosecuted by indictment or proceeded with by way of summary conviction, the Attorney General or his agent shall be deemed to have elected to proceed with the offence as an offence punishable on summary conviction.

**Orders made under s. 20.1 not included**

(5.1) For the purposes of this Act, orders made under section 20.1 shall not be taken into account in determining any time period referred to in subsection (1).

**Application to delinquency**

(6) This section applies, with such modifications as the circumstances require, in respect of records relating to the offence of delinquency under the *Juvenile Delinquents Act*, chapter J-3 of the Revised Statutes of Canada, 1970, as it read immediately prior to April 2, 1984.

R.S., 1985, c. Y-1, s. 45; R.S., 1985, c. 24 (2nd Supp.), s. 35; 1991, c. 43, s. 34; 1995, c. 19, s. 31(1–3); 1995, c. 39, ss. 187, 189(b).

*Retention of Records*

**Retention of records**

**45.01** Where, before the expiration of the period referred to in paragraph 45(1)(*e*) or (*f*) or subparagraph 45(1)(*g*)(i) or (ii), the young person is found guilty of a subsequent offence as an adult, records kept pursuant to sections 40 to 43 shall be available for inspection under section 44.1 or 44.2 and the provisions applicable to criminal records of adults shall apply.

1995, c. 19, s. 32.

*Special Records Repository*

**Special records repository**

**45.02** (1) The Commissioner of the Royal Canadian Mounted Police may establish a special records repository for records transferred pursuant to subsection 45(2.1).

**Records relating to murder**

(2) A record that relates to a conviction for the offence of first degree murder or second degree murder within the meaning of section 231 of the *Criminal Code* or an offence referred to in any of paragraphs 16(1.01)(*b*) to (*d*) may be kept indefinitely in the special records repository.

**Records relating to other serious offences**

(3) A record that relates to a conviction for an offence referred to in the schedule shall be kept in the special records repository for a period of five years and shall be destroyed forthwith at the expiration of that five year period, unless the young person to whom the record relates is subsequently found guilty of any offence referred to in the

schedule, in which case the record shall be dealt with as the record of an adult.

**Disclosure**
(4) A record kept in the special records repository shall be made available for inspection to the following persons at the following times or in the following circumstances:
(*a*) at any time, to the young person to whom the record relates and to counsel acting on behalf of the young person, or any representative of that counsel;
(*b*) where the young person has subsequently been charged with the commission of first degree murder or second degree murder within the meaning of section 231 of the *Criminal Code* or an offence referred to in the schedule, to any peace officer for the purpose of investigating any offence that the young person is suspected of having committed, or in respect of which the young person has been arrested or charged, whether as a young person or as an adult;
(*c*) where the young person has subsequently been convicted of an offence referred to in the schedule,
(i) to the Attorney General or an agent of the Attorney General,
(ii) to a parent of the young person or any adult assisting the young person,
(iii) to any judge, court or review board, for any purpose relating to proceedings relating to the young person under this Act or to proceedings in ordinary court in respect of offences committed or alleged to have been committed by the young person, whether as a young person or as an adult, or
(iv) to any member of a department or agency of a government in Canada, or any agent thereof, that is
(A) engaged in the administration of alternative measures in respect of the young person,
(B) preparing a report in respect of the young person pursuant to this Act or for the purpose of assisting a court in sentencing the young person after the young person becomes an adult or is transferred to ordinary court pursuant to section 16,
(C) engaged in the supervision or care of the young person, whether as a young person or as an adult, or in the administration of a disposition or a sentence in respect of the young person, whether as a young person or as an adult, or
(D) considering an application for parole or pardon made by the young person after the young person becomes an adult;
(*c*.1) to establish the existence of the order in any offence involving a breach of the order;
(*c*.2) for the purposes of the *Firearms Act*;
(*d*) at any time, to any employee or agent of the Government of Canada, for statistical purposes pursuant to the *Statistics Act*; or
(*e*) at any time, to any other person who is deemed, or any person within a class of persons that is deemed, by a youth court judge to have a valid interest in the record, to the extent directed by the judge, if the judge is satisfied that the disclosure is desirable in the public interest for research or statistical purposes.

1995, c. 19, s. 32; 1995, c. 39, s. 189.

*Special Fingerprints Repository*
**Special fingerprints repository**
**45.03** (1) The Commissioner of the Royal Canadian Mounted Police may establish a special fingerprints repository for fingerprints and any related information transferred pursuant to subsection 45(2.2).

**Disclosure for identification purposes**
(2) Fingerprints and any related information may be kept in the special fingerprints repository for a period of five years following the date of their receipt and, during that time, the name, date of birth and last known address of the young person to whom the fingerprints belong may be disclosed for identification purposes if a fingerprint identified as that of the young person is found during the investigation of a crime or during an attempt to identify a deceased person or a person suffering from amnesia.

**Destruction**
(3) Fingerprints and any related information in the special fingerprints repository shall be destroyed five years after the date of their receipt in the repository.

**Records of orders made under s. 20.1**
(3.1) A record that relates to an order made under section 20.1 shall be kept in the special records repository until the expiration of the order and shall be destroyed forthwith at that time.
1995, c. 19, s. 32; 1995, c. 39, s. 189.

*Disclosure in Special Circumstances*
**Where records may be made available**
**45.1** (1) Subject to subsection (1.1), a youth court judge may, on application by any person, order that any record to which subsection 45(1) applies, or any part thereof, be made available for inspection to that person or a copy of the record or part thereof be given to that person, if a youth court judge is satisfied that
(*a*) that person has a valid and substantial interest in the record or part thereof;
(*b*) it is necessary for the record, part thereof or copy thereof to be made available in the interest of the proper administration of justice; and
(*c*) disclosure of the record or part thereof or information is not prohibited under any other Act of Parliament or the legislature of a province.

**Records**
(1.1) Subsection (1) applies in respect of any record relating to a particular young person or to any record relating to a class of young persons where the identity of young persons in the class at the time of the making of the application referred

to in that subsection cannot reasonably be ascertained and the disclosure of the record is necessary for the purpose of investigating any offence that a person is suspected on reasonable grounds of having committed against a young person while the young person is, or was, serving a disposition.

**Notice**
(2) Subject to subsection (2.1), an application under subsection (1) in respect of a record shall not be heard unless the person who makes the application has given the young person to whom the record relates and the person or body that has possession of the record at least five days notice in writing of the application and the young person and the person or body that has possession has had a reasonable opportunity to be heard.

**Where notice not required**
(2.1) A youth court judge may waive the requirement in subsection (2) to give notice to a young person where the youth court is of the opinion that

(*a*) to insist on the giving of the notice would frustrate the application; or
(*b*) reasonable efforts have not been successful in finding the young person.

**Use of record**
(3) In any order under subsection (1), the youth court judge shall set out the purposes for which the record may be used.
R.S., 1985, c. 24 (2nd Supp.), s. 35; 1995, c. 19, s. 34.

**Records in the custody, etc., of archivists**
**45.2** Where records originally kept pursuant to section 40, 42 or 43 are under the custody or control of the National Archivist of Canada or the archivist for any province, that person may disclose any information contained in the records to any other person if

(*a*) the Attorney General or his agent is satisfied that the disclosure is desirable in the public interest for research or statistical purposes; and
(*b*) the person to whom the information is disclosed undertakes not to disclose the information in any form that could reasonably be expected to identify the young person to whom it relates.

R.S., 1985, c. 24 (2nd Supp.), s. 35, c. 1 (3rd Supp.), s. 12.

*Offence*
**Prohibition against disclosure**
**46.** (1) Except as authorized or required by this Act, no record kept pursuant to sections 40 to 43 may be made available for inspection, and no copy, print or negative thereof or information contained therein may be given, to any person where to do so would serve to identify the young person to whom it relates as a young person dealt with under this Act.

**Exception for employees**
(2) No person who is employed in keeping or maintaining records referred to in subsection (1) is restricted from doing anything prohibited under subsection (1) with respect to any other person so employed.

**Prohibition against use**
(3) Subject to section 45.1, no record kept pursuant to sections 40 to 43, and no copy, print or negative thereof, may be used for any purpose that would serve to identify the young person to whom the record relates as a young person dealt with under this Act after the circumstances set out in subsection 45(1) are realized in respect of that record.

**Offence**
(4) Any person who fails to comply with this section or subsection 45(2)

(*a*) is guilty of an indictable offence and liable to imprisonment for a term not exceeding two years; or
(*b*) is guilty of an offence punishable on summary conviction.

**Absolute jurisdiction of provincial court judge**
(5) The jurisdiction of a provincial court judge to try an accused is absolute and does not depend on the consent of the accused where the accused is charged with an offence under paragraph (4)(*a*).
R.S., 1985, c. Y-1, s. 46; R.S., 1985, c. 24 (2nd Supp.), s. 36.

CONTEMPT OF COURT

**Contempt against youth court**
**47.** (1) Every youth court has the same power, jurisdiction and authority to deal with and impose punishment for contempt against the court as may be exercised by the superior court of criminal jurisdiction of the province in which the court is situated.

**Exclusive jurisdiction of youth court**
(2) The youth court has exclusive jurisdiction in respect of every contempt of court committed by a young person against the youth court whether or not committed in the face of the court and every contempt of court committed by a young person against any other court otherwise than in the face of that court.

**Concurrent jurisdiction of youth court**
(3) The youth court has jurisdiction in respect of every contempt of court committed by a young person against any other court in the face of that court and every contempt of court committed by an adult against the youth court in the face of the youth court, but nothing in this subsection affects the power, jurisdiction or authority of any other court to deal with or impose punishment for contempt of court.

**Dispositions**
(4) Where a youth court or any other court finds a young person guilty of contempt of court, it may make any one of the dispositions set out in section 20, or any number thereof that are not

inconsistent with each other, but no other disposition or sentence.

**Section 708 of *Criminal Code* applies in respect of adults**
(5) Section 708 of the *Criminal Code* applies in respect of proceedings under this section in youth court against adults, with such modifications as the circumstances require.

**Appeals**
(6) A finding of guilt under this section for contempt of court or a disposition or sentence made in respect thereof may be appealed as if the finding were a conviction or the disposition or sentence were a sentence in a prosecution by indictment in ordinary court.
1980-81-82-83, c. 110, s. 47.

FORFEITURE OF RECOGNIZANCES

**Applications for forfeiture of recognizances**
**48.** Applications for the forfeiture of recognizances of young persons shall be made to the youth court.
1980-81-82-83, c. 110, s. 48.

**Proceedings in case of default**
**49.** (1) Where a recognizance binding a young person has been endorsed with a certificate pursuant to subsection 770(1) of the *Criminal Code*, a youth court judge shall,

(*a*) on the request of the Attorney General or his agent, fix a time and place for the hearing of an application for the forfeiture of the recognizance; and

(*b*) after fixing a time and place for the hearing, cause to be sent by registered mail, not less than ten days before the time so fixed, to each principal and surety named in the recognizance, directed to him at his latest known address, a notice requiring him to appear at the time and place fixed by the judge to show cause why the recognizance should not be forfeited.

**Order for forfeiture of recognizance**
(2) Where subsection (1) is complied with, the youth court judge may, after giving the parties an opportunity to be heard, in his discretion grant or refuse the application and make any order with respect to the forfeiture of the recognizance that he considers proper.

**Judgment debtors of the Crown**
(3) Where, pursuant to subsection (2), a youth court judge orders forfeiture of a recognizance, the principal and his sureties become judgment debtors of the Crown, each in the amount that the judge orders him to pay.

**Order may be filed**
(4) An order made under subsection (2) may be filed with the clerk of the superior court or, in the province of Quebec, the prothonotary and, where an order is filed, the clerk or the prothonotary shall issue a writ of *fieri facias* in Form 34 set out in the *Criminal Code* and deliver it to the sheriff of each of the territorial divisions in which any of the principal and his sureties resides, carries on business or has property.

**Where a deposit has been made**
(5) Where a deposit has been made by a person against whom an order for forfeiture of a recognizance has been made, no writ of *fieri facias* shall issue, but the amount of the deposit shall be transferred by the person who has custody of it to the person who is entitled by law to receive it.

**Subsections 770(2) and (4) of *Criminal Code* do not apply**
(6) Subsections 770(2) and (4) of the *Criminal Code* do not apply in respect of proceedings under this Act.

**Sections 772 and 773 of *Criminal Code* apply**
(7) Sections 772 and 773 of the *Criminal Code* apply in respect of writs of *fieri facias* issued pursuant to this section as if they were issued pursuant to section 771 of the *Criminal Code*.
1980-81-82-83, c. 110, s. 49.

INTERFERENCE WITH DISPOSITIONS

**Inducing a young person, etc.**
**50.** (1) Every one who

(*a*) induces or assists a young person to leave unlawfully a place of custody or other place in which the young person has been placed pursuant to a disposition,

(*b*) unlawfully removes a young person from a place referred to in paragraph (*a*),

(*c*) knowingly harbours or conceals a young person who has unlawfully left a place referred to in paragraph (*a*),

(*d*) wilfully induces or assists a young person to breach or disobey a term or condition of a disposition, or

(*e*) wilfully prevents or interferes with the performance by a young person of a term or condition of a disposition

is guilty of an indictable offence and liable to imprisonment for a term not exceeding two years or is guilty of an offence punishable on summary conviction.

**Absolute jurisdiction of provincial court judge**
(2) The jurisdiction of a provincial court judge to try an adult accused of an indictable offence under this section is absolute and does not depend on the consent of the accused.
R.S., 1985, c. Y-1, s. 50; R.S., 1985, c. 24 (2nd Supp.), ss. 37, 44(F).

APPLICATION OF THE CRIMINAL CODE

**Application of *Criminal Code***
**51.** Except to the extent that they are inconsistent with or excluded by this Act, all the provisions of the *Criminal Code* apply, with such modifications as the circumstances require, in respect of offences alleged to have been committed by young persons.
R.S., 1985, c. Y-1, s. 51; R.S., 1985, c. 24 (2nd Supp.), s. 44(F).

## PROCEDURE

**Part XXVII and summary conviction trial provisions of *Criminal Code* to apply**
52. (1) Subject to this section and except to the extent that they are inconsistent with this Act,
(*a*) the provisions of Part XXVII of the *Criminal Code*, and
(*b*) any other provisions of the *Criminal* Code that apply in respect of summary conviction offences and relate to trial proceedings

apply to proceedings under this Act
(*c*) in respect of a summary conviction offence, and
(*d*) in respect of an indictable offence as if it were defined in the enactment creating it as a summary conviction offence.

**Indictable offences**
(2) For greater certainty and notwithstanding subsection (1) or any other provision of this Act, an indictable offence committed by a young person is, for the purposes of this Act or any other Act, an indictable offence.

**Attendance of young person**
(3) Section 650 of the *Criminal Code* applies in respect of proceedings under this Act, whether the proceedings relate to an indictable offence or an offence punishable on summary conviction.

**Limitation period**
(4) In proceedings under this Act, subsection 786(2) of the *Criminal Code* does not apply in respect of an indictable offence.

**Costs**
(5) Section 809 of the *Criminal Code* does not apply in respect of proceedings under this Act. 1980-81-82-83, c. 110, s. 52.

**Counts charged in information**
53. Indictable offences and offences punishable on summary conviction may under this Act be charged in the same information and tried jointly. 1980-81-82-83, c. 110, s. 53.

**Issue of subpoena**
54. (1) Where a person is required to attend to give evidence before a youth court, the subpoena directed to that person may be issued by a youth court judge, whether or not the person whose attendance is required is within the same province as the youth court.

**Service of subpoena**
(2) A subpoena issued by a youth court and directed to a person who is not within the same province as the youth court shall be served personally on the person to whom it is directed. 1980-81-82-83, c. 110, s. 54.

**Warrant**
55. A warrant that is issued out of a youth court may be executed anywhere in Canada. 1980-81-82-83, c. 110, s. 55.

## EVIDENCE

**General law on admissibility of statements to apply**
56. (1) Subject to this section, the law relating to the admissibility of statements made by persons accused of committing offences applies in respect of young persons.

**When statements are admissible**
(2) No oral or written statement given by a young person to a peace officer or to any other person who is, in law, a person in authority on the arrest or detention of the young person or in circumstances where the peace officer or other person has reasonable grounds for believing that the young person has committed an offence is admissible against the young person unless
(*a*) the statement was voluntary;
(*b*) the person to whom the statement was given has, before the statement was made, clearly explained to the young person, in language appropriate to his age and understanding, that
(i) the young person is under no obligation to give a statement,
(ii) any statement given by him may be used as evidence in proceedings against him,
(iii) the young person has the right to consult counsel and a parent or other person in accordance with paragraph (*c*), and
(iv) any statement made by the young person is required to be made in the presence of counsel and any other person consulted in accordance with paragraph (*c*), if any, unless the young person desires otherwise;
(*c*) the young person has, before the statement was made, been given a reasonable opportunity to consult
(i) with counsel, and
(ii) a parent, or in the absence of a parent, an adult relative, or in the absence of a parent and an adult relative, any other appropriate adult chosen by the young person; and
(*d*) where the young person consults any person pursuant to paragraph (*c*), the young person has been given a reasonable opportunity to make the statement in the presence of that person.

**Exception in certain cases for oral statements**
(3) The requirements set out in paragraphs (2)(*b*), (*c*) and (*d*) do not apply in respect of oral statements where they are made spontaneously by the young person to a peace officer or other person in authority before that person has had a reasonable opportunity to comply with those requirements.

**Waiver of right to consult**
(4) A young person may waive the rights under paragraph (2)(*c*) or (*d*) but any such waiver shall be videotaped or be in writing, and where it is in writing it shall contain a statement signed by the young person that the young person has been apprised of the right being waived.

**Statements given under duress are inadmissible**
(5) A youth court judge may rule inadmissible in any proceedings under this Act a statement given

by the young person in respect of whom the proceedings are taken if the young person satisfies the judge that the statement was given under duress imposed by any person who is not, in law, a person in authority.

**Misrepresentation of age**
(5.1) A youth court judge may in any proceedings under this Act rule admissible any statement or waiver by a young person where, at the time of the making of the statement or waiver,
(*a*) the young person held himself or herself to be eighteen years of age or older;
(*b*) the person to whom the statement or waiver was made conducted reasonable inquiries as to the age of the young person and had reasonable grounds for believing that the young person was eighteen years of age or older; and
(*c*) in all other circumstances the statement or waiver would otherwise be admissible.

**Parent, etc., not a person in authority**
(6) For the purpose of this section, an adult consulted pursuant to paragraph 56(2)(*c*) shall, in the absence of evidence to the contrary, be deemed not to be a person in authority.
R.S., 1985, c. Y-1, s. 56; R.S., 1985, c. 24 (2nd Supp.), s. 38; 1995, c. 19, s. 35.

**Testimony of a parent**
57. (1) In any proceedings under this Act, the testimony of a parent as to the age of a person of whom he is a parent is admissible as evidence of the age of that person.

**Evidence of age by certificate or record**
(2) In any proceedings under this Act,
(*a*) a birth or baptismal certificate or a copy thereof purporting to be certified under the hand of the person in whose custody those records are held is evidence of the age of the person named in the certificate or copy; and
(*b*) an entry or record of an incorporated society that has had the control or care of the person alleged to have committed the offence in respect of which the proceedings are taken at or about the time the person came to Canada is evidence of the age of that person, if the entry or record was made before the time when the offence is alleged to have been committed.

**Other evidence**
(3) In the absence, before the youth court, of any certificate, copy, entry or record mentioned in subsection (2), or in corroboration of any such certificate, copy, entry or record, the youth court may receive and act on any other information relating to age that it considers reliable.

**When age may be inferred**
(4) In any proceedings under this Act, the youth court may draw inferences as to the age of a person from the person's appearance or from statements made by the person in direct examination or cross-examination.
1980-81-82-83, c. 110, s. 57.

**Admissions**
58. (1) A party to any proceedings under this Act may admit any relevant fact or matter for the purpose of dispensing with proof thereof, including any fact or matter the admissibility of which depends on a ruling of law or of mixed law and fact.

**Other party may adduce evidence**
(2) Nothing in this section precludes a party to a proceeding from adducing evidence to prove a fact or matter admitted by another party.
1980-81-82-83, c. 110, s. 58.

**Material evidence**
59. Any evidence material to proceedings under this Act that would not but for this section be admissible in evidence may, with the consent of the parties to the proceedings and where the young person is represented by counsel, be given in such proceedings.
1980-81-82-83, c. 110, s. 59.

**Evidence of a child or young person**
60. In any proceedings under this Act where the evidence of a child or a young person is taken, it shall be taken only after the youth court judge or the justice, as the case may be, has
(*a*) in all cases, if the witness is a child, and
(*b*) where he deems it necessary, if the witness is a young person,

instructed the child or young person as to the duty of the witness to speak the truth and the consequences of failing to do so.
R.S., 1985, c. Y-1, s. 60; R.S., 1985, c. 24 (2nd Supp.), s. 39.

61. [Repealed, R.S., 1985, c. 24 (2nd Supp.), s. 40]

**Proof of service**
62. (1) For the purposes of this Act, service of any document may be proved by oral evidence given under oath by, or by the affidavit or statutory declaration of, the person claiming to have personally served it or sent it by mail.

**Proof of signature and official character unnecessary**
(2) Where proof of service of any document is offered by affidavit or statutory declaration, it is not necessary to prove the signature or official character of the person making or taking the affidavit or declaration, if the official character of that person appears on the face thereof.
1980-81-82-83, c. 110, s. 62.

**Seal not required**
63. It is not necessary to the validity of any information, summons, warrant, minute, disposition, conviction, order or other process or document laid, issued, filed or entered in any proceedings under this Act that any seal be attached or affixed thereto.
1980-81-82-83, c. 110, s. 63.

SUBSTITUTION OF JUDGES

**Powers of substitute youth court judge**
**64.** (1) A youth court judge who acts in the place of another youth court judge pursuant to subsection 669.2(1) of the *Criminal Code* shall,
(*a*) if an adjudication has been made, proceed with the disposition of the case or make the order that, in the circumstances, is authorized by law; or
(*b*) if no adjudication has been made, recommence the trial as if no evidence had been taken.

**Transcript of evidence already given**
(2) Where a youth court judge recommences a trial under paragraph (1)(*b*), he may, if the parties consent, admit into evidence a transcript of any evidence already given in the case.
R.S., 1985, c. Y-1, s. 64; R.S., 1985, c. 27 (1st Supp.), s. 187.

FUNCTIONS OF CLERKS OF COURTS

**Powers of clerks**
**65.** In addition to any powers conferred on a clerk of a court by the *Criminal Code*, a clerk of the youth court may exercise such powers as are ordinarily exercised by a clerk of a court, and, in particular, may
(*a*) administer oaths or solemn affirmations in all matters relating to the business of the youth court; and
(*b*) in the absence of a youth court judge, exercise all the powers of a youth court judge relating to adjournment.
1980-81-82-83, c. 110, s. 65.

FORMS, REGULATIONS AND RULES OF COURT

**Forms**
**66.** (1) The forms prescribed under section 67, varied to suit the case, or forms to the like effect, are valid and sufficient in the circumstances for which they are provided.

**Where forms not prescribed**
(2) In any case for which forms are not prescribed under section 67, the forms set out in Part XXVIII of the *Criminal Code*, with such modifications as the circumstances require, or other appropriate forms, may be used.
R.S., 1985, c. Y-1, s. 66; R.S., 1985, c. 1 (4th Supp.), s. 43.

**Regulations**
**67.** The Governor in Council may make regulations
(*a*) prescribing forms that may be used for the purposes of this Act;
(*b*) establishing uniform rules of court for youth courts across Canada, including rules regulating the practice and procedure to be followed by youth courts; and
(*c*) generally for carrying out the purposes and provisions of this Act.
R.S., 1985, c. Y-1, s. 67; R.S., 1985, c. 24 (2nd Supp.), s. 41.

**Youth court may make rules**
**68.** (1) Every youth court for a province may, at any time with the concurrence of a majority of the judges thereof present at a meeting held for the purpose and subject to the approval of the Lieutenant Governor in Council, establish rules of court not inconsistent with this Act or any other Act of Parliament or with any regulations made pursuant to section 67 regulating proceedings within the jurisdiction of the youth court.

**Rules of court**
(2) Rules under subsection (1) may be made
(*a*) generally to regulate the duties of the officers of the youth court and any other matter considered expedient to attain the ends of justice and carry into effect the provisions of this Act;
(*b*) subject to any regulations made under paragraph 67(*b*), to regulate the practice and procedure in the youth court; and
(*c*) to prescribe forms to be used in the youth court where not otherwise provided for by or pursuant to this Act.

**Publication of rules**
(3) Rules of court that are made under the authority of this section shall be published in the appropriate provincial gazette.
1980-81-82-83, c. 110, s. 68.

YOUTH JUSTICE COMMITTEES

**Youth justice committees**
**69.** The Attorney General of a province or such other Minister as the Lieutenant Governor in Council of the province may designate, or a delegate thereof, may establish one or more committees of citizens, to be known as youth justice committees, to assist without remuneration in any aspect of the administration of this Act or in any programs or services for young offenders and may specify the method of appointment of committee members and the functions of the committees.
1980-81-82-83, c. 110, s. 69.

AGREEMENTS WITH PROVINCES

**Agreements with provinces**
**70.** Any minister of the Crown may, with the approval of the Governor in Council, enter into an agreement with the government of any province providing for payments by Canada to the province in respect of costs incurred by the province or a municipality for care of and services provided to young persons dealt with under this Act.
R.S., 1985, c. Y-1, s. 70; R.S., 1985, c. 24 (2nd Supp.), s. 42.

SCHEDULE

**(Subsections 45(2.1) and 45.02(3) and (4))**
**1.** An offence under any of the following provisions of the *Criminal Code*:
(*a*) paragraph 81(2)(*a*) (causing injury with intent);
(*b*) subsection 85(1) (using firearm in commission of offence);

(*c*) section 151 (sexual interference);
(*d*) section 152 (invitation to sexual touching);
(*e*) section 153 (sexual exploitation);
(*f*) section 155 (incest);
(*g*) section 159 (anal intercourse);
(*h*) section 170 (parent or guardian procuring sexual activity by child);
(*i*) subsection 212(2) (living off the avails of prostitution by a child);
(*j*) subsection 212(4) (obtaining sexual services of a child);
(*k*) section 236 (manslaughter);
(*l*) section 239 (attempt to commit murder);
(*m*) section 267 (assault with a weapon or causing bodily harm);
(*n*) section 268 (aggravated assault);
(*o*) section 269 (unlawfully causing bodily harm);
(*p*) section 271 (sexual assault);
(*q*) section 272 (sexual assault with a weapon, threats to a third party or causing bodily harm);
(*r*) section 273 (aggravated sexual assault);
(*s*) section 279 (kidnapping);
(*t*) section 344 (robbery);
(*u*) section 433 (arson—disregard for human life);
(*v*) section 434.1 (arson—own property);
(*w*) section 436 (arson by negligence); and
(*x*) paragraph 465(1)(*a*) (conspiracy to commit murder).

2. An offence under any of the following provisions of the *Criminal Code*, as they read immediately before July 1, 1990:
(*a*) section 433 (arson);
(*b*) section 434 (setting fire to other substance); and
(*c*) section 436 (setting fire by negligence).

3. An offence under any of the following provisions of the *Criminal Code*, chapter C-34 of the Revised Statutes of Canada, 1970, as they read immediately before January 4, 1983:
(*a*) section 144 (rape);
(*b*) section 145 (attempt to commit rape);
(*c*) section 149 (indecent assault on female);
(*d*) section 156 (indecent assault on male); and
(*e*) section 246 (assault with intent).

4. An offence under any of the following provisions of the *Controlled Drugs and Substances Act*:
(*a*) section 5 (trafficking);
(*b*) section 6 (importing and exporting); and
(*c*) section 7 (production of substance).

R.S., 1985, c. Y-1, Sch.; R.S., 1985, c. 24 (2nd Supp.), s. 43; 1995, c. 19, s. 36, c. 39, s. 189; 1996, c. 19, s. 93.1.

## RELATED PROVISIONS

– R.S., 1985, c. 24 (2nd Supp.), ss. 50, 51:

### TRANSITIONAL

**Review of dispositions under section 33 of *Young Offenders Act***
50. Any proceedings commenced under section 33 of the *Young Offenders Act* before the coming into force of section 24 of this Act shall be continued and completed as if this Act had not been enacted.

**Previous offences**
51. No person is guilty of an offence by reason only of a failure to comply with subsection 45(1), (2) or (4) of the *Young Offenders Act* as it read immediately prior to the coming into force of section 34 of this Act.

– R.S., 1985, c. 40 (4th Supp.), s. 2(4):

**Transitional—rules of court (SI/81-32 and -33)**
"(4) The Rules of Practice of the Court of the Sessions of the Peace of Quebec, Penal and Criminal Jurisdiction and the Rules of Practice of the Youth Court of the Province of Quebec, on Criminal and Penal Matters shall be deemed to have been made by the Court of Quebec with the approval of the lieutenant governor in council of that Province."

– 1991, c. 43, s. 36:

**Review**
36. (1) A comprehensive review of the provisions and operation of this Act shall be undertaken within five years after the coming into force of any provision thereof, by such committee of the House of Commons as may be designated or established for that purpose.

**Report**
(2) The committee shall submit a report of the review to the House of Commons within one year after commencing it, or within such further time as the House of Commons may authorize.

– 1992, c. 11, s. 18:

### TRANSITIONAL

**Transitional**
18. Where a young person is alleged to have committed first degree murder or second degree murder within the meaning of section 231 of the *Criminal Code* before the coming into force of this Act and
(*a*) an application was made in respect of the young person under subsection 16(1) of the *Young Offenders Act*, as that subsection read immediately before the coming into force of this Act, but no decision under that subsection had been issued before the coming into force of this Act, or
(*b*) an application is made in respect of the young person under subsection 16(1) of the *Young Offenders Act* after the coming into force of this Act,

the provisions of the *Young Offenders Act* enacted by this Act shall apply to the young person as if the offence had occurred after the coming into force of this Act.

– 1995, c. 19, s. 31(4):

**Transitional**
(4) Paragraphs 45(1)(*d*.1) to (*e*) of the Act, as enacted by subsection (2), apply in respect of a record relating to a finding of guilt made before the coming into force of that subsection only if the person to whom the record relates applies, after the coming into force of that subsection, to

the Royal Canadian Mounted Police to have those paragraphs apply.

– 1995, c. 22, s. 26:

26. For greater certainty, conduct that constituted an offence under the *Criminal Code* before the date on which this section comes into force constitutes the same offence after that date.

AMENDMENTS NOT IN FORCE

– 1992, c. 47, ss. 81 to 83:

**81. Subsection 5(1) of the *Young Offenders Act* is repealed and the following substituted therefor:**

**Exclusive jurisdiction of youth court**
5. (1) Notwithstanding any other Act of Parliament but subject to the *Contraventions Act* and the *National Defence Act* and section 16, a youth court has exclusive jurisdiction in respect of any offence alleged to have been committed by a person while a young person and any such person shall be dealt with as provided in this Act.

**82. (1) Section 9 of the said Act is amended by adding thereto, immediately after subsection (2) thereof, the following subsection:**

**Notice to parent in case of ticket**
(2.1) Subject to subsections (3) and (4), a person who serves a ticket under the *Contraventions Act* on a young person, other than a ticket served for a contravention relating to parking a vehicle, shall, as soon as possible, give or cause to be given notice in writing of the ticket to a parent of the young person.

**(2) Subsection 9(3) of the said Act is amended by striking out the word "or" at the end of paragraph (*b*) thereof, by adding the word "or" at the end of paragraph (*c*) thereof and by adding thereto, immediately after paragraph (*c*) thereof, the following paragraph:**
(*d*) on whom a ticket is served under the *Contraventions Act*, other than a ticket served for a contravention relating to parking a vehicle,

**(3) Subsection 9(4) of the said Act is repealed and the following substituted therefor:**

**Notice to spouse**
(4) A notice under this section may be given to the spouse of a young person described in paragraph (3)(*a*), (*b*), (*c*) or (*d*) instead of to a parent.

**(4) Paragraph 9(6)(*b*) of the said Act is repealed and the following substituted therefor:**

(*b*) the charge against the young person and, except in the case of a notice of a ticket served under the *Contraventions Act*, the time and place of appearance; and

**(5) Section 9 of the said Act is further amended by adding thereto, immediately after subsection (6) thereof, the following subsection:**

**Notice of ticket under *Contraventions Act***
(6.1) A notice under subsection (2.1) shall include a copy of the ticket.
1991, c. 43, s. 31(2)

**(6) All that portion of subsection 9(10) of the said Act preceding paragraph (*a*) thereof is repealed and the following substituted therefor:**

**Where notice is not served**
(10) Where there has been a failure to give a notice under subsection (1) or (2.1) in accordance with this section and none of the persons to whom the notice may be given attends court with the young person, a youth court judge or a justice before whom proceedings are held against the young person may

**83. Section 10 of the said Act is amended by adding thereto, immediately after subsection (1) thereof, the following subsection:**

**No order in ticket proceedings**
(1.1) Subsection (1) does not apply in proceedings commenced by filing a ticket under the *Contraventions Act*.

# Appendix C
## Youth Criminal Justice Act
## (Bill C-68—First Reading March 11, 1999)

RECOMMENDATION

His Excellency the Governor General recommends to the House of Commons the appropriation of public revenue under the circumstances, in the manner and for the purposes set out in a measure entitled "*An Act in respect of criminal justice for young persons and to amend and repeal other Acts.*"

SUMMARY

This enactment repeals and replaces the *Young Offenders Act* and provides principles, procedures and protections for the prosecution of young persons under criminal and other federal laws.

This enactment sets out a range of extrajudicial measures, establishes the judicial procedures and protections for young persons alleged to have committed an offence, encourages the participation of parents, victims, communities, youth justice committees and others in the youth justice system, sets out a range of sentences available to the youth justice court, establishes custody and supervision provisions, sets out the rules for the keeping of records and protection of privacy, provides transitional provisions and makes consequential amendments to other Acts.

**1st Session, 36th Parliament**
**46-47-48 Elizabeth II, 1997-98-99**
**The House of Commons of Canada**

BILL C-68

An Act in respect of criminal justice for young persons and to amend and repeal other Acts

**Preamble**

WHEREAS society should be protected from youth crime through a youth criminal justice system that commands respect, fosters responsibility and ensures accountability through meaningful consequences and effective rehabilitation and reintegration, and that reserves its most serious intervention for the most serious crimes and reduces the over-reliance on incarceration for non-violent young persons;

WHEREAS these objectives can best be achieved by replacement of the *Young Offenders Act* with a new legal framework for the youth criminal justice system;

WHEREAS members of society share a responsibility to address the developmental challenges and the needs of young persons and to guide them into adulthood;

WHEREAS communities, families, parents and others concerned with the development of young persons should, through multi-disciplinary approaches, take reasonable steps to prevent youth crime by addressing its underlying causes, to respond to the needs of young persons, and to provide guidance and support to those at risk of committing crimes;

AND WHEREAS Canada is a party to the United Nations Convention on the Rights of the Child and recognizes that young persons have rights and freedoms, including those stated in the *Canadian Charter of Rights and Freedoms* and the *Canadian Bill of Rights*, and have special guarantees of their rights and freedoms;

NOW, THEREFORE, Her Majesty, by and with the advice and consent of the Senate and House of Commons of Canada, enacts as follows:

SHORT TITLE

**Short title**
1. This Act may be cited as the *Youth Criminal Justice Act.*

INTERPRETATION

**Definitions**
2. (1) The definitions in this subsection apply in this Act.

**"adult"**
"adult" means a person who is neither a young person nor a child.

**"adult sentence"**
"adult sentence", in the case of a young person

who is found guilty of an offence, means any sentence that could be imposed on an adult who has been convicted of the same offence.

**"Attorney General"**
"Attorney General" means the Attorney General as defined in section 2 of the *Criminal Code*, read as if the reference in that definition to "proceedings" were a reference to "proceedings or extrajudicial measures", and includes an agent or delegate of the Attorney General.

**"child"**
"child" means a person who is or, in the absence of evidence to the contrary, appears to be less than twelve years old.

**"conference"**
"conference" means a group of persons who are convened to give advice in accordance with section 19.

**"confirmed delivery service"**
"confirmed delivery service" means certified or registered mail or any other method of service that provides proof of delivery.

**"custodial portion"**
"custodial portion", with respect to a youth sentence imposed on a young person under paragraph 41(2)(*n*), (*p*) or (*q*), means the period of time, or the portion of the young person's youth sentence, that must be served in custody before he or she begins to serve the remainder under supervision in the community subject to conditions under paragraph 41(2)(*n*) or under conditional supervision under paragraph 41(2)(*p*) or (*q*).

**"disclosure"**
"disclosure" means the communication of information other than by way of publication.

**"extrajudicial measures"**
"extrajudicial measures" means measures other than judicial proceedings under this Act used to deal with a young person alleged to have committed an offence.

**"extrajudicial sanction"**
"extrajudicial sanction" means a sanction that is part of a program referred to in section 10.

**"non-violent offence"**
"non-violent offence" means an offence that does not cause or create a substantial risk of causing bodily harm.

**"offence"**
"offence" means an offence created by an Act of Parliament or by any regulation, rule, order, by-law or ordinance made under an Act of Parliament other than an ordinance of the Yukon Territory or the Northwest Territories.

**"parent"**
"parent" includes, in respect of a young person, any person who is under a legal duty to provide for the young person or any person who has, in law or in fact, the custody or control of the young person, but does not include a person who has the custody or control of the young person by reason only of proceedings under this Act.

**"pre-sentence report"**
"pre-sentence report" means a report on the personal and family history and present environment of a young person made in accordance with section 39.

**"presumptive offence"**
"presumptive offence" means
(*a*) an offence under one of the following provisions of the *Criminal Code*:
(i) section 231 or 235 (first degree murder or second degree murder within the meaning of section 231),
(ii) section 239 (attempt to commit murder),
(iii) section 232, 234 or 236 (manslaughter), or
(iv) section 273 (aggravated sexual assault); or
(*b*) a serious violent offence for which an adult could be sentenced to imprisonment for more than two years committed by a young person after the coming into force of section 61, if at the time the young person committed the offence at least two judicial determinations have been made under subsection 41(8), at different proceedings, that the young person has committed a serious violent offence.

**"provincial director"**
"provincial director" means a person, a group or class of persons or a body appointed or designated by or under an Act of the legislature of a province or by the lieutenant governor in council of a province or his or her delegate to perform in that province, either generally or in a specific case, any of the duties or functions of a provincial director under this Act.

**"publication"**
"publication" means the communication of information by making it known or accessible to the general public through any means, including print, radio or television broadcast, telecommunication or electronic means.

**"record"**
"record" includes any thing containing information, regardless of its physical form or characteristics, including microform, sound recording, videotape, machine-readable record, and any copy of any of those things, that is created or kept for the purposes of this Act or for the investigation of an offence that is or could be prosecuted under this Act.

**"review board"**
"review board" means a review board referred to in subsection 86(2).

**"serious violent offence"**
"serious violent offence" means an offence that causes or creates a substantial risk of causing serious bodily harm.

**"violent offence"**
"violent offence" means an offence that causes or creates a substantial risk of causing bodily harm.

**"young person"**
"young person" means a person who is or, in the absence of evidence to the contrary, appears to be twelve years old or older, but less than eighteen years old and, if the context requires, includes any person who is charged under this Act with having committed an offence while he or she was a young person or who is found guilty of an offence under this Act.

**"youth custody facility"**
"youth custody facility" means a facility designated under subsection 84(2) for the placement of young persons and, if so designated, includes a facility for the secure restraint of young persons, a community residential centre, a group home, a child care institution and a forest or wilderness camp.

**"youth justice court"**
"youth justice court" means a youth justice court referred to in section 13.

**"youth justice court judge"**
"youth justice court judge" means a youth justice court judge referred to in section 13.

**"youth sentence"**
"youth sentence" means a sentence imposed under section 41, 50 or 59 or any of sections 93 to 95 and includes a confirmation or a variation of that sentence.

**"youth worker"**
"youth worker" means any person appointed or designated, whether by title of youth worker or probation officer or by any other title, by or under an Act of the legislature of a province or by the lieutenant governor in council of a province or his or her delegate to perform in that province, either generally or in a specific case, any of the duties or functions of a youth worker under this Act.

**Words and expressions**
(2) Unless otherwise provided, words and expressions used in this Act have the same meaning as in the *Criminal Code*.

## DECLARATION OF PRINCIPLE

**Policy for Canada with respect to young persons**
3. (1) The following principles apply in this Act:
(*a*) the principal goal of the youth criminal justice system is to protect the public by
(i) preventing crime by addressing the circumstances underlying a young person's offending behaviour,
(ii) ensuring that a young person is subject to meaningful consequences for his or her offence, and
(iii) rehabilitating young persons who commit offences and reintegrating them into society;
(*b*) the criminal justice system for young persons must be separate from that of adults and emphasize the following:
(i) fair and proportionate accountability that is consistent with the greater dependency of young persons and their reduced level of maturity,
(ii) enhanced procedural protection to ensure that young persons are treated fairly and that their rights, including their right to privacy, are protected, and
(iii) a greater emphasis on rehabilitation and reintegration;
(*c*) within the limits of fair and proportionate accountability, the measures taken against young persons who commit offences should
(i) reinforce respect for societal values,
(ii) encourage the repair of harm done to victims and the community,
(iii) be meaningful for the individual young person and, where appropriate, involve the parents, the extended family, the community and social or other agencies in the young person's rehabilitation and reintegration, and
(iv) respect gender, ethnic, cultural and linguistic differences and respond to the needs of young persons with special requirements; and
(*d*) special considerations apply in respect of proceedings against young persons and, in particular,
(i) young persons have rights and freedoms in their own right, such as a right to be heard in the course of and to participate in the processes, other than the decision to prosecute, that lead to decisions that affect them, and young persons have special guarantees of their rights and freedoms,
(ii) victims should be treated with courtesy, compassion and respect for their dignity and privacy and should suffer the minimum degree of inconvenience as a result of their involvement with the youth criminal justice system,
(iii) victims should be provided with information about the proceedings and given an opportunity to participate and be heard, and
(iv) parents should be informed of measures or proceedings involving their children and encouraged to support them in addressing their offending behaviour.

**Act to be liberally construed**
(2) This Act shall be liberally construed so as to ensure that young persons are dealt with in accordance with the principles set out in subsection (1).

## PART 1
## EXTRAJUDICIAL MEASURES

***Principles and Objectives***

**Declaration of principles**
4. The following principles apply in this Part:
(*a*) extrajudicial measures are often the most appropriate and effective way to address youth crime;
(*b*) extrajudicial measures allow for effective and timely interventions focused on correcting offending behaviour;
(*c*) extrajudicial measures are presumed to be adequate to hold a young person accountable

for his or her offending behaviour if the young person has committed a non-violent offence and has not previously been found guilty of an offence; and

(*d*) extrajudicial measures should be used if they are adequate to hold a young person accountable for his or her offending behaviour and, if the use of extrajudicial measures is consistent with the principles set out in this section, nothing in this Act precludes their use in respect of a young person who

(i) has previously been dealt with by the use of extrajudicial measures, or

(ii) has previously been found guilty of an offence.

**Objectives**

5. Extrajudicial measures should be designed to

(*a*) provide an effective and timely response to offending behaviour outside the bounds of judicial measures;

(*b*) encourage young persons to acknowledge and repair the harm caused to the victim and the community;

(*c*) encourage families of young persons—including extended families—and the community to become involved in the design and implementation of those measures;

(*d*) provide an opportunity for victims to participate in decisions related to the measures selected and to receive reparation; and

(*e*) respect the rights and freedoms of young persons and be proportionate to the seriousness of the offence.

*Warnings, Cautions and Referrals*

**Warnings, cautions and referrals**

6. (1) A police officer shall, before starting judicial proceedings or taking any other measures under this Act against a young person alleged to have committed an offence, consider whether it would be sufficient, having regard to the principles set out in section 4, to take no further action, warn the young person, administer a caution, if a program has been established under section 7, or refer the young person to a community-based program.

**Saving**

(2) The failure of a police officer to consider the options set out in subsection (1) does not invalidate any subsequent charges against the young person for the offence.

**Police cautions**

7. The Attorney General may establish a program authorizing the police to administer cautions to young persons instead of starting judicial proceedings under this Act.

**Crown cautions**

8. The Attorney General may establish a program authorizing prosecutors to administer cautions to young persons instead of starting or continuing judicial proceedings under this Act.

**Evidence of measures is inadmissible**

9. Evidence that a young person has received a warning, caution or referral mentioned in section 6, 7 or 8 or that a police officer has taken no further action in respect of an offence, and evidence of the offence, is inadmissible for the purpose of proving prior offending behaviour in any proceedings before a youth justice court in respect of the young person.

*Extrajudicial Sanctions*

**Extrajudicial sanctions**

10. (1) An extrajudicial sanction may be used to deal with a young person alleged to have committed an offence only if the young person cannot be adequately dealt with by a warning, caution or referral mentioned in section 6, 7 or 8 because of the seriousness of the offence, the nature and number of previous offences committed by the young person or any other aggravating circumstances.

**Conditions**

(2) An extrajudicial sanction may be used only if

(*a*) it is part of a program of sanctions that may be authorized by the Attorney General or authorized by a person, or a member of a class of persons, designated by the lieutenant governor in council of the province;

(*b*) the person who is considering whether to use the extrajudicial sanction is satisfied that it would be appropriate, having regard to the needs of the young person and the interests of society;

(*c*) the young person, having been informed of the extrajudicial sanction, fully and freely consents to be subject to it;

(*d*) the young person has, before consenting to be subject to the extrajudicial sanction, been advised of his or her right to be represented by counsel and been given a reasonable opportunity to consult with counsel;

(*e*) the young person accepts responsibility for the act or omission that forms the basis of the offence that he or she is alleged to have committed;

(*f*) there is, in the opinion of the Attorney General, sufficient evidence to proceed with the prosecution of the offence; and

(*g*) the prosecution of the offence is not in any way barred at law.

**Restriction on use**

(3) An extrajudicial sanction may not be used in respect of a young person who

(*a*) denies participation or involvement in the commission of the offence; or

(*b*) expresses the wish to have the charge dealt with by a youth justice court.

**Admissions not admissible in evidence**

(4) Any admission, confession or statement accepting responsibility for a given act or omission that is made by a young person as a condition of being dealt with by an extrajudicial sanction is inadmissible in evidence against any young person in civil or criminal proceedings.

**No bar to judicial proceedings**

(5) The use of an extrajudicial sanction in respect of a young person alleged to have committed an

offence is not a bar to judicial proceedings under this Act, but if a charge is laid against the young person in respect of the offence,

(*a*) the youth justice court shall dismiss the charge if it is satisfied on a balance of probabilities that the young person has totally complied with the terms and conditions of the extrajudicial sanction; and

(*b*) the youth justice court may dismiss the charge if it is satisfied on a balance of probabilities that the young person has partially complied with the terms and conditions of the extrajudicial sanction and if, in the opinion of the court, prosecution of the charge would be unfair having regard to the circumstances and the young person's performance with respect to the extrajudicial sanction.

**Laying of information, etc.**
(6) Subject to subsection (5), nothing in this section shall be construed as preventing any person from laying an information, obtaining the issue or confirmation of any process or proceeding with the prosecution of any offence in accordance with law.

**Notice to parent**
**11.** If a young person is dealt with by an extrajudicial sanction, a police officer or the Attorney General, as the case may be, shall give or cause to be given to a parent of the young person, orally or in writing, notice of the sanction taken.

**Victim's right to information**
**12.** If a young person is dealt with by an extrajudicial sanction, a police officer, the Attorney General, the provincial director or any organization established by a province to provide assistance to victims shall, on request, inform the victim of the identity of the young person and how the offence has been dealt with.

## PART 2
## ORGANIZATION OF THE YOUTH CRIMINAL JUSTICE SYSTEM

### *Youth Justice Court*

**Designation of youth justice court**
**13.** (1) A youth justice court is any court that may be established or designated by or under an Act of the legislature of a province, or designated by the Governor in Council or the lieutenant governor in council of a province, as a youth justice court for the purposes of this Act, and a youth justice court judge is a person who may be appointed or designated as a judge of the youth justice court or a judge sitting in a court established or designated as a youth justice court.

**Deemed youth justice court**
(2) When a young person elects to be tried by a judge without a jury, the judge shall be a judge as defined in section 552 of the *Criminal Code*, or if it is an offence set out in section 469 of that Act, the judge shall be a judge of the superior court of criminal jurisdiction in the province in which the election is made. In either case, the judge is deemed to be a youth justice court judge and the court is deemed to be a youth justice court for the purpose of the proceeding.

**Deemed youth justice court**
(3) When a young person elects or is deemed to have elected to be tried by a court composed of a judge and jury, the superior court of criminal jurisdiction in the province in which the election is made or deemed to have been made is deemed to be a youth justice court for the purpose of the proceeding, and the superior court judge is deemed to be a youth justice court judge.

**Court of record**
(4) A youth justice court is a court of record.

**Exclusive jurisdiction of youth justice court**
**14.** (1) Despite any other Act of Parliament but subject to the *Contraventions Act* and the *National Defence Act*, a youth justice court has exclusive jurisdiction in respect of any offence alleged to have been committed by a person while he or she was a young person, and that person shall be dealt with as provided in this Act.

**Orders**
(2) A youth justice court has jurisdiction to make orders against a young person under sections 810, 810.01 and 810.2 of the *Criminal Code*. If the young person fails or refuses to enter into a recognizance referred to in any of those sections, the court may impose any one of the sanctions set out in subsection 41(2) except that, in the case of an order under paragraph 41(2)(*n*), it shall not exceed thirty days.

**Prosecution prohibited**
(3) Unless the Attorney General and the young person agree, no extrajudicial measures shall be taken or judicial proceedings commenced under this Act in respect of an offence after the end of the time limit set out in any other Act of Parliament or any regulation made under it for the institution of proceedings in respect of that offence.

**Continuation of proceedings**
(4) Extrajudicial measures taken or judicial proceedings commenced under this Act against a young person may be continued under this Act after the person attains the age of eighteen years.

**Young persons over the age of eighteen years**
(5) This Act applies to persons eighteen years old or older who are alleged to have committed an offence while a young person.

**Powers of youth justice court judge**
(6) For the purpose of carrying out the provisions of this Act, a youth justice court judge is a justice and a provincial court judge and has the jurisdiction and powers of a summary conviction court under the *Criminal Code*.

**Powers of a judge of a superior court**
(7) A judge of a superior court of criminal jurisdiction, when deemed to be a youth justice court judge for the purpose of a proceeding, retains the

jurisdiction and powers of a superior court of criminal jurisdiction.

**Contempt against youth justice court**
**15.** (1) Every youth justice court has the same power, jurisdiction and authority to deal with and impose punishment for contempt against the court as may be exercised by the superior court of criminal jurisdiction of the province in which the court is situated.

**Jurisdiction of youth justice court**
(2) A youth justice court has jurisdiction in respect of every contempt of court committed by a young person against the youth justice court whether or not committed in the face of the court, and every contempt of court committed by a young person against any other court otherwise than in the face of that court.

**Concurrent jurisdiction of youth justice court**
(3) A youth justice court has jurisdiction in respect of every contempt of court committed by a young person against any other court in the face of that court and every contempt of court committed by an adult against the youth justice court in the face of the youth justice court, but nothing in this subsection affects the power, jurisdiction or authority of any other court to deal with or impose punishment for contempt of court.

**Youth sentence—contempt**
(4) When a youth justice court or any other court finds a young person guilty of contempt of court, it may impose as a youth sentence any one of the sanctions set out in subsection 41(2), or any number of them that are not inconsistent with each other, but no other sentence.

**Section 708 of *Criminal Code* applies in respect of adults**
(5) Section 708 of the *Criminal Code* applies in respect of proceedings under this section in youth justice court against adults, with any modifications that the circumstances require.

**Status of offender uncertain**
**16.** When a person is alleged to have committed an offence during a period that includes the date on which the person attains the age of eighteen years, the youth justice court has jurisdiction in respect of the offence and shall, on finding the person guilty of the offence,
(*a*) if it has been proven that the offence was committed before the person attained the age of eighteen years, impose a sentence under this Act;
(*b*) if it has been proven that the offence was committed after the person attained the age of eighteen years, impose any sentence that could be imposed under the *Criminal Code* or any other Act of Parliament on an adult who has been convicted of the same offence; and
(*c*) if it has not been proven that the offence was committed after the person attained the age of eighteen years, impose a sentence under this Act.

**Youth justice court may make rules**
**17.** (1) The youth justice court for a province may, subject to the approval of the lieutenant governor in council of the province, establish rules of court not inconsistent with this Act or any other Act of Parliament or with any regulations made under section 154 regulating proceedings within the jurisdiction of the youth justice court.

**Rules of court**
(2) Rules under subsection (1) may be made
(*a*) generally to regulate the duties of the officers of the youth justice court and any other matter considered expedient to attain the ends of justice and carry into effect the provisions of this Act;
(*b*) subject to any regulations made under paragraph 154(*b*), to regulate the practice and procedure in the youth justice court; and
(*c*) to prescribe forms to be used in the youth justice court if they are not otherwise provided for by or under this Act.

**Publication of rules**
(3) Rules of court that are made under the authority of this section shall be published in the appropriate provincial gazette.

*Youth Justice Committees*

**Youth justice committees**
**18.** (1) The Attorney General of Canada or a province or any other minister that the lieutenant governor in council of the province may designate may establish one or more committees of citizens, to be known as youth justice committees, to assist in any aspect of the administration of this Act or in any programs or services for young persons.

**Role of committee**
(2) The functions of a youth justice committee may include the following:
(*a*) if a police officer or the Attorney General has referred a young person alleged to have committed an offence to the youth justice committee,
(i) giving advice on the appropriate extrajudicial measure to be used in respect of the young person,
(ii) supporting any victim of the offence by soliciting his or her concerns and facilitating the reconciliation of the victim and the young person,
(iii) ensuring that community support is available to the young person by arranging for the use of facilities and services from within the community, and enlisting members of the community to provide short-term mentoring and supervision, and
(iv) when the young person is also being dealt with by a child protection agency or a community group, helping to coordinate the interaction of the agency or group with the youth criminal justice system;
(*b*) advising the federal and provincial governments on whether the provisions of this Act that grant rights to young persons, or provide

for the protection of young persons, are being complied with;
(*c*) advising the federal and provincial governments on policies and procedures related to the youth criminal justice system;
(*d*) providing information to the public in respect of this Act and the youth criminal justice system;
(*e*) acting as a conference; and
(*f*) any other functions assigned by the Attorney General.

*Conferences*

**Conferences may be convened**
19. (1) A youth justice court judge, the provincial director, a police officer or any other person may, for the purpose of making a decision required to be made under this Act, convene a conference.

**Mandate of a conference**
(2) The mandate of a conference may be, among other things, to give advice on appropriate extrajudicial measures, conditions for judicial interim release or release from custody prior to trial by a peace officer or the officer in charge, sentences, including the review of sentences, and reintegration plans.

*Justices of the Peace*

**Certain proceedings may be taken before justices**
20. (1) Any proceeding that may be carried out before a justice under the *Criminal Code*, other than a plea, a trial or an adjudication, may be carried out before a justice in respect of an offence alleged to have been committed by a young person, and any process that may be issued by a justice under the *Criminal Code* may be issued by a justice in respect of an offence alleged to have been committed by a young person.

**Orders under s. 810 of *Criminal Code***
(2) A justice has jurisdiction to make an order under section 810 of the *Criminal Code* in respect of a young person. If the young person fails or refuses to enter into a recognizance referred to in that section, the justice shall refer the matter to a youth justice court.

*Clerks of the Court*

**Powers of clerks**
21. In addition to any powers conferred on a clerk of a court by the *Criminal Code*, a clerk of the youth justice court may exercise the powers ordinarily exercised by a clerk of a court, and, in particular, may
(*a*) administer oaths or solemn affirmations in all matters relating to the business of the youth justice court; and
(*b*) in the absence of a youth justice court judge, exercise all the powers of a youth justice court judge relating to adjournment.

*Provincial Directors*

**Powers, duties and functions of provincial directors**
22. The provincial director may authorize any person to exercise the powers or perform the duties or functions of the provincial director under this Act, in which case the powers, duties or functions are deemed to have been exercised or performed by the provincial director.

## PART 3
## JUDICIAL MEASURES

*Consent to Prosecute*

**Pre-charge screening**
23. (1) The Attorney General may establish a program of pre-charge screening that sets out the circumstances in which the consent of the Attorney General must be obtained before a young person is charged with an offence.

**Pre-charge screening program**
(2) Any program of pre-charge screening of young persons that is established under an Act of the legislature of a province or by a directive of a provincial government, and that is in place before the coming into force of this section, is deemed to be a program of pre-charge screening for the purposes of subsection (1).

**Private prosecutions**
24. No prosecutions may be conducted by a prosecutor other than the Attorney General without the consent of the Attorney General.

*Right to Counsel*

**Right to counsel**
25. (1) A young person has the right to retain and instruct counsel without delay, and to exercise that right personally, at any stage of proceedings against the young person and before and during any consideration of whether, instead of starting or continuing judicial proceedings against the young person under this Act, to use an extrajudicial sanction to deal with the young person.

**Arresting officer to advise young person of right to counsel**
(2) Every young person who is arrested or detained shall, on being arrested or detained, be advised without delay by the arresting officer or the officer in charge, as the case may be, of the right to retain and instruct counsel, and be given an opportunity to obtain counsel.

**Justice, youth justice court or review board to advise young person of right to counsel**
(3) When a young person is not represented by counsel
(*a*) at a hearing at which it will be determined whether to release the young person or detain the young person in custody prior to sentencing,

(*b*) at a hearing held under section 71,
(*c*) at trial,
(*d*) at any proceedings held under subsection 97(3), 102(1), 103(1), 104(1) or 108(1),
(*e*) at a review of a youth sentence held before a youth justice court under this Act, or
(*f*) at a review of the level of custody under section 86,

the justice or youth justice court before which the hearing trial or review is held, or the review board before which the review is held, shall advise the young person of the right to retain and instruct counsel and shall give the young person a reasonable opportunity to obtain counsel.

**Trial, hearing or review before youth justice court or review board**

(4) When a young person at trial or at a hearing or review referred to in subsection (3) wishes to obtain counsel but is unable to do so, the youth justice court before which the hearing, trial or review is held or the review board before which the review is held

(*a*) shall, if there is a legal aid program or an assistance program available in the province where the hearing, trial or review is held, refer the young person to that program for the appointment of counsel; or
(*b*) if no legal aid program or assistance program is available or the young person is unable to obtain counsel through the program, may, and on the request of the young person shall, direct that the young person be represented by counsel.

**Appointment of counsel**

(5) When a direction is made under paragraph 4(*b*) in respect of a young person, the Attorney General of the province in which the direction is made shall appoint counsel, or cause counsel to be appointed, to represent the young person.

**Release hearing before justice**

(6) When a young person, at a hearing referred to in paragraph (3)(*a*) that is held before a justice who is not a youth justice court judge, wishes to obtain counsel but is unable to do so, the justice shall

(*a*) if there is a legal aid program or an assistance program available in the province where the hearing is held,
(i) refer the young person to that program for the appointment of counsel, or
(ii) refer the matter to a youth justice court to be dealt with in accordance with paragraph (4)(*a*) or (*b*); or
(*b*) if no legal aid program or assistance program is available or the young person is unable to obtain counsel through the program, refer the matter without delay to a youth justice court to be dealt with in accordance with paragraph (4)(*b*).

**Young person may be assisted by adult**

(7) When a young person is not represented by counsel at trial or at a hearing or review referred to in subsection (3), the justice before whom or the youth justice court or review board before which the proceedings are held may, on the request of the young person, allow the young person to be assisted by an adult whom the justice, court or review board considers to be suitable.

**Counsel independent of parents**

(8) If it appears to a youth justice court judge or a justice that the interests of a young person and the interests of a parent are in conflict or that it would be in the best interests of the young person to be represented by his or her own counsel, the judge or justice shall ensure that the young person is represented by counsel independent of the parent.

**Statement of right to counsel**

(9) A statement that a young person has the right to be represented by counsel shall be included in

(*a*) any appearance notice or summons issued to the young person;
(*b*) any warrant to arrest the young person;
(*c*) any promise to appear given by the young person;
(*d*) any undertaking or recognizance entered into before an officer in charge by the young person;
(*e*) any notice given to the young person in relation to any proceedings held under subsection 97(3), 102(1), 103(1), 104(1) or 108(1); or
(*f*) any notice of a review of a youth sentence given to the young person.

**Recovery of costs of counsel**

(10) Nothing in this Act prevents the lieutenant governor in council of a province or his or her delegate from establishing a program to authorize the recovery of the costs of a young person's counsel from the young person or the parents of the young person. The costs may be recovered only after the proceedings are completed and the time allowed for the taking of an appeal has expired or, if an appeal is taken, all proceedings in respect of the appeal have been completed.

**Exception for persons over the age of twenty**

(11) Subsections (4) to (9) do not apply to a person who is alleged to have committed an offence while a young person, if the person has attained the age of twenty years at the time of his or her first appearance before a youth justice court in respect of the offence; however, this does not restrict any rights that a person has under the law applicable to adults.

*Notices to Parents*

**Notice in case of arrest or detention**

**26.** (1) Subject to subsection (4), if a young person is arrested and detained in custody pending his or her appearance in court, the officer in charge at the time the young person is detained shall, as soon as possible, give or cause to be given to a parent of the young person, orally or in writing, notice of the arrest stating the place of detention and the reason for the arrest.

**Notice in other cases**

(2) Subject to subsection (4), if a summons or an appearance notice is issued in respect of a young

person, the person who issued the summons or appearance notice, or, if a young person is released on giving a promise to appear or entering into an undertaking or recognizance, the officer in charge, shall, as soon as possible, give or cause to be given to a parent of the young person notice in writing of the summons, appearance notice, promise to appear, undertaking or recognizance.

**Notice to parent in case of ticket**
(3) Subject to subsection (4), a person who serves a ticket under the *Contraventions Act* on a young person, other than a ticket served for a contravention relating to parking a vehicle, shall, as soon as possible, give or cause to be given notice in writing of the ticket to a parent of the young person.

**Notice to relative or other adult**
(4) If the whereabouts of the parents of a young person are not known or it appears that no parent is available, a notice under this section may be given to an adult relative of the young person who is known to the young person and is likely to assist the young person or, if no such adult relative is available, to any other adult who is known to the young person and is likely to assist the young person and who the person giving the notice considers appropriate.

**Notice on direction of youth justice court judge or justice**
(5) If doubt exists as to the person to whom a notice under this section should be given, a youth justice court judge or, if a youth justice court judge is, having regard to the circumstances, not reasonably available, a justice may give directions as to the person to whom the notice should be given, and a notice given in accordance with those directions is sufficient notice for the purposes of this section.

**Contents of notice**
(6) Any notice under this section shall, in addition to any other requirements under this section, include
(*a*) the name of the young person in respect of whom it is given;
(*b*) the charge against the young person and, except in the case of a notice of a ticket served under the *Contraventions Act*, the time and place of appearance; and
(*c*) a statement that the young person has the right to be represented by counsel.

**Notice of ticket under *Contraventions Act***
(7) A notice under subsection (3) shall include a copy of the ticket.

**Service of notice**
(8) Subject to subsections (10) and (11), a notice under this section that is given in writing may be served personally or be sent by confirmed delivery service.

**Proceedings not invalid**
(9) Subject to subsections (10) and (11), failure to give a notice in accordance with this section does not affect the validity of proceedings under this Act.

**Exception**
(10) Failure to give a notice under subsection (2) in accordance with this section in any case renders invalid any subsequent proceedings under this Act relating to the case unless
(*a*) a parent of the young person attends court with the young person; or
(*b*) a youth justice court judge or a justice before whom proceedings are held against the young person
(i) adjourns the proceedings and orders that the notice be given in the manner and to the persons that the judge or justice directs, or
(ii) dispenses with the notice if the judge or justice is of the opinion that, having regard to the circumstances, the notice may be dispensed with.

**Where notice is not served**
(11) Where there has been a failure to give a notice under subsection (1) or (3) in accordance with this section and none of the persons to whom the notice may be given attends court with the young person, a youth justice court judge or a justice before whom proceedings are held against the young person may
(*a*) adjourn the proceedings and order that the notice be given in the manner and to the persons that the judge or justice directs, or
(*b*) dispense with the notice if the judge or justice is of the opinion that, having regard to the circumstances, the notice may be dispensed with.

**Exception for persons over the age of twenty**
(12) This section does not apply to a person who is alleged to have committed an offence while a young person, if the person has attained the age of twenty years at the time of his or her first appearance before a youth justice court in respect of the offence.

**Order requiring attendance of parent**
27. (1) If a parent does not attend proceedings held before a youth justice court in respect of a young person, the court may, if in its opinion the presence of the parent is necessary or in the best interests of the young person, by order in writing require the parent to attend at any stage of the proceedings.

**No order in ticket proceedings**
(2) Subsection (1) does not apply in proceedings commenced by filing a ticket under the *Contraventions Act*.

**Service of order**
(3) A copy of the order shall be served by a peace officer or by a person designated by a youth justice court by delivering it personally to the parent to whom it is directed, unless the youth justice court authorizes service by confirmed delivery service.

**Failure to attend**
(4) A parent who is ordered to attend a youth justice court under subsection (1) and who fails without reasonable excuse, the proof of which lies on the parent, to comply with the order
(*a*) is guilty of contempt of court;
(*b*) may be dealt with summarily by the court; and
(*c*) is liable to the punishment provided for in the *Criminal Code* for a summary conviction offence.

**Warrant to arrest parent**
(5) If a parent who is ordered to attend a youth justice court under subsection (1) does not attend when required by the order or fails to remain in attendance as required and it is proved that a copy of the order was served on the parent, a youth justice court may issue a warrant to compel the attendance of the parent.

*Detention Before Sentencing*

**Application of Part XVI of the *Criminal Code***
**28.** Except to the extent that they are inconsistent with or excluded by this Act, the provisions of Part XVI of the *Criminal Code* apply to the detention and release of young persons under this Act.

**Detention as social measure prohibited**
**29.** (1) A youth justice court judge or a justice shall not detain a young person in custody prior to being sentenced as a substitute for appropriate child protection, mental health or other social measures.

**Detention presumed unnecessary**
(2) In considering whether the detention of a young person is necessary for the protection or safety of the public under paragraph 515(10)(*b*) of the *Criminal Code*, a youth justice court or a justice shall presume that detention is not necessary under that paragraph if the young person could not, on conviction, be committed to custody on the grounds set out in subsection 38(1), unless there is a substantial likelihood that the young person will, if released from custody, commit a criminal offence or interfere with the administration of justice.

**Designated place of temporary detention**
**30.** (1) Subject to subsection (7), a young person who is arrested and detained prior to being sentenced, or who is detained in accordance with a warrant issued under subsection 59(6), shall be detained in any place of temporary detention that may be designated by the lieutenant governor in council of the province or his or her delegate or in a place within a class of places so designated.

**Exception**
(2) A young person who is detained in a place of temporary detention under subsection (1) may, in the course of being transferred from that place to the court or from the court to that place, be held under the supervision and control of a peace officer.

**Detention separate from adults**
(3) A young person referred to in subsection (1) shall be held separate and apart from any adult who is detained or held in custody unless a youth justice court judge or a justice is satisfied that, having regard to the best interests of the young person,
(*a*) the young person cannot, having regard to his or her own safety or the safety of others, be detained in a place of detention for young persons; or
(*b*) no place of detention for young persons is available within a reasonable distance.

**Transfer to adult facility**
(4) When a young person is detained under subsection (1), the youth justice court may, on application of the provincial director made at any time after the young person attains the age of eighteen years, after giving the young person an opportunity to be heard, authorize the provincial director to direct, despite subsection (3), that the young person be temporarily detained in a provincial correctional facility for adults, if the court considers it to be in the best interests of the young person or in the public interest.

**When young person is twenty years old or older**
(5) When a young person is twenty years old or older at the time his or her temporary detention under subsection (1) begins, the young person shall, despite subsection (3), be temporarily detained in a provincial correctional facility for adults.

**Transfer by provincial director**
(6) A young person who is detained in custody under subsection (1) may, during the period of detention, be transferred by the provincial director from one place of temporary detention to another.

**Exception relating to temporary detention**
(7) Subsections (1) and (3) do not apply in respect of any temporary restraint of a young person under the supervision and control of a peace officer after arrest, but a young person who is so restrained shall be transferred to a place of temporary detention referred to in subsection (1) as soon as is practicable, and in no case later than the first reasonable opportunity after the appearance of the young person before a youth justice court judge or a justice under section 503 of the *Criminal Code*.

**Authorization of provincial authority for detention**
(8) In any province for which the lieutenant governor in council has designated a person or a group of persons whose authorization is required, either in all circumstances or in circumstances specified by the lieutenant governor in council, before a young person who has been arrested may be detained in accordance with this section, no young person shall be so detained unless the authorization is obtained.

**Determination by provincial authority of place of detention**
(9) In any province for which the lieutenant governor in council has designated a person or a

group of persons who may determine the place where a young person who has been arrested may be detained in accordance with this section, no young person may be so detained in a place other than the one so determined.

**Placement of young person in care of responsible person**

**31.** (1) A young person who has been arrested may be placed in the care of a responsible person, including the director or an employee of a program for young persons, instead of being detained in custody if a youth justice court or a justice is satisfied that

(*a*) the young person would, but for this subsection, be detained in custody under section 515 of the *Criminal Code*;

(*b*) the person is willing and able to take care of and exercise control over the young person; and

(*c*) the young person is willing to be placed in the care of that person.

**Inquiry as to availability of a responsible person**

(2) If a young person would, in the absence of a responsible person, be detained in custody, the youth justice court or the justice shall inquire as to the availability of a responsible person and whether the young person is willing to be placed in that person's care.

**Condition of placement**

(3) A young person shall not be placed in the care of a person under subsection (1) unless

(*a*) that person undertakes in writing to take care of and to be responsible for the attendance of the young person in court when required and to comply with any other conditions that the youth justice court judge or the justice may specify; and

(*b*) the young person undertakes in writing to comply with the arrangement and to comply with any other conditions that the youth justice court judge or the justice may specify.

**Removing young person from care**

(4) A young person, a person in whose care a young person has been placed or any other person may, by application in writing to a youth justice court judge or a justice, apply for an order under subsection (5) if

(*a*) the person in whose care the young person has been placed is no longer willing or able to take care of or exercise control over the young person; or

(*b*) it is, for any other reason, no longer appropriate that the young person remain in the care of the person with whom he or she has been placed.

**Order**

(5) When a youth justice court judge or a justice is satisfied that a young person should not remain in the custody of the person in whose care he or she was placed under subsection (1), the judge or justice shall

(*a*) make an order relieving the person and the young person of the obligations undertaken under subsection (3); and

(*b*) issue a warrant for the arrest of the young person.

**Effect of arrest**

(6) If a young person is arrested in accordance with a warrant issued under paragraph (5)(*b*), the young person shall be taken before a youth justice court judge or a justice without delay and dealt with under section 515 of the *Criminal Code*, unless the young person can be placed in the care of another responsible person under this section.

*Appearance*

**Appearance before judge or justice**

**32.** (1) A young person against whom an information is laid must first appear before a youth justice court judge or a justice, and the judge or justice shall

(*a*) cause the information to be read to the young person;

(*b*) if the young person is not represented by counsel, inform the young person of the right to retain and instruct counsel;

(*c*) if notified under subsection 63(2), inform the young person that the youth justice court might, if the young person is found guilty, order that an adult sentence be imposed; and

(*d*) if the young person is charged with having, after attaining the age of fourteen years, committed an offence set out in paragraph (*a*) of the definition "presumptive offence" in subsection 2(1), inform the young person in the following words of the consequences of being charged with such an offence:

> An adult sentence will be imposed if you are found guilty unless the court orders that you are not liable to an adult sentence and that a youth sentence must be imposed.

**Waiver**

(2) A young person may waive the requirements of subsection (1) if the young person is represented by counsel and counsel advises the court that the young person has been informed of that provision.

**Young person not represented by counsel**

(3) When a young person is not represented by counsel, before accepting a plea the youth justice court shall

(*a*) satisfy itself that the young person understands the charge;

(*b*) if the young person is liable to an adult sentence, explain to the young person the consequences of being liable to an adult sentence and the procedure by which the young person may apply for an order that a youth sentence be imposed; and

(*c*) explain that the young person may plead guilty or not guilty to the charge or, if the young person is liable to an adult sentence, that the young person may elect to be tried by a youth justice court judge without a jury and without having a preliminary inquiry, or to have a preliminary inquiry and be tried by a judge without a jury, or to have a preliminary inquiry and be tried by a court composed of a judge and jury.

**If youth justice court not satisfied**
(4) If the youth justice court is not satisfied that a young person understands the charge, the court shall, unless the young person must be put to his or her election under subsection 67(1), enter a plea of not guilty on behalf of the young person and proceed with the trial in accordance with subsection 35(2).

**If youth justice court not satisfied**
(5) If the youth justice court is not satisfied that a young person understands the matters set out in subsection (3), the court shall direct that the young person be represented by counsel.

*Release from or Detention in Custody*

**Application for release from or detention in custody**
33. (1) If an order is made under section 515 of the *Criminal Code* in respect of a young person by a justice who is not a youth justice court judge, an application may, at any time after the order is made, be made to a youth justice court for the release from or detention in custody of the young person, as the case may be, and the youth justice court shall hear the matter as an original application.

**Notice to prosecutor**
(2) An application under subsection (1) for release from custody shall not be heard unless the young person has given the prosecutor at least two clear days notice in writing of the application.

**Notice to young person**
(3) An application under subsection (1) for detention in custody shall not be heard unless the prosecutor has given the young person at least two clear days notice in writing of the application.

**Waiver of notice**
(4) The requirement for notice under subsection (2) or (3) may be waived by the prosecutor or by the young person or his or her counsel, as the case may be.

**Application for review under section 520 or 521 of *Criminal Code***
(5) An application under section 520 or 521 of the *Criminal Code* for a review of an order made in respect of a young person by a youth justice court judge who is a judge of a superior court shall be made to a judge or the court of appeal.

**No review**
(6) No application may be made under section 520 or 521 of the *Criminal Code* for a review of an order made in respect of a young person by a justice who is not a youth justice court judge.

**Interim release by youth justice court judge only**
(7) If a young person against whom proceedings have been taken under this Act is charged with an offence referred to in section 522 of the *Criminal Code*, a youth justice court judge, but no other court, judge or justice, may release the young person from custody under that section.

**Review by court of appeal**
(8) A decision made by a youth justice court judge under subsection (7) may be reviewed in accordance with section 680 of the *Criminal Code* and that section applies, with any modifications that the circumstances require, to any decision so made.

*Medical and Psychological Reports*

**Medical or psychological assessment**
34. (1) A youth justice court may, at any stage of proceedings against a young person, by order require that the young person be assessed by a qualified person who is required to report the results in writing to the court,
(*a*) with the consent of the young person and the prosecutor; or
(*b*) on its own motion or on application of the young person or the prosecutor, if the court believes a medical, psychological or psychiatric report in respect of the young person is necessary for a purpose mentioned in paragraphs (2)(*a*) to (*h*) and
(i) the court has reasonable grounds to believe that the young person may be suffering from a physical or mental illness or disorder, a psychological disorder, an emotional disturbance, a learning disability or a mental disability,
(ii) the young person's history indicates a pattern of repeated findings of guilt under this Act or the *Young Offenders Act*, chapter Y-1 of the Revised Statutes of Canada, 1985, or
(iii) the young person is alleged to have committed a serious violent offence.

**Purpose of assessment**
(2) A youth justice court may make an order under subsection (1) in respect of a young person for the purpose of
(*a*) considering an application under section 33;
(*b*) making its decision on an application heard under section 71;
(*c*) making or reviewing a youth sentence;
(*d*) considering an application under subsection 103(1);
(*e*) setting conditions under subsection 104(1);
(*f*) making an order under subsection 108(2);
(*g*) authorizing disclosure under subsection 126(1); or
(*h*) making an order under paragraph 41(2)(*q*).

**Custody for assessment**
(3) Subject to subsections (4) and (6), for the purpose of an assessment under this section, a youth justice court may remand a young person to any custody that it directs for a period not exceeding thirty days.

**Presumption against custodial remand**
(4) A young person shall not be remanded in custody in accordance with an order made under subsection (1) unless

(a) the youth justice court is satisfied that
(i) on the evidence custody is necessary to conduct an assessment of the young person, or
(ii) on the evidence of a qualified person detention of the young person in custody is desirable to conduct the assessment of the young person, and the young person consents to custody; or
(b) the young person is required to be detained in custody in respect of any other matter or by virtue of any provision of the *Criminal Code*.

**Report of qualified person in writing**
(5) For the purposes of paragraph (4)(a), if the prosecutor and the young person agree, evidence of a qualified person may be received in the form of a report in writing.

**Application to vary assessment order if circumstances change**
(6) A youth justice court may, at any time while an order made under subsection (1) is in force, on cause being shown, vary the terms and conditions specified in the order in any manner that the court considers appropriate in the circumstances.

**Disclosure of report**
(7) When a youth justice court receives a report made in respect of a young person under subsection (1),
(a) the court shall, subject to subsection (9), cause a copy of the report to be given to
(i) the young person,
(ii) any parent of the young person who is in attendance at the proceedings against the young person,
(iii) any counsel representing the young person, and
(iv) the prosecutor; and
(b) the court may cause a copy of the report to be given to a parent of the young person who is not in attendance at the proceedings if the parent is, in the opinion of the court, taking an active interest in the proceedings.

**Cross-examination**
(8) When a report is made in respect of a young person under subsection (1), the young person, his or her counsel or the adult assisting the young person under subsection 25(7) and the prosecutor shall, subject to subsection (9), on application to the youth justice court, be given an opportunity to cross-examine the person who made the report.

**Non-disclosure in certain cases**
(9) A youth justice court shall withhold all or part of a report made in respect of a young person under subsection (1) from a private prosecutor, if disclosure of the report or part, in the opinion of the court, is not necessary for the prosecution of the case and might be prejudicial to the young person.

**Non-disclosure in certain cases**
(10) A youth justice court shall withhold all or part of a report made in respect of a young person under subsection (1) from the young person, the young person's parents or a private prosecutor if the court is satisfied, on the basis of the report or evidence given in the absence of the young person, parents or private prosecutor by the person who made the report, that disclosure of the report or part would seriously impair the treatment or recovery of the young person, or would be likely to endanger the life or safety of, or result in serious psychological harm to, another person.

**Exception—interests of justice**
(11) Despite subsection (10), the youth justice court may release all or part of the report to the young person, the young person's parents or the private prosecutor if the court is of the opinion that the interests of justice make disclosure essential.

**Report to be part of record**
(12) A report made under subsection (1) forms part of the record of the case in respect of which it was requested.

**Disclosure by qualified person**
(13) Despite any other provision of this Act, a qualified person who is of the opinion that a young person held in detention or committed to custody is likely to endanger his or her own life or safety or to endanger the life of, or cause bodily harm to, another person may immediately so advise any person who has the care and custody of the young person whether or not the same information is contained in a report made under subsection (1).

**Definition of "qualified person"**
(14) In this section, "qualified person" means a person duly qualified by provincial law to practice medicine or psychiatry or to carry out psychological examinations or assessments, as the circumstances require, or, if no such law exists, a person who is, in the opinion of the youth justice court, so qualified, and includes a person or a member of a class of persons designated by the lieutenant governor in council of a province or his or her delegate.

***Adjudication***

**When young person pleads guilty**
**35.** (1) If a young person pleads guilty to an offence charged against the young person and the youth justice court is satisfied that the facts support the charge, the court shall find the young person guilty of the offence.

**When young person pleads not guilty**
(2) If a young person charged with an offence pleads not guilty to the offence or pleads guilty but the youth justice court is not satisfied that the facts support the charge, the court shall proceed with the trial and shall, after considering the matter, find the young person guilty or not guilty or make an order dismissing the charge, as the case may be.

***Appeals***

**Appeals**
**36.** (1) An appeal in respect of an indictable offence or an offence that the Attorney General elects to proceed with as an indictable offence lies under this Act in accordance with Part XXI of the *Criminal Code*, which Part applies with any modifications that the circumstances require.

**Appeals for contempt of court**
(2) A finding of guilt under section 15 for contempt of court or a sentence imposed in respect of the finding may be appealed as if the finding were a conviction or the sentence were a sentence in a prosecution by indictment.

**Appeal**
(3) Section 10 of the *Criminal Code* applies if a person is convicted of contempt of court under subsection 27(4).

**Appeals to be heard together**
(4) A judicial determination under subsection 41(8), or an order under subsection 72(1), 75(3) or 76(1), may be appealed as part of the sentence and, unless the court to which the appeal is taken otherwise orders, if more than one of these is appealed they must be part of the same appeal proceeding.

**Appeals for summary conviction offences**
(5) An appeal in respect of an offence punishable on summary conviction or an offence that the Attorney General elects to proceed with as an offence punishable on summary conviction lies under this Act in accordance with Part XXVII of the *Criminal Code*, which Part applies with any modifications that the circumstances require.

**Appeals where offences are tried jointly**
(6) An appeal in respect of one or more indictable offences and one or more summary conviction offences that are tried jointly or in respect of which youth sentences are jointly imposed lies under this Act in accordance with Part XXI of the *Criminal Code*, which Part applies with any modifications that the circumstances require.

**Deemed election**
(7) For the purpose of appeals under this Act, if no election is made in respect of an offence that may be prosecuted by indictment or proceeded with by way of summary conviction, the Attorney General is deemed to have elected to proceed with the offences as an offence punishable on summary conviction.

**If the youth justice court is a superior court**
(8) In any province where the youth justice court is a superior court, an appeal under subsection (5) shall be made to the court of appeal of the province.

**Appeal to the Supreme Court of Canada**
(9) No appeal lies under subsection (1) from a judgment of the court of appeal in respect of a finding of guilt or an order dismissing an information to the Supreme Court of Canada unless leave to appeal is granted by the Supreme Court of Canada.

**No appeal from youth sentence on review**
(10) No appeal lies from a youth sentence under section 59 or any of sections 93 to 95.

## PART 4
## SENTENCING

### *Purpose and Principles*

**Purpose**
37. (1) The purpose of sentencing under section 41 is to contribute to the protection of society by holding a young person accountable for an offence through the imposition of just sanctions that have meaningful consequences for the young person and that promote his or her rehabilitation and reintegration into society.

**Sentencing principles**
(2) A youth justice court that imposes a youth sentence on a young person shall determine the sentence in accordance with the following principles:
(*a*) the sentence must not result in a punishment that is greater than the punishment that would be appropriate for an adult who has been convicted of the same offence committed in similar circumstances;
(*b*) the sentence must be similar to the sentences imposed on young persons found guilty of the same offence committed in similar circumstances;
(*c*) the sentence must be proportionate to the seriousness of the offence and the degree of responsibility of the young person for that offence; and
(*d*) subject to paragraph (*c*), the sentence must
(i) be the least restrictive sentence that is capable of achieving the purpose set out in subsection (1),
(ii) be the one that is most likely to rehabilitate the young person and reintegrate him or her into society, and
(iii) promote a sense of responsibility in the young person, and an acknowledgement of the harm done to victims and the community.

**Factors to be considered**
(3) In determining a youth sentence, the youth justice court shall take into account
(*a*) the degree of participation by the young person in the commission of the offence;
(*b*) the harm done to victims and whether it was intentional or reasonably foreseeable;
(*c*) any reparation made by the young person to the victim or the community;
(*d*) the time spent in detention by the young person as a result of the offence;
(*e*) the previous findings of guilt of the young person; and
(*f*) any other aggravating and mitigating circumstances related to the young person and the offence that are relevant to the purpose and principles set out in this section.

**Restriction on committal to custody**
38. (1) A youth justice court shall not commit a young person to custody under section 41 unless
(*a*) the young person has committed a violent offence;
(*b*) the young person has failed to comply with previous non-custodial sentences;

(*c*) the young person has committed an indictable offence for which an adult could be sentenced to imprisonment for more than two years and has a history that indicates a pattern of findings of guilt under this Act or the *Young Offenders Act*, chapter Y-1 of the Revised Statutes of Canada, 1985; or

(*d*) the circumstances of the offence make the imposition of a non-custodial sentence inconsistent with the purpose and principles set out in section 37.

**Alternatives to custody**
(2) A youth justice court shall not impose a custodial sentence under section 41 unless the court has considered all alternatives to custody raised at the sentencing hearing that are reasonable in the circumstances, and determined that there is not a reasonable alternative, or combination of alternatives, that is in accordance with the purpose and principles set out in section 37.

**Factors to be considered**
(3) In determining whether there is a reasonable alternative to custody, a youth justice court shall consider submissions relating to

(*a*) the alternatives to custody that are available;

(*b*) the likelihood that the young person will comply with a non-custodial sentence, as evidenced by his or her compliance with previous non-custodial sentences; and

(*c*) the alternatives to custody that have been used in respect of young persons for similar offences committed in similar circumstances.

**Imposition of same sentence**
(4) Evidence that a particular non-custodial sentence has been imposed previously on a young person does not preclude a youth justice court from imposing the same non-custodial sentence for another offence.

**Custody as social measure prohibited**
(5) A youth justice court shall not use custody as a substitute for appropriate child protection, mental health or other social measures.

**Pre-sentence report**
(6) Before imposing a youth sentence under paragraph 41(2)(*n*), (*p*) or (*q*), a youth justice court shall consider a pre-sentence report and any sentencing proposal made by the young person or his or her counsel.

**Report dispensed with**
(7) A youth justice court may, with the consent of the prosecutor and the young person or his or her counsel, dispense with a pre-sentence report if the court is satisfied that the report is not necessary.

**Length of custody**
(8) In determining the length of a youth sentence that includes a custodial portion, a youth justice court shall be guided by the purpose and principles set out in section 37, and shall not take into consideration the fact that the supervision portion of the sentence may not be served in custody and that the sentence may be reviewed by the court under section 93.

**Reasons**
(9) If a youth justice court imposes a youth sentence that includes a custodial portion, the court shall state the reasons why it has determined that a non-custodial sentence is not adequate to achieve the purpose set out in subsection 37(1).

***Pre-sentence Report***

**Pre-sentence report**
**39.** (1) If a youth justice court considers it advisable before imposing sentence on a young person found guilty of an offence, it may, and if a youth justice court is required under this Act to consider a pre-sentence report before making an order or a sentence in respect of a young person, it shall, require the provincial director to cause to be prepared a pre-sentence report in respect of the young person and to submit the report to the court.

**Contents of report**
(2) A pre-sentence report made in respect of a young person shall, subject to subsection (3), be in writing and shall include the following, to the extent that it is relevant to the purpose and principles of sentencing set out in section 37 and to the criteria set out in section 38:

(*a*) the results of an interview with the young person and, if reasonably possible, the parents of the young person and, if appropriate and reasonably possible, members of the young person's extended family;

(*b*) the results of an interview with the victim in the case, if applicable and reasonably possible;

(*c*) the recommendations resulting from any conference;

(*d*) any information that is applicable to the case, including

(i) the age, maturity, character, behaviour and attitude of the young person and his or her willingness to make amends,

(ii) any plans put forward by the young person to change his or her conduct or to participate in activities or undertake measures to improve himself or herself,

(iii) subject to subsection 118(2), the history of previous findings of delinquency under the *Juvenile Delinquents Act*, chapter J-3 of the Revised Statutes of Canada, 1970, or previous findings of guilt for offences under the *Young Offenders Act*, chapter Y-1 of the Revised Statutes of Canada, 1985, or under this or any other Act of Parliament or any regulation made under it or under an Act of the legislature of a province or any regulation made under it or a by-law or ordinance of a municipality, the history of community or other services rendered to the young person with respect to those findings and the response of the young person to previous sentences or dispositions and to services rendered to him or her,

(iv) subject to subsection 118(2), the history of alternative measures under the *Young Offenders Act*, chapter Y-1 of the Revised Statutes of Canada, 1985, or extrajudicial sanctions used to deal with the young person and the response of the young person to those measures or sanctions,
(v) the availability and appropriateness of community services and facilities for young persons and the willingness of the young person to avail himself or herself of those services or facilities,
(vi) the relationship between the young person and the young person's parents and the degree of control and influence of the parents over the young person and, if appropriate and reasonably possible, the relationship between the young person and the young person's extended family and the degree of control and influence of the young person's extended family over the young person, and
(vii) the school attendance and performance record and the employment record of the young person;
(*e*) any information that may assist the court in determining under subsection 38(2) whether there is an alternative to custody; and
(*f*) any information that the provincial director considers relevant, including any recommendation that the provincial director considers appropriate.

**Oral report with leave**
(3) If a pre-sentence report cannot reasonably be committed to writing, it may, with leave of the youth justice court, be submitted orally in court.

**Report forms part of record**
(4) A pre-sentence report shall form part of the record of the case in respect of which it was requested.

**Copies of pre-sentence report**
(5) If a pre-sentence report made in respect of a young person is submitted to a youth justice court in writing, the court
(*a*) shall, subject to subsection (7), cause a copy of the report to be given to
(i) the young person,
(ii) any parent of the young person who is in attendance at the proceedings against the young person,
(iii) any counsel representing the young person, and
(iv) the prosecutor; and
(*b*) may cause a copy of the report to be given to a parent of the young person who is not in attendance at the proceedings if the parent is, in the opinion of the court, taking an active interest in the proceedings.

**Cross-examination**
(6) If a pre-sentence report made in respect of a young person is submitted to a youth justice court, the young person, his or her counsel or the adult assisting the young person under subsection 25(7) and the prosecutor shall, subject to subsection (7), on application to the court, be given the opportunity to cross-examine the person who made the report.

**Report may be withheld from private prosecutor**
(7) If a pre-sentence report made in respect of a young person is submitted to a youth justice court, the court may, when the prosecutor is a private prosecutor and disclosure of all or part of the report to the prosecutor might, in the opinion of the court, be prejudicial to the young person and is not, in the opinion of the court, necessary for the prosecution of the case against the young person,
(*a*) withhold the report or part from the prosecutor, if the report is submitted in writing; or
(*b*) exclude the prosecutor from the court during the submission of the report or part, if the report is submitted orally in court.

**Report disclosed to other persons**
(8) If a pre-sentence report made in respect of a young person is submitted to a youth justice court, the court
(*a*) shall, on request, cause a copy or a transcript of the report to be supplied to
(i) any court that is dealing with matters relating to the young person, and
(ii) any youth worker to whom the young person's case has been assigned; and
(*b*) may, on request, cause a copy or a transcript of all or part of the report to be supplied to any person not otherwise authorized under this section to receive a copy or a transcript of the report if, in the opinion of the court, the person has a valid interest in the proceedings.

**Disclosure by the provincial director**
(9) A provincial director who submits a pre-sentence report made in respect of a young person to a youth justice court may make all or part of the report available to any person in whose custody or under whose supervision the young person is placed or to any other person who is directly assisting in the care or treatment of the young person.

**Inadmissibility of statements**
(10) No statement made by a young person in the course of the preparation of a pre-sentence report in respect of the young person is admissible in evidence against any young person in civil or criminal proceedings except those under section 41, 59 or 71 or any of sections 93 to 95.

*Youth Sentences*

**Recommendation of conference**
**40**. When a youth justice court finds a young person guilty of an offence, the court may refer the matter to a conference for recommendations to the court on an appropriate youth sentence.

**Considerations as to youth sentence**
**41**. (1) A youth justice court shall, before imposing a youth sentence, consider any recommendations submitted under section 40, any pre-sentence

report, any representations made by the parties to the proceedings or their counsel or agents and by the parents of the young person, and any other relevant information before the court.

**Youth sentence**

(2) When a youth justice court finds a young person guilty of an offence and is imposing a youth sentence, the court shall, subject to this section, impose any one of the following sanctions or any number of them that are not inconsistent with each other and, if the offence is first degree murder or second degree murder within the meaning of section 231 of the *Criminal Code*, the court shall impose a sanction set out in paragraph (*p*) or subparagraph (*q*)(ii) or (iii) and may impose any other of the sanctions set out in this subsection that the court considers appropriate:

(*a*) reprimand the young person;

(*b*) by order direct that the young person be discharged absolutely, if the court considers it to be in the best interests of the young person and not contrary to the public interest;

(*c*) by order direct that the young person be discharged on any conditions that the court considers appropriate and be required to report to and be supervised by the provincial director;

(*d*) impose on the young person a fine not exceeding $1,000 to be paid at the time and on the terms that the court may fix;

(*e*) order the young person to pay any other person at the times and on the terms that the court may fix an amount by way of compensation for loss of or damage to property or for loss of income or support, or an amount for, in the Province of Quebec, pre-trial pecuniary loss or, in any other province, special damages, for personal injury arising from the commission of the offence if the value is readily ascertainable, but no order shall be made for other damages in the Province of Quebec or for general damages in any other province;

(*f*) order the young person to make restitution to any other person of any property obtained by the young person as a result of the commission of the offence within the time that the court may fix, if the property is owned by the other person or was, at the time of the offence, in his or her lawful possession;

(*g*) if property obtained as a result of the commission of the offence has been sold to an innocent purchaser, where restitution of the property to its owner or any other person has been made or ordered, order the young person to pay the purchaser, at the time and on the terms that the court may fix, an amount not exceeding the amount paid by the purchaser for the property;

(*h*) subject to section 53, order the young person to compensate any person in kind or by way of personal services at the time and on the terms that the court may fix for any loss, damage or injury suffered by that person in respect of which an order may be made under paragraph (*e*) or (*g*);

(*i*) subject to section 53, order the young person to perform a community service at the time and on the terms that the court may fix, and to report to and be supervised by the provincial director or a person designated by the youth justice court;

(*j*) subject to section 50, make any order of prohibition, seizure or forfeiture that may be imposed under any Act of Parliament or any regulation made under it if an accused is found guilty or convicted of that offence, other than an order under section 161 of the *Criminal Code*;

(*k*) place the young person on probation in accordance with section 54 for a specified period not exceeding two years;

(*l*) subject to subsection (3), order the young person into an intensive support and supervision program as directed by the provincial director;

(*m*) subject to subsection (3) and section 53, order the young person to attend a facility offering a program approved by the provincial director, at the times and on the terms that the court may fix, for a maximum of two hundred and forty hours, over a period not exceeding six months;

(*n*) make a custody and supervision order with respect to the young person, ordering that a period be served in custody and that a second period—which is one half as long as the first—be served, subject to sections 96 and 97, under supervision in the community subject to conditions, the total of the periods not to exceed two years from the date of the coming into force of the order or, if the young person is found guilty of an offence for which the punishment provided by the *Criminal Code* or any other Act of Parliament is imprisonment for life, three years from the date of coming into force of the order;

(*o*) subject to subsection (5), make a deferred custody and supervision order that is for a specified period not exceeding six months, subject to any conditions set out in section 54 that the court considers appropriate;

(*p*) order the young person to serve a sentence not to exceed

(i) in the case of first degree murder, ten years comprised of

(A) a committal to custody, to be served continuously, for a period that must not, subject to subsection 103(1), exceed six years from the date of committal, and

(B) a placement under conditional supervision to be served in the community in accordance with section 104, and

(ii) in the case of second degree murder, seven years comprised of

(A) a committal to custody, to be served continuously, for a period that must not, subject to subsection 103(1), exceed four years from the date of committal, and

(B) a placement under conditional supervision to be served in the community in accordance with section 104;

(*q*) subject to subsection (7), make an intensive rehabilitative custody and supervision order in respect of the young person

(i) that is for a specified period that must not exceed
(A) two years from the date of committal, or
(B) if the young person is found guilty of an offence for which the punishment provided by the *Criminal Code* or any other Act of Parliament is imprisonment for life, three years from the date of committal,
and that orders the young person to be committed into a continuous period of intensive rehabilitative custody for the first portion of the sentence and, subject to subsection 103(1), to serve the remainder under conditional supervision in the community in accordance with section 104,
(ii) that is for a specified period that must not exceed, in the case of first degree murder, ten years from the date of committal, comprising
(A) a committal to intensive rehabilitative custody, to be served continuously, for a period that must not exceed six years from the date of committal, and
(B) subject to subsection 103(1), a placement under conditional supervision to be served in the community in accordance with section 104, and
(iii) that is for a specified period that must not exceed, in the case of second degree murder, seven years from the date of committal, comprising
(A) a committal to intensive rehabilitative custody, to be served continuously, for a period that must not exceed four years from the date of committal, and
(B) subject to subsection 103(1), a placement under conditional supervision to be served in the community in accordance with section 104; and
(*r*) impose on the young person any other reasonable and ancillary conditions that the court considers advisable and in the best interests of the young person and the public.

**Agreement of provincial director**
(3) A youth justice court may make an order under paragraph (2)(*l*) or (*m*) only with the agreement of the provincial director.

**Youth justice court statement**
(4) When the youth justice court makes a custody and supervision order with respect to a young person under paragraph (2)(*n*), the court shall state the following with respect to that order:

You are ordered to serve (*state the number of days or months to be served*) in custody, to be followed by (*state one-half of the number of days or months stated above*) to be served under supervision in the community subject to conditions.

If you breach any of the conditions while you are under supervision in the community, you may be brought back into custody and required to serve the rest of the second period in custody as well.

You should also be aware that, under other provisions of the *Youth Criminal Justice Act*, a court could require you to serve the second period in custody as well.

**Deferred custody and supervision order**
(5) The court may make a deferred custody and supervision order under paragraph (2)(*o*) if
(*a*) the young person is found guilty of a non-violent offence; and
(*b*) it is consistent with the purpose and principles set out in section 37 and the criteria set out in section 38.

**Termination of order**
(6) If a young person complies with the conditions of a deferred custody and supervision order made under paragraph (2)(*o*), or any conditions as amended by section 56, for the entire period that the order is in force, the order is terminated.

**Intensive rehabilitative custody and supervision order**
(7) A youth justice court may make an intensive rehabilitative custody and supervision order under paragraph (2)(*q*) in respect of a young person only if
(*a*) the young person has been found guilty of a presumptive offence;
(*b*) the young person is suffering from a mental illness or disorder, a psychological disorder or an emotional disturbance;
(*c*) a plan of treatment and intensive supervision has been developed for the young person, and there are reasonable grounds to believe that the plan might reduce the risk of the young person repeating the offence or committing other presumptive offences; and
(*d*) the provincial director consents to the young person's participation in the program.

**Determination by court**
(8) On application of the Attorney General after a young person is found guilty of an offence, and after giving both parties an opportunity to be heard, the youth justice court may make a judicial determination that the offence is a serious violent offence and endorse the information accordingly.

**Determination is part of sentence**
(9) For the purposes of an appeal in accordance with section 36, a determination under subsection (8) is part of the sentence.

**Inconsistency**
(10) An order may not be made under paragraphs (2)(*k*) to (*m*) in respect of an offence for which a conditional discharge has been granted under paragraph (2)(*c*).

**Coming into force of youth sentence**
(11) A youth sentence or any part of it comes into force on the date on which it is imposed or on any later date that the youth justice court specifies.

**Duration of youth sentence for a single offence**
(12) No youth sentence, other than an order made under paragraph (2)(*j*), (*n*), (*p*) or (*q*), shall continue in force for more than two years and, if the

youth sentence comprises more than one sanction imposed at the same time in respect of the same offence, the combined duration of the sanctions, except in respect of an order made under paragraph (2)(*j*), (*n*), (*p*) or (*q*), shall not exceed two years.

**Duration of youth sentence for different offences**
(13) Subject to subsection (14), if more than one youth sentence is imposed under this section in respect of a young person with respect to different offences, the continuous combined duration of those youth sentences shall not exceed three years, except if one of the offences is first degree murder or second degree murder within the meaning of section 231 of the *Criminal Code*, in which case the continuous combined duration of those youth sentences shall not exceed ten years in the case of first degree murder, or seven years in the case of second degree murder.

**Duration of youth sentences made at different times**
(14) If a youth sentence is imposed in respect of an offence committed by a young person after the commencement of, but before the completion of, any youth sentences imposed on the young person,
(*a*) the duration of the sentence imposed in respect of the subsequent offence shall be determined in accordance with subsections (12) and (13);
(*b*) the sentence may be served consecutively to the sentences imposed in respect of the previous offences; and
(*c*) the combined duration of all the sentences may exceed three years and, if the offence is, or one of the previous offences was,
(i) first degree murder within the meaning of section 231 of the *Criminal Code*, the continuous combined duration of the youth sentences may exceed ten years, or
(ii) second degree murder within the meaning of section 231 of the *Criminal Code*, the continuous combined duration of the youth sentences may exceed seven years.

**Consecutive youth sentences**
(15) A youth justice court that sentences a young person may direct that terms of custody imposed on the young person be served consecutively if the young person
(*a*) is sentenced while under sentence for an offence, and the court imposes a term of custody; or
(*b*) is found guilty of more than one offence, and the court imposes terms of custody for the respective offences.

**Sentence continues when adult**
(16) Subject to sections 88, 91 and 92 of this Act and section 743.5 of the *Criminal Code*, a youth sentence imposed on a young person continues in effect in accordance with its terms after the young person becomes an adult.

**Additional youth sentences**
**42.** Subject to subsection 41(13), if a young person who is subject to a youth sentence imposed under paragraph 41(2)(*n*), (*p*) or (*q*) that has not expired receives an additional youth sentence under one of those paragraphs, the young person is, for the purposes of the *Corrections and Conditional Release Act*, the *Criminal Code*, the *Prisons and Reformatories Act* and this Act, deemed to have been sentenced to one youth sentence commencing at the beginning of the first of those youth sentences to be served and ending on the expiry of the last of them to be served.

**Custodial portion if additional youth sentence**
**43.** Subject to subsection 41(13) and section 45, if an additional youth sentence under paragraph 41(2)(*n*), (*p*) or (*q*) is imposed on a young person on whom a youth sentence had already been imposed under one of those paragraphs that has not expired and the expiry date of the youth sentence that includes the additional youth sentence, as determined in accordance with section 42, is later than the expiry date of the youth sentence that the young person was serving before the additional youth sentence was imposed, the custodial portion of the young person's youth sentence is, from the date the additional sentence is imposed, the total of
(*a*) the unexpired portion of the custodial portion of the youth sentence before the additional youth sentence was imposed, and
(*b*) the relevant period set out in subparagraph (i), (ii) or (iii):
(i) if the additional youth sentence is imposed under paragraph 41(2)(*n*), the period that is two thirds of the period that constitutes the difference between the expiry of the youth sentence as determined in accordance with section 42 and the expiry of the youth sentence that the young person was serving before the additional youth sentence was imposed,
(ii) if the additional youth sentence is a concurrent youth sentence imposed under paragraph 41(2)(*p*) or (*q*), the custodial portion of the youth sentence imposed under that paragraph that extends beyond the expiry date of the custodial portion of the sentence being served before the imposition of the additional sentence, or
(iii) if the additional youth sentence is a consecutive youth sentence imposed under paragraph 41(2)(*p*) or (*q*), the custodial portion of the additional youth sentence imposed under that paragraph.

**Supervision when additional youth sentence extends the period in custody**
**44.** (1) If a young person has begun to serve a portion of a youth sentence in the community subject to conditions under paragraph 41(2)(*n*) or under conditional supervision under paragraph 41(2)(*p*) or (*q*) at the time an additional youth sentence is imposed under one of those paragraphs, and, as a result of the application of section 43, the custodial portion of the young person's youth sentence ends on a day that is later than the day on which the young person received the additional youth sentence, the serving of a

portion of the youth sentence under supervision in the community subject to conditions or under conditional supervision shall become inoperative and the young person shall be committed to custody under paragraph 101(*b*) or 105(*b*) until the end of the extended portion of the youth sentence to be served in custody.

**Supervision when additional youth sentence does not extend the period in custody**
(2) If a youth sentence has been imposed under paragraph 41(2)(*n*), (*p*) or (*q*) on a young person who is under supervision in the community subject to conditions under paragraph 41(2)(*n*) or under conditional supervision under paragraph 41(2)(*p*) or (*q*), and the additional youth sentence would not modify the expiry date of the youth sentence that the young person was serving at the time the additional youth sentence was imposed, the young person may be remanded to the youth custody facility that the provincial director considers appropriate. The provincial director shall review the case and, no later than forty-eight hours after the remand of the young person, shall either refer the case to the youth justice court for a review under section 102 or 108 or release the young person to continue the supervision in the community or the conditional supervision.

**Supervision when youth sentence additional to supervision**
(3) If a youth sentence has been imposed under paragraph 41(2)(*n*), (*p*) or (*q*) on a young person who is under conditional supervision under paragraph 93(19)(*b*) or subsection 95(5), the young person shall be remanded to the youth custody facility that the provincial director considers appropriate. The provincial director shall review the case and, no later than forty-eight hours after the remand of the young person, shall either refer the case to the youth justice court for a review under section 102 or 108 or release the young person to continue the conditional supervision.

**Exception when youth sentence in respect of earlier offence**
45. The total of the custodial portions of a young person's youth sentences shall not exceed six years calculated from the beginning of the youth sentence that is determined in accordance with section 42 if
(*a*) a youth sentence is imposed under paragraph 41(2)(*n*), (*p*) or (*q*) on the young person already serving a youth sentence under one of those paragraphs; and
(*b*) the later youth sentence imposed is in respect of an offence committed before the commencement of the earlier youth sentence.

**Committal to custody deemed continuous**
46. (1) Subject to subsections (2) and (3), a young person who is sentenced under paragraph 41(2)(*n*) is deemed to be committed to continuous custody for the custodial portion of the sentence.

**Intermittent custody**
(2) If the sentence does not exceed ninety days, the youth justice court may order that the custodial portion of the sentence be served intermittently if it is consistent with the purpose and principles set out in section 37.

**Availability of place of intermittent custody**
(3) Before making an order of committal to intermittent custody, the youth justice court shall require the prosecutor to make available to the court for its consideration a report of the provincial director as to the availability of a youth custody facility in which an order of intermittent custody can be enforced and, if the report discloses that no such youth custody facility is available, the court shall not make the order.

**Reasons for the sentence**
47. When a youth justice court imposes a youth sentence, it shall state its reasons for the sentence in the record of the case and shall, on request, give or cause to be given a copy of the sentence and the reasons for the sentence to
(*a*) the young person, the young person's counsel, a parent of the young person, the provincial director and the prosecutor; and
(*b*) in the case of a committal to custody under paragraph 41(2)(*n*), (*p*) or (*q*), the review board.

**Warrant of committal**
48. (1) When a young person is committed to custody, the youth justice court shall issue or cause to be issued a warrant of committal.

**Exception**
(2) A young person who is committed to custody may, in the course of being transferred from custody to the court or from the court to custody, be held under the supervision and control of a peace officer or in any place of temporary detention referred to in subsection 30(1) that the provincial director may specify.

**Subsection 30(3) applies**
(3) Subsection 30(3) applies, with any modifications that the circumstances require, in respect of a person held in a place of temporary detention under subsection (2).

**Application of Part XXIII of *Criminal Code***
49. (1) Subject to section 74, Part XXIII of the *Criminal Code* does not apply in respect of proceedings under this Act except for section 722, subsection 730(2) and sections 748, 748.1 and 749, which provisions apply with any modifications that the circumstances require.

**Section 787 of *Criminal Code* does not apply**
(2) Section 787 of the *Criminal Code* does not apply in respect of proceedings under this Act.

**Mandatory prohibition order**
50. (1) Despite section 41, when a young person is found guilty of an offence referred to in any of paragraphs 109(1)(*a*) to (*d*) of the *Criminal Code*, the youth justice court shall, in addition to imposing a sentence under section 41, make an order prohibiting the young person from possessing any firearm, cross-bow, prohibited weapon,

restricted weapon, prohibited device, ammunition, prohibited ammunition or explosive substance during the period specified in the order as determined in accordance with subsection (2).

**Duration of prohibition order**
(2) An order made under subsection (1) begins on the day on which the order is made and ends not earlier than two years after the young person has completed the custodial portion of the sentence or, if the young person is not subject to custody, after the time the young person is found guilty of the offence.

**Discretionary prohibition order**
(3) Despite section 41, where a young person is found guilty of an offence referred to in paragraph 110(1)(*a*) or (*b*) of the *Criminal Code*, the youth justice court shall, in addition to imposing a sentence under section 41, consider whether it is desirable, in the interests of the safety of the young person or of any other person, to make an order prohibiting the young person from possessing any firearm, cross-bow, prohibited weapon, restricted weapon, prohibited device, ammunition, prohibited ammunition or explosive substance, or all such things, and where the court decides that it is so desirable, the court shall so order.

**Duration of prohibition order**
(4) An order made under subsection (3) against a young person begins on the day on which the order is made and ends not later than two years after the young person has completed the custodial portion of the sentence or, if the young person is not subject to custody, after the time the young person is found guilty of the offence.

**Reasons for the prohibition order**
(5) When a youth justice court makes an order under this section, it shall state its reasons for making the order in the record of the case and shall give or cause to be given a copy of the order and, on request, a transcript or copy of the reasons to the young person against whom the order was made, the counsel and a parent of the young person and the provincial director.

**Reasons**
(6) When the youth justice court does not make an order under subsection (3), or when the youth justice court does make such an order but does not prohibit the possession of everything referred to in that subsection, the youth justice court shall include in the record a statement of the youth justice court's reasons.

**Application of *Criminal Code***
(7) Sections 113 to 117 of the *Criminal Code* apply in respect of any order made under this section.

**Report**
(8) Before making an order referred to in section 113 of the *Criminal Code* in respect of a young person, the youth justice court may require the provincial director to cause to be prepared, and to submit to the youth justice court, a report on the young person.

**Review of order made under section 50**
**51.** (1) A youth justice court may, on application, review an order made under section 50 at any time after the end of the period set out in subsection 118(2) that applies to the record of the offence that resulted in the order being made.

**Grounds**
(2) In conducting a review under this section, the youth justice court shall take into account
(*a*) the nature and circumstances of the offence in respect of which the order was made; and
(*b*) the safety of the young person and of other persons.

**Decision of review**
(3) When a youth justice court conducts a review under this section, it may, after giving the young person, a parent of the young person, the Attorney General and the provincial director an opportunity to be heard,
(*a*) confirm the order;
(*b*) revoke the order; or
(*c*) vary the order as it considers appropriate in the circumstances of the case.

**New order not to be more onerous**
(4) No variation of an order made under paragraph (3)(*c*) may be more onerous than the order being reviewed.

**Application of provisions**
(5) Subsections 59(3) to (5) apply, with any modifications that the circumstances require, in respect of a review under this section.

**Funding for victims**
**52.** (1) The lieutenant governor in council of a province may order that, in respect of any fine imposed in the province under paragraph 41(2)(*d*), a percentage of the fine as fixed by the lieutenant governor in council be used to provide such assistance to victims of offences as the lieutenant governor in council may direct from time to time.

**Victim fine surcharge**
(2) If the lieutenant governor in council of a province has not made an order under subsection (1), a youth justice court that imposes a fine on a young person under paragraph 41(2)(*d*) may, in addition to any other punishment imposed on the young person, order the young person to pay a victim fine surcharge in an amount not exceeding fifteen per cent of the fine. The surcharge shall be used to provide such assistance to victims of offences as the lieutenant governor in council of the province in which the surcharge is imposed may direct from time to time.

**Where a fine or other payment is ordered**
**53.** (1) The youth justice court shall, in imposing a fine under paragraph 41(2)(*d*) or in making an order under paragraph 41(2)(*e*) or (*g*), have regard to the present and future means of the young person to pay.

**Discharge of fine or surcharge**
(2) A young person on whom a fine is imposed under paragraph 41(2)(*d*), including any percentage of a fine imposed under subsection 52(1), or on whom a victim fine surcharge is imposed under subsection 52(2), may discharge the fine or surcharge in whole or in part by earning credits for work performed in a program established for that purpose
(*a*) by the lieutenant governor in council of the province in which the fine or surcharge was imposed; or
(*b*) by the lieutenant governor in council of the province in which the young person resides, if an appropriate agreement is in effect between the government of the province in which the fine or surcharge was imposed.

**Rates, crediting and other matters**
(3) A program referred to in subsection (2) shall determine the rate at which credits are earned and may provide for the manner of crediting any amounts earned against the fine or surcharge and any other matters necessary for or incidental to carrying out the program.

**Representations respecting orders under paras. 41(2)(*e*) to (*h*)**
(4) In considering whether to make an order under any of paragraphs 41(2)(*e*) to (*h*), the youth justice court may consider any representations made by the person who would be compensated or to whom restitution or payment would be made.

**Notice of orders under paras. 41(2)(*e*) to (*h*)**
(5) If the youth justice court makes an order under any of paragraphs 41(2)(*e*) to (*h*), it shall cause notice of the terms of the order to be given to the person who is to be compensated or to whom restitution or payment is to be made.

**Consent of person to be compensated**
(6) No order may be made under paragraph 41(2)(*h*) unless the youth justice court has secured the consent of the person to be compensated.

**Orders under 41(2)(*h*), (*i*) or (*m*)**
(7) No order may be made under paragraph 41(2)(*h*), (*i*) or (*m*) unless the youth justice court is satisfied that
(*a*) the young person against whom the order is made is a suitable candidate for such an order; and
(*b*) the order does not interfere with the normal hours of work or education of the young person.

**Duration of order for service**
(8) No order may be made under paragraph 41(2)(*h*) or (*i*) to perform personal or community services unless those services can be completed in two hundred and forty hours or less and within twelve months after the date of the order.

**Community service order**
(9) No order may be made under paragraph 41(2)(*i*) unless
(*a*) the community service to be performed is part of a program that is approved by the provincial director; or
(*b*) the youth justice court is satisfied that the person or organization for whom the community service is to be performed has agreed to its performance.

**Application for further time to complete youth sentence**
(10) A youth justice court may, on application by or on behalf of the young person in respect of whom a youth sentence has been imposed under any of paragraphs 41(2)(*d*) to (*i*), allow further time for the completion of the sentence subject to any regulations made under paragraph 154(*b*) and to any rules made by the youth justice court under subsection 17(1).

**Conditions that must appear in orders**
**54.** (1) the youth justice court shall prescribe, as conditions of an order made under paragraph 41(2)(*k*) or (*l*) that the young person
(*a*) keep the peace and be of good behaviour; and
(*b*) appear before the youth justice court when required by the court to do so.

**Conditions that may appear in orders**
(2) A youth justice court may prescribe, as conditions of an order made under paragraph 41(2)(*k*) or (*l*), that a young person do one or more of the following that the youth justice court considers appropriate in the circumstances:
(*a*) report to and be supervised by the provincial director or a person designated by the youth justice court;
(*b*) notify the clerk of the youth justice court, the provincial director or the youth worker assigned to the case of any change of address or any change in the place of employment, education or training;
(*c*) remain within the territorial jurisdiction of one or more courts named in the order;
(*d*) make reasonable efforts to obtain and maintain suitable employment;
(*e*) attend school or any other place of learning, training or recreation that is appropriate, if the youth justice court is satisfied that a suitable program for the young person is available there;
(*f*) reside with a parent, or any other adult that the youth justice court considers appropriate, who is willing to provide for the care and maintenance of the young person;
(*g*) reside at a place that the provincial director may specify;
(*h*) comply with any other conditions set out in the order that the youth justice court considers appropriate, including conditions for securing the young person's good conduct and for preventing the young person from repeating the offence or committing other offences; and
(*i*) not own, possess or have the control of any weapon, ammunition, prohibited ammunition, prohibited device or explosive substance, except as authorized by the order.

**Communication of order**

(3) A youth justice court that makes an order under paragraph 41(2)(*k*) or (*l*) shall

(*a*) cause the order to be read by or to the young person bound by it;

(*b*) explain or cause to be explained to the young person the purpose and effect of the order, and confirm that the young person understands it; and

(*c*) cause a copy of the order to be given to the young person, and to any parent of the young person who is in attendance at the sentencing hearing.

**Copy of order to parent**

(4) A youth justice court that makes an order under paragraph 41(2)(*k*) or (*l*) may cause a copy to be given to a parent of the young person who is not in attendance at the proceedings if the parent is, in the opinion of the court, taking an active interest in the proceedings.

**Endorsement of order by young person**

(5) After the order has been read and explained under subsection (3), the young person shall endorse on the order an acknowledgement that the young person has received a copy of the order and had its purpose and effect explained.

**Validity of order**

(6) The failure of a young person to endorse the order or of a parent to receive a copy of the order does not affect the validity of the order.

**Commencement of order**

(7) An order made under paragraph 41(2)(*k*) or (*l*) comes into force

(*a*) on the date on which it is made; or

(*b*) if a young person receives a sentence that includes a period of continuous custody and supervision, at the end of the period of supervision.

**Effect of order in case of custody**

(8) If a young person is subject to a sentence that includes both a period of continuous custody and supervision and an order made under paragraph 41(2)(*k*) or (*l*), and the court orders under subsection 41(11) a delay in the start of the period of custody, the court may divide the period that the order made under paragraph 41(2)(*k*) or (*l*) is in effect, with the first portion to have effect from the date on which it is made until the start of the period of custody, and the remainder to take effect at the end of the period of supervision.

**Notice to appear**

(9) A young person may be given notice either orally or in writing to appear before the youth justice court under paragraph (1)(*b*).

**Warrant in default of appearance**

(10) If service of a notice in writing is proved and the young person fails to attend court in accordance with the notice, a youth justice court may issue a warrant to compel the appearance of the young person.

**Definitions**

55. (1) The definitions in this subsection apply in this section

**"optional conditions"**

"optional conditions" means the conditions referred to in subsection 54(2).

**"change"**

"change", in relation to optional conditions, includes deletions and additions.

**Amendment of order other than for breach**

(2) A youth justice court that makes an order under paragraph 41(2)(*k*) or (*l*) may, on the application of the young person or the provincial director, require the young person to appear before it and, after hearing the young person and the provincial director,

(*a*) make any changes to the optional conditions that in the opinion of the court are desirable because of a change in the circumstances of the young person since the order was made;

(*b*) relieve the young person, either absolutely or on the terms and for the period that the court considers desirable, of compliance with any optional condition; or

(*c*) cancel the order absolutely, or cancel it and substitute any other sanction set out in paragraphs 41(2)(*d*) to (*m*) that is consistent with the purpose and principles set out in section 37.

**Contravention of an order**

56. (1) If a youth justice court is satisfied that a young person has contravened a condition of an order made under paragraph 41(2)(*k*), (*l*) or (*o*) without reasonable excuse, the court may, on the application of the provincial director, require the young person to appear before it and, after hearing the young person and the provincial director,

(*a*) order that no further action be taken, if the court is satisfied that the contravention was so minor that no further action is appropriate;

(*b*) make any changes to the optional conditions that in the opinion of the court are desirable because of a change in the circumstances of the young person since the order was made;

(*c*) make any changes referred to in paragraph (*b*) and, in addition, make an attendance order under paragraph 41(2)(*m*); or

(*d*) in the case of a deferred custody and supervision order made under paragraph 41(2)(*o*), direct that the young person serve the remainder of the order as if it were a custody and supervision order made under paragraph 41(2)(*n*).

**Deferred custody and supervision order**

(2) After a court has made a direction under paragraph (1)(*d*), the provisions of this Act applicable to orders made under paragraph 41(2)(*n*) apply in respect of the deferred custody and supervision order.

**Factors to be considered**

(3) In making its decision under subsection (1), the court shall consider the length of time the

young person has been subject to the order, whether the young person has previously contravened it, and the nature of the contravention.

**Transfer of youth sentence**
57. (1) When a youth sentence has been imposed under any of paragraphs 41(2)(*d*) to (*i*), (*k*), (*l*) or (*r*) in respect of a young person and the young person or a parent with whom the young person resides is or becomes a resident of a territorial division outside the jurisdiction of the youth justice court that imposed the youth sentence, whether in the same or in another province, a youth justice court judge in the territorial division in which the youth sentence was imposed may, on the application of the Attorney General or on the application of the young person or the young person's parent, with the consent of the Attorney General, transfer to a youth justice court in another territorial division the youth sentence and any portion of the record of the case that is appropriate. All subsequent proceedings relating to the case shall then be carried out and enforced by that court.

**No transfer outside province before appeal completed**
(2) No youth sentence may be transferred from one province to another under this section until the time for an appeal against the youth sentence or the finding on which the youth sentence was based has expired or until all proceedings in respect of any such appeal have been completed.

**Transfer to a province when person is adult**
(3) When an application is made under subsection (1) to transfer the youth sentence of a young person to a province in which the young person is an adult, a youth justice court judge may, with the consent of the Attorney General, transfer the youth sentence and the record of the case to the youth justice court in the province to which the transfer is sought, and the youth justice court to which the case is transferred shall have full jurisdiction in respect of the youth sentence as if that court had imposed the youth sentence. The person shall be further dealt with in accordance with this Act.

**Interprovincial arrangements**
58. (1) When a youth sentence has been imposed under any of paragraphs 41(2)(*k*) to (*q*) in respect of a young person, the youth sentence in one province may be dealt with in any other province in accordance with any agreement that may have been made between those provinces.

**Youth justice court retains jurisdiction**
(2) Subject to subsection (3), when a youth sentence imposed in respect of a young person is dealt with under this section in a province other than that in which the youth sentence was imposed, the youth justice court of the province in which the youth sentence was imposed retains, for all purposes of this Act, exclusive jurisdiction over the young person as if the youth sentence were dealt with within that province, and any warrant or process issued in respect of the young person may be executed or served in any place in Canada outside the province where the youth sentence was imposed as if it were executed or served in that province.

**Waiver of jurisdiction**
(3) When a youth sentence imposed in respect of a young person is dealt with under this section in a province other than the one in which the youth sentence was imposed, the youth justice court of the province in which the youth sentence was imposed may, with the consent in writing of the Attorney General of that province and the young person, waive its jurisdiction, for the purpose of any proceeding under this Act, to the youth justice court of the province in which the youth sentence is dealt with, in which case the youth justice court in the province in which the youth sentence is dealt with shall have full jurisdiction in respect of the youth sentence as if that court had imposed the youth sentence.

**Review of youth sentences not involving custody**
59. (1) When a youth justice court has imposed a youth sentence in respect of a young person, other than a youth sentence under paragraph 41(2)(*n*), (*p*) or (*q*), the youth justice court shall, on the application of the young person, the young person's parent, the Attorney General or the provincial director, made at any time after six months from the date of the youth sentence or, with leave of a youth justice court judge, at any earlier time, review the youth sentence if the court is satisfied that there are grounds for a review under subsection (2).

**Grounds for review**
(2) A review of a youth sentence may be made under this section
(*a*) on the ground that the circumstances that led to the youth sentence have changed materially;
(*b*) on the ground that the young person in respect of whom the review is to be made is unable to comply with or is experiencing serious difficulty in complying with the terms of the youth sentence;
(*c*) on the ground that the terms of the youth sentence are adversely affecting the opportunities available to the young person to obtain services, education or employment; or
(*d*) on any other ground that the youth justice court considers appropriate.

**Progress report**
(3) The youth justice court may, before reviewing under this section a youth sentence imposed in respect of a young person, require the provincial director to cause to be prepared, and to submit to the youth justice court, a progress report on the performance of the young person since the youth sentence took effect.

**Subsections 93(10) to (12) apply**
(4) Subsections 93(10) to (12) apply, with any modifications that the circumstances require, in respect of any progress report required under subsection (3).

**Subsections 93(7) and (14) to (18) apply**
(5) Subsections 93(7) and (14) to (18) apply, with any modifications that the circumstances require, in respect of reviews made under this section and any notice required under subsection 93(14) shall also be given to the provincial director.

**Compelling appearance of young person**
(6) The youth justice court may, by summons or warrant, compel a young person in respect of whom a review is to be made under this section to appear before the youth justice court for the purposes of the review.

**Decision of the youth justice court after review**
(7) When a youth justice court reviews under this section a youth sentence imposed in respect of a young person, it may, after giving the young person, a parent of the young person, the Attorney General and the provincial director an opportunity to be heard,
(*a*) confirm the youth sentence;
(*b*) terminate the youth sentence and discharge the young person from any further obligation of the youth sentence; or
(*c*) vary the youth sentence or impose any new youth sentence under section 41, other than a committal to custody, for any period of time, not exceeding the remainder of the period of the earlier youth sentence, that the court considers appropriate in the circumstances of the case.

**New youth sentence not to be more onerous**
(8) Subject to subsection (9), when a youth sentence imposed in respect of a young person is reviewed under this section, no youth sentence imposed under subsection (7) shall, without the consent of the young person, be more onerous than the remainder of the youth sentence reviewed.

**Exception**
(9) A youth justice court may under this section extend the time within which a youth sentence imposed under paragraphs 41(2)(*d*) to (*i*) is to be complied with by a young person if the court is satisfied that the young person requires more time to comply with the youth sentence, but in no case shall the extension be for a period of time that expires more than twelve months after the date the youth sentence would otherwise have expired.

**Provisions applicable to youth sentences on review**
60. Subject to sections 59, 87 and 93 to 95, section 37, subsections 41(11) to (14) and (16) and sections 46, 47, 49 to 51, 53 to 58 and 91 apply, with any modifications that the circumstances require, in respect of youth sentences imposed under sections 59 and 93 to 95.

*Adult Sentences*

**Access to adult sentences**
61. An adult sentence shall be imposed on a young person who is found guilty of an offence for which an adult could be sentenced to imprisonment for more than two years, committed after the young person attained the age of fourteen years, in the following cases:
(*a*) in the case of a presumptive offence, if the youth justice court makes an order under subsection 70(2) or paragraph 72(1)(*b*); or
(*b*) in any other case, if the youth justice court makes an order under subsection 63(5) or paragraph 72(1)(*b*).

**Application by young person**
62. (1) A young person who is charged with, or found guilty of, a presumptive offence committed after he or she attained the age of fourteen years may, at any time before evidence is called as to sentence or submissions are made as to sentence, make an application for an order that he or she is not liable to an adult sentence and that a youth sentence must be imposed.

**Application unopposed**
(2) If the Attorney General gives notice to the youth justice court that the Attorney General does not oppose the application, the youth justice court shall, without a hearing, order that the young person, if found guilty, is not liable to an adult sentence and that a youth sentence must be imposed.

**Application by Attorney General**
63. (1) The Attorney General may, following an application under subsection 41(8), if any is made, and before evidence is called as to sentence or submissions are made as to sentence, make an application for an order that a young person is liable to an adult sentence if the young person is or has been found guilty of an offence, other than a presumptive offence, for which an adult could be sentenced to imprisonment for more than two years, that was committed after the young person attained the age of fourteen years.

**Notice of intention to seek adult sentence**
(2) If the Attorney General intends to seek an adult sentence for an offence by making an application under subsection (1), or by establishing that the offence is a presumptive offence within the meaning of paragraph (*b*) of the definition "presumptive offence" in subsection 2(1) committed after the young person attained the age of fourteen years, the Attorney General shall, before the young person enters a plea or with leave of the youth justice court before the commencement of the trial, give notice to the young person and the youth justice court of the intention to seek an adult sentence.

**Included offences**
(3) A notice of intention to seek an adult sentence given in respect of an offence is notice in respect of any included offence of which the young person is found guilty for which an adult could be sentenced to imprisonment for more than two years.

**Notice to young person**
(4) If a young person is charged with an offence other than an offence set out in paragraph (*a*) of the definition "presumptive offence" in subsection

2(1), committed after the young person attained the age of fourteen years, and the Attorney General intends to establish, after a finding of guilt, that the offence is a serious violent offence and a presumptive offence within the meaning of paragraph (*b*) of the definition "presumptive offence" in subsection 2(1) for which the young person is liable to an adult sentence, the Attorney General shall, before the young person enters a plea, give notice of that intention to the young person.

**Application unopposed**
(5) If the young person gives notice to the youth justice court that the young person does not oppose the application for an adult sentence, the youth justice court shall, without a hearing, order that if the young person is found guilty of an offence for which an adult could be sentenced to imprisonment for more than two years, an adult sentence must be imposed.

**Presumption does not apply**
**64.** If the Attorney General gives notice to the youth justice court that an adult sentence will not be sought in respect of a young person who is alleged to have committed an offence set out in paragraph (*a*) of the definition "presumptive offence" in subsection 2(1), the court shall order that the young person, if found guilty, is not liable to an adult sentence, and the court shall order a ban on publication of information that would identify the young person as having been dealt with under this Act.

**Procedure for application or notice**
**65.** An application under subsection 62(1) or 63(1) or a notice to the court under subsection 62(2) or 63(2) or (5) must be made or given orally, in the presence of the other party, or in writing with a copy served personally on the other party.

**No election if youth sentence**
**66.** If the youth justice court has made an order under subsection 62(2) or section 64 before a young person is required to be put to an election under section 67, the young person shall not be put to an election unless the young person is alleged to have committed first degree murder or second degree murder within the meaning of section 231 of the *Criminal Code*.

**Election—adult sentence**
**67.** (1) Subject to section 66, if a young person is charged with having, after attaining the age of fourteen years, committed an offence set out in paragraph (*a*) of the definition "presumptive offence" in subsection 2(1), or if the Attorney General has given notice under subsection 63(2) of the intention to seek an adult sentence, the youth justice court shall, before the young person enters a plea, put the young person to his or her election in the following words:

> You have the option to elect to be tried by a youth justice court judge without a jury and without having had a preliminary inquiry; or you may elect to have a preliminary inquiry and to be tried by a judge without a jury; or you may elect to have a preliminary inquiry and to be tried by a court composed of a judge and jury. If you do not elect now, you shall be deemed to have elected to have a preliminary inquiry and to be tried by a court composed of a judge and jury. How do you elect to be tried?

**Mode of trial where co-accused are young persons**
(2) When two or more young persons who are charged with the same offence are put to their election, unless all of them elect or re-elect or are deemed to have elected, as the case may be, the same mode of trial, the youth justice court judge
(*a*) may decline to record any election or re-election for trial by a youth justice court judge without a jury or a judge without a jury; and
(*b*) if the judge declines to do so, shall hold a preliminary inquiry unless a preliminary inquiry has been held prior to the election, re-election or deemed election.

**Attorney General may require trial by jury**
(3) The Attorney General may, even if a young person elects under subsection (1) to be tried by a youth justice court judge without a jury or a judge without a jury, require the young person to be tried by a court composed of a judge and jury.

**Preliminary inquiry**
(4) When a young person elects to be tried by a judge without a jury, or elects or is deemed to have elected to be tried by a court composed of a judge and jury, the youth justice court referred to in subsection 13(1) shall conduct a preliminary inquiry and if, on its conclusion, the young person is ordered to stand trial, the proceedings shall be conducted before a judge without a jury or a court composed of a judge and jury, as the case may be.

**Preliminary inquiry provisions of *Criminal Code***
(5) The preliminary inquiry shall be conducted in accordance with the provisions of Part XVIII of the *Criminal Code*, except to the extent that they are inconsistent with this Act.

**Parts XIX and XX of the *Criminal Code***
(6) Proceedings under this Act before a judge without a jury or a court composed of a judge and jury shall be conducted, with any modifications that the circumstances require, in accordance with the provisions of Parts XIX and XX of the *Criminal Code*, except that
(*a*) the provisions of this Act respecting the protection of privacy of young persons prevail over the provisions of the *Criminal Code*; and
(*b*) the young person is entitled to be represented in court by counsel if the young person is removed from court in accordance with subsection 650(2) of the *Criminal Code*.

**Proof of notice under s. 63(4)**
**68.** (1) When a young person is found guilty of an offence other than an offence set out in paragraph (*a*) of the definition "presumptive offence" in subsection 2(1), committed after he or she attained

the age of fourteen years, and the Attorney General seeks to establish that the offence is a serious violent offence and a presumptive offence within the meaning of paragraph (*b*) of the definition "presumptive offence" in subsection 2(1), the Attorney General must satisfy the youth justice court that the young person, before entering a plea, was given notice under subsection 63(4).

**Determination of serious violent offence**
(2) If the youth justice court is satisfied that the young person was given notice under subsection 63(4), the Attorney General may make an application in accordance with subsection 41(8).

**Inquiry by court and proof**
(3) If the youth justice court determines that the offence is a serious violent offence, it shall ask whether the young person admits to the previous judicial determinations of serious violent offences made at different proceedings. If the young person does not admit to any of it, the Attorney General may adduce evidence as proof of the previous judicial determinations in accordance with section 667 of the *Criminal Code*, with any modifications that the circumstances require. For the purposes of that section, a certified copy of the information endorsed in accordance with subsection 41(8) or a certified copy of a court decision is deemed to be a certificate.

**Determination by court**
(4) If the youth justice court, after making its inquiry under subsection (3), is satisfied that the offence is a presumptive offence within the meaning of paragraph (*b*) of the definition "presumptive offence" in subsection 2(1), the youth justice court shall endorse the information accordingly.

**Determination by court**
(5) If the youth justice court, after making its inquiry under subsection (3), is not satisfied that the offence is a presumptive offence within the meaning of paragraph (*b*) of the definition "presumptive offence" in subsection 2(1), the Attorney General may make an application under subsection 63(1).

**Paragraph (*a*) "presumptive offence"—included offences**
69. (1) If a young person who is charged with an offence set out in paragraph (*a*) of the definition "presumptive offence" in subsection 2(1), committed after having attained the age of fourteen years, is found guilty of committing an included offence for which an adult could be sentenced to imprisonment for more than two years, other than another presumptive offence set out in that paragraph,
(*a*) the Attorney General may make an application under subsection 63(1) without the necessity of giving notice under subsection 63(2), if the finding of guilt is for an offence that is not a presumptive offence; or
(*b*) subsections 68(2) to (5) apply without the necessity of the Attorney General giving notice under subsection 63(2) or (4), if the finding of guilt is for an offence that would be a presumptive offence within the meaning of paragraph (*b*) of the definition "presumptive offence" in subsection 2(1) if a judicial determination is made that the offence is a serious violent offence and on proof of previous judicial determinations of a serious violent offence.

**Other serious offences—included offences**
(2) If the Attorney General has given notice under subsection 63(2) of the intention to seek an adult sentence for an offence committed after the young person attained the age of fourteen years, and the young person is found guilty of committing an included offence for which an adult could be sentenced to imprisonment for more than two years, the Attorney General may make an application under subsection 63(1) or seek to apply the provisions of section 68.

**Inquiry by court to young person**
70. (1) The youth justice court, after hearing an application under subsection 41(8), if any is made, and before evidence is called or submissions are made as to sentence, shall inquire whether a young person wishes to make an application under subsection 62(1) and if so, whether the Attorney General would oppose it, if
(*a*) the young person has been found guilty of a presumptive offence committed after he or she attained the age of fourteen years;
(*b*) the young person has not already made an application under subsection 62(1); and
(*c*) no order has been made under section 64.

**No application by young person**
(2) If the young person indicates that he or she does not wish to make an application under subsection 62(1), the court shall order that an adult sentence be imposed.

**Hearing—adult sentences**
71. The youth justice court shall, at the commencement of the sentencing hearing, hold a hearing in respect of an application under subsection 62(1) or 63(1), unless the court has received notice that the application is not opposed. Both parties and the parents of the young person shall be given an opportunity to be heard at the hearing.

**Test—adult sentences**
72. (1) In making its decision on an application heard in accordance with section 71, the youth justice court shall consider the seriousness and circumstances of the offence, and the degree of responsibility, age, maturity, character, background and previous record of the young person and any other factors that the court considers relevant, and
(*a*) if it is of the opinion that a youth sentence imposed in accordance with the purpose and principles set out in section 37 would be adequate to hold the young person accountable for his or her offending behaviour, it shall order that the young person is not liable to an adult sentence and that a youth sentence must be imposed; and
(*b*) if it is of the opinion that a youth sentence

imposed in accordance with the purpose and principles set out in section 37 would not be adequate to hold the young person accountable for his or her offending behaviour, it shall order that an adult sentence be imposed.

**Onus**
(2) The onus of satisfying the youth justice court as to the matters referred to in subsection (1) is with the applicant.

**pre-sentence reports**
(3) In making its decision, the youth justice court shall consider a pre-sentence report.

**Court to state reasons**
(4) When the youth justice court makes an order under this section, it shall state the reasons for its decision.

**Appeals**
(5) For the purposes of an appeal in accordance with section 36, an order under subsection (1) is part of the sentence.

**Court must impose adult sentence**
73. (1) When the youth justice court makes an order under subsection 63(5) or 70(2) or paragraph 72(1)(*b*) in respect of a young person, the court shall, on a finding of guilt, impose an adult sentence on the young person.

**Court must impose youth sentence**
(2) When the youth justice court makes an order under subsection 62(2), section 64 or paragraph 72(1)(*a*) in respect of a young person, the court shall, on a finding of guilt, impose a youth sentence on the young person.

**Application of Parts XXIII and XXIV of the *Criminal Code***
74. (1) Parts XXIII and XXIV of the *Criminal Code* apply to a young person in respect of whom the youth justice court has ordered that an adult sentence be imposed.

**Finding of guilt becomes a conviction**
(2) A finding of guilt for an offence in respect of which an adult sentence is imposed becomes a conviction once the time allowed for the taking of an appeal has expired or, if an appeal is taken, all proceedings in respect of the appeal have been completed and the appeal court has upheld an adult sentence.

**Interpretation**
(3) This section does not affect the time of commencement of an adult sentence under subsection 719(1) of the *Criminal Code*.

**Inquiry by the court to the young person**
75. (1) If the youth justice court imposes a youth sentence in respect of a young person who has been found guilty of having, after attaining the age of fourteen years, committed a presumptive offence set out in paragraph (*a*) of the definition "presumptive offence" in subsection 2(1), or an offence under paragraph (*b*) of that definition for which the Attorney General has given notice under subsection 63(2), the court shall at the sentencing hearing inquire whether the young person or the Attorney General wishes to make an application under subsection (3) for a ban on publication.

**No application for a ban**
(2) If the young person and the Attorney General both indicate that they do not wish to make an application under subsection (3), the court shall endorse the information accordingly.

**Order for a ban**
(3) On application of the young person or the Attorney General, a youth justice court may order a ban on publication of information that would identify the young person as having been dealt with under this Act if the court considers it appropriate in the circumstances, taking into account the importance of rehabilitating the young person and the public interest.

**Appeals**
(4) For the purposes of an appeal in accordance with section 36, an order under subsection (3) is part of the sentence.

**Placement when subject to adult sentences**
76. (1) Despite anything in this Act or any other Act of Parliament, other than subsections (2) and (8) and sections 79 and 80, when a young person who is subject to an adult sentence in respect of an offence is sentenced to a term of imprisonment for the offence, the youth justice court shall, after giving the young person, a parent of the young person, the Attorney General, the provincial director and representatives of the provincial and federal correctional systems an opportunity to be heard, order that the young person serve any portion of the imprisonment in

(*a*) a youth custody facility separate and apart from any adult who is detained or held in custody;
(*b*) a provincial correctional facility for adults; or
(*c*) if the sentence is for two years or more, a penitentiary.

**When young person subject to adult penalties**
(2) The youth justice court that sentences a young person under subsection (1) shall, unless it is satisfied that to do so would not be in the best interests of the young person or would jeopardize the safety of others,

(*a*) if the young person is under the age of eighteen years at the time that he or she is sentenced, order that he or she be placed in a youth custody facility; and
(*b*) if the young person is eighteen years old or older at the time that he or she is sentenced, order that he or she not be placed in a youth custody facility and order that any portion of the sentence be served in a provincial correctional facility for adults or, if the sentence is two years or more, in a penitentiary.

**Report necessary**
(3) Before making an order under subsection (1), the youth justice court shall require that a report be prepared for the purpose of assisting the court.

**Appeals**
(4) For the purposes of an appeal in accordance with section 36, an order under subsection (1) is part of the sentence.

**Review**
(5) On application, the youth justice court shall review the placement of a young person under this section and, if satisfied that the circumstances that resulted in the initial order have changed materially, and after having given the young person, the provincial director and the representatives of the provincial and federal correctional systems an opportunity to be heard, the court may order that the young person be placed in
(*a*) a youth custody facility separate and apart from any adult who is detained or held in custody;
(*b*) a provincial correctional facility for adults; or
(*c*) if the sentence is for two years or more, a penitentiary.

**Who may make application**
(6) An application referred to in this section may be made by the young person, one of the young person's parents, the provincial director, representatives of the provincial and federal correctional systems and the Attorney General, after the time for all appeals has expired.

**Notice**
(7) When an application referred to in this section is made, the applicant shall cause a notice of the application to be given
(*a*) if the applicant is the young person or one of the young person's parents, to the provincial director, to representatives of the provincial and federal correctional systems and to the Attorney General;
(*b*) if the applicant is the Attorney General, to the young person, to a parent of the young person, to the provincial director and to representatives of the provincial and federal correctional systems; and
(*c*) if the applicant is the provincial director, to the young person, to a parent of the young person, to representatives of the provincial and federal correctional systems and to the Attorney General.

**Limit—age twenty**
(8) No young person shall remain in a youth custody facility under this section after the young person attains the age of twenty years, unless the youth justice court that makes the order under subsection (1) or reviews the placement under subsection (5) is satisfied that remaining in the youth custody facility would be in the best interests of the young person and would not jeopardize the safety of others.

**Obligation to inform—parole**
77. (1) When a young person is ordered to serve a portion of a sentence in a youth custody facility under paragraph 76(1)(*a*), the provincial director shall inform the appropriate parole board.

**Applicability of *Corrections and Conditional Release Act***
(2) For greater certainty, Part II of the *Corrections and Conditional Release Act* applies, subject to section 78, with respect to a young person who is the subject of an order under subsection 76(1).

**Appropriate parole board**
(3) The appropriate parole board for the purposes of this section is
(*a*) if subsection 112(1) of the *Corrections and Conditional Release Act* would apply with respect to the young person but for the fact that the young person was ordered into a youth custody facility, the parole board mentioned in that subsection; and
(*b*) in any other case, the National Parole Board.

**Release entitlement**
**78.** (1) For greater certainty, section 6 of the *Prisons and Reformatories Act* applies to a young person who is ordered to serve a portion of a sentence in a youth custody facility under paragraph 76(1)(*a*) only if section 743.1 of the *Criminal Code* would direct that the young person serve the sentence in a prison.

**Release entitlement**
(2) For greater certainty, section 127 of the *Corrections and Conditional Release Act* applies to a young person who is ordered to serve a portion of a sentence in a youth custody facility under paragraph 76(1)(*a*) only if section 743.1 of the *Criminal Code* would direct that the young person serve the sentence in a penitentiary.

**If person convicted under another Act**
**79.** If a person who is serving all or a portion of a sentence in a youth custody facility under paragraph 76(1)(*a*) is sentenced to a term of imprisonment under an Act of Parliament other than this Act, the remainder of the portion of the sentence being served in the youth custody facility shall be served in a provincial correctional facility for adults or a penitentiary, in accordance with section 743.1 of the *Criminal Code*.

**If person who is serving a sentence under another Act is sentenced to an adult sentence**
**80.** If a person who has been serving a sentence of imprisonment under an Act of Parliament other than this Act is sentenced to an adult sentence of imprisonment under this Act, the sentences shall be served in a provincial correctional facility for adults or a penitentiary, in accordance with section 743.1 of the *Criminal Code*.

*Effect of Termination of Youth Sentence*

**Effect of absolute discharge or termination of youth sentence**
**81.** (1) Subject to section 12 of the *Canada Evidence Act*, if a young person is found guilty of an offence, and a youth justice court directs

under paragraph 41(2)(*b*) that the young person be discharged absolutely, or the youth sentence, or any disposition made under the *Young Offenders Act*, chapter Y-1 of the Revised Statutes of Canada, 1985, has ceased to have effect, other than an order under section 50 of this Act or section 20.1 of the *Young Offenders Act*, the young person is deemed not to have been found guilty or convicted of the offence except that

(*a*) the young person may plead *autrefois convict* in respect of any subsequent charge relating to the offence;

(*b*) a youth justice court may consider the finding of guilt in considering an application under subsection 62(1) or 63(1);

(*c*) any court or justice may consider the finding of guilt in considering an application for judicial interim release or in considering what sentence to impose for any offence; and

(*d*) the National Parole Board or any provincial parole board may consider the finding of guilt in considering an application for conditional release or pardon.

**Disqualifications removed**

(2) For greater certainty and without restricting the generality of subsection (1), an absolute discharge under paragraph 41(2)(*b*) or the termination of the youth sentence or disposition in respect of an offence for which a young person is found guilty removes any disqualification in respect of the offence to which the young person is subject under any Act of Parliament by reason of a finding of guilt.

**Applications for employment**

(3) No application form for or relating to the following shall contain any question that by its terms requires the applicant to disclose that he or she has been charged with or found guilty of an offence in respect of which he or she has, under this Act or the *Young Offenders Act*, chapter Y-1 of the Revised Statutes of Canada, 1985, been discharged absolutely, or has completed the youth sentence under this Act or the disposition under the *Young Offenders Act*:

(*a*) employment in any department, as defined in section 2 of the *Financial Administration Act*;

(*b*) employment by any Crown corporation, as defined in section 83 of the *Financial Administration Act*;

(*c*) enrolment in the Canadian Forces; or

(*d*) employment on or in connection with the operation of any work, undertaking or business that is within the legislative authority of Parliament.

**Finding of guilt not a previous conviction**

(4) A finding of guilt under this Act is not a previous conviction for the purposes of any offence under any Act of Parliament for which a greater punishment is prescribed by reason of previous convictions, except for

(*a*) the purpose of establishing that an offence is a presumptive offence within the meaning of paragraph (*b*) of the definition "presumptive offence" in subsection 2(1); or

(*b*) the purpose of determining the adult sentence to be imposed.

## PART 5
## CUSTODY AND SUPERVISION

**Purpose**

**82.** (1) The purpose of the youth custody and supervision system is to contribute to the protection of society by

(*a*) carrying out sentences imposed by courts through the safe, fair and humane custody and supervision of young persons; and

(*b*) assisting young persons to be rehabilitated and reintegrated into the community as law-abiding citizens, by providing effective programs to young persons in custody and while under supervision in the community.

**Principles to be used**

(2) The following principles are to be used in achieving that purpose:

(*a*) that the least restrictive measures consistent with the protection of the public, of personnel working with young persons and of young persons be used;

(*b*) that young persons sentenced to custody retain the rights of other young persons, except the rights that are necessarily removed or restricted as a consequence of a sentence under this Act or another Act of Parliament;

(*c*) that the youth custody and supervision system facilitate the involvement of the families of young persons and members of the public;

(*d*) that custody and supervision decisions be made in a forthright and fair manner, and that young persons have access to an effective review procedure; and

(*e*) that placements of young persons where they are treated as adults not disadvantage them with respect to their eligibility for and conditions of release.

**Young person to be held apart from adults**

**83.** Subject to subsection 30(3), paragraphs 76(1)(*b*) and (*c*) and sections 88 to 92, a young person who is committed to custody shall be held separate and apart from any adult who is detained or held in custody.

**Levels of custody**

**84.** (1) In the youth custody and supervision system in each province there must be at least two levels of custody for young persons distinguished by the degree of restraint of the young persons in them.

**Designation of youth custody facilities**

(2) Every youth custody facility in a province that contains one or more levels of custody shall be designated by

(*a*) in the case of a youth custody facility with only one level of custody, being the level of custody with the least degree of restraint of the young persons in it, the lieutenant governor in council or his or her delegate; and

(*b*) in any other case, the lieutenant governor in council.

**Provincial director to specify custody level—committal to custody**

(3) The provincial director shall, when a young person is committed to custody under paragraph 41(2)(*n*), (*p*) or (*q*) or an order is made under subsection 97(3), paragraph 102(2)(*b*), subsection 103(1) or paragraph 108(2)(*b*), determine the level of custody appropriate for the young person, after having taken into account the factors set out in subsection (5).

**Provincial director to specify custody level—transfer**

(4) The provincial director may determine a different level of custody for the young person when the provincial director is satisfied that the needs of the young person and the interests of society would be better served by doing so, after having taken into account the factors set out in subsection (5).

**Factors**

(5) The factors referred to in subsections (3) and (4) are

(*a*) that the appropriate level of custody for the young person is the one that is the least restrictive to the young person, having regard to

(i) the seriousness of the offence in respect of which the young person was committed to custody and the circumstances in which that offence was committed,

(ii) the needs and circumstances of the young person, including proximity to family, school, employment and support services,

(iii) the safety of other young persons in custody, and

(iv) the interests of society;

(*b*) that the level of custody should allow for the best possible match of programs to the young person's needs and behaviour, having regard to the findings of any assessment in respect of the young person; and

(*c*) the likelihood of escape.

**Placement and transfer at appropriate level**

(6) After the provincial director has determined the appropriate level of custody for the young person under subsection (3) or (4), the young person shall be placed in the youth custody facility that contains that level of custody specified by the provincial director.

**Notice**

(7) The provincial director shall cause a notice in writing of a determination under subsection (3) or (4) to be given to the young person and a parent of the young person and set out in that notice the reasons for it.

**Procedural safeguards**

85. The provincial director shall ensure that procedures are in place to ensure that the due process rights of the young person are protected with respect to a determination made under subsection 84(3) or (4), including that the young person be

(*a*) provided with any relevant information to which the provincial director has access in making the determination;

(*b*) given the opportunity to be heard; and

(*c*) informed of any right to a review under section 86.

**Review**

86. (1) A young person may apply for a review under this section of a determination

(*a*) under subsection 84(3) that would place the young person in a facility at a level of custody that has more than a minimal degree of restraint; or

(*b*) under subsection 84(4) that would transfer a young person to a facility at a level of custody with a higher degree of restraint or increase the degree of restraint of the young person in the facility.

**Procedural safeguards**

(2) The provincial director shall ensure that procedures are in place for the review under subsection (1), including that

(*a*) the review board that conducts the review be independent;

(*b*) the young person be provided with any relevant information to which the review board has access; and

(*c*) the young person be given the opportunity to be heard.

**Factors**

(3) The review board shall take into account the factors referred to in subsection 84(5) in reviewing a determination.

**Decision is final**

(4) A decision of the review board under this section in respect of a particular determination is final.

**Functions to be exercised by youth justice court**

87. The lieutenant governor in council of a province may order that the powers conferred by subsections 84(3) and (4) be exercised by the youth justice court in that province. The following provisions of the *Young Offenders Act*, chapter Y-1 of the Revised Statutes of Canada, 1985, apply, with any modifications that the circumstances require, to the exercise of those powers:

(*a*) the definitions "review board" and "progress report" in subsection 2(1);

(*b*) section 11;

(*c*) sections 24.1 to 24.3; and

(*d*) sections 28 to 31.

**Exception if young person is twenty years old or older**

88. (1) When a young person is twenty years old or older at the time the youth sentence is imposed on him or her under paragraph 41(2)(*n*), (*p*) or (*q*), the young person shall, despite section 84, be committed to a provincial correctional facility for adults to serve the youth sentence.

**If serving youth sentence in a provincial correctional facility**

(2) If a young person is serving a youth sentence in a provincial correctional facility for adults pur-

suant to subsection (1), the youth justice court may, on application of the provincial director at any time after the young person begins to serve a portion of the youth sentence in a provincial correctional facility for adults, after giving the young person, the provincial director and representatives of the provincial and federal correctional systems an opportunity to be heard, authorize the provincial director to direct that the young person serve the remainder of the youth sentence in a penitentiary if the court considers it to be in the best interests of the young person or in the public interest and if, at the time of the application, that remainder is two years or more.

**Provisions to apply**

(3) If a young person is serving a youth sentence in a provincial correctional facility for adults or a penitentiary under subsection (1) or (2), the *Prisons and Reformatories Act* and the *Corrections and Conditional Release Act*, and any other statute, regulation or rule applicable in respect of prisoners or offenders within the meaning of those Acts, statutes, regulations and rules, apply in respect of the young person except to the extent that they conflict with Part 6 of this Act, which Part continues to apply to the young person.

**Youth worker**

**89.** (1) When a youth sentence is imposed committing a young person to custody, the provincial director of the province in which the young person received the youth sentence and was placed in custody shall, without delay, designate a youth worker to work with the young person to plan for his or her reintegration into the community, including the preparation and implementation of a reintegration plan that sets out the most effective programs for the young person in order to maximize his or her chances for reintegration into the community.

**Role of youth worker when young person in the community**

(2) When a portion of a young person's youth sentence is served in the community in accordance with section 96 or 104, the youth worker shall supervise the young person, continue to provide support to the young person and assist the young person to respect the conditions to which he or she is subject, and help the young person in the implementation of the reintegration plan.

**Reintegration leave**

**90.** (1) The provincial director of a province may, subject to any terms or conditions that he or she considers desirable, authorize, for a young person committed to a youth custody facility in the province further to an order under paragraph 76(1)(*a*) or a youth sentence imposed under paragraph 41(2)(*n*), (*p*) or (*q*),

(*a*) a reintegration leave from the youth custody facility for a period not exceeding thirty days if, in the opinion of the provincial director, it is necessary or desirable that the young person be absent, with or without escort, for medical, compassionate or humanitarian reasons or for the purpose of rehabilitating the young person or reintegrating the young person into the community; or

(*b*) that the young person be released from the youth custody facility on the days and during the hours that the provincial director specifies in order that the young person may

(i) attend school or any other educational or training institution,

(ii) obtain or continue employment or perform domestic or other duties required by the young person's family,

(iii) participate in a program specified by the provincial director that, in the provincial director's opinion, will enable the young person to better carry out employment or improve his or her education or training, or

(iv) attend an out-patient treatment program or other program that provides services that are suitable to addressing the young person's needs.

**Renewal of reintegration leave**

(2) A reintegration leave authorized under paragraph (1)(*a*) may be renewed by the provincial director for one or more thirty-day periods on reassessment of the case.

**Revocation of authorization**

(3) The provincial director of a province may, at any time, revoke an authorization made under subsection (1).

**Arrest and return to custody**

(4) If the provincial director revokes an authorization under subsection (3) or if a young person fails to comply with any term or condition of a reintegration leave or a release from custody under this section, the young person may be arrested without warrant and returned to custody.

**Transfer to adult facility**

**91.** (1) When a young person is committed to custody under paragraph 41(2)(*n*), (*p*) or (*q*), the youth justice court may, on application of the provincial director made at any time after the young person attains the age of eighteen years, after giving the young person, the provincial director and representatives of the provincial correctional system an opportunity to be heard, authorize the provincial director to direct that the young person, subject to subsection (3), serve the remainder of the youth sentence in a provincial correctional facility for adults, if the court considers it to be in the best interests of the young person or in the public interest.

**If serving youth sentence in a provincial correctional facility**

(2) The youth justice court may authorize the provincial director to direct that a young person, subject to subsection (3), serve the remainder of a youth sentence in a penitentiary

(*a*) if the youth justice court considers it to be in the best interests of the young person or in the public interest;

(*b*) if the provincial director applies for the authorization at any time after the young person begins to serve a portion of a youth sentence in a provincial correctional facility for adults further to a direction made under subsection (1);

(*c*) if, at the time of the application, that remainder is two years or more; and

(*d*) so long as the youth justice court gives the young person, the provincial director and representatives of the provincial and federal correctional systems an opportunity to be heard.

**Provisions to apply**

(3) If the provincial director makes a direction under subsection (1) or (2), the *Prisons and Reformatories Act* and the *Corrections and Conditional Release Act*, and any other statute, regulation or rule applicable in respect of prisoners and offenders within the meaning of those Acts, statutes, regulations and rules, apply in respect of the young person except to the extent that they conflict with Part 6 of this Act, which Part continues to apply to the young person.

**Placement when adult and youth sentences**

(4) If a person is subject to more than one sentence, at least one of which is a youth sentence imposed under paragraph 41(2)(*n*), (*p*) or (*q*) and at least one of which is a sentence referred to in either paragraph (*b*) or (*c*), he or she shall serve, in a provincial correctional facility for adults or a penitentiary in accordance with section 743.1 of the *Criminal Code*, the following:

(*a*) the remainder of any youth sentence imposed under paragraph 41(2)(*n*), (*p*) or (*q*);

(*b*) an adult sentence to which an order under paragraph 76(1)(*b*) or (*c*) applies; and

(*c*) any sentence of imprisonment imposed otherwise than under this Act.

**Youth sentence and adult sentence**

(5) If a young person is committed to custody under a youth sentence under paragraph 41(2)(*n*), (*p*) or (*q*) and is also already subject to an adult sentence to which an order under paragraph 76(1)(*a*) applies, the young person may, in the discretion of the provincial director, serve the sentences, or any portion of the sentences, in a youth custody facility, in a provincial correctional facility for adults or, if the unexpired portion of the sentence is two years or more, in a penitentiary.

**When young person reaches twenty years of age**

**92.** (1) When a young person who is committed to custody under paragraph 41(2)(*n*), (*p*) or (*q*) is in a youth custody facility when the young person attains the age of twenty years, the young person shall be transferred to a provincial correctional facility for adults to serve the remainder of the youth sentence, unless the provincial director orders that the young person continue to serve the youth sentence in a youth custody facility.

**If serving youth sentence in a provincial correctional facility**

(2) If a young person is serving a portion of a youth sentence in a provincial correctional facility for adults pursuant to a transfer under subsection (1), the youth justice court may, on application of the provincial director after the transfer, after giving the young person, the provincial director and representatives of the provincial and federal correctional systems an opportunity to be heard, authorize the provincial director to direct that the young person serve the remainder of the youth sentence in a penitentiary if the court considers it to be in the best interests of the young person or in the public interest and if, at the time of the application, that remainder is two years or more.

**Provisions to apply**

(3) If the provincial director makes the direction, the *Prisons and Reformatories Act* and the *Corrections and Conditional Release Act*, and any other statute, regulation or rule applicable in respect of prisoners and offenders within the meaning of those Acts, statutes, regulations and rules, apply in respect of the young person except to the extent that they conflict with Part 6 of this Act, which Part continues to apply to the young person.

**Annual review**

**93.** (1) When a young person is committed to custody pursuant to a youth sentence under paragraph 41(2)(*n*), (*p*) or (*q*) for a period exceeding one year, the provincial director of the province in which the young person is held in custody shall cause the young person to be brought before the youth justice court at the end of one year from the date of the most recent youth sentence imposed in respect of the offence—and at the end of every subsequent year from that date—and the youth justice court shall review the youth sentence.

**Annual review**

(2) When a young person is committed to custody pursuant to youth sentences imposed under paragraph 41(2)(*n*), (*p*) or (*q*) in respect of more than one offence for a total period exceeding one year, the provincial director of the province in which the young person is held in custody shall cause the young person to be brought before the youth justice court without delay at the end of one year from the date of the earliest youth sentence imposed—and at the end of every subsequent year from that date—and the youth justice court shall review the youth sentences.

**Optional review**

(3) When a young person is committed to custody pursuant to a youth sentence imposed under paragraph 41(2)(*n*), (*p*) or (*q*) in respect of an offence, the provincial director may, on the provincial director's own initiative, and shall, on the request of the young person, the young person's parent or the Attorney General, on any of the grounds set out in subsection (6), cause the young person to be brought before a youth justice court to review the youth sentence,

(*a*) when the youth sentence is for a period not exceeding one year, once at any time after the expiry of the greater of

(i) thirty days after the date of the youth sentence imposed under subsection 41(2) in respect of the offence, and

(ii) one third of the period of the youth sentence imposed under subsection 41(2) in respect of the offence; and

(*b*) when the youth sentence is for a period exceeding one year, at any time after six months after the date of the most recent youth sentence imposed in respect of the offence.

**Time for optional review**
(4) The young person may be brought before the youth justice court at any other time, with leave of the youth justice court judge.

**Review**
(5) If a youth justice court is satisfied that there are grounds for review under subsection (6), the court shall review the youth sentence.

**Grounds for review**
(6) A youth sentence imposed in respect of a young person may be reviewed under subsection (5)

(*a*) on the ground that the young person has made sufficient progress to justify a change in youth sentence;
(*b*) on the ground that the circumstances that led to the youth sentence have changed materially;
(*c*) on the ground that new services or programs are available that were not available at the time of the youth sentence;
(*d*) on the ground that the opportunities for rehabilitation are now greater in the community; or
(*e*) on any other ground that the youth justice court considers appropriate.

**No review if appeal pending**
(7) Despite any other provision of this section, no review of a youth sentence in respect of which an appeal has been taken shall be made under this section until all proceedings in respect of any such appeal have been completed.

**Youth justice court may order appearance of young person for review**
(8) When a provincial director is required under subsections (1) to (3) to cause a young person to be brought before the youth justice court and fails to do so, the youth justice court may, on application made by the young person, his or her parent or the Attorney General, or on its own motion, order the provincial director to cause the young person to be brought before the youth justice court.

**Progress report**
(9) The youth justice court shall, before reviewing under this section a youth sentence imposed in respect of a young person, require the provincial director to cause to be prepared, and to submit to the youth justice court, a progress report on the performance of the young person since the youth sentence took effect.

**Additional information in progress report**
(10) A person preparing a progress report in respect of a young person may include in the report any information relating to the personal and family history and present environment of the young person that he or she considers advisable.

**Written or oral report**
(11) A progress report shall be in writing unless it cannot reasonably be committed to writing, in which case it may, with leave of the youth justice court, be submitted orally in court.

**Subsections 39(4) to (10) to apply**
(12) Subsections 39(4) to (10) apply, with any modifications that the circumstances require, in respect of progress reports.

**Notice of review from provincial director**
(13) When a youth sentence imposed in respect of a young person is to be reviewed under subsection (1) or (2), the provincial director shall cause any notice that may be directed by rules of court applicable to the youth justice court or, in the absence of such a direction, at least five clear days notice of the review to be given in writing to the young person, a parent of the young person and the Attorney General.

**Notice of review from person requesting it**
(14) When a review of a youth sentence imposed in respect of a young person is requested under subsection (3), the person requesting the review shall cause any notice that may be directed by rules of court applicable to the youth justice court or, in the absence of such a direction, at least five clear days notice of the review to be given in writing to the young person, a parent of the young person and the Attorney General.

**Statement of right to counsel**
(15) A notice given to a parent under subsection (13) or (14) shall include a statement that the young person whose youth sentence is to be reviewed has the right to be represented by counsel.

**Service of notice**
(16) A notice under subsection (13) or (14) may be served personally or may be sent by confirmed delivery service.

**Notice may be waived**
(17) Any of the persons entitled to notice under subsection (13) or (14) may waive the right to that notice.

**If notice not given**
(18) If notice under subsection (13) or (14) is not given in accordance with this section, the youth justice court may

(*a*) adjourn the proceedings and order that the notice be given in the manner and to the persons that it directs; or
(*b*) dispense with the notice if, in the opinion of the court, having regard to the circumstances, notice may be dispensed with.

**Decision of the youth justice court after review**
(19) When a youth justice court reviews under

this section a youth sentence imposed in respect of a young person, it may, after giving the young person, a parent of the young person, the Attorney General and the provincial director an opportunity to be heard, having regard to the needs of the young person and the interests of society,

(*a*) confirm the youth sentence;

(*b*) release the young person from custody and place the young person under conditional supervision in accordance with the procedure set out in section 104, with any modifications that the circumstances require, for a period not exceeding the remainder of the youth sentence that the young person is then serving; or

(*c*) if the provincial director so recommends, convert a youth sentence under paragraph 41(2)(*q*) to a youth sentence under paragraph 41(2)(*p*) if the offence was murder or to a youth sentence under paragraph 41(2)(*n*) if the offence was an offence other than murder.

**Orders are youth sentences**

94. Orders under subsections 96(2) and 97(3), paragraph 102(2)(*b*), subsections 103(1) and 104(1) and paragraph 108(2)(*b*) are deemed to be youth sentences for the purposes of section 93.

**Recommendation of provincial director for conditional supervision of young person**

95. (1) When a young person is held in custody pursuant to a youth sentence under paragraph 41(2)(*n*), (*p*) or (*q*), the provincial director may, if satisfied that the needs of the young person and the interests of society would be better served by doing so, make a recommendation to the youth justice court that the young person be released from custody and placed under conditional supervision.

**Notice**

(2) If the provincial director makes a recommendation, the provincial director shall cause a notice to be given in writing that includes the reasons for the recommendation and the conditions that the provincial director would recommend be set under section 104 to the young person, a parent of the young person and the Attorney General and give a copy of the notice to the youth justice court.

**Application to court for review of recommendation**

(3) If notice of a recommendation is made under subsection (2) with respect to a youth sentence imposed on a young person, the youth justice court shall, if an application for review is made by the young person, the young person's parent or the Attorney General within ten days after service of the notice, review the youth sentence without delay.

**Subsections 93(7), (9) to (12) and (14) to (19) apply**

(4) Subject to subsection (5), subsections 93(7), (9) to (12) and (14) to (19) apply, with any modifications that the circumstances require, in respect of reviews made under this section and any notice required under subsection 93(14) shall also be given to the provincial director.

**If no application for review made under subsection (3)**

(5) A youth justice court that receives a notice under subsection (2) shall, if no application for a review is made under subsection (3),

(*a*) order the release of the young person and place the young person under conditional supervision in accordance with section 104, having regard to the recommendations of the provincial director; or

(*b*) if the court considers it advisable, order that the young person not be released.

For greater certainty, an order under this subsection may be made without a hearing.

**Notice when no release ordered**

(6) When a youth justice court orders that the young person not be released under paragraph (5)(*b*), it shall cause a notice of its order to be given to the provincial director without delay.

**Provincial director may request review**

(7) When the provincial director is given a notice under subsection (6), he or she may request a review under this section.

**When provincial director requests a review**

(8) When the provincial director requests a review under subsection (7),

(*a*) the provincial director shall cause any notice that may be directed by rules of court applicable to the youth justice court or, in the absence of such a direction, at least five clear days notice of the review to be given in writing to the young person, a parent of the young person and the Attorney General; and

(*b*) the youth justice court shall review the youth sentence without delay after the notice required under paragraph (*a*) is given.

**Conditions to be included in custody and supervision order**

96. (1) Every youth sentence imposed under paragraph 41(2)(*n*) shall contain the following conditions, namely, that the young person, while serving the portion of the youth sentence under supervision in the community,

(*a*) keep the peace and be of good behaviour;

(*b*) report to the provincial director and then be under the supervision of the provincial director;

(*c*) inform the provincial director immediately on being arrested or questioned by the police;

(*d*) report to the police, or any named individual, as instructed by the provincial director;

(*e*) advise the provincial director of the young person's address of residence and report immediately to the provincial director any change

(i) in that address,

(ii) in the young person's normal occupation, including employment, vocational or educational training and volunteer work,

(iii) in the young person's family or financial situation, and
(iv) that may reasonably be expected to affect the young person's ability to comply with the conditions of the sentence; and

(*f*) not own, possess or have the control of any weapon, ammunition, prohibited ammunition, prohibited device or explosive substance, except as authorized by the sentence.

**Other conditions**
(2) The provincial director may set additional conditions that promote the reintegration of the young person into the community and offer adequate protection to the public from the risk that the young person might otherwise present. The provincial director shall, in setting the conditions, take into account the nature of the offence and the ability of the young person to comply with the conditions.

**Communication of conditions**
(3) The provincial director shall

(*a*) cause the conditions to be read by or to the young person bound by them;
(*b*) explain or cause to be explained to the young person the purpose and effect of the conditions, and confirm that the young person understands them; and
(*c*) cause a copy of the conditions to be given to the young person, and to a parent of the young person.

**Provisions to apply**
(4) Subsections 54(5) and (6) apply, with any modifications that the circumstances require, in respect of conditions under this section.

**Application by provincial director**
**97.** (1) Within a reasonable time before the expiry of the custodial portion of a young person's youth sentence, the provincial director may apply to the youth justice court for an order that the young person remain in custody for a period not exceeding the remainder of the youth sentence.

**Continuation of custody**
(2) If the hearing for an application under subsection (1) cannot be completed before the expiry of the custodial portion of the youth sentence, the court may order that the young person remain in custody pending the determination of the application if the court is satisfied that the application was made in a reasonable time, having regard to all the circumstances, and that there are compelling reasons for keeping the young person in custody.

**Decision**
(3) The youth justice court may, after giving both parties and a parent of the young person an opportunity to be heard, order that a young person remain in custody for a period not exceeding the remainder of the youth sentence, if it is satisfied that there are reasonable grounds to believe that

(*a*) the young person is likely to commit a serious violent offence before the expiry of the youth sentence he or she is then serving; and
(*b*) the conditions that would be imposed on the young person if he or she were to serve a portion of the youth sentence in the community would not be adequate to prevent the commission of the offence.

**Factors**
(4) For the purpose of determining an application under subsection (1), the youth justice court shall take into consideration any factor that is relevant to the case of the young person, including

(*a*) evidence of a pattern of persistent violent behaviour and, in particular,
(i) the number of offences committed by the young person that caused physical or psychological harm to any other person,
(ii) the young person's difficulties in controlling violent impulses to the point of endangering the safety of any other person,
(iii) the use of weapons in the commission of any offence,
(iv) explicit threats of violence,
(v) behaviour of a brutal nature associated with the commission of any offence, and
(vi) a substantial degree of indifference on the part of the young person as to the reasonably foreseeable consequences, to other persons, of the young person's behaviour;

(*b*) psychiatric or psychological evidence that a physical or mental illness or disorder of the young person is of such a nature that the young person is likely to commit, before the expiry of the youth sentence the young person is then serving, a serious violent offence;
(*c*) reliable information that satisfies the youth justice court that the young person is planning to commit, before the expiry of the youth sentence the young person is then serving, a serious violent offence;
(*d*) the availability of supervision programs in the community that would offer adequate protection to the public from the risk that the young person might otherwise present until the expiry of the youth sentence the young person is then serving;
(*e*) whether the young person is more likely to reoffend if he or she serves his or her youth sentence entirely in custody without the benefits of serving a portion of the youth sentence in the community under supervision; and
(*f*) evidence of a pattern of committing offences against the person while he or she was serving a portion of a youth sentence in the community under supervision.

**Report**
**98.** (1) For the purpose of determining an application under section 97, the youth justice court shall require the provincial director to cause to be prepared, and to submit to the youth justice court, a report setting out any information of which the provincial director is aware with respect to the factors set out in subsection 97(4) that may be of assistance to the court.

**Written or oral report**
(2) A report referred to in subsection (1) shall be in writing unless it cannot reasonably be committed to writing, in which case it may, with leave of the youth justice court, be submitted orally in court.

**Provisions apply**
(3) Subsections 39(4) to (10) apply, with any modifications that the circumstances require, in respect of a report referred to in subsection (1).

**Notice of hearing**
(4) When an application is made under section 97 in respect of a young person, the provincial director shall cause to be given, to the young person and to a parent of the young person at least five clear days notice of the hearing in writing.

**Statement of right to counsel**
(5) Any notice given to a parent under subsection (4) shall include a statement that the young person has the right to be represented by counsel.

**Service of notice**
(6) A notice under subsection (4) may be served personally or may be sent by confirmed delivery service.

**When notice not given**
(7) When notice under subsection (4) is not given in accordance with this section, the youth justice court may
(*a*) adjourn the hearing and order that the notice be given in any manner and to any person that it directs; or
(*b*) dispense with the giving of the notice if, in the opinion of the youth justice court, having regard to the circumstances, the giving of the notice may be dispensed with.

**Reasons**
**99.** When a youth justice court makes an order under subsection 97(3), it shall state its reasons for the order in the record of the case and shall provide, or cause to be provided, to the young person in respect of whom the order was made, the counsel and a parent of the young person, the Attorney General and the provincial director
(*a*) a copy of the order; and
(*b*) on request, a transcript or copy of the reasons for the order.

**Review of youth justice court decision**
**100.** (1) An order made under subsection 97(3) in respect of a young person, or the refusal to make such an order, shall, on application of the young person, the young person's counsel or the provincial director made within thirty days after the decision of the youth justice court, be reviewed by the court of appeal, and that court may, in its discretion, confirm or reverse the decision of the youth justice court.

**Extension of time to make application**
(2) The court of appeal may, at any time, extend the time within which an application under subsection (1) may be made.

**Notice of application**
(3) A person who proposes to apply for a review under subsection (1) shall give notice of the application in the manner and within the period of time that may be directed by rules of court.

**Breach of conditions**
**101.** (1) If the provincial director has reasonable grounds to believe that a young person has breached or is about to breach a condition to which he or she is subject under section 96, the provincial director may, in writing,
(*a*) permit the young person to continue to serve a portion of his or her youth sentence in the community, on the same or different conditions; or
(*b*) if satisfied that the breach is a serious one that increases the risk to public safety, order that the young person be remanded to any youth custody facility that the provincial director considers appropriate until a review is conducted.

**Provisions apply**
(2) Sections 106 and 107 apply, with any modifications that the circumstances require, to an order under paragraph (1)(*b*).

**Review by youth justice court**
**102.** (1) When the case of a young person is referred to the youth justice court under section 107, the provincial director shall, without delay, cause the young person to be brought before the youth justice court, and the youth justice court shall, after giving the young person an opportunity to be heard,
(*a*) if the court is not satisfied on reasonable grounds that the young person has breached or was about to breach one of the conditions under which he or she was being supervised in the community, order that the young person continue to serve a portion of his or her youth sentence in the community, on the same or different conditions; or
(*b*) if the court is satisfied on reasonable grounds that the young person has breached or was about to breach one of the conditions under which he or she was being supervised in the community, make an order under subsection (2).

**Order**
(2) On completion of a review under subsection (1), the youth justice court
(*a*) shall order that the young person continue to serve the remainder of the youth sentence the young person is then serving in the community, and when the court does so, the court may vary the existing conditions or impose new conditions; or
(*b*) shall, despite paragraph 41(2)(*n*), order that the young person remain in custody for a period that does not exceed the remainder of the youth sentence the young person is then serving, if the youth justice court is satisfied that the breach of the conditions was serious.

**Provisions apply**
(3) Subsections 108(3) to (6) apply, with any modifications that the circumstances require, in respect of a review under this section.

**Continuation of custody**
**103.** (1) When a young person on whom a youth sentence, under paragraph 41(2)(*p*) or (*q*) has been imposed is held in custody and an application is made to the youth justice court by the Attorney General, within a reasonable time before the expiry of the custodial portion of the youth sentence, the provincial director of the province in which the young person is held in custody shall cause the young person to be brought before the youth justice court and the youth justice court may, after giving both parties and a parent of the young person an opportunity to be heard and if it is satisfied that there are reasonable grounds to believe that the young person is likely to commit an offence causing the death of or serious harm to another person before the expiry of the youth sentence the young person is then serving, order that the young person remain in custody for a period not exceeding the remainder of the youth sentence.

**Continuation of custody**
(2) If the hearing of an application under subsection (1) cannot be completed before the expiry of the custodial portion of the youth sentence, the court may order that the young person remain in custody until the determination of the application if the court is satisfied that the application was made in a reasonable time, having regard to all the circumstances, and that there are compelling reasons for keeping the young person in custody.

**Factors**
(3) For the purpose of determining an application under subsection (1), the youth justice court shall take into consideration any factor that is relevant to the case of the young person, including
(*a*) evidence of a pattern of persistent violent behaviour and, in particular,
(i) the number of offences committed by the young person that caused physical or psychological harm to any other person,
(ii) the young person's difficulties in controlling violent impulses to the point of endangering the safety of any other person,
(iii) the use of weapons in the commission of any offence,
(iv) explicit threats of violence,
(v) behaviour of a brutal nature associated with the commission of any offence, and
(vi) a substantial degree of indifference on the part of the young person as to the reasonably foreseeable consequences, to other persons, of the young person's behaviour;
(*b*) psychiatric or psychological evidence that a physical or mental illness or disorder of the young person is of such a nature that the young person is likely to commit, before the expiry of the youth sentence the young person is then serving, an offence causing the death of or serious harm to another person;
(*c*) reliable information that satisfies the youth justice court that the young person is planning to commit, before the expiry of the youth sentence the young person is then serving, an offence causing the death of or serious harm to another person; and
(*d*) the availability of supervision programs in the community that would offer adequate protection to the public from the risk that the young person might otherwise present until the expiry of the youth sentence the young person is then serving.

**Youth justice court to order appearance of young person**
(4) If a provincial director fails to cause a young person to be brought before the youth justice court under subsection (1), the youth justice court shall order the provincial director to cause the young person to be brought before the youth justice court without delay.

**Provisions to apply**
(5) Sections 98 to 100 apply, with any modifications that the circumstances require, in respect of an order made, or the refusal to make an order, under this section.

**If application denied**
(6) If an application under this section is denied, the court may, with the consent of the young person, the Attorney General and the provincial director, proceed as though the young person had been brought before the court as required under subsection 104(1).

**Conditional supervision**
**104.** (1) The provincial director of the province in which a young person on whom a youth sentence under paragraph 41(2)(*p*) or (*q*) has been imposed is held in custody or, if applicable, with respect to whom an order has been made under subsection 103(1), shall cause the young person to be brought before the youth justice court at least one month before the expiry of the custodial portion of the youth sentence. The court shall, after giving the young person an opportunity to be heard, by order, set the conditions of the young person's conditional supervision.

**Conditions to be included in order**
(2) The youth justice court shall include in the order under subsection (1) the following conditions, namely, that the young person
(*a*) keep the peace and be of good behaviour;
(*b*) appear before the youth justice court when required by the court to do so;
(*c*) report to the provincial director immediately on release, and then be under the supervision of the provincial director or a person designated by the youth justice court;
(*d*) inform the provincial director immediately on being arrested or questioned by the police;
(*e*) report to the police, or any named individual, as instructed by the provincial director;
(*f*) advise the provincial director of the young person's address of residence on release and

after release report immediately to the clerk of the youth justice court or the provincial director any change

(i) in that address,

(ii) in the young person's normal occupation, including employment, vocational or educational training and volunteer work,

(iii) in the young person's family or financial situation, and

(iv) that may reasonably be expected to affect the young person's ability to comply with the conditions of the order;

(*g*) not own, possess or have the control of any weapon, ammunition, prohibited ammunition, prohibited device or explosive substance, except as authorized by the order; and

(*h*) comply with any reasonable instructions that the provincial director considers necessary in respect of any condition of the conditional supervision in order to prevent a breach of that condition or to protect society.

**Other conditions**
(3) In setting conditions for the purposes of subsection (1), the youth justice court may include in the order the following conditions, namely, that the young person

(*a*) on release, travel directly to the young person's place of residence, or to any other place that is noted in the order;

(*b*) make reasonable efforts to obtain and maintain suitable employment;

(*c*) attend school or any other place of learning, training or recreation that is appropriate, if the court is satisfied that a suitable program is available for the young person at such a place;

(*d*) reside with a parent, or any other adult that the court considers appropriate, who is willing to provide for the care and maintenance of the young person;

(*e*) reside in any place that the provincial director may specify;

(*f*) remain within the territorial jurisdiction of one or more courts named in the order; and

(*g*) comply with any other conditions set out in the order that the court considers appropriate, including conditions for securing the young person's good conduct and for preventing the young person from repeating the offence or committing other offences.

**Temporary conditions**
(4) When a provincial director is required under subsection (1) to cause a young person to be brought before the youth justice court but cannot do so for reasons beyond the young person's control, the provincial director shall so advise the youth justice court and the court shall, by order, set any temporary conditions for the young person's conditional supervision that are appropriate in the circumstances.

**Conditions to be set at first opportunity**
(5) When an order is made under subsection (4), the provincial director shall bring the young person before the youth justice court as soon after the order is made as the circumstances permit and the court shall then set the conditions of the young person's conditional supervision.

**Report**
(6) For the purpose of setting conditions under this section, the youth justice court shall require the provincial director to cause to be prepared, and to submit to the youth justice court, a report setting out any information that may be of assistance to the court.

**Provisions apply**
(7) Subsections 98(2) to (7) and 103(4) apply, with any modifications that the circumstances require, in respect of any proceedings held under subsection (1).

**Provisions apply**
(8) Subsections 54(3) to (6), (9) and (10) and section 100 apply, with any modifications that the circumstances require, in respect of an order made under subsection (1).

**Suspension of conditional supervision**
**105.** If the provincial director has reasonable grounds to believe that a young person has breached or is about to breach a condition of an order made under subsection 104(1), the provincial director may, in writing,

(*a*) suspend the conditional supervision; and

(*b*) order that the young person be remanded to any youth custody facility that the provincial director considers appropriate until a review is conducted under section 107 and, if applicable, section 108.

**Apprehension**
**106.** (1) If the conditional supervision of a young person is suspended under section 105, the provincial director may issue a warrant in writing, authorizing the apprehension of the young person and, until the young person is apprehended, the young person is deemed not to be continuing to serve the youth sentence the young person is then serving.

**Warrants**
(2) A warrant issued under subsection (1) shall be executed by any peace officer to whom it is given at any place in Canada and has the same force and effect in all parts of Canada as if it had been originally issued or subsequently endorsed by a provincial court judge or other lawful authority having jurisdiction in the place where it is executed.

**Peace officer may arrest**
(3) If a peace officer believes on reasonable grounds that a warrant issued under subsection (1) is in force in respect of a young person, the peace officer may arrest the young person without the warrant at any place in Canada.

**Requirement to bring before provincial director**
(4) If a young person is arrested under subsection (3) and detained, the peace officer making the arrest shall cause the young person to be brought before the provincial director or a person designated by the provincial director

(*a*) if the provincial director or the designated person is available within a period of twenty-four hours after the young person is arrested, without unreasonable delay and in any event within that period; and
(*b*) if the provincial director or the designated person is not available within that period, as soon as possible.

**Release or remand in custody**
(5) If a young person is brought before the provincial director or a person designated by the provincial director under subsection (4), the provincial director or the designated person
(*a*) if not satisfied that there are reasonable grounds to believe that the young person is the young person in respect of whom the warrant referred to in subsection (1) was issued, shall release the young person; or
(*b*) if satisfied that there are reasonable grounds to believe that the young person is the young person in respect of whom the warrant referred to in subsection (1) was issued, may remand the young person in custody to await execution of the warrant, but if no warrant for the young person's arrest is executed within a period of forty-eight hours after the time the young person is remanded in custody, the person in whose custody the young person then is shall release the young person.

**Review by provincial director**
**107.** Without delay after the remand to custody of a young person whose conditional supervision has been suspended under section 105, or without delay after being informed of the arrest of such a young person, the provincial director shall review the case and, within forty-eight hours, cancel the suspension of the conditional supervision or refer the case to the youth justice court for a review under section 108.

**Review by youth justice court**
**108.** (1) If the case of a young person is referred to the youth justice court under section 107, the provincial director shall, without delay, cause the young person to be brought before the youth justice court, and the youth justice court shall, after giving the young person an opportunity to be heard,
(*a*) if the court is not satisfied on reasonable grounds that the young person has breached or was about to breach a condition of the conditional supervision, cancel the suspension of the conditional supervision; or
(*b*) if the court is satisfied on reasonable grounds that the young person has breached or was about to breach a condition of the conditional supervision, review the decision of the provincial director to suspend the conditional supervision and make an order under subsection (2).

**Order**
(2) On completion of a review under subsection (1), the youth justice court shall order
(*a*) the cancellation of the suspension of the conditional supervision, and when the court does so, the court may vary the conditions of the conditional supervision or impose new conditions; or
(*b*) the continuation of the suspension of the conditional supervision for any period of time, not to exceed the remainder of the youth sentence the young person is then serving, that the court considers appropriate, and when the court does so, the court shall order that the young person remain in custody.

**Reasons**
(3) When a youth justice court makes an order under subsection (2), it shall state its reasons for the order in the record of the case and shall give, or cause to be given, to the young person in respect of whom the order was made, the counsel and a parent of the young person and the provincial director,
(*a*) a copy of the order; and
(*b*) on request, a transcript or copy of the reasons for the order.

**Report**
(4) Before causing the young person to be brought before it, the youth justice court shall require the provincial director to cause to be prepared, and to submit to the youth justice court, a report setting out any information of which the provincial director is aware that may be of assistance to the court.

**Provisions apply**
(5) Subsections 98(2) and (4) to (7) and 104(6) apply, with any modifications that the circumstances require, in respect of a review under this section.

**Provisions apply**
(6) Section 100 applies, with any modifications that the circumstances require, in respect of an order made under subsection (2).

## PART 6
## PUBLICATION, RECORDS AND INFORMATION

*Protection of Privacy of Young Persons*

**Identity of offender not to be published**
**109.** (1) Subject to this section, no person shall publish the name of a young person, or any other information related to a young person, if it would identify the young person as a young person dealt with under this Act.

**Limitation**
(2) Subsection (1) does not apply
(*a*) in a case where the information relates to a young person who is subject to an adult sentence;
(*b*) subject to sections 64 and 75, in a case where the information relates to a young person who is subject to a youth sentence

for an offence set out in paragraph (*a*) of the definition "presumptive offence" in subsection 2(1), or an offence set out in paragraph (*b*) of that definition for which the Attorney General has given notice under subsection 63(2); and

(*c*) in a case where the publication of information is made in the course of the administration of justice, if it is not the purpose of the publication to make the information known in the community.

**Exception**
(3) A young person referred to in subsection (1) may, after he or she attains the age of eighteen years, publish or cause to be published information that would identify him or her as having been dealt with under this Act or the *Young Offenders Act*, chapter Y-1 of the Revised Statutes of Canada, 1985, provided that he or she is not in custody pursuant to either Act at the time of its publication.

***Ex parte* application for leave to publish**
(4) A youth justice court judge shall, on the *ex parte* application of a peace officer, make an order permitting any person to publish information that identifies a young person as having committed or allegedly committed an indictable offence, if the judge is satisfied that

(*a*) there is reason to believe that the young person is a danger to others; and
(*b*) publication of the information is necessary to assist in apprehending the young person.

**Order ceases to have effect**
(5) An order made under subsection (4) ceases to have effect five days after it is made.

**Application for leave to publish**
(6) The youth justice court may, on the application of a young person referred to in subsection (1), make an order permitting the young person to publish information that would identify him or her as having been dealt with under this Act or the *Young Offenders Act*, chapter Y-1 of the Revised Statutes of Canada, 1985, if the court is satisfied that the publication would not be contrary to the young person's best interests or the public interest.

**Identity of victim or witness not to be published**
**110.** (1) Subject to this section, no person shall publish the name of a child or young person, or any other information related to a child or a young person, if it would identify the child or young person as having been a victim of, or as having appeared as a witness in connection with, an offence committed or alleged to have been committed by a young person.

**Exception**
(2) A child or young person referred to in subsection (1) may, after he or she attains the age of eighteen years, publish or cause to be published information that would identify him or her as having been a victim or a witness.

**Application for leave to publish**
(3) The youth justice court may, on the application of a child or a young person referred to in subsection (1), make an order permitting the child or young person to publish information that would identify him or her as having been a victim or a witness if the court is satisfied that the publication would not be contrary to his or her best interests or the public interest.

**Non-application**
**111.** Once information is published under subsection 109(3) or (6) or 110(2) or (3), subsection 109(1) or 110(1), as the case may be, no longer applies in respect of the information.

***Fingerprints and Photographs***

***Identification of Criminals Act* applies**
**112.** (1) The *Identification of Criminals Act* applies in respect of young persons.

**Limitation**
(2) No fingerprint, palmprint or photograph or other measurement, process or operation referred to in the *Identification of Criminals Act* shall be taken of, or applied in respect of, a young person who is charged with having committed an offence except in the circumstances in which an adult may, under that Act, be subjected to the measurements, processes and operations.

***Records that May Be Kept***

**Youth justice court, review board and other courts**
**113.** A youth justice court, review board or any court dealing with matters arising out of proceedings under this Act may keep a record of any case that comes before it arising under this Act.

**Police records**
**114.** (1) A record relating to any offence alleged to have been committed by a young person, including the original or a copy of any fingerprints or photographs of the young person, may be kept by any police force responsible for or participating in the investigation of the offence.

**Police records**
(2) When a young person is charged with having committed an offence in respect of which an adult may be subjected to any measurement, process or operation referred to in the *Identification of Criminals Act*, the police force responsible for the investigation of the offence may provide a record relating to the offence to the Royal Canadian Mounted Police. If the young person is found guilty of the offence, the police force shall provide the record.

**Records held by R.C.M.P.**
(3) The Royal Canadian Mounted Police shall keep the records provided under subsection (2) in the central repository that the Commissioner of the Royal Canadian Mounted Police may, from

time to time, designate for the purpose of keeping criminal history files or records of offenders or keeping records for the identification of offenders.

**Government records**
**115.** (1) A department or an agency of any government in Canada may keep records containing information obtained by the department or agency
(*a*) for the purposes of an investigation of an offence alleged to have been committed by a young person
(*b*) for use in proceedings against a young person under this Act;
(*c*) for the purpose of administering a youth sentence or an order under the *Firearms Act* or under section 810, 810.01 or 810.2 of the *Criminal Code*;
(*d*) for the purpose of considering whether to use extrajudicial measures to deal with a young person; or
(*e*) as a result of the use of extrajudicial measures to deal with a young person.

**Other records**
(2) A person or organization may keep records containing information obtained by the person or organization
(*a*) as a result of the use of extrajudicial measures to deal with a young person; or
(*b*) for the purpose of administering or participating in the administration of a youth sentence.

*Access to Records*

**Exception—adult sentence**
**116.** Sections 117 to 128 do not apply to records kept in respect of an offence for which an adult sentence has been imposed once the time allowed for the taking of an appeal has expired or, if an appeal is taken, all proceedings in respect of the appeal have been completed and the appeal court has upheld an adult sentence. The record shall be dealt with as a record of an adult and, for the purposes of the *Criminal Records Act*, the finding of guilt in respect of the offence for which the record is kept is deemed to be a conviction.

**No access unless authorized**
**117.** (1) Except as authorized or required by this Act, no person shall be given access to a record kept under sections 113 to 115, and no information contained in it may be given to any person, where to do so would identify the young person to whom it relates as a young person dealt with under this Act.

**Exception for employees**
(2) No person who is employed in keeping or maintaining records referred to in subsection (1) is restricted from doing anything prohibited under subsection (1) with respect to any other person so employed.

**Persons having access to records**
**118.** (1) Subject to subsections (4) to (6), from the date that a record is created until the end of the applicable period set out in subsection (2), the following persons, on request, shall be given access to a record kept under section 113, and may be given access to a record kept under sections 114 and 115:
(*a*) the young person to whom the record relates;
(*b*) the young person's counsel, or any representative of that counsel;
(*c*) the Attorney General;
(*d*) the victim of the offence or alleged offence to which the record relates;
(*e*) the parents of the young person, during the course of any proceedings relating to the offence or alleged offence to which the record relates or during the term of any youth sentence made in respect of the offence;
(*f*) any adult assisting the young person under subsection 25(7), during the course of any proceedings relating to the offence or alleged offence to which the record relates or during the term of any youth sentence made in respect of the offence;
(*g*) any peace officer for
(i) law enforcement purposes, or
(ii) any purpose related to the administration of the case to which the record relates, during the course of proceedings against the young person or the term of the youth sentence;
(*h*) a judge, court or review board, for any purpose relating to proceedings against the young person, or proceedings against the person after he or she becomes an adult, in respect of offences committed or alleged to have been committed by that person;
(*i*) the provincial director, or the director of the provincial correctional facility for adults or the penitentiary at which the young person is serving a youth sentence;
(*j*) a person participating in a conference or in the administration of extrajudicial measures, if required for the administration of the case to which the record relates;
(*k*) a person acting as ombudsman, privacy commissioner or information commissioner, whatever his or her official designation might be, who in the course of his or her duties under an Act of Parliament or the legislature of a province is investigating a complaint to which the record relates;
(*l*) a coroner or a person acting as a child advocate, whatever his or her official designation might be, who is acting in the course of his or her duties under an Act of Parliament or the legislature of a province;
(*m*) a person acting under the *Firearms Act*;
(*n*) a member of a department or agency of a government in Canada, or an agent of the department or agency, who is
(i) acting in the exercise of his or her duties under this Act,
(ii) engaged in the supervision or care of the young person, whether as a young person or an adult, or in an investigation related to the young person under an Act of the legislature of a province respecting child welfare,
(iii) considering an application for conditional release or pardon made by the young person, whether as a young person or an adult,

(iv) administering a prohibition order made under an Act of Parliament or the legislature of a province, or
(v) administering a youth sentence, if the young person has been committed to custody and is serving the custody in a provincial correctional facility for adults or a penitentiary;
(*o*) a person, for the purpose of determining whether to grant security clearances required by the Government of Canada or the government of a province or a municipality for purposes of employment or the performance of services;
(*p*) an employee or agent of the Government of Canada, for statistical purposes under the *Statistics Act*;
(*q*) a person who, in the opinion of the court or the Attorney General in any proceeding against the person, must have access to the record so that the person may make a full answer and defence;
(*r*) a person or a member of a class of persons designated by order of the Governor in Council, or the lieutenant governor in council of the appropriate province, for a purpose and to the extent specified in the order; and
(*s*) any person or member of a class of persons that a youth justice court judge considers has a valid interest in the record, to the extent directed by the judge, if the judge is satisfied that access to the record is
(i) desirable in the public interest for research or statistical purposes, or
(ii) desirable in the interest of the proper administration of justice.

**Period of access**

(2) The period of access referred to in subsection (1) is
(*a*) if an extrajudicial sanction is used to deal with the young person, the period ending two years after the young person consents to be subject to the sanction in accordance with paragraph 10(2)(*c*);
(*b*) if the young person is acquitted of the offence otherwise than by reason of a verdict of not criminally responsible on account of mental disorder, the period ending two months after the expiry of the time allowed for the taking of an appeal or, if an appeal is taken, the period ending three months after all proceedings in respect of the appeal have been completed;
(*c*) if the charge against the young person is dismissed for any reason other than acquittal, the charge is withdrawn, or the young person is found guilty of the offence and a reprimand is given, the period ending two months after the dismissal, withdrawal, or finding of guilt;
(*d*) if the charge against the young person is stayed, with no proceedings being taken against the young person for a period of one year, at the end of that period;
(*e*) if the young person is found guilty of the offence and the youth sentence is an absolute discharge, the period ending one year after the young person is found guilty;
(*f*) if the young person is found guilty of the offence and the youth sentence is a conditional discharge, the period ending three years after the young person is found guilty;
(*g*) subject to paragraphs (*i*) and (*j*) and subsection (9), if the young person is found guilty of the offence and it is a summary conviction offence, the period ending three years after the youth sentence imposed in respect of the offence has been completed;
(*h*) subject to paragraphs (*i*) and (*j*) and subsection (9), if the young person is found guilty of the offence and it is an indictable offence, the period ending five years after the youth sentence imposed in respect of the offence has been completed;
(*i*) subject to subsection (9), if, during the period calculated in accordance with paragraph (*g*) or (*h*), the young person is found guilty of an offence punishable on summary conviction committed when he or she was a young person, the latest of
(i) the period calculated in accordance with paragraph (*g*) or (*h*), as the case may be, and
(ii) the period ending three years after the youth sentence imposed for that offence has been completed; and
(*j*) subject to subsection (9), if, during the period calculated in accordance with paragraph (*g*) or (*h*), the young person is found guilty of an indictable offence committed when he or she was a young person, the period ending five years after the sentence imposed for that indictable offence has been completed.

**Prohibition orders not included**

(3) Prohibition orders made under an Act of Parliament or the legislature of a province, including any order made under section 50, shall not be taken into account in determining any period referred to in subsection (2).

**Extrajudicial measures**

(4) Access to a record kept under section 114 or 115 in respect of extrajudicial measures, other than extrajudicial sanctions, used in respect of a young person, shall be given only to the following persons for the following purposes:
(*a*) a peace officer or the Attorney General, in order to a make a decision whether to again use extrajudicial measures in respect of the young person;
(*b*) a person participating in a conference, in order to decide on the appropriate extrajudicial measure; and
(*c*) a peace officer, the Attorney General or a person participating in a conference, if access is required for the administration of the case to which the record relates.

**Exception**

(5) When a youth justice court has withheld all or part of a report from any person under subsection 34(9) or (10) or 39(7), that person shall not be given access under subsection (1) to that report or part.

**Records of assessments or forensic DNA analysis**

(6) Access to a report made under section 34 or a record of the results of forensic DNA analysis of a bodily substance taken from a young person in execution of a warrant issued under section 487.05 of the *Criminal Code* may be given only under paragraphs (1)(*a*) to (*c*), (*e*) to (*h*) and (*q*) and subparagraph (1)(*s*)(ii).

**Introduction into evidence**

(7) Nothing in paragraph (1)(*h*) or (*q*) authorizes the introduction into evidence of any part of a record that would not otherwise be admissible in evidence.

**Disclosures for research or statistical purposes**

(8) When access to a record is given to a person under paragraph (1)(*p*) or subparagraph (1)(*s*)(i), the person may subsequently disclose information contained in the record, but shall not disclose the information in any form that would reasonably be expected to identify the young person to whom it relates.

**Application of usual rules**

(9) If, during the period of access to a record under any of paragraphs (2)(*g*) to (*j*), the young person is convicted of an offence committed when he or she is an adult,

(*a*) section 81 does not apply to the young person in respect of the offence for which the record is kept under sections 113 to 115;

(*b*) this Part no longer applies to the record and the record shall be dealt with as a record of an adult; and

(*c*) for the purposes of the *Criminal Records Act*, the finding of guilt in respect of the offence for which the record is kept is deemed to be a conviction.

**Records of offences that result in a prohibition order**

(10) Despite anything in this Act, when a young person is found guilty of an offence that results in a prohibition order being made, and the order is still in force at the end of the applicable period for which access to a record kept in respect of the order may be given under subsection (2), the youth justice court may disclose the record only to establish the existence of the order in any offence involving a breach of the order.

**Access to R.C.M.P. records**

**119.** (1) The following persons may, during the period set out in subsection (3), be given access to a record kept under subsection 114(3) in respect of an offence set out in the schedule:

(*a*) the young person to whom the record relates;

(*b*) the young person's counsel, or any representative of that counsel;

(*c*) an employee or agent of the Government of Canada, for statistical purposes under the *Statistics Act*;

(*d*) any person or member of a class of persons that a youth justice court judge considers has a valid interest in the record, to the extent directed by the judge, if the judge is satisfied that access is desirable in the public interest for research or statistical purposes;

(*e*) the Attorney General or a peace officer, when the young person is or has been charged with another offence set out in the schedule or the same offence more than once, for the purpose of investigating any offence that the young person is suspected of having committed, or in respect of which the young person has been arrested or charged, whether as a young person or as an adult;

(*f*) the Attorney General or a peace officer to establish the existence of an order in any offence involving a breach of the order; and

(*g*) any person for the purposes of the *Firearms Act*.

**Access for identification purposes**

(2) During the period set out in subsection (3), access to the portion of a record kept under subsection 114(3) that contains the name, date of birth and last known address of the young person to whom the fingerprints belong, may be given to a person for identification purposes if a fingerprint identified as that of the young person is found during the investigation of an offence or during an attempt to identify a deceased person or a person suffering from amnesia.

**Period of access**

(3) For the purposes of subsections (1) and (2), the period of access to a record kept under subsection 114(3) in respect of an offence is the following:

(*a*) if the offence is an indictable offence, other than a presumptive offence, the period starting at the end of the applicable period set out in paragraphs 118(2)(*h*) to (*j*) and ending five years later; and

(*b*) if the offence is an offence set out in paragraph (*a*) of the definition "presumptive offence" in subsection 2(1) or an offence set out in paragraph (*b*) of that definition for which the Attorney General has given notice under subsection 63(2), the period starting at the end of the applicable period set out in paragraphs 118(2)(*h*) to (*j*) and continuing indefinitely.

**Subsequent offences as young person**

(4) If a young person who has been found guilty of an offence set out in the schedule is, during the period of access to a record under subsection (3), found guilty of an additional offence set out in the schedule, committed when he or she was a young person, access to the record may be given to the following additional persons:

(*a*) a parent of the young person or any adult assisting the young person under subsection 25(7);

(*b*) a judge, court or review board, for a purpose relating to proceedings against the young person under this Act or any other Act of Parliament in respect of offences committed or alleged to have been committed by the young person, whether as a young person or as an adult; or (*c*) a member of a department or agency of a government in Canada, or an agent of the department or agency, that is

(i) preparing a report in respect of the young person under this Act or for the purpose of assisting a court in sentencing the young person after the young person becomes an adult,

(ii) engaged in the supervision or care of the young person, whether as a young person or as an adult, or in the administration of a sentence in respect of the young person, whether as a young person or as an adult, or

(iii) considering an application for conditional release or pardon made by the young person after the young person becomes an adult.

**Disclosure for research or statistical purposes**
(5) A person who is given access to a record under paragraph (1)(*c*) or (*d*) may subsequently disclose information contained in the record, but shall not disclose the information in any form that would reasonably be expected to identify the young person to whom it relates.

**Subsequent offences as adult**
(6) If, during the period of access to a record under subsection (3), the young person is convicted of an additional offence set out in the schedule, committed when he or she was an adult,

(*a*) this Part no longer applies to the record and the record shall be dealt with as a record of an adult and may be included on the automated criminal conviction records retrieval system maintained by the Royal Canadian Mounted Police; and

(*b*) for the purposes of the *Criminal Records Act*, the finding of guilt in respect of the offence for which the record is kept is deemed to be a conviction.

**Deemed election**
**120.** For the purposes of sections 118 and 119, if no election is made in respect of an offence that may be prosecuted by indictment or proceeded with by way of summary conviction, the Attorney General is deemed to have elected to proceed with the offence as an offence punishable on summary conviction.

**Disclosure of information and copies of record**
**121.** A person who is required or authorized to be given access to a record under section 118, 119, 122 or 123 may be given any information contained in the record and may be given a copy of any part of the record.

**Where records may be made available**
**122.** (1) A youth justice court judge may, on application by a person after the end of the applicable period set out in subsection 118(2), order that the person be given access to all or part of a record kept under sections 113 to 115 or that a copy of the record or part be given to that person,

(*a*) if the youth justice court judge is satisfied that

(i) the person has a valid and substantial interest in the record or part,

(ii) it is necessary for access to be given to the record or part in the interest of the proper administration of justice, and

(iii) disclosure of the record or part or the information in it is not prohibited under any other Act of Parliament or the legislature of a province; or

(*b*) if the youth court judge is satisfied that access to the record or part is desirable in the public interest for research or statistical purposes.

**Restriction for par. (1)(*a*)**
(2) Paragraph (1)(*a*) applies in respect of a record relating to a particular young person or to a record relating to a class of young persons only if the identity of young persons in the class at the time of the making of the application referred to in that paragraph cannot reasonably be ascertained and the disclosure of the record is necessary for the purpose of investigating any offence that a person is suspected on reasonable grounds of having committed against a young person while the young person is, or was, serving a sentence.

**Notice**
(3) Subject to subsection (4), an application for an order under paragraph (1)(*a*) in respect of a record shall not be heard unless the person who makes the application has given the young person to whom the record relates and the person or body that has possession of the record at least five days notice in writing of the application, and the young person and the person or body that has possession has had a reasonable opportunity to be heard.

**Where notice not required**
(4) A youth justice court judge may waive the requirement in subsection (3) to give notice to a young person when the judge is of the opinion that

(*a*) to insist on the giving of the notice would frustrate the application; or

(*b*) reasonable efforts have not been successful in finding the young person.

**Use of record**
(5) In any order under subsection (1), the youth justice court judge shall set out the purposes for which the record may be used.

**Disclosure for research or statistical purposes**
(6) When access to a record is given to any person under paragraph (1)(*b*), that person may subsequently disclose information contained in the record, but shall not disclose the information in any form that would reasonably be expected to identify the young person to whom it relates.

**Access to record by young person**
**123.** A young person to whom a record relates may have access to the record at any time.

*Disclosure of Information in a Record*

**Disclosure by peace officer during investigation**
**124.** (1) A peace officer may disclose to any person any information in a record kept under sec-

tion 113 or 114 that it is necessary to disclose in the conduct of the investigation of an offence.

**Disclosure by Attorney General**
(2) The Attorney General may, in the course of a proceeding under this Act or any other Act of Parliament, disclose the following information in a record kept under section 113 or 114:
(*a*) to a person who is a co-accused with the young person in respect of the offence for which the record is kept, any information contained in the record; and
(*b*) to an accused in a proceeding, if the record is in respect of a witness in the proceeding, information that identifies the witness as a young person who has been dealt with under this Act.

**Information that may be disclosed to a foreign state**
(3) The Attorney General or a peace officer may disclose to the Minister of Justice of Canada information in a record that is kept under section 113 or 114 to the extent that it is necessary to deal with a request to or by a foreign state under the *Mutual Legal Assistance in Criminal Matters Act*, or for the purposes of any extradition matter under the *Extradition Act*. The Minister of Justice of Canada may disclose the information to the foreign state in respect of which the request was made, or to which the extradition matter relates, as the case may be.

**Disclosure to insurance company**
(4) A peace officer may disclose to an insurance company information in a record that is kept under section 113 or 114 for the purpose of investigating a claim arising out of an offence committed or alleged to have been committed by the young person to whom the record relates.

**Preparation of reports**
(5) The provincial director or a youth worker may disclose information contained in a record if the disclosure is necessary for procuring information that relates to the preparation of a report required by this Act.

**Schools and others**
(6) The provincial director, a youth worker, a peace officer or any other person engaged in the provision of services to young persons may disclose to any professional or other person engaged in the supervision or care of a young person—including the representative of any school board or school or any other educational or training institution—any information contained in a record kept under sections 113 to 115 if the disclosure is necessary
(*a*) to ensure compliance by the young person with an authorization under section 90 or an order of any court concerning bail, probation, the serving of a portion of the sentence in the community under supervision or conditional supervision;
(*b*) to ensure the safety of staff, students or other persons; or
(*c*) to facilitate the rehabilitation of the young person.

**Information to be kept separate**
(7) A person to whom information is disclosed under subsection (6) shall
(*a*) keep the information separate from any other record of the young person to whom the information relates;
(*b*) ensure that no other person has access to the information except if authorized under this Act, or if necessary for the purposes of subsection (6); and
(*c*) destroy their copy of the record when the information is no longer required for the purpose for which it was disclosed.

**Time limit**
(8) No information may be disclosed under this section after the end of the applicable period set out in subsection 118(2).

**Records in the custody, etc., of archivists**
**125.** When records originally kept under sections 113 to 115 are under the custody or control of the National Archivist of Canada or the archivist for any province, that person may disclose any information contained in the records to any other person if
(*a*) the Attorney General is satisfied that the disclosure is desirable in the public interest for research or statistical purposes; and
(*b*) the person to whom the information is disclosed undertakes not to disclose the information in any form that could reasonably be expected to identify the young person to whom it relates.

**Disclosure with court order**
**126.** (1) The youth justice court may, on the application of the provincial director, the Attorney General or a peace officer, make an order permitting the applicant to disclose to the person or persons specified by the court any information about a young person that is specified, if the court is satisfied that the disclosure is necessary, having regard to the following circumstances:
(*a*) the young person has been found guilty of an offence involving serious personal injury;
(*b*) the young person poses a risk of serious harm to persons; and
(*c*) the disclosure of the information is relevant to the avoidance of that risk.

**Opportunity to be heard**
(2) Subject to subsection (3), before making an order under subsection (1), the youth justice court shall give the young person, a parent of the young person and the Attorney General an opportunity to be heard.

***Ex parte* application**
(3) An application under subsection (1) may be made *ex parte* by the Attorney General where the youth justice court is satisfied that reasonable efforts have been made to locate the young person and that those efforts have not been successful.

**Time limit**
(4) No information may be disclosed under subsection (1) after the end of the applicable period set out in subsection 118(2).

*Disposition or Destruction of Records and Prohibition on Use and Disclosure*

**Effect of end of access periods**
**127.** (1) Subject to sections 122, 123 and 125, after the end of the applicable period set out in section 118 or 119 no record kept under sections 113 to 115 may be used for any purpose that would identify the young person to whom the record relates as a young person dealt with under this Act or the *Young Offenders Act*, chapter Y-1 of the Revised Statutes of Canada, 1985.

**Disposal of records**
(2) Subject to paragraph 124(7)(*c*), any record kept under sections 113 to 115, other than a record kept under subsection 114(3), may, in the discretion of the person or body keeping the record, be destroyed or transmitted to the National Archivist of Canada or the archivist for any province, at any time before or after the end of the applicable period set out in section 118.

**Disposal of R.C.M.P. records**
(3) All records kept under subsection 114(3) shall be destroyed or, if the National Archivist of Canada requires it, transmitted to the National Archivist of Canada, at the end of the applicable period set out in section 118 or 119.

**Purging C.P.I.C.**
(4) The Commissioner of the Royal Canadian Mounted Police shall remove a record from the automated criminal conviction records retrieval system maintained by the Royal Canadian Mounted Police at the end of the applicable period referred to in section 118; however, information relating to a prohibition order made under an Act of Parliament or the legislature of a province shall be removed only at the end of the period for which the order is in force.

**Authority to inspect**
(5) The National Archivist of Canada may, at any time, inspect records kept under sections 113 to 115 that are under the control of a government institution as defined in section 2 of the *National Archives of Canada Act*, and the archivist for a province may at any time inspect any records kept under those sections that the archivist is authorized to inspect under any Act of the legislature of the province.

**Definition of "destroy"**
(6) For the purposes of subsections (2) and (3), "destroy", in respect of a record, means
(*a*) to shred, burn or otherwise physically destroy the record, in the case of a record other than a record in electronic form; and
(*b*) to delete, write over or otherwise render the record inaccessible, in the case of a record in electronic form.

**No subsequent disclosure**
**128.** No person who is given access to a record or to whom information is disclosed under this Act shall disclose that information to any other person unless the disclosure is authorized under this Act.

PART 7
GENERAL PROVISIONS

*Disqualification of Judge*

**Disqualification of judge**
**129.** (1) Subject to subsection (2), a youth justice court judge who, prior to an adjudication in respect of a young person charged with an offence, examines a pre-sentence report made in respect of the young person in connection with that offence or has, after a guilty plea or a finding of guilt, heard submissions as to sentence and then there has been a change of plea, shall not in any capacity conduct or continue the trial of the young person for the offence and shall transfer the case to another judge to be dealt with according to law.

**Exception**
(2) A youth justice court judge may, in the circumstances referred to in subsection (1), with the consent of the young person and the prosecutor, conduct or continue the trial of the young person if the judge is satisfied that he or she has not been predisposed by a guilty plea or finding of guilt, or by information contained in the pre-sentence report or submissions as to sentence.

*Substitution of Judge*

**Powers of substitute youth justice court judge**
130. (1) A youth justice court judge who acts in the place of another youth justice court judge under subsection 669.2(1) of the *Criminal Code* shall
(*a*) if an adjudication has been made, proceed to sentence the young person or make the order that, in the circumstances, is authorized by law; or
(*b*) if no adjudication has been made, recommence the trial as if no evidence had been taken.

**Transcript of evidence already given**
(2) A youth justice court judge who recommences a trial under paragraph (1)(*b*) may, if the parties consent, admit into evidence a transcript of any evidence already given in the case.

*Exclusion from Hearing*

**Exclusion from hearing**
**131.** (1) Subject to subsection (2), a court or justice before whom proceedings are carried out under this Act may exclude any person from all or part of the proceedings if the court or justice considers that the person's presence is unnecessary to the conduct of the proceedings and the court or justice is of the opinion that
(*a*) any evidence or information presented to the court or justice would be seriously injurious or seriously prejudicial to
(i) the young person who is being dealt with in the proceedings,

(ii) a child or young person who is a witness in the proceedings, or
(iii) a child or young person who is aggrieved by or the victim of the offence charged in the proceedings; or
(*b*) it would be in the interest of public morals, the maintenance of order or the proper administration of justice to exclude any or all members of the public from the court room.

**Exception**
(2) Subject to section 650 of the *Criminal Code* and except if it is necessary for the purposes of subsection 34(9) of this Act, a court or justice may not, under subsection (1), exclude from proceedings under this Act
(*a*) the prosecutor;
(*b*) the young person who is being dealt with in the proceedings, the counsel or a parent of the young person or any adult assisting the young person under subsection 25(7);
(*c*) the provincial director or his or her agent; or
(*d*) the youth worker to whom the young person's case has been assigned.

**Exclusion after adjudication or during review**
(3) A youth justice court, after it has found a young person guilty of an offence, or a youth justice court or a review board, during a review, may, in its discretion, exclude from the court or from a hearing of the review board any person other than the following, when it is being presented with information the knowledge of which might, in its opinion, be seriously injurious or seriously prejudicial to the young person:
(*a*) the young person or his or her counsel;
(*b*) the provincial director or his or her agent;
(*c*) the youth worker to whom the young person's case has been assigned; and
(*d*) the Attorney General.

**Exception**
(4) The exception set out in paragraph (3)(*a*) is subject to subsection 34(9) of this Act and section 650 of the *Criminal Code.*

*Transfer of Charges*

**Transfer of charges**
**132.** Despite subsections 478(1) and (3) of the *Criminal Code*, a young person charged with an offence that is alleged to have been committed in one province may, if the Attorney General of the province consents, appear before a youth justice court of any other province and
(*a*) if the young person pleads guilty to that offence and the youth justice court is satisfied that the facts support the charge, the court shall find the young person guilty of the offence alleged in the information; and
(*b*) if the young person pleads not guilty to that offence, or pleads guilty but the court is not satisfied that the facts support the charge, the young person shall, if he or she was detained in custody prior to the appearance, be returned to custody and dealt with according to law.

*Forfeiture of Recognizances*

**Applications for forfeiture of recognizances**
**133.** Applications for the forfeiture of recognizances of young persons shall be made to the youth justice court.

**Proceedings in case of default**
**134.** (1) When a recognizance binding a young person has been endorsed with a certificate under subsection 770(1) of the *Criminal Code*, a youth justice court judge shall,
(*a*) on the request of the Attorney General, fix a time and place for the hearing of an application for the forfeiture of the recognizance; and
(*b*) after fixing a time and place for the hearing, cause to be sent by confirmed delivery service, not less than ten days before the time so fixed, to each principal and surety named in the recognizance, directed to his or her latest known address, a notice requiring him or her to appear at the time and place fixed by the judge to show cause why the recognizance should not be forfeited.

**Order for forfeiture of recognizance**
(2) When subsection (1) is complied with, the youth justice court judge may, after giving the parties an opportunity to be heard, in his or her discretion grant or refuse the application and make any order with respect to the forfeiture of the recognizance that he or she considers proper.

**Judgment debtors of the Crown**
(3) If, under subsection (2), a youth justice court judge orders forfeiture of a recognizance, the principal and his or her sureties become judgment debtors of the Crown, each in the amount that the judge orders him or her to pay.

**Order may be filed**
(4) An order made under subsection (2) may be filed with the clerk of the superior court or, in the province of Quebec, the prothonotary and, if an order is filed, the clerk or the prothonotary shall issue a writ of *fieri facias* in Form 34 set out in the *Criminal Code* and deliver it to the sheriff of each of the territorial divisions in which any of the principal and his or her sureties resides, carries on business or has property.

**If a deposit has been made**
(5) If a deposit has been made by a person against whom an order for forfeiture of a recognizance has been made, no writ of *fieri facias* shall issue, but the amount of the deposit shall be transferred by the person who has custody of it to the person who is entitled by law to receive it.

**Subsections 770(2) and (4) of *Criminal Code* do not apply**
(6) Subsections 770(2) and (4) of the *Criminal Code* do not apply in respect of proceedings under this Act.

**Sections 772 and 773 of *Criminal Code* apply**
(7) Sections 772 and 773 of the *Criminal Code*

apply in respect of writs of *fieri facias* issued under this section as if they were issued under section 771 of that Act.

*Offences and Punishment*

**Inducing a young person, etc.**
**135.** (1) Every person who
(*a*) induces or assists a young person to leave unlawfully a place of custody or other place in which the young person has been placed in accordance with a youth sentence or a disposition imposed under the *Young Offenders Act*, chapter Y-1 of the Revised Statutes of Canada, 1985,
(*b*) unlawfully removes a young person from a place referred to in paragraph (*a*),
(*c*) knowingly harbours or conceals a young person who has unlawfully left a place referred to in paragraph (*a*),
(*d*) wilfully induces or assists a young person to breach or disobey a term or condition of a youth sentence or other order of the youth justice court, or a term or condition of a disposition or other order under the *Young Offenders Act*, chapter Y-1 of the Revised Statutes of Canada, 1985, or
(*e*) wilfully prevents or interferes with the performance by a young person of a term or condition of a youth sentence or other order of the youth justice court, or a term or condition of a disposition or other order under the *Young Offenders Act*, chapter Y-1 of the Revised Statutes of Canada, 1985,

is guilty of an indictable offence and liable to imprisonment for a term not exceeding two years or is guilty of an offence punishable on summary conviction.

**Absolute jurisdiction of provincial court judge**
(2) The jurisdiction of a provincial court judge to try an adult charged with an indictable offence under this section is absolute and does not depend on the consent of the accused.

**Failure to comply with sentence or disposition**
**136.** Every person who is subject to a youth sentence imposed under any of paragraphs 41(2)(*c*) to (*m*) or (*r*) of this Act or a disposition made under any of paragraphs 20(1)(*a*.1) to (*g*), (*j*) or (*l*) of the *Young Offenders Act*, chapter Y-1 of the Revised Statutes of Canada, 1985, and who wilfully fails or refuses to comply with that sentence or disposition is guilty of an offence punishable on summary conviction.

**Offences**
**137.** (1) Every person who contravenes subsection 109(1), 110(1), 117(1) or 127(3) or section 128 of this Act, or subsection 38(1), (1.12), (1.14) or (1.15), 45(2) or 46(1) of the *Young Offenders Act*, chapter Y-1 of the Revised Statutes of Canada, 1985,
(*a*) is guilty of an indictable offence and liable to imprisonment for a term not exceeding two years; or
(*b*) is guilty of an offence punishable on summary conviction.

**Provincial court judge has absolute jurisdiction on indictment**
(2) The jurisdiction of a provincial court judge to try an adult charged with an offence under paragraph (1)(*a*) is absolute and does not depend on the consent of the accused.

**Offence and punishment**
**138.** (1) Every person who wilfully fails to comply with section 30, or with an undertaking entered into under subsection 31(3),
(*a*) is guilty of an indictable offence and liable to imprisonment for a term not exceeding two years; or
(*b*) is guilty of an offence punishable on summary conviction.

**Offence and punishment**
(2) Every person who wilfully fails to comply with section 7 of the *Young Offenders Act*, chapter Y-1 of the Revised Statutes of Canada, 1985, or with an undertaking entered into under subsection 7.1(2) of that Act is guilty of an offence punishable on summary conviction.

**Punishment**
(3) Any person who uses or authorizes the use of an application form in contravention of subsection 81(3) is guilty of an offence punishable on summary conviction.

*Application of the Criminal Code*

**Application of *Criminal Code***
**139.** Except to the extent that it is inconsistent with or excluded by this Act, the provisions of the *Criminal Code* apply, with any modifications that the circumstances require, in respect of offences alleged to have been committed by young persons.

**Sections of *Criminal Code* applicable**
**140.** (1) Except to the extent that they are inconsistent with or excluded by this Act, section 16 and Part XX.1 of the *Criminal Code*, except sections 672.65 and 672.66, apply, with any modifications that the circumstances require, in respect of proceedings under this Act in relation to offences alleged to have been committed by young persons.

**Notice and copies to counsel and parents**
(2) For the purposes of subsection (1),
(*a*) wherever in Part XX.1 of the *Criminal Code* a reference is made to a copy to be sent or otherwise given to an accused or a party to the proceedings, the reference shall be read as including a reference to a copy to be sent or otherwise given to
(i) any counsel representing the young person,
(ii) a parent of the young person who is in attendance at the proceedings against the young person, and
(iii) a parent of the young person not in attendance at the proceedings who is, in the opinion of the youth justice court or Review Board, taking an active interest in the proceedings; and

(*b*) wherever in Part XX.1 of the *Criminal Code* a reference is made to notice to be given to an accused or a party to proceedings, the reference shall be read as including a reference to notice to be given to a parent of the young person and any counsel representing the young person.

**Proceedings not invalid**

(3) Subject to subsection (4), failure to give a notice referred to in paragraph (2)(*b*) to a parent of a young person does not affect the validity of proceedings under this Act.

**Exception**

(4) Failure to give a notice referred to in paragraph (2)(*b*) to a parent of a young person in any case renders invalid any subsequent proceedings under this Act relating to the case unless

(*a*) a parent of the young person attends at the court or Review Board with the young person; or

(*b*) a youth justice court judge or Review Board before whom proceedings are held against the young person

(i) adjourns the proceedings and orders that the notice be given in the manner and to the persons that the judge or Review Board directs, or

(ii) dispenses with the notice if the youth justice court or Review Board is of the opinion that, having regard to the circumstances, the notice may be dispensed with.

**No hospital order assessments**

(5) A youth justice court may not make an order under section 672.11 of the *Criminal Code* in respect of a young person for the purpose of assisting in the determination of a matter mentioned in paragraph (*e*) of that section.

**Considerations of court or Review Board making a disposition**

(6) Before making or reviewing a disposition in respect of a young person under Part XX.1 of the *Criminal Code*, a youth justice court or Review Board shall consider the age and special needs of the young person and any representations or submissions made by a parent of the young person.

**Cap applicable to young persons**

(7) Subject to subsection (9), for the purpose of applying subsection 672.64(3) of the *Criminal Code* to proceedings under this Act in relation to an offence alleged to have been committed by a young person, the applicable cap shall be the maximum period during which the young person would be subject to a youth sentence by the youth justice court if found guilty of the offence.

**Application to increase cap of unfit young person subject to adult sentence**

(8) If a young person is charged with a presumptive offence or notice has been given under subsection 63(2), and the young person is found unfit to stand trial, the Attorney General may apply to the court to increase the cap that will apply to the young person.

**Consideration of youth justice court for increase in cap**

(9) The youth justice court, after giving the Attorney General and the counsel and a parent of the young person in respect of whom subsection (8) applies an opportunity to be heard, shall take into consideration

(*a*) the seriousness and circumstances of the alleged offence,

(*b*) the age, maturity, character and background of the young person and any previous criminal record,

(*c*) the likelihood that the young person will cause significant harm to any person if released on expiry of the cap that applies to the young person under subsection (7), and

(*d*) the respective caps that would apply to the young person under this Act and under the *Criminal Code*.

If the court is satisfied that it would make an order under subsection 63(5) or 70(2) or paragraph 72(1)(b) if the young person were fit to stand trial, it shall apply to the young person the cap that would apply to an adult for the same offence.

***Prima facie* case to be made every year**

(10) For the purpose of applying subsection 672.33(1) of the *Criminal Code* to proceedings under this Act in relation to an offence alleged to have been committed by a young person, wherever in that subsection a reference is made to two years, there shall be substituted a reference to one year.

**Designation of hospitals for young persons**

(11) A reference in Part XX.1 of the *Criminal Code* to a hospital in a province shall be construed as a reference to a hospital designated by the Minister of Health for the province for the custody, treatment or assessment of young persons.

**Definition of "Review Board"**

(12) In this section, "Review Board" has the meaning assigned by section 672.1 of the *Criminal Code*.

**Part XXVII and summary conviction trial provisions of *Criminal Code* to apply**

**141.** (1) Subject to this section and except to the extent that they are inconsistent with this Act, the provisions of Part XXVII of the *Criminal Code*, and any other provisions of that Act that apply in respect of summary conviction offences and relate to trial proceedings, apply to proceedings under this Act

(*a*) in respect of an order under section 810, 810.01 or 810.2 of that Act or an offence under section 811 of that Act;

(*b*) in respect of a summary conviction offence; and

(*c*) in respect of an indictable offence as if it were defined in the enactment creating it as a summary conviction offence.

**Indictable offences**

(2) For greater certainty and despite subsection (1) or any other provision of this Act, an indictable offence committed by a young person is, for the purposes of this Act or any other Act of Parliament, an indictable offence.

**Attendance of young person**
(3) Section 650 of the *Criminal Code* applies in respect of proceedings under this Act, whether the proceedings relate to an indictable offence or an offence punishable on summary conviction.

**Limitation period**
(4) In proceedings under this Act, subsection 786(2) of the *Criminal Code* does not apply in respect of an indictable offence.

**Costs**
(5) Section 809 of the *Criminal Code* does not apply in respect of proceedings under this Act.

*Procedure*

**Counts charged in information**
**142.** Indictable offences and offences punishable on summary conviction may under this Act be charged in the same information and tried jointly.

**Issue of subpoena**
**143.** (1) If a person is required to attend to give evidence before a youth justice court, the subpoena directed to that person may be issued by a youth justice court judge, whether or not the person whose attendance is required is within the same province as the youth justice court.

**Service of subpoena**
(2) A subpoena issued by a youth justice court and directed to a person who is not within the same province as the youth justice court shall be served personally on the person to whom it is directed.

**Warrant**
**144.** A warrant issued by a youth justice court may be executed anywhere in Canada.

*Evidence*

**General law on admissibility of statements to apply**
**145.** (1) Subject to this section, the law relating to the admissibility of statements made by persons accused of committing offences applies in respect of young persons.

**When statements are admissible**
(2) No oral or written statement made by a young person who is less than eighteen years old, to a peace officer or to any other person who is, in law, a person in authority, on the arrest or detention of the young person or in circumstances where the peace officer or other person has reasonable grounds for believing that the young person has committed an offence is admissible against the young person unless

(*a*) the statement was voluntary;
(*b*) the person to whom the statement was made has, before the statement was made, clearly explained to the young person, in language appropriate to his or her age and understanding, that
(i) the young person is under no obligation to make a statement,
(ii) any statement made by the young person may be used as evidence in proceedings against him or her,
(iii) the young person has the right to consult counsel and a parent or other person in accordance with paragraph (*c*), and
(iv) any statement made by the young person is required to be made in the presence of counsel and any other person consulted in accordance with paragraph (*c*), if any, unless the young person desires otherwise;
(*c*) the young person has, before the statement was made, been given a reasonable opportunity to consult
(i) with counsel, and
(ii) with a parent or, in the absence of a parent, an adult relative or, in the absence of a parent and an adult relative, any other appropriate adult chosen by the young person, as long as that person is not a co-accused, or under investigation, in respect of the same offence; and
(*d*) if the young person consults a person in accordance with paragraph (*c*), the young person has been given a reasonable opportunity to make the statement in the presence of that person.

**Exception in certain cases for oral statements**
(3) The requirements set out in paragraphs (2)(*b*) to (*d*) do not apply in respect of oral statements if they are made spontaneously by the young person to a peace officer or other person in authority before that person has had a reasonable opportunity to comply with those requirements.

**Waiver of right to consult**
(4) A young person may waive the rights under paragraph (2)(*c*) or (*d*) but any such waiver
(*a*) must be recorded on video tape or audio tape; or
(*b*) must be in writing and contain a statement signed by the young person that he or she has been informed of the right being waived.

**Waiver of right to consult**
(5) When a waiver of rights under paragraph (2)(*c*) or (*d*) is not made in accordance with subsection (4), the youth justice court may admit into evidence a statement referred to in subsection (2) if it is satisfied that the young person was informed of his or her rights, and waived them.

**Admissibility of statements**
(6) When there has been a failure to comply with paragraphs (2)(*b*) to (*d*), the youth justice court may, having regard to all the circumstances and the principles and objectives of this Act, admit into evidence a statement referred to in subsection (2) if it is satisfied that admission of the statement would not bring the administration of justice into disrepute.

**Statements made under duress are inadmissible**
(7) A youth justice court judge may rule inadmissible in any proceedings under this Act a statement made by the young person in respect of whom the proceedings are taken if the young person satisfies the judge that the statement was

made under duress imposed by any person who is not, in law, a person in authority.

**Misrepresentation of age**
(8) A youth justice court judge may in any proceedings under this Act rule admissible any statement or waiver by a young person if, at the time of the making of the statement or waiver,
(*a*) the young person held himself or herself to be eighteen years old or older;
(*b*) the person to whom the statement or waiver was made conducted reasonable inquiries as to the age of the young person and had reasonable grounds for believing that the young person was eighteen years old or older; and
(*c*) in all other circumstances the statement or waiver would otherwise be admissible.

**Parent, etc., not a person in authority**
(9) For the purpose of this section, a person consulted under paragraph (2)(*c*) is, in the absence of evidence to the contrary, deemed not to be a person in authority.

**Statements not admissible against young person**
**146.** (1) Subject to subsection (2), if a young person is assessed in accordance with an order made under subsection 34(1), no statement or reference to a statement made by the young person during the course and for the purposes of the assessment to the person who conducts the assessment or to anyone acting under that person's direction is admissible in evidence, without the consent of the young person, in any proceeding before a court, tribunal, body or person with jurisdiction to compel the production of evidence.

**Exceptions**
(2) A statement referred to in subsection (1) is admissible in evidence for the purposes of
(*a*) making a decision on an application heard under section 71;
(*b*) determining whether the young person is unfit to stand trial;
(*c*) determining whether the balance of the mind of the young person was disturbed at the time of commission of the alleged offence, if the young person is a female person charged with an offence arising out of the death of her newly-born child;
(*d*) making or reviewing a sentence in respect of the young person;
(*e*) determining whether the young person was, at the time of the commission of an alleged offence, suffering from automatism or a mental disorder so as to be exempt from criminal responsibility by virtue of subsection 16(1) of the *Criminal Code*, if the accused puts his or her mental capacity for criminal intent into issue, or if the prosecutor raises the issue after verdict;
(*f*) challenging the credibility of a young person in any proceeding if the testimony of the young person is inconsistent in a material particular with a statement referred to in subsection (1) that the young person made previously;
(*g*) establishing the perjury of a young person who is charged with perjury in respect of a statement made in any proceeding;
(*h*) deciding an application for an order under subsection 103(1);
(*i*) setting the conditions under subsection 104(1);
(*j*) conducting a review under subsection 108(1); or
(*k*) deciding an application for a disclosure order under subsection 126(1).

**Testimony of a parent**
**147.** (1) In any proceedings under this Act, the testimony of a parent as to the age of a person of whom he or she is a parent is admissible as evidence of the age of that person.

**Evidence of age by certificate or record**
(2) In any proceedings under this Act,
(*a*) a birth or baptismal certificate or a copy of it purporting to be certified under the hand of the person in whose custody those records are held is evidence of the age of the person named in the certificate or copy; and
(*b*) an entry or record of an incorporated society that has had the control or care of the person alleged to have committed the offence in respect of which the proceedings are taken at or about the time the person came to Canada is evidence of the age of that person, if the entry or record was made before the time when the offence is alleged to have been committed.

**Other evidence**
(3) In the absence of any certificate, copy, entry or record mentioned in subsection (2), or in corroboration of that certificate, copy, entry or record, the youth justice court may receive and act on any other information relating to age that it considers reliable.

**When age may be inferred**
(4) In any proceedings under this Act, the youth justice court may draw inferences as to the age of a person from the person's appearance or from statements made by the person in direct examination or cross-examination.

**Admissions**
**148.** (1) A party to any proceedings under this Act may admit any relevant fact or matter for the purpose of dispensing with proof of it, including any fact or matter the admissibility of which depends on a ruling of law or of mixed law and fact.

**Other party may adduce evidence**
(2) Nothing in this section precludes a party to a proceeding from adducing evidence to prove a fact or matter admitted by another party.

**Material evidence**
**149.** Any evidence material to proceedings under this Act that would not but for this section be admissible in evidence may, with the consent of the parties to the proceedings and if the young

person is represented by counsel, be given in such proceedings.

**Evidence of a child or young person**
**150.** The evidence of a child or a young person may be taken in proceedings under this Act only after the youth justice court judge or the justice in the proceedings has
(*a*) if the witness is a child, instructed the child as to the duty to speak the truth and the consequences of failing to do so; and
(*b*) if the witness is a young person and the judge or justice considers it necessary, instructed the young person as to the duty to speak the truth and the consequences of failing to do so.

**Proof of service**
**151.** (1) For the purposes of this Act, service of any document may be proved by oral evidence given under oath by, or by the affidavit or statutory declaration of, the person claiming to have personally served it or sent it by confirmed delivery service.

**Proof of signature and official character unnecessary**
(2) If proof of service of any document is offered by affidavit or statutory declaration, it is not necessary to prove the signature or official character of the person making or taking the affidavit or declaration, if the official character of that person appears on the face of the affidavit or declaration.

**Seal not required**
**152.** It is not necessary to the validity of any information, summons, warrant, minute, sentence, conviction, order or other process or document laid, issued, filed or entered in any proceedings under this Act that any seal be attached or affixed to it.

*Forms, Regulations and Rules of Court*

**Forms**
**153.** (1) The forms prescribed under section 154, varied to suit the case, or forms to the like effect, are valid and sufficient in the circumstances for which they are provided.

**If forms not prescribed**
(2) In any case for which forms are not prescribed under section 154, the forms set out in Part XXVIII of the *Criminal Code*, with any modifications that the circumstances require, or other appropriate forms, may be used.

**Regulations**
**154.** The Governor in Council may make regulations
(*a*) prescribing forms that may be used for the purposes of this Act;
(*b*) establishing uniform rules of court for youth justice courts across Canada, including rules regulating the practice and procedure to be followed by youth justice courts; and
(*c*) generally for carrying out the purposes and provisions of this Act.

*Agreements with Provinces*

**Agreements with provinces**
**155.** Any minister of the Crown may, with the approval of the Governor in Council, enter into an agreement with the government of any province providing for payments by Canada to the province in respect of costs incurred by the province or a municipality in the province for care of and services provided to young persons dealt with under this Act.

*Programs*

**Community-based programs**
**156.** The Attorney General of Canada or a minister designated by the lieutenant governor in council of a province may establish the following types of community-based programs:
(*a*) programs that are an alternative to judicial proceedings, such as victim-offender reconciliation programs, mediation programs and restitution programs;
(*b*) programs that are an alternative to detention before sentencing, such as bail supervision programs; and
(*c*) programs that are an alternative to custody, such as intensive support and supervision programs, and programs to carry out attendance orders.

## PART 8
## TRANSITIONAL PROVISIONS

**Prohibition on proceedings**
**157.** On and after the coming into force of this section, no proceedings may be commenced under the *Young Offenders Act*, chapter Y-1 of the Revised Statutes of Canada, 1985, in respect of an offence within the meaning of that Act, or under the *Juvenile Delinquents Act*, chapter J-3 of the Revised Statutes of Canada, 1970, in respect of a delinquency within the meaning of that Act.

**Proceedings commenced under *Young Offenders Act***
**158.** (1) Subject to section 160, where, before the coming into force of this section, proceedings are commenced under the *Young Offenders Act*, chapter Y-1 of the Revised Statutes of Canada, 1985, in respect of an offence within the meaning of that Act alleged to have been committed by a person who was at the time of the offence a young, person within the meaning of that Act, the proceedings and all related matters shall be dealt with in all respects as if this Act had not come into force.

**Proceedings commenced under *Juvenile Delinquents Act***
(2) Subject to section 160, where, before the coming into force of this section, proceedings are commenced under the *Juvenile Delinquents Act*, chapter J-3 of the Revised Statutes of Canada, 1970, in respect of a delinquency within the meaning of that Act alleged to have been com-

mitted by a person who was at the time of the delinquency a child as defined in that Act, the proceedings and all related matters shall be dealt with under this Act as if the delinquency were an offence that occurred after the coming into force of this section.

**Offences committed before this section in force**
**159.** Any person who, before the coming into force of this section, while he or she was a young person, committed an offence in respect of which no proceedings were commenced before the coming into force of this section shall be dealt with under this Act as if the offence occurred after the coming into force of this section, except that

(*a*) paragraph 61(*a*) applies only if the offence is one set out in paragraph (*a*) of the definition "presumptive offence" in subsection 2(1) and the young person was at least sixteen years old at the time of its commission;

(*b*) paragraph 109(2)(*b*) does not apply in respect of the offence; and

(*c*) paragraph 41(2)(*q*) applies in respect of the offence only if the young person consents to its application.

**Applicable sentence**
**160.** (1) A person referred to in section 158 who is found guilty of an offence or delinquency, other than a person convicted of an offence in ordinary court, as defined in subsection 2(1) of the *Young Offenders Act*, chapter Y-1 of the Revised Statutes of Canada, 1985, shall be sentenced under this Act, except that

(*a*) paragraph 109(2)(*b*) does not apply in respect of the offence or delinquency; and

(*b*) paragraph 41(2)(*q*) applies in respect of the offence or delinquency only if the young person consents to its application.

The provisions of this Act applicable to sentences imposed under section 41 apply in respect of the sentence.

**Dispositions under paragraph 20(1)(*k*) of *Young Offenders Act***
(2) A young person who, on the coming into force of this section, is subject to a disposition under paragraph 20(1)(*k*) of the *Young Offenders Act*, chapter Y-1 of the Revised Statutes of Canada, 1985, shall be dealt with under this Act as if the unexpired portion of the disposition were a sentence imposed under paragraph 41(2)(*n*), and the provisions of this Act applicable to sentences imposed under paragraph 41(2)(*n*) apply in respect of the sentence.

**Dispositions under paragraph 20(1)(*k*.1) of *Young Offenders Act***
(3) A young person who, on the coming into force of this section, is subject to a disposition under paragraph 20(1)(*k*.1) of the *Young Offenders Act*, chapter Y-1 of the Revised Statutes of Canada, 1985, shall be dealt with under this Act as if the disposition were a sentence imposed under paragraph 41(2)(*p*), and the provisions of this Act applicable to sentences imposed under paragraph 41(2)(*p*) apply in respect of the sentence.

**Release by youth court on review**
(4) Subsections (2) and (3) do not apply to a young person who, before the coming into force of this section, has been released from custody in accordance with paragraph 28(17)(*c*) of the *Young Offenders Act*, chapter Y-1 of the Revised Statutes of Canada, 1985.

**Review of sentence**
(5) For greater certainty, for the purpose of determining when the sentence is reviewed under section 93, the relevant date is the one on which the disposition came into force under the *Young Offenders Act*, chapter Y-1 of the Revised Statutes of Canada, 1985.

**Proceedings commence with information**
**161.** For the purposes of sections 157 to 159, proceedings are commenced by the laying of an information.

**Application to delinquency and other offending behaviour**
**162.** Sections 113 to 128 apply, with any modifications that the circumstances require, in respect of records relating to the offence of delinquency under the *Juvenile Delinquents Act*, chapter J-3 of the Revised Statutes of Canada, 1970, and in respect of records kept under sections 40 to 43 of the *Young Offenders Act*, chapter Y-1 of the Revised Statutes of Canada, 1985.

**Agreements continue in force**
**163.** Any agreement made under the *Young Offenders Act*, chapter Y-1 of the Revised Statutes of Canada, 1985, remains in force until it expires, unless it is amended or a new agreement is made under this Act.

**Designation of youth justice court**
**164.** (1) Any court established or designated as a youth court for the purposes of the *Young Offenders Act*, chapter Y-1 of the Revised Statutes of Canada, 1985, is deemed, as of the coming into force of this section, to have been established or designated as a youth justice court for the purposes of this Act.

**Designation of youth justice court judges**
(2) Any person appointed to be a judge of the youth court for the purposes of the *Young Offenders Act*, chapter Y-1 of the Revised Statutes of Canada, 1985, is deemed, as of the coming into force of this section, to have been appointed as a judge of the youth justice court for the purposes of this Act.

**Designation of provincial directors and youth workers**
(3) Any person, group or class of persons or body appointed or designated as a provincial director for the purposes of the *Young Offenders Act*, chapter Y-1 of the Revised Statutes of Canada, 1985, and any person appointed or designated as a

youth worker for the purposes of that Act is deemed, as of the coming into force of this section, to have been appointed or designated as a provincial director or youth worker, as the case may be, for the purposes of this Act.

**Designation of review boards and youth justice committees**
(4) Any review board established or designated for the purposes of the *Young Offenders Act*, chapter Y-1 of the Revised Statutes of Canada, 1985, and any youth justice committee established for the purposes of that Act is deemed, as of the coming into force of this section, to have been established or designated as a review board or a youth justice committee, as the case may be, for the purposes of this Act.

**Alternative measures continued as extrajudicial sanctions**
(5) Any program of alternative measures authorized for the purposes of the *Young Offenders Act*, chapter Y-1 of the Revised Statutes of Canada, 1985, is deemed, as of the coming into force of this section, to be a program of extrajudicial sanctions authorized for the purposes of this Act.

**Designation of places of temporary detention and open or secure custody**
(6) Any place that was designated as a place of temporary detention or open custody for the purposes of the *Young Offenders Act*, chapter Y-1 of the Revised Statutes of Canada, 1985, and any place or facility designated as a place of secure custody for the purposes of that Act is deemed, as of the coming into force of this section, to have been designated for the purposes of this Act as
(*a*) in the case of a place of temporary detention, a place of temporary detention; and
(*b*) in the case of a place of open custody or secure custody, a youth custody facility.

**Designation of other persons**
(7) Any person designated as a clerk of the youth court for the purposes of the *Young Offenders Act*, chapter Y-1 of the Revised Statutes of Canada, 1985, or any person or group of persons who were designated under that Act to carry out specified functions and duties are deemed, as of the coming into force of this section, to have been designated as a clerk of the youth justice court, or to carry out the same functions and duties, as the case may be, under this Act.

**PART 9**
**CONSEQUENTIAL AMENDMENTS, CONDITIONAL AMENDMENTS, REPEAL AND COMING INTO FORCE**

*Consequential Amendments*

Note: Explanatory Notes have been omitted. Please see specific Acts for sections replaced and repealed by these amendments.

R.S., c. C-5
**Canada Evidence Act**

R.S., c. 19 (3rd Supp.), s. 17
**165. Subsection 4(2) of the *Canada Evidence Act* is replaced by the following:**

**Accused and spouse**
(2) The wife or husband of a person charged with an offence under subsection 135(1) of the *Youth Criminal Justice Act* or with an offence under any of sections 151, 152, 153, 155 or 159, subsection 160(2) or (3), or sections 170 to 173, 179, 212, 215, 218, 271 to 273, 280 to 283, 291 to 294 or 329 of the *Criminal Code*, or an attempt to commit any such offence, is a competent and compellable witness for the prosecution without the consent of the person charged.

1992, c. 47
**Contraventions Act**

**166. (1) The definition "youth court" in section 2 of the English version of the *Contraventions Act* is repealed.**

**(2) The definition "tribunal pour adolescents" in section 2 of the French version of the Act is replaced by the following:**

**«tribunal pour adolescents»** "youth justice court"
«tribunal pour adolescents» À l'égard d'une contravention qui aurait été commise par un adolescent sur le territoire, ou dans le ressort des tribunaux, d'une province, le tribunal établi ou désigné sous le régime d'une loi provinciale, ou encore désigné par le gouverneur en conseil ou par le lieutenant-gouverneur en conseil, afin d'exercer les attributions du tribunal pour adolescents dans le cadre de la *Loi sur le système de justice pénale pour les adolescents*.

**(3) Section 2 of the English version of the Act is amended by adding the following in alphabetical order:**

**"youth justice court" «tribunal pour adolescents»**
"youth justice court" means, in respect of a contravention alleged to have been committed by a young person in, or otherwise within the territorial jurisdiction of the courts of, a province, the court established or designated by or under an Act of the legislature of the province, or designated by the Governor in Council or lieutenant governor in council of the province, as the youth justice court for the purposes of the *Youth Criminal Justice Act*.

1996, c. 7, s. 2
**167. Section 5 of the Act is replaced by the following:**

**Relationship with *Criminal Code* and *Youth Criminal Justice Act***
5. The provisions of the *Criminal Code* relating to summary conviction offences and the provisions of the *Youth Criminal Justice Act* apply to proceedings in respect of contraventions that are commenced under this Act, except to the extent that

this Act, the regulations or the rules of court provide otherwise.

**168. Subsection 17(2) of the Act is replaced by the following:**

**Jurisdiction of adult courts over young persons**
(2) Notwithstanding the *Youth Criminal Justice Act*, a contraventions court or a justice of the peace has jurisdiction, to the exclusion of that of the youth justice court, in respect of any contravention alleged to have been committed by a young person in, or otherwise within the territorial jurisdiction of the courts of, a province the lieutenant governor in council of which has ordered that any such contravention be dealt with in ordinary court.

**169. Paragraph 62(2)(*a*) of the Act is replaced by the following:**

(*a*) for the committal of the offender to custody under the *Youth Criminal Justice Act*, for one day, if the offender is a young person; or

1992, c. 20
**Corrections and Conditional Release Act**

1995, c. 42, s. 1(2)
**170. The definition "sentence" in subsection 2(1) of the *Corrections and Conditional Release Act* is replaced by the following:**

**"sentence" «peine» ou «peine d'emprisonnement»**
"sentence" means a sentence of imprisonment and includes a youth sentence imposed under the *Youth Criminal Justice Act* and a sentence imposed by a court of a foreign state on a Canadian offender who has been transferred to Canada pursuant to the *Transfer of Offenders Act*;

**171. Subsection 15(1) of the Act is replaced by the following:**

**Newfoundland**
**15.** (1) Notwithstanding any requirement in the *Criminal Code* or under the *Youth Criminal Justice Act* that a person be sentenced, committed or transferred to penitentiary, such a person in the Province of Newfoundland shall not be received in a penitentiary without the approval of an officer designated by the Lieutenant Governor of Newfoundland.

1995, c. 22, s. 13 (Sch.II, item 4),
c. 42, par. 69(*a*)(E)
**172. The definition "offender" in subsection 99(1) of the Act is replaced by the following:**

**"offender" «délinquant»**
"offender" means
(*a*) a person, other than a young person within the meaning of the *Youth Criminal Justice Act*, who is under a sentence imposed before or after the coming into force of this section
(i) pursuant to an Act of Parliament or, to the extent that this Part applies, pursuant to a provincial Act, or
(ii) on conviction for criminal or civil contempt of court if the sentence does not include a requirement that the offender return to that court, or
(*b*) a young person within the meaning of the *Youth Criminal Justice Act* with respect to whom an order, committal or direction under section 76, 88, 91 or 92 of that Act has been made,

but does not include a person whose only sentence is a sentence being served intermittently pursuant to section 732 of the *Criminal Code*;

**173. The Act is amended by adding the following after section 99.1:**

Young persons
99.2 In this Part, a young person within the meaning of the *Youth Criminal Justice Act* with respect to whom a committal or direction under section 88, 91 or 92 of that Act has been made begins to serve his or her sentence on the day on which the sentence comes into force in accordance with subsection 41(11) of that Act.

R.S., c. C-46
**Criminal Code**

1995, c. 27, s. 1
**174. The definitions "adult", "provincial court judge" and "young person" in section 487.04 of the *Criminal Code* are replaced by the following:**

**"adult" «adulte»**
"adult" has the meaning assigned by subsection 2(1) of the *Youth Criminal Justice Act*;

**"provincial court judge"**
**«juge de la cour provinciale»**
"provincial court judge", in relation to a young person, includes a youth justice court judge within the meaning of subsection 2(1) of the *Youth Criminal Justice Act*;

**"young person" «adolescent»**
"young person" has the meaning assigned by subsection 2(1) of the *Youth Criminal Justice Act*.

1998, c. 37, s. 17
**175. The portion of subsection 487.051(1) of the Act before paragraph (*a*), as enacted by section 17 of the *DNA Identification Act*, is replaced by the following:**

**Order**
**487.051** (1) Subject to section 487.053, if a person is convicted, discharged under section 730 or, in the case of a young person, found guilty under the *Young Offenders Act*, chapter Y-1 of the Revised Statutes of Canada, 1985, or the *Youth Criminal Justice Act* of a designated offence, the court

1998, c. 37, s. 17
**176. Subsection 487.052(1) of the Act, as enacted by section 17 of the *DNA Identification***

***Act*, is replaced by the following:**

**Offences committed before *DNA Identification Act* in force**

**487.052** (1) Subject to section 487.053, if a person is convicted, discharged under section 730 or, in the case of a young person, found guilty under the *Young Offenders Act*, chapter Y-1 of the Revised Statutes of Canada, 1985, or the *Youth Criminal Justice Act*, of a designated offence committed before the coming into force of subsection 5(1) of the *DNA Identification Act*, the court may, on application by the prosecutor, make an order in Form 5.04 authorizing the taking, from that person or young person, for the purpose of forensic DNA analysis, of any number of samples of one or more bodily substances that is reasonably required for that purpose, by means of the investigative procedures described in subsection 487.06(1), if the court is satisfied that it is in the best interests of the administration of justice to do so.

1998, c. 37, s. 17

**177. Paragraph 487.053(*b*) of the English version of the Act, as enacted by section 17 of the *DNA Identification Act*, is replaced by the following:**

(*b*) by the person or young person, that they consent to the entry, in the convicted offenders index of the national DNA data bank established under that Act, of the results of DNA analysis of bodily substances that were provided voluntarily in the course of the investigation of, or taken from them in execution of a warrant that was issued under section 487.05 in respect of, the designated offence of which the person has been convicted, discharged under section 730 or, in the case of a young person, found guilty under the *Young Offenders Act*, chapter Y-1 of the Revised Statutes of Canada, 1985, or the *Youth Criminal Justice Act*, or another designated offence in respect of the same transaction.

1998, c. 37, c. 17

**178. Subsection 487.056(1) of the English version of the Act, as enacted by section 17 of the *DNA Identification Act*, is replaced by the following:**

**When collection to take place**

**487.056** (1) Samples of bodily substances referred to in sections 487.051 and 487.052 shall be taken at the time the person is convicted, discharged under section 730 or, in the case of a young person, found guilty under the *Young Offenders Act*, chapter Y-1 of the Revised Statutes of Canada, 1985, or the *Youth Criminal Justice Act*, or as soon as is feasible afterwards, even though an appeal may have been taken.

1998, c. 37, s. 20

**179. Paragraphs 487.071(1)(*a*) and (*b*) of the Act, as enacted by section 20 of the *DNA Identification Act*, are replaced by the following:**

(*a*) provided voluntarily in the course of an investigation of a designated offence by any person who is later convicted, discharged under section 730 or, in the case of a young person, found guilty under the *Young Offenders Act*, chapter Y-1 of the Revised Statutes of Canada, 1985, or the *Youth Criminal Justice Act* of the designated offence or another designated offence in respect of the same transaction and who, having been so convicted, discharged or found guilty, consents to having the results entered in the convicted offenders index;

(*b*) taken in execution of a warrant under section 487.05 from a person who is later convicted, discharged under section 730 or, in the case of a young person, found guilty under the *Young Offenders Act*, chapter Y-1 of the Revised Statutes of Canada, 1985, or the *Youth Criminal Justice Act* of the designated offence in respect of which the warrant was issued or another designated offence in respect of the same transaction and who, having been so convicted, discharged or found guilty, consents to having the results entered in the convicted offenders index;

**180. The portion of subsection 667(1) of the Act before paragraph (*b*) is replaced by the following:**

**Proof of previous conviction**

667. (1) In any proceedings,

(*a*) a certificate setting out with reasonable particularity the conviction or discharge under section 730, the finding of guilt under the *Young Offenders Act*, chapter Y-1 of the Revised Statutes of Canada, 1985, the finding of guilt under the *Youth Criminal Justice Act*, or the judicial determination under subsection 41(8) of that Act, or the conviction and sentence or finding of guilt and sentence in Canada of an offender, signed by

(i) the person who made the conviction, order for the discharge, finding of guilt or judicial determination,

(ii) the clerk of the court in which the conviction, order for the discharge, finding of guilt or judicial determination was made, or

(iii) a fingerprint examiner,

is, on proof that the accused or defendant is the offender referred to in the certificate, evidence that the accused or defendant was so convicted, so discharged or so convicted and sentenced or found guilty and sentenced, or that a judicial determination was made against the accused or defendant, without proof of the signature or the official character of the person appearing to have signed the certificate;

1997, c. 18, par. 141(*c*)

**181. Subsection 718.3(4) of the Act is replaced by the following:**

**Cumulative punishments**

(4) The court or youth justice court that sentences an accused may direct that the terms of imprisonment that are imposed by the court or the youth justice court or that result from the operation of subsection 734(4) or 743.5(1) or (2) shall be served consecutively, when

(*a*) the accused is sentenced while under sentence for an offence, and a term of imprisonment, whether in default of payment of a fine or otherwise, is imposed;
(*b*) the accused is found guilty or convicted of an offence punishable with both a fine and imprisonment and both are imposed;
(*c*) the accused is found guilty or convicted of more than one offence, and
(i) more than one fine is imposed,
(ii) terms of imprisonment for the respective offences are imposed, or
(iii) a term of imprisonment is imposed in respect of one offence and a fine is imposed in respect of another offence; or
(*d*) subsection 743.5(1) or (2) applies.

1995, c. 22, s. 6
**182. Paragraph 721(3)(*b*) of the Act is replaced by the following:**

(*b*) subject to subsection 118(2) of the *Youth Criminal Justice Act*, the history of previous dispositions under the *Young Offenders Act*, chapter Y-1 of the Revised Statutes of Canada, 1985, the history of previous sentences under the *Youth Criminal Justice Act*, and of previous findings of guilt under this Act and any other Act of Parliament;

1995, c. 22, s. 6, paras. 19(*b*), 20(*b*)
**183. Sections 743.4 and 743.5 of the Act are replaced by the following:**

**Transfer of jurisdiction when person already sentenced under *Youth Criminal Justice Act***
743.5 (1) If a young person or an adult is or has been sentenced for an offence while subject to a disposition made under paragraph 20(1)(*k*) or (*k*.1) of the *Young Offenders Act*, chapter Y-1 of the Revised Statutes of Canada, 1985, or a youth sentence imposed under paragraph 41(2)(*n*), (*p*) or (*q*) of the *Youth Criminal Justice Act*, the disposition or youth sentence shall be dealt with, for all purposes under this Act or any other Act of Parliament, as if it had been a sentence imposed under this Act.

**Transfer of jurisdiction when youth sentence imposed under *Youth Criminal Justice Act***
(2) If a disposition is made under paragraph 20(1)(*k*) or (*k*.1) of the *Young Offenders Act*, chapter Y-1 of the Revised Statutes of Canada, 1985, with respect to a person or a youth sentence is imposed on a person under paragraph 41(2)(*n*), (*p*) or (*q*) of the *Youth Criminal Justice Act* while the young person or adult is under sentence imposed under an Act of Parliament other than the *Youth Criminal Justice Act*, the disposition or youth sentence shall be dealt with, for all purposes under this Act or any other Act of Parliament, as if it had been a sentence imposed under this Act.

**Sentences deemed to constitute one sentence—section 743.1**
(3) For greater certainty, the dispositions and sentences referred to in subsections (1) and (2) are, for the purpose of section 139 of the *Corrections and Conditional Release Act*, deemed to constitute one sentence of imprisonment.

1998, c. 37, s. 24
**184. The first paragraph of Form 5.03 of the Act, as enacted by section 24 of the *DNA Identification Act*, is replaced by the following:**

Whereas (*name of offender*) has been convicted, discharged under section 730 of the *Criminal Code* or, in the case of a young person, found guilty under the *Young Offenders Act*, chapter Y-1 of the Revised Statutes of Canada, 1985, or the *Youth Criminal Justice Act* of (*offence*), an offence that is a primary designated offence within the meaning of section 487.04 of the *Criminal Code*;

1998, c. 37, s. 24
**185. The portion of the first paragraph of Form 5.04 of the Act before paragraph (*a*), as enacted by section 24 of the *DNA Identification Act*, is replaced by the following:**

Whereas (*name of offender*), in this order called the "offender", has been convicted, discharged under section 730 of the *Criminal Code* or, in the case of a young person, found guilty under the *Young Offenders Act*, chapter Y-1 of the Revised Statutes of Canada, 1985, or the *Youth Criminal Justice Act* of (*offence*), an offence that is

1998, c. 37
**DNA Identification Act**
**186. The definition "young person" in section 2 of the *DNA Identification Act* is replaced by the following:**

**"young person" «adolescent»**
"young person" has the meaning assigned by subsection 2(1) of the *Youth Criminal Justice Act*.

**187. (1) The portion of paragraph 9(2)(*c*) of the Act before subparagraph (i) is replaced by the following:**

(*c*) in the case of information in relation to a young person who has been found guilty under the *Young Offenders Act*, chapter Y-1 of the Revised Statutes of Canada, 1985, or the *Youth Criminal Justice Act* of any of the following offences, the expiry of ten years after the sentence or all dispositions made in respect of the offence have been completed, namely,

**(2) Paragraphs 9(2)(*d*) and (*e*) of the Act are replaced by the following:**

(*d*) in the case of information in relation to a young person who has been found guilty under the *Young Offenders Act*, chapter Y-1 of the Revised Statutes of Canada, 1985, or the *Youth Criminal Justice Act* of a designated offence, other than an offence referred to in any of subparagraphs (*c*)(i) to (iii) and sections 235 (first degree murder or second degree murder), 236 (manslaughter), 239 (attempt to commit murder) and 273 (aggravated sexual assault) of the *Criminal Code*, the expiry of five years after the sentence or all dispositions made in respect of the offence have been completed; and

(*e*) in the case of information in relation to a young person who has been found guilty under the *Young Offenders Act*, chapter Y-1 of the Revised Statutes of Canada, 1985, or the *Youth Criminal Justice Act* of a designated offence that is a summary conviction offence, the expiry of three years after the sentence or all dispositions made in respect of the offence have been completed.

**188. (1) The portion of paragraph 10(7)(*c*) of the Act before subparagraph (i) is replaced by the following:**

(*c*) if the person is a young person who has been found guilty under the *Young Offenders Act*, chapter Y-1 of the Revised Statutes of Canada, 1985, or the *Youth Criminal Justice Act* of any of the following offences, after the expiry of ten years after the sentence or all dispositions made in respect of the offence have been completed, namely,

**(2) Paragraphs 10(7)(*d*) and (*e*) of the Act are replaced by the following:**

(*d*) if the person is a young person who has been found guilty under the *Young Offenders Act*, chapter Y-1 of the Revised Statutes of Canada, 1985, or the *Youth Criminal Justice Act* of a designated offence, other than an offence referred to in any of subparagraphs (*c*)(i) to (iii) and sections 235 (first degree murder or second degree murder), 236 (manslaughter), 239 (attempt to commit murder) and 273 (aggravated sexual assault) of the *Criminal Code*, after the expiry of five years after the sentence or all dispositions made in respect of the offence have been completed; and

(*e*) if the person is a young person who has been found guilty under the *Young Offenders Act*, chapter Y-1 of the Revised Statutes of Canada, 1985, or the *Youth Criminal Justice Act* of a designated offence that is a summary conviction offence, after the expiry of three years after the sentence or all dispositions made in respect of the offence have been completed.

R.S., c. 30 (4th Supp.)
**Mutual Legal Assistance in Criminal Matters Act**

**189. Section 29 of the *Mutual Legal Assistance in Criminal Matters Act* is replaced by the following:**

**Exception for young persons**
29. Sections 24 to 28 do not apply in respect of a person who, at the time the request mentioned in subsection 24(1) is presented, is a young person within the meaning of the *Youth Criminal Justice Act*.

R.S., c. P-20
**Prisons and Reformatories Act**

**190. (1) Paragraph (*b*) of the definition "prisoner" in subsection 2(1) of the *Prisons and Reformatories Act* is replaced by the following:**

(*b*) a young person within the meaning of the *Youth Criminal Justice Act* with respect to whom no order, committal or direction has been made under paragraph 76(1)(*a*) or section 88, 91 or 92 of that Act,

**(2) Subsection 2(1) of the Act is amended by adding the following in alphabetical order:**

**"sentence" «peine»**
"sentence" includes a youth sentence imposed under the *Youth Criminal Justice Act*;

**191. Section 6 of the Act is amended by adding the following after subsection (7):**

**Transfer or committal to prison**
(7.1) When a prisoner is transferred from a youth custody facility to a prison under section 88, 91 or 92 of the *Youth Criminal Justice Act* or as the result of the application of section 743.5 of the *Criminal Code*, the prisoner is credited with full remission under this section for the portion of the sentence that the offender served in the youth custody facility as if that portion of the sentence had been served in a prison.

**Exceptional date of release**
(7.2) When a prisoner who was sentenced to custody under paragraph 41(2)(*p*) or (*q*) of the *Youth Criminal Justice Act* is transferred from a youth custody facility to a prison under section 91 or 92 of that Act, or is committed to imprisonment in a prison under section 88 of that Act, the prisoner is entitled to be released on the earlier of

(*a*) the date on which the prisoner is entitled to be released from imprisonment in accordance with subsection (5) of this section, and

(*b*) the date on which the custody portion of his or her youth sentence under paragraph 41(2)(*p*) or (*q*) of the *Youth Criminal Justice Act* expires.

**Effect of release**
(7.3) When a prisoner is committed or transferred in accordance with section 88, 91 or 92 of the *Youth Criminal Justice Act* and, in accordance with subsection (7.1) or (7.2) of this section, is entitled to be released,

(*a*) if the sentence was imposed under paragraph 41(2)(*n*) of that Act, sections 96 to 102 of that Act apply, with any modifications that the circumstances require, with respect to the remainder of his or her sentence; and

(*b*) if the sentence was imposed under paragraph 41(2)(*p*) or (*q*) of that Act, sections 103 to 108 of that Act apply, with any modifications that the circumstances require, with respect to the remainder of his or her sentence.

R.S., c. T-15
Transfer of Offenders Act

1993, c. 34, s. 122
**192. The portion of section 17 of the *Transfer of Offenders Act* after paragraph (*a*) is replaced by the following:**

(*b*) was, at the time of the commission of the offence of which he or she was convicted, a young person within the meaning of the Youth Criminal Justice Act,

an official designated for the purpose by the lieutenant governor in council of the province where the offender is detained may transfer the offender to a youth custody facility within the meaning of subsection 2(1) of the *Youth Criminal Justice Act*, but no person so transferred shall be detained by reason only of the sentence imposed by the foreign court beyond the date on which that sentence would terminate.

*Conditional Amendments*

1993, c. 28
**193. (1) If section 144 of Schedule III to the *Nunavut Act* comes into force before the coming into force of section 196 of this Act, the definition "offence" in subsection 2(1) of this Act is replaced by the following:**

"offence" «infraction»
"offence" means an offence created by an Act of Parliament or by any regulation, rule, by-law or ordinance made under it, other than an ordinance of the Yukon Territory or the Northwest Territories or a law made by the Legislature for Nunavut or continued by section 29 of the *Nunavut Act*.

**(2) If section 196 of this Act comes into force before the coming into force of section 144 of Schedule III to the *Nunavut Act*, section 144 of Schedule III to that Act and the heading before it are replaced by the following:**

*Youth Criminal Justice Act*

**144. The definition "offence" in subsection 2(1) is replaced by the following:**

"offence" «infraction»
"offence" means an offence created by an Act of Parliament or by any regulation, rule, by-law or ordinance made under an Act of Parliament, other than an ordinance of the Yukon Territory or the Northwest Territories or a law made by the Legislature for Nunavut or continued by section 29 of the *Nunavut Act*.

Bill C-40
**194. If Bill C-40, introduced in the first session of the thirty-sixth Parliament and entitled *An Act respecting extradition, to amend the Canada Evidence Act, the Criminal Code, the Immigration Act and the Mutual Legal Assistance in Criminal Matters Act and to amend and repeal other Acts in consequence* is assented to, then**
**(*a*) on the later of the day on which paragraph 47(*c*) of that Act comes into force and the day on which this section comes into force, paragraph 47(*c*) of that Act is replaced by the following:**

(*c*) the person was less than eighteen years old at the time of the offence and the law that applies to them in the territory over which the extradition partner has jurisdiction is not consistent with the fundamental principles governing the *Youth Criminal Justice Act*;

**(*b*) on the later of the day on which paragraphs 77(*a*) and (*b*) of that Act come into force and the day on which this section comes into force, paragraphs 77(*a*) and (*b*) of that Act are replaced by the following:**

(*a*) in respect of a prosecution or imposition of a sentence—or of a disposition under the *Young Offenders Act*, chapter Y-1 of the Revised Statutes of Canada, 1985—the Attorney General, or the Attorney General of a province who is responsible for the prosecution of the case; and
(*b*) in respect of the enforcement of a sentence or a disposition under the *Young Offenders Act*, chapter Y-1 of the Revised Statutes of Canada, 1985,
(i) the Solicitor General of Canada, if the person would serve the sentence in a penitentiary, or
(ii) the appropriate provincial minister responsible for corrections, in any other case.

**(*c*) on the later of the day on which subsection 78(1) of that Act comes into force and the day on which this section comes into force, subsection 78(1) of that Act is replaced by the following:**

Request by Canada for extradition
78. (1) The Minister, at the request of a competent authority, may make a request to a State or entity for the extradition of a person for the purpose of prosecuting the person for—or imposing or enforcing a sentence, or making or enforcing a disposition under the *Young Offenders Act*, chapter Y-1 of the Revised Statutes of Canada, 1985, in respect of—an offence over which Canada has jurisdiction.

**(*d*) on the later of the day on which paragraph 80(*a*) of that Act comes into force and the day on which this section comes into force, the portion of paragraph 80(*a*) of that Act before subparagraph (i) is replaced by the following:**

(*a*) be detained or prosecuted, or have a sentence imposed or executed, or a disposition made or executed under the *Young Offenders Act*, chapter Y-1 of the Revised Statutes of Canada, 1985, in Canada in respect of an offence that is alleged to have been committed, or was committed, before surrender other than

**(*e*) on the later of the day on which subsection 83(1) of that Act comes into force and the day on which this section comes into force, subsection 83(1) of that Act is replaced by the following:**

**Commencement of sentence**

83. (1) Subject to subsection (3), the sentence or disposition of a person who has been temporarily surrendered and who has been convicted and sentenced, or found guilty and sentenced, in Canada, or in respect of whom a disposition has been made under the *Young Offenders Act*, chapter Y-1 of the Revised Statutes of Canada, 1985, does not commence until their final extradition to Canada.

**(*f*) on the later of the day on which subsection 83(3) of that Act comes into force and the day on which this section comes into force, subsection 83(3) of that Act is replaced by the following:**

**If concurrent sentences ordered**

(3) The sentencing judge may order that the person's sentence, or the disposition under the *Young Offenders Act*, chapter Y-1 of the Revised Statutes of Canada, 1985, be executed concurrently with the sentence they are serving in the requested State or entity, in which case the warrant of committal or order of disposition shall state that the person is to be committed to custody under subsection (2) only for any portion of the sentence or disposition remaining at the time of their final extradition to Canada.

**Bill C-57**

**195. (1) If Bill C-57, introduced in the first session of the thirty-sixth Parliament and entitled *An Act to amend the Nunavut Act with respect to the Nunavut Court of Justice and to amend other Acts in consequence*, is assented to, and sections 86 to 89 of that Act come into force before section 196 of this Act,**

**(a) subsection 32(4) of this Act is replaced by the following:**

**If youth justice court not satisfied**

(4) If the youth justice court is not satisfied that a young person understands the charge, the court shall, unless the young person must be put to his or her election under subsection 67(1) or, with respect to Nunavut, subsection 67(1.1), enter a plea of not guilty on behalf of the young person and proceed with the trial in accordance with subsection 35(2).

**(*b*) section 33 of this Act is amended by adding the following after subsection (5):**

**Nunavut**

(5.1) Despite subsection (5), an application under section 520 or 521 of the *Criminal Code* for a review of an order made in respect of a young person by a youth justice court judge who is a judge of the Nunavut Court of Justice shall be made to a judge of that court.

**(*c*) section 36 of this Act is amended by adding the following after subsection (8):**

**Nunavut**

(8.1) Despite subsection (8), if the Nunavut Court of Justice is acting as a youth justice court, an appeal under subsection (5) shall be made to a judge of the Nunavut Court of Appeal, and an appeal of that judge's decision shall be made to the Nunavut Court of Appeal in accordance with section 839 of the *Criminal Code*.

**(*d*) section 67 of this Act is amended by adding the following after subsection (1):**

**Election—Nunavut**

(1.1) Subject to section 66, if a young person is charged with having, after attaining the age of fourteen years, committed an offence set out in paragraph (*a*) of the definition "presumptive offence" in subsection 2(1), or if the Attorney General has given notice under subsection 63(2) of the intention to seek an adult sentence, the youth justice court shall, before the young person enters a plea, put the young person to his or her election in the following words:

> You have the option to elect to be tried by a judge of the Nunavut Court of Justice alone, acting as a youth justice court without a jury and without a preliminary inquiry; or to have a preliminary inquiry and to be tried by a judge of the Nunavut Court of Justice, acting as a youth justice court without a jury; or to have a preliminary inquiry and to be tried by a judge of the Nunavut Court of Justice, acting as a youth justice court with a jury. If you do not elect now, you shall be deemed to have elected to have a preliminary inquiry and to be tried by a court composed of a judge and jury. How do you elect to be tried?

**(*e*) subsection 67(4) of this Act is replaced by the following:**

**Preliminary inquiry**

(4) When a young person elects to be tried by a judge without a jury, or elects or is deemed to have elected to be tried by a court composed of a judge and jury, the youth justice court referred to in subsection 13(1) shall conduct a preliminary inquiry and if, on its conclusion, the young person is ordered to stand trial, the proceedings shall be conducted

(*a*) before a judge without a jury or a court composed of a judge and jury, as the case may be; or

(*b*) in Nunavut, before a judge of the Nunavut Court of Justice acting as a youth justice court, with or without a jury, as the case may be.

**(*f*) subsection 67(6) of this Act is replaced by the following:**

**Parts XIX and XX of the *Criminal Code***

(6) Proceedings under this Act before a judge without a jury or a court composed of a judge and jury or, in Nunavut, a judge of the Nunavut Court of Justice, acting as a youth justice court, with or without a jury, shall be conducted in accordance with the provisions of Parts XIX and XX of the *Criminal Code*, with any modifications that the circumstances require, except that

(*a*) the provisions of this Act respecting the protection of privacy of young persons prevail over the provisions of the *Criminal Code*; and (*b*) the young person is entitled to be represented in court by counsel if the young person is removed from court in accordance with subsection 650(2) of the *Criminal Code*.

**(2) If Bill C-57, introduced in the first session of the thirty-sixth Parliament and entitled *An Act to amend the Nunavut Act with respect to the Nunavut Court of Justice and to amend other acts in consequence*, is assented to, and section 196 of this Act comes into force before the coming into force of sections 86 to 89 of that Act, the heading before section 86 and sections 86 to 89 of that Act are replaced by the following:**

**Youth Criminal Justice Act**

**86. Subsection 32(4) of the *Youth Criminal Justice Act* is replaced by the following:**

**If youth justice court not satisfied**
(4) If the youth justice court is not satisfied that a young person understands the charge, the court shall, unless the young person must be put to his or her election under subsection 67(1) or, with respect to Nunavut, subsection 67(1.1), enter a plea of not guilty on behalf of the young person and proceed with the trial in accordance with subsection 35(2).

**87. Section 33 of the Act is amended by adding the following after subsection (5):**

**Nunavut**
(5.1) Despite subsection (5), an application under section 520 or 521 of the *Criminal Code* for a review of an order made in respect of a young person by a youth justice court judge who is a judge of the Nunavut Court of Justice shall be made to a judge of that court.

**88. Section 36 of the Act is amended by adding the following after subsection (8):**

**Nunavut**
(8.1) Despite subsection (8), if the Nunavut Court of Justice is acting as a youth justice court, an appeal under subsection (5) shall be made to a judge of the Nunavut Court of Appeal, and an appeal of that judge's decision shall be made to the Nunavut Court of Appeal in accordance with section 839 of the *Criminal Code*.

**89. (1) Section 67 of the Act is amended by adding the following after subsection (1):**

**Election—Nunavut**
(1.1) Subject to section 66, if a young person is charged with having, after attaining the age of fourteen years, committed an offence set out in paragraph (*a*) of the definition "presumptive offence" in subsection 2(1), or if the Attorney General has given notice under subsection 63(2) of the intention to seek an adult sentence, the youth justice court shall, before the young person enters a plea, put the young person to his or her election in the following words:

You have the option to elect to be tried by a judge of the Nunavut Court of Justice alone, acting as a youth justice court without a jury and without a preliminary inquiry; or to have a preliminary inquiry and to be tried by a judge of the Nunavut Court of Justice, acting as a youth justice court without a jury; or to have a preliminary inquiry and to be tried by a judge of the Nunavut Court of Justice, acting as a youth justice court with a jury. If you do not elect now, you shall be deemed to have elected to have a preliminary inquiry and to be tried by a court composed of a judge and jury. How do you elect to be tried?

**(2) Subsection 67(4) of the Act is replaced by the following:**

**Preliminary inquiry**
(4) When a young person elects to be tried by a judge without a jury, or elects or is deemed to have elected to be tried by a court composed of a judge and jury, the youth justice court referred to in subsection 13(1) shall conduct a preliminary inquiry and if, on its conclusion, the young person is ordered to stand trial, the proceedings shall be conducted

(*a*) before a judge without a jury or a court composed of a judge and jury, as the case may be; or
(*b*) in Nunavut, before a judge of the Nunavut Court of Justice acting as a youth justice court, with or without a jury, as the case may be.

**(3) Subsection 67(6) of the Act is replaced by the following:**

**Parts XIX and XX of the *Criminal Code***
(6) Proceedings under this Act before a judge without a jury or a court composed of a judge and jury or, in Nunavut, a judge of the Nunavut Court of Justice, acting as a youth justice court, with or without a jury, shall be conducted in accordance with the provisions of Parts XIX and XX of the *Criminal Code*, with any modifications that the circumstances require, except that

(*a*) the provisions of this Act respecting the protection of privacy of young persons prevail over the provisions of the *Criminal Code*; and
(*b*) the young person is entitled to be represented in court by counsel if the young person is removed from court in accordance with subsection 650(2) of the *Criminal Code*.

**Repeal**

**Repeal of R.S., c. Y-1**
**196. The *Young Offenders Act* is repealed.**

**Coming Into Force**

**Coming into force**
**197. This Act or any of its provisions comes into force on a day or days to be fixed by order of the Governor in Council.**

# Glossary

**absolute discharge** The most lenient disposition that can be administrated by a criminal court. Once imposed, the disposition is complete, and there are no further sanctions and no criminal record.

**administrative offences** Encompasses offences such as failure to appear in court, failure to comply with a condition of bail or condition(s) of a probation order, and escape from custody.

**adolescent prostitute** Youth under the age of 16 who is involved in the prostitution trade.

**adversarial system** The procedure utilized in common-law jurisdictions in the adjudication of a case where opposing lawyers, defence and Crown, battle a case in a legal forum while the judge acts as arbiter of the legal rules.

**alternative measures** A means by which the police, Crown, or youth can divert a case from a formal court setting to some form of educational or community-service program. The intention is to avoid the damaging effects of prosecution for those cases that meet the criteria as set out in section 4 of the Young Offenders Act.

**anomie** A state of confusion with regard to norms of conduct and which of these norms should be adhered to. Anomie results when the youth experiences relocation and a loss of traditional lifestyle.

**assault** The intentional use of force on another person against his or her will. It is a type of violent crime.

**assimilation** The central pillar of the Canadian Indian policy, whereby aboriginal people were to give up their traditional lifestyles, cultures, and belief systems, and in turn were to adopt the values, beliefs, and skills of the dominant European settlers.

**Badgley Report** One of the first major reports (1984) in Canada to examine such issues as child sexual abuse and adolescent prostitution. The report found that various federal statutes were poorly equipped to ensure the protection of young people.

**Bill C-12** Proclaimed in force May 1992; it increased maximum sentences for murder from three to five years, outlined continuation of custody provisions, and clarified rules for transferring youth to adult court.

**Bill C-37** Proclaimed in force on 1 December 1995; it increased the maximum sentences for murder to ten years, created a presumption of transfer to adult court for 16- to 17-year-olds charged with serious violent offences, and allowed written victim impact statements in youth court.

**Bill C-68** Introduced in the House of Commons 11 March 1999 as the Youth Criminal Justice Act; it clearly has protection of society as its paramount goal, as well as offering more non-custodial options for minor offences.

**Bill C-106** The first proposal for amendments to the Young Offenders Act; it was introduced in the House of Commons on 30 April 1986 and ascended by the Senate on 26 June 1986. The focus was on amending seven aspects of the act—sections 22, 24, 26, 38(1), 13, 20(1), 20(4.1)—that were generally technical and procedural in nature.

***Canadian Press Stylebook*** A guide for newspaper writers and editors that sets out policy and outlines areas of concern for reporting on youth crime.

**case filtration** A situation in which cases of youth crime may be dismissed because of a lack of perceived gravity or insufficient evidence.

**cognitive-behavioural therapy** A type of therapy utilized with adolescent sexual perpetrators. A combination of social-learning theory and cognitive-development theory, it emphasizes the importance of cognitive and behavioural processes in shaping and maintaining the deviant behaviour.

**colonization** A long-term process that involves replacing traditional, self-determinant lifestyles of indigenous people with a dependent and subordinate status.

**communication law** In 1985 the Canadian Parliament passed the Anti-Communication Law, which makes public communication for the purpose of prostitution a crime. This law is applicable to both the prostitute and the "johns." See section 212 ("Procuring") in the Criminal Code.

**community change model** This "far left" model of juvenile justice represents a combination of the welfare and crime control models. The model advocates that social inequality promotes delinquency and that intervention strategies should focus more on prevention than on punishment.

**community service** A disposition available to the courts. This order can be given independently; however, it is most often combined with a probation order. Community service cannot exceed 240 hours and must be completed within a specified time period.

**conditional discharge** A conditional discharge is granted after a specified time period has elapsed and specified conditions have been met. Conditional discharge results in a criminal record.

**conflict perspective** The belief that there is very little agreement in society; the premise is that individuals and institutions have conflicting values, needs, and goals. Thus, this perspective sees deviance as behaviour that violates the status quo's rules, norms, and attitudes.

**consensus perspective** The belief that people in society share common values, needs and goals. Institutions such as family, school, and church are relied upon to maintain order and stability in society. Delinquency is regarded as dysfunctional.

**crime control model** The model of juvenile justice that emphasizes due process and protection of the community. Criminal-justice agents play a key role in the administration of juvenile justice.

**Crime prevention through social development (CPSD)** Focusses on social-development programs that address youth-crime risk factors such as poverty, dropping out of school, family violence, and substance abuse. CPSD is now widely accepted as the most effective approach to preventing crime.

**culture conflict** Describes the situation that results when aboriginal people are segregated and assimilated. The aboriginal youth is caught between two worlds: the world of the Native communities and the world of the non-Native society. As a result, the aboriginal youth is not able to function successfully in either world.

**custody (open and secure)** The most severe of youth-court dispositions. Custody can be either "open," which takes place in such settings as community residential centres, group homes, or wilderness camps, or "secure," which takes place in a jail.

**dark figure** Term coined in the 1970s to refer to the difference between true incidence of crime and the incidences discovered by police or reported by victims and witnesses.

**"Declaration of Principle"** Section 3 of the Young Offenders Act; serves as a statement of the act's spirit and intent, and provides a guide for its proper administration and the realization of its objectives.

**delinquency perspective** Those behaviours that not only conflict with societal norms, values, and morals, but also are viewed as criminal under criminal law (federal, provincial, and municipal), and are thus punishable by the state.

**deviance** A behaviour that violates a societal norm but is not necessarily sanctioned under law.

**differential intervention** An integrated approach to dealing with female youth offenders that focusses extensively on various aspects of the individual, the social environment, and societal rewards and punishments for behaviours that lead to identity development. The approach is based on interaction between all participants and acknowledgement of accountability by all participants.

**disposition** The final settlement of a criminal case; it can vary from absolute discharge to incarceration.

**due process of law** A system that ensures that individuals are afforded the legal rights guaranteed by the Charter of Rights and Freedoms.

**environmental criminology** A theoretical perspective that examines the relationship between the physical environment and its influence on human behaviour.

**exiles** Runaway youths who have been abandoned or exiled, and who still maintain some degree of dependence on their parents and family.

**extrajudicial measures** Section 4 of the Youth Criminal Justice Act that further expands the role of alternative measures. Under section 4, extrajudicial measures are divided into two categories: warnings, cautions, and referrals; and extrajudicial sanctions (as previously covered under section 4 of the Young Offenders Act).

**fine** A disposition option available to the courts when sentencing. A youth cannot be fined more than $1000, and the judge *must* consider the present and future ability of the youth to pay to avoid incurring a further charge for default of payment. This disposition is not often utilized by youth courts.

**fine-option program** A program that allows the offender to work off a fine.

**forsaken youth** Youth encouraged to leave home in order to seek an independent means of support. They tend to come from large families with low incomes; they suffer from feelings of being unwanted, unloved, and unattached to their families; and they are at a higher risk of victimization.

**Fraser Report** A 1985 report published by the conservation research group at the Fraser Institute, based in British Columbia. Although the report dealt primarily with adult prostitution, it offered a number of recommendations regarding the parameters of pornography and prostitution. Unlike the Badgley Report (see above), which emphasized the importance of social-psychological factors, this report acknowledged the role of the political economy and patriarchal social relations and how they contribute to promotion of prostitution.

**gang** A group comprising at least three or more youths; membership, though often fluid, consists of at least a stable core of members, who band together for cultural, social, or for other reasons, and impulsively or intentionally plan and commit antisocial, violent, or illegal acts.

**gang suppression** A control strategy used by U.S. communities to deal with serious gang crime and violence problems. Gang suppression relies heavily on "gang units," specially trained police officers who recognize gang activity, gather intelligence, communicate positively with gang members, and work hand-in-hand with district attorneys in gang-related cases.

**gender gap** The theoretical explanation of female delinquency that focusses on biological differences between males and females. According to this perspective, female deviance is a result of biologically based sexual problems.

**gender-role theory** A theoretical orientation that views female deviance as a result of different gender-role socialization, different gender roles, and changes in these roles.

**heterogeneity** Social diversity within a culture.

**homeless youth** Youth who have either left or have been urged to leave home with the full knowledge or approval of legal guardians. They have no alternative home to go to.

**in-and-outers** Youth that experiment with street life. These youth often run away from home several times a year, usually a period not exceeding two weeks at a time.

**judicial interim release** Section 51 of the Young Offenders Act stipulates that section 515 ("Judicial Interim (Bail) Release") of the Criminal Code applies to youth court, with necessary modifications. Basically, a young person charged with an offence who does not enter a guilty plea may be released providing the factors in section 3(1) of the YOA are met, unless the Crown can show cause as to why detention of the accused in custody is justified. See section 515(10) for primary and secondary grounds for continued detention.

**juvenile justice model** Emphasizes due process, least restrictive alternatives, and individual responsibility, while trying to respect and balance individual rights and the protection of society.

**masculinization** One of the first gender-based theoretical orientations used to explain female delinquency/crime. It refers to a perceived status that women gravitate toward, resulting from the effects of women's liberation and/or the notion that certain females lack the personality traits commonly expressed among women. Feminist theories have since debunked this paternalistic notion.

**modified justice model** A model of juvenile justice adopted in Canada; it emphasizes due process with an air of informality and has as its objective respecting individual rights while responding to individual needs.

**Native Youth-Justice Committee** A committee comprising elders and interested community members who make recommendations to the court. The focus is healing, restitution, rehabilitation, and applying cultural and traditional approaches to dealing with present-day problems of aboriginal youth.

**official statistics** Statistics are gathered by official agents, such as the police and courts, who utilize a standardized system to record information, that is, the Uniform Crime Reporting System.

**paraphilia** Encompassing sexual urges that are recurrent and intense; fantasies and behaviours that involve unusual objects; and activities or situations that cause significant distress or impairment in social, occupational, and other forms of functioning.

***parens patriae*** The state has the power to act on behalf of the child, in what the court deems to be in the child's best interest. The care and protection provided attempts to be equivalent to that of a parent.

**parole (conditional supervision)** Parole available to youth. A young offender, if charged with first- or second-degree murder, will be given conditional supervision. He or she will then serve that part of the sentence within the community under supervision (see sections 26.2(2) and (3) of the Young Offenders Act).

**participatory model** One of the more liberal models of juvenile justice; it emphasizes informality, and focusses on resocialization, community support, and volunteer efforts. The purpose of intervention is to re-educate young offenders.

**post-Newtonian** Part of the new wave of criminological theory; this theoretical perspective does not view the causes of delinquency as representing a linear model of causation, but rather as a complex interaction of different social, cultural, and individual factors.

**presumptive offence** As defined in section 2 of the Youth Criminal Justice Act, first- or second-degree murder or attempted murder, manslaughter, aggravated sexual assault, or a serious violent offence (already having two other serious violent offences on record) for which an adult could receive more than two years. Any youth over 14 years of age convicted of this offence can be sentenced as an adult (see section 57). Burden of proof is on the young person if he or she has committed a presumptive offence and opposes being treated as an adult.

**probation** The most common form of disposition imposed by youth courts. These orders can be given independently or in conjunction with other penalties (e.g., fines). There are two categories of conditions outlined in a probation order: mandatory (e.g., keep the peace and be of good behaviour) and discretionary (e.g., reporting to a probation officer) (see section 23 of the Young Offenders Act).

**rebels** Those youths who run away following authority conflicts with parents or legal guardians. These conflicts are long-standing and not easily resolved.

**recidivism** The behaviour of an individual who relapses into delinquent activity after being officially detected and is officially convicted of a new offence. However, most recently, the concept has also been extended in some cases to include young persons whose behaviour technically was not a relapse (e.g., dropping out of school, running away from home).

**reintegrative shaming** Term coined by J. Braithwaite; shaming, or an expression of community disapproval, is used constructively with young offenders to create conditions so that they are able to accept societal values and are thus reintegrated into society.

**reliability** The tendency of a test or measurement to consistently produce the same results when repeated. For example, the sun reliably rises in the east every day.

**residential schools** Schools established by the government and operated by the church from the 1800s through to the 1960s. Aboriginal children were required, under the Indian Act, to attend these schools, where the use of traditional languages and the following of cultural or spiritual beliefs were strictly forbidden.

**restorative justice** An approach that evolved out of aboriginal concepts of justice; in the 1990s, it became a popular ideology for dealing with certain types of young offenders. The focus is to reconcile offenders with those they have harmed and to help communities to reintegrate victims and offenders, thus restoring community harmony. Examples of restorative-justice programs are Family-Group Conferencing and Circle Sentencing.

**runarounds** A category of runaway youth who are escapists and tend to be highly unrestrained by their families, and are very connected to their peer groups.

**runaways** Children and youth who run away from home, at least overnight, without parental or caretaker permission. They often leave as a result of family conflict or alienation, but only after considering the option for some time.

**runners** Similar to in-and-outers, runaway youth who engage in frequent runs for short periods of time. The behaviour is often seen as a reaction to being repeatedly moved from one child-welfare placement to another.

**self-report (SR) survey** An anonymous questionnaire that attempts to survey a cross-section of the general population. Difficulties can emerge in securing the truthfulness of respondents and in obtaining a representative sample.

**sexual assault** A person forcing another person to engage in sexual contact or bribes, or tricking or coercing another person into participating in a sexual act.

**social capital** A measure of the quality of social relations and quantity of social supports. Strong social capital enables people to create opportunities for themselves, reduce risk factors that lead to criminal involvement, decrease social isolation or marginalization of members, and significantly reduce vulnerability in children and families. It is regarded as a promising approach in prevention and intervention for youth gangs and youth crime.

**social disorganization** The process that is the result of a breakdown of community, social, and leadership structures. Social disorganization threatens the personal and social welfare of individuals—their lives, safety, social relationships, and mental health—and may prompt delinquent activity.

**societal rejects** Individuals rejected by peers, family and helping organizations, who therefore may leave home in order to find acceptance, caring, and support on the streets.

**squeegee kids** A group of runaways and homeless youth who are resourceful in attempting to develop and maintain a livelihood and means of survival by offering to clean windshields at (major) intersections.

**status offence** As outlined in the Juvenile Delinquents Act, children were charged with status offences because of their status as children; they could not be charged and convicted as adults. Examples of status offences are running away, truancy, and skipping school.

**surety** A form of recognizance; a person who agrees to sign for the release of an offender and to forfeit money, or property, to the Crown if the offender violates the release conditions. This method of release is unique to youth court.

**throwaways** Children and youth asked, or encouraged, to leave home by their parents/ guardians; most leave after considering the option for a period of one week.

**triangulation** Different types of data-collection techniques used to examine the same variable (e.g., official statistics, self-report and victimization surveys). The greater the diversity of collection techniques, with consistent findings, the greater the validity of the data.

**validity** The capacity of a test or measuring instrument to predict what it was designed to measure. When something is defined as being "valid," it is considered to be an accurate reflection of what it intended to define.

**victimological perspective** Within this perspective, prostitution is seen a continuation of sexual abuse (victimization) that an adolescent experienced as a child. An individual who has previously experienced degrading and demoralizing treatment suffers from grossly diminished self-confidence.

**violent offence** Any offence judicially determined as such under section 41(8) of the Criminal Code. Any youth over 14 years of age convicted with this offence can be sentenced as an adult (see section 57 of the Youth Criminal Justice Act). The burden of proof rests with the Crown if an adult sentence is desired.

**welfare model** A model of juvenile justice that is informal and relies on child-care experts to help diagnose and offer intervention and prevention strategies. It includes a heavy emphasis on treatment and rehabilitation.

# *Notes on Contributors*

**Sibylle Artz** is Associate Professor and Director of the University of Victoria's School of Child and Youth Care. She also teaches in the Human and Social Development Multidisciplinary Masters Program. She has over 20 years of front-line experience in working with children, youth, and their families. Her research interests include the constructive use of emotions in everyday life, and family conflict and youth violence, with a specific focus on violence among adolescent females. In January 1994, her first book, *Feeling as a Way of Knowing: A Practical Guide to Working with Emotional Experience*, was published by Trifolium Books. Her second book, *Sex, Power and the Violent School Girl*, was published in the Fall of 1997 by Trifolium Books and Teacher's College Press.

**Augustine Brannigan** is Professor of Sociology at the University of Calgary and Co-director of the Research Unit for Socio-Legal Studies. He conducted a study of street prostitution in the Prairies for the Department of Justice in 1989, and a study of the Escort Services By-law in Calgary for the Alberta Law Foundation in 1992. Recently, Dr. Brannigan undertook a study of street kids in Canada with Tullio Caputo for Health and Welfare Canada.

**Gary Brayton** has been teaching in the Department of Criminology at Mount Royal College for nearly 20 years. He is a registered social worker and certified forensic counsellor. Prior to joining the college, he was involved for a number of years with Alberta Social Services and has, throughout his professional career, maintained an active practice, specializing in adolescent sex offenders.

**Donald W. Fetherston** has been an educator at high schools and technical colleges, as well as a part-time instructor at several universities. In addition, he has ten years' experience as a lawyer (LLB from the University of Alberta) and a master's degree from the University of Calgary. In 1996, he obtained his doctorate in Law and Society from the University of Hawaii. His interests include jurisprudence, ethics, and active learning strategies. He joined Mount Royal College as a full-time instructor in 1997.

**Linda Fisher** is an instructor of Criminology at Douglas College. She also teaches at the Native Education Centre in Vancouver, BC. Her research interests include aboriginal peoples and the administration of justice, the development of community-based justice programs, and professional skill development for college students.

**James Hackler** is a professor of Sociology at the University of Alberta in Edmonton, Alberta. He has frequently been reminded of his lack of talent for foreign languages while studying juvenile-justice systems in Austria, France, and Quebec. Things were somewhat easier in Australia, Fiji, and most of North America. In his book *The Great Stumble Forward: The Prevention of Youthful Crime*, Dr. Hackler argues that one should not expect a great leap forward in terms of dealing effectively with young offenders. His book *Crime and Canadian Public Policy* reviews how criminologists study crime, and the various explanations of crime, and then critically reviews the way Canadians respond to crime.

**Hannele Jantti** is Co-ordinator of the Criminal Justice Program at the Native Education Centre in Vancouver, BC. She also teaches in the Criminology Program at Douglas College. Her interests include young offenders, aboriginal justice issues, and correctional issues.

**Christine Leonard** has worked for the John Howard Society of Alberta since 1991, serving as Executive Director since 1993. She has her BA and MA in Criminology. Her research and policy interests include youth justice, dangerous offenders, corrections, and crime prevention through social development. She has appeared before the Standing Committee on Justice and Legal Affairs regarding the Young Offenders Act on three occasions, and is active in pursuing effective implementation of the Youth Criminal Justice Act.

**Bruce MacLaurin**, MSW, has worked as a manager, program evaluator, and researcher for mental-health and child-welfare services in non-profit agencies in Ontario and Alberta. He is currently a PhD candidate at the Faculty of Social Work at the University of Toronto and is employed as a research associate with the Bell Canada Child Welfare Research Unit. His current research interests are related to child-welfare effectiveness, foster-care services, and street youth, and he has published several journal articles and book chapters on these topics. He is presently involved in three research projects as co-manager of the Canadian Incidence Study of Reported Child Abuse and Neglect, research associate on the Client Outcomes in Child Welfare Project, and co-investigator on the Placement Outcomes Project.

**Fred Mathews** is a community psychologist and Director of Research and Program Development at Central Toronto Youth Services. He works as a consultant to federal, provincial, territorial, and municipal governments, and to public- and private-sector agencies on youth-at-risk and youth-violence issues, and also teaches in the Graduate School of the University of Toronto. He has chaired, given keynote addresses, and provided hundreds of workshops at local, national, and international conferences in Canada, the United States, and Venezuela. He regularly provides training to police forces, Crown attorneys, probation officers, judges, teachers and school officials, and child- and youth-care professionals. Dr. Mathews was the consultant for the Violence Free Schools Initiative of the Ontario Ministry of Education. He has written more than 50 studies, journal articles, book chapters, and resource documents on topics such as youth gangs, violence in schools, girls' violence and aggression, child abuse, and male victims. Dr. Mathews has received an Ontario Psychological Association Award of Merit, the Galen Weston Safer Communities Award, and the Bea Wickett Fund Award for his contributions to the field of psychology in education, violence prevention, and children's mental health.

**Rick Mofina** is a senior newspaper reporter with the *Ottawa Citizen* whose work has appeared in most newspapers in Canada and such publications as the *New York Times* and *Reader's Digest*.

**Tracey Morris** graduated from the University of Toronto with an MA in Criminology in 1993. Tracey has almost ten years of experience working in the criminal justice system, including the John Howard Society, the Salvation Army, and Alberta Justice. Most notably, she served as Research Manager for the John Howard Society of Alberta for four years. Tracey is currently self-employed as a research consultant.

**Philip Perry** is Former Executive Director of Wood's Homes, a comprehensive, multipurpose network of youth and family services located throughout southern Alberta that also offers services nationwide. Currently, Dr. Perry runs a treatment facility in Victoria, BC, and runs a private practice. He has authored two texts: *Beyond Content: Uncommon Interventions with People in Crisis* (1990) and *Harnessing the Power of Anger* (1992).

**Marge Reitsma-Street** has been an associate professor in the Multidisciplinary Masters' Program in Policy and Practice in the Faculty of Human and Social Development at the University of Victoria, British Columbia, since 1997. For the previous 20 years, her policy, practice, and scholarly work featured an analysis of juvenile-justice alternatives and poverty in Quebec and Ontario. She worked and published extensively in the area of female crime. Her doctoral research on girls and delinquency appeared as chapters in *Youth Injustice* (1993) and several other publications. Dr. Reitsma-Street has served several terms on the board of directors of the Elizabeth Fry Society (Hamilton, Sudbury) and the John Howard Society.

**Tony Seskus** is a reporter with the *Calgary Herald*. He has previously worked as a wire service reporter in Great Britain and Africa. He is an alumnus of the University of Regina, where he was the School of Journalism's Most Distinguished Graduate.

**John A. Winterdyk** is an instructor of Criminology at Mount Royal College in Calgary, Alberta. His current interests include alternative methods of education, comparative criminology, research methodology, and young offenders.

His recent books include *Juvenile Justice Systems: International Perspectives* (Canadian Scholars' Press, 1997); *Canadian Criminology* (Pearson, 2000); *Diversity and Justice in Canada* (Canadian Scholars' Press, 1999) with Doug King; and *Corrections in Canada* (Prentice-Hall, forthcoming). In addition, along with Karen Jensen, ND, he has co-authored *The Complete Athlete: Integrating Fitness, Nutrition, and Natural Health* (Alive Books, 1999).

# Index

## READER REPLY CARD

We are interested in your reaction to *Issues and Perspectives on Young Offenders in Canada*, Second Edition, by John A. Winterdyk. You can help us to improve this book in future editions by completing this questionnaire.

1. What was your reason for using this book?

   ☐ university course ☐ college course ☐ continuing education course
   ☐ professional development ☐ personal interest ☐ other____________________

2. If you are a student, please identify your school and the course in which you used this book.

3. Which chapters or parts of this book did you use? Which did you omit?

4. What did you like best about this book?

5. What did you like least?

6. Please identify any topics you think should be added to future editions.

7. Please add any comments or suggestions.

8. May we contact you for further information?

   Name: ______________________________

   Address: ______________________________

   Phone: ______________________________

   E-mail: ______________________________

(fold here and tape shut)

Larry Gillevet
Director of Product Development, College Group
HARCOURT CANADA
55 HORNER AVENUE
TORONTO, ONTARIO
M8Z 9Z9